the **Psychology** place

Congratulations! Included with the purchase of your new textbook is a subscription to the Special Edition of *The Psychology Place*™, a web learning environment for introductory psychology that includes activities, study and testing aids, and a wide range of content to help you succeed in your psychology course.

To activate your pre-paid subscription:

1. Launch your browser and go to http://longman.awl.com/psychzone/websites.asp

2. Select the title of the text your instructor has assigned

3. Select *The Psychology Place*™ logo

4. Enter your pre-assigned activation ID and password, exactly as they appear below, in the User ID and Password fields:

Activation ID: **PSLGST06054262**

Password: **dishes**

5. Select "Log-in"

6. Complete the online registration form to establish your personal ID and password.

7. After completing the registration form, you will receive a page confirming your personal ID and password. On this page there is a link to *The Psychology Place*™ Web site. Follow this link and bookmark the Log in page for the Web site. Whenever you wish to use *The Psychology Place*™ , access it through that bookmark or by following Steps 1, 2, and 3 above.

8. You may now Log in with your new personal user id and password.

This activation ID and password can be used only once to establish a subscription. This subscription to the Special Edition of *The Psychology Place*™ is not transferable. If you *did not* purchase this product *new* and in a shrink-wrapped package, this activation ID and password *is not* valid. However, if your instructor is recommending or requiring use of *The Psychology Place*™, you may purchase a subscription directly online or at your local college bookstore if your professor requested the stand-alone subscription be made available.

ISBN: 0-321-06042-3

Invitation to Psychology

Invitation to Psychology

Carole Wade

Dominican College of San Rafael

Carol Tavris

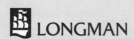LONGMAN

An Imprint of Addison Wesley Longman, Inc.

New York • Reading, Massachusetts • Menlo Park, California • Harlow, England
Don Mills, Ontario • Sydney • Mexico City • Madrid • Amsterdam

Editor in Chief: Priscilla McGeehon
Executive Editor: Rebecca Dudley
Developmental Editor: Susan Messer
Marketing Manager: Anne Wise
Supplements Editor: Cyndy Taylor
Project Manager: Donna DeBenedictis
Design Manager/Text Designer: Wendy Ann Fredericks
Cover Concept: John Odam
Cover Photo: Craig McClain
Cover Design/Photo Effects: Kay Petronio
Art Studio: Burmar
Photo Researcher: Photosearch, Inc.
Prepress Services Supervisor: Valerie Vargas
Electronic Production Specialist/Electronic Page Makeup: Joanne Del Ben
Print Buyer: Denise Sandler
Printer and Binder: World Color/Versailles
Cover Printer: The Lehigh Press, Inc.

For permission to use copyrighted material, grateful acknowledgment is made to the copyright holders on pp. C-1–C-4, which are hereby made part of this copyright page.

Library of Congress Cataloging-in-Publication Data

Wade, Carole.
    Invitation to psychology / Carole Wade, Carol Tavris
       p.   cm.
    Includes bibliographical references and indexes.
    ISBN 0-321-01285-2 (pbk.)
     1. Psychology.   I. Tavris, Carol.   II. Title.
  BF121.W265   1999
  150—dc21   98-8510
                               CIP

Please visit our website at http://longman.awl.com

ISBN 0-321-01285-2 (paperback)
ISBN 0-321-04523-8 (hard cover)

2345678910—WCV—010099

Contents at a Glance

PART ONE
YOUR SELF

At the heart of psychology lies a question: What is a person? This section shows how psychologists from five schools of thought address this question. What traits define personality, and where do they come from? What milestones occur on the way to becoming a person?

PART TWO
YOUR BODY

We cannot understand our psychological selves without understanding our physical selves. These chapters describe how brain activity, neurons, and hormones affect your psychological functioning, and how you are able to sense and perceive the world around you.

PART THREE
YOUR MIND

"I think, therefore I am," said the philosopher René Descartes. This section discusses the impressive ways in which human beings think—and why they so often fail to think and reason well—and explores the puzzles and paradoxes of memory.

PART FOUR
YOUR ENVIRONMENT

Even unsociable hermits are influenced by their surroundings and by other people. In these chapters you will learn how physical and social environments—from the immediate situation to the larger cultural context—affect your actions and attitudes.

PART FIVE
YOUR MENTAL HEALTH

At some point, many of us struggle with psychological problems, which range from everyday difficulties to incapacitating conditions. This part describes the major mental and emotional disorders and evaluates the therapies that have been designed to treat them.

PART SIX
YOUR LIFE

A satisfying life depends on having healthy emotions, coping well with stress, and knowing how to reach your goals. In these closing chapters, we see how the influences discussed in the previous units—personality, body, mind, and environment—affect your emotions, well-being, and four of life's fundamental motives: love, sex, eating, and work.

Contents

PART TWO

YOUR BODY

Neurons, Hormones, and the Brain   112

5   Sensation and Perception   148

9 Behavior in Social and Cultural Context 296

PART FIVE
YOUR MENTAL HEALTH

10 Psychological Disorders 332

11 Approaches to Treatment and Therapy 368

PART SIX
YOUR LIFE

12 Emotion, Stress, and Health   398

13 The Major Motives of Life: Love, Sex, Food, and Work   430

Appendix: Statistical Methods   464

To the Instructor

Psychology textbooks have always had a little problem with length. William James's two-volume classic, *Principles of Psychology* (1890), took him twelve long years to write and weighed in at a hefty 1,393 pages. (And today's students think *they* have it hard!) Just two years after his book was published, James followed it with *Psychology, Briefer Course,* which was much shorter, under 500 pages. But James wasn't happy with his briefer book; in a letter to his publishers, he complained that he had left out "all bibliography and experimental details, all metaphysical subtleties and digressions, all quotations, all humor and pathos, all *interest* in short...." (quoted in Weiten & Wight, 1992).

The great James was probably too hard on himself; he was entirely incapable of writing anything dull or disjointed. Nevertheless, we kept his words in mind as we were working on our own "briefer" introduction to psychology. From the outset, we were guided by a philosophy that we hoped would help us avoid some of the pitfalls of the genre:

1. A brief book should be brief—not only in terms of pages but in the number of chapters.

2. The book's organization should be appealing and meaningful.

3. Students at all levels need critical-thinking tools for evaluating psychological issues intelligently.

4. Brief or long, a textbook needs examples, analogies, lively writing, and a strong narrative sense to pull students into the material and make it meaningful to their lives.

5. Students remember more if they learn actively.

6. Research on culture, gender, and ethnicity is as integral to psychology as is research on the brain, genetics, and hormones.

In particular, here is how we have tried to translate our philosophy into reality.

1. BREVITY

Even with a brief textbook consisting of 14 or 15 chapters, instructors often feel hard-pressed to cover the material in a semester or quarter. We decided, therefore, that 13 chapters would be ideal: enough to cover all the major topics, but few enough to give instructors some breathing room. A 13-chapter book allows you to spend some extra time on topics that many students find particularly difficult, such as the brain; to develop your favorite topics in greater depth; to take time at the beginning of the semester to get to know your students; or to use time at the end of the term to summarize and review.

2. A MEANINGFUL ORGANIZATION

We wanted the organization of this book to do two things: engage students quickly and give them a framework for thinking about human behavior. The first chapter, which introduces students to psychology and to the fundamentals of critical and scientific thinking, is followed by six sections of two chapters each. The six parts focus on different aspects of human behavior or approaches to studying it:

- **Part One: Your Self** examines major theories of personality (Chapter 2) and development (Chapter 3). These are extremely high-interest topics for students and will draw them into the course right away. Moreover, starting off with these chapters allows us to avoid redundancy in coverage of the major schools of psychology—biological, learning, cognitive, sociocultural, and psychodynamic. Instead of introducing these perspectives in the first chapter and then having to explain them again in a much later personality chapter, we cover them once, in this section.

- **Part Two: Your Body** explores the many ways in which the brain, neurons, and hormones affect psychological functioning (Chapter 4); and the neurological and psychological underpinnings of sensation and perception (Chapter 5).

- **Part Three: Your Mind** discusses the impressive ways in which human beings think and reason—and why they so often fail to think and reason well (Chapter 6)—and explores the puzzles and paradoxes of memory (Chapter 7).

- **Part Four: Your Environment** covers basic principles of learning (Chapter 8) and the impact of social and cultural contexts on behavior (Chapter 9). Combining learning and social psychology in the same part is a break from convention, but we think it makes excellent sense, for these two fields share an emphasis on "extrapsychic" factors in behavior.

- **Part Five: Your Mental Health** reviews the major mental and emotional disorders (Chapter 10) and evaluates the therapies designed to treat them (Chapter 11).
- **Part Six: Your Life** shows how mind, body, and environment influence emotions, stress, and health (Chapter 12) and the fundamental motives that drive people: eating and appetite, love and sex, and work and achievement (Chapter 13).

Naturally, a brief book will not include every topic that might be found in a longer book, but we have tried to retain all of those that are truly essential to an introductory course. In most cases, you will find these topics in the chapters where you expect them to be, but there are a few exceptions, so if at first you do not see a topic that interests you, we urge you to look for it in the table of contents or the index. Because we do not have a traditional consciousness chapter, for example, sleep and dreams are covered in the chapter on the brain and nervous system (Chapter 4). Eating disorders are not discussed in the chapter on psychological disorders; instead, we discuss them in the context of the psychology and genetics of eating, overweight, and dieting (Chapter 13).

3. CRITICAL AND CREATIVE THINKING

Since we first introduced critical thinking in the first edition of our longer book a dozen years ago, we have been gratified to see its place in the study of psychology grow. Without critical-thinking skills, learning ends at the classroom door.

In this book, too, our goal is to get students to reflect on what they learn, resist leaping to conclusions on the basis of personal experience alone (so tempting in psychological matters), apply rigorous standards of evidence, and listen to competing views. As in our longer book, we introduce eight basic guidelines to critical and creative thinking right away, in the first chapter, and then teach and model these guidelines throughout the book.

We use a critical-thinking symbol—a lightbulb—together with a yellow "tab," like the one in the sample on this page, to draw the reader's attention to some (but not all) of the critical-thinking discussions in the text. The discussion may extend beyond the paragraph in which the tab appears. The tab is meant to say to students, "Listen up! As you read about this topic, you need to be especially careful about assumptions, evidence, and conclusions." The critical-thinking lightbulb also appears in Quick Quizzes to alert students to quiz items that give practice in critical thinking (see page xvii for more on this pedagogy).

True critical thinking, we have always maintained, cannot be reduced to a set of rhetorical questions or to a formula for analyzing studies. It is a *process of evaluating claims and ideas, and thus it must be woven into a book's narrative.* We try to model critical thinking for students in our evaluations not only of popular but unsupported cultural beliefs, such as in ESP, but also of popular but unsupported academic ideas, such as theories of gender differences in moral reasoning or Maslow's concept of a motivational hierarchy. Finally, we try to model the importance of critical thinking and empirical evidence in our coverage of psychological issues that often evoke emotional debate, such as children's eyewitness testimony, multiple personality disorder, "recovered" memories, the disease model of addiction, definitions of racism and sexism, and many others.

4. LIVELINESS AND RELEVANCE

Virginia Woolf once said that "Fiction is not dropped like a pebble upon the ground, but, like a spider's web, is attached to life at all four corners." The same principle applies to good textbook writing. Authors of texts at all levels have a unique opportunity to combine scholarly rigor and authority with warmth and compassion when conveying what psychologists know (and still seek to know) about the predicaments and puzzles of life.

The predicaments and puzzles that people care most about, of course, are those that arise in their own lives. **Taking Psychology with You,** a feature that concludes each chapter, draws on research reported in the chapter to tackle practical topics such as living with chronic pain (Chapter 5), becoming more creative (Chapter 6), improving study habits (Chapter 8), getting along with people of other cultures (Chapter 9), and evaluating self-help books (Chapter 11).

However, we also want students to see that psychology can deepen their understanding of events and problems that go beyond the personal. Each chapter therefore begins with a real story or incident from the news—a woman in her sixties giving birth, a court case involving recovered memories, a

---

328   PART FOUR   Your Environment

Taking Psychology with You

Travels Across the Cultural Divide

A French salesman worked for a company that was bought by Americans. When the new American manager ordered him to step up his sales within the next three months, the employee quit in a huff, taking his customers with him. Why? In France, it takes years to develop customers; in family-owned businesses, relationships with customers may span generations. The American wanted instant results, as Americans often do, but the French salesman knew this was impossible and quit. The American view was, "He wasn't up to the job; he's lazy and disloyal, so he stole my customers." The French view was, "There is no point in explaining anything to a person who is so stupid as to think you can acquire loyal customers in three months" (Hall & Hall, 1987).

Many corporations are beginning to realize that such cultural differences are not trivial and that success in a global economy depends on understanding such differences. You, too, can benefit from the psychological research on cultures, whether you plan to do business abroad, visit as a tourist, or just want to get along better in an increasingly diverse society.

• *Be sure you understand the other culture's rules,* not only of manners and customs but also of nonverbal gestures and methods of communication. If you find yourself getting angry over something a person from another culture is doing, try to find out whether your expectations and perceptions of that person's behavior are appropriate. For example, Koreans typically do not shake hands when greeting strangers, whereas most African-Americans and whites do. People who shake hands as a gesture of friendship and courtesy are likely to feel insulted if another person refuses

to do the same—unless they understand that what is going on is a cultural difference. Here's another example: Suppose you want to go shopping in Morocco or Mexico. If you are not used to bargaining, the experience may be exasperating. It will help to find a cultural "translator" who can show you the ropes. On the other hand, if you are from a culture where people bargain for everything, you will be just as exasperated in a place where everything is sold for a fixed price. "Where's the fun in this?" you'll say. "The whole human transaction of shopping is gone!"

• *When in Rome, do as the Romans do—as much as possible.* Most of the things you really need to know about a culture are not to be found in the guidebooks or travelogues. To learn the unspoken rules of a culture, keep your eyes open and your mouth shut: Look, listen, and observe. What is the pace of life like? Which is more valued in this culture, relationships or schedules? Do people regard brash individuality as admirable or embarrassing? When customers enter a shop, do they greet and chat with the shopkeeper or ignore the person as they browse?

Remember, though, that even when you know the rules, you may find it difficult to carry them out. For example, cultures differ in their tolerance for prolonged gazes (Keating, 1994). In the Middle East, two men will look directly at one another as they talk, but such direct gazes would be deeply uncomfortable to most Japanese or white Americans and a sign of insult to some African-Americans. Knowing this fact about gaze rules can help people accept the reality of different customs, but most of us will still feel uncomfortable trying to change our own ways.

• *Nevertheless, avoid stereotyping.* Try not to let your awareness of cultural differences cause you to overlook individual variations within cultures. During a dreary Boston winter, social psychologist Roger Brown (1986) went to the Bahamas for a vacation. To his surprise, he found the people he met unfriendly, rude, and sullen. He decided that the reason was that Bahamians had to deal with spoiled, critical foreigners, and he tried out this hypothesis on a cab driver. The cab driver looked at Brown in amazement, smiled cheerfully, and told him that Bahamians don't mind tourists—just *unsmiling* tourists.

And then Brown realized what had been going on. "Not tourists generally, but this tourist, myself, was the cause," he wrote. "Confronted with my unrelaxed wintry Boston face, they had assumed I had no interest in them and had responded non-committally, inexpressively. I had created the Bahamian national character. Everywhere I took my face it sprang into being. So I began smiling a lot, and the Bahamians changed their national character. In fact, they lost any national character and differentiated into individuals."

Wise travelers will use cultural findings to expand their understanding of other societies, while avoiding the trap of reducing all behavior to a matter of culture. Sociocultural research teaches us to appreciate the countless explicit and implicit rules that govern our behavior, values, and attitudes, and those of others. Yet we should not forget Roger Brown's lesson that every human being is an individual: one who not only reflects his or her culture, but who shares the common concerns of all humanity.

SUMMARY

1) Like learning theorists, social and cultural psychologists emphasize environmental influences on beh...   Social psychologists study the influence of *norms*, *roles*, and groups on behavior and cognition; cul...

3 Development over the Life Span

PSYCHOLOGY IN THE NEWS

Age Record Broken as 63-Year-Old Woman Gives Birth

The oldest woman ever to give birth, Arceli Keh, cuddles her daughter Cynthia.

LOS ANGELES, APRIL 1997. A fertility specialist at the University of Southern California has announced that a 63-year-old female patient gave birth last year to a healthy baby girl. The child was conceived through in vitro ("test tube") fertilization, with sperm from the woman's 60-year-old husband and an egg donated by a younger woman. Previously, the oldest woman on record to give birth was a 53-year-old Italian woman who had a child in 1994, using similar procedures.

Although the USC infertility program has a policy of rejecting patients over age 55, the California woman lied about her age and did not confess the truth until she was 13 weeks pregnant. The woman's own 86-year-old mother, unaware of her daughter's pregnancy until the delivery, is reportedly delighted at becoming a grandparent, and the rest of the close-knit Filipino family has also been supportive. But some fertility experts and ethicists have misgivings. Dr. Mark Sauer, who pioneered the use of donor eggs in older women, said, "I lose my comfort level after 55 because I have to believe that there are quality-of-life issues involved in raising a child at [the parent's] age. When [the baby] is 5, her mother will be 68. And I have to believe that a 78-year-old dealing with a teenager may have some problems."

How do *you* react to the idea of a 63-year-old woman having a baby? Would it make any difference if the mother were "only" 55 years old, or 50, or 45? What if she were older than 63? Do you feel the same about older fathers as you do about older mothers? Is there some "right" time to become a parent? For that matter, is there a "right" time to do anything in life—go to school, get married, retire, . . . die?

Before the Industrial Revolution in the late nineteenth century, people of different ages often inhabited the same social world. Children and teenagers worked alongside adults on farms and in factories; several generations often shared one household. Neither children nor old people were set apart from the rest of society on the grounds that they were too young or too old to participate (Chudacoff, 1990).

Then, during the first half of the twentieth century, complex social and economic changes in developed countries led to the notion that life unfolds in a progression of distinct stages. Childhood came to be seen as a special time, when powerful experiences determine the kind of adult a person will become. Adolescence, the years between the physical changes of puberty and the social markers of adulthood, became longer and longer, and its defining characteristics were said to be turmoil

---

crime of passion—and asks students how they might think critically about the issues it raises.

This **Psychology in the News** feature is not merely a "motivator" to be quickly forgotten; each story is revisited at the end of the chapter, where concepts and findings from the chapter are used to analyze and evaluate the questions raised earlier. We think this device will not only promote critical thinking, but will also help students appreciate that psychology is indeed "attached to life at all four corners."

5. ACTIVE LEARNING

One of the soundest findings about learning is that you can't just sit there and expect it to happen; you have to be actively involved, whether practicing a new skill or encoding new material. In this textbook, we have included several pedagogical features designed to encourage students to become actively involved in what they are reading.

What's Ahead introduces each major section within a chapter. This feature consists of a brief set

of family, ch__

In this chapter, we have chosen four examples to illustrate the cognitive, cultural, and biological components of human motivation: love, sex, eating, and work. As you read, see whether this information helps you understand the appeal of *Titanic*, the accusations against Sgt. Maj. McKinney, the reasons that people seek magic pills to lose weight, and the determination of Hulda Crooks to conquer towering mountains.

experiences __
ments—are __
Let me count__
Browning in__
Social scientis__
ing, although__
Let's begin o__
our terms.

| What's Ahead |

- What kind of lover defines love as jealousy and possessiveness, and what kind defines it as just the opposite—calm compatibility?

- Do men and women differ in the ability to love?

THE SOCIAL ANIMAL: MOTIVES FOR LOVE

motivation
An inferred process within a person or other animal that causes that organism to move toward a goal or away from an unpleasant situation.

need for affiliation
The motive to associate with other people, as by seeking friends, moral support, companionship, or love.

Everybody needs somebody. One of the deepest and most universal of human motives is the **need for affiliation,** the need to be with others, make friends, cooperate, love. Human survival depends on the child's ability to form attachments and learn from adults and peers, and on the adult's ability to form relationships with intimate partners, family, friends, and colleagues. The need to belong, to

T__

Do you have __
the couple fal__
ter a couple o__
pily ever afte__
able moment __
by Rhett Butl__
Gone with the __
a damn"?

Although __
they often h__
they are talki__
tion is that t__
characterized __
and *companio*__
and trust (Ha__
love is emotic__
and highly se__
fragile. Comp__
one's life, and__
stable and re__
love is the st__
first sight," a__

of questions that are not merely rhetorical but are intended to be provocative or intriguing enough to arouse students' curiosity and draw them into the material: Why do some people get depressed even though they "have it all"? Why are people who are chronically angry and mistrustful their own worst enemy? What's the difference between ordinary techniques of persuasion and the coercive techniques used by cults?

Looking Back, at the end of each chapter, lists all of the *What's Ahead* questions along with page numbers to show where the material for each question was covered. Students can check their retention and can easily review if they find that they can't answer a question. This feature also has another purpose: Students will gain a sense of how much they are learning about matters of personal and social importance, and will be able to appreciate how much more psychology offers beyond "common sense." Some instructors may want to turn some of these questions into essay or short-answer test items or written assignments.

Quick Quizzes have been retained and adapted from our longer text because of their track record in promoting active learning. These periodic self-tests encourage students to check their progress while they are reading and to go back and review if necessary. The quizzes do more than test for memorization of definitions; they tell students whether they comprehend the issues. Mindful of the common tendency to skip quizzes or to peek at the answers, we have used various formats and have included entertaining examples in order to motivate students to test themselves.

As mentioned earlier, many of the quizzes also include critical-thinking questions, identified by the critical-thinking symbol. They invite the student to reflect on the implications of findings and consider how psychological principles might illuminate real-

the pe... North America consists of... ple over the age of 85, and many of them are doing fine. The fact that people are living longer and better, however, raises crucial ethical and legal concerns about death—in particular, how and when to draw the line between death that is inevitable and death that can be delayed with technological interventions.

2. Aging has been separated from illness. People used to think that all bodily functions declined with age. Some conditions, such as osteoporosis (having extremely brittle bones) or senility (the loss of mental abilities), were assumed to be inevitable. Today we know that many such conditions are a result of malnutrition, overmedication, disease, or cellular damage from too much sun. For example,

names, dates, and ... rs. And, on average, older adults score lower on tests of reasoning and complex problem solving than do younger adults. But gerontologists disagree about exactly why these abilities tend to decline.

"Intelligence" generally takes two forms: *fluid intelligence*, the capacity for deductive reasoning and the ability to use new information to solve problems, and *crystallized intelligence*, the knowledge and skills that are built up over a lifetime—the kind that give us the ability to solve math problems, define words, or summarize the President's policy on the environment (Horn & Donaldson, 1980). Fluid intelligence is relatively independent of education and experience; it reflects an inherited predisposition, and it parallels other bio-

> **Get Involved**
>
> Ask five people—each about a decade apart in age, and one of whom is at least 70—how old they feel. (You may include yourself.) What is the gap, if any, between their chronological age and their psychological age? Is the gap larger among the oldest individuals? Ask why they perceive an "age gap" between their actual years and how old they feel.

life issues. For example: What kinds of questions should a critical thinker ask about a new drug for depression? How might a hypothetical study of testosterone and hostility be improved? How should a critical consumer evaluate some expert's claim that health is entirely a matter of "mind over matter"? Although we offer some possible responses to such questions, most of them do not have a single correct answer, and students may have valid, well-reasoned answers that differ from our own.

Get Involved exercises provide an entertaining approach to active learning. Some consist of quick demonstrations (e.g., swing a flashlight in a dark closet to see how images remain briefly in sensory memory); some are simple mini-studies (e.g., observe seating patterns in the school cafeteria); and some help students relate course material to their own lives (e.g., list the extrinsic and in-

> **??? QUICK QUIZ**
>
> A. Name the independent and dependent variables in studies designed to answer the following questions:
>
> 1. Whether sleeping after learning a poem improves memory for the poem
>
> 2. Whether the presence of other people affects a person's willingness to help someone in distress
>
> 3. Whether people get agitated from listening to heavy-metal music
>
> B. On a talk show, Dr. Blitznik announces a fabulous new program: Chocolate Immersion Therapy. "People who spend one day a week doing nothing but eating chocolate are soon cured of eating disorders, depression, drug abuse, and poor study habits," claims Dr. Blitznik. What should you find out about C.I.T. before signing up?
>
> **Answers:**
>
> A. 1. Opportunity to sleep after learning is the independent variable; memory for the poem is the dependent variable. 2. The presence of other people is the independent variable; willingness to help others is the dependent variable. 3. Exposure to heavy-metal music is the independent variable; agitation is the dependent variable. B. *Some questions to ask:* Is there research showing that people who go through C.I.T. did better than those in a control group who did not have the therapy, or who had a different therapy—say, Broccoli Immersion Therapy? If so, how many people were studied? How were they selected, and how were they assigned to the therapy and no-therapy groups? Did the person running the experiment know who was getting C.I.T. and who wasn't? How long did the "cures" last? Has the research been replicated?

trinsic reinforcers that might be involved in a diverse array of activities, from studying to prayer). Instructors may want to assign some of these exercises to the entire class and then discuss the results and what they mean.

Other pedagogical features include **graphic illustrations** of complex concepts; **summary tables;** a **running glossary** that defines boldfaced technical terms on the pages where they occur for handy reference and study; a **cumulative glossary** at the back of the book; a list of **key terms** at the end of each chapter that includes page numbers so that students can find the sections where the terms are covered; **chapter outlines;** and **chapter summaries** in numbered paragraph form to help students review major concepts.

6. COVERAGE OF HUMAN DIVERSITY

When the first edition of our longer textbook came out, some considered our goal of mainstreaming issues of gender, ethnicity, and culture into introductory psychology quite radical—either a sop to political correctness or a fluffy and superficial fad in psychology. Today, the issue is no longer whether to include these topics but how

Which woman is the chemical engineer and which is the assistant? The Western stereotype holds that (a) women are not engineers in the first place, but (b) if they are, they are Western. Actually, the engineer at this refinery is the Kuwaiti woman on the left.

best to do it. From the beginning, our own answer has been to raise relevant studies and issues about gender and culture in the main body of the text, and we continue to do so.

Are there sex differences in the brain? This controversial and fascinating issue belongs in the brain chapter (Chapter 4). Do people from all cultures experience and express emotion the same way—and do women and men differ in "emotionality"? These topics belong in the emotion chapter (Chapter 12). In addition, Chapter 9, "Behavior in Social and Cultural Context," highlights the sociocultural perspective in psychology and includes an extended discussion of ethnic identity, ethnocentrism, prejudice, and cross-cultural relations.

Findings on gender can be found, among other places, in discussions of:

Adolescent development (pp. 98–99)

Biological influences on gender (pp. 88–89)

The brain (pp. 141–143)

Changing attitudes toward gender roles (p. 322)

Child development (pp. 88–92)

Courtship and mating (pp. 438–440)

Depression (pp. 345–347)

Eating disorders (p. 449)

Emotion (pp. 410–411)

Gender schemas (pp. 90–91)

Gender socialization (pp. 89–90)

The glass ceiling (p. 457)

Hormones (pp. 124–125)

Love (pp. 435–436)

Menopause (pp. 101–102)

Meta-analysis (p. 32)

Moral reasoning (pp. 93–94)

Object-relations views of male and female development (p. 62)

Pain (p. 182)

Sexual attitudes (p. 443)

Sexual biology and behavior (pp. 437–438)

Sexual coercion (p. 440)

Sexual motives (pp. 440–444)

Sexual orientation (pp. 444–445)

Sexual scripts (pp. 442–443)

Weight and dieting (pp. 448–449)

Work motivation (p. 457)

Findings on culture and ethnicity can be found, among other places, in discussions of:

A book's coverage of gender and culture, however, cannot be adequately assessed solely in terms of the number of times group differences and characteristics are mentioned. There are hundreds of gender and cultural differences that, though reliable, are trivial and do not warrant space in an introductory textbook. We would rather devote the space to in-depth discussions of issues where diversity really matters. For example, it is not enough to say, in passing, that women are more likely than men to seek treatment for depression, or that Japanese schoolchildren have higher math scores than American children, without explaining why these differences might exist. Further, mainstreaming gender and culture also means discussing the larger controversies that the study of gender and culture raises. For example, how should we think about cultural practices, such as genital mutilation, that violate human rights (pages 318–319)? How should we assess evolutionary explanations of gender differences in sexuality and love (pages 438–440)?

SUPPLEMENTS PACKAGE

For the Instructor

Instructor's Manual

Written by Virginia Diehl of Western Illinois University, this invaluable supplement includes "teacher-to-teacher" discussions, learning objectives, chapter outlines, examples, lecture ideas, critical-thinking discussions, media materials, classroom assessment techniques, a website guide, recommended readings, in-class activities, and other resources.

Lecture Shell

The chapter outlines of the entire text are available on disk for use in creating your own customized lecture outlines.

Testbank

Written by Scott Johnson of John Wood Community College, the testbank for *Invitation to Psychol-*

ogy includes 75 multiple-choice, 10 true/false, 10 short-answer, and 2 to 3 essay questions per chapter. These questions are referenced by text topic, page number, and skill type (conceptual, application, and factual).

TestGen-EQ (with QuizMaster-EQ)

This fully networkable generation software enables you to easily view, edit, and add questions, transfer questions to tests, and print tests in a variety of fonts and forms. Search and sort features let you quickly locate questions of various formats (including short-answer, true/false, multiple-choice, essay, and matching) and arrange them in a preferred order. A built-in question editor gives you the power to create graphs, import graphics, insert mathematical symbols and templates, and insert variable numbers or text. QuizMaster-EQ automatically grades the exams, stores results on disk, and allows you to view or print a variety of reports for individual students, classes, or courses. Available in Macintosh and Windows formats.

Transparency Package

175 full-color acetates have been specially designed for clarity in large lecture halls. These transparencies both duplicate and supplement those in the textbook. An assortment of additional images can be downloaded from the Psychzone website at *http://longman.awl.com/psychzone*.

Videos

Many videos are available to accompany this text. Please contact your local sales representative for information.

Psychology Encyclopedia Laser Disks III and IV

Comprised of archival footage, documentation of contemporary demonstrations and experiments, still images, and original animation, these laser disks provide instant access to a wide variety of visuals in an easy-to-use format. Each video disk is accompanied by an annotated manual with bar code stickers.

Media Portfolio II CD-ROM

Compatible with Macintosh and Windows formats, this CD-ROM is a compilation of line art from Longman introductory texts coupled with an extensive selection of video clips and animation.

All imagery is in standard graphic file format that can be imported into major presentation software programs, including PowerPoint, Persuasion, and Astound. This CD-ROM also contains Lecture Active presentation manager software.

For the Instructor and Students

Wade/Tavris "Invitation to Psychology" Website and Psychzone

A text-specific website provides useful resources for faculty and students, including practice tests, links, visuals, activities, exercises, downloadable supplements, an author forum, a research and writing center, and much more. Please visit this site at *http://longman.awl.com/invite*.

A general introductory psychology website also provides various resources. Visit this site at *http://longman.awl.com/psychzone*.

Longman MindMatters CD-ROM

This new student-tutorial interactive CD-ROM blends interactive exercises and supporting text. Rather than rewarding memorization, this tool seeks to foster students' curiosity about psychology and their ability to integrate material. Instructors can also use this flexibly organized CD-ROM in classroom presentations.

Internet Companion for General Psychology

Written by Cheryl J. Hamel of Valencia Community College and David L. Ryan-Jones, this guide was designed to help teachers, professionals, students, and consumers take advantage of numerous psychology resources on the Internet. This helpful resource can be packaged free upon adoption of this textbook.

For the Student

Study Guide

Written by Sherri Jackson of Jacksonville University and Richard Griggs of the University of Florida, this comprehensive study guide includes such helpful features as chapter overviews, guided-study completion exercises, lists of key terms, key-term quizzes, sample answers for the "What's Ahead" questions from the text, and multiple-choice progress tests.

"Psychobabble and Biobunk" Booklet

This collection of newspaper essays by Carol Tavris applies psychological research to current issues in the news. They may be used to encourage debate in the classroom or as a basis for student papers.

StudyWizard CD-ROM

Written by Carolyn Meyer, this interactive software, also available in Windows and Macintosh formats, helps students learn and review major concepts and facts through drill and practice exercises. It provides immediate reinforcement of correct answers, provides answer explanations with textbook page references, and gives diagnostic feedback on their strengths and weaknesses. Other useful features include chapter summaries, vocabulary drill and pronunciation guide, practice tests, a glossary, and an electronic notebook.

Journey II Interactive Software

Written by Nancy Oley of the City University of New York and Jeffrey Parsons of Jersey State Community College, this software gives students an opportunity to participate in psychological experiments. It consists of "visits" to eight different labs, each containing two to four different experiments. This software also contains information on graduate schools, scholarships, and programs in psychology.

ACKNOWLEDGMENTS

Like any other cooperative effort, writing a textbook requires a support team. We are indebted to the following reviewers for their careful reading of the manuscript and their many insightful suggestions:

Paul Ackerman, Wichita State University

Ronald Baenninger, Temple University

Judith Barker, Cuyahoga East Community College

Linda M. Bastone, SUNY–Purchase College

Jim Beers, John Jay College of Criminal Justice

John Bouseman, Hillsborough Community College

Michael A. Britt, Marist College

Robert Bruel, Kean College

Dan Brunworth, Kishwaukee College

Sharon K. Calhoun, Indiana University–Kokomo

Sally Carr, Lakeland Community College

Loren Cheney, Community College of Rhode Island

Norman Culbertson, Yakima Valley College

Mark Cummins, Dawson College

William Curtis, Camden County College

Gregory Cutler, Bay de Noc Community College

Betty Davenport, Campbell University

Nat DeAnda, Los Medanos College

Virginia Diehl, Western Illinois University

Lynn Dodson, Seattle Central Community College

Laurel End, Mt. Mary College

Vivian Ferry, Community College of Rhode Island

Andrew Geoghegan, Longview Community College

Richard Girard, New Hampshire Community Technical College

Randy Gold, Cuesta College

Peter Graham, Pensacola Junior College

David Grilly, Cleveland State University

Bea Gattuso Grosh, Millersville University

Roger Harnish, Rochester Institute of Technology

James E. Hart, Edison Community College

Peter C. Hill, Grove City College

Gene Indenbaum, SUNY–Farmingdale

Sherri Jackson, Jacksonville University

Craig Johnson, Towson State University

Jim Jokerst, Aims Community College

David Klein, Stark State College of Technology

Katherine Kocel, Jackson State University

Patsy Lawson, Volunteer State Community College

Gary Levy, University of Wyoming

John F. Lindsay, Jr., Georgia College and State University

Peter Maneno, Normandale Community College

Lyla Maynard, Des Moines Area Community College

Cynthia McCormick, Armstrong Atlantic State University

Rafael Mendez, Bronx Community College

Judi Misale, Truman State University

Benjamin Newberry, Kent State University

David Perkins, College of St. Elizabeth

Wade Pickren, Southeastern Oklahoma State University

Paula M. Popovich, Ohio University

Jack Powell, University of Hartford

Shirley Pritchett, Northeast Texas Community College

Steven Richman, Nassau Community College

Mark Rittman, Cuyahoga Metro Community College

Lee Schrock, Kankakee Community College

Christina S. Sinisi, Charleston Southern University

Holly Straub, University of South Dakota

Ed Valsi, Oakland Community College

Fred Whitford, Montana State University

Edmond Zuromski, Community College of Rhode Island

We are also grateful to our superb editorial and production teams at Longman. As social psychologists have shown, cooperation in pursuit of mutual goals can strengthen the bonds of friendship, and we have indeed grown very fond of these talented, committed, and hard-working people, not one of whom ever indulged in social loafing. We especially thank our psychology editor Rebecca Dudley for her unwavering enthusiasm, her brilliant editorial suggestions, and her ability to resolve differences of opinion with grace and insight. We are also eternally indebted to our indispensable project manager Donna DeBenedictis, whose sense of humor, calm manner, and amazing organizational skills guided this project through its complicated production schedule.

In addition, our warm thanks to development director Lisa Pinto, for her many innovative ideas; our developmental editor Susan Messer for her excellent editorial skills; Shari Hatch, for her meticulous copyediting, Maddy Elliott, for her careful proofreading; and Joanne Del Ben, for creating beautiful pages from our words and art. We are also grateful to photo researcher Joan Meisel for finding us many excellent and thought-provoking photographs and cartoons.

Our special thanks to John Odam for the concept and photo and Kay Petronio for the design of this warm and inviting cover. And thanks also to Wendy Ann Fredericks who produced a clean interior design that enhances the book's readability and is stunning to look at.

As always, our greatest thanks go to Howard Williams and Ronan O'Casey, who for so many years have bolstered us with their love, humor, and good cheer, not to mention an endless supply of freshly brewed coffee.

We have enjoyed writing this book, and we hope you will enjoy reading and using it. We welcome your questions, comments, and reactions; please let us hear from you.

Carole Wade
Carol Tavris

To the Student

If you are reading this introduction, you are starting your introductory psychology course on the right foot. It helps to get a general picture of what you are about to read before charging forward.

Our goal in this book is to guide you to think critically and imaginatively about psychological issues, and to help you apply what you learn to your own life and the world around you. We ourselves have never gotten over our initial excitement about psychology, and we have done everything we can think of to make the field as absorbing for you as it is for us. However, what you bring to this book is as important as what we have written—we can pitch ideas to you, but you have to step up to the plate to connect with them. This text will remain only a collection of pages with ink on them unless you choose to read actively. The more involved you are in your own learning, the more successful the book and your course will be, and the more enjoyable, too.

GETTING INVOLVED

To encourage you to read and study actively, we have included some special features:

• Every chapter opens with **Psychology in the News,** an actual story from the media related to issues that will be discussed in the chapter. *Do not skip these stories!* We return to them at the end of the chapter to show you how findings from psychology might help you understand each story in particular and others like it that you will encounter. How do you feel about a 63-year-old woman giving birth to a baby? What's the reason for the incredible appeal of the film *Titanic?* As you read the chapter, try to link its findings and ideas to the opening story and come up with your own insights. If you do this, you will find that studying psychology will not only help you with your own problems and goals, but will also increase your understanding of the world around you.

• Each chapter contains several **Get Involved** exercises, entertaining little experiments or explorations you can do that demonstrate what you are reading about. In Chapter 2, for instance, you get to see where you fall on an inventory of basic personality traits, and in Chapter 11, we will show you how your own thoughts affect your moods. Some Get Involved exercises take only a minute;

others are "mini-studies" that you can do by observing or interviewing others.

• Before each major section, a feature called **What's Ahead** lists some preview questions to stir your curiosity and indicate what that section will cover. For example: Why does paying children for good grades sometimes backfire? Do people remember better when they're hypnotized? Why do people with the best of intentions sometimes get caught in a "cycle of distrust" with members of other ethnic groups? What do psychologists think is the "sexiest sex organ"? Do men and women differ in the ability to love? When you finish the chapter, you will encounter these questions again, under the heading **Looking Back.** Use this list as a self-test; if you can't answer a question, go to the page indicated after the question and review the material. Sample answers to these questions can be found in the Study Guide for this text.

• In Chapter 1, we will introduce you to the **basic guidelines of critical and creative thinking**—the principles we hope will help you learn the difference between unsupported claims or "psychobabble" and good, scientific reasoning. The identifying symbol for critical thinking is a lightbulb, like the one here. Throughout the book, some (but not all) of our **critical-thinking discussions** are signaled in the text by a small yellow "tab" that includes the lightbulb and the topic being critically examined (such as "Think-

Thinking Critically About Love

ing Critically About Love"). We will be telling you about many lively and passionate debates in psychology—about sex and gender differences, therapy, memory, and many other topics—and we hope our coverage of these debates will increase your involvement with the ongoing discoveries of psychology.

• Every chapter contains several **Quick Quizzes** that test your understanding, retention, and ability to apply what you have read to examples. Do not let the word "quiz" give you a sinking feeling. These quizzes are for your practical use and, we hope, for your enjoyment. When you have trouble with a question, do not go on; pause right then and there, review what you have read, and then try again.

Some of the Quick Quizzes contain a *critical-thinking item,* denoted by the lightbulb symbol. The answers we give for these items are only suggestions; feel free to come up with different ones. Quick Quizzes containing critical-thinking items are not really so quick, because they ask you to reflect on what you have read and to apply the guidelines to critical thinking described in Chapter 1. But if you take the time to respond thoughtfully to them, we think you will become more engaged with the material, learn more, and become a more sophisticated user of psychology.

• At the end of each chapter, a feature called **Taking Psychology with You** draws on research to suggest ways of applying what you have learned to everyday problems and concerns, such as how to boost your motivation, improve your memory, and become more creative, as well as more urgent ones, such as how to live with chronic pain or help a friend who seems suicidal.

HOW TO STUDY

In our years of teaching, we have found that certain study strategies can vastly improve learning, and so we offer the following suggestions. (Reading Chapter 7, on memory, and Chapter 8, on learning, will also be helpful.)

• Before starting the book, read *Contents at a Glance* (p. v) to get an overall view of the book's organization. Before starting a chapter, read the chapter title and outline to get an idea of what is in store. Browse through the chapter, looking at the pictures and reading the headings.

• Do not read the text as you might read a novel, taking in large chunks at a sitting. To get the most from your studying, we recommend that you read only a part of each chapter at a time.

• Instead of simply reading silently, nodding along saying "hmmmmm" to yourself, try to restate what you have read in your own words at the end of each major section. Some people find it helpful to write down main points on a piece of paper or on index cards. Others prefer to recite main points aloud to someone else—or even a patient pet. Do not count on getting by with just one reading of a chapter. Most people need to go through the material at least twice, and then review the main points several times before an exam.

• When you have finished a chapter, read the **Summary.** (Some students tell us they find it useful to write down their own summaries first,

then compare them with the book's.) Use the **Key Terms** list at the end of each chapter as a checklist. Try to define and discuss each term in the list to see how well you understand and remember it. If you need to review a term, a page number is given to tell you where it is first mentioned in the chapter. Finally, review the **Looking Back** questions to be sure you can answer them.

• Important new terms in this textbook are printed in **boldface** and defined in the margin of the page on which they appear or on the facing page. The **marginal glossary** permits you to find these terms and concepts easily, and will help you when you study for exams. A complete glossary also appears at the end of the book.

• The **Study Guide** for this book, available at your bookstore, is an excellent learning resource. It contains review materials, exercises, and practice tests to help you understand and apply the concepts in the book.

• If you are assigned a term project or a report, you may need to track down some references or do further reading. Throughout the book, discussions of studies and theories include *citations* that look like this: (Aardvark & Zebra, 1997). A citation tells you who the authors of a book, article, or paper are and when the work was published. The full reference can then be looked up in the alphabetical **Bibliography** at the end of the book. At the back of the book you will also find an *Author Index* and a *Subject Index*. The author index lists the name of every author cited and the pages where each person's work is discussed. If you remember the name of a psychologist but not where he or she was mentioned, look up the name in the author index. The subject index lists all the major topics mentioned in the book. If you want to review material on, say, depression, you can look up "depression" in the subject index and find each place it is mentioned.

We have done our utmost to convey our own enthusiasm about psychology, but, in the end, it is your efforts as much as ours that will determine whether you find psychology to be exciting or boring, and whether the field will make a difference in your own life. This book is our way of inviting you into the world of psychology—our warmest welcome!

Carole Wade
Carol Tavris

Carole Wade earned her Ph.D. in cognitive psychology at Stanford University. She began her academic career at the University of New Mexico; was professor of psychology for ten years at San Diego Mesa College; then taught at College of Marin; and currently teaches undergraduate courses in psychology at Dominican College of San Rafael. She is coauthor, with Carol Tavris, of *Psychology*, Fifth Edition; *Psychology in Perspective*, Second Edition; *Critical and Creative Thinking: The Case of Love and War*; and *The Longest War: Sex Differences in Perspective*. Dr. Wade has a long-standing interest in making psychology accessible to students and the general public through public lectures, workshops, general interest articles, and the electronic media. For many years she has focused her efforts on the teaching and promotion of critical-thinking skills and the enhancement of undergraduate education in psychology. She chaired the APA Board of Educational Affairs's Task Force on Diversity Issues at the Precollege and Undergraduate Levels of Education in Psychology. She is also a past chair of the APA's Public Information Committee and served on the APA's Committee on Undergraduate Education and the Steering Committee for the APA's National Conference on Enhancing the Quality of Undergraduate Education. Dr. Wade is a Fellow of the American Psychological Association, and is a charter member of the American Psychological Society.

Carol Tavris earned her Ph.D. in the interdisciplinary program in social psychology at the University of Michigan, and ever since has sought to bring research from the many fields of psychology to the public. She is author of *The Mismeasure of Woman*, which won the Distinguished Media Contribution Award from the American Association of Applied and Preventive Psychology, and the Heritage Publications Award from Division 35 of the APA. Dr. Tavris is also the author of *Anger: The Misunderstood Emotion* and coauthor with Carole Wade of *Psychology*, Fifth Edition; *Psychology in Perspective*, Second Edition; *Critical and Creative Thinking: The Case of Love and War*; and *The Longest War: Sex Differences in Perspective*. She has written on psychological topics for many magazines, journals, edited books, and newspapers, notably the *Los Angeles Times* and the *New York Times*. A highly regarded lecturer, she has given keynote addresses and workshops on, among other topics, critical thinking, pseudoscience in psychology, anger, gender, and psychology and the media. She has taught in the psychology department at UCLA and at the Human Relations Center of the New School for Social Research in New York. Dr. Tavris is a Fellow of the American Psychological Association; a charter Fellow of the American Psychological Society; and a Fellow of the Committee for the Scientific Investigation of Claims of the Paranormal.

Invitation to Psychology

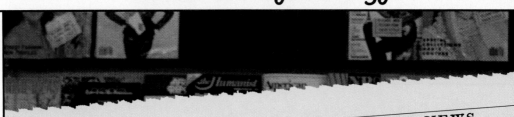

1

What Is Psychology?

PSYCHOLOGY IN THE NEWS

Linda Finch, who will re-create and complete Amelia Earhart's ill-fated flight, waves to a crowd of supporters.

Scientists Successfully Clone a Sheep

EDINBURGH, SCOTLAND. Scientists at the Roslin Institute have announced the cloning of a sheep named Dolly from the cell of an adult animal, and alarm bells are going off around the globe. People everywhere are asking: Will we soon be cloning ourselves? What will it mean to have another you in the world (not to mention another ewe)?

Child Rescued from Trapped Car

TIFTON, GA. Six men and a woman in Georgia risked their lives to rescue a 4-year-old who had become trapped in his grandmother's car when it rolled into a frigid pond. Three of the rescuers nearly drowned before one man was able to break the car window with a hammer and save the child.

Texas Woman to Re-create Earhart's Around-the-World Flight

WASHINGTON, D.C. A Texas woman, Linda Finch, 45, has announced plans to re-create the legendary flight of Amelia Earhart, the famed aviator who disappeared in 1937 in an attempt to be the first person to fly around the world at the equator. Finch said she would use the same kind of plane, in part to "teach children they can and should dream big dreams."

James Burmeister

Skinhead Convicted of Racist Murders

FAYETTEVILLE, N.C. Jurors in North Carolina today sentenced former paratrooper James Burmeister, convicted of murdering an African-American couple, to two life terms. Burmeister, 21, did not know the victims. He shot them to earn a spiderweb tattoo, a sign among skinheads at Fort Bragg that the wearer had killed a black person.

Californians Oppose Same-Sex Marriage but Support Gay Rights

SAN FRANCISCO, CA. A statewide poll finds that most Californians approve of granting family legal rights to gay and lesbian domestic partners and giving them the same pension, health, and family leave benefits as heterosexuals have. Yet over half object to laws allowing gay men and lesbians to marry members of their own sex.

San Francisco Mayor Willie Brown has conducted domestic partner ceremonies for gay and lesbian couples—but a new poll finds public disapproval of gay marriages.

If you were reading a newspaper in early 1997, you would have come across the five stories shown here. The events they describe are not terribly unusual: Newspapers and magazines are full of similar tales of heroism and courage, murder and mayhem, intellectual accomplishment and emotional controversies. So why, you may be wondering, are we beginning this book with these stories? What do they have to do with psychology? The answer is: everything.

Most people, when they hear the word *psychology*, think about mental and emotional disorders, abnormal acts and motivations, and psychotherapy. But psychologists take as their subject the entire spectrum of beautiful and brutish things that human beings do—the kinds of things you read or hear about every day. Psychologists reading the above stories would want to know what cloning might tell us about the influence of experience versus genetics on behavior. They would want to find out why some people, although perfectly pleasant to friends and relatives, burn with hatred for people of different ethnicities, religions, or nationalities; and why some people put their own lives in jeopardy to help strangers in distress. They would wonder how people can hold contradictory opinions about emotional topics such as homosexuality without recognizing any conflict. And they would be curious about the reasons that some individuals confidently pursue their dreams—such as taking a 26,000-mile journey in a two-engine plane—whereas others succumb to apathy and pessimism.

If you want to know what psychologists study, then, a newspaper is as good a place as any to start! Newspapers, of course, tend to focus on behavior that is unusual in some way; after all, that's what makes it newsworthy. Psychology, however, is not just about martyrs and murderers, heroes and haters. Psychologists are also interested in how human beings—and other animals, too—learn, remember, solve problems, perceive, feel, and get along with others. Psychologists are as likely to study commonplace experiences as exceptional ones—experiences as ordinary as rearing children, gossiping, remembering a shopping list, daydreaming, making love, and making a living.

If you have ever wondered what makes people tick, then you are in the right course. We invite you now to step into the world of psychology, the discipline that dares to explore the most complex topic on earth: *you.*

What's Ahead

- *What's the difference between psychology and plain old common sense?*

- *How old is the science of psychology?*

- *What are the five major perspectives in modern psychology?*

THE SCIENCE OF PSYCHOLOGY

psychology
The scientific study of behavior and mental processes and how they are affected by an organism's physical state, mental state, and external environment; the term is often represented by ψ, the Greek letter psi (usually pronounced "sy").

Over the years, **psychology** has been defined in various ways, but most psychologists today would define it as *the scientific study of behavior and mental processes and how they are affected by an organism's physical state, mental state, and external environment.*

This brief definition, however, is a little like defining a car as a vehicle for transporting people from one place to another, without telling you how a car differs from a train or a bus, how a Ford differs from a Ferrari, or how a catalytic converter works. To get a clearer picture of what psychology is, you are going to need to learn about its methods, its findings, and its ways of interpreting information.

Psychology, Pseudoscience, and Common Sense

Let's begin by considering what psychology is *not.* First, the psychology that you are about to study bears little relation to the popular psychology ("pop psych") found in many self-help books or on TV talk shows. Serious psychology is more complex, more informative, and, we think, far more helpful because its principles are based on rigorous research and verifiable evidence. The public's appetite for psychological information has created a huge market for what R. D. Rosen (1977) called "psychobabble"—pseudoscience and quackery covered by a veneer of psychological language. Today, more than ever, when so many simplistic pop-psych ideas have filtered into public consciousness, education, and even the law, people need to distinguish between psychobabble and serious psychology.

Second, serious psychology differs radically from such nonscientific competitors as astrology, graphology, fortune telling, and numerology. Like psychologists, promoters of these competing systems try to explain human problems and predict people's behavior; if you are having romantic problems, for example, an astrologer may advise you to choose an Aries instead of an Aquarius as your next love, and a "past-lives channeler" may say it's because you were jilted in a previous life. But when put to the test, the claims of psychics, astrologers, and the like turn out to be vague or untestable, and their predictions dead wrong (Dean, 1987; Rowe, 1993).

Third, psychology is not just a fancy name for common sense. It is true that psychological re-

Get Involved

To get an idea of just how broad a discipline psychology is, take any newspaper and circle the headlines of those stories about which psychology might be able to offer insights. Don't skip the sports, business, and "people" sections! How many headlines did you mark?

I see you as being less gullible in the future.

Studying psychology can make this prediction come true.

search sometimes confirms what people commonly believe. When that happens, it may be tempting to conclude that scientific studies are a waste of time and money. Often, though, the obviousness of a psychological finding is only an illusion. Armed with the wisdom of hindsight, people may maintain that they "knew it all along" when in fact they did not.

Indeed, psychological research often produces findings that contradict common sense. For example, according to popular belief, early experiences determine how a person turns out, for better or for worse; people speak of their "formative years" and the supposedly lifelong effects of childhood traumas. Yet, as we will see in later chapters, many abilities and attributes can change throughout life in response to new situations; and even children traumatized by abuse, neglect, or war can become happy, secure adults if their circumstances improve (Garmezy, 1991; Werner, 1989).

You will be learning about many other findings that violate current "common sense." Are unhappy memories "repressed" and then accurately recalled years later, as if they had been tape recorded? Are most abused children destined to become abusive parents themselves? Do policies of abstinence from alcohol reduce rates of alcoholism? All of these common beliefs are contradicted by the evidence.

On the other hand, psychological findings do not have to be surprising to be important. Psychologists also seek to extend and deepen our understanding of generally accepted facts. After all, long before the laws of gravity were discovered, people knew that an apple would fall to the ground if it dropped from a tree. But it took Isaac Newton to discover the principles that explain why the apple falls and why it travels at a particu-

lar speed while falling. Psychologists, too, strive to deepen our understanding of an already familiar world.

The Birth of Modern Psychology

Most of the great thinkers of history, from Aristotle to Zoroaster, raised questions that today would be called psychological. They wanted to know how people take in information through their senses, solve problems, and become motivated to act in brave or villainous ways. They wondered about the elusive nature of emotion and whether it controls us or is something we can control. Like modern psychologists, they wanted to *describe, predict, understand,* and *modify* behavior in order to add to human knowledge and increase human happiness. But unlike modern psychologists, scholars of the past did not rely heavily on **empirical** evidence—evidence gathered by careful observation, experimentation, and measurement. Often, their observations were based simply on anecdotes or descriptions of individual cases.

This does not mean that the forerunners of modern psychology were always wrong. Even without scientific methods, the great thinkers of history often had insights and made observations that were verified by later work. Hippocrates (c. 460 B.C.–c. 377 B.C.), the Greek physician known as the founder of modern medicine, observed patients with head injuries and inferred that the brain must be the ultimate source of "our pleasures, joys, laughter, and jests as well as our sorrows, pains, griefs, and tears." And so it is. In the first century A.D., the Stoic philosophers observed that people do not become angry or sad or anxious because of actual events but because of their explanations of those events. And so they do. In the seventeenth century, the French philosopher René Descartes (1596–1650) helped to promote scientific thinking by searching for physical explanations of behavior. Later in the same century, the English philosopher John Locke (1643–1704) argued that the mind works by associating ideas arising from experience, a notion that continues to influence many psychologists today.

But without empirical methods, the forerunners of psychology also committed some terrible blunders. A good example comes from the early 1800s, when the theory of *phrenology* (Greek for "study of the mind") became wildly popular. Inspired by the writings and lectures of Austrian physician Joseph Gall (1758–1828), phrenologists

empirical

Relying on or derived from observation, experimentation, or measurement.

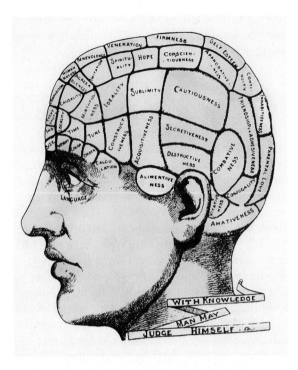

Bumpy logic? Phrenology, a nineteenth-century fad that was unsupported by any empirical evidence, linked bumps on the skull with character traits. On this phrenological "map," notice the tiny space allocated to self-esteem and the large one devoted to cautiousness!

argued that different brain areas accounted for specific character and personality traits, such as "stinginess" and "religiosity," and that such traits could be "read" from bumps on the skull. Thieves, for example, supposedly had large bumps above the ears. When phrenologists examined people who had "stealing bumps" but who were *not* thieves, they explained away this counterevidence by saying that other bumps represented positive traits that were holding the person's thieving impulses in check. Phrenology was a classic pseudoscience—sheer nonsense.

During the nineteenth century, several pioneering researchers began to study psychological issues using scientific methods. And in 1879, the first psychological laboratory was officially established, in Leipzig, Germany, by Wilhelm Wundt (VIL-helm Voont). Wundt, who was trained in medicine and philosophy, promoted a method called *trained introspection,* in which specially trained volunteers carefully observed, analyzed, and described their own sensations, mental images, and emotional reactions. Once trained, Wundt's introspectors might take as long as 20 minutes to report their inner experiences during a 1.5-second experiment. The goal was to break be-

havior down into its most basic elements, much as a chemist might analyze water into hydrogen plus oxygen. Eventually, most psychologists rejected trained introspection as too subjective, but Wundt still gets the credit for formally initiating the movement to make psychology into a science.

Another early approach to scientific psychology, called **functionalism,** emphasized the function, or purpose, of behavior, instead of its analysis and description. One of functionalism's leaders was William James (1842–1910), an American philosopher, physician, and psychologist. Attempting to grasp the nature of the mind through introspection, wrote James (1890/1950), is "like seizing a spinning top to catch its motion, or trying to turn up the gas quickly enough to see how the darkness looks." Inspired in part by the evolutionary theories of British naturalist Charles Darwin (1809–1882), James and other functionalists instead asked how various actions help a person or animal adapt to the environment. This emphasis on the causes and consequences of behavior was to set the course of psychological science.

Psychology also has roots in Vienna, Austria, where it first developed as a method of psychotherapy. As Sigmund Freud, who was a neurologist by training, listened to his patients' reports of depression, nervousness, and obsessive habits, he became convinced that many of their symptoms had mental, not bodily, causes. His patients' distress was due, he concluded, to conflicts, memories, and emotional traumas going back to early childhood. Freud's ideas eventually evolved into a broad theory of personality, and both his theory and his methods of treating people with emotional problems became known as *psychoanalysis.*

From these early beginnings in philosophy, natural science, and medicine, psychology has grown into a complex field encompassing different specialties, perspectives, methods, and training. Psychology today is like a large, sprawling family. The members of this family share common great-grandparents, but some of the cousins have formed alliances, some are quarreling, and a few are barely speaking to one another!

Psychology's Present

Five major theoretical perspectives now predominate in psychology. These approaches reflect different questions that psychologists ask about human behavior, different assumptions about how the mind works, and, most important, different kinds of explanations of why people do what they do.

functionalism

An early psychological approach that emphasized the function or purpose of behavior and consciousness.

1. The *biological perspective* focuses on how bodily events affect behavior, feelings, and thoughts. Electrical impulses shoot along the intricate pathways of the nervous system. Hormones course through the bloodstream, signaling internal organs to slow down or speed up. Chemical substances flow across the tiny gaps that separate one microscopic brain cell from another. *Biological psychologists* want to know how these bodily events interact with events in the external environment to produce perceptions, memories, and behavior.

2. The *learning perspective* is concerned with how the environment and experience affect our actions. Within this perspective, *behaviorists* focus on the environmental conditions—the rewards and punishers—that maintain or discourage specific behaviors. Behaviorists do not invoke the mind to explain behavior; they prefer to stick to what they can observe and measure directly. *Social-learning theorists,* on the other hand, combine elements of classic behaviorism with research on thoughts, values, and intentions. They believe that people learn not only by adapting their behavior to the environment, but also by imitating others and by thinking about the events happening around them.

3. The *cognitive perspective* emphasizes what goes on in people's heads—how people reason, remember, understand language, solve problems, explain experiences, and form beliefs. (The word *cognitive* comes from the Latin for "to know.") One of the most important contributions of this perspective has been to show that our explanations and perceptions affect what we do and feel. All of us are constantly seeking to make sense of the world and of our own physical and mental states. Our ideas may not always be realistic or sensible, but they continually influence our actions and choices.

4. The *psychodynamic perspective* deals with unconscious dynamics within the individual, such as inner forces, conflicts, or instinctual energy. This approach is associated most closely with psychoanalysis, but many other psychodynamic theories also exist. Psychodynamic psychologists try to dig below the surface of a person's behavior to get to the roots of personality; they think of themselves as archeologists of the mind. As we will see, psychodynamic psychology is the thumb on the hand of psychology—connected to the other fingers, but also set apart from them because it differs radically from the others in its language, methods, and standards of acceptable evidence.

5. The *sociocultural perspective* goes beyond the study of the individual, focusing on how social and cultural forces shape every aspect of human behavior, from how (and whether!) we kiss to what and where we eat. Most of us underestimate the impact of other people, group affiliations, and cultural rules on our actions. We are like fish that are unaware they live in water, so obvious is water in their lives. Sociocultural psychologists study the water—the social and cultural environment we "swim" in every day.

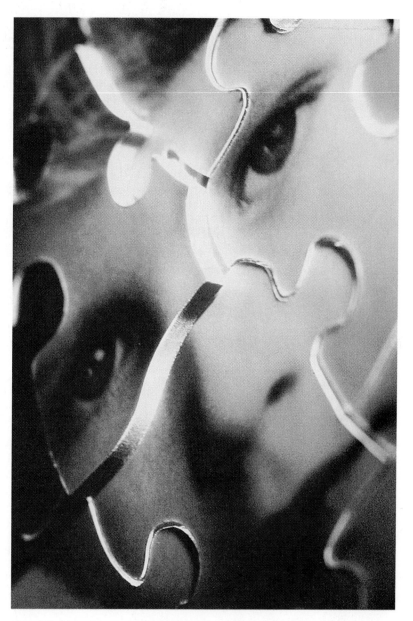

What makes us who we are? Psychologists approach questions about human behavior from five major perspectives: biological, learning, cognitive, psychodynamic, and sociocultural.

We will be encountering the major findings and methods of these five approaches in the rest of this book. The differences among these schools of thought are very real; a psychoanalyst's explanation of your personality will not be the same as a cognitive psychologist's, and neither account will be the same as a biological or learning psychologist's.

However, not all psychologists feel they must swear allegiance to one approach or another. Many, if not most, psychologists are *eclectic*, using what they believe to be the best features of diverse schools of thought. Moreover, whatever their theoretical convictions, most psychological scientists agree on certain basic guidelines about what is and what is not acceptable in their discipline. Nearly all reject supernatural explanations of events—evil spirits, psychic forces, miracles, and so forth. Most believe in the importance of gathering empirical evidence and not relying on hunches or personal belief. This insistence on rigorous standards of proof is what sets psychology apart from other, nonscientific explanations of human experience.

??? QUICK QUIZ

Anxiety is a common problem. To find out whether you understand the five major perspectives in psychology, match each possible explanation of anxiety on the left with a perspective on the right.

1. Anxious people often think about the future in distorted ways.

2. Anxiety is due to forbidden, unconscious desires.

3. Anxiety symptoms often bring hidden rewards, such as being excused from exams.

4. Excessive anxiety can be caused by a chemical imbalance.

5. A national emphasis on competition and success promotes anxiety about failure.

a. behavioral

b. psychodynamic

c. sociocultural

d. biological

e. cognitive

Answers:
1.e 2.b 3.a 4.d 5.c

What's Ahead

- *If someone tells you that he or she is a psychologist, why can't you assume the person is a therapist?*

- *If you decided to call yourself a "psychotherapist," would doing so be legal?*

- *How can you distinguish a clinical psychologist from a psychiatrist?*

WHAT PSYCHOLOGISTS DO

Now you know the main viewpoints that guide psychologists in their work. But what do they actually do with their time between breakfast and dinner?

The professional activities of psychologists generally fall into three broad categories: (1) teaching and doing research in colleges and universities; (2) providing health or mental health services, often referred to as *psychological practice;* and (3) conducting research and applying its findings in nonacademic settings such as business, sports, government, law, and the military (see Table 1.1). Many psychologists move flexibly across these areas. Some, for instance, do research and also provide counseling services in a mental health setting, such as a research hospital. Some work in universities and also serve as professional consultants in legal cases or to government policymakers.

Psychological Research

Most psychologists who do research have doctoral degrees (Ph.D.s or Ed.D.s, doctorates in educa-

Table 1.1	What Is a Psychologist?	
A psychologist has an advanced degree; many psychologists are psychotherapists (clinicians), but others do research, teach, work in business, or consult.		
Academic/Research Psychologists	**Clinical Psychologists**	**Psychologists in Industry, Law, or Other Settings**
Specialize in areas of pure or applied research, such as:	*May work in any of these settings, or in some combination:*	*Do research or serve as consultants to institutions on, for example:*
Human development	Private practice	Sports
Psychometrics (testing)	Mental health clinics or services	Consumer issues
Health	Hospitals	Advertising
Education	Research laboratories	Organizational problems
Industrial/organizational psychology	Colleges and universities	Environmental issues
Consumer psychology		Public policy
Physiological psychology		Survey research and opinion polls
Perception and sensation		

tion). Some, seeking knowledge for its own sake, work in **basic psychology;** others, concerned with the practical uses of knowledge, work in **applied psychology.** A psychologist doing basic research might ask, "How do children, adolescents, and adults differ in their approach to moral issues such as honesty?" An applied psychologist might ask, "How can knowledge about moral development be used to prevent teenage violence?" A psychologist in basic science might ask, "Can a chimpanzee or a gorilla learn to use sign language?" An applied psychologist might ask, "Can techniques used to teach sign language to a chimpanzee be used to help mentally impaired or disturbed children who do not speak?"

Most of the findings you will be reading about in this book come from the efforts of research psychologists, so you can get a good idea of what they study by scanning the Table of Contents on pages vii to xi. Psychologists doing basic and applied research have made important contributions in areas as diverse as health, education, child development, testing, conflict resolution, marketing, industrial design, worker productivity, and urban planning.

Psychological Practice

Psychological practitioners, whose goal is to understand and improve physical and mental health,
work in mental hospitals, general hospitals, clinics, schools, counseling centers, and private practice. Since the late 1970s, the proportion of psychologists who are practitioners has steadily increased; today, practitioners account for well over two-thirds of new psychology doctorates and members of the American Psychological Association (APA), psychology's largest professional organization (Shapiro & Wiggins, 1994). Some practitioners are *counseling psychologists,* who generally help people deal with problems of everyday life, such as test anxiety, family conflicts, or low job motivation. Others are *school psychologists,* who work with parents, teachers, and students to enhance students' performance and resolve emotional difficulties. The majority, however, are *clinical psychologists,* who diagnose, treat, and study mental or emotional problems. Clinical psychologists are trained to do psychotherapy with severely disturbed people, as well as with those who are simply unhappy and want to learn to handle their problems better.

In almost all states, a license to practice clinical psychology requires a doctorate. Most clinical psychologists have a Ph.D., some have an Ed.D., and a smaller but growing number have a Psy.D. (doctorate in psychology, pronounced "sy-dee"). Clinical psychologists typically do four or five years of graduate work in psychology, plus at least a year's internship under the direction of a practicing psychologist. Clinical programs leading to a Ph.D. or

basic psychology
The study of psychological issues in order to seek knowledge for its own sake rather than for its practical application.

applied psychology
The study of psychological issues that have direct practical significance and the application of psychological findings.

Ed.D. are usually designed to prepare a person both as a scientist and as a clinical practitioner; they require completion of a dissertation, a major research project that contributes to knowledge in the field. Programs leading to a Psy.D. focus on professional practice and do not usually require a dissertation, although they do require the student to complete a research study, theoretical paper, literature review, or other scholarly project.

People often confuse the terms *psychotherapist, psychoanalyst, clinical psychologist,* and *psychiatrist,* but these terms mean different things. A *psychotherapist* is anyone who does any kind of psychotherapy. The term is not legally regulated; in fact, in most states, anyone can say that he or she is a "therapist" of one sort or another without having any training at all. A *psychoanalyst* is a person who practices one particular form of therapy, psychoanalysis. To call yourself a psychoanalyst, you must have an advanced degree (usually an M.D. or Ph.D.), get specialized training at a psychoanalytic institute, and undergo extensive psychoanalysis yourself. *Psychiatrists* are medical doctors (M.D.s) who have done a three-year residency in psychiatry, to learn to diagnose and treat mental disorders under the supervision of more experienced physicians. Some psychiatrists go on to do research on mental problems, such as depression or schizophrenia, rather than work with patients.

Psychiatrists and clinical psychologists do similar work, but psychiatrists, because of their medical training, tend to focus on possible biological causes of mental disorders and to treat these problems with medication. They can write prescriptions, and clinical psychologists cannot (at least not yet; in many states, psychologists are pressing for prescription-writing privileges). Psychiatrists, however, are often untrained in psychological theories and methods. These differences can affect approaches to diagnosis and treatment. For example, if a patient is depressed, a psychiatrist will tend to look for biochemical causes. A clinical psychologist is more likely to look for psychological and social origins of the depression.

Social workers, school counselors, and marriage, family, and child counselors also do mental-health work. These professionals ordinarily treat general problems in adjustment, rather than serious mental disturbance, although their work may bring them into contact with people with serious problems who would not otherwise seek professional help—violent delinquents, sex offenders, individuals involved in domestic and child abuse. Licensing requirements vary from state to state but usually include a master's degree in psychology or social work and one or two years of supervised experience. (For a summary of the types of psychotherapists and the training they receive, see Table 1.2.)

Many research psychologists are worried about an increase in poorly trained psychotherapists across America (Dawes, 1994; Poole et al., 1995). Many of these therapists are unschooled in research methods and the empirical findings of psychology, and they use therapy techniques that have not been tested and validated. Some practitioners, too, are concerned about the lack of a uniform, national standard of professional education (Fox, 1994). Such concerns contributed to the formation, in 1987, of the American Psychological

Table 1.2	Types of Psychotherapists
Psychotherapist	A person who does psychotherapy; may have anything from no degree to an advanced professional degree; the term is unregulated
Clinical psychologist	Has a Ph.D., Ed.D., or Psy.D.
Psychoanalyst	Has specific training in psychoanalysis after an advanced degree (M.D. or Ph.D.)
Psychiatrist	A medical doctor (M.D.) with a specialty in psychiatry
Licensed social worker (LSW); school psychologist; marriage, family, and child counselor (MFCC)	Licensing requirements vary; generally has at least an M.A. in psychology or social work

Society, an organization devoted to the needs and interests of psychology as a science. Many practitioners, on the other hand, argue that psychotherapy is an art, and that therefore research findings are largely irrelevant to the work they do with clients. In Chapter 11, we will return to the important issue of the widening gap in training and attitudes between scientists and some therapists.

Partly because of these tensions, and partly because the media and the public persist in equating "psychologist" with "psychotherapist," some psychological scientists think it is time to use other labels to describe what they do and to yield the word *psychologist* to its popular meaning. Research psychologists, they say, should call themselves "cognitive scientists," "behavioral scientists," "neuroscientists," and so forth, depending on their area of study. This change in language is already underway. At present, however, the word *psychologist* still embraces all the cousins in psychology's sprawling family.

Psychology in the Community

In recent decades, psychology has expanded rapidly in terms of scholars, publications, and specialties. The American Psychological Association now has 50 divisions. Some of these divisions represent major fields such as developmental psychology and physiological psychology. Others represent specific research or professional interests, such as the psychology of women, ethnic minority issues, sports, the arts, environmental concerns, gay and lesbian issues, peace, psychology and the law, and health.

As psychology has expanded, many psychologists have found ways to contribute to their communities in about as many fields as you can think of. They consult with companies to improve worker satisfaction. They establish programs to improve race relations and reduce ethnic tensions. They advise commissions on how pollution and noise affect mental health. They do research for

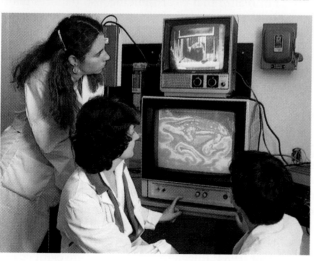

Psychological researchers and practitioners work in many settings, from classrooms to courtrooms. Clockwise, from lower left: Patricia Goldman-Rakic and her colleagues use technology to study the brain mechanisms underlying memory; a clinical psychologist helps a couple in therapy; and Louis Herman studies a dolphin's ability to understand an artificial language comprised of hand signals. In response to the gestural sequence "person" and "over," the dolphin will leap over the person in the pool.

the military. They do rehabilitation training for people who are physically or mentally disabled. They educate judges and juries about the reliability of eyewitness testimony. They assist the police in emergencies involving hostages or disturbed persons. They conduct public-opinion surveys.

They run suicide-prevention hot lines. They advise zoos on the care and training of animals. They help coaches improve the athletic performances of their teams. And on and on.

Is it any wonder that many people are a little fuzzy about what a psychologist is?

??? QUICK QUIZ

Can you match the specialties on the left with their defining credentials and approaches on the right?

1. psychotherapist

2. psychiatrist

3. clinical psychologist

4. research psychologist

5. psychoanalyst

a. Has M.D. or Ph.D. and training in an approach started by Freud

b. Has Ph.D., Psy.D., or Ed.D. and does research on, or psychotherapy for, mental-health problems

c. May have any credential or none

d. Has advanced degree (usually a Ph.D.) and does applied or basic research

e. Has M.D.; tends to take a medical approach to emotional problems

Answers: 1.c 2.e 3.b 4.d 5.a

| What's Ahead |

- *What guidelines can you use to tell whether a psychological claim is merely psychobabble?*

- *Why is a psychological theory unscientific if it explains anything that could conceivably happen?*

- *What's wrong with drawing conclusions about behavior from a collection of anecdotes?*

CRITICAL AND SCIENTIFIC THINKING IN PSYCHOLOGY

One of the greatest benefits of studying psychology is that you learn not only how the brain works in general but also how to use yours in particular—by thinking critically. **Critical thinking** is the ability and willingness to assess claims and make objective judgments on the basis of well-supported reasons. It is the ability to look for flaws in arguments and to resist claims that have no

supporting evidence. Critical thinking, however, is not merely negative thinking. It also requires the ability to be *creative and constructive*—to come up with possible explanations for events, think of implications of research findings, and apply new knowledge to social and personal problems.

These days, most people know that you have to exercise the body to keep it in shape, but they may not realize that clear thinking also requires effort and practice—that unlike breathing, it's not automatic. All around us we can see examples of flabby thinking. Sometimes people justify their mental laziness by proudly telling you they are open-minded. "It's good to be open-minded," philosopher Jacob Needleman once replied, "but not so open that your brains fall out."

Critical thinking is not only indispensable in ordinary life; it is also the basis of all science, including psychological science. By exercising critical-thinking skills, you will be able to distinguish true psychology from the psychobabble that clutters the airwaves and bookstores. Some of these skills involve the rules of logic, but others are also important (Ennis, 1985; Halpern, 1995; Levy, 1997; Paul, 1984; Ruggiero, 1991). Here are eight essen-

critical thinking

The ability and willingness to assess claims and to make objective judgments on the basis of well-supported reasons.

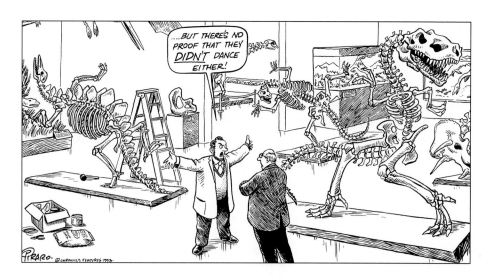

It is not enough to say that something "could be" true; critical thinkers demand that claims be supported by evidence.

tial critical-thinking guidelines that we will be emphasizing throughout this book.

Ask Questions; Be Willing to Wonder.   What is the one kind of question that most exasperates parents of young children? "Why is the sky blue, Mommy?" "Why doesn't the plane fall?" "Why don't pigs have wings?" Unfortunately, as children grow up, they tend to stop asking "why" questions. (Why do you think this is?)

"The trigger mechanism for creative thinking is the disposition to be curious, to wonder, to inquire," observed Vincent Ruggiero (1988). "Asking 'What's wrong here?' and/or 'Why is this the way it is, and how did it come to be that way?' leads to the identification of problems and challenges." We hope that you will not approach psychology as received wisdom but will ask many questions about the theories and findings we present in this book. Be on the lookout, too, for questions about human behavior that are not answered. If you do that, you will not only be learning psychology, but you will also be learning to think the way psychologists do.

Define Your Terms.   Once you have raised a question, the next step is to identify the issues in clear, concrete terms. Vague or inadequate terms in a question can lead to misleading or incomplete answers. For example, asking, "Can animals learn language?" allows for only two possible answers: yes or no. But putting the question another way—"Which aspects of language might certain animals be able to acquire?"—takes into account the fact that language requires many abilities, and that cognitive differences exist among species.

For scientists, defining terms means being precise about just what it is that they're studying. Researchers often start out with a **hypothesis,** a statement that attempts to describe or explain a given behavior, and initially, this hypothesis may be stated quite generally, as in, say, "Misery loves company." But before any research can be done, the hypothesis must be made more precise. For example, "Misery loves company" might be rephrased as "People who are anxious about a threatening situation tend to seek out others facing the same threat." A hypothesis, in turn, leads to explicit predictions about what will happen in a particular situation. In a prediction, terms such as *anxiety* or *threatening situation* are given **operational definitions,** specifications about how the phenomena in question are to be observed and measured. *Anxiety* might be defined operationally as a score on an anxiety questionnaire; *threatening situation* might be defined as the threat of an electric shock. The prediction might be, "If you raise people's anxiety scores by telling them they are going to receive electric shocks, and then you give them the choice of waiting alone or with others in the same situation, they will be more likely to choose to wait with others than they would be if they were not anxious." The prediction can then be tested.

Examine the Evidence.   Have you ever heard someone in the heat of argument exclaim, "I just know it's true, no matter what you say" or "That's my opinion; nothing's going to change it"? Have you ever made such statements yourself? Accepting a conclusion without evidence, or expecting others to do so, is a sure sign of uncritical thinking. A critical thinker asks, "What evidence supports or

hypothesis

A statement that attempts to predict or to account for a set of phenomena; scientific hypotheses specify relationships among events or variables and are empirically tested.

operational definition

A precise definition of a term in a hypothesis, which specifies the operations for observing and measuring the process or phenomenon being defined.

refutes this argument and its opposition? How reliable is the evidence?" If the critical thinker cannot check the reliability of the evidence directly, the person considers whether it came from a reliable source.

In scientific research, an idea may initially generate excitement because it is plausible, imaginative, or appealing, but eventually it must be backed by empirical evidence if it is to be taken seriously. A collection of anecdotes or an appeal to authority will not do.

Here's an example involving childhood autism, a serious mental disorder. Autistic children often will not look you in the eye; they live in a silent world of their own, cut off from normal social interaction. They may rock back and forth for hours, and sometimes they do self-destructive things, such as poking pencils in their ears. At one time, many clinicians thought that autism was caused by a rejecting, cold "refrigerator mother." They were influenced by the writings of the eminent psychoanalyst Bruno Bettelheim, especially his

principle of falsifiability
The principle that a scientific theory must make predictions that expose the theory to the possibility of disconfirmation; that is, the theory must predict not only what will happen, but also what will not happen.

When demonstrating "levitation" and other "magical phenomena," illusionists such as André Kole exploit people's tendency to trust the evidence of their own eyes even when such evidence is misleading. Critical thinkers ask questions about the nature and reliability of the evidence for a phenomenon.

book *The Empty Fortress* (1967). Bettelheim's only evidence consisted of case studies of 3 autistic children whose mothers had a history of psychological problems, and brief allusions to 37 other cases he said he had treated—and he vastly exaggerated the number of children he cured (Pollak, 1997). Yet Bettelheim's authority was so great that many people accepted his claims despite his meager data.

Then some researchers began to have doubts about Bettelheim's ideas. They compared the parents of autistic children with parents who did not have an autistic child, using standardized tests of psychological adjustment and analyzing their data statistically. The results were clear: The two groups of parents did not differ in terms of personality traits or family life (DeMyer, 1975; Koegel et al., 1983). Bruno Bettelheim had been wrong, and because of his advice, thousands of parents had mistakenly felt responsible for their children's disorder, suffering needless guilt and remorse. Today, scientists generally agree that autism stems from a neurological problem rather than from any psychological problems of the parents.

Analyze Assumptions and Biases. Critical thinkers evaluate assumptions and biases in the books they read, the political speeches they hear, and the ads that bombard them every day. In science, too, a questioning attitude toward assumptions is an important step on the path toward understanding. Some of the greatest scientific advances have been made by those who dared to doubt what everyone else assumed to be true: that the sun revolves around the earth, that illness can be cured by applying leeches to the skin, that madness is a sign of demonic possession.

Critical thinkers are also willing to analyze and test their *own* assumptions (which is a lot harder than criticizing someone else's). In psychology, researchers put their assumptions to the test by stating a hypothesis in such a way that it can be *refuted*, or disproved by counterevidence. This principle, known as the **principle of falsifiability,** does not mean that the hypothesis *will* be disproved, only that it *could* be if contrary evidence were to be discovered. Another way of saying this is that a scientist must risk disconfirmation by predicting not only what will happen, but also what will *not* happen. In the "misery loves company" study, the hypothesis would be refuted if most anxious people went off alone to sulk and worry, or if anxiety had no effect on their behavior (see Figure 1.1). A willingness to make "risky" predictions forces the scientist to take such negative evi-

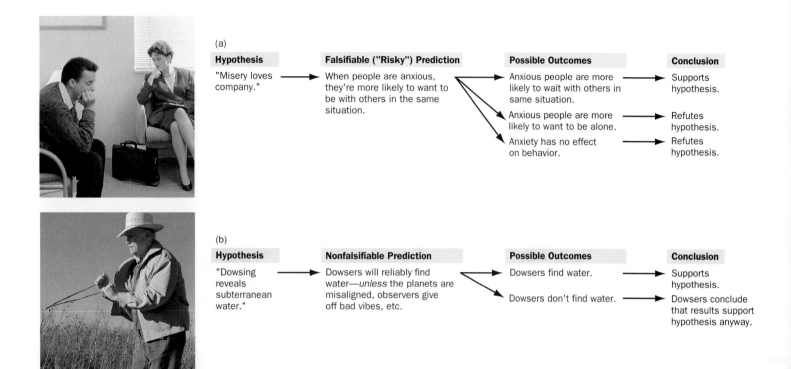

Figure 1.1

The Principle of Falsifiability

The scientific method requires researchers to expose their ideas to possible counterevidence, as in row *a*. In contrast, pseudoscientists and people claiming psychic powers, such as dowsers (who say they can find underground water with a "dowsing rod" that bends when water is present), typically interpret *all* possible outcomes as support for their assertions, as in row *b*. Therefore, their claims are untestable.

dence seriously and to abandon mistaken assumptions. Any researcher who refuses to go out on a limb and risk disconfirmation is not a true scientist; and any theory that purports to explain everything that could conceivably happen is unscientific.

If you keep your eyes open, you will find many violations of the principle of falsifiability by non-scientists. For example, some police officers and therapists believe that murderous satanic cults are widespread, even though research psychologists, the FBI, and police investigators have been unable to substantiate this claim (Goodman et al., 1995; Hicks, 1991). Believers say they are not surprised by the lack of evidence because satanic cults cover up their activities by eating bodies or burying them. The FBI's failure to find the evidence is "proof," they say, that the FBI is part of a conspiracy to support the satanists. To believers, then, the lack of evidence of satanic cults is actually a sign of the cults' success. But think about that claim. If a lack of evidence can count as evidence, then what could possibly count as *counter*evidence?

Avoid Emotional Reasoning: "If I Feel This Way, It Must Be True."   Emotion has a place in everyday critical thinking and in science, too. Passionate commitment to a view is the fuel of progress; it motivates people to think boldly, to defend unpopular ideas, and to seek evidence for creative new theories. But emotional conviction alone cannot settle arguments. As Nobel Prize–winning scientist Peter Medawar (1979) wrote, "The intensity of the conviction that a hypothesis is true has no bearing on whether it is true or not."

You probably already hold strong beliefs about child rearing, drugs, the causes of crime, racism, the origins of intelligence, gender differences, homosexuality, and many other issues of concern to psychologists. As you read this book, you may find yourself quarreling with findings that you dislike. Disagreement is fine; it means that you are reading actively. All we ask is that you think about why you are disagreeing: Is it because the results conflict with an assumption you hold dear or because the evidence is unpersuasive?

Don't Oversimplify. A critical thinker looks beyond the obvious, resists easy generalizations, and rejects either/or thinking. For example, is it better to feel you have control over what happens to you, or to accept with tranquility whatever life serves up? Either answer oversimplifies. As we will see in Chapter 12, control has many important benefits, but sometimes it's best to "go with the flow."

Often, in a disagreement, you will hear someone *arguing by anecdote*—generalizing from a personal experience or a few examples to everyone. One crime committed by a paroled ex-convict means that parole should be abolished; one friend who hates his or her school means that everybody who goes there hates it. Anecdotes are often the source of stereotyping as well: One dishonest welfare mother means they are all dishonest; one encounter with an unconventional Californian means they are all flaky. Critical and scientific thinkers want more evidence than one or two stories before drawing such sweeping conclusions.

Consider Other Interpretations. A critical thinker creatively formulates hypotheses that offer reasonable explanations of the topic at hand. In science, the goal is to arrive at a **theory,** an organized system of assumptions and principles that purports to explain certain phenomena and how they are related. A scientific theory is not just someone's personal opinion, as people imply when they say "It's only a theory." Theories that come to be accepted by the scientific community make as few assumptions as possible and account for many empirical findings (Stanovich, 1996).

Before settling on an explanation of some behavior, however, critical thinkers are careful not to shut out alternative possibilities. They generate as many interpretations of the evidence as they can before settling on the most likely one. For example, suppose a news bulletin reports that people who are chronically depressed are more likely than nondepressed people to develop cancer. Before you can conclude that depression causes cancer, you'll want to consider other possibilities. Perhaps the depressed people who were studied were more likely to smoke and drink too much, and those unhealthful habits caused the cancer. Or perhaps an early, undetected cancer was responsible for the feelings of depression.

Tolerate Uncertainty. Ultimately, learning to think critically teaches us one of the hardest lessons of life: how to live with uncertainty. Ex-

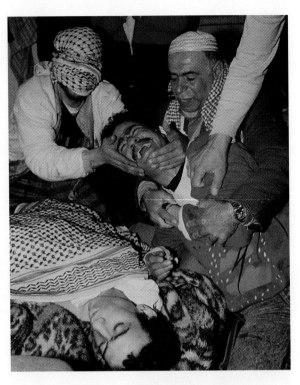

Critical thinkers consider competing explanations. For example, many North Americans believe that men are "naturally" less emotionally expressive than women, but cultural rules have a powerful influence on how men and women express their feelings, as we will see in Chapter 12. This Palestinian man, grieving over his dead son, does not fit Western stereotypes of male emotionality. (And your own culture's rules may be affecting how you react emotionally to this scene.)

amining the evidence before drawing conclusions is important, but sometimes there is little or no evidence available to examine. Sometimes the evidence permits only tentative conclusions. And sometimes the evidence seems good enough to permit strong conclusions . . . until, exasperatingly, new evidence throws our beliefs into disarray. Critical thinkers are willing to accept this state of uncertainty. They are not afraid to say, "I don't know" or "I'm not sure."

In science, tolerating uncertainty means that researchers are supposed to avoid drawing firm conclusions until other researchers have repeated, or *replicated,* their studies and verified their findings. A big "no-no" in science is to be secretive about your work; you must be willing to tell others where you got your ideas and how you tested them so that others can challenge you if they think you're wrong. Replication is an essential part of the scientific process because sometimes

theory
An organized system of assumptions and principles that purports to explain a specified set of phenomena and their interrelationships.

what seems to be a fabulous phenomenon turns out to be only a fluke.

The need to accept a certain amount of uncertainty does not mean that we must abandon all assumptions, beliefs, and convictions. That would be impossible, in any case: We all need values and principles to guide our actions. As Vincent Ruggiero (1988) wrote, "It is not the embracing of an idea that causes problems—it is the refusal to relax that embrace when good sense dictates doing so."

As you read this book, you will have many opportunities to think critically about psychological theories and about the personal and social issues that affect us all. From time to time, a yellow tab with a lightbulb symbol (like the one shown here) will highlight a discussion where one or more of the critical thinking guidelines just discussed is especially relevant. Also, in Quick Quizzes, the lightbulb will indicate questions that give you practice in applying the guidelines. Keep in mind, however, that critical thinking is important throughout the book, not only where the lightbulb appears.

Thinking Critically About . . .

Critical thinking is a tool to guide us on a life-long quest for understanding—a tool that we must keep sharpening. And it is as much an attitude as it is a set of skills. True critical thinking, in the words of philosopher Richard W. Paul (1984), is "fair-mindedness brought into the heart of every-day life."

??? QUICK QUIZ

Can you identify how the guidelines to critical thinking were violated in each of the following cases?

1. For years, writer Norman Cousins told how he had cured himself of a rare, life-threatening disease through a combination of humor and vitamins. In a best-selling book, he related his experience and recommended the same approach to others.

2. Benjamin Rush, a physician and signer of the Declaration of Independence, believed that yellow fever should be treated by bloodletting. Many of his patients died, but Rush did not lose faith in his approach; he attributed each case of improvement to his treatment and each death to the severity of the disease (Stanovich, 1996).

Answers:

1. Cousins oversimplified, arguing by anecdote instead of examining evidence from controlled studies that included cases in which people were *not* helped by humor and vitamins; and he may have been reasoning emotionally because of his own dramatic recovery.   2. Rush failed to analyze and test his assumptions; he violated the principle of falsifiability, interpreting a patient's survival as support for his hypothesis and explaining away each death by saying that the person had been too ill for the treatment to work. Thus there was no possible counterevidence that could refute the theory (which, by the way, was completely wrong—the "treatment" was actually as dangerous as the disease).

What's Ahead

- *When are psychological case studies informative, and when are they useless?*
- *Why do psychologists often do research in laboratories instead of observing people in their everyday lives?*
- *Why should you be skeptical about psychological tests in magazines and newspapers?*
- *What's the difference between a psychological survey and a poll of listeners by your local radio talk-show host?*

DESCRIPTIVE STUDIES: ESTABLISHING THE FACTS

Psychologists gather evidence to support their hypotheses by using different methods, depending on the kinds of questions they want to answer. These methods are not mutually exclusive, however. Just as a police detective may use a magnifying glass *and* a fingerprint duster *and* interviews of suspects to figure out "who done it," psychological sleuths often draw on different techniques at different stages of an ongoing investigation. (As you read about these methods, you might want to list their advantages and disadvantages, to help you remember them.)

Let's begin with **descriptive methods,** which allow a researcher to describe and predict behavior but not necessarily to choose one explanation over other, competing ones. Some descriptive methods are used primarily by clinicians to describe and understand the behavior of individuals; others are used primarily by researchers to compare groups of people and arrive at generalizations about behavior; and some methods can be used in either way.

Case Studies

A **case study** (or *case history*) is a detailed description of a particular individual. It may be based on careful observation or on formal psychological testing. It may include information about the person's childhood, dreams, fantasies, experiences, relationships, and hopes—anything that will provide insight into the person's behavior. Case studies are most commonly used by clinicians, but sometimes academic researchers use them as well, especially when they are just beginning to study a topic or when practical or ethical considerations prevent them from gathering information in other ways.

For example, suppose you want to know whether the first few years of life are critical for acquiring language. Can children who have missed out on hearing speech (or, in the case of deaf children, seeing signs) "catch up" later? Psychologists who are interested in this question obviously cannot answer it by isolating children and seeing what happens, so instead they have studied unusual cases of language deprivation. One such case involved a 13-year-old girl who had been locked up in a small room since infancy. Her mother, a battered wife, barely cared for her, and no one in the family spoke a word to her. If she made the slightest sound, her severely disturbed father beat her with a large piece of wood. When she was finally rescued, "Genie," as researchers called her, did not know how to chew or to stand erect, and her only sounds were high-pitched whimpers. Eventually, she began to use words and understand short sentences, but even after many years, her grammar and pronunciation remained abnormal. She never learned to use pronouns correctly, ask questions, produce proper negative sentences, or use the little word endings that communicate tense, conjunction, and possession (Curtiss, 1977, 1982; Rymer, 1993). This sad case, along with similar ones, suggests that a criti-

This picture, drawn by Genie, a young girl who endured years of isolation and mistreatment, shows one of her favorite pastimes: listening to researcher Susan Curtiss play the piano. Genie's drawings were used along with other case material to study her mental and social development.

cal period exists for language development, with the likelihood of mastering a first language declining steadily after early childhood and falling off drastically at puberty.

Case studies illustrate psychological principles in a way that abstract generalizations and cold statistics never can, and they produce a more detailed picture of an individual than other methods do. Their main drawback for psychological researchers is that the person who is the focus of a case study may be *unrepresentative* of the people about whom a researcher would like to draw conclusions; for example, it is possible that Genie was born with mental deficits that made her unlike most other children. That is why case studies are usually only sources, rather than tests, of hypotheses. You should be extremely cautious about pop-psych books and TV programs that present only testimonials and vivid case histories as evidence.

Observational Studies

In **observational studies,** the researcher systematically observes, measures, and records behavior while remaining as unobtrusive as possible and taking care not to interfere with the people (or animals) being observed. The primary purpose of *naturalistic observation* is to find out how people or

descriptive methods
Methods that yield descriptions of behavior but not necessarily causal explanations.

case study
A detailed description of a particular individual being studied or treated.

observational study
A study in which the researcher carefully and systematically observes and records behavior without interfering with the behavior; it may involve either naturalistic or laboratory observation.

other animals act in their normal social environments. Psychologists use naturalistic observation wherever people happen to be—at home, on playgrounds or streets, in schoolrooms, or in offices. Often, however, researchers prefer making their observations in a laboratory setting. In *laboratory observation,* the psychologist has more control. He or she can use sophisticated equipment, determine how many people will be observed at once, maintain a clear line of vision while observing, and so forth.

Suppose that you wanted to know how infants of different ages respond when left with a stranger. The most efficient approach might be to have parents and their infants come to your laboratory, observe them playing together for a while through a one-way window, then have a stranger enter the room and, a few minutes later, have the parent leave. You could record signs of distress, interactions with the stranger, and other behavior, checking your observations against those of others to ensure accuracy. If you did this, you would find that very young infants carry on cheerfully with whatever they are doing when the parent leaves. However, by the age of about 8 months, children often burst into tears or show other signs of what child psychologists call "separation anxiety" (Ainsworth, 1979).

One shortcoming of laboratory observation is that the presence of researchers and special equipment may cause subjects to behave differently than they would in their usual surroundings. Further, observational studies, like other descriptive studies, are more useful for *describing* behavior than for *explaining* it. If we observe infants protesting whenever a parent leaves the room, we cannot be sure *why* they are protesting. Is it because they have become attached to their parents and want them nearby, or have they learned from experience that crying brings attention and affection? It is hard to answer such questions on the basis of observational studies alone.

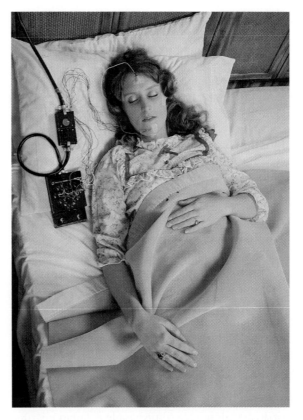

Slumbering for science: By sleeping in the laboratory instead of in the natural environment of their own homes, volunteers can provide researchers with valuable information about brain and muscle activity during sleep. One important finding is that people awakened during periods of rapid eye movement (REM) are likely to say they have been dreaming.

Tests

Psychological tests, sometimes called *assessment instruments,* are procedures for measuring and evaluating personality traits, emotional states, aptitudes, interests, abilities, and values. Typically, such tests require people to answer a series of written or oral questions. The answers may then be

psychological tests

Procedures used to measure and evaluate personality traits, emotional states, aptitudes, interests, abilities, and values.

Get Involved

Try a little naturalistic observation of your own. Go to a public place where people voluntarily seat themselves near others, such as a movie theater or a cafeteria with large tables. If you choose a setting where many people enter at once, you might recruit some friends to help you; you can divide the area into sections and assign each observer one section to observe. As individuals and groups sit down, note how many seats they leave between themselves and the next person. On the average, how far do people tend to sit from strangers? Once you have your results, see how many possible explanations you can come up with.

totaled to yield a single numerical score, or a set of scores. *Objective tests,* also called "inventories," measure beliefs, feelings, or behaviors of which an individual is aware; *projective tests* are designed to tap unconscious feelings or motives (see Chapter 10).

At one time or another, you have probably taken a psychological test, such as an intelligence test, achievement test, or vocational-aptitude test. Hundreds of psychological tests are used in industry, education, the military, and the helping professions. Some are given to individuals, others to large groups. These measures help clarify differences among individuals, as well as differences in the reactions of the same individual on different occasions or at different stages of life. They may be used to promote self-understanding, to evaluate treatments and programs, or, in scientific research, to draw generalizations about human behavior. Well-constructed psychological tests are a great improvement over simple self-evaluation because many people have a distorted view of their own abilities and traits.

One test of a good test is whether it is **standardized**—that is, whether uniform procedures exist for giving and scoring the test. It would hardly be fair to give some people detailed instructions and plenty of time and others only vague instructions and limited time. Those who administer the test must know exactly how to explain the tasks involved, how much time to allow, and what materials to use. Scoring is usually done by referring to **norms,** or established standards of performance. The usual procedure for developing norms is to give the test to a large group of people who resemble those for whom the test is intended. Norms tell users of the test which scores can be considered high, low, or average.

Test construction, administration, and interpretation present many challenges. For one thing, the test must be **reliable**—that is, it must produce the same results from one time and place to the next. A vocational-interest test is not reliable if it tells Tom that he would make a wonderful engineer but a poor journalist, and then it gives different results when Tom retakes the test a week later. Nor is it reliable if alternate forms of the test, intended to be comparable, yield different results when given to the same people.

To be useful, a test must also be **valid;** that is, it must measure what it sets out to measure. A creativity test is not valid if what it actually measures is verbal sophistication. The validity of a test is often measured by its ability to predict other, independent measures, or criteria, of the trait in question. The criterion for a scholastic aptitude test might be college grades; the criterion for a test of shyness might be behavior in social situations.

Among psychologists, controversy exists about the validity of even some widely used tests. For example, a recent critique of the Graduate Record Exam (GRE) found that it was somewhat useful for predicting first-year grades in graduate psychology programs, but *not* second-year grades, professors' ratings of students, or the quality of students' dissertations (Sternberg & Williams, 1997). Criticisms and reevaluations of psychological tests help keep psychological assessment scientifically rigorous and can lead to better, more sophisticated testing. In contrast, the pseudoscientific psychological tests frequently found in magazines and newspapers usually have not been evaluated for either validity or reliability. These questionnaires often have inviting headlines such as "Are You Self-destructive?" or "The Seven Types of Lover," but they are only lists of questions that someone thought sounded good.

Surveys

Psychological tests usually generate information about people indirectly. In contrast, **surveys** are questionnaires and interviews that gather information by asking people *directly* about their experiences, attitudes, or opinions. Most of us are familiar with surveys in the form of national opinion polls, such as the Gallup and Roper polls. Surveys have been done on many topics, from consumer preferences to sexual preferences. They produce bushels of data—but they are not easy to do well.

The biggest hurdle is getting a **representative sample,** a group of subjects that is representative of the larger population that the researcher wishes to describe. Suppose you wanted to know about drug use among college sophomores. It would not be practical to question every college sophomore in the country; instead, you would choose a sample. Special selection procedures could be used to ensure that this sample contained the same proportion of women, men, blacks, whites, poor people, rich people, Catholics, Jews, and so on as in the general population of college sophomores.

A sample's size is less critical than its representativeness; a small but representative sample may yield extremely accurate results, whereas a survey or poll that fails to use proper sampling methods may yield questionable results, no matter how large the sample. For example, a radio station that asks

standardize

In test construction, to develop uniform procedures for giving and scoring a test.

norms

In test construction, established standards of performance.

reliability

In test construction, the consistency of scores derived from a test, from one time and place to another.

validity

The ability of a test to measure what it was designed to measure.

surveys

Questionnaires and interviews that ask people directly about their experiences, attitudes, or opinions.

representative sample

A group of subjects selected from a population for study, which matches the population on important characteristics such as age and sex.

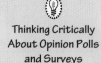

Thinking Critically About Opinion Polls and Surveys

its listeners to vote yes or no by telephone on a controversial question is hardly conducting a scientific poll. Only those who feel quite strongly about the issue *and* who happen to be listening to that particular station are likely to call in, and those who feel strongly may be likely to take a particular side. A psychologist or statistician would say that the poll suffers from a **volunteer bias:** Those who volunteer probably differ from those who stay silent. When you read about a survey (or any other kind of study), always ask what sorts of people participated. A biased, nonrepresentative sample does not necessarily mean that a survey is worthless or uninteresting, but it does mean that the results may not hold for other groups.

Another problem with surveys is that people sometimes lie—especially when the survey is about a touchy topic ("What? Me do that disgusting/dishonest/fattening thing? Never!"). The likelihood of lying is reduced when respondents are guaranteed anonymity. Also, there are ways to check for lying—for example, by asking a question several times with different wording. But not all surveys use these techniques, and even when people are trying to be truthful, they may misinterpret the survey questions or misremember the past.

When you hear about the results of a survey or opinion poll, it is important to think about how the questions were phrased. Political pollsters often design questions to produce the results they

want. A Republican might ask people whether they support "increasing the amount spent on Medicare at a slower rate," whereas a Democrat might ask whether people favor "cuts in the projected growth of Medicare." The two phrases mean the same thing, but respondents are likely to react more negatively when the word "cuts" is used (Kolbert, 1995).

As you can see, although surveys can be extremely informative, they must be conducted and interpreted carefully.

volunteer bias

A shortcoming of findings derived from a sample of volunteers instead of a representative sample.

??? QUICK QUIZ

A. Which descriptive method would be most appropriate for studying each of the following topics? (All of these topics, by the way, have been investigated by psychologists.)

1. Ways in which the games of boys differ from those of girls
2. Changes in attitudes toward nuclear disarmament after a television movie about nuclear holocaust
3. The math skills of children in the United States versus Japan
4. Physiological changes that occur when people watch violent movies
5. The development of a male infant who was reared as a female after his penis was accidentally burned off during a routine surgery

a. case study
b. naturalistic observation
c. laboratory observation
d. survey
e. test

B. Professor Flummox gives his new test of aptitude for studying psychology to his psychology students at the start of the year. At the end of the year, he finds that those who did well on the test averaged only a C in the course. The test lacks _____.

Answers:
A. 1.b 2.d 3.e 4.c 5.a B. validity

What's Ahead

- *If two things are "negatively" correlated, like grades and TV watching, what's the relationship between them?*

- *If depression and illness are correlated, does that mean depression causes illness?*

CORRELATIONAL STUDIES: LOOKING FOR RELATIONSHIPS

correlational study

A descriptive study that looks for a consistent relationship between two phenomena.

correlation

A measure of how strongly two variables are related to one another.

variables

Characteristics of behavior or experience that can be measured or described by a numeric scale; variables are manipulated and assessed in scientific studies.

positive correlation

An association between increases in one variable and increases in another.

negative correlation

An association between increases in one variable and decreases in another.

In descriptive research, psychologists often want to know whether two or more phenomena are related and, if so, how strongly. To find out, they do **correlational studies.** For example, a correlational study might examine the relationship between the number of hours spent by students in front of the television set and students' grade-point averages.

The word **correlation** is often used as a synonym for relationship. Technically, however, a correlation is a numerical measure of the *strength* of the relationship between two things. The "things" may be events, scores, or anything else that can be recorded and tallied. In psychological studies, such things are called **variables** because they can vary in quantifiable ways. Height, weight, age, income, IQ scores, number of items recalled on a memory test, number of smiles in a given time period—anything that can be measured, rated, or scored can serve as a variable.

A **positive correlation** means that high values of one variable are associated with high values of the other, and that low values of one variable are associated with low values of the other:

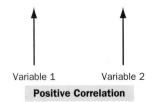

Height and weight are positively correlated, for example; so are IQ scores and school grades. Rarely is a correlation perfect, however. Some tall people weigh less than some short ones; some people with average IQs are superstars in the classroom, and some with high IQs get poor grades. Figure 1.2a shows a positive correlation between men's educational level and their annual income.

A **negative correlation** means that high values of one variable are associated with *low* values of the other:

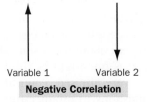

Figure 1.2b shows a negative correlation between average income and the incidence of dental disease for groups of 100 families; in general, as you

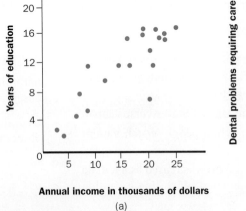

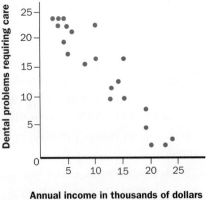

Figure 1.2

Correlations

Graph (a) shows a positive correlation; in general, the more education people have, the higher their income. Graph (b) shows a negative correlation; in general, the higher people's income, the fewer dental problems they have. (From Wright, 1976.)

can see, the higher the income, the fewer the dental problems. In the automobile business, the older the car, the lower the price, except for antiques and models favored by collectors. As for human beings, in general, the older adults are, the fewer miles they can run, the fewer crimes they are likely to commit, and the fewer hairs they have on their heads. And remember that correlation between hours spent watching TV and grade point averages? It's a negative one: Lots of hours in front of the television are associated with lower grades (Potter, 1987; Ridley-Johnson, Cooper, & Chance, 1983). See whether you can think of other variables that are negatively correlated. Remember, though, a negative correlation means that a certain kind of relationship exists. If there is no relationship between two variables, we say that they are *uncorrelated.* Shoe size and IQ scores are uncorrelated.

The statistic used to express a correlation is called the **coefficient of correlation.** This number conveys both the size of the correlation and its direction. A perfect positive correlation has a coefficient of +1.00, and a perfect negative correlation has a coefficient of −1.00. Suppose you weighed ten people and listed them in order, from lightest to heaviest. Then suppose you measured their heights and listed them in order, from shortest to tallest. If the names on the two lists were in exactly the same order, the correlation between weight and height would be +1.00. If you hear that the correlation between two variables is +.80, it means that the two are very strongly related. If you hear that the correlation is −.80, the relationship is just as strong, but it is negative. When there is no association between two variables, the coefficient is zero or close to zero.

Correlational studies in the social sciences are common and are often reported in the news. But beware; correlations can be misleading. The important thing to remember is that *a correlation does not show causation.* It is easy to assume that if A predicts B, A must be causing B—that is, making B happen—but that is not necessarily so. The number of storks nesting in some European villages is reportedly correlated (positively) with the number of human births in those villages. Therefore, knowing when the storks nest allows you to predict when more births than usual will occur. But that doesn't mean that storks bring babies or that babies attract storks! Human births seem to be somewhat more frequent at certain times of the year

Thinking Critically About Correlation and Causation

(you might want to speculate on the reasons), and the peaks just happen to coincide with the storks' nesting periods.

The coincidental nature of the correlation between nesting storks and human births is obvious, but in other cases, unwarranted conclusions about causation are more tempting. For example, television watching is positively correlated with children's aggressiveness. Therefore, many people assume that watching television (A), with its violent programs, causes aggressiveness (B):

But it is also possible that being highly aggressive (B) causes children to watch more television (A):

And there is yet another possibility—growing up in a violent household (C) could cause children both to be aggressive *and* to watch television:

Psychologists are still debating which of these relationships is the strongest; actually, there is evidence for all three (APA Commission on Violence and Youth, 1993; Eron, 1982, 1995).

The moral of the story: When two variables are associated, one variable may or may not be causing the other.

coefficient of correlation
A measure of correlation that ranges in value from −1.00 to +1.00.

??? QUICK QUIZ

A. Are you clear about correlations? Find out by identifying each of the following correlations as positive or negative:

1. The higher a male monkey's level of the hormone testosterone, the more aggressive he is likely to be.

2. The older people are, the less frequently they tend to have sexual intercourse.

3. The hotter the weather, the more crimes against persons (such as muggings) tend to occur.

 B. Now see whether you can generate two or three alternative explanations for each of these findings.

Answers:

A. 1. positive 2. negative 3. positive B. 1. The hormone may cause aggressiveness, or acting aggressively may stimulate hormone production. 2. Older people may have less interest in sex than younger people, may have less energy, or may think they are supposed to have less interest in sex and behave accordingly; older people may also have trouble finding sexual partners. 3. Hot temperatures may make people edgy and cause them to commit crimes; potential victims may be more plentiful in warm weather because more people stroll outside and go out at night; criminals may find it more comfortable to be out committing their crimes in warm weather than in cold. (Our explanations for these correlations are not the only ones possible.)

What's Ahead

- *Why do psychologists rely so heavily on experiments?*

- *What, exactly, do control groups control for?*

- *In a double-blind experiment, who is "blind," and what aren't they supposed to "see"?*

THE EXPERIMENT: HUNTING FOR CAUSES

Researchers often propose explanations of behavior on the basis of descriptive studies, but to actually track down the causes of behavior, they rely heavily on the experimental method. An **experiment** allows the researcher to *control* or manipulate the situation being studied. Instead of being a passive recorder of what is going on, the researcher actively does something that he or she thinks will affect the subjects' behavior and then observes what happens. These procedures allow the experimenter to draw conclusions about cause and effect.

All psychological studies must conform to certain ethical guidelines, but such guidelines are especially important in experimental research because of this element of manipulation. In most

experiment

A controlled test of a hypothesis in which the researcher manipulates one variable to discover its effect on another.

colleges and universities, an ethics committee must approve all proposed studies. In addition, the American Psychological Association (APA) has a code of ethics, stating that human subjects must voluntarily consent to participate in a study and must know enough about it to make an intelligent decision, a doctrine known as *informed consent*. Investigators must protect participants from physical and mental discomfort or harm, and if any risk exists, they must warn the subjects in advance and give them an opportunity to withdraw at any time. The APA's code also covers the humane treatment of research animals, which are used in only a small minority of psychological studies but are crucial to progress in some fields, especially psychobiology and behavioral research. Because of heated debates over animal rights and welfare, guidelines for using animals have been made more comprehensive in recent years, and stronger federal regulations have been established. Every experiment involving vertebrates must now be reviewed by a committee that includes representatives from the research institution and the community.

Experimental Variables

Suppose you are a psychologist and you come across reports that cigarette smoking improves performance on simple reaction-time tasks. You do not question these findings, but you have a hunch that nicotine may have the opposite effect on more demanding kinds of behavior, such as driving—so you decide to do an experiment. In a laboratory, you ask smokers to "drive" using a computerized driving simulator equipped with a stick shift and a gas pedal. The object, you tell them, is to maximize distance by driving as fast as possible on a winding road while avoiding collisions. At your request, some of the subjects smoke a cigarette immediately before climbing into the driver's seat. Others do not. You are interested in comparing how many collisions the two groups have. The basic design of this experiment is illustrated in Figure 1.3, which you may want to refer back to as you read the next few pages.

The aspect of an experimental situation manipulated or varied by the researcher is known as the **independent variable.** The reaction of the subjects—the behavior that the researcher tries to predict—is the **dependent variable.** Every experiment has at least one independent and one dependent variable. In our example, the independent variable is nicotine use: one cigarette versus none. The dependent variable is the number of collisions.

Ideally, everything about the experimental situation *except* the independent variable is held constant—that is, kept the same for all subjects. You

independent variable
A variable that an experimenter manipulates.

dependent variable
A variable that an experimenter predicts will be affected by manipulations of the independent variable.

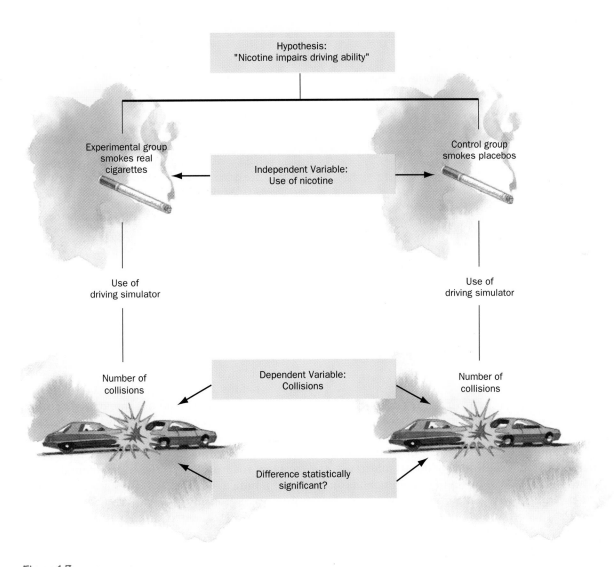

Figure 1.3
Do Smoking and Driving Mix?
The text describes this experimental design to test the hypothesis that nicotine in cigarettes impairs driving skills.

would not have some people use a stick shift and others an automatic, unless shift type were an independent variable. Similarly, you would not have some people go through the experiment alone and others perform in front of an audience. Holding everything but the independent variable constant ensures that whatever happens is due to the researcher's manipulation and nothing else. It allows you to rule out other interpretations.

Understandably, students often have trouble keeping independent and dependent variables straight. You might think of it this way: The dependent variable—the outcome of the study—*depends* on the independent variable. When psychologists set up an experiment, they think, "If I do (such and such), the subjects in my study will do (such and such)." The first "such and such" represents the independent variable; the second represents the dependent variable:

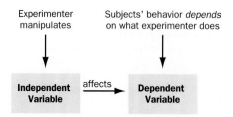

Most variables may be either independent or dependent, based on what the experimenter is manipulating and trying to predict. If you want to know whether eating chocolate makes people nervous, then the amount of chocolate eaten is the independent variable. If you want to know whether feeling nervous makes people eat chocolate, then the amount of chocolate eaten is the dependent variable.

Experimental and Control Conditions

Experiments usually require both an experimental condition and a comparison, or **control condition.** In the control condition, subjects are treated exactly like those in the experimental condition, except that they are not exposed to the same treatment, or manipulation of the independent variable. Without a control condition, you can't be sure that the behavior you are interested in would not have occurred anyway, even without your manipulation. In some studies, the same

Why control groups matter: According to practitioners of "facilitated communication," autistic children who have never spoken can peck out messages on keyboards or letter grids when an adult places a hand on the child's to "facilitate" the child's response. But studies using control groups find that it is the adult, not the child, who is doing the communicating. For example, when facilitators and children see different pictures, the child will type out a description of what the facilitator sees—not what the child sees (Jacobson, Mulick, & Schwartz, 1995). The facilitator is unconsciously nudging the child's hand to produce the desired response (Burgess et al., 1998; Spitz, 1997).

subjects can be used in both the control and the experimental conditions; they are said to serve as their own controls. In other studies, subjects are assigned to either an *experimental group* or a *control group.*

In the nicotine experiment, the people who smoke before driving make up the experimental group, and those who do not smoke make up the control group. We want these two groups to be roughly the same in terms of average driving skill. It wouldn't do to start out with a bunch of reckless roadrunners in the experimental group and a bunch of tired tortoises in the control group. We probably also want the two groups to be similar in average intelligence, education, smoking history, and other characteristics so that none of these variables will affect our results. One way to accomplish this is to *randomly assign* people to one group or another; if we have

control condition

In an experiment, a comparison condition in which subjects are not exposed to the same treatment as in the experimental condition.

enough participants in our study, individual differences among them are likely to be roughly balanced in the two groups.

We now have two groups. We also have a problem. In order to smoke, the experimental subjects must light up and inhale. These acts might set off certain expectations—of feeling relaxed, getting nervous, feeling confident, or whatever. These expectations, in turn, might affect driving performance. It would be better to have the control group do everything the experimental group does except use nicotine.

Therefore, let's change our experimental design a bit. Instead of having the control subjects refrain from smoking, we will give them a **placebo,** a fake treatment. Placebos, which are used frequently in drug research, often take the form of pills or injections containing no active ingredients. Assume that it's possible for us to use phony cigarettes that taste and smell like the real thing but that contain no active ingredients. Our control subjects will not know their cigarettes are fake and will have no way of distinguishing them from real ones. Now if they have substantially fewer collisions than the experimental group, we will feel safe in concluding that nicotine increases the probability of an accident.

Experimenter Effects

Because expectations can influence the results of a study, subjects should not know whether they are in an experimental or a control group. When this is so (as it usually is), the experiment is said to be a **single-blind study.** But subjects are not the only ones who bring expectations to the laboratory; so do researchers. Their expectations and hopes for a particular result may cause them to inadvertently influence the participants' responses through facial expressions, posture, tone of voice, or some other cue.

Many years ago, Robert Rosenthal (1966) demonstrated how powerful such **experimenter effects** can be. He had students teach rats to run a maze. Half the students were told that their rats had been bred to be "maze bright," and half were told that their rats had been bred to be "maze dull." In reality, there were no genetic differences between the two groups of rats, yet the supposedly brainy rats actually did learn the maze more quickly, apparently because of the way the students treated them. If an experimenter's expectations can affect a rodent's behavior, reasoned Rosenthal, they can also affect a human being's. He went on to demonstrate this point in many other studies (Rosenthal, 1994). Even an experimenter's friendly smile can affect people's responses in a study.

One solution to the problem of experimenter effects is to do a **double-blind study.** In such a study, the person running the experiment, the one having actual contact with the subjects, does not know which subjects are in which groups until the data have been gathered. Double-blind procedures are standard in drug research. Different doses of a drug are coded in some way, and the person administering the drug is kept in the dark about the code's meaning until after the experiment. To run our nicotine study in a double-blind fashion, we would keep the person dispensing the cigarettes from knowing which ones were real and which were placebos. In psychological research, double-blind studies are often more difficult to design than those that are single-blind. The goal, however, is always to control everything possible in an experiment.

placebo
An inactive substance or fake treatment used as a control in an experiment or given by a medical practitioner to a patient.

single-blind study
An experiment in which subjects do not know whether they are in an experimental or a control group.

experimenter effects
Unintended changes in subjects' behavior due to cues inadvertently given by the experimenter.

double-blind study
An experiment in which neither the subjects nor the individuals running the study know which subjects are in the control group and which are in the experimental group until after the results are tallied.

Get Involved

Prove to yourself how easy it is for experimenters to affect the behavior of a study's participants by giving off nonverbal cues. As you walk around campus or sit in the library, quickly glance at individuals approaching you and either smile or maintain a neutral expression. Try to keep the duration of your glance the same whether you smile or not. You might record the results on a piece of paper as you collect them instead of relying on your memory. Chances are that people to whom you smile will smile back, whereas those whom you approach with a neutral expression will do the same. What does this tell you about the importance of doing double-blind studies?

Advantages and Limitations of Experiments

Because experiments allow conclusions about cause and effect, they have long been the method of choice in psychology. However, like all methods, the experiment has its limitations. Just as in case studies and surveys, the participants are not always representative of the larger population. Most volunteers in academic experiments are college stu-

dents, who differ in many ways from people who are not in school. Moreover, in an experiment, the researcher determines what the questions are and which behaviors will be recorded, and the participants try to do as they are told. In their desire to cooperate, advance scientific knowledge, or present themselves in a positive light, they may act in ways that they ordinarily would not (Kihlstrom, 1995). Thus, research psychologists confront a dilemma: The more control they exercise over the situation,

Table 1.3 Research Methods in Psychology: Their Advantages and Disadvantages

Method	Advantages	Disadvantages
Case study	Good source of hypotheses Provides in-depth information on individuals Unusual cases can shed light on situations or problems that are unethical or impractical to study in other ways	Individual may not be representative or typical Difficult to know which subjective interpretation is best
Naturalistic observation	Allows description of behavior as it occurs in the natural environment Often useful in first stages of a research program	Allows researcher little or no control of the situation Observations may be biased Does not allow firm conclusions about cause and effect
Laboratory observation	Allows more control than naturalistic observation Allows use of sophisticated equipment	Allows researcher only limited control of the situation Observations may be biased Does not allow firm conclusions about cause and effect Behavior in the laboratory may differ from behavior in the natural environment
Test	Yields information on personality traits, emotional states, aptitudes, abilities	Difficult to construct tests that are valid and reliable
Survey	Provides a large amount of information on large numbers of people	If sample is nonrepresentative or biased, it may be impossible to generalize from the results Responses may be inaccurate or untrue
Correlational study	Shows whether two or more variables are related Allows general predictions	Does not permit identification of cause and effect
Experiment	Allows researcher to control situation Permits researcher to identify cause and effect	Situation is artificial, and results may not generalize well to the real world Sometimes difficult to avoid experimenter effects

the more unlike real life it may be. For this reason, many psychologists are calling for more *field research,* the careful study of behavior in natural contexts such as schools and the workplace, using both descriptive and experimental methods.

Now that we have come to the end of our discussion of research methods, how did you do on your list of their advantages and disadvantages? You can find out by comparing your list with the one in Table 1.3 on the previous page.

??? QUICK QUIZ

A. Name the independent and dependent variables in studies designed to answer the following questions:

1. Whether sleeping after learning a poem improves memory for the poem

2. Whether the presence of other people affects a person's willingness to help someone in distress

3. Whether people get agitated from listening to heavy-metal music

 B. On a talk show, Dr. Blitznik announces a fabulous new program: Chocolate Immersion Therapy. "People who spend one day a week doing nothing but eating chocolate are soon cured of eating disorders, depression, drug abuse, and poor study habits," claims Dr. Blitznik. What should you find out about C.I.T. before signing up?

Answers:

A. 1. Opportunity to sleep after learning is the independent variable; memory for the poem is the dependent variable. 2. The presence of other people is the independent variable; willingness to help others is the dependent variable. 3. Expo- sure to heavy-metal music is the independent variable; agitation is the dependent variable. B. *Some questions to ask:* Is there research showing that people who go through C.I.T. did better than those in a control group who did not have the therapy, or who had a different therapy—say, Broccoli Immersion Therapy? If so, how many people were studied? How were they selected, and how were they assigned to the therapy and no-therapy groups? Did the person running the ex- periment know who was getting C.I.T. and who wasn't? How long did the "cures" last? Has the research been replicated?

What's Ahead

- *How can psychologists tell whether a finding is impressive or trivial?*

- *Why are some findings significant statistically but insignificant in practical terms?*

EVALUATING THE FINDINGS

If you are a psychologist who has just done an observational study, a survey, or an experiment, your work has only just begun. Once you have some results in hand, you must do three things with them: (1) describe them, (2) assess how reliable and meaningful they are, and (3) figure out how to explain them.

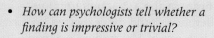

Why Psychologists Use Statistics

Let's say that 30 people in the nicotine experiment smoked real cigarettes, and 30 smoked placebos.

We have recorded the number of collisions for each person on the driving simulator. Now we have 60 numbers. What can we do with them?

The first step is to summarize the data. The world does not want to hear how many collisions each person had. It wants to know what happened in the nicotine group as a whole, compared with what happened in the control group. To provide this information, we need numbers that sum up our data. Such numbers, known as **descriptive statistics,** are often depicted in graphs and charts.

A good way to summarize the data is to compute group averages. The most commonly used type of average is the **arithmetic mean.** (For two other types, see the Appendix.) The mean is calculated by adding up all the individual scores and dividing the result by the number of scores. We can compute a mean for the nicotine group by adding up the 30 collision scores and dividing the sum by 30. Then we can do the same for the control group. Now our 60 numbers have been boiled

descriptive statistics
Statistics that organize and summarize research data.

arithmetic mean
An average that is calculated by adding up a set of quantities and dividing the sum by the total number of quantities in the set.

Averages can be misleading if you don't know the extent to which events deviated from the mean and how they were distributed.

down to 2. For the sake of our example, let's assume that the nicotine group had an average of 10 collisions, whereas the control group's average was only 7.

We must be careful, however, about how we interpret these averages. It is possible that no one in our nicotine group actually had 10 collisions. Perhaps half the people in the group were motoring maniacs and had 15 collisions, whereas the others were more cautious and had only 5. Perhaps almost all the subjects had 9, 10, or 11 collisions. Perhaps accidents were evenly distributed between 0 and 15. The mean does not tell you about such variation in subjects' responses. For that, there are other statistics. For example, the **variance** tells you how clustered or spread out the individual scores are around the mean; the more spread out they are, the less "typical" the mean is. (For details, see the Appendix.) Unfortunately, when research is reported in newspapers or on the nightly news, you usually hear only about the mean.

At this point in our nicotine study, we have one group with an average of 10 collisions and another with an average of 7. Should we break out the champagne? Try to get on TV? Call our mothers? Better hold off. Perhaps if one group had an average of 15 collisions and the other an average of 1, we could get excited. But rarely does a psychological study hit you between the eyes with a sensationally clear result. In most cases, there is some possibility that the difference between the two groups was due simply to chance. Perhaps the people in the nicotine group just happened to be a little more accident-prone, and their behavior had nothing to do with the nicotine.

To find out how impressive the data are, the psychologist uses **inferential statistics.** These statistics do not merely describe or summarize the data; they permit a researcher to draw *inferences* (conclusions based on evidence) about how

meaningful the findings are. Like descriptive statistics, inferential statistics involve the application of mathematical formulas to the data (see the Appendix). The most commonly used inferential statistics are *significance tests* that tell researchers how likely a result was to have occurred by chance. In our nicotine study, a significance test will tell us how likely it is that the difference between the nicotine group and the placebo group occurred by chance. It is impossible to rule out chance entirely, but if the likelihood that a result occurred by chance is extremely low, we say that the result is **statistically significant.** This means that the probability that the difference is "real" is overwhelming—not certain, mind you, but overwhelming.

By convention, psychologists consider a result to be significant if it would be expected to occur by chance 5 or fewer times in 100 repetitions of the study. Another way of saying this is that the result is significant at the .05—"point oh five"—level. If the difference could be expected to occur by chance in 6 out of 100 studies, we would have to say that the results failed to support the hypothesis—that the difference we obtained might well have occurred merely by chance—although we might still want to do further research to be sure. You can see that psychologists refuse to be impressed by just any old result.

By the way, a nicotine study similar to our hypothetical example, but with somewhat more complicated procedures, has actually been done (Spilich, June, & Renner, 1992). Smokers who lit up before driving got a little farther on the simulated road, but they also had significantly more rear-end collisions on average (10.7) than did temporarily abstaining smokers (5.2) or non-smokers (3.1). After hearing about this research, the head of Federal Express banned smoking on the job among all of the company's 12,000 drivers (George Spilich, personal communication).

variance

A measure of the dispersion of scores around the mean.

inferential statistics

Statistical tests that assess how likely it is that a study's results occurred merely by chance.

statistically significant

A term used to refer to a result that is extremely unlikely to have occurred by chance.

???QUICK QUIZ

Check your understanding of the descriptive–inferential distinction by placing a check in the appropriate column for each phrase:

	Descriptive statistics	Inferential statistics
1. Summarize the data	_____	_____
2. Give likelihood of data occurring by chance	_____	_____
3. Include the mean	_____	_____
4. Give measure of statistical significance	_____	_____
5. Tell you whether to call your mother about your results	_____	_____

Answers:
1. descriptive 2. inferential 3. descriptive 4. inferential 5. inferential

From the Laboratory to the Real World

The last step in any study is to figure out what the findings mean. Trying to understand behavior from uninterpreted findings is like trying to become fluent in Swedish by reading a Swedish–English dictionary. Just as you need the grammar of Swedish to tell you how the words fit together, the psychologist needs hypotheses and theories to explain how to fit together the facts that emerge from research.

Choosing the Best Explanation.   Sometimes it is hard to choose between competing explanations. Does nicotine disrupt driving by impairing coordination, by increasing a driver's vulnerability to distraction, by interfering with the processing of information, or by distorting the perception of danger? In interpreting any study, we must not go too far beyond the facts. Several explanations may fit those facts equally well, which means that more research will be needed to determine the best explanation.

Sometimes the best interpretation does not emerge until a hypothesis has been tested in different ways. If the findings of studies using different methods converge, there is greater reason to be confident about them. On the other hand, if they conflict, researchers will know they must modify their hypotheses or do more research.

As an example, when psychologists compare the mental-test scores of young people and old people, they usually find that younger people outscore older ones. This type of research, in which groups are compared at a given time, is called **cross-sectional:**

Cross-sectional Study

Different groups compared at one time:

Group A (20-year-olds)
Group B (50-year-olds)   compared
Group C (80-year-olds)

Other researchers, however, have used **longitudinal studies** to investigate mental abilities across the life span. In a longitudinal study, the same people are followed over a period of time and are reassessed at regular intervals:

Longitudinal Study

Same group compared at different times:

Group A at age 20 ⟶ Group A at age 50 ⟶ Group A at age 80

In contrast to cross-sectional studies, longitudinal studies find that as people age, they often continue to perform as well as they ever did on many types of mental tests. A general decline in ability does not usually occur until the seventh or eighth decade of life, if at all (Baltes & Graf, 1996; Schaie, 1993). Why do results from the two types of studies conflict? Apparently, cross-sectional studies measure generational differences; younger generations tend to outperform older ones on many tests, perhaps because they are better educated or more familiar with the types of items used on the tests. Without longitudinal studies, we might falsely conclude that mental ability inevitably declines sharply with age.

cross-sectional study
A study in which subjects of different ages are compared at a given time.

longitudinal study
A study in which subjects are followed and periodically reassessed over a period of time.

Judging the Result's Importance. Sometimes psychologists agree on the reliability and meaning of a finding, but not on its ultimate relevance for theory or practice. Statistical significance alone does not provide the answer. A result may be statistically significant at the "point oh five level" but at the same time be small and of minor consequence in everyday life. On the other hand, a result may not quite reach statistical significance yet be worth following up on (Falk & Greenbaum, 1995; Hunter, 1996). As a result, many psychologists now prefer other statistical procedures that reveal how powerful the independent variable really is—how much of the variation in the data the variable accounts for.

One increasingly popular statistical technique, called **meta-analysis,** combines and analyzes data from many studies, instead of assessing each study's results separately. Meta-analysis tells the researcher how much of the variation in scores across *all* the studies examined can be explained by a particular variable. For example, a meta-analysis of nearly 50 years of research found that gender accounts for a good deal of the variance in performance on certain spatial–visual tasks, with males doing better than females on the average (Voyer, Voyer, & Bryden, 1995). In contrast, other meta-analyses have shown that gender accounts for only 1 to 5 percent of the variance on tests of verbal ability, math ability, and aggressiveness (Eagly & Carli, 1981; Feingold, 1988; Hyde, 1981, 1984; Hyde, Fennema, & Lamon, 1990; Hyde & Linn, 1988). Gender differences on these tests are reliable, but small, and the scores for males and females greatly overlap.

Techniques such as meta-analysis are useful because rarely does one study prove anything, in psychology or any other field. That is why you should be suspicious of headlines that announce a sudden, major scientific breakthrough. Scientific progress usually occurs gradually, not in one fell swoop.

Thinking Critically About "Significant" Findings

meta-analysis

A procedure for combining and analyzing data from many studies; it determines how much of the variance in scores across all studies can be explained by a particular variable.

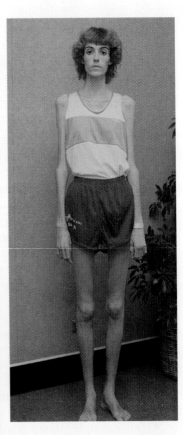

Psychologists use the methods described in this chapter to study many puzzles of behavior—why people dress up in funny outfits; pursue their goals in the face of enormous obstacles; develop life-threatening eating disorders; or join cults such as Japan's Aum Shinrikyo ("Supreme Truth"), whose members are shown here obliterating their individual identities by wearing masks of their leader's face.

Now that you have finished the first chapter of this book, you are ready to explore more deeply what psychologists have learned about human behavior. We hope you will resist the temptation to skip descriptions of how these findings were obtained because what we know about human behavior cannot be separated from how we know it.

At the start of each of the remaining chapters, we will present a real story from the news, one that raises some intriguing psychological questions. Then, at the end of the chapter, we will revisit the story to show how the material you have learned can help answer those questions. If you are ready to share the excitement of studying the puzzles of human behavior; if you love mysteries and want to know not only who did it but also why they did it; if you are willing to reconsider what you think you think . . . then you are ready to read on.

What Psychology Can Do for You—and What It Can't

If you intend to become a psychologist or a mental-health professional, you have an obvious reason for taking a course in psychology. But psychology can contribute to your life in many ways, whether you plan to work in the field or not. Here are a few things psychology can do for you:

• *Make you a more informed person.* One purpose of education is to acquaint people with their cultural heritage and with humankind's achievements in literature, the humanities, and science. Because psychology plays a large role in contemporary society, being a well-informed person requires knowing something about psychological methods and findings.

• *Satisfy your curiosity about human nature.* When the Greek philosopher Socrates admonished his students to "know thyself," he was only telling them to do what they wanted to do anyway. The topic that fascinates human beings most is human beings. Psychology, along with the other social sciences, literature, history, and philosophy, can contribute to a better understanding of yourself and others.

• *Help you increase control over your life.* Psychology cannot solve all your problems, but it does offer techniques that may help you handle your emotions, improve your memory, and eliminate unwanted habits. It can also foster an attitude of objectivity that is useful for analyzing your behavior and your relationships with others.

• *Help you on the job.* A bachelor's degree in psychology is useful for getting a job in a help-

ing profession, for example, as a welfare caseworker or a rehabilitation counselor. Anyone who works as a nurse, doctor, member of the clergy, police officer, or teacher can also put psychology to work on the job. So can waiters, flight attendants, bank tellers, salespeople, receptionists, and others whose jobs involve customer service. Finally, psychology can be useful to those whose jobs require them to predict people's behavior—for example, labor negotiators, politicians, advertising copywriters, managers, product designers, buyers, market researchers, magicians. . . .

• *Give you insights into political and social issues.* Crime, drug abuse, discrimination, and war are not only social issues but also psychological ones. Psychological knowledge alone cannot solve the complex political, social, and ethical problems that plague every society, but it can help you make informed judgments about them. For example, if you know that involuntary crowding often leads to stress, hostility, and difficulty concentrating, this knowledge may affect your views on which programs to support for schools and prisons.

We are optimistic about psychology's role in the world, but we want to caution you that sometimes people expect things from psychology that it can't deliver. For example, psychology can't tell you the meaning of life. A philosophy about the purpose of life requires not only knowledge but also reflection and a willingness to learn from life's experiences. Nor does psychological understanding relieve people of responsibility for their actions. Knowing

that your short temper is a result, in part, of your unhappy childhood doesn't give you a green light to yell at your family. Similarly, understanding the origins of child beating may help us to reduce child abuse and treat offenders, but we can still hold child beaters accountable for their behavior.

Most important, psychology will not provide you with simple answers to complex questions. You have already learned that psychologists, like other scientists, often disagree among themselves. This disagreement is a normal result of their differing perspectives and methods, and it reflects the fact that most human phenomena—from violence to love—do not lend themselves to one-note explanations. Therefore, rather than becoming attached to any one approach ("Medication will one day cure all mental illnesses"; "With the right environment, any child can become a Mozart"), the critical thinker will try to integrate the best contributions of each. In the final chapter of this book, we suggest how findings from several perspectives might help us understand some of the most fundamental activities and motives of life.

Despite the complexity of behavior and the lack of simple answers to human problems, psychologists have made enormous progress in unraveling the secrets of the human brain, mind, and heart. At the end of each chapter, starting with the next one, the "Taking Psychology with You" feature will suggest ways to apply psychological findings to your own life—at school, on the job, or in your relationships.

SUMMARY

The Science of Psychology

1) *Psychology* is the study of behavior and mental processes and how they are affected by an organism's external and internal environment. In its methods and its reliance on evidence, psychology differs from pseudoscience and "psychobabble."

2) Psychological findings sometimes confirm, but often contradict, common sense. In any case, a result does not have to be surprising to be scientifically important.

3) Psychology's forerunners made valid observations and had useful insights, but until the late 1800s, psychology was not a science. A lack of *empirical* evidence often led to serious errors in the description and explanation of behavior.

4) The official founder of scientific psychology was Wilhelm Wundt, who emphasized the analysis of experience into basic elements, through *trained introspection*. A competing approach, *functionalism*, emphasized the purpose of behavior; one of its leading proponents was William James. Psychology as a method of psychotherapy was born in Vienna, with the work of Sigmund Freud.

5) Five points of view predominate today in psychology: The *biological perspective* emphasizes bodily events associated with actions, thoughts, and feelings. The *learning perspective* emphasizes the study of observable behavior and rejects mentalistic explanations (*behaviorism*), or combines elements of behaviorism with the study of thoughts, values, and intentions (*social-learning theory*). The *cognitive perspective* emphasizes mental processes in perception, problem solving, belief formation, and other human activities. The *psychodynamic perspective*, which originated with Freud's theory of *psychoanalysis*, emphasizes unconscious motives, conflicts, and desires. The *sociocultural perspective* explores how other people and cultural rules affect an individual's beliefs and behavior. Each approach has made important contributions to psychology, but many, if not most, psychologists are eclectic, drawing on more than one school of thought.

What Psychologists Do

6) Psychologists do research and teach in colleges and universities, provide mental-health services (*psychological practice*), and conduct research and apply findings in a wide variety of nonacademic settings. *Applied psychologists* are concerned with the practical uses of psychological knowledge. *Basic psychologists* are concerned with knowledge for its own sake.

7) *Psychotherapist* is an unregulated word for anyone who does therapy, including even persons who have no credentials or training at all. Licensed therapists differ according to their training and approach: *Clinical psychologists* have a Ph.D., an Ed.D., or a Psy.D.; *psychiatrists* have an M.D.; *psychoanalysts* are trained in psychoanalytic institutes; and social workers, counseling and school psychologists, and marriage and family counselors may have a variety of postgraduate degrees.

Critical and Scientific Thinking in Psychology

8) One of the greatest benefits of studying psychology is the development of *critical thinking* skills and attitudes. The critical thinker asks questions, defines terms and issues clearly and accurately, examines the evidence, analyzes assumptions and biases, avoids emotional reasoning, avoids oversimplification, considers alternative interpretations, and tolerates uncertainty. These activities are not only useful in ordinary life, but are also the basis of the scientific method. For example, scientists are required to state hypotheses and predictions precisely ("Define your terms"), to gather empirical evidence, to comply with the *principle of falsifiability* ("analyze assumptions"), and to resist drawing firm conclusions until results are replicated ("tolerate uncertainty").

Descriptive Studies: Establishing the Facts

9) *Descriptive methods* allow a researcher to describe and predict behavior but not necessarily to choose one explanation over others. Such methods include case studies, observational studies, psychological tests, surveys, and correlational methods.

10) *Case studies* are detailed descriptions of individuals. They are often used by clinicians, and they can be valuable in exploring new research topics and addressing questions that would otherwise be difficult or impossible to study. But because the person under study may not be representative of people in general, case studies are typically sources rather than tests of hypotheses.

11) In *observational studies*, the researcher systematically observes and records behavior without interfering in any way with the behavior. *Naturalistic observation* is used to find out how subjects behave in their natural environments. *Laboratory observation* allows more control and the use of special equipment; behavior in the laboratory, however, may differ in certain ways from behavior in natural contexts.

12) *Psychological tests* are used to measure and evaluate personality traits, emotional states, aptitudes, interests, abilities, and values. A good test is one that has been *standardized* and is both *valid* and *reliable*. Critics have questioned the reliability and validity of even some widely used tests.

13) *Surveys* are questionnaires or interviews that ask people directly about their experiences, attitudes, and opinions. Researchers must take precautions to obtain a sample that is *representative* of the larger population that the researcher wishes to describe and that yields results that are not skewed by a *volunteer bias*. Findings can be affected by the fact that respondents sometimes lie, misremember, or misinterpret the questions.

Correlational Studies: Looking for Relationships

14) In descriptive research, studies that look for relationships between phenomena are known as *correlational*. A *correlation* is a measure of the strength of a positive or negative relationship between two variables. A correlation does *not* demonstrate a causal relationship between the variables.

The Experiment: Hunting for Causes

15) *Experiments* allow researchers to control the situation being studied, manipulate an *independent variable*, and assess the effects of the manipulation on a *dependent variable*. Experimental studies usually require a comparison or *control* condition. *Single-blind* and *double-blind* procedures can be used to prevent the expectations of the subjects or the experimenter from affecting the results. Because experiments allow conclusions about cause and effect, they have long been the method of choice in psychology. However, like laboratory observations, experiments create a special situation that may call forth behavior not typical in other environments.

Evaluating the Findings

16) Psychologists use *descriptive statistics*, such as the *arithmetic mean* and *variance*, to summarize data. They use *inferential statistics* to find out how impressive the data are. *Significance tests* tell the researcher how likely it is that the results of a study occurred merely by chance. The results are said to be *statistically significant* if this likelihood is very low.

17) Choosing among competing interpretations of a finding can be difficult, and care must be taken to avoid going beyond the facts. Sometimes the best interpretation does not emerge until a hypothesis has been tested in more than one way—for example, by using both *cross-sectional* and *longitudinal* methods.

18) Statistical significance does not always imply real-world importance because the amount of variation in the data accounted for by a particular variable may be small. Conversely, a result that does not quite reach significance may be potentially useful. Therefore, many psychologists are now turning to other statistical measures. The technique of *meta-analysis*, for example, reveals how much of the variation in scores across many different studies can be explained by a particular variable.

KEY TERMS

Use this list to check your understanding of terms and people in this chapter. If you have trouble with a term, you can find it on the page listed.

psychology 4	functionalism 6	biological perspective 7
empirical 5	William James 6	learning perspective 7
Wilhelm Wundt 6	Sigmund Freud 6	behaviorists 7
trained introspection 6	psychoanalysis 6	social-learning theorists 7

LOOKING BACK

Now that you have read this chapter, see whether you can answer the "What's Ahead" questions that preceded each major section. By using these questions to "look back," you can find out how much you have learned—and what you may need to review.

- *What's the difference between psychology and plain old common sense? (pp. 4–5)*

- *How old is the science of psychology? (p. 6)*

- *What are the five major perspectives in modern psychology? (p. 7)*

- *If someone tells you that he or she is a psychologist, why can't you assume the person is a therapist? (pp. 8–9)*

- *If you decided to call yourself a "psychotherapist," would doing so be legal? (p. 10)*

- *How can you distinguish a clinical psychologist from a psychiatrist? (p. 10)*

- *What guidelines can you use to tell whether a psychological claim is merely psychobabble? (pp. 13–17)*

- *Why is a psychological theory unscientific if it explains anything that could conceivably happen? (pp. 14–15)*

- *What's wrong with drawing conclusions about behavior from a collection of anecdotes? (p. 16)*

- *When are psychological case studies informative, and when are they useless? (p. 18)*

- *Why do psychologists often do research in laboratories instead of observing people in their everyday lives? (p. 19)*

- *Why should you be skeptical about psychological tests in magazines and newspapers? (p. 20)*

- *What's the difference between a psychological survey and a poll of listeners by your local radio talk-show host? (pp. 20–21)*

- *If two things are "negatively" correlated, like grades and TV watching, what's the relationship between them? (p. 22)*

- *If depression and illness are correlated, does that mean depression causes illness? (p. 23)*

- *Why do psychologists rely so heavily on experiments? (p. 24)*

- *What, exactly, do control groups control for? (p. 26)*

- *In a double-blind experiment, who is "blind," and what aren't they supposed to "see"? (p. 27)*

- *How can psychologists tell whether a finding is impressive or trivial? (p. 30)*

- *Why are some findings significant statistically but insignificant in practical terms? (p. 32)*

2 Theories of Personality

Dennis Rodman's costumes and antics amuse some people and appall others.

Rodman Continues to Outrage Foes, Delight Fans

CHICAGO, JULY 1997. Dennis ("the Worm") Rodman, the controversial Chicago Bulls' basketball player, today became a free agent, amid speculation about who—if anyone—will offer him a contract. Fans of the flamboyant rebounder hail him as a bril-

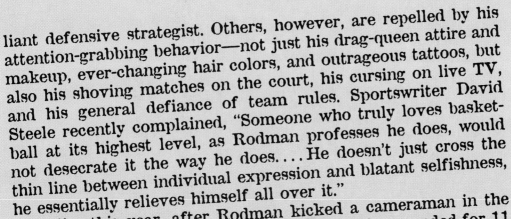

liant defensive strategist. Others, however, are repelled by his attention-grabbing behavior—not just his drag-queen attire and makeup, ever-changing hair colors, and outrageous tattoos, but also his shoving matches on the court, his cursing on live TV, and his general defiance of team rules. Sportswriter David Steele recently complained, "Someone who truly loves basketball at its highest level, as Rodman professes he does, would not desecrate it the way he does. . . . He doesn't just cross the thin line between individual expression and blatant selfishness, he essentially relieves himself all over it."

Earlier this year, after Rodman kicked a cameraman in the groin for no apparent reason and got himself suspended for 11 games, his own coach compared his actions to those of a 4-year-old who has had his toys taken away. Remarked teammate Scottie Pippen, "I'm not sure he's capable of learning any lessons from his suspensions. I don't expect him ever to change because if he did, he wouldn't be the Worm, the personality he has invented for himself."

*C*an Dennis Rodman change? Was he born to be an outlandish exhibitionist, or is that merely a persona he cleverly created to make himself famous? Which personality traits best describe him: hardworking, savvy, and effective, or outlandish, childish, and silly? Do his actions, which offend so many people, stem from some deep-seated, perhaps unconscious aspect of his personality, or is he just being "playful"? Will the real Dennis Rodman please stand up?

In psychology, **personality** refers to a distinctive pattern of behavior, thoughts, motives, and emotions that characterizes an individual over time. This pattern reflects a particular set of **traits**, characteristics that are assumed to describe the person across many situations: shy, brave, reliable, friendly, hostile, confident, sullen, and so on. The schools of psychology that we discussed in Chapter 1 differ in the traits they consider most important, and in their views of the origins and stability of personality. Biological psychologists seek evidence for genetically influenced qualities that remain entrenched throughout life. In the learning tradition, many behavioral psychologists argue that people are influenced more by their learning histories and immediate circumstances than by any permanent, individual traits. Cognitive social-learning theorists, who draw on both the learning and the cognitive perspectives, emphasize the perceptions, values, and beliefs that contribute to an individual's distinctive personality. Cultural psychologists trace the cultural origins of traits and typical ways of behaving. Psychodynamic psychologists search for personality in the dark, unconscious recesses of the mind. And humanists, who belong to a modern philosophical branch of psychology, regard personality as the private self, the "true self" behind the masks that people wear in daily life.

In this chapter, we will describe these major approaches to personality, and when we are done, we will return to Dennis Rodman, to speculate on what makes him tick—and tick people off. As you read, ask yourself: Is personality really stable, or are some qualities and traits changeable? Are we, by nature, aggressive, loving, cooperative, or hostile, or are these qualities learned? To what extent are we conscious of the motives and conflicts that shape our personalities? And which has more influence on our behavior: our personality or the situation we are in?

The four basic personality types.

What's Ahead

- *How can psychologists tell which personality traits "clump together"?*

- *Which five dimensions of personality seem to describe people the world over?*

THE ELEMENTS OF PERSONALITY

Psychological tests provide information about specific aspects of personality, such as needs, values, interests, and typical ways of responding to situations. Using these tests, psychologists have identified a broad array of personality traits, from sensation seeking (the enjoyment of risk) to "erotophobia" (the fear of sex).

One of the most influential trait theorists was Gordon Allport (1897–1967). Allport observed that most members of a society share certain traits that their culture expects and rewards. To understand why two people differ, said Allport (1937, 1961), we must look beyond these shared traits, to the individual characteristics that make each of them unique. *Cardinal traits* are of overwhelming importance to an individual and influence almost everything the person does. We

might say that Mohandas Gandhi (called Mahatma, or "wise one") and Martin Luther King, Jr., had the cardinal trait of nonviolence. But few people, said Allport, have cardinal traits. Instead, most of us have five to ten *central* (or global) *traits* that reflect a characteristic way of behaving, dealing with others, and reacting to new situations. Allport (1961) wrote, "For some the world is a hostile place where men are evil and dangerous; for others it is a stage for fun and frolic. It may appear as a place to do one's duty grimly; or a pasture for cultivating friendship and love." *Secondary traits*, in contrast, are more changeable aspects of personality. They include preferences (for foods, colors, music, movies), habits, casual opinions, and the like.

Another important theorist, Raymond B. Cattell, advanced the study of personality traits by applying a statistical method called **factor analysis.** This procedure identifies clusters of correlated items that seem to be measuring some common, underlying factor. Using questionnaires, life descriptions, and observations, Cattell (1965, 1973) measured dozens of personality traits in hundreds of people. He called these descriptive qualities *surface traits* because they are visible in a person's words or deeds. He believed that factor analysis would identify *source traits*, the underlying sources of surface qualities. For example, you might have the surface traits of assertiveness, courage, and ambition; the source trait linking all three might

personality

A distinctive and relatively stable pattern of behavior, thoughts, motives, and emotions that characterizes an individual.

trait

A descriptive characteristic of an individual, assumed to be stable across situations and time.

factor analysis

A statistical method for analyzing the intercorrelations among various measures or test scores; clusters of measures or scores that are highly correlated are assumed to be measuring the same underlying trait, ability, or aptitude (factor).

be dominance. Cattell and his associates investigated many aspects of personality, including humor, intelligence, creativity, leadership, and emotional disorder. Out of these, he developed a 16 Personality Factors (16 PF) Questionnaire. Later in his career, he noted that only 6 of these factors had been repeatedly confirmed, but the 16 PF test remained popular for many years (Digman, 1996).

By the mid-1980s, researchers, using diverse methods to reduce surface traits into basic clusters, had identified five fundamental traits, called the *Big Five* (Digman, 1996; Goldberg, 1993; McCrae & Costa, 1996; Wiggins, 1996):

1. *Introversion versus extroversion* describes the extent to which people are outgoing or shy. It includes such traits as being talkative or silent, sociable or reclusive, adventurous or cautious, eager to be in the limelight or inclined to stay in the shadows. Extroversion is associated with a tendency to be enthusiastic, lively, and cheerful.

2. *Neuroticism,* or emotional instability, includes such traits as anxiety and an inability to control impulses, a tendency to have unrealistic ideas, and general instability and negativity. Neurotic individuals are worriers, complainers, and defeatists, even when they have no major problems. They complain about different things at different ages,

Extroversion–introversion is a stable dimension of personality. This merry dancer kicking up her heels has probably been outgoing and demonstrative since childhood.

but they are always ready to see the sour side of life and none of its sweetness. Neuroticism is sometimes called *negative emotionality* because of the neurotic person's tendency to feel anger, scorn, revulsion, guilt, anxiety, and other negative emotions (Watson & Clark, 1992).

3. *Agreeableness* describes the extent to which people are good-natured or irritable, gentle or head-

---

Get Involved

Using the Big Five, rate your own personality traits along a five-point scale by mentally marking the appropriate space with an X. Refer to the text for a description of the specific qualities making up each dimension.

introverted ___ / ___ / ___ / ___ / ___ extroverted

neurotic ___ / ___ / ___ / ___ / ___ emotionally stable

agreeable ___ / ___ / ___ / ___ / ___ stubborn

conscientious ___ / ___ / ___ / ___ / ___ undependable

open to experience ___ / ___ / ___ / ___ / ___ prefer the familiar

How did you come out? Are there some traits on which you fall at one end of the scale or the other?

Now choose one of these traits and find out how well it actually predicts your behavior. Over a period of time—a day may be enough, or you may need several days—keep notes about when your behavior is consistent with the trait and when it is not. For example, if you rated yourself as introverted, notice whether you are as introverted with your friends as you are in class. In which situations, if any, are your actions at odds with the way you described yourself? What might be the explanation?

Here's something else to try. Have a friend or relative rate you on the Big Five. How closely does this rating match your own? If there's a discrepancy, what might be the reason for it?

strong, cooperative or abrasive, secure or suspicious and jealous. It reflects the capacity for friendly relationships or the tendency to have hostile ones.

4. *Conscientiousness* describes the degree to which people are responsible or undependable, persevering or likely to quit easily, steadfast or fickle, tidy or careless, scrupulous or unscrupulous.

5. *Openness to experience,* which in some personality measures is called *imagination,* describes the extent to which people are original, imaginative, questioning, artistic, and capable of creative thinking—or are conforming, unimaginative, and predictable.

Not everyone subscribes to the Big Five model. Some researchers think there are fewer basic traits; others think there are more, or different ones. Yet evidence for the Big Five continues to turn up from many sources, including studies of

children and adults, using Chinese, Dutch, Japanese, Spanish, Filipino, Hawaiian, German, Tagalog, Russian, and Australian samples (Benet & Waller, 1995; Digman & Shmelyov, 1996; Katigbak, Church, & Akamine, 1996; Yang & Bond, 1990). Moreover, within individuals, the Big Five traits are as persistent as crabgrass. You might think (and hope) that people would become more open-minded and agreeable and less neurotic as they mature. But longitudinal studies of men and women ages 21 to 96 find that no matter how you measure them, these traits remain quite stable, year after year (Costa & McCrae, 1994).

Measures of the essential dimensions of personality are useful for probing the origins of human diversity, and psychologists have identified some of the key qualities that form the foundation of an individual's character. The logical next question is, "Where do those traits come from?"

??? QUICK QUIZ

1. Raymond Cattell advanced the study of personality with his method of (a) case-study analysis, (b) factor analysis.

2. Which of the following are *not* among the "Big Five" traits in personality? (a) introversion, (b) agreeableness, (c) psychoticism, (d) openness to experience, (e) intelligence, (f) neuroticism, (g) conscientiousness

Answers: 1.b 2.c,e

What's Ahead

- *Is it possible to be born touchy or easygoing?*
- *How do psychologists measure the "heritability" of a trait?*
- *To what extent are personality differences among people influenced by their genetic differences?*
- *Are people who have highly heritable personality traits stuck with them forever?*

THE BIOLOGICAL TRADITION

temperaments
Characteristic styles of responding to the environment that are present in infancy and are assumed to be innate.

A mother we know was describing her two children. "My daughter has always been emotionally intense and a little testy," she said, "but my son is the opposite, placid and good-natured. They came

out of the womb that way." A biological psychologist would probably agree with her conclusion. Let's see why.

Heredity and Temperament

One way to explore the biological underpinnings of personality is to study **temperaments,** relatively stable, characteristic styles of responding to the environment that appear in infancy or early childhood. Developmental psychologists have found that even in the first weeks after birth, infants differ in activity level, mood, responsiveness, soothability, and attention span (Belsky, Hsieh, & Crnic, 1996; Kagan, 1994). Some are irritable and cranky; others are docile and sweet-natured. Some will cuddle up in any adult's arms and snuggle; others squirm and fidget as if they can't stand being held. Some smile easily; others fuss and cry. Because such differences appear so early, most psychologists believe they have a genetic basis (although prenatal factors such as the mother's hormone levels could also play a role).

How can genes affect a baby's temperament? **Genes,** the basic units of heredity, are made up of elements of *DNA* (deoxyribonucleic acid). These elements form chemical codes for the synthesis of proteins, and proteins, in turn, affect virtually all of the structural and biochemical characteristics of an organism, including the nervous system.

Jerome Kagan and his colleagues have been studying the physiological correlates of two specific temperamental styles, which they call "inhibited" and "uninhibited." (These temperaments are extremes; most children fall somewhere in between.) Inhibited children are shy and timid; they react negatively to novel situations, such as being introduced to a group of unfamiliar children. In contrast, uninhibited children are talkative and spontaneous. In the absence of intervention, these temperamental styles tend to remain stable throughout childhood, as you can see in Figure 2.1 (Kagan, 1994).

Kagan's group has found that during mildly stressful mental tasks, socially inhibited 5-year-olds are more likely than uninhibited children to show signs of activity in the sympathetic nervous system, the part of the nervous system associated with physiological arousal (see Chapter 4). These signs include increased heart rate, dilation of the pupils, characteristic patterns of brain activity, and high levels of two hormones—norepinephrine and cortisol. In white children (most of the children studied have been white), inhibition is associated to some extent with having blue eyes and allergies, or having close relatives with these characteristics (Kagan & Snidman, 1991).

Interestingly, Stephen Suomi (1987, 1991) has found exactly the same physiological attributes in shy, anxious infant rhesus monkeys (except for the blue eyes). Suomi calls the inhibited monkeys "uptight" and the uninhibited ones "laid back." Starting early in life, uptight monkeys respond with anxiety to novelty and challenge, just as Kagan's inhibited children do. Like Kagan's human subjects, Suomi's monkeys have high heart rates and elevated levels of cortisol, and they are more likely to have allergic reactions starting in infancy. When uptight rhesus monkeys grow up, they usually continue to be anxious when challenged, and they act traumatized even though they have experienced no traumas (Higley et al., 1991).

Genetically based temperaments, then, seem to influence later personality traits. However, they do not provide a fixed, unchangeable blueprint for personality. Consistency in a given temperament depends in part on how extreme that trait is in infancy. Kagan (1994) found that children who are

genes
The functional units of heredity; they are composed of DNA and specify the structure of proteins.

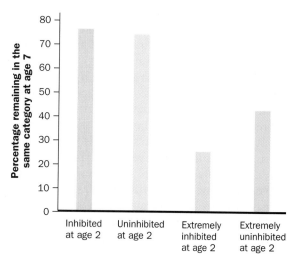

Figure 2.1

The Persistence of Temperament

In research on temperament, three-fourths of 2-year-old children classified as inhibited or uninhibited remained in those categories at the age of 7. Of those children who were extremely inhibited at age 2, 25 percent remained so five years later; of those who were extremely uninhibited, 42 percent remained at that extreme.

Figure 2.2

Overcoming Shyness

On the left, a timid infant rhesus monkey cowers behind a friend in the presence of an outgoing stranger. Such socially inhibited behavior seems to be biologically based in monkeys, as it is in human beings (Suomi, 1989). But a nurturant foster mother (center) can help an infant monkey overcome its timidity. At first, the infant clings to her; a few days later (right) the same young monkey has become more adventurous.

shy at age 2 tend to be quiet, cautious, and inhibited at age 7; and those who are sociable and uninhibited at age 2 are usually talkative and sociable at age 7. But most children, who fall somewhere in the middle, show far less consistency over time.

Consistency in temperament also depends on how parents and others respond to an infant. In his work with monkeys, Stephen Suomi (1989) showed that a highly inhibited infant is likely to overcome its timidity if it is reared by an extremely nurturant foster mother (see Figure 2.2). In human beings, the "fit" between a child's nature and the parents' is critical: Not only do parents affect the baby, but the baby also affects the parents. Imagine a high-strung parent with a child who is difficult and sometimes slow to respond to affection. The parent may begin to feel desperate, angry, or rejected. Over time, the parent may withdraw from the child or use excessive punishment, which in turn makes the child even more difficult to live with. In contrast, a more easygoing parent may have a calming effect on a difficult child or may persist in showing affection even when the child holds back, leading the child to become more responsive.

heritability

A statistical estimate of the proportion of the total variance in some trait within a group that is attributable to genetic differences among individuals within the group.

Heredity and Traits

Another way to study the biological basis of personality is to estimate the **heritability** of specific traits within groups of children or adults. This method is favored by *behavioral geneticists*, scientists concerned with the genetic bases of ability and personality. Within any group, individuals will vary in their degree of shyness, cheerfulness, impulsiveness, or any other quality. "Heritability" gives us a statistical estimate of *the proportion of the total variation in a particular trait that is attributable to genetic variation among individuals within a group.* Because it is expressed as a proportion, the maximum value it can have is 1.0.

We know that heritability is a tough concept to understand at first, so here's an example. Suppose that your entire psychology class took a test of shyness, and you computed an average shyness score for the group. Some individuals' scores would be close to the average, whereas others' scores would be much higher or lower than the average. Heritability would give you an estimate of the extent to which this variation in shyness was due to genetic differences among the students who took the test. Note, however, that this estimate would apply only to the group as a whole. It would not tell you anything about the impact of genetics on any *particular* individual's shyness or extroversion. You might be shy primarily because of your genes, but Henrietta might be shy because she comes from a culture that values modesty and social reserve in females.

One obvious example of a highly heritable trait is height: Within a group of equally well-nourished individuals, most of the variation among them will be accounted for by their genetic differences. In contrast, table manners have low heritability because most variation among individuals is accounted for by differences in upbringing. Even highly heritable traits, however, can be modified by the environment. For example, although height is highly heritable, malnourished children may not grow up to be as tall as they would with sufficient food. Conversely, if children eat a supernutritious diet, they may grow up to be taller than anyone thought they could.

Computing Heritability.   Scientists have no way to estimate the heritability of a trait or behavior directly, so they must *infer* it by studying people whose degree of genetic similarity is known. You might think that the simplest approach would be to compare blood relatives within families; everyone knows of families that are famous for some talent or personality trait. But the fact that a trait "runs" in a family doesn't tell us much because close relatives usually share environments, as well as genes. If Carlo's parents and siblings all love lasagna, that doesn't mean a taste for lasagna is heritable. The same applies if everyone in Carlo's family is shy, neurotic, or moody.

A better approach is to study adopted children (e.g., Loehlin, Horn, & Willerman, 1996; Plomin & DeFries, 1985). Such children share half of their genes with each birth parent, but they grow up in a different environment. On the other hand, they share an environment with their adoptive parents and siblings, but not their genes. Researchers can compare correlations between the children's traits and those of their biological and adoptive relatives and can then use the results to estimate heritability.

Another approach is to compare **identical (monozygotic) twins** with **fraternal (dizygotic) twins.** Identical twins develop when a fertilized egg (zygote) divides into two parts that then become separate embryos. Because the twins come from the same fertilized egg, they share all their genes, barring genetic mutations or other accidents. (They may be slightly different at birth, however, because of birth complications, differences in the blood supply to the two fetuses, or other chance factors.) In contrast, fraternal twins develop when a woman's ovaries release two eggs instead of one, and each egg is fertilized by a different sperm. Fraternal twins are wombmates, but they are no more alike genetically than any other two siblings, and they may be of different sexes. Behavioral geneticists often estimate heritability of a trait by comparing groups of same-sex frater-

nal twins with groups of identical twins. The assumption is that if identical twins are more alike than fraternal twins, then the increased similarity must be genetic.

Perhaps, however, environments shared by identical twins differ from those shared by fraternal twins. People may treat identical twins, well, identically, or they may go to the other extreme by emphasizing the twins' differences. To avoid these problems, investigators have studied identical twins who were separated early in life and reared apart. (Until recently, adoption policies and attitudes toward illegitimacy permitted such separations to occur.) In theory, separated identical twins share all their genes but not their environments. Any similarities between them should be primarily genetic and should permit a direct estimate of heritability.

In one important project, begun in 1979, an interdisciplinary team at the University of Minnesota has tested and interviewed hundreds of identical and fraternal twins reared apart (Bouchard, 1984, 1995, 1996; Bouchard et al., 1990, 1991; Tellegen et al., 1988). Subjects have undergone comprehensive psychological and medical monitoring and have answered thousands of written questions. Information is now available on many sets of reunited twins and also on many twins reared together.

identical (monozygotic) twins
Twins that develop when a fertilized egg divides into two parts that become separate embryos.

fraternal (dizygotic) twins
Twins that develop from two separate eggs fertilized by different sperm; they are no more alike genetically than any other pair of siblings.

Identical twins Gerald Levey (left) and Mark Newman, separated shortly after birth, have been studied at the Minnesota Center for Twin and Adoption Research. When Gerald and Mark were reunited at age 31, they discovered that they shared some astounding similarities. Both men are volunteer firefighters, wear mustaches, and are bachelors. Both like to hunt, watch old John Wayne movies, and eat Chinese food after a night on the town. They also drink the same brand of beer, hold the can with the little finger curled under it, and crush the can when it is empty. The challenge for researchers is to determine which of these traits and behaviors are influenced strongly by heredity, which result mainly from environmental factors such as social class and upbringing, and which are due merely to chance.

How Heritable Are Personality Traits?   Here is the remarkable and consistent conclusion from adoption studies and twin studies: Whether the trait in question is selflessness, aggression, one of the Big Five, overall well-being, or even religious attitudes, heritability is typically between .40 and .60 (Bouchard, 1995; Loehlin, 1992; Lykken & Tellegen, 1996; Tellegen et al., 1988; Waller et al., 1990). This means that within a group of people, 40 to 60 percent of the variance in such traits is attributable to genetic differences among the individuals in the group. Geneticists and biological psychologists hope that the actual genes underlying these traits will one day be discovered. Indeed, one group believes it has already found one of several genes involved in neuroticism, pessimism, and anxiety (Lesch et al., 1996).

Some researchers have even reported high heritability for such specific behaviors as getting divorced (McGue & Lykken, 1992) and watching a lot of television in childhood (Plomin et al., 1990)! These results are astounding; how can divorce and TV watching be heritable? Our prehistoric ancestors didn't get married, let alone divorced, and they certainly didn't watch TV. What could be the personality traits or temperaments underlying these behaviors? And here's another startling finding: The only environmental contribution to personality differences comes from experiences not shared with other family members, such as having a particular teacher in the fourth grade or winning the lead in the school play (Bouchard, 1995; Loehlin, 1992). Shared environment and parental child-rearing practices seem to have no significant effect on adult personality traits!

Drawing by Chas. Addams; © 1981 The New Yorker Magazine, Inc.

Separated at birth, the Mallifert twins meet accidentally.

Understandably, behavioral geneticists are excited about these results, which have major implications for the age-old debate over the relative contributions of "nature" (genetic dispositions) and "nurture" (upbringing and environment) to the development of personality. They believe this evidence undermines the conventional wisdom that child-rearing practices are central to personality development. "It will doubtless seem incredible to many readers that variables such as social class, educational opportunities, religious training, and parental love and discipline have no substantial influence on adult personality," wrote Robert McCrae and Paul Costa (1988), "but imagine for a moment that it is correct. What will it mean for research in developmental psychology? How will clinical psychology and theories of therapy be changed?"

Good questions! What would these findings, if true, mean for education, for raising children, or for psychotherapy and the treatment of personality problems?

Evaluating Genetic Theories

Before we conclude that differences in personality are based almost entirely on differences in heredity, we need to consider some of the problems that arise in measuring heritability.

One problem is that measures of environmental factors are still pretty crude, often relying on vague, grab-bag categories such as "social class" or "religious training." Thus these measures probably fail to detect some important environmental influences. Because heritability tells us only the *relative* impact **Thinking Critically About Genes and Personality** of genetics versus the environment on any trait, underestimating the influence of the environment inevitably means overestimating the influence of heritability.

Another problem is that most separated twins have grown up in fairly similar settings, in terms of opportunities, stimulation, and experiences. Whenever environmental differences are few, heritability estimates will automatically be inflated.

A third problem is one of interpretation. Although the findings on the heritability of personality traits are impressive, they do not mean that genes are the whole story. If heredity accounts for only part of why people differ in their traits, then the environment (and random errors in measurement) must account for the rest. As Robert Plomin (1989), a leading behavioral geneticist, has observed, "The wave of acceptance of genetic influence on behavior is growing into a tidal wave that threatens to engulf the second message of this research: These same data provide the best available evidence for the importance of environmental influences."

We must consider, too, that heritability (the relative influence of genes versus the environment) can change over a person's lifetime. Over the years, correlations between twins in most personality traits tend to decrease (McCartney, Harris, & Bernieri, 1990). And for some traits, experiences at certain periods in life become particularly influential. For example, an analysis of data from nearly 15,000 Finnish twins, ages 18 to 59, found that the heritability of extroversion decreases (and thus the impact of the environment *increases*) from the late

teens and early 20s to the late 20s—a time when young people tend to leave home, marry, and establish independent adult lives (Viken et al., 1994).

Finally, even if some traits have a heritable component, this does not mean that these qualities are rigidly fixed. An initial tendency may be strengthened, or diminished, by a child's experiences. As Kagan (1994) observed in his own research with temperamentally inhibited children, "a fearful child can learn to control the urge to withdraw from a stranger or a large dog. . . . The role of the environment is more substantial in helping a child overcome the tendency to withdraw than in making that child timid in the first place." Every child, he reminds us, is always part of a context in which biology and experience are inextricably intertwined.

??? QUICK QUIZ

We hope the trait of conscientiousness will motivate you to take this quiz.

1. What two broad areas of investigation support the hypothesis that personality differences are due in part to genetic differences?

2. In behavioral genetic studies, the heritability of personality traits, including the Big Five, is typically about (a) .40 to .60, (b) .90, (c) .10, (d) zero.

3. Diane hears that generosity and stinginess are highly heritable. She concludes that her own stinginess must be due mostly to genes and that there's nothing she can do about it. What's wrong with her reasoning?

4. A newspaper headline announces "Couch Potatoes Born, Not Made: Kids' TV Habits May Be Hereditary." Why is this headline misleading? What other explanations of the finding are possible? What aspects of TV watching *could* have a hereditary component?

Answers:
1. research on temperaments and on heritability   2. a   3. Heritability applies only to differences among individuals within a group, not to particular individuals. Also, a trait may be highly heritable *and* still be susceptible to modification.   4. The headline implies that there is a "TV-watching gene," but the writer is failing to consider other explanations. Perhaps some temperaments dispose people to be sedentary or passive, and this disposition can lead to a tendency to watch a lot of television.

What's Ahead

- *Why do behaviorists regard labels such as "aggressive" or "shy" as meaningless for explaining behavior?*

- *Why did cognitive social-learning theorists break away from radical behaviorists in explaining personality?*

- *What's the difference between people who think they control their own destiny—and those who think destiny controls them?*

THE LEARNING TRADITION

On a hot summer day, James Peters shot and killed his next-door neighbor, Ralph Galluccio. Peters had reached the end of his patience in a ten-year dispute with Galluccio over their common property line. Shocked friends said that the intensity of this feud was not predictable from the men's personalities. Galluccio, his employer reported, was "a likable person with a good, even disposition." Peters, said his employer, was a "very mild-mannered, cooperative" man, an "all-around good guy."

A biological psychologist might say that this violent episode demonstrates the aggressive capacity of human nature in general and of violence-prone personalities in particular. A learning theorist, however, would emphasize each man's past learning and present environment. In Chapter 8, we will discuss in detail the principles that govern learning and the major findings of this approach. Here we will be concerned only with what psychologists from the learning perspective have had to say about personality.

The Behavioral School

In 1913, a psychologist named John B. Watson (1878–1958) published a paper that rocked the still-young science of psychology. In "Psychology as the Behaviorist Views It," Watson argued that if psychology were ever to be as objective as physics, chemistry, and biology, psychologists would have to avoid terms such as *mental state* and *mind,* and stick to what they could observe and measure directly—acts and events taking place in the environment. In short, they should give up mentalism for **behaviorism.**

In his own research, Watson focused on reflexive behavior, such as trembling and sweating when you are scared. Later, B. F. Skinner (1904–1990) extended the behavioral view, but with important modifications. Calling his approach *radical behaviorism,* Skinner emphasized **operant conditioning** as the fundamental form of learning. In operant conditioning, which involves voluntary rather than reflexive behavior, the consequences of any act powerfully affect the probability that the act will occur again. In brief, acts followed by pleasant consequences (**reinforcers**) are more likely to be repeated, whereas acts followed by unpleasant consequences (punishment or withdrawal of reinforcers) are likely to decrease. For Skinner, the explanation of behavior was to be found primarily by looking outside the individual, rather than within.

In this approach, personality amounts to a collection of acquired behavioral patterns. Labels such as "aggressive," "ambitious," or "conscientious" do not explain behavior; they are simply shorthand descriptions of responses that tend to occur in particular situations. We may say that one job applicant, for example, is "calm and confident," whereas another is "anxious and shy," but all this means is that the two applicants tend to respond differently when being interviewed for a

In the behavioral view, personality traits stem from an individual's history of reinforcement and punishment. Because of past experiences, one person in an unemployment line may have low self-esteem and be pessimistic, whereas another may be more hopeful.

job. Skinner would say that if we looked into the behavioral histories of the two applicants, we would discover different patterns of reinforcement and punishment. For the first person, calm, confident behavior probably paid off in the past. For the second person, attempts at self-expression in school or at home may have been met with ridicule or sarcasm.

Behaviorists do not deny that people have feelings, thoughts, or values. However, they believe that these mental states are as subject to the laws of learning as, say, riding a bike. In this view, mental states, values, and personality traits do not explain behavior; they are behaviors to be explained. Thus Skinner would say that it is meaningless to say that "Juanita works hard because she is ambitious" or that "Gary procrastinates because he's lazy." Instead, he would say, hard work probably earns rewards for Juanita, which is why she continues to work hard, and procrastination may get Gary sympathy when he fails, which is why he continues to avoid finishing his work.

The Cognitive Social-Learning School

Behaviorism was the predominant American school of psychological research until the early 1960s. In that decade, a "cognitive revolution" swept psychology, and researchers began to focus

behaviorism
An approach to psychology that emphasizes the study of observable behavior and the role of the environment as a determinant of behavior.

operant conditioning
The process by which a response becomes more likely to occur or less so, depending on its consequences.

reinforcer
A stimulus or event that strengthens or increases the probability of the response it follows.

on the ways in which thoughts and beliefs affect behavior. But even earlier, some psychologists within the learning tradition had begun to doubt that behavioral principles were sufficient to explain behavior and personality. Eventually, these doubts led to an outgrowth of behaviorism known as **social-learning theory** (today often called *cognitive social-learning theory*).

Habits, Beliefs, and Behavior.   As we will see in more detail in Chapter 8, cognitive social-learning theorists depart from classic behaviorism by emphasizing three things: (1) observational learning and the role of models, (2) cognitive processes such as perceptions and interpretations of events, and (3) motivating values, emotions, and beliefs, such as enduring expectations of success or failure or confidence in your ability to achieve goals.

Whereas behaviorists see personality as a set of habits and beliefs that have been rewarded over a person's lifetime, cognitive social-learning theorists maintain that these habits and beliefs eventually acquire a life of their own, coming to exert their own effects on behavior. For example, you may grow up to be emotionally restrained because your parents rarely expressed their emotions and rewarded you for controlling your feelings; but once you have this trait, it will influence how you respond to others, whom you associate with, and many other aspects of your behavior (Bandura, 1994; Mischel & Shoda, 1995).

Cognitive social-learning theorists also emphasize how mental processes, such as thoughts, values, and goals, affect what individuals will do at any given moment and, more generally, the kinds of personalities they develop. A behaviorist would say that a man who is quick to behave aggressively has learned to do so because his actions get him what he wants. But a cognitive social-learning theorist would add that aggressive people also have characteristic perceptions and beliefs that fuel their behavior. They assume that people are insulting them, even in the absence of evidence. If someone does something they dislike, they attribute the action to the person's meanness and malice. They see provocation everywhere. In contrast, nonviolent people are able to take another person's perspective. If someone does something they dislike, they are apt to say, "He's had a rotten day" instead of "He's a rotten person."

Perceptions of Control.   One of the most important personality traits studied by cognitive social-learning theorists is the extent to which peo-

ple believe they have control over their lives. Much of the original work on this topic was done by Julian Rotter (1966, 1982, 1990), who started out as a behaviorally oriented experimentalist. During the 1950s, Rotter was working as both a psychotherapist and a researcher, trying to apply behavioral principles to his patients' troubling emotions and irrational beliefs (Hunt, 1993). Rotter saw that his clients had formed entrenched attitudes as a result of their lifetimes of experience, and that these attitudes were affecting their decisions and actions.

Over time, Rotter concluded, people learn that some acts will be rewarded and others punished, and thus they develop *generalized expectancies* about which situations and acts will be rewarding. A child who studies hard and gets good grades, attention from teachers, admiration from friends, and loving praise from parents will come to expect that hard work in other situations will also pay off. A child who studies hard and gets poor grades, is ignored by teachers, is rejected by friends for being a grind, or earns no support or praise from parents will come to expect that hard work isn't worth it. Once acquired, these expectations often create a *self-fulfilling prophecy:* The person's expectations lead to behavior that makes the expectation come true (Maddux, 1995). You expect to succeed, so you work hard—and succeed. Or you expect to fail, so you don't do much work, and as a result you do poorly.

Rotter and his colleagues demonstrated the power of expectancies in many experiments. At the same time, both in his private practice and in his research, Rotter was observing people whose expectations of success never went up, even when they were actually successful. "Oh, that was just a fluke," they would say, or "I was lucky; it will never happen again." Rotter concluded that people's feelings or beliefs about the factors that govern their behavior are as important as the actual reinforcers and punishers in the environment. He chose the term **locus of control** to refer to people's beliefs about whether the results of their actions are under their own control. People who have an *internal locus of control* ("internals") tend to believe that they are responsible for what happens to them, that they control their own destiny. People who have an *external locus of control* tend to believe that they are victims (or sometimes beneficiaries) of luck, fate, or other people. To measure these traits, Rotter (1966) developed an Internal/External (I/E) Scale consisting of pairs of statements. People had to choose the statement in

social-learning theory
A theory that emphasizes how behavior is learned and maintained through observation and imitation of others, positive consequences, and cognitive processes such as plans, expectations, and motivating beliefs.

locus of control
A general expectation about whether the results of your actions are under your own control (internal locus) or beyond your control (external locus).

each pair with which they most strongly agreed, as in these two items:

1. a. Many of the unhappy things in people's lives are partly due to bad luck.
   b. People's misfortunes result from mistakes they make.
2. a. Becoming a success is a matter of hard work; luck has little or nothing to do with it.
   b. Getting a good job depends mainly on being in the right place at the right time.

Research on locus of control took off like a shot, and over the years more than 2,000 studies based on the I/E scale (including a version for children) have been published, involving people of all ages and from many different ethnic groups. They show that an internal locus of control emerges at an early age and is associated with many aspects of life—including health, academic achievement, and political activism (Nowicki & Strickland, 1973; Strickland, 1989). (In Chapter 12, we will discuss in greater detail how a sense of control affects health.)

But a person's locus of control can change, depending on his or her status and experiences in society. During the 1960s, when the civil-rights movement was gathering steam, civil-rights activists and black student leaders were more likely to score at the "internal" end of the scale than control groups of people who were uninvolved in civil-rights efforts (Gore & Rotter, 1963; Strickland, 1965). By the 1970s, however—after the assassinations of Martin Luther King, Jr., Malcolm X, and both John and Robert Kennedy; after riots had devastated many black communities; and after the nation had become embroiled in the Vietnam War—American self-confidence in social progress was deeply shaken. Accordingly, scores on the locus-of-control scale changed. Civil-rights leaders and college students became less internal—that is, less confident that they, as individuals, could improve social conditions (Phares, 1976; Strickland, 1989).

Where would you place your own locus of control today? How do you think it influences your actions? How does it affect your beliefs about the possibility of personal and social change?

Evaluating Learning Theories

Why did James Peters kill Ralph Galluccio? Behaviorists would investigate why these two men failed to learn the skills to negotiate their differences, and how each had learned over time that aggressive actions would make other people knuckle under. Cognitive social-learning theorists would investigate not only the environmental conditions of the quarrel, but also each man's perceptions of it, and why Peters and Galluccio thought there was no way out other than violence. Both learning approaches would have no trouble explaining how these two men, who were so hostile toward each other, could be described by their friends and employers as mild-mannered and likeable. A behaviorist would say that different situations evoke and reinforce different "traits." A cognitive social-learning theorist would say that a person can be hostile and obnoxious in one situation and pleasant and friendly in another, depending on how the person interprets the two situations.

Some psychologists criticize the behavioral branch of the learning perspective for implying that individuals are as soft as jellyfish, and that with the right environment, anyone can become anything. They also complain that behaviorism treats people as passive recipients of environmental events. These common charges are not really fair. Skinner, for instance, often stated that people's genetic constitutions and temperaments

These members of the Communications Workers Union have an internal locus of control and are motivated to protest their city's budget cuts. What social forces might promote an internal locus of control, and which ones might reduce it?

Get Involved

Think back to the last time you did well on a test, or on some task you set yourself. Which of the following phrases best describes how you explained your success to yourself?

- I'm really competent (or smart, skillful, etc.).

- I worked hard, and it paid off.

- I was lucky.

- The test (or task) was pretty easy.

- I did well, but only because someone else helped me.

Now think about a time you did *not* do well on a test or task. Which phrase best describes how you accounted for your disappointing performance?

- I'm just not good at this.

- I didn't work (or try) hard enough.

- I was unlucky.

- I did poorly, but the test (or task) wasn't fair.

- I did poorly, but only because I got bad instruction or too little help.

What do your answers tell you about your locus of control? Do you tend to be internal for success, or external? What about for failure? Do your beliefs about the results of your actions motivate you to further effort, or do they cause you to become discouraged?

---

place limits on what they can learn, and he argued that people can choose to change their environments and thus their own behavior.

A more valid criticism is that learning approaches to personality sometimes attribute be-

Thinking Critically About the Environment and Personality

havior to the "environment" without defining exactly what the environment consists of or how it affects people. Or they explore one influence on learning at a time: a parental model, a teacher's reactions, the pattern of reinforcers in a given situation, media messages, and so forth. In real life, though, people are surrounded by hundreds of interacting influences. This fact poses a serious problem for learning theories: When nearly anything can have an influence on you, it can be frustratingly difficult to show that any one thing actually is having an influence. It's like trying to grab a fistful of fog; you know it's there, but somehow it keeps getting away from you.

For example, how strongly do images of women and men in the media influence how the sexes see themselves and how they behave? For many people, the answer is obvious—"very strongly." Yet not everyone reacts to the same images in the same way. Some men watch Arnold Schwarzenegger terminate the bad guys and want to rush out and commit a little mayhem themselves, but others see the same movie and conclude he's an overpaid weight lifter who should take acting lessons. Some women see gaunt models and think they should look that way too, but others are repelled by these images and want to buy the models a decent meal. Thus it is difficult to specify *which* media images are having an effect, and on whom; and it is difficult to disentangle the effects of the media from all the other events that influence people's ideas about how men and women should behave.

Nevertheless, the learning approach to personality makes an essential point: In the most general sense, people must learn by observation and reinforcement what the rules of their culture and community are, and which personality traits are encouraged or discouraged.

??? QUICK QUIZ

Do you have a generalized expectancy of answering these questions correctly?

1. In the behavioral view, labels for personality traits are simply shorthand descriptions of _____.

2. What is the essential difference between behavioral and social-learning approaches to personality?

3. Anika usually takes credit for doing well on her work assignments and blames her failures on lack of effort or errors in judgment. She probably (a) has a history of being punished for working hard; (b) has an internal locus of control; (c) depends on environmental reinforcers.

Answers:

1. behavioral responses that tend to occur in specific situations   2. Behaviorists regard personality as a set of habits and beliefs that have been rewarded over a person's lifetime; social-learning theorists maintain that these habits and beliefs eventually come to exert their own effects on behavior.   3. b

What's Ahead

- *How does belonging to an individualist or collectivist culture influence your personality—and even whether you think you have a stable "self"?*

- *Why might an Arab and a Swede agree on everything the other is saying—and still feel uncomfortable with each other?*

- *Why are punctuality and tardiness more than just individual personality traits?*

THE CULTURAL TRADITION

Are you the kind of person who likes taking risks? How likely are you to smoke cigarettes, drive 100 mph on the highway, drive without a seatbelt, have unprotected sex with a stranger, or decide to live near a nuclear-power plant?

Most Western psychologists who study personality regard "risk taking" and "risk avoidance" as individual personality traits—qualities embedded in an individual, perhaps because of a genetic predisposition or a lifetime of rewarded experiences. But those in the *cultural tradition* are interested in how cultures affect the behavior, attitudes, motives, and emotions that make up "personality." Cultural values, for example, affect people's feelings about risk: People in the Netherlands or Britain are more likely than Germans and Austrians to be risk takers and less likely to favor rules and regulations that are intended to promote public safety, such as the requirement to carry citizen

identification cards (Cvetkovich & Earle, 1994). The reason, according to cultural psychologists, is that Germany and Austria (among other cultures) place a high value on avoiding uncertainty and thus welcome rules and regulations that reduce individual and social risk.

A **culture** can be defined as (1) a program of shared rules that govern the behavior of members of a community or society, and (2) a set of values, beliefs, and attitudes shared by most members of that community (Lonner, 1995). In this section, we will consider some of the contributions of the cultural approach to understanding personality.

Culture and Personality

People learn their culture's rules as effortlessly as they learn its language. Just as they can speak without being able to state the rules of grammar, most people follow their culture's prescriptions without being consciously aware of them. But these rules are major contributors to the package of traits we call personality.

It can be hard to see this because the power of culture often feels less real than our private sense of self. But here's a demonstration. Who are you? Take as much time as you like to complete this sentence: "I am _____."

Your response to the "who am I?" test will be greatly influenced by your cultural background. One important way in which cultures differ is in their emphasis on individualism or community (Hofstede & Bond, 1988; Markus & Kitayama,

culture

A program of shared rules that govern the behavior of members of a community or society, and a set of values, beliefs, and attitudes shared by most members of that community.

Collectivist Chinese workers in Beijing do their morning T'ai Chi exercises in identical, harmonious fashion; individualistic Americans exercise by running, walking, bicycling, and skating, in different directions and wearing different clothes.

1991; Triandis, 1995, 1996). In **individualist cultures,** the independence of the individual takes precedence over the needs of the group, and the "self" is often defined as a collection of personality traits ("I am outgoing, agreeable, and ambitious") or in occupational terms ("I am a clinical psychologist"). In **collectivist cultures,** group harmony takes precedence over the wishes of the individual, and the "self" is defined in the context of relationships and the larger community ("I am the son of a farmer, descended from three generations of storytellers on my mother's side and five generations of farmers on my father's side, and their ancestors came to this village 200 years ago . . . .").

As Table 2.1 shows, individualist and collectivist ways of defining the self influence which personality traits we value, how we express emotions, and how much we value having relationships or maintaining freedom (Campbell et al., 1996; Kashima et al., 1995). Individualist and

individualist cultures

Cultures in which the self is regarded as autonomous, and individual goals and wishes are prized above duty and relations with others.

collectivist cultures

Cultures in which the self is regarded as embedded in relationships, and harmony with one's group is prized above individual goals and wishes.

| Table 2.1 | *Some Average Differences Between Individualist and Collectivist Cultures* |

Members of Individualist Cultures	Members of Collectivist Cultures
Define the self as autonomous, independent of groups	Define the self as an interdependent part of groups
Give priority to individual, personal goals	Give priority to the needs and goals of the group
Value independence, leadership, achievement, "self-fulfillment"	Value group harmony, duty, obligation, security
Give more weight to an individual's attitudes and preferences than to group norms as explanations of behavior	Give more weight to group norms than to individual attitudes as explanations of behavior
Attend to the benefits and costs of relationships; if costs exceed advantages, a person is likely to drop a relationship	Attend to the needs of group members; if a relationship is beneficial to the group but costly to the individual, the individual is likely to stay in the relationship

Source: Triandis, 1996.

collectivist outlooks even affect whether we believe that personality is stable across situations. In a revealing study comparing Japanese and Americans, the Americans reported that their sense of self changes only 5 to 10 percent in different situations, whereas the Japanese said that 90 to 99 percent of their sense of self changes (de Rivera, 1989). For the group-oriented Japanese, it is important to enact *tachiba,* to perform your social roles correctly so that there will be harmony with others. Americans, in contrast, tend to value "being true to your self" and having a "core identity." Thus even basic ideas about what "personality" means and whether it is consistent across situations are deeply affected by culture.

Because they fail to understand the power of culture on behavior, many people attribute another person's mysterious or annoying actions to personality when they are really due to cultural norms. Consider, for example, *conversational distance:* how close people usually stand to one another when they are speaking (Hall, 1959, 1976). Arabs like to stand close enough to feel your breath, touch your arm, and see the pupils of your eyes—a distance that makes white Americans, Canadians, and northern Europeans uneasy, unless they are talking intimately with a lover. The English and the Swedes stand farthest apart when they converse; southern Europeans stand closer; and Latin Americans and Arabs stand the closest (Keating, 1994; Sommer, 1969). One of our students from the Middle East told us he always thought his Anglo classmates were cold and aloof, even prejudiced against him, because they kept moving away from him in conversation. They, in turn, thought he had a "pushy" personality. Each was simply trying to reestablish the conversational distance that made them comfortable.

Cultural psychologists have studied many personality traits that are heavily influenced by cultural values and norms. Take cleanliness. How often do you take baths or showers? Do you regard baths as healthy and invigorating, or as a disgusting wallow in dirty water? How often, and where, do you wash your hands—or feet? A person who might seem obsessively "clean" in one culture might seem an appalling slob in another (Fernea & Fernea, 1994).

Or consider tardiness. Individuals differ in whether they try to be places "on time" or are always late, but cultural norms affect how individuals regard time in the first place. In **monochronic cultures,** such as those of northern Europe,

Canada, and the United States, time is organized into linear segments in which people do one thing "at a time" (Hall, 1983; Hall & Hall, 1990). The day is divided into appointments, schedules, and routines, and because time is a precious commodity, people don't like to "waste" time or "spend" too much time on any one activity. In such cultures, therefore, it is considered the height of rudeness (or high status) to keep someone waiting.

But the further south you go in Europe, the Americas, and Africa, the more likely you are to find **polychronic cultures.** Here, time is organized along parallel lines. People do many things at once, and the needs of friends and family supersede those of the appointment book. People in Latin America and the Middle East think nothing of waiting all day, or even a week, to see someone. The idea of having to be somewhere "on time," as if time were more important than a person, is unthinkable.

In culturally diverse North America, the two time systems keep bumping into each other. Business, government, and other institutions are organized monochronically, but Native Americans, Latinos, African-Americans, and other people tend to operate on polychronic principles. The result is repeated misunderstandings. A white judge in Miami got into hot water when he observed that "Cubans always show up two hours late for weddings"—late in his culture's terms, that is. The judge was accurate in his observation; the problem was his implication that something was wrong with Cubans for being "late." And "late" compared to what, by the way? The Cubans were perfectly on time for Cubans.

Evaluating Cultural Theories

A woman we know, originally from England, married a Lebanese man. They were happy together but had the usual number of marital misunderstandings and squabbles. After a few years, they visited his home town in Lebanon, where she had never been. "I was stunned," she told us. "All the things I thought he did because of his *personality* turned out to be because he's *Lebanese!* Everyone there was just like him!"

Our friend's reaction illustrates both the contributions and the limitations of cultural theories of personality. She was right in recognizing that some of her husband's behavior was attributable to his culture—for example, his Lebanese notions of time were very different from her English no-

---

monochronic cultures

Cultures in which time is organized sequentially; schedules and deadlines are valued over people.

polychronic cultures

Cultures in which time is organized horizontally; people tend to do several things at once and value relationships over schedules.

tions. But she was wrong to infer that the Lebanese are all "like him": Individuals are affected by their culture, but they vary within it.

Cultural psychologists face the key problem of how to describe cultural influences on personality without stereotyping (Church & Lonner, 1998). As one student of ours put it, "How come when we students speak of 'the' Japanese or 'the' blacks or 'the' whites or 'the' Latinos, it's called stereotyping, and when you do it, it's called 'cross-cultural psychology'?" This question shows excellent critical thinking! The study of culture does not rest on the assumption that all members of a culture behave the same way. As we have already seen in this chapter, individuals vary according to their temperaments, beliefs, and learning histories, and this variation occurs within every culture. But the fact that individuals vary within a culture does not negate the existence of cultural rules that, on average, make Swedes different from Bedouins or Cambodians different from Italians.

Thinking Critically About Culture and Personality

Cultural theories of personality remind us, therefore, that what we value, how we behave, the qualities we like in ourselves and the ones we would like to root out all start with the culture or ethnic group in which we are raised.

??? QUICK QUIZ

Are you from a culture that values taking quizzes?

1. Are cultures whose members regard the "self" as a collection of stable personality traits individualist or collectivist?

2. Are cultures whose members do many things at once and value relationships over schedules and appointments monochronic or polychronic?

3. Which of the terms in items 1 and 2 apply to the majority culture in the United States and Canada?

Answers:
1. individualist   2. polychronic   3. individualist, monochronic

We turn now to approaches to personality that depart from mainstream empirical psychology, in both theory and methods. Psychodynamic and humanist views of the person regard the objective measurement of traits and the piece-by-piece approach of biological, learning, and cultural theories of personality as fragmented and incomplete. Instead, they propose global theories of personality that emphasize the development of the whole person.

What's Ahead ➤

- *In Freud's theory of personality, why are the id and the superego always at war?*

- *When people tell you that you're being "defensive," what defenses might they be thinking of?*

- *How do psychologists regard Freud today— as a genius or a fraud?*

- *What would Carl Jung have to say about Darth Vader?*

- *What are the "objects" in the object-relations approach to personality?*

THE PSYCHODYNAMIC TRADITION

Of all the theories of personality, the psychodynamic approach is the one most embedded in popular culture. A man apologizes for "displacing" his frustrations at work onto his family. A woman suspects that she is "repressing" a childhood trauma. An alcoholic reveals that he is no longer in "denial" about his dependence on drinking. A newspaper columnist advises readers to "sublimate" their anger or risk becoming ill. A teacher informs a divorcing couple that their 8-year-old child is "regressing" to immature behavior. All of this language—about displacing, repressing, denying, sublimating, and regressing—can be traced to the first psychodynamic theory of personality, Sigmund Freud's **psychoanalysis.**

Freud's theory is called **psychodynamic** because it emphasizes the movement of psychological energy within the person, in the form of attachments, conflicts, and motivations. Today many psychodynamic theories exist, differing from Freudian theory and from one another, but they all share five general elements:

1. An emphasis on unconscious **intrapsychic** dynamics, the movement of psychic forces within the mind.

2. An assumption that adult behavior and ongoing problems are determined primarily by experiences in early childhood.

3. A belief that psychological development occurs in fixed stages, during which predictable mental events occur and unconscious issues or crises must be resolved.

4. A focus on fantasies and symbolic meanings of events as the unconscious mind perceives them—a person's *psychic reality*—as the main motivators of personality and behavior.

5. A reliance on subjective rather than objective methods of getting at the truth of a person's life—for example, through analysis of dreams, myths, folklore, symbols, and, most of all, the revelations uncovered in psychotherapy.

In this section, we will introduce you to Freud's ideas, and to two of the many psychodynamic theories that have added new rooms and levels to the original Freudian edifice. Then we will try to show you why attitudes toward Freud range from reverence to contempt—and why he evokes such controversy.

Freud and Psychoanalysis

To enter the world of Sigmund Freud (1856–1939) is to enter a realm of unconscious motives, passions, guilty secrets, unspeakable yearnings, and conflicts between desire and duty. These unseen forces, Freud believed, have far more power over human behavior than consciousness does. The unconscious reveals itself, said Freud, in dreams, in *free association*—talking about anything that pops into your head, without worrying about what anyone will think of you—and in jokes, apparent accidents, and slips of the tongue. The British member of Parliament who referred to the "honourable member from Hell" when he meant to say "Hull," said Freud (1920/1960), was revealing his actual, unconscious appraisal of his colleague.

The Structure of Personality.

In Freud's theory, personality consists of three major systems: the id, the ego, and the superego (see Table 2.2). Any action we take or problem we have results from the interaction and degree of balance among these systems (Freud, 1905b, 1920/1960, 1923/1962).

The **id,** which is present at birth, is the reservoir of unconscious psychological energies and instincts. To Freud, the id was the true psychic reality because it represents the inner world of subjective experience. It operates according to the *pleasure principle,* seeking to reduce tension, avoid pain, and obtain pleasure. The id contains two competing groups of instincts: the life, or sexual, instincts (fueled by psychic energy called the **libido**) and the death, or aggressive, instincts. As energy builds up in the id, tension results. The id may discharge this tension in the form of reflex actions, physical symptoms, or wishful thinking—uncensored mental images and unbidden thoughts.

The **ego,** the second system to emerge, is a referee between the needs of instinct and the demands of society. It obeys the *reality principle,* putting a rein on the id's desire for sex and aggression until a suitable, socially appropriate outlet for them can be found. The ego, said Freud, is both conscious and unconscious, and it represents "reason and good sense."

The **superego,** the last system of personality to develop, represents morality, the rules of parents and society, and the power of authority; it includes the conscience, the inner voice that says you did something wrong. The superego, which is partly conscious but largely unconscious, judges the activities of the id, handing out good feelings (pride, satisfaction) when you do something well and handing out miserable feelings (guilt, shame) when you break the rules.

An old joke summarizes the role of the id, ego, and superego this way: The id says, "I want, and I want it now"; the superego says, "You can't have it; it's bad for you"; and the ego, the rational mediator, says, "Well, maybe you can have some of it—later." According to Freud, the healthy personality must keep all three systems in balance. Someone who is too controlled by the id is gov-

Marginal glossary

psychoanalysis

A theory of personality and a method of psychotherapy developed by Sigmund Freud; it emphasizes unconscious motives and conflicts.

psychodynamic theories

Theories that explain behavior and personality in terms of unconscious energy dynamics within the individual.

intrapsychic

Within the mind (psyche) or self.

id

In psychoanalysis, the part of personality containing inherited psychological energy, particularly sexual and aggressive instincts.

libido

In psychoanalysis, the psychic energy that fuels the sexual or life instincts of the id.

ego

In psychoanalysis, the part of personality that represents reason, good sense, and rational self-control.

superego

In psychoanalysis, the part of personality that represents conscience, morality, and social standards.

Table 2.2	Summary of Freud's Model of the Mind		
	Id	**Ego**	**Superego**
What it does	Expresses sexual and aggressive instincts; follows the pleasure principle	Mediates between desires of the id and demands of the superego; follows the reality principle; uses defense mechanisms to ward off unconscious anxiety	Represents conscience and the rules of society; follows internalized moral standards
How conscious it is	Entirely unconscious	Partly conscious, partly unconscious	Partly conscious, mostly unconscious
When it develops	Present at birth	Emerges after birth, with early formative experiences	Last system to develop; becomes internalized after the Oedipal stage
Example	"I'm so mad I could kill you" (felt unconsciously)	Might make a conscious choice ("Let's talk about this") or resort to an unconscious defense mechanism, such as denial ("What, me angry? Never")	"Thou shalt not kill"

erned by impulse and selfish desires. Someone who is too controlled by the superego is rigid, moralistic, and bossy. Someone who has a weak ego is unable to balance personal needs and wishes with social duties and realistic limitations.

If a person feels anxious or threatened when the wishes of the id conflict with social rules, the ego has weapons at its command to relieve the tension. These weapons, called **defense mechanisms,** have two characteristics: They deny or distort reality, and they operate unconsciously. According to Freud, ego defenses are necessary to protect us from conflict and the stresses of reality; they become unhealthy only when they cause self-defeating behavior and emotional problems. Freud described 17 defense mechanisms; later, other psychoanalysts expanded and modified his list. Here are some of the primary defenses identified by Freud's daughter Anna (1946), who became a psychoanalyst herself, and by most contemporary psychodynamic psychologists (Vaillant, 1992):

1. *Repression* occurs when a threatening idea, memory, or emotion is blocked from consciousness. A woman who had a frightening childhood experience that she cannot remember, for example, is said to be repressing her memory of it.

2. *Projection* occurs when a person's own unacceptable or threatening feelings are repressed and then attributed to someone else. A boy who dislikes his father, for instance, may feel anxious about disliking someone he depends on. So he may project his feelings onto his father, conclud-

ing that "he hates me." Or a person who is embarrassed about having sexual feelings toward members of a different ethnic group may project this discomfort onto them, saying, "Those people are dirty-minded and oversexed."

3. *Displacement* occurs when people direct their emotions (especially anger) toward things, animals, or other people that are not the real object of their feelings. A boy who is forbidden to express anger at his father, for example, may "take it out" on his toys or his younger sister. When displacement serves a higher cultural or socially useful purpose, as in the creation of art or inventions, it is called *sublimation*. Freud argued that society has a duty to help people sublimate their unacceptable impulses, for the sake of civilization. Thus aggressive impulses might be displaced in sports competition instead of directly expressed in war, and sexual impulses might be displaced in the creation of passionate poetry and literature.

4. *Reaction formation* occurs when a feeling that produces unconscious anxiety is transformed into its opposite in consciousness. A woman who is afraid to admit to herself that she doesn't love her husband may cling to the belief that she loves him deeply. A person who is aroused by erotic images may angrily assert that pornography is disgusting. How does such a transformed emotion differ from a true emotion? In reaction formation, the professed feeling is excessive: The person "protests too much" and is extravagant and compulsive about demonstrating it. ("Of course I love him! I *never* have any bad thoughts about him! He's perfect!")

defense mechanisms
Methods used by the ego to prevent unconscious anxiety or threatening thoughts from entering consciousness.

"I'm sorry, I'm not speaking to anyone tonight.
My defense mechanisms seem to be out of order."

5. *Regression* occurs when a person reverts to a previous phase of psychic development. As we will see, Freud believed that personality develops in a series of stages from birth to maturity. People may regress to an earlier stage if they suffer a traumatic experience in a later one. An 8-year-old boy who is anxious about his parents' divorce may regress to earlier habits of thumb sucking or clinging. Adults may regress to immature behavior when they are under pressure—for example, by having a temper tantrum if they don't get their way.

6. *Denial* occurs when people refuse to admit that something unpleasant is happening or that they are experiencing a "forbidden" emotion. Some people deny that they are angry; alcoholics may deny that they depend on liquor. Denial protects a person's self-image or preserves the illusion of invulnerability ("It can't happen to me").

The Development of Personality. Freud maintained that personality develops in a series of stages. He called these stages *psychosexual* because he believed that psychological development depends on the changing expression of sexual energy in different parts of the body as the child matures. Each new step, however, produces a certain amount of frustration, conflict, and anxiety. If these become too great, normal development may be halted, and the child may remain *fixated*, or stuck, at the current stage.

1. *The oral stage* marks the first year of life. Babies take in the world, as well as their nourishment, through their mouths, so the mouth, said Freud, is the focus of sensation at this stage.

Adults who remain fixated at the oral stage (because they were either overindulged as infants when nursing or weaned too abruptly) may seek oral gratification in smoking, drinking, overeating, nail biting, chewing on pencils, and the like. Like a nursing child, they may be clinging and dependent, or they may deny their dependence by acting brash and tough.

2. *The anal stage*, at about age 2 to 3, marks the start of ego development, as the child becomes aware of the self and of the demands of reality. The major issue at this stage, said Freud, is control of bodily wastes, a lesson in self-control that the child learns during toilet training. People who remain fixated at this stage, he thought, become "anal retentive," holding everything in, obsessive about neatness and cleanliness. Or they become just the opposite, "anal expulsive"—that is, messy and disorganized.

Is she fixated at the oral stage?

3. *The phallic (or Oedipal) stage* lasts roughly from age 3 to age 5 or 6. Now sexual sensation is located in the penis, for boys, and in the clitoris, for girls. The child, said Freud, unconsciously wishes to possess the parent of the other sex and to get rid of the parent of the same sex. Children of this age often announce proudly that "I'm going to marry Daddy (or Mommy) when I grow up," and they reject the same-sex "rival." Freud (1924a, 1924b) labeled this phenomenon the **Oedipus complex,** after the Greek legend of King Oedipus, who unwittingly killed his father and married his mother.

Boys and girls, Freud believed, go through the Oedipal stage differently. Boys at this stage are discovering the pleasure and pride of having a penis. When they see a naked girl for the first time, they are horrified. Their unconscious exclaims (in effect), "Her penis has been cut off! Who could have done such a thing to her? Why, it must have been her powerful father. And if he could do it to her, my father could do it to me!" This realization, said Freud, causes the boy to repress his desire for his mother and identify with his father. He accepts his father's authority and the father's standards of conscience and morality; the superego has emerged.

Freud admitted that he didn't quite know what to make of girls, who, lacking the penis, couldn't go through the same steps. He speculated that a girl, upon discovering male anatomy, would panic that she had only a puny clitoris instead of a stately penis. She would conclude, said Freud, that she already had lost her penis. As a result, girls don't have the powerful motivating fear that boys do to give up their Oedipal feelings and develop a strong superego; they have only a lingering sense of "penis envy."

By about age 5 or 6, when the Oedipus complex is resolved, said Freud, the child's personality patterns are formed. Unconscious conflicts with parents, unresolved fixations and guilts, and attitudes toward the same and the other sex will continue to replay themselves throughout life.

4. *The latency stage,* said Freud, lasts from the end of the phallic stage until puberty. The mental conflicts of the Oedipal complex are repressed; the child settles down, goes to school, develops self-confidence, and learns the social rules for appropriate male or female behavior. (Freud thought that during this period, sexual feelings are dormant—but modern sex research has shown him to be wrong.)

5. *The genital stage* begins at puberty and marks the beginning of what Freud considered mature adult sexuality. Sexual energy is now located in the genitals and eventually is directed toward sexual intercourse.

To sum up: In Freud's view, your adult personality is shaped by how you progressed through the psychosexual stages of development; which defense mechanisms you have learned to use to reduce anxiety; and whether your ego is strong enough to balance the conflict between the id (what you'd like to do) and the superego (your conscience).

As you might imagine, Freud's ideas were not exactly received with yawns. Sexual feelings in infants and children! Repressed longings in the most respectable adults! Unconscious meanings in dreams! Penis envy! Sexual sublimation! This was strong stuff, and before long, psychoanalysis had captured the public imagination in Europe and America. But it also produced a sharp rift with the emerging schools of empirical psychology (Hornstein, 1992).

This rift continues to divide psychologists today. Many revere Freud as a hero who bravely battled public censure and ridicule in his unwavering pursuit of scientific truth (Gay, 1988). Others acknowledge that some of Freud's ideas have proved faulty, but they believe that the overall framework of his theory is timeless and brilliant. Others, especially scientifically oriented psychologists, think psychoanalytic theory is, frankly, nonsense, with little empirical support. Citing recently uncovered documents, these critics argue that Freud was not the brilliant theoretician, impartial scientist, or even the successful clinician that he claimed to be. On the contrary, Freud often pressured his patients into accepting his explanations of their symptoms; and many of his most famous patients would today have every ground to sue him for malpractice and unethical behavior (Cioffi, 1974; Crews, 1995; Esterson, 1993; Powell & Boer, 1994, 1995; Sulloway, 1992; Webster, 1995).

One such patient was "Dora" (Ida Bauer), an 18-year-old who had been spurning the explicit sexual advances made by her father's friend, "Herr K," since she was 14 (Lakoff & Coyne, 1993). Dora finally complained to her father. But her father wanted her to accept Herr K's overtures, perhaps because he himself was having an affair with Herr K's wife; so he sent her off to Freud, who attempted to cure her of her "hysterical" refusal to have sex with Herr K. Freud tried to convince Dora that it was not the ugly situation involving her father and his friend that was distressing her, but her own *repressed desires* for sex.

Oedipus complex
In psychoanalysis, a conflict in which a child desires the parent of the other sex and views the same-sex parent as a rival; this is the key issue in the phallic stage of development.

Dora angrily left treatment after three months, and Freud was never able to accept her "obstinate" refusals to believe his analysis of her symptoms. If only Herr K had learned, said Freud, "that the slap Dora gave him by no means signified a final 'No' on her part," and if he had resolved "to press his suit with a passion which left room for no doubts, the result might very well have been a triumph of the girl's affection for him over all her internal difficulties."

Sigmund Freud was thus a man of contradictions—a mix of intellectual vision and blindness, sensitivity and arrogance (Hunt, 1993). His provocative ideas and his approach to therapy left a powerful legacy to psychology. And it was one that others began to tinker with immediately.

??? QUICK QUIZ

Which Freudian concepts do these events suggest?

1. A 4-year-old girl wants to snuggle on Daddy's lap but refuses to kiss her mother.

2. A celibate priest writes poetry about sexual passion.

3. A man who is angry at his boss shouts at his kids for making noise.

4. A woman who was molested by her stepfather for many years assures her friends that she adores him and thinks he is perfect.

5. A racist justifies segregation by saying that black men are only interested in sex with white women.

6. A 9-year-old boy who moves to a new city starts having tantrums.

Answers:
1. Oedipus complex   2. sublimation   3. displacement   4. reaction formation   5. projection   6. regression

---

Two Other Psychodynamic Approaches

Some of Freud's followers stayed in the psychoanalytic tradition and modified Freud's theories from within. Karen Horney [HORN-eye], for example, argued that it is insulting philosophy and bad science to claim that half the human race is dissatisfied with its anatomy. When women feel inferior to men, she said, we should look for explanations in the disadvantages that women live with and their second-class status. In fact, said Horney, if anyone has an envy problem, it is men. Men have "womb envy": They envy women's ability to bear and nurse children.

Others broke away from Freud, or were actively rejected by him, and went off to start their own schools. Today, there are many psychodynamic approaches, but two are especially popular: the work of Carl Jung and that of the object-relations theorists.

Jungian Theory.   Carl Jung (1875–1961) was originally one of Freud's closest friends, but by 1914 he had left Freud's inner circle. His greatest difference with Freud concerned the nature of the unconscious. In addition to the individual's own unconscious, said Jung (1967), there is a **collective unconscious** containing universal memories, symbols, and images that are the legacy of human history. In his studies of myths, art, and folklore in cultures all over the world, Jung identified a number of these common themes, which he called **archetypes.**

An archetype, he said, can be a picture, such as the "magic circle," called a *mandala* in Eastern religions, which Jung thought symbolizes the unity of life and "the totality of the self." Or it can be a mythical figure, such as the Hero, the Nurturing Mother, the Powerful Father, or the Wicked Witch. It can even be an aspect of the self. For example, the *persona* is the public personality, the aspects of yourself that you reveal to others, the role that society expects you to play. The *shadow* archetype reflects the prehistoric fear of wild animals and represents the sinister, evil side of human nature. Although most psychologists feel that Jung's idea of the collective unconscious is a mystical concept rather than a scientific one, they recognize that some basic archetypes, such as the

collective unconscious

To Carl Jung, the universal memories and experiences of humankind, represented in the unconscious images and symbols of all people.

archetypes (AR-ki-tipes)

In Jungian theory, universal, symbolic images that appear in myths, art, dreams, and other expressions of the collective unconscious.

To Jungians, Dracula can never be killed because he represents the shadow archetype, the evil side of human nature.

Hero and the Earth Mother, do appear in virtually every society, taking different forms (Campbell, 1949/1968; Neher, 1996). Jung would recognize dragons, Darth Vader, and Dracula as expressions of the shadow archetype.

Two of the most important archetypes, in Jung's view, are those of maleness and femaleness. Jung (like Freud) recognized that human beings are psychologically bisexual—that is, that "masculine" and "feminine" qualities exist in both sexes. The *anima* represents the feminine archetype in men; the *animus* represents the masculine archetype in women. Problems can arise, however, if a person tries to repress his or her internal, opposite archetype: that is, if a man totally denies his softer "feminine" side or if a woman denies her "masculine" aspects. People also create problems in relationships when they expect the partner to behave like the ideal archetypal man or woman, instead of a human being who has both sides (Young-Eisendrath, 1993).

Although Jung shared with Freud a fascination with the unconscious side of the personality, he (along with several other dissenters from Freudian orthodoxy) had confidence in the positive, forward-moving strengths of the ego. For Jung, people are motivated not only by past conflicts, but also by their future goals and their desire to fulfill themselves. This emphasis anticipated the humanist movement by several decades. Jung also accurately anticipated modern trait research by

many years when he identified introversion–extroversion as a central personality orientation.

Some Jungians are interested in how universal images and stories affect the way people see their own lives. When Dan McAdams (1988) asked 50 people to tell their life stories in a two-hour session, he found that people tended to report a common archetype, a mythic character, at the heart of their life narratives. For example, many individuals told stories that could be symbolized by the myth of the Greek god Dionysus, the pleasure seeker who escapes responsibility. Archetypes, says McAdams, represent "the main characters in the life stories we construct as our identities."

The Object-Relations School.

In the late 1950s, John Bowlby (1958), a British psychoanalyst, contested the Freudian view that an infant's attachment to its mother is due to her ability to gratify the baby's oral needs. Bowlby observed that infants who were deprived of normal contact with parents and other adults suffered catastrophically, and he argued for the primacy of attachment needs—social stimulation, warmth, and contact. Bowlby's work influenced other psychoanalysts to acknowledge the fundamentally social nature of human development. Although the need for social contact in infancy now seems obvious, this change in emphasis was a significant departure from the classic Freudian view, for Freud essentially regarded the baby as if it were an independent little organism ruled by its own instinctive desires.

Today, an emphasis on relationships is associated with the **object-relations school,** which was developed in Great Britain by Melanie Klein, W. Ronald Fairbairn, and D. W. Winnicott (Horner, 1991; Hughes, 1989). In contrast to Freud's emphasis on the Oedipal period, object-relations theorists hold that the first two years of life are the most critical for development of the inner core of personality. Freud emphasized the child's fear of the powerful father; object-relations analysts emphasize the child's need for the powerful mother, who is usually the baby's caregiver in the first critical years. Freud's theory was based on the dynamics of inner drives; object-relations theory holds that the basic human drive is not impulse gratification but the need to be in relationships.

The reason for the clunky word "object" in object-relations theory (instead of the warmer word "human" or even "parent") is that the infant's attachment isn't only to a person but also to the infant's evolving perception of the person. In this theory, the child initially "takes in" a *representation*

object-relations school
A psychodynamic approach that emphasizes the importance of the infant's first two years of life and the baby's formative relationships.

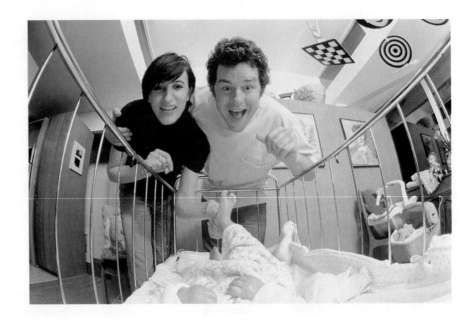

According to object-relations theory, a baby constructs unconscious representations of his or her parents—representations that will later influence the child's relations with others.

of the mother—someone who is kind or fierce, protective or rejecting—that is not literally the same as the woman herself. "Object relations" reflect both the numerous representations of the self and others that the child eventually constructs, and the psychodynamic interplay among them (Horner, 1991). These representations, whether realistic or distorted, may unconsciously affect the individual's personality throughout life, influencing how the person relates to others—with trust or suspicion, acceptance or criticism.

In Freudian theory, as we saw, the central dynamic tension is the shifting of psychic energy—sexual and aggressive energy in particular—within the individual. Other people are relevant only insofar as they gratify our drives or block them. But to object-relations theorists, other people are important as sources of attachment. Therefore the central dynamic tension is the constantly changing balance between independence and connection to others. This balance requires constant adjustment to separations and losses: small ones that occur during quarrels, moderate ones such as leaving home for the first time, and major ones such as divorce or death. In object-relations theory, the way we react to these separations is largely determined by our experiences in the first two years of life, and some theorists would say in the first months.

The object-relations school also departs from Freudian theory regarding the nature of male and female development (Chodorow, 1978; Sagan, 1988; Winnicott, 1957/1990). In the object-relations view, children of both sexes identify first with the mother. Girls, who are the same sex as the mother, do not need to separate from her; the mother treats a daughter as an extension of herself. But boys, if they are to develop a masculine identity, must break away from the mother; the mother encourages a son to be independent and separate. Some object-relations theorists believe that this process is inevitable because women are biologically suited to be the primary nurturers. But others, such as Nancy Chodorow (1978, 1992), argue that the process is culturally determined, and that if men played a greater role in the nurturing of infants and small children, the sex difference in the need for separation from the mother would fade.

In either case, in the object-relations view, a man's identity is less secure than a woman's identity because it is based on *not* being like women. Men develop more rigid *ego boundaries* between themselves and other people, whereas women's boundaries are more permeable. Later in life, runs this argument, the typical psychological problem for women is how to increase their autonomy and independence, so they can assert their own needs and abilities in close relationships. In contrast, the typical problem for men is permitting close attachments (Gilligan, 1982).

Evaluating Psychodynamic Theories

Although modern psychodynamic theorists differ in many ways, they share Freud's general approach to personality and his assumptions about uncon-

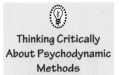

Thinking Critically About Psychodynamic Methods

scious dynamics. Many psychologists in other fields, however, regard psychodynamic ideas as descriptive metaphors, more poetic than scientific. More specifically, empirical psychologists accuse psychodynamic approaches to personality of three scientific failings:

1. *Violating the principle of falsifiability.* As we saw in Chapter 1, a theory that is impossible to disconfirm in principle is not scientific. Many psychodynamic ideas about unconscious motivations are, in fact, impossible to confirm or disconfirm. If your experience seems to support these ideas, it is taken as evidence of their correctness, but if you doubt them or offer disconfirming evidence, you must be "defensive," or (a favorite accusation) you are "in denial." This way of responding to criticism is neither scientific nor fair!

2. *Drawing universal principles from the experiences of a few atypical patients.* Freud and most of his followers generalized from a few individuals, often patients in therapy, to all human beings. Of course, the problem of overgeneralizing from small samples also occurs in other areas of psychology, and sometimes valid insights about human behavior can be obtained from case studies. The problem occurs when the observer fails to confirm these observations by studying other samples and incorrectly infers that what applies to some individuals must apply to all. For example, to confirm Freud's ideas about penis envy, you would need to observe or talk to many young children. Freud himself did not do this; however, when research psychologists interview preschool-

age children, they typically find that many children of *both* sexes envy one another. In one charming study of 65 preschool-age boys and girls, 45 percent of the girls had fantasized about having a penis or being male in other ways—and 44 percent of the boys had fantasized about being pregnant (Linday, 1994).

3. *Basing theories of development on the retrospective accounts and fallible memories of patients.* Most psychodynamic theorists have not observed random samples of children at different ages, as modern child psychologists do, to construct their theories of development. Instead they have worked backward, creating theories based on themes in adults' recollections. The analysis of memories can be an illuminating way to achieve insights about our lives; in fact, it is the only way we can think about our own lives! But as we will see in Chapter 7, memory is often inaccurate, influenced as much by what is going on in a person's current life as by what actually happened. If you are currently not getting along with your mother, you may remember all the times in your childhood when she seemed to treat you unkindly and forget the counterexamples of her kindness.

Retrospective analysis also has another problem: It creates an *illusion of causality* between events. People often assume, without justification, that if A came before B, then A must have caused B. For example, if your mother spent three months in the hospital when you were 5 years old and today you are having trouble in school, you might draw a connection between the two facts. (An object-relations analyst probably would.) But a lot of other things in your present circumstances could also be causing your school difficulties.

Some psychodynamic ideas can be tested empirically. To Freudians, for example, sports such as football and hockey permit the displacement of aggressive energy into a socially accepted activity, thereby reducing aggressiveness. But behavioral research repeatedly finds that such sports actually stimulate hostility and violence among players, and among spectators like these soccer fans.

In response to the concerns of critics, some psychodynamic psychologists are turning to empirical methods and research findings to reformulate and refine their theories and clinical assessments. For example, some are developing objective tests of defense mechanisms to find out how these strategies protect self-esteem and reduce anxiety (Margo et al., 1993; Plutchik et al., 1988). Psychologists in other fields are also investigating psychodynamic concepts, such as nonconscious processes in thought and memory (Epstein, 1994; Kihlstrom, Barnhardt, & Tataryn, 1992).

Psychodynamic ideas will continue to be controversial, but these ideas have encouraged researchers to tackle large, fascinating, and difficult questions: why some symbols are universal; why men and women regard each other as often with envy and animosity as with love; why individuals are sometimes unaware of their own motives; and why people unconsciously repeat patterns of behavior that seem irrational to others.

??? QUICK QUIZ

Find out whether the correct response to each of these questions is in the conscious part of your mind.

1. An 8-year-old boy is behaving aggressively in class, hitting other children, and refusing to obey the teacher. Match each explanation of his behavior with the appropriate theorist: Freud, Jung, or object-relations theorists.

   a. The boy has repressed his internal *anima* archetype.

   b. The boy is expressing the aggressive energy of the id and has not developed enough ego control.

   c. The boy has had unusual difficulty separating emotionally from his mother and is compensating by behaving aggressively.

2. In the 1950s and 1960s, many psychoanalysts, observing unhappy gay men who had sought therapy, concluded that homosexuality was a mental illness. What violation of the scientific method were they committing?

Answers:

1. a. Jung   b. Freud   c. object-relations theorists   2. The analysts were drawing inappropriate conclusions from atypical patients in therapy, failing to test these conclusions with a sample of gay men who were not in therapy or with a sample of heterosexuals in therapy. When such research was actually done, by the way, it turned out that gay men were not more mentally disturbed or depressed than heterosexuals (Hooker, 1957).

What's Ahead

- *How does the humanist vision of human nature differ from the visions of behaviorism and psychoanalysis?*

- *In the humanist view, what's wrong with saying to a child, "I love you because you've been good"?*

THE HUMANIST TRADITION

humanist psychology

A psychological approach that emphasizes personal growth and the achievement of human potential rather than the scientific understanding and assessment of behavior.

A final way to look at personality starts with the person's own view of the world—his or her subjective interpretation of what is happening right now. Psychologists who take a *humanist* approach to personality believe that personality is influenced less by our genes, past learning, or unconscious conflicts than by our uniquely human capacity to shape our own futures. It is defined, they say, by the human abilities that separate us from other animals: freedom of choice and free will.

The Inner Experience

Humanist psychology was launched as a movement within psychology in the early 1960s. Humanists rejected the psychoanalytic emphasis on hostility, instincts, and conflict. They also rejected the fragmented approach of behaviorism, with its emphasis on pieces of the person. The movement's chief leaders—Abraham Maslow (1908–1970), Rollo May (1909–1994), and Carl

Rogers (1902–1987)—argued that it was time for a "third force" in psychology, one that would deal with people's real problems and draw a fuller picture of human potential.

The trouble with psychology, said Maslow (1971), was that it had forgotten many of the positive aspects of human nature, such as joy, laughter, love, happiness, and *peak experiences* (rare moments of rapture caused by the attainment of excellence or the drive toward higher values). The traits that Maslow thought most important to personality were not the Big Five, but rather the qualities of the *self-actualized person*—the person who strives for a life that is meaningful, challenging, and productive. Personality development could be viewed, he thought, as a gradual progression toward a state of self-actualization. As Maslow (1971) wrote, "When you select out for careful study very fine and healthy people, strong people, creative people, saintly people, sagacious people . . . then you get a very different view of mankind. You are asking how tall can people grow, what can a human being become?"

Carl Rogers, like Freud, derived many of his ideas from observing his clients in therapy. As a clinician, Rogers (1951, 1961) was interested not only in why some people cannot function well, but also in what he called the fully functioning individual. How you behave depends on your subjective reality, Rogers said, not on the external reality around you. Fully functioning people experience *congruence,* or harmony, between their self-image and their true feelings, perceptions, and wishes. Such people are trusting, warm, and open instead of defensive or intolerant. Their beliefs about themselves are realistic.

To become fully functioning people, Rogers maintained, we all need **unconditional positive regard,** love and support for the people we are, without strings (conditions) attached. This doesn't mean that Winifred should be allowed to kick her brother when she is angry with him or that Wilbur may throw his dinner out the window because he doesn't like pot roast. In these cases, a parent can correct the child's behavior without withdrawing love from the child. The child can learn that the behavior, not the child, is what is bad. "House rules are 'no violence,' Winifred," is a very different message from "You are a horrible person, Winifred."

Unfortunately, Rogers observed, many children are raised with *conditional* positive regard. The condition is "I'll love you if you behave well, and I won't love you if you behave badly." Adults often treat each other this way, too. People

In the humanist view, many individuals disguise their real selves from others—and from themselves. Fully functioning people, however, are able to be open, honest, and authentic, and need not mask their true personalities.

treated with conditional regard begin to suppress or deny feelings or actions that they believe are unacceptable to those they love. The result, said Rogers, is the sensation of being "out of touch with your feelings," of not being true to your "real self." The suppression of feelings and parts of oneself produces low self-regard, defensiveness, and unhappiness. The result is an individual who scores high on neuroticism—who is bitter, unhappy, and negative.

Not all humanists have been optimistic about human nature. Rollo May emphasized some of the inherently difficult and tragic aspects of the human condition, including loneliness, anxiety, and alienation. In books such as *The Meaning of Anxiety, Existential Psychology,* and *Love and Will,* May brought to American psychology elements of the European philosophy of *existentialism.* This doctrine holds that we have free will and freedom of choice, which confers on us responsibility for our actions. Freedom, and its burden of responsibility, carries a price in anxiety and despair, which is why so many people try to escape from freedom into narrow certainties and blame others for their misfortunes. Our personalities reflect the ways we cope with what existentialist therapist Irvin Yalom (1989) calls the

unconditional positive regard

To Carl Rogers, love or support given to another person, with no conditions attached.

66   PART ONE   Your Self

"givens of existence"—the inevitable struggle to find meaning in life, to use our freedom wisely, and to face suffering and death with courage.

Humanist psychologists depart from many other schools of psychology in maintaining that our lives are not inevitably determined by our parents, our pasts, or our present circumstances; we have the power to choose our own destinies, even when fate delivers us into tragedy.

Evaluating Humanist Theories

As with psychodynamic theories, the major criticism of humanist psychology is that because it is closer to philosophy than to science, many of its assumptions are untestable. Freud looked at humanity and saw destructive drives, selfishness, and lust. Maslow and Rogers looked at humanity and saw cooperation, selflessness, and love. May looked at humanity and saw fear of freedom, loneliness, and the struggle for meaning. These differences, say the critics, may tell us more about the observers than about the observed.

Many humanist concepts, although intuitively appealing, are hard to define operationally (see Chapter 1). How can we know whether a person is self-fulfilled or self-actualized? How can we

Thinking Critically About Testing Humanist Ideas

tell whether a woman's decision to quit her job and become a professional rodeo rider represents an "escape from freedom" or a freely made choice? And what exactly is unconditional positive regard? If it is interpreted as unquestioned support of a child's efforts at mastering a new skill, or as assurance that the child is loved in spite of his or her mistakes, then it's clearly a good idea. But in the popular culture, it has often been interpreted as an unwillingness ever to say "no" to a child, offer constructive criticism, or set limits—all of which, as we will see in the next chapter, children need.

Despite such concerns, humanist psychologists have added balance to the study of personality. Influenced in part by the humanists, scientific psychologists in other perspectives are studying many positive human traits, such as creativity, helpfulness to others, the motivation to excel, and self-confidence. Stress researchers have discovered the healing powers of humor and hope. Developmental psychologists have shown how parents can foster or crush a child's empathy and creativity. Thus humanist ideas have drawn attention to some previously ignored facets of personality.

??? QUICK QUIZ

Exercise free will and choose to take this quiz.

1. According to Carl Rogers, a man who loves his wife only when she is looking her best is giving her positive regard that is (a) conditional or (b) unconditional.

2. The humanist who described the importance of having peak experiences was (a) Rollo May, (b) Abraham Maslow, (c) Carl Rogers.

3. A humanist and a psychoanalyst are arguing about human nature. What underlying assumptions about psychology and human potential are they likely to bring to their discussion, and what do their assumptions overlook?

Answers:

1. a 2. b 3. The analyst assumes that human nature is basically selfish and destructive, that it is basically loving and life-affirming. Their assumptions overlook the facts that human beings have both capacities, and the situation often determines which capacity is expressed.

Together, the five approaches to personality discussed in this chapter portray a complex constellation of qualities that make up a human being. Biological research teaches us to appreciate the genetic influences on a person's typical ways of behaving in the world. Learning theories remind us that experiences also influence us, and that people do not behave the same way across all

situations or throughout their lives. Cognitive social-learning research shows how beliefs, values, and expectations, such as those involved in locus of control, become internalized as stable aspects of personality. Cultural approaches show us that traits, beliefs, and behavior are influenced by cultural rules and expectations. Psychodynamic theories contribute an appreciation of the uncon-

Table 2.3	Competing Explanations of Personality				
	Basic method of inquiry	Basic units of study	Basic view of human nature	Possibility of personal change	Influence of culture on behavior
Biological theories	Empirical	Genes, traits, temperament	Neutral	Limited by temperament and genetically influenced traits	Interacts with genetic dispositions
Learning theories { Behaviorism	Empirical	Behavior in a given situation	Neutral	Good, if environment changes	Affects what a society wants its members to learn and value
Cognitive social-learning theories	Empirical	Behavior, cognitions, internalized beliefs and values	Neutral	Good because of ability for self-regulation	
Cultural theories	Empirical	Behavior, cognitions, beliefs and values	Neutral	Limited by cultural norms, practices, and attitudes toward individual expression	Heavily influences many aspects of personality
Psychodynamic theories { Freud	Subjective	Unconscious dynamics	Pessimistic	Limited by unconscious motives and early formative experiences	Largely irrelevant; unconscious forces are universal
Modern schools	Usually subjective, some empirical research	Unconscious dynamics	Varies; some more optimistic than classical psychoanalysis		
Humanist theories	Subjective, but some ideas have influenced empirical research	Conscious self	Generally optimistic	Good, if person exercises free will and takes responsibility for change	All human beings share basic needs and must face the inherent dilemmas of life

scious motives and defenses that affect people's behavior and create distinctive, sometimes destructive, ways of coping with life. And humanist approaches draw our attention to the uplifting possibilities of human nature, as well as to the universal struggle to make sense of what it means to be human. (For a summary of these five approaches to personality, see Table 2.3.)

One way to integrate these perspectives lies in recognizing that personality has two dimensions. Each of us has a public personality that we present to the world, consisting of our characteristic habits and temperaments and our basic traits. This is the personality that biological, learning, and cultural theories address. But we also have a private personality that reflects our interior sense of self, consisting of the subjective experience of emotions, memories, dreams, wishes, and worries (Hermans, 1996; Singer, 1984). This is the personality that psychodynamic and humanistic theories address. Each of us weaves these two dimensions of personality together in the narratives we tell to explain our lives, our inconsistencies, our failures and successes.

How are these dimensions woven together in Dennis Rodman, whose controversial personality was described in the news item at the start of this chapter? The biological approach suggests that some of Rodman's traits probably have a genetic basis, in particular his extroversion (one of the Big Five personality traits) and perhaps his pugnaciousness, as well. We do not know what Rodman was like as a little boy, but it's highly unlikely that he was a wallflower—or that he'll ever become one.

A learning theorist, however, would remind us that our knowledge of Rodman is based only on his public appearances and the media's coverage of those appearances. We would understand him a lot better if we knew how he behaves with close friends and relatives, or when he is discussing strategy with his teammates or relaxing after a hard day. As we have seen, people are not always consistent; their behavior depends in part on the situation. So Dennis Rodman may be hardworking, smart, and efficient, as his supporters argue, *and* outlandish, childish, and silly, as his detractors complain.

Psychologists who take a learning perspective would also point out that any innate tendencies Rodman had to be flamboyant were undoubtedly rewarded by attention. Today his outlandish behavior puts him in the limelight and earns him millions of dollars—pretty powerful reinforcers. He is able to get these rewards, the cultural perspective tells us, because American culture values and encourages individual expression. In a group-oriented culture, where fitting in with the group is more important, people would respond to Rodman's antics by snubbing or shunning him.

Psychodynamic and humanist psychologists would agree that the private Dennis Rodman, the one that lives inside his skin and not inside his glittering outfits, could be quite different from the Dennis Rodman we see on the basketball court or on TV. A psychodynamic theorist might even speculate that Rodman's outrageous posturing is a defense mechanism that masks inner feelings of insecurity and inadequacy, and reflects a desperate need for approval. Like the learning approach, psychodynamic and humanistic approaches teach us to be wary of forming impressions of celebrities solely on the basis of the images they create for public consumption.

Ultimately, then, we can only guess at who the "real" Dennis Rodman is. All of us, however, can use the insights of the theorists in this chapter to better understand ourselves and the people in our lives. Genetic influences, learned habits, cultural norms, unconscious fears and conflicts, and visions of possibility, filtered through our interior sense of self and our life story, give each of us the stamp of our personality . . . one that is as distinctive as a fingerprint.

Taking Psychology with You

How to Avoid the Barnum Effect

How well does the following paragraph describe you?

Some of your aspirations tend to be pretty unrealistic. At times you are extroverted, affable, sociable, while at other times you are introverted, wary, and reserved. You have found it unwise to be too frank in revealing yourself to others. You pride yourself on being an independent thinker and do not accept others' opinions without satisfactory proof. You prefer a certain amount of change and variety, and you become dissatisfied when hemmed in by restrictions and limitations. At times you have serious doubts as to whether you have made the right decision or done the right thing.

When people believe that this description was written just for them—the result of a personalized horoscope, "personality profile," or handwriting analysis—they all say the same thing: "It's me! It describes me *exactly!*" The reason is that this description is vague enough to apply to almost everyone and flattering enough to get almost anyone to accept it (French et al., 1991). The magician James Randi often gives audiences of college students a similar "personalized profile" and asks them to rate it for its accuracy. Audience members invariably rate their profiles as highly accurate—until Randi asks them to exchange profiles with a neighbor, and they realize that all the descriptions are identical.

It is sad but true that people are more willing to believe flattering statements about themselves than statements that are scientifically accurate (Thiriart, 1991). And if they must pay money for a profile, take the time to write away for it, or give detailed information about themselves, they are all the more likely to believe that the profile is "eerily accurate." A French psychologist once advertised himself as an astrologer. In reply to the hundreds of people who wrote to him for his services, he sent out the same vague horoscope. More than 200 recipients sent him thank-you notes praising his accuracy and perceptiveness (Snyder & Shenkel, 1975).

This is why many psychologists worry about people who fall prey to the "P. T. Barnum effect." Barnum was the great circus showman who said, "There's a sucker born every minute." He knew that the formula for success was to "have a little something for everybody"—which is what unscientific personality profiles, horoscopes, and handwriting tests have in common. To help you avoid the Barnum effect, research offers a few strategies:

• *Beware of all-purpose descriptions that could apply to anyone*. We know a couple who were terribly impressed when an astrologer told them that "each of you needs privacy and time to be independent," along with "but don't become too independent, or you will lose your bond." Such observations, which play it safe by playing it both ways, apply to just about all couples.

• *Beware of your own selective perceptions*. Most of us are so impressed when a horoscope or supposed psychic gets something right that we overlook all the descriptions that are plain wrong.

• *Resist flattery*. This is the hard one. Most of us would reject a profile that described us as being nasty, sullen, and stupid, or unoriginal and eager to steal other people's ideas. But many of us fall for profiles that tell us how wonderful and smart we are, or how modest we are about our abilities.

If you keep your critical faculties with you, you won't end up paying hard cash for soft answers, pawning the piano because Geminis should invest in gold this month, or taking a job you despise because it fits your "personality type." In other words, you will prove Barnum wrong.

SUMMARY

The Elements of Personality

1) *Personality* is usually defined as an individual's distinctive and relatively stable pattern of behavior, motives, thoughts, and *traits*, characteristics that describe a person across situations.

2) Gordon Allport argued that personality consists of cardinal, central, and secondary traits. Raymond Cattell used *factor analysis* to distinguish *surface traits* from *source traits*, which he considered the basic components of personality. Although researchers are debating how many basic components there are, one leading theory proposes the *Big Five:* extroversion versus introversion, neuroticism (negative emotionality), agreeableness, conscientiousness, and openness to experience.

The Biological Tradition

3) Individual differences in *temperaments* or ways of reacting to the environment emerge early in life and can influence subsequent personality development. Temperamental differences in shyness and inhibition, found in children and monkeys, may be due to variations in the responsiveness of the sympathetic nervous system to change and novelty.

4) Data from twin and adoption studies suggest that the *heritability* of many adult personality traits is around .40 to .60. But caution is warranted in drawing conclusions about the heritability of traits because of the vagueness with which environment has been measured, the similarity of environments of even separated twins, the interaction of a child's temperament and the environment, and the diminishing effect of genes over time.

The Learning Tradition

5) Learning theories of personality emphasize the role of experience. *Radical behaviorists* argue that personality is only a convenient fiction because behavior depends on environmental reinforcers and punishers. *Cognitive social-learning theorists* agree with behaviorists that personality consists of acquired patterns, but they argue that learned expectations, habits, and beliefs come to influence and regulate behavior, even when external reinforcers are no longer present. One of the most important self-regulating traits that influence behavior is the extent to which people believe they have control over their lives (*locus of control*).

6) One problem with learning theories of personality is that behavior is sometimes attributed to a vague category called "the environment" without specifying which aspects of it are having effects. Another problem is that so many situational factors influence people's behavior that it can be difficult to single out the impact of any one of them.

The Cultural Tradition

7) Many qualities that Western psychologists treat as individual personality traits are heavily influenced by culture. People from *individualist* cultures define themselves in different terms than those from *collectivist* cultures, and they perceive

their "selves" as more stable across situations. People from *monochronic cultures* are more concerned with punctuality and doing things "one at a time" than are people from *polychronic cultures*, who value relationships above time schedules.

8) Cultural theories of personality face the problem of describing broad cultural characteristics without promoting stereotypes.

The Psychodynamic Tradition

9) Sigmund Freud was the founder of *psychoanalysis*, which was the first *psychodynamic* theory. Modern psychodynamic theories share an emphasis on intrapsychic dynamics, the formative role of childhood experiences and conflicts, the idea that psychological development occurs in stages, a person's "psychic reality" as determined by the unconscious, and subjective methods of understanding a person's life and personality.

10) To Freud, the personality consists of the *id* (the source of *libido* or sexual energy and the aggressive instinct), the *ego* (the source of reason), and the *superego* (the source of conscience). *Defense mechanisms* protect the ego from unconscious anxiety. They include, among others, repression, projection, displacement (one form of which is sublimation), reaction formation, regression, and denial.

11) Freud believed that personality develops in a series of *psychosexual stages:* oral, anal, phallic (Oedipal), latency, and genital. During the phallic stage, Freud believed, the *Oedipus complex* occurs, in which the child desires the parent of the other sex and feels rivalry with the same-sex parent. When the Oedipus complex is resolved, the child identifies with the same-sex parent and settles into the latency stage, but females retain a lingering sense of inferiority and "penis envy"—a notion contested by another psychoanalyst, Karen Horney.

12) Carl Jung believed that people share a *collective unconscious* that contains universal mem-

ories and images, or *archetypes*. Jung also identified extroversion–introversion as a key personality trait.

13) The *object-relations school* differs from classical Freudian theory in emphasizing the importance of the first two years of life, rather than the Oedipal phase; the infant's relationships to important figures, especially the mother, rather than sexual needs and drives; and the problem in male development of breaking away from the mother.

14) Current attitudes about Freud and his work range from reverence to contempt. Psychodynamic theories have been criticized for violating the principle of falsifiability; for overgeneralizing from atypical patients to everyone; and for being based on the unreliable memories and retrospective accounts of patients. But some psychodynamic ideas, especially about nonconscious processes and defenses, are being studied empirically.

The Humanist Tradition

15) *Humanist psychologists* focus on the person's subjective sense of self and free will to change. They emphasize human potential and the strengths of human nature, as in Abraham Maslow's concepts of *peak experiences* and *self-actualization*. Carl Rogers stressed the importance of *unconditional positive regard* in creating a "fully functioning" person. Rollo May added the element of *existentialism* to American psychology, emphasizing the inherent dilemmas of human existence, such as the search for meaning in life. Critics observe that these ideas are subjective, elusive, and difficult to measure, but they have added depth to the study of personality.

16) Biological, learning, and cultural theories of personality tend to emphasize the public personality that we present to the world; psychodynamic and humanist theories tend to emphasize the private, "interior" personality. Together these approaches portray a complex vision of human personality.

KEY TERMS

personality 39	surface and source traits 40	identical and fraternal twins 45
trait 39	the "Big Five" personality traits 41	
Gordon Allport 40		John B. Watson 48
cardinal, central, and secondary traits 40	temperament 42	behaviorism 48
	genes 43	B. F. Skinner 48
Raymond Cattell 40	heritability 44	operant conditioning 48
factor analysis 40	behavioral genetics 44	reinforcer 48

LOOKING BACK

- *How can psychologists tell which personality traits are basic? (p. 40)*

- *Which five dimensions of personality seem to describe people the world over? (pp. 41–42)*

- *Is it possible to be born touchy or easygoing? (pp. 42–43)*

- *How do psychologists measure the "heritability" of a trait? (p. 45)*

- *To what extent are personality differences among people influenced by their genetic differences? (p. 46)*

- *Are people who have highly heritable personality traits stuck with them forever? (p. 47)*

- *Why do behaviorists regard labels such as "aggressive" or "shy" as meaningless for explaining behavior? (p. 48)*

- *Why did cognitive social-learning theorists break away from radical behaviorists in explaining personality? (p. 49)*

- *What's the difference between people who think they control their own destiny—and those who think destiny controls them? (pp. 49–50)*

- *How does belonging to an individualist or collectivist culture influence your personality—and even whether you think you have a stable "self"? (pp. 53–54)*

- *Why might an Arab and a Swede agree on everything the other is saying—and still feel uncomfortable with each other? (p. 54)*

- *Why are punctuality and tardiness more than just individual personality traits? (p. 54)*

- *In Freud's theory of personality, why are the id and the superego always at war? (p. 56)*

- *When people tell you that you're being "defensive," what defenses might they be thinking of? (pp. 57–58)*

- *How do psychologists regard Freud today—as a genius or a fraud? (p. 59)*

- *What would Carl Jung have to say about Darth Vader? (pp. 60–61)*

- *What are the "objects" in the object-relations approach to personality? (pp. 61–62)*

- *How does the humanist vision of human nature differ from the visions of behaviorism and psychoanalysis? (pp. 64–65)*

- *In the humanist view, what's wrong with saying to a child, "I love you because you've been good"? (p. 65)*

Development over the Life Span

PSYCHOLOGY IN THE NEWS

Age Record Broken as 63-Year-Old Woman Gives Birth

The oldest woman ever to give birth, Arceli Keh, cuddles her daughter Cynthia.

LOS ANGELES, APRIL 1997. A fertility specialist at the University of Southern California has announced that a 63-year-old female patient gave birth last year to a healthy baby girl. The child was conceived through in vitro ("test tube") fertilization, with sperm from the woman's 60-year-old husband and an egg donated by a younger woman. Previously, the oldest woman on record to give birth was a 53-year-old Italian woman who had a child in 1994, using similar procedures.

Although the USC infertility program has a policy of rejecting patients over age 55, the California woman lied about her age and did not confess the truth until she was 13 weeks pregnant. The woman's own 86-year-old mother, unaware of her daughter's pregnancy until the delivery, is reportedly delighted at becoming a grandparent, and the rest of the close-knit Filipino family has also been supportive. But some fertility experts and ethicists have misgivings. Dr. Mark Sauer, who pioneered the use of donor eggs in older women, said, "I lose my comfort level after 55 because I have to believe that there are quality-of-life issues involved in raising a child at [the parent's] age. When [the baby] is 5, her mother will be 68. And I have to believe that a 78-year-old dealing with a teenager may have some problems."

How do *you* react to the idea of a 63-year-old woman having a baby? Would it make any difference if the mother were "only" 55 years old, or 50, or 45? What if she were older than 63? Do you feel the same about older fathers as you do about older mothers? Is there some "right" time to become a parent? For that matter, is there a "right" time to do anything in life—go to school, get married, retire, . . . die?

Before the Industrial Revolution in the late nineteenth century, people of different ages often inhabited the same social world. Children and teenagers worked alongside adults on farms and in factories; several generations often shared one household. Neither children nor old people were set apart from the rest of society on the grounds that they were too young or too old to participate (Chudacoff, 1990).

Then, during the first half of the twentieth century, complex social and economic changes in developed countries led to the notion that life unfolds in a progression of distinct stages. Childhood came to be seen as a special time, when powerful experiences determine the kind of adult a person will become. Adolescence, the years between the physical changes of puberty and the social markers of adulthood, became longer and longer, and its defining characteristics were said to be turmoil

In some eras, children were regarded as "little adults," as this painting of Sir Walter Raleigh and his son shows. The idea of childhood as a developmentally special time is a relatively new one.

and turbulence. Adulthood was conceptualized as a series of predictable events, from marriage and parenthood to retirement. Elderly people were increasingly separated from the rest of society on the grounds that they could not keep up with the fast-moving world.

Today we are undergoing another revolution in the way we think about the universal human journey from birth to death. Because of improvements in health care, a changing economy, a high divorce rate, and advances in reproductive technology, events over the life span are no longer as predictable as they were just a few decades ago. Many individuals still have their first child in their 20s, but others become first-time parents in their 40s. Most college students are still in their late teens or their 20s, but many are older. A person might marry or start a career at 25, and do so again at 55.

Psychologists are probably no better equipped than anyone else to address the thorny ethical issues raised by these changes—such as whether a woman should forgo pregnancy if she can't realistically expect to be around until her child grows up. But *developmental psychologists,* who study universal aspects of life-span development as well as the cultural and individual variations, can help us think critically about the question of "natural" life stages. In this chapter, we will explore some of their findings, starting at the very beginning, with the period from conception to birth. As you read, ask yourself which years of life clearly involve predictable stages and which do not. What does it mean, in psychological terms, to be young, middle-aged, or old? And why do so many people feel uneasy about the prospect of postmenopausal motherhood?

What's Ahead

- *How can a pregnant woman reduce the risk of damage to the embryo or fetus?*

- *Given a choice, what do newborns prefer to look at?*

- *Why is cuddling so important for infants (not to mention adults)?*

- *If you have a 1-year-old, why shouldn't you worry if your baby cries when left with a new babysitter?*

- *How does culture affect how a baby matures physically and socially?*

FROM CONCEPTION TO THE FIRST YEAR

A baby's development, before and after birth, is a marvel of *maturation,* the sequential unfolding of genetically influenced behavior and physical characteristics. In only 9 months of a mother's pregnancy, a cell grows from a dot this big (.) to a squalling bundle of energy that looks just like Aunt Sarah. In another 15 months, that bundle of energy grows into a babbling toddler who is curious about everything. No other time in human development brings so many changes, so fast.

Prenatal Development

Prenatal development is divided into three stages: the germinal, the embryonic, and the fetal. The *germinal stage* begins at conception, when the male sperm unites with the female ovum (egg). A day or so after conception, the fertilized egg, or *zygote,* begins to divide into two parts and, in 10 to 14 days, it attaches itself to the wall of the uterus. The outer portion of the zygote will form part of the placenta and umbilical cord, and the inner portion becomes the embryo. The placenta, connected to the embryo by the umbilical cord, serves as the growing embryo's link for food from the mother; it allows nutrients to enter and wastes to exit, and it screens out some, but not all, harmful substances.

Once implantation of the zygote is completed, about two weeks after conception, the *embryonic stage* begins, lasting until the eighth week after conception. The embryo develops webbed fingers and toes, a tail, eyes, ears, a nose, a mouth, a heart and circulatory system, and a spinal cord—although at 8 weeks, the embryo is only 1½ inches long. During the fourth to eighth week, the hormone testosterone is secreted by the rudimentary testes in embryos that are genetically male; without this hormone, the embryo will develop to be anatomically female.

After eight weeks, the *fetal stage* begins. The organism, now called a *fetus,* further develops the organs and systems that existed in rudimentary form in the embryonic stage. By 28 weeks, the nervous and respiratory systems are developed enough to allow most fetuses to live if born prematurely. (New medical technology allows many to survive if born even earlier, but the risks are much higher.) The greatest gains in brain and nervous system development and in fetal weight occur during the last 12 weeks of a full-term pregnancy.

Although the womb is a fairly sturdy protector of the growing embryo or fetus, some harmful influences can cross the placental barrier. These influences, which are particularly damaging during the embryonic stage, include the following:

- *German measles* (rubella), especially early in the pregnancy, can affect the fetus's eyes, ears, and heart. The most common consequence is deafness. Rubella is preventable if the mother has been vaccinated, which can be done in adulthood, up to three months before pregnancy.

- *X-rays or other radiation,* or *toxic chemicals* such as lead, can cause fetal abnormalities and deformities. Exposure to lead is also associated with attention problems and reduced IQ scores, as we will see in Chapter 6.

- *Sexually transmitted diseases* can cause mental retardation, blindness, and other physical disorders. Genital herpes affects the fetus only if the mother has an outbreak at the time of delivery, which exposes the newborn to the virus as the baby passes through the birth canal. This risk can be avoided by having a cesarean section, in which the baby is removed surgically through the uterus. Although the AIDS virus can be transmitted to the fetus, not all babies born to HIV-infected mothers themselves become infected; estimates range from 13 percent in a European study to 30 percent in U.S. studies (Bee, 1997).

- *Cigarette smoking* during pregnancy increases the likelihood of miscarriage, premature birth, abnormal fetal heartbeat, and an underweight baby. The negative effects may last long after birth, showing up in increased rates of infant sickness, sudden infant death syndrome (SIDS), and, in later childhood, hyperactivity and difficulties in school.

- *Having more than two alcoholic drinks a day* significantly increases the risk of a baby having *fetal alcohol syndrome (FAS)*. FAS infants are smaller than normal, have smaller brains, have facial deformities, are less coordinated, and are mentally retarded. Even when babies do not have FAS, exposure to alcohol during pregnancy can affect their mental abilities and concentration as children (Streissguth et al., 1991). The most dangerous stage for these effects is the first trimester (first 12 weeks). But the consequences of lighter drinking—say, a drink or two a day—are not quite as clear; some longitudinal studies find no effects, whereas others find small but significant intellectual deficits (Forrest et al., 1991; Hunt et al., 1995; Streissguth et al., 1991).

- *Drugs* can be harmful to the fetus, whether they are illicit ones such as morphine, cocaine, and heroin, or commonly used legal substances such as

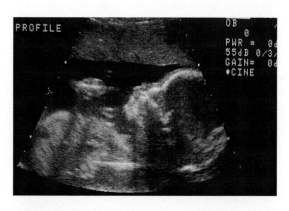

The first picture that many parents have of their offspring is a fetal sonogram, like this one taken during the twenty-third week of pregnancy.

antibiotics, antihistamines, tranquilizers, acne medication, and diet pills. (Fathers' drug use can also cause fetal defects; cocaine, for example, does so by binding to sperm [Yazigi, Odem, & Polakoski, 1991].) In the 1960s, pregnant women who took the tranquilizer thalidomide gave birth to fetuses with missing or deformed limbs. Until 1971, many women were given the hormone diethylstilbestrol (DES) to prevent miscarriages; daughters of these women had an unusually high risk of developing vaginal and cervical cancer during adolescence, and sons were prone to testicular problems.

The lesson is clear. A pregnant woman does well to abstain completely from smoking, to avoid alcohol or drink very little of it, and to take no other drugs of any kind unless they are medically necessary and have been adequately tested for safety—and then to accept the fact that her child will never be properly grateful for all that sacrifice!

The Infant's World

Newborn babies could never survive on their own, but they are far from being passive and inert. As a result of evolution, many abilities, tendencies, and characteristics are universal in human beings and are present at birth or develop very early, given certain experiences.

Physical Abilities.   Newborns begin life with several *motor reflexes,* automatic behaviors that are necessary for survival (see Table 3.1). For example, they will grasp tightly a finger pressed on their palms; and they will turn their heads toward a touch on the cheek or corner of the mouth and search for something to suck on, a handy "rooting reflex" that allows them to find the breast or bottle. Many of these reflexes eventually disappear, but others—such as the knee-jerk, eye-blink, and sneeze reflexes—remain.

Babies are also equipped with a set of inborn perceptual abilities. They can see, hear, touch, smell, and taste (bananas and sugar water are in; rotten eggs are out). A newborn's visual focus range is only about 8 inches, the average distance between the baby and the face of the person holding the baby, but visual ability develops rapidly. Newborns open their eyes wide to investigate what is around them, even in the dark. They can distinguish contrasts, shadows, and edges. They can discriminate their mother or other primary caregiver on the basis of smell, sight, or sound almost immediately (Bee, 1997). Within a couple of months, they show evidence of depth perception (see Chapter 5).

By observing what infants look at, given a choice, and how long they gaze at it, psychologists have identified many inborn infant preferences. Infants reveal a surprising interest in looking at and listening to unfamiliar things—which, of course, includes most of the world. A baby will even stop nursing if someone new enters his or her range of vision. Infants are also primed to re-

Table 3.1	Reflexes of the Newborn Baby

Reflex	Description
Rooting	An infant touched on the cheek or corner of the mouth will turn toward the touch and search for something to suck on.
Sucking	An infant will suck on anything suckable, such as a nipple or finger.
Swallowing	An infant can swallow, though this reflex is not yet well coordinated with breathing.
Moro or "startle"	In response to a loud noise or a physical shock, an infant will throw its arms outward and arch back.
Babinski	In response to a touch on the bottom of the foot, the infant's toes will splay outward and then curl in. (In adults, the toes just curl in.)
Grasp	In response to a touch on the palm of the hand, an infant will grasp.
Stepping	If held so that the feet just touch the ground, an infant will show "walking" movements, alternating the feet in steps.

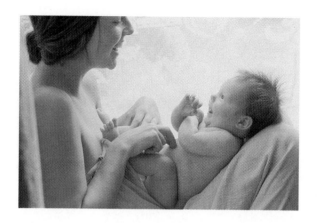 

Babies are born with a special delight in looking at and studying human faces. Within a few weeks, many can even imitate adult facial expressions.

spond to human faces. Babies who are only *9 minutes old* will turn their heads to watch a drawing of a face if it moves in front of them, but they will not turn if the "face" consists of scrambled features or is only the outline of a face (Goren, Sarty, & Wu, 1975; Johnson et al., 1991). A preference for faces over other stimuli in the environment may have survival value because it helps babies recognize where their next meal is likely to come from.

Despite such commonalities, however, many aspects of children's maturation depend on cultural customs that govern how their parents hold, touch, feed, and talk to them (Super & Harkness, 1994). For example, in the United States, babies are expected to sleep for eight uninterrupted hours by the age of 4 or 5 months. This milestone is considered a sign of neurological maturity, although many babies wail when the parent puts them in the crib at night and leaves the room. But among Mayan Indians, rural Italians, African villagers, and urban Japanese, this nightly clash of wills never occurs because the infant sleeps with the mother for the first few years of life, waking and nursing about every four hours. Although many American parents worry about the "right" or "wrong" sleep arrangements for an infant, neither custom is better than the other. These differences reflect cultural and parental values. Mayan mothers believe it is important to sleep with the baby in order to forge a close bond with the child; many American parents believe it is important to foster the child's independence as soon as possible (Morelli et al., 1992).

Cultural customs even influence physical development. Infants in many African cultures surpass American infants in their rate of learning to sit and to walk, but not in learning to crawl or climb stairs. The reason is that the African parents routinely bounce babies on their feet, exercise the newborn's walking reflex, prop young infants in

sitting positions, and discourage crawling (Cole & Cole, 1993).

Attachment.   Emotional attachment is a universal capacity of all primates, all through life. By becoming attached to a caregiver, children gain a secure base from which they can explore the environment, and a haven of safety to return to when they are afraid (Bowlby, 1973).

Emotional attachment begins with physical attachment: touching and cuddling between infant and parent. Margaret and Harry Harlow first demonstrated the importance of touching, or **contact comfort,** by raising infant rhesus monkeys with two kinds of artificial mothers (Harlow,

contact comfort

In primates, the innate pleasure derived from close physical contact; it is the basis of an infant's first attachment.

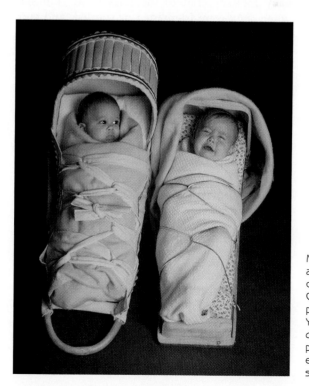

Most Navaho babies calmly accept being strapped to a cradle board (left), whereas Caucasian babies will often protest vigorously (right). Yet despite cultural differences in such practices, babies everywhere eventually sit, crawl, and walk.

 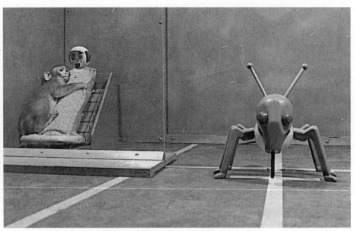

Figure 3.1

The Comfort of Contact

Infants need cuddling as much as they need food. In Margaret and Harry Harlow's studies, infant rhesus monkeys were reared with a cuddly terry cloth "mother" and with a bare wire "mother" that provided milk (see photo on left). The infants would cling to the terry cloth mother when they weren't being fed, and when they were frightened (as by the toy spider on the right), it was the terry cloth mother they ran to.

1958; Harlow & Harlow, 1966). The first was a forbidding construction of wires and warming lights, with a milk bottle connected to it. The second was constructed of wire and covered in foam rubber and cuddly terry cloth (see Figure 3.1). At the time, psychologists thought that babies become attached to their mothers because their moms provide food and warmth. But the Harlows' baby monkeys ran to the terry-cloth "mother" when they were frightened or startled, and cuddling up to it calmed them down. Human children, too, often seek contact comfort when they are in an unfamiliar situation, are scared by a nightmare or surprised by a bouncy dog, or fall and hurt themselves.

Once babies are emotionally attached to the mother or other caregiver, separation can be a wrenching experience. Between 7 and 9 months of age, many babies become wary or fearful of strangers, a reaction called *stranger anxiety*. They wail if they are put in an unfamiliar setting or are left with an unfamiliar person. And they show *separation anxiety* if the primary caregiver temporarily leaves the room. This reaction usually continues until the middle of the second year, but many children show signs of distress at parental separation until they are about 3 years old. Virtually all children go through this phase.

To determine the nature of the attachment between mothers and babies, Mary Ainsworth (1973, 1979; Ainsworth et al., 1978) devised an experimental method called the *Strange Situation.* A mother brings her baby into an unfamiliar room containing lots of toys. After a while a stranger comes in and attempts to play with the child. The mother leaves the baby with the stranger. She then returns and plays with her child, and the stranger leaves. Finally, the mother leaves the baby alone for three minutes and then returns. In each case, observers carefully note how the baby behaves—with the mother, with the stranger, and when the baby is alone.

Ainsworth divided children into three categories on the basis of the children's reactions to the Strange Situation. Some babies are *securely attached:* They cry or protest if the parent leaves the room; they welcome her back and then play happily again; they are clearly more attached to the mother than to the stranger.

Other babies are *insecurely attached,* and this insecurity can take either of two forms. The child may be *avoidant,* not caring whether the mother leaves the room, making little effort to seek contact with her on her return, and treating the stranger about the same as the mother. Or the child may be *anxious or ambivalent,* resisting contact with the mother at reunion but protesting loudly if she leaves. Anxious or ambivalent babies may cry to be picked up and then demand to be put down, or they may behave as if they are angry with the mother and resist her efforts to comfort them.

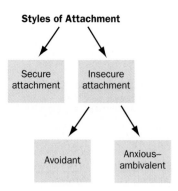

Styles of Attachment

When infants are consistently deprived of social contact, affection, and cuddling, the effects can be disastrous and long-lasting. Insecurely attached infants often grow into children who have behavioral and cognitive problems (Jacobsen, Edelstein, & Hofmann, 1994; Posada, Lord, & Waters, 1995; Speltz, Greenberg, & Deklyen, 1990; Waters et al., 1995). They may have low self-esteem and a poor self-image, and they are at increased risk for depression (Mikulincer, 1995; Roberts, Gotlib, & Kassel, 1996). Eventually they may grow into adults who are anxious or avoidant in their own close relationships.

Ainsworth argued that the differences among secure, avoidant, and anxious attachment lie primarily in the way mothers treat their babies during the first few months. Mothers of securely attached babies, she believes, are sensitive to their babies' needs and the meanings of their cries; they are affectionate and demonstrative. Mothers of avoidant babies are irritated by their infants, express controlled anger toward them, and are rejecting; they dislike or are uncomfortable with close physical contact with their children. Mothers of anxious–ambivalent babies are insensitive and inept but are not rejecting. They don't know what to do to relieve their babies' distress and are uncomfortable and awkward when handling them.

The quality and stability of a baby's attachment are not determined solely by the caregiver's sensitivity, however. Babies can become insecurely attached because they are temperamentally difficult—fearful and prone to crying—which can test the patience of the most well-intentioned adult (Belsky, Hsieh, & Crnic, 1996; Seifer et al., 1996). Attachment patterns are also affected by events: Children are likely to shift from secure to insecure attachment if their families are undergoing a period of change, chronic stress, or illness.

Cultural variations in child-rearing practices also influence the strength of separation anxiety

and how long it lasts (see Figure 3.2). Cultures differ in whether they expect attachment to occur between infant and mother, infant and both parents, or infant and extended family. Among the Efe of Africa, for example, babies spend about half their time, and 3-year-olds spend fully 70 percent of their time, away from their mothers, in the care of older children and other adults (Tronick, Morelli, & Ivey, 1992). Efe children do not experience the one-on-one intense attachment that Western children do, and they develop a sense of self that is tied more closely to other people and the larger group.

Cultural differences such as these show that infants can thrive in many kinds of environments, and that "good care" covers a lot of territory and many different customs. It does not matter whether babies sleep with their parents or in their own cribs; or whether they are cared for at home, by relatives, or in good child-care settings (NICHD Early Child Care Research Network, 1996). As long as caregivers are sensitive, affectionate, and responsive, most babies get along fine.

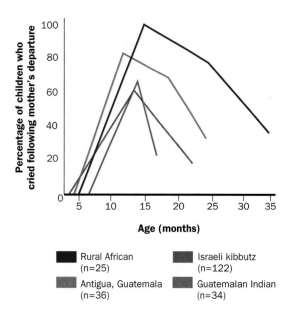

Figure 3.2

The Rise and Fall of Separation Anxiety

A baby's separation anxiety—distress when the mother or primary caregiver leaves the room—typically peaks at about a year of age and then steadily declines. But notice how the proportion of children responding to their mothers' departure varies across cultures, from a high among rural African children to a low among children raised in a communal Israeli kibbutz, where children become attached to many adults (Kagan, Kearsley, & Zelazo, 1978.)

What's Ahead

- *What important accomplishment is an infant revealing when the infant learns to play "peekaboo"?*

- *Why will most 5-year-olds choose a tall, narrow glass of lemonade over a short, fat one containing the same amount?*

- *Can a 4-year-old understand that others experience the world from a different perspective?*

- *How are a toddler's first word combinations similar to the language in a telegram?*

- *Why do many psychologists believe that children's brains are equipped with a "language acquisition device"?*

COGNITIVE DEVELOPMENT

Our friend Joel reports how thrilled he was when his 13-month-old daughter Alison looked at him one day and said, for the first time, "Daddy!" His delight was deflated somewhat, though, when the doorbell rang and she ran to the door, calling, "Daddy!" And his delight was completely shattered when the phone rang and Alison ran to it, shouting, "Daddy!" Later Joel learned that there was a 2-year-old child in Alison's child-care group whose father would call her on the telephone during the day and ring the doorbell when he picked her up. Alison had acquired her friend's enthusiasm for phones and doorbells but didn't quite get the hang of "Daddy." She will soon enough, though, and that is the mystery of language. Eventually, she will also be able to imagine, reason, and see the world from Daddy's viewpoint, and that is the mystery of thought.

The Ability to Think

As anyone who has ever observed a young child knows, children do not think the way adults do. At age 2, they may call all large animals by one name (say, *horsie*) and all small animals by another (say, *bug*). At 4, they may protest that a sibling has "more" fruit juice when it is only the shapes of the glasses that differ, not the amount of juice.

In the 1920s, the Swiss psychologist Jean Piaget [Zhan Pee-ah-ZHAY] (1896–1980) proposed a new theory of cognitive development to explain these childish mistakes. Piaget was to child development what Freud was to psychoanalysis and Skinner to behaviorism: a figure of towering influence (Brainerd, 1996; Flavell, 1996). His keen observations of children and his brilliant ideas caused a revolution in thinking about how thinking develops and have inspired thousands of studies by investigators all over the world.

Piaget's great insight was that children's errors are as interesting as their correct responses. Children will say things that seem cute or wildly illogical to adults, but the strategies children use to think and solve problems, said Piaget, are not random or meaningless; they reflect a predictable interaction between the child's maturational stage and the child's experience in the world.

Piaget's Cognitive Stages.   According to Piaget (1929/1960, 1952, 1984), mental functioning depends on two inborn processes. One is *organization:* All human beings are designed to organize their observations and experiences into a coherent set of meanings. The other is *adaptation* to new observations and experiences. Adaptation, said Piaget, takes two forms, which he called assimilation and accommodation.

Assimilation is what you do when you fit new information into your present system of knowledge and beliefs or into your mental *schemas* (networks of associations, beliefs, and expectations about categories of things and people). Suppose that little Harry learns a schema for "dog" by playing with the family schnauzer. If he then sees the neighbor's collie and says "doggie!" he has assimilated the new information about the neighbor's pet into his schema for dogs. **Accommodation** is what you do when, as a result of undeniable new information, you must change or modify your existing schemas. If Harry sees the neighbor's Siamese cat and still says "doggie!" his parents are likely to laugh and correct him. Harry will have to modify his schema for *dogs* to exclude cats, and he will have to create a schema for *cats.* In this way, he accommodates the new information that a Siamese cat is not a dog.

Using these concepts, Piaget proposed that all children go through four stages of cognitive development:

1. *The sensorimotor stage (birth to age 2).* In this stage, the infant learns through concrete actions: looking, touching, hearing, putting things in the mouth, sucking, grasping. "Thinking" consists of coordinating sensory information with bodily movements. Soon these movements become more purposeful, as the child explores the environment and learns that specific movements will produce specific results. Swatting a cloth away will reveal a hidden toy; letting go of a fuzzy toy duck will cause it to drop out of reach; banging on the table with a spoon will produce dinner (or Mom, taking the spoon away).

A major accomplishment at this stage, said Piaget, is **object permanence,** the understanding that something continues to exist even if you can't see it or touch it. In the first few months, he observed, infants seem to follow the motto "out of sight, out of mind." They will look intently at a little toy, but if you hide it behind a piece of paper they will not look behind the paper or make an effort to get the toy. By about 6 months of age, in-

fants begin to grasp the idea that a toy exists and the family cat exists, whether or not they can see the toy or the cat. If a baby of this age drops a toy from her playpen, she will look for it; she also will look under a cloth for a toy that is partially hidden. By 1 year of age, most babies have developed an awareness of the permanence of (some) objects. This is when they love to play peekaboo.

Object permanence, said Piaget, represents the beginning of *representational thought,* the capacity to use mental imagery and other symbolic systems. For the first time, the child is able to hold a concept in mind, to learn that the word *fly* represents an annoying, buzzing creature, and that *Daddy* represents a friendly, playful one.

2. *The preoperational stage (ages 2 to 7).* In this stage, the use of symbols and language accelerates, in play and in imitation of adult behavior. A 2-year-old is able to pretend, for instance, that a large box is a house, table, or train. But Piaget described this stage largely in terms of what (he thought) the child cannot do. Although children can think, said Piaget, they cannot reason, and they lack the mental abilities necessary for understanding abstract principles or cause and effect. Piaget called these missing abilities **operations,** by which he meant *reversible* actions that the child performs in the mind. An operation is a sort of "train of thought" that can be run backward or forward. Multiplying 2 times 6 to get 12 is an operation; so is the reverse operation, dividing 12 by 6 to get 2.

Children at the preoperational stage, Piaget believed, rely on primitive reasoning based on the evidence of their own senses, which can be misleading. If a tree moves in the wind, it must be alive; if the wind blows while the child is walking, then walking must make the wind blow. Piaget also believed—mistakenly, as we will see—that children of this age cannot take another person's point of view because their thinking is **egocentric.** They see the world only from their own frame of reference. They cannot imagine that you see things differently, that events happen to other people that do not happen to them, or that the world does not exist solely for them. "Why are there mountains [with lakes]?" Piaget asked a preoperational Swiss child. "So that we can skate," answered the child.

Further, said Piaget, preoperational children cannot grasp the concept of **conservation**—the notion that physical properties do not change when their forms or appearances change. These children are unable to understand that an amount

assimilation

In Piaget's theory, the process of absorbing new information into existing cognitive structures.

accommodation

In Piaget's theory, the process of modifying existing cognitive structures in response to experience and new information.

object permanence

The understanding, which develops late in the first year after birth, that an object continues to exist even when you can't see it or touch it.

operations

In Piaget's theory, mental actions that are cognitively reversible.

egocentric thinking

Seeing the world from only your own point of view; the inability to take another person's perspective.

conservation

The understanding that the physical properties of objects—such as the number of items in a cluster or the amount of liquid in a glass—can remain the same even when their form or appearance changes.

Figure 3.3
Piaget's Principle of Conservation

In a typical test for conservation of number (left), the child must say whether one of the sets of blocks has "more." His answer shows whether he understands that the two sets contain the same number, even though the larger blocks in one set take up more space. In a test for conservation of quantity (right), the child is shown two short, fat glasses with equal amounts of liquid. Then the contents of one glass are poured into a tall, narrow beaker, and the child is asked whether one container now has more. Her answer shows whether she understands that pouring liquid from a short, fat glass into a tall, narrow one leaves the amount of liquid unchanged.

of liquid, a number of pennies, or a length of rope remains the same even if you pour the liquid from one glass to another, stack the pennies, or coil the rope (see Figure 3.3). If you pour liquid from a short, fat glass into a tall, narrow glass, preoperational children will say there is more liquid in the second glass. They attend to the appearance of the liquid (its height in the glass) instead of its fixed quantity.

3. *The concrete operations stage (about age 6 or 7 to 11).* During this stage, according to Piaget, the nature and quality of children's thinking change significantly. They come to understand the principles of conservation, reversibility, and cause and effect. They understand the nature of *identity;* for example, they know that a girl doesn't turn into a boy by wearing a boy's hat, and that a brother will always be a brother, even if he grows up. They learn mental operations, such as addition, subtraction, multiplication, division, and categorization of objects, people, events, and actions. They learn a few abstract concepts, such as *serial order-*

ing, the idea that things can be ranked from smallest to largest, lightest to darkest, shortest to tallest. But, according to Piaget, children's thinking at this age is still grounded primarily in concrete experiences and concepts, rather than in abstractions or logical deductions.

4. *The formal operations stage (age 12 to adulthood).* This stage, said Piaget, marks the beginning of abstract reasoning. Teenagers understand that ideas can be compared and classified, just as objects can. They are able to reason about situations they have not experienced firsthand, and they can think about future possibilities. They are able to search systematically for answers to problems. They are able to draw logical conclusions from premises common to their culture and experience. (Table 3.2 summarizes Piaget's stages of cognitive development.)

Evaluating Piaget. Piaget transformed the field of developmental psychology, providing an entirely new vision of the nature of children. Be-

Get Involved

If you know any young children, try one of Piaget's conservation experiments. A simple one is to make two rows of seven buttons or pennies, aligned identically. Ask the child whether one row has more. Now simply spread out the buttons in one row, and ask the child again whether one has more. If the child says "Yes," ask which one—and why. Try to do this experiment with a 3-year-old and a 7- or 8-year-old. You will probably see a big difference in their answers.

Table 3.2	Summary of Piaget's Stages of Cognitive Development
Stage	**Major Accomplishments**
Sensorimotor (0–2)	Object permanence Beginning of representational thought
Preoperational (2–7)	Accelerated use of symbols and language
Concrete operations (6 or 7–11)	Understanding of conservation Understanding of identity Understanding of serial ordering
Formal operations (12–adulthood)	Abstract reasoning Ability to compare and classify ideas

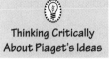

Thinking Critically About Piaget's Ideas fore summarizing the lasting contributions of his theory, however, we want to consider some findings that challenge some of Piaget's ideas:

1. *The changes from one stage to another are neither as clear-cut nor as sweeping as Piaget implied.* In particular, there is no abrupt shift from preoperational to concrete-operational thought. At any given age, a child may use several different strategies in trying to solve a problem, some more complex or accurate than others—a finding that has prompted one researcher to suggest that cognitive ability develops in overlapping waves rather than discrete steps (Siegler, 1996). Moreover, children's reasoning ability often depends on the circumstances—who is asking them questions, the specific words used, the materials used, and what they are reasoning *about*—not just on the stage they are in.

2. *Children can understand far more than Piaget gave them credit for.* Taking advantage of the fact that infants look longer at novel than at familiar stimuli, psychologists have designed delightfully imaginative methods of testing what babies know. In a typical experiment, infants are shown a possible event and an impossible event that violates expectations of reality (see Figure 3.4). The idea is that if infants possess the belief or expectation being tested—for example, "it is impossible for a box to float on air"—they will perceive the impossible event as being more unusual and surprising than the possible event and, thus, will look at it longer.

Using this method, one research team found that infants as young as 4 months seem to understand some basic principles of physics! Babies that young will look longer at a ball if it seems to roll through a solid barrier, or leap between two platforms, or hang in midair, than they do when an action obeys the laws of physics. And infants as young as 2½ to 3½ months are aware that objects continue to exist even when masked by other objects and that one object cannot move through the space occupied by another (Baillargeon, 1994). Such results suggest that babies may be biologically programmed to understand some things about how the world works.

Possible event

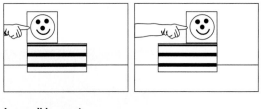

Impossible event

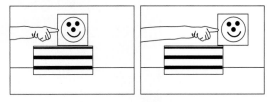

Figure 3.4

Testing Infants' Knowledge

In one method for studying infants' understanding of whether an object needs physical support, the baby sees a hand pushing a box from left to right along a striped platform. The box is pushed until it reaches the end of the platform (a possible event) or until only a bit of it rests on the platform (an impossible event). Babies look longer at the impossible event, suggesting that it surprises them (Baillargeon, 1994).

Children also advance rapidly in their symbolic abilities earlier than Piaget thought—between the ages of 2½ and 3. Within that six-month period, toddlers become able to think of a miniature model of a room in two ways at once: as a room in its own right and as a symbol of the larger room it represents (DeLoache, 1995). This ability is a big step toward adult symbolic thought, in which anything can stand for anything else—a flag for a country, a logo for a company.

3. *Preschoolers are not as egocentric as Piaget thought.* A large body of evidence shows that most 3- and 4-year-olds *can* take another person's perspective. When 4-year-olds play with 2-year-olds, for example, they modify and simplify their speech so the younger children will understand (Shatz & Gelman, 1973). Further, even very young children are capable of charming acts of empathy, and they often realize that people experience things differently (Flavell, 1993). One 5-year-old we know showed her teacher a picture she had drawn of a cat and an unidentifiable blob. "The cat is lovely," said the teacher, "but what is this thing here?" "That has nothing to do with you," said the child. "That's what the *cat* is looking at."

4. *Children's cognitive development occurs in a social and cultural context.* Pierre Dasen (1994) spent years testing Piaget's theory in different cultures: among the Aborigines in Australia, the Inuit in Canada, the Ebri and the Baoulé in the Ivory Coast, and the Kikuyu in Kenya. Traditional no-madic hunting peoples, such as the Inuit and the Aborigines, do not quantify things and do not need to. The Aborigines have number words only up to five; after that, all quantities are described as "many." In such cultures, the cognitive ability to understand the conservation of quantity or number develops late, if at all. But nomadic hunting tribes rely on their spatial orientation—knowing where water holes and successful hunting routes are—and so spatial abilities develop rapidly. In contrast, children who live in settled agricultural communities, such as the Baoulé, develop rapidly in the domain of quantification and much more slowly in spatial reasoning. Experiences with school affect cognitive development, too: Many unschooled children of the Wolof, a rural group in Senegal, do not acquire an understanding of conservation, as do their peers who attend school, but brief training can speed its development (Greenfield, 1976).

5. *Just as Piaget underestimated the cognitive skills of young children, he overestimated those of many adults.* As we will see in Chapter 6, not all adolescents and adults develop the ability for formal reasoning and reflective judgment. Many continue to show the magical thinking typical of preoperational children (concluding, for example, that "If X comes before Y, then X must have caused Y"). Some people never develop the capacity for formal operations, and others continue to think concretely unless a specific problem requires abstract thought.

Experience and culture influence cognitive development. Children who work with clay, wood, and other materials, such as this young potter in India, tend to understand the concept of conservation sooner than children who have not had this practical experience.

Although these important findings have required significant modifications in Piaget's theory, the general sequence of cognitive development that he described does hold up across cultures. Most psychologists today accept Piaget's major point, that new reasoning abilities depend on the emergence of previous ones: You can't learn algebra before you can count, and you can't learn philosophy before you understand logic. Piaget's assimilation–accommodation model correctly emphasizes the ongoing interaction between the cognitive structures that children are born with and the child's continuing adaptation to the environment (Flavell, 1996). It is largely due to Piaget that developmental psychologists (and parents) now understand that children are not passive vessels into which education and experience are poured. Children actively interpret their worlds, using their perceptions and developing schemas to assimilate new information and to try to figure things out.

The Ability to Speak

Try to read this sentence aloud:

Kamaunawezakusomamanenohayawewenimtuwa maanasana.

Can you tell where one word begins and another ends? Unless you know Swahili, the syllables of this sentence will sound like gibberish.*

Well, to a baby learning its native tongue, *every* sentence must, at first, be gibberish. How, then, does an infant pick out discrete syllables and words from the jumble of sounds in its environment, much less figure out what those words mean? And how is it that in only a few short years, children not only understand thousands of words, but can also produce and understand an endless number of new word combinations?

The process begins in the first months, with crying and cooing. Even at this early stage, babies are highly responsive to the pitch, intensity, and sound of language, and to the emotions in people's voices. As Anne Fernald (1990) puts it, for babies, "the melody is the message." Adults seem to know this; when they speak to babies, their pitch is typically higher and more varied than usual, and their intonation is more exaggerated. Speaking to infants in "baby talk" is not universal, but it is widespread, as investigators in France, Italy, Japan, rural South Africa, Britain, Canada, and China have found.

By 4 to 6 months of age, babies have learned many key consonant and vowel sounds (phonemes) of their native language and can distinguish such sounds from those of a foreign language (Kuhl et al., 1992). They can also recognize their own names and other words that are regularly spoken with emotion, such as "mommy" and "daddy." Over time, exposure to the baby's native language reduces his or her ability to perceive speech sounds in other languages. Thus Japanese infants can hear the difference between the English sounds "la" and "ra," but Japanese adults cannot because this contrast does not exist in their language and so they are no longer sensitive to it.

Between 6 months and 1 year, infants become increasingly familiar with the sound structure of their native language, and soon they are able to distinguish words from the unbroken flow of speech. They will listen longer to native words that violate their expectations of what words should sound like (Jusczyk, 1993; Jusczyk et al., 1993). They start to babble, making many "ba-ba" and "goo-goo" sounds, endlessly repeating sounds and syllables. At about a year of age (though the timing varies considerably), children begin to name things. They already have mental concepts for familiar objects and people, and their first words represent these concepts ("mama," "doggie," "bug").

Starting at about 11 months, babies begin to develop a repertoire of symbolic *gestures*, another important tool of communication. They use these gestures to refer to objects (e.g., sniffing to indicate "flower"), to request things (smacking the lips for "food," moving the hands up and down for "play the piano"), to describe objects (blowing or waving a hand for "hot," raising the arms for "big"), and to reply to questions (opening the palms or shrugging the shoulders for

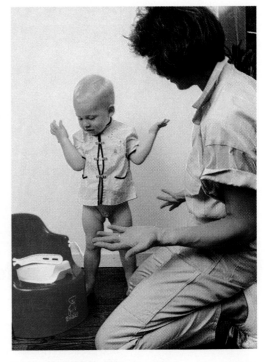

Symbolic gestures emerge early! This mother and her son are clearly having a "conversation."

Kama unaweza kusoma maneno haya, wewe ni mtu wa maana sana means, in Swahili, "If you can read these words, you are a remarkable person."

"I don't know"). Parents who encourage their babies to use gestures actually spur their children's language learning; their babies turn out to be more alert, better listeners, and less frustrated in their efforts to communicate than babies who are not encouraged to use gestures (Goodwyn & Acredolo, 1993).

Between the ages of 18 months and 2 years, toddlers begin to produce words in two- or three-word combinations ("Mama here," "go 'way bug," "my toy"). The child's first combinations of words have a common quality: They are **telegraphic.** When people had to pay for every word in a telegram, they quickly learned to drop unnecessary articles (*a, an,* or *the*) and auxiliary verbs (such as *is* or *are*), but they still conveyed the message. Similarly, the two-word "telegrams" of toddlers omit articles, auxiliary verbs, other parts of speech, and word endings, but they are still remarkably accurate in conveying meanings (Slobin, 1985). Toddlers can name things ("that chair"), make demands ("more milk"), negate actions ("no want," "allgone milk"), describe events ("Bambi go"), modify objects ("pretty dress"), and ask questions ("Where Daddy?"). Pretty good for a little kid, don't you think?

How do children do all this? At one time, many psychologists assumed that children learned to

telegraphic speech
A child's first word combinations, which omit (as a telegram does) unnecessary words.

Human beings appear to have an inborn facility for acquiring language, even when they cannot hear speech. In North America, hearing-impaired people use American Sign Language (ASL) to express not only everyday meanings but also poetic and musical ones. Deaf children learn to sign in ASL as easily as hearing children learn to speak.

speak—or in the case of deaf children, to use the gestures of American Sign Language (ASL) or other gestural languages—by imitating adults and paying attention when adults corrected their mistakes. Then along came linguist Noam Chomsky (1957, 1980), who argued that language was far too complex to be learned bit by bit, as one might learn a list of world capitals or the rules of algebra. Language, he noted, is not just any old communication system. It is a system that enables us to combine elements that are themselves meaningless into utterances that convey meaning—and to reject utterances that are not acceptable in our native tongue. It permits us to express and comprehend an infinite number of novel utterances, created on the spot—and this is essential, because except for a few fixed phrases ("How are you?" "Get a life"), most of the utterances we produce or hear over a lifetime are new.

Chomsky observed that children not only figure out which sounds form words but they can also take the *surface structure* of a sentence—the way the sentence is actually spoken or signed—and apply rules of grammar (*syntax*) to infer an underlying *deep structure* that contains meaning. For example, although "Mary kissed John" and "John was kissed by Mary" have different surface structures, any 5-year-old knows that the two sentences have essentially the same deep structure, in which Mary is the actor and John the recipient of the action. The human brain, said Chomsky, must therefore contain a *language acquisition device,* a mental module that allows young children to develop language if they are exposed to an adequate sampling of conversation. Just as a bird is designed to fly, human beings are designed to use language.

Over the years, Chomsky and others have presented several kinds of evidence to support this position (Crain, 1991; Pinker, 1994):

1. *Children everywhere go through similar stages of linguistic development.* For example, they will often use double negatives ("He don't want no milk"; "Nobody don't like me"), even when their language does not allow such constructions (Klima & Bellugi, 1966; McNeill, 1966). These commonalities suggest that children are born with a sort of "universal grammar," which is another way of saying that the brain is disposed to notice the features common to all languages (nouns, verbs, phrase structures, and so forth), as well as the variations that can occur.

CARTOONISTS & WRITERS SYNDICATE

RICHTER
USA

"It's like learning a new language. You can't say 'ain't,' you don't end a sentence with a preposition, a sentence must have a subject and a predicate, you can't . . ."

Why is it that children have trouble learning the formal rules of "proper" language, yet by the time they start school they can all apply the grammatical rules of their language to produce and understand new utterances?

2. *Children combine words in ways that adults never would, so they could not simply be imitating adults.* They reduce a parent's sentences ("Let's go to the store!") to their own two-word version ("Go store!") and make errors an adult would not ("The alligator goed kerplunk," "Daddy taked me," "Hey, Horton heared a Who") (Ervin-Tripp, 1964; Marcus et al., 1992). Such errors are not random; they show that the child has grasped a grammatical rule ("add the *t* or *d* sound to make a verb past tense, as in *walked* and *hugged*") and is merely overgeneralizing it (*taked, goed*). These *overregularizations* show that children are actively seeking regular, predictable rules of language.

3. *Adults do not consistently correct their children's syntax.* Learning explanations of language acquisition assume that children are rewarded for saying the right words and punished for making errors. But parents don't stop to correct every error in their children's speech, so long as they can understand what the child is trying to say (Brown, Cazden, & Bellugi, 1969). Indeed, parents often *reward* children for incorrect statements! The 2-year-old who says "Want milk!" is likely to get it; most parents would not wait for a more gram-

matical (or polite) request. Yet by the tender age of 3, as Steven Pinker (1994) writes, the child has become "a grammatical genius—master of most constructions, obeying rules far more often than flouting them, respecting language universals, erring in sensible, adultlike ways, and avoiding many kinds of errors altogether."

Chomsky's ideas completely changed the way researchers think about language development, and even the terms they use (language "acquisition" replaced language "learning"). Although he himself has avoided the evolutionary implications, others have argued that the capacity for language evolved in human beings because it permitted our ancestors to convey precise information about time, space, objects, and events, and to negotiate alliances that were necessary for survival (Pinker, 1994).

But as we saw in Chapter 2, in our discussion of genes and personality, nature and nurture normally interact. Parents may not go around correcting their children's speech all day, but neither do they ignore their children's errors. For example, they are more likely to repeat verbatim a child's well-formed sentence than a sentence with errors ("That's a horse, mommy!" "Yes, that's a horse"). And when the child makes a mistake or produces a clumsy sentence, parents almost invariably respond by recasting it or expanding its elements ("Monkey climbing!" "Yes, the monkey is climbing the tree") (Bohannon & Stanowicz, 1988). In turn, children are more likely to imitate adult recasts and expansions, suggesting that they are learning from them (Bohannon & Symons, 1988). They also imitate their parents' accents, inflections, and tone of voice, and they will repeat some words that the parent tries to teach ("This is a ball, Erwin." "Baw").

Language therefore depends on both biological readiness and social experience. Children who are abandoned and abused, and who are not exposed to language for years (such as Genie, whom we mentioned in Chapter 1), rarely speak normally. Such sad evidence suggests a *critical period* in language development, during the first few years of life or possibly the first decade (Curtiss, 1977; Lenneberg, 1967; Tartter, 1986). During these years, children do not need to hear *speech*—deaf children's acquisition of sign language parallels the development of spoken language—but they do need close relationships and practice in conversation.

??? QUICK QUIZ

Please use language (and thought) to answer these questions.

1. Understanding that two rows of six pennies are equal in number, even if one row is flat and the other is stacked up, is an example of _____.

2. Understanding that a toy exists even after Mom puts it in her purse is an example of _____, which develops during the _____ stage.

3. The belief that a car moves because you are riding in it shows _____ thinking.

4. Name five findings that challenge aspects of Piaget's theory.

5. "More cake!" and "Mommy come" are examples of _____ speech.

6. Name three arguments for the existence of an innate "universal grammar."

Answers: 1. conservation   2. object permanence; sensorimotor   3. egocentric   4. The changes from one stage to another are not as clear as Piaget implied; children know more and know it earlier than Piaget thought; they are less egocentric than Piaget thought; their cognitive development is affected by their culture; and not all adolescents and adults achieve the ability for formal operations.   5. telegraphic   6. Children everywhere seem to go through similar stages of linguistic development; children combine words in ways that adults never would; adults do not consistently correct their children's syntax.

What's Ahead

- *How would a biologically oriented psychologist explain why little boys and girls are often so "sexist" in their choice of toys?*

- *How do teachers often unintentionally reinforce aggressiveness in boys?*

- *If a little girl "knows" that girls can't be doctors, does this mean she will never go to med school?*

GENDER DEVELOPMENT

Most babies, unless they have rare abnormalities, are born unambiguously male or female—an anatomical and physiological distinction. But how do children learn the rules of masculinity and femininity—the things that boys do that are supposedly different from what girls do? Why, as one psychologist we know put it, do most preschool children act like the Gender Police, rigidly insisting, say, that boys can't be nurses and girls can't be doctors?

To distinguish what is anatomically given from what is learned, many psychologists distinguish *sex* from *gender* (Deaux, 1985; Lott, 1997). *Sex* is used to refer to the physiological or anatomical attributes of the sexes; thus we might speak of a "sex difference" in the frequency of baldness or color blindness. *Gender* is used to refer to the cultural and psychological attributes that children learn

are appropriate for the sexes; thus, we might speak of a "gender difference" in sexual attitudes, dishwashing, and fondness for romance novels.

As we will see shortly, early in life, most children learn to label themselves as male or female and are able to distinguish the two sexes. It takes them longer, however, to get the hang of **gender roles,** the rules and expectations governing male and female attitudes and behavior. And not until the age of 4 or 5 do most children develop a secure **gender identity,** a fundamental sense of maleness or femaleness that exists regardless of what one wears or does. Only then do they understand that *what boys and girls do* is not necessarily the same as *what sex they are*—that a girl remains a girl even if she can climb a tree, and a boy remains a boy even if he has a ponytail.

Developmental psychologists study the biological factors, principles of learning, and cognitive processes that might explain why children's behavior is often so sex-stereotyped and how children learn what it means to be "masculine" or "feminine."

Gender and Biology

Biological psychologists hold that some differences between the sexes are largely a matter of prenatal hormones, genes, and possibly brain organization: especially differences in aggression, occupational

gender role

A social position governed by rules and standards for male or female attitudes and behavior.

gender identity

The fundamental sense of being male or female; it is independent of whether the person conforms to the social and cultural rules of gender.

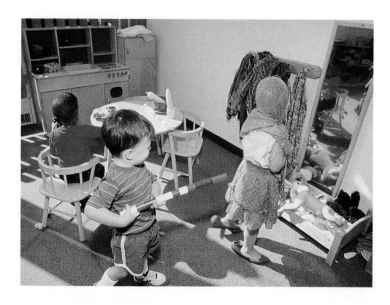

Look familiar? In a scene typical of many nursery schools, the boy builds a gun out of anything he can, and the girl dresses up in any pretty thing she can find. Psychologists (and parents) debate whether such sex-typed behaviors are biologically based or are a result of subtle reinforcements and cultural expectations (see the cartoon below).

interests (e.g., math or nursing), and skills (e.g., flying airplanes or knitting sweaters). Girls who were exposed to prenatal androgens (masculinizing hormones) in the womb, they note, are later more likely than nonexposed girls to prefer "boys' toys," such as cars, fire engines, and Lincoln logs (Berenbaum & Snyder, 1995). And in all primate species, young males are more likely than females to go in for physical roughhousing.

Biologically oriented researchers point out that some gender differences emerge regardless of what parents and teachers do; parents may treat their sons and daughters equally, or try to, yet their sons still prefer mechanical toys and their daughters still want tea sets. A meta-analysis of 172 studies showed that in 18 domains of parental treatment of children—including responsiveness and warmth, encouragement of achievement or

dependency, use of reasoning, restrictiveness, and amount of interaction—parents treated sons and daughters no differently (Lytton & Romney, 1991). Yet the children often acted out gender stereotypes anyway, leading the researchers to conclude that toy and play preferences have a biological basis.

Gender and Learning

Behavioral and social-learning theorists investigate the many subtle and not-so-subtle reinforcers that teach children what "girls" do and what "boys" do. In the learning view, most differences between boys and girls are a result of **gender socialization,** sometimes called *sex typing:* the psychological process by which boys and girls learn

gender socialization

The process by which children learn the behaviors, attitudes, and expectations associated with being masculine or feminine in their culture; also called sex typing.

cathy®   **by Cathy Guisewite**

what it means to be masculine or feminine. This process begins at the moment of birth, when the newborn is enveloped in the clothes, colors, and toys the parents think are appropriate for its sex. No parent ever excitedly calls a relative to exclaim, "Guess what? It's a baby! It's a $7\frac{1}{2}$-pound, black-haired baby!" Adults respond to babies and toddlers differently, depending on whether the child is a male or female—even when the adults think they are treating boys and girls alike.

For example, Beverly Fagot and her colleagues (1985) observed the reactions of teachers to "assertive acts" (such as efforts to get an adult's attention) and "communicative acts" of 12- to 16-month-old children. Although the boys and girls did not differ in the frequency of these acts, the teachers responded far more often to assertive boys than to shy ones, and to verbal girls than to less verbal ones. When the researchers observed the same children a year later, a gender difference was now apparent, with boys behaving more assertively and girls talking more to teachers.

Similarly, the aggressiveness of boys gets more attention and other rewards from teachers and peers than does aggressiveness in girls, even when the children start out being equally aggressive. In one observational study of preschool children, peers or teachers paid attention to the aggression of boys 81 percent of the time, compared to only 24 percent of the time for the girls' aggression. When girls and boys behaved dependently, however—say, by calling for help from the teacher—the girls got attention far more often than the boys did (Fagot, 1984).

Children also learn to adjust their behavior, making it more or less sex-typed, depending on the situation and the social context. For example, preschool girls are seldom passive with each other; however, when paired with boys, girls typically stand on the sidelines and let the boys monopolize the toys. The reason, it seems, is that when a boy and girl compete for a shared toy, the boy tends to dominate—unless an adult is in the room. Girls in mixed classrooms may stay nearer to the teacher not because they are more dependent but because they want a chance at the toys! Girls play as independently as boys when they are in all-girl groups, and they will actually sit farther from the teacher than boys in all-boy groups do (Maccoby, 1990).

The hidden messages conveyed by parents, teachers, and other adults affect older children, as well as younger ones, as a longitudinal study of seventh- and ninth-grade children's math achievement revealed (Jacobs & Eccles, 1985). At the start of the study, the children were equal in math ability, as determined by test scores and teachers' evaluations. But over time, parents who believed that boys are naturally superior in math unintentionally communicated this message to their children. These parents might tell a son who did well in math, "You're a natural math whiz, Johnny!" But if their daughters got identically good grades, the parents would say, "Wow, you really worked hard in math, Janey, and it shows!" The implication, not lost on the children, was clear: When girls do well, it is because of concerted effort; when boys do well, it is because they have a natural gift. This attitude was related to the reduced likelihood that the girls would take further math courses, remain interested in math, and value math in general. Why should they, if the subject is going to be so hard and isn't natural to females anyway? Similarly, parents' stereotypical expectations about their children's talents in English and sports strongly influence their children's performance and feelings of competence in these areas (Eccles, 1993; Eccles, Jacobs, & Harold, 1990).

Gender and Cognition

Another approach to gender development emphasizes the role of children's unfolding cognitive abilities. As children mature, they develop a **gender schema,** a mental network of beliefs,

gender schema

A cognitive schema (mental network) of knowledge, beliefs, metaphors, and expectations about what it means to be male or female.

Get Involved

If you woke up tomorrow and found that you had been transformed into a member of the other sex, how would your life change, if at all? Would anything be different about your attitudes, behavior, habits, experiences, choices, preferences, and feelings? Write down your first reactions, and then ask a few of your male and female friends the same question. If possible, ask young children, too. Do their answers differ depending on their sex? If so, how? What does this exercise reveal about gender socialization?

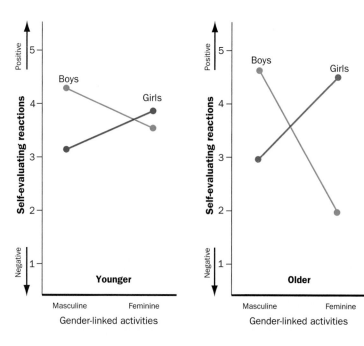

Figure 3.5

The Internalization of Gender Roles

In a study of gender socialization, 3-year-old children did not expect to feel significantly different about themselves if they played with "masculine" or "feminine" toys (left graph). But 4-year-olds, especially boys, anticipated feeling much better about playing with toys associated with their own sex than those associated with the other sex (right graph). These self-evaluations accurately predicted which toys the children actually played with (Bussey & Bandura, 1992).

metaphors, and expectations about what it means to be male or female (Bem, 1985, 1993; Fagot, 1985; Spence, 1985). These gender schemas in turn influence a child's behavior.

Gender schemas depend on the ability to notice that there are two sexes—an ability that starts to emerge even before children can speak. By the age of 9 months, most babies can discriminate male from female faces (Fagot & Leinbach, 1993), and they can match female faces with female voices (Poulin-Dubois et al., 1994). Once children acquire the ability to distinguish male and female, they soon label themselves as "boy" or "girl." And once they do that, they begin to prefer same-sex playmates and sex-typed toys, without being explicitly taught to do so. "Early labelers" are more sex-typed in their toy play, motor activity, aggressiveness, and verbal skills than children who still cannot consistently label males and females. But late-labeling children eventually catch up in their ability to distinguish the two sexes, and then their behavior becomes similarly sex-typed (Fagot, 1993).

The period between ages 2 and 4 is especially important for the development of gender schemas. Later, these schemas expand far beyond preferences for dolls or jungle gyms to include all sorts of meanings and associations—for example, that rough, spiky, black, or mechanical things are "male" and that soft, pink, fuzzy, or flowery things are "female" (Fagot & Leinbach, 1993).

In general, however, boys express stronger pref-

erences for "masculine" toys and activities than girls do for "feminine" ones, and boys are harsher on themselves if they fail to behave in sex-typed ways (see Figure 3.5). One reason may be that society values masculine activities, occupations, and traits more than feminine ones, and in general gives males higher status. Preschoolers are already aware of these facts. When asked to watch two furry rabbit puppets acting out a story, 4- and 5-year-olds thought that the rabbit that was deferent, had its opinions overruled, and was less likely to have its advice followed was . . . a female (Ward, 1994). So when boys behave like (or play with) girls they lose status, and when girls behave like boys they gain status (Serbin, Powlishta, & Gulko, 1993).

With increasing experience, knowledge, and cognitive sophistication, children construct their own standards of what boys and girls may or may not do. Eventually, they become aware of the exceptions to their gender schemas—for instance, that women can be engineers and men can be cooks. From middle childhood through adolescence, many become more flexible about what they think they can do as males or females, especially if they have friends of the other sex and if their families, jobs, or cultures encourage such flexibility (Katz & Ksansnak, 1994). Others carry fairly rigid gender schemas into adolescence and adulthood, and thus feel uncomfortable or even angry when they see a male nurse or a female drill sergeant (Eagly, Makhijani, & Klonsky, 1990). How flexible are your own gender schemas?

In today's fast-moving world, all theories of gender development must deal with the fact that the rules of masculinity and femininity keep changing. Because of these changes, gender differences acquired in childhood do not necessarily last. A meta-analysis of 65 studies, involving more than 9,000 people, found that gender differences in personality, moral reasoning, maturity of thought, conformity, and other characteristics were greatest among junior- and senior-high-school students (Cohn, 1991). But these differences declined significantly among college-age adults and disap-peared entirely among older men and women.

Because people's schemas, attitudes, and behavior change as they have new experiences and as society changes, gender development is a life-long process. Children may act like the "Gender Police" when they are 3, when they are trying to figure out what it means to be male or female; but most will have become far more flexible by the time they are 23 or 43. Children can grow up in an extremely sex-typed family and yet, as adults, find themselves in careers or relationships they might never have imagined for themselves.

??? QUICK QUIZ

Whether you are a male or female, you should take this quiz.

1. A biological psychologist would say that a 3-year-old boy's love of going "vroom, vroom" with his truck collection is probably a result of _____; a learning theorist would say that it results from _____ by parents and teachers.

2. Two-year-old Jeremy thinks that if he changed from wearing pants to wearing dresses, he could become a girl; he still lacks a stable _____.

3. Which statement about gender schemas is *false*? (a) They are present in early form by 1 year of age; (b) they are permanent conceptualizations of what it means to be masculine or feminine; (c) they eventually expand to include many meanings and associations with being male and female.

Answers:
1. biological factors such as hormones or brain processes; reinforcement (or more generally, gender socialization)   2. gender identity   3. b

What's Ahead ▬ ▬ ▬ ▬ ▬

- *According to a leading theory, why is moral reasoning based on law, justice, and duty* not *the pinnacle of moral development?*

- *When reasoning about moral dilemmas, are women more concerned with compassion and caring than men are?*

- *Are college students more moral than young children?*

- *What's wrong with "because I say so" as a way of getting children to behave?*

MORAL DEVELOPMENT

Do you think it is morally acceptable to steal something you desperately need if you can't afford to pay for it? If you visited your lonely grand-mother, but only because you hoped to inherit her estate, would your act be moral? If you could help a friend cheat on a test, would you do it? How would you feel about it? As these questions suggest, morality is a complex phenomenon involving empathy for others, the cognitive ability to evaluate moral dilemmas, the inner voice of conscience, and behaving in considerate and responsible ways (Kurtines & Gewirtz, 1995).

Moral Judgments: Reasoning About Morality

Much of the research on moral development has focused on how children make moral judgments. Piaget (1932) was the first psychologist to divide the development of moral reasoning into stages based on the child's cognitive maturity. In the 1960s, Lawrence Kohlberg (1964, 1966), drawing on Piaget's ideas, outlined his own theory of stages in moral reasoning, which became highly influential. Your moral stage, said Kohlberg, can be determined by the answers you give to hypothetical moral dilemmas. For example, suppose a man's wife is dying and needs a special drug. The man can't afford the drug and the druggist won't lower his price. Should the man steal the drug? What if he no longer loves his wife? If the man is caught, should the judge be lenient? To Kohlberg, the reasoning behind the answers was more important than the decisions themselves.

Kohlberg (1964, 1976, 1984) proposed three levels of moral development, each divided into two stages. He believed that the stages were universal and occurred in an invariant order; a person would not reach the highest stages, however, without having certain key experiences. At Kohlberg's first level, *preconventional morality,* young children obey rules because they fear being punished if they disobey (Stage 1), and later because they think it is in their best interest to obey (Stage 2). Stage 2 reasoning is also hedonistic, self-centered, and lacking in empathy; what is "right" is what feels good. At about age 10 or 11, according to Kohlberg, children shift to the second level, the *conventional morality* of adult society. At Stage 3, conventional morality is based on trust, conformity, and loyalty to others; morality means "don't hurt others; don't rock the boat." Most people then advance to Stage 4, a "law-and-order" orientation, based on understanding the social order, law, justice, and duty.

Late in adolescence and early in adulthood, said Kohlberg, some people realize that some laws—such as those that segregate ethnic groups or that legitimize the systematic mistreatment of minorities—are themselves immoral. Such awareness moves them to the highest level, *postconventional ("principled") morality.* At Stage 5, they realize that values and laws are relative, that people hold different standards, and that laws are important but can be changed. Kohlberg thought that only a few great individuals reach Stage 6, developing a moral standard based on universal human rights. When faced with a conflict between law and conscience, such people follow conscience, even at great personal risk.

Hundreds of studies have been done, all over the world, to test Kohlberg's theory (Eckensberger, 1994; Shweder, Mahapatra, & Miller, 1990; Snarey, 1985). The results show that although Stages 5 and 6 are rare, the others do tend to develop sequentially in many cultures, and therefore Kohlberg's theory remains an influential one in developmental psychology (Bee, 1997).

In the early 1980s, Carol Gilligan (1982) countered Kohlberg's theory of moral reasoning with one of her own. She argued that men tend to base their moral choices on abstract principles of law and justice, asking questions such as "Whose rights should take precedence here?" whereas

To many people, Martin Luther King, Jr. (center), shown here leading a civil rights march in 1965, exemplified the highest stage of moral reasoning. The rare individuals who reach this stage, argued Lawrence Kohlberg, follow conscience rather than law when the law oppresses entire groups of people. King's commitment to justice and equality for black Americans cost him his life.

women tend to base their moral decisions on principles of compassion and caring, asking questions such as "Who will be hurt least?" Some studies have supported Gilligan's view, but most find no gender differences, especially when people are allowed to rank *all* the reasons behind their moral judgments (Clopton & Sorell, 1993; Cohn, 1991; Friedman, Robinson, & Friedman, 1987; Thoma, 1986). Both sexes usually say that they base their moral decisions on compassion *and* on abstract principles of justice; they worry about feelings *and* fairness. Both sexes tend to use "justice" reasoning when they are thinking about highly abstract ethical dilemmas, and "care" reasoning when they are thinking about intimate dilemmas in their own lives (Clopton & Sorell, 1993; Walker, de Vries, & Trevethan, 1987).

Thinking Critically About Stages of Moral Reasoning

Kohlberg's and Gilligan's theories of moral reasoning have generated much research and animated discussion. People enjoy speculating about their own stages and whether the sexes differ in how they think about moral problems. Some psychologists, however, regard all stage theories of moral judgment as inherently limited, for three reasons:

1. *Stage theories tend to overlook educational and cultural influences on moral reasoning.* College-educated people tend to give "higher-level" explanations of moral decisions than people who have not attended college, but all that shows, say Kohlberg's critics, is that college-educated people are more verbally sophisticated. Stage theories also ignore cultural differences (Shweder, Mahapatra, & Miller, 1990). In Iceland and Germany, for example, concern for others is far more important than the theory would predict among children supposedly at only Stage 2; and because Stage 4 is heavily based on formal legal conceptions, unschooled members of many cultures do not achieve it (Eckensberger, 1994).

2. *People's moral reasoning is often inconsistent across situations.* In research using Kohlberg's moral dilemmas, and in most people's lives, moral reasoning depends on the situation and on the nature of the dilemma. For example, you might show conventional morality by overlooking a racial slur at a dinner party because you don't want to upset anyone but reveal postconventional reasoning by protesting a governmental policy you regard as immoral. In one study using Kohlberg's dilemmas, most of the participants gave responses spanning three to six substages, and only one young man based all his judgments on the same stage (Wark & Krebs, 1996).

3. *Moral reasoning is often unrelated to moral behavior.* Stage theories of moral reasoning do not necessarily predict whether people will actually behave in kind, fair, and responsible ways. Moral reasoning increases during the school years, but so do cheating, lying, cruelty, and the cognitive ability to rationalize these actions (Kagan, 1993). College students usually draw on "higher" principles of justice and fair play to justify moral decisions, yet about one-third of American and Canadian college men say they would force a woman into sexual acts if they could get away with it—the lowest form of moral reasoning (Malamuth & Dean, 1990). As Thomas Lickona (1983) wryly summarized, "We can reach high levels of moral reasoning, and still behave like scoundrels."

Because of such problems, some psychologists concentrate not on moral reasoning, but on the emergence of conscience and the development of "moral emotions" such as shame, guilt, and empathy (Hoffman, 1990). The basic capacity for moral feeling, like that for language, seems to be inborn. As Jerome Kagan (1984) wrote, "Without this fundamental human capacity, which nineteenth-century observers called a *moral sense,* the child could not be socialized." The "moral sense" must be nurtured, however. Its development depends on children becoming attached to their parents, motivated to adopt their parents' standards of right and wrong, and concerned about disappointing their parents or losing their parents' love.

Moral Behavior: Rearing a Moral Child

Even moral emotions, however, do not inevitably lead to moral behavior; we can feel really miserable about treating each other horribly—and do it anyway. In Chapter 9 we will look at some of the social processes, such as conformity and obedience, that affect moral behavior. Here we want to consider how children develop into helpful members of society. How do they learn to avoid the temptations to steal, lie, cheat, and otherwise behave as they might like to?

Learning theorists answer that children's moral actions depend on the rewards, punishments, and examples they get as they grow up. When children are rewarded for aggressive or selfish acts, such behavior will prevail over cooperation and altruism. Role models are also important—what they do, and what they "get away with." Does a public figure commit an illegal act and then earn a fortune from movie deals? Does a sports celebrity get away with cheating, violence, or rape?

Parents, of course, are important role models and sources of rewards and punishments, but children learn as much from *how* their parents interact with them as from the content of their parents' lessons. When you did something wrong as a child, for example, did the adults in your family shout at you, punish you, or explain the error of your ways?

One of the most common methods used by parents to enforce moral standards is **power assertion,** which includes threats, physical punishment, depriving the child of privileges, and generally taking advantage of being bigger, stronger, and more powerful ("Do it because I say so"). Yet power assertion, which is based on the child's fear of punishment, is associated with a lack of moral feeling and behavior in children, poor self-control, and a failure to internalize moral values.

Longitudinal studies show how power assertion by parents can lead to aggressiveness and poor impulse control in children. Parents of aggressive children do a lot of shouting, scolding, and spanking, but they fail to clearly connect the punishment with the child's behavior. They do not state clear rules, require compliance, consistently punish violations, or praise good behavior. Instead, they nag and shout at the child, occasionally and unpredictably tossing in a slap or a loss of privileges. This combination of power assertion with a pattern of intermittent discipline causes the child's aggressiveness to increase and eventually get out of hand. The child becomes withdrawn, manipulative, and difficult to control, which causes the parents to try to assert their power even more forcefully, which makes the child angrier . . . and a vicious cycle is generated (Patterson, 1994; Patterson, Reid, & Dishion, 1992).

A far more successful method for teaching moral behavior is **induction,** in which the parent appeals to the child's own resources, helpful nature, affection for others, and sense of responsibility. A parent using induction might explain to a misbehaving child that the child's actions could harm, inconvenience, or disappoint another person ("You made Doug cry; it's not nice to bite"; "You must never poke anyone's eyes because that could hurt them seriously"). Or the parent might

power assertion

A method of child rearing in which the parent uses punishment and authority to correct the child's misbehavior.

induction

A method of child rearing in which the parent appeals to the child's own resources, abilities, sense of responsibility, and feelings for others in correcting the child's misbehavior.

Power Assertion

Parent uses threats, physical force, or other kinds of power to get child to obey.

Example:
"Do it because I say so"; "Stop that right now."

Result:
Child obeys, but only when parent is present; child often feels resentful.

Induction

Parent appeals to child's good nature, empathy, love of parent, and sense of responsibility to others; offers explanations of rules.

Example:
"You're too grown-up to behave like that"; "Fighting hurts your little brother."

Result:
Child tends to internalize reasons for good behavior.

appeal to the child's own helpful inclinations ("I know you're a person who likes to be good to others"), which is far more effective than citing external reasons to be good ("You'd better be nice or you won't get dessert") (Eisenberg, 1995). Children whose parents use induction tend to feel guilty if they hurt others. They internalize standards of right and wrong, confess rather than lie if they misbehave, accept responsibility for their misbehavior, and act considerately toward others (Hoffman & Saltzstein, 1967; Radke-Yarrow, Zahn-Waxler, & Chapman, 1983).

In a program of research spanning three decades, Diana Baumrind (1966, 1971, 1973, 1989, 1991), expanding on the concepts of induction and power assertion, has identified three overall styles of child rearing and their results. (We discuss methods of child rearing further in "Taking Psychology with You.")

1. *Authoritarian* parents rely too much on power assertion and give too little nurturance. Communication is all one way: The parent issues orders ("Stop that!" "Do it because I say so!"), and the child is expected to listen and obey. The children of these parents tend to be less socially skilled than other children, have lower self-esteem, and do more poorly in school. Some are overly timid, and others are overly aggressive.

2. *Permissive* parents are nurturant, but they exercise too little control and don't make strong demands for mature and responsible behavior on the part of their children. They fail to state rules clearly and enforce them consistently, and they have poor communication with their kids. Their children, compared with the offspring of other kinds of parents, are likely to be impulsive, immature, irresponsible, and academically unmotivated.

3. *Authoritative* parents travel a middle road, knowing when and how to discipline their children. They have high but reasonable expectations and teach their children how to meet them. They also give their children emotional support and encourage two-way communication. Their children tend to have good self-control, high self-esteem, and self-confidence; to be independent yet cooperative; to do better than average in school; and to be socially mature, cheerful, thoughtful, and helpful.

The parent's methods of discipline, however, always interact with the child's temperament, cognitive abilities, and perceptions of the parent's intentions (Grusec & Goodnow, 1994). The methods used by a parent in an impoverished or dangerous community may seem harsh and "authoritarian" to an outsider, but the child may interpret the parent's behavior as evidence of love and concern (Baumrind, 1991). Some parents may become "authoritarian" because they are dealing with a difficult child whose temperament is aggressive and antisocial from the outset (Henry et al., 1996).

Ultimately, the greatest influence on children's moral behavior is what others expect of them (Eisenberg, 1995). In a cross-cultural study of children in Kenya, India, Mexico, Okinawa, the Philippines, and the United States, Beatrice and John Whiting (1975) measured how often children behaved altruistically (offering help, support,

In many cultures, children are expected to contribute to the family income and to take care of their younger siblings. These experiences encourage helpfulness and empathy.

or unselfish suggestions) or egoistically (seeking help and attention or wanting to dominate others). This research was later reanalyzed, and five new cultures were added (Whiting & Edwards, 1988). American children were the least altruistic on all three study measures and the most egoistic. Altruistic children came from societies in which children are assigned many tasks, such as caring for younger children and gathering and preparing food. The children knew that their work made a genuine contribution to the well-being or eco-nomic survival of the family. Mothers had many responsibilities inside and outside the home, and children respected the parents' authority to set rules and limits.

In summary, whether children learn to become kind, helpful, and responsible members of society depends on (1) their emerging cognitive capacities to evaluate complex moral issues; (2) styles of child rearing that foster or inhibit moral standards, emotions, and behavior; and (3) the behavior that is expected and required of children every day.

??? QUICK QUIZ

To rear children who are kind and helpful, parents and parents-to-be should be able to answer the following questions.

1. Margo says she pays her taxes because she believes in obeying the law. According to Kohlberg, what level of moral reasoning is she showing?

2. Two psychologists noted that in Kohlberg's system, the cruelest lawyer could get a higher moral-reasoning score than the kindest 8-year-old (Schulman & Mekler, 1994). What did the psychologists mean?

3. Which method of parental discipline tends to create children who have internalized values of helpfulness and empathy? (a) induction, (b) punishment, (c) power assertion

4. Which form of family life tends to create helpful children? (a) Every family member "does his or her own thing," (b) parents insist that children obey, (c) children contribute to the family welfare, (d) parents remind children often about the importance of being helpful.

5. In Chapter 2, you read that the Big Five personality traits have a genetic component, are resistant to change, and emerge almost regardless of what parents do. Now here we are offering evidence that what parents do often *does* make a difference. How might these two lines of research be reconciled?

Answers:
1. conventional morality 2. A person's score reflects verbal ability and education, and not necessarily actual behavior. 3. a 4. c 5. We can avoid either-or thinking by asking which qualities may be due largely to genetic influences (such as extroversion) and which are strongly affected by parental lessons (such as aggressiveness and empathy). Also, how a child turns out depends on the interaction between a child's temperament and the parents' reactions. And perhaps the relative impact of temperament and parental techniques changes as the child matures.

What's Ahead

- *What are the advantages and disadvantages of experiencing puberty earlier than most of your classmates do?*

- *During adolescence, are extreme turmoil and unhappiness the exception or the rule?*

- *When teenagers and their parents quarrel, what is it typically about?*

ADOLESCENCE

Adolescence refers to the period of development between **puberty,** the age at which a person becomes capable of sexual reproduction, and adulthood. In some cultures, the time span between puberty and adulthood is only a few months; a sexually mature boy or girl is soon expected to marry and assume adult tasks. In modern Western societies, adolescence lasts several years. Teen-

puberty
The age at which a person becomes capable of sexual reproduction.

agers are not considered emotionally mature enough to be full-fledged adults with all the rights, responsibilities, and roles of adulthood. The long span of adolescence is new to this century. In the past, societies needed the labor of young people and could not afford to have them spend a decade in school or in "self-discovery."

The Physiology of Adolescence

Until puberty, boys and girls produce roughly the same levels of "male" hormones (androgens) and "female hormones" (estrogens). At puberty, the brain's pituitary gland begins to stimulate hormone production in the adrenal and other endocrine glands and in the reproductive glands (see Chapter 4). As a result, from puberty on, boys have a higher level of androgens than girls do, and girls have a higher level of estrogens than boys do.

In boys, the reproductive glands are the testes (testicles), which produce sperm; in girls, the reproductive glands are the ovaries, which release eggs, or ova. During puberty, these sex organs mature and the individual becomes capable of reproduction. In girls, the onset of menstruation, called **menarche,** and the development of breasts are

menarche (men-ARR-kee)
The onset of menstruation.

signs of sexual maturity. In boys, the signs are the onset of nocturnal emissions and the growth of the testes, scrotum, and penis. Hormones are also responsible for the emergence of *secondary sex characteristics,* such as a deepened voice and facial and chest hair in boys and pubic hair in both sexes.

The dramatic physical changes of puberty are part of the last "growth spurt" on the child's road to adulthood. For girls, the adolescent growth spurt begins, on average, at age 10, peaks at 12 or 13, and stops at about age 16, by which time most girls are sexually mature. For boys, the average adolescent growth spurt starts at about age 12 and ends at about age 18. This difference in rates of development is often a source of misery to adolescents, for most girls mature sooner than most boys.

The timing of the changes of puberty depends on both genetic and environmental factors. The onset of menarche, for example, can be affected by nutrition, stress, and exercise; indeed, better nutrition may help explain why the average age of menarche has been declining in Europe and North America since the mid-1800s. A study of more than 17,000 girls found that almost 15 percent of white girls and about 48 percent of African-American girls now show signs of pubic hair or breast development by age 8 (Herman-Giddens, 1997). The onset of puberty seems to be occurring earlier for males, too. Decades ago, the average American man did not reach his maximum height until the age of 26; today this marker of the end of puberty occurs, on average, at age 18 (Cole & Cole, 1993).

Individuals vary enormously, however, in the onset and length of puberty. Some girls first menstruate as early as age 8 and others as late as 16. One 15-year-old male may be as developed as an adult man and another may still be a boy. In addition, mischievous nature has made growth a jumpy, irregular business, with different parts of the body maturing at different rates. A girl may have undeveloped breasts but adult-size hands and feet. A boy may be tall and gangly but have no trace of a longed-for beard. Eventually, everything catches up.

If you entered puberty before most of your classmates, or if you matured much later than they did, you know that your experience of adolescence was different from that of the average teenager (whoever that is). Some psychologists believe that the *timing* of puberty is more important in an adolescent's development than the specific biological events themselves. Early-maturing boys generally have a more positive view of their bodies, and their relatively greater size and strength gives them a

Children typically reach puberty at different times, often to their embarrassment. These girls are all the same age, but they differ considerably in physical maturity.

boost in sports and the prestige that being a good athlete brings young men. But they are also more likely to smoke, drink, use illicit drugs, and break the law than later-maturing boys, and to have less self-control and emotional stability (Duncan et al., 1985). Late-developing boys feel the worst about themselves in the seventh grade, but by the twelfth grade they usually end up as the psychologically healthiest group (Petersen, 1989).

Likewise, some early-maturing girls have the prestige of being socially popular, but, partly because others in their peer group regard them as being sexually precocious, they are also more likely to have conflict with their parents, have behavioral problems, drop out of school, have a negative body image, and have emotional problems (Caspi & Moffitt, 1991; Stattin & Magnusson, 1990). Girls who go through puberty relatively late, in contrast, have a more difficult time at first, but by the end of adolescence many are happier with their appearance and more popular than their early-maturing classmates.

A longitudinal study of 501 girls in New Zealand found that girls who entered menarche before the age of 12 subsequently had the most problems (Caspi & Moffitt, 1991). Because the researchers had been observing these teenagers since childhood, they were able to show that early menarche itself wasn't the problem; rather, it tended to accentuate the *existing* behavioral

problems and family conflicts the girls had had in childhood. The group with the most troubles throughout adolescence were early maturers who had a history of behavioral problems in childhood.

During times of transition—whether a biological change such as puberty or a social change such as starting college—existing personality traits and problems are magnified. Biological changes alone, even the hormonal changes of adolescence, do not produce the same psychological consequences for everyone (Eccles et al., 1993; Jessor, 1993).

The Psychology of Adolescence

Recently, we came across a high-school textbook on adolescence that painted the bleakest picture of teenage life we've ever seen. To be an adolescent, according to this book, is to suffer depression, anxiety, insecurity, horrible fights with parents, loneliness, identity conflicts, and all-around misery. Reading this book, you wouldn't have a clue that teenagers ever felt good about themselves, held jobs, did well in school, had friends, or got along with their parents. Yet in studies using representative samples, only a minority of teenagers conform to the stereotype of the troubled, angry, unhappy

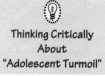

Thinking Critically About "Adolescent Turmoil"

Adolescence can be a time of turmoil and rebellion (left), but most teens feel good about themselves and their communities, as do the young people on the right who have volunteered to remove graffiti.

adolescent. Most teenagers have supportive families, a sense of purpose and self-confidence, good friends, and the skill to cope with their problems. Extreme turmoil and unhappiness are the exception, not the rule (Bee, 1997; Offer & Sabshin, 1984; Steinberg, 1990).

Still, adolescence can be a difficult and challenging time. Teenagers must learn the rules of adult sexuality, morality, work, and family. They are beginning to develop their own standards and values, and often they do so by trying on the styles, actions, and attitudes of their peers, in contrast to those of their parents. They are questioning adult life, even as they are rehearsing for it. For some teenagers—especially those who have experienced parental divorce, the death of a close relative, or serious illness, or are grappling with issues of sexual identity—these changes can feel overwhelming and can lead to loneliness, depression, and anxiety. Some succumb to psychological problems typical of their sex as they struggle to fit their peers' and society's views of masculinity or femininity: During adolescence, "externalizing" problems (such as aggression and other antisocial behavior) become substantially higher in boys than in girls, and "internalizing" problems (such as depression and eating disorders) become higher in girls than in boys (Zahn-Waxler, 1996). Also, rates of suicide among adolescent males are a serious, growing problem in North America and Europe (Garland & Zigler, 1994).

During the transition from childhood to adulthood, conflicts and misunderstandings with adults typically focus on the adolescent's increased desire for autonomy. The Michigan Study of Adolescent Life Transitions followed some 1,500 adolescents as they moved from the sixth grade (elementary school) to the seventh (junior high). Those pre-teens whose motivation dwindled and misconduct increased were reacting to specific changes in their environments. Their teachers were no longer encouraging active classroom participation and decision making as they had in elementary school but were instead requiring rote learning; and their parents, perhaps worried about their maturing children's sexuality and possible drug use, were using increasingly punitive measures of controlling them. Thus, the researchers concluded, just when adolescents' cognitive abilities are maturing to enable them to do more complex academic tasks and make personal decisions, some teachers and parents are stifling these needs.

When teenagers have conflicts with their parents over autonomy, they are usually trying to *individuate*, to develop their own opinions and values, rather than sever the connection entirely. In one study, adolescents described quarrelling over issues like these: "why my mother manipulates the conversation to get me to hate her"; "how much of a bastard my father is to my sister"; "how ugly my mom's taste is"; "how pig-headed my mom and dad are" (Csikszentmihalyi & Larson, 1984). But these fights—over what is important, who should set the rules, differences of opinion and taste, and the like—rarely reflected a true rift between parent and adolescent. Likewise, in a study of 65 ethnically diverse mother–daughter pairs in Britain and the United States, most of the teenage girls reported plenty of quarrels with their mothers, but they also named their mothers as the person they felt closest to (Apter, 1990). For young men and women in Western societies, then, quarrels with parents tend to signify a change from one-sided parental authority to a more reciprocal, adult relationship (Laursen & Collins, 1994; Steinberg, 1990).

??? QUICK QUIZ

If you're not feeling rebellious, try these questions.

1. The onset of menstruation is called _____.
2. *True or false:* Puberty is the same thing as adolescence.
3. Extreme turmoil and rebellion in adolescence are (a) nearly universal, (b) the exception rather than the rule, (c) rare.
4. When teenagers have conflicts with their parents, the conflicts are typically over issues of _____.

Answers:
1. menarche   2. false (can you say why?)   3. b   4. autonomy or individuation

| What's Ahead |

- *Does menopause make most women depressed or irrational?*

- *Do men experience a male version of menopause?*

- *What intellectual skills often decline in old age—and which ones don't?*

- *What's wrong with thinking of life as a series of predictable stages?*

- *What feelings are common when people fail to marry, start working, or have children at the "right" time?*

ADULTHOOD

According to ancient Greek legend, the Sphinx was a monster—half lion, half woman—who terrorized passersby on the road to Thebes. The Sphinx would ask each traveler a question and then murder those who failed to answer correctly. (The Sphinx was a pretty tough grader.) The question was this: What animal walks on four feet in the morning, two feet at noon, and three feet in the evening? Only one traveler, Oedipus, knew the solution to the riddle. The animal, he said, is Man, who crawls on all fours as a baby, walks upright as an adult, and limps in old age with the aid of a staff.

The Sphinx was the first life-span theorist. Since then, many philosophers, writers, and scientists have speculated on the course of adult life, expanding the Sphinx's three stages into seven, eight, or ten. The idea of stages is terrifically appealing. Everyone can see that children go through stages of physical and mental maturation, so people have assumed that adults go through stages, too. But do they? In this section, we will consider this question, as we examine the biological and psychological influences on adult development.

The Biological Clock

The biology of aging affects people all through life, as a 27-year-old "aging" tennis champion can tell you. For most people, though, after puberty the next significant chiming of the biological clock rings at midlife. Many people think that menopause, which usually occurs between ages 45 and 55, is a traumatic "deficiency disease" that causes women to become depressed, irritable, and

irrational, and that men go through the emotional equivalent, a "midlife crisis." Many people also believe that after midlife, it's all downhill—that the older you get, the more you lose, biologically speaking: your memory, your brain cells, your intelligence. Let's look at the scientific evidence on these assumptions.

Menopause and Midlife.   **Menopause** is the midlife cessation of menstruation, which occurs when the ovaries stop producing estrogen and progesterone. Menopause does produce physical symptoms in many women, notably "hot flashes," as the vascular system adjusts to the decrease in estrogen. But only about 10 percent of all women have unusually severe physical symptoms.

The negative view of menopause as a syndrome that causes depression and other emotional reactions is based on women who have had an early menopause following a hysterectomy (removal of the uterus) or who have had a lifetime history of depression. But these women are not typical. In a large survey of more than 8,000 healthy, randomly chosen women, most viewed menopause positively (with relief that they no longer had to worry about pregnancy or menstrual periods) or with no particular feelings at all. Only 3 percent reported regret at having reached menopause. The vast majority had only a few, temporarily bothersome symptoms and did not suffer from depression. Most women said that menopause is no big deal (McKinlay, McKinlay, & Brambilla, 1987). Other large-scale studies of normal populations have confirmed that menopause itself has no effect on most women's mental and emotional health (Matthews et al., 1990).

Thinking Critically About Menopause

For most educated women, the midlife years are actually the best and happiest. American women in their 50s today are more likely than those in any other age group to describe their lives as being "first-rate" and to report having a high quality of life (Mitchell & Helson, 1990). They tend to have higher incomes than women in other age groups; their children are often grown and launched; and they are more likely than other women to have struck a balance between their needs for intimacy and for autonomy, feeling close to others yet also in charge of their lives.

What about men? Although testosterone seems to peak during adolescence, men lack a biological equivalent to menopause. Testosterone never drops as sharply in men as estrogen does in

menopause
The cessation of menstruation and of the production of ova; usually a gradual process lasting up to several years.

women, and men do not lose their fertility, although their sperm count may slowly decline. For both sexes, the physical changes of midlife and the biological fact of aging do not predict how people will feel about aging or how they will respond to it (Ryff & Keyes, 1995). Whether a man or a woman will have a "midlife crisis" has little to do with their hormones and more to do with how satisfied they are with their lives.

The Coming of Age.   What does it mean to be old? The popular image in Western cultures is of a person who is forgetful, somewhat senile, and physically and mentally feeble. On television and in the movies, old people are usually portrayed as objects of amusement, sympathy, or scorn. But *gerontologists*—people who study aging and the old—have been challenging these stereotypes. By distinguishing the processes that are part of normal aging from those due to preventable conditions, they have dramatically changed our understanding of old age in several ways:

1. *The definition of "old" has gotten older.* "Old age" is no longer just a matter of chronological years, but of how well a person is able to function. Not long ago you would have been considered old in your 60s. Today, the fastest-growing segment of the population in North America consists of people over the age of 85, and many of them are doing fine. The fact that people are living longer and better, however, raises crucial ethical and legal concerns about death—in particular, how and when to draw the line between death that is inevitable and death that can be delayed with technological interventions.

2. *Aging has been separated from illness.* People used to think that all bodily functions declined with age. Some conditions, such as osteoporosis (having extremely brittle bones) or senility (the loss of mental abilities), were assumed to be inevitable. Today we know that many such conditions are a result of malnutrition, overmedication, disease, or cellular damage from too much sun. For example, an alarmingly high number of older people are given too many drugs for different problems, in combinations that can cause confusion, senility, or even psychosis. Many take over-the-counter drugs, such as sleeping pills and antihistamines, that can cause similar problems.

3. *The biology of aging has been separated from its psychology.* Imagine that you are taken from your home, your friends, and your work, and put in a residence where you know no one and have nothing to do. Your relatives live too far away to visit. You aren't allowed to make decisions, decorate your room, keep a pet, have a lover, or choose your food. What would happen to you? Probably you would become depressed, bored, and forgetful. You would become, in a word, "old." Many problems once thought to be an inherent part of aging are now recognized to be the result of social losses, not physical ones—the loss of loved ones, close friends, meaningful activity, intellectual stimulation, and control over events (Langer, 1989; Schaie, 1994).

The picture of old age that emerges from research is not entirely positive, of course; some aspects of intelligence, memory, and other forms of mental functioning do decline (Craik & Salthouse, 1992). As people age, it takes them longer to retrieve names, dates, and other facts. And, on average, older adults score lower on tests of reasoning and complex problem solving than do younger adults. But gerontologists disagree about exactly why these abilities tend to decline.

"Intelligence" generally takes two forms: *fluid intelligence*, the capacity for deductive reasoning and the ability to use new information to solve problems, and *crystallized intelligence*, the knowledge and skills that are built up over a lifetime—the kind that give us the ability to solve math problems, define words, or summarize the President's policy on the environment (Horn & Donaldson, 1980). Fluid intelligence is relatively independent of education and experience; it reflects an inherited predisposition, and it parallels other bio-

Get Involved

Ask five people—each about a decade apart in age, and one of whom is at least 70—how old they feel. (You may include yourself.) What is the gap, if any, between their chronological age and their psychological age? Is the gap larger among the oldest individuals? Ask why they perceive an "age gap" between their actual years and how old they feel.

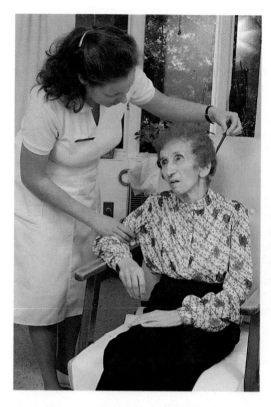

Stereotypes about older people are breaking down as more and more people live long, healthy lives. Although some people in their 80s are ailing and infirm, or suffer from brain diseases such as Alzheimer's disease (left), many remain healthy, energetic, and active.

logical capacities in its growth and, in later years, decline (Baltes & Graf, 1996). Crystallized intelligence, in contrast, depends heavily on culture, education, and experience, and it tends to remain stable or even improve over the life span. This is why physicians, lawyers, teachers, farmers, musicians, insurance agents, politicians, psychologists, and people in many other occupations can continue working well into old age. Fortunately, a person's crystallized intelligence may compensate for the brain's declining efficiency late in life (Baltes & Graf, 1996).

Some of the decline in fluid intelligence stems from physical changes that occur because of illness, medication, or normal deterioration. But the decline may also appear to be steeper than it really is because of generational differences in nutrition, education, and current levels of intellectual stimulation. That may be why *cross-sectional* studies, which compare people of different ages at the same time, often find a steady decline in mental abilities, whereas *longitudinal* studies, which compare the same people as they age, often do not find this decline until extreme old age (see Chapter 1).

In Chapter 6, we will see that differences in general cognitive functioning among people, what-

ever their age, are due in part to genetic differences. But just as training programs can boost the intelligence scores of children, they can also boost the intellectual and memory skills of older people. Older adults can do as well on memory tests as people in their 20s, when given guidance and cues for retrieving memories—for example, when they are taught to use encoding strategies rather than making lists (Loewen, Shaw, & Craik, 1990). Short-term training programs for people between ages 60 and 80 produce gains in mental-test scores that are as large as the losses typical for that particular age group (Baltes, Sowarka, & Kliegl, 1989; Willis, 1987).

Many researchers who study cognition and aging are therefore optimistic. From studies of healthy rats and of elderly people who live in stimulating, enriched environments, they conclude that brain function does not inevitably decay (Diamond, 1993; Kolb, 1996). In this view, people who have challenging occupations and interests, and who adapt flexibly to change, are likely to maintain their cognitive abilities in old age. Other researchers, however, are less optimistic. They are worried about the fact that more people are living to extreme old age, when rates of cognitive impairment and dementia rise dramatically (Baltes &

Graf, 1996). The challenge for society, and for us as individuals, is to make sure that the many people who will be living into their 90s can keep using their brains instead of losing them.

The Social Clock

Since the 1970s, popular books have tried to identify the predictable "passages," "seasons," and "transformations" of adult life. It is always fun to try to figure out what stage you are in. And it is natural for people to look for a guide through the uncharted territory of the future. Let's look more closely at this notion of adult stages.

Stages and Ages.   As we saw in Chapter 2, Freud believed that personality is formed by age 5 or 6, when the Oedipus complex is resolved. A fuller theory of development, stretching from birth to death, was proposed by psychoanalyst Erik H. Erikson (1902–1994). Erikson (1950/1963, 1982, 1987) wrote that all individuals go through eight stages in their lives, resolving an inevitable "crisis" at each one:

1. *Trust versus mistrust* is the crisis that occurs during the baby's first year, when the baby de-

According to Erik Erikson, children must resolve the crisis of competence and older adults must resolve the crisis of generativity. This child and her grandmother are certainly meeting their respective developmental tasks—but are these tasks confined to a particular stage of life?

pends on others to provide food, comfort, cuddling, and warmth. If these needs are not met, the child may never develop the essential trust necessary to get along in the world, especially in relationships.

2. *Autonomy (independence) versus shame and doubt* is the crisis that occurs when the child is a toddler. The young child is learning to be independent and must do so without feeling too ashamed or doubtful of his or her actions.

3. *Initiative versus guilt* is the crisis that occurs as the preschooler is acquiring new physical and mental skills, setting goals, and enjoying newfound talents. At the same time, the child must also learn to control impulses and energies, without developing too strong a sense of guilt over his or her fantasies, growing abilities, and childish instincts.

4. *Competence versus inferiority* is the crisis for school-age children, who are learning to make things, use tools, and acquire the skills for adult life. Children who fail these lessons of mastery and competence risk feeling inadequate and inferior.

5. *Identity versus role confusion* is the crisis of adolescence, when teenagers must decide what they are going to be and what they hope to make of their lives. The term *identity crisis* describes what Erikson considered to be the primary conflict of this stage. Those who resolve this crisis will come out of this stage with a strong identity, ready to plan for the future. Those who do not will sink into confusion, unable to make decisions.

6. *Intimacy versus isolation* is the crisis of young adulthood. Once you have decided who you are, said Erikson, you must share yourself with another and learn to make commitments. No matter how successful you are in work, you are not complete until you are capable of intimacy.

7. *Generativity versus stagnation* is the crisis of the middle years. Now that you know who you are and have an intimate relationship, will you sink into complacency and selfishness, or will you experience generativity, the pleasure of creativity and renewal? Parenthood is the most common means for the successful resolution of this stage, but people can be productive, creative, and nurturant in other ways, in their work or their relationships with the younger generation.

8. *Ego integrity versus despair* is the crisis of old age. As they age, people strive to reach the ultimate goal—wisdom, spiritual tranquility, an acceptance of their lives. Just as the healthy child will not fear life, said Erikson, the healthy adult will not fear death.

Erikson recognized that cultural and economic factors affect psychological development. Some societies, for example, make the passage between stages relatively easy. If you know you are going to be a farmer like your mother and father and you have no alternative, then moving from adolescence into young adulthood is not a terribly painful step (unless you hate farming). If you have many choices, however, as adolescents in urban societies often do, the transition can become prolonged. Some people put off making choices indefinitely and never resolve their "identity crisis." Similarly, cultures that place a high premium on independence and individualism will make it difficult for many of their members to resolve Erikson's sixth crisis, that of intimacy versus isolation.

The Transitions of Life.

Erikson showed that development is never finished; it is an ongoing process, and the unconscious issues of one stage may be reawakened during another. His work was important because he placed adult development in the context of family and society, and he specified the essential concerns of adulthood: trust, competence, identity, generativity, and the ability to enjoy life and accept death.

During the past two decades or so, however, researchers have shown that Erikson's stages are far from universal, and they do not occur in the same order for everyone. Although in Western societies adolescence *is* often a time of confusion about identity and aspirations, an "identity crisis" is not limited to the teen years. A man who has worked in one job all his life, and then is laid off and must find an entirely new career, may have an identity crisis, too. Likewise, competence is not

Thinking Critically About Life-Stage Theories

mastered once and for all in childhood. People learn new skills and lose old ones throughout their lives, and their sense of competence rises and falls accordingly. Erikson omitted women from his original work, and when they were later studied, they seemed to be doing things out of order—for example, going through "generativity" by having families before they faced the matter of professional "identity" (Peterson & Stewart, 1993).

For these reasons, today's theories of adult development emphasize the *transitions* and milestones that mark adult life instead of a rigid developmental sequence (Baltes, 1983; Schlossberg, 1984). According to these theories, the fact of having a child has stronger effects on you than the age at which you have a child; entering the workforce affects self-esteem and ambition regardless of when you start work.

Yet in spite of the growing unpredictability of changes in adult life, most people still unconsciously evaluate their transitions according to a *social clock* that determines whether they are "on time" for their age or "off time" (Helson & McCabe, 1993; Neugarten, 1979). The social clock creates special pressures for young adults, who are often making many rapid transitions—from home to college, from college to work, from work to close relationships—and who often feel "under the gun" in comparison to their peers: "I'm a junior and haven't declared a major," "I'm almost 30 and not even in a serious relationship" (Helson & McCabe, 1993).

All cultures have social clocks that define the "right" time to marry, start work, and have children, but these clocks vary greatly. In some societies young men and women are supposed to marry and start having children right after

People don't always progress steadily through life's stages; some return to earlier ones.

puberty, and work responsibilities come later. In others, a man may not marry until he has shown that he can support a family, which might not be until his 30s. Society's reactions to people who are "off time" vary as well, from amused tolerance ("Oh, when will he grow up?") to pity, scorn, and outright rejection.

Doing the right thing at the right time, compared to your friends and age-mates, can make you feel satisfied and normal. When nearly everyone in your group goes through the same experience or enters a new role at the same time—going to school, driving a car, voting, marrying, having a baby, retiring—adjusting to these *anticipated transitions* is relatively easy. Increasingly, though, you may have to face *unanticipated transitions*—the events that happen without warning, such as be-

ing fired from a job or becoming too ill to finish school. In addition, you are likely to have to deal with *"nonevent" transitions*—the changes you expect to happen that don't: For example, you don't get married at the age you expected to; you learn that you can't have children; you aren't promoted; you hoped to retire but can't afford to (Schlossberg & Robinson, 1996). People who wish to do things "on time" and cannot, for reasons out of their control, may feel inadequate, depressed, and anxious.

Perhaps they would feel better if they realized that, as one developmental psychologist put it, "There is not one process of aging, but many; there is not one life course followed, but multiple courses. . . . The variety is as rich as the historic conditions people have faced and the current circumstances they experience" (Pearlin, 1982).

??? QUICK QUIZ

This quiz provides a nice transition to the end of the chapter.

1. Most women react to menopause by (a) feeling depressed, (b) regretting the loss of femininity, (c) feeling relieved or neutral, (d) going a little crazy.

2. Almost overnight, your 80-year-old grandmother has become confused and delusional. Before concluding that old age has made her senile, what other explanations should you rule out?

3. Which of these statements about the decline of mental abilities in old age is *false?* (a) It can often be reversed with training programs; (b) it inevitably happens to all old people; (c) it is often a result of malnutrition or disease, rather than aging; (d) it is slowed when people live in stimulating environments.

4. The key psychological issue during adolescence, said Erikson, is a(n) _____ crisis.

5. Frank wants to go to law school but is failing his prelaw classes. Frank is about to undergo a(n) _____ transition.

 6. You are reading a best-seller called *Levels,* which describes five levels of adult development: preconscious, barely aware, conscious, hyperconscious, and, for a select few, "evolved." What is likely to be a problem with the assumptions of this book, and how might you critically evaluate its argument?

Answers:

1. c 2. You should rule out the possibility that she is taking too many medications or taking drugs that can be hazardous in older people. 3. b 4. identity 5. nonevent 6. Adult development does not occur in predictable, clear-cut phases that apply to everyone. People may move back and forth between "stages," depending on changing circumstances. You would also want to know the evidence for this theory: Was it based on a representative sample of men and women from different cultures? How does the author define and measure vague terms such as "evolved"?

Has our review of events across the life span helped you to clarify your thoughts about the woman who gave birth at age 63? The concept of the social clock can help us understand why so many people feel queasy about a woman getting pregnant so late in life: She is obviously "off time"! We have also seen that age can bring cognitive, not to mention physical, changes, and it seems legitimate to worry about whether elderly parents—of either sex—will have the mental resources and energy to guide their children through the many hurdles of childhood and adolescence (although plenty of older people, re-

quired by circumstances to rear their grandchildren, have done so successfully).

But we have also learned that the whole concept of "natural stages" is far more valid for children than for adults. Children do go through predictable stages in their cognitive, linguistic, and social development. But the terrain of adulthood can vary tremendously, depending on a person's genes, culture, generation, and individual experiences. Reaching a certain age has few if any inevitable consequences; increasingly, in adulthood, age is what we make of it.

In the years to come, we are likely to see more and more people charting their travels through life in ways that challenge conventional notions of what the guiding road map should look like. In the absence of clear signposts, will they get disoriented and lose their way? Or will the result be a more creative and satisfying adventure?

Taking Psychology with You

Bringing Up Baby

How should you treat your children? Should you be strict or lenient, powerful or permissive? Should you require your child to stop having tantrums, to clean up his or her room, to be polite? According to the research described in this chapter, the following guidelines are effective in teaching children to control aggressive impulses and to be confident, considerate, and helpful:

• *Set high expectations that are appropriate to the child's age, and teach the child how to meet them* (Damon, 1995). Some parents make few demands on their children, either unintentionally or because they believe a parent should not impose standards. Others make many demands, such as requiring children to be polite, help with chores, control their anger, be thoughtful of others, and do well in school. The children of parents who make few demands tend to be aggressive, impulsive, and immature. The children of parents who have high expectations tend to be helpful and above average in competence and self-confidence. But the demands must be appropriate for the child's age. You can't expect 2-year-olds to dress themselves, and before you can expect children to get up on time. they have to know how to work an alarm clock.

• *Explain, explain, explain.* Induction—telling a child why you have applied a rule—teaches a child to be responsible. Punitive methods ("Do it or I'll spank you") may result in compliance, but the child will tend to disobey as soon as you are out of sight. Explanations also teach children how to reason and understand; they reward curiosity and open-mindedness. This doesn't mean you have to argue with a 4-year-old about the merits of table manners. But, while setting standards for your children, you can also allow them to express disagreements and feelings.

• *Encourage empathy.* Call the child's attention to the effect of his or her actions on others, appeal to the child's sense of fair play and desire to be good, and teach the child to take another person's point of view. Vague orders, such as "Don't fight," are less effective than showing the child how fighting disrupts and hurts others. For boys especially, aggression and empathy are strongly and negatively related: the higher the one, the lower the other (Eisenberg et al., 1996; Feshbach & Feshbach, 1986).

• *Notice, approve of, and reward good behavior.* Many parents tend to punish the behavior

they dislike, a form of attention that may actually be rewarding to the child (see Chapter 8). It is much more effective to praise the behavior you do want, which teaches the child what is right.

We know that many people get huffy at the notion of using induction with their children, saying "My parents hit me and I turned out okay, so why shouldn't I do the same with my kids?" Some people scoff at the idea of explaining family rules to a 6-year-old. People often care deeply for even the most authoritarian of parents, and they may equate criticisms of the authoritarian approach with criticisms of their parents, who, after all, may only have been doing their best. But if we are willing to examine the evidence and question some assumptions, we will be open to the lessons that developmental psychology has to offer.

Of course, even the best parental practices cannot create the "ideal child"—that is, one who is an exact replica of you. But you can expect the best from your children—their best, not yours.

SUMMARY

From Conception to the First Year

1) Prenatal development consists of the *germinal, embryonic,* and *fetal* stages. Certain harmful influences can adversely affect the fetus's development; they include German measles, toxic chemicals, some sexually transmitted diseases, cigarettes, alcohol (which in excess can cause *fetal alcohol syndrome*), illegal drugs, and even over-the-counter medications.

2) Babies are born with certain physical abilities, including motor reflexes necessary for survival and a number of perceptual abilities. Newborns are naturally attracted to novelty and to human faces. But despite such commonalities, many aspects of maturation depend on cultural practices, such as whether the baby sleeps alone or with the mother, and how parents handle the child.

3) Babies' survival depends on physical and emotional attachment to their caregivers. Their innate need for *contact comfort* gives rise to emotional attachment to their caregivers, and by the age of 7 to 9 months, they begin to feel *stranger anxiety* and *separation anxiety*. Studies of the *Strange Situation* have identified three styles of infant attachment: secure, avoidant, and anxious–ambivalent. Children whose parents are hostile, neglectful, rejecting, or simply uncomfortable handling them may become insecurely attached and develop long-term cognitive and behavioral problems. Cultural variations in child-rearing practices affect the nature of parent–child attachment.

Cognitive Development

4) Jean Piaget argued that cognitive development depends on an interaction between maturation and a child's experiences in the world. Children's thinking changes and adapts through *assimilation* and *accommodation*. Piaget proposed four stages of cognitive development: *sensorimotor* (birth to age 2), during which the child learns *object permanence; preoperational* (ages 2 to 7), during which language and symbolic thought develop; *concrete operations* (ages 6 or 7 to 11), during which the child comes to understand *conservation,* identity, and serial ordering; and *formal operations* (age 12 to adulthood), during which abstract reasoning develops.

5) Researchers have found that the changes from one stage to another are not as clear-cut as Piaget implied; that young children have more cognitive abilities, at earlier ages, than Piaget thought; and that young children are not always egocentric in their thinking. Further, cultural practices affect the pace and content of cognitive development, and not all adults develop the ability for formal operations. But the general sequence of development that Piaget observed does hold up.

6) Infants are responsive to the pitch, intensity, and sound of language, which may be why adults in many cultures speak to babies in higher-pitched tones, with exaggerated intonation. At 4 to 6 months of age, babies begin to recognize the sounds of their own language; and they go through a "babbling phase" from age 6 months to 1 year. At about 1 year, one-word utterances begin, as do symbolic gestures. At age 2, children speak in two- or three-word *telegraphic* sentences that convey a variety of messages.

7) Language allows us to express and comprehend an infinite number of novel utterances. Noam Chomsky argued that the ability to take the *surface structure* of any utterance and apply rules of *syntax* to infer its underlying *deep structure* must depend on an innate faculty for language, a universal grammar. Many others have supported this view and have explored its evolutionary implications. Nonetheless, parental practices, such as repeating correct sentences verbatim and recasting incorrect ones, appear to aid in language acquisition. Case studies of children deprived of exposure to language suggest that a *critical period* exists for acquiring a first language.

Gender Development

8) Biological psychologists account for gender differences in behavior in terms of genetics, hormones, and brain organization. Learning theorists study (a) the rewards, punishments, and models that cause children to become sex typed during the process of *gender socialization,* and (b) the situations that can affect their gender-related behavior. Cognitive psychologists study how children develop *gender schemas* of "male" and "female" categories and qualities, which in turn shape their sex-typed behavior.

9) As children mature, their notions of gender often become more flexible. In adulthood, many differences between men and women decline and eventually even disappear.

Moral Development

10) Lawrence Kohlberg's theory of moral development involves three levels of moral reasoning, each with two stages: *preconventional morality* (based on rules, punishment, and self-interest), *conventional morality* (based on relationships and rules of justice and law), and *postconventional* ("principled") morality (based on higher principles of human rights). Carol Gilligan has argued that women tend to base moral decisions on principles of compassion, whereas men tend to base theirs on abstract principles of justice; most research, however, finds no gender differences in moral reasoning.

11) Evidence supports the universality of Kohlberg's first four stages. However, cognitive stage theories of moral reasoning have three limitations: (1) They tend to overlook the influence of culture and education; (2) moral reasoning is often inconsistent across situations; and (3) moral reasoning and moral behavior are often unrelated. Because of these problems, many developmental researchers focus not on moral reasoning but on moral emotions, such as empathy, and on moral behavior.

12) Parental discipline methods have different consequences for a child's moral behavior. *Power assertion* is associated with children who have a sense of external control, are aggressive and destructive, and show a lack of empathy and moral behavior. *Induction* is associated with children who develop empathy and internalized moral standards and who can resist temptation. In general, *authoritative* parents have better results with their children than do *authoritarian* or *permissive* parents. Altruistic children tend to come from families in which they contribute to the family's well-being, carry out many tasks, and respect parental authority, and in which parents set limits without being arbitrary.

Adolescence

13) *Adolescence* begins with the physical changes of *puberty*. In girls, puberty is signaled by *menarche* and the development of breasts; in boys, it begins with the onset of nocturnal emissions and the development of the testes and scrotum. Boys and girls who enter puberty early tend to have a more difficult later adjustment than do those who enter puberty later than average. One reason may be that early puberty intensifies already existing problems from childhood.

14) Most adolescents do not go through extreme emotional turmoil, anger, or rebellion. However, for some teenagers, the changes of adolescence can seem overwhelming and lead to psychological problems such as aggression, anxiety, or depression.

15) One of the main challenges at this stage is developing autonomy and a balanced, adult relationship with parents. "Separation" from parents usually means becoming an independent individual, not undergoing a complete rift.

Adulthood

16) In women, *menopause* begins in the late 40s or early 50s. Many women have temporary physical symptoms, such as hot flashes, but most do not regret the end of fertility, do not become depressed and irritable, and report a high quality of life. In middle-aged men, hormone production slows down, but fertility continues.

17) Ideas about old age have been revised now that old people are living longer and healthier lives. Many supposedly inevitable results of aging, such as senility and cognitive decline, are often the result of disease, overmedication, poor nutrition, lack of education, and lack of stimulation and control of the environment. *Fluid intelligence*, which is relatively independent of education and experience, parallels other biological capacities in its eventual decline. *Crystallized intelligence*, in contrast, depends heavily on culture, education, and experience, and it tends to remain stable or even improve over the life span.

18) Erik Erikson proposed an influential theory of life-span development. He argued that life consists of eight stages, each with a unique psychological crisis that must be resolved, such as an *identity crisis* in adolescence. Erikson made an important contribution by recognizing the essential concerns of adulthood and by showing that development is a lifelong process. However, psychologists have learned that unlike stages of child development, adult "stages" are not universal and

are not confined to particular chronological periods or sequences.

19) The *transitions* approach to development emphasizes the changes in people's lives regardless of when they occur: *anticipated transitions,* *unanticipated transitions,* and *"nonevent" transitions.* Adults often evaluate their development according to a *social clock* that determines whether they are "on time" or "off time" for a particular event.

KEY TERMS

maturation   74

germinal, embryonic, fetal stages   74

fetal alcohol syndrome (FAS)   75

motor reflexes   76

contact comfort   77

separation anxiety   78

secure, avoidant, and anxious–ambivalent kinds of attachment   78

Jean Piaget   80

assimilation   81

accommodation   81

sensorimotor stage   81

object permanence   81

representational thought   81

preoperational stage   81

operations   81

egocentric thinking   81

conservation   81

concrete operations stage   82

formal operations stage   82

telegraphic speech   86

syntax   86

surface structure and deep structure   86

language acquisition device   86

universal grammar   86

overregularizations   87

critical period (for language acquisition)   87

gender role   88

gender identity   88

gender socialization (sex typing)   89

gender schema   90

preconventional, conventional, and postconventional levels of moral reasoning (Kohlberg)   93

care-based versus justice-based types of moral reasoning (Gilligan)   93

power assertion   95

induction   95

authoritarian, permissive, and authoritative parenting styles (Baumrind)   96

puberty   97

menarche   98

secondary sex characteristics   98

menopause   101

gerontology   102

fluid versus crystallized intelligence   102

Erik Erikson's stage theory   104

identity crisis   104

social clock   105

transitions: anticipated, unanticipated, and nonevent   106

LOOKING BACK

- *How can a pregnant woman reduce the risk of damage to the embryo or fetus? (pp. 75–76)*

- *Given a choice, what do newborns prefer to look at? (pp. 76–77)*

- *Why is cuddling so important for infants (not to mention adults)? (pp. 77–78)*

- *If you have a 1-year-old, why shouldn't you worry if your baby cries when left with a new babysitter? (p. 78)*

- *How does culture affect how a baby matures physically and socially? (pp. 77, 79)*

- *What important accomplishment is an infant revealing when the infant learns to play "peekaboo"? (p. 81)*

- *Why will most 5-year-olds choose a tall, narrow glass of lemonade over a short, fat one containing the same amount? (pp. 81–82)*

- *Can a 4-year-old understand that others experience the world from a different perspective? (p. 84)*

- *How are a toddler's first word combinations similar to the language in a telegram? (p. 86)*

- *Why do many psychologists believe that children's brains are equipped with a "language acquisition device"? (pp. 86–87)*

- *How would a biologically oriented psychologist explain why little boys and girls are often so "sexist" in their choice of toys? (pp. 88–89)*

- *How do teachers often unintentionally reinforce aggressiveness in boys? (p. 90)*

- *If a little girl "knows" that girls can't be doctors, does this mean she will never go to med school? (pp. 91–92)*

- *According to a leading theory, why is moral reasoning based on law, justice, and duty* not *the pinnacle of moral development? (p. 93)*

- *When reasoning about moral dilemmas, are women more concerned with compassion and caring than men are? (p. 94)*

- *Are college students more moral than young children? (p. 94)*

- *What's wrong with "because I say so" as a way of getting children to behave? (pp. 95, 96)*

- *What are the advantages and disadvantages of experiencing puberty earlier than most of your classmates do? (pp. 98–99)*

- *During adolescence, are extreme turmoil and unhappiness the exception or the rule? (pp. 99–100)*

- *When teenagers and their parents quarrel, what is it typically about? (p. 100)*

- *Does menopause make most women depressed or irrational? (p. 101)*

- *Do men experience a male version of menopause? (pp. 101–102)*

- *What intellectual skills often decline in old age—and which ones don't? (pp. 102–103)*

- *What's wrong with thinking of life as a series of predictable stages? (p. 105)*

- *What feelings are common when people fail to marry, start working, or have children at the "right" time? (p. 106)*

PSYCHOLOGY IN THE NEWS

Mystery Man Claiming Amnesia Found on Beach

Amnesia victim Philip Cutajar, who thought he was someone called William D'Souza, has been using the Internet to search for information about his identity.

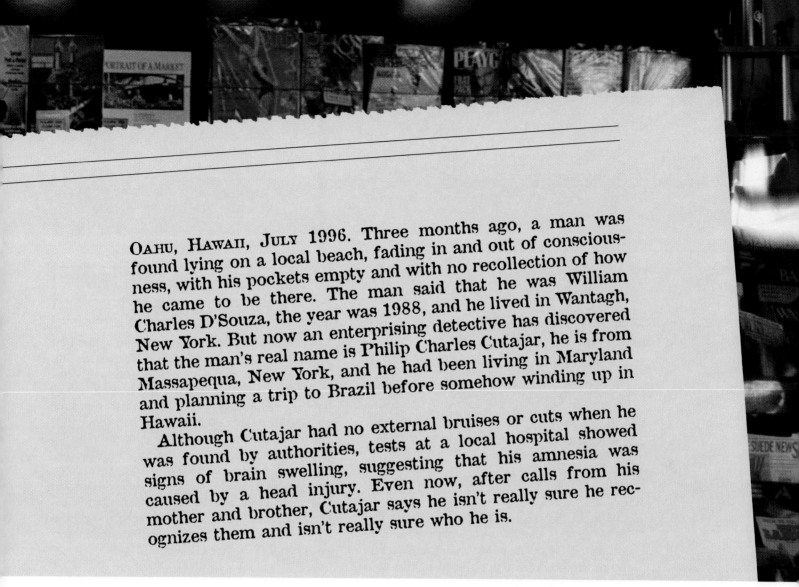

OAHU, HAWAII, JULY 1996. Three months ago, a man was found lying on a local beach, fading in and out of consciousness, with his pockets empty and with no recollection of how he came to be there. The man said that he was William Charles D'Souza, the year was 1988, and he lived in Wantagh, New York. But now an enterprising detective has discovered that the man's real name is Philip Charles Cutajar, he is from Massapequa, New York, and he had been living in Maryland and planning a trip to Brazil before somehow winding up in Hawaii.

Although Cutajar had no external bruises or cuts when he was found by authorities, tests at a local hospital showed signs of brain swelling, suggesting that his amnesia was caused by a head injury. Even now, after calls from his mother and brother, Cutajar says he isn't really sure he recognizes them and isn't really sure who he is.

Cases like this one, which appear in the news every few years, dramatically demonstrate that the brain is the bedrock of behavior and mental activity. Change the brain and you inevitably change the person—sometimes as profoundly as in the case of Philip Charles Cutajar. Neuropsychologists, along with neuroscientists from other disciplines, excavate the bedrock by analyzing the brain and the rest of the nervous system, in hopes of gaining a better understanding of consciousness, perception, memory, emotion, stress, mental disorders, and even self-identity.

At this very moment, your own brain, assisted by other parts of your nervous system, is busily taking in these words. Whether you are excited, curious, or bored, your brain is registering some sort of emotional reaction. As you continue reading, your brain will (we hope) store away much of the information in this chapter. Later on, your brain may enable you to smell a flower, climb the stairs, greet a friend, solve a personal problem, or chuckle at a joke. But the brain's most startling accomplishment is its knowledge that it is doing all these things. This self-awareness makes brain research different from the study of anything else in the universe. Scientists must use the cells, biochemistry, and circuitry of their own brains to understand the cells, biochemistry, and circuitry of brains in general.

the MIND-BRAIN Question

"THEN IT'S AGREED—YOU CAN'T HAVE A MIND WITHOUT A BRAIN, BUT YOU CAN HAVE A BRAIN WITHOUT A MIND."

Because the brain is the site of consciousness, people disagree about what language to use in discussing it. If we say that your brain stores events or registers emotions, where is the "you" that is "using" that brain? But if we leave "you" out of the picture and just say the brain does these things, we risk implying that brain mechanisms alone explain behavior (which is untrue), and we lose sight of the person—a dilemma that no one has ever resolved.

William Shakespeare called the brain "the soul's frail dwelling house." Actually, this miraculous organ is more like the main room in a house filled with many alcoves and passageways—the "house" being the nervous system as a whole. Before we can understand the windows, walls, and furniture of this house, we need to become acquainted with the overall floor plan. It's a pretty technical plan, which means that you will be learning many new terms, but you will need to know these terms in order to understand how biological psychologists go about explaining psychological topics. As you read, keep the strange case of Philip Charles Cutajar in mind. How can a person's very sense of self reside in a blob of tissue in the head? Which parts of Cutajar's brain were probably affected by his injury? If we knew everything about this man's brain, would we know then who he was?

central nervous system (CNS)
The portion of the nervous system consisting of the brain and spinal cord.

spinal cord
A collection of neurons and supportive tissue running from the base of the brain down the center of the back, protected by a column of bones (the spinal column).

What's Ahead

- *Why do you automatically pull your hand away from something hot, "without thinking"?*
- *Is it possible to consciously control your heartbeat or blood pressure?*
- *In an emergency, which part of your nervous system whirls into action?*

THE NERVOUS SYSTEM: A BASIC BLUEPRINT

The function of a nervous system is to gather and process information, produce responses to stimuli, and coordinate the workings of different cells. Even the lowly jellyfish and the humble worm have the beginnings of such a system. In very simple organisms that do little more than move, eat, and eliminate wastes, the "system" may be no more than one or two nerve cells. In human beings, who do such complex things as dance, cook, and take psychology courses, the nervous system contains billions of cells. Scientists divide this intricate network into two main parts: the central nervous system and the peripheral (outlying) nervous system (see Figure 4.1).

The Central Nervous System

The **central nervous system (CNS)** receives, processes, interprets, and stores incoming sensory information—information about tastes, sounds, smells, color, pressure on the skin, the state of internal organs, and so forth. It also sends out messages destined for muscles, glands, and internal organs. The CNS is usually conceptualized as having two components: the brain, which we will consider in detail later, and the **spinal cord.** The spinal cord is actually an extension of the brain. It runs from the base of the brain down the center of the back, protected by a column of bones (the spinal column), and it acts as a bridge between the brain and the parts of the body below the neck.

The spinal cord produces some behaviors on its own, without any help from the brain. These *spinal reflexes* are automatic, requiring no conscious effort. For example, if you accidentally touch a hot iron, you will immediately pull your hand away, even before your brain has had a chance to register what has happened. Nerve im-

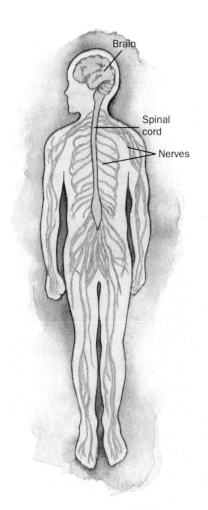

Figure 4.1

The Central and Peripheral Nervous Systems

The central nervous system, shown in yellow, includes the brain and the spinal cord. The peripheral nervous system, shown in red, consists of 43 pairs of nerves that transmit information to and from the central nervous system. Twelve pairs of cranial nerves in the head enter the brain directly; 31 pairs of spinal nerves enter the spinal cord at the spaces between the vertebrae of the spine.

pulses bring a message to the spinal cord (hot!), and the spinal cord immediately sends out a command via other nerve impulses, telling muscles in your arm to contract and to pull your hand away from the iron. (Reflexes above the neck, such as sneezing and blinking, involve the lower part of the brain, rather than the spinal cord.)

The neural circuits underlying many spinal reflexes are linked to other neural pathways that run up and down the spinal cord, to and from the brain. Because of these connections, reflexes can sometimes be influenced by thoughts and emotions. An example is erection in men, a spinal reflex that can be inhibited by anxiety or distracting thoughts, and initiated by erotic thoughts. Some reflexes can be brought under conscious control. If you concentrate, you may be able to keep your knee from jerking when it is tapped, as it normally would. Similarly, most men can learn to voluntarily delay ejaculation, another spinal reflex.

The Peripheral Nervous System

The **peripheral nervous system (PNS)** handles the central nervous system's input and output. It contains all portions of the nervous system outside the brain and spinal cord, right down to nerves in the tips of the fingers and toes. If your brain could not collect information about the world by means of a peripheral nervous system, it would be like a radio without a receiver. In the peripheral nervous system, *sensory nerves* carry messages from special receptors in the skin, muscles, and other internal and external sense organs to the spinal cord, which sends them along to the brain. These nerves put us in touch with both the outside world and the activities of our own bodies. *Motor nerves* carry orders from the central nervous system to muscles, glands, and internal organs. They enable us to move, and they cause glands to contract and to secrete substances, including chemical messengers called *hormones*.

Scientists further divide the peripheral nervous system into two parts: the somatic (bodily) nervous system and the autonomic (self-governing) nervous system. The **somatic nervous system,** sometimes called the *skeletal nervous system*, consists of nerves that are connected to sensory receptors and to the skeletal muscles that permit voluntary action. When you sense the world around you, or when you turn off a light or write your name, your somatic system is active. The **autonomic nervous system** regulates the functioning of blood vessels, glands, and internal (visceral) organs such as the bladder, stomach, and heart. When you happen upon the secret object of your desire, and your heart pounds, your hands get sweaty, and your cheeks feel hot, you can blame your autonomic nervous system.

The autonomic nervous system works more or less automatically, without a person's conscious control. However, some people can learn to heighten or suppress their autonomic responses intentionally. In India, some yogis can slow their heartbeats and metabolisms so dramatically that they can survive in a sealed booth long after most of us would have died of suffocation. During the

peripheral nervous system (PNS)

All portions of the nervous system outside the brain and spinal cord; it includes sensory and motor nerves.

somatic nervous system

The subdivision of the peripheral nervous system that connects to sensory receptors and to skeletal muscles; sometimes called the *skeletal nervous system*.

autonomic nervous system

The subdivision of the peripheral nervous system that regulates the internal organs and glands.

1960s and 1970s, Neal Miller and his colleagues showed that many other people can also learn to control their visceral responses by using a technique called *biofeedback* (Miller, 1978).

In biofeedback, monitoring devices track the bodily process in question and produce a signal, such as a light or a tone, whenever a person makes the desired response. The person may either use a prearranged method to produce the desired response or simply try to increase the signal's frequency in any way that he or she chooses. Using biofeedback, some people have learned to control such autonomic responses as blood pressure, blood flow, heart rate, and skin temperature. Some clinicians are therefore using biofeedback training to treat high blood pressure, asthma, and migraine headaches, although there is controversy about success rates and about what, exactly, is being controlled—the actual autonomic responses, or responses that can be voluntarily produced, such as breathing, which then in turn affect the autonomic system.

The autonomic nervous system is itself divided into two parts: the **sympathetic nervous system** and the **parasympathetic nervous system.** These two parts work together, but in opposing ways, to adjust the body to changing circumstances (see Figure 4.2). To simplify, the sympathetic system acts like the accelerator of a car, mobilizing the body for action and an output of energy. It makes you blush, sweat, and breathe more deeply, and it pushes up your heart rate and blood pressure. As we will see in Chapter 12, when you are in a situation that requires you to fight, flee, or cope, the sympathetic nervous system whirls into action. The parasympathetic system is more like a brake: It does not stop the body, but it does tend to slow things down or keep them running smoothly. It enables the body to conserve and store energy. If you have to jump out of the way of a speeding motorcyclist, sympathetic nerves increase your heart rate. Afterward, parasympathetic nerves slow it down again and keep its rhythm regular.

sympathetic nervous system

The subdivision of the autonomic nervous system that mobilizes bodily resources and increases the output of energy during emotion and stress.

parasympathetic nervous system

The subdivision of the autonomic nervous system that operates during relaxed states and that conserves energy.

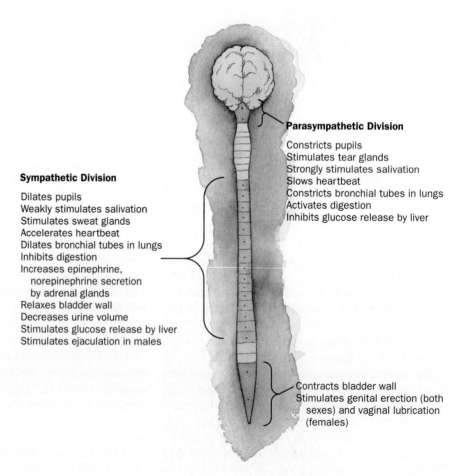

Sympathetic Division

Dilates pupils
Weakly stimulates salivation
Stimulates sweat glands
Accelerates heartbeat
Dilates bronchial tubes in lungs
Inhibits digestion
Increases epinephrine,
     norepinephrine secretion
     by adrenal glands
Relaxes bladder wall
Decreases urine volume
Stimulates glucose release by liver
Stimulates ejaculation in males

Parasympathetic Division

Constricts pupils
Stimulates tear glands
Strongly stimulates salivation
Slows heartbeat
Constricts bronchial tubes in lungs
Activates digestion
Inhibits glucose release by liver

Contracts bladder wall
Stimulates genital erection (both
     sexes) and vaginal lubrication
     (females)

Figure 4.2

The Autonomic Nervous System

In general, the sympathetic division of the autonomic nervous system prepares the body to expend energy, and the parasympathetic division restores and conserves energy. Sympathetic nerve fibers exit from areas of the spinal cord shown in purple in this illustration; parasympathetic fibers exit from the base of the brain and from spinal cord areas shown in green.

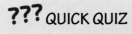QUICK QUIZ

Pause now to test your memory by mentally filling in the missing parts of the nervous system "house." Then see whether you can briefly describe what each part of the system does.

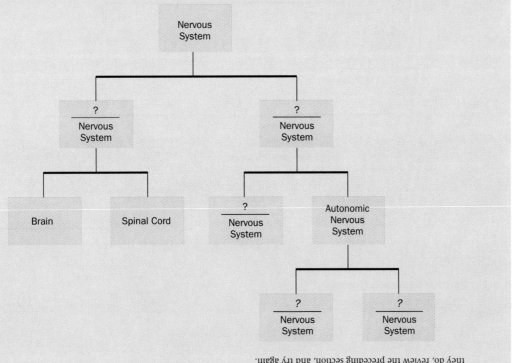

Answers:
Check your answers against Figure 4.3 on the next page. If you had difficulty, or if you could label the parts but forgot what they do, review the preceding section, and try again.

What's Ahead

- *Which nervous-system cells are "communication specialists"—and how do they "talk" to each other?*

- *How do learning and experience alter the brain's circuits?*

- *Why do neural impulses travel more slowly in babies than in adults?*

- *What happens when levels of brain chemicals called neurotransmitters are too low or too high?*

- *Which substances in the brain mimic the effects of morphine by dulling pain and promoting pleasure?*

- *Which hormones can improve your memory?*

COMMUNICATION IN THE NERVOUS SYSTEM

The blueprint we have just described provides only a general idea of the nervous system's structure. Now let's turn to the details.

The nervous system is made up in part of **neurons,** or *nerve cells.* These neurons are held in place by *glial cells* (from the Greek for "glue"). Glial cells, which greatly outnumber neurons, also provide the neurons with nutrients, insulate the neurons, and remove cellular debris when the neurons die. Many neuroscientists suspect that glial cells carry electrical or chemical signals between parts of the nervous system, and that these signals somehow influence the activity of neighboring neurons. It is the neurons, however, that are the communication specialists, transmitting signals to, from, or within the central nervous system.

neuron

A cell that conducts electrochemical signals; the basic unit of the nervous system; also called a *nerve cell.*

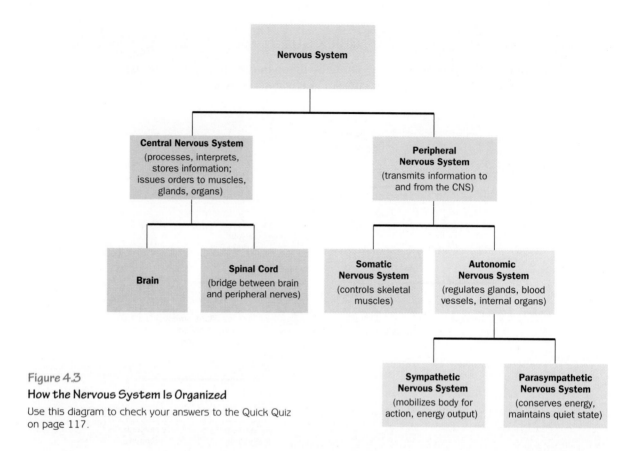

Figure 4.3

How the Nervous System Is Organized

Use this diagram to check your answers to the Quick Quiz on page 117.

Although neurons are often called the building blocks of the nervous system, in structure they are more like snowflakes than blocks, exquisitely delicate and differing from one another greatly in size and shape (see Figure 4.4). In the giraffe, a neuron that runs from the spinal cord down the animal's hind leg may be nine feet long! In the human brain, neurons are microscopic. No one is sure how many neurons the human brain contains, but a typical estimate is 100 billion, about the same number as there are stars in our galaxy—and some estimates go much higher.

dendrites

A neuron's branches that receive information from other neurons and transmit it toward the cell body.

cell body

The part of the neuron that keeps it alive and determines whether it will fire.

The Structure of the Neuron

As you can see in Figure 4.5, a neuron has three main parts: *dendrites,* a *cell body,* and an *axon.* The **dendrites** look like the branches of a tree; indeed, the word *dendrite* means "little tree" in Greek. Dendrites act like antennas, receiving messages from as many as 10,000 other nerve cells and transmitting these messages toward the cell body. The **cell body,** which is shaped roughly like a sphere or a pyramid, contains the biochemical machinery for keeping the neuron alive. As we will see later, it

Figure 4.4

Different Kinds of Neurons

Neurons vary in size and shape, depending on their location and function. More than 200 types of neurons have been identified in mammals.

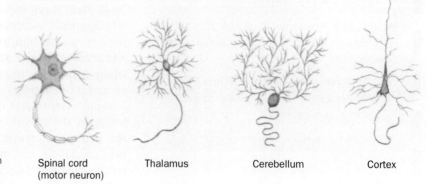

Spinal cord   Thalamus   Cerebellum   Cortex
(motor neuron)

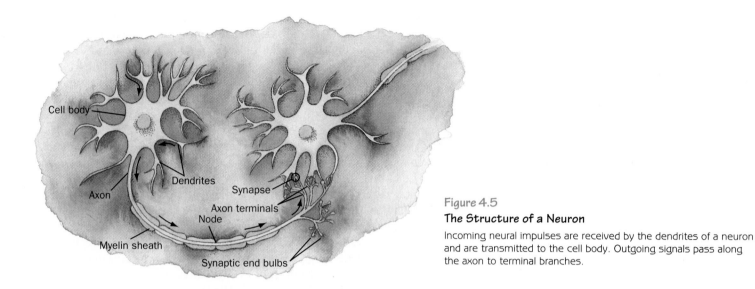

Figure 4.5

The Structure of a Neuron

Incoming neural impulses are received by the dendrites of a neuron and are transmitted to the cell body. Outgoing signals pass along the axon to terminal branches.

also determines whether the neuron should "fire"—that is, transmit a message to other neurons—based on the number of inputs from other neurons. The **axon** (from the Greek for "axle") transmits messages away from the cell body to other neurons or to muscle or gland cells. Axons commonly divide at the end into branches, called *axon terminals.* In adult human beings, axons vary from only four thousandths of an inch to a few feet in length. Dendrites and axons give each neuron a double role: As one researcher put it, a neuron is first a catcher, then a batter (Gazzaniga, 1988).

Many axons, especially the larger ones, are insulated by a surrounding layer of fatty material called the **myelin sheath,** which is derived from glial cells. This covering is divided into segments that make it look a little like a string of link sausages (see Figure 4.5). One of its purposes is to prevent signals in adjacent cells from interfering with each other. Another, as we will see shortly, is to speed up the conduction of neural impulses. In individuals with multiple sclerosis, loss of myelin causes erratic nerve signals, leading to loss of sensation, weakness or paralysis, lack of coordination, or vision problems.

In the peripheral nervous system, the fibers of individual neurons (axons and sometimes dendrites) are collected together in bundles called **nerves,** rather like the lines in a telephone cable. The human body has 43 pairs of peripheral nerves; one nerve from each pair is on the left side of the body, and the other is on the right. Most of these nerves enter or leave the spinal cord, but the 12 pairs that are in the head, the *cranial nerves,* connect directly to the brain. In Chapter 5, we will

discuss three cranial nerves involved in sensory processing: the *olfactory nerve,* involved in smell; the *auditory nerve,* involved in hearing; and the *optic nerve,* involved in vision.

Until a decade ago, neuroscientists thought that neurons in the central nervous system could neither reproduce (multiply) nor regenerate (grow back). The assumption was that we are born with nearly all the CNS neurons we are ever going to have, and that if these cells were injured or damaged, nothing could be done. But then animal studies showed that severed axons in the spinal cord *can* regrow if you block the effects of some nervous-system chemicals and stimulate the production of others (Schnell & Schwab, 1990). What's more, Canadian neuroscientists discovered that "precursor" cells from the brains of mice, when immersed in a growth-promoting protein in the laboratory, will produce new neurons, which

axon

A neuron's extending fiber that conducts impulses away from the cell body and transmits them to other neurons.

myelin sheath

A fatty insulation that may surround the axon of a neuron.

nerve

A bundle of nerve fibers (axons and sometimes dendrites) in the peripheral nervous system.

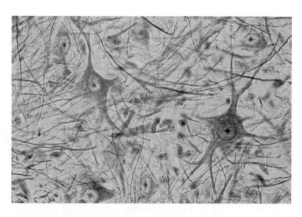

This photograph, taken through a microscope, reveals the delicate fibers of human motor neurons.

then continue to divide and multiply (Reynolds & Weiss, 1992). One of the researchers, Samuel Weiss, said that this result was hard to believe at first: "It challenged everything I had read; everything I had learned when I was a student" (quoted in Barinaga, 1992).

Since then, scientists have learned that the human brain contains similar precursor cells, and that these cells also give rise to new neurons when treated in the laboratory (Kirschenbaum et al., 1994). Even more astonishing, researchers recently demonstrated for the first time that new neurons are produced in the brains of adult primates. Working with marmoset monkeys, they found that precursor cells in a brain area associated with learning and memory continue to divide and mature, suggesting that human brains may also continue to produce new neurons during adulthood (Gould et al., 1998).

So far, no one has been able to get severed nerve fibers to regrow in large quantities, nor has anyone used neurons grown from precursor cells to replace brain cells lost through disease. But each year brings ever more exciting findings on neurons. Eventually, these results may lead to new treatments for neurological damage—treatments that promise to be among the most stunning contributions of biological research.

How Neurons Communicate

Neurons do not directly touch each other, end to end. Instead, they are separated by a minuscule space called the *synaptic cleft,* where the axon terminal of one neuron nearly touches a dendrite or the cell body of another. The entire site—the axon terminal, the cleft, and the covering membrane of the receiving dendrite or cell body—is called a **synapse.** Because a neuron's axon may have hundreds or even thousands of terminals, a single neuron may have synaptic connections with a great many others. As a result, the number of communication links in the nervous system runs into the trillions or perhaps even the quadrillions.

When we are born, most of these synapses have not yet formed (see Figure 4.6). Throughout life, axons and dendrites continue to grow, and tiny projections on dendrites called *spines* increase both in size and in number, producing more complex connections among the brain's nerve cells. New learning leads to new synaptic connections, with stimulating environments producing the greatest changes (Diamond, 1993; Greenough & Anderson, 1991; Greenough & Black, 1992; Rosenzweig, 1984). Conversely, some unused synaptic connections are lost as cells or their branches die and are not replaced. Thus, the brain's circuits are not fixed and permanent; they are continually changing in response to information, challenges, and changes in the environment. This remarkable *plasticity* (flexibility) helps explain why people with brain damage sometimes experience amazing recoveries—why individuals who cannot recall simple words after a stroke may be speaking normally within a matter of months, and why patients who cannot move an arm after a head injury may regain full use of it after physical therapy.

Neurons speak to one another, or in some cases to muscles or glands, in an electrical and chemical language. When a nerve cell is stimulated, a change in electrical potential occurs between the inside and the outside of the cell. The physics of this process involves the sudden, momentary inflow of positively charged sodium ions across the

synapse

The site where transmission of a nerve impulse from one nerve cell to another occurs; it includes the axon terminal, the synaptic cleft, and receptor sites in the membrane of the receiving cell.

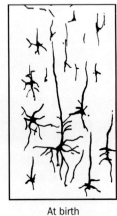 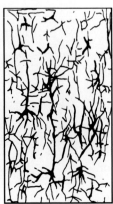 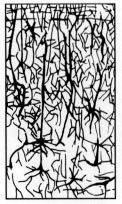 

At birth   3 months   6 months   15 months

Figure 4.6

Getting Connected

Neurons in a newborn's brain are widely spaced, but they immediately begin to form connections. These drawings show the marked increase in the size and number of neurons from birth to age 15 months.

cell's membrane, followed by the outflow of positively charged potassium ions. The result is a brief change in electrical voltage—*an action potential*—which produces an electrical current or impulse.

If an axon is unmyelinated, the action potential at each point in the axon gives rise to a new action potential at the next point; thus, the action potential travels down the axon somewhat as fire travels along the fuse of a firecracker. In myelinated axons, the process is a little different. Conduction of a neural impulse beneath the sheath is impossible, in part because sodium and potassium ions cannot cross the cell's membrane except at the breaks (nodes) between the myelin's "sausages." Instead, the action potential "hops" from one node to the next. (More specifically, positively charged ions flow down the axon at a very fast rate, causing regeneration of the action potential at each node.) This arrangement allows the impulse to travel faster than it could if the action potential had to be regenerated at every point along the axon. Nerve impulses travel more slowly in babies than in older children and adults because when babies are born, the myelin sheaths on their axons are not yet fully developed.

When a neural impulse reaches the axon terminal's buttonlike tip, it must get its message across the synaptic cleft to another cell. At this point, *synaptic vesicles,* tiny sacs in the tip of the axon terminal, open and release a few thousand molecules of a chemical substance called a **neurotransmitter.** Like sailors carrying a message from one island to another, these molecules then diffuse across the synaptic cleft (see Figure 4.7).

When they reach the other side, the neurotransmitter molecules bind briefly with *receptor sites,* special molecules in the membrane of the receiving neuron, fitting these sites much as a key fits a lock. Changes occur in the receiving neuron's membrane, and the ultimate effect is either *excitatory* (a voltage shift in a positive direction) or *inhibitory* (a voltage shift in a negative direction), depending on which receptor sites have been activated. If the effect is excitatory, the probability that the receiving neuron will fire increases; if it is inhibitory, the probability decreases. Inhibition in the nervous system is extremely important. Without it, we could not sleep or coordinate our movements. Excitation of the nervous system would be overwhelming, producing convulsions.

neurotransmitter

A chemical substance that is released by a transmitting neuron at the synapse and that alters the activity of a receiving neuron.

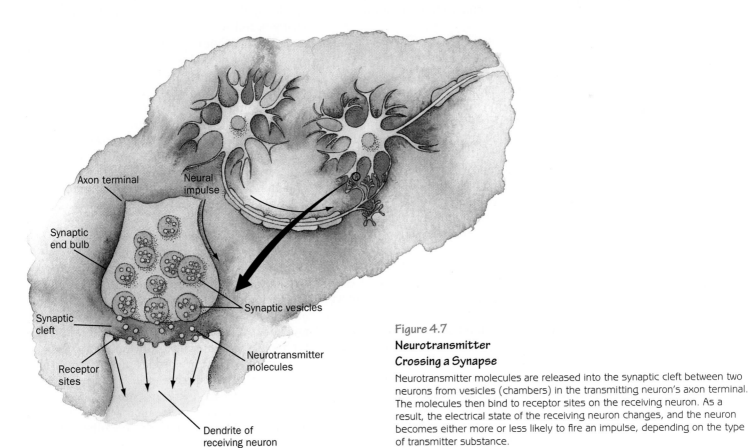

Figure 4.7

Neurotransmitter Crossing a Synapse

Neurotransmitter molecules are released into the synaptic cleft between two neurons from vesicles (chambers) in the transmitting neuron's axon terminal. The molecules then bind to receptor sites on the receiving neuron. As a result, the electrical state of the receiving neuron changes, and the neuron becomes either more or less likely to fire an impulse, depending on the type of transmitter substance.

What any given neuron does at any given moment depends on the net effect of all the messages being received from other neurons. Only when the cell's voltage reaches a certain threshold will it fire. Thousands of messages, both excitatory and inhibitory, may be coming into the cell. Essentially, the neuron must average them. But how it does this, and how it "decides" whether to fire, is still a puzzle. The message that reaches a final destination depends on the rate at which individual neurons are firing, how many are firing, what types of neurons are firing, and where the neurons are located. It does *not* depend on how strongly the neurons are firing, however, because a neuron always either fires or it doesn't. Like the turning on of a light switch, the firing of a neuron is an *all-or-none* event.

Chemical Messengers in the Nervous System

The nervous system "house" would remain forever dark and lifeless without chemical couriers such as the neurotransmitters. Let's look more closely now at these substances, and at two other types of chemical messengers: endorphins and hormones.

Neurotransmitters: Versatile Couriers.   As we have seen, neurotransmitters make it possible for one neuron to excite or inhibit another. Hundreds of substances are known or suspected to be neurotransmitters, and the number keeps growing. Each substance binds only to specific types of receptor sites. This means that if some of those "sailors" we mentioned (the neurotransmitter molecules) get off course and reach the wrong "islands" (receiving neurons), their messages will not be heard (no binding will occur). The existence of different neurotransmitters and receptor sites ensures that messages go where they are supposed to go.

Neurotransmitters exist not only in the brain, but also in the spinal cord, the peripheral nerves, and certain glands. Through their effects on specific nerve circuits, these substances can affect mood, memory, and well-being. The nature of the effect depends on the level of the neurotransmitter and its location. Our understanding of most neurotransmitters is still quite hazy. Here are a few of the better understood neurotransmitters and some of their known or suspected effects:

- *Serotonin* affects neurons involved in sleep, appetite, sensory perception, temperature regulation, pain suppression, and mood.

- *Dopamine* affects neurons involved in voluntary movement, learning, memory, and emotion.
- *Acetylcholine* affects neurons involved in muscle action, cognitive functioning, memory, and emotion.
- *Norepinephrine* affects neurons involved in increased heart rate and the slowing of intestinal activity during stress, and neurons involved in learning, memory, dreaming, waking from sleep, and emotion.
- *GABA* (gamma-aminobutyric acid) functions as the major inhibitory neurotransmitter in the brain.

Harmful effects can occur when neurotransmitter levels are too high or too low. Low levels of serotonin and norepinephrine have been associated with severe depression. Abnormal GABA levels have been implicated in sleep and eating disorders and in convulsive disorders, including epilepsy (Bekenstein & Lothman, 1993). Elevated levels of serotonin, along with other biochemical and brain abnormalities, have been implicated in childhood autism (du Verglas, Banks, & Guyer, 1988). People with *Alzheimer's disease,* a devastating condition that leads to memory loss, personality changes, and eventual disintegration of all physical and mental abilities, lose brain cells responsible for producing acetylcholine, and this deficit may help account for their memory problems.

The degeneration of brain cells that produce and use another neurotransmitter, dopamine, appears to cause the symptoms of *Parkinson's disease,* a condition characterized by tremors, muscular spasms, and increasing muscular rigidity. Patients with advanced Parkinson's may "freeze" for minutes or even hours. Injections of dopamine do not help because dopamine molecules cannot cross the *blood–brain barrier,* a system of densely packed capillary and glial cells, whose function is to prevent potentially harmful substances from entering the brain. Symptoms can be lessened by the administration of levodopa (L-dopa), which is a *precursor* (building block) of dopamine, but patients must take larger and larger doses to achieve the desired result. After a while, adverse effects, including depression, confusion, and even episodes of psychosis, may be worse than the disease itself.

During the past few years, surgeons have pioneered a dramatic new approach to treating Parkinson's disease and potentially other diseases as well. They have grafted dopamine-producing brain tissue from aborted fetuses into the brains of

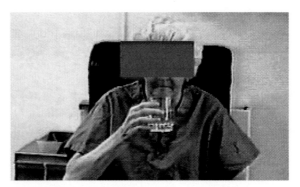

Fetal brain-tissue transplants have allowed some Parkinson's patients to perform daily tasks of living for the first time in years (Redmond et al., 1993). Before the procedure, the woman in these video images could not pick up a glass of water (left), but one year later, she had no trouble (right).

Parkinson's patients and patients who developed symptoms similar to those of Parkinson's after using a botched synthetic mood-altering drug that killed their dopamine-producing cells (Freed et al., 1993; Lindvall et al., 1994; Uchida & Toya, 1996; Widner et al., 1993). Not all patients have improved, but some who were virtually helpless before the operation can now move freely and even dress and feed themselves. Although the long-term risks and benefits of brain-tissue transplants are not yet known, and although at present the technique is not feasible on any large scale, this work has generated a lot of excitement.

We want to warn you, however, that pinning down the relationship between neurotransmitter abnormalities and behavioral abnormalities is extremely difficult. Each neurotransmitter plays multiple roles, and the functions of different substances often overlap. Further, it is always possible that something about a disorder leads to abnormal neurotransmitter levels, instead of the other way around. Although drugs that boost or decrease levels of particular neurotransmitters are sometimes effective in treating disorders, that does not necessarily mean that abnormal neurotransmitter levels are *causing* the disorders. After all, aspirin can relieve a headache, but headaches are not caused by a lack of aspirin!

While scientists try to unravel the relationships between neurotransmitters and medical and psychological disorders, many of us are already doing things that affect our own neurotransmitters, usually without knowing it. For example, most recreational drugs produce their effects by blocking or enhancing the actions of neurotransmitters. Even ordinary foods can influence the availability of neurotransmitters in the brain (although more subtly than do drugs), as we discuss in "Taking Psychology with You."

Endorphins: The Brain's Natural Opiates. Another intriguing group of chemical messengers is known collectively as *endogenous opioid peptides,* or more popularly as **endorphins.** Endorphins have effects similar to those of natural opiates; that is, they reduce pain and promote pleasure. They are also thought to play a role in appetite, sexual activity, blood pressure, mood, learning, and memory. Some endorphins function as neurotransmitters, but most act primarily as *neuromodulators,* which alter the effects of neurotransmitters—for example, by limiting or prolonging those effects.

Endorphins were identified in the early 1970s. Candace Pert and Solomon Snyder (1973) were doing research on morphine, a pain-relieving and mood-elevating opiate derived from heroin, which is made from poppies. They found that morphine works by binding to receptor sites in the brain. This seemed odd. As Snyder later recalled, "We doubted that animals had evolved opiate receptors just to deal with certain properties of the poppy plant" (quoted in Radetsky, 1991). Pert and Snyder reasoned that if opiate receptors exist, then the body must produce its own internally generated, or *endogenous,* morphinelike substances, which they named "endorphins." Soon they and other researchers confirmed this hypothesis.

Endorphin levels seem to shoot up when an animal or a person is afraid or under stress. This is no accident; by making pain bearable in such situations, endorphins give a species an evolutionary advantage. When an organism is threatened, it needs to do something fast. Pain, however, can interfere with action: A mouse that pauses to lick a wounded paw may become a cat's dinner; a soldier who is overcome by an injury may never get off the battlefield. But, of course, the body's built-in system of counteracting pain is only partly successful, especially when painful stimulation is prolonged.

endorphins (en-DOR-fins) Chemical substances in the nervous system that are similar in structure and action to opiates; they are involved in pain reduction, pleasure, and memory, and are known technically as *endogenous opioid peptides.*

A link also seems to exist between endorphins and the pleasures of social contact. In a series of studies, Jack Panksepp and his colleagues (1980) gave low doses of morphine or endorphins to young puppies, guinea pigs, and chicks. After the injections, the animals showed much less distress than usual when separated from their mothers. (In all other respects, they behaved normally.) The injections seemed to provide a biochemical replacement for the mother, or, more precisely, for the endorphin surge presumed to occur during contact with her. Conversely, when young guinea pigs and chicks received a chemical that *blocks* the effects of opiates, their crying increased. These findings suggest that endorphin-stimulated euphoria may be a child's initial motive for seeking affection and cuddling—that, in effect, a child attached to a parent is a child addicted to love.

Hormones: Long-Distance Messengers.

Hormones, which make up the third class of chemical messengers, are substances that are produced in one part of the body and affect another. Hormones originate primarily in **endocrine glands** and are released directly into the bloodstream, which carries them to organs and cells that may be far from their point of origin. Hormones have dozens of jobs, from promoting bodily growth to aiding digestion to regulating metabolism.

Neurotransmitters and hormones are not always chemically distinct; the two classifications are like clubs that admit some of the same members. A particular chemical, such as norepinephrine, may belong to more than one classification, depending on where it is located and what function it is performing. Nature has been efficient, giving some substances more than one task to perform.

The following hormones, among others, are of particular interest to psychologists:

1. **Melatonin,** which is secreted deep within the brain by the *pineal gland,* promotes sleep. It also helps to regulate a "biological clock" in the brain that coordinates an array of bodily rhythms, including the 24-hour wake–sleep cycle (Haimov & Lavie, 1996). Melatonin is produced during the hours of darkness, and the pineal gland responds to light and dark via complex connections that originate in the back of the eye. Melatonin treatments have been used to synchronize the disturbed sleep–wake cycles of blind people who lack light perception (Tzischinsky et al., 1992). They can also help some sighted people who suffer from chronic insomnia, especially older peole, who often show a decline in the hormone (Garfinkel et al., 1995; Haimov & Lavie, 1996).

2. Certain **adrenal hormones,** which are produced by the *adrenal glands* (organs perched right above the kidneys), are involved in emotion and stress (see Chapter 12). These hormones also rise in response to nonemotional conditions, such as heat, cold, pain, injury, burns, and physical exercise, and in response to some drugs, such as caffeine and nicotine. The outer part of each adrenal gland produces *cortisol,* which increases blood-sugar levels and boosts energy. The inner part produces *epinephrine* (popularly known as adrenaline) and *norepinephrine.* When adrenal hormones are released in your body, they activate the sympathetic nervous system, which in turn increases your arousal level and prepares you for action.

Adrenal hormones also enhance memory. If you give people a drug that prevents their adrenal glands from producing these hormones, they will remember less about emotional stories they heard than will control subjects (Cahill et al., 1994). Conversely, if you give epinephrine to animals right after learning, their memories will improve (McGaugh, 1990). This effect occurs, however, only when the hormones are at moderate levels. If the dosages are too high, memory suffers. Thus a moderate level of emotional arousal is probably best when you are learning and need to encode events in memory. If you want to remember information well, you should aim for an arousal level somewhere between "hyper" and "laid back."

3. **Sex hormones,** which are secreted by tissue in the gonads (testes in men, ovaries in women), and also by the adrenal glands, include three main types, all occurring in both sexes but in differing amounts and proportions in males and females after puberty. *Androgens* (the most important of which is *testosterone*) are masculinizing hormones produced mainly in the testes but also in the ovaries and the adrenal glands. Androgens set in motion the physical changes males experience at puberty—for example, a deepened voice and facial and chest hair—and cause pubic and underarm hair to develop in females. Testosterone also influences sexual arousal in both sexes. *Estrogens* are feminizing hormones that bring on the physical changes females experience at puberty, such as breast development and the onset of menstruation, and that influence the course of the menstrual cycle. *Progesterone* contributes to the growth and maintenance of the uterine lining in preparation for a fertilized egg, among other functions.

hormones

Chemical substances, secreted by organs called *glands,* that affect the functioning of other organs.

endocrine glands

Internal organs that produce hormones and release them into the bloodstream.

melatonin

A hormone, secreted by the pineal gland, that is involved in the regulation of daily biological rhythms.

adrenal hormones

Hormones that are produced by the adrenal glands and that are involved in emotion and stress.

sex hormones

Hormones that regulate the development and functioning of reproductive organs and that stimulate the development of male and female sexual characteristics; they include androgens, estrogens, and progesterone.

Estrogens and progesterone are produced mainly in the ovaries but also in the testes and the adrenal glands. Researchers are now studying the possible involvement of sex hormones in behavior not directly related to sex and reproduction, such as memory and mental functioning. For example, one adrenal androgen, which increases significantly in both sexes at about age 10, may be related to cognitive changes at that age (McClintock & Herdt, 1996).

??? QUICK QUIZ

You can activate your neurotransmitters by taking this quiz.

A. Which word in parentheses best fits each of the following definitions?

1. Basic building blocks of the nervous system (*nerves/neurons*)

2. Cell parts that receive nerve impulses (*axons/dendrites*)

3. Site of communication between neurons (*synapse/myelin sheath*)

4. Opiatelike substance in the brain (*dopamine/endorphin*)

5. Chemicals that make it possible for neurons to communicate (*neurotransmitters/hormones*)

6. Hormone closely associated with emotional excitement (*epinephrine/estrogen*)

B. *True or false:* Hormone research suggests that if you want to remember the material in this chapter well, you should be as relaxed as possible while learning it.

 C. Imagine that you are depressed, and you hear about a treatment for depression that affects the levels of several neurotransmitters thought to be involved in the disorder. Based on what you have learned, what questions would you want to ask before deciding whether to try the treatment?

Answers:

A. 1. neurons 2. dendrites 3. synapse 4. endorphin 5. neurotransmitters 6. epinephrine B. false C. You might want to ask, among other things, about side effects (each neurotransmitter has several functions, all of which might be affected by the treatment); about evidence that the treatment works; and about whether there is any reason to believe that your own neurotransmitter levels are abnormal or whether there may be other reasons for your depression.

What's Ahead

- *Why are patterns of electrical activity in the brain called "brain waves"?*

- *What two techniques allow psychologists to view changes in the brain while people listen to music or solve math problems?*

MAPPING THE BRAIN

We come now to the main room of the nervous system "house": the brain. A disembodied brain stored in a formaldehyde-filled container is unexciting, a putty-colored, wrinkled glob of tissue that looks a little like an oversized walnut. It takes an act of imagination to envision this modest-looking organ writing *Hamlet,* discovering radium, or inventing the paper clip.

In a living person, of course, the brain is encased in a thick protective vault of bone. How, then, can scientists study it? One approach is to study patients who have had a part of the brain damaged or removed because of disease or injury. Another, called the *lesion method,* involves damaging or removing sections of brain in animals, then observing the effects.

The brain can also be probed by using devices called *electrodes.* Some electrodes are

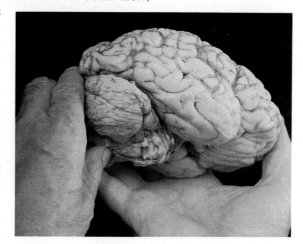

The human brain's modest appearance gives no hint of its extraordinary powers.

coin-shaped and are simply pasted or taped onto the scalp. They detect the electrical activity of millions of neurons in particular regions of the brain and are widely used in research and medical diagnosis. The electrodes are connected by wires to a machine that translates the electrical energy from the brain into wavy lines on a moving piece of paper or visual patterns on a screen. That is why electrical patterns in the brain are known as "brain waves." Different wave patterns are associated with sleep, relaxation, and mental concentration.

A brain-wave recording is called an **electroencephalogram (EEG).** A standard EEG is useful but not very precise because it reflects the activities of many cells at once. "Listening" to the brain with an EEG machine is like standing outside a sports stadium: You know when something is happening, but you can't be sure what it is or who is doing it. Fortunately, computer technology can be combined with EEG technology to get a clearer picture of brain activity patterns associated with specific events and mental processes; the computer suppresses all the background "noise," leaving only the pattern of electrical response to the event being studied.

For even more precise information, researchers use *needle electrodes,* very thin wires or hollow glass tubes that can be inserted into the brain, either directly in an exposed brain or through tiny holes in the skull. Only the skull and the membranes covering the brain need to be anesthetized; the brain itself, which processes all sensation and feeling,

paradoxically feels nothing when touched. Therefore, a human patient or an animal can be awake and not feel pain during the procedure. Needle electrodes can be used both to record electrical activity from the brain and to stimulate the brain with weak electrical currents. Stimulating a given area often results in a specific sensation or movement. *Microelectrodes* are so fine that they can be inserted into single cells.

Since the mid-1970s, even more amazing doors to the brain have opened. The **PET scan (positron-emission tomography)** goes beyond anatomy to record biochemical changes in the brain as they are happening. One type of PET scan takes advantage of the fact that nerve cells convert glucose, the body's main fuel, into energy. A researcher can inject a patient with a glucoselike substance that contains a harmless radioactive element. This substance accumulates in brain areas that are particularly active and are consuming glucose rapidly. The substance emits radiation, which is a telltale sign of activity, like cookie crumbs on a child's face. The radiation is detected by a scanning device, and the result is a computer-processed picture of biochemical activity on a display screen, with different colors indicating different activity levels (see Figure 4.8).

electroencephalogram (EEG)

A recording of neural activity detected by electrodes.

PET scan (positron-emission tomography)

A method for analyzing biochemical activity in the brain, using injections of a glucoselike substance containing a radioactive element.

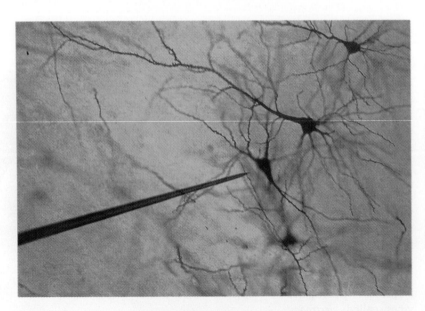

A microelectrode is used to record the electrical impulses generated by a single cell in the brain of a monkey.

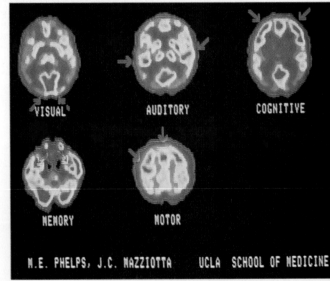

Figure 4.8

PET Scans of Metabolic Activity in the Brain

In these PET scans, red indicates areas of highest activity and violet areas of lowest activity. Clockwise starting from the upper left, the arrows point to regions that are most active when the person looks at a complicated visual scene, listens to a sound, performs a mental task, moves the right hand, or recalls stories heard previously.

PET scans, which were originally designed to diagnose abnormalities, have produced evidence that certain brain areas in people with emotional disorders are either unusually quiet or unusually active. But PET technology can also show which parts of the brain are active during ordinary activities and emotions. It lets researchers see which areas are busiest when a person hears a song, recalls a sad memory, works on a math problem, or shifts attention from one task to another.

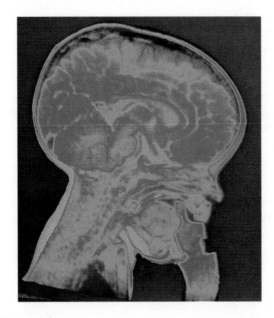

Figure 4.9
MRI of a Child's Brain
This MRI shows a child's brain—and the bottle he was drinking from while the image was obtained.

Another technique, **MRI (magnetic resonance imaging),** allows the exploration of "inner space" without injecting chemicals. Powerful magnetic fields and radio frequencies are used to produce vibrations in the nuclei of atoms making up body organs, and the vibrations are then picked up as signals by special receivers. A computer analyzes the signals, taking into account their strength and duration, and converts them into a high-contrast picture (see Figure 4.9). Like the PET scan, MRI is used both for diagnosing disease and for studying normal brains. Breakthroughs in computer hardware and software have led to faster techniques that can capture brain changes during specific mental activities, such as thinking of a word or looking at a scene (Rosen et al., 1993). These techniques detect blood flow by picking up magnetic signals from blood that has given up its oxygen to active brain cells. We will be reporting some of the incredible findings revealed by MRI research throughout this book—findings on memory, sex differences, depression, schizophrenia, and even how psychotherapy affects brain activity.

One of the newest brain-scan techniques combines EEG and MRI technology and provides something like a movie of ongoing changes in brain-cell activity (Gevins et al., 1994) (see Figure 4.10). And additional techniques are becoming available with each passing year. Thus, the brain can no longer hide from researchers behind the fortress of the skull. It is now possible to get a clear visual image of our most enigmatic organ without so much as lifting a scalpel.

MRI (magnetic resonance imaging)

A method for studying body and brain tissue, using magnetic fields and special radio receivers.

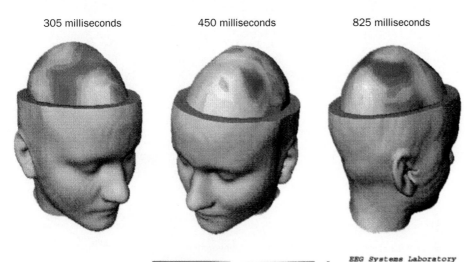

305 milliseconds   450 milliseconds   825 milliseconds

− |███████| |███████| +   *EEG Systems Laboratory & SAM Technology, Inc.*

Figure 4.10
Brain Activity in 3-D
By combining a new technology, MRI, with an old one, the EEG, researchers can monitor electrical changes in brain cells from moment to moment while a person works on a task. These computer models show changes on the brain's surface during a 1-second interval as the person compares the location of a stimulus with the location of another one seen moments before.

brain stem

The part of the brain at the top of the spinal cord, consisting of the medulla and the pons.

medulla

A structure in the brain stem responsible for certain automatic functions, such as breathing and heart rate.

pons

A structure in the brain stem involved in, among other things, sleeping, waking, and dreaming.

reticular activating system (RAS)

A dense network of neurons found in the core of the brain stem; it arouses the cortex and screens incoming information.

cerebellum

A brain structure that regulates movement and balance, and that is involved in the learning of certain kinds of simple responses.

What's Ahead

- *Which brain part acts as a "traffic officer" for incoming sensations?*

- *Which brain part is the "gateway to memory"—and what cognitive catastrophe occurs when it is damaged?*

- *Why is it a good thing that the outer covering of the human brain is so wrinkled?*

- *How did a bizarre nineteenth-century accident illuminate the role of the frontal lobes?*

A TOUR THROUGH THE BRAIN

All modern brain theories assume that different brain parts perform different (though overlapping) tasks. This concept, known as *localization of function,* goes back at least to Joseph Gall (1758–1828), the Austrian anatomist who thought that person-ality traits were reflected in the development of specific areas of the brain (see Chapter 1). Gall's theory of *phrenology* was completely wrong-headed (so to speak), but his general notion of specialization in the brain had merit.

To learn about what the various brain structures do, let's take an imaginary stroll through the brain. Pretend, now, that you have shrunk to a microscopic size and that you are wending your way through the "soul's frail dwelling house," starting at the lower part, just above the spine. In general, the more reflexive or automatic a behavior is, the more likely it is to involve lower brain areas; and the more complex a behavior, the more likely it is to involve areas that are higher up (although some lower areas also appear to be involved in some "higher" mental functions). Figure 4.11 shows the major structures we will encounter along the tour; you may want to refer to it as we proceed.

The Brain Stem

We begin at the base of the skull with the **brain stem,** which began to evolve some 500 million

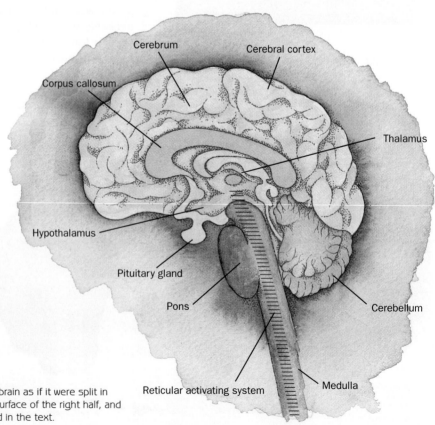

Figure 4.11

The Human Brain

This cross section depicts the brain as if it were split in half. The view is of the inside surface of the right half, and shows the structures described in the text.

years ago in segmented worms. The brain stem looks like a stalk rising out of the spinal cord. Pathways to and from upper areas of the brain pass through its two main structures: the **medulla** and the **pons.** The pons is involved in (among other things) sleeping, waking, and dreaming. The medulla is responsible for bodily functions that do not have to be consciously willed, such as breathing and heart rate. Hanging has long been used as a method of execution because when it breaks the neck, nervous pathways from the medulla are severed, stopping respiration.

Extending upward from the core of the brain stem is the **reticular activating system (RAS).** This dense network of neurons, which extends above the brain stem into the center of the brain and has connections with higher areas, screens incoming information and arouses the higher centers when something happens that demands their attention. Without the RAS, we could not be alert or perhaps even conscious.

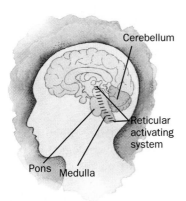

The Cerebellum

Standing atop the brain stem and looking toward the back part of the brain, we see a structure about the size of a small fist. It is the **cerebellum,** or "lesser brain," which contributes to a sense of balance and coordinates the muscles so that movement is smooth and precise. If your cerebellum were damaged, you would probably become exceedingly clumsy and uncoordinated. You might have trouble using a pencil, threading a needle, or riding a bicycle. In addition, this structure is involved in remembering certain simple skills and acquired reflexes (Krupa, Thompson, & Thompson, 1993; Thompson, 1986). Some researchers think that the cerebellum also plays a role in analyzing sensory information and in some complex mental tasks, such as solving a puzzle or generating words (Fiez, 1996; Gao et al., 1996).

The Thalamus

Deep in the brain's interior, we can see the **thalamus,** the busy traffic officer of the brain. As sensory messages come into the brain, the thalamus directs them to higher centers. For example, the sight of a sunset sends signals that the thalamus directs to a vision area, and the sound of an oboe sends signals that the thalamus sends on to an auditory area. The only sense that completely bypasses the thalamus is the sense of smell, which has its own private switching station, the *olfactory bulb.* The olfactory bulb lies near areas involved in emotion. Perhaps that is why particular odors—the smell of fresh laundry, gardenias, a steak sizzling on the grill—often rekindle memories of important personal experiences.

The Hypothalamus and the Pituitary Gland

Beneath the thalamus sits a structure called the **hypothalamus** (*hypo* means "under"). It is involved in drives associated with the survival of both the individual and the species—hunger, thirst, emotion, sex, and reproduction. It regulates body temperature by triggering sweating or shivering, and it controls the complex operations of the autonomic nervous system. Hanging down from the hypothalamus, connected to it by a short stalk, is a cherry-sized endocrine gland called the **pituitary gland.** The pituitary is often called the body's "master gland" because the hormones it secretes affect many other endocrine glands. The master, however, is really only a supervisor. The true boss is the hypothalamus, which sends chemicals to the pituitary that tell it when to "talk" to the other endocrine glands. The pituitary, in turn, sends hormonal messages out to these glands.

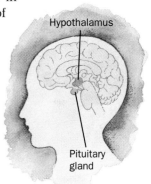

The Limbic System

The hypothalamus has many connections to a set of loosely interconnected structures called the **limbic system,** shown in Figure 4.12. (*Limbic* comes from the Latin for "border": These structures form a sort of border between the higher and lower parts of the brain.) Some anatomists include

thalamus

A brain structure that relays sensory messages to the cerebral cortex.

hypothalamus

A brain structure involved in emotions and drives vital to survival, such as fear, hunger, thirst, and reproduction; it regulates the autonomic nervous system.

pituitary gland

A small endocrine gland at the base of the brain, which releases many hormones and regulates other endocrine glands.

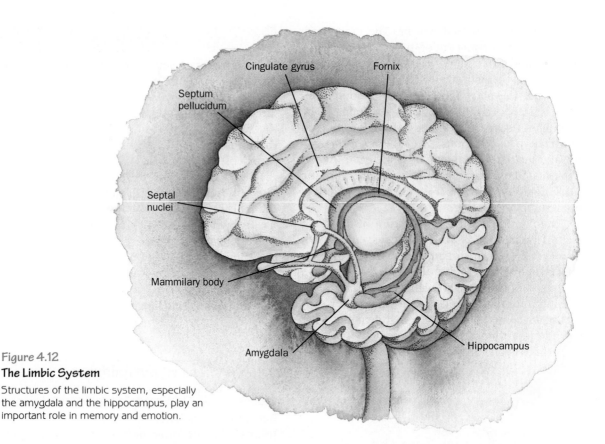

Cingulate gyrus

Fornix

Septum
pellucidum

Septal
nuclei

Mammilary body

Amygdala

Hippocampus

Figure 4.12
The Limbic System
Structures of the limbic system, especially
the amygdala and the hippocampus, play an
important role in memory and emotion.

the hypothalamus and parts of the thalamus in the limbic system. Although the usefulness of speaking of the limbic system as an integrated set of structures is now in dispute (LeDoux, 1996), it's clear that structures in this region are heavily involved in emotions, such as rage and fear, that we share with other animals (MacLean, 1993).

Many years ago, James Olds and Peter Milner argued that there were "pleasure centers" in the limbic system (Olds, 1975; Olds & Milner, 1954). They trained rats to press a lever in order to get a buzz of electricity delivered through tiny electrodes to the limbic system. Some rats would press the bar thousands of times an hour, for 15 or 20 hours at a time, until they collapsed from exhaustion. When they revived, they went right back to the bar. When forced to make a choice, the hedonistic rodents opted for electrical stimulation over such temptations as water, food, and even an attractive rat of the other sex that was making provocative gestures. Today, researchers believe that brain stimulation activates neural pathways rather than discrete "centers," and that changes in neurotransmitter or neuromodulator levels are involved.

The Amygdala.   One limbic structure that especially concerns psychologists is the **amygdala,** which appears to be responsible for evaluating sensory information, quickly determining its emotional importance, and contributing to the initial decision to approach or withdraw from a person or situation (see Chapter 12). The amygdala also plays an important role in mediating anxiety and depression; PET scans find that depressed and anxious patients show increased neural activity in this structure (Schulkin, 1994).

The Hippocampus.   Another important limbic area is the **hippocampus,** which has a shape that must have reminded someone of a sea horse, for that is what its name means. This structure has been called the "gateway to memory" because, along with adjacent brain areas, it enables us to form new memories about facts and events—the kind of information you need to identify a flower, tell a story, or recall a vacation trip. The information is then stored in the cerebral cortex, which we will be discussing shortly. For example, when you recall meeting someone yesterday, varous aspects of the memory—information about the per-

limbic system

A group of brain areas involved in emotional reactions and motivated behavior.

amygdala

A brain structure involved in the arousal and regulation of emotion and the initial emotional response to sensory information.

hippocampus

A brain structure involved in the storage of new information in memory.

son's greeting, tone of voice, appearance, and location—are probably stored in different locations in the cortex (Damasio et al., 1996; Squire, 1987). But without the hippocampus, the information would never get to these destinations (Mishkin et al., 1997; Squire & Zola-Morgan, 1991).

We know about the "gateway" function of the hippocampus in part from research on brain-damaged patients with severe memory problems. The case of one man, known to researchers as H. M., is thought to be the most intensely studied in the annals of medicine (Corkin, 1984; Corkin et al., 1997; Milner, 1970; Ogden & Corkin, 1991). In 1953, when H. M. was 27, surgeons removed most of his hippocampus, along with part of the amygdala. The operation was a last-ditch effort to relieve H. M.'s severe and life-threatening epilepsy. People who have epilepsy, a neurological disorder that has many causes and takes many forms, often have seizures. Usually, the seizures are brief, mild, and controllable by drugs, but in H. M.'s case, they were unrelenting and uncontrollable.

The operation did achieve its goal: Afterward, the young man's seizures were milder and could be managed with medication. His memory, however, had been affected profoundly. Although H. M. continued to recall most events that had occurred before the operation, he could no longer remember new experiences for much longer than 15 minutes; they vanished like water down the drain. With sufficient practice, H. M. could acquire new manual or problem-solving skills, such as playing tennis or solving a puzzle, but he could not remember the training sessions in which he learned these skills. He would read the same magazine over and over without realizing it. He could not recall the day of the week, the year, or even his last meal. Today, many years later, he will occasionally recall an unusually emotional event, such as the assassination of someone named Kennedy. He sometimes remembers that both his parents are dead, and he knows he has memory problems. But, according to Suzanne Corkin, who has studied H. M. extensively, these "islands of remembering" are the exceptions in a vast sea of forgetfulness. This good-natured man still does not know the scientists who have studied him for decades. He thinks he is much younger than he is, and he can no longer recognize a photograph of his own face; he is stuck in a time warp from the past.

Scientists are starting to understand just what happens in the hippocampus and in nearby structures during the formation of a long-term memory. For example, it appears that some synaptic pathways become more easily excitable and therefore more receptive to further impulses (McNaughton & Morris, 1987). But these changes and others take time, which may explain why memories remain vulnerable to disruption for a while after they are stored. Just as concrete takes time to set, memories require a period of *consolidation*, or stabilization, before they solidify.

The Cerebrum

At this point in our tour, the largest part of the brain still looms above us. It is the cauliflower-like **cerebrum,** where the higher forms of thinking take place. The complexity of the human brain's circuitry far exceeds that of any computer in existence, and much of its most complicated wiring is packed into this structure. Compared with many other creatures, we humans may be ungainly, feeble, and thin-skinned, but our well-developed cerebrum enables us to overcome these limitations and creatively control our environment (and, some would say, to mess it up).

The cerebrum is divided into two separate halves, or **cerebral hemispheres,** connected by a large band of fibers called the **corpus callosum.** In general, the right hemisphere is in charge of the left side of the body and the left hemisphere is in charge of the right side of the body. As we will see shortly, the two hemispheres also have somewhat different tasks and talents, a phenomenon known as **lateralization.**

The Cerebral Cortex.   Working our way right up through the top of the brain, we find that the cerebrum is covered by several thin layers of densely packed cells known collectively as the **cerebral cortex.** Cell bodies in the cortex, as in many other parts of the brain, produce a grayish tissue; hence the term *gray matter*. In other parts of the brain (and in the rest of the nervous system), long, myelin-covered axons prevail, providing the brain's *white matter*. Although the cortex is only about 3 millimeters thick, it contains almost three-fourths of all the cells in the human brain. The cortex has many deep crevasses and wrinkles, which enable it to contain its billions of neurons without requiring us to have the heads of giants—heads that would be too big to permit us to be born. In other mammals, which have fewer neurons, the cortex is less crumpled; in rats, it is quite smooth.

cerebrum (suh-REE-brum)
The largest brain structure, consisting of the upper part of the brain; divided into two hemispheres, it is in charge of most sensory, motor, and cognitive processes. From the Latin for "brain."

cerebral hemispheres
The two halves of the cerebrum.

corpus callosum
The bundle of nerve fibers connecting the two cerebral hemispheres.

lateralization
Specialization of the two cerebral hemispheres for particular operations.

cerebral cortex
A collection of several thin layers of cells covering the cerebrum; it is largely responsible for higher mental functions. *Cortex* is Latin for "bark" or "rind."

Lobes of the Cortex.   On each cerebral hemisphere, especially deep fissures divide the cortex into four distinct regions, or lobes (see Figure 4.13):

- The *occipital lobes* (from the Latin for "in back of the head") are at the lower back part of the brain. Among other things, they contain the *visual cortex,* where visual signals are processed. Damage to the visual cortex can cause impaired visual recognition or blindness.

- The *parietal lobes* (from the Latin for "pertaining to walls") are at the top of the brain. They contain the *somatosensory cortex,* which receives information about pressure, pain, touch, and temperature from all over the body. The areas of the somatosensory cortex that receive signals from the hands and the face are disproportionately large because these body parts are particularly sensitive.

- The *temporal lobes* (from the Latin for "pertaining to the temples") are at the sides of the brain, just above the ears, behind the temples. They are involved in memory, perception and emotion, and they contain the *auditory cortex,* which processes sounds. An area of the left temporal lobe known as *Wernicke's area* is involved in language comprehension.

- The *frontal lobes,* as their name indicates, are located toward the front of the brain, just under the skull in the area of the forehead. They contain the *motor cortex,* which issues orders to the 600 muscles of the body that produce voluntary movement. In the left frontal lobe, a region known as *Broca's area* handles speech production. During short-term memory tasks, areas in the frontal lobes are especially active (Goldman-Rakic, 1996). The frontal lobes are also involved in the ability to make plans, think creatively, and take initiative.

When a surgeon probes these four pairs of lobes with an electrode, different things tend to happen (although there is some overlap). If current is applied to the somatosensory cortex in the parietal lobes, the patient may feel tingling in the skin or a sense of being gently touched. If the visual cortex in the occipital lobes is stimulated, the person may report a flash of light or swirls of color. But in most areas of the cortex, nothing happens as a result of electrical stimulation. These "silent" areas, sometimes called the *association cortex,* appear to be responsible for higher mental processes.

The silent areas of the cortex are finally beginning to reveal their secrets. Psychologists are espe-

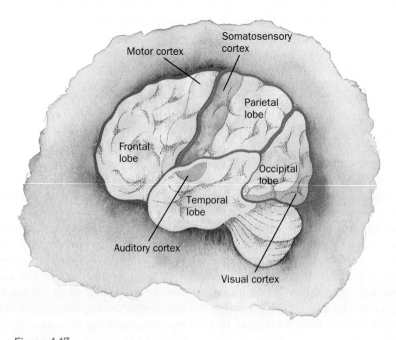

Figure 4.13
Lobes of the Cerebral Cortex
Deep fissures divide the cortex of each cerebral hemisphere into four regions.

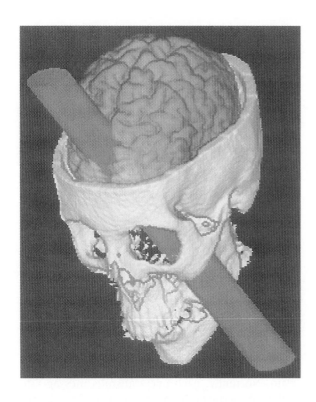

Figure 4.14

A Famous Skull

When an iron rod penetrated Phineas Gage's skull, his behavior and personality changed dramatically. The exact location of the brain damage remained controversial for almost a century and a half, until Hanna and Antonio Damasio and their colleagues (1994) used measurements of Gage's skull and MRIs of normal brains to plot possible trajectories of the rod. This reconstruction shows that the damage occurred in an area of the prefrontal cortex thought to be involved in emotional processing and rational decision making.

cially interested in the forwardmost part of the frontal lobes, the *prefrontal cortex*. This area barely exists in mice and rats and takes up only 3.5 percent of the cerebral cortex in cats, about 7 percent in dogs, and 17 percent in chimpanzees. In human beings, it accounts for fully 29 percent of the cortex.

Scientists have long known that the frontal lobes, and the prefrontal cortex in particular, must have something to do with personality. The first clue appeared in 1848, when a bizarre accident drove an inch-thick, 3½-foot-long iron rod clear through the head of a young railroad worker named Phineas Gage. As you can see in Figure 4.14, the rod (which is still on display at Harvard University, along with Gage's skull) entered beneath the left eye and exited through the top of the head, destroying much of the prefrontal cortex (H. Damasio et al., 1994). Miraculously, Gage survived this trauma and retained the ability to speak, think, and remember. But his friends complained that he was "no longer Gage." In a sort of Jekyll-and-Hyde transformation, he had changed from a mild-mannered, friendly, efficient worker into a foul-mouthed, ill-tempered, undependable lout who could not hold a steady job or stick to a plan. His employers had to let him go, and he was reduced to exhibiting himself as a circus attraction.

This sad case and others suggest that parts of the frontal lobes are involved in social judgment, rational decision making, and the ability to set goals and to make and carry through plans—or what is commonly called "will." As neurologist Antonio Damasio (1994) wrote, "Gage's unintentional message was that observing social convention, behaving ethically, and, in general, making decisions advantageous to one's survival and progress, require both knowledge of rules and strategies and the integrity of specific brain systems." Interestingly, the mental deficits that characterize damage to these areas are accompanied by a flattening out of emotion and feeling, which suggests that normal emotions are necessary for everyday reasoning and decision making.

The frontal lobes also govern the ability to do a series of tasks in the proper sequence and to stop doing them at the proper time. The pioneering Soviet psychologist Alexander Luria (1980) studied many cases in which damage to the frontal lobes disrupted these abilities. One man observed by Luria kept trying to light a match after it was already lit. Another planed a piece of wood in the hospital carpentry shop until it was gone, and then went on to plane the workbench!

What's Ahead

- *If the two cerebral hemispheres were out of touch, would they feel different emotions and think different thoughts?*

- *Why do researchers often refer to the left hemisphere as "dominant"?*

- *Should you sign up for a program that promises to perk up your right brain?*

THE TWO HEMISPHERES OF THE BRAIN

We have seen that the cerebrum is divided into two hemispheres that control opposite sides of the body. Although similar in structure, these hemispheres have somewhat separate talents, or areas of specialization.

Split Brains: A House Divided

In a normal brain, the two hemispheres communicate with one another across the corpus callosum, the bundle of fibers that connects them. Whatever happens in one side of the brain is instantly flashed to the other side. What would happen, though, if the two sides were cut off from one another?

In 1953, Ronald E. Myers and Roger W. Sperry took the first step toward answering this question by severing the corpus callosum in cats. They also cut parts of the nerves leading from the eyes to the brain. Normally, each eye transmits messages to both sides of the brain. After this procedure, a cat's left eye sent information only to the left hemisphere and its right eye sent information only to the right hemisphere.

At first, the cats did not seem to be affected much by this drastic operation. But Myers and Sperry showed that something profound had happened. They trained the cats to perform tasks with one eye blindfolded. For example, a cat might have to push a panel with a square on it to get food but ignore a panel with a circle. Then the researchers switched the blindfold to the cat's other eye and tested the animal again. Now the cats behaved as if they had never learned the trick. Apparently, one side of the brain didn't know what the other side was doing. It was as if the animals had two minds in one body. Later studies confirmed this result with other species, including monkeys (Sperry, 1964).

In all the animal studies, ordinary behavior, such as eating and walking, remained normal. Encouraged by this finding, a team of surgeons led by Joseph Bogen decided in the early 1960s to try cutting the corpus callosum in patients with debilitating, uncontrollable epilepsy. In severe forms of this disease, disorganized electrical activity spreads from an injured area to other parts of the brain. The surgeons reasoned that cutting the connection between the two halves of the brain might stop the spread of electrical activity from one side to the other. As in the case of H. M., operating was a last resort.

Get Involved

Have a right-handed friend tap on a paper with a pencil held in the right hand, for one minute. Then have the person do the same with the left hand, using a fresh sheet of paper. Finally, repeat the procedure, having the person talk at the same time as tapping. For most people, talking will decrease the rate of tapping—but more for the right hand than for the left, probably because both activities involve the same hemisphere, and there is "competition" between them. (Left-handed people vary more in terms of which hemisphere is dominant for language, so the results for them will be more variable.)

The results of this *split-brain surgery* generally proved successful. Seizures were reduced and sometimes disappeared completely. As an added bonus, these patients gave scientists a chance to find out what each half of the brain can do when it is quite literally cut off from the other. It was already known that the two hemispheres are not mirror images of each other. In most people, language is largely handled by the left hemisphere; thus, a person who suffers brain damage because of a stroke—a blockage in or rupture of a blood vessel in the brain—is much more likely to have language problems if the damage is in the left side than if it is in the right. How would splitting the brain affect language and other abilities?

In their daily lives, split-brain patients did not seem much affected by the fact that the two sides of their brains were incommunicado. Their personalities and general intelligence remained intact; they could walk, talk, and in general lead normal lives. Apparently, connections in the undivided brain stem kept body movements normal. But in a series of ingenious studies, Sperry and his colleagues (and later other researchers) showed that perception and memory had been affected, just as they had been in earlier animal research. In 1981, Sperry won a Nobel Prize for his work.

To understand this research, you must know how nerves connect the eyes to the brain. (The human patients, unlike Myers and Sperry's cats, did not have these nerves cut.) If you look straight ahead, everything in the left side of the scene before you—the "visual field"—goes to the right half of your brain, and everything in the right side of the scene goes to the left half of your brain. This is true for *both* eyes (see Figure 4.15).

The procedure was to present information only to one or the other side of the subjects' brains. In one early study (Levy, Trevarthen, & Sperry, 1972), the researchers took photographs of different faces, cut them in two, and pasted different halves together. The reconstructed photographs

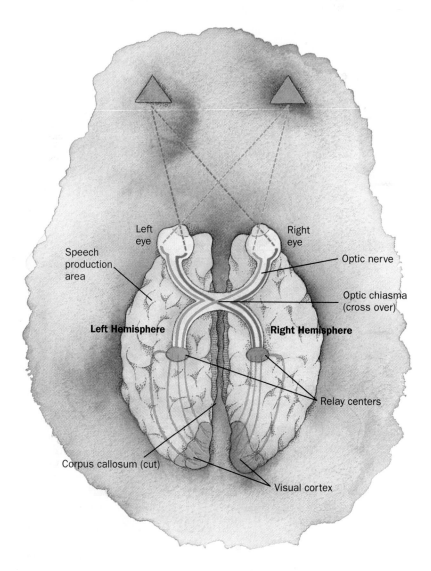

Figure 4.15

Visual Pathways

Each brain hemisphere receives information from the eyes about the opposite side of the visual field. Thus, if you stare directly at the corner of a room, everything to the left of the juncture is represented in your right cerebral hemisphere and vice versa. This is so because half the axons in each optic nerve cross over (at the optic chiasma) to the opposite side of the brain. Normally, each hemisphere immediately shares its information with the other one, but in split-brain patients, severing the corpus callosum prevents such communication.

were then presented on slides. The person was told to stare at a dot on the middle of the screen, so that half the image fell to the left of this point and half to the right. Each image was flashed so quickly that the person had no time to move his or her eyes. When the subjects were asked to say what they had seen, they named the person in the right part of the image (which would be the little boy in Figure 4.16). But when they were asked to *point* with their left hands to the face they had seen, they chose the person in the left side of the image (the mustached man in Figure 4.16). Further, they claimed they had noticed nothing unusual about the original photographs! Each side of the brain saw a different half-image and automatically filled in the missing part. Neither side knew what the other side had seen.

Why did the patients name one side of the picture but point to the other? Speech centers are in the left hemisphere. When the person responded with speech, it was the left side of the brain doing the talking. When the person pointed with the left hand, which is controlled by the right side of the brain, the right hemisphere was giving *its* version of what the person had seen.

In another study, the researchers presented slides of ordinary objects and then suddenly flashed a slide of a nude woman. Both sides of the brain were amused, but because only the left side has speech, the two sides responded differently. When the picture was flashed to one woman's left hemisphere, she laughed and identified it as a nude. When it was flashed to her right hemisphere, she said nothing but began to chuckle. Asked what she was laughing at, she said, "I don't know . . . nothing . . . oh—that funny machine." The right hemisphere could not describe what it had seen, but it reacted emotionally, just the same (Gazzaniga, 1967).

A Question of Dominance

Several dozen people have undergone the split-brain operation since the mid-1960s, and research on left–right differences has also been done with people whose brains are intact. Electrodes and PET scans have been used to gauge activity in the left and right hemispheres while people perform different tasks. The results confirm that nearly all

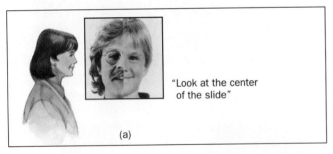

"Look at the center of the slide"

(a)

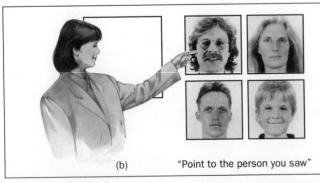

(b)   "Point to the person you saw"

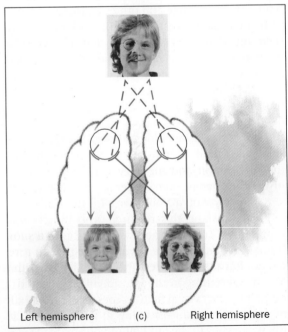

Left hemisphere   (c)   Right hemisphere

Figure 4.16

Divided Brain, Divided View

When split-brain patients were shown composite photographs (a) and were then asked to pick out the face they had seen from a series of intact photographs (b), they said they had seen the face on the right side of the composite—yet they pointed with their left hands to the face that had been on the left. Because the two hemispheres of the brain could not communicate, the verbal left hemisphere was aware of only the right half of the picture, and the relatively mute right hemisphere was aware of only the left half (c).

The snack for your left brain.

FI-BAR simply makes more sense than the sugary sweets you usually reach for.

Because it's full of smart stuff like oat bran and up to twelve different dietary fibers.

FI-BAR's cholesterol free. Low in calories, low in saturated fat.

With absolutely no artificial anything.

In fact, FI-BAR is a scientifically balanced, highly nutritious snack that's down-right good for kids and grown-ups alike.

The snack for your right brain.

You know something? This stuff tastes like a candy bar.

It's easy to exaggerate the differences between the left and right brain hemispheres.

right-handed people and a majority of left-handers process language mainly in the left hemisphere. The left side is also more active during some logical, symbolic, and sequential tasks, such as solving math problems and understanding technical material. Because of its cognitive talents, many researchers refer to the left hemisphere as *dominant*. They believe that the left hemisphere usually exerts control over the right hemisphere. One well-known split-brain researcher, Michael Gazzaniga (1983), has argued that without help from the left side, the right side's mental skills would probably be "vastly inferior to the cognitive skills of a chimpanzee." He and others also believe that a mental "module" in the left hemisphere is constantly trying to explain actions and emotions generated by brain parts whose workings are nonverbal and outside of awareness.

You can see in split-brain patients how the left brain concocts such explanations. In one classic example, a picture of a chicken claw was flashed to a patient's left hemisphere, a picture of a snow scene to his right. The task was to point to a related image for each picture from an array, with a chicken the correct choice for the claw and a shovel for the snow scene. The patient chose the shovel with his left hand and the chicken with his right. When asked to explain why, he responded (with his left hemisphere) that the chicken claw went with the chicken, and the shovel was for cleaning out the chicken shed. The left brain had seen the left hand's response but did not know about the snow scene, so it interpreted the response by using the information it did have (Gazzaniga, 1988). In people with intact brains, says

Gazzaniga, the left brain's interpretations account for the sense of a unified, coherent identity.

Other researchers, including Sperry (1982), have rushed to the right hemisphere's defense. The right side, they point out, is no dummy. It is superior in problems requiring spatial–visual ability, the ability you use to read a map or follow a dress pattern, and it excels in facial recognition and the ability to read facial expressions. It is active during the creation and appreciation of art and music. It recognizes nonverbal sounds, such as a dog's barking. The right brain also has some language ability. Typically, it can read a word briefly flashed to it and can understand an experimenter's instructions. In a few split-brain patients, right-brain language ability has been quite well developed.

Some researchers have credited the right hemisphere with having a cognitive style that is intuitive and holistic (in which things are seen as wholes), in contrast to the left hemisphere's more rational and analytic mode. However, many researchers are concerned about popular misinterpretations of this conclusion. Books and programs that promise to make you more "right-brained," they observe, tend to oversimplify and exaggerate hemispheric differences. The differences are relative, not absolute—a matter of degree. In most real-life activities, the two hemispheres cooperate naturally, with each making a valuable contribution (Kinsbourne, 1982; J. Levy, 1985). As Sperry (1982) himself once noted, "The left–right dichotomy . . . is an idea with which it is very easy to run wild."

Thinking Critically About "Right Brain/Left Brain" Theories

What's Ahead

- *How do biological theories of dreaming differ from the familiar Freudian view?*
- *Do men talk about sports and women about feelings because their brains are different?*

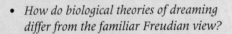
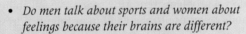

TWO STUBBORN ISSUES IN BRAIN RESEARCH

If you have mastered the definitions and descriptions in this chapter, you are prepared to read popular accounts of advances in neuropsychology. But many mysteries remain about how the brain works, and we will end this chapter with two of them.

Why Do We Dream?

One of the oldest mysteries about the brain is why it seems to "shut down" for sleep yet remains active by providing us with strange and colorful nightly dreams.

The purposes of sleep itself are still not entirely understood. Most likely, sleep creates a "time-out" period so that the body can eliminate waste products from muscles, repair cells, strengthen the immune system, and recover physical abilities lost during the day. Our nightly slumbers also appear to help the brain function efficiently. After the loss of even a single night's sleep, mental flexibility, attention, memory for new facts, and creativity

all suffer (Dement, 1992; Horne, 1988). Chronic sleepiness, which many experts think is commonplace in busy modern nations, can lead to automobile and work accidents (Coren, 1996; Maas, 1998). And after several days of sleep deprivation, people become extremely irritable and begin to have hallucinations and delusions (Dement, 1978).

Sleep, then, is obviously necessary for alert mental functioning. But what in the world is the purpose of dreaming? Why do we spend a good part of each night flying through the air, battling monsters, or having weird conversations in the fantasy world of our dreams? Biological research is beginning to reveal the answers.

The Realms of Sleep. Until the early 1950s, little was known about dreaming. Then a breakthrough occurred in the laboratory of physiologist Nathaniel Kleitman, who at the time was the only person in the world who had spent an entire career studying sleep. Kleitman had given one of his graduate students, Eugene Aserinsky, the tedious task of finding out whether the slow, rolling eye movements that characterize the onset of sleep continue throughout the night. To both men's surprise, eye movements did indeed occur, but they were rapid, not slow (Aserinsky, & Kleitman, 1955). Using the electroencephalograph to measure the brain's electrical activity, these researchers, along with another of Kleitman's students, William Dement, were able to correlate the rapid eye movements with changes in sleepers' brain-wave patterns (Dement, 1992). Adult volunteers were soon spending their nights sleeping in laboratories while scientists observed them and measured changes in their brain activity, muscle tension, breathing, and other physiological responses.

As a result of this research, today we know that during sleep, periods of **rapid eye movement (REM)** alternate with periods of fewer eye movements, or *non-REM* (NREM), in a cycle that recurs about every 90 minutes or so. The REM periods last from a few minutes to as long as an hour, averaging about 20 minutes. Whenever they begin, the pattern of electrical activity from the sleeper's brain changes to resemble that of alert wakefulness. Non-REM periods are themselves divided into four shorter stages, each associated with a particular brain-wave pattern.

In the first stage, you feel yourself drifting on the edge of consciousness. In the second, you are sleeping soundly enough to be undisturbed by minor noises. In the third, your brain waves, breathing, and pulse have slowed down considerably, and you are hard to arouse. And in the fourth, you are in deep sleep and are difficult to awaken (though, oddly, this is when sleeptalking and sleepwalking are most likely to occur).

Then you move back up the ladder, from stage 4 to 3 to 2 to 1. At that point, about 70 to 90 minutes after the onset of sleep, something peculiar happens. Stage 1 does not turn into drowsy wakefulness, as one might expect. Instead, your brain begins to emit long bursts of very rapid, somewhat irregular waves, similar to those produced during stage 1. Your heart rate increases, your blood pressure rises, and your breathing becomes faster and more irregular. Small twitches in the face and fingers may occur. In men, the penis becomes somewhat erect as vascular tissue relaxes and blood fills the genital area faster than it exits. In women, the clitoris enlarges and vaginal lubrication increases. At the same time, most of your skeletal muscles go as limp as a rag doll, preventing your aroused brain from producing physical movement. You have entered the realm of REM.

Because the brain is extremely active while the body is entirely inactive, REM sleep has also been called "paradoxical sleep." It is during these periods that you are most likely to dream. Even people who claim they never dream at all will report dreams if awakened in a sleep laboratory during REM sleep. Dreaming is also reported during non-REM sleep, but less often, and the images tend to be somewhat less vivid and more realistic than those reported during REM sleep.

REM and non-REM sleep continue to alternate throughout the night, with the REM periods tend-

Because cats sleep so much—up to 80 percent of the time—it is easy to catch them in the various stages of slumber. A cat in non-REM sleep (left) remains upright, but during the REM phase (right), its muscles go limp and it flops onto its side.

ing to get longer and closer together as the hours pass. An early REM period may last only a few minutes, whereas a later one may go on for 20 or 30 minutes and sometimes as long as an hour—which is why people are likely to be dreaming when the alarm clock goes off in the morning.

The Dreaming Brain.   In the past, most theories of dreaming were entirely psychological. Sigmund Freud, for example, proposed that we dream in order to gratify unconscious wishes and longings, often sexual or violent in nature (Freud, 1900/1953). If the dream arouses anxiety, said Freud, the rational part of the mind disguises its message; otherwise the dream would intrude into consciousness and waken the dreamer. To Freud, every dream had a hidden meaning, no matter how absurd the images might seem.

Some contemporary dream researchers have emphasized instead the ongoing *conscious* preoccupations of waking life, such as concerns over relationships, work, sex, or health (Siegel, 1991; Webb & Cartwright, 1978). They believe that the symbols and images in a dream convey its true meaning, rather than disguising it. During a crisis, emotional concerns activate images in memory and our dream machinery goes into high gear (Cartwright & Lloyd, 1994). For example, in people who recover most quickly from the grief of divorce—in contrast to those remaining depressed—the first dream of the night often comes sooner, the dream lasts longer, and it is more emotional and storylike. This pattern suggests that the "successful" dreamers are working to resolve issues of loss in their dreams. The researcher who reported this finding, Rosalind Cartwright (1990), concluded that getting through a divorce (and, by implication, other

rapid eye movement (REM) sleep

Sleep periods characterized by eye movement, loss of muscle tone, and dreaming.

crises) takes "time, good friends, good genes, good luck, and a good dream system."

In contrast, biological researchers believe that dreams originate not in the psyche but in the physiological workings of the brain. For example, Francis Crick and Graeme Mitchison (1995) argue that during REM sleep, synaptic connections that are unneeded are weakened, making memory more efficient and accurate. In this view, dreams are merely mental garbage, and there's no point in trying to remember them or analyze them for their "meanings," whether hidden or obvious. REM sleep may also *strengthen* synaptic connections associated with recently stored memories; memories for a new skill usually improve for a while after initial learning, during the period of consolidation that we mentioned earlier—but not if you are deprived of REM sleep (Karni et al., 1994).

Probably the most influential biological theory is the **activation-synthesis theory,** proposed by Allan Hobson (1988, 1990). To Hobson, dreams have a most unromantic source: neurons that are firing spontaneously in the lower part of the brain, in the pons. These neurons control eye movement, gaze, balance, and posture, and they send messages to sensory and motor areas of the cortex

activation-synthesis theory

The theory that dreaming results from the cortical synthesis and interpretation of neural signals triggered by activity in the lower part of the brain.

responsible during wakefulness for visual processing and voluntary action. According to the activation-synthesis theory, such signals have no psychological meaning in themselves. But the cortex tries to make sense of them by *synthesizing,* or combining, them with existing knowledge and memories to produce some sort of coherent interpretation—just as it would if the signals had come from sense organs during ordinary wakefulness. When neurons fire in the part of the brain that handles balance, for instance, the cortex may generate a dream about falling. When signals occur that would ordinarily produce running, the cortex may manufacture a dream about being chased. Because the signals themselves lack coherence, the interpretation—the dream—is also likely to be incoherent and confusing. And because cortical neurons that control initial storage of new memories are turned off during sleep (because certain neurotransmitter levels are low), we typically forget our dreams upon waking unless we write them down or immediately recount them to someone else.

Hobson's theory explains why REM sleep and dreaming do not occur continuously through the night. Giant cells in the reticular activating system of the pons, cells that are sensitive to the neurotransmitter acetylcholine, appear to initiate REM sleep. They then proceed to fire in unrestrained bursts, like a machine gun. Eventually, however, the gun's magazine is emptied, and other neurons, which inhibit REM sleep, take over. Only when the neurons "reload" can firing, and REM sleep, resume.

Wishes, in this view, do not cause dreams; brain-stem mechanisms do. But that doesn't mean that dreams are meaningless. Hobson (1988) argued that the brain "is so inexorably bent upon the quest for meaning that it attributes and even creates meaning when there is little or none to be found in the data it is asked to process." By studying these attributed meanings, you can learn about your unique perceptions, conflicts, and concerns—not by trying to dig below the surface of the dream, as Freud would, but by examining the surface itself. Or you can relax and enjoy the nightly entertainment that dreams provide.

Advocates of psychological explanations of dreams, however, have not conceded defeat. We all know from experience that dreams differ: Some seem related to daily problems, some are vague and incoherent, and some are "anxiety dreams" that occur when we are tense and worried (for example, you arrive to take your psychology exam, and the questions are all about Chinese culture

Activation-Synthesis Theory of Dreams

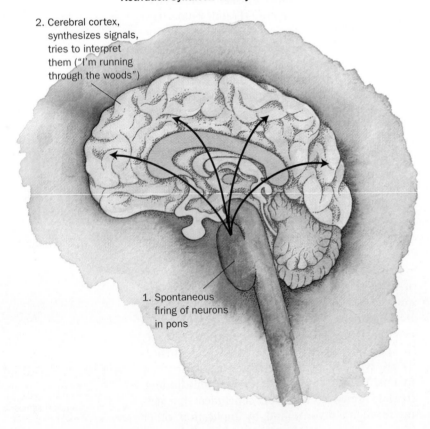

2. Cerebral cortex, synthesizes signals, tries to interpret them ("I'm running through the woods")

1. Spontaneous firing of neurons in pons

during the Ming dynasty). Perhaps different kinds of dreams have different purposes and origins. Much remains to be learned about the functions of dreaming and even of sleep itself.

Are There "His" and "Hers" Brains?

A second stubborn issue concerns the existence of sex differences in the brain. Historically, findings on male–female brain differences have often flip-flopped in a most suspicious manner, a result of the biases of the observers rather than the biology of the brain (Shields, 1975). For example, three decades ago, scientists speculated that women were more "right-brained" and men were more "left-brained," which supposedly explained why men were "rational" and women "intuitive." Then, when the virtues of the right hemisphere were discovered, some researchers decided that *men* were more right-brained. But it is now clear that the abilities popularly associated with the two sexes do not fall neatly into the two hemispheres of the brain. The left side is more verbal (presumably a "female" trait), but it is also more mathematical (presumably a "male" trait). The right side is more intuitive ("female"), but it is also more spatially talented ("male").

To evaluate the issue of sex differences in the brain intelligently, we need to ask two questions: Do male and female brains differ physically? And if so, what, if anything, does this difference have to do with behavior?

Let's consider the first question. Several anatomical and biochemical sex differences have been found in animal brains, especially in areas related to reproduction, such as the hypothalamus (McEwen, 1983). Human sex differences, however, have been more elusive. Of course, we would expect to find male–female brain differences that are related to the regulation of sex hormones and other aspects of reproduction. But many researchers want to know whether there are differences that affect how men and women think or behave—and here, the picture is murkier.

For example, in 1982, two anthropologists autopsied 14 human brains and reported an average sex difference in the size and shape of the *splenium*, a small section at the end of the corpus callosum, the bundle of fibers dividing the cerebral hemispheres (de Lacoste-Utamsing & Holloway, 1982). The researchers concluded that women's brains are less lateralized for certain tasks than men's are—that men rely more heavily on one or the other side of the brain, whereas women tend to use both sides. This conclusion quickly made its way into newspapers, magazines, and even textbooks as a verified sex difference.

Now that more than a decade of research has passed, the picture has changed. In a review of the available studies, neuroscientist William Byne (1993) found that only the 1982 study reported the splenium to be larger in women. Two very early studies (in 1906 and 1909) found that it was larger in men, and 21 later studies found no sex difference at all. Moreover, a Canadian analysis of 49 studies found only trivial differences between the two sexes, differences that paled in comparison with the huge individual variations *within* each sex (Bishop & Wahlsten, 1997). Most people are unaware of these findings because studies that find no differences rarely make headlines.

Researchers are now looking for other sex differences in the brain, such as in the density of neurons in specific areas. Sandra Witelson and her colleagues, who studied nine brains from autopsied bodies, found that the women had an average of 11 percent more cells in areas of the cortex associated with the processing of auditory information; all of the women had more of these cells than did any of the men (Witelson, Glazer, & Kigar, 1994). Other researchers are using high-tech methods to search for average sex differences in the brain areas that are active when people work on a particular task. In one study (Shaywitz et al., 1995), 19 men and 19 women (all right-handed) were asked to say whether pairs of nonsense words rhymed, a task that required them to process and compare sounds. MRI scans showed that in both sexes an area at the front of the left hemisphere was activated. But in 11 of the women and none of the men, the corresponding area in the right hemisphere was also active (see Figure 4.17 on the next page). These findings are further evidence for a sex difference in lateralization, at least for this one type of language function. This could help explain why left-hemisphere damage is less likely to cause language problems in women than in men after a stroke (Inglis & Lawson, 1981; McGlone, 1978).

Over the next few years, research may reveal additional anatomical and information-processing differences in the brains of males and females. But even if such differences exist, we must then ask our second question: *What do the differences mean for the behavior of men and women in real life?*

Some popular writers have been quick to assume that brain differences explain, among other things,

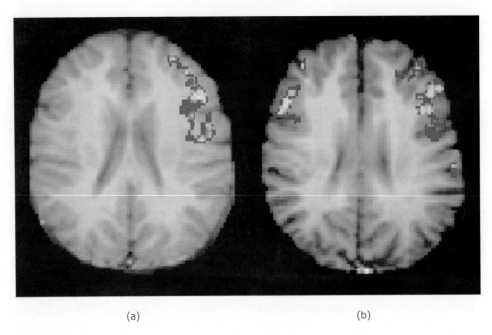

(a)   (b)

Figure 4.17

Gender and the Brain

These MRIs show that men and women tended to function differently during a task requiring the comparison of sounds. (Because of the orientation of the MRIs, the left hemisphere is seen on the right and vice versa.) During the first step in the task, the sounding out of words, Broca's area—the left-hemisphere area associated with speech production—was active in the men's brains (a). Eight women had this same pattern, but the brains of the other 11 showed activity in both hemispheres (b). The two sexes performed equally well on the task, leading the researchers to conclude that nature has provided the brain with different routes to the same ability (Shaywitz et al., 1995). However, the results might help explain why women seem to compensate better than men do for reading disabilities.

Thinking Critically About Sex Differences in the Brain

women's allegedly superior intuition, women's love of talking about feelings and men's love of talking about sports, women's greater verbal ability, men's edge in math ability, and why men won't ask for directions when they're lost. But there are at least three problems with these conclusions:

1. *These supposed gender differences are stereotypes;* in each case, the overlap between the sexes is greater than the difference between them. As we saw in Chapter 1, even differences that are statistically significant are often quite small in practical terms.

2. *A biological difference does not necessarily have behavioral implications.* In the rhyme-judgment study, for example, both sexes performed equally well, despite the differences in their MRIs. When it comes to explaining how brain differences are related to more general abilities, speculations are

as plentiful as ants at a picnic, but at present they remain just that—speculations (Hoptman & Davidson, 1994). To know whether sex differences in the brain translate into significant behavioral differences, we would need to know much more about how brain organization and chemistry affect human abilities and traits.

3. *Sex differences in the brain could be the result rather than the cause of behavioral differences.* Remember that experiences in life are constantly sculpting the circuitry of the brain, affecting the way brains are organized and how they function—and males and females often have different experiences.

Thus the answer to our second question, whether physical differences are linked to behavior, is "No one really knows." It is important to keep an open mind about new findings on sex differences in the brain, but because the practical significance of these findings (if any) is not clear, it is also important to be cautious and aware of how such results might be exaggerated and misused.

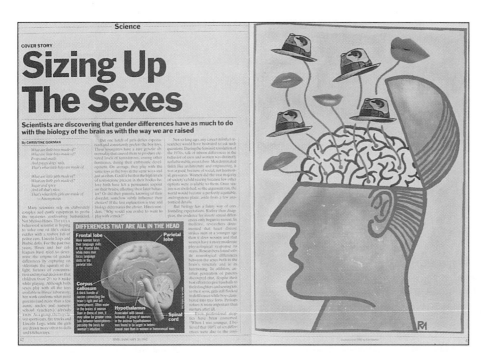

The press has been quick to run stories on differences in male and female brains. Articles, such as this one from *Time*, often conclude from interesting but tentative findings that gender differences in behavior must be biologically based. Is this conclusion justified? Why do you think the media give so much less attention to studies reporting similarities between the sexes?

Speaking of caution . . . we should also be cautious in thinking about the mysterious case of Philip Charles Cutajar, which opened this chapter. People can have many motives for "forgetting" who they are, leaving their pasts behind them, making up a new identity, and trying to start over in a strange place where no one knows them. But assuming that Cutajar's amnesia was real and not feigned, we might speculate that it had something to do with injury to the cortex, where memories for events are stored. (If you guessed that it was his hippocampus that was damaged, remember that the hippocampus is involved in the *formation* of long-term memories and is not thought to be the site of their actual storage.)

We might also speculate that the damage occurred in the left hemisphere. Many researchers today believe that the brain is organized as a loose confederation of independent modules, or mental systems, all working in parallel (Dennett, 1991; Gazzaniga, 1985; Restak, 1994). As we saw earlier, Michael Gazzaniga (1985) has proposed that the sense of having a unified self—a personal identity—occurs because the one verbal module, an "interpreter" usually located in the left hemisphere, is constantly coming up with theories to explain the actions, moods, and thoughts of the other modules. (Recall how in split-brain patients,

the left hemisphere constructed theories to explain the actions and emotions generated by the right hemisphere.) Perhaps, then, the trauma suffered by Cutajar impaired the brain module responsible for his very sense of identity.

This is one mystery, however, that has no pat answers. The brain is a complex organ, and any number of problems might have contributed to Cutajar's amnesia, including a disruption in neurotransmitter production, injury to a pathway linking specific brain parts, and impairment of the brain's ability to pull the bits and pieces of a memory together to form a coherent whole. But even if we knew everything there is to know about Cutajar's brain and how it was damaged, we would still be left with the puzzle of how and why he assumed an entirely different identity, that of "William Charles D'Souza," and why on earth he thought he was from Wantagh, New York. To solve that puzzle, we would want to know a great deal more about this man's previous history, his relationships, and whether emotional problems could have contributed to his memory loss.

There is a larger moral here: Analyzing a human being in terms of physiology alone is like analyzing the Taj Mahal solely in terms of the materials that were used to build it. Even if we could monitor every cell and circuit of the brain, we would still not know how we come to be who we are. We would still need to understand the circumstances, thoughts, and cultural rules that affect whether we are gripped by hatred, consumed by grief, lifted by love, or transported by joy.

Food for Thought: Diet and Neurotransmitters

"Vitamin improves sex!" "Mineral boosts brainpower!" "Chocolate chases the blues!" Claims such as these have long given nutritional theories of behavior a bad reputation. In the late 1960s, when Nobel laureate Linus Pauling proposed that some mental disorders be treated with massive doses of vitamins, few researchers listened. Mainstream medical authorities classified Pauling's vitamin therapy with such infamous cure-alls as snake oil and leeches.

Today, most mental-health professionals remain skeptical of nutritional cures for mental illness. But the underlying premise of nutritional treatments, that diet affects the brain and therefore behavior, is getting a second look. Claims that sugar or common food additives lead to undesirable behavior in otherwise normal people remain doubtful, but in some cases of disturbance, diet may make a difference. In one double-blind study, researchers asked depressed patients to abstain from refined sugar and caffeine. Over a three-month period, these patients showed significantly more improvement in their symptoms than did another group of patients who refrained from eating red meat and using artificial sweeteners instead (Christensen & Burrows, 1990).

Some of the most exciting work on diet and behavior has looked at the role played by nutrients in the synthesis of neurotransmitters, the brain's chemical messengers. *Tryptophan*, an amino acid found in protein-rich foods (dairy products, meat, fish, and poultry), is a precursor (building block) of serotonin. *Tyrosine*, another amino acid found in proteins, is a precursor of norepinephrine, epinephrine, and dopamine. *Choline*, a component of the lecithin found in egg yolks, soy products, and liver, is a precursor of acetylcholine.

In the case of tryptophan, the path between the dinner plate and the brain is indirect. Tryptophan leads to the production of serotonin, which appears to reduce alertness, promote relaxation, and hasten sleep. Because tryptophan is found in protein, you might think that a high-protein meal would make you drowsy and that carbohydrates (sweets, bread, pasta, potatoes) would leave you relatively alert. Actually, the opposite is true. High-protein foods contain several amino acids, not just tryptophan, and they all compete for a ride on carrier molecules headed for brain cells. Because tryptophan occurs in foods in small quantities, it doesn't stand much of a chance *if* all you eat is protein. It is in the position of a tiny child trying to push aside a crowd of adults for a seat on the subway. Carbohydrates, however, stimulate the production of the hormone insulin, and insulin causes all the other amino acids to be drawn out of the bloodstream while having little effect on tryptophan. So carbohydrates increase the odds that tryptophan will make it to the brain (Wurtman, 1982). Paradoxically, then, a high-carbohydrate, no-protein meal is likely to make you relatively calm or lethargic and a high-protein one is likely to promote alertness, all else being equal (Spring, Chiodo, & Bowen, 1987; Wurtman & Lieberman, 1982–1983).

How else might nutrition affect mental and physical performance? In a report commissioned by the U.S. Army, the National Academy of Sciences reviewed existing animal and human studies on this question (Marriott, 1994). These studies suggest that (1) tyrosine can reduce symptoms that occur in extreme cold and at high altitudes, such as fuzzy thinking, headache, and nausea; (2) carbohydrates can prolong endurance under stressful conditions, increase fine-motor coordination, improve mood, and help people sleep; (3) choline can enhance memory and strengthen muscles and the immune system; and (4) caffeine improves alertness and mental performance (although in high doses it can cause anxiety and insomnia).

We need to keep in mind, though, that many other factors also influence mood and behavior; the effects of nutrients are subtle; and some of these effects depend on a person's age, the circumstances, and the time of day when a meal is eaten. Further, nutrients interact with each other in complex ways. If you don't eat protein, you won't get enough tryptophan, but if you go without carbohydrates, the tryptophan found in protein will be useless. And trying to rev yourself up with too many nutritional supplements can actually be dangerous. The moral of the story: If you're looking for brain food, you are most likely to find it in a well-balanced diet.

SUMMARY

1) The brain is the "bedrock" of consciousness, perception, memory, emotion, and self-awareness.

The Nervous System: A Basic Blueprint

2) The function of the nervous system is to gather and process information, produce responses to stimuli, and coordinate the workings of different cells. Scientists divide it into the *central nervous system (CNS)* and the *peripheral nervous system (PNS)*. The CNS, which includes the brain and spinal cord, receives, processes, interprets, and stores information and sends messages destined for muscles, glands, and organs. The PNS transmits information to and from the CNS by way of sensory and motor nerves.

3) The peripheral nervous system consists of the *somatic nervous system*, which permits sensation and voluntary actions, and the *autonomic nervous system*, which regulates blood vessels, glands, and in-

ternal (visceral) organs. The autonomic system usually functions without conscious control, although some people can learn to heighten or suppress autonomic responses, using *biofeedback* techniques.

4) The autonomic nervous system is divided into the *sympathetic nervous system,* which mobilizes the body for action, and the *parasympathetic nervous system,* which conserves energy.

Communication in the Nervous System

5) *Neurons* are the basic units of the nervous system. Each neuron consists of *dendrites,* a *cell body,* and an *axon.* In the peripheral nervous system, axons (and sometimes dendrites) are collected together in bundles called *nerves.* Many axons are insulated by a *myelin sheath* that speeds up the conduction of neural impulses and prevents signals in adjacent cells from interfering with one another. Recent research has challenged the old assumption that neurons in the human central nervous system cannot be induced to regenerate or multiply.

6) Communication between two neurons occurs at the *synapse.* Many synapses have not yet formed at birth. During development, axons and dendrites continue to grow as a result of both physical maturation and experience with the world, and throughout life, new learning results in new synaptic connections in the brain. Thus, the brain's circuits are not fixed and immutable but are continually changing in response to information, challenges, and changes in the environment.

7) When a wave of electrical voltage (*action potential*) reaches the end of a transmitting axon, *neurotransmitter* molecules are released into the *synaptic cleft.* When these molecules bind to receptor sites on the receiving neuron, that neuron becomes either more or less likely to fire. The message that reaches a final destination depends on how frequently particular neurons are firing, how many are firing, what types are firing, and where they are located.

8) Through their effects on neural circuits, neurotransmitters play a critical role in mood, memory, and psychological well-being. Abnormal levels of neurotransmitters have been implicated in several disorders, including depression, childhood autism, Alzheimer's disease, and Parkinson's disease.

9) *Endorphins,* which act primarily as *neuromodulators* that affect the action of neurotransmit-
ters, reduce pain and promote pleasure. Endorphin levels seem to shoot up when an animal or person is afraid or is under stress. Endorphins may also be linked to the pleasures of social contact.

10) *Hormone* levels affect, and are affected by, the nervous system. Psychologists are especially interested in *melatonin,* which promotes sleep and appears to regulate a "biological clock" that coordinates bodily rhythms; *adrenal hormones* such as *epinephrine* and *norepinephrine,* which are involved in emotions, memory; and stress; and the *sex hormones,* which are involved in the physical changes of puberty, the menstrual cycle (estrogens and progesterone), and sexual arousal (testosterone).

Mapping the Brain

11) Researchers study the brain by observing patients with brain damage; by using the *lesion method* with animals; and by using such techniques as electroencephalograms (*EEGs*), positron emission tomography (*PET scans*), and magnetic resonance imaging (*MRI*).

A Tour Through the Brain

12) All modern brain theories assume *localization of function.* In the lower part of the brain, the *brain stem* controls automatic functions such as heartbeat and breathing, and the *reticular activating system (RAS)* screens incoming information and is responsible for alertness. The *cerebellum* contributes to balance and muscle coordination and may also play a role in some higher mental operations.

13) The *thalamus* directs sensory messages to appropriate higher centers. The *hypothalamus* is involved in emotion and in drives associated with survival, controls the operations of the autonomic nervous system, and sends out chemicals that tell the *pituitary gland* when to "talk" to other endocrine glands.

14) The *limbic system* is involved in emotions that we share with other animals, and it contains pathways involved in pleasure. Within this system, the *amygdala* is responsible for evaluating sensory information and quickly determining its emotional importance, and for the initial decision to approach or withdraw from a person or situation. The *hippocampus* has been called the "gateway to memory" because it plays a critical role in the formation of long-term memories for facts and events.

15) Much of the brain's circuitry is packed into the *cerebrum*, which is divided into two hemispheres and is covered by thin layers of cells known collectively as the *cerebral cortex*. The *occipital, parietal, temporal*, and *frontal lobes* of the cortex have specialized (but partially overlapping) functions. The *association cortex* appears to be responsible for higher mental processes. The frontal lobes, particularly areas in the *prefrontal cortex*, are involved in social judgment, the making and carrying out of plans, and decision making.

The Two Hemispheres of the Brain

16) Studies of split-brain patients, who have had the *corpus callosum* cut, show that the two cerebral hemispheres have somewhat different talents. In most people, language is processed mainly in the left hemisphere, which generally is specialized for logical, symbolic, and sequential tasks. The right hemisphere is associated with spatial–visual tasks, facial recognition, and the creation and appreciation of art and music. In most mental activities, however, the two hemispheres cooperate as partners, with each making a valuable contribution.

Two Stubborn Issues in Brain Research

17) Sleep appears to be necessary not only for bodily restoration but also for normal brain function. During sleep, periods of *rapid eye movement, or REM*, alternate with non-REM sleep. Dreams are reported most often during the REM periods. Freud argued that dreams arise because of unconscious wishes and longings, and many contemporary sleep researchers believe that dreaming provides an opportunity to work through emotional issues. Biological theories, however, emphasize the physiological origins of dreams. For example, the *activation-synthesis theory* holds that dreams occur when the cortex tries to make sense of spontaneous neural firing initiated in the pons.

18) Sex differences have been observed in anatomical and biochemical studies of animal brains. Sex differences in human brains, however, have been more elusive, and there is controversy about their existence and their meaning. Biological differences do not necessarily explain behavioral ones, and sex differences in experience could affect brain organization rather than the other way around.

19) In evaluating research on the brain and behavior, it is important to remember that findings about the brain are most illuminating when they are integrated with psychological and cultural ones.

KEY TERMS

central nervous system   114
spinal cord   114
spinal reflex   114
peripheral nervous system   115
sensory nerves   115
motor nerves   115
somatic nervous system   115
autonomic nervous system   115
biofeedback   116
sympathetic nervous system   116
parasympathetic nervous system   116
neuron   117
glial cells   117

dendrites   118
cell body   118
axon   119
axon terminals   119
myelin sheath   119
nerve   119
synaptic cleft   120
synapse   120
plasticity   120
action potential   121
synaptic vesicles   121
neurotransmitter   121
receptor sites   121
endorphins   123
neuromodulators   123

hormones   124
endocrine glands   124
melatonin   124
adrenal hormones   124
cortisol   124
epinephrine and norepinephrine   124
sex hormones (androgens, estrogens, progesterone)   124
electrodes   125
electroencephalogram (EEG)   126
PET scan   126
magnetic resonance imaging (MRI)   127

LOOKING BACK

- *Why do you automatically pull your hand away from something hot, "without thinking"? (p. 114)*

- *Is it possible to consciously control your heartbeat or blood pressure? (pp. 115–116)*

- *In an emergency, which part of your nervous system whirls into action? (p. 116)*

- *Which nervous-system cells are "communication specialists"—and how do they "talk" to each other? (pp. 117, 120–121)*

- *How do learning and experience alter the brain's circuits? (p. 120)*

- *Why do neural impulses travel more slowly in babies than in adults? (p. 121)*

- *What happens when levels of brain chemicals called neurotransmitters are too low or too high? (p. 122)*

- *Which substances in the brain mimic the effects of morphine by dulling pain and promoting pleasure? (p. 123)*

- *Which hormones can improve your memory? (p. 124)*

- *Why are patterns of electrical activity in the brain called "brain waves"? (p. 126)*

- *What two techniques allow psychologists to view changes in the brain while people listen to music or solve math problems? (pp. 126–127)*

- *Which brain part acts as a "traffic officer" for incoming sensations? (p. 129)*

- *Which brain part is the "gateway to memory"— and what cognitive catastrophe occurs when it is damaged? (p. 130)*

- *Why is it a good thing that the outer covering of the human brain is so wrinkled? (p. 131)*

- *How did a bizarre nineteenth-century accident illuminate the role of the frontal lobes? (p. 133)*

- *If the two cerebral hemispheres were out of touch, would they feel different emotions and think different thoughts? (pp. 135–136)*

- *Why do researchers often refer to the left hemisphere as "dominant"? (p. 137)*

- *Should you sign up for a program that promises to perk up the right side of your brain? (p. 137)*

- *How do biological theories of dreaming differ from the familiar Freudian view? (p. 140)*

- *Do men talk about sports and women about feelings because their brains are different? (p. 142)*

5 Sensation and Perception

PSYCHOLOGY IN THE NEWS

Hundreds of people have traveled to view this shellacked cinnamon bun, said to form a likeness of Mother Teresa.

Mother Teresa's Image in Cinnamon Bun Draws Crowds

NASHVILLE, TENN. MAY 1997. Mother Teresa, the Albanian nun who is famous for her work with the poor and the dying, has asked the Bongo Java coffee shop in Nashville to stop capitalizing on her likeness. Last October, a customer thought he saw Mother Teresa's image in the folds of a cinnamon bun. The shop's owner had the pastry shellacked and enshrined in a counter display; since then, hundreds of people have come to view it, and have bought T-shirts, mugs, prayer cards, and other items inscribed with pictures of the "nun bun." But Mother Teresa, who forbids the commercial use of her name, voice, or image, has personally asked the coffee shop to desist, and for the time being, at least, it is complying. "We're not trying to be martyrs," said the proprietor. "We're just trying to run a little business and have a little fun."

We've all heard stories similar to this one about the late Mother Teresa. Someone "sees" the face of Jesus on an apartment building wall or spots a "spaceship" that turns out to be a weather balloon or military jet. Many of us laugh when we hear such accounts, yet we can all be fooled about the nature of reality. Who has not seen nonexistent water on a hot highway, or heard a nonexistent ring when expecting a phone call, or felt a nonexistent insect on the skin after merely thinking about bugs? In this chapter, we will try to understand these common experiences by exploring how our sense organs take in information from the environment and how the brain uses this information to construct a model of the world—a model that is not always accurate.

Sensation is the detection of physical energy emitted or reflected by physical objects. The cells that do the detecting, called **sense receptors,** are located in the *sense organs*—the eyes, ears, tongue, nose, skin, and internal body tissues. Sensory processes produce an immediate awareness of sound, color, form, and other building blocks of consciousness. They tell us what is happening, both inside our bodies and in the world beyond our own skins. Without sensation, we would lose touch—literally—with reality. Yet sensation alone is not sufficient for making sense

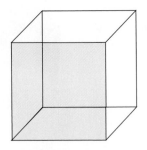

If you stare at this cube, the surface on the outside and front will suddenly be on the inside and back, or vice versa, because your brain can interpret the sensory image in two different ways.

of the world impinging on our senses; for that, we also need **perception,** a set of processes that organize sensory impulses into meaningful patterns. Our sense of vision produces a two-dimensional image on the back of the eye, but we *perceive* the world in three dimensions. Our sense of hearing brings us the sound of a C, an E, and a G played simultaneously on the piano, but we *perceive* a C-major chord.

Psychologists study sensation and perception because these processes are the foundation of learning, thinking, and acting. Research on these topics can often be put to practical use—for example, in the design of hearing aids and of robots that "see," "hear," and "feel"; and in the training of flight controllers, astronauts, and others who must make important decisions based on what they sense and perceive. An understanding of sensation and perception can also enhance our ability to think critically about our own experiences. As you read this chapter, ask yourself why people sometimes perceive things that aren't there, such as a nun's face in a cinnamon bun; and, conversely, why they sometimes miss things that *are* there—looking without seeing, listening without hearing.

What's Ahead

- *What kind of "code" in the nervous system helps explain why a pinprick and a kiss feel different?*

- *Why does your dog hear a "silent" doggie whistle when you can't?*

- *What kind of bias can influence whether you think you hear the phone ringing in the other room?*

- *What happens when people are deprived of all external sensory stimulation?*

OUR SENSATIONAL SENSES

At some point you probably learned that there are five senses, corresponding to five sense organs: vision (eyes), hearing (ears), taste (tongue), touch (skin), and smell (nose). Actually, there are more than five senses, though scientists disagree about the exact number. The skin, which is the organ of touch or pressure, also senses heat, cold, and pain, not to mention itching and tickling. The ear, which is the organ of hearing, also contains receptors that account for a sense of balance. And the skeletal muscles contain receptors responsible for a sense of bodily movement.

All of our senses evolved to help us survive. Even pain, which causes so much human misery, is an indispensable part of our evolutionary heritage, for it alerts us to illness and injury. Sensory experiences also contribute immeasurably to our quality of life, even when they are not directly helping us stay alive. They entertain us, amuse us, soothe us, inspire us. If we really pay attention to our senses, said poet William Wordsworth, we can "see into the life of things" and hear "the still, sad music of humanity."

The Riddle of Separate Sensations

Sensation begins with the sense receptors. When these receptors detect an appropriate stimulus—light, mechanical pressure, or chemical molecules—they convert the energy of the stimulus into electrical impulses that travel along nerves to the brain. Sense receptors are like military scouts who scan the terrain for signs of activity. These scouts cannot make many decisions on their own. They must transmit what they learn to field officers—sensory neurons in the peripheral nervous system. The field officers in turn must report to generals at a command center—the cells of the brain. The generals are responsible for analyzing the reports, combining information brought in by different scouts, and deciding what it all means.

The "field officers" in the sensory system all use exactly the same form of communication: a neural impulse. It is as if they must all send their messages on a bongo drum and can only go "boom." How, then, are we able to experience so many different kinds of sensations? The answer is that the nervous system *encodes* the messages. One kind of code, which is *anatomical,* was first described as far back as A.D. 150 by the Greek physician Galen, and in 1826 the German physiologist Johannes Müller elaborated on it in his *doctrine of specific nerve energies.* According to this doctrine, different sensory modalities (such as vision and hearing) exist because signals received by the sense organs stimulate different nerve pathways leading to different areas of the brain. Signals from the eye cause impulses to travel along the optic nerve to the visual cortex. Signals from the ear cause impulses to travel along the auditory nerve to the

sensation

The detection of physical energy emitted or reflected by physical objects; it occurs when energy in the external environment or the body stimulates receptors in the sense organs.

sense receptors

Specialized cells that convert physical energy in the environment or the body to electrical energy that can be transmitted as nerve impulses to the brain.

perception

The process by which the brain organizes and interprets sensory information.

auditory cortex. Light and sound waves produce different sensations because of these anatomical differences.

The doctrine of specific nerve energies implies that what we know about the world ultimately reduces to what we know about the state of our own nervous system. Therefore, if sound waves could stimulate nerves that end in the visual part of the brain, we would "see" sound. In fact, a similar sort of crossover does occur when you close your right eye, press lightly on the right side of the lid, and "see" a flash of light seemingly coming from the left. The pressure produces an impulse that travels up the optic nerve to the visual area in the right side of the brain, where it is interpreted as coming from the left side of the visual field.

Anatomical encoding, however, does not completely solve the riddle of separate sensations. For one thing, linking the different skin senses to distinct nerve pathways has proven difficult. The doctrine of specific nerve energies also fails to explain variations of experience within a particular sense—the sight of pink versus red, the sound of a piccolo versus the sound of a tuba, or the feel of a pinprick versus the feel of a kiss. An additional kind of code is therefore necessary.

This second kind of code has been called *functional* (Schneider & Tarshis, 1986). Functional codes rely on the fact that sensory receptors and neurons fire, or are inhibited from firing, only in the presence of specific sorts of stimuli. At any particular time, then, some cells in the nervous system are firing, and some are not. Information about *which* cells are firing, *how many* cells are firing, the *rate* at which cells are firing, and the *patterning* of each cell's firing constitutes a functional code. You might think of such a code as the neurological equivalent of the Morse code. Functional encoding may occur all along a sensory route, starting in the sense organs and ending in the brain. As we will see, much remains to be learned about how functional encoding allows us to form an overall perception of an object.

Measuring the Senses

Just how sensitive are our senses? The answer comes from the field of *psychophysics,* which is concerned with how the physical properties of stimuli are related to our psychological experience of them. Drawing on principles from both physics and psychology, psychophysicists have studied how the strength or intensity of a stimulus affects the strength of sensation in an observer.

Absolute Thresholds.   One way to find out how sensitive the senses are is to show people a series of signals that vary in intensity and ask them to say which signals they can detect. The smallest amount of energy that a person can detect reliably is known as the **absolute threshold.** The word *absolute* is a bit misleading because people detect borderline signals on some occasions and miss them on others. "Reliable" detection is said to occur when a person can detect a signal 50 percent of the time.

If you were having your absolute threshold for brightness measured, you might be asked to sit in a dark room and look at a wall or screen. You would then be shown flashes of light, varying in brightness, one flash at a time. Your task would be to say whether you noticed a flash. Some flashes you would never see. Some you would always see. And sometimes you would miss seeing a flash, even though you had noticed one of equal brightness on other trials. Such errors seem to occur in part because of random firing of cells in the nervous system, which produces fluctuating background noise, something like the background noise in a stereo system.

By studying absolute thresholds, psychologists have found that our senses are very sharp indeed. If you have normal sensory abilities, you can see a candle flame on a clear, dark night from 30 miles away. You can hear a ticking watch in a perfectly quiet room from 20 feet away. You can taste a teaspoon of sugar diluted in two gallons of water, smell a drop of perfume diffused through a three-room apartment, and feel the wing of a bee falling on your cheek from a height of 1 centimeter (Galanter, 1962).

Yet despite these impressive sensory skills, our senses are tuned in to only a narrow band of physical energies. For example, we are visually sensitive to only a tiny fraction of all electromagnetic energy; we do not see radio waves or microwaves (see Figure 5.1). Other species can pick up signals that we cannot. Dogs can detect high-frequency sound waves that are beyond our range, as you know if you have ever called your pooch with a "silent" doggie whistle. Bats and porpoises can hear sounds two octaves beyond our range.

Difference Thresholds.   Psychologists also study sensory sensitivity by having people

absolute threshold

The smallest quantity of physical energy that can be reliably detected by an observer.

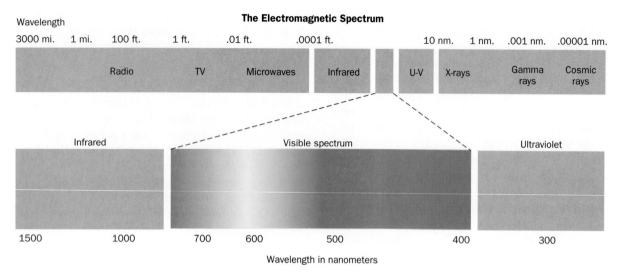

Figure 5.1

Visible Spectrum of Electromagnetic Energy

Our visual system detects only a small fraction of the electromagnetic energy around us.

compare two stimuli and judge whether they are the same or different. A subject might be asked to compare the weight of two blocks, the brightness of two lights, or the saltiness of two liquids. The smallest difference in stimulation that a person can detect reliably (again, half of the time) is called the **difference threshold,** or *just noticeable difference* (jnd). When you compare two stimuli, A and B, the difference threshold will depend on the intensity or size of A. The larger or more intense A is, the greater the change must be before you can detect a difference. If you are comparing the weights of two pebbles, you might be able to detect a difference of only a fraction of an ounce,

but you would not be able to detect such a subtle difference if you were comparing two massive boulders.

In everyday life, we may sometimes think we can detect a difference between stimuli when we can't. For example, many people say they prefer one of the two leading colas to the other, and ads often capitalize on that claim. Years ago, as a class project, undergraduate students at Williams College put cola preference claims to the test. They offered tasters three glasses of cola, two of one leading brand and one of the other (or vice versa), and asked them which drink they liked most and least. Each taster was given three trials. Most of

The flower on the left was photographed in normal light. The one on the right, photographed under ultraviolet light, is what a butterfly might see, because butterflies have ultraviolet receptors. The hundreds of tiny bright spots are nectar sources.

the tasters were inconsistent in their preferences, indicating that they had trouble telling the two brands apart (Solomon, 1979). Apparently, the difference between the two tastes exceeded the students' difference thresholds.

Signal-Detection Theory.

Despite their usefulness, the procedures we have described have a serious limitation. Measurements for any given individual may be affected by the person's general tendency, when uncertain, to respond, "Yes, I noticed a signal (or a difference)" or "No, I didn't notice anything." Some people are habitual yea-sayers, willing to gamble that the signal was really there. Others are habitual naysayers, cautious and conservative. In addition, alertness, motives, and expectations can influence how a person responds on any given occasion. If you are in the shower and you're expecting an important call, you may think you heard the telephone ring when it didn't. In laboratory studies, when observers want to impress the experimenter, they may lean toward a positive response.

Fortunately, these problems of *response bias* are not insurmountable. According to **signal-detection theory,** an observer's response in a detection task can be divided into a *sensory process,* which depends on the intensity of the stimulus, and a *decision process,* which is influenced by the observer's response bias. Methods are available for separating these two components. For example, the researcher can include some trials in which no stimulus is present and others in which a weak stimulus is present. Yea-sayers will have more "hits" than naysayers when a weak stimulus is present, but they will also have more "false alarms" when there is no stimulus. This information can be fed into a mathematical formula that yields separate estimates of a person's response bias and sensory capacity. The individual's true sensitivity to a signal of any particular intensity can then be predicted.

The old method of measuring thresholds assumed that a person's ability to detect a stimulus depended solely on the stimulus. Signal-detection theory assumes that at any given moment, a person's sensitivity to a stimulus depends on a decision that he or she actively makes—that there is no single "threshold." Signal-detection methods have many real-world applications, from screening applicants for jobs requiring keen hearing to training air-traffic controllers, whose decisions about the presence or absence of a blip on a radar screen may mean the difference between life and death.

Sensory Adaptation

Variety, they say, is the spice of life. It is also the essence of sensation, for our senses are designed to respond to change and contrast in the environment (see Figure 5.2). When a stimulus is unchanging or repetitious, sensation often fades or disappears. Receptors or nerve cells higher up in the sensory system get "tired" and fire less frequently. The resulting decline in sensory responsiveness is called **sensory adaptation.** Such adaptation is usually useful because it spares us from having to respond to unimportant information; for example, most of the time you have no need to feel your watch sitting on your wrist. Sometimes, however, adaptation can be hazardous, as when you no longer smell a gas leak that you noticed when you first entered the kitchen.

We never completely adapt to extremely intense stimuli—a terrible toothache, the odor of ammonia, the heat of the desert sun. And we rarely adapt completely to visual stimuli, whether they are weak or intense. Eye movements, voluntary and involuntary, cause the location of an object's image on the back of the eye to keep changing, so that visual receptors don't have a chance to "fatigue." But in the laboratory, researchers can stabilize the image of a simple pattern, such as a line, at a particular point on the back of a person's eye. They use an ingenious device consisting of a

signal-detection theory

A psychophysical theory that divides the detection of a sensory signal into a sensory process and a decision process.

sensory adaptation

The reduction or disappearance of sensory responsiveness that occurs when stimulation is unchanging or repetitious.

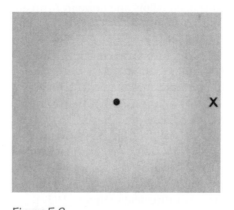 

Figure 5.2

Now You See It, Now You Don't

Sensation depends on change and contrast in the environment. Hold your hand over one eye and stare steadily at the dot in the middle of the circle on the right. You should have no trouble maintaining an image of the circle. However, if you do the same with the circle on the left, the image will fade. The gradual change from light to dark does not provide enough contrast to keep the visual receptors in your eye firing at a steady rate. The circle reappears only if you close and reopen your eye or you shift your gaze to the X.

The effects of sensory deprivation depend on the circumstances. Being isolated against your will can be terrifying, but many people find an hour alone in a flotation tank to be pleasantly relaxing.

tiny projector mounted on a contact lens. Although the eyeball moves, the image of the object stays focused on the same receptors. In minutes, the image begins to disappear.

What would happen if our senses adapted to *most* incoming stimuli? Would we sense nothing, or would the brain substitute its own images for the sensory experiences no longer available by way of the sense organs? In early studies of **sensory deprivation,** researchers studied this question by isolating male volunteers from all patterned sight and sound. Vision was restricted by a translucent visor; hearing by a U-shaped pillow and noise from an air conditioner and fan; and touch by cotton gloves and cardboard cuffs. The volunteers took brief breaks to eat and use the bathroom, but otherwise, they lay in bed, doing nothing. The results were dramatic. Within a few hours, many of the men felt edgy. Some were so disoriented that they quit the study the first day. Those who stayed longer became confused, restless, and grouchy. Many reported bizarre visions, such as a squadron of marching squirrels or a procession of marching eyeglasses. Few were willing to remain in the study for more than two or three days (Heron, 1957).

But the notion that sensory deprivation is unpleasant or even dangerous turned out to be an oversimplification (Suedfeld, 1975). In many of the studies, the experimental procedures themselves probably aroused anxiety: Participants were told about "panic buttons" and were asked to sign "release from legal liability" forms. Later research, using better methods, showed that hallucinations are less dramatic and less disorienting than at first thought. In fact, many people enjoy time-limited periods of deprivation, and some perceptual and intellectual abilities actually improve. The response to sensory deprivation is affected by a person's expectations and interpretations of what is happening. Reduced sensation can be scary if you are locked in a room for an indefinite period, but relaxing if you have retreated to that room voluntarily for a little time out—or if you are paying cash money for a session in a "relaxation chamber."

Still, it is clear that the human brain requires a minimum amount of sensory stimulation in order to function normally. This need may help explain why people who live alone often keep the radio or television set running continuously and why prolonged solitary confinement is used as a form of punishment or even torture.

Sensory Overload

If too little stimulation can be bad for you, so can too much. Excessive stimulation can lead to fatigue and mental confusion. If you have ever felt exhausted, nervous, and headachy after a day crammed with hectic activities—feeling you have too much to do with too little time to do it—you know firsthand about sensory overload.

When people find themselves in a state of overload, they often cope by blocking out unimportant sights and sounds and focusing only on those they find interesting or useful. Psychologists have dubbed this the "cocktail party phenomenon" because at a cocktail party, a person typically focuses on just one conversation, ignoring other voices, the clink of ice cubes, music, and bursts of laughter across the room. The competing sounds all enter the nervous system, enabling the person to pick up anything important—such as the person's own name, spoken by someone several yards away. Unimportant sounds, though, are not fully processed by the brain.

The capacity for **selective attention** protects us in daily life from being overwhelmed by all the sensory signals impinging on our receptors. The brain is not forced to respond to everything the sense receptors send its way. The "generals" in the brain can choose which "field officers" get past the command center's gates. Those that don't seem to have anything important to say are turned back.

sensory deprivation
The absence of normal levels of sensory stimulation.

selective attention
The focusing of attention on selected aspects of the environment and the blocking out of others.

Thinking Critically
About Sensory
Deprivation

??? QUICK QUIZ

If you're not overloaded, try answering these questions.

1. Even on the clearest night, some stars cannot be seen by the naked eye because they are below the viewer's _____ threshold.

2. If you jump into a cold lake, but moments later the water no longer seems so cold, sensory _____ has occurred.

3. If you are immobilized in a hospital bed, with no roommate and no TV or radio, and you feel edgy and disoriented, you may be suffering the effects of _____.

4. During a break from your job as a waiter, you decide to read. For 20 minutes, you are so engrossed that you fail to notice the clattering of dishes or orders being called out to the cook. This is an example of _____.

 5. In real-life detection tasks, is it better to be a "naysayer" or a "yea-sayer"?

Answers:
1. absolute 2. adaptation 3. sensory deprivation 4. selective attention 5. Neither: it depends on the consequences of a "miss," or a "false alarm," and the probability of an event occurring. You might want to be a "yea-sayer" if you're just out the door, you think you hear the phone ringing, and you're expecting a call about a job interview. You might want to be a "naysayer" if you're just out the door, you think you hear the phone, and you're on your way to a job interview and don't want to be late.

What's Ahead

- *How does the eye differ from a camera?*

- *Why can we describe a color as bluish green but not as reddish green?*

- *If you were blind in one eye, why might you misjudge the distance of a painting on the wall but not of buildings a block away?*

- *As a friend approaches, her image on your retina grows larger; then why do you continue to see her as the same size?*

- *Why are perceptual illusions so valuable to psychologists?*

VISION

Vision is the most frequently studied of all the senses, and with good reason. More information about the external world comes to us through our eyes than through any other sense organ. (Perhaps that is why people say "I see what you mean" instead of "I hear what you mean.") Because we are most active in the daytime, we are "wired" to take advantage of the sun's illumination. Animals that are active at night tend to rely more heavily on hearing.

What We See

The stimulus for vision is light; even cats, raccoons, and other creatures famous for their ability to get around in the dark need *some* light to see. Visible light comes from the sun and other stars and from lightbulbs; it is also reflected off objects. Light travels in the form of waves, and the way we see the world is affected by the characteristics of these waves: hue, brightness, and saturation.

1. **Hue,** the dimension of visual experience specified by color names, is related to the *wavelength* of light—that is, to the distance between the crests of a light wave. Shorter waves tend to be seen as violet and blue, and longer ones as orange and red. (We say "tend to" because other factors also affect color perception, as we will see later.) The sun produces white light, a mixture of all the visible wavelengths. Sometimes, drops of moisture in the air act like a prism: They separate the sun's white light into the colors of the visible spectrum, and we are treated to a rainbow.

hue

The dimension of visual experience specified by color names and related to the wavelength of light.

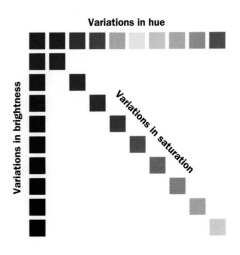

Variations in hue

Variations in brightness

Variations in saturation

2. **Brightness** is the dimension of visual experience related to the amount, or *intensity,* of the light an object emits or reflects. Intensity corresponds to the amplitude (maximum height) of the wave. Generally speaking, the more light an object reflects, the brighter it appears. However, brightness is also affected by wavelength: Yellows appear brighter than reds and blues when physical intensities are actually equal. (For this reason, some fire departments have switched from red engines to yellow ones.)

3. **Saturation** (colorfulness) is the dimension of visual experience related to the *complexity of light*—that is, to how wide or narrow the range of wavelengths is. When light contains only a single wavelength, it is said to be "pure," and the resulting color is said to be completely saturated. At the other extreme is white light, which lacks any color and is completely unsaturated. In nature, pure light is extremely rare. Usually we sense a mixture of wavelengths, and we see colors that are duller and paler than completely saturated ones.

Note that hue, brightness, and saturation are all *psychological* dimensions of visual experience, whereas wavelength, intensity, and complexity are all *physical* properties of the visual stimulus, light.

brightness

Lightness or luminance; the dimension of visual experience related to the amount of light emitted from or reflected by an object.

saturation

Vividness or purity of color; the dimension of visual experience related to the complexity of light waves.

retina

Neural tissue lining the back of the eyeball's interior, which contains the receptors for vision.

An Eye on the World

Light enters the visual system through the eye, a wonderfully complex and delicate structure. As you read this section, examine Figure 5.3. Notice that the front part of the eye is covered by the transparent *cornea.* The cornea protects the eye and bends incoming light rays toward a *lens* located behind it. A camera lens focuses incoming light by moving closer to or farther from the shutter opening. However, the lens of the eye works by subtly changing its shape, becoming more or less curved to focus light from objects that are close by or far away. The amount of light that gets into the eye is controlled by muscles in the *iris,* the part of the eye that gives it color. The iris surrounds the round opening, or *pupil,* of the eye. When you enter a dim room, the pupil widens, or dilates, to let more light in. When you emerge into bright sunlight, the pupil gets smaller, contracting to allow in less light. You can see these changes by watching your eyes in a mirror as you change the lighting.

The visual receptors are located in the back of the eye, or **retina.** In a developing embryo, the retina forms from tissue that projects out from the brain, not from tissue destined to form other parts

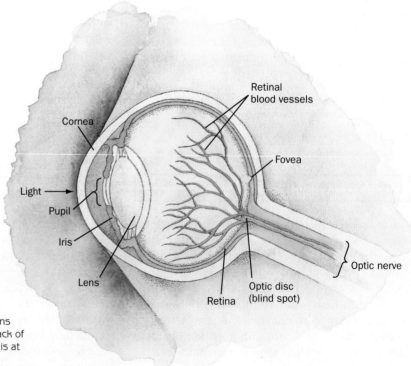

Figure 5.3
Major Structures of the Eye
Light passes through the pupil and lens and is focused on the retina at the back of the eye. The point of sharpest vision is at the fovea.

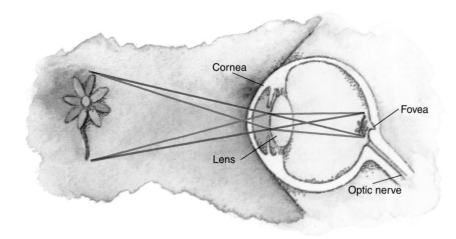

Figure 5.4
The Retinal Image

When we look at an object, the light pattern on the retina is upside down. René Descartes was probably the first person to demonstrate this fact. He cut a piece from the back of an ox's eye and replaced the piece with paper. When he held the eye up to the light, he saw an upside-down image of the room on the paper!

of the eye; thus the retina is actually an extension of the brain. As Figure 5.4 shows, when the lens of the eye focuses light on the retina, the result is an upside-down image (which can actually be seen with an instrument used by eye specialists). Light from the top of the visual field stimulates light-sensitive receptor cells in the bottom part of the retina, and vice versa. The brain interprets this up-side-down pattern of stimulation as something that is right side up.

About 120 to 125 million receptors in the retina are long and narrow and are called **rods.** Another 7 or 8 million receptors are cone-shaped and are called, appropriately enough, **cones.** The center of the retina, or *fovea,* where vision is sharpest, contains only cones, clustered densely together. From the center to the periphery, the ratio of rods to cones increases, and the outer edges contain virtually no cones.

Rods are more sensitive to light than cones are. They enable us to see in dim light and at night. (Cats see well in dim light in part because they have a high proportion of rods.) Because rods occupy the outer edges of the retina, they also handle peripheral (side) vision. That is why you can sometimes see a star from the corner of your eye even though it is invisible to you when you gaze straight at it. But rods cannot distinguish different wavelengths of light and therefore are not sensitive to color. That is why it is often hard to distinguish colors clearly in dim light. The cones, on the other hand, are differentially sensitive to specific wavelengths of light and allow us to see colors. However, the cones need much more light than rods do to respond. Therefore they don't help us much when we are trying to find a seat in a darkened movie theater.

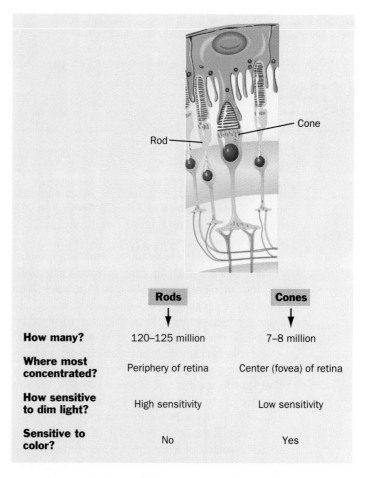

	Rods	Cones
How many?	120–125 million	7–8 million
Where most concentrated?	Periphery of retina	Center (fovea) of retina
How sensitive to dim light?	High sensitivity	Low sensitivity
Sensitive to color?	No	Yes

We have all noticed that it takes some time for our eyes to adjust fully to dim illumination. This process of **dark adaptation** involves chemical changes in the rods and cones, and occurs in two stages. The cones adapt quickly, within 10 minutes or so, but they never become very sensitive to the dim illumination. The rods adapt more slowly, taking 20 minutes or longer, but are

rods

Visual receptors that respond to dim light.

cones

Visual receptors involved in color vision.

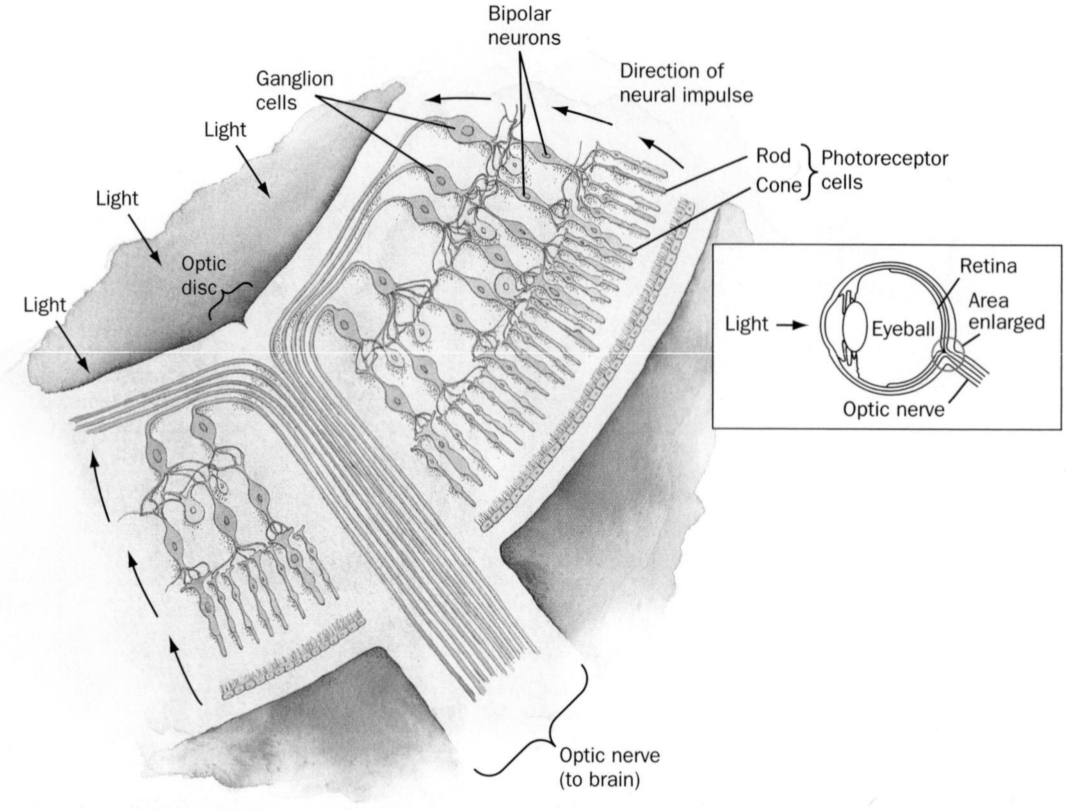

Figure 5.5
The Structures of the Retina
For clarity, all cells in this drawing are greatly exaggerated in size. In order to reach the receptors for vision (the rods and cones), light must pass through the ganglion cells and bipolar neurons as well as the blood vessels that nourish them (not shown). Normally we do not see the shadow cast by this network of cells and blood vessels because the shadow always falls on the same place on the retina, and such stabilized images are not sensed. But when an eye doctor shines a moving light into your eye, the treelike shadow of the blood vessels falls on different regions of the retina and you may see it—a rather eerie experience.

dark adaptation

A process by which visual receptors become maximally sensitive to dim light.

ganglion cells

Neurons in the retina of the eye, which gather information from receptor cells (by way of intermediate bipolar cells); their axons make up the optic nerve.

feature detectors

Cells in the visual cortex that are sensitive to specific features of the environment.

ultimately much more sensitive. After the first phase of adaptation, you can see better but not well; after the second phase, your vision is as good as it will get.

Rods and cones are connected by synapses to *bipolar neurons,* which in turn communicate with neurons called **ganglion cells** (see Figure 5.5). The axons of the ganglion cells converge to form the *optic nerve,* which carries information out through the back of the eye and on to the brain. Where the optic nerve leaves the eye, at the *optic disc,* there are no rods or cones. The absence of receptors produces a blind spot in the field of vision. Normally, we are unaware of the blind spot because (1) the image projected on the spot is hitting a different, "nonblind" spot in the other eye; (2) our eyes move so fast that we can pick up the complete image; and (3) the brain tends to fill in the gap. You can find your blind spot by following the instructions in the Get Involved exercise on the next page.

Why the Visual System Is Not a Camera

Because the eye is often compared with a camera, it is easy to assume that the visual world is made up of a mosaic of dots, as in a photograph. But unlike a camera, the visual system is not a passive recorder of the external world. Instead of simply registering spots of light and dark, neurons in the system build up a picture of the world by detecting its meaningful features.

Ganglion cells and cells in the thalamus of the brain respond to simple features in the environment, such as spots of light and dark. In mammals, special **feature-detector** cells in the visual cortex respond to more complex features. This fact was first demonstrated by David Hubel and Torsten Wiesel (1962, 1968), who painstakingly recorded impulses from individual cells in the brains of cats and monkeys. (In 1981, they received a Nobel Prize for their work.) Hubel and Wiesel found that different neurons were sensitive to different patterns projected on a screen in front of the animal's eyes. Most cells responded maximally to moving or stationary lines that were oriented in a particular direction and located in a particular part of the visual field. One type of cell might fire most rapidly in response to a horizontal line in the lower right part of the visual field, another to a diagonal line at an angle in the upper left part of the visual field. In the real world, such features make up the boundaries and edges of objects.

Get Involved

A blind spot exists where the optic nerve leaves the back of your eye. Find the blind spot in your left eye by closing your right eye and looking at the magician. Then slowly move the book toward and away from yourself. The rabbit should disappear when the book is between 9 and 12 inches from your eye.

Since this pioneering work was done, scientists have found that other cells in the visual system have more complex kinds of specialties. For example, in primates, the visual cortex contains cells that respond maximally to bull's-eyes, spirals, or concentric circles (Gallant, Braun, & Van Essen, 1993), and the temporal lobe contains visual cells that "prefer" a starlike shape (Sáry, Vogels, & Orban, 1993). Even more intriguing, some cells in the temporal lobe respond maximally to *faces* (Desimone, 1991; Young & Yamane, 1992). But no one is sure whether cells that respond to such complex forms are responding to the overall form or to some specific component of it. And to complicate matters further, it is not only the frequency of a cell's firing that provides information to the brain but also the *pattern* or *rhythm* with which it fires (Richmond & Optican, 1990).

The brain's job is to take fragmentary information about lines, angles, shapes, motion, brightness, texture, and other features of what we see, and come up with a unified view of the world. How on earth does it do this? We saw in Chapter 4 that as neurons converge at a synapse, their overall pattern of firing determines whether the neuron on the other side of the synapse is excited or inhibited. The firing (or inhibition) of that neuron, then, actually conveys information to the *next* neuron along the sensory route about what was happening in many other cells. Eventually, a single "hypercomplex" cell in the cortex of the brain may receive information that was originally contained in the firing of thousands of different visual receptors. But most researchers believe that the perception of a visual stimulus ultimately depends not just on the firing of a single hypercomplex cell but on the simultaneous activation of many cells in different parts of the brain, and the overall pattern of firing of these groups of cells. Researchers are now using computer models to try to figure out how this intricate process might take place.

How We See Colors

For 300 years, scientists have been trying to figure out why we see the world in living color. One approach, the **trichromatic theory** (also known as the *Young–Helmholtz theory*), assumed that three mechanisms in the visual system, each especially sensitive to a range of wavelengths, interacted in some way to produce all the different color sensations. Another approach, the **opponent-process theory,** assumed that the visual system treated particular pairs of colors—blue/yellow and red/green—as opposing or antagonistic, which would explain why we can describe a color as bluish green or yellowish green but not as reddish green or yellowish blue. Both views, it turns out, are valid; each explains a different level of processing.

The trichromatic theory applies to the first level of processing, which occurs in the retina. The retina contains three types of cones. One type responds maximally to blue (or more precisely, to a

trichromatic theory

A theory of color perception that proposes three mechanisms in the visual system, each sensitive to a certain range of wavelengths; their interaction is assumed to produce all the different experiences of hue.

opponent-process theory

A theory of color perception that assumes that the visual system treats pairs of colors as opposing or antagonistic.

range of wavelengths near the short end of the spectrum, which give rise to the experience of blue), another to green, and a third to red. The hundreds of colors we see result from the combined activity of these three types of cones.

Total color blindness is usually due to a genetic variation that causes cones of the retina to be absent or malfunctional. The visual world then consists of black, white, and shades of gray. Many animal species are totally color-blind, but the condition is extremely rare in human beings. Most "color-blind" people are actually *color deficient.* Usually, the person is unable to distinguish red and green; the world is painted in shades of blue, yellow, brown, and gray. In rarer instances, a person may be blind to blue and yellow and may see only reds, greens, and grays. Color deficiency is found in about 8 percent of white men, 5 percent of Asian men, and 3 percent of black men and Native American men (Sekuler & Blake, 1994). Because of the way the condition is inherited, it is very rare in women.

The opponent-process theory applies to the second stage of color processing, which occurs in ganglion cells in the retina and in neurons in the thalamus and visual cortex of the brain. These cells, known as *opponent-process cells,* either respond to short wavelengths but are inhibited from firing by long wavelengths, or vice versa (DeValois & DeValois, 1975). Some opponent-process cells respond in opposite fashion to red and green; they fire in response to one and turn off in response to the other. Others respond in opposite fashion to blue and yellow. (A third system responds in opposite fashion to white and black and thus yields information about brightness.) The net result is a color code that is passed along to the higher visual centers.

Opponent-process cells that are *inhibited* by a particular color seem to produce a burst of firing when the color is removed, just as they would if the opposing color were present. Similarly, cells that *fire* in response to a color stop firing when the color is removed, just as they would if the opposing color were present. These facts seem to explain why we are susceptible to *negative afterimages* when we stare at a particular hue—why we see, for instance, red after staring at green (see the Get Involved exercise on this page). A sort of neural rebound effect occurs: The cells that switch on or off to signal the presence of "green" send the opposite signal ("red") when the green is removed—and vice versa.

Unfortunately, two-stage theories do not yet provide a complete explanation of color vision. The perceived color of an object also depends on the wavelengths reflected by *everything around it*—

Get Involved

Opponent-process cells that switch on or off in response to green send an opposite message—"red"—when the green is removed, producing a negative afterimage. Stare at the black dot in the middle of this heart for at least 20 seconds. Then shift your gaze to a white piece of paper or a white wall. Do you get a "change of heart"? You should see an image of a red heart with a blue border.

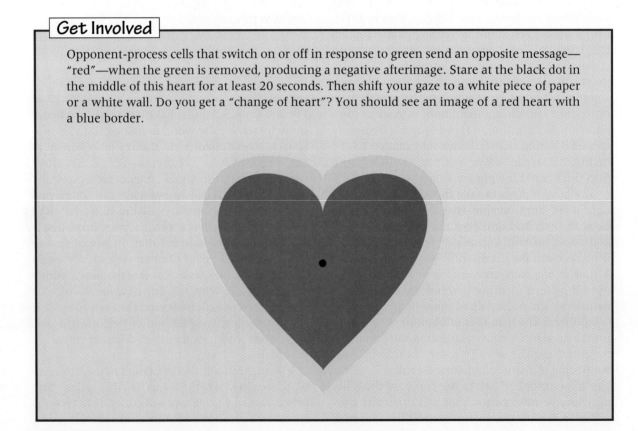

Figure 5.6

Color in Context

The way you perceive a color depends on the colors around it. In this work by Joseph Albers, the adjacent Xs in each pair are actually the same color, but against different backgrounds they look different.

a fact well known to artists and interior designers (see Figure 5.6.) Thus you never see a good, strong red unless other objects in the surroundings reflect the green and blue part of the spectrum. Edwin Land (1959), inventor of the Polaroid camera, worked out precise rules that predict exactly how an object will appear, given the wavelengths reflected by all the objects in a scene. Researchers are now working to understand how the brain uses such information (Brainard, Wandell, & Chichilnisky, 1993).

Constructing the Visual World

We do not see a retinal image; that image is merely grist for the mill of the mind, which actively interprets the image and constructs the world from the often fragmentary data of the senses. In the brain, sensory signals that give rise to vision, hearing, taste, smell, and touch are combined from moment to moment to produce a unified model of the world. This is the process of perception.

Form Perception.   To make sense of the world, we must know where one thing ends and another begins, and we must do this in all our sensory modalities. In vision, we must separate the teacher from the lectern; in hearing, we must separate the piano solo from the orchestral accompaniment; and in taste, we must separate the marsh-

mallow from the hot chocolate. This process of dividing up the world occurs so rapidly and effortlessly that we take it completely for granted—until we must make out objects in a heavy fog or words in the rapid-fire conversation of someone speaking a foreign language.

The *Gestalt psychologists,* who belonged to a movement that began in Germany and was influential in the 1920s and 1930s, were among the first to study how people organize the world visually into meaningful units and patterns. In German, *gestalt* means "pattern" or "configuration." The Gestalt psychologists' motto was "The whole is more than the sum of its parts." They observed that when we perceive something, properties emerge from the whole configuration that are not found in any particular component. When you watch a movie, for example, the motion you "see" is nowhere in the film, which consists of separate static frames projected at 24 frames per second.

The Gestalt psychologists noted that we always organize the visual field into *figure* and *ground*. The figure stands out from the rest of the environment (see Figure 5.7). Some things stand out as figure by virtue of their intensity or size; it is hard to ignore the blinding flash of a camera or a tidal wave approaching your piece of beach. Unique objects also stand out, such as a banana in a bowl of oranges. Moving objects in an otherwise still

Figure 5.7

Figure and Ground

Do you see goblins or angels? The woodcut *Heaven and Hell* by M. C. Escher shows both, depending on whether you see the black or white sections as figure or ground.

environment, such as a shooting star, will usually be seen as figure. Indeed, it is hard to ignore a sudden change of any kind in the environment because our brains are geared to respond to change and contrast. However, selective attention, the ability to concentrate on some stimuli and to filter out others, gives us some control over what we perceive as figure and ground.

Here are some other *Gestalt principles* that the visual system uses to group sensory building blocks into perceptual units:

1. *Proximity*. Things that are near each other tend to be grouped together. Thus you perceive the dots on the left as two groups of dots, not as 8 separate, unrelated ones. Similarly, you perceive the pattern on the right as vertical columns of dots, not as horizontal rows:

2. *Closure*. The brain tends to fill in gaps in order to perceive complete forms. This is fortunate because we often need to decipher less than perfect images. The following figures are easily perceived as a triangle, a face, and the letter e, even though none of the figures is complete:

3. *Similarity*. Things that are alike in some way (for example, in color, shape, or size) tend to be perceived as belonging together. In the figure on the left, you see the circles as forming an *x*. In the one on the right, you see horizontal bars rather than vertical columns because the horizontally aligned stars share the same color:

4. *Continuity*. Lines and patterns tend to be perceived as continuing in time or space. You perceive the figure on the left as a single line partially cov-

ered by an oval rather than as two separate lines touching an oval. In the figure on the right, you see two lines, one curved and one straight, instead of two curved and two straight lines, touching at one focal point:

Consumer products are sometimes designed with little thought for visual principles such as those formulated by the Gestalt psychologists, which is why it can be a major challenge to figure out how to use a new camera or VCR (Norman, 1988). Good design requires, among other things, that crucial distinctions be visually obvious. For instance, knobs and switches with different functions should differ in color, texture, or shape, and they should stand out as "figure." But on many VCRs, it is hard to tell the rewind button from the fast-forward button!

Depth and Distance Perception.　Ordinarily we need to know not only what something is, but also where it is. Touch gives us this information directly, but vision does not, so we must *infer* an object's location by estimating its distance or depth.

To perform this remarkable feat, we rely in part on **binocular cues**—cues that require the use of two eyes. One is **convergence,** the turning of the eyes inward, which occurs when they focus on a nearby object. The closer the object, the greater the convergence (as you know if you have ever tried to appear "cross-eyed" by looking at your own nose). As the angle of convergence changes, the corresponding muscular changes provide information to the brain about distance.

The two eyes also receive slightly different retinal images of the same object. You can easily prove this by holding a finger about 12 inches in front of your face and looking at it with only one eye at a time. Its position will appear to shift when you change eyes. Now hold up two fingers, one closer to your nose than the other. Notice that the amount of space between the two fingers appears to change when you switch eyes. The slight difference in lateral (sideways) separation between two objects as seen by the left eye and the right eye is called **retinal disparity.** Because retinal disparity increases as the distance between two objects increases, the brain can use this disparity to infer depth and calculate distance.

Binocular cues help us estimate distances up to about 50 feet. For objects farther away, we only

---

binocular cues

Visual cues to depth or distance requiring two eyes.

convergence

The turning inward of the eyes, which occurs when they focus on a nearby object.

retinal disparity

The slight difference in lateral separation between two objects as seen by the left eye and the right eye.

use **monocular cues,** cues that do not depend on using both eyes. One such cue is *interposition:* When an object is interposed between the viewer and a second object, partly blocking the view of the second object, the first object is perceived as being closer. Another monocular cue is *linear per-*

spective: When two lines known to be parallel appear to be coming together or converging, they imply the existence of depth. For example, if you are standing between railroad tracks, they appear to converge in the distance. These and other monocular cues are illustrated in Figure 5.8.

monocular cues

Visual cues to depth or distance, which can be used by one eye alone.

(a)   (b)   (c)

(d)   (e)   (f)

Figure 5.8
Monocular Cues to Depth

Most cues to depth do not depend on having two eyes. Some monocular (one-eyed) cues are:
(a) **Interposition** (partial overlap). An object that partly blocks or obscures another one must be in front of the other one and is therefore seen as closer. (b) **Motion parallax.** When an observer is moving, objects appear to move at different speeds and in different directions. The closer an object, the faster it seems to move; and close objects appear to move backward, whereas distant ones seem to move forward. (c) **Light and shadow.** Both attributes give objects the appearance of three dimensions.
(d) **Relative size.** The smaller an object's image on the retina, the farther away the object appears.
(e) **Relative clarity.** Because of particles in the air—from dust, fog, or smog—distant objects tend to look hazier, duller, or less detailed. (f) **Texture gradients.** Distant parts of a uniform surface appear denser; that is, its elements seem spaced more closely together. (g) **Linear perspective.** Parallel lines will appear to be converging in the distance; the greater the apparent convergence, the greater the perceived distance—a cue often exaggerated by artists to convey an impression of depth.

(g)

Visual Constancies: When Seeing Is Believing.
You might be able to see what things are and
where they are, but your perceptual world would
be a confusing place without another important
perceptual skill. Lighting conditions, viewing angles, and the distances of stationary objects are all
continually changing as we move about, yet we
rarely confuse these changes with changes in the
objects themselves. This ability to perceive objects
as stable or unchanging even though the sensory
patterns they produce are constantly shifting is
called **perceptual constancy.** The best-studied
constancies are visual, and they include the following:

1. *Shape constancy.* We continue to perceive objects as having a constant shape even though the
shape of the retinal image produced by an object
changes when our point of view changes. If you
hold a Frisbee directly in front of your face, its image on the retina will be round. When you set the
Frisbee on a table, its image becomes elliptical, yet
you continue to identify the Frisbee as round.

2. *Location constancy.* We perceive stationary objects as remaining in the same place, even though
the retinal image moves about as we move our
eyes, heads, and bodies. As you drive along the
highway, telephone poles and trees fly by—on
your retina. But you know that objects such as
telephone poles and trees move by themselves
only in cartoons, and you also know that your
body is moving, so you perceive the poles and
trees as staying put.

3. *Size constancy.* We continue to see an object as
having a constant size even when its retinal image
becomes smaller or larger. A friend approaching
on the street does not seem to be growing; a car
pulling away from the curb does not seem to be
shrinking. Size constancy depends in part on familiarity with objects. You *know* people and cars
don't change size just like that. It also depends on
the apparent distance of an object. When you
move your hand toward your face, your brain registers the fact that the hand is getting closer, and
you correctly perceive its unchanging size. There
is, then, an intimate relationship between perceived size and perceived distance.

4. *Brightness constancy.* We continue to see objects as having a relatively constant brightness,
even though the amount of light they reflect
changes as the overall level of illumination
changes. Snow remains white even on a cloudy
day. In fact, it is possible for a black object in
strong sunlight to reflect more light than a white

BIZARRO   By DAN PIRARO

When size constancy fails.

object in the shade. We are not fooled, though,
because the brain registers the total illumination
in the scene, and we automatically take this information into account in the perception of any particular object's brightness.

5. *Color constancy.* We see an object as maintaining its hue despite the fact that the wavelength of
light reaching our eyes from the object may
change somewhat as the illumination changes.
For example, outdoor light is "bluer" than indoor
light, and objects outdoors therefore reflect more
"blue" light than those indoors. Conversely, indoor light from a lamp is rich in long wavelengths
and is therefore "yellower." Yet objects usually
look the same color in both places. The explanation involves sensory adaptation, which we discussed earlier. Outdoors, we quickly adapt to
short-wavelength (bluish) light, and indoors, we
adapt to long-wavelength light. As a result, our visual responses are similar in the two situations.
Also, as we saw earlier, the brain takes into account all the wavelengths in the visual field when
computing the color of a particular object. If a
lemon is bathed in bluish light, so, usually, is
everything else around it. The increase in blue
light reflected by the lemon is "canceled" in the visual cortex by the increase in blue light reflected

perceptual constancy
The accurate perception of
objects as stable or unchanged
despite changes in the sensory
patterns they produce.

by the lemon's surroundings, and so the lemon continues to look yellow.

Visual Illusions: When Seeing Is Misleading.

Perceptual constancies allow us to make sense of the world. Occasionally, however, we can be fooled, and the result is a **perceptual illusion.** For psychologists, illusions are valuable because they are *systematic* errors that provide us with hints about the perceptual strategies of the mind.

Although illusions can occur in any sensory modality, visual illusions have been studied more than other kinds. Visual illusions sometimes occur when the strategies that normally lead to accurate perception are overextended to situations where they don't apply. Compare the lengths of these two lines:

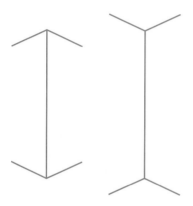

If you are like most people, you perceive the line on the right as slightly longer than the one on the left. Yet if you measure the lines, you will find that they are exactly the same length. This is the Müller–Lyer illusion, named after the German sociologist who first described it in 1889.

One explanation for the Müller–Lyer illusion is that the figures contain perspective cues that normally suggest depth (Gregory, 1963). The line on the left is like the near edge of a building; the one on the right is like the far corner of a room, as in the drawing that follows this paragraph. Although the two lines produce the same-size retinal image, the one with the outward-facing branches suggests greater distance. We are fooled into perceiving it as longer because we automatically apply a rule about the relationship between size and distance that is normally very useful: When two objects produce the same-size retinal image and one is farther away, the farther one is larger. The problem, in this case, is that there is no actual differ-

ence in the distance of the two lines, so the rule is inappropriate.

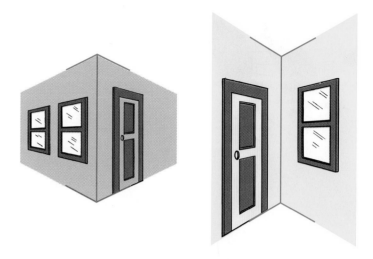

Just as there are size, shape, location, brightness, and color constancies, so there are size, shape, location, brightness, and color illusions. Some illusions are simply a matter of physics. Thus a chopstick in a half-filled glass of water looks bent because water and air refract light differently. Other illusions occur due to misleading messages from the sense organs, as in sensory adaptation. Still others, like the Müller–Lyer illusion, seem to occur because the brain misinterprets sensory information. Figure 5.9 on the following page shows other startling illusions.

In everyday life, most illusions are harmless, or even useful or entertaining. Occasionally, however, an illusion interferes with the normal performance of some skill. In baseball, two types of pitches that drive batters batty are the rising fastball, in which the ball seems to jump a few inches when it reaches home plate, and the breaking curveball, in which the ball seems to loop toward the batter and then plummet at the last moment. Both of these pitches are physical impossibilities; according to one explanation, they are illusions that occur when batters misestimate a ball's speed and momentarily shift their gaze to where they think it will cross home plate (Bahill & Karnavas, 1993). Illusions may also lead to industrial and automobile accidents. For example, because large objects often appear to move more slowly than small ones, drivers sometimes underestimate the speed of onrushing trains at railroad crossings and think they can "beat" the train, with tragic results.

perceptual illusion
An erroneous or misleading perception of reality.

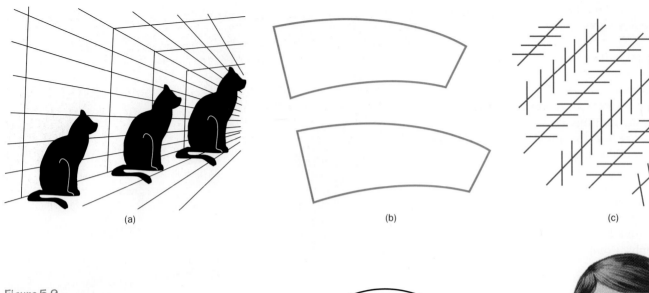

(a)   (b)   (c)

Figure 5.9

Some Visual Illusions

Although perception is usually accurate, we can be fooled. In (a) the cats as drawn are all the same size; in (b) the two figures are the same size; in (c) the diagonal lines are all parallel; and in (d) the sides of the square are all straight. To see the illusion depicted in (e), hold your index fingers 5 to 10 inches in front of your eyes as shown, then focus straight ahead. Do you see a floating "fingertip frankfurter"? Can you make it shrink or expand? Why does this illusion occur?

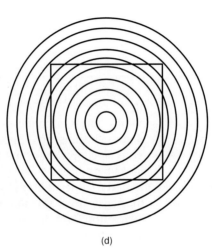

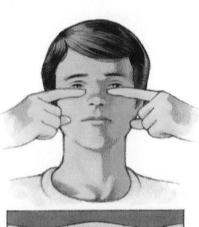

(d)   (e)

??? QUICK QUIZ

Can you accurately perceive these questions?

1. How can two Gestalt principles help explain why you can make out the Big Dipper on a starry night?

2. *True or false:* Binocular cues help us locate objects that are very far away.

3. Hold one hand about 12 inches from your face and the other one about 6 inches away. (a) Which hand will cast the smaller retinal image? (b) Why don't you perceive that hand as smaller?

Answers:

1. *Proximity* of certain stars encourages you to see them as clustered together to form a pattern; *closure* allows you to "fill in the gaps" and see the contours of a "dipper."   2. false   3. a. The hand that is 12 inches away will cast a smaller retinal image.   b. Your brain takes the differences in distance into account in estimating size; also, you know how large your hands are.

- *Why does a note played on a flute sound different from the same note on an oboe?*
- *If you habitually listen to loud music through headphones, what kind of hearing impairment are you risking?*
- *To locate the source of a sound, why does it sometimes help to turn or tilt your head?*

HEARING

Like vision, the sense of hearing, or *audition,* provides a vital link with the world around us. When people lose their hearing, they sometimes come to feel socially isolated because social relationships rely so heavily on hearing others. That is why many hearing-impaired people feel strongly about teaching deaf children American Sign Language (ASL), which allows them to communicate normally with and forge close relationships with other signers.

What We Hear

The stimulus for sound is a wave of pressure created when an object vibrates (or, sometimes, when compressed air is released, as in a pipe organ). The vibration (or release of air) causes molecules in a transmitting substance to move together and apart. This movement produces variations in pressure that radiate in all directions. The transmitting substance is usually air, but sound waves can also travel through water and solids, as you know if you have ever put your ear to the wall to hear voices in the next room.

As with vision, psychological aspects of our auditory experience are related in a predictable way to physical characteristics of the stimulus—in this case, a sound wave:

1. **Loudness** is the dimension of auditory experience related to the *intensity* of a wave's pressure. Intensity corresponds to the amplitude, or maximum height, of the wave. The more energy contained in the wave, the higher it is at its peak. Perceived loudness is also affected by how high or low a sound is. If low and high sounds produce waves with equal amplitudes, the low sound may seem quieter.

Sound intensity is measured in units called *decibels* (dB). A decibel is one-tenth of a *bel,* a unit named for Alexander Graham Bell, the inventor of the telephone. The average absolute threshold of hearing in human beings is zero decibels. Decibels are not equally distant, as inches on a ruler are. A 60-decibel sound (such as that of a sewing machine) is not 50 percent louder than a 40-decibel sound (such as that of a whisper); it is 100 times louder. Table 5.1 on the next page shows the intensity in decibels of some common sounds.

2. **Pitch** is the dimension of auditory experience related to the frequency of the sound wave and, to some extent, its intensity. *Frequency* refers to how rapidly the air (or other medium) vibrates—that is, the number of times per second the wave cycles through a peak and a low point. One cycle per second is known as 1 *hertz* (Hz). The healthy ear of a young person normally detects frequencies in the range of 16 Hz (the lowest note on a pipe organ) to 20,000 Hz (the scraping of a grasshopper's legs).

3. **Timbre** is the distinguishing quality of a sound. It is the dimension of auditory experience related to the *complexity* of the sound wave—to the relative breadth of the range of frequencies that make up the wave. A pure tone consists of only one frequency, but in nature, pure tones are extremely rare. Usually what we hear is a complex wave consisting of several subwaves with different frequencies. A particular combination of frequencies results in a particular timbre. Timbre is what makes a note played on a flute, which produces relatively pure tones, sound different from the same note played on an oboe, which produces very complex sounds.

When many frequencies are present but are not in harmony, we hear noise. When all the frequencies of the sound spectrum occur, they produce a hissing sound called *white noise.* White noise is named by analogy to white light. Just as white light includes all wavelengths of the visible light spectrum, so white noise includes all frequencies of the sound spectrum.

An Ear on the World

As Figure 5.10 on page 169 shows, the ear has an outer, a middle, and an inner section. The soft, funnel-shaped outer ear is well designed to collect sound waves, but hearing would still be quite good without it. The essential parts of the ear are hidden from view, inside the head.

A sound wave passes into the outer ear and through an inch-long canal to strike an oval-shaped membrane called the *eardrum.* The eardrum is so

loudness
The dimension of auditory experience related to the intensity of a pressure wave.

pitch
The dimension of auditory experience related to the frequency of a pressure wave; height or depth of a tone.

timbre
The distinguishing quality of a sound; the dimension of auditory experience related to the complexity of the pressure wave.

Table 5.1	**Sound Intensity Levels in the Environment**

The following decibel levels apply at typical working distances. Each ten-point increase on the decible scale represents a tenfold increase in sound intensity over the previous level. Even some everyday noises can be hazardous to hearing if exposure goes on for too long a time.

Typical Level (Decibels)	Examples	Dangerous Time Exposure
0	Lowest sound audible to human ear	
30	Quiet library, soft whisper	
40	Quiet office, living room, bedroom away from traffic	
50	Light traffic at a distance, refrigerator, gentle breeze	
60	Air conditioner at 20 feet, conversation, sewing machine	
70	Busy traffic, noisy restaurant (constant exposure)	Critical level begins
80	Subway, heavy city traffic, alarm clock at 2 feet, factory noise	More than 8 hours
90	Truck traffic, noisy home appliances, shop tools, lawn mower	Less than 8 hours
100	Chain saw, boiler shop, pneumatic drill	Less than 2 hours
120	Rock concert in front of speakers, sandblasting, thunderclap	Immediate danger
140	Gunshot blast, jet plane at 50 feet	Any length of exposure time is dangerous
180	Rocket launching pad	Hearing loss inevitable

Source: Reprinted with permission from the American Academy of Otolaryngology—Head and Neck Surgery, Washington, D.C.

sensitive that it can respond to the movement of a single molecule! A sound wave causes it to vibrate with the same frequency and amplitude as the wave itself. This vibration is passed along to three tiny bones in the middle ear, the smallest bones in the human body. These bones, known informally as the "hammer," the "anvil," and the "stirrup," move one after the other, which has the effect of intensifying the force of the vibration. The innermost bone, the stirrup, pushes on a membrane that opens into the inner ear.

The actual organ of hearing, the *organ of Corti,* is a chamber inside the **cochlea,** a snail-shaped structure within the inner ear. The organ of Corti plays the same role in hearing that the retina plays in vision. It contains the all-important receptor cells, which in this case look like bristles and are called hair cells, or *cilia.* Exposure to extremely loud noise for a brief period, or more moderate levels of noise for a sustained period, can damage these fragile cells (see Table 5.1). They flop over, like broken blades of grass, and if the damage reaches a critical point, hearing loss occurs. In our society, with its ubiquitous office machines, automobiles, power saws, leaf blowers, jackhammers, and stereos (often played at full blast and listened to through headphones), such impairment is common. Many college students already have impaired hearing because of damage to the cilia.

The hair cells of the cochlea are embedded in the rubbery *basilar membrane,* which stretches across the interior of the cochlea. When pressure reaches the cochlea, it causes wavelike motions in fluid within the cochlea's interior. These motions push on the basilar membrane, causing it to move in a wavelike motion, too. Just above the hair cells is yet another membrane. As the hair cells rise and fall, their tips brush against it, and they bend. This

cochlea (KOCK-lee-uh)

A snail-shaped, fluid-filled organ in the inner ear, containing the receptors for hearing.

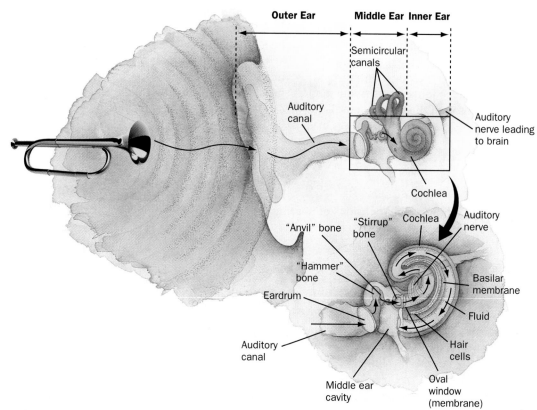

Outer Ear **Middle Ear** **Inner Ear**

Semicircular canals

Auditory canal

Auditory nerve leading to brain

Cochlea

Cochlea

"Anvil" bone

"Stirrup" bone

Auditory nerve

"Hammer" bone

Basilar membrane

Eardrum

Fluid

Auditory canal

Hair cells

Middle ear cavity

Oval window (membrane)

Figure 5.10

Major Structures of the Ear

Sound waves collected by the outer ear are channeled down the auditory canal, causing the eardrum to vibrate. These vibrations are then passed along to the tiny bones of the middle ear. Movement of these bones intensifies the force of the vibrations and funnels them to a small membrane separating the middle and inner ear. The receptor cells for hearing (hair cells), located in a small organ within the snail-shaped cochlea, initiate nerve impulses that travel along the auditory nerve to the brain.

causes the hair cells to initiate a signal that is passed along to the *auditory nerve*, which then carries the message to the brain. The particular pattern of hair-cell movement is affected by the manner in which the basilar membrane moves. This pattern determines which neurons fire and how rapidly they fire, and the resulting code in turn determines the sort of sound we hear. For example, we discriminate high-pitched sounds largely on the basis of where activity occurs along the basilar membrane; activity at different sites leads to different neural codes. We discriminate low-pitched sounds largely on the basis of the frequency of the basilar membrane's vibration; again, different frequencies lead to different neural codes.

Could anyone ever imagine such a complex and odd arrangement of bristles, fluids, and snail shells if it didn't already exist?

Constructing the Auditory World

Just as we do not see a retinal image, so we do not hear a chorus of brushlike tufts bending and swaying in the dark recesses of the cochlea. Just as we do not see a jumbled collection of lines and colors, so we do not hear a disconnected cacophony of pitches and timbres. Instead, we use our perceptual powers to organize patterns of sound and to construct a meaningful auditory world.

For example, in class, your psychology instructor hopes you will perceive his or her voice as *figure* and the hum of a passing airplane, cheers from the athletic field, or distant sounds of a construction crew as *ground*. Whether these hopes are realized will depend, of course, on where you choose to direct your attention. Other Gestalt principles also seem to apply to hearing. The *proximity* of notes in a melody tells you which notes go together to form phrases; *continuity* helps you follow a melody on one violin when another violin is playing a different melody; *similarity* in timbre and pitch helps you pick out the soprano voices in a chorus and hear them as a unit; *closure* helps you understand a radio announcer's words even when static makes some of the individual sounds unintelligible.

Besides needing to organize sounds, we also need to know where they are coming from. We can estimate the *distance* of a sound's source by using loudness as a cue. For example, we know that a train sounds louder when it is 20 yards away than when it is a mile off. To locate the *direction* a sound is coming from, we depend in part on the fact that we have two ears. A sound arriving from the right reaches the right ear a fraction of a second sooner than it reaches the left ear, and vice versa. The sound may also provide a bit more energy to the right ear (depending on its frequency) because it has to get around the head to reach the left ear. Localizing sounds that are coming from directly in back of you or from directly above your head is hard because such sounds reach both ears at the same time. When you turn or cock your head, you are actively trying to overcome this problem. Many animals don't have to do this; they can move their ears independently of their heads.

??? QUICK QUIZ

How well can you detect the answers to these questions on hearing?

1. Which psychological dimensions of hearing correspond to the intensity, frequency, and complexity of the sound wave?

2. Willie Nelson has a nasal voice, and Ray Charles has a gravelly voice. Which psychological dimension of hearing describes the difference?

3. An extremely loud or sustained noise can permanently damage the _____ of the ear.

4. During a lecture, a classmate draws your attention to a buzzing fluorescent light that you had not previously noticed. What will happen to your perception of figure and ground?

Answers:

1. loudness, pitch, timbre   2. timbre   3. hair cells (cilia)   4. The buzzing sound will become figure and the lecturer's voice will become ground, at least momentarily.

What's Ahead

- *Why do saccharin and caffeine taste bitter to some people but not to others?*

- *Why do you have trouble tasting your food when you have a cold?*

- *Why do people often continue to "feel" limbs that have been amputated?*

OTHER SENSES

Psychologists have been particularly interested in vision and audition because of the importance of these senses to human survival. However, research on the other senses is growing dramatically, as awareness of how they contribute to our lives increases and new ways are found to study them.

Taste: Savory Sensations

Taste, or *gustation*, occurs because chemicals stimulate thousands of receptors in the mouth. These receptors are located primarily on the tongue, but some are also found in the throat, inside the cheeks, and on the roof of the mouth. If you look at your tongue in a mirror, you will notice many tiny bumps; they are called **papillae** (from the Latin for "pimple"), and they come in several forms. In all but one form, **taste buds** line the sides of each papilla (see Figure 5.11). The buds, which up close look a little like a segmented orange, are commonly referred to, mistakenly, as the receptors for taste. The actual receptor cells are *inside* the buds, 15 to 50 to a bud. These cells send tiny fibers out through an opening in the bud; the receptor sites are on these fibers. The receptor cells are replaced by new cells about every 10 days. However, after age 40 or so, the total number of taste buds (and therefore receptors) declines, which is probably why older people can often enjoy strong tastes that children may detest.

There appear to be four basic tastes: *salty, sour, bitter,* and *sweet,* each produced by a different type of chemical. Until recently, most textbooks included a "tongue map," showing areas supposedly most sensitive to these tastes. But then physiological psychologist Linda Bartoshuk (1993) found

---

papillae (pa-PILL-ee)
Knoblike elevations on the tongue, containing the taste buds. (Singular: *papilla.*)

taste buds
Nests of taste-receptor cells.

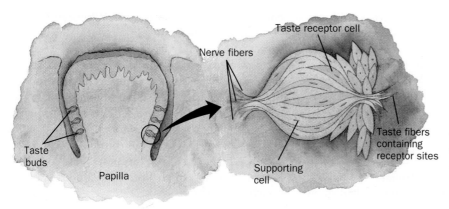

Figure 5.11
Taste Receptors

The illustration on the left shows taste buds lining the sides of a papilla on the tongue's surface. The illustration on the right shows an enlarged view of a single taste bud.

that the map was based on a misleading graph published in 1942—and it was simply wrong. The four basic tastes can be perceived at any spot on the tongue that has receptors, and differences among the areas are small. Interestingly, the center of the tongue contains no taste buds, and so it cannot produce *any* sort of taste sensation. But you will not usually notice the lack of sensation because the brain fills in the gap.

When you bite into an egg or a piece of bread or an orange, its unique flavor is composed of some combination of the four basic taste types. The physiological details, however, are still not well understood. For example, it is not clear whether the four tastes are really points on a continuum, as colors are, or are distinct and are associated with different types of nerve fibers.

Some taste preferences, such as a liking for sweets, are universal, a part of our evolutionary heritage (Bartoshuk & Beauchamp, 1994). Others are a matter of culture. For example, many North Americans who enjoy raw oysters, raw smoked salmon, and raw herring are nevertheless put off by other forms of raw seafood that are popular in Japan, such as sea urchin and octopus. Individual tastes also vary; within a given culture, some people will greedily gobble up a dish that makes others turn green. These differences are due in part to learning (see Chapter 7). But they are also related to genetic differences in the density of taste buds; human tongues can have as few as 500 or as many as 10,000 taste buds (Miller & Reedy, 1990).

Genetic differences make people more or less sensitive to the chemicals in particular foods (Bartoshuk, 1993). For example, some people experience a bitter taste from saccharin, caffeine, and other substances, but others do not. People who are "supertasters" for bitter substances have more taste buds than do "nontasters," who are less sensitive to such substances. Further, in supertasters, papillae

of a certain type are smaller, are more densely packed, and look different than those in nontasters (Anliker et al., 1991; Reedy et al., 1993).

The attractiveness of a food can also be affected by its temperature and texture. As Goldilocks found out, a bowl of cold porridge isn't nearly as delicious as one that is properly heated. And any peanut butter fan will tell you that chunky and smooth peanut butters just don't taste the same. Even more important for taste is a food's odor (see Figure 5.12). Subtle flavors such as chocolate and

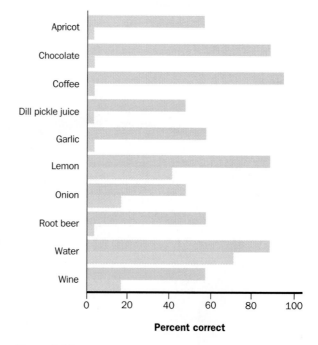

Percent correct

Figure 5.12
Taste Test

The beige bars show the percentages of people who could identify a substance dropped on the tongue when they were able to smell it. The purple bars show the percentages who could identify a substance when they were prevented from smelling it. (From Mozell et al., 1969.)

vanilla would have little taste if we could not smell them. The dependence of taste on smell explains why you have trouble tasting your food when you have a stuffy nose. Most people who chronically have trouble tasting things have a problem with smell, not taste per se.

Smell: The Sense of Scents

The great author and educator Helen Keller, who was blind and deaf from infancy, once called smell "the fallen angel of the senses." Yet our sense of smell, or *olfaction*, although seemingly crude when compared to a bloodhound's, is actually quite good—and more useful than most people realize. People can detect thousands of odors. And they can smell some substances before odor-sensitive machines detect them, which is why human beings are often hired to detect odors in chemical plants and laboratories and to detect the freshness of fish at fish markets.

The receptors for smell are specialized neurons embedded in a tiny patch of mucous membrane in the upper part of the nasal passage, just beneath the eyes (see Figure 5.13). These receptors, about 5 million of them in each nasal cavity, respond to chemical molecules in the air. When you inhale, you pull these molecules into the nasal cavity, but they can also enter from the mouth, wafting up the throat like smoke up a chimney. Somehow, these molecules trigger responses in the receptors that combine to yield the yeasty smell of freshly baked bread or the spicy fragrance of a eucalyptus tree. Signals from the receptors are carried to the brain's olfactory bulb by the olfactory nerve, which is made up of the receptors' axons. But the neural code for smell, like that for taste, is still poorly understood.

One complicating factor in the study of olfaction is that so many words exist for describing smells (rotten, burned, musky, fruity, spicy, flowery, resinous, putrid, . . .), and researchers do not agree on which smells, if any, are basic. Also, as many as a *thousand* receptor types may exist (Buck & Axel, 1991). This kind of system is quite unlike the one involved in vision, where only three basic receptor cell types are involved, or the one involved in taste, where there seem to be four basic types.

Although smell is less vital for human survival than for the survival of other animals, it is still important. We sniff out danger by smelling smoke, food spoilage, or poison gases. Thus, a deficit in

Figure 5.13

Receptors for Smell

Airborne chemical molecules (vapors) enter the nose and circulate through the nasal cavity, where the smell receptors are located. The receptors' axons make up the olfactory nerve, which carries signals to the brain. When you sniff, you draw more vapors into the nose and speed their circulation. Vapors can also reach the nasal cavity through the mouth by way of a passageway from the throat.

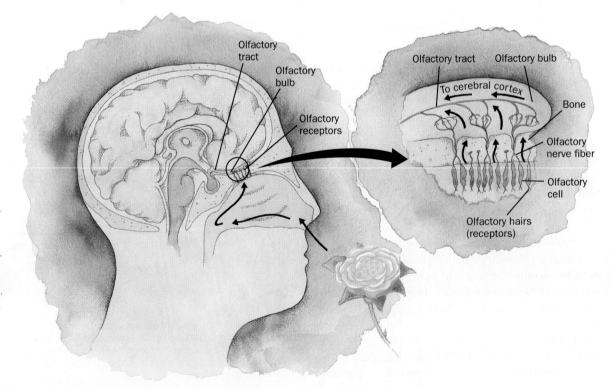

the sense of smell is nothing to turn up your nose at. Such a loss can come about because of infection or disease, or because of cigarette or pipe smoking. In one study in which people took a whiff of 40 common odors, such as pizza, motor oil, and banana, smokers were nearly twice as likely as nonsmokers to show impaired ability. The researchers also found that a person who has smoked two packs a day for 10 years must abstain from cigarettes for 10 more years before odor detection will return to normal (Frye, Schwartz, & Doty, 1990).

Human odor preferences, like taste preferences, vary. In some societies, people use rancid fat as a hair pomade, but anyone in North America who did so would quickly have a social problem. Within a particular culture, context and experience are all-important. The very same chemicals that contribute to unpleasant body odors and bad breath also contribute to the pleasant bouquet and flavor of cheese.

Senses of the Skin

The skin's usefulness is more than just skin deep. Besides protecting our innards, our 2 square yards of skin help us identify objects and establish intimacy with others. By providing a boundary between ourselves and everything else, the skin also gives us a sense of ourselves as distinct from the environment.

The skin senses include *touch* (or pressure), *warmth, cold,* and *pain.* At one time, it was thought that these four senses were associated with four distinct kinds of receptors, or "end organs," but this view is now in doubt. The skin does contain spots that are particularly sensitive to cold, warmth, pressure, and pain. But except in the case of pressure, no simple correspondence exists between the sensation a person feels at a given spot and the type of receptor found there. Recent research has therefore concentrated more on the neural codes involved in the skin senses than on the receptors themselves.

Smell has not only evolutionary but also cultural significance. These pilgrims in Japan are purifying themselves with holy incense for good luck and health. Incense has always been an important commodity; in the New Testament, the gifts of the Magi included frankincense and myrrh.

Pain, which is both a skin sense and an internal sense, has come under special scrutiny. Pain differs from other senses in an important way: When the stimulus producing pain is removed, the sensation may continue—sometimes for years. Chronic pain disrupts lives, puts stress on the body, keeps people from their jobs, and causes depression and despair. (For ways of coping with pain, see "Taking Psychology with You.")

According to the **gate-control theory** of pain, the experience of pain depends partly on whether pain impulses get past a "gate" in the spinal cord and thus reach the brain (Melzack & Wall, 1965). The gate is made up of neurons that can either transmit or block pain messages from the skin, muscles, and internal organs. Pain fibers (like other kinds of fibers in the nervous system) are always active. When injury to tissue occurs, certain fibers open the gate. Normally, though, the gate is closed, either by impulses coming into the spinal cord from larger fibers that respond to pressure or by signals coming down from the brain itself. According to the gate-control theory, chronic pain occurs when disease, infection, or injury damages the fibers that ordinarily close the gate, and pain messages are able to reach the brain unchecked.

The gate-control theory may help explain the strange phenomenon of *phantom pain,* in which a person continues to feel pain that seemingly comes from an amputated limb, or from a breast or internal organ that has been surgically removed. Although sense receptors that were in the body part no longer exist, the pain can nonetheless be excruciating. An amputee may feel the same aching, burning, or sharp pain from gangrenous ulcers, calf cramps, throbbing toes, surgical wounds, or even ingrown toenails that he or she endured before the surgery (Katz & Melzack, 1990).

One explanation of phantom pain is that impulses normally responsible for closing the pain "gate" are reduced or eliminated by the amputation or operation. Without these inhibitory impulses, pain fibers near the spinal cord are able to get their messages through, and pain pathways are permanently activated. Another possibility is that in the absence of normal sensory inputs from the missing limb or organ, the level of activity in certain brain circuits increases, generating pain sensations that continue on their own (Melzack, 1997). That would explain why even amputees who undergo complete transection (horizontal cutting) of the spinal cord often continue to report phantom pain from areas below the break.

Since the late 1960s, researchers have learned that the occurrence of pain involves the release of several chemicals at the site of tissue damage and in the spinal cord and brain. Thus, pain is far more complex physiologically than scientists thought when the gate-control theory was first proposed. However, in its general outlines, the theory remains useful. It correctly predicts that mild pressure, as well as other types of stimulation, can interfere with severe or protracted pain by closing the spinal gate, either directly or by means of signals sent from the brain. When we vigorously rub a banged elbow, or put ice packs, heat, or stimulating salves on injured areas, we are applying this principle.

Much remains to be learned, not only about the four basic skin sensations, but also about itch, tickle, sensitivity to vibration, the sensation of wetness, and different types of pain. Researchers are trying to break the neural codes that explain why gently pricking pain spots with a needle produces itch; why lightly touching adjacent pressure spots in rapid succession produces tickle; and why the simultaneous stimulation of warm and cold spots produces not a lukewarm sensation but the sensation of heat. Decoding the messages of the skin senses will eventually tell us how we are able to distinguish sandpaper from velvet and glue from grease.

The Environment Within

We usually think of our senses as pipelines to the "outside" world, but two senses keep us informed about the movements of our own bodies. **Kinesthesis** tells us where our body parts are located and lets us know when they move. This information is provided by pain and pressure receptors located in the muscles, joints, and tendons (tissues that connect muscles to bones). Without kinesthesis, you could not touch your finger to your nose with your eyes shut. In fact, you would have trouble with any voluntary movement. Think of how hard walking is when your leg has "fallen asleep" or how clumsy chewing is when a dentist has numbed your jaw with novocaine.

Equilibrium, or the sense of balance, gives us information about our bodies as a whole. Along with vision and touch, it lets us know whether we are standing upright or on our heads and tells us when we are falling or rotating. Equilibrium relies primarily on three **semicircular canals** in the inner ear (see Figure 5.10 on page 169). These thin tubes are filled with fluid that moves and presses on hairlike receptors whenever the head rotates. The receptors initiate messages that travel through

gate-control theory
The theory that the experience of pain depends in part on whether pain impulses get past a neurological "gate" in the spinal cord and thus reach the brain.

kinesthesis
(KIN-es-THEE-sis)
The sense of body position and movement of body parts; also called *kinesthesia.*

equilibrium
The sense of balance.

semicircular canals
Sense organs in the inner ear that contribute to equilibrium by responding to rotation of the head.

a part of the auditory nerve that is not involved in hearing.

Normally, kinesthesis and equilibrium work together to give us a sense of our own physical reality, something we take utterly for granted but shouldn't. Oliver Sacks (1985) tells the heartbreaking story of a young British woman named Christina, who suffered irreversible damage to her kinesthetic nerve fibers because of a mysterious inflammation. At first, Christina was as floppy as a rag doll; she could not sit up, walk, or stand. Then, slowly, she learned to do these things, relying on visual cues and sheer willpower. But her movements remained unnatural; she had to grasp a fork with painful force or she would drop it. More important, despite her remaining sensitivity to light touch on the skin, she could no longer experience herself as physically embodied: "It's like something's been scooped right out of me, right at the centre. . . ."

With equilibrium, we come, as it were, to the end of our senses. Every second, millions of sensory signals reach the brain, which combines and integrates them to produce a model of reality from moment to moment. How does it know how to do this? Are our perceptual abilities inborn, or must we learn them? We turn next to this issue.

Olympic gold medalist Greg Louganis executes a winning dive that requires precise positioning of each part of his body. "I have a good kinesthetic awareness," Louganis once said, with considerable understatement. "I am aware of where I am in space."

??? QUICK QUIZ

Can you make some sense out of the following sensory problems?

1. April always has trouble tasting foods, especially those with subtle flavors. What's the most likely explanation of her difficulty?

2. May has chronic shoulder pain. How might the gate-control theory explain it?

3. June, a rock musician, discovers she can't hear as well as she used to. What's a likely explanation?

Answers:

1. An impaired sense of smell, possibly due to disease, illness, or cigarette smoking. 2. Nerve fibers that normally close the pain "gate" may have been damaged. Or it may be that pain-producing activity in the brain is, for some reason, continuing even without pain impulses from the spinal cord. 3. Hearing impairment has many causes, but in June's case, we might suspect that prolonged exposure to loud music has damaged the hair cells of her cochlea.

What's Ahead

- *Do babies see the world the way adults do?*

- *Why does one person think a cloud is a cloud, and another think it's a spaceship?*

PERCEPTUAL POWERS: ORIGINS AND INFLUENCES

What happens when babies first open their eyes? Do they see the same sights, hear the same sounds, smell the same smells, taste the same tastes? Are their strategies for organizing the world wired into their brains from the beginning? Or is an infant's world, as William James once suggested, only a "blooming, buzzing confusion," waiting to be organized by experience and learning? The truth lies somewhere between these two extremes.

Inborn Abilities and Perceptual Lessons

One way to study the origins of perceptual abilities is to see what happens when the usual perceptual experiences of early life fail to take place. To do so, researchers study animals whose sensory and perceptual systems are similar to our own, such as cats. What they find is that without certain experiences during critical periods of development, perception develops abnormally.

Researchers studying vision, for example, have discovered that when newborn animals are reared in total darkness for weeks or months, or are fitted with translucent goggles that permit only diffuse light to get through, or are allowed to see only one visual pattern and no others, visual development is impaired. In one famous study, kittens were exposed to either vertical or horizontal black and white stripes. Special collars kept them from seeing anything else, even their own bodies. After several months, the kittens exposed only to vertical stripes seemed blind to all horizontal contours; they bumped into horizontal obstacles, and they ran to play with a bar that an experimenter held vertically but not to a bar held horizontally. In contrast, those exposed only to horizontal stripes bumped into vertical obstacles and ran to play with horizontal bars but not vertical ones (Blakemore & Cooper, 1970).

You might conclude that animals and humans need to see certain stimuli in order to develop normal vision. But physiological studies suggest that in many cases these experiences merely ensure the survival of skills *already present* at birth in rudimentary form. For example, the brains of newborn kittens are equipped with exactly the same kinds of feature-detector cells that adult cats have; when kittens are kept from seeing lines of a particular orientation, such as horizontal or vertical ones, cells sensitive to those orientations deteriorate or change, and perception suffers (Hirsch & Spinelli, 1970; Mitchell, 1980).

From such findings, psychologists have concluded that human infants are probably born with an ability to detect and discriminate the edges and angles of objects. And infants have other visual talents, as well. They can discriminate sizes and colors very early, possibly at birth. They can distinguish contrasts, shadows, and complex patterns after only a few weeks. Even some depth perception may be present from the beginning.

Testing an infant's perception of depth requires considerable ingenuity. One clever procedure that was used for decades was to place infants on a device called a *visual cliff* (Gibson & Walk, 1960). The "cliff" is a pane of glass covering a shallow surface and a deep one (see Figure 5.14). Both surfaces are covered by a checkerboard pattern. The infant is placed on a board in the middle, and the child's mother tries to lure the baby across either the shallow or the deep side. Babies as young as 6 months of age will crawl to their mothers across the shallow side but will refuse to crawl out over the "cliff." Their hesitation shows that they have depth perception.

Of course, by 6 months of age, a baby has had quite a bit of experience with the world. But infants younger than 6 months, even though they are unable to crawl, can also be tested on the visual cliff. At only 2 months of age, babies show a drop in heart rate when placed on the deep side of the cliff, but no change when they are placed on the shallow side. A slowed heart rate is usually a sign of increased attention. Thus, although these infants may not be frightened the way an older infant would be, it seems they can perceive the difference between the "shallow" and "deep" sides of the cliff (Banks & Salapatek, 1984).

We have been talking only about vision, but other sensory abilities are also inborn or develop very early, as we saw in Chapter 3. Infants can distinguish salty from sweet and can discriminate among odors. They can distinguish a person's voice from other kinds of sounds. And they will startle to a loud noise and turn their heads toward its source, showing that they perceive sound as being localized in space. Because neurological connections in their brains and sensory systems are not completely formed, their senses are less acute than an adult's. However, an infant's world is far from the blooming, buzzing confusion that William James took it to be.

Psychological and Cultural Influences on Perception

The fact that some perceptual processes appear to be innate does not mean that all people perceive the world in the same way. A camera doesn't care

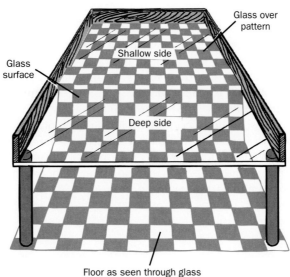

Glass over pattern

Shallow side

Glass surface

Deep side

Floor as seen through glass

Figure 5.14

A Cliff-hanger

Infants as young as 6 months usually hesitate to crawl past the apparent edge of a visual cliff, which suggests that they are able to perceive depth.

what it "sees." A tape recorder doesn't ponder what it "hears." A robot arm on a factory assembly line holds no opinion about what it "touches." But because we human beings care about what we see, hear, taste, smell, and feel, psychological factors can influence what we perceive and how we perceive it. Here are a few of them:

1. *Needs.* When we need something, have an interest in it, or want it, we are especially likely to perceive it. For example, hungry individuals are faster than others at seeing words related to hunger when the words are flashed briefly on a screen (Wispé & Drambarean, 1953).

2. *Beliefs.* What we hold to be true about the world can affect the interpretation of ambiguous sensory signals. Suppose you spot a round object hovering high in the sky. If you believe that extraterrestrials occasionally visit Earth, you may

"see" the object as a spaceship. But if you think such beliefs are hogwash, you are more likely to see a weather balloon or a cloud.

3. *Emotions.* Emotions can also influence our interpretation of sensory information. A small child afraid of the dark may see a ghost instead of a robe hanging on the door, or a monster instead of a beloved doll. Pain, in particular, is affected by emotion. Soldiers who are seriously wounded often deny being in much pain, even though they are alert and are not in shock. Their relief at being alive may offset the anxiety and fear that contribute so much to pain (although other explanations are also possible). Conversely, negative emotions such as anger, fear, sadness, or depression can prolong and intensify a person's pain (Fernandez & Turk, 1992; Fields, 1991).

4. *Expectations.* Previous experiences often affect how we perceive the world (Lachman, 1996). The tendency to perceive what you expect is called a **perceptual set.** Perceptual sets can come in handy; they help us fill in words in sentences, for example, when we haven't really heard every one. But perceptaul sets can also cause misperceptions. In Center Harbor, Maine, local legend has it that veteran newscaster Walter Cronkite was sailing into port one day when he heard a small crowd on shore shouting "Hello, Walter . . . Hello, Walter." Pleased, he waved and took a bow. Only when he ran aground did he realize what they had really been shouting: "Low water . . . low water."

Is this a UFO? See page 181.

perceptual set

A habitual way of perceiving, based on expectations.

By the way, there is a misspelled word in the previous paragraph. Did you notice it? If not, probably it was because you expected all the words in this book to be spelled correctly.

Our needs, beliefs, emotions, and expectations are all affected, in turn, by the culture we live in. Different cultures give people practice with different environments. In a classic study done in the 1960s, researchers found that members of some African tribes were much less likely to be fooled by the Müller–Lyer illusion and other geometric illusions than were Westerners. In the West, the researchers observed, people live in a "carpentered" world, full of rectangular structures built with the aid of saws, planes, straight edges, and carpenter's squares. Westerners are also used to interpreting two-dimensional photographs and perspective drawings as representations of a three-dimensional world. Therefore, they interpret the kinds of angles used in the Müller–Lyer illusion as right angles extended in space—just the sort of habit that would increase susceptibility to the illusion. The rural Africans in the study, living in a less carpentered environment and in round huts, seemed more likely to take the lines in the figures literally, as two-dimensional, which could explain why they were less susceptible to the illusion (Segall, Campbell, & Herskovits, 1966).

This research was followed by a flurry of replications in the 1970s, showing that it was indeed culture that produced the differences between groups (Segall, 1994; Segall et al., 1990). Since then, there has been little further work on the fascinating intersection of culture and visual illusions. However, culture affects perception in many other ways: by shaping our stereotypes, directing our attention, and telling us what is important to notice and what is not.

What's Ahead

- *Can "subliminal perception" tapes help you lose weight or reduce your stress?*

- *Why are most psychologists skeptical about ESP?*

PUZZLES OF PERCEPTION

We come, finally, to two intriguing questions about perception that have captured the public's imagination for years. First, can we perceive what is happening in the world without being conscious that we are doing so? Second, can we pick up signals from the world or from other people without using our usual sensory channels at all?

Conscious and Nonconscious Perception

Many aspects of perception occur outside of awareness. As we have seen, before we can recognize or identify something, we must analyze its basic features. In the case of vision, we must make out edges, colors, textures, and differences in the reflectance of light. We must separate figure from ground, calculate distance or depth, and adjust for changing patterns of stimulation on the retina. All this we do without any conscious intention or awareness.

What about more complicated perceptual tasks, such as registering and deciphering speech? As we saw earlier in our discussion of the "cocktail party phenomenon," even when people are oblivious to speech sounds, they are processing and recognizing those sounds at some level. But these sounds would be *above* the absolute threshold if a person were consciously attending to them. Is it also possible to perceive and respond to messages that are *below* the threshold—too quiet to be consciously heard (in the case of hearing) or too brief or dim to be consciously seen (in the case of vision), even when you are trying your best to hear or see them? Perhaps you have seen ads for products that will allow you to take advantage of such "subliminal perception." Or perhaps you have heard that subliminal perception doesn't really exist. What are the facts?

First, considerable evidence exists that a simple visual stimulus *can* affect a person's responses to a task even when the person has no awareness of seeing the stimulus. For example, in one study, people subliminally exposed to a face tended to prefer that face over one they did not "see" in this way (Bornstein, Leone, & Galley, 1987). In another study, words were briefly flashed on a screen and were then immediately masked by a pattern of X's and O's. Subjects said they could not read the words or even tell whether a word had appeared at all. But when an "invisible" word (e.g., *bread*) was followed by a second, visible word that was either related in meaning (e.g., *butter*) or unrelated (e.g., *bubble*), the subjects were able to read the related word more quickly (Dagenbach, Carr, & Wilhelmsen, 1989).

Findings such as these have convinced many psychologists that people often know more than they know they know (Greenwald, 1992; Moore, 1992). In fact, nonconscious processing appears to occur not only in perception, but also in memory, thinking, and decision making, as we will see in Chapters 6 and 7. However, the real-world implications of subliminal perception are not as dramatic as you might think. Even in the laboratory, where researchers have considerable control, the phenomenon is hard to demonstrate. The strongest evidence comes from studies using simple stimuli (faces or single words, such as *bread*), rather than complex stimuli such as sentences

("Eat whole-wheat bread, not white bread"). And even with single words, the influence of the subliminal stimulus is short-lived—in one recent study, only 100 milliseconds (Greenwald, Draine, & Abrams, 1996). Some psychoanalytic researchers have reported that the sentence "Mommy and I are one," presented subliminally, can make anxious, depressed, or disturbed patients feel better (Silverman & Weinberger, 1985). However, serious questions exist about the methods used by these researchers, and most psychologists remain skeptical about these claims. Timothy Moore, one such skeptic, told us he will be convinced when the "Mommy" stimulus gets positive results in comparison to a control stimulus that merely changes two letters: "Tommy and I ate one."

Thinking Critically About Subliminal Perception

Moreover, while visual *subliminal perception* may occur under certain conditions, subliminal *persuasion,* the subject of many popular books and magazine articles, is quite another matter. Empirical research has uncovered no basis whatsoever for believing that advertisers can seduce us into buying soft drinks or voting for political candidates by flashing subliminal slogans on television, or by slipping subliminal images into magazine ads.

Nor is there any evidence for the belief that subliminal messages in music or movies can corrupt anyone or inspire destructive acts. In 1990, when parents of two troubled teenagers sued the rock group Judas Priest, claiming that the subliminal message "Do it" had caused their sons to commit suicide, they lost their suit.

As for the countless subliminal tapes that promise, among other things, to help you slim down, stop smoking, relieve stress, read faster, lower your cholesterol, stop biting your nails, overcome jet lag, stop taking drugs, stop swearing, and enlarge your bust, they, too, are based on claims that have no support. In study after study, "placebo" tapes—tapes that don't really contain any messages even though participants think they do—are just as "effective" as subliminal tapes (Eich & Hyman, 1992; Greenwald et al., 1991; Merikle & Skanes, 1992; Moore, 1995).

If advertisers want you to buy something, therefore, they would do better to spend their money on *above*-threshold messages that you can consciously evaluate. And if you want to improve yourself or your life, we encourage you to do so—but you'll probably have to do it the old-fashioned way: by working at it.

??? QUICK QUIZ

Suppose you hear about a study that appeared to find evidence of "sleep learning"—the ability to perceive and retain material played on an audiotape while a person sleeps. What would you want to know about this research before deciding to tape this chapter and play it by your bedside all night instead of studying it in the usual way?

Answer:

You might ask about the kinds of stimuli used (in studies of other kinds of nonconscious perception, positive results have been obtained with very simple stimuli, not whole sentences); whether the results were large enough to have practical consequences; and most important, how it was determined that the subjects were really asleep while the tape was playing. When EEG measurements are used to verify that subjects are actually sleeping, no "sleep learning" takes place. So if you want to learn the material in this chapter, you'll have to stay awake!

Extrasensory Perception: Reality or Illusion?

Eyes, ears, mouth, nose, skin—we rely on these organs for our experience of the external world. Some people, however, claim they can send and receive messages about the world without relying on the usual sensory channels, by using *extrasensory perception (ESP)*.

Reported ESP experiences (also known as *Psi,* a shortening of "psychic phenomena") fall into four general categories: (1) *Telepathy* is direct communication from one mind to another without the usual visual, auditory, and other sensory signals. If you try to guess what number someone is thinking or what card a person is holding, you are attempting telepathy. (2) *Clairvoyance* is the perception of an event or fact without normal sensory input. If a man suddenly "knows" that his wife has just died, yet no one has informed him of the death, he might be called clairvoyant. (3) *Precognition* is the perception of an event that has not yet happened. Fortune-tellers make their livings by claiming to read the future in tea leaves or in a person's palm. (4) *Out-of-body experiences* involve the perception of one's own body from "outside," as an observer might see it. Such experiences are often reported by persons who have been near death, but some people say they can bring them on at will.

Evidence—or Just Coincidence?

Much of the "evidence" for extrasensory perception comes from

THE FAR SIDE   By GARY LARSON

10th Annual
PSYCHICS
CONFERENCE

For the most part, the meeting was quite successful. Only a slight tension filled the air, stemming from the unforeseen faux pas of everyone wearing the same dress.

anecdotal accounts. Unfortunately, people are not always reliable reporters. They often embellish and exaggerate, or recall only parts of an experience. They also tend to forget incidents that don't fit their beliefs, such as "premonitions" of events that fail to occur. Many ESP experiences could merely be unusual coincidences that are memorable because they are dramatic. What passes for telepathy, clairvoyance, or precognition could also be based on what a person knows or deduces through ordinary means. If Joanne's father has had two heart attacks, her premonition that her father will die shortly (followed, in fact, by her father's death) may not be so impressive.

The scientific way to establish a phenomenon is to produce it under controlled conditions. Extrasensory perception has been studied extensively by researchers in the field of **parapsychology.** In a typical study, a person might be asked to guess which of five symbols will appear on a card presented at random. A "sender" who has already seen the card tries to transmit a mental image of the symbol to the person. Although most people do no better than chance at guessing the symbols, in some studies, a few people have consistently done somewhat better than chance. But ESP studies have often been poorly designed, with inadequate precautions against fraud and improper statistical analysis. When skeptical researchers try to repeat the studies, they get negative results. After an exhaustive review, the National Research Council concluded that there was "no scientific justification . . . for the existence of parapsychological phenomena" (Druckman & Swets, 1988).

The issue has not gone away, however. A few years ago, a well-known social psychologist, Daryl Bem, made waves in the psychological community when he reported a series of ESP studies car-

Thinking Critically
About ESP

ried out with the late Charles Honorton, a British parapsychologist. Bem and Honorton (1994) studied telepathy (they called it the "anomalous process of information transfer") by using a variation of a method known as the *ganzfeld* ("total field") procedure. A sender sits in a soundproof room and concentrates on a picture or video clip selected at random by a computer. A receiver sits in another soundproof room. At the end of the transmission period, the receiver is shown four pictures or video clips and is asked to pick out the one that most closely matched his or her mental imagery during the transmission period. If the receiver selects the stimulus that was "sent," that trial is counted as a "hit." Bem and Honorton reported an overall hit rate of about 33 percent, whereas chance would predict only 25 percent.

Of course, these findings have been the subject of much critical interpretation. Although the methods used by Bem and Honorton were better than those used by previous researchers, Ray Hyman (1994), a leading critic of parapsychology, has pointed out possible flaws in the way the target stimuli were randomized and selected. And everyone agrees that the findings need to be replicated in other laboratories. It will be interesting to see what happens, although we think it is safe to say that caution is warranted. The history of research on psychic phenomena has been one of initial enthusiasm followed by disappointment when results cannot be replicated, and the thousands of studies done since the late 1940s have failed to make a convincing case for ESP.

Lessons from a Magician.

Despite the lack of evidence for ESP, about half of all Americans say they believe in it. Perhaps you yourself have had an experience that seemed to involve ESP or have seen a convincing demonstration by someone else. Surely you can trust the evidence of your own eyes—or can you? We will answer with a true story that contains an important lesson, not only about ESP but about ordinary perception as well.

During the 1970s, physician Andrew Weil set out to investigate the claims of a self-proclaimed psychic named Uri Geller (Weil, 1974a, 1974b). Geller seemed able to bend keys without touching them, start broken watches, and guess the nature of simple drawings hidden in sealed envelopes. Although he had performed as a stage magician in Israel, his native country, he denied using trickery. His powers, he said, came from energy from another universe.

Weil, who believed in telepathy, felt that ESP might be explained by principles of modern physics and was receptive to Geller's claims. When he met Geller at a private gathering, he was not disappointed. Geller correctly identified a cross and a Star of David sealed inside separate envelopes. He made a stopped watch start running and a ring sag into an oval shape, apparently without touching them. He made keys change shape in front of Weil's very eyes. Weil came away a convert. What he had seen with his own eyes seemed impossible to deny . . . until he met The Amazing Randi.

James Randi is a well-known magician who is dedicated to educating the public about psychic deception. To Weil's astonishment, Randi was able to duplicate much of what Geller had done. He, too, could bend keys and guess the contents of sealed envelopes. But Randi's feats were tricks, and he was willing to show Weil exactly how they were done. Weil suddenly experienced "a sense of how strongly the mind can impose its own interpretations on perceptions; how it can see what it expects to see, but not see the unexpected."

parapsychology
The study of purported psychic phenomena such as ESP and mental telepathy.

These odd objects may look like flying saucers, but they are really lenticular (lens-shaped) clouds over Santos, Brazil. When people have a strong need to believe in UFOs, or anything else, they may see what they want to see and ignore alternative interpretations.

Weil was dis-illusioned—literally. He was forced to admit that the evidence of one's own eyes is not always reliable. Even when he knew what to look for in a trick, he could not catch The Amazing Randi doing it. Weil learned that our sense impressions of reality are not the same as reality. Our eyes, our ears, and especially our brains can play tricks on us.

The great Greek philosopher Plato once said that "knowledge is nothing but perception." But in fact, simple perception is *not* always the best path to knowledge. As we have seen throughout this chapter, we do not passively register the world "out there"; we mentally construct it. The truth about human behavior, then, is most likely to emerge if we are aware of how our beliefs and assumptions shape and alter our perceptions.

This means that we should be careful about drawing conclusions when people report seeing things that are unlikely (such as spaceships and aliens) or that seem "miraculous" (such as the image of Mother Teresa described at the start of this chapter). Some people, as we have learned, are habitual "yea-sayers" who, because of their expectations, are quick to think they saw something that wasn't there. And all of us have needs and beliefs that can fool us into seeing things that we *want* to see, or cause us to read meanings into sensory experiences that are not inherent in the experience itself.

On the other hand, we should also not be too quick to rule out some aspect of reality just because we can't perceive it directly. Because our sense organs evolved for particular purposes, our sensory windows on the world are partly shuttered. We can use reason, ingenuity, and technology, however, to pry open those shutters. Ordinary perception tells us that the sun circles the earth, but the great astronomer Copernicus was able to figure out nearly five centuries ago that the opposite is true. Ordinary perception will never let us see ultraviolet and infrared rays directly (unless evolution or genetic engineering drastically changes the kind of organism we are), but we know they are there, and we can measure them. If science can enable us to overturn the everyday evidence of our senses, who knows what surprises about reality are still in store for us?

Taking Psychology with You

Living with Pain

Temporary pain is an unpleasant but necessary part of life, a warning of disease or injury. Chronic pain, which is ongoing or recurring, is another matter, a serious problem in itself. Back injuries, arthritis, migraine headaches, serious illnesses such as cancer—all can cause unrelieved misery to pain sufferers and their families. Chronic pain can also impair the immune system (Page et al., 1993), and such impairment can put patients at risk of further complications from their illnesses.

At one time, the only way to combat pain was with drugs or surgery, which were not always effective. Today, we know that the experience of pain is affected by attitudes, actions, emotions, and circumstances, and that treatment must take into account psychology as well as biology. Even social roles can influence a person's response to pain. For example, although women tend to report greater pain than men do, a real-world study of people who were in pain for more than six months found that men suffered more severe psychological distress than women, possibly because the male role made it hard for them to admit their pain (Snow et al., 1986).

Many pain-treatment programs encourage patients to manage their pain themselves instead of relying entirely on health-care professionals. Usually, these programs combine several strategies:

• *Painkilling medication.* Doctors often worry that patients will become addicted to painkillers or will develop a tolerance to the drugs. The physicians will therefore give a minimal dose, then wait until the effects wear off and the patient is once again in agony before giving more. This approach is ineffective and ignores the fact that addiction depends in part on the motives for which a drug is taken and the circumstances under which it is used. The method now recommended by experts (although doctors and hospitals do not always follow the advice) is to give pain sufferers a continuous dose of painkiller in whatever amount is necessary to keep them pain-free, and to allow them to do this for themselves when they leave the hospital. This strategy leads to *reduced* dosages rather than larger ones and does not lead to drug dependence (Hill et al., 1990; Portenoy, 1994).

• *Spouse or family involvement.* When a person is in pain, friends and relatives understandably tend to sympathize and to excuse the sufferer from regular responsibilities. The sufferer takes to bed, avoids physical activity, and focuses on the pain. As we will see in Chapter 8, attention from others is a powerful reinforcer of whatever behavior produces the attention. Also, focusing on pain tends to increase it, and inactivity can lead to shortened muscles, muscle spasms, and fatigue. So sympathy and attention can sometimes backfire and may actually prolong the agony (Flor, Kerns, & Turk, 1987).

For this reason, many pain experts now encourage family members to resist rewarding or reinforcing the pain and to reward activity, exercise, and wellness instead. This approach, however, must be used carefully, preferably under the direction of a medical or mental-health professional, because a patient's complaints about pain are an important diagnostic tool for the physician (Rodgers, 1988).

• *Self-management.* When patients learn to identify how, when, and where their pain occurs, this knowledge helps them determine whether the pain is being maintained by external events. Just having a sense of control over pain can have a powerful pain-reducing effect. In one study, students who monitored their pain while one hand was submerged in freezing water showed more rapid recovery from the pain than did students who had tried to suppress their awareness of pain sensations or distract themselves, apparently because the monitoring students had a sense of control (Cioffi & Holloway, 1993). Patients also need muscle "reeducation"; instead of tensing muscles in response to pain, which only makes the pain worse, patients can learn to relax them (Keefe & Gil, 1986).

• *Biofeedback, hypnosis, and guided relaxation.* These techniques have all been successful with some patients. It is unclear, however, whether biofeedback and guided relaxation are applicable to all types of chronic pain.

• *Cognitive-behavioral therapy.* Cognitive-behavioral strategies teach people to (a) recognize the connections among thoughts, feelings, and pain; (b) substitute adaptive thoughts for negative ones; and (c) use coping strategies such as distraction, relabeling of sensations, and imagery to alleviate suffering (see Chapter 11). All these techniques increase feelings of control and reduce feelings of inadequacy.

For further information about help for pain, you can contact pain clinics or services in teaching hospitals and medical schools. There are many reputable clinics around the country, some specializing in specific disorders, such as migraines or back injuries. But take care: There are also many untested therapies and quack practitioners who only prey on people's pain.

SUMMARY

1) *Sensation* is the detection and direct experience of physical energy as a result of environmental or internal events. *Perception* is the process by which sensory impulses are organized and interpreted.

Our Sensational Senses

2) Sensation begins with the sense receptors, which convert the energy of a stimulus into electrical impulses that travel along nerves to the brain. Separate sensations can be accounted for by *anatomical codes* (the *doctrine of specific nerve energies*) and *functional codes* in the nervous system.

3) Psychologists in the area of *psychophysics* have studied sensory sensitivity by measuring *absolute* and *difference thresholds*. *Signal-detection theory*, however, holds that responses in a detection task consist of both a sensory process and a decision process and will vary with the person's motivation, alertness, and expectations. This theory has led to improved methods for estimating individual sensitivity to stimuli.

4) Our senses are designed to respond to change and contrast in the environment. When stimulation is unchanging, *sensory adaptation* occurs. Too little stimulation can cause *sensory deprivation*, and too much stimulation can cause *sensory overload*, which is why we exercise *selective attention*.

Vision

5) Vision is affected by the wavelength, frequency, and complexity of light, which produce the psychological dimensions of visual experience—*hue, brightness,* and *saturation.* The visual receptors, *rods* and *cones,* are located in the *retina* of the eye. Rods are responsible for vision in dim light; cones are responsible for color vision. The visual world is not a mosaic of light and dark spots but a collection of lines and angles detected and integrated by special *feature-detector cells* in the visual areas of the brain. The eye is not a camera; the brain takes in fragmentary information about lines, angles, shapes, motion, brightness, texture, and other features of what we see, and it comes up with a unified view of the world.

6) The *trichromatic* and *opponent-process* theories of color vision apply to different stages of processing. In the first stage, three types of cones in the retina respond selectively to different wavelengths of light. In the second, *opponent-process cells* in the retina and the thalamus respond in opposite fashion to short and long wavelengths of light.

7) Perception involves the active construction of a model of the world from moment to moment. The *Gestalt principles* (e.g., *figure and ground, proximity, closure, similarity*, and *continuity*) describe visual strategies used in form perception.

8) We localize objects in visual space by using both *binocular* and *monocular* cues to depth. Binocular cues include *convergence* and *retinal disparity*. Monocular cues include interposition, linear perspective, and relative size. *Perceptual constancies* allow us to perceive objects as stable despite changes in the sensory patterns they produce. *Perceptual illusions* occur when sensory cues are misleading or when we misinterpret cues.

Hearing

9) Hearing (*audition*) is affected by the intensity, frequency, and complexity of pressure waves in the air or other transmitting substance, corresponding to the experience of loudness, pitch, and timbre of the sound. The receptors for hearing are hair cells (cilia) embedded in the *basilar membrane*, in the interior of the *cochlea*. The sounds we hear are determined by patterns of hair-cell movement, which produce different neural codes. When we localize sounds, we use as cues subtle differences in how pressure waves reach each of our ears.

Other Senses

10) Taste (*gustation*) is a chemical sense. Elevations on the tongue, called *papillae*, contain many *taste buds*. There are four basic tastes—salty, sour, bitter, and sweet. Responses to a particular taste depend on culture, genetic differences among individuals, the texture and temperature of the food, and above all, the food's smell.

11) Smell (*olfaction*) is also a chemical sense. No basic odors have been identified, and the neural code for smell remains to be worked out. There may be as many as a thousand different receptor types for smell. Cultural and individual differences affect people's responses to particular odors.

12) The skin senses include touch (pressure), warmth, cold, and pain. Except in the case of pressure, no simple correspondence seems to exist between these four senses and different types of receptors. Pain is both a skin sense and an internal sense. According to the *gate-control theory*, the experience of pain depends on whether neural impulses get past a "gate" in the spinal cord and reach the brain.

13) *Kinesthesis* tells us where our body parts are located, and *equilibrium* tells us the orientation of the body as a whole. Together, these two senses provide us with a feeling of physical embodiment.

Perceptual Powers: Origins and Influences

14) Studies of animals and human infants suggest that many fundamental perceptual skills are inborn or acquired shortly after birth. By using the *visual cliff*, for example, psychologists have learned that babies have depth perception by the age of 6 months and possibly even earlier. However, without certain experiences early in life, cells in the nervous system deteriorate, change, or fail to form appropriate neural pathways, and perception is impaired.

15) Psychological influences on perception include needs, beliefs, emotions, and expectations. These influences are affected by culture, which gives people practice with certain kinds of experiences. Because psychological factors affect the way we construct the perceptual world, the evidence of our senses is not always reliable.

Puzzles of Perception

16) Many perceptual processes occur outside of awareness and without conscious intention. In the laboratory, simple visual subliminal messages can influence behavior, at least briefly. However, there is no evidence that complex behaviors can be altered by subliminal-perception tapes or other subliminal techniques.

17) *Extrasensory perception (ESP)* refers to paranormal abilities such as telepathy, clairvoyance, precognition, and out-of-body experiences. Believers in ESP tend to overlook disconfirming evidence. To date, the evidence for ESP is not convincing. Many so-called psychics take advantage of people's desire to believe in ESP, but what they do is no different from the tricks of any good magician. The story of ESP illustrates a central fact about human perception: that it does not merely capture objective reality, but also reflects our needs, biases, and beliefs.

KEY TERMS

LOOKING BACK

- *What kind of "code" in the nervous system helps explain why a pinprick and a kiss feel different? (p. 151)*

- *Why does your dog hear a "silent" doggie whistle when you can't? (p. 151)*

- *What kind of bias can influence whether you think you hear the phone ringing in the other room? (p. 153)*

- *What happens when people are deprived of all external sensory stimulation? (p. 154)*

- *How does the eye differ from a camera? (p. 158)*

- *Why can we describe a color as bluish green but not as reddish green? (p. 159)*

- *If you were blind in one eye, why might you misjudge the distance of a painting on the wall but not of buildings a block away? (pp. 162–163)*

- *As a friend approaches, her image on your retina grows larger; then why do you continue to see her as the same size? (p. 164)*

- *Why are perceptual illusions so valuable to psychologists? (p. 165)*

- *Why does a note played on a flute sound different from the same note on an oboe? (p. 167)*

- *If you habitually listen to loud music through headphones, what kind of hearing impairment are you risking? (p. 168)*

- *To locate the source of a sound, why does it sometimes help to turn or tilt your head? (p. 170)*

- *Why do saccharin and caffeine taste bitter to some people but not to others? (p. 171)*

- *Why do you have trouble tasting your food when you have a cold? (pp. 171–172)*

- *Why do people often continue to "feel" limbs that have been amputated? (p. 174)*

- *Do babies see the world the way adults do? (p. 176)*

- *Why does one person think a cloud is a cloud, and another think it's a spaceship? (p. 177)*

- *Can "subliminal perception" tapes help you lose weight or reduce your stress? (p. 179)*

- *Why are most psychologists skeptical about ESP? (pp. 180–181)*

PSYCHOLOGY IN THE NEWS

Supercomputer Defeats World Chess Champion

Chess champion Garry Kasparov ponders his next move in his historic match with Deep Blue.

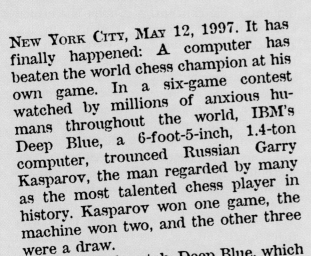

NEW YORK CITY, MAY 12, 1997. It has finally happened: A computer has beaten the world chess champion at his own game. In a six-game contest watched by millions of anxious humans throughout the world, IBM's Deep Blue, a 6-foot-5-inch, 1.4-ton computer, trounced Russian Garry Kasparov, the man regarded by many as the most talented chess player in history. Kasparov won one game, the machine won two, and the other three were a draw.

In the final match, Deep Blue, which can analyze 200 million chess positions per second, took only 88 minutes to declare victory. The exhausted Kasparov was not gracious in defeat, at first accusing IBM of secretly providing the machine with help from grandmasters hidden behind a screen. ("Look at the printouts!" he shouted.) His loss, he said, had "nothing to do about science." Before the match, however, Kasparov had said he was "defending human superiority in a purely intellectual field ... that defines human beings."

As soon as the final game ended, morose messages began to appear on the Internet. "It's over for mankind," sulked one writer. "This is the moment in which human beings begin to take to the sidelines," remarked another gloomily. Deep Blue had no comment but was no doubt pleased, as IBM's stock immediately jumped $5 a share.

Does Deep Blue's achievement mean that human beings aren't as smart as they think? Can a machine think—and therefore be said to have a mind? Is it really "over for mankind"? To answer those questions intelligently, we need to have a clear understanding of what thinking and intelligence are.

Each day, in the course of ordinary living, we all make plans, draw inferences, concoct explanations, analyze relationships, and organize and reorganize the flotsam and jetsam of our mental world. Descartes' famous declaration, "I think, therefore I am," could just as well have been reversed: "I am, therefore I think." Our powers of thought and intelligence inspired our forebears to give our species the immodest name *Homo sapiens,* Latin for wise or rational man. But just how "sapiens" are we, really?

Certainly the human mind, which has managed to come up with poetry, penicillin, and panty hose, is a miraculous thing. But the human mind has also managed to come up with traffic jams, junk mail, and war. To better understand why the same species that figured out how to get to the moon is also capable of breathtaking bumbling here on earth, we will examine in this chapter how people reason, solve problems, and grow in intelligence, as well as some sources of their mental shortcomings.

What's Ahead

- *When you think of a bird, why are you more likely to recall a robin than a penguin?*

- *How are visual images like images on a television screen?*

- *What's happening mentally when you mistakenly take your geography notes to your psychology class?*

THOUGHT: USING WHAT WE KNOW

Think for a moment about what *thinking* does for you. It frees you from the confines of the immediate present: You can think about a trip taken three years ago, a party planned for next Saturday, or the War of 1812. It carries you beyond the boundaries of reality: You can imagine unicorns and utopias, Martians and magic. Because people think, they do not need to grope their way blindly through their problems but, with some effort and knowledge, can solve them intelligently and creatively.

To explain such abilities, many cognitive psychologists liken the human mind to an information processor, somewhat analogous to a computer but far more complex. Information-processing approaches capture the fact that the brain does not passively record information but actively alters and organizes it. When we take action, we physically manipulate the environment; when we think, we *mentally* manipulate internal representations of objects, activities, and situations.

The Elements of Cognition

One type of mental representation, or unit of thought, is the **concept.** A concept is a mental category that groups objects, relations, activities, abstractions, or qualities having common properties. The instances of a concept are seen as roughly similar. For example, *golden retriever, cocker spaniel,* and *Weimaraner* are instances of the concept *dog;* and *anger, joy,* and *sadness* are instances of the concept *emotion.* Concepts simplify and summarize information about the world so that it is manageable, and so that we can make decisions quickly and efficiently. You may never have seen a *basenji* or eaten *escargots,* but if you know that the first is an instance of *dog* and the second an instance of *food,* you will know, roughly, what to do with them (unless you do not like to eat snails, which is what escargots are).

Not all the qualities associated with a concept necessarily apply to every instance: Some apples are not red; some dogs do not bark; some birds do not fly or perch on trees. But all the instances of a concept do share a "family resemblance." When we need to decide whether something belongs to a concept, we are likely to compare it to a **prototype,** a representative example of the concept (Rosch, 1973). For instance, which dog is doggier— a golden retriever or a chihuahua? Which fruit is more fruitlike—an apple or a pineapple? Which activity is more representative of sports—football or

concept

A mental category that groups objects, relations, activities, abstractions, or qualities having common properties.

prototype

An especially representative example of a concept.

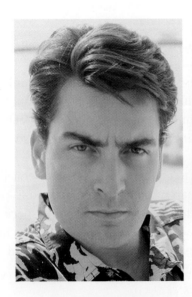
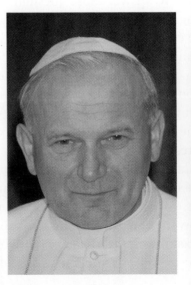

Some instances of a concept are more representative, or prototypical, than others. For example, actor Charlie Sheen clearly qualifies as a "bachelor," an unmarried man (at least, as of 1998). But is the Pope a bachelor? What about Robert Redford, who is divorced and has not remarried?

weight lifting? Most people within a culture can easily tell you which instances are most representative, or *prototypical,* of a given concept.

Concepts are the building blocks of thought, but they would be of limited use if we merely stacked them up mentally. We must also represent their relationships to one another. One way we accomplish this may be by storing and using **propositions,** units of meaning that are made up of concepts and that express a unitary idea. A proposition can express nearly any sort of knowledge (*Hortense raises basenjis*) or belief (*Basenjis are beautiful*). Propositions, in turn, are linked together in complicated networks of knowledge, associations, beliefs, and expectations. These networks, which psychologists call **cognitive schemas,** serve as mental models of aspects of the world. For example, gender schemas represent a person's beliefs and expectations about what it means to be male or female (see Chapter 3). People also have schemas about cultures, occupations, animals, geographical locations, and many other features of the social and natural environment.

Most cognitive psychologists believe that **mental images** are also important in thinking and in the construction of cognitive schemas—especially visual images, pictures in what Shakespeare called the "mind's eye." Although no one can directly "see" another person's visual images, psychologists are able to study them indirectly. One method is to measure how long it takes people to rotate an image, scan from one point to another in an image, or read off some detail from an image. The results suggest that visual images function something like images on a television screen: We can manipulate them, they occur in a mental "space" of a fixed size, and small ones contain less detail than larger ones (Kosslyn, 1980; Shepard & Metzler, 1971).

In addition to visual images, most people report auditory images (for instance, a song, slogan, or poem you can hear in your "mind's ear"), and many report images in other sensory modalities— touch, taste, smell, or pain. Some even report kinesthetic images, feelings in the muscles and joints. Athletes often imagine themselves performing a skill, such as diving or sprinting, and this visual and kinesthetic rehearsal seems to improve actual performance (Druckman & Swets, 1988). Brain scans show that such mental practice activates most of the brain circuits involved in the activity itself (Stephan et al., 1995).

Albert Einstein relied heavily on visual and kinesthetic imagery in formulating his ideas. The happiest thought of his life, he once recalled, occurred in 1907, when he suddenly imagined a man falling freely from the roof of a house and realized that the man would not experience a gravitational field in his immediate vicinity. This insight led eventually to Einstein's formulation of the principle of relativity, and physics was never again the same.

The elements of cognition, then, can be summarized as follows:

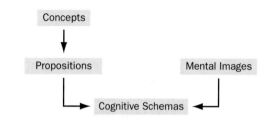

How Conscious Is Thought?

When we think about thinking, most of us have in mind those mental activities, such as solving problems or making decisions, that are carried out in a deliberate way with a conscious goal in mind. However, not all mental processing is conscious.

Subconscious processes lie outside of awareness but can be brought into consciousness with little effort when necessary. These processes allow us to handle more information and to perform more complex tasks than if we depended entirely on conscious thought, and they enable us to perform more than one task simultaneously (Kahneman &

proposition
A unit of meaning that is made up of concepts and expresses a single idea.

cognitive schema
An integrated mental network of knowledge, beliefs, and expectations concerning a particular topic or aspect of the world.

mental image
A mental representation that mirrors or resembles the thing it represents; it can occur in many and perhaps all sensory modalities.

subconscious processes
Mental processes occurring outside of conscious awareness but accessible to consciousness when necessary.

Some well-learned tasks, such as holding a baby, do not require much conscious thought, so this father can do other things at the same time—at least until the baby hits "Delete."

Treisman, 1984). Consider all the automatic routines performed "without thinking," though they might once have required careful, conscious attention: knitting, typing, driving a car, decoding the letters in a word in order to read it. Because of the capacity for automatic processing, with proper training, people can even learn to perform simultaneously such complex tasks as reading and taking dictation (Hirst, Neisser, & Spelke, 1978).

Nonconscious processes, unlike subconscious ones, remain outside of awareness, but nonetheless affect behavior. For example, most of us have had the odd experience of having a solution to a problem "pop into mind" after we have given up trying to find one; apparently, a mental search was going on that we were unaware of. Similarly, people will often say they rely on intuition rather than conscious reasoning to solve a problem. Intuition may actually be an orderly process involving two stages (Bowers et al., 1990). In the first stage, clues in the problem automatically activate certain memories or knowledge, and you begin to see a pattern or structure in the problem, although you can't yet say what it is. This nonconscious process guides you toward a hunch or a hypothesis. Then, in the second stage, your thinking becomes conscious, and you become aware of a possible solution. This stage may feel like a sudden revelation ("Aha, I've got it!"), but considerable mental work has already occurred, even though you are not aware of it. (Most modern cognitive psychol-

nonconscious processes
Mental processes occurring outside of and not available to conscious awareness.

ogists distinguish these nonconscious processes from Freud's notion of the unconscious, which he believed contained sexual and other threatening thoughts and wishes.)

Usually, of course, much of our thinking is conscious—but we may not be thinking very *hard*. We may act, speak, and make decisions out of habit, without stopping to analyze what we are doing or why we are doing it. This sort of mental inertia, which Ellen Langer (1989) has called *mindlessness,* keeps people from recognizing when a change in context requires a change in behavior.

In one study by Langer and her associates, a researcher approached people as they were about to use a photocopier and made one of three requests: "Excuse me, may I use the Xerox machine?" "Excuse me, may I use the Xerox machine, because I have to make copies," or "Excuse me, may I use the Xerox machine, because I'm in a rush." Normally, people will let someone go before them only if the person has a legitimate reason, as in the third request. In this study, however, people also complied when the reason sounded like an authentic explanation but was actually meaningless ("because I have to make copies"). They heard the form of the request, but not its content, and they mindlessly stepped aside (Langer, Blank, & Chanowitz, 1978).

The mindless processing of information has benefits: If we stopped to think twice about everything we did, we would get nothing done ("Okay, now I'm reaching for my toothbrush; now I'm putting toothpaste on it; now I'm brushing my upper-right molars"). But mindlessness can also lead to errors and mishaps, ranging from the trivial (putting the butter in the dishwasher or locking yourself out of your apartment) to the serious (driving carelessly while on "automatic pilot").

Jerome Kagan (1989) argues that fully conscious awareness is needed only when we must make a deliberate choice, when events happen that can't be handled automatically, and when unexpected moods and feelings arise. "Consciousness," he says, "can be likened to the staff of a fire department. Most of the time, it is quietly playing pinochle in the back room; it performs [only] when the alarm sounds." That may be so, but most of us would probably benefit if our mental firefighters paid a little more attention to their jobs. Cognitive psychologists have, therefore, devoted a great deal of study to mindful, conscious thought and the capacity to reason.

Drawing by Weber; © 1989 The New Yorker Magazine, Inc.

"This CD player costs less than players selling for twice as much."

This salesman knows all about mindlessness.

??? QUICK QUIZ

1. Stuffing your mouth with cotton candy, licking a lollipop, and chewing on a piece of beef jerky are all instances of the _____ *eating.*

2. Which example of the concept *chair* is prototypical: *high chair, rocking chair, dining-room chair?*

3. In addition to concepts and images, _____, which express a unitary idea, have been proposed as a basic form of mental representation.

4. Peter's mental representation of *Thanksgiving* includes associations (e.g., to turkeys), attitudes ("It's a time to be with relatives"), and expectations ("I'm going to gain weight from all that food"). They are all part of his _____ for the holiday.

5. Zelda discovers that she has dialed her boyfriend's number instead of her mother's, as she intended. Her error can be attributed to _____.

Answers:

1. concept 2. a plain, straight-backed dining-room chair will be prototypical for most people 3. propositions 4. cognitive schema 5. mindlessness

---

What's Ahead

- *Mentally speaking, why is making a cake, well, a piece of cake?*

- *Why can't logic solve all problems?*

- *What kind of reasoning do juries need to be good at?*

- *When people say that all opinions and claims are equally valid, what error are they making?*

REASONING RATIONALLY

Reasoning is purposeful mental activity that involves operating on information in order to reach conclusions. Unlike impulsive or nonconscious responding, reasoning requires us to draw specific inferences from observations, facts, or assumptions.

Formal Reasoning: Algorithms and Logic

In *formal reasoning problems*—the kind you might find, say, on an intelligence test or a college entrance exam—the information needed for drawing a conclusion or a solution is specified clearly, and there is a single right (or best) answer.

In some types of formal problems and well-defined tasks, all we have to do is apply an **algorithm,** a set of procedures guaranteed to produce a solution even if we don't really know how it works. To solve a problem in long division, for example, we need only apply a series of operations that we all learned in the fourth grade. To make a cake, we need only apply an algorithm called a *recipe*.

For other formal problems, the tools of formal logic are crucial weapons to have in your mental arsenal. These tools include (among others) the processes of deductive and inductive reasoning. In *deductive reasoning*, a conclusion *necessarily* follows from certain propositions or *premises;* for example, if the premises "All human beings are mortal" and "I am a human being" are true, then the conclusion "I am mortal" must necessarily follow. In contrast, in *inductive reasoning*, a conclusion *probably* follows from certain propositions or premises, but it could conceivably be false. For example, if your premises are "I had a delicious meal at Joe's Restaurant on Monday," "I had a delicious meal there again on Tuesday," and "I had another delicious meal there on Wednesday," you might reasonably reach the conclusion that "Joe's Restaurant consistently serves good food." Deductive and inductive reasoning may seem

reasoning
The drawing of conclusions or inferences from observations, facts, or assumptions.

algorithm
A problem-solving strategy guaranteed to produce a solution even if the user does not know how it works.

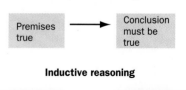

Deductive reasoning

Premises true → Conclusion must be true

Inductive reasoning

Premises true → Conclusion probably true

pretty straightforward, but many of us have trouble thinking logically in our lives.

Informal Reasoning: Heuristics and Dialectical Thinking

Unfortunately, logic and algorithms cannot solve all of life's problems. In *informal reasoning problems,* there may be no clearly correct solution (Galotti, 1989). Information may be incomplete, or people may disagree on what the premises should be. Your position on the controversial issue of abortion, for example, will depend on your premises about when meaningful human life begins, what rights an embryo has, and what rights a woman has to control her own body. People on opposing sides of this issue even disagree on how the premises should be phrased because they have different emotional reactions to terms such as "rights," "meaningful life," and "control over one's body."

In informal reasoning problems, many approaches, viewpoints, or possible solutions may compete, and you may have to decide which one is most reasonable, based on what you know (see Table 6.1). In some cases, the answer is to apply a **heuristic**—a rule of thumb that suggests a course of action without guaranteeing an optimal solution. Anyone who has ever played chess or a card game such as Bridge or Hearts is familiar with heuristics (e.g., "Get rid of high cards first"); in

heuristic

A rule of thumb that suggests a course of action or guides problem solving but does not guarantee an optimal solution.

dialectical reasoning

A process in which opposing facts or ideas are weighed and compared, with a view to determining the best solution or to resolving differences.

these games, working out all the possible sequences of moves would take too long and be too difficult. Heuristics, however, are also useful to an investor trying to predict the stock market, a renter trying to decide whether to lease an apartment, a doctor trying to determine the best treatment for a patient, a marriage counselor advising a troubled couple, and a factory owner trying to boost production: All are faced with incomplete information on which to base a decision and may therefore resort to rules of thumb that have proven effective in the past.

In thinking about real-life problems, a person must also be able to think dialectically. **Dialectical reasoning** is the ability to evaluate opposing points of view. Philosopher Richard Paul (1984) has described it as a process of moving "up and back between contradictory lines of reasoning, using each to critically cross-examine the other":

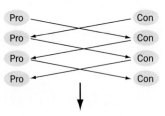

Dialectal reasoning

Arguments:

Most reasonable conclusion based on evidence and logic

Table 6.1	Two Kinds of Reasoning

In formal reasoning, we apply rules of logic to solve well-specified problems. In informal, everyday reasoning, we must solve problems that are less clearly defined. Here are some differences between the two modes of thought:

Formal	Informal
All premises are supplied.	Some premises are implicit and some are not supplied at all.
There is typically one correct answer.	There are typically several possible answers that vary in quality.
Established methods often exist for solving the problem.	Established procedures of inference that apply to the problem rarely exist.
You usually know when the problem is solved.	It is often unclear whether the current solution is good enough.
The problem is often of limited real-world interest.	The problem typically has personal relevance.
Problems are solved for their own sake.	Problems are often solved as a means of achieving other goals.

Source: Adapted from Galotti, 1989.

Deductive and inductive reasoning alone will not enable the members of this jury to reach a conclusion. They will also need to reason dialectically, weighing the evidence for and against guilt or innocence and judging the reasonableness of the attorneys' arguments.

Dialectical reasoning is what juries are supposed to do to arrive at a verdict: consider arguments for and against the defendant's guilt, point and counterpoint. It is also what voters are supposed to do when thinking about whether the government should raise taxes or lower them, or about the best way to improve public education.

Reflective Judgment

Many adults clearly have trouble thinking dialectically. Evidence comes from the research of Karen Kitchener and Patricia King, who for many years have been asking adolescents and adults of all ages and occupations where they stand on such issues as nuclear power, the safety of food additives, and the objectivity of the news media. Kitchener and King are not interested in how much people know about these issues, or even how they feel about them, but rather in how they

think. More specifically, these researchers want to know whether people use reflective judgment in thinking about everyday problems (King & Kitchener, 1994; Kitchener & King, 1990). *Reflective judgment* is basically what we have called critical thinking: the ability to evaluate and integrate evidence, relate that evidence to a theory or opinion, and reach a conclusion that can be defended as reasonable or plausible. To think reflectively, you must question assumptions, consider alternative interpretations, and stand ready to reassess your conclusions in the face of new information.

King and Kitchener and their colleagues have interviewed more than 1,700 adolescents and adults, ranging in age from 14 to 65. (Some of this research has followed the same individuals for up to a decade.) First the researchers provide the interviewee with statements that describe opposing viewpoints on various topics. Then the interviewer asks, What do you think about these statements? How did you come to hold that point of

Get Involved

Here's some practice in dialectical reasoning. Choose a controversial topic, such as whether marijuana should be legalized or whether the right to abortion should be revoked. First, list all the arguments you can think of that support your own position. Then list all the arguments you can think of on the *other side* of the issue. You do not have to agree with these arguments; just list them. Do you feel a mental block or emotional discomfort while doing this? Can you imagine how opponents of your position would answer your arguments? Having strong opinions is fine; you should have an (informed) opinion on matters of public interest. But does that opinion get in the way of even imagining a contrary point of view or of altering your view if the evidence warrants?

view? On what do your base your position? Can you ever know for sure that your position is correct? Why do you suppose disagreement exists about this issue?

King and Kitchener have identified seven cognitive stages on the road to reflective thought, some occurring in childhood and others unfolding throughout adolescence and adulthood. At each stage, people make different kinds of assumptions about how things are known and use different ways of justifying or defending their beliefs. Each stage builds on the skills of the prior one and lays a foundation for successive ones.

We will not be concerned here with the details of these stages, but only with their broad outlines. In general, people in the two early, *prereflective* stages assume that a correct answer always exists and that it can be obtained directly through the senses ("I know what I've seen") or from authorities ("They said so on the news"; "That's what I was brought up to believe"). If authorities don't yet have the truth, prereflective thinkers tend to reach conclusions on the basis of what "feels right" at the moment. They do not distinguish between knowledge and belief, or between belief and evidence, and they don't see any reason for justifying a belief (King & Kitchener, 1994):

INTERVIEWER: Can you ever know for sure that your position [on evolution] is correct?

RESPONDENT: Well, some people believe that we evolved from apes and that's the way they want to believe. But I would never believe that way and nobody could talk me out of the way I believe because I believe the way that it's told in the Bible.

During the three *quasi-reflective* stages, people recognize that some things cannot be known with absolute certainty, but they are not sure how to deal with these situations. They realize that judgments should be supported by reasons, but they pay attention only to evidence that fits what they already believe. They know that there are alternative viewpoints, but they seem to think that because knowledge is uncertain, any judgment about the evidence is purely subjective. Quasi-reflective thinkers will defend a position by saying that "We all have a right to our own opinion," as if all opinions are created equal. Here is the response of a college student who uses quasi-reflective reasoning:

INTERVIEWER: Can you say you will ever know for sure that chemicals [in foods] are safe?

STUDENT: No, I don't think so.

INTERVIEWER: Can you tell me why you'll never know for sure?

STUDENT: Because they test them in little animals, and they haven't really tested them in humans, as far as I know. And I don't think anything is for sure.

INTERVIEWER: When people differ about matters such as this, is it the case that one opinion is right and one is wrong?

STUDENT: No. I think it just depends on how you feel personally because people make their decisions based upon how they feel and what research they've seen. So what one person thinks is right, another person might think is wrong. . . . If I feel that chemicals cause cancer and you feel that food is unsafe without it, your opinion might be right to you and my opinion is right to me.

In the last two stages, a person becomes capable of reflective judgment. He or she understands that although some things can never be known with certainty, some judgments are more valid than others because of their coherence, their fit with the evidence, their usefulness, and so on. People at these stages are willing to consider evidence from a variety of sources and to reason dialectically. At the very highest stage, they are able to defend their conclusions as representing the most complete, plausible, or compelling understanding of an issue, based on currently available evidence. This interview with a graduate student illustrates reflective thinking:

INTERVIEWER: Can you ever say you know for sure that your point of view on chemical additives is correct?

STUDENT: No, I don't think so [but] I think that we can usually be reasonably certain, given the information we have now, and considering our methodologies.

INTERVIEWER: Is there anything else that contributes to not being able to be sure?

STUDENT: Yes. . . . It might be that the research wasn't conducted rigorously enough. In other words, we might have flaws in our data or sample, things like that.

INTERVIEWER: How then would you identify the "better opinion"?

STUDENT: One that takes as many factors as possible into consideration. I mean one that uses the higher percentage of the data that we have, and perhaps that uses the methodology that has been most reliable.

INTERVIEWER: And how do you come to a conclusion about what the evidence suggests?

STUDENT: I think you have to take a look at the different opinions and studies that are offered by different groups. Maybe some studies offered by the chemical industry, some studies by the government, some private studies. . . . You wouldn't trust, for instance, a study funded by the tobacco industry that proved that cigarette smoking is not harmful . . . you have to try to interpret people's motives and that makes it a more complex soup to try to strain out.

Most people do not show evidence of reflective judgment until their middle or late twenties—if at all. That doesn't mean they're incapable of it; most studies have measured people's typical performance, not their *optimal* performance. When students get support for thinking reflectively and opportunities to practice it, their reasoning processes tend to become more complex, sophisticated, and well-grounded (Kitchener et al., 1993). This may be one reason that higher education seems to move people gradually closer to reflective judgment. Most undergraduates, whatever their age, tend to score at Stage 3 during their first year of college, and at Stage 4 as seniors; most graduate students score at Stage 4 or 5; and many advanced doctoral students perform consistently at Stage 6 (King & Kitchener, 1994). (Longitudinal studies show that these differences do not occur only because lower-level thinkers are more likely to drop out of school along the way.)

The gradual development of thinking skills among undergraduates, said Barry Kroll (1992), represents an abandonment of "ignorant certainty" in favor of "intelligent confusion." It may not seem so, but this is a big step forward! You can see why, in this book, we emphasize thinking about and evaluating psychological findings, and not just memorizing them.

??? QUICK QUIZ

Put on your thinking cap to answer these questions.

1. Most of the items Mervin bought as holiday gifts this year cost more than they did last year, so he concludes that inflation is increasing. Is he using inductive, deductive, or dialectical reasoning?

2. Yvonne is arguing with Henrietta about whether real estate is a better investment than stocks. "You can't convince me," says Yvonne. "I just know I'm right." Yvonne needs training in _____ reasoning.

3. Seymour thinks the media have a liberal political bias, and Sophie thinks they're too conservative. "Well," says Seymour, "I have my truth and you have yours. It's purely subjective." Which of King and Kitchener's levels of thinking is Seymour at?

 4. What kind of evidence might resolve the issue that Seymour and Sophie are arguing about?

Answers:
1. inductive 2. dialectical 3. quasi-reflective 4. Researchers might have raters watch a random sample of TV news shows and measure the amount of time devoted to conservative and liberal politicians or viewpoints. Or raters could read a random sample of newspaper editorials from all over the country and evaluate the editorials as liberal or conservative in outlook. You can probably think of other strategies as well. However, having people judge whether entire TV programs or newspapers are slanted in one direction or the other, based solely on their own subjective impressions, might not be informative because people often perceive only what they want or expect to perceive.

What's Ahead

- *Why do people worry about dying in an airplane crash but ignore dangers that are far more likely?*

- *How might your physician's choice of words affect which treatment you choose?*

- *When "Monday morning quarterbacks" say they knew all along who would win Sunday's big game, what bias might they be showing?*

- *Why will a terrible hazing make you more loyal to the group that hazed you?*

BARRIERS TO REASONING RATIONALLY

In spite of the human ability to think logically, reason dialectically, and make judgments reflectively, it is abundantly clear that most of us don't always

Thinking Critically About Why We Don't Think Critically

do so. One obstacle to rational thinking may be the need to be right. We all have our convictions, of course, but if your self-esteem depends on being right all the time, you will find it hard to listen with an open mind to competing views. Another obstacle may be a sort of mental laziness traceable in part to the replacement of reading by television watching. Television news often gives us sound bites instead of fully developed arguments, encouraging us to form quick, impulsive opinions instead of carefully considered ones. As writer Mitchell Stephens

availability heuristic
The tendency to judge the probability of a type of event by how easy it is to think of examples or instances.

(1991) said, "All television demands is our gaze."

Human thought processes are also subject to many normal, predictable biases and errors that affect personal, economic, and political decision making (Simon, 1973; Tversky & Kahneman, 1986). Psychologists have studied dozens of these cognitive pitfalls; here we report just a few of them.

Exaggerating the Improbable

One common bias is the inclination to exaggerate the probability of very rare events—a bias that helps explain why so many people enter lotteries and why they buy airline disaster insurance. People are especially likely to exaggerate the likelihood of a rare event if its consequences are catastrophic. One reason is the **availability heuristic,** the tendency to judge the probability of an event by how easy it is to think of examples or instances (Tversky & Kahneman, 1973). Catastrophes stand out in our minds and are therefore more "available" than other kinds of negative events. In one study, people overestimated the frequency of deaths from tornadoes and underestimated the frequency of deaths from asthma, which occur 20 times as often but do not make headlines. These same people estimated deaths from accidents and disease to be equally frequent, even though 16 times as many people die each year from disease as from accidents (Lichtenstein et al., 1978).

People will sometimes work themselves into a froth about highly unlikely events, such as dying in an airplane crash, yet they will irrationally ignore dangers to human life that are harder to visualize,

Many of us overestimate the chances of dying in a plane crash and underestimate the chances of dying in a car crash. One reason, as the text explains, is the availability heuristic: Although airline disasters are rare, we remember them better than the automobile accidents that take place every day.

such as a growth in skin-cancer rates due to depletion of the ozone layer in the earth's atmosphere. Similarly, parents are often more frightened about real but unlikely threats to their children, such as being kidnapped by a stranger or dying from a routine immunization shot (both horrible but extremely rare), than they are about problems more common in children, such as depression, delinquency, and poor grades (Stickler et al., 1991).

Avoiding Loss

In general, people making decisions try to avoid or minimize risks, losses, and negative outcomes. So when a choice is framed in terms of risk, they will respond more cautiously than when the *same* choice is framed in terms of gain. They will, for example, choose a ticket that has a 10 percent chance of winning a raffle to one that has a 90 percent chance of losing! Or they will rate a condom as effective when they are told it has a 95 percent success rate in protecting against the AIDS virus, but not when they are told it has a 5 percent failure rate—which is logically the same thing (Linville, Fischer, & Fischhoff, 1992).

Here's another example. Suppose you had to choose between two health programs to combat a disease expected to kill 600 people. Which would you prefer, a program that would definitely save 200 people, or one with a one-third probability of saving all 600 people and a two-thirds probability of saving none? (Figure 6.1a illustrates this choice.) When asked this question, most people, including physicians, say they prefer the first program. In other words, they reject the riskier though potentially more rewarding solution in favor of a sure gain. However, people *will* take a risk if they see it as a way to *avoid loss*. Suppose now that you have to choose between a program in which 400 people will definitely die and a program in which there is a one-third probability of nobody dying and a two-thirds probability that all 600 will die. If you think about it, you will see that the alternatives are exactly the same as in the first problem; they are merely worded differently (see Figure 6.1b). Yet this time, most people choose the second solution. They reject risk when they think of the outcome in terms of lives saved but accept risk when they think of the outcome in terms of lives lost (Tversky & Kahneman, 1981).

Few of us will have to face a decision involving hundreds of lives, but we may have to choose between different medical treatments for ourselves

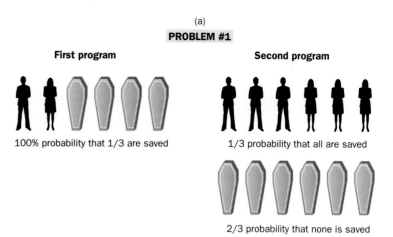

(a)

PROBLEM #1

First program

100% probability that 1/3 are saved

Second program

1/3 probability that all are saved

2/3 probability that none is saved

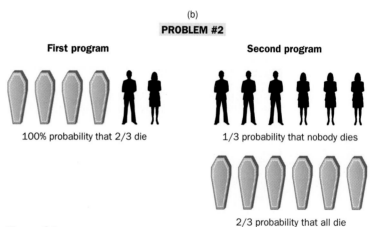

(b)

PROBLEM #2

First program

100% probability that 2/3 die

Second program

1/3 probability that nobody dies

2/3 probability that all die

Figure 6.1

A Matter of Wording

People's decisions depend on how the alternatives are framed. When asked to choose between the programs in (a), which are described in terms of lives saved, most people choose the first program. When asked to choose between the programs in (b), which are described in terms of lives lost, most people choose the second program. Yet the alternatives in (a) are actually identical to those in (b).

or a relative. Our decision may be affected by whether the doctor frames the choice in terms of chances of surviving or chances of dying.

The Confirmation Bias

When people want to make the most accurate judgment possible, they usually try to consider all of the relevant information. But when they are thinking about issues they already feel strongly about, they tend to give in to the **confirmation bias,** paying attention only to evidence that confirms what they want to believe, and finding fault with evidence or arguments that point in a different direction

confirmation bias

The tendency to look for or pay attention only to information that confirms one's own belief.

(Edwards & Smith, 1996; Kunda, 1990). We rarely hear someone say, "Oh, thank you for explaining to me why my lifelong philosophy of child raising (or politics, or investing) is wrong. I'm so grateful for the facts!" The person usually says, "Oh, buzz off, and take your cockamamie ideas with you."

You can see the confirmation bias at work in yourself, your friends, politicians, and editorial writers—whenever people are defending their beliefs and seeking to confirm them. Politicians, for example, are likely to accept economic news that confirms their philosophies and dismiss counterevidence as biased or unimportant. Police officers who are convinced of a suspect's guilt are likely to take anything the suspect says or does as evidence that confirms it. Unfortunately, the con-

firmation bias also affects many jury members. In one study, people listened to an audiotaped reenactment of an actual murder trial and then said how they would have voted and why. Instead of considering and weighing possible verdicts in light of the evidence, many people quickly constructed a story about what had happened and then considered only the evidence that supported their version of events. These same people were the most confident in their decisions and were most likely to vote for an extreme verdict (Kuhn, Weinstock, & Flaton, 1994).

The confirmation bias can also affect how students react to what they learn. When students read about scientific findings that dispute one of their own cherished beliefs or that challenge the

---

Get Involved

Suppose someone deals out four cards, each with a letter on one side and a number on the other. You can only see one side of each card:

E	J	6	7

Your job is to find out whether the following rule is true: "If a card has a vowel on one side, then it has an even number on the other side." Which two cards do you need to turn over to find out?

The vast majority of people say they would turn over the E and the 6, but they are wrong. You do need to turn over the E (a vowel) because if the number on the other side is even, it confirms the rule, and if it's odd, the rule is false. However, the card with the 6 tells you nothing. The rule doesn't say that a card with an even number must always have a vowel on the other side. So it doesn't matter whether the 6 has a vowel or a consonant on the other side. The card you *do* need to turn over is the 7, because if it has a vowel on the other side, that fact disconfirms the rule.

People do poorly on this problem because they are biased to look for confirming evidence and because they ignore the possibility of disconfirming evidence. Don't feel too bad if you missed it. Most judges, lawyers, and people with doctorates do, too. On the other hand, everyone does better when the problem is more realistic. Try this one (from Griggs & Cox, 1982):

Drinking beer	Drinking cola	16 years old	22 years old

Rule: If a person is drinking beer, then
the person is over 19 years of age.

Which two cards must you turn over? The answer is on page 224.

wisdom of their own actions, they tend to acknowledge but minimize the strengths of the research. In contrast, when a study supports their view, they will acknowledge any flaws (such as a small sample or a reliance on self-reports) but will give these flaws less weight than they would otherwise (Sherman & Kunda, 1989). In thinking critically, people apply a double standard: They think most critically about results they don't like. Even psychologists do this!

Biases Due to Mental Sets

Another roadblock on the way to rational thinking is the development of a **mental set,** a tendency to try to solve new problems by using the same heuristics, strategies, and rules that worked in the past on similar problems. Mental sets make human learning and problem solving efficient; because of them, we do not have to keep reinventing the wheel. But mental sets are not helpful when a problem calls for fresh insights and methods. They cause us to cling rigidly to the same old assumptions, hypotheses, and strategies, blinding us to better or more rapid solutions. (The Get Involved exercise on this page illustrates this point.)

One common mental set is the tendency to find patterns in events. The quest for meaningful patterns is adaptive because it helps us understand and exert some control over life's events. But it also leads us to see meaningful patterns even when they don't exist. For example, many people with arthritis think that their symptoms follow a pattern dictated by the weather. They suffer more, they say, when the barometric pressure changes, or when it's damp or humid out. But when Donald Redelmeier and Amos Tversky (1996) followed 18 arthritis patients for 15 months, they found *no* association between weather conditions and the patients' self-reported pain levels, their ability to function in daily life, or a doctor's evaluation of their joint tenderness. (The patients, by the way, refused to believe these results.)

The Hindsight Bias

Would you have been able to predict, beforehand, that the movie *Titanic* would become a smashing success instead of the box-office disaster forecast by many in Hollywood? Would you have known, beforehand, that the underdog Denver Broncos would win the 1998 Super Bowl instead of the heavily favored Green Bay Packers? People who learn the outcome of an event or the answer to a question tend to be sure that they "knew it all along." Armed with the wisdom of hindsight, they see the outcome that actually occurred as inevitable, and they overestimate their ability to have predicted what happened. Compared with judgments made *before* an event takes place, their judgments about their ability to have predicted the event in advance are inflated (Fischhoff, 1975; Hawkins & Hastie, 1990).

mental set
A tendency to solve problems using procedures that worked before on similar problems.

Get Involved

Copy the following figure and see whether you can connect the dots by using no more than four straight lines, without lifting your pencil or pen. A line must pass through each point. Can you do it?

Most people have difficulty with this problem because they have a mental set to interpret the arrangement of dots as a square. Once having done so, they then assume that they can't extend a line beyond the "boundaries" of the square. Now that you know this, you might try again if you haven't yet solved the puzzle. Some possible solutions are given on page 225.

This **hindsight bias** shows up in all kinds of after-the-fact assessments—political ("I always knew my candidate would win"), medical ("I could have told you that mole was cancerous"), and military ("The generals should have known the Japanese were going to attack Pearl Harbor"). Sometimes this bias helps us learn efficiently: When we're trying to make sense of the past, explaining outcomes that didn't occur can be a waste of time. But as Scott Hawkins and Reid Hastie (1990) wrote, "hindsight biases represent the dark side of successful learning and judgment" because when we are sure we knew something "all along," we are less willing to find out what we need to know in order to make accurate predictions in the future. In medical conferences, for example, when doctors are told what the postmortem findings were for a patient who died, they tend to think the case was easier than it actually was ("I would have known it was a brain tumor"), and so they learn less from the case than they should (Dawson et al., 1988).

Perhaps you feel that we're not telling you anything new because you have always known about the hindsight bias. If so, could you have a hindsight bias about the hindsight bias?

Cognitive-Dissonance Reduction

In 1994, Americans were stunned when football legend O. J. Simpson was charged with murdering his former wife Nicole Brown and her friend Ron Goldman. Glued to their television sets, viewers watched in shock as Simpson, who had always seemed the quintessential nice guy, was pursued by a caravan of police on a Los Angeles freeway, then arrested at his home and led away in handcuffs. Some reacted by quickly revising their opinion of their fallen hero. Others, however, groped to make sense of the unimaginable. Perhaps Simpson had run from the police because he was suicidal with grief over his ex-wife's death. Perhaps one of the police investigators had planted incriminating evidence (an argument later used successfully by the defense attorneys). Perhaps the media were exploiting the case by exaggerating the evidence against Simpson. Perhaps he did kill Nicole, but only after she provoked the attack.

To psychologists, such strategies for coming to terms with information that conflicts with existing ideas are predictable. They can be explained, said Leon Festinger (1957), by the theory of **cognitive dissonance.** "Dissonance," the opposite of consistency ("consonance"), is a state of tension that occurs when a person simultaneously holds either two cognitions (beliefs, thoughts, attitudes) that are psychologically inconsistent or a belief that is incongruent with the person's behavior. This tension is uncomfortable, and someone in a state of dissonance will therefore be motivated to reduce it—by rejecting or changing a belief, by changing a behavior, by adding new beliefs, or by rationalizing (Harmon-Jones et al., 1996).

For example, cigarette smoking is dissonant with the awareness that smoking causes illness. If you smoke, you might try to reduce the dissonance by trying to quit; by rejecting the evidence that smoking is bad; by persuading yourself that you will quit later on ("after these exams"); by emphasizing the benefits of smoking ("A cigarette helps me relax"); or by deciding that you don't want a long life, anyhow ("It will be shorter, but sweeter"). Cigarette manufacturers are equally talented at reducing dissonance. When the president of one tobacco company was told that smoking during pregnancy increases the chances of having a low-birthweight baby, he replied, "Some women would prefer having smaller babies" (quoted in Kluger, 1996).

You can also see cognitive-dissonance reduction at work among people who believe that doomsday is at hand. Do you ever wonder what happens to true believers when a doomsday prophecy fails? Do they ever say, "Boy, what a jerk I was"? What would dissonance theory predict?

Many years ago, Festinger and two associates explored people's reactions to failed prophecies by

hindsight bias

The tendency to overestimate one's ability to have predicted an event once the outcome is known; the "I knew it all along" phenomenon.

cognitive dissonance

A state of tension that occurs when a person simultaneously holds two cognitions that are psychologically inconsistent, or when a person's belief is incongruent with his or her behavior.

This police photo of O. J. Simpson, taken after his arrest for murder, put millions of his fans into a state of cognitive dissonance, forcing them to search for ways to resolve their conflicting feelings.

infiltrating a group of people who thought the world would end on December 21 of that year (Festinger, Riecken, & Schachter, 1956). The group's leader, whom the researchers called Marian Keech, promised that the faithful would be picked up by a flying saucer and whisked to safety at midnight on December 20. Many of her followers quit their jobs and spent all their savings, waiting for the end. What would they do or say, Festinger and his colleagues wondered, to reduce the dissonance between "The world is still muddling along on the 21st" and "I predicted the end of the world and sold all my worldly possessions"?

The researchers predicted that believers who had made no public commitment to the prophecy, who awaited the end of the world by themselves at home, would simply lose their faith. But those who had acted on their conviction, waiting with Keech for the spaceship, would be in a state of dissonance. They would, said the researchers, have to *increase* their religious belief to avoid the intolerable realization that they had behaved foolishly. That is just what happened. At 4:45 A.M., long past the appointed hour of the saucer's arrival, the leader had a new vision. The world had been spared, she said, because of the impressive faith of her little band.

Cognitive-dissonance theory thus predicts that people will resist or rationalize information that conflicts with their existing ideas. Here are three of the conditions under which you are particularly likely to try to reduce dissonance (Aronson, Wilson, & Akert, 1997; Taylor, Peplau, & Sears, 1997):

1. *When you feel that you have freely made a decision.* If you think you freely chose to join a group, sell your possessions, or smoke a cigarette, you will feel dissonance if these actions prove misguided. There is no dissonance, however, between "The Army drafted me; I had no choice" and "I hate basic training."

2. *When what you do violates your self-concept.* If you are in a political discussion at a party and you pretend to agree with the majority's position for the sake of harmony, you will experience dissonance only if you have a concept of yourself as always honest and true to your convictions. If you lie frequently and you know it (and don't care), you won't feel dissonance, even if your words contradict your beliefs (Thibodeau & Aronson, 1992).

3. *When you put a lot of effort into a decision, only to find the results less than you had hoped for.* The harder you work to reach a goal, or the more you suffer for it, the more you will try to convince yourself that you value the goal, even if the goal isn't so great after all (Aronson & Mills, 1959). This explains why hazing, whether in social clubs or in the military, turns new recruits into loyal members. The cognition "I went through a lot of awful stuff to join this group" is dissonant with the cognition "only to find I hate the group." Therefore, people must decide either that the hazing wasn't so bad or that they really like the group. This mental reevaluation is called the *justification of effort,* and it is one of the most popular methods of reducing dissonance.

Cognitive-dissonance theory has its limitations. It can be hard to know when two cognitions are inconsistent: What is dissonant to you may be neutral or pleasingly paradoxical to another. Moreover, some people reduce dissonance by admitting their mistakes instead of rationalizing them. Still, there is vast evidence of a motive for cognitive consistency under some conditions, and this motive can lead to irrational decisions and actions.

As you can see, the decisions and judgments that people make, and the feelings of regret or pleasure

Cognitive-dissonance theory predicts the "justification of effort." The more you must endure to reach a goal, the more highly you will value it—which may be one reason fraternities often subject pledges to disgusting, frightening, or even dangerous hazing. These initiates, blindfolded and forced to wear vomit-drenched T-shirts, were also covered with molasses and were urinated on by their new fraternity brothers. They probably became devoted members.

that follow, are not always logical. This fact has enormous implications for decision makers in the legal system, business, medicine, government—in fact, in all areas. But before you despair about the human ability to think clearly and rationally, we should tell you that the situation is not hopeless. People are not equally irrational in all situations. When they are doing things they have some expertise in, or making decisions that have serious consequences, cognitive biases often diminish. Accountants who audit companies' books, for example, are less subject to the confirmation bias than are undergraduates in psychology experiments, perhaps because auditors can be sued if they overestimate a firm's profitability or economic health (Smith & Kida, 1991).

Further, once we understand a bias, we may be able to reduce or eliminate it. For example, we have seen that doctors are vulnerable to the hind-sight bias if they already know what caused a patient's death. But Hal Arkes and his colleagues (1988) were able to reduce a similar bias in neuropsychologists. The psychologists were given a case study and asked to state one reason why each of three possible diagnoses—alcohol withdrawal, Alzheimer's disease, and brain damage—might have been applicable. This procedure forced the psychologists to consider all the evidence, not just evidence that supported the correct diagnosis. The hindsight bias evaporated, presumably because the psychologists realized that the correct diagnosis had not been so obvious at the time the patient was being treated.

Some people, of course, seem to think more clearly than others habitually; we call them "intelligent." But just what is intelligence, and how can we measure and refine it? We take up that question next.

??? QUICK QUIZ

Think rationally to answer these questions.

1. Stu takes a study break and meets a young woman at the student cafeteria. They hit it off, start to see each other regularly, and eventually get married. Says Stu, "I knew that day, when I headed for the cafeteria, that something special was about to happen." What cognitive bias is affecting Stu's thinking?

2. In a classic study of cognitive dissonance (Festinger & Carlsmith, 1959), students did some boring, repetitive tasks and then had to tell another student, who was waiting to participate in the study, that the work was interesting and fun. Half the students were offered $20 for telling this lie and the others only $1. Which students who lied decided later on that the tasks had been fun after all?

Answers:
1. the hindsight bias   2. The students who got only $1: They were in a state of dissonance because "the task was as dull as dishwater" is dissonant with "I said I enjoyed it—and for a mere dollar, at that." Those who got $20 could rationalize that the large sum (which was *really* large in 1956) justified the lie.

What's Ahead

- *Is it possible to design intelligence tests that aren't influenced by culture?*

- *Why do some psychologists oppose traditional intelligence testing and others defend it?*

- *What kind of intelligence allows you to master the unspoken rules for academic success?*

- *What's your "EQ"—and why is it as important as IQ?*

INTELLIGENCE

The educator Sylvia Ashton-Warner once called intelligence "the tool to find the truth—a tool that must be kept sharpened." Yet much as we all desire to possess this tool, it is hard to agree on just what it is. Some psychologists equate it with the ability to reason abstractly, others with the ability to learn and profit from experience in daily life. Some emphasize the ability to think rationally, others the ability to act purposefully. These qualities are all probably part of what most people mean by **intelligence,** but theorists weigh them differently.

One of the longest-running debates in psychology is whether a global quality called "intelligence" even exists. A typical intelligence test asks you to do several things: provide a specific bit of information, notice similarities between objects, solve arithmetic problems, define words, fill in the missing parts of incomplete pictures, arrange pictures in a logical order, arrange blocks to resemble a design, assemble puzzles, use a coding scheme, or judge what behavior would be appropriate in a particular situation. Researchers use a statistical method called *factor analysis* to try to identify which basic abilities underlie performance on the various items. As we saw in Chapter 2, this procedure identifies clusters of correlated items that seem to be measuring some common ability, or factor. Many scientists believe that a general ability, or **g factor,** underlies many specific abilities and talents (Herrnstein & Murray, 1994; Spearman, 1927; Wechsler, 1955). Others dispute the existence of a g factor, arguing that a person can excel in some tasks yet do poorly in others (Gould, 1994; Guilford, 1988). Disagreements over how to define intelligence have led some writers to suggest, only half-jokingly, that intelligence is "whatever intelligence tests measure."

Measuring Intelligence: The Psychometric Approach

The traditional approach to intelligence, the **psychometric** approach, focuses on how well people perform on standardized aptitude tests. The tests you take in your courses are called *achievement tests* because they are designed to measure skills and knowledge that have been explicitly taught. *Aptitude tests,* in contrast, are designed to measure the ability to acquire skills or knowledge in the future. For example, vocational aptitude tests can help you decide whether you will do better as a mechanic or a musician, and IQ tests do a pretty good job of predicting school performance. But all mental tests are in some sense achievement tests because they assume past learning or experience with particular objects, words, or situations. The difference between achievement tests and aptitude tests is one of degree and intended use.

Binet's Brainstorm.   The first intelligence test was devised in 1904, when the French Ministry of Education asked psychologist Alfred Binet (1857–1911) to design a test that would identify children who were slow learners and who therefore would benefit from remedial work. The ministry was reluctant to let teachers identify such children because the teachers might have prejudices about poor children or might assume that shy or disruptive children were retarded. Wrestling with the problem, Binet had a great insight: In the classroom, the responses of "dull" children resembled those of ordinary children of younger ages. Bright children, on the other hand, responded like children of older ages. The thing to measure, then, was a child's **mental age (MA),** or level of intellectual development relative to other children's. Then instruction could be tailored to the child's capabilities.

The test devised by Binet and his colleague, Theophile Simon, measured memory, vocabulary, and perceptual discrimination. Items ranged from those that most young children could do easily to those that only older children could handle, as determined by the testing of large numbers of children. A scoring system developed later by others used a formula in which the child's mental age was divided by the child's chronological age (CA) to yield an **intelligence quotient,** or **IQ.** Thus a child of 8 who performed like the average 6-year-old would have a mental age of 6 and an IQ of 75 (6 divided by 8, times 100); and a child of 8 who scored like an average 10-year-old would have a mental age of 10 and an IQ of 125 (10 divided by 8, times 100). All average children, regardless of age, would have an IQ of 100 because MA and CA would be the same. (In actual calculations, months were used, not years, to yield a more precise figure.)

This method of figuring IQ had serious flaws. At one age, scores might cluster tightly around the average, whereas at another age they might be more dispersed. As a result, the score necessary to be in the top 10 or 20 or 30 percent of your age group varied, depending on your age. Also, the IQ formula did not make much sense for adults: a 50-year-old who scores like a 30-year-old does not have low intelligence! Today, therefore, intelligence tests are scored differently. The average is usually set arbitrarily at 100, and tests are constructed so that about two-thirds of all people score between 85 and 115. Individual scores are computed from tables based on established norms. These scores are still informally referred to as "IQs," and they still reflect how a person compares with other people, either children of a particular age or adults in general. At all ages, the distribution of scores approximates a normal (bell-shaped) curve, with scores near the average

intelligence

An inferred characteristic of an individual, usually defined as the ability to profit from experience, acquire knowledge, think abstractly, act purposefully, or adapt to changes in the environment.

g factor

A general intellectual ability assumed by many theorists to underlie specific mental abilities and talents.

psychometrics

The measurement of mental abilities, traits, and processes.

mental age (MA)

A measure of mental development expressed in terms of the average mental ability at a given age.

intelligence quotient (IQ)

A measure of intelligence originally computed by dividing a person's mental age by his or her chronological age and multiplying the result by 100; now derived from norms provided for standardized intelligence tests.

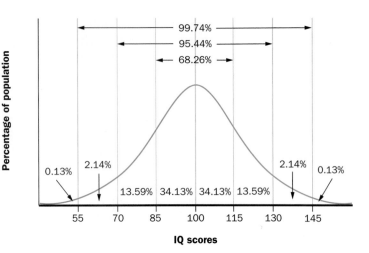

Figure 6.2

Expected Distribution of IQ Scores

In a large population, IQ scores tend to be distributed on a normal (bell-shaped) curve. On most tests, about 68 percent of all people will score between 85 and 115; about 95 percent will score between 70 and 130; and about 99.7 percent will score between 55 and 145. In any actual sample, however, the distribution will depart somewhat from the theoretical ideal.

(mean) most common and very high or very low scores rare (see Figure 6.2).

Binet recognized that all children taking his test in France had similar cultural backgrounds, but that this might not be true elsewhere. He also emphasized that the test merely *sampled* intelligence and did not measure everything covered by that term. A test score, he said, could be useful, along with other information, for predicting school performance under ordinary conditions, but it should not be confused with intelligence itself. The purpose of testing was to identify children with learning problems, not to rank children.

In the United States, Stanford psychologist Lewis Terman revised Binet's test and established norms for American children. His version, the Stanford-Binet Intelligence Scale, was first published in 1916 and has been updated several times since. (For some sample items, see Table 6.2.) Two decades later, David Wechsler, chief psychologist at Bellevue Hospital in New York City, designed another test, expressly for adults, which became the Wechsler Adult Intelligence Scale (WAIS). It was followed by the Wechsler Intelligence Scale for Children (WISC). Although the Wechsler tests produce a general IQ score, they also provide specific scores for different kinds of ability. Verbal items test a person's vocabulary, arithmetic abilities, immediate memory span, ability to recognize similarities (e.g., "How are books and movies

alike?"), and general knowledge and comprehension (e.g., "Who was Thomas Jefferson?" "Why do people who want a divorce have to go to court?"). "Performance" items test a range of nonverbal skills (see Figure 6.3).

When intelligence testing was brought from France to the United States, however, its original purpose got lost at sea. In France, Binet's test had been given to each child individually, so the test giver could see whether a child was ill or nervous, had poor vision, or was not trying. In America, the Wechsler tests and the revised Binet test were also given to individuals, but other intelligence tests were given to huge groups of people, usually students or soldiers, and the advantages of individualized testing were lost. Americans also used the tests for a different purpose than did the French: not to bring slow learners up to the average, but to categorize people in school and in the armed services according to their presumed "natural ability." The testers overlooked the fact that in America, with its many ethnic groups, people did not all share the same background and experience (Gould, 1981/1996).

Intelligence tests developed between World War I and the 1960s for use in schools favored city children over rural ones, middle-class children over poor ones, and white children over minority children. One item, for example, asked whether the Emperor Concerto was written by Beethoven, Mozart, Bach, Brahms, or Mahler. (The answer is Beethoven.) Critics complained that the tests did not measure the kinds of knowledge and skills that are intelligent in a minority neighborhood or in the hills of Appalachia (Scarr, 1984). They also pointed out that because teachers thought IQ scores revealed the limits of a child's potential, low-scoring children might not get the educational attention or encouragement they needed.

Culture-Free and Culture-Fair Tests. In the 1970s, group intelligence testing became a public issue. School boards and employers were sued for restricting the opportunities of low scorers. Some states prohibited the use of group tests for classifying children. Several test makers responded by trying to construct tests that were *culture-free.* Such tests were usually nonverbal; in some, instructions were even pantomimed. Test constructors soon found, however, that culture can affect performance in unexpected ways. In one case, children who had emigrated from Arab countries to Israel were asked to show which detail was missing from a picture of a face with no mouth (Ortar, 1963). The children, who were not used to

Table 6.2	**Sample Items from the Stanford-Binet Intelligence Test, Form L-M**

The older the test taker is, the more the test requires in the way of verbal comprehension and fluency.

Age	Task
4	Fills in the missing word when asked, "Brother is a boy; sister is a ___."
	Answers correctly when asked, "Why do we have houses?"
9	Answers correctly when examiner says, "In an old graveyard in Spain they have discovered a small skull which they believe to be that of Christopher Columbus when he was about 10 years old." What is foolish about that?
	Examiner presents folded paper; child draws how it will look unfolded.
12	Completes "The streams are dry . . . there has been little rain."
	Tells what is foolish about statements such as "Bill Jones's feet are so big that he has to put his trousers on over his head."
Adult	Can describe the difference between *misery* and *poverty*, *character* and *reputation*, *laziness* and *idleness*.
	Explains how to measure 3 pints of water with a 5-pint and a 2-pint can.

Source: From Lewis M. Terman and Maud A. Merrill, *Stanford-Binet Intelligence Scale* (1972 norms ed.). Boston: Houghton Mifflin, 1973. (Currently published by the Riverside Publishing Company.) Items are copyright 1916 by Lewis M. Terman, 1937 by Lewis M. Terman and Maud A. Merrill, © 1960, 1973 by the Riverside Publishing Company. Reproduced or adapted by permission of the publisher.

Picture arrangement
(Arrange the panels to make a meaningful story)

Object assembly
(Put together a jigsaw puzzle)

Digit symbol
(Using the key at the top, fill in the appropriate symbol beneath each number)

Picture completion
(Supply the missing feature)

Block design
(Copy the design shown, using another set of blocks)

Figure 6.3

Performance Tasks on the Wechsler Tests

Nonverbal items such as these are particularly useful for measuring the abilities of those who have poor hearing, are not fluent in the tester's language, have limited education, or resist doing classroom-type problems. A large gap between a person's verbal score and performance score on a Wechsler test sometimes indicates a specific learning problem. (Object assembly, digit symbol, and picture completion adapted from Cronbach, 1990.)

An intelligence test is useful only if it is used intelligently. Testing by the U.S. army during World War I often occurred under noisy, crowded, and confusing conditions, and many items were culturally loaded. Nevertheless, many people concluded from the results that a high proportion of army recruits were "morons."

thinking of a drawing of a head as a complete picture, said that the *body* was missing!

Psychologists then tried to design tests that were *culture-fair*. Their aim was not to eliminate the influence of culture, but to find items that incorporate knowledge and skills common to many different cultures. This approach, too, was less successful than originally hoped, because cultural values affect a person's attitude toward taking tests, comfort while being tested, motivation, rapport with the test giver, competitiveness, and experience in solving problems independently rather than with others (Anastasi, 1988; López, 1995).

Moreover, cultures differ in the problem-solving strategies they emphasize (Serpell, 1994). For example, in the West, children from white, middle-class families typically learn to classify things by category—to say that an apple and a peach are similar because they are both fruits, and that a saw and a rake are similar because they are both tools. But children who are not trained in middle-class ways of sorting things may classify objects according to their sensory qualities or functions. They will say that an apple and a peach are similar because they taste good. That's a charming and innovative answer, but it is one that test administrators interpret as less intelligent (Miller-Jones, 1989).

In theory, it should be possible to establish test norms that are not based on white urban children, by throwing out items on which such children get higher scores than others. A similar strategy was actually used years ago to eliminate sex differ-

ences in IQ. On early tests, girls scored higher than boys at every age (Samelson, 1979). No one was willing to conclude that males were intellectually inferior, so in the 1937 revision of the Stanford-Binet test, Lewis Terman simply deleted the items on which boys had done poorly. Poof! No sex differences.

But few people seem willing to do for cultural differences what Terman did for sex differences, and the reason reveals a dilemma at the heart of intelligence testing. Intelligence tests put some groups of children at a disadvantage, yet they also measure skills and knowledge useful in the classroom. How can educators recognize and accept cultural differences and, at the same time, require students to demonstrate mastery of the skills, knowledge, and attitudes that will help them succeed in school and in the larger society? How can they eliminate bias from tests, while preserving the purpose for which the tests were designed? Anne Anastasi (1988), an eminent testing specialist, has argued that concealing the effects of cultural disadvantage by rejecting conventional tests is "equivalent to breaking a thermometer because it registers a body temperature of 101." Instead, she believes, special help should be given to any child who needs it. Others feel that conventional mental tests do more harm than good. Sociologist Jane Mercer (1988) tried for years to get testers to understand that children can be *ignorant* of information required by IQ tests without being *stupid*, but she finally gave up, resolving instead to "kill the IQ test."

Beyond the IQ Test.   The resolution of this debate may depend on whether test users can learn to use intelligence tests more intelligently. Most educators feel that the tests have value, as long as a person's background is kept in mind and the results are interpreted cautiously. IQ tests predict school performance fairly well: Correlations between IQ scores and current or future school grades range between .40 and .60. IQ tests often identify not only the mentally retarded, but also gifted students who have not previously considered higher education.

In some schools, a child's placement in a special education program now depends not only on an IQ score, but also on tests of specific abilities, medical data, and the child's demonstrated inability to get along in the family and community. And some schools are returning to Binet's original concept. Instead of using group tests to label and categorize children, they give individual tests to identify a child's strengths and weaknesses so that teachers can design individualized programs that will boost the child's performance.

This change in emphasis reflects an increasing awareness that the intellect—and IQ scores—can be improved, even in the mentally retarded (Butterfield & Belmont, 1977; Feuerstein, 1980; Sternberg, 1986). Educators also now realize that a person may have a **learning disability**—a problem with a specific mental skill, such as reading or arithmetic—without having a general intellectual impairment. Many children with learning

disabilities have normal or even superior intelligence and can overcome or compensate for their handicaps.

Critics of traditional approaches to measuring intelligence, however, argue that when a child's abilities don't match those expected by teachers and testers, the best solution may be to modify the classroom or the test. Anthropologist Shirley Brice Heath (1983) has shown how this approach can work. In a study of a small African-American community in a southern city, Heath found that black parents were less likely than white parents to ask their children "what," "where," "when," and "who" questions—the sorts of questions found on standardized tests and in schoolbooks ("What's this story about?" "Who is this?"). Black parents preferred to ask analogy questions ("What's that like?") and story-starter questions ("Did you hear about . . . ?"). Teachers in the community used this information to modify their teaching strategies. They encouraged their black pupils to ask "school-type questions," but they also incorporated analogy and story-starter questions into their lessons. Soon the black children, who had previously been uncomfortable and quiet, became eager, confident participants.

Critics also point out that standardized tests don't reveal *how* a person goes about answering questions and solving problems. Nor do they explain why people with low scores on IQ tests often behave intelligently in real life—making smart consumer decisions, winning at the racetrack, and making wise personal choices (Ceci, 1996). Some researchers, therefore, have rejected the psychometric approach to the study and measurement of intelligence in favor of a cognitive approach.

Dissecting Intelligence: The Cognitive Approach

Cognitive psychologists, thinking critically about the very meaning of "intelligence," have questioned prevailing assumptions about the nature of intelligence and the best way to define and measure it. Intelligent behavior, they argue, involves, among other things, encoding problems, noticing similarities and differences, spotting fallacies, and "reading" the environment and other people. In contrast to the psychometric approach to intelligence, which is concerned with how many answers a person gets right on a test, the cognitive approach

Thinking Critically About What It Means to be Smart

Children with Down syndrome, who score low on standard IQ tests, are accomplishing more academically than anyone once thought they could—showing that intellectual ability is not as fixed and immutable as many people assume.

learning disability
A difficulty in the performance of a specific mental skill, such as reading or arithmetic; sometimes linked to perceptual or memory problems.

emphasizes the *strategies* people use when thinking about problems and arriving at a solution.

The Triarchic Theory.

One well-known cognitive theory, Robert Sternberg's *triarchic theory of intelligence* (1988, 1995), distinguishes three aspects of intelligence:

1. *Componential intelligence* refers to the information-processing strategies that go on inside your head when you are thinking intelligently about a problem. These mental "components" include recognizing the problem, selecting a method for solving it, mastering and carrying out the strategy, and evaluating the result. Some of these operations require **metacognition,** the knowledge or awareness of your own cognitive processes and the ability to monitor and control those processes. Students who are weak in metacognition fail to notice when a passage in a textbook is especially difficult or they haven't understood it; as a result, they don't spend enough time on difficult material, and they spend too much time on material they already know (Nelson & Leonesio, 1988). In contrast, students who are strong in metacognition check their comprehension by restating what they have read, backtracking when necessary, and questioning what they are reading (Bereiter & Bird, 1985). (If they are reading this textbook, they also take the Quick Quizzes!)

2. *Experiential intelligence* refers to how creative you are and how well you transfer skills to new situations. People with experiential intelligence cope well with novelty and learn quickly to make new tasks automatic; those who are lacking in this area perform well only under a narrow set of circumstances. For example, Selena may do well in school, where assignments have specific due dates and feedback is immediate, but be less successful after graduation if her job requires her to set her own deadlines and her employer doesn't tell her how she is doing.

3. *Contextual intelligence* refers to the practical application of intelligence, which requires you to take into account the different contexts in which you find yourself. If you are strong in contextual intelligence, you know when to adapt to the environment (you are in a dangerous neighborhood, so you become more vigilant); when to change environments (you had planned to be a teacher but discover that you don't enjoy working with kids, so you switch to accounting); and when to fix the situation (your marriage is rocky, so you and your spouse go for counseling). Without contextual intelligence, you won't acquire *tacit knowledge*—practical strategies for success that usually are not formally taught but must instead be inferred (Sternberg et al., 1995). In studies of college professors, business managers, and salespeople, scores on tests of tacit knowledge do not correlate strongly with conventional ability-test scores, but they do predict effectiveness on the job (Sternberg, Wagner, & Okagaki, 1993). Tacit knowledge about how to be a good student predicts academic success in college as well as entrance exams do (Sternberg & Wagner, 1989).

Most intelligence tests do not measure the experiential and contextual aspects of intelligence, yet these aspects have a powerful effect on personal and occupational success.

Domains of Intelligence.

In other ways, too, cognitive approaches are expanding our understanding of what it means to be intelligent. Howard Gardner (1983), in his *theory of multiple intelligences,* suggests that there are seven "intelligences," or domains of talent: *linguistic, logical-mathematical, spatial, musical, bodily-kinesthetic* (which actors, athletes, and dancers have), *intrapersonal* (insight into yourself), and *interpersonal* (understanding of others). These talents are relatively independent, and each may even have its own neural structures. People with brain damage

metacognition
The knowledge or awareness of one's own cognitive processes.

┌ Get Involved ┐

How good is your tacit knowledge about how to be a student? List as many strategies for success as you can think of. Consider what the successful student does when listening to lectures, participating in class discussions, communicating with professors, preparing for exams, writing term papers, and dealing with an unexpectedly low grade. Many of these strategies are never explicitly taught. You may want to do this exercise with a friend and compare lists. Are there some strategies that one of you thought of and the other didn't?

Intelligence is more than what IQ tests measure. A singer has musical intelligence, a surveyor has spatial intelligence, and a compassionate friend has emotional intelligence.

often lose one of the seven without losing their competence in the others. And some autistic and retarded individuals, once known by the insensitive label "idiot savants" (*savant* means "learned" in French), have exceptional talents in one area, such as music, art, or rapid mathematical computation, despite poor functioning in all others.

Gardner's last two "intelligences" correspond to what some psychologists call *emotional intelligence:* the ability to identify your own and other people's emotions accurately, express your emotions clearly, and regulate emotions in yourself and others (Goleman, 1995; Mayer & Salovey, 1997). People with high emotional intelligence (familiarly known as "EQ") use their emotions to motivate themselves and others, to spur creative thinking, and to deal empathically with others. People who are low in emotional intelligence are often unable to identify their own emotions; they may insist that they're not depressed when a relationship ends, for example, but meanwhile they start drinking too much, become extremely irritable, and stop going out with friends. They express emotions inappropriately, such as by acting violently or impulsively when they are angry or worried. And they misread nonverbal signals from others; for example, they will give a long-winded account of all their problems even when the listener is obviously bored.

Emotional intelligence contributes to school achievement. Children who have difficulty in interpreting nonverbal emotional signals from others are less likely to do well academically, and this is especially true of boys (Nowicki & Duke, 1989). One study compared children whose parents had taught them to analyze and manage feelings of anger with children who had comparable IQs and socioeconomic backgrounds but whose parents were not good "emotional coaches." Those who had learned to understand their own emotions as preschoolers tended at age 8 to score higher on math and reading tests and to have longer attention spans (Hooven, Gottman, & Katz, 1995). Perhaps children who can't read emotional cues from their teachers and classmates, or who can't regulate their own emotions, have trouble learning because they feel anxious, confused, or angry (Goleman, 1995).

People with emotional intelligence are skilled at reading nonverbal emotional cues. Which of these boys do you think feels the cockiest, and which is most anxious? What cues are you using to answer?

??? QUICK QUIZ

How intelligent are you about intelligence?

1. In a sense, all mental tests are (aptitude/achievement) tests.

2. *True or false:* Culture-fair tests have eliminated group differences that show up on traditional IQ tests.

3. What goal do cognitive theories of intelligence have that psychometric theories do not?

4. Logan understands the material in his statistics class, but on tests, he plans his time poorly, spending the entire period on the most difficult problems and never even getting to the problems he can solve easily. According to the triarchic theory of intelligence, which aspect of intelligence does he need to improve?

5. Tracy does not have an unusually high IQ and she was not an A student in school, but at work, she was quickly promoted because she knew how to set priorities, communicate with management, and make others feel valued. Tracy has _____ intelligence and possesses _____ knowledge.

 6. What's wrong with defining intelligence as "whatever intelligence tests measure"?

Answers:

1. achievement 2. false 3. to understand people's strategies for solving problems and use this information to improve mental performance 4. componential intelligence (including metacognition) 5. contextual, tacit 6. The definition is circular. How do we know someone is intelligent? Because he or she scored high on an intelligence test. Why did the person score high? Because the person is intelligent. The definition also discourages criticisms of the tests and efforts to improve them. People are led to assume that a low score must be entirely the scorer's fault rather than the test's. But the test taker may be intelligent in ways that the test fails to measure, and the test may be measuring traits other than intelligence.

What's Ahead

- *If intelligence is highly heritable, does that mean that group differences in IQ are genetic?*

- *Is a child with a low IQ destined to have a low score throughout life?*

- *Some gifted people are professionally successful and others aren't; what makes the difference?*

- *Why do Asian children perform so much better in school than American students do, even though Asian classes are larger, with worse facilities?*

THE ORIGINS OF INTELLIGENCE

"Intelligence," as we have seen, can mean many things. But however we define it, clearly some people think and behave more intelligently than others. What accounts for these differences?

Genes and Intelligence

Behavioral geneticists approach this question by doing heritability studies. In Chapter 2, we saw that *heritability* is the proportion of the total variance in a trait within a group that is attributable to genetic variation within the group. This proportion, which can have a maximum value of 1.0, is usually estimated by doing twin and adoption studies.

Behavioral-genetic studies show that the kind of intelligence that produces high IQ scores is highly heritable. For children and adolescents, heritability estimates average around .50; that is, about half of the variance in IQ scores, give or take a few percentage points, is explainable by genetic differences (Chipuer, Rovine, & Plomin, 1990; Devlin, Daniels, & Roeder, 1997; Plomin, 1989). For adults, the estimates are usually higher—in the .60 to .80 range (Bouchard, 1995; McGue et al., 1993; McClearn et al., 1997). Although the precise estimates range widely across studies, depending on the methods used, the scores of identical twins are always more highly correlated than those of fraternal twins. In fact,

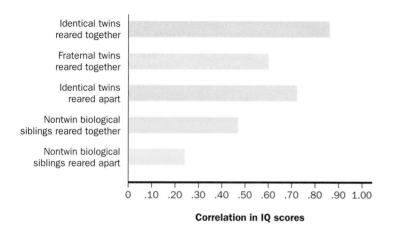

Figure 6.4

Correlations in Siblings' IQ Scores

The IQ scores of identical twins are highly correlated, even when they are reared apart. The figures represented in the graph are based on average correlations across many studies (Bouchard & McGue, 1981).

the scores of identical twins reared *apart* are more highly correlated than those of fraternal twins reared *together,* as you can see in Figure 6.4. And in adoption studies, the scores of adopted children are more highly correlated with those of their birth parents than with those of their biologically unrelated adoptive parents. As adopted children grow into adolescence, the correlation between their IQ scores and those of their biologically unrelated family members diminishes, and in adulthood the correlation is *zero* (Bouchard, 1997b; Scarr, 1993; Scarr & Weinberg, 1994).

These are dramatic findings, but they do not mean that genes determine IQ. In Chapter 2, we saw that if heredity accounts for only part of why people differ on some trait, then the environment must account for the rest. We also saw that a highly heritable trait can nonetheless be highly modifiable by the environment. Thus, even though the IQ scores of adopted children correlate more highly with their birth parents' scores than with those of their adoptive parents (that is, the higher the birth parents' scores, the higher the child's score is likely to be), in *absolute* terms, a child's IQ may differ considerably from the scores of his or her birth parents. Indeed, on average, adopted children have IQs that are 10 to 20 points higher than those of their birth parents (Scarr & Weinberg, 1977). Most psychologists believe that this difference exists because adoptive families are generally smaller, wealthier, and better educated than other families—and these environmental factors are associated with higher IQs in children.

Many people mistakenly infer that if genes influence individual differences in intelligence, genes must also help account for differences between groups. Naturally, this issue has tremendous politi-

cal and social importance, so we are going to look at it closely. Most of the focus has been on black–white differences, because African-American children score, on average, some 10 to 15 points lower on IQ tests than do white children. (Keep in mind that we are talking about *averages;* the distributions of scores for black children and white children overlap considerably.) A few psychologists have proposed a genetic explanation of this difference (Jensen, 1969, 1981; Rushton, 1988). Unfortunately, racists often cite such theories to justify their own hatreds, and politicians have used them to argue for cuts in programs that would benefit blacks and other minorities. It is vital, therefore, that we all know how to evaluate genetic theories of group differences. What are the facts?

One fatal flaw in genetic theories of black–white differences is their use of heritability estimates based mainly on white samples to estimate the role heredity plays in *group* differences. This problem sounds pretty technical, but it is not really difficult to understand, so stay with us.

Thinking Critically About Group Differences in IQ

Consider, first, not people but tomatoes. (This "thought experiment," illustrated in Figure 6.5 on the next page, is based on Lewontin, 1970.) Suppose you have a bag of tomato seeds that vary genetically; all things being equal, some will produce tomatoes that are puny and tasteless, and some will produce tomatoes that are plump and delicious. Now you take a bunch of these seeds in your left hand and another bunch from the same bag in your right hand. Though one seed differs genetically from another, there is no *average* difference between the seeds in your left hand and those in your right. You plant the left hand's seeds in pot A, with some soil that you have doctored

Poor soil   Rich soil

Figure 6.5

The Tomato Plant Experiment

In the hypothetical experiment described in the text, even if the differences among plants within each pot were due entirely to genetics, the average difference *between* pots could be environmental. The same general principle applies to individual and group differences among human beings.

with nitrogen and other nutrients, and you plant the right hand's seeds in pot B, with soil from which you have extracted nutrients. When the tomato plants grow, they will vary *within* each pot in terms of height, the number of tomatoes produced, and the size of the tomatoes, purely because of genetic differences. But there will also be an average difference between the plants in pot A and those in pot B: The plants in pot A will be healthier and bear more tomatoes. This difference *between* pots is due entirely to the different soils—even though the heritability of the *within*-pot differences is 100 percent.

The principle is the same for people as it is for tomatoes. Although intellectual differences *within* groups are at least partly genetic, that does not mean that differences *between* groups are genetic. Blacks and whites do not grow up, on average, in the same "pots" (environments). Because of a long legacy of racial discrimination and de facto segregation, black children (as well as Latino and other minority children) often receive far fewer nutrients—literally, in terms of food, and figuratively, in terms of education, encouragement by society, and intellectual opportunities. This point is often forgotten or overlooked. For example, in

the much-discussed book *The Bell Curve: Intelligence and Class Structure in American Life* (1994), the late psychologist Richard Herrnstein and conservative political theorist Charles Murray cited heritability studies done mostly with whites to imply that the gap in IQ scores between the average white and the average black child can never be closed.

Doing research on the origins of group differences is nearly impossible in the United States, where racism affects the lives of even affluent, successful African-Americans (Cose, 1994; Parker, 1997; Staples, 1994). However, the handful of studies that have overcome past methodological problems fail to reveal any genetic differences between blacks and whites in whatever it is that IQ tests measure. One study found, for example, that children fathered by black and white American soldiers in Germany after World War II and reared in similar German communities by similar families did not differ significantly in IQ (Eyferth, 1961). Another showed that degree of African ancestry (which can be roughly estimated from skin color, blood analysis, and genealogy) was not related to measured intelligence, as a genetic theory of black–white differences would predict (Scarr et al., 1977).

An intelligent reading of the research on intelligence, therefore, does not direct us to conclude that differences among cultural, ethnic, or national groups are permanent, genetically determined, or signs of any group's superiority. On the contrary, the research suggests that we should make sure that all children grow up in the best possible soil, with room for the smartest and the slowest to find a place in the sun.

The Environment and Intelligence

Let's look more closely now at the kinds of environmental deficits that hinder intellectual development, and the environmental "nutrients" that promote it. Here are some of the influences associated with reduced mental ability:

- *Poor prenatal care.* If a pregnant woman is malnourished, contracts infections, takes certain drugs, smokes, drinks excessively, or is exposed to environmental pollutants, the fetus is at risk of having learning disabilities and a reduced IQ.

- *Malnutrition.* The average IQ gap between severely malnourished and well-nourished children can be as high as 20 points (Stoch & Smythe, 1963; Winick, Meyer, & Harris, 1975).

• *Exposure to toxins.* Lead, for example, can damage the nervous system, producing attention problems, lower IQ scores, and poor school achievement (Needleman et al., 1990, 1996). Nearly 9 percent of all children in the United States ages 1 to 5 are exposed to dangerous levels of lead from lead paint and old lead pipes, and for black children ages 1 and 2, the percentage rises to 21.6 (Brody et al., 1994).

• *Large family size.* The average IQ in a family tends to decline as the number of children rises (Belmont & Marolla, 1973). Birth order also makes a difference: IQ tends to decline slightly in each successive child (Zajonc & Markus, 1975). Most researchers attribute these facts to the reduced time parents with many children can spend with each child.

• *Stressful family circumstances.* The Rochester Longitudinal Study has examined family risk factors in the development of several hundred children, from birth through early adolescence (Sameroff et al., 1987; Sameroff & Seifer, 1989). Factors that predict reduced intellectual competence include a father who does not live with the family, a mother with a history of mental illness, limited parental work skills, and a history of stressful events during the child's early life. On average, each risk factor reduces a child's IQ score by 4 points. Children with no risk factors score more than *30 points higher* than those with seven risk factors (see Figure 6.6).

Parents can play a vital role in their children's intellectual development by reading to them, asking them questions, and providing books and games that arouse their curiosity.

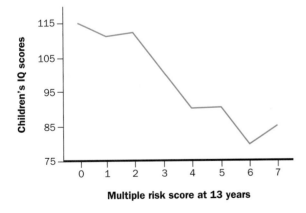

Figure 6.6

Family Risk Factors and IQ

The greater the number of stressful family circumstances, the lower a child's IQ score is likely to be (Sameroff & Seifer, 1989). An enormous gap exists between the average IQ scores of children with no stressful family circumstances and the scores of those with many, as you can see from this graph.

In contrast, a healthy and stimulating environment can raise mental performance. In a longitudinal study called the Abecedarian Project, inner-city children who got lots of mental enrichment at home and in child care or school, starting in infancy and lasting throughout childhood, had higher IQs by age 12 than did children in a control group (Campbell & Ramey, 1994, 1995). The increases were not trivial: They averaged 15 to 30 points.

In school, individual experiences, such as having an inspiring teacher or winning a prize in a science fair, can affect a child's aptitudes and achievements (Dunn & Plomin, 1990). Children's mental abilities also improve when parents spend time with them, encourage them to think things through, read to them, provide toys and field trips, talk to them about many topics, answer their questions, describe things fully, and expect them to do well (Bee et al., 1982; Bradley & Caldwell, 1984; Clarke-Stewart, VanderStoep, & Killian, 1979).

Fortunately, these parenting skills can be taught. In one study, 30 middle-class parents learned during two brief training sessions to ask open-ended questions when reading to their toddlers ("What is the cat doing?") instead of merely asking the children to point out objects or answer yes–no questions ("Is the cat asleep?"). The parents also learned

The children of migrant workers (left) often spend long hours in backbreaking field work and may miss out on the educational opportunities and intellectual advantages available to middle-class children (right).

to expand on the children's answers, correct inaccurate responses, and give plenty of praise. Parents in a control group read just as often to their children but did not get the special instruction. After only a month, the children in the experimental group were 8½ months ahead of those in the control group in their expressive-language skills and 6 months ahead of them in vocabulary skills (Whitehurst et al., 1988). A similar study, in which parents and teachers read interactively with low-income children, also produced highly significant vocabulary enhancement (Whitehurst et al., 1994). The implications are enormous when you consider that by one estimate, the average low-income child enters first grade with only 25 hours of one-on-one picture-book reading, compared with 1,000 to 1,700 hours for middle-class children (Adams, 1990).

Probably the best evidence for the importance of the environment in cognitive growth is the fact that IQ scores in developed countries have been climbing for at least three generations (Flynn, 1987) (see Figure 6.7). Genes in these countries can't possibly have changed enough to account for this rise in scores. The causes are still being debated, but most cognitive psychologists believe they include improvements in education, an increasing emphasis on the skills required by technology, and better nutrition (Neisser et al., 1996).

We see, then, that although heredity may provide the range of a child's intellectual potential—a Forrest Gump can never become an Einstein—many other factors affect where in that range the child will fall.

Figure 6.7

Climbing IQ Scores

Raw scores on IQ tests have been rising in developed countries for many decades, at a rate much too steep to be accounted for by genetic changes. Because test norms are periodically readjusted to set the average score at 100, most people are unaware of the increase. On this graph (adapted from Horgan, 1995), average scores are calibrated according to 1989 norms. As you can see, performance was much lower in 1918 than in 1989.

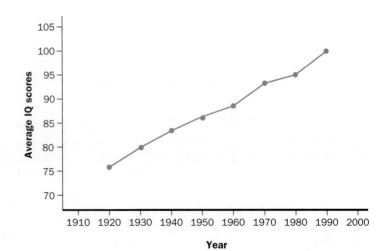

Attitudes, Motivation, and Intelligence

You could have a high IQ, think logically, have emotional intelligence, be talented, and "know your way around"; you could have genetic and environmental advantages; but without a few other qualities, you might still get nowhere at all. Talent, unlike cream, does not inevitably rise to the top; success depends on drive and determination.

Consider a finding from one of the longest-running psychological studies ever conducted. Since 1921, researchers at Stanford University have been following 1,528 people with childhood IQ scores in the top 1 percent of the distribution. As boys and girls, these subjects were nicknamed "Termites," after Lewis Terman, who originally directed the research. The Termites started out bright, physically healthy, sociable, and well adjusted. As they entered adulthood, most became successful in the traditional ways of the times: men in careers and women as homemakers (Sears & Barbee, 1977; Terman & Oden, 1959). However, some gifted men failed to live up to their early promise, dropping out of school or drifting into low-level work. When the researchers compared the 100 most successful men in the Stanford study with the 100 least successful, they found that motivation made the difference. The successful men were ambitious, were socially active, had many interests, and were encouraged by their parents. The least successful drifted casually through life. There was *no* average difference in IQ between the two groups.

Motivation to work hard at intellectual tasks depends in turn on a person's beliefs about the origins of intelligence and values regarding achievement. For many years, Harold Stevenson and his colleagues have been studying such beliefs and values by doing cross-cultural studies in Asia and the United States. The researchers began in 1980 by comparing large samples of first- and fifth-grade children, their parents, and their teachers in Minneapolis, Sendai (Japan), and Taipei (Taiwan). In another project, they compared children from 20 schools in Chicago and 11 schools in Beijing (Stevenson & Stigler, 1992). In 1990, Stevenson, along with Chuansheng Chen and Shin-Ying Lee (1993), revisited the original schools to collect new data on fifth-graders, and they also retested many of the children who had been in the 1980 study and who were now in the eleventh grade. Their results have much to teach us about the cultivation of intellect.

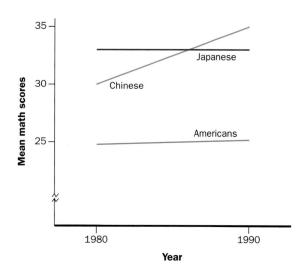

Figure 6.8

Mathematical Performance of Asian and American Children

In 1980 and again in 1990, the math performance of fifth-graders in Taiwan and Japan far outstripped that of children in the United States. This graph shows the gap on one of the tests given (Stevenson, Chen, & Lee, 1993). The performance differences were associated with differences in attitudes, standards, and effort.

In 1980, the Asian children far outperformed the American children on a broad battery of mathematical tests. (A similar gap existed between the Taiwanese and American children on reading tests.) On computations and word problems, there was virtually no overlap between schools, with the lowest-scoring Beijing schools doing better than the highest-scoring Chicago schools. By 1990, the gap between the Asian and American children had grown even greater (see Figure 6.8). Only 4 percent of the Chinese children and 10 percent of the Japanese children had scores as low as those of the *average* American child. These differences could not be accounted for by educational resources: The Chinese had worse facilities and larger classes than the Americans, and on average, the Chinese parents were poorer and less educated than the American parents. Nor did it have anything to do with intellectual ability in general because the American children were just as knowledgeable and capable as the Asian children on tests of general information.

But, this research found, Asians and the Americans are worlds apart in their attitudes, expectations, and efforts:

• *Beliefs about intelligence.* American parents, teachers, and children are far and away more likely than Asians to believe that mathematical ability is innate. They think that if you "have it," you don't have to work hard, and if you don't have it, there's no point in trying. When Japanese teachers were asked to choose the most important factor in math performance, 93 percent of them chose "studying hard," compared with only 26 percent of the American teachers. Students pick up these attitudes: 72 percent of the Japanese but only 27 percent of the American eleventh-graders thought studying hard was the key to success in math.

• *Standards.* American parents have far lower standards for their children's performance than Asian parents do. The Americans said they would be satisfied with scores barely above average on a 100-point test; most felt that their children were doing fine in math and that the schools were doing a good or excellent job. In contrast, the Chinese and Japanese parents said they would be happy only with very high scores, and most were not highly satisfied with their children's schools or even with their children's excellent performance.

• *Conflicts.* American students have more stressful, conflicting demands on their time than their Asian counterparts do. Chinese and Japanese students are expected to devote themselves to their studies, but American students are expected to be "well-rounded"—to have after-school jobs (74 percent of them did, compared with only 21 percent of the Asians), to have dates and an active social life (85 percent to 37 percent), and to have time for sports and other activities. Contrary to the stereotype of the stressed and overworked Japanese student, it is American students who are most likely to report that school is a source of stress and academic anxiety (Crystal et al., 1994). Japanese eleventh-graders actually had the lowest incidence of stress, depression, insomnia, aggression, and physical symptoms.

• *Values.* American students do not value education as much as Asian students do, and they are more complacent about mediocre work. When asked what they would wish for if a wizard could give them anything they wanted, more than 60 percent of the Chinese fifth-graders named something related to their education. Can you guess what the American children wanted? A majority said money or possessions.

The moral is clear: When it comes to intellect, it's not just what you've got that counts, but what you do with it. Complacency, fatalism, or low standards can prevent people from recognizing what they don't know and reduce their efforts to learn.

??? QUICK QUIZ

Show that you are not complacent by taking this quiz.

1. On average, behavioral-genetic studies estimate the heritability of intelligence to be (a) about .90, (b) low at all ages, (c) about .50 for children and adolescents.

2. *True or false:* If a trait such as intelligence is highly heritable within a group, then differences between groups must also be due mainly to heredity.

3. The available evidence (does/does not) show that ethnic differences in average IQ scores are due to genetic differences.

4. Name five environmental factors associated with reduced mental ability.

Answers:

1. c 2. false (can you say why, using the tomato-plant analogy?) 3. does not 4. poor prenatal care, malnutrition, exposure to toxins, large family size, and stressful family circumstances.

What's Ahead

• *Why do some researchers think that animals can think, and others remain skeptical?*

• *Everyone loves to talk to their pets—but can their pets learn to talk back?*

ANIMAL MINDS

A green heron swipes some bread from a picnicker's table and scatters the crumbs on a nearby stream. When a minnow rises to the bait, the heron strikes, swallowing its prey before you can say "hook, line, and sinker." A sea otter, floating

How smart is this otter?

calmly on its back, bangs a mussel shell against a stone that is resting on its stomach. When the shell cracks apart, the otter devours the tasty morsel inside, tucks the stone under its flipper, and dives for another shell, which it will open in the same way. In Africa, a lioness chases a herd of wildebeests toward a ditch. Another lioness, lying in wait at the ditch, leaps up and kills one of the passing wildebeests. The first lioness then joins her companion for the feast.

Incidents such as these, summarized nicely in Donald Griffin's *Animal Minds* (1992), have convinced some scientists that humans are not the only intelligent animals on the planet—that "dumb beasts" are far smarter than we may think.

Animal Intelligence

For many years, any scientist who claimed that animals could think was likely to get laughed at, or worse; today, the interdisciplinary field of **cognitive ethology,** the study of cognitive processes in nonhuman animals, is gaining increased attention (Gould & Gould, 1995; Ristau, 1991). (*Ethology* is the study of animal behavior, especially in natural environments.) Cognitive ethologists argue that some animals can anticipate future events, make plans and choices, and coordinate their activities with those of their comrades. The versatility of these animals in meeting new challenges in the environment, say these researchers, suggests that they are, indeed, capable of thought.

Other scientists are not so sure, noting that even complex behavior can be genetically prewired. The assassin bug of South America catches termites by gluing nest material on its back as camouflage, but it is hard to imagine how the bug's tiny dab of brain tissue could enable it to plan this strategy

consciously. Even many cognitive ethologists are cautious about how much cognition they are willing to read into an animal's behavior. An animal could be aware of its environment and know some things, they say, without knowing that it knows and without being able to think about its own thoughts in the way that human beings do—in short, without having metacognition (Cheney & Seyfarth, 1990; Crook, 1987).

But explanations of animal behavior that leave out any sort of consciousness at all and that attribute animals' actions entirely to instinct leave many questions unanswered. Like the otter who uses a stone to crack mussel shells, many animals are capable of using objects in the natural environment as rudimentary tools. For example, mother chimpanzees occasionally show their young how to use stone tools to open hard nuts (Boesch, 1991). In the laboratory, too, nonhuman primates have accomplished some truly surprising things. In one study, chimpanzees compared two pairs of food wells containing chocolate chips. One pair might contain, say, five chips and three chips, the other four chips and three chips. Allowed to choose which pair they wanted, the chimps almost always chose the one with the higher total, showing some sort of summing ability (Rumbaugh, Savage-Rumbaugh, & Pate, 1988). Other chimps have learned to use numerals to label quantities of items and simple sums (Boysen & Berntson, 1989; Washburn & Rumbaugh, 1991).

Animals and Language

Have you ever wished you could ask your pooch what it's like to be a dog—and be able to understand the answer? If only animals could speak!

A primary ingredient of human cognition is *language,* the ability to combine elements that are themselves meaningless into an infinite number of utterances that convey meaning. As we saw in Chapter 3, language allows us to express and comprehend an infinite number of novel utterances, created on the spot. We seem to be the only species that evolved to do this naturally. Other primates use a variety of grunts and screeches to warn each other of danger, to attract attention, and to express emotions, but the sounds are not combined to produce original sentences (at least, as far as we can tell). Bongo may make a certain sound when he finds food, but he cannot say, "The bananas in the next grove are a lot riper than the ones we ate last week and sure beat our usual diet of termites."

cognitive ethology
The study of cognitive processes in nonhuman animals.

Perhaps, however, some animals could acquire language if they got a little help from their human friends. Dozens of researchers have tried to provide apes, especially chimpanzees, with just such help. Because the vocal tract of an ape does not permit speech, early efforts, which focused on trying to teach speech to chimpanzees, were failures, though some comprehension on the part of the animals did occur. During the 1960s and 1970s, researchers tried innovative approaches that relied on visual symbols or gestures, rather than speech. In one project, chimpanzees learned to use as words various geometric plastic shapes arranged on a magnetic board (Premack & Premack, 1983). In another, they learned to punch symbols on a computer-monitored keyboard (Rumbaugh, 1977). In yet another, they learned hundreds of signs from American Sign Language (ASL) (Fouts & Rigby, 1977; Gardner & Gardner, 1969). All these animals learned to follow instructions, answer questions, and make requests. More important, they combined individual signs or symbols into longer utterances that they had never seen before. In general, their linguistic abilities resembled those of a 2-year-old child.

As you can imagine, accounts of the apes' abilities caused quite a stir. The animals were apparently using their newfound skills to apologize for being disobedient, scold their trainers, and even talk to themselves. Koko, a lowland gorilla, reportedly used signs to say that she felt happy or sad, to refer to past and future events, to mourn for her dead pet kitten, and to convey her yearning for a baby. She even lied on occasion, when she did something naughty (Patterson & Linden, 1981).

The animals in these studies were lovable, the findings appealing—so it was easy for emotional reasoning to prevail over critical thinking. But soon skeptics and some of the researchers themselves began to point out serious problems (Seidenberg & Petitto, 1979; Terrace, 1985). In their desire to talk to the animals and their affection for their

Thinking Critically About Apes and Language

primate friends, researchers had not always been objective. They had overinterpreted the animal's utterances, reading all sorts of meanings and intentions into a single sign or symbol. In videotapes, they could be seen unwittingly giving nonverbal cues that might enable the apes to respond correctly. Further, the animals appeared to be stringing signs and symbols together in no particular order, instead of using grammatical rules to produce novel utterances; "Me eat banana" seemed to be no different for them than "Banana eat me."

Researchers took these criticisms to heart and improved their procedures. Today, carefully controlled experiments have established that with training, chimps can indeed acquire the ability to use symbols to refer to objects. In some projects, chimpanzees have spontaneously used signs to converse with each other, suggesting that they are not merely imitating or trying to get a reward (Van Cantfort & Rimpau, 1982). Bonobos (sometimes misleadingly called "pygmy chimps") are even more adept at language than are chimpanzees. One bonobo named Kanzi has learned to understand English words and short sentences, and to understand keyboard symbols, *without formal training* (Savage-Rumbaugh & Lewin, 1994;

Kanzi, a bonobo with the most advanced linguistic skills yet acquired by a nonhuman primate, answers questions and makes requests by punching symbols on a specially designed computer keyboard. He can also understand short English sentences.

Savage-Rumbaugh, Shanker, & Taylor, 1996). Kanzi responds correctly to commands such as "Put the key in the refrigerator" and "Go get the ball that is outdoors." He picked up language as children do—by observing others using it, and through normal social interaction. He has also learned, with training, to manipulate keyboard symbols to request particular foods or activities (games, TV, visits to friends) or to announce his intentions, and he seems to use some simple grammatical ordering rules to convey meaning.

Certain nonprimates also seem able to acquire some aspects of language. In Hawaii, Louis Herman and his colleagues have taught dolphins to respond to requests made in two artificial languages, one consisting of computer-generated whistles and another of hand and arm gestures (Herman, 1987; Herman, Kuczaj, & Holder, 1993). To interpret a request correctly, the dolphins must take into account both the meaning of the individual symbols in a string of whistles or gestures and the order of the symbols (syntax). For example, they must understand the difference between "To left Frisbee, right surfboard take" and "To right surfboard, left Frisbee take."

In another fascinating project, Irene Pepperberg (1990, 1994) has taught an African gray parrot named Alex to count, classify, and compare objects by vocalizing English words. When the bird is shown up to six items and is asked how many there are, he responds with spoken (squawked?) English phrases, such as "two cork(s)" or "four key(s)." He can even respond correctly to questions about items specified on two dimensions, as in "How many blue key(s)?" Alex also makes requests ("Want pasta") and answers simple questions about objects ("What color [is this]?" "Which is bigger?"). When presented with a blue cork and a blue key and asked "What's the same?" he will correctly respond "Color." He actually scores slightly better with new objects than with familiar ones, suggesting that he is not merely memorizing a set of stock phrases.

These recent results on animal language and cognition are impressive, but scientists are still divided over just what the animals in these studies are doing. Do they have true language? Are they "thinking," in human terms? On one side are those who worry about *anthropomorphism,* the tendency to falsely attribute human qualities to nonhuman beings. They tell the story of Clever Hans, a "wonder horse" at the turn of the century, who was said to possess mathematical and other

Alex is one clever bird—but how clever? His abilities raise intriguing questions about the intelligence of animals and their capacity for specific aspects of language.

abilities (Spitz, 1997). Clever Hans would answer math problems by stamping his hoof the appropriate number of times and other problems by tapping in an established code. But a little careful experimentation by a psychologist, Oskar Pfungst (1911/1965), revealed that when Hans was prevented from seeing his questioners, or when they did not know the answers themselves, his "powers" left him. It seems that questioners were staring at the animal's feet and leaning forward expectantly after stating the problem, then lifting their eyes and relaxing as soon as he completed the right number of taps. Clever Hans was indeed clever, but not at math or other human skills. He was merely responding to nonverbal signals that people were inadvertently providing.

On the other side are those who warn against *anthropocentrism,* the tendency to think, mistakenly, that human beings have nothing in common with other animals. The need to see our own species as unique, they say, may keep us from recognizing that other species, too, have cognitive abilities, even if not as intricate as our own. Those who take this position point out that most modern researchers have gone to great lengths to avoid the Clever Hans problem.

The outcome of this debate is bound to have an effect on how we view ourselves and our place among other species. As Donald Griffin (1992) wrote, "Cognitive ethology presents us with one of the supreme scientific challenges of our times, and it calls for our best efforts of critical and imaginative investigation."

We human beings have always thought of ourselves as the smartest species around. Yet, as this chapter has shown, we are not always as wise in our thinking as we might think, and we may not even be the only animal capable of thought. As if that weren't bad enough, now some people are saying that machines are gaining on us in the mental abilities department. Should we let Deep Blue, whose accomplishments in chess opened this chapter, give us the blues? Today a computer can beat a world champion at a challenging board game; tomorrow, will computers also take over such tasks as setting public policy, planning sports strategies, and deciding what should be on the fall TV schedule?

That's hardly likely. Deep Blue's accomplishments—or more accurately, the accomplishments of the human programmers who wrote the software for the machine—are certainly impressive. However, we have seen that real intelligence is more than the capacity to compute chess moves with lightning speed. It involves the ability to deal with informal reasoning problems, reason dialectically and reflectively, devise mental shortcuts, read emotions, acquire tacit knowledge, invent endless new gizmos, and use language to create everything from puns to poetry. And it involves mental efficiency: Human beings are intelligent not because they can consider 200 chess positions a second, but because they don't have to!

During the contest between Kasparov and Deep Blue, the machine, in a sense, cheated (Klopfenstein, 1997). The Russian was prevented by the traditional rules of play from consulting any books or experts; the machine had access to a complete historical library of chess strategy, stored in its electronic memory banks. Kasparov couldn't touch any pieces until he was ready to move one; the machine could mentally "touch" as many pieces as it wanted to. But its raw calculating power disguised its inefficiency; the machine could not "prune" moves that were likely to be ineffective or draw analogies with moves that had been duds in similar circumstances. The only way it could win was to reject the same moves millions of times (McCarthy, 1997).

Deep Blue wasn't the least bit troubled by its lack of cleverness because it lacks a mind to be troubled. As computer scientist David Gelernter (1997) wrote, "How can an object that wants nothing, fears nothing, enjoys nothing, needs nothing, and cares about nothing have a mind?" Lacking a mind, the machine lacks a trait that distinguishes human beings not only from computers but also from other species: *We try to understand our own misunderstandings*. We want to know what we don't know; we are motivated to overcome our mental shortcomings—and this capacity for self-examination is probably the best reason to remain optimistic about our cognitive capacities.

Taking Psychology with You

Becoming More Creative

Take a few moments to answer these items from the Remote Associates Test. Your task is to come up with a fourth word that is associated with each item in a set of three words (Mednick, 1962). For example, an appropriate answer for the set *news–clip–wall* is *paper*. Got the idea? Now try these (the answers are given on page 224):

1. piggy–green–lash

2. surprise–line–birthday

3. mark–shelf–telephone

4. stick–maker–tennis

5. blue–cottage–cloth

Associating elements in new ways by finding a common connection among them is an important component of creativity. People who are uncreative rely on *convergent thinking*, following a particular set of steps that they think will converge on one correct solution. Once they have solved a problem, they tend to develop a mental set.

Creative people, in contrast, exercise *divergent thinking;* instead of stubbornly sticking to one tried-and-true path, they explore some side alleys and generate several possible solutions. They come up with new hypotheses, imagine other interpretations, and look for connections that may not be immediately obvious. As a result, they are able to use familiar concepts in unexpected ways. Creative thinking can be found in the auto mechanic who invents a new tool, the mother who designs and makes her children's clothes, or the office manager who devises a clever way to streamline work flow (Richards, 1991).

Interestingly, having a high IQ does not guarantee creativity. Personality characteristics seem more important, especially these three essential ones (MacKinnon, 1962, 1968; McCrae, 1987; Schank, 1988):

1. *Nonconformity.* Creative individuals are not overly concerned about what others think of them. They are willing to risk ridicule by proposing ideas that may initially appear foolish or off the mark. Geneticist Barbara McClintock's research was ignored or belittled by many for nearly 30 years. But she was sure she could show how genes move around and produce sudden changes in heredity. In 1983, McClintock was vindicated: She won the Nobel Prize. The judges called her work the second greatest genetic discovery of our time, after the discovery of the structure of DNA.

2. *Curiosity.* Creative people are open to new experiences; they notice when reality contradicts expectations, and they are curious about the reason. For example, Wilhelm Roentgen, a German physicist, was studying cathode rays when he noticed a strange glow on one of his screens. Other people had seen the glow, but they ignored it because it didn't jibe with then-current understanding of cathode rays. Roentgen studied the glow, found it to be a new kind of radiation, and thus discovered X rays (Briggs, 1984).

3. *Persistence.* This is perhaps the most important attribute of the creative person. After that imaginary lightbulb goes on over your head, you still have to work hard to make the illumination last. Or, as Thomas Edison, who invented the real lightbulb, reportedly put it, "Genius is one-tenth inspiration and nine-tenths perspiration." No invention or work of art springs forth full-blown from a person's head. There are many false starts and painful revisions along the way.

In addition to traits that foster creativity, there are *circumstances* that do so. For example, cheerful situations can loosen up creative associations. The performance of students on creativity tests improved significantly after they watched a funny film or received a gift of candy, which put them in a good mood. In contrast, watching an upsetting film on concentration camps, watching a neutral film on math, or exercising to boost energy had no effect on creativity (Isen, Daubman, & Nowicki, 1987).

Another situational factor is the encouragement of *intrinsic* rather than *extrinsic* motivation. Intrinsic motives include a sense of accomplishment, intellectual fulfillment, the satisfaction of curiosity, and the sheer love of the activity. Extrinsic motives include a desire for money, fame, and attention, or the wish to avoid punishment. In one study, artworks created for extrinsic reasons (they were commissioned by art collectors) were judged to be less creative than works done by the same artists for the intrinsic pleasure of creation. This was true whether the works were judged by the artists themselves or by judges who were blind to the condition under which a work had been completed. And it was true even when the person commissioning the work allowed the artists complete freedom (Amabile, Phillips, & Collins, 1993).

Creativity also flourishes when people have control over how to perform a task or solve a problem; are evaluated unobtrusively, instead of being constantly observed and judged; and work independently (Amabile, 1983). And organizations encourage creativity when they let people take risks, give them plenty of time to think about problems, and welcome innovation.

In sum, if you hope to become more creative, there are two things you can do. One is to cultivate the personal qualities that lead to creativity. The other is to seek out the kinds of situations that permit you to express them.

SUMMARY

Thought: Using What We Know

1) *Thinking* is the mental manipulation of information. Our mental representations simplify and summarize information from the environment.

2) A *concept* is a mental category that groups objects, relations, activities, abstractions, or qualities that share certain properties. *Prototypical* instances of a concept are more representative than others. *Propositions* are made up of concepts and express a unitary idea. They may be linked together to form *cognitive schemas,* which serve as mental models of aspects of the world. Mental images also play a role in thinking.

3) Not all mental processing is conscious. *Subconscious processes* lie outside of awareness but can be brought into consciousness when necessary. *Nonconscious processes* remain outside of awareness but nonetheless affect behavior and may be involved in what we call "intuition." Conscious processing may be carried out in a mindless fashion if we overlook changes in context that call for a change in behavior.

Reasoning Rationally

4) *Reasoning* is purposeful mental activity that involves drawing inferences and conclusions from observations, facts, or assumptions (premises).

5) *Formal reasoning problems* can often be solved by applying an *algorithm,* a set of procedures guaranteed to produce a solution, or by using logical processes, such as *deductive* and *inductive* reasoning.

6) In *informal reasoning problems,* there may be no clearly correct solution. People may disagree about basic premises, and information may be incomplete; many viewpoints may compete. In thinking about such problems, people may apply *heuristics,* rules of thumb that suggest a course of action without guaranteeing an optimal solution. They also need to be able to think *dialectically* about opposing points of view.

7) Studies of *reflective judgment* show that many people have trouble thinking dialectically. People in the *prereflective* stages assume that a correct answer always exists; they do not distinguish between knowledge and belief, or between belief and evidence. Those in the *quasi-reflective* stages think that because knowledge is sometimes uncertain, any judgment about the evidence is purely subjective. Those who think *reflectively* understand that although some things cannot be known with certainty, some judgments are more valid than others, depending on their coherence, usefulness, fit with the evidence, and so on. Higher education seems to move people gradually closer to reflective judgment.

Barriers to Reasoning Rationally

8) The need to be right is an obstacle to rational thinking, and the replacement of reading by television watching may promote mental laziness. The ability to reason clearly and rationally is also affected by many *cognitive biases.* People tend to exaggerate the likelihood of improbable events, in part because of the *availability heuristic;* to be swayed in their choices by the desire to *avoid loss* and by the way a choice is framed; to attend mostly to evidence that confirms what they want to believe (the *confirmation bias*); to be mentally rigid, forming *mental sets* and seeing patterns where none exists; and to overestimate their ability to have made accurate predictions (the *hindsight bias*). The theory of *cognitive dissonance* holds that people are also motivated to reduce the tension that exists when two cognitions are in conflict—by rejecting or changing a belief, changing their behavior, or rationalizing. People are not always rational, but once we understand a bias, we may be able to reduce or eliminate it.

Intelligence

9) Although we all wish to think intelligently, intelligence is hard to define. Some theorists believe that a general ability (a *g factor*) underlies the many specific abilities tapped by intelligence tests, whereas others do not.

10) The traditional approach to intelligence, the *psychometric* approach, focuses on how well people perform on standardized mental tests. The *intelligence quotient,* or *IQ,* represents how a person has done on an intelligence test, compared to other people. Alfred Binet designed the first widely used intelligence test for the purpose of identifying children who could benefit from remedial work. But in the United States, people assumed that intelligence tests revealed "natural ability," and they used the tests to categorize people in school and in the armed services.

11) IQ tests have been criticized for being biased in favor of white, middle-class people. However, efforts to construct culture-free and culture-fair tests have been disappointing. Some critics would like to dispense with IQ tests because they are so often interpreted unintelligently. Critics also argue that when a child's abilities don't match those expected by teachers and testers, the best solution may be to modify the classroom or the test. Others consider the tests useful for predicting school performance and diagnosing learning difficulties, as long as test scores are combined with other information.

12) In contrast to the psychometric approach, *cognitive approaches* to intelligence emphasize the strategies people use to solve problems, not just whether they get the right answers. Sternberg's *triarchic theory of intelligence* proposes three aspects of intelligence: *componential* (including *metacognition*), *experiential,* and *contextual.* Most conventional intelligence tests do not measure experiential and contextual intelligence, or people's *tacit knowledge,* yet these help determine an individual's personal and occupational success.

13) Howard Gardner's *theory of multiple intelligences* holds that there are actually seven "intelligences": linguistic, logical-mathematical, spatial, musical, bodily-kinesthetic, intrapersonal, and interpersonal. The last two correspond roughly to

emotional intelligence, which is related to personal and academic success.

The Origins of Intelligence

14) Behavioral-genetic studies estimate the heritability of intelligence to be high: about .50 for children and adolescents and .60 to .80 for adults. But these results do not mean that genes determine intelligence, or that *group* differences in intelligence are genetic. It is not valid to draw conclusions about ethnic differences in intelligence from estimates based on differences within a group. The available evidence fails to support genetic explanations of these differences.

15) Environmental factors such as poor prenatal care, malnutrition, exposure to toxins, large family size, and stressful family circumstances are associated with lower performance on mental tests; a healthy and stimulating environment can raise performance.

16) Intellectual achievement is also affected by motivation and attitudes. Cross-cultural work shows that beliefs about the origins of mental abilities, parental standards, and attitudes toward education can help account for differences in academic performance.

Animal Minds

17) Some researchers argue that nonhuman animals have greater cognitive abilities than is usually thought. Some animals can use objects as rudimentary tools. Chimpanzees have learned to use numerals to label quantities of items and symbols to refer to objects. Several researchers have used visual symbol systems or American Sign Language (ASL) to teach primates language skills, and some animals (even some nonprimates) seem able to use simple grammatical ordering rules to convey or comprehend meaning. However, scientists are still divided as to how to interpret these findings.

KEY TERMS

thinking   188

concept   188

prototype   188

proposition   189

cognitive schema   189

mental image   189

subconscious processes   189

nonconscious processes   190

mindlessness   190

reasoning   191

formal reasoning problems   191

algorithm   191

deductive reasoning   191

premise   191

inductive reasoning   191

informal reasoning problems   192

heuristic   192

dialectical reasoning   192

reflective judgment   193

prereflective and quasi-reflective judgment   194

availability heuristic   196

avoidance of loss   197

confirmation bias   197

mental set   199

hindsight bias   199

cognitive dissonance   200

justification of effort   201

intelligence   202

factor analysis   203

g factor   203

psychometric approach to intelligence   203

achievement versus aptitude tests   203

mental age (MA)   203

intelligence quotient (IQ)   203

Stanford-Binet Intelligence Scale   204

Wechsler Adult Intelligence Scale (WAIS)   204

Wechsler Intelligence Scale for Children (WISC)   204

culture-free and culture-fair tests   204

learning disability   207

cognitive approaches to intelligence   207

triarchic theory of intelligence   208

componential intelligence   208

metacognition   208

experiential intelligence   208

contextual intelligence   208

tacit knowledge   208

theory of multiple intelligences   208

emotional intelligence   209

heritability   210

cognitive ethology   217

anthropomorphism   219

anthropocentrism   219

convergent versus divergent thinking   220

intrinsic versus extrinsic motivation   221

LOOKING BACK

- *When you think of a bird, why are you more likely to recall a robin than a penguin? (pp. 188–189)*

- *How are visual images like images on a television screen? (p. 189)*

- *What's happening mentally when you mistakenly take your geography notes to your psychology class? (p. 190)*

- *Mentally speaking, why is making a cake, well, a piece of cake? (p. 191)*

- *Why can't logic solve all problems? (p. 192)*

- *What kind of reasoning do juries need to be good at? (p. 193)*

- *When people say that all opinions and claims are equally valid, what error are they making? (p. 194)*

- *Why do people worry about dying in an airplane crash but ignore dangers that are far more likely? (pp. 196–197)*

- *How might your physician's choice of words affect which treatment you choose? (p. 197)*

- *When "Monday morning quarterbacks" say they knew all along who would win Sunday's big game, what bias might they be showing? (pp. 199–200)*

- *Why will a terrible hazing make you more loyal to the group that hazed you? (p. 201)*

- *Is it possible to design intelligence tests that aren't influenced by culture? (pp. 204, 206)*

- *Why do some psychologists oppose traditional intelligence testing and others defend it? (p. 206)*

- *What kind of intelligence allows you to master the unspoken rules for academic success? (p. 208)*

- *What's your "EQ"—and why is it as important as IQ? (p. 209)*

- *If intelligence is highly heritable, does that mean that group differences in IQ are genetic? (pp. 211–212)*

- *Is a child with a low IQ destined to have a low score throughout life? (pp. 213–214)*

- *Some gifted people are professionally successful and others aren't; what makes the difference? (p. 215)*

- *Why do Asian children perform so much better in school than American students do, even though Asian classes are larger, with worse facilities? (pp. 215–216)*

- *Why do some researchers think that animals can think, and others remain skeptical? (p. 217)*

- *Everyone loves to talk to their pets—but can their pets learn to talk back? (pp. 218–219)*

Answer to the Problem in the Get Involved exercise on page 198:

You need to turn over the cards that say "Drinking beer" and "16 years old."

Answers to the Creativity Test on page 220:

back, party, book, match, cheese

Some Solutions to the Nine-Dot Problem in the Get Involved exercise on page 199 (from Adams, 1986):

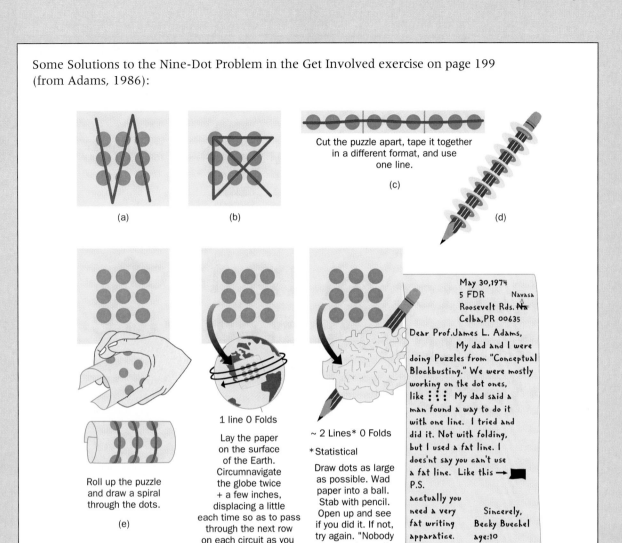

(a)

(b)

Cut the puzzle apart, tape it together in a different format, and use one line.

(c)

(d)

Roll up the puzzle and draw a spiral through the dots.

(e)

1 line 0 Folds

Lay the paper on the surface of the Earth. Circumnavigate the globe twice + a few inches, displacing a little each time so as to pass through the next row on each circuit as you "Go West, young man."

(f)

~ 2 Lines* 0 Folds

*Statistical

Draw dots as large as possible. Wad paper into a ball. Stab with pencil. Open up and see if you did it. If not, try again. "Nobody loses: play until you win."

(g)

May 30, 1974
5 FDR   Navasa
Roosevelt Rds. N.
Celba, PR 00635
Dear Prof. James L. Adams,
    My dad and I were
doing Puzzles from "Conceptual
Blockbusting." We were mostly
working on the dot ones,
like ⋮⋮⋮ My dad said a
man found a way to do it
with one line. I tried and
did it. Not with folding,
but I used a fat line. I
does'nt say you can't use
a fat line. Like this → ▰
P.S.
actually you
need a very   Sincerely,
fat writing   Becky Buechel
apparatice.   age:10

(h)

7

Memory

Man Convicted of Murder on Basis of Daughter's Recovered Memory

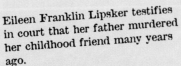
Eileen Franklin Lipsker testifies in court that her father murdered her childhood friend many years ago.

REDWOOD CITY, CA., NOVEMBER 30, 1990. In a case that has drawn national attention, a jury today convicted retired fire-fighter George Franklin, 51, of first-degree murder on the ba-

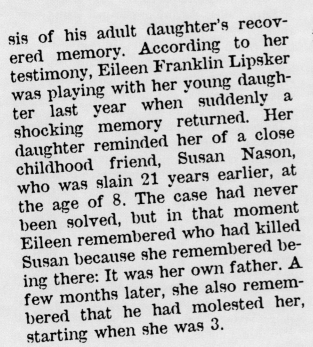

sis of his adult daughter's recovered memory. According to her testimony, Eileen Franklin Lipsker was playing with her young daughter last year when suddenly a shocking memory returned. Her daughter reminded her of a close childhood friend, Susan Nason, who was slain 21 years earlier, at the age of 8. The case had never been solved, but in that moment Eileen remembered who had killed Susan because she remembered being there: It was her own father. A few months later, she also remembered that he had molested her, starting when she was 3.

Prosecutor Elaine Tipton burst into tears of relief at the verdict, and Eileen and Margaret Nason, Susan's mother, embraced each other and wept. Doug Horngrad, Franklin's defense attorney, expressed dismay at the verdict, telling reporters that Eileen was a disturbed and vindictive woman who had changed her story numerous times before the trial began. He vowed to appeal the verdict.

Numerous other recovered memories, mostly of sexual abuse, are being reported across North America. Experts predict that a wave of criminal charges and lawsuits will follow.

A wave of charges and lawsuits did, indeed, follow George Franklin's conviction. In one typical case, a woman named Laura B. sued her father, claiming that he had molested her from the ages of 5 to 23 and had even raped her just days before her wedding. Laura B. said she had no memories of these events until they emerged during therapy (Loftus, 1995).

A bitter controversy has raged for years about whether such accusations should be believed, and whether they provide sufficient evidence, in the absence of corroboration, to convict the alleged perpetrators. One side—we'll call it the *recovered-memory school*—believes that false memories are rare; that traumatic memories are commonly blocked from consciousness; and that virtually all recovered memories of trauma or abuse should be taken seriously (Harvey & Herman, 1994). In this view, people who raise doubts about such memories are betraying victims and abetting child molesters. The other side—we'll call it the *pseudomemory school*—argues that although real abuse occurs, many false memories of victimization are being encouraged by naïve or uninformed therapists (Loftus & Ketcham, 1994). Emotions run high because much is at stake: finding justice for people who have been victimized by punishing perpetrators of abuse and other crimes, while also protecting adults from false charges that can destroy their lives.

At the end of this chapter, we'll tell you what ultimately happened in the Franklin case and in the Laura B. case. Meanwhile, in thinking about this issue, ask yourself, How reliable is memory? We all forget a great deal, of course: We watch the evening news and half an hour later can't recall the main story; we enjoy a meal and quickly forget what we ate; we study our heads off for an exam, only to find that some of the information isn't there when we need it most. Do we also "remember" things that never happened? Are we really likely to forget traumatic events that *did* happen? Are memory malfunctions the exception to the rule, or could they be the norm? And if memory is not always reliable, how can any of us hope to know the story of our own life? How can we hope to understand the past?

| What's Ahead |

- *What's wrong with thinking of memory as a mental movie camera?*
- *If you have a strong emotional reaction to a remembered event, does that mean your memory is accurate?*
- *Do people remember better when they're hypnotized?*
- *Why do "flashbulb memories" of surprising or shocking events sometimes have less wattage than we assume?*
- *Can the question a person asks you about a past event affect what you remember about it?*

RECONSTRUCTING THE PAST

Memory refers both to the capacity to retain and retrieve information and to the structures that account for this capacity. Human beings are capable of astonishing feats of memory. Most of us can easily remember who fought whom in World War II, the tune of our national anthem, the procedure for using an automated teller machine, the most embarrassing experience we ever had, and hundreds of thousands of other bits of information, without hesitation. A mathematician once calculated that over the course of a lifetime, we store 500 times as much information as there is in the entire *Encyclopaedia Britannica* (Griffith, in Horn & Hinde, 1970).

Memory confers competence; without it, we would be as helpless as newborns, unable to negotiate even the most trivial of our daily tasks. Memory also confers a sense of personal identity; we are each the sum total of our personal recollections, which is why we feel so threatened when others challenge our memories. Individuals and cultures alike rely on a remembered history for a sense of coherence and meaning; memory gives us our past and guides our future.

In ancient times, philosophers compared memory to a tablet of hot wax that would preserve anything that chanced to make an imprint on it. Then, with the advent of the printing press, they began to think of memory as a gigantic library, storing specific events and facts for later retrieval. Today, in the audiovisual age, many people compare memory to a tape recorder or a movie camera, automatically recording each and every moment of their lives. Popular and appealing though this belief about memory is, however, it is utterly, absolutely wrong. Not everything that happens to us or impinges on our senses is tucked away for later use. If it were, our minds would be cluttered with all sorts of mental junk—the temperature at noon Thursday, the price of turnips two years ago, a phone number needed only once. Memory must be selective. And recovering a memory is not at all like replaying a film of an event; it is more like watching a few unconnected frames and then figuring out what the rest of the scene must have been like.

One of the first scientists to make this point was the British psychologist Sir Frederic Bartlett (1932). Bartlett asked people to read lengthy, unfamiliar stories from other cultures and then tell the stories back to him. As the volunteers tried to recall the stories, they made interesting errors: They often eliminated or changed details that did not make sense to them, and they added other details to make the story coherent, sometimes even adding a moral. Memory, Bartlett concluded, must therefore be largely a *reconstructive* process. (Psychologists today sometimes call this process *confabulation.*) We may reproduce some kinds of simple information by rote, said Bartlett, but when we remember complex information, we typically alter it in ways that help us make sense of the material, based on what we already know, or think we know. Since Bartlett's time, hundreds of studies have found his conclusion to be true for

Films and novels reflect and influence popular assumptions about memory. When Alfred Hitchcock made "Spellbound" in 1945, psychoanalytic ideas held sway. In the film, amnesia patient Gregory Peck is suspected of murder, and the clues to the identity of the real killer appear in a dream he has. The surrealistic dream sequences, designed by artist Salvador Dali, conveyed the idea that painful memories are never forgotten but are merely locked away in the unconscious with all the details intact, waiting to be recovered—a notion that modern research has questioned.

everything from stories to conversations to personal experiences (Schacter, 1996).

In reconstructing their memories, people often draw on many sources. Suppose, for example, that someone asks you to describe one of your early birthday parties. You may have some direct recollection of the event, but you may also incorporate information gleaned from family stories, photographs, or home videos, and even from accounts of other people's birthdays and reenactments of birthdays on television. You take all these bits and pieces and build one integrated account. Later, though, you may not be able to separate your original experience from what you added after the fact—a phenomenon called **source amnesia,** or *source misattribution.*

A dramatic instance of reconstruction once occurred in the sad case of H. M., whom we described briefly in Chapter 4 (page 131). Ever since 1953, when much of H. M.'s hippocampus and the adjacent cortex were surgically removed, he has suffered from the inability to form lasting memories for new events and facts. He cannot learn new words, songs, stories, or faces, and therefore he does not remember much of anything that has happened since his operation (Hilts, 1995; Ogden & Corkin, 1991). To cope with his devastating condition, H. M. will sometimes resort to confabulation. On one occasion, after eating a large chocolate Valentine's Day heart, H. M. stuck the shiny red wrapping in his shirt pocket. Two hours later, while searching for his handkerchief, he pulled out the paper and looked at it in puzzlement. When researcher Jenni Ogden asked why he had the paper in his pocket, he replied, "Well, it could have been wrapped around a big chocolate heart. It must be Valentine's Day!" Ogden could hardly contain her excitement about H. M.'s possible recall of a recent episode. But a short time later, when she asked him to take out the paper again and say why he had it in his pocket, he replied, "Well, it might have been wrapped around a big chocolate rabbit. It must be Easter!"

Of course, H. M. *had* to reconstruct the past; his damaged brain could not recall it in any other way. But those of us with normal memory abilities also reconstruct, far more often than we realize.

The Conditions of Confabulation

False memories of events or experiences, or misremembering of the particulars of an event, are especially likely to occur under the following circumstances (Garry, Manning, & Loftus, 1996; Hyman & Pentland, 1996; Johnson, 1995):

• *You have thought about the imagined event many times.* Suppose that at family gatherings you keep

source amnesia
The inability to distinguish what you originally experienced from what you heard or were told about an event later.

Get Involved

Select an incident in your childhood that stands out in your memory, and write down as much as you can about it. Now ask a friend or family member who was present at the time to write a description of the same event. Compare the two accounts; do they differ? If so, can one of you convince the other that his or her recollection is the correct one? What does this exercise tell you about the nature of memory?

hearing about the time that Uncle Sam scared everyone at a New Year's Eve party by pounding a hammer into the wall with such force that the wall collapsed. It's such a colorful story that you can practically see Uncle Sam in your mind's eye. The more you think about this event, the more likely you are to believe that you were actually there, even if you were sound asleep in another house.

• *The image of the event contains a lot of details.* Ordinarily, we can distinguish an imagined event from a real one by the amount of detail we recall; real events tend to produce more details. However, the longer you think about an imagined event, the more details you are likely to add— what Sam was wearing, the fact that he'd had too much to drink, the crumbling plaster, people standing around in party hats—and these details may in turn persuade you that the event really happened and that you have a direct memory of it.

• *The event is easy to imagine.* If forming an image of an event takes little effort (as does visualizing a

man pounding a wall with a hammer), then we tend to think that our memory is real. In contrast, when we have to make an effort to form an image—for example, of being in a place we have never seen or doing something that is utterly foreign to us—the cognitive operations we perform apparently serve as a cue that the event did not really take place, or that we were not there when it did.

• *You focus on your emotional reactions to the event rather than on what actually happened.* Emotional reactions to an imagined event can resemble those that would have occurred in response to a real event, and so they can mislead us. This means that your feelings about an event, no matter how strongly you hold them, are not a reliable cue to the event's reality. Let's return to our Sam story, which happens to be true. A woman we know believed for years that she had been present in the room as an 11-year-old child when her uncle destroyed the wall. Because the story was so vivid and upsetting to her, she felt angry at him for

A memory may be striking or emotionally significant, and still be wrong. A student of ours recalls a wonderful trip to Ireland with his father when he was a preschooler; he has vivid visual memories of their travels together. There is only one problem: He was blind for the first few years of his life, and his father died before the son regained his sight!

what she thought was his mean and violent behavior, and she assumed that she must have been angry at the time as well. Then, as an adult, she learned that she wasn't at the party at all but had merely heard about it repeatedly over the years; and that Sam hadn't pounded the wall in anger, but as a joke—to inform the assembled guests that he and his wife were about to remodel their home. Nevertheless, our friend's family has had a hard time convincing her that her "memory" of this event is entirely wrong, and they aren't sure she believes them yet.

As the Sam story illustrates, and as laboratory research verifies, false memories can be as stable over time as true ones (Brainerd, Reyna, & Brandse, 1995; Poole, 1995; Roediger & McDermott, 1995). But what about all those apparent cases of superb recall under hypnosis that we hear about, and all those stories about perfect recollections of emotionally powerful events? Don't these accounts mean that memories are permanently stored somewhere in the brain with perfect accuracy, after all? Let's look more closely at the evidence.

Hypnosis and Memory

Consider, first, the frequent claim that under hypnosis, people can remember information that appears to have been lost. Sometimes, hypnosis can indeed be used successfully to jog people's memories. After the 1976 kidnapping of a busload of schoolchildren in Chowchilla, California, the bus driver was able, under hypnosis, to recall all but one of the license plate numbers on the kidnappers' car; that clue provided a breakthrough in the investigation. But in other cases, hypnotized witnesses, despite feeling completely confident about their memories, have been completely mistaken. It turns out that although hypnosis does sometimes boost the amount of information recalled, it also increases errors, perhaps because hypnotized people are more willing than others to guess, or because they mistake vividly imagined possibilities for actual memories (Dinges et al., 1992; Kihlstrom, 1994; Nash & Nadon, 1997). Because pseudomemories and errors are so common in hypnotically induced recall, the American Psychological Association and the American Medical Association oppose the use of "hypnotically refreshed" testimony in courts of law.

Thinking Critically About Hypnosis and Memory

When it comes to reliving very early memories under hypnosis—so-called "age regression"—the evidence is even more negative. Michael Nash (1987) reviewed six decades of scientific research on age regression. He found that the mental and moral performance of people supposedly regressed to an earlier age remain "essentially adult in nature," and their memories are often wrong. They are basically playing a role, and they will do the same when they are hypnotically *progressed* ahead—say, to age 70 or 80—or regressed to "past lives."

Unfortunately, some psychotherapists who use hypnosis in their practice are unaware of these findings. In a survey of 869 members of the American Association of Marriage and Family Therapists, more than half mistakenly thought that "hypnosis can be used to recover memories from as far back as birth," and a third agreed that "the mind is like a computer, accurately recording events that actually occurred" (Yapko, 1994). Moreover, between one-fourth and one-third of all therapists are using hypnosis and other suggestive techniques to try to uncover their clients' supposedly repressed memories, without knowing much about the limitations of these methods (Poole et al., 1995).

In a fascinating program of research that dramatically demonstrated how fantasy and role playing can lead to false memories under hypnosis, Nicholas Spanos and his colleagues (Spanos et al., 1991) directed hypnotized Canadian university students to regress *past* their own birth to a previous life. About a third of the students reported that they could do so. But when they were asked, while supposedly "reliving" a past life, to name the leader of their country, say whether the country was at peace or at war, or describe the money used in their community, the students were at a loss. One young man, who thought he was Julius Caesar, said the year was A.D. 50 and he was emperor of Rome—but Caesar died in 44 B.C. and was never crowned emperor, and besides, dating years as A.D. or B.C. did not begin until several centuries later. Many of the hypnotized students wove events, places, and persons from their present lives into their accounts, and their descriptions were also influenced by what the hypnotist told them. The researchers concluded that the act of "remembering" another "self" involves the construction of a fantasy that accords not only with the remember's own beliefs but also with the beliefs of others—in this case, the authoritative hypnotist.

The Fading Flashbulb

Of course, some surprising, shocking, or tragic events, such as earthquakes or accidents, seem to hold a special place in memory, especially when we are personally involved. Such events seem frozen in time, with all the details intact (Conway et al., 1994; Neisser, Winograd, & Weldon, 1991). Years ago, Roger Brown and James Kulik (1977) labeled the vivid recollections of these events "flashbulb memories" because that term captures the surprise, illumination, and seemingly photographic detail that characterize them. Brown and Kulik speculated that the capacity for flashbulb memories may have evolved because such memories had survival value. Remembering the details of a surprising or dangerous experience could have helped our ancestors avoid similar situations.

Despite their intensity, however, even flashbulb memories are not always complete or accurate records of the past. Many people who were alive when President John F. Kennedy was killed swear that they saw the assassination on television, as he was riding in his motorcade. In reality, no television cameras were present, and the only film of the event, made by a bystander, was not shown until much later. Similarly, many people over the age of 25 say that they know exactly where they were and what they were doing when they learned of the 1986 explosion of the space shuttle *Challenger,* as well as who told them the news and what their own reactions were. Yet even "unforgettable" memories such as these often grow dim with time (Wright, 1993). In one study, college students, on the morning after the *Challenger* tragedy, reported how they had heard the news. Three years later, when they again recalled how they learned of the incident, not one student was entirely correct and a third of them were *completely wrong,* although they felt confident that they were remembering accurately (Neisser & Harsch, 1992).

Even with flashbulb memories, then, facts tend to get mixed with a little fiction. The conclusion is inescapable: Remembering is an *active* process, one that involves not only dredging up stored information but also putting two and two together to reconstruct the past.

The Eyewitness on Trial

The reconstructive nature of memory helps the mind work efficiently. Instead of cramming our brains with zillions of specific details, we can store the essentials of an experience, then use our knowledge of the world to figure out the specifics when we need them. But sometimes the same process gets us into hot water, and this raises some thorny problems in legal cases that involve eyewitness testimony. The accounts of eyewitnesses play a vital role in any justice system; without them, many guilty people would go free. But because memory is reconstructive, eyewitness testimony is not always reliable, even when the witness is certain about the accuracy of his or her report (Bothwell, Deffenbacher, & Brigham, 1987; Sporer et al., 1995). As a result, convictions based solely or mostly on such testimony occasionally turn out to be tragic mistakes. Errors are especially likely to occur when the suspect's ethnicity differs from that of the witness, perhaps because prejudices or lack of familiarity prevent people from attending to the distinctive features of members of other ethnic groups (Brigham & Malpass, 1985; Chance & Goldstein, 1995).

To complicate matters further, eyewitness accounts are heavily influenced by the way in which questions are put to the witness. In a classic study of leading questions, Elizabeth Loftus and John

THE FAR SIDE   By GARY LARSON

More facts of nature: All forest animals, to this very day, remember exactly where they were and what they were doing when they heard that Bambi's mother had been shot.

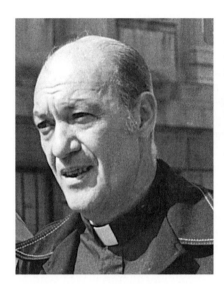 

The legal system relies on the memories of eyewitnesses, but sometimes witnesses make mistakes. Seven people identified Father Bernard Pagno (left) as having committed a series of armed robberies, but Robert Clouser (right) later confessed to the crimes.

Palmer (1974) showed people short films depicting car collisions. Afterward, the researchers asked some of the viewers, "About how fast were the cars going when they hit each other?" Other viewers were asked the same question, but with the verb changed to *smashed, collided, bumped,* or *contacted.* Estimates of how fast the cars were going varied, depending on which word was used. *Smashed* produced the highest average speed estimates (40.8 mph), followed by *collided* (39.3 mph), *bumped* (38.1 mph), *hit* (34.0 mph), and *contacted* (31.8 mph).

In a similar study, the researchers asked some participants, "Did you see a broken headlight?" but asked of others "Did you see the broken headlight?" (Loftus & Zanni, 1975). The question with *the* presupposes a broken headlight and merely asks whether the witness saw it, whereas the question with *a* makes no such presupposition. People who received questions with *the* were far

more likely to report having seen something that had not really appeared in the film than were those who received questions with *a.* If a tiny word like *the* can lead people to "remember" what they never saw, you can imagine how the leading questions of police detectives and lawyers might influence a witness's recall.

In more recent research, people have been induced by leading questions to reconstruct complicated personal events that never happened. In one study, 7 out of 24 subjects were induced to falsely remember being lost in a shopping mall or other public place at the age of about 5 (Loftus & Pickrell, 1995). Other researchers have implanted false memories of such distinctive events as being hospitalized for a high fever, or spilling punch all over the mother of the bride at a wedding (Hyman & Pentland, 1996).

The power of suggestion can affect anyone, but many people are especially concerned about its

Leading questions can affect recall. Students saw the face of a young man with straight hair, then heard a description of the face supposedly written by another witness—one that wrongly mentioned light, curly hair. When they reconstructed the face using a kit of facial features, 33 percent of their reconstructions contained the misleading detail, whereas only 5 percent contained it when curly hair was not mentioned. On the left is one person's reconstruction in the absence of the misleading information; on the right is another person's reconstruction of the same face after exposure to the misleading information (Loftus & Greene, 1980).

impact on children being questioned about possible sexual abuse. For many decades, most adults believed that children's memories could not be trusted—that children confuse fantasy with reality and tend to say whatever adults expect. Then, as the issue of child abuse came to public attention in the 1970s and 1980s, some people began to argue that no child would ever lie about or misremember such a traumatic experience.

After carefully reviewing the more than 100 studies of children's eyewitness testimony done since 1979, Stephen Ceci and Maggie Bruck (1993, 1995) concluded that both of these positions are wrong. Ceci and Bruck found that most young children *do* recollect accurately most of what they've observed or experienced, including potentially embarrassing experiences such as genital examinations at a doctor's office. More specifically, most children do not report that their genitals were touched if they were not touched, even when the children are asked leading questions (Goodman et al., 1990; Saywitz et al., 1991). This finding is important because without a few leading questions, some young children who have been abused will not volunteer information that they feel is embarrassing or shameful. On the other hand, some children *will* say that something happened when it did not. Like adults, they can be influenced to report an event in a certain way, depending on the frequency of the suggestions and the insistence of the person making them.

Therefore, instead of asking, "Are children suggestible?" or "Are children's memories accurate?"

Thinking Critically About Children's Suggestibility

Ceci and Bruck suggest asking a more useful question: "Under what conditions are children apt to be suggestible?" One such condition is age. Preschoolers' memories are more vulnerable to suggestion than are those of school-age children and adults. And the boundary between reality and fantasy may blur for very young children, especially in emotionally charged situations, making it more likely that their accounts will include confabulations of imagined events.

In addition, children's memories, just like adults' memories, can be influenced by pressure to conform to the interviewer's expectations and by the desire to please the interviewer. In one study, 3- and 6-year-old children played with an unfamiliar man for five minutes while seated across the table from him. Four *years* later, the researchers interviewed the children, telling them that they were being questioned about "an important event" and that they would "feel better once they told about it." Of course, by then, few children remembered the episode. Yet 5 of the 15 children, in response to a leading question, said that the man had hugged or kissed them; two "remembered" that he had taken pictures of them in the bathroom; and one little girl agreed that he had given her a bath (Goodman et al., 1989).

In sum, children, like adults, can be accurate in what they report; and, also like adults, they can distort, forget, fantasize, and be misled. As research shows, their memory processes are only human.

??? QUICK QUIZ

See whether you can reconstruct what you have read in order to answer these questions.

1. Memory is like (a) a wax tablet, (b) a giant file cabinet, (c) a video recorder, (d) none of these.

2. In the children's game "telephone," one person tells another person a story, the second person relates the story to a third, and so on. By the end of the game, the story will have changed considerably, which illustrates the principle that memory is _____.

3. *True or false:* Hypnosis reduces errors in memory.

 4. In psychotherapy, hundreds of people have claimed to recall long-buried memories of having taken part in satanic rituals involving animal and human torture and sacrifice. Yet law-enforcement investigators and psychologists have been unable to confirm any of these reports (Goodman et al., 1995). Based on what you have learned so far, how might you explain such "memories"?

What's Ahead

- *In general, which is easier: a multiple-choice question or a short-answer essay question—and why?*

- *Can you know something without knowing that you know it?*

MEASURING MEMORY

Now that we have seen how memory *doesn't* work—namely, like a tape recorder, an infallible filing system, or a journal written in indelible ink—we turn to studies of how it *does* work. The ability to remember is not an absolute talent; it depends on the type of performance being called for. Students who express a preference for multiple-choice, essay, or true–false exams already know this.

Conscious recollection of an event or an item of information is called **explicit memory.** It is usually measured using one of two methods. The first tests for **recall,** the ability to retrieve and reproduce information encountered earlier. Essay and fill-in-the-blank exams and memory games such as Trivial Pursuit or Jeopardy require recall. The second tests for **recognition,** the ability to identify information you have previously observed, read, or heard about. The information is given to

you, and all you have to do is say whether it is old or new, or perhaps correct or incorrect, or pick it out of a set of alternatives. The task, in other words, is to compare the information you are given with the information stored in your memory. True–false and multiple-choice tests call for recognition.

As all students know, recognition tests can be tricky, especially when false items closely resemble correct ones. Under most circumstances, however, recognition is easier than recall. Recognition for visual images is particularly impressive; if you show people more than 2,500 slides of faces and places, and later you ask them to identify which ones they saw out of a larger set, they will be able to identify over 90 percent of the original slides accurately (Haber, 1970).

The superiority of recognition over recall was once demonstrated in a study of people's memories of their high school classmates (Bahrick, Bahrick, & Wittlinger, 1975). The subjects, ages 17 to 74, first wrote down the names of as many classmates as they could remember. Recall was poor; most recent graduates could write only a few dozen names, and those out of school for 40 years or more recalled an average of only 19. Even when prompted with yearbook pictures, the youngest participants failed to name almost 30 percent of their classmates, and the oldest ones failed to name more than 80 percent. Recognition,

explicit memory

Conscious, intentional recollection of an event or of an item of information.

recall

The ability to retrieve and reproduce from memory previously encountered material.

recognition

The ability to identify previously encountered material.

Get Involved

You can try this test of recall if you are familiar with the Christmas song "Rudolph the Red-Nosed Reindeer." In the song, Rudolph has eight reindeer friends; name as many of them as you can. After you have done your best, turn to the Get Involved exercise on page 236 for a recognition test on the same information.

however, was far better. The task was to look at ten cards, each containing five photographs, and to say which picture on each card was that of a former classmate. Recent graduates were right 90 percent of the time, but so were people who had graduated 35 years earlier! Even those out of high school for *more than 40 years* could identify three-fourths of their classmates, and the ability to recognize names was nearly as impressive.

Sometimes information that we have encountered affects our thoughts and actions even though we do not consciously or intentionally remember it—a phenomenon known as **implicit memory** (Graf & Schacter, 1985; Schacter, Chiu, & Ochsner, 1993). To get at this subtle sort of knowledge, researchers must rely on indirect methods, instead of the direct ones used to measure explicit memory. One common method, **priming,** asks you to read or listen to some information and then tests you later to see whether the information affects your performance on another type of task:

Priming

Exposure to information	influences →	Responses to *different* task
TASK 1		**TASK 2**

For example, suppose that you had to read a list of words, some of which began with the letters *def* (such as *define, defend,* or *deform*). Later you might be asked to complete word stems (such as *def-*) with the first word that comes to mind. Even if you could not recognize or recall the original words very well, you would be more likely to complete the word fragments with words from the list than you would be if you had not seen the list. In this procedure, the original words "prime" (make more available) certain responses on the word-completion task, showing that people can retain more knowledge about the past than they realize. They know more than they know that they know (Richardson-Klavehn & Bjork, 1988; Roediger, 1990).

Another method of measuring memory, the **relearning method,** or *savings method,* straddles the boundary between implicit and explicit memory tests. Devised by Hermann Ebbinghaus (1885/1913) over a century ago, the relearning method requires you to relearn information or a task that you learned earlier. If you master it more quickly the second time around, you must be remembering something from the first experience:

Relearning

Exposure to information	Relearn *same* task later
TASK 1	**TASK 2**

An eminent memory researcher we consulted said that he considers the relearning method to be a test of explicit memory. But another maintained that it can function as a test of implicit memory if the learner is unaware that the material being relearned was ever learned earlier.

implicit memory
Unconscious retention in memory, as evidenced by the effect of a previous experience or previously encountered information on current thoughts or actions.

priming
A method for measuring implicit memory in which a person reads or listens to information and is later tested to see whether the information affects performance on another type of task.

relearning method
A method for measuring retention that compares the time required to relearn material with the time used in the initial learning of the material.

What's Ahead

- *Why is the computer often used as a metaphor for the mind?*

- *Why is short-term memory like a leaky bucket?*

- *When a word is on the tip of your tongue, what errors are you likely to make in recalling it?*

- *What's the difference between "knowing how" and "knowing that"?*

THE THREE-BOX MODEL OF MEMORY

Although people usually refer to memory as a single faculty, as in "I must be losing my memory" or "He has a memory like an elephant's," the term *memory* actually covers a complex collection of abilities, processes, and mental systems. If tape recorders or video cameras aren't accurate metaphors for capturing these diverse components of memory, then what metaphor would be better?

Memory as Information Processing

As we saw in Chapter 6, many cognitive psychologists liken the mind to an information processor, along the lines of a computer, though more complex. They have constructed *information-processing*

models of cognitive processes, borrowing liberally from the language of computer programming such terms as *inputs, output, accessing,* and *information retrieval.* In a computer, when you type something on your keyboard, the machine encodes the information into an electronic language, stores it on a disk, and retrieves it when you need to use it. Similarly, in information-processing models of memory, we *encode* information (convert it to a form that the brain can process and use), *store* the information (retain it over time), and *retrieve* the information (recover it for use). In storage, the information may be represented as concepts, propositions, images, or schemas. (If you can't retrieve the meanings of these terms, see Chapter 6.)

In most information-processing models, storage takes place in three interacting memory systems, which you can think of as clusters of mental processes occurring at different stages. *Sensory memory* retains incoming sensory information for a second or two, until it can be processed further. *Short-term memory (STM)* holds a limited amount of information for a brief period of time, perhaps up to 30 seconds or so, unless a conscious effort is made to keep it there longer. *Long-term memory (LTM)* accounts for longer storage—from a few minutes to decades (Atkinson & Shiffrin, 1968, 1971). Information can pass from sensory memory to short-term memory and in either direction between short-term and long-term memory, as illustrated in Figure 7.1.

This model, which is often informally called the "three-box model," has dominated research on memory for more than three decades. However,

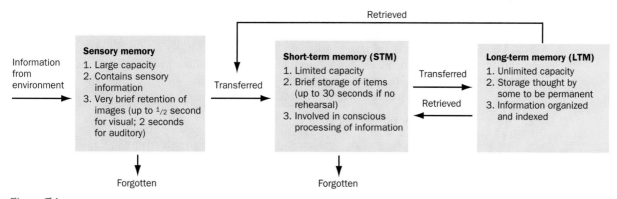

Figure 7.1

Three Memory Systems

In the "three-box model" of memory, information that does not transfer out of sensory memory or short-term memory is assumed to be forgotten forever. Once in long-term memory, information can be retrieved for use in analyzing incoming sensory information or performing mental operations in short-term memory.

competing information-processing models also exist. Some of their advocates question the notion of distinct memory systems. They argue that just one system exists, with different mental processes called on for different tasks.

Further, although many psychologists agree with Philip Johnson-Laird (1988) that "the computer is the last metaphor for the mind," others note that the human brain does not operate like your average computer. Most computers process instructions sequentially and work on a single stream of data. In contrast, the human brain performs many operations simultaneously—that is, in parallel. It recognizes patterns all at once, rather than as a sequence of information bits. It monitors bodily functions, perceives the environment, produces speech, and searches memory all at the same time. It can do this because millions of neurons are active at once, and each neuron communicates with thousands of others, which in turn communicate with millions more. Although no single neuron is terribly smart or terribly fast, millions of them working at the same time produce the complexities of cognition.

parallel distributed processing (PDP)

An alternative to the information-processing model of memory, in which knowledge is represented as connections among thousands of interacting processing units, distributed in a vast network, and all operating in parallel.

Because of these differences between human beings and machines, some cognitive scientists have rejected the traditional information-processing approach altogether in favor of a **parallel distributed processing (PDP)**, or *connectionist*, model (McClelland, 1994; Rumelhart, McClel-

land, & the PDP Research Group, 1986). In PDP models, knowledge is represented not as propositions or images but as connections among thousands and thousands of interacting processing units, distributed in a vast network and all operating in parallel—just like the neurons of the brain. As new information enters the system, the ability of these units to excite or inhibit each other is constantly adjusted to reflect new knowledge.

Memory researchers are still arguing about whether the connectionist approach is an improvement on information-processing models. PDP models have the virtue of resembling the brain's actual wiring, and they are applicable not just to memory but also to perception, language, and decision making. On the other hand, information-processing models are better at explaining why well-learned information is sometimes forgotten when new information is learned (Ratcliff, 1990).

In this chapter, we have decided to retain the information-processing model of three separate memory systems—sensory, short-term, and long-term—because it offers a convenient way to organize the major findings on memory, does a good job of accounting for these findings, and is consistent with the biological facts about memory described in Chapter 4. But keep in mind that the computer metaphor could one day be as outdated as the metaphor of memory as a camera.

??? QUICK QUIZ

How well have you encoded what you just learned?

1. Alberta solved a crossword puzzle a few days ago. She no longer recalls the words in the puzzle, but while playing a game of Scrabble with her brother, she unconsciously tends to form words that were in the puzzle, showing that she has _____ memories of some of the words.

2. The three basic memory processes are _____, storage, and _____.

3. Do the preceding two questions ask for recall, recognition, or relearning? (And what about *this* question?)

4. One objection to traditional information-processing theories of memory is that unlike most computers, which process information _____, the brain performs many independent operations _____.

Answers:

1. implicit   2. encoding, retrieval   3. The first two questions both measure recall; the third question measures recognition.   4. sequentially; simultaneously, or in parallel

Sensory Memory: Fleeting Impressions

In the three-box model, all incoming sensory information must make a brief stop in **sensory memory,** the entryway of memory. Sensory memory includes a number of separate memory subsystems, or **sensory registers**—as many as there are senses. Information in sensory memory is short-lived. Visual images, or *icons,* remain in a visual register for a maximum of half a second. Auditory images, or *echoes,* remain in an auditory register for a slightly longer time, by most estimates up to two seconds or so.

Sensory memory acts as a holding bin, retaining information until we can select items for attention from the stream of stimuli bombarding our senses. It gives us a brief time to decide whether information is extraneous or important; not everything detected by our senses warrants our attention. *Pattern recognition,* the preliminary identification of a stimulus on the basis of information already contained in long-term memory, occurs during the transfer of information from sensory memory to short-term memory. Information that does not go on to short-term memory vanishes forever, like a message written in disappearing ink.

Images in sensory memory are fairly detailed and complete. How do we know that? In a clever experiment, George Sperling (1960) briefly showed people visual arrays of letters that looked like this:

$$
\begin{array}{cccc}
X & K & C & Q \\
N & D & X & G \\
T & F & R & J
\end{array}
$$

In previous studies, subjects had been able to recall only four or five letters, no matter how many they initially saw. Yet many people insisted that they had actually seen more items. Some of the letters, they said, seemed to slip away from memory before they could retrieve and report them. To overcome this problem, Sperling devised a method of "partial report." He had people report the first row of letters when they heard a high tone, the middle row when they heard a medium tone, and the third row when they heard a low tone:

X	K	C	Q	←	High tone
N	D	X	G	←	Medium tone
T	F	R	J	←	Low tone

If the tone occurred right after they saw the array, people could recall about three letters from a row. Because they did not know beforehand which row they would have to report, they therefore must have had most of the letters in sensory memory right after viewing them. However, if the tone occurred after a delay of even one second, people remembered little of what they had seen. The letters had slipped away. In normal processing, too, sensory memory needs to clear quickly to prevent sensory "double exposures."

Short-term Memory: Memory's Work Area

Like sensory memory, **short-term memory (STM)** retains information only temporarily—for up to about 30 seconds by most estimates, although some researchers think that the maximum interval

sensory memory
A memory system that momentarily preserves extremely accurate images of sensory information.

sensory registers
Subsystems of sensory memory; most memory models assume a separate register for each sensory modality.

short-term memory (STM)
In the three-box model of memory, a limited-capacity memory system involved in the retention of information for brief periods; also used for holding information retrieved from long-term memory for temporary use.

Get Involved

Go into a dark room or closet and swing a flashlight rapidly in a circle. You will see an unbroken circle of light instead of a series of separate points. The reason: the successive images remain briefly in sensory memory.

may extend to a few minutes. In short-term memory, the material is no longer an exact sensory image but is an encoding of one, such as a word or a phrase. This material either transfers into long-term memory or decays and is lost forever.

Cases of brain injury demonstrate the importance of transferring new information from short-term memory into long-term memory. H. M.'s case is again instructive. H. M., you will recall, can store information on a short-term basis; he can hold a conversation and appears normal when you first meet him. He also retains implicit memories. However, for the most part, H. M. cannot retain explicit information about new facts and events for longer than a few minutes. His terrible memory deficits involve a problem in transferring explicit memories from short-term storage into long-term storage. With a great deal of repetition and drill, H. M. can learn some new visual information, retain it in long-term memory, and recall it normally (McKee & Squire, 1992). But usually information does not get into long-term memory in the first place.

Besides retaining new information for brief periods while we are learning it, short-term memory also holds information that has been retrieved from long-term memory for temporary use, providing the mental equivalent of a scratch pad. For this reason, short-term memory is often referred to as *working memory*. When you do an arithmetic problem, working memory contains the numbers and the instructions for doing the necessary operations

chunk
A meaningful unit of information; may be composed of smaller units.

("Add the right-hand column, carry the 2"), plus the intermediate results from each step. The ability to bring information from long-term memory into working memory is not disrupted in patients such as H. M. They can do arithmetic, converse, relate events that predate their injury, and do anything else that requires retrieval of information from long-term into short-term memory. Their problem is with the flow of information in the other direction, from short-term memory to long-term.

People such as H. M. fall at the extreme end on a continuum of forgetfulness, but even those of us with normal memories know from personal experience how frustratingly brief short-term retention can be. We look up a telephone number, are distracted for a moment, and find that the number has vanished from our minds. We meet a woman at a meeting and two minutes later find ourselves groping unsuccessfully for her name. Is it any wonder that short-term memory has been called a "leaky bucket"?

According to most memory models, if the bucket did not leak, it would quickly overflow because at any given moment, short-term memory can hold only so many items. Years ago, George Miller (1956) estimated its capacity to be "the magical number 7 plus or minus 2." Five-digit zip codes and 7-digit telephone numbers fall conveniently in this range; 16-digit credit card numbers do not. Some researchers have questioned whether Miller's magical number is so magical after all; estimates of STM's capacity have ranged from 2 items to 20, with most of the estimates at the lower end. Everyone agrees, however, that the number of items that short-term memory can handle at any one time is small.

If this is so, then how do we remember the beginning of a spoken sentence until the speaker reaches the end? After all, most sentences are longer than just a few words. According to most models of memory, we overcome this problem by grouping small bits of information into larger units, or **chunks.** The real capacity of STM, it turns out, is not a few bits of information but a few chunks. A chunk may be a word, a phrase, a sentence, or even a visual image, and it depends on previous experience. For most of us, the acronym *FBI* is one chunk, not three, and the date *1492* is one chunk, not four. In contrast, the number *9214* is four chunks and *IBF* is three—unless your address is 9214 or your initials are IBF. Take another, more visual example: If you are not familiar with football and look at a field full of players, you probably won't be able to remember their positions when you look away. But if you are a

If you don't play chess, you probably won't be able to recall the positions of these chess pieces after looking away. But experienced chess players, in the middle of a game, can remember the position of every piece after glancing only briefly at the board. They are able to "chunk" the pieces into a few standard configurations, instead of trying to memorize where each piece is located.

fan of the game, you may see a single chunk of information—say, a wishbone formation—and be able to retain it.

Even chunking cannot keep short-term memory from eventually filling up. Fortunately, much of the information we take in during the day is needed for only a few moments. If you are multiplying two numbers, you need to remember them only until you have the answer. If you are talking to someone, you need to keep the person's words in mind only until you have understood them. But some information is needed for longer periods and must be transferred to long-term memory. Items that are particularly meaningful, have an emotional impact, or relate to something already in long-term memory may enter long-term storage easily, with only a brief stay in STM. The destiny of other items depends on how soon new information displaces them in short-term memory. Material in short-term memory is easily displaced unless we do something to keep it there—as we will discuss shortly.

Long-term Memory: Final Destination

The third box in the three-box model of memory is **long-term memory (LTM).** The capacity of long-term memory seems to have no practical limits. The vast amount of information stored there enables us to learn, get around in the environment, and build a sense of identity and personal history.

Organization in Long-term Memory.   Because long-term memory contains so much information, we cannot search through it exhaustively, as we can through short-term memory. According to most models of memory, the information must be organized and indexed in some way, so that we can find it. One way to index words (or the concepts they represent) is by the semantic categories to which they belong. *Chair,* for example, belongs to the category *furniture.* In a classic study, people had to memorize 60 words that came from four semantic categories: animals, vegetables, names, and professions. The words were presented in random order, but when people were allowed to recall the items in any order they wished, they tended to recall them in clusters corresponding to the four categories (Bousfield, 1953). This finding has been replicated many times.

Evidence on the storage of information by semantic category also comes from cases of people with brain damage. In one such case, a patient called M. D. appeared to have made a complete recovery two years after suffering several strokes, with one odd exception: He had trouble remembering the names of fruits and vegetables. M. D. could easily name a picture of an abacus or a sphinx but drew a blank when he saw a picture of an orange or a carrot. He could sort pictures of animals, vehicles, and other objects into their appropriate categories but did poorly with pictures of fruits and vegetables. On the other hand, when M. D. was *given* the names of fruits and vegetables, he immediately pointed to the corresponding pictures (Hart, Berndt, & Caramazza, 1985). Apparently, M. D. still had information about fruits and vegetables, but his brain lesion prevented him from using their names to get to the information when he needed it, unless the names were provided by someone else. This evidence suggests that information about a particular concept (such as *orange*) is linked in some way to information about the concept's semantic category (such as *fruit*).

Many models of long-term memory represent its contents as a vast network or grid of interrelated concepts and propositions (Anderson, 1990; Collins & Loftus, 1975). A small part of a conceptual grid for *animals* might look something like the one in Figure 7.2. *Network models* assume that semantic networks are a universal way of

long-term memory (LTM)
In the three-box model of memory, the memory system involved in the long-term storage of information.

Culture affects the encoding, storage, and retrieval of information in long-term memory. Navaho healers, who use stylized, symbolic sand paintings in their rituals, must be able to commit to memory dozens of intricate visual designs because no exact copies are made and the painting is destroyed after each ceremony.

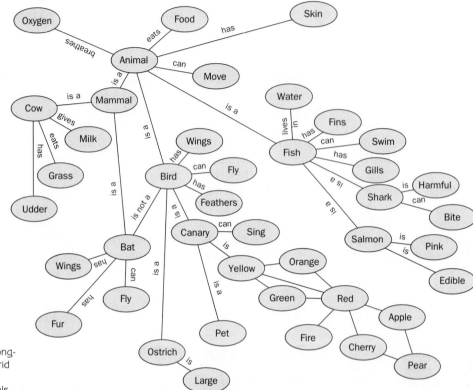

Figure 7.2
Part of a Conceptual Grid in Long-term Memory

Many models of memory represent the contents of long-term semantic memory as an immense network or grid of concepts and the relationships among them. This illustration shows part of a hypothetical grid for *animals*.

organizing information. The way people use these networks, however, depends on experience and education. For example, studies of rural children in Liberia and Guatemala have shown that the more schooling children have, the more likely they are to use semantic categories in recalling lists of objects (Cole & Cole, 1993). This makes sense because in school, children must memorize a lot of information in a short time, and semantic grouping can help. Unschooled children, having less need to memorize lists, do not cluster items and do not remember them as well. But this does not mean that unschooled children have poor memories. When the task is meaningful to them—say, recalling objects that were in a story or a village scene—they remember extremely well (Mistry & Rogoff, 1994).

We organize information in long-term memory not only by semantic groupings but also in terms of the way words sound or look. Have you ever tried to recall some word that was on the "tip of your tongue"? Nearly everyone experiences such *tip-of-the-tongue (TOT) states*, especially when trying to recall the names of acquaintances or famous

persons, the names of objects and places, or the titles of movies or books (Burke et al., 1991). TOT states are reported even by users of sign language, who call them tip-of-the-finger experiences!

One way to study this frustrating state is to have people record tip-of-the-tongue episodes in daily diaries. Another is to give people the definitions of uncommon words and ask them to supply the words. When a word is on the tip of the tongue, people tend to come up with words that are similar in meaning to the right one before they finally recall it. For example, for "patronage bestowed on a relative, in business or politics" a person might say "favoritism" rather than the correct response, "nepotism." But verbal information in long-term memory also seems to be indexed by sound and form, and it is retrievable on that basis. Thus, incorrect guesses often have the correct number of syllables, the correct stress pattern, the correct first letter, or the correct prefix or suffix (A. Brown, 1991; R. Brown & McNeill, 1966). For example, for the target word *sampan* (an Asian boat), a person might say "Siam" or "sarong."

Information in long-term memory may also be organized by its familiarity, relevance, or association with other information. The method a person uses in any given instance probably depends on the nature of the memory; you would no doubt store information about the major cities of Europe differently from information about your first date. To understand the organization of long-term memory, then, we must know what kinds of information can be stored there.

The Contents of Long-term Memory. Most theories of memory distinguish skills or habits ("knowing how") from abstract or representational knowledge ("knowing that"). **Procedural memories** are memories of knowing how—for example, knowing how to comb your hair, use a pencil, solve a jigsaw puzzle, knit a sweater, or swim. Some researchers consider procedural memories to be implicit because once skills and habits are well learned, they do not require much conscious processing. **Declarative memories** are memories of "knowing that," and they are usually assumed to be explicit.

Declarative memories, in turn, come in two varieties: semantic memories and episodic memories (Tulving, 1985). **Semantic memories** are internal representations of the world, independent of any particular context. They include facts, rules, and concepts—items of general knowledge. On the basis of your semantic memory of the concept *cat,* you can describe a cat as a small, furry mammal that typically spends its time eating, sleeping,

prowling, and staring into space, even though a cat may not be present when you give this description, and you probably won't know how or when you first learned it. **Episodic memories,** on the other hand, are internal representations of personally experienced events. When you remember how your cat once surprised you in the middle of the night by pouncing on your face as you slept, you are retrieving an episodic memory.

You might draw on procedural memories to ride a bike, semantic memories to identify a bird, and episodic memories to recall your wedding. Figure 7.3 summarizes these distinctions. Can you come up with other examples for each memory type?

From Short-term to Long-term Memory: A Riddle. The three-box model of memory has often been invoked to explain an interesting phenomenon called the **serial-position effect.** If you are shown a list of items and are then asked immediately to recall them, your retention of any particular item will depend on its position in the list (Glanzer & Cunitz, 1966). Recall will be best for items at the beginning of the list (the *primacy effect*) and at the end of the list (the *recency effect*). When retention of all the items is plotted, the result will be a U-shaped curve, as shown in Figure 7.4 on the next page. A serial-position effect occurs when you are introduced to a roomful of people and find you can recall the names of the first few people and the last, but almost no one in the middle.

procedural memories
Memories for the performance of actions or skills ("knowing how").

declarative memories
Memories of facts, rules, concepts, and events ("knowing that"); include semantic and episodic memories.

semantic memories
Memories of general knowledge, including facts, rules, concepts, and propositions.

episodic memories
Memories of personally experienced events and the contexts in which they occurred.

serial-position effect
The tendency for recall of the first and the last items on a list to surpass recall of items in the middle of the list.

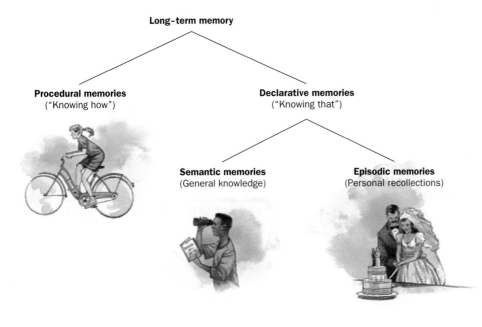

Long-term memory

Procedural memories
("Knowing how")

Declarative memories
("Knowing that")

Semantic memories
(General knowledge)

Episodic memories
(Personal recollections)

Figure 7.3
Types of Long-term Memories
Memories fall into different categories. Perhaps this figure will help you remember them.

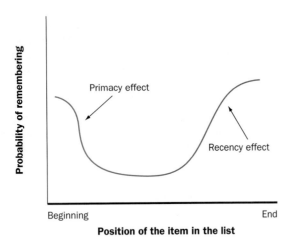

Figure 7.4

The Serial-Position Effect

When people try to recall a list of items immediately after learning it, they tend to remember the first and last items best and the ones in the middle worst.

to compete with other ones to make it into long-term memory. They were thoroughly processed, so they remain memorable. The last few items are remembered for a different reason: At the time of recall, they are still sitting in short-term memory. The items in the middle of a list, however, are not so well retained because by the time they get into short-term memory, it is already crowded. As a result, many of these items drop out of short-term memory before they can be stored in long-term memory.

This explanation makes sense except for one thing: Under some conditions, the last items on a list are well remembered even when the test is delayed past the time when short-term memory has presumably been "emptied" and filled with other information (Greene, 1986). In other words, the recency effect occurs even when, according to the three-box model, it should not. Therefore, the serial-position curve remains something of a puzzle.

According to the three-box model, the first few items on a list are remembered well because short-term memory was relatively "empty" when they entered. Therefore, these items did not have

??? QUICK QUIZ

Find out whether the findings just discussed have transferred from your short-term memory to your long-term memory.

1. _____ memory holds visual images for a fraction of a second.

2. For most people, the abbreviation *U.S.A.* consists of _____ informational chunk(s).

3. Suppose you must memorize a long list of words that includes the following: *desk, pig, gold, dog, chair, silver, table, rooster, bed, copper,* and *horse.* If you can recall the words in any order you wish, how are you likely to group them in recall? Why?

4. When you in-line skate, are you relying on procedural, semantic, or episodic memory? How about when you recall the months of the year? How about when you remember falling off your in-line skates on an icy January day?

5. If a child is trying to memorize the alphabet, which sequence should present the greatest difficulty: *abcdefg, klmnopq,* or *tuvwxyz?* Why?

Answers:

1. sensory   2. one   3. *Desk, chair, table,* and *bed* would probably form one cluster; *pig, dog, rooster,* and *horse* a second; and *gold, silver,* and *copper* a third. Concepts tend to be organized in long-term memory in terms of semantic categories, such as *furniture, animals,* and *metals.*   4. procedural; semantic; episodic   5. *klmnopq,* because of the serial-position effect

What's Ahead

- *What's wrong with trying to memorize in a rote fashion when you're studying—and what's a better strategy?*
- *Memory tricks are fun—but are they always useful?*

HOW WE REMEMBER

Once we understand how memory works, we can use that understanding to remember better—to encode and store information so that it "sticks" and will be there when we need it. What are the best strategies to use?

Effective Encoding

Our memories, as we have seen, are not exact replicas of experience. Sensory information is summarized and encoded—for example, as words or images—almost as soon as it is detected. When you hear a lecture, for example, you may hang on every word (we hope you do!), but you do not memorize those words verbatim. You extract the main points and encode them.

To remember information well, you have to encode it accurately in the first place. With some kinds of information, accurate encoding takes place automatically, without effort. Think about where you usually sit in your psychology class. When were you last there? You can probably provide this information easily, even though you never made a deliberate effort to encode it. In general, people automatically encode their location in space and time and the frequency with which they do certain things (Hasher & Zacks, 1984). But other kinds of information require *effortful* encoding. To retain such information, you might have to select the main points, label concepts, associate the information with personal experiences or with material you already know, or rehearse it until it is familiar. A friend of ours tells us that in her ballet class, she knows exactly what to do when asked to perform a *pas de bourrée*, yet she often has trouble recalling the term itself. Because she rarely uses it, she probably has not bothered to encode it well.

Unfortunately, people sometimes count on automatic encoding when effortful encoding is needed. For example, some students wrongly assume that they can encode the material in a textbook as effortlessly as they encode where they usually sit in the classroom. Or they assume that the ability to remember and perform well on tests is innate and that effort won't make any difference (Devolder & Pressley, 1989). As a result, they wind up in trouble at test time. Experienced students know that most of the information in a college course requires effortful encoding.

Rehearsal

An important technique for keeping information in short-term memory and increasing the chances of long-term retention is *rehearsal,* the review or practice of material while you are learning it. When people are prevented from rehearsing, the contents of their short-term memories quickly fade.

Encoding classroom material for later recall usually takes a deliberate effort. Which of these students do you think will remember best?

In an early study of this phenomenon, people had to memorize meaningless groups of letters. Immediately afterward, they had to start counting backward by threes from an arbitrary number; this counting prevented them from rehearsing the letter groups. Within only 18 seconds, the subjects forgot most of the items (see Figure 7.5). But when they did not have to count backward, their performance was much better, probably because they

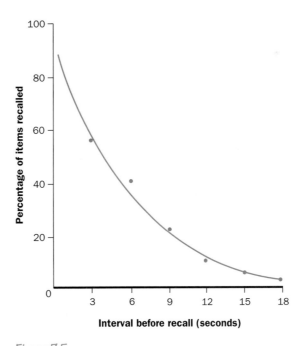

Figure 7.5

Going, Going, Gone

As this graph shows, without rehearsal, the ability to recall information in short-term memory quickly falls off. (From Peterson & Peterson, 1959.)

were rehearsing the items to themselves (Peterson & Peterson, 1959). You are taking advantage of rehearsal when you look up a telephone number and then repeat it over and over in order to keep it in short-term memory until you no longer need it.

A dramatic and poignant demonstration of the power of rehearsal once occurred during a session with H. M. (Ogden & Corkin, 1991). The experimenter gave H. M. five digits to repeat and remember, but then she was unexpectedly called away. When she returned after more than an hour, H. M. was able to repeat the five digits correctly. He had been rehearsing them the entire time!

Short-term memory holds many kinds of information, including visual information and abstract meanings. In fact, some theorists believe that there are several STMs, each specializing in a particular type of information. But most people—or at least most hearing people—seem to favor speech for encoding and rehearsing the contents of short-term memory. The speech may be spoken aloud or to oneself. When people make errors on short-term memory tests that use letters or words, they often confuse items that sound the same or similar, such as *b* and *t*, or *bear* and *bare*. These errors suggest that they have been rehearsing verbally.

Some strategies for rehearsing are more effective than others. **Maintenance rehearsal** involves merely the rote repetition of the material. This kind of rehearsal is fine for keeping information in STM, but it will not always lead to long-term retention. A better strategy if you want to re-

member for the long haul is **elaborative rehearsal,** also called *elaboration of encoding* (Cermak & Craik, 1979; Craik & Tulving, 1975). Elaboration involves associating new items of information with material that has already been stored or with other new facts. It can also involve analyzing the physical, sensory, or semantic features of an item.

Suppose, for example, that you are studying the hypothalamus in Chapter 4. Simply rehearsing the definition of the hypothalamus in a rote manner is unlikely to transfer the information you need from short-term to long-term memory. Instead, when going over (rehearsing) the concept, you could encode the information in Figure 7.6. The more you elaborate the concept of the hypothalamus, the better you will remember it.

A related strategy for prolonging retention is **deep processing,** or the processing of meaning. If you process only the physical or sensory features of a stimulus, such as how the word *hypothalamus* is spelled and how it sounds, your processing will be shallow even if it is elaborated. If you recognize patterns and assign labels to objects or events ("The hypothalamus is below the thalamus"), your processing will be somewhat deeper. If you fully analyze the meaning of what you are trying to remember (for example, by encoding the functions, location, and importance of the hypothalamus), your processing will be deeper yet. Sometimes, shallow processing is useful; when you memorize a poem, for instance, you will want to pay attention to (and elaborately encode) the

maintenance rehearsal

Rote repetition of material in order to maintain its availability in memory.

elaborative rehearsal

Association of new information with already stored knowledge and analysis of the new information to make it memorable.

deep processing

In the encoding of information, the processing of meaning rather than of simply the physical or sensory features of a stimulus.

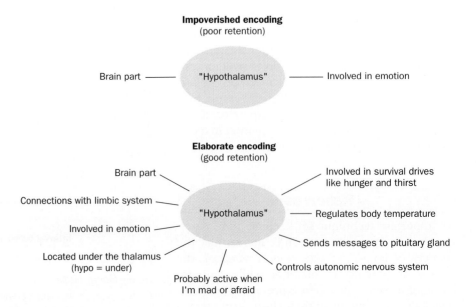

Figure 7.6

Elaboration of Encoding

In elaborated encoding, you encode the features of an item and its associations with other items in memory. When you studied the hypothalamus in Chapter 4, was your encoding elaborated or impoverished?

sounds of the words and the patterns of rhythm in the poem, and not just the poem's meaning. Usually, however, deep processing is more effective. Unfortunately, students (and other people) often try to memorize information that has little or no meaning for them, which explains why the information doesn't stick.

Mnemonics

In addition to using elaborative rehearsal and deep processing, people who want to give their powers of memory a boost sometimes employ **mnemonics** [neh-MON-iks], formal strategies and tricks for encoding, storing, and retaining information. (Mnemosyne [neh-MOZ-eh-nee] was the ancient Greek goddess of memory.) Some mnemonics take the form of easily memorized rhymes (e.g., "Thirty days hath September / April, June, and November . . ."). Others use formulas (e.g., "**E**very **g**ood **b**oy **d**oes **f**ine" for remembering which notes are on the lines of the treble clef in musical notation). Still others use visual images or word associations, which increase retention.

The best mnemonics force you to encode material actively and thoroughly. They may also reduce the amount of information by chunking it (as in the phone number 466-3293, which corresponds to the letters in GOOD-BYE—appropriate, perhaps, for a travel agency). Or they may make the material meaningful and thus easier to store and retrieve; facts and words to be memorized are often more memorable, for example, if they are woven into a coherent story (Bower & Clark, 1969). If you needed to remember the parts of the digestive system for a physiology course, you could construct a narrative about what happens to a piece of food after it enters a person's mouth,

"YOU SIMPLY ASSOCIATE EACH NUMBER WITH A WORD, SUCH AS 'TABLE' AND 3,476,029."

then repeat the narrative aloud to yourself or to a study partner.

Some stage performers with amazing recall rely on more complicated mnemonics. We are not going to spend time on them here because for ordinary memory tasks, such tricks are often no more effective than rote rehearsal, and sometimes they are actually worse (Wang, Thomas, & Ouellette, 1992). Most memory researchers do not use such mnemonics themselves (Park, Smith, & Cavanaugh, 1990). After all, why bother to memorize a grocery list using a fancy mnemonic when you can write down what you need to buy? The fastest route to a good memory is to follow the principles suggested by the findings in this section and by research reviewed in the "Taking Psychology with You" feature at the end of this chapter.

mnemonics
Strategies and tricks for improving memory, such as the use of a verse or a formula.

??? VERY QUICK QUIZ

 Camille is furious with her history professor. "I read the chapter three times, but I still failed the quiz," she fumes. "The quiz must have been unfair." What's wrong with Camille's reasoning, and what are some other possible explanations for her poor performance, based on principles of critical thinking and what you have learned so far about memory?

Answer:

Camille is reasoning emotionally and is not examining the assumptions underlying her explanations. Perhaps she relied on automatic rather than effortful encoding, used maintenance instead of elaborative rehearsal, and used shallow instead of deep processing when she studied. She may also have tried to encode everything, instead of being selective.

WHY WE FORGET

Have you ever, in the heat of some deliriously happy moment, said to yourself, "I'll never forget this, never, *never*, NEVER"? Do you find that you can more clearly remember saying those words than the deliriously happy moment itself? Sometimes you encode an event, you rehearse it, you analyze its meaning, you tuck it away in long-term storage—and still you forget it. Is it any wonder that most of us have wished, at one time or another, for a "photographic memory"?

Actually, having a perfect long-term memory is

Thinking Critically About Having a Perfect Memory

not the blessing that you might suppose. The Russian psychologist Alexander Luria (1968) once told of a journalist, S., who could remember giant grids of numbers and could reproduce them both forward and backward, even after the passage of 15 years. S. also remembered the exact circumstances under which he had originally learned the material. To accomplish his astonishing feats, he used mnemonics, especially the formation of visual images. But you shouldn't envy him, for he had a serious problem: He could not forget even when he wanted to. Along with the diamonds of experience, he kept dredging up the pebbles. Images he had formed in order to remember kept creeping into consciousness, distracting him and interfering with his ability to concentrate. At times he even had trouble holding a conversation because the other person's words would set off a jumble of associations. In fact, Luria called him "rather dull-witted." Eventually, unable to work at his profession, S. took to supporting himself by traveling from place to place, demonstrating his mnemonic abilities for audiences.

Like remembering, then, a certain degree of forgetting contributes to our survival and our sanity. (Think back; would you really want to recall every angry argument, every embarrassing episode, every painful moment in your life? Could it be that self-confidence and optimism depend on locking some follies and grievances in a back drawer of memory?) Nonetheless, most of us forget more than we would like to, and we would like to know why.

Over a century ago, in an effort to measure pure memory loss independent of personal experience, Hermann Ebbinghaus (1885/1913) memorized long lists of nonsense syllables, such as *bok, waf,* or *ged,* and then tested his retention over a period of several weeks. Most of his forgetting occurred soon after the initial learning and then leveled off (see Figure 7.7a). Ebbinghaus's method of studying memory was adopted by generations of psychologists, even though it didn't tell them much about the kinds of memories that people care about most.

A century later, Marigold Linton decided to find out how people forget real events rather than nonsense syllables. Like Ebbinghaus, she used herself as a subject, but she charted the curve of forgetting over years, rather than days. Every day for 12 years she recorded on a 4- × 6-inch card two or more things that had happened to her that day. Eventually, she accumulated a catalogue of thousands of discrete events, both trivial ("I have dinner at the Canton Kitchen: delicious lobster dish") and significant ("I land at Orly Airport in Paris"). Once a month, she took a random sampling of all the cards accumulated to that point, noted whether she could remember the events on them, and tried to date the events. Reporting on the results from the first six years of the study, Linton (1978) told how she had expected the kind of rapid forgetting reported by Ebbinghaus. Instead, as you can see in Figure 7.7b, she found that long-term forgetting was slower and proceeded at a much more constant pace, as details gradually dropped out of her memories.

Of course, some memories, especially those that mark important transitions (marriage, getting a first job), are more memorable than others. But why did Marigold Linton, like the rest of us, forget so many details? Psychologists have proposed five mechanisms to account for forgetting: decay, replacement of old memories by new ones, interference, motivated forgetting, and cue-dependent forgetting.

The Decay Theory

One commonsense view, the **decay theory,** holds that memory traces fade with time if they are not "accessed" now and then. We have al-

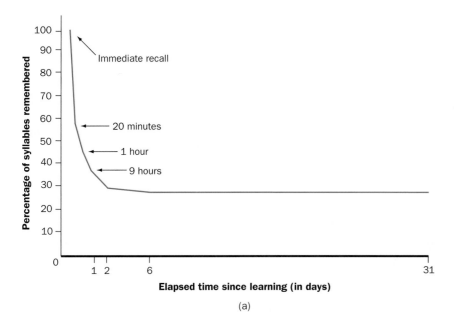

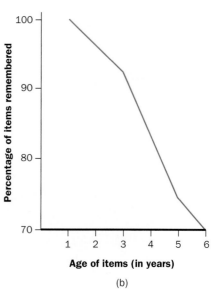

(a)

(b)

Figure 7.7

Two Kinds of Forgetting Curves

When Hermann Ebbinghaus tested his own memory for nonsense syllables, forgetting was rapid at first and then tapered off (a). In contrast, when Marigold Linton tested her own memory for personal events over a period of several years, her retention was excellent at first, but then it fell off at a gradual but steady rate (b).

ready seen that decay occurs in sensory memory and that it occurs in short-term memory as well, if we don't rehearse the material. However, the mere passage of time does not account so well for forgetting in long-term memory. People commonly forget things that happened only yesterday while remembering events from many years ago. Indeed, some memories, both procedural and declarative, remain accessible for a lifetime. If you learned to swim as a child, you will still know how to swim at age 30, even if you haven't been in a pool or lake for 22 years. We are also happy to report that some lessons learned in school have great staying power. In one study, people did well on a Spanish test as long as 50 years after taking Spanish in high school, even though most had hardly used Spanish at all in the intervening years (Bahrick, 1984). Decay alone, then, cannot explain lapses in long-term memory.

New Memories for Old

Another explanation of forgetting holds that new information can completely wipe out old information, just as rerecording on an audiotape or videotape will obliterate the original material. In one

Motor skills, which are stored as procedure memories, can last a lifetime.

When people who saw a car with a yield sign (top) were later asked if they had seen "the stop sign" (a misleading question), many said they had. Similarly, when those shown a stop sign were asked if they had seen "the yield sign," many said yes. These false memories persisted even after the researchers revealed their use of misleading questions, suggesting that the misleading information had erased the subjects' original mental representations of the signs (Loftus, 1980).

study supporting this view, researchers showed people slides of a traffic accident and used leading questions to get them to think that they had seen a stop sign when they had really seen a yield sign, or vice versa. People in a control group who were not misled in this way were able to identify the sign they had actually seen. Later, all the subjects were told the purpose of the study and were asked to guess whether they had been misled. Almost all of those who had been misled continued to insist that they had *really, truly* seen the sign whose existence had been planted in their minds (Loftus, Miller, & Burns, 1978). These findings suggest that the subjects had not just been trying to please the researchers, and that their original perceptions had in fact been "erased" by the misleading information.

Interference

A third theory holds that forgetting occurs because similar items of information interfere with one another in either storage or retrieval; the information may get into memory, but it becomes confused with other information. Such interference, which occurs in both short- and long-term memory, is especially common when you have to recall isolated facts—names, addresses, personal identification numbers, passwords, access numbers, area codes, credit card numbers, and the like.

retroactive interference

Forgetting that occurs when recently learned material interferes with the ability to remember similar material stored previously.

proactive interference

Forgetting that occurs when previously stored material interferes with the ability to remember similar, more recently learned material.

Suppose you are at a party and you meet someone named Julie. A half-hour later you meet someone named Judy. You go on to talk to other people, and after an hour, you again bump into Julie, but by mistake you call her Judy. The second name has interfered with the first. This type of interference, in which new information interferes with the ability to remember old information, is called **retroactive interference:**

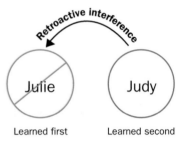

This type of interference is sometimes illustrated by a story about an absent-minded professor of ichthyology (the study of fish) who complained that whenever he learned the name of a new student, he forgot the name of a fish.

Because new information is constantly entering memory, we are all vulnerable to the effects of retroactive interference—or at least *most* of us are. H. M. is an exception; his memories of childhood and adolescence are unusually detailed, clear, and unchanging. H. M. can remember actors and singers famous when he was a child, the films they were in, and who their costars were. He knows the names of friends from the second grade. Presumably, these early declarative memories have not been subject to interference from memories acquired since the operation because no new memories have been acquired!

Interference also works in the opposite direction. Old information (such as the Spanish you learned in high school) may interfere with the ability to remember new information (such as the French you're trying to learn now). This type of interference is called **proactive interference:**

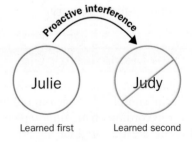

Over a period of weeks, months, and years, proactive interference may cause more forgetting than retroactive interference does because we have stored up so much information that can potentially interfere with anything new.

Motivated Forgetting

Sigmund Freud maintained that people forget because they block from consciousness those memories that are too threatening or painful to live with, and he called this self-protective process *repression* (see Chapter 2). Today, many psychologists prefer a more general term, **motivated forgetting,** and they argue that people might be motivated to forget events for many reasons, including embarrassment, guilt, shock, and a desire to protect their own pride. (In Chapter 10 we will discuss *dissociative amnesia,* in which people selectively forget a stressful or traumatic experience that is threatening to the self.)

The concepts of repression and motivated forgetting are based mostly on clinical reports of people in psychotherapy who appear to recall long-buried memories, typically of traumatic events in childhood—as in the case of Eileen Franklin Lipsker. Only rarely, however, have such memories been corroborated by objective evidence, so it is difficult and often impossible to determine their accuracy. It is also difficult to distinguish "repression" from other kinds of forgetting or from a simple refusal to think about an upsetting experience. We will return to this issue at the end of this chapter.

Cue-dependent Forgetting

Often, when we need to remember, we rely on *retrieval cues,* items of information that can help us find the specific information we're looking for. When we lack such cues, we may feel as if we have lost the call number for an entry in the mind's library. In long-term memory, this type of memory failure, called **cue-dependent forgetting,** may be the most common type of all. Willem Wagenaar (1986), who, like Marigold Linton, recorded critical details about events in his life, found that within a year, he had forgotten 20 percent of those details, and after five years, he had forgotten 60 percent. However, when he gathered cues from witnesses about ten events that he thought he had forgotten, he was able to recall something about all ten, which suggests that some of his forgetting was cue dependent.

Retrieval cues may work by getting us into the general area of memory where an item is stored, or by making a match with information that is linked in memory with the item in question. Thus, if you are trying to remember the last name of an actor, it might help to know the person's first name or the name of a recent movie the actor starred in.

Cues that were present at the time you learned a new fact or had an experience are apt to be especially useful as retrieval aids. That may explain why remembering is often easier when you are in the same physical environment as you were when an event occurred: Cues in the present context match those from the past. Some people have suggested that the overlap between present and past cues may also lead to a *false* sense of having been in exactly the same situation before; this is the eerie phenomenon of *déjà vu* (which means "already seen" in French). Ordinarily, however, contextual cues help us remember the past more accurately.

Your mental or physical state may also act as a retrieval cue, evoking a **state-dependent memory.** For example, if you are intoxicated when something happens, you may remember it better when you once again have had a few drinks than

motivated forgetting
Forgetting that occurs because of a desire to eliminate awareness of painful, embarrassing, or otherwise unpleasant experiences.

cue-dependent forgetting
The inability to retrieve information stored in memory because of insufficient cues for recall.

state-dependent memory
The tendency to remember something when the rememberer is in the same physical or mental state as during the original learning or experience.

Charlie Chaplin's film *City Lights* provides a classic illustration of state-dependent memory. After Charlie saves the life of a drunken millionaire, the two spend the rest of the evening in boisterous merrymaking. But the next day, after sobering up, the millionaire fails to recognize Charlie and gives him the cold shoulder. Then, once again, the millionaire gets drunk—and once again he greets Charlie as a pal.

when you are sober. (This is not an endorsement of drunkenness! Your memory will be best if you are sober during both encoding and recall.) Likewise, if your emotional arousal is especially high or low at the time of an event, you may remember that event best when you are once again in the same emotional state. When victims of violent crimes have trouble recalling details of the experience, it may be in part because they are far less emotionally aroused than they were at the time of the crime (Clark, Milberg, & Erber, 1987).

Retrieval of a memory may also be more likely when your *mood* is the same as it was when you first encoded and stored the memory, presumably because mood serves as a retrieval cue. Findings on this notion, however, have been frustratingly inconsistent, possibly because the effect depends on many factors, such as the strength of the mood, the nature of the event, and the way the memory is retrieved (Eich, 1995). What really counts is probably the match between your current mood and the *kind of material* you are trying to remember, especially when you are feeling happy. In other words, you are likely to remember happy events better when you are feeling happy than when you are sad (Mayer, McCormick, & Strong, 1995). Perhaps that is one reason that depressed people become stuck in their bleak moods: They are less likely than others to retrieve the pleasant memories that might help them feel better.

??? QUICK QUIZ

If you haven't repressed what you just read, try these questions.

1. Ever since she read *Even Cowgirls Get the Blues* many years ago, Wilma has loved the novels of Tom Robbins. Later, she developed a crush on actor Tim Robbins, but every time she tries to recall his name, she calls him "Tom." Why?

2. When a man at his twentieth high school reunion sees his old friends, he recalls incidents he had thought were long forgotten. Why?

Answers:

1. proactive interference   2. The sight of his friends provides retrieval cues for the incidents.

What's Ahead

- *Why are the first few years of life a mental blank?*
- *Which periods of life tend to stand out in memory?*

AUTOBIOGRAPHICAL MEMORIES

Memory provides each of us with a sense of identity that evolves and changes as we build up a store of episodic memories about events we have experienced firsthand. For most of us, the memories we have of our own lives—our *autobiographical memories*—are by far the most fascinating. We use them as entertainment ("Did I ever tell you about the time . . . ?"); we manipulate them—some people even publish them—in order to create an image of ourselves; we analyze them to learn more about who we are.

childhood (infantile) amnesia

The inability to remember events and experiences that occurred before ages 2 or 3.

Childhood Amnesia: The Missing Years

One curious aspect of autobiographical memory is that most adults cannot recall any events from earlier than the third or fourth year of life. A few people apparently can recall momentous experiences that occurred when they were as young as 2 years old, such as the birth of a sibling, but not events that occurred earlier (Usher & Neisser, 1993). As adults, we cannot remember having our parents feed us during infancy, taking our first steps, or uttering our first halting sentences. We are victims of **childhood amnesia** (sometimes called *infantile amnesia*).

People often find childhood amnesia difficult to accept. There is something disturbing about the fact that our early years are beyond recall—so disturbing that some people adamantly deny it, claiming to remember events from the second or even the first year of life. But like other false memories, these recollections are merely recon-

Thinking Critically About Childhood Amnesia

structions based on photographs, family stories, and imagination. Indeed, the "remembered" event may not even have taken place. Swiss psychologist Jean Piaget (1951) once reported a memory of being nearly kidnapped at the age of 2. Piaget remembered sitting in his pram, watching his nurse as she bravely defended him from the kidnapper. He remembered the scratches she received on her face. He remembered a police officer with a short cloak and white baton who finally chased the kidnapper away. There was only one small problem: None of it happened. When Piaget was 15, his nurse wrote to his parents confessing that she had made up the entire story. Piaget noted, "I therefore must have heard, as a child, the account of this story . . . and projected it into the past in the form of a visual memory, which was a memory of a memory, but false." (This incident, by the way, is also a good example of source amnesia.)

Of course, we all retain procedural memories from the toddler stage, when we first learned to use a fork, drink from a cup, build a tower from blocks, and pull a wagon. We also retain semantic memories acquired early in life: the rules of counting, the names of people and things, knowledge about all manner of objects in the world. Further, toddlers who are only 1 to 2 years old can often remember past experiences, and some 4-year-olds can remember experiences that occurred before age 2½ (Bauer & Dow, 1994; McDonough & Mandler, 1994). The mystery is why our early episodic memories do not survive into later childhood or adulthood.

Sigmund Freud thought that childhood amnesia was due to repression (see Chapter 2). Today, however, some biological researchers argue that repression has nothing to do with it; childhood amnesia, they say, occurs because brain areas involved in the formation or storage of events are not well developed until a few years after birth (McKee & Squire, 1993; Nadel & Zola-Morgan, 1984). And other psychologists have proposed various cognitive explanations for the amnesia of the first years:

• *Lack of a sense of self.* In one view, we can't have an autobiographical memory of our*selves* until we have a self to remember. Indeed, autobiographical memories do not begin until the emergence of a self-concept, an event that occurs at somewhat different ages for different children, but

This infant, who is learning to kick in order to make a mobile move, may remember the trick a week later. However, she will not remember the experience itself when she is older. Like the rest of us, she will fall victim to childhood amnesia.

not before the age of 2 (Howe, Courage, & Peterson, 1994).

• *Differences between early and later cognitive schemas.* Only after we enter school do we learn to think as adults do, using language to organize our memories and storing not only events but also our reactions to them. Schemas formed in late childhood or adulthood, therefore, are not necessarily useful for reconstructing early events from the memory fragments we stored at the time (Howe & Courage, 1993).

• *Impoverished encoding.* Preschoolers probably encode experiences far less elaborately than adults do because their information-processing abilities are still limited. Young children have not yet mastered the social conventions for reporting events; they do not know what is important and interesting to others. Instead, they tend to rely on adults' questions to provide retrieval cues ("Where did we go for breakfast?" "Who did you go trick-or-treating with?"), and this dependency on adults may prevent them from building up a stable core of remembered material that will be available when they are older (Fivush & Hamond, 1991).

• *A focus on the routine.* Preschoolers tend to focus on the routine, familiar aspects of an experience, such as eating lunch or playing with toys, rather than the distinctive aspects that will provide retrieval cues and make an event memorable in the long run (Fivush & Hamond, 1991; White & Pillemer, 1979).

Whatever the explanation for childhood amnesia, our first memories, even when they are not accurate, may provide some useful insights into our personalities, basic concerns, ambitions, and attitudes toward life (Kihlstrom & Harackiewicz, 1982). The early psychologist Lloyd Morgan once wrote that an autobiography "is a story of oneself in the past, read in the light of one's present self." That is just what our private memories are.

Memory and Narrative: The Stories of Our Lives

Communications psychologist George Gerbner (1988) once observed that our species is unique because we tell stories . . . and live by the stories we tell. This view of human beings as the "story-telling animal" has had a huge impact on cognitive psychology and related fields. The *narratives* we compose to make sense of our lives can have a profound influence on us: Our plans, memories, love affairs, hatreds, ambitions, and dreams are all guided by plot outlines.

Human beings construct and preserve the past in many imaginative ways. The Hmong of Laos have created needlework narratives that tell of their long, dangerous flight from their homeland in the early 1970s, at the end of the war in Southeast Asia, and of the celebrations and daily events in their former villages. If you had the sewing skills of the Hmong, what tapestry would you create of your own life?

Thus we say, "I am this way because, as a small child, this happened to me, and then my parents . . . ." We say, "Let me tell you the story of how we fell in love." We say, "When you hear what happened, you'll understand why I felt entitled to take such cold-hearted revenge." These stories are not necessarily fictions, as in the child's meaning of "tell me a story." Rather, they are narratives that provide a unifying theme to organize the events of our lives and give them meaning. But because these narratives rely heavily on memory, and because memories are reconstructed and dynamic, constantly shifting in response to present needs, beliefs, and experiences, our stories are also, to some degree, works of interpretation and imagination. Adult memories thus reveal as much about the present as they do about the past.

An understanding of the importance of narrative helps us to appreciate some features of how autobiographical memory works and why it sometimes fails. As we age, certain periods of our lives tend to stand out; old people remember more from adolescence and early adulthood than from midlife, a phenomenon known as the "reminiscence bump" (MacKavey, Malley, & Stewart, 1991). Perhaps the younger years are especially memorable because they are full of memorable transitions. Or perhaps people are especially likely to weave events from their youth into a coherent story and thus remember them better ("After I graduated from college I met the love of my life, who dumped me in the most cruel and heartless fashion, and before I knew it. . . .")

Yet, as we have seen throughout this chapter, many details about events, even those transitions we are sure we remember clearly, are probably added after the fact. By now, you should not be surprised that memory can be as fickle as it can be accurate. As cognitive psychologists have shown repeatedly, we are not merely actors in our personal life dramas. We also write the scripts.

Now that you know about the reconstructive nature of memory, you are ready to reconsider Eileen Franklin Lipsker's accusation against her father, George Franklin. Eileen, you'll recall, claimed that a long-forgotten memory of her friend's murder had returned in a flash, with perfect accuracy. Yet as we have seen, research disputes the belief that memories can be preserved for years in a pristine, uncontaminated state of "repression"; most memories, even of shocking experiences, are vulnerable to distortion, error, and influence by others. Further, leading questions and suggestive interrogation methods such as hypnosis can encourage memories for events that never happened. And, unfortunately, a person's confidence in his or her memory is not a reliable guide to a memory's accuracy.

The recovered-memory school argues that these findings do not apply to memories of something as horrible as murder or incest. Yet the Franklin case, which launched the recovered-memory phenomenon, eventually fell apart. In 1996, George Franklin's conviction was reversed on the grounds that Eileen's testimony could have been based on information she read in the newspapers rather than on her own memories, which provided no new details or incriminating evidence. It also turned out that Eileen's "memories" had emerged under hypnosis during psychotherapy, not spontaneously as she initially claimed. And her accusations escalated: After accusing her father of murdering her friend, she "remembered" seeing him murder two other girls. An investigation completely exonerated him.

In an important ruling in the case of Laura B., the woman who said she had repressed the memory of 18 years of molestation by her father, the judge wrote that her recovered memories would not be admissible evidence because "the phenomenon of memory repression, and the process of therapy used in these cases to recover the memories, have not gained general acceptance in the field of psychology; and are not scientifically reliable" (*State of New Hampshire* v. *Joel Hungerford*, May 23, 1995). Many other courts across the country have reached similar decisions.

Of course, all psychologists realize that people can and do forget troubling, embarrassing, and painful experiences, and that with the right cues, these memories may return. Obviously, then, not all "recovered" memories are false. It would be wonderful to have a litmus test for distinguishing real memories from false ones, and perhaps someday we will. In a recent PET-scan study, false and true memories for words heard in lists triggered different patterns of brain activity (Schacter et al., 1996). But no one knows yet whether these results will generalize to memories for real events and experiences.

How, then, should we respond to an individual's claim to have recovered memories of abuse or other traumas? Based on the research in this chapter, we should be skeptical if the person says that, thanks to therapy, he or she now has memories from the first year or two of life. We should be skeptical if, over time, the person's memories become more and more implausible—for instance, the person says that sexual abuse continued day and night for 15 years without ever being remembered and without anyone else in the household noticing anything amiss. And we should hear alarm bells if a therapist used suggestive techniques such as hypnosis or guided imagery to "help" a patient recall the alleged abuse. In contrast, a person's recollections are more likely to be trustworthy if there is corroborating evidence from medical records or the recollections of other family members; if the person revealed signs of trauma, such as nightmares and disturbed behavior, at the time the remembered event is said to have occurred; and if the person spontaneously recalled the event without pressure from others or the use of suggestive techniques in therapy.

In many ways, we are our memories; what we remember, and what we choose to forget, are the hallmarks of our personalities. Shared memories—real or distorted—bind families, and sometimes destroy them. Private memories—real or distorted—make up the narratives that guide our lives. Psychological research on this hugely complex and fascinating topic can give us greater respect for our ability to remember—and greater humility when we fail to remember accurately.

Taking Psychology with You

How to . . . Uh . . . Remember

Someday, drugs may help people with memory deficiencies and may increase normal memory performance. For the time being, however, those of us who hope to improve our memories must rely on mental strategies. Some simple mnemonics can be useful, but as we have seen, complicated ones are often more bother than they're worth. A better approach is to follow some general guidelines based on the principles in this chapter:

• *Pay attention!* It seems obvious, but often we fail to remember because we never encoded the information in the first place. For example, which of these is the real Lincoln penny?

Most Americans have trouble recognizing the real penny because they have never attended to the details of a penny's design (Nickerson & Adams, 1979). We are not advising you to do so, unless you happen to be a coin collector or a counterfeiting expert. Just keep in mind that when you do have something to remember, such as the material in this book, you will do better if you encode it well. (The real penny, by the way, is the left one in the bottom row.)

• *Encode information in more than one way.* The more elaborate the encoding of information, the more memorable it will be. Use your imagination! For instance, in addition to remembering a telephone number by the sound of the individual digits, you might note the spatial pattern they make as you punch them in on a touch-tone phone.

• *Add meaning.* The more meaningful the material, the more likely it is to link up with information already in long-term memory. Meaningfulness also reduces the number of chunks of information you have to learn. Common ways of adding meaning include making up a story about the material (fitting the material into a cognitive schema) and forming visual images. (Some people find that the odder the image, the better.) If your license plate happens to be 236MPL, you might think of 236 maples. If you are trying to re- member the concept of procedural memory from this chapter, you might make the concept meaningful by thinking of an example from your own life, such as your ability to ride a mountain bike, and then imagine a "P" superimposed on an image of yourself on your bike.

• *Aim for a moderate arousal level.* As we saw in Chapter 4, hormones released by the adrenal glands during stress and emotional arousal, including epinephrine (adrenaline) and certain steroids, appear to enhance memory—but only if the hormones remain at moderate levels (Cahill et al., 1994; McGaugh, 1990). Thus, if you want to remember information well, you should try not to be too worked up *or* too relaxed.

• *Take your time.* Just as concrete takes time to set, the neural and synaptic changes in the brain that underlie long-term memory take time to develop (see Chapter 4). Memories, therefore, require a period of *consolidation,* or stabilization, before they solidify. That fact may help explain why leisurely learning, spread out over several sessions, usually produces better results than harried cramming (although *reviewing* material just before a test can be helpful). In terms of hours spent, "distributed" (spaced) learning sessions are more efficient than "massed" ones; in other words, three separate one-hour study sessions may result in more retention than one session of three hours.

• *Take time out.* If possible, minimize interference by using study breaks for rest or recreation. Sleep is the ultimate way to reduce interference. In a classic study, students who slept for eight hours after learning lists of nonsense syllables retained them better than students who went about their usual business (Jenkins & Dallenbach, 1924). Sleep is not always possible, of course, but periodic mental relaxation usually is.

• *Overlearn.* You can't remember something you never learned well in the first place. Overlearning—studying information even after you think you already know it—is one of the best ways to ensure that you'll remember it.

• *Monitor your learning.* By testing yourself frequently, rehearsing thoroughly, and reviewing periodically, you will have a better idea of how you are doing. Don't just evaluate your learning immediately after reading the material, though; because the information is still in short-term memory, you are likely to feel a false sense of confidence about your ability to recall it later. If you delay making a judgment for at least a few minutes, your evaluation will probably be more accurate (Nelson & Dunlosky, 1991).

Whatever strategies you use, you will find that active learning produces more comprehension and better retention than does passive reading or listening. The mind does not gobble up information automatically; you must make the material digestible. Even then, you should not expect to remember everything you read or hear. Nor should you want to. Piling up facts without distinguishing the important from the trivial is just confusing. Popular books and tapes that promise a "perfect," "photographic" memory, or "instant recall" of everything you learn, fly in the face of what psychologists know about how the mind operates. Our advice: Forget them.

SUMMARY

Reconstructing the Past

1) Unlike a tape recorder or video camera, human memory is highly selective and is *reconstructive:* People add, delete, and change elements in ways that help them make sense of information and events. Sometimes they confuse imagined events with actual ones, especially when (a) they have thought about the imagined event many times; (b) the image of the event contains many details; (c) the event is easy to imagine; and (d) the focus of attention is on emotional reactions to the event.

2) People who hold the mistaken belief that all memories are permanently stored with perfect accuracy often cite cases of recall under hypnosis and of emotionally powerful memories that seem to be permanent (*flashbulb memories*). Under hypnosis, however, people confabulate. Even flashbulb memories are often embellished or distorted and tend to change over time.

3) The reconstructive nature of memory raises problems in legal cases involving eyewitness testimony. Errors are especially likely when the suspect's ethnicity differs from that of the witness and when leading questions are put to witnesses.

4) Findings on memory help clarify the issues in the debate about whether children are capable of making up accounts of sexual abuse. Children, like adults, are often able to remember the essential aspects of an important event with great accuracy. However, like adults, they can also be suggestible, especially when they are very young, are in emotionally charged situations that blur the line between fantasy and reality, are asked leading questions, or have a desire to please the interviewer.

Measuring Memory

5) The ability to remember depends in part on the type of performance being called for. In tests of *explicit memory* (conscious recollection), *recognition* is usually better than *recall.* In tests of *implicit memory,* which is measured by indirect methods such as *priming,* past experiences may affect current thoughts or actions, even when these experiences are not consciously and intentionally remembered. The *relearning method* seems to straddle the boundary between explicit and implicit tests of memory.

The Three-Box Model of Memory

6) In *information-processing models,* memory involves the *encoding, storage,* and *retrieval* of information. In most information-processing models, storage occurs in three interacting systems: *sensory memory, short-term memory,* and *long-term memory.*

7) The "three-box model" has dominated research on memory for more than three decades, but competing models also exist. Some cognitive scientists prefer a *parallel distributed processing (PDP)* or *connectionist* model, which represents knowledge as connections among numerous interacting processing units, distributed in a vast network and all operating in parallel. Nonetheless, the three-box

model continues to offer a convenient way to organize the major findings on memory, and it is consistent with findings on the biology of memory.

8) In the three-box model, incoming sensory information makes a brief stop in *sensory memory*, which momentarily retains it in the form of literal sensory images, such as *icons* and *echoes*. *Pattern recognition* occurs during the transfer of information from sensory memory to short-term memory. Sensory memory gives us a little time to decide whether information is important enough to warrant further attention.

9) *Short-term memory (STM)* retains new information for up to 30 seconds by most estimates (unless rehearsal takes place) and also serves as a *working memory* for the processing of information retrieved from long-term memory for temporary use. The capacity of STM is extremely limited but can be extended if information is organized into larger units by *chunking*. Items that are meaningful, have an emotional impact, or link up to something already in long-term memory may enter long-term storage easily, with only a brief stay in STM.

10) *Long-term memory (LTM)* contains a vast amount of information that must be organized and indexed. For example, words (or the concepts they represent) seem to be organized by semantic categories. *Network models* of LTM represent its contents as a network of interrelated concepts. The way people use these networks depends on experience and education. Words are also indexed in LTM in terms of sound and form.

11) *Procedural memories* ("knowing how") are memories for how to perform specific actions; *declarative memories* ("knowing that") are memories for abstract or representational knowledge. Declarative memories include *semantic memories* and *episodic memories.*

12) The three-box model has often been invoked to explain the *serial-position effect* in memory, but it cannot explain why a *recency effect* sometimes occurs even when it shouldn't.

How We Remember

13) In order to remember material well, we must encode it accurately in the first place. Some kinds of information, such as material in a college course, require effortful, as opposed to automatic, encoding.

14) Rehearsal of information keeps it in short-term memory and increases the chances of long-term retention. *Elaborative rehearsal* is more likely to result in transfer to long-term memory than is *maintenance rehearsal,* and *deep processing* is usually a more effective retention strategy than *shallow processing.*

15) *Mnemonics* can also enhance retention by promoting elaborative encoding and making material meaningful, but for ordinary memory tasks, complex memory tricks are often ineffective or even counterproductive.

Why We Forget

16) Forgetting can occur for several reasons. Information in sensory and short-term memory appears to *decay* if it does not receive further processing. New information may "erase" old information in long-term memory. *Proactive* and *retroactive interference* may take place. Some lapses in memory may be due to *motivated forgetting,* although it is difficult to confirm the validity of "repressed" memories that are then "recovered." Finally, *cue-dependent forgetting* may occur when retrieval cues are inadequate. The most effective retrieval cues are those that were present at the time of the initial experience. A person's mood or physical state may also act as a retrieval cue, evoking a *state-dependent memory.*

Autobiographical Memories

17) Because of *childhood amnesia,* most people cannot recall any events from earlier than the third or fourth year of life. The reason may be partly biological, but many cognitive explanations have also been proposed: the lack of a sense of self in the first few years of life; the child's reliance on cognitive schemas that differ from schemas used later; the fact that young children encode experiences less elaboratively than older people do; and children's focus on routine rather than distinctive aspects of an experience.

18) A person's narrative or "life story" organizes the events of his or her life and gives them meaning. Narratives change as people build up a store of episodic memories. Many memories seem to be based on people's current traits and beliefs. Life stories are, to some degree, works of interpretation and imagination.

19) Findings on memory suggest that we exercise caution in evaluating claims of recovered memories of past trauma, especially when such memories emerge after suggestive techniques have been used in therapy; the memories are for events that allegedly occurred very early in life; and the memories become increasingly implausible over time.

KEY TERMS

LOOKING BACK

- *What's wrong with thinking of memory as a mental movie camera? (p. 228)*
- *If you have a strong emotional reaction to a remembered event, does that mean your memory is accurate? (p. 230)*
- *Do people remember better when they're hypnotized? (p. 231)*
- *Why do "flashbulb memories" of surprising or shocking events sometimes have less wattage than we assume? (p. 232)*
- *Can the question a person asks you about a past event affect what you remember about it? (pp. 232–233)*
- *In general, which is easier: a multiple-choice question or a short-answer essay question—and why? (p. 235)*
- *Can you know something without knowing that you know it? (p. 236)*
- *Why is the computer often used as a metaphor for the mind? (p. 237)*
- *Why is short-term memory like a leaky bucket? (p. 240)*
- *When a word is on the tip of your tongue, what errors are you likely to make in recalling it? (p. 242)*
- *What's the difference between "knowing how" and "knowing that"? (p. 243)*
- *What's wrong with trying to memorize in a rote fashion when you're studying—and what's a better strategy? (p. 246)*
- *Memory tricks are fun—but are they always useful? (p. 247)*
- *How might new information erase old memories? (pp. 249–250)*
- *What theory explains why you keep dialing an old area code instead of the one that has replaced it? (p. 250)*
- *Why is it easier to recall experiences from elementary school if you see pictures of your classmates? (p. 251)*
- *Why are the first few years of life a mental blank? (pp. 253–254)*
- *Which periods of life tend to stand out in memory? (p. 255)*

8

Learning

Ignoring World Opinion, Singapore Will Punish American Teen Vandal by Flogging

Michael Fay, accompanied by his stepfather, enters Singapore's high court to appeal his sentence.

SINGAPORE, APRIL, 1994. Despite requests for clemency from President Clinton and others, Singapore authorities have announced that they will proceed with the flogging of Michael Fay, an 18-year-old American recently convicted of spray-painting cars, throwing eggs, and possessing stolen property. In addition to a four-month prison term and a fine, Fay will receive six blows on the bare buttocks with a moistened rattan cane, administered by a jailer trained in the martial arts. The punishment is more severe than it sounds: Although padding will protect Fay's spine and kidneys from injury, flogging has been known to cause shock from loss of blood, and it can leave permanent scars.

In the United States, reactions have ranged from applause to outrage. The American Chamber of Commerce said it was "shaken" by the harsh sentence, and the U.S. chargé d'affaires for Singapore publicly criticized the penalty. But some politicians, including former New York mayor Ed Koch, have expressed support for a moderate form of caning, and in op-ed pages around the country, citizens fed up with graffiti, hooliganism, and violence have voiced their approval of Fay's punishment. Responding to the controversy, former prime minister Lee Kuan Yew, Singapore's patriarch, said that "the punishment does what it is supposed to do, to remind the wrongdoer that he should never do it again."

Is Yew's claim valid? Do severe penalties deter wrongdoers? In 1996, inspired in part by the Fay case, California state Assemblyman Mickey Conroy introduced a bill permitting judges to order the paddling of youthful graffiti vandals. "I want these juveniles to know they'll be held accountable for their actions," Conroy said. On the other side of the issue, Assemblywoman Sheila Kuehl argued that "violence begets violence" and that "beating a child does not teach the child the difference between right and wrong." The bill ultimately went down to defeat, but the debate over the corporal punishment of children and young offenders promises to be with us for a long time.

At the core of this debate is a more general question: What are the best ways to get people to behave well and to discourage them from behaving badly? This question is a central one for researchers who study **learning,** which to psychologists means any relatively permanent change in behavior that occurs because of experience (excluding changes due to fatigue, injury, or disease). Experience is the great teacher, providing the essential link between the past and the future and enabling an organism to adapt to changing circumstances in order to survive and thrive.

Research on learning has been heavily influenced by **behaviorism,** the school of psychology that accounts for behavior in terms of observable events, without reference to such hypothetical mental entities as "mind" or "will." Behaviorists have focused on a basic kind of learning called **conditioning,** which involves associations between environmental stimuli and responses. They have shown that two types of conditioning—*classical conditioning* and *operant conditioning*—can explain much of human behavior. But as we will see, other approaches, collectively known as *social-learning theories,* hold that omitting mental processes from explanations of human learning is like omitting passion from descriptions of sex: You may explain the form, but you miss the substance. To social-learning theorists and cognitive theorists, learning is not so much a change in behavior as a change in *knowledge* that has the *potential* for affecting behavior.

As you read about the principles of conditioning and learning in this chapter, ask yourself what they can teach us about the use of punishment to control unwanted behavior. Should Singapore's system be imported into North America? Are there any good alternatives to punishment? How can we most effectively modify other people's behavior—and our own?

learning

A relatively permanent change in behavior (or behavioral potential) due to experience.

behaviorism

An approach to psychology that emphasizes the study of observable behavior and the role of the environment as a determinant of behavior.

conditioning

A basic kind of learning that involves associations between environmental stimuli and the organism's responses.

What's Ahead

- *Why would a dog salivate when it sees a lightbulb or hears a buzzer, even though they are inedible?*

- *How can classical conditioning help explain prejudice?*

- *If you have learned to fear collies, why might you also be scared of sheepdogs?*

CLASSICAL CONDITIONING

At the turn of the century, the great Russian physiologist Ivan Pavlov (1849–1936) was studying salivation in dogs, as part of a research program on digestion. His work would shortly win him the Nobel Prize in physiology and medicine. One of Pavlov's procedures was to make a surgical opening in a dog's cheek and insert a tube that conducted saliva away from the animal's salivary gland so that the saliva could be measured. To stimulate the reflexive flow of saliva, Pavlov placed meat powder or other food in the dog's mouth. This procedure was later refined by others (see Figure 8.1).

Pavlov was a truly dedicated scientific observer. Many years later, as he lay dying, he even dictated his sensations for posterity! During his salivation studies, Pavlov noticed something that most people would have overlooked or dismissed as trivial. After a dog had been brought to the laboratory a number of times, it would start to salivate *before* the food was placed in its mouth. The sight or

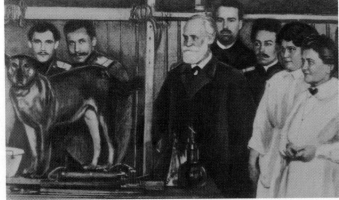

Figure 8.1

A Modification of Pavlov's Method

In the apparatus on the right, which was based on Pavlov's techniques, saliva from a dog's cheek flowed down a tube and was measured by the movement of a needle on a revolving drum. In the photo above, you can see Ivan Pavlov himself in the center, flanked by his students and a canine subject.

smell of the food, the dish in which the food was kept, even the sight of the person who delivered the food each day or the sound of the person's footsteps were enough to start the dog's mouth watering. This new salivary response clearly was not inborn, so it had to have been acquired through experience.

At first, Pavlov treated the dog's drooling as merely an annoying "psychic secretion." But after reviewing the literature on reflexes, he realized that he had stumbled onto an important phenomenon, one that he came to believe was the basis of all learning in human beings and other animals. He called that phenomenon a "conditional" reflex—conditional because it depended on environmental conditions. Later, an error in the translation of his writings transformed "conditional" into "conditioned," the word most commonly used today.

Pavlov soon dropped what he had been doing and turned to the study of conditioned reflexes, to which he devoted the last three decades of his life. Why were his dogs salivating to aspects of the environment other than food?

New Reflexes from Old

Pavlov decided that it was entirely pointless to speculate about his dogs' thoughts, wishes, or memories. Instead, he analyzed the environment in which the conditioned reflex arose. The original salivary reflex, according to Pavlov, consisted of an **unconditioned stimulus (US),** food, and an **unconditioned response (UR),** salivation. By an *unconditioned stimulus,* Pavlov meant an event or thing that elicits a response automatically or reflexively. By an *unconditioned response,* he meant the response that is automatically produced:

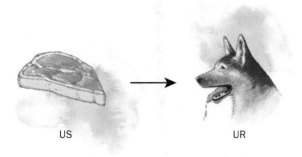

Learning occurs, Pavlov said, when some neutral stimulus is regularly paired with an uncondi-

tioned stimulus. The neutral stimulus then becomes a **conditioned stimulus (CS),** which elicits a learned or **conditioned response (CR)** that is usually similar to the original, unlearned one. In Pavlov's laboratory, the sight of the food dish, which had not previously elicited salivation, became a CS for salivation:

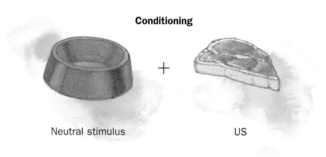

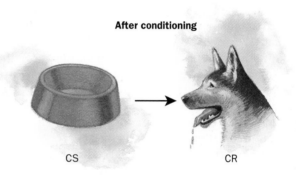

The procedure by which a neutral stimulus becomes a conditioned stimulus eventually became known as **classical conditioning** and is also sometimes called *Pavlovian* or *respondent conditioning.* In his research, Pavlov went on to show that many diverse things can become conditioned stimuli for salivation if they are paired with food—the ticking of a metronome, the musical tone of a tuning fork, the vibrating sound of a buzzer, a triangle drawn on a large card, even a pinprick or an electric shock. Moreover, salivation is not the only response that can be classically conditioned. Since Pavlov's day, researchers have established that nearly any automatic, involuntary response can do so—for example, heartbeat, stomach secretions, blood pressure, reflexive movements, blinking, or muscle contractions. The optimal interval between the presentation of the neutral stimulus and the presentation of the US depends on the kind of response involved; in the laboratory, the interval is often less than a second.

unconditioned stimulus (US)

The classical-conditioning term for a stimulus that elicits a reflexive response in the absence of learning.

unconditioned response (UR)

The classical-conditioning term for a reflexive response elicited by a stimulus in the absence of learning.

conditioned stimulus (CS)

The classical-conditioning term for an initially neutral stimulus that comes to elicit a conditioned response after being associated with an unconditioned stimulus.

conditioned response (CR)

The classical-conditioning term for a response that is elicited by a conditioned stimulus; occurs after the conditioned stimulus is associated with an unconditioned stimulus.

classical conditioning

The process by which a previously neutral stimulus acquires the capacity to elicit a response through association with a stimulus that already elicits a similar or related response.

Get Involved

Try out your behavioral skills by conditioning an eye-blink response in a friend, using classical conditioning procedures. You'll need a drinking straw and something to make a ringing sound—a spoon tapped on a water glass works well. Tell your friend that you're going to blow in his or her eye through the straw, but don't say why. Immediately before each puff of air, make the ringing sound. Repeat this procedure ten times. Then make the ringing sound while holding the straw up to the person's eye, but *don't* puff. Your friend will probably blink anyway and may continue to do so for one or two more repetitions of the sound before the response fades. Can you identify the US, the UR, the CS, and the CR in this exercise?

What's Really Learned in Classical Conditioning?

For effective classical conditioning to occur, the stimulus to be conditioned must *precede* the unconditioned stimulus rather than follow it or occur simultaneously with it. This makes sense because in classical conditioning, the conditioned stimulus becomes a kind of signal for the unconditioned stimulus. It enables the organism to *prepare* for an event that is about to happen. In Pavlov's studies, for instance, a bell or buzzer was a signal that meat was coming, and the dog's salivation was preparation for digesting food.

Indeed, today many psychologists contend that what an animal or person actually learns in classical conditioning is not merely an association between two paired stimuli that occur close together in time, but rather *information* conveyed by one stimulus about another. In this view, the mere pairing of an unconditioned stimulus and a neutral stimulus is not sufficient to produce learning; to become a conditioned stimulus, the neutral stimulus must reliably *signal*, or *predict*, the unconditioned stimulus.

Suppose you are a budding behaviorist and you want to teach a rat to fear a tone. Following the usual procedure, you repeatedly sound the tone before an unconditioned stimulus for fear, such as a mild electric shock: tone, shock, tone, shock, tone, shock, ... After 20 such pairings, the rat shows signs of fear on hearing the tone. Now suppose you do this experiment again—on 20 trials the tone precedes the shock—but this time you randomly intersperse an additional 20 trials in which the shock occurs *without* the tone. With this method, the tone precedes the shock just as often as before, but it signals shock only half of the time. In other words, the tone does not affect the probability that the shock will occur. Robert Rescorla (1968, 1988) showed that under these conditions, when the tone does not provide any information about the shock, little if any conditioning occurs. (The same is true if you present the tone without the shock on half the trials.)

In everyday life, too, a potential CS may sometimes predict an unconditioned stimulus and sometimes not, so conditioning is less certain than when the CS and US always occur together in the laboratory. Paul Chance (1994) gives this example. Suppose you are a stock clerk who is allowed to receive routine calls from store personnel. However, a telephone switchboard operator (this is a low-tech store) has instructions to route outside calls to you only in an emergency. During your first day on the job, your sweetheart calls to jilt you; the police to report that your new car was stolen; and your landlord to tell you that a broken water pipe has ruined your belongings. If these were the only calls you got, the next time you heard the phone ring (the CS) you might freak out (the CR). But if they occurred randomly among 50 routine calls for supplies, the phone's ringing would probably not upset you because it would not necessarily signal another disaster.

From his findings, Rescorla (1988) concluded that "Pavlovian conditioning is not a stupid process by which the organism willy-nilly forms associations between any two stimuli that happen to co-occur. Rather, the organism is better seen as an information seeker using logical and perceptual relations among events, along with its own preconceptions, to form a sophisticated representation of its world." Not all learning theorists agree with this conclusion; an orthodox behaviorist would say that it is silly to talk about the preconceptions of a rat. The important point, however, is that for many researchers, concepts such as "information seeking," "preconceptions," and "representations of the world" have opened the door to a more cognitive view of classical conditioning.

??? QUICK QUIZ

The terminology of classical conditioning can be hard to learn, so be sure to pause for this quiz before going on.

A. Name the unconditioned stimulus, unconditioned response, conditioned stimulus, and conditioned response in these two situations:

1. Five-year-old Samantha is watching a storm from her window. A huge bolt of lightning is followed by a tremendous thunderclap, and Samantha jumps at the noise. This happens several more times. There is a brief lull and then another lightning bolt. Samantha jumps in response to the bolt.

2. Gregory's mouth waters whenever he eats anything with lemon in it. One day, while reading an ad that shows a big glass of lemonade, Gregory notices his mouth watering.

B. In the view of many modern learning theorists, pairing a neutral and unconditioned stimulus is not enough to produce learning; the neutral stimulus must _____ the unconditioned stimulus in order for classical conditioning to occur.

Answers:

A. 1. US = the thunderclap; UR = jumping elicited by the noise; CS = the sight of the lightning; CR = jumping elicited by the lightning. 2. US = the taste of lemon; UR = salivation elicited by the taste of lemon; CS = the picture of a glass of lemonade; CR = salivation elicited by the picture. B. signal or predict

Principles of Classical Conditioning

The processes involved in classical conditioning are common to all species, from worms to *Homo sapiens*. Let's look more closely at how some of the most important of these processes work: extinction, higher-order conditioning, and stimulus generalization and discrimination.

Extinction.   Conditioned responses do not necessarily last forever. If, after conditioning, the conditioned stimulus is repeatedly presented without the unconditioned stimulus, the conditioned response eventually disappears, and **extinction** is said to have occurred (see Figure 8.2). Suppose that you train a dog to salivate to the sound of a bell, but then you ring the bell every five minutes and do *not* follow it with food. The dog will salivate less and less to the bell and will soon stop salivating altogether; salivation has been extinguished. However, if you come back the next day and ring the bell, the dog may salivate again for a few trials. The reappearance of the response, which is called **spontaneous recovery,** explains why completely eliminating a conditioned response usually requires more than one extinction session.

extinction

The weakening and eventual disappearance of a learned response; in classical conditioning, occurs when the conditioned stimulus is no longer paired with the unconditioned stimulus.

spontaneous recovery

The reappearance of a learned response after its apparent extinction.

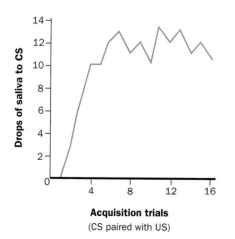

Acquisition trials
(CS paired with US)

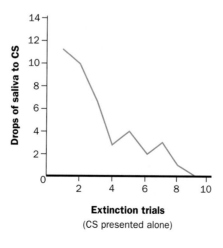

Extinction trials
(CS presented alone)

Figure 8.2

Acquisition and Extinction of a Salivary Response

When a neutral stimulus is consistently followed by an unconditioned stimulus for salivation, the neutral stimulus also comes to elicit salivation (left); that is, it becomes a conditioned stimulus. When the conditioned stimulus is repeatedly presented without the unconditioned stimulus, the conditioned salivary response weakens and eventually disappears (right); it has been extinguished.

Higher-order conditioning

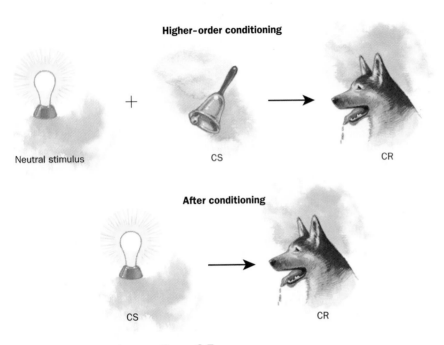

Neutral stimulus   CS   CR

After conditioning

CS   CR

Figure 8.3
Higher-order conditioning

In this illustration of higher-order conditioning, the light becomes a conditioned stimulus for salivation when it is associated with an already established conditioned stimulus for that response (the bell).

Higher-order Conditioning. Sometimes a neutral stimulus can become a conditioned stimulus by being paired with an already established CS, a procedure known as **higher-order conditioning.** Say a dog has learned to salivate to the ringing of a bell. Now you present a flash of light before ringing the bell. With repeated pairings of the light and the bell, the dog may learn to salivate to the light, although the light will probably elicit less salivation than the bell does. The procedure for higher-order conditioning is illustrated in Figure 8.3.

It may be that words acquire their emotional meanings through a process of higher-order conditioning. When they are paired with objects or other words that already elicit some emotional response, they, too, may come to elicit that response (Chance, 1994; Staats & Staats, 1957). For example, a child may learn a positive response to the word *birthday* because of its association with gifts and attention. Conversely, the child may learn a negative response to ethnic or national labels, such as *Swede, Turk,* or *Jew,* if those words are paired with already disagreeable words, such as *dumb* or *dirty.* Higher-order conditioning, in other words, may contribute to the formation of prejudices.

higher-order conditioning

In classical conditioning, a procedure in which a neutral stimulus becomes a conditioned stimulus through association with an already established conditioned stimulus.

stimulus generalization

After conditioning, the tendency to respond to a stimulus that resembles one involved in the original conditioning; in classical conditioning, occurs when a stimulus that resembles the conditioned stimulus elicits the conditioned response.

stimulus discrimination

The tendency to respond differently to two or more similar stimuli; in classical conditioning, occurs when a stimulus similar to the CS fails to evoke the CR.

Stimulus Generalization and Discrimination. After a stimulus becomes a conditioned stimulus for some response, other, similar stimuli may produce a similar reaction—a phenomenon known as **stimulus generalization.** For example, a dog conditioned to salivate to middle C on the piano may also salivate to D, which is one tone above C, even though D was not paired with food. Stimulus generalization is described nicely by an old English proverb: "He who hath been bitten by a snake fears a rope."

The mirror image of stimulus generalization is **stimulus discrimination,** in which *different* responses are made to stimuli that resemble the conditioned stimulus in some way. Suppose that you condition your poodle to salivate to middle C on the piano by repeatedly pairing the sound with food. Now you play middle C on a guitar, *without* following it by food (but you continue to follow C on the piano by food). Eventually, the dog will learn to salivate to a C on the piano and not to salivate to the same note on the guitar; that is, the animal will discriminate between the two sounds.

| What's Ahead |

- *If you eat licorice and then happen to get the flu, how might your taste for licorice change?*

- *Why do advertisers often include pleasant music and gorgeous scenery in ads for their products?*

- *How would a classical-conditioning theorist explain your irrational fear of heights or mice?*

- *Why might a drug dose that is ordinarily safe kill you if you take it in a new place?*

CLASSICAL CONDITIONING IN REAL LIFE

If a dog can learn to salivate to the ringing of a bell, so can you. In fact, you probably have learned to salivate to the sound of a lunch bell, not to mention the sight of the refrigerator, the phrase *hot fudge sundae,* "mouth-watering" pictures of food in magazines, the sight of a waiter in a restaurant, and a voice calling out "Dinner's ready!" But the role of classical conditioning goes far beyond the learning of simple reflexive responses; conditioning affects us every day in many ways.

Accounting for Taste

We probably learn to like and dislike many foods and odors through a process of classical conditioning. In the laboratory, researchers have taught animals to dislike foods or odors by pairing them with drugs that cause nausea or other unpleasant symptoms. One researcher trained slugs to associate the smell of carrots, which slugs normally like, with a bitter-tasting chemical that they detest. Soon the slugs were avoiding the smell of carrots. The researcher then demonstrated higher-order conditioning by pairing the smell of carrots with the smell of potato. Sure enough, the slugs began to avoid the smell of potato as well (Sahley, Rudy, & Gelperin, 1981).

Many people have learned to dislike a food after eating it and then falling ill, even though the two events were unrelated. The food, previously a neutral stimulus, becomes a conditioned stimulus for nausea or for other symptoms produced by the illness. Martin Seligman, who has studied learned behavior in the laboratory for many years, once told how he himself was conditioned to hate béarnaise sauce. One night, shortly after he and his wife ate a delicious filet mignon with béarnaise sauce, he came down with the flu. Naturally, he

Whether we say "yum" or "yuck" to certain foods may depend on a past experience involving classical conditioning.

felt wretched. His misery had nothing to do with the béarnaise sauce, of course, yet the next time he tried it, he found he disliked the taste (Seligman & Hager, 1972).

Learning to Like

Classical conditioning can help explain how we acquire emotional responses to objects, events, and places. One of the first psychologists to recognize this fact was John B. Watson, who founded American behaviorism and was an enthusiastic promoter of Pavlov's ideas. Watson believed that emotions were no more than collections of gut-level muscular and glandular responses to stimuli. A few of these reactions are inborn, said Watson, but most develop when stimuli in the environment are paired with positive unconditioned stimuli such as stroking and cuddling or negative ones such as loud noises. Watson's views were later derided by detractors as "muscle-twitch psychology" (Hunt, 1993), and today we know that emotions involve a lot more than conditioned reflexes (see Chapter 12). However, his premise that classical conditioning helps determine what we feel emotional *about* is correct.

For example, classical conditioning helps explain why feelings of fondness, pride, or sentimentality sweep over us when we see certain objects or symbols, such as a school mascot, a national flag, or the logo of the Olympic games. And many of Madison Avenue's techniques for getting us to like certain products are based on the principles first demonstrated by Pavlov, whether advertising executives realize it or not.

In one study that explored the classical conditioning techniques that often underlie advertising, college students looked at slides of either a beige pen or a blue pen. During the presentation, half the students heard a song from a recent musical film, and half heard a selection of traditional music from India. (The experimenter made the reasonable assumption that the show tune would be more appealing to the young Americans participating in the study.) Later the students were allowed to choose one of the pens. Almost three-fourths of those who heard the popular music chose a pen that was the same color as the one they had seen in the slides. An equal number of those who heard the Indian music chose a pen that *differed* in color from the one they had seen (Gorn, 1982). In classical-conditioning terms, the music was an unconditioned stimulus for internal responses associated with pleasure or displeasure, and the pens became conditioned stimuli for similar responses. You can see why television commercials often pair their products with music, attractive people, or other appealing sounds and images.

Learning to Fear

Dislikes and negative emotions such as fear can also be classically conditioned. Cancer patients, for example, sometimes develop a classically conditioned fear of places and objects that have been associated with their chemotherapy treatments—the sound of a nurse's voice, the smell of rubbing alcohol, the waiting room of the clinic. In one study (Jacobsen et al., 1995), patients who drank lemon-lime Kool-Aid before their chemotherapy sessions developed an anxiety response to the drink, and they continued to feel anxious even when the drink was offered in their homes rather than at the clinic.

When a fear of an object or situation is irrational and interferes with normal activities, it qualifies as a *phobia*. To demonstrate how a phobia might be acquired, John Watson and Rosalie Rayner (1920) deliberately established a rat phobia in an 11-month-old boy named Albert. The ethics, procedures, and findings of their study have since been questioned, and no researcher today would perform such a demonstration. Nevertheless, the study remains a classic, and its main conclusion, that fears can be conditioned, is still well accepted.

"Little Albert" was a rather placid tyke who rarely cried. When Watson and Rayner gave him a furry white rat to play with (a live one, not a toy), Albert showed no fear; in fact, he was delighted. However, like most children, Albert was afraid of loud noises. As a result, when the researchers made a loud noise behind his head by striking a steel bar with a hammer, he would jump and fall sideways onto the mattress he was sitting on. The noise made by the hammer was an unconditioned stimulus for the unconditioned response of fear.

Having established that Albert liked rats, Watson and Rayner set about teaching him to fear them. Again they offered him a rat, but this time, as Albert reached for it, one of the researchers struck the steel bar. Startled, Albert fell onto the mattress. The researchers repeated this procedure several times. Albert began to whimper and trem-

ble. Finally, the rat was offered alone, without the noise. Albert fell over, cried, and crawled away as fast as he could; the rat had become a conditioned stimulus for fear:

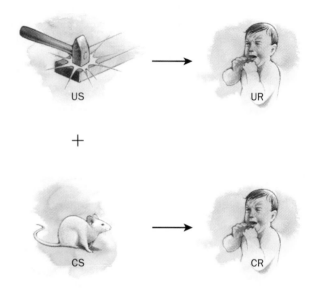

Further tests showed that Albert's fear had generalized to other hairy or furry objects, including white rabbits, cotton wool, a Santa Claus mask, and even John Watson's hair.

Unfortunately, Watson and Rayner did not have an opportunity to reverse the conditioning, for reasons that are unclear. Later, however, Watson and Mary Cover Jones did accomplish a reversal in a 3-year-old named Peter (Jones, 1924). Peter was deathly afraid of rabbits. His fear was, as Watson put it, "home-grown" rather than psychologist induced. Watson and Jones eliminated it with a method called **counterconditioning,** in which a conditioned stimulus is paired with some other stimulus that elicits a response incompatible with the unwanted response. In this case, the rabbit (the CS) was paired with a snack of milk and crackers, and the snack produced pleasant feelings incompatible with the conditioned response of fear. At first, the researchers kept the rabbit some distance from Peter, so that his fear would remain at a low level. Otherwise, Peter might have learned to fear milk and crackers! But gradually, over several days, they brought the rabbit closer and closer. Eventually Peter was able to sit with the rabbit in his lap, playing with it with one hand while he ate with the other. A variation of this procedure, called *systematic desensitization*, was later devised for treating phobias in adults (see Chapter 11).

counterconditioning

In classical conditioning, the process of pairing a conditioned stimulus with a stimulus that elicits a response that is incompatible with an unwanted conditioned response.

Reacting to Drugs

Many researchers believe that classical conditioning has important implications for understanding aspects of drug addiction (Goodison & Siegel, 1995; Poulos & Cappell, 1991; Siegel, 1990). In their view, a drug's effect is the unconditioned stimulus for a *compensatory* bodily response, a response that opposes the drug's effect in order to restore a normal biological state. For example, when morphine causes numbness to pain, the body compensates by becoming increasingly sensitive to pain. Environmental cues that are paired with the drug's effect, such as needles or a particular location, may then become conditioned stimuli for this compensatory response:

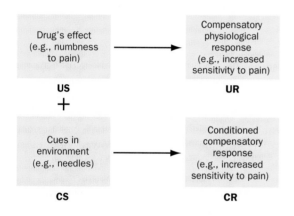

This analysis can help explain why *tolerance* to drugs—the increasing resistance to a drug's effects—often develops. In the presence of environmental cues associated with drug taking, a compensatory response occurs, so more and more of the drug is needed to produce the usual effects. On the other hand, a drug dose that would ordinarily be safe, given an addict's tolerance level, may be lethal when the drug is used in novel circumstances because the usual conditioned compensatory response does not occur. The result may be sudden and seemingly inexplicable death.

Experiments with both animals and human beings, using many different drugs, support this theory. In one study, male college students drank large amounts of beer at the same place on each of four consecutive days. On the fifth day, some of the students downed their beers at a new place. Students who remained at the original location scored higher on tests of intellectual and perceptual-motor skills, apparently because their bodies had learned to moderate the effects of alcohol in

the presence of familiar cues (Lightfoot, 1980). In another study, researchers gave rats a strong dose of heroin. Some of the rats were already experienced with the drug. In inexperienced rats, the injection was almost always fatal, but in experienced ones, the outcome depended on the setting: Two-thirds of the rats injected while in a strange environment died, versus only one-third of those who remained in a familiar place (Siegel et al., 1982).

The importance of environmental cues may help explain why in-hospital drug treatment programs often fail: When people return to the neighborhoods where they used to take drugs, conditioned stimuli elicit the usual compensatory responses. In the absence of the drug, such responses are now experienced as a return of unpleasant withdrawal symptoms, and a craving for the drug again develops (Siegel, 1990). The implication is that people who want to overcome drug dependence must either move to a new environment or get treatment that systematically exposes them to familiar features of their usual environment until their conditioned physiological responses to these cues are extinguished.

We see, then, that many seemingly "natural" or biological responses—food preferences, fears, addictions—may have their origins in classical conditioning. Conversely, in recent decades, behavioral researchers have acknowledged the importance of innate tendencies and have integrated biological factors into their theories.

These factors, for example, can help us understand the story of the psychologist who learned to hate béarnaise sauce. Unlike conditioning in the laboratory, this learning occurred after only one pairing of the sauce with illness and with a considerable delay between the conditioned and the unconditioned stimuli. In addition, neither the psychologist's wife nor his dinner plate became conditioned stimuli for nausea, though they, too, were paired with illness. Apparently many animals (including psychologists) are biologically primed to associate sickness with taste (Garcia & Koelling, 1966; Seligman & Hager, 1972). This tendency enhances the species' survival: Eating bad food is more likely to be followed by illness than are, say, particular sights or sounds. Likewise, in human beings, it is easier to condition a fear of spiders, snakes, or heights than of butterflies, flowers, or toasters, no doubt because during human evolution, the former objects presented a danger.

??? QUICK QUIZ

We hope that you don't have a classically conditioned fear of quizzes. See whether you can supply the correct term to describe the outcome in each of these situations:

1. After a child learns to fear spiders, he also responds with fear to ants, beetles, and other crawling bugs.

2. A toddler is afraid of the bath, so her father puts just a little water in the tub and gives the child a lollipop to suck on while she is being washed. Soon, the little girl loses her fear of the bath.

3. A factory worker notices that his mouth waters whenever a noontime bell signals the beginning of his lunch break. One day, the bell goes haywire and rings every half hour. By the end of the day, the worker has stopped salivating to the bell.

Answers:
1. stimulus generalization   2. counterconditioning   3. extinction

---

What's Ahead

- *What do praise and the cessation of nagging have in common?*

- *What's the best way to discourage a friend from interrupting you while you're studying?*

- *How do trainers teach guide dogs to do the amazing things they do for their owners?*

- *How can operant principles account for the popularity of good-luck charms?*

OPERANT CONDITIONING

At the end of the nineteenth century, in the first known scientific effort to study anger, G. Stanley Hall (1899) asked people to describe angry episodes they had experienced or observed. One informant told of a 3-year-old girl who broke out in furious, seemingly uncontrollable sobs when she was punished by being kept home from a ride. In the middle of her tantrum, the child suddenly stopped crying and asked in a perfectly calm voice if her father was in. Told no, she immediately resumed her sobbing.

Children, of course, cry for many valid reasons—pain, discomfort, fear, illness, fatigue—and these cries deserve an adult's sympathy and attention. However, even infants only a few weeks old will also learn to cry when they are *not* in physical distress if adults respond to such cries (Gewirtz & Peláez-Nogueras, 1991). The child in Hall's study

had learned, from prior experience, that an outburst of sobbing would bring her attention and possibly the ride she wanted—that her tears stood a reasonable chance of working. Her behavior, which some might label "naughty," was perfectly understandable because it followed one of the most basic laws of learning: *Behavior becomes more likely or less so, depending on its consequences.*

An emphasis on environmental consequences is at the heart of **operant conditioning** (also called *instrumental conditioning*), the second type of conditioning studied by behaviorists. In classical conditioning, the animal's or person's behavior does not have such consequences; in Pavlov's procedure, the dog got food, whether it salivated or not. But in operant conditioning, the organism's

the neighborhood. Jerry Van Amerongen

Reprinted with special permission of King Features Syndicate.

An instantaneous learning experience.

---

operant conditioning

The process by which a response becomes more likely to occur or less so, depending on its consequences.

response (the little girl's sobbing, for example) *operates* (produces effects) on the environment. These effects, in turn, influence whether the response will occur again. Classical and operant conditioning also tend to differ in the types of responses they involve. In classical conditioning, the response is reflexive, an automatic reaction to something happening in the environment, such as the sight of food or the sound of a bell. Generally, responses in operant conditioning are complex and are not reflexive, and they involve the entire organism—for instance, riding a bicycle, writing a letter, climbing a mountain, . . . or throwing a tantrum.

Operant conditioning has been studied since the early twentieth century, although it wasn't called "operant" until later. Edward Thorndike (1898), then a young doctoral candidate, set the stage by observing cats as they tried to escape from a "puzzle box" to reach a scrap of fish that was just outside the box. At first, the cat would engage in trial and error, scratching, biting, or swatting at parts of the cage in an unorganized way. Then, after a few minutes, the cat would chance on the successful response (loosening a bolt, pulling a string, or hitting a button) and rush out to get the reward. Placed in the box again, the cat now took a little less time to escape, and after several trials, the animal immediately made the correct response. According to Thorndike's *law of effect,* the correct response had been "stamped in" by its satisfying effects (getting the food). In contrast, annoying or unsatisfying effects "stamped out" behavior. Behavior, said Thorndike, is controlled by its consequences.

This general principle was elaborated and extended to more complex forms of behavior by B. F. (Burrhus Frederic) Skinner, whose ideas we introduced in Chapter 2. Skinner argued that to understand behavior we should focus on the external causes of an action and the action's consequences. He was careful to avoid such terms as "satisfying" and "annoying," which reflect assumptions about what an organism feels and wants. To explain behavior, he said, we should look outside the individual, not inside.

Skinner has often been called the greatest of American psychologists, and certainly he is one of the best known. Yet despite his fame, his position is often distorted by the general public, psychology students, and even some psychologists. For example, many people think Skinner denied the existence of human consciousness and the value of studying it. It is true that Skinner's predecessor

John Watson thought that psychologists should study only public (external) events, not private (internal) ones. But Skinner maintained that we *can* study private events, by observing our own sensory responses, the verbal reports of others, and the conditions under which such events occur. For Skinner, the private events we "see" when we examine our own "consciousness" are simply the early stages of behavior, before the behavior begins to act on the environment. These private events are as real or physical as public ones, Skinner said, although they are less accessible and harder to describe (Skinner, 1972, 1990).

Whereas some psychologists, notably the humanists, have argued for the existence of free will, Skinner regarded free will as an illusion and steadfastly supported the *determinist* view that we are shaped by our environments and our genetic heritage. Skinner refused to credit personal traits, such as curiosity, or mental events, such as goals and motives, for his own or anyone else's accomplishments. Indeed, he regarded himself not as a

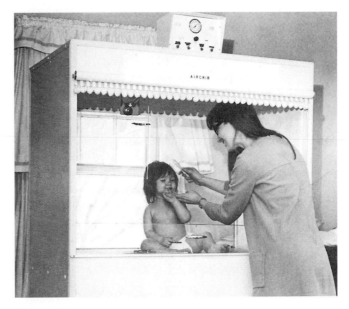

B. F. Skinner invented an enclosed "living space," the Air-Crib, for his daughter Deborah. It had temperature and humidity controls to eliminate the usual discomforts babies suffer: heat, cold, wetness, and confinement by blankets. The Air-Crib reflected Skinner's belief that to change someone's behavior—say, a baby's cries of discomfort—you must change the environment. But many people imagined, incorrectly, that the Skinners were leaving Deborah in the box all the time without cuddling and holding her, and rumors later circulated that she had gone insane or killed herself. Actually, both of Skinner's daughters grew up to be perfectly normal and very successful. The baby in this Air-Crib is Skinner's granddaughter Lisa, with her mother Julie.

"self" but as a "repertoire of behaviors" resulting from an environment that encouraged looking, searching, and investigating (Bjork, 1993). "So far as I know," he wrote in the third volume of his autobiography (Skinner, 1983), "my behavior at any given moment has been nothing more than the product of my genetic endowment, my personal history, and the current setting."

Reinforcement and Punishment: The Carrot and the Stick

In Skinner's analysis, which has inspired an immense body of research, a response ("operant") can lead to one of three types of consequences. The first type is neutral as far as future behavior is concerned: It neither increases nor decreases the probability that the behavior will recur. If a door handle squeaks each time you turn it, and the sound does not affect whether you turn the door handle in the future, the squeak is a neutral consequence.

A second type of consequence involves **reinforcement** (see Figure 8.4). In reinforcement, a reinforcing stimulus, or *reinforcer,* strengthens or increases the probability of the response that it follows. When you are training your dog to heel, and you praise her or give her a pat on the head when she keeps pace with you, you are trying to reinforce the good behavior. Reinforcers are roughly equivalent to rewards, and many psychologists have no objection to the use of the words *reward* and *reinforcer* as approximate synonyms. However, strict behaviorists avoid *reward.* The word *reward* usually refers to something earned that results in happiness or satisfaction, but a stimulus is

a reinforcer if it strengthens the behavior it follows, whether or not the organism experiences pleasure or any other positive state. Conversely, no matter how pleasurable a stimulus is, it is not a reinforcer if it does not increase the likelihood of a response. It's pleasurable to get a paycheck, but if you get paid regardless of the effort you put into your work, the money will not reinforce "hardwork behavior."

The third type of consequence involves **punishment,** which occurs when the stimulus or event that follows a response weakens it or makes it less likely to recur. Any aversive (unpleasant) stimulus or event may be a *punisher.* A dog that runs into the street and is injured by a passing car will be less likely to run into the street in the future when cars are around.

Here is a visual summary of the difference between a reinforcer and a punisher:

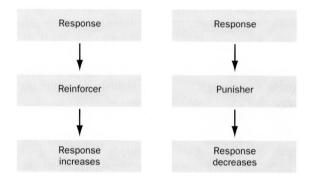

Of course, what an animal can learn through operant conditioning depends first and foremost on its physical characteristics; a fish cannot be trained to climb a ladder. And operant-condition-

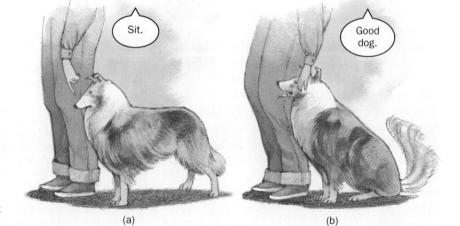

Figure 8.4
Reinforcement in Action

If the command "sit" (a) results in the desired response and the response is followed by a reinforcer (b), the probability of the response occurring in the future will be strengthened. Pet owners, take heed!

(a)   (b)

ing procedures, like classical ones, work best when they capitalize on inborn tendencies. Years ago, Keller and Marian Breland (1961), psychologists who became animal trainers, described what happens when biological constraints are ignored. The Brelands found that animals often had trouble learning tasks that should have been easy. For example, a pig was supposed to drop large wooden coins in a box. Instead, the pig would drop the coin, push at it with its snout, throw it in the air, and push at it some more. This odd behavior actually delayed delivery of the reinforcer, so it was hard to explain in terms of operant principles. Apparently the pig's rooting instinct—its tendency to use its snout to uncover edible roots—was keeping it from learning the task. The Brelands called such a reversion to instinctive behavior **instinctive drift.**

Positive and Negative Reinforcers and Punishers

Reinforcement and punishment may seem to be the proverbial carrot and stick, but they are not quite so simple as they seem. In our example of reinforcement in dog training, something pleasant

(praise or a pat on the dog's head) followed the dog's response (heeling). This type of procedure is known as **positive reinforcement.** But there is another brand of reinforcement, **negative reinforcement,** which involves the *removal* of something *unpleasant:*

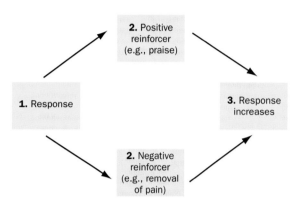

If you politely ask your roommate to turn off some music you can't stand, and your roommate immediately complies, the likelihood of your being polite when making similar requests will probably increase. Your politeness has been strengthened (negatively reinforced) by the removal of the unpleasant music. As Table 8.1 shows, the

reinforcement

The process by which a stimulus or event strengthens or increases the probability of the response that it follows.

punishment

The process by which a stimulus or event weakens or reduces the probability of the response that it follows.

instinctive drift

The tendency of an organism to revert to an instinctive behavior over time; can interfere with learning.

positive reinforcement

A reinforcement procedure in which a response is followed by the presentation of, or increase in intensity of, a reinforcing stimulus; as a result, the response becomes stronger or more likely to occur.

negative reinforcement

A reinforcement procedure in which a response is followed by the removal, delay, or decrease in intensity of an unpleasant stimulus; as a result, the response becomes stronger or more likely to occur.

| Table 8.1 | Types of Reinforcement and Punishment |

In operant conditioning, a response increases or decreases in likelihood, depending on its consequences. The occurrence of a pleasant stimulus or the removal of an unpleasant one reinforces the response. The occurrence of an unpleasant stimulus or the removal of a pleasant one constitutes punishment, which weakens the response.

What event follows the response?

		Stimulus presented	Stimulus removed
What happens to the response?	Response increases	**Positive reinforcement** For example, completion of homework assignments increases when followed by praise.	**Negative reinforcement** For example, use of aspirin increases when followed by reduction of headache pain.
	Response decreases	**Positive punishment** For example, nail biting decreases when followed by the taste of a bitter substance painted on the nails.	**Negative punishment** For example, parking in a "no parking" zone decreases when followed by loss of money (a fine).

positive–negative distinction can also be applied to punishment: Something unpleasant may occur (positive punishment), or something *pleasant* may be *removed* (negative punishment).

The distinction between positive and negative reinforcement has been a source of confusion and frustration for generations of students. It has been known to turn strong and confident people into quivering heaps. We can assure you that if we had been around when these irksome terms were first coined, we would have complained loudly. But now we are stuck with them.

You will master these terms more quickly if you understand that in reinforcement, "positive" and "negative" have nothing to do with "good" or "bad." They refer to *procedures*—giving something or taking something away. *With either positive or negative reinforcement, a response becomes more likely.* If you praise Ludwig for doing his homework and he starts studying more, that is positive reinforcement (of studying). If you have been nagging Ludwig to study more, and you stop the nagging when he starts his homework, that is negative reinforcement (of studying). In both cases, his studying has been reinforced. With positive reinforcement, he gets praise; with negative reinforcement, he stops getting nagged at. Think of a positive reinforcer as something pleasant that is added or obtained, and a negative reinforcer as avoidance of or escape from something unpleasant.

Recall again what happened with Little Albert. Albert learned to fear rats through a process of classical conditioning. Then, after he acquired this fear, crawling away (an operant behavior) was negatively reinforced by escape from the now-fearsome rodent. The negative reinforcement that results from escaping or avoiding something unpleasant explains why so many fears are long-lasting. When you evade a feared object or situation, you also cut off all opportunities for extinguishing your fear.

Understandably, people often confuse negative reinforcement with positive punishment because both involve an unpleasant stimulus. To keep the two straight, remember that punishment—positive or negative—*decreases* the likelihood of a response. Reinforcement—positive or negative—*increases* it. In real life, punishment and negative reinforcement often go hand in hand. If you use a choke collar on your dog to teach it to heel, a yank on the collar punishes the act of walking, but release of the collar negatively reinforces the act of standing still by your side.

You can positively reinforce your studying of this material by taking a refreshment break. And as you master the material, a decrease in your anxiety will negatively reinforce studying. But don't punish your efforts by telling yourself "I'll never get it" or "It's too hard"!

Primary and Secondary Reinforcers and Punishers

Food, water, light stroking of the skin, and a comfortable air temperature are naturally reinforcing because they satisfy biological needs. They are therefore known as **primary reinforcers.** Similarly, pain and extreme heat or cold are inherently punishing and are therefore known as **primary punishers.** Primary reinforcers and punishers are very effective for controlling behavior, but they also have their drawbacks. For one thing, the organism may have to be in a deprived state for a stimulus to act as a primary reinforcer; a glass of water isn't much of a reward to someone who just drank three glasses. Also, there are ethical problems with using primary punishers or taking away primary reinforcers.

Fortunately, behavior can be controlled just as effectively by **secondary reinforcers** and **secondary punishers,** which are learned. Money, praise, applause, good grades, awards, and gold stars are common secondary reinforcers. Criticism, demerits, catcalls, scoldings, fines, and bad grades are common secondary punishers. Most behaviorists believe that secondary reinforcers and punishers acquire their ability to influence behavior by being paired with primary reinforcers and punishers. If that reminds you of classical conditioning, reinforce your excellent thinking with a pat on the head! Indeed, secondary reinforcers and punishers are often called *conditioned* reinforcers and punishers.

Just because a reinforcer (or punisher) is a secondary one doesn't mean it is any less potent than a primary one. Money has considerable power over most people's behavior; not only can it be exchanged for primary reinforcers such as food and shelter, but it also brings with it other secondary reinforcers, such as praise and respect. Still, like any conditioned stimulus, a secondary reinforcer such as money will eventually lose its ability to affect behavior if it cannot be paired at least occasionally with one of the stimuli originally associated with it. In 1930, a child who found a penny would be thrilled at the goodies it could buy. Today, U.S. pennies are so worthless that millions of them go out of circulation each year because people leave them on the ground when they drop.

primary reinforcer

A stimulus that is inherently reinforcing, typically satisfying a physiological need; an example is food.

primary punisher

A stimulus that is inherently punishing; an example is electric shock.

secondary reinforcer

A stimulus that has acquired reinforcing properties through association with other reinforcers.

secondary punisher

A stimulus that has acquired punishing properties through association with other punishers.

??? QUICK QUIZ

What kind of consequence will follow if you can't answer these questions?

1. A child nags her father for a cookie; he keeps refusing, but she keeps pleading. Finally, unable to stand the "aversive stimulation" any longer, he hands over the cookie. For him, the ending of the child's pleas is a _____. For the child, the cookie is a _____.

2. A hungry toddler gleefully eats his oatmeal with his hands after being told not to. His mother promptly removes the cereal and takes the messy offender out of the high chair. The removal of the cereal is a _____.

3. Which of the following are secondary (conditioned) reinforcers: quarters spilling from a slot machine, a winner's blue ribbon, a piece of candy, an A on an exam, "frequent-flyer" points.

4. During "happy hours" in bars and restaurants, typically held in the late afternoon, drinks are sold at a reduced price, and appetizers are often free. What undesirable behavior may be rewarded by this practice?

Answers:
1. negative reinforcer; positive reinforcer   2. punisher—or more precisely, a negative punisher—because playing with the oatmeal is likely to decrease after the behavior is punished by removal of the food (assuming the child wants the oatmeal).   3. All but the candy are secondary reinforcers.   4. One possible answer: The reduced prices, free appetizers, and convivial atmosphere all reinforce heavy alcohol consumption just before the commuter rush hour, thus possibly contributing to drunk driving (see Geller & Lehman, 1988).

Principles of Operant Conditioning

Thousands of studies have been done on operant conditioning, many using animals. A favorite experimental tool is the *Skinner box,* a cage equipped with a device that delivers food into a dish when an animal makes a desired response (see Figure 8.5). A *cumulative recorder* connected to the cage automatically records each response and produces a graph showing how many responses have been made up to any given point in time.

Early in his career, Skinner (1938) used the Skinner box for a classic demonstration of operant conditioning. A rat that had previously learned to eat from the pellet-releasing device was placed in the box. Because no food was present, the animal proceeded to do typical ratlike things, scurrying about the box, sniffing here and there, and randomly touching parts of the floor and walls. Quite by accident, it happened to press a lever mounted on one wall, and immediately, a pellet of tasty rat food fell into the food dish. The

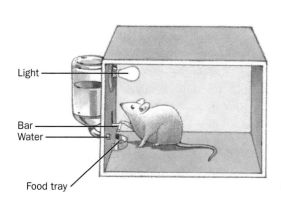

Light

Bar

Water

Food tray

Figure 8.5

The Skinner Box

When a rat in a Skinner box presses a bar, a food pellet or drop of water is automatically released. The photo shows Skinner at work on one of the boxes.

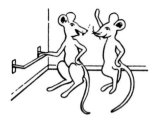

"Boy, do we have this guy conditioned. Every time I press the bar down he drops a pellet in."

rat continued its movements and again happened to press the bar, causing another pellet to fall into the dish. With additional repetitions of bar pressing followed by food, the animal began to behave less randomly and to press the bar more consistently. Eventually, Skinner had the rat pressing the bar as fast as it could. By using the Skinner box and similar devices, behavioral researchers have discovered many techniques and applications of operant conditioning.

Extinction.   In operant conditioning, as in classical, **extinction** is a procedure that causes a previously learned response to stop. In operant conditioning, extinction takes place when the reinforcer that maintained the response is removed or is no longer available. At first, there may be a spurt of responding, but then the responses gradually taper off and eventually cease. Suppose you put a coin in a vending machine and get nothing back. You may throw in another coin, or perhaps even two, but then you will probably stop trying. The next day, you may put in yet another coin, an example of *spontaneous recovery*. Eventually, however, you will give up on that machine. Your response will have been extinguished.

Immediate Versus Delayed Consequences. In general, the sooner a reinforcer or punisher follows a response, the greater its effect. This principle applies especially to animals and children, but human adults also respond more reliably when they don't have to wait too long for a paycheck, a smile, or a grade. When there is delay, other responses occur in the interval, and the connection between the desired or undesired response and the consequence may not be made.

Stimulus Generalization and Discrimination. In operant conditioning, as in classical, **stimulus generalization** may occur. That is, responses may generalize to stimuli that were not present during the original learning situation but resemble the original stimuli. For example, a pigeon that has been trained to peck at a picture of a circle may also peck at a slightly oval figure. But if you wanted to train the bird to discriminate between the two shapes, you would present both the circle and the oval, giving reinforcers whenever the bird pecked at the circle and withholding reinforcers when it pecked at the oval. Eventually, **stimulus discrimination** would occur.

Sometimes an animal or human being learns to respond to a stimulus only when some other stim-

ulus, called a **discriminative stimulus,** is present. The discriminative stimulus signals whether a response, if made, will "pay off." In a Skinner box containing a pigeon, a light may serve as a discriminative stimulus for pecking at a circle. When the light is on, pecking brings a reward; when it is off, pecking is futile. The light is said to exert **stimulus control** over the pecking by setting the occasion for reinforcement to occur if the response is made. However, the response is not *compelled*, as salivation was compelled by the ringing of the bell in Pavlov's classical-conditioning studies. It merely becomes more probable (or occurs at a greater rate) in the presence of the discriminative stimulus.

Human behavior is controlled by many discriminative stimuli, both verbal ("Store hours are 9 to 5") and nonverbal (traffic lights, doorbells, the ring of a telephone, the facial expressions of others). Learning to respond correctly when such stimuli are present is an essential part of a person's socialization. In a public place, if you have to go to the bathroom, the words *Women* and *Men* are discriminative stimuli for entering one door or the other. One word tells you the response will be rewarded by the opportunity to empty a full bladder, the other that it will be punished by the jeers or protests of other people.

Learning on Schedule.   Reinforcers can be delivered according to different schedules, or patterns over time. When a response is first acquired, learning is usually most rapid if the response is reinforced each time it occurs; this procedure is called **continuous reinforcement.** However, once a response has become reliable, it will be more resistant to extinction if it is rewarded on a **partial** or **intermittent schedule of reinforcement,** which involves reinforcing only some responses, not all of them. Skinner (1956) reported that he first happened on this property of partial reinforcement when he ran short of food pellets for his rats and was forced to deliver reinforcers less often. (Not all scientific discoveries are planned!) Years later, when he was asked how he could tolerate being misunderstood so often, he replied that he only needed to be understood three or four times a year—his own intermittent schedule of reinforcement.

Many kinds of intermittent schedules have been studied. Some deliver a reinforcer only after a certain number of responses have occurred. Others deliver a reinforcer only if a response is made after a certain amount of time has passed

Get Involved

If you have a pet, you can use operant-conditioning principles to teach your animal a desired behavior. Choose something simple. (Shaping complex behavior can be difficult unless you have special training.) One student we know taught her cat to willingly enter the garage for the night by feeding the animal a special treat there each evening at the same time. Soon the cat was "asking" to get into the garage at bedtime! Another student taught her pastured horse to come to her and submit willingly to the halter by rewarding the animal's occasional approach with a carrot. Soon the horse was approaching regularly and could be put on an intermittent schedule of reinforcement. Be creative, and see whether you can make your pet better behaved or more cooperative in some way.

since the last reinforcer. The number of responses that must occur or the amount of time that must pass may be fixed (e.g., three responses or five seconds) or may vary around some average. These patterns of reinforcement affect the rate, form, and timing of behavior. The details are beyond the scope of this book, but here's an example. Suppose your sweetheart sends you ten e-mail messages each day, playfully spacing them at unpredictable intervals, although they come on average every hour or so. You will probably check your e-mail regularly, at a low but steady rate. But if your sweetheart sends you just one e-mail every day, at around dinnertime, you'll probably start checking frequently around 5:00 P.M., keep doing so until the message arrives (your reward), and then stop looking at all until the next evening.

A basic principle of operant conditioning is that if you want a response to persist after it has been learned, you should reinforce it intermittently, not continuously. If an animal has been receiving continuous reinforcement for some response and then the reinforcement suddenly stops, the animal will soon stop responding. Because the change in reinforcement is large, from continuous to none at all, the animal can easily discern the change. But if reinforcement has been intermittent, the change will not be so dramatic, and the animal will keep responding for some period of time. Pigeons, rats, and people on intermittent schedules of reinforcement have responded in the laboratory thousands of times without reinforcement before throwing in the towel, especially when the timing of the reinforcer varies. Animals will sometimes work so hard for an unpredictable, infrequent bit of food that the energy they expend is greater than that gained from the reward; theoretically, the animal could actually work itself to death.

It follows that if you want to get rid of a response, you should be careful *not* to reinforce it

intermittently. If you are going to extinguish undesirable behavior by ignoring it—a child's tantrums, a friend's midnight phone calls, a parent's unasked-for advice—you must be absolutely consistent in withholding reinforcement (your attention). Otherwise, you will probably only make matters worse. The other person will learn that if he or she keeps up the screaming, calling, or advice giving long enough, it will eventually be rewarded. One of the most common errors people make, from a behavioral point of view, is to reward intermittently the responses they would like to eliminate.

Shaping. For a response to be reinforced, it must first occur. But suppose you want to train a rat to pick up a marble, a child to use a knife and fork properly, or a friend to play terrific tennis. Such behaviors, and most others in everyday life, have almost no probability of appearing spontaneously. You could grow old and gray waiting for them to occur so that you could reinforce them. The operant solution to this dilemma is a procedure called **shaping.**

In shaping, you start by reinforcing a tendency in the right direction, and then you gradually require responses that are more and more similar to the final, desired response. The responses that you reinforce on the way to the final one are called *successive approximations*. In the case of the rat and the marble, you might deliver a food pellet if the rat merely turned toward the marble. Once this response was well established, you might then reward the rat for taking a step toward the marble. After that, you could reward it for approaching the marble, then for

shaping
An operant-conditioning procedure in which successive approximations of a desired response are reinforced; used when the desired response has a low probability of occurring spontaneously.

Animals can learn to do some surprising things, with a little help from their human friends and the application of operant-conditioning techniques.

touching the marble, then for putting both paws on the marble, and finally for holding it. With the achievement of each approximation, the next one would become more likely, making it available for reinforcement.

Using shaping and other techniques, Skinner was able to train pigeons to play Ping-Pong with their beaks and to "bowl" in a miniature alley, complete with a wooden ball and tiny bowling pins. Rats have learned equally impressive behaviors (see Figure 8.6). Animal trainers routinely use shaping to teach dogs to act as the "eyes" of the blind and to act as the "limbs" of people with spinal-cord injuries by turning on light switches, opening refrigerator doors, and reaching for boxes on supermarket shelves. Shaping works with people, too. According to one story (probably fictitious), some university students once used eye contact as a reinforcer to shape the behavior of a famous professor who was an expert on operant conditioning. They decided to get him to deliver his lecture from a corner of the room. Each time he moved in that direction, they looked at him; otherwise, they averted their gaze. Eventually, the

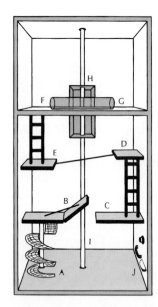

Figure 8.6
A Rat's Route
To demonstrate shaping and other operant procedures, a researcher trained a rat to perform a long sequence of activities in an apparatus resembling this one. Starting at point A, the rat climbs a ramp to B, crosses a drawbridge to C, climbs a ladder to D, crosses a tightrope to E, climbs another ladder to F, crawls through a tunnel to G, runs to H and enters an elevator, descends to I, and runs out of the elevator to J, where it presses a lever and finally receives some well-deserved food. (After Cheney, in Chance, 1994.)

professor was backed into the corner, never suspecting that his behavior had been shaped.

Superstition.   Do you cross your fingers when you're waiting for good news? Have you ever avoided walking under a ladder because doing so brings bad luck? Do you have a lucky charm in your car to protect you against accidents? Why do people hold such superstitions?

The answer, say behaviorists, has to do partly with the nature of reinforcement, which can be effective even when it is entirely coincidental. Skinner (1948) first demonstrated this fact by putting eight pigeons in boxes and rigging the boxes so that food was delivered every 15 seconds, even if the bird didn't lift a feather. Pigeons, like rats, are often in motion, so when the food came, each animal was likely to be doing *something.* That something was then reinforced by delivery of the food. The behavior, of course, was reinforced entirely by chance, but it still became more likely to occur, and thus to be reinforced again. Within a short time, six of the pigeons were practicing some sort of consistent ritual—turning in counterclockwise circles, bobbing the head up and down, swinging the head to and fro, or making brushing movements toward the floor. None of these activities had the least effect on the delivery of the reinforcer; the birds were behaving "superstitiously." It was as if they thought their movements were responsible for bringing the food.

You can see how coincidental reinforcement might account for some human superstitions. A baseball pitcher happens to scratch his left ear, then strikes out a star batter on the other team; ever after, he scratches his left ear before pitching. A student uses a purple pen on the first exam of the semester, gets an A, and from then on uses only purple pens for taking tests. Why, though, don't such superstitions extinguish? After all, the pitcher isn't going to strike out every batter, nor is the student always going to be brilliant. One answer: Intermittent reinforcement may make the response particularly resistant to extinction. If coincidental reinforcement occurs occasionally, the superstitious behavior may continue indefinitely. Ironically, the fact that our little rituals only "work" some of the time ensures that we will keep using them.

Of course, you don't have to have an accident after walking beneath a ladder, spilling the salt, or breaking a mirror to believe that these actions bring bad luck. Many superstitions are reinforced

Thinking Critically About Superstitions

by the agreement or attention of others, or by the feeling of control they provide. And once you have acquired a superstition, you may notice evidence that justifies it but ignore contrary evidence. As long as nothing awful happens when you are carrying a good-luck charm, for example, you can credit it with protective powers; but if something bad does occur, you can always say that the charm has lost its powers (a violation of the principle of falsifiability!). Even when we know the reasons for our superstitions, they can be hard to shake. As behaviorist Paul Chance (1988) wrote, "A black cat means nothing to me now, nor does a broken mirror. There are no little plastic icons on the dashboard of my car, and I carry no rabbit's foot. I am free of all such nonsense, and I am happy to report no ill effects—knock wood."

??? QUICK QUIZ

Can you apply the principles of operant conditioning? In each of the following situations, choose the best alternative, and give your reason for choosing it.

1. You want your 2-year-old to ask for water with a word instead of a grunt. Should you give him water when he says "wa-wa" or wait until his pronunciation improves?

2. Your roommate keeps interrupting you while you are studying even though you have asked her to stop. Should you ignore her completely or occasionally respond for the sake of good manners?

3. Your father, who rarely writes to you, has finally sent a letter. Should you reply quickly or wait a while so he will know how it feels to be ignored?

Answers:

1. You should reinforce "wa-wa," an approximation of *water,* because complex behaviors need to be shaped. 2. From a behavioral view, you should ignore her completely because intermittent reinforcement (attention) could cause her interruptions to persist. 3. If you want to encourage letter writing, you should reply quickly because immediate reinforcement is more effective than delayed reinforcement.

What's Ahead

- *Why do efforts to "crack down" on wrongdoers often go awry?*

- *What's the best way to discourage a child from throwing tantrums?*

- *Why does paying children for good grades sometimes backfire?*

OPERANT CONDITIONING IN REAL LIFE

Operant principles can clear up many mysteries of behavior. We could give you thousands of examples, but here are just a couple. In some countries, such as the United States and Norway, many victims of "fender-bender" automobile accidents complain of whiplash symptoms (neck pain and headaches) that last for months or even years. In other countries, such as Lithuania, whiplash is virtually unknown; there is no difference between car-accident victims and controls in frequency of chronic headaches and neck pain. A Norwegian research team, concerned about the epidemic of whiplash lawsuits in Norway, compared Norwegians and Lithuanians and discovered the reason: Few Lithuanians have personal-injury insurance, and the government pays most medical bills (Schrader et al., 1996). In other words, when there are no reinforcers for labeling or reporting chronic whiplash, the "syndrome" disappears!

Operant principles also help us understand why people don't always behave as they would like. In this age of self-improvement, for example, personal-growth and motivational workshops provide participants with lots of reinforcement for emotional expressiveness and self-disclosure. Participants often feel that their way of interacting with others has been transformed. But when they return home and to work, where the environment is full of the same old reinforcers, punishers, and discriminative stimuli, they are often disappointed to find that their new responses have failed to generalize. A grumpy boss or a cranky spouse may still be able to "push their buttons"—a relapse that is predictable from behavioral principles.

If we could understand the environmental circumstances that control our behavior, say behaviorists, we could design a world more to our liking. Over the years, behaviorists have carried operant principles out of the narrow world of the Skinner box and into the wider world of the classroom, athletic field, prison, mental hospital, nursing home, rehabilitation ward, child-care center, factory, and office. The use of operant techniques (and classical ones) in such real-world settings is called **behavior modification.**

Many behavior-modification programs rely on a technique called the **token economy.** Tokens are secondary reinforcers, such as points or scrip money, that have no real value in themselves but that are exchangeable for primary reinforcers or other secondary reinforcers. They provide an easy way to reinforce behavior on a continuous schedule. Once a particular behavior is established, tokens can be phased out and replaced by more natural intermittent reinforcers, such as praise.

Behavior modification has had some enormous successes. Behaviorists have taught parents how to toilet train their children in only a few sessions (Azrin & Foxx, 1974). They have taught autistic

Behavioral principles have many useful applications. This capuchin monkey has been trained to assist her paralyzed owner by picking up objects, opening doors, helping with feeding, and performing other everyday tasks.

children who have never before spoken to use a vocabulary of several hundred words (Lovaas, 1977). They have trained disturbed and mentally retarded adults to communicate, mingle socially with others, and earn a living (Lent, 1968; McLeod, 1985). They have taught brain-damaged patients to control inappropriate behavior, focus their attention, and improve their language abilities (McGlynn, 1990). And they have helped ordinary folk eliminate unwanted habits, such as smoking and nail biting, or acquire wanted ones, such as practicing the piano or studying.

Yet when people try to apply the principles of conditioning to commonplace problems, their efforts sometimes fail or backfire. Both punishment and reinforcement have their pitfalls, as we are about to see.

The Problem with Punishment

In his novel *Walden Two* (1948/1976), Skinner imagined a utopia in which reinforcers were used so wisely that undesirable behavior was rare. Un-

behavior modification

The application of conditioning techniques to teach new responses or to reduce or eliminate maladaptive or problematic behavior.

token economy

A behavior-modification technique in which secondary reinforcers called *tokens*, which can be collected and exchanged for primary or other secondary reinforcers, are used to shape behavior.

fortunately, we do not live in a utopia; bloopers, bad habits, and antisocial acts abound, and we are faced with how to get rid of them.

An obvious approach might seem to be punishment. Most Western countries have banned corporal (physical) punishment of schoolchildren by principals and teachers, but in the United States, the physical punishment of children has roots in the religious belief that you must beat children or their innate wickedness will land them in hell (Greven, 1991). Many states still permit corporal punishment for disruptive behavior, graffiti vandalism, and other problems that plague many schools. Boys, minority children, and poor white children are the most likely to be hit (I. Hyman, 1994).

The American penal system, too, has become more severe in the punishments it metes out for crime; the United States has a higher proportion of its citizens in jail for nonviolent crimes (such as drug use) than any other developed country. And of course in daily life, people punish one another constantly, by yelling, scolding, fining, and sulking. Many people feel rewarded by a temporary feeling of control and power when they punish others in these ways. But does all this punishment work?

Sometimes punishment is unquestionably effective. Some highly disturbed children have been known to chew their own fingers to the bone, stick objects in their eyes, or tear out their hair. You can't ignore such behavior because the children will seriously injure themselves. You can't respond with concern and affection because you may unwittingly reward the behavior. In this case, punishment works: Immediately punishing the self-destructive behavior eliminates it (Lovaas, 1977; Lovaas, Schreibman, & Koegel, 1974). Mild punishers, such as a spray of water in the face, are often just as effective as strong ones, such as electric shock; sometimes they are even more effective. A firm "No!" can also be established as a conditioned punisher.

Thinking Critically About Punishment

The effects of punishment, however, are far less predictable than many people realize, and simplistic efforts to "crack down" on wrongdoers by punishing them often fail. Laboratory and field studies suggest why:

1. *People often administer punishment inappropriately or when rage prevents them from thinking through what they are doing and how they are doing it.* They swing blindly or yell wildly, applying punishment so broadly that it covers all sorts of irrelevant behaviors. And even when people are not carried away by anger, they often misunderstand the proper application of punishment. One student told us his parents used to punish their children before leaving them alone for the evening because of all the naughty things they were *going* to do. Naturally, the children didn't bother to behave like angels!

2. *The recipient of punishment often responds with anxiety, fear, or rage.* Through a process of classical conditioning, these emotional side effects may then generalize to the entire situation in which the punishment occurs—the place, the person delivering the punishment, and the circumstances. Negative emotional reactions tend to create new problems. A teenager who has been severely punished may strike back or run away. A spouse who is constantly abused will feel bitter and resentful, and is likely to retaliate with small acts of hostility. As the California legislator who opposed corporal punishment in our opening story noted, violence breeds violence, which may help explain why the physical punishment of

Harried parents often resort to physical punishment without being aware of the many negative consequences for themselves and their children. Based on your reading of this chapter, what alternatives does this mother have?

children is correlated with high rates of violence in children (I. Hyman, 1994; McCord, 1991; Straus, 1991; Weiss et al., 1992).

3. *The effects of punishment are sometimes temporary, depending heavily on the presence of the punishing person or circumstances.* All of us can probably remember some transgressions of childhood that we never dared commit when our parents were around but that we promptly resumed as soon as they were gone. All that we learned was not to get caught.

4. *Most misbehavior is hard to punish immediately.* Recall that punishment, like reward, works best if it quickly follows a response, especially with animals and children. Outside the laboratory, immediate punishment is often hard to achieve.

5. *Punishment conveys little information.* If it immediately follows the misbehavior, it may tell the recipient what *not* to do. But it doesn't communicate what the person *should* do. For example, spanking a toddler for messing in her pants will not teach her to use the potty chair. As Skinner (1968) wrote, "We do not teach [a student] to learn quickly by punishing him when he learns slowly, or to recall what he has learned by punishing him when he forgets, or to think logically by punishing him when he is illogical."

6. *An action intended to punish may instead be reinforcing because it brings attention.* Indeed, in some cases angry attention may be just what the offender is after. If a mother yells at a child who is throwing a tantrum, the very act of yelling may give him what he wants—a reaction from her. In the schoolroom, teachers who scold children in front of other students, thus putting them in the limelight, often unwittingly reward the very misbehavior they are trying to eliminate.

Because of these drawbacks, most psychologists believe that punishment, especially severe punishment, is a poor way to eliminate unwanted behavior in most situations. When punishment must be used, it should not involve physical abuse, it should be accompanied by information about what kind of behavior would be appropriate, and it should be followed, whenever possible, by the reinforcement of desirable behavior.

Fortunately, a good alternative to punishment exists: extinction of the responses you want to discourage. Of course, extinction is sometimes difficult to achieve. It is hard to ignore the child nagging for a cookie before dinner, the roommate interrupting your concentration, or the dog barking its lungs out. Moreover, the simplest form of

Why do so many people ignore warnings and threats of punishment?

extinction—ignoring the behavior—is not always appropriate. A teacher cannot ignore a child who is hitting a playmate. The dog owner who ignores Fido's backyard barking may soon hear "barking" of another sort—from the neighbors. A parent whose child is a TV addict can't ignore the behavior because television is rewarding to the child. One solution: Combine extinction of undesirable acts with reinforcement of alternative ones. If a child is addicted to TV, the parent might ignore the child's pleas for "just one more program" and at the same time encourage behavior that is incompatible with television watching, such as playing outdoors or building a model airplane.

It is also important to understand the reasons for a person's misbehavior before deciding how to respond to it. For example, when autistic and other disturbed children throw tantrums, attack their teachers, or do self-destructive things such as punching or poking themselves, it is often because difficult demands are being placed on them or because they are bored and frustrated. Their bizarre behavior is a way of saying, "Hey, let me out of here!" And because the behavior often works, or is reinforced by attention from adults, it tends to persist. When these children are taught to use words to ask for praise or help ("Am I doing good work?" "I don't understand"), their problem behavior decreases and often even disappears (Carr & Durand, 1985). Similarly, a child screaming in a supermarket may be saying, "I'm going out of my head with boredom. Help!" A lover who sulks may be saying, "I'm not sure you really care about me; I'm frightened." Once we understand the purpose or meaning of behavior we dislike, we may be more effective in dealing with it.

The Problem with Reward

Researchers have conditioned rats thousands of times, and as far as we know, none of the rats ever refused to cooperate or felt that they were being manipulated. Human beings are different. A little girl we know came home from school one day in a huff after her teacher announced that good performance would be rewarded with play money that could later be exchanged for privileges. "Doesn't she think I can learn without being bribed?" the child asked her mother indignantly.

This child's reaction illustrates a complication in the use of reinforcers. Most of our examples of operant conditioning have involved **extrinsic reinforcers,** which come from an outside source and are not inherently related to the activity being reinforced. Money, praise, gold stars, applause, hugs, and thumbs-up signs are all extrinsic reinforcers. But people (and probably some other animals, too) also work for **intrinsic reinforcers,** such as enjoyment of the task and the satisfaction of accomplishment. As psychologists have applied operant conditioning in real-world settings, they have sometimes found that extrinsic reinforcement, if you focus on it exclusively, can become too much of a good thing: In some circumstances it can kill the pleasure of doing something for its own sake.

Thinking Critically About Rewards

Consider what happened when psychologists gave nursery-school children the chance to draw with felt-tipped pens (Lepper, Greene, & Nisbett, 1973). The children already liked this activity and readily took it up during free play. First, the researchers recorded how long each child spontaneously played with the pens. Then they told some of the children that if they would draw with felt-tipped pens for a man who had come "to see what kinds of pictures boys and girls like to draw with Magic Markers," they would get a prize, a "Good Player Award" complete with gold seal and red ribbon. After drawing for six minutes, each child got the award, as promised. Other children did not expect a reward and were not given one. A week later, the researchers again observed the children's free play. Those children who had expected and received a reward were spending much less time with the pens than they had before the start of the experiment. In contrast, children who were not given an award continued to show as much interest in the activity as they had shown initially, as you can see in Figure 8.7. Similar results occurred when older children were or were not rewarded for working on academic tasks.

Because promised rewards (otherwise known as bribes) can be effective in the short term and can sometimes increase test scores by boosting students' motivation, some educators advocate using more of them (O'Neil, Sugrue, & Baker, 1995/1996). But being motivated to do well on a test is not the same thing as being motivated to learn. In a study of 9-year-olds and their mothers, half the mothers were told to encourage learning for the intrinsic pleasure of it, and half the mothers were told to reward high grades and punish low ones. A year later, those in the first group had higher motivation and better school performance. For those in the second group, however, extrinsic rewards and punishments actually seemed to impede academic achievement (Gottfried, Fleming, & Gottfried, 1994).

extrinsic reinforcers

Reinforcers that are not inherently related to the activity being reinforced, such as money, prizes, and praise.

intrinsic reinforcers

Reinforcers that are inherently related to the activity being reinforced, such as enjoyment of the task and the satisfaction of accomplishment.

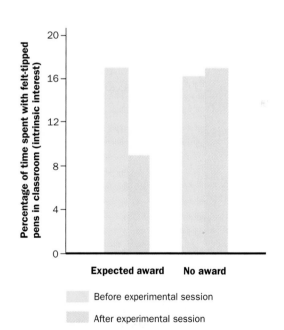

Figure 8.7

Turning Play Into Work

Extrinsic rewards can sometimes reduce the intrinsic pleasure of an activity. When preschoolers were promised a prize for drawing with felt-tipped pens, the behavior temporarily increased, but after receiving the prize, the children spent less time with the pens than they had before the study began.

Drawing by Lorenz; © 1986 The New Yorker Magazine, Inc.

"That is the correct answer, Billy,
but I'm afraid you don't win
anything for it."

Why should extrinsic rewards undermine intrinsic motivation? One possibility is that when we are paid for an activity, we interpret it as work. It is as if we say to ourselves, "I'm doing this because I'm being paid for it. Since I'm being paid, it must be something I wouldn't do if I didn't have to." When the reward is withdrawn, we refuse to "work" any longer. Another possibility is that extrinsic rewards are seen as controlling, and therefore they reduce a person's sense of autonomy and choice ("I guess I should just do what I'm told to do—and *only* what I'm told to do") (Deci & Ryan, 1987). A third, more behavioral explanation is that extrinsic reinforcement sometimes raises the rate of responding above some optimal, enjoyable level. Then the activity really does become work.

There is a trade-off, then, between the short-term effectiveness of extrinsic rewards and the long-term effectiveness of intrinsic ones. Extrinsic rewards work: How many people would trudge off to work every morning if they never got paid? In the classroom, a teacher who offers incentives to an unmotivated student may be taking the only course of action open. If a behavior is to last when the teacher isn't around, however, extrinsic reinforcers eventually must be phased out. As one mother once wrote in a *Newsweek* essay, "The winners [of prizes for schoolwork] will . . . suffer if they don't discover for themselves that they can gain the pleasure of health and strength from exercise, the joy of music from songs, the power of

Get Involved

Which of your actions are controlled primarily by extrinsic reinforcers and which by intrinsic ones? Fill in this checklist:

Activity	Reinforcers mostly extrinsic	Reinforcers mostly intrinsic	Reinforcers about equally extrinsic and intrinsic
Studying	_____	_____	_____
Housework	_____	_____	_____
Worship	_____	_____	_____
Grooming	_____	_____	_____
Job	_____	_____	_____
Dating	_____	_____	_____
Attending class	_____	_____	_____
Reading unrelated to school	_____	_____	_____
Sports	_____	_____	_____
Cooking	_____	_____	_____

Is there an area of your life in which you'd like intrinsic reinforcement to play a larger role? What can you do to make that happen?

mathematics from counting and all of human wisdom from reading" (Skreslet, 1987).

We do not want to leave the impression, however, that extrinsic reinforcers always decrease the pleasure of an activity. If you get money, a high grade, or a trophy for doing a task *well,* rather than for just doing it, your intrinsic motivation won't decline (Dickinson, 1989; Eisenberger & Cameron, 1996). And if you have always loved to read or play the piano, you're likely to keep on reading or playing even when

your teacher no longer grades you or gives you gold stars (Mawhinney, 1990). Many educators and employers have learned to avoid the trap of either–or thinking by recognizing that most people do their best work when they get tangible rewards *and* when they have interesting, challenging, and varied kinds of work to do.

Effective behavior modification, as you can see, is not only a science but an art. In "Taking Psychology with You," we offer further guidelines for mastering that art.

??? QUICK QUIZ

A. According to behavioral principles, what is happening here?

1. An adolescent whose parents have hit him for minor transgressions since he was small runs away from home.

2. A young woman whose parents paid her to clean her room while she was growing up is a slob when she moves to her own apartment.

3. Two parents scold their young daughter every time they catch her sucking her thumb. The thumb sucking continues anyway.

 B. In a fee-for-service system of health care, doctors are paid for each visit by a patient or for each service performed, and the longer the visit, the higher the fee. In contrast, some health maintenance organizations (HMOs) pay their doctors a fixed amount per patient for the entire year. If the amount actually expended is less, the physician gets a bonus, and in some systems, if the amount expended is more, the physician is financially penalized. Given what you know about operant conditioning, what are the potential advantages and disadvantages of each system?

Answers:

A. 1. The physical punishment was painful, and through a process of classical conditioning, the situation in which it occurred also became unpleasant. Because escape from an unpleasant stimulus is negatively reinforcing, the boy ran away. 2. Extrinsic reinforcers are no longer available, so room-cleaning behavior has been extinguished. Also, extrinsic rewards may have displaced the intrinsic satisfaction of having a tidy room. 3. Punishment has failed, possibly because the scolding brings attention or because thumb sucking continues to bring the child pleasure when the parents aren't around. B. In a fee-for-service system, the doctor is likely to provide the attention and tests that ill patients need. However, this system also rewards doctors for unnecessary tests and patient visits, contributing to the explosion in health-care costs. The policies of the HMOs help contain these costs, but because doctors are rewarded for reducing costs and in some cases are penalized for running up charges, some patients may not get the attention or services they need.

What's Ahead

- *How might watching violence on TV make (some) people more aggressive?*

- *Why do parents who yell at their children to be quiet tend to produce children who are yellers?*

- *Why do two people often learn different lessons from exactly the same experience?*

SOCIAL-LEARNING THEORIES

For half a century, most American learning theories held that learning could be explained by specifying the behavioral "ABCs"—*antecedents* (events preceding behavior), *behaviors,* and *consequences.* Yet even during the early glory years of behaviorism, a few behaviorists rebelled against explanations of behavior that relied solely on conditioning principles.

In the 1940s, two social scientists proposed a modification they called *social-learning theory* (Dollard & Miller, 1950). In human beings, they argued, most learning is social—that is, acquired by observing other people in a social context, rather than through standard conditioning procedures. By the 1960s and 1970s, social-learning theory was in full bloom, and a new element had been added: the human capacity for higher-level cognitive processes. Its proponents agreed with behaviorists that human beings, along with the rat and the rabbit, are subject to the laws of operant and classical conditioning. But they added that human beings, unlike the rat and the rabbit, are full of attitudes, beliefs, and expectations that affect the way they acquire information, make decisions, reason, and solve problems. All these mental processes affect what individuals will do at any given moment and also, more generally, the kinds of people they become.

Orthodox behaviorists regard environmental factors and behavior as a two-way street, like this:

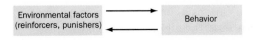

But social-learning theorists regard the environment, behavior, *and* a person's internalized motives and cognitions as forming a circle in which all elements mutually affect each other (Bandura, 1986):

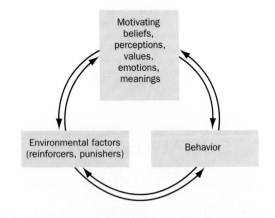

We speak of **social-learning theories** in the plural because they do not represent a single unified approach to behavior in the way that traditional behaviorism does; they differ in how much emphasis they place on cognitive processes and in

how much they distance themselves from behaviorism. Some researchers continue to call themselves social-learning theorists, but the two leading advocates of this approach, Walter Mischel and Albert Bandura, call their theories *cognitive social learning* (Mischel, 1973) and *social cognitive theory* (Bandura, 1986, 1994). In general, however, social-learning theories emphasize two topics of research that distinguish them from traditional behaviorism: (1) observational learning and the role of models, and (2) cognitive processes such as perceptions and interpretations of events.

Observational Learning: The Copycat Syndrome

Late one night, a friend who lives in a rural area was awakened by a loud clattering and banging. Her whole family raced outside to find the source of the commotion. A raccoon had knocked over a "raccoon-proof" garbage can and seemed to be demonstrating to an assembly of other raccoons how to open it: If you jump up and down on the can's side, the lid will pop off.

According to our friend, the observing raccoons learned from this episode how to open stubborn garbage cans, and the observing humans learned how smart raccoons can be. In short, they all benefited from **observational learning** (which behaviorists call *vicarious conditioning*): learning by watching what others do and what happens to them for doing it. Social-learning theorists emphasize that operant conditioning often occurs vicariously, when an animal or person observes a *model* (another animal or person) behaving in certain ways and experiencing the consequences (Bandura, 1977). Sometimes the learner imitates the responses shortly after observing them. At other times the learning remains latent until circumstances allow or require it to be expressed in performance. A little boy may observe a parent setting the table, threading a needle, or tightening a screw, but he may not act on this learning for years. Then the child finds he knows how to do these things, even though he has never before done them. He did not learn by doing, but by watching.

None of us would last long without observational learning. We would have to learn to avoid oncoming cars by walking into traffic and suffering the consequences or learn to swim by jumping into a deep pool and flailing around. Learning would be not only dangerous but also inefficient.

social-learning theories

Theories that emphasize how behavior is learned and maintained through observation and imitation of others, positive consequences, and cognitive processes such as plans, expectations, and motivating beliefs.

observational learning

A process in which an individual learns new responses by observing the behavior of another (a model) rather than through direct experience; sometimes called *vicarious conditioning*.

Like father, like daughter. Parents can be powerful role models.

Parents and teachers would be busy 24 hours a day shaping children's behavior. Bosses would have to stand over their employees' desks, rewarding every little link in the complex behavioral chains we call typing, report writing, and accounting. Observational learning also explains why parents who hit their children tend to rear hitters, and why yellers ("Be quiet!") tend to rear yellers. Children often do as their parents do, not as their parents say (Grusec, Saas-Kortsaak, & Simutis, 1978).

Many years ago, Albert Bandura and his colleagues showed just how important observational learning is, especially for children who are learning the rules of social behavior (Bandura, Ross, & Ross, 1963). The researchers had nursery-school children watch a short film of two men, Rocky and Johnny, playing with toys. (Apparently the children did not think this behavior was odd.) In the film, Johnny refuses to share his toys, and Rocky responds by clobbering him. Rocky's actions are rewarded because he winds up with all the toys. Poor Johnny sits dejectedly in the corner, while Rocky marches off with a sack full of his loot and a hobbyhorse under his arm. After viewing the film, each child was left alone for 20 minutes in a playroom full of toys, including some of the items shown in the film. Watching through a one-way mirror, the researchers found that the children played much more aggressively with the toys than did children who had not seen the film. Sometimes their behavior was almost a direct imitation of Rocky's. At the end of the session, one little girl even asked the experimenter for a sack!

Of course, children imitate positive activities too. Matt Groening, the creator of the cartoon *The Simpsons*, decided it would be funny if the Simpsons' 8-year-old daughter Lisa played the baritone sax. Sure enough, across the country little girls began imitating her. Cynthia Sikes, a saxophone teacher in New York, told the *New York Times* (January 14, 1996) that "when the show started, I got an influx of girls coming up to me saying, 'I want to play the saxophone because Lisa Simpson plays the saxophone.'" Groening says his mail regularly includes photos of girls holding up their saxophones.

Behaviorists have always acknowledged the importance of observational learning; they just think it can be explained in stimulus–response terms. But social-learning theorists believe that in human beings, observational learning cannot be fully understood without taking into account the thought processes of the learner (Meltzoff & Gopnik, 1993).

Cognitive Processes: Peering into the "Black Box"

Early behaviorists liked to compare the mind to an engineer's hypothetical "black box," a device whose workings must be inferred because they can't be observed directly. To them, the box contained irrelevant wiring; it was enough to know that pushing a button on the box would produce a predictable response.

But even as early as the 1930s, a few behaviorists could not resist peeking into that black box. Edward Tolman (1938) committed virtual heresy at the time by noting that his rats, when pausing at turning points in a maze, seemed to be *deciding* which way to go. In his studies, Tolman found that sometimes the animals didn't behave as conditioning principles would predict. Sometimes the animals were clearly learning without any obvious behavioral change. What, he wondered, was going on in their little rat brains that might account for this puzzle?

In a classic experiment, Tolman and his colleague Chase Honzik (1930) placed three groups of rats in mazes and observed the rats' behavior each day for more than two weeks. The rats in Group 1 always found food at the end of the maze. Group 2 never found food. Group 3 found no food for ten days but then received food on the eleventh. The Group 1 rats, whose behavior had been reinforced with food, quickly learned to head straight for the end of the maze without going down blind alleys, whereas Group 2 rats did not learn to go to the end. But the Group 3 rats were different. For ten days they appeared to follow no particular route. Then, on the eleventh day, when food was introduced, they quickly learned to run to the end of the maze. As Figure 8.8 shows, by the next day, they were doing as well as Group 1.

Group 3 had demonstrated **latent learning,** learning that is not immediately expressed. A great deal of human learning also remains latent until circumstances allow or require it to be expressed, as we saw in our discussion of observational learning. But latent learning poses problems for behavioral theories. Not only does it occur in

latent learning
A form of learning that is not immediately expressed in an overt response; occurs without obvious reinforcement.

cognitive map
A mental representation of the environment.

the absence of any obvious reinforcer, but it also raises questions about what, exactly, is learned during learning. The rats that were not given food until the eleventh day had no reason to run toward the end during their first ten days in the maze. Yet clearly they had learned *something*.

Tolman (1948) argued that this "something" was a **cognitive map,** a mental representation of the spatial layout of the environment. You have a cognitive map of your neighborhood, which is what allows you to find your way to Fourth and Kumquat Streets even if you have never done so before. More generally, according to social-learning theories, what a learner learns in observational and latent learning is not a specific response but *knowledge* about responses and their consequences. We learn how the world is organized and which actions produce which payoffs, and this knowledge permits us to be creative and flexible in reaching our goals.

Social-learning theories also emphasize the importance of people's *perceptions* in what they learn: perceptions of the models they observe and also perceptions of themselves. Two people may observe the same event and come away with entirely different interpretations of it; they have learned, we might say, two different lessons from it. Individuals also bring different knowledge and assumptions to an event, and they notice and pay attention to different aspects of a situation. Imagine two people trying to learn how to do a perfect "tush push" in country-western line dancing: One is paying careful attention to the instructor who is modeling the complex steps, but the other is distracted by an appealing tush-pusher down the line. And of course the two novices may differ in how much they want to learn the new dance. People make thousands of observations every day and theoretically could learn something from all of them; but if they don't *want* to learn what is being modeled, they could watch a hundred teachers and not get anywhere at all (Bandura, 1986, 1994).

Individual differences in perceptions and interpretations help explain why violent television programs do not have the same impact on all children. As the results of the Rocky and Johnny study would predict, some children—and adults— do, unquestionably, imitate the incessant aggression they observe on television and in movies (APA Commission on Violence and Youth, 1993; Comstock et al., 1978; Eron, 1995). But the personal qualities people bring with them when they are watching TV also play a role. While seeing

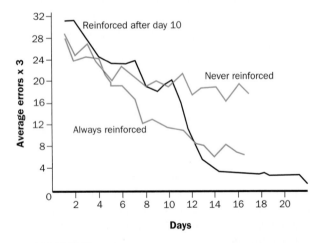

Figure 8.8
Latent Learning

In a classic experiment, rats that always found food in a maze made fewer and fewer errors in reaching the food, as shown by the blue curve on this graph. Rats that never found food showed little improvement, as shown by the red curve. Rats in a third group found no food for ten days, and then were given food on the eleventh. As the black curve shows, these animals showed rapid improvement from then on, quickly equaling the performance of the rats that had received food from the start. This result suggests that learning involves cognitive changes that can occur in the absence of reinforcement and that may not be acted on until a reinforcer becomes available (Tolman & Honzik, 1930).

people being "blown away," one viewer may learn that violence is cool and masculine; another may conclude that violence is ugly, stupid, and self-defeating. In general, the more aggressive a person is to begin with, the more likely the person is to seek out violent shows and movies and be affected by them (Bushman, 1995).

Behaviorists would say that personality traits such as aggressiveness are simply sets of habits and beliefs that have been rewarded over a person's lifetime. Social-learning theorists, however, maintain that these habits and beliefs come to exert their own effects on behavior (see Chapter 2). For example, to understand why some people work hard and persist even after failing many times, whereas others give up, we need to understand not only the effects of rewards and punishers, but also the degree of control people feel over their lives and their confidence in their own abilities. We will be discussing the influence of motivating beliefs and internalized goals further in Chapters 12 and 13.

??? QUICK QUIZ

How latent is your learning?

1. After watching her teenage sister put on some lipstick, a little girl takes a lipstick and applies it to her own lips. She has acquired this behavior through a process of _____.

2. Your friend asks you to meet her at a new restaurant across town; you have never been to this specific address, but you find your way there anyway because you have a good _____ of your town.

3. To a social-learning theorist, the phenomenon of latent learning shows that we learn not specific responses but rather _____.

Answers:

1. observational learning 2. cognitive map 3. knowledge about responses and their consequences

---

What's Ahead

- *Can an ape show "insight" into a problem?*
- *Can a pigeon show insight? What would a behaviorist say?*

BEHAVIOR AND THE MIND: THE QUESTION OF INSIGHT

Today, most psychologists allow for cognitions in their theories and explanations of behavior. However, to the true behaviorist, mental explanations are misleading fictions, and nothing is to be gained by using them. As behaviorist William Baum (1994) has written, "I no more have a mind than I have a fairy godmother. I can talk to you about my mind or about my fairy godmother; that cannot make either of them less fictional. No one has ever seen either one . . . such talk is no help in a science."

The tension between behaviorism and cognitive approaches to psychology can be seen in how the two approaches treat the interesting problem of insight. **Insight** is learning or problem solving that appears to occur in a flash: You suddenly "see" how to solve an equation, assemble a cabinet that came with unintelligible instructions, or finish a puzzle. The human species is not the only one capable of insight. In studies done during World War I, Wolfgang Köhler (1925) put chimpanzees in situations in which some tempting bananas were just out of reach, then watched to see what the apes would do. Most did nothing, but a few turned out to be both enterprising and creative. If the bananas were outside the cage, the animal might pull them in with a stick. If the bananas were hung overhead, and there were boxes in the cage, the chimpanzee might pile up the boxes and climb on top of them to reach the fruit. Often, the solution came after the animal had been sitting quietly without actively trying to reach the bananas. It appeared as though the animal had been thinking about the problem and suddenly saw the answer.

insight

A form of problem solving that appears to involve the (often sudden) understanding of how elements of a situation are related or can be reorganized to achieve a solution.

(a)   (b)   (c)

Figure 8.9

Smart Bird?

"Now, let's see . . . ." A pigeon looks at a cluster of toy bananas strung overhead (a), pushes a small box beneath the bananas (b), and then climbs on the box to peck at them (c). The bird had previously learned separate components of this sequence through a process of operant conditioning. Behaviorists view this accomplishment as evidence against the cognitive view of insight. What do you think?

Thinking Critically About Insight

To most people, insight seems to be an entirely cognitive phenomenon—a new way of perceiving logical and cause-and-effect relationships, in which a person or animal does not simply respond to a stimulus but instead solves a problem. But behaviorists argue that insight can be explained in terms of an organism's reinforcement history, without resorting to mentalistic concepts (Windholz & Lamal, 1985). Insight, they say, is just a label for the combination of previously learned patterns; it does not *explain* the behavior.

Behaviorists point out that even animals not usually credited with higher mental processes seem capable of what looks suspiciously like "insight," under some conditions. In one ingenious study, Robert Epstein and his colleagues (1984) taught four pigeons three separate behaviors, during different training sessions: to push boxes in a particular direction, to climb onto a box, and to peck at a toy banana in order to obtain grain. The birds were also taught not to fly or jump at the banana; those behaviors were extinguished. Then the pigeons were left alone with the toy banana suspended just out of reach overhead and the box at the edge of the cage. Just as Köhler's chimps had done, the birds quickly solved their feeding problem by pushing the box beneath the banana and climbing onto it (see Figure 8.9). Yet few people would want to credit pigeons with complex thought processes. Cognitive researchers, however, are not convinced; just because the behavior of a pigeon looks some-

thing like that of a human being, they say, does not mean its origins are the same. Cognitive studies, they maintain, show that in human beings (and possibly chimpanzees), insight requires *mentally* combining previously learned responses in new ways.

The debates between behaviorists and their critics over insight and many other kinds of learning promise to continue. But in practice, behavioral and cognitive approaches are sometimes treated as different levels of analysis, rather than as conflicting approaches. Many therapists, for example, combine behavioral principles with cognitive ones to treat people in psychotherapy (see Chapter 11). And even researchers who concentrate on the vast country of the mind want to know how the external environment affects the geography of that country—a topic we are about to explore further, as we examine the impact of society and culture on an individual's behavior.

How can the principles covered in this chapter help us think about the unhappy case of Michael Fay, which opened this chapter? Most Americans and Canadians would probably not want to emulate Singapore by hanging every person convicted of armed robbery or drug trafficking (which in that island nation can mean possession of half an ounce of heroin or an ounce of cocaine). Nor would they want to dispense with jury trials and other aspects of due process, as Singapore has done. But surveys show that many Americans do favor stiffer penalties for crime, and a majority think that juveniles should be treated as harshly as adults.

The problem, as we saw in this chapter and in our discussion of power assertion in Chapter 3, is that punishment brings its own set of problems and is not always a successful deterrent. In Singapore, armed robberies and kidnappings have plummeted since the death penalty was made mandatory, but the number of drug addicts has been rising, despite stringent laws against drug use. David Marshall, the country's first elected chief minister when it was under British rule, told the *Los Angeles Times* that each year he sees the number of death sentences increase, which suggests that the penalty is not an effective deterrent overall.

One of our critical-thinking guidelines, "Consider other interpretations," directs us to examine more closely the apparent connection between harsh punishment and low crime rates in countries like Singapore. It's true that Singapore's streets are safe and clean; muggings are rare, and gang warfare, which was once common, is now nonexistent. But the reason may have as much to do with the absence of poverty in that country, its low unemployment (at least until recently), and its excellent educational system as with the punitiveness of its legal code. As a professor of management observed in a letter to the *Los Angeles Times*, "A population with good opportunities for jobs at rising wages will not be crime-prone." From a learning perspective, the explanation is clear: Good wages and job opportunities reinforce socially responsible, law-abiding behavior.

Cultural factors probably also play a role. Among the ethnic Chinese who make up most of Singapore's population, family life is central, children remain at home until marriage, and public shame is a powerful deterrent to antisocial behavior. Hong Kong, which also has a largely Chinese population, has even lower rates of violent crime than Singapore (though not of other types of crime)—and Hong Kong does not impose the death penalty or use caning in its legal system.

The principles of learning certainly do not rule out all use of punishment. But to reduce antisocial behavior, we also need to identify the rewards and payoffs that promote such behavior, withdraw those rewards and payoffs, and reinforce cooperative, friendly behavior instead. In addition, we need to be aware of the kinds of messages conveyed by role models, including parents and media heroes. A society that truly wishes to reduce violence and criminality will not celebrate bullies or lawless vigilantes, glorify violence in sports, or look the other way when parents model violence in the home by using it against their children or each other.

The real world, alas, will never be as peaceful and law-abiding as Skinner's Walden Two. But learning principles do give us cause for optimism about our ability to change for the better by fashioning better environments for ourselves, our families, and our fellow human beings. In Skinner's book, the main protagonist, Frazier, exclaims, "The Good Life is waiting for us—here and now! We have the necessary techniques, both material and psychological, to create a full and satisfying life for everyone." Frazier was overstating his case, which was his prerogative as a character in a utopian novel. But the rest of us can take with us his ultimate message: that with patience, care, and forethought, we can learn to apply the principles of learning in our own lives and in our communities.

Taking Psychology with You

Shape Up!

Operant conditioning can seem deceptively simple—a few rewards here, a bit of shaping there, and you're done. In practice, though, behavior modification can be full of unwanted surprises, even in the hands of experts. Here are a few things to keep in mind if you want to modify someone's behavior:

• *Accentuate the positive.* Most people notice bad behavior more than good and therefore miss opportunities to use reinforcers. Parents, for example, often scold a child for bedwetting but fail to give praise for dry sheets in the morning; or they punish a child for poor grades but fail to reward studying.

• *Reinforce small improvements.* A common error is to withhold reinforcement until behavior is perfect (which may be never). Has your child's grade in math improved from a D to a C? Has your favorite date, who is usually an awful cook, managed to serve up a half-decent omelette? Has your messy roommate left some dirty dishes in the sink but vacuumed the rug? It's probably time for shaping behavior with a reinforcer. On the other hand, you don't want to overdo praise or give it insincerely. Gushing about every tiny step in the right direction will cause your praise to lose its value, and soon nothing less than a standing ovation will do.

• *Find the right reinforcers.* You may have to experiment a bit to find which reinforcers a person (or animal) actually wants. In general, it is good to use a variety of reinforcers because the same one used again and again can get boring. Reinforcers, by the way, do not have to be *things.* You can also use valued activities, such as going out to dinner, to reinforce other behavior.

• *Always examine what you are reinforcing.* It is easy to reinforce undesirable behavior simply by responding to it. Suppose someone is always yelling at you at the slightest provocation, and you want the shouting to stop. If you respond to it at all, whether by crying, apologizing, or yelling back, you are likely to reinforce it unintentionally. An alternative might be to explain in a calm voice that you will henceforth not respond to complaints unless they are communicated without yelling— and then, if the yelling continues, leave. When the person does speak civilly, you can reward this behavior with your attention and goodwill.

Because you are with yourself more than with anyone else, it may be easier to modify your own behavior than someone else's. You may wish to reduce your nibbling, eliminate a smoking habit, or become more outgoing. Let's assume, for the sake of discussion, that you aren't studying enough. How can you increase the time you spend with your books? Some hints:

• *Analyze the situation.* Are there circumstances that keep you from studying, such as a friend who is always pressuring you to go out or a rock band that practices next door? If so, you need to change the discriminative stimuli in your environment during study periods. Try to find a comfortable, cheerful, quiet place. Not only will you concentrate better, but you may also have positive emotional responses to the environment that may generalize to the activity of studying.

• *Set realistic goals.* Goals should be demanding but achievable. If a goal is too vague, as in "I'm going to work harder," you don't know what action to take to reach it or how to know when you get there (what does "harder" mean?). If your goal is focused, as in "I am going to study two hours every evening instead of one, and read 25 pages instead of 15," you have specified both a course of action and a goal you can achieve (and reward!).

• *Reinforce getting started.* The hardest part of studying can be getting started. (This is true of many other activities, too, as writers, joggers, and taxpayers who prepare their own returns can tell you.) You might give yourself a small bit of candy or some other reward just for sitting down at your desk or, if you study at the library, reward yourself for getting there early.

• *Keep records.* Chart your progress in some way, perhaps by constructing a daily graph. This will keep you honest, and the progress you see on the graph will serve as a secondary reinforcer.

• *Don't punish yourself.* If you didn't study enough last week, don't brood about it or berate yourself with self-defeating thoughts, such as "I'll never be a good student" or "I'm a failure." Think about the coming week instead.

Above all, be patient. Shaping behavior is a creative skill that takes time to learn and apply. Like Rome, new habits cannot be built in a day.

SUMMARY

1) Research on learning has been heavily influenced by *behaviorism,* which accounts for behavior in terms of observable events without reference to such hypothetical mental entities as "mind" or "will." Behaviorists have focused on two types of *conditioning:* classical conditioning and operant conditioning.

Classical Conditioning

2) *Classical conditioning* was first studied by Russian physiologist Ivan Pavlov. In this type of learning, when a neutral stimulus is paired with an *unconditioned stimulus (US)* that elicits some reflexive *unconditioned response (UR),* the neutral stimulus comes to elicit a similar or related response. The neutral stimulus is then called a *conditioned stimulus (CS),* and the response it elicits is a *conditioned response (CR).* Nearly any kind of involuntary response can become a CR.

3) Many theorists believe that what an animal or person learns in classical conditioning is not just an association between the unconditioned and the conditioned stimulus, but information conveyed by one stimulus about another. They cite evidence that the neutral stimulus does not become a CS unless it reliably signals or predicts the US.

4) In *extinction,* the conditioned stimulus is repeatedly presented without the unconditioned stimulus, and the conditioned response eventually disappears. In *higher-order conditioning,* a neutral stimulus becomes a conditioned stimulus by being paired with an already established conditioned

stimulus. In *stimulus generalization,* after a stimulus becomes a conditioned stimulus for some response, other, similar stimuli may produce the same reaction. In *stimulus discrimination,* different responses are made to stimuli that resemble the conditioned stimulus in some way.

Classical Conditioning in Real Life

5) Classical conditioning may account for the acquisition of likes and dislikes, emotional responses to objects and events, and fears and phobias. John Watson showed how fears may be learned and then unlearned through a process of *counterconditioning.* Classical conditioning may also be involved in such aspects of drug addiction as tolerance and withdrawal.

Operant Conditioning

6) The basic principle of *operant conditioning* is that behavior becomes more likely to occur or less so, depending on its consequences. Responses in operant conditioning are generally not reflexive and are more complex than in classical conditioning. Research in this area is closely associated with B. F. Skinner.

7) In the Skinnerian analysis, a response ("operant") can lead to neutral, reinforcing, or punishing consequences. *Reinforcement* strengthens or increases the probability of a response. *Punishment* weakens or decreases the probability of a response. Reinforcement (and punishment) may be positive or negative. *Positive reinforcement* occurs when something pleasant follows a response. *Negative reinforcement* occurs when something unpleasant is removed. Reinforcement is called *primary* when the reinforcer is naturally reinforcing (e.g., because it satisfies a biological need) and *secondary* when the reinforcer has acquired its ability to strengthen a response through association with other reinforcers. A similar distinction is made for punishers.

8) Behaviorists have shown that extinction, stimulus generalization, and stimulus discrimination occur in operant, as well as in classical, conditioning. They also find that immediate consequences usually have a greater effect on a response than do delayed consequences.

9) The pattern of responding in operant conditioning depends in part on the *schedule of reinforcement. Continuous reinforcement* leads to the most rapid learning, but *intermittent,* or *partial,* reinforcement makes a response more resistant to extinction. One of the most common errors people make is to reward intermittently the responses they would like to eliminate.

10) *Shaping* is used to train behaviors with a low probability of occurring spontaneously. Reinforcers are given for *successive approximations* to the desired response, until the desired response is achieved.

11) Accidental or coincidental reinforcement can effectively strengthen behavior and can help account for both the learning and the persistence of superstitions.

Operant Conditioning in Real Life

12) *Behavior modification,* the application of conditioning principles, has been used successfully in many settings, often by applying a *token economy.* But reinforcement and punishment both have their pitfalls.

13) Punishment is sometimes effective in eliminating undesirable behavior. However, it is often administered inappropriately because of the emotion of the moment; it may produce rage and fear; its effects are often only temporary; it is hard to administer immediately; it conveys little information about what kind of behavior is desired; and it may bring attention that is rewarding. Extinction of undesirable behavior, combined with reinforcement of desired behavior, is generally preferable to the use of punishment. It is also important to understand the reasons for a person's misbehavior instead of simply trying to get rid of it without knowing why it occurs.

14) An exclusive reliance on *extrinsic reinforcement* can sometimes undermine the power of *intrinsic reinforcement.* But money and praise do not usually interfere with intrinsic pleasure when a person is rewarded for succeeding or making progress rather than for merely participating in an activity, or when a person is already extremely interested in the activity.

Social-Learning Theories

15) The 1960s and 1970s saw the increased influence of *social-learning theories,* which focus on the ways in which the environment, behavior, and a person's internalized motives and cognitions interact. Social-learning theorists emphasize *observational learning,* in which the learner imitates the behavior of a model; performance may

be either immediate or delayed (*latent learning*). These theorists also emphasize the role of people's perceptions and motivating beliefs in explaining behavior.

Behavior and the Mind: The Question of Insight

16) The tension between behaviorism and cognitive approaches to psychology can be seen in how the two approaches treat *insight,* learning that seems to occur suddenly and that involves the solving of a problem. Behaviorists believe insight can be understood in terms of the conditioning history of the organism. Cognitive psychologists believe that what is learned is knowledge rather than behavior. The behavioral and cognitive approaches are quite different, but many psychologists treat them as different levels of analysis and use concepts and techniques from both.

KEY TERMS

learning   261

behaviorism   261

conditioning   262

unconditioned stimulus (US)   263

unconditioned response (UR)   263

conditioned stimulus (CS)   263

conditioned response (CR)   263

classical conditioning   263

extinction (in classical conditioning)   265

spontaneous recovery   265

higher-order conditioning   266

stimulus generalization (in classical conditioning)   266

stimulus discrimination (in classical conditioning)   266

phobia   268

counterconditioning   268

operant conditioning   270

law of effect   271

free will versus determinism   271

reinforcement and reinforcers   272

punishment and punishers   272

instinctive drift   273

positive and negative reinforcement and punishment   273

primary reinforcers and punishers   274

secondary (conditioned) reinforcers and punishers   274

Skinner box   275

extinction (in operant conditioning)   276

stimulus generalization (in operant conditioning)   276

stimulus discrimination (in operant conditioning)   276

discriminative stimulus   276

stimulus control   276

continuous reinforcement   276

intermittent (partial) reinforcement   276

shaping   277

successive approximations   277

behavior modification   280

token economy   280

extrinsic versus intrinsic reinforcers   283

behavioral "ABCs"   285

social-learning theories   286

observational (vicarious) learning   286

latent learning   288

cognitive map   288

insight   289

LOOKING BACK

- *Why would a dog salivate when it sees a lightbulb or hears a buzzer, even though they are inedible? (pp. 263–264)*

- *How can classical conditioning help explain prejudice? (p. 266)*

- *If you have learned to fear collies, why might you also be scared of sheepdogs? (p. 266)*

- *If you eat licorice and then happen to get the flu, how might your taste for licorice change? (p. 267)*

- *Why do advertisers often include pleasant music and gorgeous scenery in ads for their products? (pp. 267–268)*

- *How would a classical-conditioning theorist explain your irrational fear of heights or mice? (p. 268)*

- *Why might a drug dose that is ordinarily safe kill you if you take it in a new place? (p. 269)*

- *What do praise and the cessation of nagging have in common? (pp. 273–274)*

- *What's the best way to discourage a friend from interrupting you while you're studying? (p. 277)*

- *How do trainers teach guide dogs to do the amazing things they do for their owners? (pp. 277–278)*

- *How can operant principles account for the popularity of good-luck charms? (pp. 278–279)*

- *Why do efforts to "crack down" on wrongdoers often go awry? (pp. 281–282)*

- *What's the best way to discourage a child from throwing tantrums? (p. 282)*

- *Why does paying children for good grades sometimes backfire? (pp. 283–284)*

- *How might watching violence on TV make (some) people more aggressive? (p. 287)*

- *Why do parents who yell at their children to be quiet tend to produce children who are yellers? (p. 287)*

- *Why do two people often learn different lessons from exactly the same experience? (pp. 288–289)*

- *Can an ape show "insight" into a problem? (pp. 289–290)*

- *Can a pigeon show insight? What would a behaviorist say? (p. 290)*

PSYCHOLOGY IN THE NEWS

Homeowner Fatally Shoots Exchange Student in Cultural Misunderstanding

Slain exchange student Yoshihiro Hattori posed with his new American friends after arriving in the United States.

BATON ROUGE, LA., NOVEMBER 1, 1992. A mistake over the address of a Halloween party yesterday had tragic consequences. Sixteen-year-old Japanese exchange student Yoshihiro Hattori and his friend Webb Haymaker stopped at the wrong house while looking for the party. When no one answered the doorbell, Hattori went to see if the party might be in the back yard. The homeowner, Bonnie Peairs, then opened the front door, saw Haymaker in his Halloween costume, and spotted Hattori running back toward her waving an object (which turned out to be a camera). She panicked and called for her husband to get his gun; Rodney Peairs then grabbed a loaded .44 Magnum and shouted at Yoshihiro to "freeze." The young student, not understanding the command, kept running, and Peairs shot him in the heart, killing him instantly.

Little more than a minute passed between the time that Yoshihiro Hattori rang the doorbell and the time that Rodney Peairs shot him to death.

How would you explain the actions taken by Bonnie and Rodney Peairs? A learning theorist might seek an explanation in their individual histories, in the role models of violence that all Americans see in the media, and in the ways that handguns literally trigger aggressive behavior. Similarly, researchers in the fields of *social psychology* and *cultural psychology* address the many puzzles of human behavior by emphasizing the external environment rather than internal personality dynamics or individual pathology. But social and cultural psychologists broaden our vision by examining the entire sociocultural context in which an individual lives. *Social* psychologists study how social roles, attitudes, relationships, and groups influence people to do things they would not necessarily do on their own—act bravely, mindlessly, aggressively, or even cruelly. *Cultural* psychologists study the origins of roles, attitudes, and group norms in people's larger cultural worlds—their ethnic, regional, and national communities.

Together, social and cultural psychology cover a lot of territory, from first impressions on meeting a stranger to international diplomacy. In this book, we have already reported on sociocultural influences on child-rearing practices, moral development, and intelligence test scores. In later chapters we will discuss other areas of sociocultural research, including love and attachment, social processes in psychotherapy, and the communication of emotion.

In this chapter, however, we will focus on the basic social and cultural forces that affect behavior and make human beings less independent than they might think. As you read, ask yourself whether *you* would ever "shoot now and ask questions later," as Rodney Peairs did. Could a social situation or cultural attitude ever induce you to behave in a way that violates your code of ethics? Would you vote to convict Rodney Peairs or acquit him, and how does your culture affect your answer?

When Bonnie Peairs took the witness stand, she wept. "There was no thinking involved," she said. "I wish I could have thought. If I could have just thought." An awareness of social and cultural influences might help us all to act more mindfully and think more critically.

consists of social **norms,** rules about how we are supposed to act, enforced by threats of punishment if we violate them and promises of reward if we follow them (Kerr, 1995). Norms are the conventions of everyday life that make interactions with other people predictable and orderly. Every culture has norms, passed from one generation to another, for just about everything in the human-made environment: for conducting courtships, for raising children, for making decisions, for behavior in public places. Some norms are matters of law, such as, "A person may not beat up another person, except in self-defense." Some are unspoken cultural understandings, such as, "A man may beat up another man who insults his masculinity." And some are tiny, invisible regulations that people learn to follow unconsciously, such as, "You may not sing at the top of your lungs on a public bus."

Within any society, people fill a variety of social **roles,** positions that are regulated by norms about how people in those positions should behave. Gender roles define the proper behavior for a man and a woman. Occupational roles determine the correct behavior for a manager and an employee, a professor and a student. Family roles set tasks for parent and child, husband and wife.

Most people follow their culture's prescriptions without being conscious of them. When one of these prescriptions is violated, however, a person is likely to feel extremely uncomfortable. Other people may respond, whether intentionally or not, by making the violator feel guilty or inadequate. For instance, in your family, whose job is it to buy gifts for parents, send greeting cards to friends, organize parties, prepare the food, remember an aunt's birthday, and call friends to see how they're doing? Chances are you are thinking of a woman. These duties are considered part of the woman's role in most cultures, and women are usually blamed if they are not carried out (di Leonardo, 1987; Lott & Maluso, 1993). Similarly,

What's Ahead

- *How do social rules guide behavior—and what is likely to happen when you violate them?*

- *Do you have to be mean or disturbed to inflict pain on someone just because an authority tells you to?*

- *How can ordinary college students be transformed into sadistic prison guards?*

- *How can people be "entrapped" into violating their moral principles?*

ROLES AND RULES

norms (social)
Social conventions that regulate human life, including explicit laws and implicit cultural standards.

role
A given social position that is governed by a set of norms for proper behavior.

"We are all fragile creatures entwined in a cobweb of social constraints," social psychologist Stanley Milgram once said. The cobweb he referred to

Get Involved

Either alone or with a friend, try a mild form of "norm violation"—nothing alarming, obscene, dangerous, or offensive. For example, stand backward in line at the grocery store or cafeteria; sit right next to a stranger in the library or at a movie, even when other seats are available; sing or hum loudly for a couple of minutes in a public place; face the back wall of an elevator instead of the doors. Notice the reactions of onlookers, as well as your own feelings, while you violate this norm. (If you do this exercise with someone else, one of you can be the "violator" and the other can note the responses of onlookers; then switch places.) Was it easy to do this exercise? Why or why not?

Many roles in modern life require us to give up individuality, as conveyed by this dazzling image of white-suited referees at the Seoul Olympics. If each referee behaved out of role, the games could not continue. When is it appropriate to suppress your personal desires for the sake of the role, and when not?

what is likely to happen to a man who reveals his fears and worries although his culture's male gender role condemns such revelations as signs of weakness? Men who deviate from the masculine role by disclosing their emotions and fears are frequently regarded by both sexes as being "too feminine" and "poorly adjusted" (Peplau & Gordon, 1985; Taffel, 1990).

Naturally, people bring their own personalities and interests to the roles they play. Although two actresses who play the role of Cleopatra must follow the same script, you can bet that Kate Winslet and Whitney Houston will have different interpretations. In the same way, you will impose your own interpretation on the role of friend, parent, student, or employer. Nonetheless, the requirements of a social role affect nearly everyone who fills it, and they may even cause you to behave in ways that shatter your fundamental sense of who you are. We turn now to two classic and controversial studies that illuminate the power of social roles in our lives.

The Obedience Study

In the early 1960s, Stanley Milgram (1963, 1974) designed a study that was to become one of the most famous in all of psychology. Milgram wanted to know how many people would obey an authority figure when directly ordered to violate their own ethical standards. Participants in the study thought they were taking part in an experiment on the effects of punishment on learning.

Each was assigned, apparently at random, to the role of "teacher." Another person, introduced as a fellow volunteer, played the role of "learner." Whenever the learner, seated in an adjoining room, made an error in reciting a list of word pairs he was supposed to have memorized, the teacher had to give him an electric shock by depressing a lever on a machine (see Figure 9.1). With each error, the voltage (marked from 0 to 450) was to be increased by another 15 volts. The shock levels on the machine were labeled from SLIGHT SHOCK to DANGER—SEVERE SHOCK and, finally, ominously, XXX. In reality, the learners were confederates of Milgram and did not receive any shocks, but none of the teachers ever realized this during the experiment. The actor–victims played their parts convincingly: As the study continued, they shouted in pain and pleaded to be released, all according to a prearranged script.

When Milgram first designed this study, he asked a number of psychiatrists, students, and middle-class adults how many people they thought would "go all the way" to XXX on orders from the experimenter. The psychiatrists predicted that most people would refuse to go beyond 150 volts, the point at which the learner first demanded to be freed, and that only one person in a thousand, someone who was emotionally disturbed and sadistic, would administer the highest voltage. The nonprofessionals agreed with this prediction, and all of them said that they personally would disobey early in the experiment.

That's not the way the results turned out, however. Every single subject administered some

Figure 9.1
The Milgram Obedience Experiment
On the left is Milgram's original shock machine; in 1963, it looked pretty ominous. On the right, the "learner" is being strapped into his chair by the experimenter and the "teacher."

shock to the learner, and about two-thirds of the participants, of all ages and from all walks of life, obeyed to the fullest extent. Many protested to the experimenter, but they backed down when he merely asserted, "The experiment requires that you continue." They obeyed no matter how much the victim shouted for them to stop and no matter how painful the shocks seemed to be. They obeyed even when they themselves were anguished about the pain they believed they were causing. They obeyed even as they wept and implored the experimenter to release them from further participation. As Milgram (1974) noted, participants would "sweat, tremble, stutter, bite their lips, groan, and dig their fingernails into their flesh"—but still they obeyed.

More than 1,000 participants at several American universities eventually went through the Milgram study. Most of them, men and women equally, inflicted what they thought were dangerous amounts of shock to another person (Blass, 1993). Researchers in at least eight other countries have also found high percentages of obedience, ranging to more than 90 percent in Spain and the Netherlands (Meeus & Raaijmakers, 1995; Smith & Bond, 1993/1994).

Milgram and his team subsequently set up several variations of the study to determine the circumstances under which people might disobey the experimenter. They found that virtually nothing the victim did or said changed the likelihood of the person's compliance—even when the victim said he had a heart condition, screamed in agony, or stopped responding entirely as if he had collapsed. However, people *were* more likely to disobey under the following conditions:

- *When the experimenter left the room.* Many people then subverted authority by giving low levels of

shock while reporting that they had followed orders.

- *When the victim was right there in the room,* and the teacher had to administer the shock directly to the victim's body.

- *When two experimenters issued conflicting demands* to continue the experiment or to stop at once. In this case, no one kept inflicting shock.

- *When the person issuing the orders was an ordinary man,* apparently another volunteer, instead of the authoritative experimenter.

- *When the subject worked with peers who refused to go further.* Seeing someone else rebel gave participants the courage to disobey.

Obedience, Milgram concluded, was more a function of the situation than of the particular personalities of the participants. "The key to [their] behavior," Milgram (1974) summarized, "lies not in pent-up anger or aggression but in the nature of their relationship to authority. They have given themselves to the authority; they see themselves as instruments for the execution of his wishes; once so defined, they are unable to break free."

The Milgram experiment has had its critics. Some consider it unethical because people were kept in the dark about what was really happening until the session was over (of course, telling them in advance would have invalidated the findings) and because many suffered emotional pain (Milgram countered that they wouldn't have felt pain if they had disobeyed instructions). Others question the conclusion that the situation often overrules personality; they note that some personality traits, such as hostility and authoritarianism, do predict obedience to authority in real life (Blass, 1993).

Some psychologists also object strenuously to the parallel Milgram drew between the behavior of his experimental volunteers and the brutality of Nazi doctors, concentration-camp executioners, and soldiers who massacre civilians. As John Darley (1995) noted, the people in Milgram's study obeyed only when the experimenter was hovering right there, and many of them felt enormous discomfort and conflict; in contrast, the defining characteristic of those who commit atrocities is that they do so without supervision by authorities, without external pressure, and without feelings of anguish.

Nevertheless, this experiment has had a tremendous influence on public awareness of the dangers of uncritical obedience. As Darley himself observed, "Milgram shows us the beginning of a path by means of which ordinary people, in the grip of social forces, become the origins of atrocities in the real world."

The Prison Study

Imagine that one day, as you are walking home from school, a police car pulls up. Two uniformed officers get out, arrest you, and take you to a prison cell. There you are stripped of your clothes, sprayed with delousing fluid, assigned a uniform, photographed with a prison number, and put behind bars. You feel a bit queasy, but you are not panicked because you have agreed to play the part of prisoner for two weeks and your arrest is merely part of the script. Your prison cell, while apparently authentic, is located in the basement of a university building.

So began an effort to discover what happens when ordinary college students take on the roles of prisoners and guards (Haney, Banks, & Zimbardo, 1973). The young men who volunteered for this study were paid a nice daily fee. They were randomly assigned to be prisoners or guards, but they were given no instructions about how to behave. The results were dramatic. Within a short time, the prisoners became distressed, helpless, and panicky. They developed emotional symptoms and physical ailments. Some became depressed and apathetic; others became rebellious and angry. After a few days, half of the prisoners begged to be let out. They were more than willing to forfeit their pay to gain an early release.

Within an equally short time, the guards adjusted to their new power. Some tried to be nice, helping the prisoners and doing little favors for them. Some were "tough but fair," holding strictly to "the rules." But about a third became tyrannical. Although they had complete freedom to use any method to maintain order, they almost always chose to be abusive, even when the prisoners were not resisting in any way. One guard, unaware that he was being observed by the researchers, paced the corridor while the prisoners were sleeping, pounding his nightstick into his hand. Another put a prisoner in solitary confinement (a small closet) and tried to keep him there all night, concealing this information from the researchers, who, he thought, were "too soft" on the prisoners. Many guards were willing to work overtime without additional pay.

The researchers, who had not expected such a speedy and terrifying transformation of normal college students, ended this study after only six days. The prisoners were relieved by this decision, but most of the guards were disappointed. They had enjoyed their short-lived authority.

Critics of this research maintain that you can't learn much from such an artificial setup. They argue that the volunteers already knew, from movies, TV, and games, how they were supposed to behave. They acted their parts to the hilt, in order to have fun and not disappoint the researchers. Their behavior was no more surprising than if young men had been dressed in football gear and then had been found to be willing to bruise each other. For all its drama, say the critics, the study provided no new information (Festinger, 1980).

Philip Zimbardo, who designed the prison study, responds that this dramatization illustrated the power of roles in a way that no ordinary lab experiment could. After all, real prisoners and

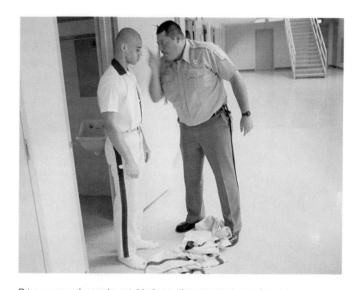

Prisoners and guards quickly learn their respective roles, as they have done at this correctional facility.

guards know their parts, too. Moreover, if the students were having so much fun, why did the prisoners beg for early release? Why did the guards lose sight of the "game" and behave as if it were a real job? Twenty-five years after the prison study was done, Zimbardo (1996) reflected on its contribution to psychology and to public awareness of how situations can outweigh personality in influencing behavior. The study showed, said Zimbardo, that roles can transform people as profoundly as the potion that transformed Dr. Jekyll into Mr. Hyde, especially when people cannot call upon past experience to guide their behavior and when their own habitual ways of behaving are not reinforced.

The Power of Roles

The two imaginative studies we have described vividly demonstrate the power of social roles and obligations to influence the behavior of individuals. The behavior of the prisoners and guards varied—some prisoners were more rebellious than others, some guards were more abusive than others—but ultimately, what the students did depended on the roles they were assigned. And whatever their personal traits, when people in the Milgram experiment believed they had to follow the legitimate orders of authority, most of them put their private values aside.

Obedience, of course, is not always harmful or bad. A certain amount of routine compliance with rules is necessary in any group, and obedience to authority can have constructive as well as destructive results (Darley, 1995). A nation could not operate if all its citizens ignored traffic signals, cheated on their taxes, dumped garbage wherever they chose, or assaulted each other. An organization could not function if its members came to work only when they felt like it. But obedience also has a darker aspect. Throughout history, the plea "I was only following orders" has been offered to excuse actions carried out on behalf of orders that were foolish, destructive, or illegal. The writer C. P. Snow once observed that "more hideous crimes have been committed in the name of obedience than in the name of rebellion."

Most people follow orders because of the obvious consequences of disobedience: They can be suspended from school, fired from their jobs, or arrested. They may also obey because they respect the authority who is giving the orders; because

they want to be liked; or because they hope to gain advantages. But what about all those obedient people in Milgram's experiment who felt they were doing wrong, who wished they were free, but who could not untangle themselves from the cobweb of social constraints? Why do people obey when it is not in their interests, or when obedience requires them to ignore their own values or even commit a crime?

Social psychologists Herbert Kelman and Lee Hamilton (1989) have studied "crimes of obedience," ranging from military massacres of civilians to bureaucratic crimes such as Watergate (in which Richard Nixon and his advisors tried to cover up the attempted theft of files from a Democratic headquarters) and the Iran–Contra scandal (in which Ronald Reagan's administration sold arms to Iran in order to unlawfully fund the Contra forces in Nicaragua). They and other researchers draw our attention to several factors that cause people to obey when they would rather not:

1. *Legitimization of the authority* allows people to absolve themselves of accountability for their actions. In Milgram's study, many of those who administered the highest levels of shock relinquished responsibility to the experimenter. A 37-year-old welder explained that the experimenter was responsible for any pain the victim might suffer "for the simple reason that I was paid for doing this. I had to follow orders." In contrast, individuals who refused to give high levels of shock took responsibility for their actions and refused to grant the authority legitimacy. "One of the things I think is very cowardly," said a 32-year-old engineer, "is to try to shove the responsibility onto someone else. See, if I now turned around and said, 'It's your fault . . . it's not mine,' I would call that cowardly" (Milgram, 1974).

2. *Routinization* is the process of defining an activity in terms of routine duties and roles so that your behavior becomes normalized, a job to be done, and there is little opportunity to raise doubts or ethical questions. In the Milgram study, some people became so fixated on the "learning task" that they shut out any moral concerns about the learner's demands to be let out. Routinization is typically the mechanism by which governments get citizens to aid and abet programs of genocide: German bureaucrats kept meticulous records of every Nazi victim, and in Cambodia, the Khmer Rouge recorded the names and histories of the millions of victims they tortured and

The routinization of horror enables people to commit or collaborate in atrocities. More than 16,000 political prisoners were tortured and killed at Tuol Sleng prison by members of Cambodia's Khmer Rouge, during the regime of Pol Pot. Prison authorities kept meticulous records and photos of each victim in order to make their barbarous activities seem mundane and normal. This man, Ing Pech, was one of only seven survivors, spared because he had skills useful to his captors. He now runs a memorial museum at the prison.

killed. "I am not a violent man," said Sous Thy, one of the clerks who recorded these names, to a reporter from the *New York Times*. "I was just making lists."

3. *The rules of good manners* smooth over the rough spots of social interaction, making relationships and civilization possible; but once people are caught in what they perceive to be legitimate roles and are obeying an authority, good manners ensnare them into further obedience. Most people don't like to rock the boat, challenge the experts, or appear to be rude because they know they will be disliked for doing so (Collins, 1993). And many lack the words to explain or justify disobedience. One woman in the Milgram study kept apologizing to the experimenter, trying not to offend him with her worries for the victim: "Do I go right to the end, sir? I hope there's nothing wrong with him there." (She did go right to the end.) A man repeatedly protested and questioned the experimenter, but he too obeyed, even when the victim had apparently collapsed in pain. "He thinks he is killing someone," Milgram (1974) commented, "yet he uses the language of the tea table."

4. *Entrapment* is a process in which individuals increase their commitment to a course of action in order to justify their investment in it (Brockner & Rubin, 1985). The first steps of entrapment pose no difficult choices, but one step leads to another, and before you realize it, you have become committed to a course of action that poses problems, and it is hard to free yourself. In Milgram's study, once participants had given a 15-volt shock, they had committed themselves to the experiment.

The next level was "only" 30 volts. Unless they resisted the authority soon afterward, they were likely to go on to administer what they believed were dangerously strong shocks. At that point, it was difficult to explain a sudden decision to quit (Modigliani & Rochat, 1995).

A chilling study of entrapment was conducted with 25 men who had served in the Greek military police during the authoritarian regime that ended in 1974 (Haritos-Fatouros, 1988). A psychologist who interviewed the men identified the steps used in training them to use torture when questioning prisoners. First the men were ordered to stand guard outside the interrogation cells. Then they stood guard in the detention rooms, where they observed the torture of prisoners. Then they "helped" beat up prisoners. Once they had obediently followed these orders and became actively involved, the torturers found their actions easier to carry out.

Many people expect solutions to moral problems to fall into two clear categories, with right on one side and wrong on the other. Yet in everyday life, as in the Milgram study, people often set out on a path that is morally ambiguous, only to find that they have traveled a long way toward violating their own principles. From Greece's cruel torturers to the Khmer Rouge's dutiful clerks to Milgram's "well-meaning" volunteers, people share the difficult task of drawing a line beyond which they will not go. Those who mindlessly succumb to the power of roles are less likely to hear the voice of conscience.

entrapment

A gradual process in which individuals escalate their commitment to a course of action to justify their investment of time, money, or effort.

??? QUICK QUIZ

Step into your role as student to answer these questions.

1. About what percentage of the people in Milgram's obedience study administered the highest level of shock? (a) two-thirds, (b) one-half, (c) one-third, (d) one-tenth

2. Which of the following actions by the "learner" reduced the likelihood of being shocked by the "teacher" in Milgram's study? (a) protesting noisily, (b) screaming in pain, (c) complaining of having a heart ailment, (d) nothing he did made a difference

3. In the Milgram and Zimbardo studies, the participants' behavior was predicted most strongly by (a) their personality traits, (b) the dictates of conscience, (c) their assigned roles, (d) norms codified in law.

4. Suppose that a friend of yours, who is moving, asks you to bring over a few boxes. Since you are there anyway, he asks you to fill them with books, and before you know it, you have packed up his entire kitchen, living room, and bedroom. What social-psychological process is at work here?

5. Sam is having dinner with a group of fellow students when one of his friends tells a joke about how dumb women are. Sam is angry and disgusted but doesn't say anything. What social-psychological concept might help explain his silence?

Answers:

1. a 2. d 3. c 4. entrapment 5. the rules of good manners (and perhaps Sam also lacks the words to protest effectively)

What's Ahead

- *In what ways do people balance their ethnic identity and membership in the larger culture?*

- *What's one of the most common mistakes people make when explaining the behavior of others?*

- *What is the "Big Lie"—and why does it work so well?*

- *What's the difference between ordinary techniques of persuasion and the coercive techniques used by cults?*

IDENTITY, ATTRIBUTIONS, AND ATTITUDES

social cognition

An area in social psychology concerned with social influences on thought, memory, perception, and other cognitive processes.

social identity

The part of a person's self-concept that is based on identification with a nation, culture, or ethnic group or with gender or other roles in society.

Social psychologists are interested not only in what people do in social situations, but also in what goes on in their heads while they're doing it. Researchers in the area of **social cognition** examine how the social environment and relationships influence thoughts, beliefs, and memories; and how people's perceptions of themselves and one another affect their relationships (A. Fiske & Haslam, 1996). We will consider three important topics in this area: self-identity, attributions (explanations) about behavior, and the formation of attitudes.

Self-identity

Each of us, while growing up, develops a *personal identity,* a sense of who we are that is based on our own unique traits and history. In addition, we develop **social identities,** aspects of our self-concepts that are based on nationality, ethnicity, religion, and social roles (Brewer & Gardner, 1996; Hogg & Abrams, 1988). In Chapter 2, we saw that *collectivist cultures* and *individualist cultures* differ in how they balance the independence of the individual with social harmony within groups. But in all cultures, including individualist ones, social identities are an important part of people's self-concepts because they provide a feeling of place and position in the world. Without them, most of us would feel like loose marbles rolling around in an unconnected universe.

Table 9.1	**Patterns of Ethnic Identity and Acculturation**		

		Ethnic identity is	
		Strong	**Weak**
Acculturation is	**Strong**	Bicultural	Assimilated
	Weak	Separatist	Marginal

In multicultural societies such as the United States, different social identities sometimes collide. In particular, people often face the dilemma of balancing an **ethnic identity,** a close identification with a religious or ethnic group, with **acculturation,** an identification with the dominant culture (Cross, 1971; Phinney, 1996; Spencer & Dornbusch, 1990). As Table 9.1 shows, four outcomes are possible, depending on whether ethnic identity is strong or weak, and whether identification with the larger culture is strong or weak (Berry, 1994; Phinney, 1990).

People who are *bicultural* have strong ties both to their ethnicity and to the larger culture: They say, "I am proud of my ethnic heritage, but I identify just as much with my new country." They can alternate easily between their culture of origin and the majority culture, slipping into the customs and language of each, as circumstances dictate (LaFromboise, Coleman, & Gerton, 1993). People who choose *assimilation* have weak feelings of ethnicity but a strong sense of acculturation: Their attitude, for example, might be "I'm an American, period." *Ethnic separatists* have a strong sense of ethnic identity but weak feelings of acculturation: They may say, "My ethnicity comes first; if I join the mainstream, I'm betraying my origins." And some people feel *marginal,* connected to neither their ethnicity nor the dominant culture: They may say, "I'm an individual and don't identify with any group" or "I don't belong anywhere."

Some of the conflicts between cultural groups in North America stem from disagreements about how (or even whether) acculturation and ethnic identity should be balanced. These tensions are reflected in the touchy subject of what groups should be called. Because this issue is understandably emotional for many people, they fail to question their own assumptions—and fail to realize that even within ethnic groups, there are different views. For example, the label *Hispanic* is used by the U.S. government to include all Spanish-speaking groups, but many "Hispanics" dislike the term. Some prefer *Latino* and *Latina,* or, for Mexican-Americans, *Chicano* and *Chicana;* others prefer national-origin labels such as Cuban or Cuban-American, or just

Thinking Critically About Ethnic Labels

These children are observing the December festival of Kwanza, an African-American holiday that celebrates traditional African spiritual values. In a culturally diverse society, many people maintain a strong attachment to their ethnic heritage.

ethnic identity

A person's identification with a racial, religious, or ethnic group.

acculturation

The process by which members of minority groups come to identify with and feel part of the mainstream culture.

The tension in America between ethnic identity and acculturation was apparent during the 1996 Hispanic March on Washington, when thousands of Hispanic Americans demanded rights for immigrants—while waving flags from their countries of origin. To the demonstrators, the flags symbolized pride in their heritage, but many other Americans regarded the flags as evidence of the demonstrators' lack of commitment to the United States. What would be your interpretation?

American (de la Garza et al., 1992). Similarly, although *African-American* is now widely accepted, some blacks reject the term because they feel no special kinship to Africa. For that matter, not all white Americans want to be called Anglos, which refers to a British heritage, or European-American, as if all European countries, from Greece to Norway, France to Poland, were the same. And the growing numbers of people of multiethnic backgrounds are exasperated by society's efforts to squeeze them into a single category—which is why the U.S. government has finally decided to include a multiethnic category in its census. Debates about ethnic labels, and about the proper balance between ethnicity and acculturation, are likely to continue, as ethnic groups struggle to define their place in a medley of cultures.

attribution theory

The theory that people are motivated to explain their own and other people's' behavior by attributing causes of that behavior to a situation or a disposition.

fundamental attribution error

The tendency, in explaining other people's behavior, to overestimate personality factors and underestimate the influence of the situation.

Attributions

Detective stories are known as "whodunits," but real life is a "*why*dunit": Everyone wants to know *why* people do what they do. Is it something in people's genes, their upbringing, or their current circumstances? According to **attribution theory,** the explanations we make of our own behavior and the behavior of others generally fall into two categories. When we make a *situational attribution,* we are identifying the cause of an action as something in the environment: "Joe stole the money because his family is starving." When we make a *dispositional attribution,* we are identifying the cause of an action as something in the person, such as a trait or a motive: "Joe stole the money because he is a born thief."

Social psychologists have discovered some of the conditions in which people prefer situational or dispositional attributions. For example, when people are trying to find reasons for someone else's behavior, one of the most common mistakes they make is to overestimate personality factors and underestimate the influence of the situation (Nisbett & Ross, 1980). This tendency has been called the **fundamental attribution error.** Were the hundreds of people who obeyed Milgram's experimenters sadistic by nature? Were the student guards in the prison study basically mean and the prisoners basically cowardly? Those who think so are committing the fundamental attribution error.

People are especially likely to overlook situational attributions when they are distracted or preoccupied and don't have time to ask themselves, for example, "Why, exactly, *is* Aurelia behaving like a dork today?" Instead, they leap to the easiest attribution, which is dispositional: Aurelia simply has a dorky personality.

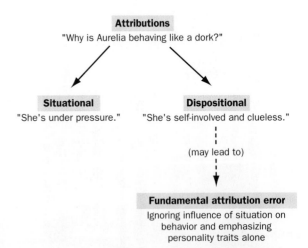

So powerful is this bias that people will often make a dispositional attribution even when they know that a person had no choice about how to act in a particular setting (Taylor, Peplau, & Sears, 1997).

The fundamental attribution error is especially prevalent in Western nations, where middle-class people tend to believe that individuals are responsible for their own actions. In countries such as India, where everyone is deeply embedded in caste and family networks, and in Japan, China, and Hong Kong, where people are more group oriented than in the West, people are more likely to recognize situational constraints on behavior (Lee, Hallahan, & Herzog, 1996; Morris & Peng, 1994). Thus if someone is behaving oddly, makes a mistake at work, or plays badly in a soccer match, an Indian or Chinese, unlike a Westerner, is more likely to make a situational attribution of the person's behavior ("He's under pressure") than a dispositional one ("He's incompetent").

Westerners do not always prefer dispositional attributions, however. When it comes to explaining their *own* behavior, they often have a **self-serving bias:** They tend to choose attributions that are favorable to them, taking credit for their good actions (a dispositional attribution) but letting the situation account for their bad ones. For instance, most Westerners, when angry, will say, "I am furious for good reason—this situation is intolerable." They are less likely to say, "I am furious because I am an ill-tempered grinch." On the other hand, if they do something admirable, such as donating money to charity, they are likely to attribute their motives to a personal disposition ("I'm so generous") instead of the situation ("That guy on the phone pressured me into it").

Like the fundamental attribution error, the self-serving bias is more common in some situations and cultures than in others. For example, in Japan, heads of companies are expected to take responsibility not only for their own failings, but also for the failings of their employees or products—and they do (Hamilton & Sanders, 1992; Markus & Kitayama, 1991). In the United States, in contrast, the common practice is for heads of corporations to get huge salaries and bonuses even when the company is doing poorly, and to blame the economy, government policies, or their employees if something goes wrong. (Of course, many Americans also deny responsibility for their mistakes because they fear lawsuits.)

People's attributions are also affected by the need to believe that the world is fair, that good people are rewarded and villains punished. According to the **just-world hypothesis** (Lerner, 1980), the belief in a just world helps people make sense out of senseless events and feel safe in the presence of threatening events. It often leads to a

dispositional attribution called *blaming the victim.* If a friend loses his job, if a woman is raped, if a prisoner is tortured, it is reassuring to think that they all must have done something to deserve what happened, or at least to cause it. This kind of attribution was apparent in the Milgram study: Many of the "teachers" spoke harshly of the learner. "Such comments as, 'He was so stupid and stubborn he deserved to get shocked,' were common," wrote Milgram (1974).

Of course, most human actions are determined both by personality and by environment. Therefore, attributing someone else's behavior to a disposition, or explaining your own behavior in terms of noble motives, is not always an error. The point to keep in mind is that attributions, whether they are accurate or not, have important consequences for decisions, actions, emotions, and everyday relations. Happy couples, for example, tend to attribute their partners' occasional lapses to something in the situation ("Poor Harold is under a lot of stress at work"), whereas unhappy couples tend to make dispositional attributions ("Harold is a thoughtless, selfish skunk") (Fincham & Bradbury, 1993; Karney et al., 1994). As you can imagine, your attributions about your partner will make a big difference in how the two of you get along—and how long you'll put up with the person!

Attitudes

People hold attitudes about all sorts of things—politics, people, food, children, movies, sports heroes, you name it. An *attitude* is a relatively stable opinion containing a cognitive element (perceptions and beliefs about the topic) and an emotional element (feelings about the topic, which can range from negative and hostile to positive and loving).

Where Do Attitudes Come From?   Most people think their attitudes are based on reasoned conclusions about how things work. Sometimes, of course, that's true. But social psychologists have found that some attitudes are a result of not thinking at all. They are a result of conformity, habit, rationalization, economic self-interest, and many subtle social and environmental influences.

Some attitudes, for example, arise by virtue of the *cohort effect.* Each generation, or age cohort, has its own experiences and economic concerns, and therefore its own characteristic opinions about the world. The ages of 16 to 24 appear to be critical for the formation of these attitudes; a

self-serving bias

The tendency, in explaining one's own behavior, to take credit for one's good actions and rationalize one's mistakes.

just-world hypothesis

The notion that many people need to believe that the world is fair and that justice is served; that bad people are punished and good people rewarded.

survey of the American population found that the major political events and social changes that occur during these years make deeper impressions and exert a more lasting influence than those that happen later in a person's life (Schuman & Scott, 1989). Some of the key events that have affected American generational cohorts in this century include the Great Depression (1930s), World War II (1940s), the dropping of the atomic bomb on Hiroshima (1945), the rise of the civil rights movement (1950s–1960s), the assassination of John F. Kennedy (1963), the Vietnam War (1965–1973), the rebirth of the women's rights movement (1970s), and the legalization of abortion (1973). People who were between 16 and 24 when these events occurred regard them as "peak memories" that have shaped their political philosophy, values, and attitudes about life. (What do you think might be the critical generational events affecting the attitudes of your own cohort?)

Psychologists have argued for years about which comes first, attitudes or behavior. Of course, attitudes often dispose people to behave in certain ways (Kraus, 1995); if you have a positive attitude toward martial-arts movies, you'll go to as many as you can, and if you hate them, you'll probably stay away from them. But it also works the other way around: Changing behavior can lead to a change in attitude because the new behavior alters a person's knowledge or experience. Suppose you dislike exercise and have always avoided it, but your friend persuades you to begin jogging with her. Once you get the hang of it, you may find that you enjoy it and that your attitude has completely changed.

A change in behavior may also lead to a change in attitudes because of **cognitive dissonance,** which we discussed in Chapter 6. Cognitive dissonance is the uncomfortable feeling that occurs when two attitudes, or an attitude and behavior, are in conflict (are dissonant). People are often motivated to resolve this dissonance by changing their attitudes. For example, if a politician or celebrity you admire does something immoral or illegal, you can reduce the dissonance by changing your attitude toward the person ("Guess he's not such a swell guy after all") or toward the person's behavior ("It's not so bad; everyone does it").

Friendly Persuasion.   All around you, every day, people are trying to get you to change your attitudes. One weapon they use is the drip, drip, drip of a repeated idea. Repeated exposure even to a nonsense syllable such as *zug* is enough to make a person feel more positive toward it (Zajonc, 1968). The effectiveness of familiarity has long been known to politicians and advertisers: Repeat something often enough, even the basest lie, and eventually the public will believe it. Indeed, the Nazis called this phenomenon the "Big Lie." Its formal name is the **validity effect.**

In a series of experiments, Hal Arkes and his associates demonstrated how the validity effect operates (Arkes, 1991; Arkes, Boehm, & Xu, 1991; Boehm, 1994). In a typical study, people read a list of statements, such as "Mercury has a higher boiling point than copper" or "Over 400 Hollywood films were produced in 1948." The participants had to rate each statement for its validity, where "1" meant that the rater thought the statement was definitely false and "7" that it was definitely true. A week or two later, they again rated the validity of some of these statements and also rated others they hadn't seen previously. The result: Mere repetition increased the perception that the familiar statements were true. The same effect also

cognitive dissonance
A state of tension that occurs when a person simultaneously holds two cognitions that are psychologically inconsistent, or when a person's belief is incongruent with his or her behavior.

validity effect
The tendency of people to believe that a statement is true or valid simply because it has been repeated many times.

LIFESTYLE

Lounging: *Have an hour? Make it happy hour.*

Young Fogies

Bored with the present and uneasy about the future, Gen X toasts the good old days

Each age group has a generational identity that stems from shared experiences and values. What, if any, are the defining experiences of "Generation X," those who are in their twenties today, or of the as-yet-nameless generation of those who are now in their teens? The news media keep trying to find the answer!

occurred for unverifiable opinions (e.g., "At least 75 percent of all politicians are basically dishonest"), opinions that people initially felt were true, and even opinions that they initially felt were false. "Note that no attempt has been made to persuade," wrote Arkes (1991). "No supporting arguments are offered. We just have subjects rate the statements. Mere repetition seems to increase rated validity. This is scary."

Another effective technique for getting people to change their minds is to have your arguments presented by someone who is admired or attractive—which is why advertisements are full of beautiful models, sports heroes, and "experts" (Cialdini, 1993). Persuaders may also try to link their message with a good feeling. In one classic study, students who were given peanuts and Pepsi while listening to a speaker's point of view were more likely to be convinced by it than were students who listened without the pleasant munchies and soft drinks (Janis, Kaye, & Kirschner, 1965). Perhaps this explains why so much business is conducted over lunch, and so many courtships over dinner!

In sum, here are 3 good ways to affect attitudes:

Effective Ways to Influence Attitudes

- Repetition of an idea or assertion (the validity effect)
- Endorsement by an admired or attractive person
- Association of the message with a good feeling

In contrast, the emotion of fear can cause people to resist arguments that are in their own best interest (Pratkanis & Aronson, 1992). Fear tactics are often used to try to persuade people to quit smoking or abusing other drugs, drive only when sober, use condoms, check for signs of cancer, and prepare for earthquakes. However, fear works only if people become moderately anxious, not scared to death, *and* if the message also provides information about how to avoid the danger (Leventhal & Nerenz, 1982). When messages about a potential disaster are too terrifying and when people believe that they can do nothing to avoid it, they tend to deny the danger.

Coercive Persuasion. Sometimes, efforts to change attitudes go beyond exposing people to a new idea and persuading them to accept it. The

Would this ad keep you from drinking and driving? Ads that arouse fear often backfire. Successful campaigns to prevent drunk driving include increased penalties, efforts to change social norms by making drunk driving "uncool," promoting the use of designated drivers, and providing other transportation, such as free cab rides.

manipulator uses harsh tactics, not just hoping that people will change their minds, but attempting to force them to. These tactics are sometimes referred to as *brainwashing,* a term first used during the Korean War to describe techniques used on American prisoners of war to get them to collaborate with their Chinese Communist captors and to endorse anti-American propaganda. Most psychologists, however, prefer the phrase *coercive persuasion.* "Brainwashing," they argue, implies that a person has a sudden change of mind and is unaware of what is happening. 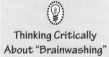 *Thinking Critically About "Brainwashing"* It sounds mysterious and powerful. In fact, the methods involved are neither mysterious nor unusual. The difference between "persuasion" and "brainwashing" is often only a matter of degree and the observer's bias, just as a group that is a crazy cult to one person may be a group of devoutly religious people to another.

How, then, might we distinguish coercive persuasion from the usual techniques of persuasion that occur in daily life? Studies of religious, political, and other cults have identified some of the processes by which individuals can be coerced by these groups (Galanter, 1989; Mithers, 1994; Ofshe & Watters, 1994; Singer, Temerlin, & Langone, 1990; Zimbardo & Leippe, 1991):

1. *The person is put under physical or emotional distress.* The individual may not be allowed to eat, sleep, or exercise; may be isolated in a dark room with no stimulation or food; or may be induced into a trancelike state through repetitive chanting, hypnosis, or deep relaxation.

2. *The person's problems are defined simplistically, and simple answers are offered repeatedly.* There are as many of these answers as there are persuasive groups. Here are some actual examples: Are you afraid or unhappy? It all stems from the pain of being born. Are you worried about homeless earthquake victims? It's not your problem; victims are responsible for everything that happens to them. Are you struggling financially? It's your fault for not wanting to be rich fervently enough.

3. *The leader offers unconditional love, acceptance, and attention.* A new recruit may be given a "love bath" from the group—constant praise, support, applause, and affection. Positive emotions of euphoria and well-being are generated. In exchange, the leader demands everyone's attachment, adoration, and idealization.

4. *A new identity based on the group is created.* The recruit is told that he or she is part of the chosen, the elite, the redeemed. To foster this new identity, many cults have their members wear identifying clothes or eat special diets, and they assign each member a new name. All members of the Philadelphia group MOVE were given the last name "Africa"; all members of the Church of Armageddon took the last name "Israel."

5. *The person is subjected to entrapment.* At first, the person agrees only to small things, but gradually the demands become greater: for example, to spend a weekend with the group, then take weekly seminars, then advanced courses. During the Korean War, the Chinese first got the American POWs to agree with mild remarks, such as "The United States is not perfect." Then the POWs had to add their own examples of the imperfections. At the end, they were signing their names to anti-American broadcasts (Schein, Schneier, & Barker, 1961).

6. *The person's access to information is severely controlled.* As soon as a person is a committed believer or follower, the group limits the person's choices, denigrates critical thinking, makes fun of doubts, and insists that any private distress is due to lack of belief in the group. The person may be isolated from the outside world and thus from antidotes to the leader's ideas. Members may be taught to hate certain "evil" enemies: parents, capitalists, blacks, whites, nonbelievers. Total conformity is demanded.

Even in groups that allow members to leave freely, you can see many of these strategies in operation. In the Heaven's Gate cult, for example, the leader, Marshall Applewhite, offered members a new identity (as extraterrestrials in human bodies) and a simplistic solution to their problems (suicide would free them to be whisked away to a spaceship hiding in the tail of the Hale-Bopp comet). He encouraged members to sever their relationships with friends and relatives, had them dress alike, and censored all dissenting opinions. By all accounts, his followers were pleasant, nice people, and many were well-educated. Most of them would probably not have considered killing themselves when they first joined the group. Yet eventually, 38 men and women, along with Applewhite, did just that.

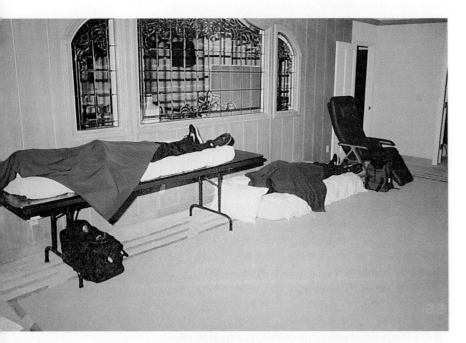

Cults persuade their members to suppress all signs of individual identity and yield to the will of the leader—even when the leader requires mass suicide, as he did in the Heaven's Gate cult. Police found 39 identically clad bodies laid out on beds or tables, all but 2 of them covered by purple cloths and each with a packed suitcase nearby. The members all had close-cropped hair, and despite their differences in age and sex, they looked so much alike that at first the police mistakenly thought they were all young men.

Research on persuasion, like the research on roles, shows us that you do not have to be evil to do evil things, stupid to do self-destructive things, or crazy to do irrational things. Some peo- ple may be more vulnerable than others to coer- cive tactics, but these techniques are powerful enough to overwhelm even strong, well-edu- cated individuals.

??? QUICK QUIZ

Now, how can we persuade you to take this quiz without using coercion?

1. Frank, an African-American student, finds himself caught between two philoso- phies on his campus. One holds that blacks should move toward full integration into mainstream culture. The other holds that blacks should immerse themselves in the history, values, and contributions of African culture. Frank is caught between his _____ and _____.

2. In each of the following cases, what kind of attribution is being made—situational or dispositional? (a) A man says, "My wife has sure become a grouchy person." (b) The same man says, "I'm grouchy because I've had a bad day at the office." (c) A woman reads about high unemployment in inner-city communities and says, "Well, if those people weren't so lazy, they would find work."

3. What principles of attribution theory are suggested by the items in the preceding question?

4. Candidate Carson spends $3 million to make sure his name is seen and heard fre- quently, and to repeat unverified charges that his opponent is a thief. What psycho- logical phenomenon is he relying on to win?

5. Your best friend urges you to join a "life-renewal" group called "The Feeling Life." Your friend has been spending increasing amounts of time with her fellow Feelies, and you have some doubts about them. What questions would you want to have answered before joining up?

Answers:

1. ethnic identity and acculturation 2. a. dispositional b. situational c. dispositional 3. Item *a* illustrates the funda- mental attribution error; *b*, the self-serving bias; and *c*, blaming the victim because of the just-world hypothesis. 4. the va- lidity effect 5. A few things to consider: Is there an autocratic leader who tolerates no dissent or criticism, while rational- izing this practice as a benefit for members? ("Doubt and disbelief are signs that your feeling side is being repressed.") Have long-standing members given up their friends, families, interests, and ambitions for this group? Does the leader offer sim- ple but unrealistic promises to repair your life and all that troubles you? Are members required to make extreme sacrifices by donating large amounts of time and money?

What's Ahead

- *Why do people in groups often go along with the majority even when the majority is dead wrong?*

- *How can "groupthink" lead to bad—even catastrophic—decisions?*

- *Why is it common for a group of people to hear someone shout for help without one of them calling the police?*

- *What enables some people to dissent, take moral action, or blow the whistle on wrong- doers?*

INDIVIDUALS IN GROUPS

Even when a group is not at all coercive, some- thing happens to individuals when they join a bunch of other people. They act differently than they would on their own, regardless of whether the group has convened to solve problems and make decisions, has gathered to have fun, consists of anonymous bystanders, or is just a loose collec- tion of individuals waiting around in a room. The decisions group members make and the actions they take may depend less on their own desires than on the structure and dynamics of the group itself.

Conformity

One thing people in groups do is conform, taking action or adopting attitudes as a result of real or imagined pressures.

Suppose that you are required to appear at a psychology laboratory for an experiment on perception. You join seven other students seated in a room. You are shown a 10-inch line and asked which of three other lines is identical to it:

Test line   A   B   C

The correct answer, line A, is obvious, so you are amused when the first person in the group chooses line B. "Bad eyesight," you say to yourself. "He's off by 2 whole inches!" The second person also chooses line B. "What a dope," you think. But by the time the fifth person has chosen line B, you are beginning to doubt yourself. The sixth and seventh students also choose line B, and now you are worried about *your* eyesight. The experimenter looks at you. "Your turn," he says. Do you follow the evidence of your own eyes or the collective judgment of the group?

This was the design for a series of famous studies of conformity conducted by Solomon Asch (1952, 1965). The seven "nearsighted" students were actually Asch's confederates. Asch wanted to know what people would do when a group unanimously contradicted an obvious fact. He found that when people made the line comparisons on their own, they were almost always accurate. But in the group, only 20 percent of the students remained completely independent on every trial, and often they were apologetic for not going along. One-third conformed to the group's incorrect decision more than half the time, and the rest conformed at least some of the time. Whether they conformed or not, the students often felt uncertain of their decision. As one participant later said, "I felt disturbed, puzzled, separated, like an outcast from the rest."

Asch's experiment has been replicated many times over the years, in the United States and in many other countries. A meta-analysis of 133 studies in 17 countries revealed three general findings (Bond & Smith, 1996). First, in America, conformity has declined since Asch's work in the 1950s, suggesting that conformity reflects prevailing social norms. Second, people in individualistic cultures, such as that of the United States, are less likely to conform than are people in group-oriented cultures, where social harmony is more highly valued than individual assertiveness. Third, regardless of culture, conformity increases as the stimulus becomes more ambiguous, as the number of accomplices giving the wrong answer increases, and as members of the group become more alike in age, ethnicity, gender, and so on.

Like obedience, conformity has both its positive and its negative sides. Society runs more smoothly

Sometimes people like to conform in order to feel part of the group . . .

. . . and sometimes they like to rebel a little in order to assert their individuality.

when people know how to behave in a given situation and when they go along with cultural rules of dress and manners. But conformity can also suppress critical thinking and creativity. In a group, many people will deny their private beliefs, agree with silly notions, and violate their own values (Aronson, 1995; Cialdini, 1993). Some do so because they identify with group members and want to be like them in dress, attitudes, or behavior. Some want to be liked and know that disagreeing with a group can make them unpopular. Some believe the group has knowledge or abilities that are superior to their own. And some go along out of pure self-interest—to keep their jobs, win promotions, or win votes.

Groupthink

Close, friendly groups usually work well together, but they also face the problem of how to get the best ideas and efforts of their members while reducing the risk of conformity. In particular, members of such groups must avoid a problem called **groupthink,** the tendency for all members to think alike and to suppress dissent. According to Irving Janis (1982, 1989), groupthink occurs when a group's need for total agreement overwhelms its need to make the wisest decision, and when the members' needs to be liked and accepted overwhelm their ability to disagree with a bad decision.

Throughout history, groupthink has resulted in disastrous military decisions, as two American examples illustrate. In 1961, President John F. Kennedy, after meeting with his advisers, approved a CIA plan to invade Cuba at the Bay of Pigs and overthrow the government of Fidel Castro; the invasion was a humiliating disaster. In the mid-1960s, President Lyndon Johnson and his cabinet escalated the war in Vietnam in spite of obvious signs that further bombing and increased troops were not bringing the war to an end. Janis (1982) examined the historical records pertaining to these two decisions and identified typical features of groups that are susceptible to groupthink: They are highly cohesive; they are isolated from other viewpoints; they feel under pressure from outside forces; and they have a strong, directive leader. Under these conditions, the following symptoms of groupthink tend to appear:

- *An illusion of invulnerability.* The group believes that it can do no wrong, that it is 100 percent correct in its decisions.

- *Self-censorship.* Dissenters decide to keep quiet in order not to rock the boat, offend their friends, or risk being ridiculed. For example, Arthur Schlesinger, a college professor who was one of Kennedy's advisers, decided not to express his doubts about the Bay of Pigs invasion because he feared others would regard him as presumptuous for disagreeing with high government officials.

- *Direct pressure on dissenters to conform,* either by the leader or other group members. For example, President Johnson, who favored increased bombing of North Vietnam, ridiculed his adviser Bill Moyers by greeting him with "Well, here comes Mr. Stop-the-Bombing."

- *An illusion of unanimity.* By discouraging dissent, leaders and group members create an illusion of consensus. Arthur Schlesinger did eventually voice his doubts to the secretary of state, who passed them along to Kennedy, who was not pleased. When it came time to vote on whether to invade, Kennedy asked each of his advisers to voice an opinion—except for Schlesinger.

Fortunately, groupthink can sometimes be counteracted by creating conditions that explicitly encourage and reward the expression of doubt and dissent—for example, by basing decisions on majority rule instead of unanimity (Kameda & Sugimori, 1993). President Kennedy apparently learned this lesson from the Bay of Pigs decision. In his next major foreign policy decision, during the 1962 crisis over missiles placed in Cuba by the Soviet Union, Kennedy brought in outside experts to advise his inner circle, often absented himself from the group so as not to influence their discussions, and encouraged free debate between the "hawks" and the "doves" (Aronson, Wilson, & Akert, 1997; May & Zelikow, 1997). The crisis, one of the most dangerous in post–World War II history, was resolved peacefully.

groupthink

In close-knit groups, the tendency for all members to think alike for the sake of harmony and to suppress dissent.

Of course, it is easy to see *after the fact* how conformity contributed to a bad decision or open debate led to a good one. If we want to predict whether a group will make good or bad decisions in the future, however, we need to know its history, the nature of the decision to be made, the characteristics of the leader, and many other things (Aldag & Fuller, 1993). Nevertheless, Janis put his finger on a phenomenon that many people have experienced: individual members of a group suppressing their real opinions and doubts so as to be good team players.

The Anonymous Crowd

Many years ago, in an incident that received much public attention, a woman named Kitty Genovese was stabbed repeatedly in front of her apartment building. She screamed for help for more than half an hour, but not one of the 38 neighbors who heard her, who came to their windows to watch, even called the police. Kitty Genovese was a victim of a process called the **diffusion of responsibility,** in which responsibility for an outcome is diffused, or spread, among many people, and individuals fail to take action because they believe that someone else will do so. The many reports of *bystander apathy* in the news—people watching as a woman is attacked, as a man struggles with a stalled car on a freeway, as a child is eventually beaten to death by disturbed parents—reflect the diffusion of responsibility on a large scale.

In work groups, the diffusion of responsibility sometimes takes the form of *social loafing:* Each member of a team slows down, letting others work harder (Karau & Williams, 1993; Latané,

diffusion of responsibility

In organized or anonymous groups, the tendency of members to avoid taking responsibility for actions or decisions, assuming that others will do so.

deindividuation

In groups or crowds, the loss of awareness of one's own individuality and the abdication of mindful action.

Williams, & Harkins, 1979). This slowdown of effort and abdication of responsibility does not happen in all groups. It occurs primarily when individual group members are not accountable for the work they do; when people feel that working harder would only duplicate their colleagues' efforts; when workers feel exploited; or when the work itself is uninteresting (Shepperd, 1995). When the challenge of the job is increased or when each member of the group has a different, important job to do, the sense of individual responsibility rises, and loafing declines. Loafing also declines when people know their group's performance will be evaluated against that of another group, or if they are working on a group project that really matters to them (Harkins & Szymanski, 1989; Williams & Karau, 1991).

The most extreme instances of the diffusion of responsibility occur when members of a group lose all awareness of their individuality and sense of self, a state called **deindividuation** (Festinger, Pepitone, & Newcomb, 1952). Deindividuated people "forget themselves"; they are more likely to act mindlessly, and their behavior becomes disconnected from their values. They may do destructive things: break store windows, loot, get into fights, riot at a sports event, or commit rape. Or they may become more friendly; think of all the chatty people on buses and planes who reveal things to their seatmates they would never tell anyone they knew. Not surprisingly, deindividuation increases in situations that make people feel anonymous. It is more likely to occur when a person is in a large city rather than a small town; in a faceless mob rather than an intimate group; when signs of individuality are covered by uniforms or masks; or in a large and impersonal class of hundreds of students rather than a small class of only 15.

Wearing a uniform or disguise can increase deindividuation and mindlessness. In one study, when women wore these Ku Klux Klan-like white disguises, they delivered twice as much apparent shock to another woman as did women who were undisguised and wore large name tags (Zimbardo, 1970).

Get Involved

For this exercise in deindividuation, choose two situations: one in which you are one of many people, perhaps hundreds (as in a large classroom or a concert audience); and one in which you are one of a few (as in a small discussion group). In both situations, close your eyes and pretend to fall asleep. Is this easier to do in one context than in the other? Why? In each case, what is the reaction of other people around you?

Just as extreme deindividuation has its hazards, so does extreme *individuation,* which can cause people to become too self-aware and self-focused, and to forget their dependence on others. Cultures that emphasize the importance of individual action consider deindividuation a bad thing, but those that emphasize the importance of social cohesiveness see it differently. Asians are on the average less individuated than whites, blacks, and Latinos, reflecting the Asian cultural emphasis on social harmony (Maslach, Stapp, & Santee, 1985).

Courage and Nonconformity

We have seen how social roles and cultural norms can cause people to obey orders or conform to ideas that they believe are wrong. Sometimes, however, people have disobeyed such orders or have gone against prevailing beliefs, and their actions have changed the course of history. Many blacks and whites disobeyed the laws of segregation. Many individuals have stopped conforming to traditional gender roles. Many men and women have decided to "blow the whistle" on company or government practices they consider immoral or unfair, risking their jobs and friendships to do so (Glazer & Glazer, 1990).

Dissent and *altruism,* the willingness to take selfless or dangerous action on behalf of others, are in part a matter of personal convictions and conscience. The Quakers and other white abolitionists who risked their lives to help blacks escape their captors before the Civil War did so because they believed in the inherent evil of slavery. In the former Soviet Union, a KGB officer named Viktor Orekhov secretly informed political dissidents of planned KGB action against them, thereby saving hundreds of people from arrests and grueling interrogations. Orekhov was eventually caught and spent eight years in a Soviet jail. On his release, he explained why he felt he had to help the protest-ers: "I was afraid that [unless I acted] my children would be ashamed of me" (Fogelman, 1994).

However, just as there are many external reasons for obedience and conformity, so there are many external influences on a person's decision to dissent, take moral action, or help a stranger in trouble. Instead of condemning bystanders and conformists for their laziness or cowardice, social psychologists have identified the social and situational factors that predict independent actions such as whistle-blowing, voicing a minority opinion, or helping others:

1. *The individual perceives the need for intervention or help.* It may seem obvious, but before people can take independent action, they must realize that such action is necessary. Unfortunately, sometimes people willfully blind themselves to this need in order to justify their own inaction. During World War II, the German citizens of Dachau didn't "see" the local concentration camp, although it was in plain view. Similarly, many employees choose not to see flagrant examples of bribery and other illegal actions. Blindness to the need for action also occurs when people have too many demands on their attention. Workers who must juggle many demands on their time cannot stop to correct every problem they notice. Likewise, residents of crowded, densely populated cities cannot stop to offer help to everyone who seems to need it (Levine et al., 1994). Crowding increases the sensory overload on people and makes them more deindividuated.

2. *The individual decides to take responsibility.* In a large crowd or a large organization, it is easy for people to avoid action because of the diffusion of responsibility. When people are alone and hear someone call for help, they usually do intervene (Latané & Darley, 1976). But the decision to take responsibility also depends on the degree of risk involved. For example, helping a stranger in trouble can sometimes be dangerous, even fatal. A Good Samaritan in San Francisco intervened in an

Many people retain their individuality and courage even at great risk to themselves. On the left, Terri Barnett and Gregory Alan Williams are honored at Los Angeles City Hall for rescuing white people during the violence that followed the 1992 acquittal of four white police officers who beat black motorist Rodney King. On the right are Ria Solomon, Sylvia Robins, and Al Bray, three whistle-blowers from Rockwell International who tried to inform NASA that the space shuttle *Challenger* was unsafe.

angry dispute between two men in the street and was stabbed to death as a consequence; he had interrupted a quarrel between drug dealers. In cities where homeless persons number in the thousands, many people are feeling "compassion fatigue": How many can they help? What kind of help is best? It is easier to be a whistle-blower or to protest a company policy when you know it will be easy to find another job, but what if jobs in your field are scarce and you have a family to support?

3. *The individual decides that the costs of doing nothing outweigh the costs of getting involved.* The cost of helping or protesting might be embarrassment and wasted time or, more seriously, lost income, loss of friends, and even physical danger. The cost of not helping or remaining silent might be guilt, blame from others, loss of honor, or, in some tragic cases, responsibility for the injury or death of others. Although three courageous whistle-blowers from Rockwell International tried to inform NASA that the space shuttle *Challenger* was not safe, the NASA authorities remained silent. No one was prepared to take responsibility for the costly decision to postpone the launch. The price of their silence was an explosion that caused the deaths of the entire crew.

4. *The individual has an ally.* In Asch's conformity experiment, the presence of one other person who gave the correct answer was enough to overcome agreement with the majority. In Milgram's experiment, the presence of a peer who disobeyed the experimenter's order to shock the learner sharply increased the number of people who disobeyed. One dissenting member of a group may be viewed as a troublemaker, but two dissenters are a coalition. Having an ally reassures a person of the rightness of the protest. Allies also make minority members seem less deviant or rebellious and make their ideas seem more legitimate (Wood et al., 1994).

5. *The individual becomes entrapped.* Once having taken the initial step of getting involved, most people will increase their commitment to taking action. In one study, 8,587 federal employees were asked whether they had observed any wrongdoing at work, whether they had told anyone about it, and what happened if they had told. Nearly half of the sample had observed some serious cases of wrongdoing, such as someone stealing federal funds, accepting bribes, or creating a situation that was dangerous to public safety. Of that half, 72 percent had done nothing at all, but the other 28 percent reported the problem to their immediate supervisors. Once they had taken that step, nearly 60 percent of the whistle-blowers eventually took the matter to higher authorities (Graham, 1986).

As you can see, independent action is not just the spontaneous or selfless expression of a desire to do the right thing. Certain social conditions make altruism, whistle-blowing, and dissent more likely to occur, just as certain conditions suppress them. What anyone does in a given situation depends on a constellation of beliefs and perceptions, personality traits, and aspects of the situation itself. This is why a man may leap into a frozen river to rescue a child on Monday and keep silent on Tuesday when his employer orders him to ignore worker-safety precautions at a factory because they are too expensive.

How do you think you would behave if you were faced with a conflict between social pressure

and conscience? Would you blow the whistle on a fellow student who cheated, call 911 if you saw someone being injured in a fight, or voice your true opinion in class even though everyone else disagreed? Would you act to rescue someone from persecution or discrimination? What aspects of the situation would influence your responses?

??? QUICK QUIZ

No matter how your fellow students feel about quizzes, you should answer this one.

A. See whether you can name the social-psychological phenomenon represented by each of the following situations.

1. The president's closest advisers are afraid to disagree with his views on arms negotiations.

2. You are at a Halloween party wearing a silly gorilla suit. Although you usually don't play practical jokes, when you see a chance to play one on your host, you do it.

3. Walking down a busy street, you see that fire has broken out in a store window. "Someone must have called the fire department," you say, and walk on.

B. What five conditions tend to encourage independent action such as dissent, whistle-blowing, and altruism?

Answers:
A. 1. groupthink 2. deindividuation 3. diffusion of responsibility B. Seeing the need for action, deciding to take responsibility, deciding that the costs of inaction outweigh the costs of involvement, having an ally, and becoming entrapped

What's Ahead

- *How do stereotypes benefit us—and how do they distort reality?*
- *Why does prejudice increase in times of social and economic unrest?*
- *Why do well-intentioned people sometimes get caught up in a "cycle of distrust" with other ethnic groups?*
- *Why isn't mere contact between cultural groups enough to resolve their conflicts? What would work?*

CROSS-CULTURAL RELATIONS

By now, we hope you're persuaded that all of us are affected by the social roles we play in society and the cultural norms we are expected to follow. Most people rarely pause to question these roles and norms, assuming instead that their own cul-

ture's way of doing things is logical, normal, and right—and that other people's cultural rules and norms are irrational, peculiar, and wrong. **Ethnocentrism,** the belief that your own culture or ethnic group is superior to all others, is universal, probably because it aids survival by increasing people's attachment to their own group and willingness to work on its behalf. Ethnocentrism is even embedded in some languages: The Chinese word for China means "the center of the world" and the Navajo and the Inuit call themselves simply "The People."

Ethnocentrism rests on a fundamental social identity: Us. As soon as people have created a category called "us," however, they invariably perceive everybody else as "not-us." It almost does not matter what the "us" category is, as Henri Tajfel and his colleagues (1971) demonstrated in an experiment with British schoolboys. Tajfel showed the boys slides with varying numbers of dots on them and asked the boys to guess how many dots there were. The boys were then arbitrarily told that they were "overestimators" or

ethnocentrism

A person's belief that his or her own ethnic group, nation, or religion is superior to all others.

"underestimators." On a subsequent task, they had a chance to give points to other boys identified as overestimators or underestimators. The researchers had created in-group favoritism: Although each boy worked alone in his cubicle, almost every single one assigned far more points to boys he thought were like him, an overestimator or an underestimator. As the boys emerged from their rooms, they were asked, "Which were you?"—and the answer received a mix of cheers and boos from the others.

Because of ethnocentrism, the possibility of harmonious relations among ethnic groups and cultures often looks bleak. All over the world, cultural animosities perpetually erupt in bloody battles. And in multicultural societies, differences in customs, values, and beliefs can produce a clash between the laws of the majority and the practices of minorities. In California, a man from Laos killed a puppy—a sacrifice he believed would help his wife recover from illness but one that enraged his neighbors and violated the animal-cruelty laws. In Nebraska, two Iraqi men, ages 34 and 28, married 13-year-old Iraqi girls—a normal custom to them, but statutory rape under Nebraska law. Some immigrants from Africa, the Middle East, and Indonesia are determined to continue their tradition of female genital mutilation—cutting off a girl's clitoris and often the rest of the external genitals as well—a practice they believe ensures a girl's chastity before marriage and her fidelity after-

ward; the United States (and other Western nations) have outlawed the procedure.

Some people take a *relativist* position on these differences, arguing that cultures should be judged strictly on their own terms—that we should not pass judgment on the customs of others even when those customs cause suffering or death. Others take an *absolutist* position, maintaining that when cultures violate certain universal human rights, the correct response is moral indignation and censure. Cultural psychologists try to help us reconcile these two views (Adamopoulos & Lonner, 1994). It is important, most would say, to morally oppose customs that violate universal human rights (although not every culture will agree on what those are—for example, whether all children are entitled to an education, whether all women are entitled to sexual pleasure, or whether torture and genocide are reprehensible). But cultural psychologists also caution us to be wary of our own ethnocentrism, the impulse to judge other cultures' practices as immoral simply because they differ from our own. We need to understand that customs are not arbitrary; they are adaptations to specific kinds of kinship systems and economic arrangements. In countries that practice genital mutilation, for example, the tradition ensures women a secure place in society; most women who do not have the operation will remain unmarried and unprotected by their extended families. This is why efforts to eliminate

Faces of the enemy: In every country, propaganda posters stereotype the enemy as ugly, aggressive, brutish, and greedy. These examples show the Soviet depiction of the United States in the 1930s as a greedy capitalist (a) and an American depiction of the German enemy in World War I as a "mad brute" (b).

(a)   (b)

female genital mutilation without also raising the status and economic security of women have failed (Dawit & Mekuria, 1993).

Social and cultural psychologists strive to understand not only the functions of cultural practices, but also the conditions that promote harmony or conflict between cultures. We turn now to their findings on stereotypes and prejudice, which so often fuel the flames of cultural misunderstanding and intolerance.

Stereotypes

A **stereotype** is a summary impression of a group of people in which all members of the group are viewed as sharing a common trait or traits. Stereotypes may be negative, positive, or neutral. There are stereotypes of people who drive Jeeps or BMWs, of men who wear earrings and of women who wear business suits, of engineering students and art students, of feminists and fraternities.

Stereotypes have a valid role to play in human thinking. They help us quickly process new information and retrieve memories. They allow us to organize experience, make sense of differences among individuals and groups, and predict how people will behave. They are, as some psychologists have called them, useful "tools in the mental toolbox"—energy-saving devices that allow us to make efficient decisions (Macrae, Milne, & Bodenhausen, 1994).

The problem is that stereotypes also distort reality in three ways (Judd et al., 1995). First, *they exaggerate differences between groups,* making the stereotyped group seem odd, unfamiliar, or dangerous. Second, *they produce selective perception;* people tend to see only what fits the stereotype and to reject any perceptions that do not fit. Third, *they underestimate differences within other groups.* People realize that their own groups are made up of all kinds of individuals, but stereotypes create the impression that all members of other groups (say, all Texans or all teenagers) are the same.

Many stereotypes have a grain of truth, capturing with some accuracy something about a group (Allport, 1954/1979). The difficulties occur when people assume that the grain of truth is the whole seashore. For example, many American whites have a stereotype about blacks that is based on the troubling statistics in the news, such as the number of young black men who are in prison. But recent decades have also seen an enormous expansion of blacks into the middle class and into

Which woman is the chemical engineer and which is the assistant? The Western stereotype holds that (a) women are not engineers in the first place, but (b) if they are, they are Western. Actually, the engineer at this refinery is the Kuwaiti woman on the left.

integrated occupations and communities, and many whites have not assimilated these positive changes into their racial stereotypes. For their part, many blacks hold negative stereotypes about whites, whom they often see as unvarying in their attributes and prejudices (Judd et al., 1995).

Stereotypes, both positive and negative, affect the way we react to the behavior of someone from the stereotyped group (Peabody, 1985). If you have a positive stereotype of Scots, for example, you might decide that a Scottish uncle of yours is "thrifty"; but if your stereotype is negative, you might think of him as "stingy." Likewise, depending on whether your stereotypes are positive or negative, you may see the behavior of others as "exuberant" or "noisy," "family-oriented" or "clannish" (Peabody, 1985).

Positive and negative stereotypes, in turn, depend on the values, cultural norms, and attributions of the observer. For example, students in Mexico and African-American students are significantly more accepting of heavy people and less concerned about their own weight than are white American students. Whites tend to have strongly negative stereotypes about fat people, which stem from a cultural ideology that individuals are responsible for what happens to them and for how they look (Crandall & Martinez, 1996).

Differences in ideology and values also affect how people from different cultures evaluate the same event (Taylor & Porter, 1994). Is coming late to class good, bad, or neutral? Is it good or bad to

stereotype

A cognitive schema or a summary impression of a group, in which a person believes that all members of the group share a common trait or traits (positive, negative, or neutral).

argue with your parents about grades? Chinese students in Hong Kong, where communalism and respect for one's elders are highly valued, and students in Australia, where individualism is highly valued, give entirely different interpretations of these two actions (Forgas & Bond, 1985). It is a small step from different interpretations to negative stereotypes: "Australians are selfish and disrespectful of adults"; "The Chinese are mindless slaves of authority." And it is a small step from negative stereotyping to prejudice.

Prejudice

A *prejudice* consists of a negative stereotype and a strong, unreasonable dislike or hatred of a group or a cultural practice. Feelings of prejudice violate the spirit of critical thinking because they resist rational argument and evidence. In his classic book *The Nature of Prejudice,* Gordon Allport (1954/1979) described the responses characteristic of a prejudiced person when confronted with evidence contradicting his or her beliefs:

MR. X: The trouble with Jews is that they only take care of their own group.

MR. Y: But the record of the Community Chest campaign shows that they give more generously, in proportion to their numbers, to the general charities of the community, than do non-Jews.

MR. X: That shows they are always trying to buy favor and intrude into Christian affairs. They think of nothing but money; that is why there are so many Jewish bankers.

MR. Y: But a recent study shows that the percentage of Jews in the banking business is negligible, far smaller than the percentage of non-Jews.

MR. X: That's just it; they don't go in for respectable business; they are only in the movie business or run night clubs.

Notice that Mr. X doesn't even try to respond to Mr. Y's evidence; he just moves along to another reason for his dislike of Jews. That is the nature of prejudice.

THE MANY FACES OF PREJUDICE

Prejudice has a long history in the United States. Hotels and job ads used to make it clear that "Gentiles only" were wanted, and anti-Semitism still exists today. In the 1920s and during World War II, anti-Japanese feelings ran high, . . .

The Origins of Prejudice. One reason for the persistence of prejudice lies in its ability to ward off feelings of doubt and fear. Prejudiced persons often project their fears or feelings of insecurity onto the target group. For example, a person who has doubts or anxieties about his own sexuality may develop a hatred toward gay people. In uncertain times, prejudice allows people to reduce complex problems to one cause, using the target group as a scapegoat: "Those people are the source of all my troubles." Most important, as research on samples from many nations has repeatedly confirmed, prejudice is a tonic for low self-esteem: People puff up their own low feelings of self-worth by disliking or hating groups they see as inferior (Islam & Hewstone, 1993; Stephan et al., 1994; Tajfel & Turner, 1986).

Not all prejudices have deep-seated psychological roots, however. As social-learning theorists have shown, some people acquire prejudices from advertising, entertainment shows, and news reports that perpetuate derogatory images and stereotypes of groups such as old people and fat people. Some prejudices are acquired mindlessly in the process of socialization; parents may communicate subtle messages to their children that say, "We don't associate with people like that," sometimes without either generation having ever met the object of their dislike. Pressures to conform can make it difficult for people to break away from the prejudices of their friends, families, and associates.

Perhaps the most important reason for prejudice, in the sociocultural view, is that it brings economic benefits and justifies the majority group's dominance (Sidanius, Pratto, & Bobo, 1996). That is why prejudice always rises when groups are in direct competition for jobs. In the nineteenth century, when Chinese immigrants in the United States were working in the gold mines, local whites described them as depraved, vicious, and bloodthirsty. Just a decade later, when the Chinese began working on the transcontinental railroad—doing difficult and dangerous jobs that few white men wanted—prejudice against them declined. Whites described them as hard-working, industrious, and law-abiding. Then, after the railroad was finished and the Chinese had to compete with Civil War veterans for scarce jobs, white

. . . and hostility returned during the economic recession of the early 1990s, when Iranians and other immigrants also became targets. Native Americans have been objects of hatred since Europeans first arrived on the continent. Segregated facilities for blacks were legal until the 1950s, and today many neighborhoods and schools remain separate and unequal. . . .

attitudes changed again. Whites now considered the Chinese to be "criminal," "crafty," "conniving," and "stupid" (Aronson, 1995).

Years ago, a classic study confirmed the strong link between economic conditions and scapegoating in America. Data from 14 states showed a strong negative correlation between the number of black lynchings in the American South and the economic value of cotton: the poorer the economic conditions for whites, the greater the number of lynchings (Hepworth & West, 1988; Hovland & Sears, 1940). More recently, another project examined several measures of economic and social insecurity (including the unemployment rate, the rate of serious crimes, the number of work stoppages, and income levels) and of prejudice (including the number of anti-Semitic incidents, activities by the Ku Klux Klan, and attitudes toward other groups). Again, during times of high social and economic threat, prejudice increased significantly (Doty, Peterson, & Winter, 1991).

Varieties of Prejudice. Studies that define prejudice in terms of people's expressed attitudes

report that prejudice in the United States and Canada is declining. White attitudes toward integration have become steadily more favorable, and the belief that blacks are inferior to whites has become much less prevalent (Devine, 1995). Similarly, men's endorsement of gender equality has steadily increased. The number of men openly expressing prejudice toward women executives declined from 41 percent in 1965 to only 5 percent in 1985 (Tougas et al., 1995), and between 1970 and 1995 antiwoman attitudes in general dropped sharply (Twenge, 1996).

Thinking Critically About the Prevalence of Prejudice

However, some social scientists believe that these statistics are misleading. Overt attitudes, they say, are not an accurate measure of prejudice because people know they should not admit feeling prejudiced (Bell, 1992; Tougas et al., 1995). These observers maintain that racial animosity and sexism are undiminished. Prejudice toward blacks, they argue, lurks behind a mask of *symbolic racism*, in which whites focus not on dislike of black individuals but on issues such as "reverse

. . . Despite great gains by women, anti-female prejudice remains widespread, as does anger against gay men and lesbians. Why do new prejudices keep emerging and why do some old ones persist?

Get Involved

Are you prejudiced against a specific group of people? Is it a group defined by gender, ethnicity, sexual orientation, nationality, religion, physical appearance, or political views? Write down your deepest thoughts and feelings about this group. Take as long as you want, and do not censor yourself or say what you think you ought to say. Now reread what you have written. Which of the many reasons for prejudice discussed in the text might be supporting your views? Do you feel that your attitudes toward the group are legitimate, or are you uncomfortable about them?

discrimination," "hard-core criminals," or "welfare abuse." In this view, such issues have become code words for the continuing animosity that many whites have for blacks.

The way to measure racism, according to this argument, is by using unobtrusive measures rather than direct attitude questionnaires. You might observe how people behave when they are with a possible object of prejudice; do they sit farther away than they normally would? You might observe how quickly people come up with positive or negative associations to pictures of people from different races—a possible measure of unconscious prejudice (Fazio et al., 1995). You might observe how people who say they are unprejudiced behave when they are emotionally upset (Jones, 1991).

In one such experiment, students administered shock to confederates in an apparent study of biofeedback. White students initially showed *less* aggression toward blacks than toward whites. But as soon as the white students were angered by overhearing derogatory remarks about themselves, they showed *more* aggression toward blacks than toward whites (Rogers & Prentice-Dunn, 1981). This finding implies that whites may be willing to control their negative feelings toward blacks or other targets of prejudice under normal conditions. But as soon as they are angry, stressed, provoked, or suffer a blow to their self-esteem, their real prejudice reveals itself.

One complication in measuring prejudice is that not all people are prejudiced in the same way. Some people are unapologetically racist, sexist, or antigay. Others have a patronizing but unconscious sense of superiority over other groups. And some people hold remnants of prejudices that were acquired in childhood but feel guilty about having such feelings. Gordon Allport (1954/1979) observed that "defeated intellectually, prejudice lingers emotionally." That is, a person might realize that prejudice against a certain group is unwarranted, yet still feel uncomfortable with members of that group. Should we put this person in the same category as one who is an outspoken bigot or who actively discriminates against others because of their sex, culture, sexual orientation, weight, disability, or skin color? What if a person is ignorant of another culture or group and mindlessly blurts out a remark that reflects that ignorance? Does that count as prejudice or mere thoughtlessness?

Can Cultures Get Along?

Given the many sources and definitions of prejudice, no one method of reducing it is likely to work (Monteith, 1996). That is why social and cultural psychologists have designed different programs to try to reduce misunderstanding and prejudice, depending on the origins of a given conflict.

For example, according to Patricia Devine (1995), people who are actively trying to break their "prejudice habit" should not be lumped together with bigots. Their discomfort could reflect an honest effort to put old prejudices aside or simple unfamiliarity with another group's ways. When people are unfamiliar or uncomfortable with members of another group, a "cycle of distrust" and animosity can emerge even when individuals start off with the best intentions to get along. Some majority-group members, although highly motivated to work well with minorities, may be self-conscious and anxious about doing "the wrong thing." Their anxiety makes them behave awkwardly, for instance by blurting out dumb remarks and avoiding eye contact with minority-group members. The minority members, based on their own history of discrimination, may interpret the majority-group members' behavior as evidence of hostility and respond with withdrawal, aloofness, or anger. The majority members, not understanding that their own anxieties have been interpreted as evidence of prejudice,

Some doubts and insecurities felt by minority-group members.

Some doubts and insecurities felt by majority-group members.

regard the minority members' behavior as unreasonable or mysterious, so they reciprocate the hostility or withdraw. This behavior confirms the minority members' suspicions about the majority's true feelings and prejudices (Devine, Evett, & Vasquez-Suson, 1996).

By understanding this cycle, Devine argues, people of goodwill can learn to break it. Majority members can become aware of the discrepancy between their intentions and their actual behavior. They can learn to reduce their discomfort with people unlike themselves and acquire the skills that will lessen their anxiety. But breaking the cycle of distrust and hostility is not just the majority's problem. Minorities can become part of the solution too, for example, by recognizing their possible biases in seeing the majority members' behavior only in a negative light. Both sides, Devine (1995) emphasizes, should remember that reducing prejudice is a *process;* it does not happen overnight. It is important, she argues, to reward people who are making an effort to change their biases, instead of condemning them for not being perfect.

What happens, however, when two groups really do bear enormous animosity toward each other, for historical, economic, or emotional reasons? How then might their conflicts be reduced? Sociocultural research emphasizes the importance of changing people's circumstances, rather than waiting around for individuals to undergo a moral or psychological conversion.

One line of attack is to change the laws that make discrimination—the official endorsement of prejudice against certain groups—acceptable. Integration of public facilities in the American South would never have occurred if civil-rights advocates had waited for segregationists to have a change of heart. Women would never have gotten the right to vote, attend college, or do "men's work" without persistent challenges to the laws that permitted discrimination. Laws, however, do not necessarily change attitudes if all they do is produce unequal contact between groups or if economic competition for jobs continues. Even with legal reforms, de facto segregation of schools and neighborhoods is still the rule in the United States and other countries, and racial prejudices are still deeply felt.

Another approach, based on the *contact hypothesis,* holds that the best way to end prejudice is to bring members of both sides together and let them get acquainted; in this way, they will discover their shared humanity. The contact hypothesis had a moment of glory during the 1950s and 1960s, when contact between blacks and whites did reduce hostility in some settings, such as newly integrated housing projects (Deutsch & Collins, 1951; Wilner, Walkley, & Cook, 1955). However, as is apparent at most big-city high schools today, desegregation and opportunities to socialize are often unsuccessful. Ethnic groups still form cliques and gangs, fighting other groups and defending their own ways.

A third approach is to go directly into desegregated schools and businesses and set up cooperative situations in which antagonistic groups have to work together for a common goal. The importance of cooperation was demonstrated years ago, when Muzafer Sherif and his colleagues conducted an experiment in a natural setting, a Boy Scout camp called Robbers Cave (Sherif, 1958; Sherif et al., 1961). Sherif randomly assigned 11- and 12-year-old boys to two groups: the Eagles and the Rattlers. To build team spirit, he had each group work on communal projects, such as making a rope bridge and building a diving board. Sherif then put the teams in competition for prizes. During fierce games of football, baseball, and tug-of-war, the boys developed a competitive fever that spilled off of the playing fields. They began to raid each other's cabins, call each other names, and start fistfights. No one dared to have a friend from the rival group. Before long, the Rattlers and the Eagles were as hostile toward each other as any two rival gangs fighting for turf, any two siblings fighting for a parent's attention, and any two nations fighting for dominance. Their hostility continued even when they were just sitting around together watching movies.

To undo the hostility he had created, Sherif set up a series of predicaments in which the Eagles and the Rattlers had to work together to reach a desired goal. The boys had to cooperate to get the water-supply system working. They had to pool their resources to get a movie they all wanted to see. When the staff truck broke down on a camping trip, they all had to join forces to pull the truck up a steep hill and get it started again. This policy of *interdependence in reaching mutual goals* was highly successful in reducing the boys' competitiveness and hostility. The boys eventually made friends with their former enemies.

Several years later, another team of researchers used a similar strategy, the "jigsaw method," to try to reduce ethnic conflict among white, Chicano, and black children in Texas elementary schools (Aronson et al., 1978). Classes were divided into groups of six students of mixed ethnicity, and every group worked together on a shared task that was broken up like a jigsaw puzzle. Each child needed the contributions of the others to put the assignment together; for instance, each child might be given one paragraph of a six-paragraph biography and be asked to learn the whole story. The cooperative students, in comparison to classmates in regular classes, had greater self-esteem, liked their classmates better, showed a decrease in prejudice, and improved their grades.

These findings, and studies of other versions of cooperative learning, have been replicated in many classrooms (Aronson, Wilson, & Akert, 1997; Johnson & Johnson, 1989). However, cooperation doesn't work when members of a group have unequal status, blame one another for loafing or "dropping the ball," or perceive that their teachers or employers are playing favorites.

Because the origins of tensions between groups in today's world are so complex, no single arrow is likely to hit the bull's-eye of prejudice. Each of the strategies we have described can be effective—making discrimination illegal, increasing contact and

In the first stage of the Robbers Cave study, a harmonious atmosphere was created by having campers cooperate and function as a team—for example, by having them work together carrying canoes to the lake (left). In the second stage, competitive games such as tug-of-war (right) fostered stereotyping and hostility between the Rattlers and the Eagles. Eventually, peace among the boys was again established when the two groups had to work together on problems such as the repair of the camp's water-supply system.

Cultural and ethnic tensions tend to subside when people from different groups work together on a common goal. Here, volunteers from Habitat for Humanity, a group that constructs housing for low-income people, build a new home in the Watts area of Los Angeles.

economic opportunity, prejudice can continue. Thus, simply putting blacks and whites in the same situation won't necessarily reduce conflict if the whites have all the decision-making authority and economic resources.

2. *Both sides must cooperate, working together for a common goal,* an enterprise that reduces us–them thinking and creates an encompassing social identity ("We're all in this together"). If one side tries to bully and dominate the other, if one side passively capitulates or withdraws, or if both sides compete to see who will win, the conflict will continue (Rubin, 1994).

3. *Both sides must have the moral, legal, and economic support of authorities,* such as teachers, employers, the judicial system, government officials, and the police. In other words, the larger culture must support the goal of equality in its laws and in the actions of its officials.

4. *Both sides must have opportunities to work and socialize together, formally and informally.* Prejudice declines when people have the chance to get used to one another's food, music, customs, and attitudes (Fisher, 1994).

cooperation between antagonistic groups—but for any of them to have its greatest impact, four conditions must be met (Amir, 1994; Fisher, 1994; Rubin, 1994; Staub, 1996; Stephan & Brigham, 1985):

1. *Both sides must have equal status and equal economic standing.* If one side has more power or greater

Perhaps one reason that cultural conflicts have been so persistent around the world is that these four conditions are rarely met all at the same time.

??? QUICK QUIZ

Try to overcome your prejudice against quizzes by taking this one.

A. Which concept—ethnocentrism, stereotyping, or prejudice—is illustrated by each of the following statements?

    1. Juan believes that all Anglos are uptight and cold, and he won't listen to any evidence that contradicts his belief.

    2. John knows and likes the Mexican minority in his town, but he privately believes that Anglo culture is superior to all others.

    3. Jane believes that Honda owners are thrifty and practical. June believes that Honda owners are stingy and dull.

B. What strategy does the Robbers Cave study suggest for reducing hostility between groups?

 C. Surveys find that large percentages of African-Americans, Asian-Americans, and Latinos hold negative stereotypes of one another and resent other minorities almost as much as they resent whites. What are some of the reasons that people who have themselves been victims of stereotyping and prejudice would hold the same attitudes toward others?

Answers:
A. 1. prejudice 2. ethnocentrism 3. stereotypes B. the fostering of interdependence in reaching mutual goals C. socialization by parents and messages in the larger society; conformity with friends who share these prejudices; and economic competition for jobs and other resources

If ever an incident illustrated the power of social norms and cultural differences, the shooting of Yoshihiro Hattori is it. When Rodney Peairs's case came to trial, the jury acquitted him of manslaughter after only three hours of deliberation. The Japanese were appalled at this verdict. To them, it illustrated everything that is wrong with America. In their view, the United States is a nation rife with guns and violence—a "developing nation," as one news commentator put it, that is still growing out of its Wild-West past. Japanese television reporters, in amazement, showed their viewers American gun stores, restaurants that display guns on the walls, and racks of gun magazines. The Japanese cannot imagine a nation in which private individuals are allowed to keep guns, and the murder rate in Japan is a tiny percentage of what it is in America.

"I think for Japanese the most remarkable thing is that you could get a jury of Americans together, and they could conclude that shooting someone before you even talked to him was reasonable behavior," Masako Notoji, a professor of American cultural studies in Tokyo, told the *New York Times* (May 25, 1993). "We are more civilized. We rely on words." In contrast, the citizens of Baton Rouge were surprised that the case came to trial at all. What is more right and natural, they asked, than protecting yourself and your family from intruders? "A man's home is his castle," said one potential juror, expressing puzzlement that Peairs had even been arrested. A local man, joining the many sympathizers of Rodney Peairs, said, "It would be to me what a normal person would do under those circumstances."

But what is normal? As findings in cultural psychology have shown, what is normal in some cultures—emphasizing group harmony over individual rights, prohibiting individuals from owning guns or encouraging gun use, excising the genitals of women, killing a puppy for religious sacrifice—may be considered abnormal, immoral, or unnatural in other cultures.

Moreover, as findings in social psychology have shown, even within a culture, "normal" people can do some terribly disturbing things when norms and roles encourage or require them to do so—when the situation "takes over" and, like Bonnie Peairs, they don't stop to think critically and ask questions. Normal people may join self-destructive cults, harm others, and go along with the crowd, even when the crowd is performing brutal acts. They may then call upon self-serving attributions to rationalize their behavior; they may even blame the victims of their actions.

Philosopher Hannah Arendt (1963) used the phrase "the banality of evil" to describe how it was possible for "normal" people in Nazi Germany to commit the monstrous acts they did. (*Banal* means "commonplace" or "unoriginal.") The compelling evidence for the banality of evil is, perhaps, the hardest lesson in psychology. Most people want to believe that harm to others is done only by evil people who are bad down to their bones, or that wars are started only by evil cultures that don't have a single good custom to recommend them. It is reassuring to divide the world into those who are good or bad, kind or cruel, moral or immoral.

Of course, some people do stand out as particularly cruel or particularly kind. But from the standpoint of social and cultural psychology, all human beings, like all cultures, contain the potential for both good and bad. All of us, depending on circumstances, are susceptible to mindless obedience and conformity, bystander apathy, groupthink, deindividuation, ethnocentrism, stereotyping, and prejudice. All of us are subject to the same psychological, social, and economic forces that foster tolerance or animosity, conformity or dissent, courage or cowardice.

The findings from cultural and social psychology suggest that ethnocentrism and cultural conflict will always be with us, as long as economic, cultural, and status differences exist among groups. But this research can also help us formulate realistic goals for living in a diverse world. For example, because of cross-cultural findings, businesses are now hiring cultural advisers to help them make the best use of their employees' diversity and do better business with other countries. And research on bystander intervention is being used in the training of police officers in California, to encourage them to intervene when their colleagues use too much force. (The man hired to design the program is Ervin Staub, whose family was saved from the Nazis in 1944—by concerned bystanders.)

By recognizing that conflicts and misunderstandings will always occur, we can turn our attention to finding nonviolent ways of resolving them. By identifying the social conditions that have created the banality of evil, we can create others that foster the "banality of virtue"—everyday acts of kindness, selflessness, and generosity.

Taking Psychology with You

Travels Across the Cultural Divide

A French salesman worked for a company that was bought by Americans. When the new American manager ordered him to step up his sales within the next three months, the employee quit in a huff, taking his customers with him. Why? In France, it takes years to develop customers; in family-owned businesses, relationships with customers may span generations. The American wanted instant results, as Americans often do, but the French salesman knew this was impossible and quit. The American view was, "He wasn't up to the job; he's lazy and disloyal, so he stole my customers." The French view was, "There is no point in explaining anything to a person who is so stupid as to think you can acquire loyal customers in three months" (Hall & Hall, 1987).

Many corporations are beginning to realize that such cultural differences are not trivial and that success in a global economy depends on understanding such differences. You, too, can benefit from the psychological research on cultures, whether you plan to do business abroad, visit as a tourist, or just want to get along better in an increasingly diverse society.

• *Be sure you understand the other culture's rules*, not only of manners and customs but also of nonverbal gestures and methods of communication. If you find yourself getting angry over something a person from another culture is doing, try to find out whether your expectations and perceptions of that person's behavior are appropriate. For example, Koreans typically do not shake hands when greeting strangers, whereas most African-Americans and whites do. People who shake hands as a gesture of friendship and courtesy are likely to feel insulted if another person refuses

to do the same—unless they understand that what is going on is a cultural difference. Here's another example: Suppose you want to go shopping in Morocco or Mexico. If you are not used to bargaining, the experience may be exasperating. It will help to find a cultural "translator" who can show you the ropes. On the other hand, if you are from a culture where people bargain for everything, you will be just as exasperated in a place where everything is sold for a fixed price. "Where's the fun in this?" you'll say. "The whole human transaction of shopping is gone!"

• *When in Rome, do as the Romans do—as much as possible.* Most of the things you really need to know about a culture are not to be found in the guidebooks or travelogues. To learn the unspoken rules of a culture, keep your eyes open and your mouth shut: Look, listen, and observe. What is the pace of life like? Which is more valued in this culture, relationships or schedules? Do people regard brash individuality as admirable or embarrassing? When customers enter a shop, do they greet and chat with the shopkeeper or ignore the person as they browse?

Remember, though, that even when you know the rules, you may find it difficult to carry them out. For example, cultures differ in their tolerance for prolonged gazes (Keating, 1994). In the Middle East, two men will look directly at one another as they talk, but such direct gazes would be deeply uncomfortable to most Japanese or white Americans and a sign of insult to some African-Americans. Knowing this fact about gaze rules can help people accept the reality of different customs, but most of us will still feel uncomfortable trying to change our own ways.

• *Nevertheless, avoid stereotyping.* Try not to let your awareness of cultural differences cause you to overlook individual variations within cultures. During a dreary Boston winter, social psychologist Roger Brown (1986) went to the Bahamas for a vacation. To his surprise, he found the people he met unfriendly, rude, and sullen. He decided that the reason was that Bahamians had to deal with spoiled, critical foreigners, and he tried out this hypothesis on a cab driver. The cab driver looked at Brown in amazement, smiled cheerfully, and told him that Bahamians don't mind tourists—just *unsmiling* tourists.

And then Brown realized what had been going on. "Not tourists generally, but this tourist, myself, was the cause," he wrote. "Confronted with my unrelaxed wintry Boston face, they had assumed I had no interest in them and had responded non-committally, inexpressively. I had created the Bahamian national character. Everywhere I took my face it sprang into being. So I began smiling a lot, and the Bahamians changed their national character. In fact, they lost any national character and differentiated into individuals."

Wise travelers will use cultural findings to expand their understanding of other societies, while avoiding the trap of reducing all behavior to a matter of culture. Sociocultural research teaches us to appreciate the countless explicit and implicit rules that govern our behavior, values, and attitudes, and those of others. Yet we should not forget Roger Brown's lesson that every human being is an individual: one who not only reflects his or her culture, but who shares the common concerns of all humanity.

SUMMARY

1) Like learning theorists, social and cultural psychologists emphasize environmental influences on behavior, but they broaden their attention to include the entire sociocultural context. Social psychologists study the influence of *norms*, *roles*, and groups on behavior and cognition; cultural psychologists study the cultural origins of and variations in norms and roles.

Roles and Rules

2) Two classic studies illustrate the power of roles to affect individual actions. In Milgram's obedience study, most people in the role of "teacher" inflicted what they thought was extreme shock on another person because an authoritative experimenter told them to. In Zimbardo's prison study, college students quickly fell into the role of "prisoner" or "guard."

3) A certain amount of routine obedience to authority is necessary for the smooth running of any society, but obedience can also lead to actions that are deadly, foolish, or illegal. People follow orders because of the obvious consequences of disobedience, out of respect for authority, and to gain advantages. Even when they would rather not obey, they may do so because they believe the authority is *legitimate*; because their role is *routinized* into duties that are performed mindlessly; because they are embarrassed to violate the rules of good manners; or because they have been *entrapped*.

Identity, Attributions, and Attitudes

4) In addition to having their own individual identities, people develop *social identities*, aspects of self-identity that are based on nationality, ethnicity, and social roles. Social identities provide a feeling of place and connection in the world.

5) In culturally diverse societies, many people face the problem of balancing their *ethnic identity* with *acculturation* into the larger society. Depending on whether ethnic identity and acculturation are strong or weak, a person may become *bicultural*; choose *assimilation*; become an *ethnic separatist*; or feel *marginal*.

6) According to *attribution theory*, people are motivated to search for causes to which they can attribute their own and other people's behavior. These attributions may be *situational* or *dispositional*. The *fundamental attribution error* occurs when people overestimate personality traits as a cause of behavior and underestimate the influence of situation. A *self-serving bias* allows people to take credit for their good deeds and to excuse their own mistakes by blaming the situation. According to the *just-world hypothesis*, most people need to believe that the world is fair and that people get what they deserve; to preserve this belief, they may blame victims of abuse or injustice instead of the perpetrators.

7) People hold many *attitudes*, which are composed of cognitions and feelings about a subject. Some attitudes are a result of conformity, habit, rationalization, economic self-interest, and subtle social and environmental influences, including the *cohort effect*. Although attitudes influence behavior, a change in behavior can also lead to a change in attitudes, often as a result of *cognitive dissonance*.

8) One way to persuade others to change their attitudes is to take advantage of the *validity effect:* Simply repeating a statement over and over again makes it seem more believable. Other everyday techniques of attitude change include associating a product or message with someone who is famous, attractive, or expert, and linking the product with good feelings. Fear tactics, however, tend to backfire.

9) Some methods of attitude change are intentionally manipulative. Tactics of *coercive persuasion* include putting a person under stress; defining problems and their solutions simplistically; offering unconditional love and acceptance in exchange for unquestioning loyalty; creating a new identity for the person; using entrapment; and controlling access to outside information.

Individuals in Groups

10) In groups, individuals may conform to social pressure because they identify with the group, trust the group's judgment or knowledge, hope for personal gain, or wish to be liked. They may even conform mindlessly and self-destructively, violating their own preferences and values because "everyone else is doing it."

11) Cohesive, friendly groups are particularly vulnerable to *groupthink*, the tendency of group members to think alike, censor themselves, actively suppress disagreement, and feel that their decisions are invulnerable. Groupthink can produce faulty decisions because group members fail to seek disconfirming evidence for their ideas. However, groups can be structured to discourage groupthink.

12) *Diffusion of responsibility* in a group can lead to inaction on the part of individuals—to *bystander apathy* and, in work groups, *social loafing*. The most extreme instances of the diffusion of responsibility occur when people are in a state of *deindividuation*, losing awareness of their individuality. Deindividuation increases under conditions of anonymity.

13) Although the willingness to speak up for an unpopular opinion, blow the whistle, or help a stranger is in part a matter of personal belief and conscience, social and situational factors are also important. Dissent, moral action, and altruism increase when individuals are able to recognize a need for intervention or help; decide to take responsibility; conclude that the costs of inaction outweigh the costs of getting involved; have an ally; and become entrapped in a commitment.

Cross-cultural Relations

14) *Ethnocentrism*, the belief that your own ethnic group or culture is superior to all others, promotes "us–them" thinking. Because of ethnocentrism and genuine differences in values and beliefs, cultural animosities and conflicts are common throughout the world.

15) *Stereotypes* help people rapidly process new information and retrieve memories, but they also distort reality by exaggerating differences between groups; producing selective perception; and underestimating the differences within groups. Positive and negative stereotypes affect whether we see the behavior of another person in a positive or negative light—for example, as thrifty or stingy.

16) A *prejudice* is an unreasonable negative feeling toward a category of people or a cultural practice. Prejudice reduces anxiety by allowing people to feel superior; bolsters self-esteem when they feel threatened; and provides a simple explanation of complex problems. Some people acquire prejudices from media images or from their parents. Prejudice protects economic interests and justifies the majority group's dominance. During times of social and economic insecurity, prejudice rises significantly.

17) Overtly prejudiced and sexist attitudes are declining in the United States and Canada, but scientists disagree on the significance of this fact. Some argue that prejudice toward African-Americans lurks behind a mask of *symbolic racism.* In studies, expressed attitudes toward other groups are sometimes at odds with actual behavior. Debates over whether prejudice is declining are complicated by the fact that not all prejudiced people are prejudiced in the same way. Some people may feel guilty about their discomfort with members of other groups and may wish to overcome such feelings.

18) When prejudice arises from a "cycle of distrust," people can learn to break the cycle by recognizing their biases and learning to reduce their discomfort with members of the other group. But when two groups feel animosity toward each other for historical, economic, or emotional reasons, four conditions are necessary for prejudice to decline: The groups must have equal status and economic standing; they must cooperate for a common goal; they must have the legal, moral, and economic support of authorities; and, as the *contact hypothesis* would predict, they must have opportunities to work and socialize together.

19) Social and cultural psychology show that under certain conditions, good people can be induced to do bad things; normal sociocultural processes can lead to bystander apathy, groupthink, and conflict. But the sociocultural context can also be designed to encourage selflessness, group harmony, and constructive dissent.

KEY TERMS

social psychology   297
cultural psychology   297
norms (social)   298
role   298
routinization   302
entrapment   303
social cognition   304
social identity   304

individualist versus collectivist
   cultures   304
ethnic identity   305
acculturation   305
bicultural identity   305
assimilation   305
ethnic separatism   305
marginal identity   305

attribution theory   306
situational attributions   306
dispositional attributions   306
fundamental attribution error
   306
self-serving bias   307
just-world hypothesis   307
blaming the victim   307

LOOKING BACK

- *How do social rules guide behavior—and what is likely to happen when you violate them? (pp. 298–299)*

- *Do you have to be mean or disturbed to inflict pain on someone just because an authority tells you to? (pp. 299–300)*

- *How can ordinary college students be transformed into sadistic prison guards? (p. 301)*

- *How can people be "entrapped" into violating their moral principles? (p. 303)*

- *In what ways do people balance their ethnic identity and membership in the larger culture? (p. 305)*

- *What's one of the most common mistakes people make when explaining the behavior of others? (p. 306)*

- *What is the "Big Lie"—and why does it work so well? (pp. 308–309)*

- *What's the difference between ordinary techniques of persuasion and the coercive techniques used by cults? (p. 310)*

- *Why do people in groups often go along with the majority even when the majority is dead wrong? (p. 313)*

- *How can "groupthink" lead to bad—even catastrophic—decisions? (p. 313)*

- *Why is it common for a group of people to hear someone shout for help without one of them calling the police? (p. 314)*

- *What enables some people to dissent, take moral action, or blow the whistle on wrongdoers? (pp. 315–316)*

- *How do stereotypes benefit us—and how do they distort reality? (p. 319)*

- *Why does prejudice increase in times of social and economic unrest? (pp. 321–322)*

- *Why do well-intentioned people sometimes get caught in a "cycle of distrust" with members of other ethnic or cultural groups? (pp. 323–324)*

- *Why isn't mere contact between groups enough to resolve cultural conflict? What would work? (pp. 324, 326)*

10

Psychological Disorders

Writer Caught Plagiarizing, Blames "Psychological Problem"

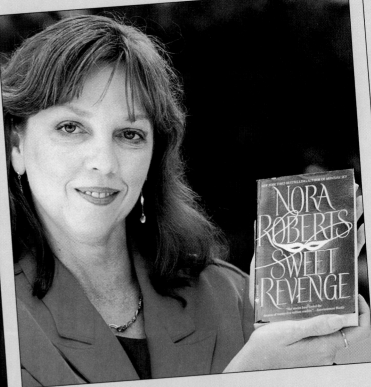

Romance writer Janet Dailey (left) admits that she lifted passages from books by Nora Roberts (right), but blames a stress-induced psychological disorder.

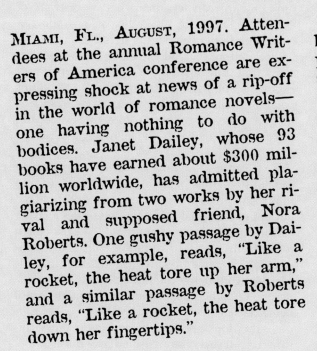

MIAMI, FL., AUGUST, 1997. Attendees at the annual Romance Writers of America conference are expressing shock at news of a rip-off in the world of romance novels—one having nothing to do with bodices. Janet Dailey, whose 93 books have earned about $300 million worldwide, has admitted plagiarizing from two works by her rival and supposed friend, Nora Roberts. One gushy passage by Dailey, for example, reads, "Like a rocket, the heat tore up her arm," and a similar passage by Roberts reads, "Like a rocket, the heat tore down her fingertips."

Dailey has publicly apologized and has asked Roberts to forgive her, explaining that she was under great stress when she lifted Roberts' words. At the time, her husband had lung cancer, she had lost two brothers to cancer, and her dog had died. Her acts, she says, are "attributable to a psychological problem that I never even suspected I had. I have already begun treatment for the disorder and have been assured that, with treatment, this behavior can be prevented in the future." Roberts, however, doesn't buy the story and has announced that she is "continuing to evaluate her options," including a lawsuit.

Would you buy Dailey's excuse? Was she psychologically disturbed when she helped herself to Roberts' words and ideas, or just unscrupulous? Where would you draw the line between a psychological disorder and plain old rotten behavior? When does difficulty coping with life's stresses and tragedies diminish a person's responsibility for actions that are harmful to others?

You don't have to be a psychologist to recognize the more extreme forms of abnormal behavior. A homeless woman stands on a street corner every night between midnight and 3:00 A.M., screaming obscenities and curses; by day, she is calm. A man in a shop tells you confidentially that his shoes have been bugged by the FBI, his phone is wiretapped, and his friends are spying on him for the CIA. When people think of "mental illness," they usually think of individuals like these. But most psychological problems are far less dramatic and far more common. One person may go through episodes of complete inability to function, yet get along pretty well between those episodes. Another may be able to function adequately every day, yet suffer chronic feelings of melancholy—always feeling somewhat "below par" in terms of mood.

One of the most common worries that people have is "Am I normal?" It is normal to fear being abnormal—especially when you are reading about psychological problems! We all occasionally have difficulties that seem overwhelming, that make us feel as though we cannot cope, and it is often difficult to pinpoint precisely when "normal" problems shade into "abnormal" ones on the spectrum of human behavior. In this chapter, you will learn how mental health professionals define disorder and how they diagnose a wide range of psychological problems.

What's Ahead

- *Why were slaves who dreamed of freedom once considered to have a "mental disorder"?*

- *What's wrong with using tests such as the famous "inkblot" test to diagnose disorders?*

- *Why is the standard guide to the diagnosis of mental disorders so controversial?*

DEFINING AND DIAGNOSING DISORDER

Many people tend to confuse the terms *abnormal behavior*—behavior that deviates from the norm—and *mental disorder,* but the two are not the same. A person may behave in ways that are statistically

People the world over paint their bodies, but what is normal in one culture may be considered abnormal or eccentric in another. The Samburu tribesman of Kenya on the left has adorned his face in ways that might seem odd to North Americans but that are typical in his society. The tattoos of the American bikers on the right might seem abnormal to most Americans but are perfectly normal in the biking subculture. Do you think these examples of body decoration are beautiful, amusing, disgusting, or creepy? Why?

rare (collecting ceramic pigs, being a genius at math, committing murder) without having a mental illness. Conversely, some mental disorders, such as depression or anxiety, are extremely common. If frequency of the problem isn't a guide, how then should we define mental disorder?

In the law, the definition of mental disorder rests primarily on whether a person is aware of the consequences of his or her actions and can control his or her behavior. If not, the person may be declared insane and therefore incompetent to stand trial. But *insanity* is a legal term only; psychologists and psychiatrists do not use the terms *sanity* or *insanity* in either research or diagnosis. Instead, when defining disorder, mental health professionals emphasize the following criteria:

1. *Violation of cultural standards.* Every society sets up standards for its members to follow, and those who break the rules are usually considered deviant or disturbed. Many of these rules are specific to a particular time or group. For example, in most North American cultural groups, having visions of a deceased relative (though not uncommon) is considered abnormal; bereaved people tend to keep their hallucinations secret, for fear of being labeled "crazy" (Bentall, 1990). But the Chinese, the Hopi, and members of many other cultures regard such visions as perfectly normal.

Sometimes, a society's notions of mental disorder serve the interests of those in power. In the early years of the nineteenth century, for instance, a physician named Samuel Cartwright argued that many slaves were suffering from *drapetomania,* an urge to escape from slavery. As Hope Landrine (1988) has noted, "Sanity for a slave was synonymous with submission, and protest and seeking freedom were the equivalent of psychopathology." Thus doctors could assure slave owners that a mental illness, not the intolerable condition of slavery, made slaves seek freedom. Today, of course, psychologists consider "drapetomania" foolish and cruel. But decisions about what should count as a mental disorder sometimes still depend on the prevailing cultural climate, as we will see later in this chapter.

2. *Maladaptive behavior.* Another approach to defining mental disorder emphasizes the negative consequences of a person's behavior. Some behavior is harmful to the individual—for example, the behavior of a woman who is so afraid of crowds that she cannot leave her house, a man who drinks so much that he cannot keep a job, or a student who is so anxious that he cannot take exams. In other cases, the individual may report

feeling fine and deny that anything is wrong but behave in ways that are disruptive or dangerous to the community, or out of touch with reality—as when a child sets fires, a compulsive gambler loses the family savings, or a man hears voices telling him to kill people.

3. *Emotional distress.* A third approach identifies mental disorder in terms of a person's suffering. By this criterion, according to nationwide surveys, about 28 percent of all Americans in any given year have one or more mental disorders, including depression, anxiety, incapacitating fears, and alcohol or other drug problems (Kessler et al., 1994; Regier et al., 1993). This definition recognizes that a behavior that is unendurable or upsetting for one person, such as lack of interest in sex, may be acceptable and normal for another. But it does not cover the behavior of people who are clearly disturbed and dangerous to others, yet are not troubled about their actions.

In this chapter, we will define **mental disorder** broadly, as any behavior or emotional state that causes an individual great suffering or worry; is self-defeating or self-destructive; or is maladaptive and disrupts either the person's relationships or the larger community. By this definition, many people will have some mental-health problem in the course of their lives, or their loved ones will.

Assessing Mental Disorders

Deciding on a general definition of mental disorder is one thing; translating it into practice is quite

another. Clinicians usually base their assessment of a person's mental and emotional state on interviews and observations of the person's behavior, and many also use psychological tests to help them arrive at a diagnosis.

Projective tests are designed to reveal unconscious motives, feelings, and conflicts—aspects of personality that may not be apparent in a person's actions. These tests consist of ambiguous pictures, patterns, sentences, or stories for the test taker to interpret or complete. A child or adult may be asked to draw a person, a house, or some other object, or to complete a sentence (such as "My father . . ." or "Women are . . ."). The assumption behind all projective tests is a psychodynamic one: that the person's unconscious thoughts and feelings will be "projected" onto the test materials and revealed in the person's responses.

Projective tests help clinicians establish rapport with their clients and can encourage clients to open up about anxieties and conflicts they might be ashamed to discuss. But the evidence is mounting that most of these tests have low *reliability* (give inconsistent results) when they are used for assessment or diagnosis—to decide, say, whether a patient has an anxiety disorder or a child has been sexually abused (Dawes, 1994). One reason for their low reliability is that different clinicians often interpret the same person's scores differently, perhaps because the clinicians themselves are "projecting" their own beliefs and assumptions when they decide what a specific response means. The tests also have low *validity;* that is, they often fail to measure what they claim to measure. The

mental disorder
Any behavior or emotional state that causes an individual great suffering or worry; is self-defeating or self-destructive; or is maladaptive and disrupts the person's relationships or the larger community.

projective tests
Psychological tests used to infer a person's motives, conflicts, and unconscious personality dynamics from the person's interpretations of ambiguous or unstructured stimuli.

Get Involved

This drawing was made by a young man who had bludgeoned his girlfriend with a hammer in a jealous rage. A psychologist has interpreted the drawing as follows: The upraised hands represent aggression and preparation to strike; the short legs represent feelings of inadequacy, and possible feelings of sexual inadequacy; and the red shirt represents passion, violence, and impulsivity. Rank the plausibility of this analysis on the following scale:

Very high _____ / _____ / _____ / _____ / _____ Very low

What other features of the drawing seem to reflect the young man's personality? Consider movement, color, form, and content.

When you have finished this exercise, turn the page—but not before!

reason is that a person's responses can be affected by sleepiness, hunger, drugs, worry, verbal ability, the clinician's instructions, the clinician's own personality (friendly and warm, or cool and neutral), and events occurring in the person's life that day (Anastasi, 1988).

All of these problems are apparent in the **Rorschach Inkblot Test,** which was devised by Swiss psychiatrist Hermann Rorschach in 1921. The test consists of ten cards with symmetrical abstract patterns, originally formed by spilling ink on paper and folding the paper in half. The test taker reports what he or she sees in the inkblots, and the clinician interprets the answers subjectively, taking into account the symbolic meanings emphasized by psychodynamic theories. One kind of response, for example, might be interpreted as a sign of dependency, and another as a sign of self-involvement. The Rorschach is enormously popular among clinicians, but efforts by independent investigators to confirm its reliability and validity have repeatedly failed. And many studies by advocates, supposedly supporting the test, have remained unpublished and unreplicated (Dawes, 1994; Wood, Nezworski, & Stejskal, 1996).

Another popular projective test, the **Thematic Apperception Test (TAT)** (Morgan & Murray, 1935), has the test taker make up stories about ambiguous drawings and pictures of people doing something. What is happening? What are the characters thinking and feeling? What will happen next? A standardized scoring system considers the themes raised in each story, the characters the

What do you see in this Rorschach inkblot?

test taker identifies with, the motives attributed to the characters, and the endings given to the stories. The TAT has greater reliability and validity than other projective tests, but *only* when it is used to measure specific motives rather than general mental disorders (see Chapter 13).

Many therapists also use *objective tests,* or **inventories.** These are standardized questionnaires that ask about the test taker's behavior and feelings. Some inventories, such as the Beck Depression Inventory, the Spielberger State-Trait Anger Inventory, and the Taylor Manifest Anxiety Scale, assess specific problems. The most widely used objective test, the **Minnesota Multiphasic Personality Inventory (MMPI),** is organized into hundreds of clinical categories, or *scales,* covering such problems as depression, paranoia, schizophrenia, and introversion.

Rorschach Inkblot Test
A projective test that asks respondents to interpret abstract, symmetrical inkblots.

Thematic Apperception Test (TAT)
A projective test that asks respondents to interpret a series of drawings showing ambiguous scenes of people.

inventories
Standardized objective questionnaires requiring written responses; typically include scales on which people are asked to rate themselves.

Minnesota Multiphasic Personality Inventory (MMPI)
A widely used objective personality test.

Get Involved

This drawing was made by a young man recently hospitalized following a suicide attempt. A psychologist has interpreted the drawing as follows: The upraised hands represent helplessness and loss; the short legs represent diminished stature, an inability to "measure up"; and the red shirt represents anger turned toward himself. Rank the plausibility of this analysis on the following scale:

Very high _____ / _____ / _____ / _____ / _____ Very low

What other features of the drawing seem to reflect the young man's personality? Consider movement, color, form, and content.

What does this exercise, combined with the one on the previous page, tell you about how prior knowledge about a person might affect the interpretation of the person's performance on a projective test, such as the Rorschach Inkblot Test?

Inventories are more reliable and more valid than either projective methods or subjective clinical judgments based on observations and interviews (Anastasi, 1988; Dawes, 1994). But inventories also have their problems. For example, critics of the MMPI feel that in spite of recent revisions, the test's standards of normality do not sufficiently reflect differences among cultural, ethnic, and socioeconomic groups. Two psychologists who reviewed the history and validity of the MMPI concluded that correctly interpreting it requires "substantial experience and sophistication" (Helmes & Reddon, 1993), and, unfortunately, this condition is not always met.

Diagnosis: Art or Science?

Because of the problems we have discussed, the value of psychological testing for clinical diagnosis has been hotly debated. But this debate is a whisper compared with the noisy controversy about the categories used for classifying disorders in the first place.

The standard guide for diagnosing mental disorders is the *Diagnostic and Statistical Manual of Mental Disorders* (DSM), published by the American Psychiatric Association. The first edition of the DSM, in 1952, was only 86 pages long and contained only a few basic categories, including brain disorders, "mental deficiency," and personality problems. The latest edition, the DSM-IV (1994), is nearly 900 pages long and contains more than 300 mental disorders. The DSM's primary aim is descriptive: to provide clear diagnostic categories, so that clinicians and researchers can agree on which disorders they are talking about and can study and treat them. (For a list of the DSM's major categories, see Table 10.1.)

The DSM lists the symptoms of each disorder and, wherever possible, gives information about the typical age of onset, predisposing factors, course of the disorder, prevalence of the disorder, sex ratio of those affected, and cultural issues that might affect diagnosis. In addition, rather than just assigning a global label such as "depression," clinicians are encouraged to evaluate each client according to five *axes,* or dimensions:

1. The primary clinical problem, such as depression.

2. Ingrained aspects of the client's personality that may affect the person's ability to be treated, such as self-involvement or dependency.

3. General medical conditions that are relevant to the disorder, such as respiratory or digestive problems.

4. Social and environmental problems that can make the disorder worse, such as job and housing troubles or loss of a support group.

5. A global assessment of the client's overall level of functioning in work, relationships, and leisure time, including whether the problem is of recent origin or of long duration, and how incapacitating it is.

The DSM has had an extraordinary impact worldwide. Virtually all textbooks in psychiatry and psychology base their discussions of mental disorders on the DSM. Insurance companies require clinicians to assign their clients an appropriate DSM code number for the diagnosed disorder, which puts pressure on compilers of the manual to add more diagnoses so that physicians and psychologists will be compensated. Attorneys and judges often refer to the manual's list of mental disorders, even though the DSM warns that its categories "may not be wholly relevant to legal judgments."

Because of the DSM's influence, it is important to be aware of its limitations. Critics point to the following concerns about efforts to classify and label mental disorders in general, and the DSM's efforts in particular:

Thinking Critically About Diagnosing Disorders

1. *The danger of overdiagnosis.* "If you give a small boy a hammer," wrote Abraham Kaplan (1967), "it will turn out that everything he runs into needs pounding." In the same way, say critics, the DSM encourages the overuse of diagnostic categories. Consider dissociative identity disorder, commonly known as "multiple personality disorder." Before 1980, fewer than 200 cases had ever been diagnosed. Since 1980, when the DSM-III included new criteria for this diagnosis, thousands of cases have been reported, almost all of them in North America (Nathan, 1994; Piper, 1997). Does this mean that the disorder is being better identified, or that it is being overdiagnosed by North American clinicians who are looking for it? (We will return to this question later in this chapter.)

2. *The power of diagnostic labels.* Once a person has acquired a label—for example, once an impulsive, troubled teenager is diagnosed as having "oppositional defiant disorder"—other people may ignore changes in the individual's behavior and fail

Table 10.1	Major Diagnostic Categories in the DSM-IV

Disorders usually first diagnosed in infancy, childhood, or adolescence include mental retardation, attention deficit disorders (such as hyperactivity or an inability to concentrate), eating disorders, and developmental problems.

Delirium, dementia, amnesia, and other cognitive disorders are those resulting from brain damage, degenerative diseases such as syphilis or Alzheimer's, toxic substances, or drugs.

Substance-related disorders are problems associated with excessive use of or withdrawal from alcohol, amphetamines, caffeine, cocaine, hallucinogens, nicotine, opiates, or other drugs.

Schizophrenia and other psychotic disorders are disorders characterized by delusions, hallucinations, and severe disturbances in thinking and emotion.

Mood disorders include major depression, bipolar disorder (manic depression), and dysthymia (chronic depressed mood).

Anxiety disorders include generalized anxiety disorder, phobias, panic attacks with or without agoraphobia, posttraumatic stress disorder, and obsessive thoughts or compulsive rituals.

Somatoform disorders involve physical symptoms (e.g., paralysis, heart palpitations, or dizziness) for which no organic cause can be found. This category includes hypochondria (an extreme preoccupation with health and the unfounded conviction that one is ill), and conversion disorder (in which a physical symptom, such as a paralyzed arm or blindness, serves a psychological function).

Dissociative disorders include dissociative amnesia (in which important events cannot be remembered after a traumatic event) and dissociative identity disorder (formerly "multiple personality disorder," characterized by the presence of two or more distinct identities or personality states).

Sexual and gender identity disorders include problems of sexual (gender) identity, such as transsexualism (wanting to be the other gender), problems of sexual performance (such as premature ejaculation, lack of orgasm, or lack of desire), and paraphilias (unusual or bizarre imagery or acts that are necessary for sexual arousal, as in fetishism, sadomasochism, or exhibitionism).

Impulse-control disorders involve an inability to resist an impulse to perform some act that is harmful to the individual or to others, as in pathological gambling, stealing (kleptomania), setting fires (pyromania), or having violent rages.

Personality disorders are inflexible and maladaptive patterns that cause distress to the individual or impair the person's ability to function; they include paranoid, narcissistic, and antisocial personality disorders.

Additional conditions that may be a focus of clinical attention include "problems in living" such as bereavement, academic difficulties, religious or spiritual problems, and acculturation problems.

---

to consider other explanations of it (maybe the teenager is defiant because he is bored or because his parents never listen to him).

In a famous study, David Rosenhan (1973) demonstrated just how powerful psychiatric labels can be. Eight normal, healthy adults—a housewife, a painter, a pediatrician, a graduate student, a psychiatrist, and three psychologists, including Rosenhan himself—appeared at 12 different hospitals, claiming to have heard hazy voices that seemed to be saying "hollow," "empty," and "thud." Apart from this lie, they all gave honest personal histories. One was diagnosed as manic–depressive and the others as schizophrenic, and all eight were quickly admitted. At that point, the pseudopatients stopped faking any symptoms and behaved normally. Nonetheless, the hospital staff regarded everything they did as further signs of emotional disorder. For example, all of the pseudopatients took frequent notes on their experiences. Several nurses recorded this act in the records without asking them what they were writing about. One nurse wrote "patient engages in writing behavior," as if writing were an odd thing to do. Upon their release, after a period ranging from 7 to 52 days, the pseudopatients were labeled as being "in remission" (without symptoms)—but they were not labeled "recovered" or "well."

Of course, Rosenhan and his colleagues knew they didn't have schizophrenia, but in the real world, a psychiatric diagnosis can also have powerful effects on the individual who receives it. Diagnostic labels can be reassuring ("Whew! So *that's* what I've got!"), but they can also create a self-fulfilling prophecy: The client tries to conform to the assigned diagnosis, and the clinician then interprets everything the client does as confirmation of the diagnosis (Maddux, 1996).

3. *Confusion of serious mental disorders with normal problems.* The DSM is not called "The Diagnostic and Statistical Manual of Mental Disorders and a Whole Bunch of Everyday Problems." Yet the compilers of the DSM keep adding everyday problems. The latest version actually contains "disorder of written expression" (having trouble writing clearly), "mathematics disorder" (not doing well in math), and "caffeine-induced sleep disorder" (which at least is easy to cure, by just laying off the coffee). Some critics fear that by lumping together such normal difficulties with true mental illnesses, such as schizophrenia, the DSM implies that everyday problems are comparable to disorders— and equally likely to require treatment (Kutchins & Kirk, 1997; Maddux, 1993; Szasz, 1961/1967).

4. *The illusion of objectivity.* Finally, some critics argue that the whole enterprise of the DSM is a vain attempt to impose a veneer of science on an inherently subjective process (Kutchins & Kirk, 1997; Maddux, 1993; Tiefer, 1995). Many decisions about what to include as a diagnosis, say the critics, are based not on empirical evidence, but on group consensus. For example, when the American Psychiatric Association decided in the early 1970s to remove homosexuality from the DSM, it did not base its decision on the research showing that homosexuals were no more disturbed than heterosexuals. Rather, it took a vote of its members. Over the years, psychiatrists have quite properly rejected many other "disorders" that reflected cultural prejudices, such as drapetomania, lack of vaginal orgasm, childhood masturbation disorder, and nymphomania (Wakefield, 1992). But they have also voted in new disorders that reflect today's prejudices and values, such as "hypo-

Harriet Tubman (on the left) poses with some of the people she helped to escape from slavery on her "underground railroad." Slaveholders welcomed the idea that Tubman and others who insisted on their freedom had a "mental disorder" called "drapetomania."

active sexual desire disorder"—not wanting to have sex often enough.

Defenders of the DSM point out that new studies are improving empirical support for many of its categories. They argue that when the manual is used carefully and correctly, it improves the accuracy of diagnosis (Barlow, 1991; Spitzer & Williams, 1988; Wittchen et al., 1995). The DSM's labels, its supporters feel, help people identify the source of their unhappiness so they can get proper treatment (Kessler et al., 1994). As for the problem of subjectivity, advocates point out that not all diagnoses reflect society's biases (Wakefield, 1992). In cultures around the world, from the Inuit of Alaska to the Yorubas of Nigeria, some individuals have delusions, are severely depressed, or can't control their behavior; in every culture, such individuals are considered to have mental illnesses (Kleinman, 1988).

We will return to these controversies as we examine some of the DSM's major categories of disorder.

What's Ahead

- *What's the difference between ordinary anxiety and an anxiety disorder?*

- *Why is the most disabling of all phobias known as the "fear of fear"?*

- *When is checking the stove before leaving home a sign of caution—and when does it signal a disorder?*

ANXIETY DISORDERS

Anyone who is facing a dangerous, unfamiliar, or stressful situation, such as making a first parachute jump or waiting for important news, quite sensibly feels *anxiety* (a general state of apprehension or psychological tension) or *fear* (apprehension about a specific threat). In the short run, these emotions are adaptive because they energize and motivate us to cope with danger—they ensure, for example, that we don't make that first jump without knowing how to operate the parachute.

But in some individuals, fear and anxiety become detached from any apparent danger, or they don't turn off when danger is past. Such individuals may be suffering from *generalized anxiety disorder,* marked by long-lasting feelings of apprehension and doom; *panic attacks,* short-lived but intense feelings of spontaneous anxiety; *phobias,* excessive fears of specific things or situations; or *obsessive–compulsive disorder,* in which repeated thoughts and rituals are used to ward off anxious feelings.

Fear is normal when you jump out of a plane for the first time—but people with anxiety disorders feel as if they are jumping out of planes all the time.

Anxiety States

The chief characteristic of **generalized anxiety disorder** is continuous, uncontrollable anxiety or worry—a feeling of foreboding and dread—that occurs on a majority of days during a six-month period and that is not brought on by physical causes such as disease, drugs, or drinking too much coffee. Symptoms include restlessness or

generalized anxiety disorder

A continuous state of anxiety marked by feelings of worry and dread, apprehension, difficulties in concentration, and signs of motor tension.

feeling keyed up, being easily fatigued, difficulty concentrating, irritability, muscle tension and jitteriness, and sleep disturbance.

Some people have *predisposing factors*—qualities in their own makeup or experience—that increase their susceptibility to generalized anxiety disorder: for example, a hereditary predisposition, poor coping skills, or impractical goals or unreasonable beliefs that foster worry and fear. And often (but not always), an anxiety disorder is set off and sustained by *precipitating factors,* upsetting one-time events or continuing, unsettling situations—for example, not knowing from day to day whether your job is secure, your partner will leave you, or you'll get through school.

People who survive uncontrollable and unpredictable dangers—such as war, rape, torture, or natural disasters—may suffer afterward from **posttraumatic stress disorder (PTSD).** Typical symptoms include reliving the trauma in recurrent, intrusive thoughts or dreams; "psychic numbing," a sense of detachment from others and an inability to feel happy or loving; and increased physiological arousal, reflected in difficulty concentrating, insomnia, and irritability. These symptoms can occur either immediately after a trauma or after a delay of many months, and episodes may recur for months, years, or even decades. A random survey of 5,877 Americans found that nearly 1 person in 12 has suffered from PTSD in his or her life, and in more than one-third of the cases, the symptoms lasted for at least 10 years (Kessler et al., 1995).

Another kind of anxiety disorder is **panic disorder,** in which a person has sudden attacks of intense fear or panic, with feelings of impending doom. The attacks may last from a few minutes to (more rarely) several hours and may involve such intense symptoms as trembling and shaking, dizziness, chest pain or discomfort, heart palpitations, feelings of unreality, hot and cold flashes, sweating, and a fear of dying, going crazy, or losing control.

People who have panic disorder are found throughout the world, although culture influences the particular symptoms of a panic attack (Barlow, 1990). Feelings of choking or being smothered, numbness, and fear of dying are most common in Latin America and southern Europe; fear of public places is most common in northern Europe and the United States; and a fear of going crazy is more common in the Americas than in Europe. In Greenland, some fishermen suffer from "kayak-angst": a sudden attack of dizziness and fear that occurs while they are fishing in small, one-person kayaks (Amering & Katschnig, 1990).

Although panic attacks seem to occur out of nowhere, they are often related to stress, prolonged emotion, exercise, drugs such as caffeine or nicotine, specific worries, or traumatic experiences (Barlow, 1990; Beck, 1988). For example, a friend of ours was on a plane that was the target of a bomb threat. He coped beautifully at the time, but two weeks later, seemingly "out of nowhere," he had a panic attack. Such delayed attacks in the aftermath of life-threatening scares are common; the essential difference between people who go on to develop a disorder and those who do not lies in *how they interpret their bodily reactions* (Barlow, 1990; McNally, 1994). Healthy people who have occasional panic attacks see them correctly as a result of a passing crisis or period of stress, comparable to another person's migraines. But people who develop a full-fledged panic disorder regard the attack as a sign of impending death or disaster, and they begin to live their lives in restrictive ways, trying to avoid future attacks.

Fears and Phobias

Are you afraid of bugs, snakes, or dogs? Are you so afraid that you can't stand to be around one, or are you just vaguely uncomfortable? A **phobia** is an exaggerated fear of a specific situation, activity, or thing. The susceptibility to some common phobias, such as fear of heights (acrophobia), thunder (brontophobia), closed spaces (claustrophobia), snakes, and insects, may have evolved in human beings because these fears were adaptive for the species. Other, more idiosyncratic phobias, such as a fear of bunnies or the color purple (porphyrophobia), may be acquired through classical conditioning, as we saw in Chapter 8. Still other phobias, such as fear of dirt and germs (mysophobia) and the number 13 (triskaidekaphobia), reflect personality preferences or cultural norms. A phobia, whatever its specific nature, is truly frightening and often incapacitating for its sufferer. It is not just a tendency to say "ugh" at tarantulas or skip the snake display at the zoo.

People who have a *social phobia* have a persistent fear of situations in which they will be observed by others. They worry that they will do or say something that will humiliate or embarrass them. Common social phobias are fears of speaking or per-

posttraumatic stress disorder (PTSD)
An anxiety disorder in which a person who has experienced a traumatic or life-threatening event has symptoms such as psychic numbing, reliving of the trauma, and increased physiological arousal.

panic disorder
An anxiety disorder in which a person experiences intense periods of fear and feelings of impending doom, accompanied by physiological symptoms such as rapid breathing and pulse, and dizziness.

phobia
An exaggerated fear of a specific situation, activity, or object.

THE FAR SIDE   By GARY LARSON

Luposlipaphobia: The fear of being pursued by timber wolves around a kitchen table while wearing socks on a newly waxed floor.

agoraphobia

A set of phobias, often set off by a panic attack, involving the basic fear of being away from a safe place or person.

obsessive–compulsive disorder (OCD)

An anxiety disorder in which a person feels trapped in repetitive, persistent thoughts (obsessions) and repetitive, ritualized behaviors (compulsions) designed to reduce anxiety.

business, and religious center of town, the public meeting place away from home. The fundamental fear in agoraphobia is of being alone in a public place, where escape might be difficult or where help might be unavailable. Individuals with agoraphobia report many specific fears—of public buses, driving in traffic or tunnels, eating in restaurants, or going to parties—but the underlying fear is of being away from a safe place, usually home, or a safe person, usually a parent or spouse.

Agoraphobia may begin with a series of panic attacks that seem to come out of the blue. The attack is so unexpected and so scary that the agoraphobic-to-be begins to avoid situations that he or she thinks may provoke another one. After a while, any sort of emotional arousal, from whatever source, feels too much like anxiety, and the person with agoraphobia will try to avoid it. Because so many of the actions associated with this phobia are designed to help the person avoid a panic attack, researchers often describe agoraphobia as a "fear of fear" rather than a fear of places (Chambless, 1988).

forming in public, using public restrooms, eating in public, and writing in the presence of others. Again, these phobias are more severe forms of ordinary problems, such as the occasional shyness and social anxiety that everyone experiences.

By far the most disabling fear disorder is **agoraphobia,** which accounts for more than half of the phobia cases for which people seek treatment. In ancient Greece, the *agora* was the social, political,

Obsessions and Compulsions

Obsessive–compulsive disorder (OCD) is characterized by recurrent, persistent, unwished-for thoughts or images (*obsessions*) and by repetitive, ritualized, stereotyped behaviors that the person feels must be carried out to avoid disaster (*compulsions*). Of course, many people have trivial compulsions and practice superstitious rituals; as we noted in Chapter 8, baseball players are famous for them. Obsessions and compulsions become serious—a disorder—when they trouble the individual and interfere with the person's life.

Get Involved

Everyone fears something. Stop for a moment to think about what you fear most. Is it heights? Snakes? Speaking in public? Ask yourself these questions:

- How long have I feared this thing or situation?

- How would I respond if I could not avoid this thing or situation?

- How much would I be willing to rearrange my life (my movements, schedule, activities) to avoid this feared thing or situation?

After considering these questions, would you regard your fear as a full-blown phobia or merely a normal source of apprehension? What are your criteria for deciding?

The Disease Germ Is More Dangerous Than the Mad Dog

What is a normal concern with hygiene in one culture could seem an abnormal compulsion in another. This Lysol ad played on Americans' fears of disease by warning about the "unseen menace—more threatening, more fatal, more cruel than a million mad dogs— . . . the disease germ."

Obsessive thoughts are often experienced as frightening or repugnant. For example, the person may have repetitive thoughts of killing a child, of becoming contaminated by shaking hands, or of having unknowingly hurt someone in a traffic accident. Obsessive thoughts take many forms, but they are alike in reflecting maladaptive ways of reasoning and processing information. In one case, a man had repeated images of hitting his 3-year-old son with a hammer. Unable to explain his horrible thoughts about his beloved son, he assumed he was going insane. Most parents, in fact, have occasional negative feelings about their children and may even entertain a fleeting thought of murder, but they recognize that these brief feelings are not the same as actions. The man, it turned out, felt that his son had usurped his place in his wife's affections, but he was unable to reveal his anger and hurt to his wife directly (Carson, Butcher, & Mineka, 1996).

People who suffer from compulsions likewise feel they have no control over them. The most common compulsions are hand washing, counting, touching, and checking. A woman *must* check the furnace, lights, locks, oven, and fireplace three times before she can sleep; or a man *must* wash his hands and face precisely eight times before he leaves the house. Most sufferers of OCD do not enjoy such rituals and realize that the behavior is senseless. But if they try to forgo the ritual, they feel mounting anxiety that is relieved only by giving in to it.

For one young man with OCD, stairs became a treadmill he could not get off: "At first I'd walk up and down the stairs only three or four times," he recalled. "Later I had to run up and down 63 times in 45 minutes. If I failed, I had to start all over again from the beginning. Then other weird behaviors, such as compulsive washing, started to kick in. . . . They took on a life of their own and became the enemy" (quoted in King, 1989).

Some cases of obsessive–compulsive disorder may involve a brain abnormality. PET scans find that several parts of the brain are hyperactive in people with OCD. One area of the frontal lobes, the *orbital cortex* (which lies just above the eye sockets), apparently sends messages of impending danger to the *caudate nucleus,* an area involved in controlling the movement of the limbs, and to other structures involved in preparing the body to feel afraid and respond to external threats. Normally, once danger is past or a person realizes that there is no real cause for fear, the caudate nucleus switches off the alarm signals. In people with OCD, however, the orbital cortex sends out repeated false alarms; then the emotional networks send out mistaken "fear!" messages, and the caudate nucleus fails to turn them off. The sufferer feels in a constant state of danger and tries repeatedly to reduce the resulting anxiety (Schwartz et al., 1996).

Anxiety disorders, uncomfortable or painful as they can be, are at least a sign of commitment to the future: The person can anticipate the future enough to worry about it. But sometimes people's hopes for the future become extinguished. They are no longer anxious that something may go wrong; they are convinced it will go wrong, and that there is nothing they can do about it. This belief is a sign of depression, to which we turn next.

??? QUICK QUIZ

We hope you don't feel anxious about matching each term on the left with its description on the right:

1. social phobia
2. generalized anxiety disorder
3. posttraumatic stress disorder
4. agoraphobia
5. compulsion
6. obsession

a. need to perform ritual
b. fear of fear; of being trapped in public
c. continuing sense of doom and worry
d. repeated, unwanted thoughts
e. fear of meeting new people
f. anxiety following severe shock

Answers:
1. e 2. c 3. f 4. b 5. a 6. d

What's Ahead

- *How can you tell whether you have major depression or just the blues?*
- *What are the "poles" in bipolar disorder?*
- *How do some people think themselves into depression?*

MOOD DISORDERS

The writer William Styron, who fought and recovered from severe depression, used the beginning of Dante's classic poem, *The Divine Comedy,* to convey his suffering:

> In the middle of the journey of our life
> I found myself in a dark wood.
> For I had lost the right path.

"For those who have dwelt in depression's dark wood," wrote Styron in *Darkness Visible,* "and known its inexplicable agony, the return from the abyss is not unlike the ascent of the poet, trudging upward and upward out of hell's black depths and at last emerging into what he saw as 'the shining world.' "

Although most people say they feel "depressed" from time to time, their sadness is very far removed from the anguish of people like William Styron. Depression becomes a disorder when it goes beyond ordinary sadness over life's problems, such as the end of a love affair, or even the wild grief that accompanies tragedy and bereavement. In the DSM, the category of "Mood Disorders" includes disturbances in mood that range from extreme depression to extreme mania.

major depression

A mood disorder involving disturbances in emotion (excessive sadness), behavior (loss of interest in one's usual activities), cognition (thoughts of hopelessness), and body function (fatigue and loss of appetite).

Depression and Mania

Depression is so widespread that it has been called the common cold of psychiatric problems. Some people suffer from a chronic form of depression called *dysthymia,* in which they function adequately but nearly always report their mood as sad or "down in the dumps." Others suffer from **major depression,** which involves emotional, behavioral, and cognitive changes severe enough to disrupt a person's usual functioning. People with this disorder report despair and hopelessness. They may think often of death or suicide. They lose interest or pleasure in their usual activities. They feel unable to get up and do things; it takes an enormous effort just to get dressed. Their thinking patterns feed their bleak moods. They exaggerate minor failings, ignore or discount positive events ("She didn't mean that compliment; she was only being polite"), and interpret any little thing that goes wrong as evidence that nothing will ever go right. Emotionally healthy people who are sad or grieving do not see themselves as completely worthless and unlovable, and they know at some level that their sadness or grief will pass. But depressed people have low self-esteem: They interpret losses as signs of personal failure and conclude that they will never be happy again.

Depression is accompanied by physical changes as well. The depressed person may overeat or stop eating, have difficulty falling asleep or sleeping through the night, lose sexual desire, have trouble concentrating, and feel tired all the time. Some sufferers have other physical reactions, such as inexplicable pain or headaches.

The hallmarks of depression are despair and hopelessness.

About half of all those who go through a period of major depression will do so only once; others have recurrent bouts. Some people have episodes that are many years apart; others have clusters of depressive episodes over a few years. Alarmingly, depression and suicide rates among young people have increased rapidly in recent years (see "Taking Psychology with You").

At the opposite pole from depression is *mania,* an abnormally high state of exhilaration. You might think it's impossible to feel too good, but mania is not the normal joy of being in love or winning the Pulitzer Prize. Someone in a manic state is expansive to an extent that is out of character. The symptoms are exactly the opposite of those in depression. Instead of feeling fatigued and listless, the person is full of energy. Instead of feeling hopeless and powerless, the person feels full of ambitions, plans, and power. The depressed person speaks slowly, monotonously, without inflection. The manic person speaks rapidly, dramatically, often with many jokes and puns. The depressed person has low self-esteem. The manic person has inflated self-esteem.

When people experience episodes of both depression and mania, they are said to have **bipolar disorder** (formerly called *manic–depressive disorder*). Unlike depression, which affects approximately 15 percent of Americans at some time in their lives, bipolar disorder is rare, affecting only 1.5 percent (Kessler et al., 1994). The great humorist Mark Twain had bipolar disorder, which he described as "periodical and sudden changes of mood . . . from deep melancholy to half-insane tempests and cyclones."

Although bipolar disorder occurs equally in both sexes, major depression is overrepresented among women of all ethnicities (McGrath et al., 1990). Some psychologists think that women are truly more likely to become depressed than men are, but others think the difference is more apparent than real. Because the sexes often express feelings differently (see Chapter 12), depression in males may be overlooked or misdiagnosed. Some researchers, for example, believe that drug abuse and violence in men often masks depression or anxiety (Canetto, 1992; Kessler et al., 1994).

Theories of Depression

Explanations of depression generally emphasize five possible causes: biological predispositions, social conditions, problems with close attachments, cognitive habits, or a combination of individual vulnerability and stress.

1. *Biological explanations emphasize genetics and brain chemistry.* These explanations seem especially plausible in cases of depression that do not involve reactions to actual crises or losses, but which instead seem to come from nowhere or to occur in response to minor stresses.

Although the search for the gene or genes that might be involved in depression and bipolar disorder has so far proved fruitless, studies of adopted children and twins support the notion that these disorders sometimes have a genetic component (DiLalla et al., 1996; Nurnberger & Gershon, 1992; Tsuang & Faraone, 1990). Studies of neurotransmitters suggest that a biochemical imbalance plays a role. As we saw in Chapter 4, neurotransmitters permit messages to be transmitted from one neuron to another in the brain. In the view of some researchers, depression is caused by a deficient production of the neurotransmitter serotonin and/or norepinephrine, and manic moods are caused by excessive levels of norepinephrine. Drugs that increase the levels of serotonin and norepinephrine sometimes alleviate symptoms of depression, and drugs that reduce norepinephrine sometimes alleviate the symptoms of mania. (However, as we will see in the next chapter, these drugs do not help everyone.)

bipolar disorder

A mood disorder in which episodes of both depression and mania (excessive euphoria) occur.

Researchers are now using brain-scan technologies to identify changes that occur in the brain during depressive and manic episodes (see Figure 10.1). In general, the brains of depressed people seem less active, especially the frontal lobes, which are involved in positive emotions (Davidson, 1992). However, brain scans alone do not tell us whether brain changes cause the disorder, or having the disorder changes the brain.

2. *Social explanations emphasize the circumstances of people's lives.* In the social view, women are more likely than men to suffer from depression because they have less satisfying work and family lives, lower status than men in work and society, and higher rates of sexual victimization. Men are nearly twice as likely as women to be married and working full time, a combination of activities that is strongly associated with mental health (Brown, 1993; Golding, 1988). In a random sample of 1,111 men and women in Boston, virtually all of the differences between men and women in their reported levels of depression could be accounted for by their different states of marriage and employment (Gore & Mangione, 1983). Mothers are especially vulnerable to depression: The more children a woman has, the more likely she is to become depressed (McGrath et al., 1990).

Other likely social factors in the origins of depression include sexual abuse and other forms of violence. Women who have suffered sexual trauma are more likely than other women to be depressed, and their symptoms are more severe than those of depressed women who have not been sexually traumatized (Bryer et al., 1987; Burnam et al., 1988). In the United States, inner-city adolescents of both sexes who are exposed to high rates of violence report higher levels of depression and more thoughts of—and efforts to commit—suicide than those who are not subjected to violence in their lives or communities (Mazza, Reynolds, & Grover, 1995). Social analyses, however, fail to explain why most victims of violence do not become clinically depressed. Nor do they explain why some people become depressed even though their lives are comfortable, safe, and secure.

3. *Attachment explanations emphasize problems with affiliation and close relationships.* In this view, depression results from disturbed relationships; separations and losses, both past and present; and a history of insecure attachments (Klerman et al., 1984; Roberts, Gotlib, & Kassel, 1996). This explanation is supported by the fact that depressive episodes are most frequently set off by disruption of a primary relationship (Barnett & Gotlib, 1988). However, attachment theories raise an interesting cause-and-effect problem: Has a broken relationship caused depression, or was the relationship broken because one partner was depressed? Depressed people sometimes seem demanding and "depressing" to family and friends, who may feel angry or sad around them and eventually break away (Gotlib & Hooley, 1988; Joiner & Metalsky, 1995).

4. *Cognitive explanations emphasize particular habits of thinking and interpreting events.* Two decades ago, the theory of "learned helplessness" proposed that people become depressed when their efforts to avoid pain or control the environment fail (Seligman, 1975). But this explanation had a fatal flaw: Not all depressed people have actually failed in their lives, and some seem to have everything they could want. Yet these people believe that nothing they do will be successful. Modifications were therefore made in the theory, which in its current form holds that depression often results from having a *pessimistic explanatory style* (see Chapter 12). People who are habitually pessimistic do not just feel helpless; they also feel hopeless, regardless of the actual circumstances of their lives. They believe that nothing good will ever happen to them—that the future is bleak and they can't do anything to change it (Abramson, Metalsky, & Alloy, 1989; Seligman, 1991).

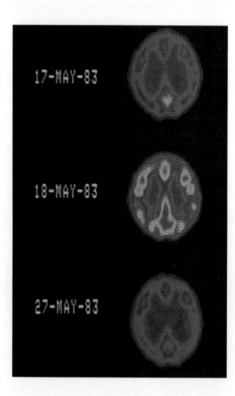

Figure 10.1

The Bipolar Brain

These PET scans show changes in the metabolism of glucose, the brain's energy supply, in a patient with bipolar disorder. On May 17 and 27, the patient was depressed, and glucose metabolism throughout the brain was lower than normal. On May 18, the patient became manic, and metabolic activity increased to near normal levels. Keep in mind that such changes do not show the direction of cause and effect: A drop in glucose might bring on depression, but depression might also cause a drop in glucose levels.

Other cognitive bad habits are also associated with depression. People who focus inward and brood endlessly about their negative feelings—who have a "ruminating response style"—tend to have longer and more intense periods of depression than do those who are able to distract themselves, look outward, and seek solutions to their problems. Women are more likely than men to develop such a ruminating, introspective style, beginning in adolescence, and this tendency may contribute both to longer-lasting depressions in women and to the sex difference in reported rates (Bromberger & Matthews, 1996; Nolen-Hoeksema, 1991; Nolen-Hoeksema & Girgus, 1994). Of course, when you are already feeling sad, gloomy ideas come more easily. Negative thinking, therefore, can be both a cause and a result of depression (Hilsman & Garber, 1995).

5. *"Vulnerability–stress" explanations draw on all four explanations just discussed.* They hold that depression and other disorders result from an *interaction* between individual vulnerabilities—in personality traits, habits of thinking, genetic predispositions, and so forth—and environmental stress or sad events:

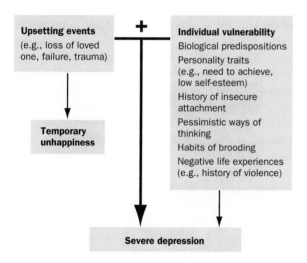

Interaction models are an improvement over theories implying that everyone is equally vulnerable to depression, given a certain experience or biological disposition. These models try to specify which personality traits interact with which events to produce depression. In one study, for example, students who got worse grades than they expected reported feeling depressed (not a surprise), but this mood persisted only in those who *also* had a depressive way of explaining events ("I'm stupid and always will be") *and* low self-esteem. In this case, depression resulted from a combination of having a pessimistic explanatory style, low self-esteem, and an experience with failure, leading to a sense of hopelessness (Metalsky et al., 1993).

In assessing these different approaches critically, keep in mind that depression comes in varying degrees of intensity, and it may have different causes in different people. One person may have

> **Thinking Critically About Causes of Depression**

been abandoned in childhood and may therefore feel insecurely attached in current relationships. Another may have a pessimistic explanatory style that fosters depressive interpretations of even happy events ("Yeah, yeah, I've met this great person but it will never last"). A third may have a biological predisposition to respond to stress with depression. And a fourth may lack satisfying work or love, or may have been subjected to violence or other trauma.

That is why we must avoid either–or explanations of depression—it's biochemical *or* it's psychological. By understanding depression as an interaction among an individual's biology, personality, and experiences, we can see why the same precipitating event, such as a minor setback or even the loss of a loved one, might produce ordinary sadness in one person and extreme depression in another.

??? QUICK QUIZ

We hope you won't perceive this quiz in a way that depresses you.

1. In the view of some biological researchers, depression involves a deficit in _____ and/or _____.

2. Depression is most likely to occur if you (a) are habitually optimistic, (b) think a lot about your negative feelings, (c) are married and are employed full time, (d) have inflated self-esteem.

3. Vulnerability–stress theories attribute depression to an interaction between _____ and _____.

 4. A newspaper headline announces that a single gene has been identified as the cause of depression, but when you read the fine print, you learn that other studies have failed to support this research. What explanations can you think of to explain these contradictory findings?

Answers:

1. serotonin, norepinephrine   2. b   3. individual vulnerabilities; environmental stress or sad events   4. The conflicting evidence may mean, among other possibilities, that if a genetic predisposition for depression does exist, it is not due to a single specific gene, but involves several genes working in the context of environmental events. It may mean that the right gene has not yet been identified. Or it may mean that genes are not a factor in all forms of depression.

What's Ahead

- *When does being self-centered become a disorder?*

- *What do a charming but heartless tycoon and a remorseless killer have in common?*

- *Why are some people seemingly incapable of feeling guilt and shame?*

PERSONALITY DISORDERS

Personality disorders involve rigid, maladaptive traits that cause great distress or an inability to get along with others. The DSM-IV describes such a disorder as "an enduring pattern of inner experience and behavior that deviates markedly from the expectations of the individual's culture." This pattern is not caused by depression, a drug reaction, or a situation that temporarily induces a person to behave in ways that are out of character.

Problem Personalities

One personality disorder, **paranoid personality disorder,** involves pervasive, unfounded suspiciousness and mistrust of other people; irrational jealousy; secretiveness; and doubt about the loyalty of others. People with paranoid personalities have delusions of being persecuted by everyone from their closest relatives to government agencies, and their beliefs are immune to disconfirming evidence.

Another personality disorder, **narcissistic personality disorder,** involves an exaggerated sense of self-importance and self-absorption. Narcissism gets its name from the Greek myth of Narcissus, a beautiful boy who fell in love with his

own image. Individuals who are narcissistic are preoccupied with fantasies of unlimited success, power, brilliance, or ideal love. They demand constant attention and admiration and feel entitled to special favors, without being willing to reciprocate. They fall in love quickly and out of love just as fast, when the beloved proves to have some human flaw.

Notice that although these descriptions evoke flashes of recognition ("I know that type!"), they involve general qualities that depend on subjective labels and value judgments (Maddux & Mundell,

Narcissus fell in love with his own image, and now he has a personality disorder named after him—just what a narcissist would expect!

---

personality disorders
Rigid, maladaptive personality patterns that cause personal distress or an inability to get along with others.

paranoid personality disorder
A disorder characterized by habitually unreasonable and excessive suspiciousness, jealousy, or mistrust.

narcissistic personality disorder
A disorder characterized by an exaggerated sense of self-importance and self-absorption.

1997). Culture influences the decision to classify an individual as having one of these disorders. For example, American society often encourages people to pursue dreams of unlimited success and ideal love, but such dreams might be considered signs of serious disturbance in a more group-oriented society. Where would you draw the line between having a "narcissistic personality disorder" and being a normal member of a group or culture that encourages "looking out for number one" and puts a premium on youth and beauty?

The Antisocial Personality

Throughout history, most societies have recognized and feared the few members in their midst who lack all human connection to anyone else—who can cheat, con, and kill without flinching. In the 1830s these individuals were said to be afflicted with "moral insanity," and in the twentieth century they came to be called "psychopaths" or "sociopaths." The DSM, trying to avoid such emotionally charged terms, refers to **antisocial personality disorder.** By any name, this condition is a fascinating and frightening one because of the great harm these people inflict on their victims and on society.

People with antisocial personality disorder lack the emotions that link human beings to one another: empathy, the ability to take another person's perspective; shame for actions that hurt others; and guilt, the ability to feel remorse or sorrow for immoral actions. They are without conscience and have no regard for the rights of others. They can lie, charm, seduce, and manipulate others and then drop them without a qualm. If caught in a lie or a crime, they may seem sincerely sorry and promise to make amends, but it is all just an act. They are often sexually promiscuous, unable to maintain attachments, and irresponsible in their obligations to others. Some antisocial persons are sadistic, with a history of criminal or cruel behavior that began in childhood. They can kill anyone—an intended victim, a child, a bystander—without a twinge of regret. Others direct their energies into con games or career advancement, abusing other people emotionally or economically rather than physically. These individuals may be quite "sociable," charming everyone around them, but they have no emotional connection to others or guilt about their wrongdoing.

For unknown reasons, antisocial personality disorder is more common in males than in females; according to the DSM-IV and survey evidence, it occurs in 3 to 5 percent of all males and less than 1 percent of all females (Robins, Tipp, & Przybeck, 1991). Antisocial individuals create a lot of havoc; they may account for more than half of all serious crimes committed in the United States (Hare, 1993). In a review of longitudinal research, Terrie Moffitt (1993) found that the troubling behavior of such individuals starts early and continues through adolescence and adulthood: "biting and hitting at age 4, shoplifting and truancy at age 10, selling drugs and stealing cars at age 16, robbery and rape at age 22, and fraud and child abuse at age 30 . . . [such] persons lie at home, steal from shops, cheat at school, fight in bars, and embezzle at work."

antisocial personality disorder

A disorder (sometimes called psychopathy or sociopathy) characterized by antisocial behavior such as lying, stealing, manipulating others, and sometimes violence; a lack of social emotions (guilt, shame, and empathy); and impulsivity.

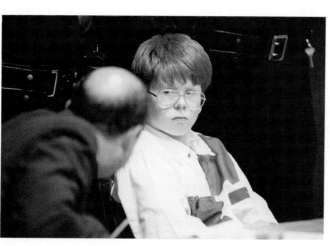

Some people with antisocial personalities use charm and elaborate con games to deceive others. Giovanni Vigliotto (left) married 105 women over 33 years, seized their assets, and then abandoned them. But other people with APD are sadistic and violent, starting in childhood. At age 13, Eric Smith (right) bludgeoned and strangled a 4-year-old boy to death. He was tried as an adult and sentenced to a prison term of nine years to life.

Antisocial individuals do not respond to punishments that would make most people anxious (Hare, 1965, 1993). Normally, when a person is anticipating danger, pain, or punishment, the electrical conductance of the skin changes—a classically conditioned response that indicates anxiety or fear. But in several experiments, people with antisocial personality disorder were slow to develop such responses (see Figure 10.2). It may be that people with this disorder are unable to feel the anxiety necessary for learning that their actions will have unpleasant consequences. Their inability to feel emotional arousal—empathy, guilt, fear of punishment, anxiety under stress—suggests some abnormality in the central nervous system.

Some researchers believe that people who are antisocial, hyperactive, addicted, or impulsive share a common inherited disorder (Luengo et al., 1994; Newman, Widom, & Nathan, 1985). These conditions all involve problems in *behavioral inhi-*

bition—the ability to control responses to frustration or to inhibit a pleasurable action that may have unpleasant repercussions. The biological children of parents with antisocial personality disorder, substance-abuse problems, or impulsivity disorders are at greater than normal risk of developing these disorders themselves, even when these children are reared by others (Nigg & Goldsmith, 1994).

Many children who become violent and antisocial have suffered neurological impairments, a result not of genetics but of physical battering and subsequent brain injury (Milner & McCanne, 1991; Moffitt, 1993). Consider the chilling results of a study that compared two groups of delinquents: violent boys who had been arrested for repeated incidents of vicious assault, rape, or murder; and boys whose violence was limited to fistfights. Nearly all of the extremely violent boys (98.6 percent) had at least one neurological abnormality, and many had more than one, compared with 66.7 percent of the less violent boys. More than three-fourths of the violent boys had suffered head injuries as children, had a history of serious medical problems, or had been beaten savagely by their parents, compared with one-third of the others (Lewis, 1981).

Other research supports a *vulnerability–stress model*, which holds that brain damage interacts with social deprivation and other experiences to produce individuals who are impulsively violent. A study of 4,269 boys, followed from birth to age 18, found that many of those who became violent offenders had experienced two risk factors: birth complications that caused damage to the prefrontal cortex, and early maternal rejection. Their mothers hadn't wanted the pregnancy, and the babies were put in public institutional care for at least four months during their first year. Although only 4.4 percent of the boys had both risk factors, these boys accounted for 18 percent of all violent crimes committed by the sample as a whole (Raine, Brennan, & Mednick, 1994).

Clearly, cultures and environments can make antisocial behavior either more likely or less so (Moffitt, 1993; Patterson, 1994; Persons, 1986). Societies or corporations that place a premium on individual achievement and "success at all costs" may reward the qualities of selfishness, professional ruthlessness, and emotional hard-heartedness. In contrast, small, close-knit cultures that depend on each member's cooperation and consideration for others would find selfishness and coldness intolerable.

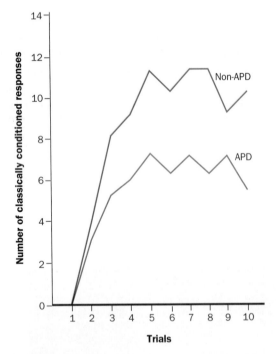

Figure 10.2

Emotional Flatness and Antisocial Personality Disorder

In several experiments, people with antisocial personality disorder (APD) were slow to develop classically conditioned responses to anticipated danger, pain, or shock—responses that indicate normal anxiety (Hare, 1965). This deficit may be related to the ability of people with APD to behave in destructive ways without remorse or regard for the consequences (Hare, 1993).

It seems, then, that several routes lead to the development of antisocial personality disorder: having a genetic disposition toward impulsivity, addiction, or hyperactivity, which leads to rule breaking and crime; being neglected or rejected by parents; having brain damage as a result of birth complications or physical abuse in childhood; and living in a culture or environment that rewards and fosters antisocial traits. These multiple origins may explain why the incidence of antisocial personality disorder varies within and across societies and history.

??? QUICK QUIZ

A. Can you diagnose each of the following disorders?

1. Ann can barely get out of bed in the morning. She feels that life is hopeless and despairs of ever feeling good about herself.

2. Connie constantly feels a sense of impending doom; for many weeks, her heart has been beating rapidly and she can't relax.

3. Damon is totally absorbed in his own feelings and wishes.

4. Edna believes that everyone is out to get her and no one can be trusted.

 B. Suppose you read about an unusually brutal assault committed by a young man during a robbery. Should you assume he has an antisocial personality disorder? Why or why not?

Answers:

A 1. major depression 2. generalized anxiety disorder 3. narcissistic personality disorder 4. paranoid personality disorder B. You should not assume the man has APD; behaving antisocially is not the same thing as having an antisocial *personality*. Many factors could have influenced the young man to be violent, including his perceptions of danger, the support of his peer group, and feelings of anger or panic, to name only a few.

What's Ahead

- *What causes otherwise healthy people to forget who they are?*
- *Why are many clinicians and researchers skeptical about multiple personality disorder?*

DISSOCIATIVE DISORDERS

Have you ever been out driving on a highway and suddenly realized you have lost all track of time and distance? This is a small but common everyday example of "dissociation," a split in awareness: Part of you is driving the car and attending to other drivers, and part of you is daydreaming. Dissociation also occurs when we must deal with stress or shock and we feel temporarily cut off from ourselves—strange, dazed, or "unreal." In **dissociative disorders,** however, consciousness, behavior, and identity are severely split or altered. The symptoms are intense, last a long time, and appear to be out of the individual's control. Like posttraumatic stress disorder, dissociative disorders often occur in response to upsetting or harmful events. But whereas people with PTSD cannot get the trauma out of their minds and waking thoughts, people with dissociative disorders apparently escape the trauma by putting it out of their minds, erasing it from memory (Cardeña et al., 1994).

Amnesia and Fugue

Amnesia, according to the DSM-IV, is an inability to remember important personal information, usually of a traumatic or stressful nature, that cannot be explained by ordinary forgetfulness. Amnesia can result from organic conditions such as head injury. When no physical causes are apparent, and when the person forgets only selective information that is threatening to the self, the amnesia is considered *dissociative* or *psychogenic* (psychological in origin). In one case, a young man temporarily forgot that he had been in an automobile accident in which a pedestrian was killed. The shock of the experience and his fear that he might have been responsible set off the

dissociative disorders

Conditions in which consciousness or identity is split or altered.

amnesia (dissociative)

When no organic causes are present, a dissociative disorder involving partial or complete loss of memory for threatening information or traumatic experiences.

amnesia. After a few days, he awoke in great distress, and eventually he recalled the incident.

Dissociative amnesia is a controversial diagnosis among psychologists. Its proponents assume that traumatic memories are "repressed" or "cut off." However, as we saw in Chapter 7, the concept of repression is the subject of much academic debate, and no clear procedures exist for distinguishing it from ordinary forgetting.

Dissociative **fugue,** an even more fascinating disorder, is equally controversial. The word *fugue* [pronounced "fewg"] comes from the Latin for "flight." A person in a fugue state forgets his or her identity and also gives up customary habits and wanders far from home (as seems to have been the case with Philip Charles Cutajar, whose story opened Chapter 4). The person may take on a new identity, remarry, get a new job, and live contentedly until he or she suddenly "wakes up"—puzzled and often with no memory of the fugue experiences. The fugue state may last anywhere from a few days to many years. James McDonnell, Jr., left his family in New York in 1971 and wandered to New Jersey, where he took a new name and a new job. Fifteen years later, he woke up and made his way back to his wife, who (apparently) greeted him with open arms.

Skeptics, however, point out that it is often difficult to determine when people in fugue states have a true disorder and when they are faking. This problem also arises in the curious disorder of multiple personality.

In the 1950s the book and film *The Three Faces of Eve*, based on a reported case of multiple personality, spawned dozens of imitators, such as the film *Lizzie*. Stories about MPD then faded from the public eye, and so did individuals who claimed to have the disorder. In the mid-1970s, MPD returned in the form of several highly publicized books and case studies, and since then thousands of cases have been reported. But there is now strong evidence that most of these cases were caused by unwitting therapist influence and sensational stories in the media.

Dissociative Identity Disorder ("Multiple Personality")

The DSM-IV uses the term **dissociative identity disorder** to describe the appearance, within one person, of two or more distinct identities. In our discussion, however, we will retain the more commonly used term, *multiple personality disorder* (MPD). In this disorder, each identity appears to have its own memories, preferences, personality traits, and even medical problems.

Cases of multiple personality portrayed in the films *The Three Faces of Eve* and *Sybil* have captivated the public for years. Among mental health professionals, however, two competing and incompatible views of MPD exist. On one side are those who think that MPD is common, but often unrecognized or misdiagnosed. On the other side are those who believe that most cases of MPD are generated by clinicians themselves, in unwitting collusion with vulnerable and suggestible clients, and that if the condition exists at all, it is extremely rare.

Those in the MPD-is-real camp believe that it originates in childhood, as a means of coping with unspeakable, continuing traumas, such as torture (Gleaves, 1996; Kluft, 1993; Ross, 1995). In this view, the trauma produces a mental "splitting"; one personality emerges to handle everyday experiences and another emerges to cope with the bad ones. MPD patients are frequently described as having lived for years with several personalities of which they were unaware, until hypnosis and other techniques in therapy revealed them.

Those who are skeptical about MPD, however, have shown that most of the research used to support the diagnosis is seriously flawed (Merskey, 1995; Piper, 1997). For instance, claims that MPD patients show different physiological responses (e.g.,

Thinking Critically About "Multiple Personalities"

fugue

A dissociative disorder in which a person flees home and forgets his or her identity.

dissociative identity disorder

A controversial disorder marked by the appearance within one person of two or more distinct personalities, each with its own name and traits; also called *multiple personality disorder*.

different EEG patterns) for each personality rest mostly on anecdotes or studies that lacked control groups (Brown, 1994). When researchers have corrected these flaws by comparing MPD patients with healthy people who are merely role-playing different personalities, they find physiological differences between "personalities" in the healthy people, too (Miller & Triggiano, 1992). Apparently, people can alter physiological measures such as brain-wave activity by changing their moods, energy levels, and concentration, so these measures are not a valid way to verify the existence of MPD.

Clinicians and researchers who are doubtful about this diagnosis also worry that some clinicians may actually be creating the disorder in their clients through the power of suggestion (McHugh, 1993a; Merskey, 1992, 1995; Piper, 1997; Spanos, 1996). For example, one advocate of the MPD diagnosis, Richard Kluft (1987), maintains that efforts to determine the presence of MPD—that is, to get the person to reveal a dissociated personality—may require "between 2½ and 4 hours of continuous interviewing. Interviewees must be prevented from taking breaks to regain composure. . . . In one recent case of singular difficulty, the first sign of dissociation was noted in the 6th hour, and a definitive spontaneous switching of personalities occurred in the 8th hour." After eight hours of "continuous interviewing" without a single break, how many of us wouldn't do what the interviewer wanted? Do psychologists who operate this way *permit* another personality to reveal itself, or do they actively *create* such a personality by pressing for it to be revealed?

An alternative, *sociocognitive explanation* of multiple personality disorder is that it is an extreme form of the ability we all have to present different aspects of our personalities to others (Merskey, 1995; Spanos, 1996). In this view, the diagnosis of MPD provides a way for some troubled people to make sense of their problems—or to account for embarrassing, regretted, or unacceptable behavior ("My other personality did it"). In turn, therapists who are looking for MPD reward such patients by paying attention to their symptoms and personalities, thus further influencing the patients to reorganize their memories and make them consistent with the diagnosis (Ofshe & Watters, 1994). When Canadian psychiatrist Harold Merskey (1992) reviewed several famous cases of MPD, including those of Eve and Sybil, he was unable to find a single case in which a patient developed MPD without being influenced by the therapist's sug-

gestions or reports about the disorder in books and the media.

Of course, the fact that MPD is controversial and has little empirical evidence to support it does not mean that no legitimate cases exist. But caution is warranted because of the epidemic of cases reported since the mid-1970s—and because so many of those cases have turned out to be a result of psychiatrist malpractice (Piper, 1997). The story of MPD teaches us to think critically and to demand good evidence for a diagnosis, so that people with real mental disorders can be helped and dangerous fads can be avoided.

What's Ahead

- *Why can two people drink the same amount of wine and have two different physical reactions to it?*

- *Why is alcoholism more common in Ireland than in Italy?*

- *Why don't policies of total abstinence from alcohol always work?*

- *If you take morphine to control chronic pain, does that mean you'll become addicted to it?*

DRUG ABUSE AND ADDICTION

Perhaps no topic better illustrates the problem of finding the point at which normal blurs into abnormal than that of drug abuse and addiction. Most people use drugs (legal, illegal, or prescription) in moderation and for short-lived effects, but some people overuse them. Every drug—including aspirin, cough medicine, and coffee—can be dangerous and even lethal if taken in excess. The question is: How do we define "overuse" and "excess"?

The DSM-IV answers by defining *substance abuse* as "a maladaptive pattern of substance use leading to clinically significant impairment or distress." Symptoms of such impairment include the failure to fulfill obligations at work, home, or school (e.g., the person cannot hold a job, care for children, or complete schoolwork because of excessive drug use); use of the drug in hazardous situations (e.g., while driving a car or operating machinery); recurrent arrests for drug use; and persistent conflicts with others about use of the drug or as a result of using the drug.

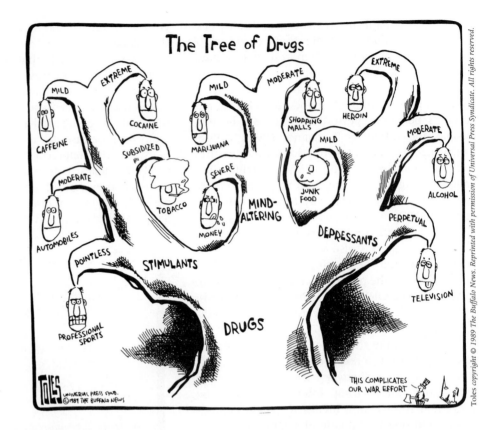

By poking fun at the things people do to alter consciousness and make themselves feel better, this cartoon reminds us that many "addictions" are neither chemical nor illegal.

Why are some people able to use drugs moderately, whereas others abuse them? In this section, focusing on the example of alcoholism, we will consider the two dominant approaches to understanding addiction and drug abuse—the biological model and the learning model—and conclude with an effort to integrate the contributions of both.

The Biological Model

In 1960, a book was published that profoundly changed the way most people thought about alcoholics. In *The Disease Concept of Alcoholism*, E. M. Jellinek argued that alcoholism is a disease over which an individual has no control and from which he or she never recovers. Drunkenness is not an inevitable property of alcohol, he said, but a characteristic of some people who have an inborn vulnerability to liquor; for them, complete abstinence is the only solution. The disease theory of alcoholism transformed the moral condemnation of the addict as a bad and sinful person into concern for someone who is sick.

Today, many people continue to regard alcoholism as a disease, and the *biological model* of ad-diction is widely accepted by researchers and the public. The biological model holds that addiction, whether to alcohol or any other drug, is due primarily to a person's biochemistry, metabolism, and genetic predisposition. In the biological view, just as some individuals and ethnic groups cannot physically tolerate the lactose in milk, some individuals and ethnic groups have a low tolerance for alcohol. Thus women generally will get drunker than men on the same amount of alcohol because women are smaller, on average, and their bodies metabolize alcohol differently (Fuchs et al., 1995). Similarly, many Asians have a genetically determined adverse reaction to even small amounts of alcohol, which can cause severe headaches and diarrhea (Cloninger, 1990).

But why are some people in every group more likely than others to become alcoholic? Twin and adoption studies, and other family studies, suggest that alcoholism may sometimes involve an inherited vulnerability (Cloninger, 1990; Goodwin et al., 1994; Schuckit & Smith, 1996). *Type I alcoholism*, which begins in adulthood, is not associated with genetic factors; but *Type II alcoholism*, which begins in adolescence and is linked to impulsivity, antisocial behavior, and violent criminality, does seem to be partly heritable (Bohman et al., 1987; McGue, Pickens, & Svikis, 1992). Type II alcoholics have a lowered activity of the enzyme MAOB (monoamine oxidase-B) in their blood cells, compared with nonalcoholics. Low levels of MAOB are not a direct cause of addiction, but they may reflect an underlying physiological deficiency leading to severe alcoholism and other psychiatric problems (Devor et al., 1994).

Researchers are trying to identify the key genes or biological anomalies that might be involved in alcoholism (Blum, 1991; Kendler et al., 1992; Polich, Pollock, & Bloom, 1994). As with so many other disorders, however, tracking down those genes has been difficult. At first it appeared that alcoholics might be more likely than nonalcoholics to have a gene that affects the functioning of dopamine, a neurotransmitter that helps regulate pleasure-seeking actions (Noble et al., 1991). However, several studies have found no difference between alcoholics and controls in the presence of this gene (Baron, 1993; Gelernter et al., 1991).

At present, then, we cannot conclude that a single gene causes alcoholism (or any other addiction) directly. It is possible that several genes in combination affect the response to alcohol, the compulsive use of alcohol and other mood-altering drugs, or the progression of alcohol-related diseases such as cirrhosis of the liver. It is possible that genes contribute to temperament or traits that predispose some people to become alcoholics. And it is possible that genes affect how the liver metabolizes alcohol. But it is also possible that genes have little to do with alcoholism, and that alcoholism results, basically, from alcohol! Heavy drinking alters brain function, reduces the level of painkilling endorphins, produces nerve damage, shrinks the cerebral cortex, and damages the liver. In the view of some researchers, these changes then create biological dependence, an inability to metabolize alcohol, and psychological problems.

The Learning Model

The biological model, popular though it is, has been challenged by another approach. According to the *learning model,* addiction to any drug is neither a sin nor a disease but "a central activity of the individual's way of life" that depends on learning and culture (Fingarette, 1988). Proponents marshal four arguments in support of this view:

1. *Addiction patterns vary according to cultural practices and the social environment.* Alcoholism, for example, is much more likely to occur in societies that forbid children to drink but condone drunkenness in adults (as in Ireland) than in societies that teach children how to drink responsibly and moderately but condemn adult drunkenness (as in Italy, Greece, and France). In cultures with low rates of alcoholism (except for those committed to a religious rule that forbids use of all psychoactive drugs), adults demonstrate correct drinking habits to their children, gradually introducing them to alcohol in safe family settings. These lessons are maintained by adult customs. Alcohol is not used as a rite of passage into adulthood, nor is it associated with masculinity and power (Peele & Brodsky, 1991; Vaillant, 1983). Drinking is considered neither a virtue nor a sin. Abstainers are not sneered at, and

In cultures in which people drink moderately with meals, and children learn the rules of social drinking from their families, alcoholism rates are much lower than in cultures in which drinking occurs mainly in bars, in binges, or in privacy.

drunkenness is not considered charming, comical, or manly; it is considered stupid or obnoxious.

Within a particular country, addiction rates can rise or fall rapidly in response to cultural changes. In colonial America, the average person actually drank two to three times the amount of liquor consumed today, yet alcoholism was not the serious social problem it is now. Drinking was a universally accepted social activity. Families drank and ate together. Alcohol was believed to produce pleasant feelings and relaxation. The Puritan minister Cotton Mather even called liquor "the good creature of God." If a person committed a crime or became violent while drunk, the colonials did not conclude that liquor was to blame. Rather, they assumed that the person's own immoral tendencies led both to drunkenness and crime (Critchlow, 1986). Then, between 1790 and 1830, when the American frontier was expanding, drinking came to symbolize masculine independence, high-spiritedness, and toughness. The saloon became the place for drinking away from home, and, as the learning model would predict, alcoholism rates shot up.

Substance abuse and addiction problems increase not only when people fail to learn how to take drugs in moderation, but also when they move from their own culture of origin into another that has different drinking rules (Westermeyer, 1995). For example, in most Latino cultures, such as those of Mexico and Puerto Rico, drinking and drunkenness are considered male activities. Thus Latina women tend to drink little, if at all, and they have few drinking problems—until they move into an Anglo environment, when their rates of alcoholism rise (Canino, 1994).

2. *Policies of total abstinence tend to increase rates of addiction rather than reduce them.* In the United States, the temperance movement of the early twentieth century held that drinking inevitably leads to drunkenness, and drunkenness causes crime. The solution it proposed, and won for the Prohibition years (1920 to 1933), was national abstinence. But this victory backfired: As the learning model would predict, Prohibition actually increased rates of alcoholism. Because people were denied the opportunity to learn to drink moderately, they drank excessively when given the chance (McCord, 1989). Something similar happened in Canada with the Inuit and other native groups, who were prohibited from drinking alcohol until 1951 (and would therefore drink as much as they could if they could get hold of it) and then were permitted to drink only in licensed bars (and would therefore drink as much as they

For over a century, the temperance movement in the United States promoted total abstinence from alcoholic beverages, and for a brief period (1920–1933), Prohibition was the law of the land. But the legal ban on alcohol proved unenforceable, and was actually associated with *increased* alcoholism rates, as the text explains.

could while in a bar). Both policies were guaranteed to create drunkenness. (The 1951 law was repealed in 1960.)

3. *Not all addicts have withdrawal symptoms when they stop taking a drug.* When heavy users of a drug stop taking it, they often suffer such unpleasant symptoms as nausea, abdominal cramps, muscle spasms, depression, and sleep problems, depending on the drug. But these symptoms are far from universal. During the Vietnam War, nearly 30 percent of American soldiers were taking heroin in doses far stronger than those available on the streets of U.S. cities. These men believed themselves to be addicted, and experts predicted a drug-withdrawal disaster among the returning veterans. It never materialized; over 90 percent of the men simply gave up the drug, without withdrawal pain, when they came home to new circumstances (Robins, Davis, & Goodwin, 1974). Similarly, most people who are addicted to cigarettes, tranquilizers, or painkillers are able to stop taking these drugs, without outside help and without withdrawal symptoms (Prochaska, Norcross, & DiClemente, 1994).

Get Involved

If you drink, why do you do so? Check all of the motives that apply to you:

_____ to relax	_____ to conform to peer pressure
_____ to be sociable	_____ to rebel against authority
_____ to escape from worries, stress	_____ to relieve boredom
_____ to handle feelings of depression	_____ to have an excuse to express anger
_____ to enhance a good meal	_____ other (specify)
_____ to get drunk and lose control	

Do your reasons for drinking promote abuse or responsible use? How do you respond physically to alcohol? What have you learned about drinking from your family, your friends, and cultural messages? What do your answers tell you about your own vulnerability to addiction?

---

4. *Addiction does not depend on the drug alone, but also on the reason for taking it.* Addicts use drugs to escape from the real world, but people living with chronic pain use some of the same drugs, including morphine and other opiates, in order to function in the real world—and they do not become addicted (Portenoy, 1994). In a study of 100 hospital patients who had been given strong doses of narcotics for postoperative pain, 99 had no withdrawal symptoms upon leaving the hospital (Zinberg, 1974). And of 10,000 burn patients who received narcotics as part of their hospital care, not one became an addict (Perry & Heidrich, 1982).

To understand why people abuse drugs, therefore, the learning model focuses on the reasons they take the drugs. In the case of alcohol, most people drink simply to be sociable or to conform to the group they are with, but others drink in order to regulate their emotions. "Coping drinkers" drink to reduce negative feelings when they are anxious, depressed, or tense; "enhancement drinkers" drink to increase positive feelings when they are tired, bored, or stressed. Coping drinkers have significantly more drinking problems than enhancement drinkers do (Cooper et al., 1995).

Debating Theories of Addiction

The biological and learning models both contribute to our understanding of drug abuse and addiction. Yet these views have become quite polarized, as you can see in Table 10.2. What we have here is a case of either–or thinking on a national scale, with passions running high because of the implications for the treatment of alcoholics and other addicts.

The argument is most heated in the debate over whether former alcoholics can learn to drink moderately without becoming intoxicated and dependent once again on alcohol. Those who advocate the biological or disease model say there is no such thing as a "former" alcoholic; once an addict has even a single drink, he or she will not be able to stop. In this view, problem drinkers who learn to cut back to social-drinking levels were never true alcoholics in the first place. Those who champion the learning model, on the other hand, argue that once a person no longer *needs* to become drunk, he or she can learn to drink socially and in moderation (Marlatt, 1996). Longitudinal studies find that this shift is quite common, a result of maturation, changing environments, and changing reasons for drinking (Vaillant, 1983).

How can we assess these two positions critically? Can we locate a common ground between them? Because alcoholism and problem drinking occur for many reasons, neither model offers the only solution. Many alcoholics, perhaps most, cannot learn to drink moderately, especially if they have had drinking problems for many years (Vaillant, 1995). On the other hand, although the total-abstinence policies of groups like Alcoholics Anonymous have unquestionably saved lives, they do not work for everyone. According to its own surveys, one-third to one-half of those who join AA drop out, and many of those dropouts benefit from programs such as Rational Recovery, Moderation Management, and DrinkWise, which teach people how to drink moderately and keep their drinking under control (Marlatt, 1996; Peele & Brodsky, 1991; Rosenberg, 1993).

Thinking Critically About Models of Addiction

Table 10.2	Two Models of Addiction	

The biological and learning models of addiction differ in how they explain drug abuse and the solutions they propose:

The Biological Model	The Learning Model
Addiction is genetic, biological.	Addiction is a way of coping.
Once an addict, always an addict.	A person can grow beyond the need for alcohol or other drugs.
An addict must abstain from the drug forever.	Most problem drinkers can learn to drink in moderation.
A person is either addicted or not.	The degree of addiction will vary, depending on the situation.
The solution is medical treatment and membership in groups that reinforce one's permanent identity as a recovering addict.	The solution involves learning new coping skills and changing one's environment.
An addict needs the same treatment and group support forever.	Treatment lasts only until the person no longer abuses the drug.

Source: Adapted from Peele & Brodsky, 1991.

The factors that predict whether an alcoholic or problem drinker will be able to learn to control excessive drinking include previous severity of dependence on the drug; social stability (not having a criminal record, having a stable work history, being married); and beliefs about the necessity of maintaining abstinence (Rosenberg, 1993). Alcoholics who believe that one drink will set them off—those who accept the alcoholics' creed, "first drink, then drunk"—are in fact more likely to behave that way, compared with those who believe that controlled drinking is possible. Ironically, then, the course that alcoholism takes may reflect, in part, a person's belief in the disease model or the learning model.

In sum, abuse and addiction reflect an interaction of physiology and psychology, person and culture. Problems with alcohol or other drugs are most likely to occur when

- a person has a genetic or physiological vulnerability to a drug;
- a person believes he or she has no control over the drug;
- laws or customs encourage or teach people to take a drug in binges, and moderate use is neither encouraged nor taught;
- a person comes to rely on a drug as a way of coping with problems, relieving pain, avoiding stress, or gaining a sense of power and self-esteem; and
- members of a person's peer group drink heavily or use other drugs excessively.

??? QUICK QUIZ

If you are addicted to passing exams, try these questions:

1. What seems to be the most reasonable conclusion about the role of genes in alcoholism? (a) Without a key gene, a person cannot become alcoholic; (b) the presence of a key gene or genes will almost always cause a person to become alcoholic; (c) genes may work in combination to increase a person's vulnerability to some kinds of alcoholism.

2. Which cultural practice is associated with low rates of alcoholism? (a) drinking in family or group settings, (b) infrequent but binge drinking, (c) drinking as a rite of passage, (d) regarding alcohol as a sinful drink

3. *True or false:* Policies of total abstinence reduce alcoholism rates.

Answers:
1. c 2. a 3. false

What's Ahead

- *What's the difference between schizophrenia and a "split personality"?*

- *Why do most researchers consider schizophrenia a brain disorder?*

- *Could schizophrenia begin in the womb?*

SCHIZOPHRENIA

To be schizophrenic is best summed up in a repeating dream that I have had since childhood. In this dream I am lying on a beautiful sunlit beach but my body is in pieces. This fact causes me no concern until I realize that the tide is coming in and that I am unable to gather the parts of my dismembered body together to run away. The tide gets closer and just when I am on the point of drowning I wake up screaming in panic. This to me is what schizophrenia feels like; being fragmented in one's personality and constantly afraid that the tide of illness will completely cover me. (Quoted in Rollin, 1980)

In 1911, Swiss psychiatrist Eugen Bleuler coined the term **schizophrenia** to describe cases in which the personality loses its unity. People with schizophrenia do not have a "split" or "multiple personality," however. As the above quotation illustrates, schizophrenia is a fragmented condition in which words are split from meaning, actions from motives, perceptions from reality. It is an example of a **psychosis,** a mental condition that involves distorted perceptions of reality and an inability to function in most aspects of life.

Symptoms of Schizophrenia

If depression is the common cold of psychological disorder, said psychiatrist Donald Klein (1980), schizophrenia is its cancer: elusive, complicated, varying in form. In general, schizophrenia produces two categories of symptoms. *Active* or *positive* symptoms involve an exaggeration or distortion of normal thinking processes and behavior. These symptoms are called "positive" symptoms because they are *additions* to normal behavior; healthy people do not have delusions that their brains are receiving Martian signals. In contrast, *negative symptoms* involve the *loss* or absence of normal traits and abilities, such as the ability to speak flu-

ently and feel warm emotions, as you can see in this chart:

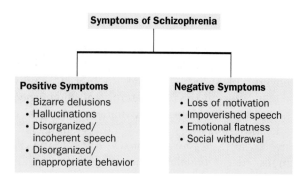

Symptoms of Schizophrenia

Positive Symptoms
- Bizarre delusions
- Hallucinations
- Disorganized/ incoherent speech
- Disorganized/ inappropriate behavior

Negative Symptoms
- Loss of motivation
- Impoverished speech
- Emotional flatness
- Social withdrawal

The most common active symptoms include the following:

1. *Bizarre delusions* (false beliefs), such as the belief that dogs are extraterrestrials disguised as pets. Some people have paranoid delusions, taking innocent events—a stranger's cough, a helicopter overhead—as evidence that the world is plotting against them. Some have "delusions of identity," believing that they are Moses, Jesus, Joan of Arc, or some other famous person.

2. *Hallucinations* (sensory experiences in the absence of sensory stimulation) that feel intensely real and believable to the person having them. Schizophrenic hallucinations usually take the form of voices speaking garbled, odd words; a running conversation in the head; or two or more voices conversing with each other. But some hallucinations are tactile (e.g., feeling insects crawling over the body) or visual (e.g., seeing a famous actress in the mirror).

3. *Disorganized, incoherent speech* consisting of an illogical jumble of ideas and symbols, linked by meaningless rhyming words or by remote associations called *word salads.* A patient of Bleuler's wrote, "Olive oil is an Arabian liquor-sauce which the Afghans, Moors and Moslems use in ostrich farming. The Indian plantain tree is the whiskey of the Parsees and Arabs. Barley, rice and sugar cane called artichoke, grow remarkably well in India. The Brahmins live as castes in Baluchistan. The Circassians occupy Manchuria and China. China is the Eldorado of the Pawnees" (Bleuler, 1911/1950).

4. *Grossly disorganized and inappropriate behavior* that may range from childlike silliness to unpredictable and violent agitation. The person may wear three overcoats and gloves on a hot day, start collecting garbage, or hoard scraps of food. Some people with schizophrenia completely withdraw into a private world, sitting for hours without

schizophrenia

A psychotic disorder or group of disorders marked by positive symptoms (e.g., delusions, hallucinations, disorganized and incoherent speech, and inappropriate behavior) and negative symptoms (e.g., emotional flatness and loss of motivation).

psychosis

An extreme mental disturbance involving distorted perceptions and irrational behavior; it may have psychological or organic causes. (Plural: *psychoses.*)

moving, a condition called *catatonic stupor*. In *Autobiography of a Schizophrenic Girl,* Marguerite Sechehaye wrote, "A wall of brass separates me from everybody and everything. In the midst of desolation, in indescribable distress, in absolute solitude, I am terrifyingly alone."

Negative symptoms include loss of motivation; poverty of speech (making only brief, empty replies in conversation, because of diminished thought, rather than an unwillingness to speak); and, most notably, emotional flatness—unresponsive facial expressions, poor eye contact, and diminished emotionality. One man set fire to his house, and then sat down calmly to watch TV. These negative symptoms may appear months before active ones do, and they often persist when the active symptoms are in remission.

Cases of schizophrenia vary enormously in severity, duration, and likelihood of recovery. In some individuals, the symptoms appear abruptly, often in response to a stressful situation; in such cases, the prognosis for recovery is relatively good. In other individuals, the onset is more insidious; negative symptoms gradually emerge, and friends and family report a slow change in personality.

The person may stop working or bathing, become isolated and withdrawn, and start behaving in peculiar ways. In these cases, the outlook is far less certain. The more breakdowns and relapses the individual has had, the poorer are the chances for complete recovery (Eaton et al., 1992a, 1992b). Yet many people suffering from this illness learn to control the symptoms, while working and having good family relationships. Some even seem to "outgrow" their symptoms (Eaton et al., 1992b; Harding, Zubin, & Strauss, 1992).

The mystery of schizophrenia is that we could go on listing symptoms and variations all day and never finish. Some people with schizophrenia are almost completely impaired in all spheres; others do extremely well in certain areas. Some have normal moments of lucidity in otherwise withdrawn lives. One adolescent crouched in a rigid catatonic posture in front of a television for the month of October; later, he was able to report on all the highlights of the World Series he had seen. A middle-aged man, hospitalized for 20 years, believing he was a prophet of God and that monsters were coming out of the walls, was able to interrupt his ranting to play a good game of chess (Wender & Klein, 1981).

When people with schizophrenia are asked to draw pictures, their drawings are often distorted, lack color, include words, and reveal flat emotion. One patient was asked to copy a picture of flowers from a magazine (left). The initial result is shown in the center. The drawing on the right shows how much the patient improved after several months of treatment.

Theories of Schizophrenia

As you might imagine, any disorder that has so many variations and symptoms will pose many problems for diagnosis and explanation. One psychologist concluded that the concept of schizophrenia is "almost hopelessly in tatters" (Carson, 1989), and some psychologists would like to drop the label entirely (Sarbin, 1992). But others argue that the label is worth keeping because in cultures around the world, the same core signs of the disorder appear: hallucinations, bizarre delusions, inappropriate behavior, and disorders of thought and sensation.

Using brain-imaging techniques, dissections of autopsied brains, and longitudinal studies, scientists are beginning to unravel the mysteries of schizophrenia. They are searching for genetic factors, abnormalities in the brain, abnormalities in prenatal development, and the interaction between biological abnormalities and a person's life experiences. Here we cover just a few of their many findings.

1. *Structural brain abnormalities.* Some individuals with schizophrenia show decreased brain weight, a decrease in the volume of the temporal lobe or limbic regions, reduced numbers of neurons in the prefrontal cortex, or enlargement of the *ventricles,* the spaces in the brain filled with cerebrospinal fluid (see Figure 10.3). These may all be signs of cerebral damage (Akbarian et al., 1996; Andreasen et al., 1994; Heinrichs, 1993; Raz & Raz, 1990). Men with schizophrenia are also

more likely than controls to have abnormalities in the thalamus, the traffic-control center for incoming sensations (Andreasen et al., 1994). This finding might explain why the brains of some people with schizophrenia are overly sensitive to everyday stimuli, causing them to retreat into an inner world.

2. *Neurotransmitter abnormalities.* Many people with schizophrenia have high levels of activity in brain areas where the neurotransmitter dopamine is found. Moreover, autopsy studies find that a particular kind of dopamine receptor is far more common in the brains of patients with schizophrenia than in those of other people (Seeman et al., 1993; Wong et al., 1986). Many researchers, therefore, suspect that some of the symptoms of schizophrenia are brought on by a high level of dopamine activity. Serotonin may also play a role; serotonin inhibits dopamine activity, so if serotonin levels are low, activity in brain areas served by dopamine will increase (Pickar et al., 1991; Spoont, 1992). As we will see in the next chapter, drugs that reduce dopamine levels tend to reduce schizophrenic symptoms—and drugs that both reduce dopamine levels and increase serotonin levels tend to be the most effective.

3. *Genetic predispositions.* As Figure 10.4 on the next page shows, a person has a considerably greater risk of schizophrenia if an identical twin develops the disorder, and this is true even if the person is reared apart from the affected sibling (Gottesman, 1991, 1994). Moreover, children with one schizophrenic parent have a lifetime risk of 12 percent, and children with two schizophrenic

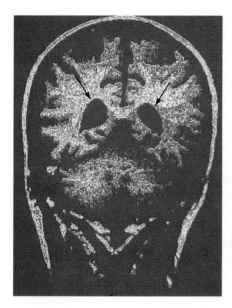 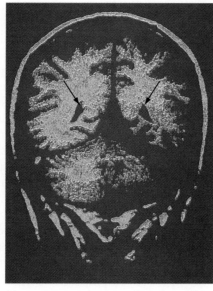

Figure 10.3
Schizophrenia and the Brain
MRI scans show that a person with schizophrenia (left) is more likely than a healthy person (right) to have enlarged ventricles, or spaces, in the brain (see arrows) (Andreasen et al., 1994).

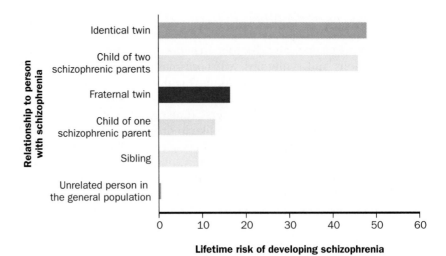

Figure 10.4

Genetic Vulnerability to Schizophrenia

This graph, based on combined data from 40 European twin and adoption studies conducted over nearly seven decades, shows that the closer the genetic relationship to a person with schizophrenia, the higher the risk of developing the disorder. (Based on Gottesman, 1991.)

parents have a lifetime risk of 35–46 percent, compared to a risk in the general population of only 1–2 percent (Goldstein, 1987). These and other findings indicate the existence of a genetic contribution to the disorder. Just as with alcoholism and bipolar disorder, however, tracking down the genes involved and determining the extent of their influence has proven difficult (Holzman & Matthysse, 1990). And clearly, genes alone cannot predict who will develop schizophrenia. Even among identical twins, when one twin develops the disorder, the chances that the other will do so are slightly less than half (Torrey et al., 1994). Nearly 90 percent of all persons with schizophrenia do *not* have a schizophrenic parent, and nearly 90 percent of all children with one such parent do not develop the disorder.

4. *Prenatal abnormalities.* Evidence is mounting that damage to the fetal brain increases the likelihood of schizophrenia (and some other mental disorders). In some cases, the damage may occur because of severe malnutrition: Babies conceived during times of famine have twice the schizophrenia rate as babies conceived when their mothers ate normal diets during pregnancy (Susser et al., 1996).

Another culprit may be, remarkably, an infectious virus during prenatal development (Torrey, 1988; Torrey et al., 1994). The virus theory can account for many odd aspects of schizophrenia. It explains why symptoms may not emerge until a person reaches adolescence or young adulthood: Viruses can attack specific areas of the brain, leaving other areas untouched, yet remain latent for many years before causing symptoms to appear. It explains why the births of schizophrenic children show seasonal fluctuations; viruses, too, are sea-

sonal. And it explains why sometimes only one twin of a genetically identical pair later becomes schizophrenic: Only one was affected prenatally by a virus. A longitudinal study that began decades ago found a significant association between exposure to influenza virus during the second trimester of prenatal development—when the brain is forming crucial connections—and the onset of adult schizophrenia 20 to 30 years later (Bracha et al., 1991; Mednick, Huttunen, & Machón, 1994).

5. *The vulnerability–stress model.* Although the evidence for brain abnormalities in schizophrenia is compelling, many researchers believe that this disorder—like depression, antisocial personality disorder, and addiction—is best explained by an interactive theory (Gottesman, 1991). In this view, genes or brain damage alone will not inevitably produce schizophrenia, and a vulnerable person who lives in a good environment may go through life without ever showing full-fledged signs of the disorder.

For many years, the Copenhagen High-Risk Project has followed 207 children at high risk for schizophrenia (because of having a schizophrenic parent) and a control group of 104 low-risk children. The project has identified several factors that, *in combination,* increase the likelihood of schizophrenia: the existence of schizophrenia in the family; physical trauma during childbirth that might damage the brain; exposure to the flu virus or other prenatal trauma during the second trimester of gestation; unstable, stressful environments in childhood and adolescence; and having emotionally disturbed parents (Mednick, Parnas, & Schulsinger, 1987; Olin & Mednick, 1996).

Some researchers hope that a single cause of all the kinds of schizophrenia may yet be discovered. After all, rheumatic fever also seemed to be several different diseases—of the nervous system, the heart, the joints, and the skin—until bacteriolo- gists identified its common source. But other in- vestigators believe that schizophrenia is really sev- eral disorders with different causes, and that no one culprit is likely to be found. The riddle of schizophrenia remains to be solved.

??? QUICK QUIZ

The following quiz is not a hallucination.

1. A patient with schizophrenia hears voices in her head when no one is around. Is this an example of a positive symptom or a negative one?

2. Name as many brain abnormalities associated with schizophrenia as you can.

3. *True or false:* Most people with schizophrenia have a schizophrenic parent.

Answers:
1. positive 2. Abnormalities include decreased brain weight, decreased volume of the temporal lobe or limbic regions, re- duced numbers of neurons in the prefrontal cortex, enlargement of the ventricles, and abnormalities in the thalamus. 3. false

---

We have come to the end of a long walk along the spectrum of mental disorders. Have you formed your own opinion about when normal problems become disorders, and when those disorders ab- solve people of responsibility for their actions?

Romance writer Janet Dailey, as you'll recall, felt that her plagiarism of her rival's words should be forgiven because she was under unusual stress and had a "psychological problem." Certainly, Dailey was coping with some difficult circum- stances. By this reasoning, however, nearly every hurtful or annoying thing that people do when they are stressed out or in psychological pain could be excused, and there would be no negative consequences for bad behavior. So where do we draw the line?

One answer takes into account the severity of the purported disorder. On one side of the line, we might put problems such as anxiety, mild depres- sion, and "caffeine-induced sleep disorder." On the other, we might put disabling conditions such as schizophrenia. But this still leaves a large gray area. Does obsessive–compulsive disorder absolve you of responsibility for your actions? What about antisocial personality disorder or drug addiction?

The Janet Dailey case was a civil matter involv- ing money, and it quickly disappeared from the news. But the issue of diminished responsibility also arises in far more serious cases involving criminal behavior, such as stalking, arson, rape, and murder. In the United States, in order to claim diminished responsibility for such crimes, the de- fense must show clear and convincing evidence that the defendant had a severe mental condition and not just a personality defect or a bad day at work. If the strategy is successful, the accused per- son is usually sentenced to a mental institution in- stead of prison. Few lawyers take advantage of the insanity defense; in fact, it is used in only 0.9 per- cent of all felony cases, and succeeds in only about a quarter of those cases (Silver, Cirincione, & Steadman, 1994). Nonetheless, some defense at- torneys, aided by the testimony of psychiatrists and psychologists, keep trying to expand the legal grounds for diminished responsibility, searching for mental disorders that might lessen the severity of the sentence a guilty person receives.

Because of the subjective nature of diagnosis, many trials involving diminished-responsibility arguments end up as a battle of the experts, and the jury must decide which side to believe. A few years ago, in the sensational case of Lyle and Erik Menendez, who shot their wealthy parents to death, some psychologists argued that the broth- ers were suffering from a form of posttraumatic stress disorder resulting from years of abuse. But others thought that if the brothers had any mental disorder at all, their cold-bloodedness indicated an antisocial personality disorder. It is hard for juries to decide among such competing views when the experts can't. (In the Menendez case, after two long and expensive trials, a jury rejected the diminished-responsibility argument altogether. Lyle and Erik were convicted of murder and sentenced to life in prison without the possibility of parole.)

When thinking about the relationship between mental disorder and personal responsibility, we are faced with a dilemma. Most legal and mental health professionals believe that people who are mentally incompetent, delusional, or disturbed should not be judged by the same standards as mentally healthy individuals, and should receive treatment rather than punishment. At the same time, society has an obligation to protect innocent individuals from harm, reject easy excuses for violations of the law, and bring wrongdoers to justice. To balance these two positions, we need to find ways to ensure that people who commit crimes or behave reprehensibly face the consequences of their behavior; and also to ensure that people who are suffering from psychological problems have the compassionate support of society in their search for help. After all, psychological problems of one kind or another are problems that all of us will have at some time in our lives.

Taking Psychology with You

When a Friend Is Suicidal

Suicide can be frightening to those who find themselves fantasizing about it, and it is devastating to the family, friends, and acquaintances of those who go through with it. In North America, most people who commit suicide are over the age of 45, but suicide rates are rapidly increasing among young people. Between 1960 and 1988, the rate among adolescents rose by more than 200 percent, increasing especially among white males (Garland & Zigler, 1994). Between 1980 and 1995, however, the suicide rate among black male teenagers jumped 146 percent, and the gap between the rates of white and black teenage suicides is narrowing significantly (*New York Times*, March 20, 1998).

People who attempt suicide have different motives. Some believe they have no reason to live; some feel like failures in a world where they think everyone else is happy and successful; some want revenge against those who they think have made them suffer. In the African-American community, risk factors include parental drug abuse, family losses and low levels of family cohesion, exposure to violence, and being a teenage mother (Summerville, Kaslow, & Doepke, 1996). All suicidal people share the belief that life is unendurable. This belief may be rational in the case of people who are terminally ill and in pain, but more often it reflects the distorted thinking of someone suffering from depression. Often, suicidal individuals don't really want to die; they just want to escape intolerable emotions and despair (Baumeister, 1990).

Friends and family members can help prevent a suicide by knowing the difference between fact and fiction and by recognizing the danger signs.

• *Don't assume you can identify a "suicidal type."* Most adolescents who try to commit suicide or are vulnerable to it are isolated and lonely. Many are children of divorced or alcoholic parents. Some have problems in school and feel like failures. But others are college students who are perfectionistic and self-critical. The former may feel like ending their lives because they can foresee no future. The latter may feel suicidal because they do not like the futures they foresee.

• *Take all suicide threats seriously.* Some people assume they can't doing anything about it when a friend talks about committing suicide. "He'll just do it at another place, another time," they think. In fact, most suicides occur during an acute crisis. Once the person gets through the crisis, the desire to die fades. One researcher tracked down 515 people who had attempted suicide by jumping off the Golden Gate Bridge many years earlier. Less than 5 percent had actually committed suicide in the subsequent decades (Seiden, 1978).

Some people believe that if a friend is talking about suicide, he or she won't really do it. This belief is also false. Few people commit suicide without signaling their intentions. Most are ambivalent: "I want to kill myself, but I don't want to be dead—at least not forever." Most suicidal people want relief from the terrible pain of feeling that nobody cares, that life is not worth living. Getting these thoughts and fears out in the open is an important first step.

• *Know the danger signs.* A depressed person may be at risk of trying to commit suicide if he or she has tried to do it before; has become withdrawn, apathetic, and isolated; has a history of depression; reveals specific plans for carrying out the suicide or begins to give away cherished possessions; expresses no concern about the usual deterrents to suicide, such as consideration for one's family, adherence to religious rules, or the fact that suicide is irreversible; and has access to a lethal method, such as a gun (Garland & Zigler, 1994).

• *Take constructive action.* If you believe a friend is in danger of suicide, do not be afraid to ask, "Are you thinking of suicide?" This question does not "put the idea" in anyone's mind. If your friend is contemplating the action, he or she will probably be relieved to talk about it, and you will know that it is time to get help. Let your friend talk without argument or disapproval. Don't try to talk your friend out of it by debating whether suicide is right or wrong, and don't put on phony cheerfulness. If your friend's words or actions scare you, say so. By listening nonjudgmentally, you are showing that you care. By allowing your friend to unburden his or her grief, you help the person get through the immediate crisis.

Most of all, don't leave your friend alone. If necessary, get the person to a counselor, health professional, or emergency room of a hospital; or call a local suicide hot line. Don't worry about doing the wrong thing. In an emergency, the worst thing you can do is nothing at all.

SUMMARY

Defining and Diagnosing Disorder

1) The prevalence of a behavior does not indicate whether it is disordered. When defining *mental disorder,* mental health professionals emphasize the violation of cultural standards; whether the behavior is maladaptive for the individual or society; and the emotional suffering caused by the behavior.

2) In diagnosing psychological disorders, clinicians often use *projective tests* such as the Thematic Apperception Test and the Rorschach Inkblot Test, which are based on psychodynamic assumptions, and *objective tests or inventories,* such as the MMPI. In general, objective tests have better reliability and validity than projective ones.

3) *The Diagnostic and Statistical Manual of Mental Disorders* (DSM), which is used throughout the world, is designed to provide objective criteria and categories for diagnosing mental disorder. Critics argue that the manual fosters overdiagnosis; overlooks the influence of diagnostic labels on clients and therapists; confuses serious disorders with normal problems; and disguises the inherently subjective nature of diagnosis. Supporters of the DSM believe that when the DSM criteria are used correctly, reliability in diagnosis improves; and that although some diagnoses are subjective and culture-specific, not all diagnoses reflect society's biases.

Anxiety Disorders

4) *Generalized anxiety disorder* involves continuous, chronic anxiety, with signs of nervousness, worry, and irritability. When anxiety results from exposure to uncontrollable or unpredictable danger, it can lead to *posttraumatic stress disorder,* which involves such symptoms as mentally reliving the trauma, "psychic numbing," and increased physiological arousal. *Panic disorder* involves sudden, intense attacks of profound fear, with feelings of impending doom. Panic attacks are common in the aftermath of stress or frightening experiences; those who go on to develop a disorder tend to interpret the attacks as a sign of impending disaster.

5) *Phobias* are exaggerated fears of specific situations, activities, or things. *Agoraphobia,* the fear of being away from a safe place or person, is the most disabling phobia. It often begins with a series of panic attacks, which the person tries to avoid in the future by staying close to "safe" places.

6) *Obsessive–compulsive disorder* (OCD) involves recurrent, unwished-for thoughts or images (obsessions) and repetitive, ritualized behaviors (compulsions) that a person feels unable to control. Several parts of the brain having to do with fear and response to threat are more active than normal in people with OCD.

Mood Disorders

7) Symptoms of *major depression* include distorted thinking patterns, low self-esteem, physical ailments such as fatigue and loss of appetite, and prolonged grief and despair. In *bipolar disorder,* a person experiences episodes of both depression and *mania* (excessive euphoria). Women are more likely than men to be treated for major depression, but psychologists disagree on whether the sex difference is real or due to misdiagnosis of men's symptoms.

8) *Biological* explanations of depression emphasize low levels of the neurotransmitters serotonin and norepinephrine, and the role of genetic predispositions. *Social* explanations emphasize the circumstances of people's lives, such as work and family life, motherhood, and the experience of sexual abuse and other forms of violence. *Attachment* theories argue that depression results from broken or conflicted relationships or a history of insecure attachment. *Cognitive* explanations attribute depression to a pessimistic explanatory style, distorted thoughts, and habits of brooding or rumination. *Vulnerability–stress models* look at specific interactions between individual vulnerabilities (genetic dispositions, cognitive habits, and personality traits) and environmental stress.

Personality Disorders

9) *Personality disorders* are characterized by rigid, self-destructive traits that cause distress or an inability to get along with others. They include *paranoid, narcissistic,* and *antisocial personality disorders.* A person with antisocial personality disorder (sometimes also called a psychopath or sociopath) lacks guilt, shame, and empathy; is oblivious to punishment; and is impulsive and lacks self-control. The disorder may involve a neurological defect that is genetic or is caused by central-nervous-system damage at birth or during childhood; parental rejection and abuse; and living in environments that reward antisocial traits and behaviors.

Dissociative Disorders

10) *Dissociative disorders* involve a split in consciousness or identity. They include *amnesia, fugue states*, and *dissociative identity disorder* (*multiple personality disorder*, or *MPD*). In MPD, two or more distinct personalities and identities appear within one person. Considerable controversy surrounds the validity and nature of MPD. Some clinicians think it is common, often goes undiagnosed, and originates in childhood trauma. Others hold a *sociocognitive* explanation, arguing that most cases are manufactured in unwitting collusion between therapists who believe in the disorder and suggestible patients who find it a congenial explanation for their problems.

Drug Abuse and Addiction

11) The effects of drugs depend on whether they are used moderately or are abused. Signs of *substance abuse* include impaired ability to work or get along with others, use of the drug in hazardous situations, recurrent arrests for drug use, and conflicts with others caused by drug use.

12) According to the *biological or disease model* of addiction, some people have a biological vulnerability to alcoholism and other addictions, due to a genetic factor that affects their metabolism, biochemistry, or personality traits. But advocates of the *learning model* of addiction point out that addiction patterns vary according to culture, learning, and accepted practice; that many people can stop taking drugs without experiencing withdrawal symptoms; that drug abuse depends on the reasons for taking a drug; and that abuse increases when people are not taught moderate use. Although the biological and learning models are polarized on many issues, the evidence suggests that addiction and abuse result from an interaction between biological and psychological vulnerability and a person's culture, learning history, and situation.

Schizophrenia

13) *Schizophrenia* is a psychotic disorder involving *positive* or *active* symptoms such as delusions, hallucinations, disorganized speech (*word salads*), and grossly inappropriate behavior; and *negative symptoms* such as loss of motivation, poverty of speech, and emotional flatness. Cases of schizophrenia vary in severity, duration, and prognosis. Research on causes of this disorder is focusing on structural brain abnormalities, neurotransmitter abnormalities, genetic predispositions, abnormalities of prenatal development resulting from viral infection or other causes during the second trimester, and—in the *vulnerability–stress model*—interactions between such factors and a person's environment during childhood or young adulthood.

KEY TERMS

insanity   334

mental disorder   335

projective tests   335

Rorschach Inkblot Test   336

Thematic Apperception Test (TAT)   336

objective tests (inventories)   336

Minnesota Multiphasic Personality Inventory (MMPI)   336

Diagnostic and Statistical Manual of Mental Disorders (DSM)   337

generalized anxiety disorder   340

posttraumatic stress disorder (PTSD)   341

panic disorder   341

panic attack   341

phobia   341

social phobia   341

agoraphobia   342

obsessive–compulsive disorder (OCD)   342

dysthymia   344

major depression   344

mania   345

bipolar disorder   345

vulnerability–stress model of depression   347

personality disorders   348

paranoid personality disorder   348

narcissistic personality disorder   348

antisocial personality disorder (APD)   349

vulnerability–stress model of APD   350

LOOKING BACK ←

- *Why were slaves who dreamed of freedom once considered to have a "mental disorder"? (p. 334)*

- *What's wrong with using tests such as the famous "inkblot" test to diagnose disorders? (pp. 335–336)*

- *Why is the standard guide to the diagnosis of mental disorders so controversial? (pp. 337–339)*

- *What's the difference between ordinary anxiety and an anxiety disorder? (p. 340)*

- *Why is the most disabling of all phobias known as the "fear of fear"? (p. 342)*

- *When is checking the stove before leaving home a sign of a caution—and when does it signal a disorder? (p. 342)*

- *How can you tell whether you have major depression or just the blues? (p. 344)*

- *What are the poles in bipolar disorder? (p. 345)*

- *How do some people think themselves into depression? (pp. 346–347)*

- *When does being self-centered become a disorder? (p. 348)*

- *What do a charming but heartless tycoon and a remorseless killer have in common? (p. 349)*

- *Why are some people seemingly incapable of feeling guilt and shame? (p. 350)*

- *What causes otherwise healthy people to forget who they are? (p. 351)*

- *Why are many clinicians and researchers skeptical about multiple personality disorder? (pp. 352–353)*

- *Why can two people drink the same amount of wine and have two different physical reactions to it? (pp. 354–355)*

- *Why is alcoholism more common in Ireland than in Italy? (pp. 355–356)*

- *Why don't policies of total abstinence from alcohol always work? (p. 356)*

- *If you take morphine to control chronic pain, does that mean you'll become addicted to it? (p. 357)*

- *What's the difference between schizophrenia and a "split personality"? (p. 359)*

- *Why do most researchers consider schizophrenia a brain disorder? (pp. 361–362)*

- *Could schizophrenia begin in the womb? (p. 362)*

PSYCHOLOGY IN THE NEWS

Malpractice or Innovative Psychotherapy?

Psychotherapist Richard Corriere (right) enters the California state office building with his attorney.

LOS ANGELES, CA., SEPTEMBER, 1986. The longest and costliest psychotherapy malpractice case in California history continues this month with an inquiry into the now-defunct Hollywood Center for Feeling Therapy. Psychologist Richard J. (Riggs) Corriere, the center's cofounder, and several of his colleagues are defending their treatment methods in license-revocation hearings by the state. Earlier this year, a lawsuit against the center by former patients was settled for several million dollars.

The defense says that the center was an innovative "therapeutic community" that encouraged confused young adults to develop healthier lifestyles. In contrast, the prosecution portrays the "commu-

nity" as a cult that brainwashed patients into submissiveness.

Corriere, who was unlicensed when the clinic was first established, stands accused of having sex with one patient, striking several others, using ethnic and religious slurs, pressuring patients to make financial donations, and controlling patients' lives. Corriere responds that these charges are distortions by disturbed individuals who do not understand the unorthodox methods used by "feeling therapy" to help patients work through the pain of parental rejection.

Berkeley psychologist Margaret Singer, an expert on cults, testified that the center's alleged techniques are "extreme departures from the standards of practice of psychology." But two other expert witnesses, professors of psychiatry and psychology at the University of Southern California and Harvard University, respectively, said that the defendants' handling of therapeutic situations indicates "no extreme departures from the standard of practice (of psychology) and would demonstrate a very good, excellent, practice."

Were the techniques used by Richard Corriere and his colleagues "excellent practice"? How is an informed user of psychological services supposed to tell the difference between good therapy and bad? When does psychotherapy help people with their problems and when does it do emotional damage?

These questions remain as pressing today as they were during the Corriere case. "Therapeutic cults," in which patients are told they must "detach" from their "toxic" parents and partners and make their primary allegiance to the therapist, continue to pop up from time to time. In Pennsylvania in 1997, 13 former patients of Genesis Associates filed lawsuits claiming that they had been victims of such mind-control techniques. In recent years, numerous psychotherapists have been convicted of malpractice for using coercive or suggestive techniques to convince patients that they had multiple personality disorder and had participated in satanic cults. Typically, the treatment consisted of persistent pressure on patients to "remember" satanic rituals while they were hypnotized or drugged, isolated from relatives and friends, physically restrained, and deprived of sleep. In 1997, Chicago's Rush Presbyterian–St. Luke's Medical Center and two well-known psychiatrists agreed to pay a record $10.6 million to one former patient and her family, although the psychiatrists did not admit any negligence or renounce the unorthodox techniques that they had used.

Fortunately, these cases are not the norm. Many legitimate, well-tested therapies are available for treating psychological problems ranging from normal life difficulties (such as marital conflict or fear of public speaking) to the delusions of schizophrenia. In this chapter, we will evaluate three major approaches to treatment. *Biological treatments* include drugs or direct intervention in brain function; they are prescribed by psychiatrists or other physicians in a hospital or on an outpatient basis. *Psychotherapy* covers an array of psychological approaches, including psychodynamic therapies, cognitive and behavioral therapies, family therapy, and humanist therapies. *Self-help groups* provide support, and *community alternatives* provide skills training, rehabilitation counseling, and community interventions.

Each of these approaches can successfully treat some problems but not others. As you read what psychologists have learned about the effectiveness of drugs, psychotherapy, self-help, and community alternatives, see whether you can come up with some things you would want to know when evaluating any form of therapy, including unorthodox ones such as "feeling therapy."

What's Ahead

- *What kinds of drugs are used to treat psychological disorders?*

- *Are antidepressants always the best treatment for depression?*

- *Why is "shock therapy" hailed by some clinicians but condemned by others?*

BIOLOGICAL TREATMENTS

Over the centuries, individuals trying to understand and treat psychological disorders have often taken a biological (*organic*) approach, viewing mental disorders as diseases that can be treated medically. Today organic approaches are enjoying a resurgence, in part because of growing evidence that some disorders have a genetic component or involve a biochemical or neurological abnormality (see Chapter 10), and in part because of the failure of traditional psychotherapies to help chronic sufferers of some disorders.

antipsychotic drugs
Drugs used primarily in the treatment of schizophrenia and other psychotic disorders.

antidepressant drugs
Drugs used primarily in the treatment of mood disorders, especially depression and anxiety.

The Question of Drugs

The most widespread biological treatment is medication. Because drugs are so widely prescribed these days, both for severe disorders such as schizophrenia and for more common problems such as anxiety and depression, consumers need to understand what these drugs are, how they can best be used, and what their limitations are. The main classes of drugs used in the treatment of mental and emotional disorders are these:

1. **Antipsychotic drugs,** also called *neuroleptics*—such as chlorpromazine (Thorazine), haloperidol (Haldol), and clozapine (Clozaril)—are used in the treatment of schizophrenia and other psychoses. As we saw in Chapter 10, many researchers believe that some of the symptoms of schizophrenia are brought on by high levels of dopamine activity. Antipsychotic drugs block or reduce the sensitivity of brain receptors that respond to dopamine. Some also increase levels of serotonin, a neurotransmitter that inhibits dopamine activity. Antipsychotic drugs can reduce a patient's agitation, delusions, and other symptoms, and they can shorten schizophrenic episodes. (Before these drugs were introduced, hospitals controlled psychotic patients with physical restraints, including straitjackets, or put them in padded cells to keep them from hurting others or themselves.) Antipsychotics are not a cure, however. They cannot restore normal thought patterns or relationships. Although they allow many people to be released from hospitals, these individuals cannot always care for themselves, and they often fail to take their medication because of its unpleasant unintended effects. The overall success of antipsychotic drugs is modest, and some individuals diagnosed as schizophrenic deteriorate when they take them (Breggin, 1991; Karon, 1994).

2. **Antidepressant drugs** are used primarily in the treatment of depression, anxiety, phobias, and obsessive–compulsive disorder. *Monoamine oxidase (MAO) inhibitors,* such as Nardil, elevate the levels of norepinephrine and serotonin in the brain by blocking or inhibiting an enzyme that deactivates these neurotransmitters. *Tricyclic antidepressants,* such as Elavil, boost norepinephrine and serotonin levels by preventing the normal reabsorption, or "reuptake," of these substances by the cells that have released them. *Selective serotonin reuptake inhibitors (SSRIs),* such as Prozac, work on the same principle as the tricyclics but specifically target serotonin.

These photos show the effects of antipsychotic drugs on the symptoms of a young man with schizophrenia. In the photo on the left, he was unmedicated; in the photo on the right, he had taken medication. However, drug treatments do not help all people with psychotic disorders.

3. **Tranquilizers,** such as Valium and Xanax, increase the activity of the neurotransmitter gamma-aminobutyric acid (GABA). These drugs are most often prescribed by physicians for patients who complain of depressed mood, panic, or anxiety. However, they are not effective for depression or panic disorder, and while they may help an anxious person temporarily feel calmer during an acute experience of anxiety, they are not considered the treatment of choice over a long period of time. One reason is that a significant percentage of people who take tranquilizers overuse the drugs and develop problems with withdrawal and tolerance (i.e., they need larger and larger doses) (Lader & Morton, 1991). Xanax can also result in rebound panic attacks if it is not taken exactly on schedule. That is why antidepressants are generally preferable to tranquilizers in treating mood and anxiety disorders.

4. A special category of drug, a salt called *lithium carbonate,* often helps people who suffer from bipolar disorder (depression alternating with manic euphoria). It may produce its effects by moderating levels of norepinephrine. It must be given in exactly the right dose, and the patient's blood levels of lithium must be carefully monitored, because too little won't help and too much is toxic.

The increasing popularity of drugs as a method of treatment poses a problem for clinical psychologists,

tranquilizers
Drugs commonly but often inappropriately prescribed for patients who complain of unhappiness, anxiety, or worry.

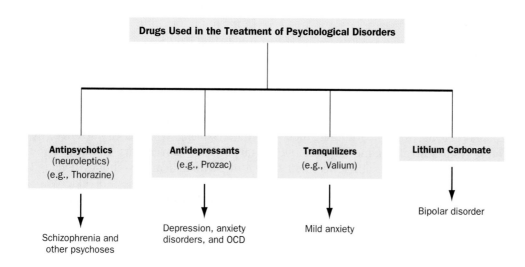

Drugs Used in the Treatment of Psychological Disorders

Antipsychotics (neuroleptics) (e.g., Thorazine)
↓
Schizophrenia and other psychoses

Antidepressants (e.g., Prozac)
↓
Depression, anxiety disorders, and OCD

Tranquilizers (e.g., Valium)
↓
Mild anxiety

Lithium Carbonate
↓
Bipolar disorder

who, unlike psychiatrists, are not currently licensed to prescribe medication. Many psychologists are now lobbying for prescription rights, arguing that they should have access to the full range of treatment possibilities (DeLeon & Wiggins, 1996). But they have run into resistance from the medical profession, which argues that even with increased training, psychologists will not be qualified to prescribe medication, and also from psychologists who are concerned about the medicalizing of their field and who want psychology to remain a distinct alternative to psychiatry (DeNelsky, 1996).

Drugs have helped many people who have gone from therapy to therapy without relief. Although medication cannot magically eliminate people's problems, it can be a useful first step in treatment. By improving sleep patterns, appetite, and energy, it can help people concentrate on solving their problems. Yet, despite these benefits, some words of caution are in order. Many psychiatrists and drug companies are trumpeting the benefits of medication without informing the public of its limitations. Here are some of those limitations:

Thinking Critically About Drug Treatments

1. *The placebo effect.* New drugs, like new psychotherapies, often promise quick and effective cures, as was the case with the arrival of Clozaril, Xanax, and Prozac. But the placebo effect (see Chapter 1) ensures that some people will respond positively to new drugs just because of the enthusiasm surrounding them. After a while, when placebo effects decline, many drugs turn out to be neither as effective as promised nor as widely applicable. This has happened repeatedly with each new generation of tranquilizer and is happening again with antidepressants.

The belief that antidepressants are the treatment of choice for depression is widespread, so we were as surprised as anyone to discover the large amount of evidence questioning that belief. One meta-analysis found that clinicians considered antidepressants helpful, but patients' ratings showed no advantage for the drugs beyond the placebo effect (Greenberg et al., 1992). Another meta-analysis, of 39 studies involving more than 3,000 depressed patients, found little difference in the effectiveness of medication versus psychotherapy. Moreover, 73 percent of the drugs' effectiveness was due to the placebo effect or other nonchemical factors (Sapirstein & Kirsch, 1996). Studies of the much-heralded Prozac show that it is no more effective than the older generation of antidepressants (Greenberg et al., 1994).

2. *High relapse and dropout rates.* A person may have short-term success with antipsychotic or antidepressant drugs. However, in part because these medications have some unpleasant physical effects, between 50 and 67 percent of people stop taking them (McGrath et al., 1990; Torrey, 1988). Individuals who take antidepressants without learning how to cope with their problems are also more likely to relapse and again become depressed (Antonuccio, Danton, & DeNelsky, 1995).

3. *Dosage problems.* The challenge with drugs is to find the "therapeutic window," the amount that is enough but not too much. Many questions remain about which drug best suits which problem, what the proper dose should be, how long the drug should and can be taken, and so forth (Gutheil, 1993). To complicate matters, the same dose of a drug may be metabolized differently in men and women, old people and young people, and different ethnic groups (Strickland et al., 1991, 1995; Willie et al., 1995). When psychiatrist Keh-Ming Lin moved from Taiwan to the United States, he was amazed to learn that the dosage of antipsychotic drugs given to American patients with schizophrenia was often 10 times higher than the dose for Chinese patients. In subsequent studies, Lin and his colleagues confirmed that Asian patients require significantly lower doses of the medication for optimal treatment (Lin, Poland, & Chien, 1990; Lin et al., 1989). Similarly, African-Americans suffering from depression or bipolar disorder seem to need lower dosages of tricyclic antidepressants and lithium than other ethnic groups do (Strickland et al., 1991, 1995). Groups may differ in the dosages they can tolerate because of variations in metabolic rates, amount of body fat, the number or type of drug receptors in the brain, or cultural practices such as smoking and eating habits.

4. *Long-term risks, known and unknown.* Antipsychotic drugs are among the safest in medicine, but they can have some dangerous effects if they are taken over many years. One is the development of a neurological disorder called *tardive* (late-appearing) *dyskinesia,* which is characterized by involuntary muscle movements. About one-fourth of all adults who take antipsychotics develop this disorder, and fully one-third of elderly patients do (Saltz et al., 1991). Another is *neuroleptic malignant syndrome,* which occurs in a small percentage of cases and produces fever, delirium, coma, and sometimes death (Keck, McElroy, & Pope, 1991).

Antidepressants are assumed to be safe, and they are nonaddictive, but they can produce unpleasant physical reactions, including dry mouth, headaches, constipation, nausea, restlessness, gastrointestinal problems, weight gain, and, in as many as one-third of all patients, decreased sexual desire and blocked or delayed orgasm. The effects of taking antidepressants for many years are still unknown.

The general public and even many physicians do not realize that new drugs are often tested on only a few hundred people for only a few weeks or months, even when the drug is one that patients might take for many years. For example, Clozapine was tested in controlled trials that lasted only six weeks (*FDA Drug Bulletin,* 1990). Many psychiatrists, relying on such short-term tests, overlook the possibility of negative long-term effects.

As we will see later in this chapter, certain psychotherapies work as well as drugs do, or even better, for most people who have panic attacks, phobias, anxiety, or depression. And biological treatments are not necessarily the only appropriate ones even when a disorder appears to have biological origins. A PET-scan study of people with obsessive–compulsive disorder found that cerebral glucose metabolic rates changed in patients who were taking Prozac, suggesting that the drug was having a beneficial effect on the brain. But two studies found the *same* brain changes in patients who were getting cognitive-behavior therapy and no medication (Baxter et al., 1992; Schwartz et al., 1996). These findings remind us that although the brain affects behavior, behavior (including the behavior that takes place in therapy) can also affect the brain (see Figure 11.1).

Without question, drugs have rescued some people from emotional despair, suicide, or years in a mental hospital. They have enabled severely depressed or disturbed people to function and even to be able to respond to psychotherapy. But we need to think critically about drug therapies because many doctors prescribe them routinely, often without accompanying psychotherapy for the person's problems. The overprescription of drugs is partly a result of pressure from managed-care organizations, which prefer to pay for one patient visit for a prescription rather than ten visits for psychotherapy, and from drug companies, which are spending fortunes to market and promote these highly profitable products (Antonuccio, Danton, & DeNelsky, 1995; Critser, 1996). At one

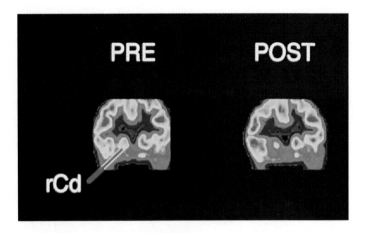

Figure 11.1

Psychotherapy and the Brain

These PET scans show the brain of a person with obsessive–compulsive disorder before and after treatment with behavior therapy. Before therapy, the glucose metabolic rates in the right caudate nucleus (rCd) were elevated; after therapy, this area "calmed down," becoming less active (Schwartz et al., 1996).

conference we attended, a psychiatrist warned that because of the ease of prescribing antidepressants and tranquilizers, "It is not unusual for [psychiatrists] to see anywhere from six to eight patients per client hour. This is not being involved with your patient in any meaningful way."

In sum, drugs used for treating psychological problems are neither totally miraculous nor totally worthless. Their effectiveness depends on the individual, the problem, and whether medication is combined with psychotherapy.

Surgery and Electroshock

For centuries, physicians treated mental illness by trying to change brain function directly. In the seventeenth century, for example, physicians tried to release the "psychic pressures" they believed were causing a person's symptoms by drilling holes in the person's skull—a method called *trepanning.* **Psychosurgery**—surgery designed to destroy selected areas of the brain thought to be responsible for emotional disorders or disturbed behavior—continued well into this century.

The most famous form of modern psychosurgery was invented in 1935, when a Portuguese neurologist, Egas Moniz, drilled two holes into the skull of a mental patient and used a specially designed instrument to cut or crush nerve

psychosurgery

Any surgical procedure that destroys selected areas of the brain believed to be involved in emotional disorders or violent, impulsive behavior.

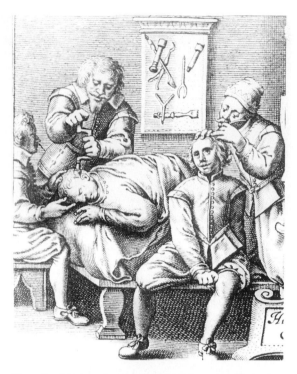

Throughout history, healers have tried to root out behavior they considered abnormal—sometimes literally. An engraving from 1634 shows trepanning, an ancient method of drilling holes in the skull to release "psychic pressures" supposedly causing mental illness.

fibers running from the prefrontal lobes to other areas. This operation, called a *prefrontal lobotomy,* was supposed to reduce the patient's emotional symptoms without impairing intellectual ability. The procedure—which, incredibly, was never assessed or validated scientifically—was performed on tens of thousands of people. In America, the lobotomy was popularized by Walter Freeman, who personally performed more than 3,500 operations. Tragically, lobotomies left many patients apathetic, withdrawn, and unable to care for themselves (Valenstein, 1986). Yet Moniz won a Nobel Prize for his work.

With the advent of antipsychotic drugs in the 1950s, the number of lobotomies declined, but other forms of psychosurgery took their place. These surgeries, too, had unpredictable and often devastating consequences for the patient (Breggin, 1991; Valenstein, 1986). Today, psychosurgery is rarely used, although the rapid development of new technologies for probing the brain may mean that we will see its resurgence in the future.

Another controversial procedure that *has* made a dramatic return is **electroconvulsive therapy (ECT),** or "shock therapy," which is used for the treatment of severe depression. An electrode is placed on one or both sides of the head, and a current is turned on briefly. The current triggers a seizure that typically lasts one minute, causing the body to convulse. A colleague told us about a man who was given ECT in the early 1950s: The convulsions sent the man flying off the table and shattered his legs. Cases such as this reinforced the public impression of ECT as a barbaric and painful practice, and the method lost favor, especially when drugs seemed so promising. Then, when drugs proved to have limited effectiveness and to take time to work, and when new ways of measuring brain activity appeared, researchers began to reexamine ECT.

Today, the technique has been vastly modified and the voltage reduced. Patients are given muscle relaxants and anesthesia, so that they can sleep through the procedure and their convulsions are minimized. But the controversy about ECT remains. It indeed can be effective with suicidally depressed people, for whom there is a risk in waiting until antidepressants or psychotherapy can take effect, because the results of ECT are immediate

electroconvulsive therapy (ECT)

A procedure used in cases of prolonged and severe major depression, in which a brief brain seizure is induced.

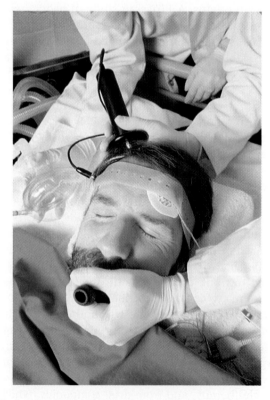

Electroconvulsive therapy has been used successfully to treat severe depression that has not responded to other treatments, but supporters and critics continue to disagree vehemently about its use.

(Holmes, 1997). But, although there are many theories, no one knows how or why ECT works. And it is *ineffective* with other disorders, such as schizophrenia or alcoholism, though it is sometimes misused for these conditions.

ECT's supporters argue that it is foolish to deny suffering, depressed patients a way out of their misery, especially if their misery is making them suicidal. They cite research showing that when

ECT is used properly, it is safe and effective and causes no long-term cognitive impairment, memory loss, or detectable brain damage (Coffey, 1993; Devanand et al., 1994; Endler, 1991). Critics reply that ECT is too often used improperly, and that it can indeed damage the brain (Breggin, 1991). One psychiatrist has called its use "like hitting [someone] with a two-by-four" (Fisher, 1985). ECT continues to inspire passion, pro and con.

??? QUICK QUIZ

A. Match these treatments with the problems for which they are typically used.

1. antipsychotic drugs
2. antidepressant drugs
3. lithium carbonate
4. electroconvulsive therapy

a. suicidal depression
b. bipolar disorder
c. schizophrenia
d. depression and anxiety
e. obsessive–compulsive disorder

B. Give four reasons why the public should be cautious about concluding that drugs for psychological disorders are miracle cures.

 C. Jezebel has had occasional episodes of depression that seem to be getting worse. Her physician prescribes an antidepressant. Before taking it, what questions should Jezebel ask herself—and the doctor?

Answers:

A. 1. c 2. d, e 3. b 4. a B. (1) Placebo effects are common; (2) dropout and relapse rates are high; (3) appropriate dosages can be difficult to determine and can vary by sex, age, and ethnicity; and (4) some drugs have unknown or long-term risks. C. Jezebel might want to ask these questions: Has the physician taken her full medical and psychological history or prescribed the drug casually? Has the physician explored with her the possible reasons for her depression or referred her to a mental-health professional who will do so? Would psychotherapy be appropriate, either with or without medication? Does the medication have any unpleasant physical effects or long-term risks? Will the doctor continue to monitor her reactions to the drug on a regular basis?

What's Ahead

- *Why are psychodynamic therapies called "depth" therapies?*

- *How can therapies based on learning principles help you change your bad habits?*

- *How do cognitive therapists help people get rid of self-defeating thoughts?*

- *Why do humanist therapists focus on the "here and now" instead of the "why and how"?*

- *Why do family therapists prefer to treat families rather than individuals?*

KINDS OF PSYCHOTHERAPY

All good psychotherapists want to help clients think about their lives in new ways and find solutions to the problems that plague them. In this section we will consider the major schools of psychotherapy and some of their offshoots. To illustrate the philosophy and methods of each approach, we will focus on a fictional fellow named Murray, a smart guy whose problem is all too familiar to many students. Murray procrastinates. He just can't seem to settle down and write his term papers. He keeps getting incompletes, and before long the incompletes turn to F's. Why does Murray procrastinate, manufacturing his own misery? What kind of therapy might help him?

Psychodynamic Therapy

Sigmund Freud was the father of the "talking cure," as one of his patients called it. He believed that intensive probing of the past and of the mind would produce *insight*—the patient's awareness of the reason for his or her symptoms and anguish. With insight and emotional release, the symptoms would disappear. Freud's original method of *psychoanalysis* has evolved into many different forms of therapy, which are called *psychodynamic* because they share the goal of exploring the unconscious dynamics of personality, such as defenses and conflicts (see Chapter 2). These approaches are considered by their proponents to be "depth" therapies because the goal is to delve for unconscious processes rather than concentrate on "superficial" symptoms and conscious beliefs.

In psychoanalysis and some other psychodynamic therapies, the client lies on a couch, facing away from the analyst, and engages in **free association,** saying whatever comes to mind. For example, by free associating to his dreams, his fantasies about work, and his early memories, our friend Murray might gain the insight that he procrastinates as a way of expressing anger toward his parents. He might realize that he is angry because they insist that he study for a career he dislikes. Ideally, Murray will come to this insight by himself. If the analyst suggests it, Murray might feel too defensive to accept it.

Another major element of psychodynamic therapy is **transference,** the client's transfer (displacement) of emotional elements of his or her inner life—usually feelings about the parents—outward onto the analyst. Have you ever found yourself responding to a new acquaintance with unusually quick affection or dislike and later realized it was because the person reminded you of a loved or loathed relative? That experience is similar to transference. A woman who failed to resolve her Oedipal love for her father might seem to fall in love with the analyst. A man who is unconsciously angry at his mother for rejecting him might become furious with his analyst for going on vacation. Through analysis of transference, psychodynamic therapists believe, clients can resolve their emotional conflicts.

However, psychodynamic therapies, especially

"HAVE A COUPLE OF DREAMS, AND CALL ME IN THE MORNING."

Analyzing dreams is a major element of psychoanalytic therapy.

psychoanalysis, do not expressly aim to solve an individual's immediate problem. In fact, a person may come in complaining of a symptom such as anxiety or headaches, and the therapist may not get around to that symptom for months or even years. The analyst views the symptom as only the tip of the mental iceberg. Some traditional analysts don't attempt cures at all. The goal, they say, is understanding, not change.

Today, many psychodynamic therapists use ideas derived from Freudian theory but reject traditional psychoanalytic methods. They face the client; they participate more; and they are more goal-directed. In orthodox psychoanalysis, the client may meet with the therapist more than once a week, over a period of many years. (In the old film *Sleeper,* when a character played by Woody Allen awakens after two centuries of suspended animation, his first thought is, "I haven't seen my analyst in 200 years! He was a strict Freudian—if I'd been going all this time I'd probably almost be cured by now.") But many psychodynamic therapists are now practicing time-limited or *brief psychodynamic therapy,* consisting of 15, 20, or 25 sessions. Without delving into the client's entire history, the therapist listens to the client's problems and formulates the main issue, or *dynamic focus* (Strupp & Binder, 1984). The rest of the therapy focuses on the person's self-defeating habits and recurring problems. The therapist

free association

In psychoanalysis, a method of uncovering unconscious conflicts by saying freely whatever comes to mind.

transference

In psychodynamic therapies, a critical step in which the client transfers unconscious emotions or reactions, such as emotional feelings about his or her parents, onto the therapist.

looks for clues in the client's behavior in therapy to identify and change these patterns.

Behavioral and Cognitive Therapy

Unlike psychodynamic therapists, psychologists who practice behavioral or cognitive therapy (or, more commonly, a mixture of the two) would focus on helping Murray change his current behavior and attitudes rather than on striving for insight. "Mur," they would say, "you have lousy study habits. And you have a set of beliefs about studying, writing papers, and success that are woefully unrealistic." Such therapists would not worry much about Murray's past, his parents, or his unconscious anxieties.

Behavioral Techniques.

A behavior therapist might draw on techniques such as the following, which are derived from the behavioral principles of classical and operant conditioning discussed in Chapter 8. (You may want to review those principles before going on.)

1. *Behavioral records and contracts* help clients identify the reinforcers (rewarding consequences) that are keeping their unwanted habits going. For example, a man who wants to curb his overeating may not be aware of how much he eats throughout the day to relieve tension; a behavioral record might show that he eats more junk food than he realized in the late afternoon. Once the unwanted behavior is identified, along with the reinforcers that have been maintaining it, a treatment program can be designed to change it; the man might find other ways to reduce stress and be sure that he is nowhere near junk food in the late afternoon. The therapist helps the person set *behavioral goals,* small step by small step, perhaps with a behavioral contract. For instance, a husband and wife who fight over housework might be asked to draw up a contract indicating who will do what, with specified rewards for carrying out their duties. With such a contract, they can't fall back on accusations such as "You never do anything around here."

2. *Systematic desensitization* is a step-by-step process of desensitizing a client to a feared object or experience. It is based on the classical-conditioning procedure of *counterconditioning,* in which a stimulus for an unwanted response (such as fear) is paired with some other stimulus or situation that elicits a response incompatible with the undesirable one (see Chapter 8). In this case, the incompatible response is usually relaxation. The client learns to relax deeply while imagining or looking at a sequence of feared stimuli, arranged in a hierarchy ranging from the least frightening to the most frightening. The sequence for a person who is terrified of flying might be to read about airplane safety, look at pictures or models of airplanes, visit an airport and watch planes taking off, sit in a plane while it is on the ground, take a short flight, and then take a long flight. At each step the person must become relaxed and comfortable before going on. Eventually, the fear responses are extinguished.

3. *Aversive conditioning* substitutes punishment for the reinforcement that has perpetuated a bad habit. Suppose a woman who bites her nails is reinforced each time she does so by relief from her anxiety and a brief good feeling. A behavior therapist might have her wear a rubber band around her wrist and ask her to snap it (hard!) each time she bites her nails or feels the desire to do so. The

Get Involved

In Chapter 10, a Get Involved exercise asked you to identify your greatest fear. Now see whether systematic desensitization procedures will help you conquer your fear. Write down a list of situations that evoke your fear, starting with one that produces little anxiety (e.g., seeing a photo of a tiny brown spider) and ending with the most frightening one possible (e.g., looking at live tarantulas at the pet store). Then find a quiet room where you will have no distractions or interruptions (no TV!), sit in a comfortable reclining chair, and relax all the muscles of your body. Breathe slowly and deeply. Imagine the first, easiest scene, remaining as relaxed as possible. Do this until you can confront the image without becoming the least bit anxious. When that happens, go on to the next scene in your hierarchy. Don't try this all at once; space out your sessions over time. Does it work?

IN THE BLEACHERS   By Steve Moore

Batters overcoming bonkinogginophobia, *a fear of the ball.*

Exposure therapy at work.

goal is to make sure that she receives no continuing rewards for the undesirable behavior.

4. *Flooding or exposure treatments* take the client right into a feared situation, with the therapist going along to show that the situation isn't going to kill either of them. For example, a person suffering from agoraphobia would be taken into the very situation that he or she fears most—a department store, say, or a subway—and would remain there, with the therapist, until the panic and anxiety declined. Notice how different this approach is from a psychodynamic one, in which the goal is to uncover the presumably unconscious reason that the agoraphobic feels afraid of going out.

5. *Skills training* provides practice in behaviors that are necessary for achieving the person's goals. It's not enough to tell someone "Don't be shy" if the person doesn't know how to make small talk with others; skills training would teach the shy person how to converse in social settings (for example, by focusing on other people rather than on his or her own insecurity). Countless skills-training programs are available—for parents who don't know how to discipline children, for people who don't know how to manage anger, for children and

adults who don't know how to express their wishes clearly, and so on.

A behaviorist would treat Murray's procrastination in several ways. Murray might not be aware of how he actually spends his time when he is avoiding his studies. Afraid that he hasn't time to do everything, he does nothing. Keeping a behavioral diary would let Murray know exactly how he spends his time, and how much time he should realistically allot to a project. Instead of having a vague, impossibly huge goal, such as "I'm going to reorganize my life," Murray would establish specific small goals, such as reading the two books necessary for an English paper and writing one page of an assignment. The therapist might also offer skills training to make sure Murray knows how to reach these goals.

Cognitive Techniques. Of course, people's thoughts, feelings, and motivations can influence their behavior. *Cognitive therapy* aims to help clients identify the beliefs and expectations that might be unnecessarily prolonging their unhappiness, conflicts, and other problems. To a cognitive therapist, expressing emotions is not enough to get rid of them if the thoughts behind the emotions remain (Greenberger & Padesky, 1995).

For example, in Chapter 10 we saw that mood problems often involve distorted thoughts and perceptions. In particular, depression often involves three habits of thinking:

1. *Internality.* Depressed people tend to believe that the reason for their misery is internal—something in them, an entrenched aspect of their personality. They will say, for example, "I'm unattractive and awkward; no wonder I'm not making friends." They rarely consider external explanations, such as "This school is so big and impersonal it's hard to meet new people" (Anderson et al., 1994).

2. *Stability.* Depressed people tend to believe that their situation is permanent ("Nothing good will ever happen to me"; "I'll never fall in love"). This belief can create a vicious cycle: Expecting nothing to get better, they do nothing to improve their lives, and therefore they remain lonely and sad.

3. *Control.* Depressed people tend to believe that they have no control over their emotions or the situations that caused those emotions ("I'm depressed because I'm ugly and horrible and I can't do anything about it").

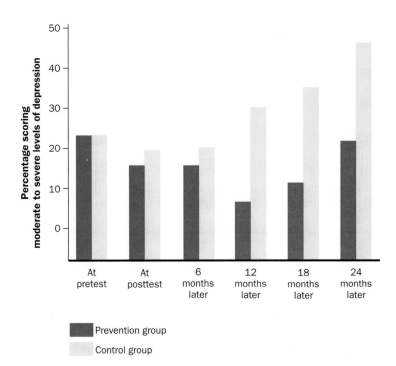

Figure 11.2

Inoculating Children Against Depression

This graph shows the percentage of children who were at moderate to high risk of depression (pretest), and their depression scores after a cognitive intervention (posttest) and during four follow-up assessments. Notice that the effects of the intervention were still strong two years later, as the children entered adolescence (Gillham et al., 1995).

A cognitive therapist would help a depressed person substitute positive thoughts for self-defeating ones and encourage the person to seek out situations that confirm the new ways of thinking.

One of the oldest and best-known schools of cognitive therapy is Albert Ellis's rational emotive therapy, now called *rational emotive behavior therapy* (Ellis, 1993). In this approach, the therapist uses rational arguments to directly challenge a client's unrealistic beliefs or expectations. Another popular cognitive strategy, devised by Aaron Beck (1976, 1991), does not involve any direct challenge to the client's beliefs; instead, the therapist simply encourages the person to test those beliefs against the evidence.

Cognitive interventions can prevent mood disorders from developing in the first place. One remarkable program targeted 69 fifth- and sixth-grade children who were considered at risk of depression because they scored high on a children's depression inventory, came from homes with high levels of parental conflict, or both. The children were taught to identify pessimistic beliefs, examine the evidence for and against those beliefs, and generate more realistic alternatives. A control group of children who were also at risk of depression did not get this training. As you can see in Figure 11.2, after the training, children in the intervention group had lower depression scores than did those in the control group at all four follow-up sessions. The differences still held two years later, when the children were entering adolescence and when depression rates in the control group shot up steeply (Gillham et al., 1995).

A cognitive therapist might treat Murray's procrastination by having Murray write down his thoughts about work, read the thoughts as if someone else had said them, and then write a rational response to each one. This technique would encourage Murray to examine the validity of his assumptions and beliefs. Many procrastinators are perfectionists; if they can't do something perfectly, they won't do it at all. Unable to accept their limitations, they set impossible standards and "catastrophize":

Negative Thought	Rational Response
This paper isn't good enough; I'd better rewrite it for the twentieth time.	Good enough for what? It won't win a Pulitzer Prize, but it is a pretty good paper.
If I don't get an A+ on this paper, my life will be ruined.	My life will be a lot worse if I keep getting incompletes. It's better to get a B or even a C than to do nothing at all.
My professor is going to think I'm an idiot when he reads this. I'll feel humiliated by his criticism	He's not accused me of being an idiot yet. If he makes some criticisms, I can learn from them and do better next time.

Get Involved

Try this exercise to see whether cognitive therapy techniques can help you control your moods. Think of a time recently when you had particularly strong feelings, such as depression, anger, or anxiety. On a piece of paper, record (1) the situation—who was there, what happened, and when; (2) your feelings at the time, rating each one as weak, moderate, or strong; and (3) the thoughts that were going through your mind (e.g., "She never cares about what I want to do"; "I hate being angry"; "He's going to leave me"). Now examine your thoughts and ask yourself, What do these thoughts reveal about me? What am I afraid might happen? What is the worst thing that could happen if my thought is true? Is there another way to think about this situation or the other person's behavior? If you practice this exercise repeatedly, you may learn how your thoughts affect your moods—and find out that you have more control over your feelings than you realized (from Greenberger & Padesky, 1995).

As you may recall from Chapter 8, strict behaviorists consider thoughts to be "behaviors" that are modifiable by learning principles; they do not regard thoughts as causes of behavior. But most psychologists believe that thoughts and behavior influence each other, which is why cognitive-behavioral therapy is more common than either form alone.

Humanist and Existential Therapy

Humanist therapies, like their parent philosophy humanism, start from the assumption that people seek self-actualization and self-fulfillment. These therapies generally do not delve into past conflicts but aim instead to help people feel better about themselves and free themselves from self-imposed limits. To humanists, the most important thing to know is how a person subjectively perceives his or her own situation, and the important thing to work for is the will to bring about change. That is why they explore what is going on "here and now," not the issues of "why and how."

In *client-centered* or nondirective therapy, developed by Carl Rogers, the therapist's role is to listen sympathetically, to offer what Rogers called *unconditional positive regard*, to be an "ideal parent" (see Chapter 2). Whatever the client's specific complaint is, the goal is to build the client's self-esteem and help the person feel that he or she is loved and respected no matter what. Thus a Rogerian might assume that Murray's procrastination masks his low self-regard, and that Murray is out of touch with his real feelings and wishes. Perhaps he isn't working to pass his courses because he is trying to please his parents by majoring in prelaw, when he'd secretly rather become an artist.

Rogers (1961) believed that effective therapists must be warm, genuine, and honest in expressing their feelings, and they must show accurate, empathic understanding of the client's problems. The therapist's support for the client, according to Rogers, will eventually be adopted by the client, who will become more self-accepting. Once that is accomplished, the person can accept the limitations of others too.

Existential therapy helps clients explore the meaning of existence and face with courage the great questions of life, such as death, freedom, free will, alienation from oneself and others, loneliness, and meaninglessness. Existential therapists, like humanist therapists, believe that our lives are not inevitably determined by our pasts or our circumstances—that we have the power to choose our own destinies. As Irvin Yalom (1989) explained, "The crucial first step in therapy is the patient's assumption of responsibility for his or her life predicament. As long as one believes that one's problems are caused by some force or agency outside oneself, there is no leverage in therapy."

Some observers believe that, ultimately, all therapies are existential. In different ways, therapy helps people determine what is important to them, what values guide them, and what changes they will have the courage to make. An existential therapist might help Murray think about the significance of his procrastination, what his ultimate goals in life are, and how he might find the strength to carry out his ambitions.

Family Therapy

Murray's situation is getting worse. His father has begun to call him Tomorrow Man, which upsets his mother, and his younger brother the math major has been calculating how much tuition money Murray's incompletes are costing. His older sister Isabel, the biochemist who never had an incomplete in her life, now proposes that all of them go to a family therapist. "Murray's not the only one in this family with complaints," she says.

Family therapists would maintain that Murray's problem developed in a social context, that it is sustained by a social context, and that any change he makes will affect that context. One leading family therapist, Salvador Minuchin (1984), compared the family to a kaleidoscope, a changing pattern of mosaics in which the pattern is larger than any one piece. In this view, efforts to isolate and treat one member of the family without the others are doomed. Only if all family members reveal their differing perceptions of each other can mistakes and misperceptions be identified. A teenager, for instance, may see his mother as crabby and nagging when actually she is tired and worried. A parent may see a child as rebellious when in fact the child is lonely and desperate for attention.

Family members are usually unaware of how they influence one another. By observing the entire family (or, in the case of couples, both partners), the family therapist hopes to discover tensions and imbalances in power and communication. For example, in some families a child may develop an illness or a psychological problem that affects the workings of the whole family. One parent may become overinvolved with the sick child while the other parent retreats, and each may start blaming the other. The child, in turn, may cling to the illness as a way of expressing anger, keeping the parents together, getting the parents' attention, or asserting control (Luepnitz, 1988).

Some family therapists look for patterns of behavior across generations (Kerr & Bowen, 1988). The therapist and client may create a *genogram,* a family tree of psychologically significant events across as many generations as possible (Carter & McGoldrick, 1988; Coupland, Serovich, & Glenn, 1995). This method often reveals the origins of current problems and conflicts. The genogram of

Family therapist Alan Entin uses photographs to help people identify themes in their family histories and put their feelings in perspective. When one woman was asked to talk about a photo of her parents (left), she began to cry; she felt that it revealed her father's alienation from her and the rest of his family. Does the picture on the right convey a happy cohesive family to you, or a divided one? Shortly after it was taken, the couple divorced; the father took custody of the children . . . and the mother kept the dog (Entin, 1992).

Figure 11.3

The Family Genogram of Playwright Eugene O'Neill

Genograms can reveal patterns of behavior across several generations within a family. The O'Neill family shows patterns of estrangement between father and children, multiple marriages, and addiction. Both Eugene and his older brother Jamie were alienated from their father; in turn, Eugene was estranged from his two sons, and he never spoke to his daughter Oona again after she married Charlie Chaplin. Eugene attempted suicide, and both of his sons killed themselves. Eugene's grandfather, father, older brother, and sons were alcoholics; his mother, a morphine addict for 26 years, was later cured. Eugene had problems with alcohol too but quit drinking at age 37. (From McGoldrick & Gerson, 1985.)

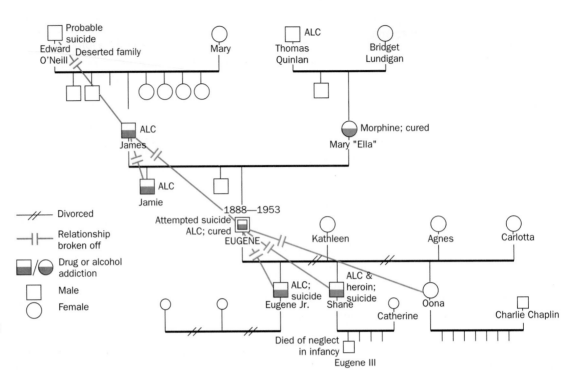

the playwright Eugene O'Neill, for instance, shows a pattern of drug abuse and estrangement between father and children for three generations (see Figure 11.3).

Even when it is not possible to treat the whole family, some therapists will treat individuals from a *family systems* perspective (Bowen, 1978; Carter & McGoldrick, 1988). Clients learn that if they change in any way, even for the better, their families may protest noisily or may send subtle messages that read, "Change back!" Why? Because when one family member changes, each of the others must change too. As the saying goes, it takes two to tango, and if one dancer stops, so must the other. But most people don't like change. They are comfortable with old patterns and habits, even those that cause them trouble. They want to keep tangoing, even if their feet hurt.

In general, family therapists would observe how Murray's procrastination fits his family dynamics. Perhaps it allows Murray to get his father's attention and his mother's sympathy. Perhaps it keeps Murray from facing his greatest fear: that if he does finish his work, it won't measure up to his father's high standards. The therapist will not only help Murray change his work habits, but will help his family deal with a changed Murray.

Psychotherapy in Practice

The four approaches to psychotherapy that we have discussed may seem quite different. In theory, they are, and so are the techniques resulting from them (see Table 11.1). Yet in practice, most psychotherapists draw on methods and ideas from

Get Involved

Using the example of a genogram in Figure 11.3, draw a diagram of a trait or behavior that has recurred in your family. It might be a problem, such as alcoholism, violence, or parental abandonment; an illness or disability that affected family dynamics, such as asthma or diabetes; or a positive quality, such as creativity or musical ability. What does this exercise show you about patterns across generations?

Table 11.1	The Major Schools of Therapy Compared	
	Primary goal	**Methods**
Psychodynamic	Insight into unconscious motives and feelings	Probing the unconscious through dream analysis, free association, transference, other forms of "talk therapy"
Cognitive-behavioral	Modification of behavior and irrational beliefs	Behavioral techniques such as systematic desensitization and flooding; exercises to identify and change faulty beliefs
Humanist	Insight; self-acceptance and self-fulfillment	Providing a safe, nonjudgmental setting in which to discuss life issues
Family	Modification of individual habits and family patterns	Working with couples, families, and sometimes individuals to identify and change patterns that perpetuate problems

various approaches, avoiding strong allegiances to any one theory or school of thought (Lambert & Bergin, 1994). This flexibility enables them to treat clients with whatever methods are most appropriate and effective.

Some therapists also take advantage of a lesson from social psychology—namely, that the influence of other people may accomplish what a single therapist cannot. In *group therapy,* people with the same or different problems are put together to find solutions. Members learn that their problems are not unique. They also learn that they cannot get away with their usual excuses because others in the group have tried them all (Yalom, 1995). Group therapies are commonly used in institutions, such as prisons and mental hospitals. They are also popular among people who have a range of social difficulties, such as shyness and anxiety, or who share a common traumatic experience, such as sexual assault (Becker et al., 1984). (Keep in mind that therapy groups are not the same as self-help groups, which we will discuss in the next section, or motivational or spiritual programs designed for personal growth rather than psychotherapy.)

All successful therapies seem to share some common elements (Lambert & Hill, 1994; Mahoney, 1991; Orlinsky & Howard, 1994). One is what George Howard (1991) calls "story repair": Good therapists try to replace a client's self-defeating, pessimistic, or unrealistic life story, or personal narrative, with one that is more hopeful and attainable. Some therapists are making this "story repair" an explicit focus of treatment, using the *narrative method* to help clients form new stories about themselves (Freedman & Combs, 1996; White & Epston, 1990). The therapist may write a letter to the client, framing the problem as the therapist sees it and inviting the client to write a reply. As cognitive therapists would predict, this exercise allows people to identify their irrational or unsupported beliefs and find other interpretations of their experiences.

One proponent of the narrative method, David Epston, wrote a long letter to Marisa, an immigrant woman who had been abused and rejected all her life. It said, in part, "Telling me, a virtual stranger, your life story, which turned out to be a history of exploitation, frees you to some extent from it. To tell a story about your life turns it into a history, one that can be left behind, and makes it easier for you to create a future of your own design" (quoted in O'Hanlon, 1994). Marisa replied that his letter helped her to tell a new story about her life and future. Instead of seeing the tragedies that had befallen her as evidence that she was a worthless victim, as she always had, she now saw the same events as evidence of her strength and endurance. In short, she transformed her victim narrative into a story of triumph. "My life has a future now," she wrote back to him. "It will never be the same again."

??? QUICK QUIZ

Match each method with the therapy most likely to use it.

1. free association
2. systematic desensitization
3. facing the fear of death
4. reappraisal of thoughts
5. unconditional positive regard
6. genogram
7. contract specifying duties

a. cognitive therapy
b. psychoanalysis
c. humanist therapy
d. behavior therapy
e. family therapy
f. existential therapy

Answers:
1.b 2.d 3.f 4.a 5.c 6.e 7.d

What's Ahead

- *What community resources can help people who have serious mental disorders?*
- *What can a self-help group offer a person that relatives, friends, and psychotherapists can't?*

ALTERNATIVES TO PSYCHOTHERAPY

Psychotherapy is used for all sorts of problems, but sometimes it is not enough and sometimes it is too much. *Community and rehabilitation programs* aim to help people who are seriously mentally ill or who have disabilities and need more than psychotherapy. *Self-help groups* are designed for people who have problems that do not require individual or group therapy guided by professionals.

The Community and Rehabilitation Movements

Many people assume that most individuals who are seriously mentally ill live in hospitals and other institutions, but in the United States, this is not true. The Community Mental Health Centers Act of 1963 called for a nationwide network of mental health centers to replace mental hospitals, which often merely served as warehouses for the mentally ill. But the law was never funded, and sadly, thousands of patients were simply "dumped." Be-

tween 1955 and 1992 the number of people in mental institutions plummeted from 559,000 to 90,000 (Shogren, 1994). Today, the vast majority of those with severe mental disorders spend most of their lives in boarding houses, hotel rooms, hostels, jails, hallways, abandoned buildings, halfway houses, or the streets. The question of how best to treat them is crucial to these individuals, their families, and society.

One answer has been provided by *community psychologists* and other mental-health workers who set up programs to help people who are mentally ill, in their own communities rather than in hospitals (Dion & Anthony, 1987; Orford, 1992). These programs emphasize community support, including outpatient services at local clinics and close contact with family and friends (Harding, Zubin, & Strauss, 1987). The nature of the support depends on the nature of the disorder or disability.

For example, people with schizophrenia need a comprehensive program. Traditional psychotherapies are not effective for most of them. And although drugs are helpful—even essential—they are not sufficient; a drug can reduce symptoms but cannot teach a person how to get a job. Psychologists have experimented with many different solutions. One successful approach is the *clubhouse model*, a program for mentally ill people that provides rehabilitation counseling, job and skills training, and a support network. Members may live at the clubhouse until they are ready to be on their own, and they may visit the clubhouse at any time. New York City's Fountain House, one of the oldest such programs in the country, has an

At halfway houses such as Fountain House in New York City, people with mental disorders live "halfway" between hospitalization and complete independence. They learn to take care of themselves and others, they get job training, and they receive some therapy until they are able to live on their own.

excellent track record in helping its members find work, return to school, and establish friendships (Beard, Propst, & Malamud, 1982; Foderaro, 1994). Other community approaches include family therapy, foster care and family home alternatives, and family support groups (Hatfield & Lefley, 1987; Orford, 1992).

We want to emphasize that community approaches are not available for all who need them. Many chronic mental patients live in private nursing homes and board-and-care homes that are unregulated and poorly staffed. For the most part, patients are no better off in these types of facilities than they were in state institutions (Shadish, Lurigio, & Lewis, 1989). And unfortunately, general hospitals, which are burdened with people who have psychotic disorders, often give patients medication and release them even when there are no services and families to care for them. Back on the street, many patients stop taking their medication. Their psychotic symptoms return, they are rehospitalized, and the revolving-door cycle continues.

Rehabilitation psychologists are concerned with the assessment and treatment of people who are physically disabled, either temporarily or permanently. They work primarily with people who have chronic pain, severe physical injuries, epilepsy, arthritis, cancer, and addictions. They conduct research to find the best ways to teach disabled people to work and live independently, overcome motivational slumps, improve their sex lives, and follow healthy regimens. Their approach to treatment is flexible, often including

behavior therapy, group counseling, job training, and community intervention. Because more people are surviving traumatic injuries and living long enough to develop chronic medical conditions, rehabilitation is one of the fastest-growing areas of health care (Frank, Gluck, & Buckelew, 1990).

The Self-help Movement

Not all psychological problems require the aid of a professional. Nowadays, thousands of books and programs are designed to help people help themselves. More than 2,000 self-help books are published every year. (For some guidelines to use when evaluating such books, see "Taking Psychology with You.") In addition, an estimated 7 to 15 million adults belong to self-help groups (Christensen & Jacobson, 1994). Such groups are available for alcoholics, people who live with alcoholics, abusive parents, people suffering from depression or schizophrenia, gay fathers, divorced people, women who have had mastectomies, parents of murdered children, rape victims, diabetics, widows, widowers, stepparents, cancer patients, relatives of patients, and people with just about any other concern you can think of.

A survey of 1,900 randomly selected Americans found that about 40 percent participate regularly in a small group that provides emotional support for its members. About two-thirds of these groups are organized around prayer or Bible study, and

Formal and informal support groups provide a setting for sharing concerns and exchanging constructive advice, as these men with AIDS are doing.

the others around shared problems or interests. But regardless of the kind of group, members say that the primary benefits are the awareness that they are not alone, encouragement when they are feeling down, and help in feeling better about themselves (Wuthnow, 1995).

Thinking Critically About Self-help Groups

Self-help groups offer understanding, empathy, and solutions to shared problems. Such groups can be reassuring and supportive in ways that family, friends, and psychotherapists sometimes may not be (Dunkel-Schetter, 1984; Wyatt & Mickey, 1987). For example, people with disabilities face unique challenges that involve not only coping with physical problems but also coping with the condescension, hostility, and prejudice of many nondisabled people (Linton, 1998; Robertson, 1995). Other disabled people, who share these challenges, may be able to offer useful advice.

Self-help groups, however, do not provide psychotherapy for specific problems, and they are not designed to help people with serious psychological difficulties. Moreover, unlike group therapies, which are usually supervised by a licensed therapist, self-help groups are not regulated by law or by professional standards, and they vary widely in their philosophies and methods. Some are accepting and tolerant, offering support, cohesiveness, and spiritual guidance. Others are confrontational and coercive, and members who disagree with the premises of the group may be made to feel de-

viant, crazy, or "in denial." If you choose to become part of a support group, you need to be sure it falls in the first category.

What's Ahead

- *What is the "scientist–practitioner gap"— and why has it been widening?*

- *What does research tell us about the effectiveness of psychotherapy?*

- *What sorts of people make the best therapists—and the best clients?*

- *Which form of psychotherapy is most likely to help you if you are anxious or depressed?*

- *Under what conditions can psychotherapy be harmful?*

EVALUATING PSYCHOTHERAPY AND ITS ALTERNATIVES

Poor Murray! He's getting a little baffled by all these therapeutic possibilities. He's tempted to spend a weekend with the Nature Walk "Trek to Truth" self-help group, but that will really put him behind. He'd like to make a choice soon, but he wonders, will therapy help him? Is it even possible to evaluate psychotherapy's effectiveness?

The Scientist–Practitioner Gap

Thinking Critically About the Relevance of Research to Therapy

Many psychotherapists believe that trying to evaluate psychotherapy using the standard methods of empirical research is an exercise in futility. Psychotherapy is an art, they say, not a science; and laboratory and survey studies capture only a small and shadowy image of the complex exchange that takes place between a therapist and a client (Edelson, 1994; Elliott & Morrow-Bradley, 1994). Clinical experience is therefore more valuable to therapists than research is.

Scientific psychologists agree that research has little to say about the existential aims of therapy, such as helping people come to terms with illness and death or helping them choose which values to live by (Cushman, 1995). But scientists are concerned that when therapists fail to keep up with empirical findings in the field—findings on the most beneficial methods for particular problems, on ineffective or potentially harmful techniques, and on topics relevant to their practice, such as memory, hypnosis, and child development—their clients may pay the price (Dawes, 1994).

Over the years, the breach between scientists and therapists has widened on this issue of the relevance and importance of research findings, leading to what some psychologists call the *scientist–practitioner gap*. This gap can have powerful individual and social consequences, as we saw in earlier chapters, when we discussed the controversy about repressed memories of sexual abuse (Chapter 7), and the popularity of unvalidated projective tests (Chapter 10).

Yet despite the skepticism about research on the part of many clinicians, good research on clinical practice is increasing. Economic pressures and the rise of managed-care health programs now require psychotherapists to produce clear, research-based guidelines for which therapies are most effective, which therapies are best for which disorders, and which therapies are ineffective or potentially harmful (Barlow, 1996; Chambless, 1995). To develop these guidelines, clinical researchers conduct *controlled clinical trials,* in which people with a given problem or disorder are randomly assigned to one or more treatment groups or to a control group. Hundreds of studies have been designed to test the effectiveness of different kinds of therapy, counseling, and self-help groups (Lambert & Hill, 1994). Here are the overall results to date:

1. *Psychotherapy is better than doing nothing at all.* People who receive almost any professional treatment improve more than people who do not get help (Lambert & Bergin, 1994; Lipsey & Wilson, 1993; Maling & Howard, 1994; Robinson, Berman, & Neimeyer, 1990; Smith, Glass, & Miller, 1980; Weisz et al., 1995).

2. *People who have less serious problems and are motivated to improve do the best in psychotherapy.* Emotional disorders, self-defeating habits, and problems coping with crises are more successfully treated than are long-standing personality problems and psychotic disorders (Kopta et al., 1994). Clients who make the best use of therapy tend to have more adaptive levels of functioning to begin with, are prepared for treatment, and are ready to change (Orlinsky & Howard, 1994; Strupp, 1982).

3. *For the common emotional problems of life, short-term treatment is usually sufficient.* Most psychodynamic therapists believe that the longer therapy

Drawing by M. Twohy; © 1991 The New Yorker Magazine, Inc.

THE SEVEN DWARFS AFTER THERAPY

How much can therapy change a person?

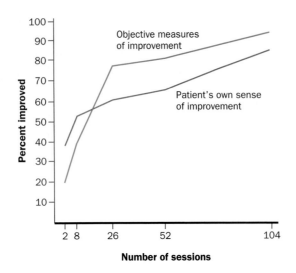

Figure 11.4

Is More Therapy Better?

In one study, about half of all patients improved in only 8 sessions and about three-fourths improved by the 26th session (Howard et al., 1986). Other research confirms that the benefits of therapy occur within 8 to 11 sessions for half of all clients, and most of the rest need no more than a year of treatment (Kopta et al., 1994).

goes on, the more successful it will be. Of course, people with severe mental disorders do often require and benefit from continued therapeutic care. But for most problems, shorter treatments are enough. About half of all people in therapy improve within 8 to 11 sessions, according to self-reports and objective measures of improvement. And 76 percent improve within six months to a year; after that, further change is minimal (Howard et al., 1986; Kopta et al., 1994) (see Figure 11.4).

4. *In some cases, psychotherapy is harmful because of the therapist's incompetence, biases, unethical behavior, or lack of knowledge* (Brodsky, 1982; Garnets et al., 1991; Lambert & Bergin, 1994; López, 1989; McHugh, 1993b; Peterson, 1992). Individual therapists can do great harm by behaving unethically, incompetently, or prejudicially. Some psychologists are concerned that therapeutic malpractice may be increasing because of the recent surge in the number of poorly trained, unlicensed therapists who use unvalidated methods (Dawes, 1994).

Because of these findings, most of the new research on psychotherapy is directed toward three questions: What are the common ingredients in all successful therapies? Which kinds of therapy are best suited for which problems? And under what conditions can therapy be harmful?

When Therapy Helps

Psychotherapy is a social exchange, and like all such exchanges, its success depends on the qualities of the participants and the fit between them.

Successful Clients and Therapists.   Clients who are likely to do well in therapy have a strong sense of self and are also distressed enough to want to work on their problems. They tend to have support from their families and a personal style of dealing actively with problems instead of avoiding them (Gaston et al., 1989). Basic personality traits also influence whether a person will be able to change in therapy. As we saw in Chapter 2, some people are characteristically negative and bitter; others are more agreeable and positive,

The most successful therapists communicate warmth, empathy, and respect for the client.

even in the midst of emotional crises. Hostile, negative individuals are more resistant to treatment and are less likely to benefit from it (Orlinsky & Howard, 1994).

The personality of the therapist is also critical to the success of any therapy, particularly the qualities that Carl Rogers praised: empathy, expressiveness, warmth, and genuineness. The most successful therapists make their clients feel respected, accepted, and understood. They are actively invested in the interaction with the client, instead of detached in the manner of Freud (Orlinsky & Howard, 1994).

Apart from the individual qualities of the client and the therapist, successful therapy depends on the bond they establish between them, called the **therapeutic alliance.** In a good therapeutic alliance, both parties respect and understand one another, feel reaffirmed, and work toward a common goal.

Cultural and Group Differences.

To establish a successful therapeutic alliance, the therapist and client do not have to share the same ethnicity, sex, sexual orientation, or religion (Howard, 1991). But both parties do have to try to identify and avoid potential misunderstandings that might result from ignorance, dissimilar qualities, or prejudice (Comas-Díaz & Greene, 1994; Cross & Fhagen-Smith, 1996; Franklin, 1993). For example, some white therapists misunderstand not only their black clients' psychological concerns, but also their clients' body language. These therapists regard lack of eye contact and frequent glancing around as the client's attempt to avoid revelations, instead of as signs of discomfort and an effort to get oriented (Brodsky, 1982). For their part, African-American clients often misunderstand or distrust the white therapist's demand for self-disclosure. A lifetime of experience with racism may have made them reluctant to reveal feelings that they believe a white person would not understand or accept. And black therapists frequently have to deal with clients and co-workers who are bigoted or uncomfortable with them, or who fail to understand or accept them (Boyd-Franklin, 1989; Markowitz, 1993).

In establishing a bond with clients, therapists must distinguish normal cultural patterns from individual psychological problems (Pedersen et al., 1996). Monica McGoldrick and John Pearce (1982), Irish-American clinicians, described some problems that are typical of Irish-American families. These problems arise from Irish history and religious beliefs, and they are deeply ingrained.

"In general, the therapist cannot expect the family to turn into a physically affectionate, emotionally intimate group, or to enjoy being in therapy very much," they observed. "The notion of Original Sin—that you are guilty before you are born—leaves them with a heavy sense of burden. Someone not sensitized to these issues may see this as pathological. It is not. But it is also not likely to change and the therapist should help the family tolerate this inner guilt rather than try to get rid of it."

More and more psychotherapists are becoming "sensitized to the issues" caused by cultural differences. For example, Latino and Asian clients are likely to react to a formal interview with a therapist with relative passivity and deference, leading some therapists to diagnose a shyness problem that is only a cultural norm. Latinos may respond to catastrophic stress with an *ataque nervioso*, a nervous attack of screaming, swooning, and agitation. The attack is a culturally determined response, but an uninformed clinician might label it as a sign of pathology (Malgady, Rogler, & Costantino, 1987). Similarly, *susto*, or "loss of the soul," is a syndrome common in Latin American cultures as a response to extreme grief or fright; the person believes his or her soul has departed along with that of the deceased relative. A psychiatrist unfamiliar with this culturally determined response might conclude that the sufferer was delusional or psychotic!

The American Psychiatric Association (1994) recommends that therapists consider a person's cultural background when making a diagnosis or suggesting treatment. For example, one New York psychiatrist, originally from Peru, treated a woman who was suffering from *susto* by prescribing a tradition important in her culture: a mourning ritual to help her accept the loss of her uncle. This ritual "was quite powerful for her," the psychiatrist told the *New York Times* (December 5, 1995). "She didn't need any antidepressants, and within a few meetings, including two with her family, her symptoms lifted and she was back participating fully in life once again."

Being aware of cultural differences, however, does not mean that the therapist should stereotype clients (Sue, 1991). Some Asians, after all, do have problems with excessive shyness, some Latinos do have emotional disorders, and some Irish don't feel the burden of guilt! It does mean that therapists must do what is necessary to ensure that the client will find the therapist to be trustworthy and effective, and that clients must be aware of their prejudices too.

therapeutic alliance
The bond of confidence and mutual understanding established between therapist and client, which allows them to work together to solve the client's problems.

Some psychotherapists fit their approach to the client's cultural background. The therapists on the right, for example, are using traditional Puerto Rican stories, such as the tales of Juan Bobo (left), to teach Puerto Rican children to control aggression, understand right from wrong and delay gratification. The children and their mothers watch a videotape of the folktale, discuss it together, and later role-play its major themes. This method has been more successful than traditional therapies in reducing children's anxiety and improving their attention spans and imaginations (Costantino, Malgady, & Rogler, 1986).

Which Therapy for Which Problem?

By now, Murray is really motivated to change. He just read a study showing that procrastinators not only get worse grades than other students, but they also have more stress and illness during the semester (Tice & Baumeister, 1997). It is time to choose a therapeutic approach.

Recently the APA's Division of Clinical Psychology convened a task force to assess the research evaluating specific methods for specific problems (Barlow, 1996; Chambless, 1995; Chambless et al., 1996). To qualify as an empirically validated treatment, a method had to meet stringent criteria. For example, it had to have been tested repeatedly against a placebo or another treatment, and it had to have its efficacy demonstrated by at least two different investigators. Although the task force could not assess every therapy in existence, one key finding emerged clearly: *For many problems and emotional disorders, behavior and cognitive therapies are the method of choice.* These therapies are particularly effective for the following problems:

• *Anxiety disorders,* including panic attacks, phobias, and obsessive–compulsive disorder. For example, exposure techniques are more effective than any other treatment for reducing severe phobias (Kaplan, Randolph, & Lemli, 1991). Systematic de-

sensitization is most effective with simple phobias, such as fear of speaking to a group. And cognitive-behavioral therapy is recommended for panic disorder, generalized anxiety disorder, and obsessive–compulsive disorder (Schwartz et al., 1996).

• *Depression.* Cognitive therapy's greatest success has been in the treatment of mood disorders, especially depression (Black et al., 1993; Greenberger & Padesky, 1995). Cognitive therapy is often more effective than treatment with antidepressant drugs alone, and it is more likely to prevent relapses (Antonuccio, Danton, & DeNelsky, 1995; McNally, 1994; Robinson, Berman, & Neimeyer, 1990; Whisman, 1993).

• *Health problems.* These include chronic pain, chronic fatigue syndrome, headaches, irritable bowel syndrome, and eating disorders such as bulimia (Butler et al., 1991; J. Skinner et al., 1990; Wilson & Fairburn, 1993).

• *Childhood and adolescent behavior problems.* Researchers who conducted a meta-analysis of more than 100 outcome studies of children and adolescents reported that "Behavioral treatments proved more effective than nonbehavioral treatments regardless of client age, therapist experience, or treated problem" (Weisz et al., 1987).

Of course, as the APA task force acknowledged, these important findings don't tell the whole story (nor have we listed every effective therapy the task force identified). Cognitive-behavioral therapies are designed for specific, identifiable problems, but sometimes people seek therapy for less clearly defined reasons. They may wish to introspect about their feelings and lives, find solace and courage, or explore moral issues. "Depth" approaches may be well suited for such individuals. Moreover, in spite of their many successes, behavior and cognitive therapies have had their failures, especially with personality disorders and psychoses (Brody, 1990; Foa & Emmelkamp, 1983). These therapies are not particularly helpful for sex offenders. They are also not highly effective with people who do not really want to change and who are not motivated to carry out a behavioral or cognitive program.

Some problems, and some clients, are immune to any single kind of therapy but may respond to *combined* methods. For example, people who have mood disorders, obsessive–compulsive disorder, or drug-abuse problems sometimes respond better to a combination of antidepressants and cognitive-behavioral therapy than to either method alone (Bowers, 1990; Carroll et al., 1994; Leonard et al., 1993). The most promising treatment for sex offenders combines cognitive therapy, aversive conditioning, sex education, group therapy, reconditioning of sexual fantasies, and social-skills training (Abel et al., 1988; Kaplan, Morales, & Becker, 1993). Young adults with schizophrenia often do best with a combination of medication and family therapy that helps their parents learn to cope with the illness constructively (Goldstein & Miklowitz, 1995).

Figure 11.5 summarizes the factors contributing to successful therapy—qualities of the partici-pants, the nature of the therapy, and the affinity between therapist and client.

When Therapy Harms

Every treatment and intervention carries risks, and so does psychotherapy. Some people are seriously harmed or unduly influenced by the treatment or by the therapist. Their emotional state may deteriorate and their symptoms may worsen. Some clients become excessively dependent, relying on the therapist for all decisions; and some therapists actively foster this dependency for financial or psychological motives (Johnson, 1988). Clients can also be harmed by the following:

Thinking Critically About Poor Therapeutic Practices

• *Coercion to accept the therapist's advice, sexual intimacies, or other unethical behavior* (Gabbard, 1989; Peterson, 1992). Some therapists abuse their clients' trust, pressuring them, in subtle or overt ways, to behave in ways the clients find reprehensible. As we saw at the start of this chapter, some therapy groups even acquire cultlike attributes, persuading their members that their mental health depends on staying in the group and severing their connections to their families (Mithers, 1994). Such "psychotherapy cults" are created by the therapist's use of techniques that foster the client's dependency and isolation, prevent the client from terminating therapy, and reduce the client's ability to think critically (Temerlin & Temerlin, 1986).

• *Bias on the part of a therapist who does not understand the client because of the client's gender, culture,*

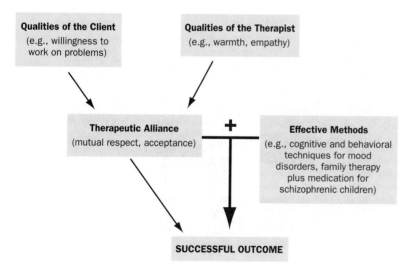

Figure 11.5

Factors in Successful Therapy

As this summary chart shows, the outcome of psychotherapy depends not only on the methods used but also on the qualities of, and relationship between, the therapist and the client.

religion, or sexual orientation. A therapist may try to induce the client to conform to the therapist's standards and values, even if they are not appropriate to the client or in the client's best interest (Brodsky, 1982; López, 1989). For example, for many years gay men and lesbians who entered therapy were told that homosexuality is a mental illness that should be "cured," and some of the so-called treatments were quite savage (Bayer, 1981).

● *Therapist-induced disorders resulting from inadvertent suggestions or influence.* In a healthy therapeutic alliance, therapists and clients seek a common explanation for the client's problems. Of course, the therapist will influence this explanation, according to his or her training and philosophy. This is why Freudian patients have dreams of phallic symbols, and patients in Jungian therapy have dreams of archetypes! However, some therapists so zealously believe in the prevalence of certain problems that they inadvertently induce the client to produce the symptoms they are looking

for (McHugh, 1993b; Merskey, 1995; Ofshe & Watters, 1994). In Chapter 10 we discussed how such therapist influence might be one reason for the growing number of people diagnosed with multiple personality disorder. It is also the mechanism by which people create *pseudomemories*, constructed memories about events that did not happen—why people in primal scream therapy "remember" being born, people in fetal therapy "remember" their lives in the womb, and people in past-lives therapy "remember" being Julius Caesar (or whomever) (Spanos, 1996).

The risk of therapist influence increases when a therapist uses hypnosis, sodium amytal (a barbiturate misleadingly called "truth serum"), guided imagery, and other techniques that enhance the client's suggestibility. As we noted in Chapter 7, a significant minority of therapists—between one-fourth and one-third—are using one or more of these techniques (Poole et al., 1995). And these were the techniques used in the malpractice cases mentioned at the beginning of this chapter.

??? QUICK QUIZ

Are you learning to be an educated consumer of psychotherapy?

1. The most important predictor of successful therapy is (a) how long it lasts, (b) the insight it provides the client, (c) the bond between therapist and client, (d) whether the therapist and client are matched according to gender, ethnicity, and culture.

2. The most important attribute of a good therapist is (a) years of training, (b) warmth and empathy, (c) objective detachment, (d) intellectual ability.

3. In general, anxiety and depression are most effectively treated by which type of psychotherapy?

4. What are three possible sources of harm in psychotherapy?

5. Ferdie, who spends all his free time playing softball, joins a self-help group called "Sportaholics Anonymous" (SA). The group tells him he is suffering from sport addiction and that the only cure is SA. After a few months, Ferdie announces that the group doesn't seem to be helping him and he's going to quit. The other members reply with personal testimonials of how SA has helped them. They tell Ferdie that he is in denial, and that his doubts about the group are actually a sign that it's working. What are some problems with their argument?

Answers:

1. c 2. b 3. cognitive-behavioral 4. coercion, bias, and therapist-induced disorders 5. The group members have violated the principle of falsifiability (see Chapter 1): That is, they will accept no evidence that disproves their claims. If a person is helped by the group, they say it works; if a person is not helped by the group, they still say it works but the person doesn't know it yet or is "denying" its benefits. They are also arguing by anecdote: Ferdie is not hearing testimonials from people who have dropped out of the group and were not helped by it. Arguing by anecdote is not scientific reasoning, nor is it a way to determine a group's or therapy's effectiveness.

Now that we have reviewed some of the benefits and hazards of psychotherapy, let's return to the issues raised by the malpractice case against Richard Corriere and the Hollywood Center for Feeling Therapy. The main issue it raises is protection for consumers against harmful therapeutic practices. It is certainly true that some troubled individuals may make false accusations against therapists because they misinterpreted a therapist's techniques or remarks or because they are disturbed and are having paranoid fantasies. However, it is also true that some unconventional therapies may pose a threat to the mental well-being of the very people they are supposed to help. How can you, as a potential consumer of psychological services, distinguish between techniques that are beneficial and techniques that can do harm?

As we saw in Chapter 1, a person must have an advanced degree and a period of supervised training to become a licensed psychologist, psychiatrist, or social worker. However, the word *therapy* is unregulated; anyone can set up any kind of program and call it "therapy." Moreover, the fact that someone has a license does not guarantee that he or she is competent, reputable, or ethical. To protect yourself, and to get the best possible help, you will need to think critically and to ask some questions about the therapist and about the approach the therapist takes:

- Has the therapy been validated by controlled clinical studies?

- Is the therapist warm, empathic, and supportive? Does the therapist treat you with attention and respect?

- Has the therapist suggested that a sexual relationship with him or her will help you with a problem? This is always unethical, and it is illegal in many states.

- Does the therapist show sensitivity to differences in culture, ethnicity, religion, gender, and sexual orientation?

- Is the therapy consistent with what researchers know about memory and personality change, or does it ignore those findings (for example, by promising to help you recall the experience of being born, or guaranteeing to change you from an introvert to an extrovert)?

- Does the therapist help you find ways to be happier at work and at home, or does he or she invite you to join a "community" that isolates you from friends and family and fosters dependency, a technique of coercive persuasion associated with cults?

- Does the therapist encourage you to blame your parents for everything wrong in your life, or even to break away from them entirely? Some parents may be cruel and neglectful, but others merely commit human mistakes; does the therapist help you to tell the difference?

- Does the therapist or therapy group discourage you from leaving even when the problems that originally brought you to therapy have been solved?

- Most important, does the therapist encourage you to think for yourself, or instead pressure you to passively accept his or her beliefs and interpretations?

In the case of the Hollywood Center for Feeling Therapy, the California Board of Medical Quality Assurance was not satisfied with the answers to such questions. Corriere and 12 colleagues—one physician, five psychologists, one psychiatric technician, and five marriage, family and child counselors—lost or surrendered their licenses.

Besides choosing a therapist carefully, consumers need to be realistic about what they expect of psychotherapy. In the hands of an empathic and knowledgable practitioner, psychotherapy can help you make decisions and clarify your values and goals. It can teach you new skills and new ways of thinking. It can help you get along better with your family and break out of destructive family patterns. It can get you through bad times when no one seems to care or to understand what you are feeling. It can teach you how to manage depression, anxiety, and anger.

However, despite its benefits, psychotherapy cannot transform you into someone you're not. It cannot cure a disorder overnight. It cannot provide a life without problems. And it is not intended to substitute for experience—for work that is satisfying, relationships that are sustaining, activities that are enjoyable. As Socrates knew, the unexamined life is not worth living. But as an anonymous philosopher added, the unlived life is not worth examining.

How to Evaluate a Self-help Book

If you wander through the psychology section of your local bookstore (perhaps called "psychology and self-help" or "personal growth"), you will find rows of books promising to fix anything that ails you. They will tell you how to make money, how to use your mind to cure your body, how to recover from heartbreak, and how to find happiness in seven easy steps. They will keep you from being too independent, too dependent, or too codependent. They will help you find a relationship, fix a relationship, or end a relationship. People in the United States and Canada, countries with long historical traditions of self-improvement and do-it-yourself attitudes, consume self-help books like peanuts—by the handful. Which are helpful, which are harmful, and which are just innocuous?

Some self-help books, if they propose a specific program for the reader to follow, can be as effective as treatment administered by a therapist (Christensen & Jacobson, 1994). The problem is that many readers fail to follow through. Also, not all books are good ones—and the fact that a book has been written by a psychologist or a program has been endorsed by the American Psychological Association is no guarantee of its merit.

After serving as chair of the APA's Task Force on Self-Help Therapies, which investigated the proliferation and promises of self-help books and tapes, Gerald Rosen (1981) concluded, "Unfortunately, the involvement of psychologists in the development, assessment, and marketing of do-it-yourself treatment programs has often been less than responsible. Psychologists have published untested materials, advanced exaggerated claims, and accepted the use of misleading titles that encourage unrealistic expectations regarding outcome." The situation remains the same today.

Rosen recognizes that self-help books and programs can be effective in helping people, however, and thus offers consumers some research-based criteria for evaluating a self-help book:

- *The authors should be qualified,* which means that they have conducted good research or are thoroughly versed in the field. Personal testimonials by people who have survived difficulties or tragedy can be helpful and inspirational, of course, but an author's own experience is not grounds for generalizing to everyone.

- *The book's advice should be based on sound scientific theory,* not on the author's hunches, pseudoscientific theories, or armchair observations. This criterion rules out, among other kinds of books, all the weight-loss manuals based on crash diets or goofy nutritional advice ("Eat popcorn and watermelon for a week").

- *The book should include evidence of the program's effectiveness* and not simply the author's unsupported assertions that it works. Many self-help books offer programs that have not been tested for efficacy.

- *The book should not promise the impossible.* This lets out books that promise you perfect sex, total love, or high self-esteem in 30 days. It also lets out books, programs, or tapes that promote techniques whose effectiveness has been disconfirmed by psychological research, such as "subliminal" tapes, discussed in Chapter 5 (Moore, 1995).

- *The advice should be organized in a systematic program,* step by step, not as a vague pep talk to "take charge of your life" or "find love in your heart"; and the reader should be told how to evaluate his or her progress.

Some books do meet all these criteria. One is *Changing for Good* (Prochaska, Norcross, & DiClemente, 1994), which describes the common ingredients of effective change that apply to people in and out of therapy. But as long as people yearn for a magic bullet to cure their problems—a pill, a book, a subliminal tape—quick-fix solutions will find a ready audience.

Biological Treatments

1) Over the centuries, people trying to understand and treat psychological disorders have often taken a biological (*organic*) approach, and today, biological approaches are enjoying a resurgence.

2) Medications most commonly prescribed for mental disorders include *antipsychotic drugs,* used in treating schizophrenia and other psychotic disorders; *antidepressants,* used in treating depression, anxiety disorders, and obsessive–compulsive disorder; *tranquilizers,* often prescribed for emotional problems; and *lithium,* a salt used to treat bipolar disorder. Antidepressants are generally more effective for mood disorders than are tranquilizers, which can become addictive.

3) Drawbacks of drug treatment include the *placebo effect;* high dropout and relapse rates among people who take medications without also learning how to cope with their problems; the difficulty of finding the correct dose (the *therapeutic window*) for each individual, compounded by the fact that a person's ethnicity, sex, and age can in-

fluence a drug's effectiveness; and the long-term risks of medication, known and unknown. Medication can be helpful and can even save lives, but it should not be prescribed mindlessly and routinely, especially when nondrug therapies can work as well as drugs for many mood and behavioral problems.

4) When drugs or psychotherapy have failed to help seriously disturbed people, some psychiatrists have intervened directly in the brain. *Psychosurgery* destroys selected areas of the brain thought to be responsible for a psychological problem; it is rarely done today. *Electroconvulsive therapy* (ECT), in which a current is sent briefly through the brain, has been used successfully to treat suicidal depression. However, controversy exists about its effects on the brain and the appropriateness of its use.

Kinds of Psychotherapy

6) The hundreds of existing psychotherapies basically fall into four schools: (1) *Psychodynamic ("depth") therapies* include Freudian psychoanalysis and its modern variations, which explore unconscious dynamics. Brief psychodynamic therapy is a time-limited version that focuses on one major dynamic issue. (2) *Therapies based on cognitive and behavioral techniques* draw on cognitive and learning principles. *Behavior therapies* use such methods as behavioral contracts, systematic desensitization, aversive conditioning, flooding or exposure, and skills training. *Cognitive therapies* aim to change the irrational thoughts involved in negative emotions and self-defeating actions. (3) *Humanist and existential therapies* attempt to help people feel better about themselves by focusing on here-and-now issues and helping people cope with philosophical dilemmas, such as the meaning of life and the fear of death. (4) *Family therapies* share the view that individual problems develop in the context of the whole family network. Some family therapists look for patterns of behavior across generations.

7) In practice, most therapists are flexible, drawing on many methods and ideas. And whatever their nature, successful therapies share some elements in common, such as efforts to help clients form more adaptive "life stories."

Alternatives to Psychotherapy

8) People who have severe mental disorders, such as schizophrenia, or who have physical dis-

abilities resulting from disease or injury, may benefit from alternatives to individual psychotherapy. *Community psychologists* set up programs in the community to treat mental-health problems, using many strategies, including the *clubhouse model. Rehabilitation psychologists* are concerned with the assessment and treatment of people who are physically disabled. *Self-help groups* are organized around a specific problem or common interest; they can be immensely helpful, but they vary widely in their methods and results.

Evaluating Psychotherapy and Its Alternatives

9) A *scientist–practitioner gap* has developed because of the different assumptions held by researchers and many clinicians regarding the value of research for formulating psychotherapy approaches and assessing the effectiveness of psychotherapy.

10) Controlled clinical trials show that overall, psychotherapy is better than no treatment at all; that it is most effective with people who have the least serious disorders and who are motivated to improve; that for problems other than chronic mental disorders, short-term treatment is as effective as long-term therapy; and that sometimes therapy can be harmful.

11) The clients who benefit most from psychotherapy are motivated to solve their problems and willing to take responsibility for them. Good therapists are empathic, warm, and constructive. Successful therapy requires a *therapeutic alliance* between the therapist and the client, so that they understand each other and can work together. They do not need to be matched in terms of gender, ethnicity, or sexual orientation, but both parties must try to avoid bias, stereotyping, and cultural misunderstandings.

12) Some therapies are demonstrably better than others for specific problems. Behavioral and cognitive-behavioral therapies are the most effective for anxiety disorders, depression, certain health problems and eating disorders, and childhood and adolescent behavior problems. Depth therapies may be most effective for people who want to introspect about their lives. And some problems, such as sex offenses and schizophrenia, respond best to combined techniques.

13) In some cases, therapy is harmful. The therapist may foster the client's dependency; be coercive, biased, or unethical; or inadvertently

create disorders through undue influence or suggestion, as in the case of therapist-induced *pseudomemories.*

14) Consumers need to choose a therapist carefully and be realistic about what they expect

of psychotherapy. Therapy can help people in many ways, but it cannot transform you into something you are not, and it cannot substitute for the family, friends, and work that everyone needs.

KEY TERMS

LOOKING BACK

- What kinds of drugs are used to treat psychological disorders? (pp. 370–371)
- Are antidepressants always the best treatment for depression? (pp. 372–373)
- Why is "shock therapy" hailed by some clinicians but condemned by others? (p. 375)
- Why are psychodynamic therapies called "depth" therapies? (p. 376)
- How can therapies based on learning principles help you change your bad habits? (p. 377)
- How do cognitive therapists help people get rid of self-defeating thoughts? (pp. 378–379)
- Why do humanist therapists focus on the "here and now" instead of the "why and how"? (p. 380)
- Why do family therapists prefer to treat families rather than individuals? (p. 381)
- What community resources can help people who have serious mental disorders? (pp. 384–385)

- *What can a self-help group offer a person that relatives, friends, and psychotherapists can't? (p. 386)*

- *What is the "scientist–practitioner gap"—and why has it been widening? (p. 387)*

- *What does research tell us about the effectiveness of psychotherapy? (pp. 387–388)*

- *What sorts of people make the best therapists— and the best clients? (pp. 388–389)*

- *Which form of psychotherapy is most likely to help you if you are anxious or depressed? (p. 390)*

- *Under what conditions can psychotherapy be harmful? (pp. 391–392)*

12 Emotion, Stress, and Health

PSYCHOLOGY IN THE NEWS

Road rage is a growing problem on U.S. highways.

Road Rage on the Rise

WASHINGTON, D.C., JULY 18, 1997. Motorists on the nation's highways are increasingly tailgating, making obscene gestures, leaning on their horns, shouting insults, cutting in front of other drivers, and even shooting at each other, experts report. According to a study by the American Automobile Association Foundation for Traffic Safety, incidents of "road rage"—overt

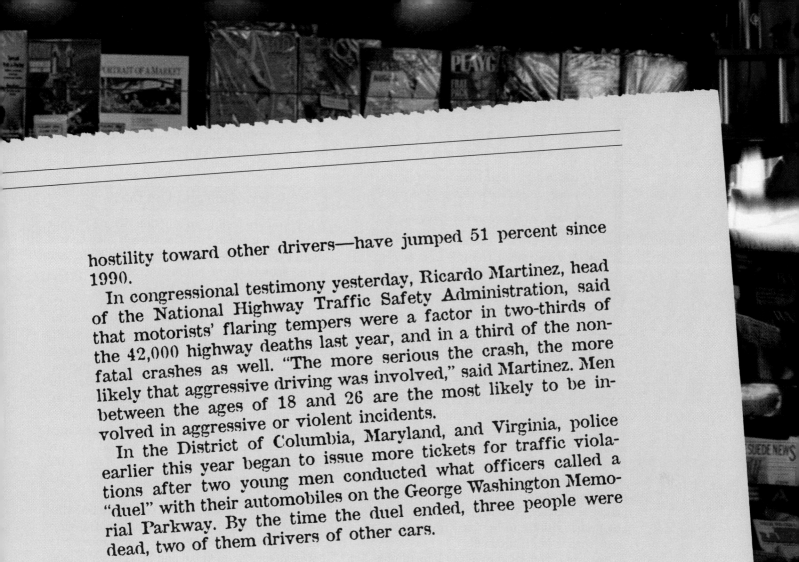

hostility toward other drivers—have jumped 51 percent since 1990.

In congressional testimony yesterday, Ricardo Martinez, head of the National Highway Traffic Safety Administration, said that motorists' flaring tempers were a factor in two-thirds of the 42,000 highway deaths last year, and in a third of the non-fatal crashes as well. "The more serious the crash, the more likely that aggressive driving was involved," said Martinez. Men between the ages of 18 and 26 are the most likely to be involved in aggressive or violent incidents.

In the District of Columbia, Maryland, and Virginia, police earlier this year began to issue more tickets for traffic violations after two young men conducted what officers called a "duel" with their automobiles on the George Washington Memorial Parkway. By the time the duel ended, three people were dead, two of them drivers of other cars.

Why do so many people "lose it" when they get behind the wheel, whereas others are able to keep things in perspective and stay cool under the pressures of the road? More generally, why do some people respond to the inevitable stresses of life by losing control of their emotions, whereas others are able to keep unpleasant feelings from turning into abusive or self-destructive actions?

In this chapter we will examine two fundamental experiences in everyone's life—emotions and stress—and the links between them. Prolonged negative emotions such as anger can certainly be stressful, and, as stories of road rage tell us, stress can produce negative emotions. To understand emotion and stress, and how they interact, we will need to draw on all of the psychological perspectives described in this book: We will need to consider the biology of the brain and body, the mental processes of perception and belief, and the situational and cultural contexts that shape experience. As you read, keep in mind all those drivers exploding in dangerous road rage, and see whether you can come up with some ideas for reducing unpleasant emotions and stressful experiences in your own life.

What's Ahead

- *Which facial expressions of emotion do people the world over recognize?*

- *Which side of your brain is most active when you're filled with joy—or despair?*

- *Which two hormones can make you "too excited to eat"?*

- *In a competition, who is likely to be happier, the third-place winner or the second-place winner?*

- *Why can't an infant feel shame or guilt?*

THE NATURE OF EMOTION

Without emotions, you would be unmoved by the magic of music. You would never care about losing someone you love, not only because you would not know sadness but also because you would not know love. You would never laugh because nothing would strike you as funny. And you would be a social klutz because without "emotional intelligence," you could not identify other people's feelings. Yet people often curse their emotions, wishing to be freed from anger, jealousy, shame, guilt, and grief.

Because emotions can get us into trouble, for centuries emotion was regarded as the opposite of thinking, and an inferior opposite at that. The heart (emotion) was said to go its own way, in spite of what the head (reason) wanted. Today, psycholo-

Thinking Critically About Emotions and Rationality

gists avoid such either–or thinking. As we saw in Chapters 6 and 7, normal thought processes involve many "irrational" bi-ases, such as the confirmation bias, the hindsight bias, and biases in the construction of memories. Conversely, emotions are not always irrational, even when they are uncomfortable. Emotions bind people together, motivate them to achieve their goals, and help them make decisions and plans (Damasio, 1994; Oatley, 1990). When you are faced with a decision between two appealing and justifiable career alternatives, for example, your sense of which one "feels right" emotionally may help you make the best choice. Emotions themselves, then, are not a problem. Too much emotionality, however, can lead to trouble and can even threaten your health.

The full experience of **emotion** is like a tree: The *biological* capacity for emotion is the trunk;

emotion

A state of arousal involving facial and bodily changes, brain activation, cognitive appraisals, subjective feelings, and tendencies toward action.

thoughts and explanations create the many branches; and *culture* is the gardener that shapes the tree and prunes it, cutting off some limbs and cultivating others. Let's begin with the trunk.

Emotion and the Body

When you are feeling an emotion, where in your body are you feeling it? The answer may be just about everywhere—on the face, in the brain, and in the activity of the autonomic nervous system.

The Face of Emotion.   The most obvious place to look for emotion is on the face, where emotions are often visibly expressed. In his classic book *The Expression of the Emotions in Man and Animals* (1872/1965), Charles Darwin argued that basic human facial expressions—the smile, the frown, the grimace, the glare—are as "wired in" as the wing flutter of a frightened bird, the purr of a contented cat, and the snarl of a threatened wolf. Such expressions evolved, he said, because they allowed our forebears to tell at a glance the difference between a friendly stranger and a hostile one.

Modern psychologists have supported Darwin's idea by showing that certain emotional displays are recognized the world over (see Figure 12.1). For example, Paul Ekman and his colleagues have gathered abundant evidence for the universality of seven basic facial expressions of emotion: anger, happiness, fear, surprise, disgust, sadness, and contempt (Ekman, 1994; Ekman & Heider, 1988; Ekman et al., 1987). In every culture they have studied—in Brazil, Chile, Estonia, Germany, Greece, Hong Kong, Italy, Japan, New Guinea, Scotland, Sumatra, Turkey, and the United States—a large majority of people recognize the emotional expressions portrayed by those in other cultures. Even most members of isolated tribes that have never watched a movie or read *People* magazine, such as the Foré of New Guinea or the Minangkabau of West Sumatra, can recognize the emotions expressed in pictures of people who are entirely foreign to them, and we can recognize theirs.

These findings do not mean that everybody in a society can recognize the same expressions in all situations. Ekman (1994) calls his theory *neurocultural* to emphasize that two factors are involved in facial expression: a universal neurophysiology in the facial muscles associated with certain emotions, and culture-specific variations in the ex-

Figure 12.1

Some Universal Expressions

Can you tell what feelings are being conveyed here? Most people around the world can readily identify expressions of surprise, disgust, happiness, sadness, anger, fear, and contempt—no matter what the age, culture, or historical epoch of the person conveying the emotion.

pression of emotion. Thus, while most people in most cultures do recognize basic emotions as portrayed in photographs, sometimes a large minority does not. Across 20 studies of Western cultures, for example, fully 95 percent of the participants agreed in their judgments of happy faces, but only 78 percent agreed on expressions of sadness and anger; and across 11 non-Western societies, 88 percent recognized happiness, but only 74 percent agreed on sadness and 59 percent on anger.

One emotion that nicely illustrates the neurocultural approach is disgust. Make an expression of disgust and notice what you are doing: You are probably wrinkling your nose, dropping the corners of your mouth, or retracting your upper lip. These universal reactions may have originated in the "distaste" response of infants to bitter tastes

and may serve as a warning against eating tainted food. But the *content* of what produces disgust changes as the infant matures, and it varies from culture to culture. People may acquire feelings of disgust in response to particular foods, as well as to bugs, sex, gore, dirt, death, "contamination" by contact with undesirable strangers, or violations of moral rules, such as those governing incest (Rozin, Lowery, & Ebert, 1994).

Of course, people do not always reveal their emotions on their faces. Most of us do not go around scowling and clenching our jaws whenever we are angry. We can grieve and feel enormously sad without weeping. We can feel worried and tense, yet put on a happy face. People use facial expressions, in short, to lie about their feelings as well as to express them.

Facial expressions do not always convey the emotion being felt. A posed, social smile like this one may have nothing to do with true feelings of happiness. Cover this woman's smile with your hand and you'll see that her "smile" doesn't reach her eyes.

To get around the human ability to mask emotions, Ekman and his associates developed a way to peek under the mask. A special coding system allows researchers to analyze and identify each of the nearly 80 muscles of the face, as well as the combinations of muscles associated with various emotions. When people try to hide their real emotions, they use different groups of muscles. For example, when people try to pretend that they feel grief, only 15 percent manage to get the eyebrows, eyelids, and forehead wrinkle exactly right, mimicking the way grief is expressed spontaneously. Authentic smiles last only two seconds; false smiles may last ten seconds or more (Ekman, 1994; Ekman, Friesen, & O'Sullivan, 1988).

Even though some emotional expressions are probably universal, the interpretation of an expression is not automatic: It depends on the specific *context* in which an observer sees it. Look at the photograph of the woman in the margin; what emotion would you say she is feeling? Suppose we tell you that this woman has been waiting over an hour for a table at a ritzy restaurant, in spite of having made reservations months earlier. Trendy-looking couples are being seated immediately, but she has been told that she will have to wait another hour. Now, what emotion do you think she is expressing? Although this woman is supposed to be displaying universal signs of fear, most people, after hearing about her situation, will say that her staring eyes and open mouth reveal anger. Similarly, people who see an "angry" face in a sit-

What emotion is this woman expressing?

uation that would normally provoke fear are likely to decide that the person is afraid (Carroll & Russell, 1996).

Facial expressions not only express internal states, but also help us communicate our intentions to others. You can see this even in infants. A baby's expressions of misery, angry frustration, happiness, or disgust send a clear message to most parents, who respond by soothing an uncomfortable baby, feeding a hungry one, and cuddling a happy one (Izard, 1994b; Stenberg & Campos, 1990). Babies, in turn, react to the facial expressions of their parents; American, German, Greek, Japanese, Trobriand Island, and Yanomamo mothers all "infect" their babies with happy moods by displaying happy expressions (Keating, 1994).

Starting at the end of their first year, babies begin to alter their own behavior after observing their parents' emotions and reactions, and this ability has survival value. Do you recall the visual-cliff studies described in Chapter 5 (see p. 176)? These studies were originally designed to test for depth perception, which emerges early in infancy. But in one experiment, 1-year-old babies were put on a more ambiguous visual cliff that did not drop off sharply and thus did not automatically evoke fear, as the original one did. In this case, 74 percent of the babies crossed the cliff when their mothers showed a happy, reassuring expression, but not a single one crossed when their mothers showed an expression of fear (Sorce et al., 1985). If you have ever watched a toddler take a tumble and then look at his or her parent before deciding whether to cry or forget it, you will understand the influence of parental facial expressions.

Interestingly, facial expressions may also help people communicate with themselves, so to speak, by enabling them to more readily identify their own emotions. According to the *facial-feedback hypothesis,* the facial muscles send messages to the brain about the basic emotion being expressed; a smile tells us that we're happy, a frown that we're angry or perplexed (Izard, 1990; Tomkins, 1981). When people are asked to contort their facial muscles into various patterns, they often report that their emotions have changed to fit the pattern. As one young man put it, "When my jaw was clenched and my brows down, I tried not to be angry but it just fit the position" (Laird, 1974). What's more, when people are told to contract the facial muscles involved in smiling (though not actually instructed to smile) and then look at cartoons, they find the cartoons funnier than if they are contracting their muscles in a way

Get Involved

See whether "facial feedback" works for you. Next time you are feeling sad or afraid, try purposely smiling—even if no one is around. Keep smiling. Does your facial expression affect your mood? Is it true, as Anna sings in *The King and I*, that when we fool the people we meet—by wearing a happy smile or whistling a happy tune to disguise fear—we fool ourselves as well?

that is incompatible with smiling (Strack, Martin, & Stepper, 1988). (Does smiling affect your own reaction to the cartoon on this page?)

Facial expressions, however, do not always correspond with our internal emotional states, suggesting that their primary purpose is communication with others (Fridlund, 1994). A study of 22 Olympic gold medalists, observed as they stood on the podium during the awards ceremonies, found that the athletes smiled only when they were interacting with officials or the public, not when they were standing alone—though presumably they were equally happy the whole time (Fernández-Dols & Ruiz-Belda, 1995). Similarly, when you are

Great moms have always understood the importance of facial feedback.

sitting at home by yourself, you may be feeling perfectly happy, but it is unlikely that you will be smiling. You will save your smiles until you have an audience—and even then your smile might not mean "I'm happy," but rather "I'm glad to meet you" or "Don't be mad at me." Later we will see that cultures and circumstances play an important role in when and how people express their feelings.

Emotion and the Brain. Another line of research seeks to identify parts of the brain responsible for the many components of emotional experience: recognizing another person's emotion, feeling intensely aroused, labeling an emotion, deciding what to do about it, and so forth. Many aspects of emotion are associated with specific brain locations. For example, people with a rare condition called *prosopagnosia* are often able to recognize facial expressions but are unable to identify individual faces (Sacks, 1985). The reason is that recognizing expressions and identifying faces are handled in different areas of the right hemisphere; people with prosopagnosia have damage only in the area involved in facial identification (Damasio, 1994).

Interestingly, the two cerebral hemispheres play different roles in the experience of emotions (Davidson, 1992). Regions of the left hemisphere appear to be specialized for positive emotions such as happiness, whereas regions of the right hemisphere are specialized for negative emotions such as fear and sadness. People with damage to the left hemisphere sometimes experience excessive anger or depression; people with damage to the right hemisphere may experience mania and laugh excessively. And people whose brains are undamaged but who are clinically depressed have less activation in the left frontal regions than nondepressed people do (Henriques & Davidson, 1991).

In recent years psychologists have discovered that the *amygdala,* a small structure in the brain's limbic system, plays a key role in emotion (see Chapter 4). The amygdala appears to be responsible for evaluating sensory information, determining its emotional importance, and making the initial decision to approach or withdraw from a person or situation (LeDoux, 1994, 1996). The amygdala quickly assesses danger or threat, which is a good thing because otherwise you could be standing in the street asking, "Is it wise to cross now, while that very large truck is coming toward me?" The amygdala's initial response may then be "overridden" by a more accurate appraisal from the cerebral cortex (LeDoux, 1996). This is why you jump with fear when you suddenly feel a hand on your back in a dark alley, and why your fear evaporates when the cortex registers that the hand belongs to a friend whose lousy idea of humor is to scare you in a dark alley.

Second, the cerebral cortex generates a more complete picture; it can override signals sent by the amygdala ("It's only Mike in a down coat").

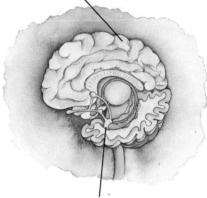

First, the amygdala scrutinizes information for its emotional importance ("It's a bear! Be afraid! Run!").

If either the amygdala or critical areas of the cortex are damaged, emotional abnormalities result. A rat with a damaged amygdala "forgets" to be afraid when it should be; and people with damage to the amygdala often have difficulty recognizing fear in themselves or others (Damasio, 1994). But rats or people with damage to critical areas of the cortex often lose the capacity to put aside their fear when the emotion is no longer necessary. The result can be constant, irrational feelings of impending doom and anxiety, and obsessive thoughts of danger—as is the case in obsessive–compulsive disorder, which we discussed in Chapter 10 (Schulkin, 1994; Schwartz et al., 1996).

The Energy of Emotion.

A third line of physiological research focuses on hormones, which produce the energy of emotion. In particular, the inner part of the adrenal gland, the medulla, sends out two hormones, *epinephrine* and *norepinephrine* (see Chapter 4). These chemical messengers activate the sympathetic division of the autonomic nervous system and produce a state of arousal and alertness. The pupils dilate, widening to allow in more light; the heart beats faster; breathing speeds up; and blood sugar rises, providing the body with more energy. Digestion slows down, so that blood flow can be diverted from the stomach and intestines to the muscles and surface of the skin—which is why, when you are excited, scared, furious, or wildly in love, you may not want to eat. The ultimate purpose of all this physiological arousal is to prepare the body to respond quickly (Frijda, 1988; Lang, 1995). When you feel an emotion, you generally feel motivated to do something specific: embrace the person who instills joy in you, yell at the person who is angering you, or run from the situation that is frightening you.

The adrenal glands produce epinephrine and norepinephrine in response to many challenges in the environment. These hormones will surge if you are laughing at a comedian, playing a video game, worrying about an exam, cheering at a sports event, reacting to an insult, or driving on a hot day in terrible traffic. Epinephrine in particular provides the energy of an emotion—that familiar tingle, excitement, and sense of animation. At high levels, it can create the sensation of being "seized" or "flooded" by an emotion that is out of your control. In a sense, the release of epinephrine does cause us to lose control because few people can consciously alter their heart rates, blood pressures, and digestive tracts. However, people can learn to control their actions when they are under the sway of an emotion. And no emotion, no matter how urgent or compelling, lasts forever. As arousal subsides, a "hot" emotion turns into its "cool" counterpart. Anger may pale into annoyance, ecstasy into contentment, fear into suspicion, past emotional whirlwinds into calm breezes.

Although epinephrine and norepinephrine are released during many emotions, physiological differences among emotions also exist. The brain has a variety of chemical messengers at its disposal—neurotransmitters, hormones, and neuromodulators—and these play different roles in different emotions (Oatley & Jenkins, 1996). Moreover, fear, disgust, anger, sadness, surprise, and happiness are associated with somewhat different patterns of autonomic nervous system activity, involving such measures as heart rate, electrical conductivity of the skin (galvanic skin responses, or GSR), and finger temperature (Levenson, 1992; Levenson, Ekman, & Friesen, 1990). These distinctive patterns of arousal may explain why people say they feel "hot and bothered" when they are angry, but "cold and clammy" when they are afraid.

To sum up: Emotions involve characteristic facial expressions; activity in specific parts of the brain, notably the amygdala and the cerebral cortex; and sympathetic nervous system activity that prepares the body for action. But the physical changes involved in emotion cannot explain why, of two students about to take an exam, one feels psyched up and the other feels overwhelmed by anxiety. Different patterns of hemispheric activation in cheerful and depressed people won't tell us why the former see the world through rose-tinted glasses and the latter through foggy gray ones. And hormones alone won't tell you whether you are thrilled or frightened, sick or just in love.

??? QUICK QUIZ

We hope that a little surge of hormonal energy will help you answer these questions.

1. A 3-year-old sees her dad dressed as a gorilla and runs away in fear. What brain structure is probably involved in her withdrawal from him?

2. Casey is watching "Hatchet Murders in the Dorm: Sequel XVII." What hormones cause his heart to pound and his palms to sweat when the murderer is stalking an unsuspecting victim?

3. Melissa is watching an old Laurel and Hardy film, which makes her chuckle and puts her in a good mood. Which hemisphere of her brain is likely to be most active?

Answers:
1. the amygdala   2. epinephrine, norepinephrine   3. the left

---

Emotion and the Mind

What gives you the feeling of a feeling? What would happen if you were injected with the hormones that create the physical arousal associated with emotion, but while you were sitting in a quiet, boring room with no *reason* to feel an emotion? In the 1960s, Stanley Schachter and Jerome Singer proposed a **two-factor theory of emotion** to answer this question (Schachter, 1971; Schachter & Singer, 1962). They argued that bodily changes are necessary to experience an emotion but are not enough. Emotion, they said, depends on two things: *physiological arousal* and a *cognitive interpretation* of that arousal. Your body may be churning away in high gear, but unless you can interpret, explain, and label those changes, you will not feel a true emotion.

Schachter and Singer's own studies investigating this theory were never successfully replicated, but their ideas had an electrifying effect on emotion research. The two-factor theory spurred other investigators to study how emotions are created or influenced by beliefs, perceptions of the situation, expectations, and *attributions*—the explanations that people make of their own and other people's behavior (see Chapter 9). Human beings, after all, are the only species that can say, "The more I thought about it, the madder I got." That remark shows that we can think ourselves into an emotional state—in this case, anger—and by implication, we can think ourselves out of it.

Psychologists have studied the role of cognitions in all kinds of emotions, from joy to sadness. For example, imagine that you get an A on your psychology midterm; how will you feel? Or perhaps you get a D on that midterm; how will you feel then? The answers aren't so obvious; the emotions you will feel in response to your grade will depend more on how you *explain* your grade than on what you actually get—on whether you attribute your grade to your own efforts (or lack of effort), to the teacher, or to fate. In one series of experiments, students who believed they did well because of their own efforts tended to feel proud, competent, and satisfied. Those who believed they did well because of a lucky fluke or chance tended to feel gratitude, surprise, or guilt ("I don't deserve

two-factor theory of emotion

The theory that emotions depend on both physiological arousal and a cognitive interpretation of that arousal.

As the text explains, third-place winners tend to be happier about their performance than those who come in second. Certainly Olympic fencing bronze medalist Jean-Michel Henry of France (left) is happier than silver-medalist Pavel Kolobkov of the Unified Team (right)! (Eric Strecki, center, won the gold for France.)

this"). Those who believed their failures were their own fault tended to feel regretful, guilty, or resigned. And those who blamed others tended to feel angry or hostile (Weiner, 1986).

Here is another interesting example of how thoughts affect emotions. Of two Olympic contenders, one who wins a second-place silver medal and one who wins a third-place bronze medal, which will feel happier? Won't it be the silver medalist? Nope. In a study of athletes' reactions to placing second and third in the 1992 Olympics and the 1994 Empire State games, the bronze medalists were happier than the silver medalists (Medvec, Madey, & Gilovich, 1995). Apparently, the athletes were comparing their performance to "what might have been." The second-place winners, comparing themselves to the gold medalists, were unhappy that they didn't get the gold; but the third-place winners, comparing themselves to those who did worse than they, were happy that they earned a medal at all!

Cognitive research on emotion helps explain a puzzle of emotional experience: why people sometimes feel an emotion that is inappropriate to the situation. The reason is that they mislabel their own physical state, making an incorrect attribution. For example, people sometimes decide that they are suffering from anxiety because they can't sleep and have a rapid, pounding heartbeat,

when their symptoms are really due to too much coffee or to partying late. Or they may decide that they are feeling a particular emotion, when in reality their physical arousal is due to exercise, heat, cold, crowds, stress, traffic, and the like (Sinclair, 1994). Mislabeling explains why a person who has just exercised is more likely to interpret someone else's irritating behavior as an intentional insult and thus to feel angry. Unaware of the real reason for the arousal, the person seeks one in the environment or in the behavior of others (Averill, 1982; Zillman, 1983). Misattributions may also explain why the driver of a car feels angrier at other drivers than a passenger does ("That jerk tried to kill me"). Presumably, the jerky other driver could have killed the passenger as well as the driver, but only the driver is already tense and physically worked up from handling the car.

Cognitions play a greater role in some emotions than in others. A conditioned sentimental response to a patriotic symbol or a warm fuzzy feeling toward a familiar object involves only a simple, nonconscious reaction (Murphy, Monahan, & Zajonc, 1995). Other emotions require complex cognitive capacities, such as the ability to decide that you have been flattered, constructively criticized, humiliated, or betrayed. Infants cannot feel shame or guilt because these emotions require a sense of self and the ability to perceive that you have behaved badly or let down another person (Baumeister, Stillwell, & Heatherton, 1994; Tangney et al., 1996). With increasing mental maturity, the child's cognitive evaluations of a situation, and therefore the child's emotions, become

This baby will not feel an ounce of remorse for keeping her parents up all night—or gratitude for their care. Remorse and gratitude require the capacity for complex cognitive appraisals.

more complex (Malatesta, 1990; Oatley & Jenkins, 1996).

Today, almost all theories of emotion hold that attributions, beliefs, and the meanings people give to events are essential to the creation of most emotions. But where do these attributions, beliefs, and meanings come from? When people decide that it is shameful for a man to dance on a table with a lampshade on his head, or for a woman to walk down a street with her arms and legs uncovered, where do their ideas about shame originate? If you are the sort of motorist who curses others for driving too slowly, where did you learn that cursing is acceptable on the highway? To answer these questions, we turn to the third major aspect of emotional experience: the role of culture.

??? QUICK QUIZ

How are your thoughts affecting your feelings about this quiz?

1. What are the two factors in Schachter and Singer's two-factor theory of emotion?

2. Dara and Dinah get B's on their psychology midterm, but Dara is ecstatic and proud, and Dinah is furious. What expectations and attributions are probably affecting their emotional reactions?

3. At a party, you see a stranger flirting with your date. Suddenly you are flooded with jealousy. What cognitions might be causing this emotion? *Be specific.* What alternative thoughts might reduce the jealousy?

Answers:
1. physiological arousal and a cognitive interpretation of that arousal   2. Dara was probably expecting a lower grade and is attributing her B to her own efforts; Dinah was probably expecting a higher grade and is attributing her B to the instructor's unfairness, bad luck, or other external reasons.   3. Possible thoughts causing jealousy are "My date finds other people more attractive," "That person is trying to steal my date," or "My date's behavior is humiliating me." But you could be saying, "It's a compliment to me that other people find my date attractive" or "It pleases me that my date is getting such deserved attention."

What's Ahead

- *Are the "basic" emotions basic everywhere?*

- *Do Germans, Japanese, and Americans always mean the same thing when they smile at others?*

- *Why do people feel obliged to show sadness at funerals even when they're not feeling sad?*

- *Are women really more emotional than men?*

EMOTION AND CULTURE

A young wife leaves her house one morning to draw water from the local well as her husband watches from the porch. On her way back from the well, a male stranger stops her and asks for some water. She gives him a cupful and then invites him home to dinner. He accepts. The husband, wife, and guest have a pleasant meal together. The husband, in a gesture of hospitality, invites the guest to spend the night—with his wife. The guest accepts. In the morning, the husband leaves early to bring home breakfast. When he returns, he finds his wife again in bed with the visitor.

The question is, At what point in this story does the husband feel angry? The answer is, It depends on the culture to which he belongs (Hupka, 1981, 1991). A North American husband would feel rather angry at a wife who had an extramarital affair, and a wife would feel rather angry at being offered to a guest as if she were a lamb chop. But these reactions are not universal. A Pawnee husband of the nineteenth century would be enraged at any man who dared ask his wife for water. An Ammassalik Inuit husband finds it perfectly honorable to offer his wife to a stranger, but only once; he would be angry to find his wife and the guest having a second encounter. And a Toda husband at the turn of the century in India would not be angry at all because the Todas allowed both husband and wife to take lovers. Both spouses might feel angry, though, if one of them had a *sneaky* affair, without announcing it publicly.

As this example illustrates, people in most cultures experience anger as a response to insult and the violation of social rules; they just disagree about what an insult or the correct rule is. In this section, we will explore how culture influences the emotions we feel and the ways in which we express them.

The Varieties of Emotion

Earlier we saw that certain emotional expressions are recognizable throughout the world. Many psychologists believe that the emotions corresponding to these expressions—fear, anger, sadness, joy, surprise, disgust, and contempt—are universal and biologically based. These **primary emotions** are evoked by the same situations everywhere: Sadness follows perception of loss, fear follows perception of threat and bodily harm, anger follows perception of insult or injustice (Scherer & Wallbott, 1994). People in different cultures even give similar physical descriptions of these emotions, saying, for example, that they feel hot in response to anger and have a "lump in the throat" in response to sadness (Mesquita & Frijda, 1993; Oatley & Duncan, 1994).

In this view, **secondary emotions** are the cultural variations. Germans, for example, talk about *schadenfreude,* a feeling of joy at another's misfortune. The Japanese have *ijirashii,* a feeling associated with seeing an admirable person overcoming an obstacle, and *hagaii,* helpless anguish tinged with frustration. *Litost* is a Czech word that combines grief, sympathy, remorse, and longing; the Czech writer Milan Kundera used it to describe "a state of torment caused by a sudden insight into one's own miserable self."

Other psychologists, however, think that the effort to distinguish primary and secondary emotions masks the profound influence of culture on *every* aspect of emotional experience, starting with which feelings a culture considers "basic." For example, anger is a basic emotion in the United States, which emphasizes independence and personal rights, but it is caused and experienced quite differently in community-oriented cultures, where shame and loss of face are more central (Kitayama & Markus, 1994). On the tiny Micronesian atoll of Ifaluk, everyone would say that *fago* is the most fundamental emotion. *Fago,* translated as "compassion/love/sadness," reflects the sad feeling one has when a loved one is absent or in need, and the pleasurable sense of compassion in being able to care and help (Lutz, 1988).

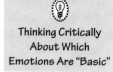
Thinking Critically About Which Emotions Are "Basic"

What, then, would theories of primary emotions look like from a non-Western perspective? They might start with shame or *fago,* which are far from central in Western emotion research.

Even if some basic emotions do prove to be hard-wired biologically, cultures clearly determine much of what people feel emotional *about.* Among the Bedouins and other "shame-oriented" cultures, shame is produced by violations of a complex code of honor; on Bali and Java, shame and embarrassment are generated by perceived challenges to one's status (Mesquita & Frijda, 1993). In Ifaluk, it is cause for anger if someone next to you is smoking without offering you the cigarette; it means the smoker is unwilling to share—a terrible offense (Lutz, 1988). Increasingly in the United States and Canada, it is cause for anger if someone is smoking at all! To nonsmokers, smoking means an infringement on their right to clean air.

Communicating Emotions

We could go on all day giving examples of cultural differences in emotion, but perhaps the most striking difference lies in how emotions are expressed. Suppose that someone who was dear to you died. Would you mourn privately and quietly, or publicly and noisily? Your answer will depend in part on your culture's **display rules** for emotion (Ekman et al., 1987). In some cultures, grief is expressed by wailing and weeping; in others, by tearless resignation; and in still others by dance, drink, and song. The death of Diana, Princess of Wales, revealed a major shift in England's display rules for grief—from "keep a stiff upper lip" (don't express your grief publicly) to "let it all hang out."

Even the smile, recognized the world over as a sign of friendliness, has many meanings and uses that are not universal and that depend on a culture's display rules. Americans tend to smile more frequently than Germans do; this does not mean that Americans are friendlier than Germans, but that they differ in their notions of when a smile is appropriate. After a German-American business session, Americans often complain that their German counterparts are cold and aloof. For their part, Germans often complain that Americans are

primary emotions
Emotions that are considered to be universal and biologically based; they generally include fear, anger, sadness, joy, surprise, disgust, and contempt.

secondary emotions
Emotions that are specific to certain cultures.

display rules
Social and cultural rules that regulate when, how, and where a person may express (or suppress) emotions.

Certain emotions are universal, but the rules for expressing them are not. The rule for a formal Japanese wedding portrait is "no expressions of emotion"—but not every member of this family has learned that rule yet.

excessively cheerful, hiding their real feelings under the mask of a smile (Hall & Hall, 1990). The Japanese smile even more than Americans, to disguise embarrassment, anger, or other negative emotions whose public display is considered rude and incorrect.

Display rules also govern emotional *body language,* including nonverbal signals of body movement, posture, gesture, and gaze (Birdwhistell, 1970). Some signals of body language, like some facial expressions, seem to be "spoken" universally. Across cultures, people generally recognize body movements that reveal pleasure or displeasure, liking or dislike, tension or relaxation, high status or low status, and primary emotions such as sadness, anger, and fear (Buck, 1984; Keating, 1994). When people are depressed, it shows in their walk, stance, and head position. However, most aspects of body language are specific to particular spoken languages and cultures, which makes even the simplest gesture subject to misunderstanding and offense. The sign of the University of Texas football team, the Longhorns, is to extend the second finger and the pinkie. In Italy and other parts of Europe, this gesture means a man's wife has been unfaithful to him—a serious insult.

Cultural misunderstandings of emotional display rules can lead to hostilities and even war (Triandis, 1994). On January 9, 1991, the Foreign Minister of Iraq, Tariq Aziz, met with the American Secretary of State, James Baker, to discuss Iraq's invasion of Kuwait. Seated next to Aziz was the half-brother of Iraq's president, Saddam Hussein. Baker said, "If you do not move out of Kuwait we will attack you." An unmistakable statement, right? But his *nonverbal* language was that of an American diplomat, moderate and

---

Get Involved

What are your culture's display rules for showing emotion in public places? Visit several different locations—a supermarket checkout line, a bus stop, your student union, an elevator in an apartment or office building—and notice people's emotional expressions. In general, are they showing much emotion, or are they "blank"? Do they make eye contact with strangers and smile at them, or avoid looking at anyone? If you do see someone expressing an emotion, such as anger or happiness, what is the person doing that conveys this feeling? To whom is the person expressing it? Under what conditions?

restrained. He didn't shout, stamp his feet, or wave his hands. Saddam Hussein's brother, for his part, behaved like a normal Iraqi. He paid attention to Baker's nonverbal language, which he considered the important form of communication. He reported to Saddam Hussein that Baker was "not at all angry. The Americans are just talking, and they will not attack." Saddam therefore instructed Aziz to be inflexible and to yield nothing. This misunderstanding contributed to the outbreak of a bloody war in which untold thousands of people died.

Just as people can speak without being able to state the rules of grammar, most people express or suppress their emotions without being aware of the display rules they are following (Keating, 1994). These rules tell us not only what to do when we are feeling an emotion, but also how and when to show an emotion we do not feel. Acting out an emotion we don't really feel, or trying to create the right emotion for the occasion, has been called **emotion work.** People are expected to demonstrate sadness at funerals, happiness at weddings, and affection toward relatives,

emotion work
Expression of an emotion, often because of a role requirement, that a person does not really feel.

Smiling to convey friendliness is part of the job description for flight attendants, whether they are male or female—but not necessarily for the passengers they serve.

whether they feel these emotions or not (which explains why Queen Elizabeth drew criticism when she didn't immediately display grief over the death of Princess Diana, even though everyone knew that the relationship between the two women was chilly). Sometimes emotion work is a job requirement: Flight attendants must "put on a happy face" to convey cheerfulness, even if they are angry about a rude or drunken passenger, and bill collectors must put on a stern face to convey threat, even if they feel sorry for the person they are collecting money from (Hochschild, 1983).

Differing display rules for communicating emotion help explain why many people in Western cultures think women are more "emotional" than men are. There is little evidence that one sex *feels* emotions more often than the other (Hatfield & Rapson, 1996; Oatley & Duncan, 1994; Shaver & Hazan, 1987; Shields, 1991).

Thinking Critically About Gender Differences in Emotionality

However, women in North America do tend to smile more than men do, gaze at their listeners more, have more emotionally expressive faces, use more expressive hand and body movements, and both touch other people more and be touched by others more (DePaulo, 1992). Women are also more likely to talk about their emotions—especially emotions that reveal vulnerability and helplessness, such as fear, sadness, loneliness, shame, and guilt (Fischer, 1993; Grossman & Wood, 1993; Nolen-Hoeksema, 1990). In contrast, most North American men are permitted to express only one emotion more freely than women: anger in public.

Women in North America tend to be involved in the flight-attendant side of emotion work, persuading others that they are friendly, happy, and warm, conveying deference, and making sure that others are happy (DePaulo, 1992; Henley, 1995). Women who don't smile when others expect them to do so are often disliked, even if they are actually smiling as often as men would. Men tend to be involved in the bill-collection side, persuading others that they are stern, aggressive, and unemotional. They are more likely than women to be rejected and disliked if they admit they are lonely or reveal emotions of "weakness" (Borys & Perlman, 1985).

These North American gender differences, however, are by no means universal. In most Asian cultures, *both* sexes are taught to control emotional expression (Buck & Teng, 1987). In

Europe, the Middle East, and South America, the display rules for women and men vary, depending on the country and the emotion. British, Spanish, Swiss, and German women are more likely than their male counterparts to inhibit feelings of sadness. Overall, European women are not more expressive than men; the differences are greater between cultures than between the sexes (Wallbott, Ricci-Bitti, & Bänninger-Huber, 1986).

Even within a culture, the influence of a particular situation often overrides gender rules. An American man is as likely as an American woman to control his temper when the target of anger is someone with higher status or power; few people, no matter how angry, will readily sound off at a professor, police officer, or employer. In the home, men and women are equally likely to express anger by sulking, discussing matters outright, or being verbally abusive (Averill, 1982; Gelles & Straus, 1988; Thomas, 1993). And you won't usually find gender differences in emotional expressiveness at a football game!

The emotion "tree," as we have seen, can take many shapes, depending on physiology, cognitive processes, and cultural rules. Next we will see how these three factors can help us understand those difficult situations in which stress and negative emotions threaten to overwhelm us and even to make us ill.

In some cultures, the expression worn by this grieving Israeli father would be regarded as "mature and manly," whereas in others it might be seen as "cold and uptight." Emotional display rules for men and women depend on both the culture and the emotion being expressed.

??? QUICK QUIZ

1. In Western theories of emotion, anger would be called a _____ emotion whereas *fago* would be called a _____ emotion.

2. Maureen is working in a fast-food restaurant and is becoming irritated with a customer who isn't ordering fast enough. She is supposed to be pleasant to all customers, but instead she snaps, "Hey, whaddaya want to order, slowpoke?" To keep her job and her temper, Maureen needs practice in _____.

3. In a class discussion of family traditions, a student from one culture says something that upsets a student from another. The second student smiles to disguise his discomfort; the first student thinks he is not being taken seriously and gets angry. What concepts from this section might explain this misunderstanding?

4. *True or false:* Throughout the world, women are more emotionally expressive than men.

Answers:

1. primary, secondary   2. emotion work   3. The students may come from cultures with different emotional display rules for discomfort and anger, and different customs governing nonverbal communication.   4. false

What's Ahead

- *Why are you more likely to get a cold when you're "stressed out"?*

- *Which stressors pose the greatest hazard to your health?*

- *Why do optimists tend to live longer than pessimists?*

- *When is a sense of control good for you, and when is it not?*

THE NATURE OF STRESS

No life is entirely free of stress. We are all vulnerable to conflicts that annoy us, traumatic experiences that shatter our sense of safety, continuing pressures that seem beyond our control, and small irritations that wear us down. The question that most fascinates laypeople and professionals alike is whether these *stressors* are linked to illness, and whether, by controlling our emotional reactions to events, we can improve health and well-being.

Stress and the Body

In his groundbreaking 1956 book *The Stress of Life,* Canadian physician Hans Selye (1907–1982) showed that many environmental stressors—heat, cold, pain, toxins, viruses, and so on—force an organism to mobilize its physiological resources and prepare to either fight or escape (this is commonly known as the "fight or flight response"). Drawing on data from animal studies, Selye concluded that "stress" consists of a series of physiological reactions that occur in three predictable phases:

1. *The alarm phase,* in which the body mobilizes to meet the threat with a package of physiological responses. These responses allow you to escape from danger no matter what the stressor is—crossing a busy street or dealing with deadline pressures at work.

2. *The resistance phase,* in which the organism attempts to resist or cope with a threat that cannot be avoided. During this phase, the body's physiological responses are in high gear, but unfortunately, these very responses make the body more susceptible to other stressors. For example, when your body has mobilized to fight off the flu, you may find that you are more easily annoyed by minor frustrations. In most cases, the body will eventually adapt to the stressor and return to normal.

3. *The exhaustion phase,* in which persistent stress causes depletion of energy and therefore increases vulnerability to physical problems and eventually illness. The same reactions that allow the body to resist short-term stressors are unhealthy as long-range responses. Tense muscles can cause headache and neck pain. Increased blood pressure can become chronic hypertension. Closing off of digestion can eventually lead to digestive disorders.

Selye did not believe that people should aim for a stress-free life. Some stress, which Selye called *eustress* (YOO-stress), is positive and productive, even if it also requires the body to produce short-term energy: competing in an athletic event, falling in love, working hard on a project you enjoy. And some negative stress is simply unavoidable. The goal is to minimize wear and tear on the system, not get rid of it entirely.

Selye recognized that psychological stressors, such as a fight with a loved one or grief over loss, can have as great an impact on health as do physical stressors, such as heat, crowds, or noise. But by and large, he concentrated on the biological responses that result from a person's or animal's attempts to adapt to environmental demands. A diagram of his view would look like this:

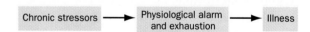

Of the many bodily systems affected by stress, one of the most intensively studied has been the immune system, which enables the body to fight disease and infection. The white blood cells of the immune system are designed to do two things: (1) recognize foreign substances (*antigens*), such as flu viruses, bacteria, and tumor cells; and (2) destroy or deactivate those substances. When an antigen invades the body, the immune system deploys different kinds of white blood cells as weapons, depending on the nature of the enemy.

Prolonged stress can suppress some or many of these white blood cells. In one study of medical students who had the herpes virus, herpes outbreaks were more likely to occur when the students were feeling lonely or were under pressure from exams. Loneliness and tension apparently suppress the immune system's capabilities, permitting the existing herpes virus to erupt (Kiecolt-Glaser et al., 1985a). In another study, 420 heroic volunteers in the war against the common cold used either ordinary nose drops or nose drops

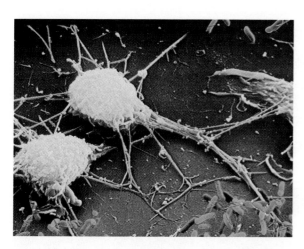

Like a fantastical Hollywood creature, a white blood cell reaches out with extended "arms" to ensnare unwitting bacteria.

containing viruses known to cause a cold's miserable symptoms. Everyone was then quarantined for a week. The results: People exposed to the virus who were under high stress, who felt their lives were "unpredictable, uncontrollable, and overwhelming," were twice as likely to develop colds as exposed people reporting low levels of stress (Cohen, Tyrrell, & Smith, 1993).

Stressors Affecting the Body.

Some kinds of stressors are especially likely to affect the immune, cardiovascular, and endocrine systems, and thus to increase the risk of illness or poor health:

1. *Bereavement and loss.* One of the most powerful stressors is the loss of a loved one or a close relationship, especially through death or divorce. In the two years following bereavement, widowed people are more susceptible to illness and physical ailments, and their mortality rate is higher than expected. Divorce can also take a long-term health toll: Divorced adults have higher rates of heart disease, pneumonia, and other diseases than their counterparts who are not divorced (Laudenslager, 1988). Bereaved and divorced people may be vulnerable to illness in part because, feeling unhappy, they don't sleep well, they stop eating properly, and they consume more drugs and cigarettes. But broken attachments also seem to affect the body at a cellular level, producing cardiovascular changes, a lowered number of white blood cells, and other abnormal responses of the immune system (Stroebe et al., 1996). Unhappily married individuals show the same physiological impairments as divorced people (Kiecolt-Glaser et al., 1993).

2. *Noise, crowding, and hassles.* When people speak of being under stress, they are often thinking of everyday hassles: thoughtless friends, traffic jams, bad weather, endless paperwork, quarrels, broken plumbing, lost keys, a computer that dies when a deadline is near. Psychologists used to think that hassles posed a major threat to health, but it turns out that these short-term stressors are hazardous primarily for anxious people who are quick to overreact (Kohn, Lafreniere, & Gurevich, 1991). For most other people, hassles don't pose a long-term risk to health unless they become *chronic* (recurring or constant).

One unhealthy chronic stressor is loud noise. Children in noisy schools, such as those near airports, tend to have higher blood pressure, to be more distractible, and to have more learning difficulties than do children in quieter schools (Cohen et al., 1980; Evans, Hygge, & Bullinger, 1995). In adults, noise contributes to cardiovascular problems, ulcers, irritability, fatigue, and aggressiveness, probably because of overstimulation of the autonomic nervous system (Staples, 1996). The noise that is most stressful to people, however, is noise they cannot control. The rock song that you choose to listen to with the volume all the way up may be pleasurable to you but intolerable—stressful—to anyone who does not share your musical taste.

Another chronic stressor is crowding, which, like noise, is most harmful to health and mental performance when it curtails your sense of control—when you feel trapped or are forced to endure interactions that are unwanted, intrusive, and inescapable (Evans, Lepore, & Schroeder, 1996; Taylor, 1995). Feelings about being crowded are in turn affected by your culture. North Americans associate crowded cities with stress and social tensions that lead to urban problems, such as crime. But in Tokyo, where the population density exceeds that of any U.S. city, people are accustomed to crowding, and it is not associated with tensions or crime.

3. *Poverty and powerlessness.* People at the lower end of the socioeconomic ladder have worse health and higher mortality rates for almost every disease and medical condition than do those on the upper rungs (Adler et al., 1994). One obvious reason is that poor people cannot afford good medical care, healthy food, and preventive examinations. Another, however, has to do with the continuous stressors that low-income people often live with: higher crime rates, fewer community services, run-down housing, fewer recreational

Who has more stress: corporate managers and white-collar workers or assembly-line workers and blue-collar laborers? People in highly competitive and complicated jobs, or people in boring and predictable jobs? Researchers find that "It is not the bosses but the bossed who suffer most from job stress" (Karasek & Theorell, 1990).

facilities, and greater exposure to environmental hazards (Taylor, Repetti, & Seeman, 1997).

In the United States, these conditions affect urban blacks disproportionately and may help account for the high incidence of hypertension (high blood pressure) among African-Americans (Anderson, 1991; Krieger & Sidney, 1996). But environmental factors interact with dietary practices, such as eating fast foods that are high in sodium, and with a genetic susceptibility to the negative effects of salt. (African-Americans are more likely to be salt sensitive.) When people with such a genetic vulnerability eat a high-salt diet *and* live in a high-stress environment, the result is high blood pressure (Weder & Schork, 1994).

In the workplace, the employees who suffer most from job stress and who are at greatest risk of a variety of illnesses are not executives and managers, but those who have little opportunity to exercise initiative and who are trapped doing repetitive tasks (Karasek & Theorell, 1990). For example, the women who are most at risk of heart disease are clerical workers who feel they have no support from their bosses, who are stuck in low-paying jobs without hope of promotion, and who have financial problems at home (Haynes & Feinleib, 1980).

The Stress–Illness Mystery.   The stressors we have discussed are all risk factors in the onset of disease, but none of them leads in a direct, simple way to illness or affects everyone in the same

way. Of two people exposed to a flu virus, one may be sick all winter and the other may not even get the sniffles. Some people have impaired immune function as a result of bereavement, interminable noise, or boring work, but others show no immune changes at all (Manuck et al., 1991). Some people show heightened blood pressure and heart rate when faced with an exam or high-pressure work, but others do not (Uchino et al., 1995).

Today, therefore, Selye's model of stress has been considerably modified and expanded (Basic Behavioral Science Task Force, 1996; Taylor, Repetti, & Seeman, 1997). Unlike Selye, who defined stress narrowly as the body's response to any environmental threat, health psychologists now take into account psychological qualities of the individual and how the individual copes (Taylor, 1995):

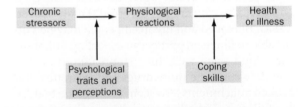

In this more complicated view, **psychological stress** is caused by an interaction of the person and the environment, in which the person believes that the situation strains or overwhelms his or her resources and is endangering his or her

psychological stress

The result of a relationship between the person and the environment, in which the person believes the situation is overwhelming and threatens his or her ability to cope.

ability to cope. Earlier we saw that emotions involve not only the body but also the mind and a person's social context; the same is true for reactions to stress.

Stress and the Mind

Some people manufacture their own misery. Send them to Tahiti for a week to escape the pressures of civilization, and they bring along a suitcase full of worries and irritations. Others have a talent for staying serene in the midst of chaos and conflict. These two kinds of people are distinguished by how they explain events and by the degree of control they think they exert over events.

Optimism and Pessimism. When something bad happens, what's your first reaction? Do you tell yourself that you'll somehow come through it okay, or do you gloomily think to yourself, "If something can go wrong for me, it will"? These two responses reflect *pessimistic* and *optimistic explanatory styles,* and as far as health is concerned,

the optimistic style is a lot better for you (Scheier & Carver, 1992; Seligman, 1991). The pessimistic style is associated with lower self-esteem, less achievement, more illness, and slower emotional recovery from trauma. It's not what happens to you, but how you think about what happens to you, that makes the most difference to your state of mind and your physical well-being.

If you are a pessimist, you will probably protest that optimism is just a *result,* not a cause, of good health or good fortune; after all, it's easy to think positively when you feel good! But optimism actually seems to produce good health. In an imaginative study of baseball Hall-of-Famers who had played between 1900 and 1950, 30 players were rated according to their explanatory style. A pessimist would attribute a bad performance to a permanent failing in himself, as in: "We didn't win because my arm is shot, and it'll never get better." An optimist would attribute the same performance to external and changing conditions, as in: "We didn't win because we got a couple of lousy calls, just bad luck in this game, but we'll be great tomorrow." The optimists were significantly more

Zack Wheat, an outfielder for the Brooklyn Dodgers, had an optimistic explanatory style: "I'm a better hitter than I used to be because my strength has improved and my experience has improved." Wheat lived to be 83.

Walter Johnson, a star pitcher for the Washington Senators, had a pessimistic explanatory style: "I can't depend on myself to pitch well. I'm growing old. I have had my day." Johnson died at age 59.

likely to have lived well into old age than were the pessimists (Seligman, 1991).

Many pessimists, naturally, think that optimists are just poor judges of reality. They may be right, but a little unrealistic optimism can be a good thing. Health and well-being often depend on having "positive illusions"—overly positive self-evaluations, exaggerated perceptions of control or mastery, and unrealistic optimism (Taylor & Brown, 1988, 1994). People who are optimistic and have positive illusions do not deny their problems; they acknowledge bad news when it comes. But they are more likely than pessimists to be active problem solvers and to seek information that can help them (Aspinwall & Taylor, 1997). They keep their senses of humor, plan for the future, and reinterpret the situation in a positive light (Aspinwall & Brunhart, 1996; Carver et al., 1993a). They probably also take better care of themselves when they have minor ailments, such as colds, and when they have life-threatening illnesses, such as AIDS (Taylor, 1995). Pessimists, in contrast, often do self-destructive things: They drink too much, smoke, fail to wear seat belts, or refuse to take medication for illness.

Pessimism, however, is not associated with poor outcomes for everyone. Some people adopt a stance called "defensive pessimism": "I expect the worst, but I'll work hard to avoid it, so if it happens anyway it won't be my fault." Edward Chang (1996) finds this attitude to be more common in Asian cultures than in Western ones. Although pessimism is associated with poorer coping strategies among Westerners, it is associated with stronger problem-solving strategies among Asians. By anticipating the worst, Chang argues, many Asians paradoxically take action to avoid it.

Can the risky form of pessimism be "cured"? Optimists, naturally, think so. In Chapter 11, we described an intervention program that inoculated elementary-school children against pessimism and depression by teaching them optimistic explanatory styles (Gillham et al., 1995). We also saw that in cognitive therapy, people can learn to question their belief that the world will collapse if they get a C in biology or that no one will ever love them. A third method worked for psychologist Rachel Hare-Mustin, whose mother cured her childhood pessimism with humor. "Nobody likes me," Rachel lamented. "Don't say that," her mother said. "Everybody hasn't met you yet."

The Sense of Control.   Optimism is related to another important cognitive ingredient in psycho-

logical and physical health: having an internal locus of control (Marshall et al., 1994). **Locus of control,** as we saw in Chapter 2, refers to your general expectation about whether you can control what happens to you. People who have an *internal* locus of control ("internals") tend to believe that they are responsible for what happens to them; those who have an *external* locus of control ("externals") tend to believe that they are the victims of circumstance.

People can tolerate years of difficulty if they believe they can control events or at least predict and prepare for them. Feeling in control helps to reduce pain, improve adjustment to surgery and illness, and speed up recovery from some diseases (Shapiro, Schwartz, & Astin, 1996; E. Skinner, 1996). In a group of patients recovering from heart attack, for example, those who thought their illness was due to bad luck or fate—factors outside their control—were less likely to generate active plans for recovery and more likely to resume their old unhealthy habits. In contrast, those who thought the heart attack occurred because they smoked, didn't exercise, or had a stressful job were more likely to change their bad habits and recover more quickly (Affleck et al., 1987; Ewart, 1995).

A sense of control actually affects the neuroendocrine and immune systems, which may explain why it is so beneficial to old people, whose immune systems normally decline (Rodin, 1988). When elderly residents of nursing homes are given more choices over their activities and more control over day-to-day events—even small but engrossing activities such as tending plants—the results are dramatic: They become more alert, more active, and happier, and they live longer (Langer, 1983).

Overall, then, a sense of control is a good thing. But the question must always be asked: control over what? The kind of control that is related to good health is *self-efficacy:* the belief that you are basically in charge of your own life and well-being, and

Thinking Critically
About Being
"in Control"

that if you become sick you can take steps to get better (Marshall, 1991). Health and well-being are not enhanced by other, more unrealistic forms of control, such as self-blame ("Whatever goes wrong with my health is my fault") or the belief that all disease can be prevented by doing the right thing ("If I eat right and work out, I'll never get sick"). If an unrealistically confident person tries to control the uncontrollable ("I'm going to be a

locus of control
A general expectation about whether the results of your actions are under your own control (internal locus) or beyond your control (external locus).

Sometimes life serves up a disaster, as it has for many farm families who have lost their lands and livelihoods because of a changing economy. When is it realistic to believe we can control what happens to us and when is it not?

movie star in 60 days"), the person's inevitable failure may lead to a sense of helplessness or incompetence, rather than better health (E. Skinner, 1996).

Ideas about control are strongly influenced by culture. In general, Western cultures celebrate **primary control,** in which people try to influence existing reality by changing other people, events, or circumstances: If you don't like a situation, you're supposed to change it, fix it, or fight it. The Eastern approach emphasizes **secondary control,** in which people try to accommodate to reality by changing their own aspirations or de-

sires: If you have a problem, you're supposed to live with it or act in spite of it (Rothbaum, Weisz, & Snyder, 1982).

A Japanese psychologist offered some examples of Japanese proverbs that teach the benefits of yielding to the inevitable (Azuma, 1984): *To lose is to win* (giving in, to protect the harmony of a relationship, demonstrates the superior trait of generosity); *Willow trees do not get broken by piled-up snow* (no matter how many problems pile up in your life, flexibility will help you survive them); and *The true tolerance is to tolerate the intolerable* (some "intolerable" situations are facts of life that no amount of protest will change). You can imagine how long "to lose is to win" would survive on an American football field, or how long most Americans would be prepared to tolerate the intolerable!

People who are ill or under stress can reap the benefits of both Western and Eastern forms of control by avoiding either–or thinking—by taking responsibility for future actions, while not blaming themselves unduly for past ones (Thompson, Nanni, & Levine, 1994). Among women coping with cancer, for example, adjustment is related to a woman's belief that she is not to blame for getting sick but that she is in charge of taking care of herself from now on (Taylor, Lichtman, & Wood, 1984). "I felt that I had lost control of my body somehow," said one woman, "and the way for me to get back some control was to find out as much as I could." This way of thinking allows you to avoid guilt and self-blame while retaining a sense of self-efficacy. Most problems require us to decide what we can change and accept what we cannot; perhaps the secret of healthy control lies in knowing the difference.

primary control

An effort to modify reality by changing other people, the situation, or events; a "fighting back" philosophy.

secondary control

An effort to accept reality by changing your own attitudes, goals, or emotions; a "learn to live with it" philosophy.

??? QUICK QUIZ

We hope these questions are not sources of stress for you.

1. Steve is unexpectedly called on in class to discuss a question. He hasn't the faintest idea of the answer, and he feels his heart start to pound and his palms to sweat. According to Selye, Steve is in the _____ phase of his stress response.

2. Which stressor has the strongest relationship to immune problems and illness? (a) listening to loud music in your room, (b) listening to your roommate's rotten choice of loud music in your room, (c) being swept up in a crowd of people celebrating New Year's Eve, (d) having a high-paying job that requires you to make many important but rapid decisions

3. Maria has worked as a file clerk for 17 years. Which aspect of the job is likely to be most stressful for her? (a) the speed of the work, (b) the predictable routine, (c) feeling trapped, (d) the daily demands from her boss

4. "I'll never find anyone else to love because I'm not good-looking; that one romance was a fluke" illustrates a(n) _____ explanatory style.

 5. On television, a self-described health expert explains that "no one gets sick if they don't want to be sick," because we can all control our bodies. As a critical thinker, how should you assess this claim?

Answers:
1. alarm 2. b 3. c 4. pessimistic 5. Skeptically. First, you would want to define your terms: What does "control" mean, and what kind of control? People can control some things, such as the decision to exercise and quit smoking, and they can control some aspects of treatment once they become ill; but they do not have control over everything that happens to them. Second, this "expert" assumes that control is always a good thing, but the belief that we have total control over our lives could lead to depression and unwarranted self-blame when illness strikes.

What's Ahead

- *Why are people who are chronically angry and mistrustful their own worst enemy?*

- *Which disease is depression most clearly linked to?*

- *How can revealing your unresolved feelings about a past trauma help your health?*

STRESS AND EMOTION

Have you ever heard people say things like, "She was so depressed, it's no wonder she got cancer" or "He worried himself into an ulcer over that job"? When we are under stress, we are usually "worked up" emotionally. Are emotions such as anger, anxiety, and depression hazardous to health?

Hostility and Depression

One of the first modern efforts to link emotions and illness was research on the *Type A personality*, a set of qualities proposed in the 1970s as a predictor of heart disease (Friedman & Rosenman, 1974). The Type A pattern describes people who are determined to achieve, have a sense of time urgency, are irritable, and are impatient at anyone who gets in their way. Type B people are calmer and less intense. It seemed logical that Type A's would be at greater risk of heart trouble than Type B's.

It turned out, however, that being highly reactive to stress and challenge is not in itself a risk factor in heart disease (Krantz & Manuck, 1984). Type A people do set themselves a fast work pace and a heavy workload, but many cope better than Type B people who have a lighter workload. Further, people who are highly involved in their jobs, even if they work hard, have a low incidence of heart disease. "There'd be nothing wrong with us fast-moving Type A's," said a friend of ours, "if it weren't for all those slow-moving Type B's."

The next round of research uncovered what it was about the behavior of some Type A's that *is* dangerous: hostility. We're not talking about the

Which is more stressful for this Type A man—his workload or his emotional reaction to it?

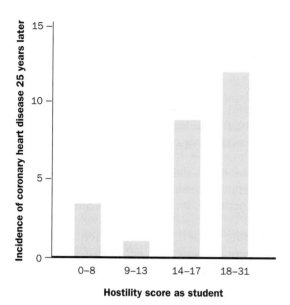

Figure 12.2

Hostility and Heart Disease

This graph shows that men who had the highest hostility scores as young medical students were the most likely to have coronary heart disease 25 years later (Williams, Barefoot, & Shekelle, 1985).

irritability or anger that everyone feels on occasion. The toxic kind is *cynical* or *antagonistic hostility,* which characterizes people who are mistrustful of others and quick to have mean, furious arguments (Marshall et al., 1994; Miller et al., 1996). As you can see in Figure 12.2, men who are chronically angry and resentful and who have a hostile attitude are five times as likely as nonhostile men to get heart disease, even when other risk factors, such as smoking and a poor diet, are controlled for (Ewart & Kolodner, 1994; Williams, Barefoot, & Shekelle, 1985). (The relationship between hostility and heart disease in women is less clear, in part because many longitudinal studies have included only men [Miller et al., 1996; Thomas, 1993].)

A second emotional suspect in the risk of illness is depression. In a recent longitudinal study of 1,551 people, those who were clinically depressed at the start of the study were four times more likely to have a heart attack in the ensuing 13 years than nondepressed people—even after controlling for all other risk factors, including high blood pressure and smoking (Pratt et al., 1996). It is still not known, however, whether depression increases the risk of heart attack because many depressed people fail to take care of themselves or because depression has direct biochemical effects on the body.

There is a common belief that depression is associated with other diseases as well, notably cancer and AIDS, but here the evidence is conflicting. Some studies find no links among depression, immune function, and either cancer or AIDS; others do. At present, therefore, the best conclusion is that chronic depression is a risk factor for heart disease and *possibly* other diseases as well.

Emotional Inhibition

Quick! Don't think of a white bear! Are you not thinking of it?

You might assume by now that the best thing to do when you feel a negative emotion is to suppress it. The problem is that when you actively try to avoid a thought, you are likely to process it more frequently. (How are you doing with that white bear?) That is why, when you are obsessed with someone you were once romantically involved with, trying not to think of the person actually prolongs your emotional responsiveness to him or her (Wegner & Gold, 1995).

Most people try to suppress feelings some of the time, but some people do so almost all of the time; they have the personality trait of *emotional inhibition* (Basic Behavioral Science Task Force, 1996). People with this trait, who are called "repressors," tend to deny feelings of anxiety, anger, or fear and pretend that everything is fine. Yet, when they are in stressful or emotion-producing situations, their physiological responses, such as heart rate and blood pressure, rise sharply. Repressors are at greater risk of becoming ill than people who can acknowledge their fears. Once they contract a serious disease, they may even die sooner: When women diagnosed with breast cancer were divided according to their style of coping—positive/confronting, fatalistic, hopeless/helpless, or denial/avoidance—the "positive/confronting" style was associated with the greatest longevity, regardless of the severity of the illness (Burgess, Morris, & Pettingale, 1988).

Why should emotional inhibition increase the risk of having health problems? One possibility is that the prolonged inhibition of thoughts and emotions requires physical effort that is stressful to the body (Pennebaker, 1995; Pennebaker & Harber, 1993). Another is that the inability or unwillingness to confide important or traumatic events may place continuing stress on the immune system. If that is so, then divulging private thoughts and feelings that make you ashamed or depressed may be helpful.

Everyone has private moments of sad reflection. But when you feel sad, anxious, or fearful for too long, keeping your feelings to yourself may increase your stress and the risk of health problems.

donment, but most had never discussed their feelings with anyone. The researchers took blood samples from the students to test for the immune activity of white blood cells. They also collected data on the students' physical symptoms, emotions, and visits to the health center. On every measure, the students who wrote about traumatic experiences were better off than those who did not (Pennebaker, Kiecolt-Glaser, & Glaser, 1988). Some of them showed short-term increases in anger and depression; writing about an unpleasant experience was disturbing. But over time, their health and well-being improved.

Writing about the same experience for several days may be beneficial because it produces insight and emotional distance, ending the mental repetition of obsessive thoughts and unresolved feelings. One woman, who had been molested at the age of 9 by a boy a year older, at first wrote about her feelings of embarrassment and guilt. By the third day, she was writing about how angry she felt at the boy. By the last day, she had begun to see the whole event differently; he was young, too, after all. When the study was over, she said, "Before, when I thought about it, I'd lie to myself. . . . Now, I don't feel like I even have to think about it because I got it off my chest. I finally admitted that it happened."

Consider what happened when college students were assigned to write about either a personal, traumatic experience or a trivial topic for 20 minutes a day for four days. Those students who were asked to reveal their deepest thoughts and feelings about a traumatic event all had something to talk about. Many told stories of sexual coercion, physical beatings, humiliation, and parental aban-

How strong, overall, is the link between emotion and illness? Some researchers believe that personality traits involving the expression or suppression of emotion play a key role in the onset of illness, and even that specific emotions can be tied to particular illnesses, such as cancer or heart disease (Eysenck, 1993; Grossarth-Maticek et al., 1991). Others caution against exaggerating the role of emotional styles in health, arguing that we must not overlook the stronger influences of chronic stressors, the biology of the disease, and the individual's health habits, such as smoking (Greenwald, 1992; Jorgensen et al., 1996).

Get Involved

To see whether the research on the benefits of confession will benefit you, take a moment to jot down your "deepest thoughts and feelings" about being in college, your past, a secret, your future . . . anything you've never told anyone. Do this again tomorrow, and again for a few days in a row. Note your feelings after writing. Are you upset? Troubled? Sad? Relieved? Does your account change over time? Research suggests that if you do this exercise now, you may have fewer colds, headaches, and trips to the doctor next year.

Both sides, however, agree that the links among emotions, stress, and health should not be oversimplified. Living all the time with unresolved negative emotions can be stressful to the body, but a life of constant stress also tends to foster negative emotions. Depression and anxiety may contribute to illness in some individuals, but illness also makes some people depressed or anxious. Chronic emotional inhibition is hazardous to some people's health, but so is constant emotional ventilation, which violates social and cultural rules and can alienate others (Kelly & McKillop, 1996). Health psychology suggests a middle path: learning to identify and deal with our negative emotions, without ruminating on them and letting them dominate our lives or erode our relationships.

Thinking Critically About Emotions and Health

??? QUICK QUIZ

You'll reduce stress and experience positive emotions if you can answer these questions.

1. Which aspect of Type A behavior seems most hazardous to men's health? (a) working hard, (b) being in a hurry, (c) cynical hostility, (d) high physical reactivity to work, (e) general grumpiness

2. Valerie has many worries about being in college, but she is afraid to tell anyone. What might be the healthiest solution for her? (a) exercise, (b) writing down her feelings in a diary, (c) talking frequently to strangers who won't judge her, (d) expressing her hostility whenever she feels it

Answers:
1. c 2. b

What's Ahead

- *When you're feeling overwhelmed, what are some ways to calm yourself?*

- *Why is it important to move beyond the emotions caused by a problem and deal with the problem itself?*

- *How can you learn to rethink your problems?*

- *When do friends reduce your stress, and when do they just make matters worse?*

EMOTIONS, STRESS, AND HEALTH: HOW TO COPE

Remarkably, most people who are under stress—even those living in the toxic environments of war and poverty, or living through long, emotionally draining episodes of anger or grief—do not become ill. In this section, we will consider some of the most effective methods of coping with and recovering from the troubles of life.

Cooling Off

The most immediate way to cope with the physiological tension of stress and negative emotions is to calm down: to take time out and reduce the body's physical arousal.

One of the best ways to calm yourself is to use conscious relaxation techniques. *Relaxation training*—learning to alternately tense and relax the muscles, to lie or sit quietly, or to meditate by clearing your mind and banishing worries of the day—has beneficial effects on the body, lowering stress hormones and enhancing immune function (Baum, Herberman, & Cohen, 1995). Studies of many different groups, including elderly residents of retirement homes and women with first-stage breast cancer, find that people who reduce stress by using relaxation techniques show significantly improved immune activity (Gruber et al., 1993; Kiecolt-Glaser et al., 1985b). Relaxation is also helpful for people who feel chronically angry or anxious.

Another buffer between stressors and physical symptoms is exercise. A low level of physical activity is associated with decreased life expectancy for both sexes and contributes independently to the development of many chronic diseases (Dubbert, 1992). As you can see in Figure 12.3, when people are experiencing the same objective pressures, those who are physically fit have fewer health problems than people who are less fit; they also show less physiological arousal to stressors and pay fewer visits to the doctor (Brown, 1991). The more that people exercise, the less anxious, depressed, and irritable they are, and the fewer physical symptoms and colds they have (Hendrix et al., 1991).

Perhaps you can think of other ways to cool off when you're hot and bothered. Many people respond beneficially to the soothing touch of massage (Field, 1995). Others listen to calm music, take a refreshing walk, or bake bread. Such activities give the physiological symptoms of stress and intense negative emotions a chance to subside. However, you can't always jog away from your problems. Relaxation is not going to change the fact that you may lose your job, your best friend has betrayed a confidence, or you need a serious operation. Other coping strategies are also necessary.

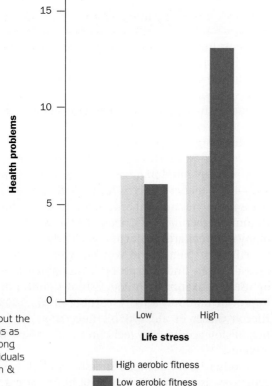

Figure 12.3
Fitness and Health

Among people with low stress, aerobically fit individuals had about the same number of health problems as those who were less fit. But among people with high stress, fit individuals had fewer health problems (Roth & Holmes, 1985).

Solving the Problem

A woman we know, whom we will call Nancy, was struck by tragedy when she was 22. She and her new husband were driving home one evening when a car went out of control and crashed into them. When Nancy awoke in a hospital room, she learned that her husband had been killed and that she herself had permanent spinal injury and would never walk again. For many months, Nancy reacted with understandable rage and despair. "Get it out of your system," her friends said. "You need to get in touch with your feelings." "But I know I'm miserable," Nancy lamented. "What do I *do?*"

Nancy's friends' advice and her reply illustrate the difference between *emotion-focused* and *problem-focused coping* (Lazarus & Folkman, 1984). Emotion-focused coping concentrates on the emotions the problem has caused, whether anger, anxiety, or grief. For a period of time after any personal tragedy or traumatic natural disaster, it is normal to give in to these emotions and feel overwhelmed by them. In this stage, people often need to talk obsessively about the event in order to come to terms with it, make sense of it, and decide what to do about it (Pennebaker & Harber, 1993). Eventually, though, most people become ready to move beyond their emotional state and concentrate on the problem itself. The specific steps in problem-focused coping depend on the nature of the problem: whether it is a pressing but one-time decision; a continuing difficulty, such as living with a disability; or an anticipated event, such as having an operation.

Once the problem is identified, the coper can learn as much as possible about it from professionals, friends, books, and others in the same predicament. In Nancy's case, she learned more about her medical condition and prognosis, how other accident victims had coped, and the occupations that were possible for her. Nancy stayed in school, remarried, got a Ph.D. in psychology, and now does research and counseling with disabled people.

Problem-focused coping tends to increase your sense of self-efficacy (D'Zurilla & Sheedy, 1991). It encourages you to think critically by considering alternatives and resisting emotional reasoning. People who think concretely and creatively about their problems are better able to solve them, avoid negative emotions such as anger and anxiety, and even reduce physiological arousal (Katz & Epstein, 1991).

Rethinking the Problem

A third method of coping with stress and negative emotions is to think about your problems in new ways, in order to feel more optimistic and in control. Some of the most effective "rethinking" strategies are these:

1. *Reappraisal.* You may not be able to eliminate a stressor, but you can choose to reassess its meaning. Problems can be turned into challenges, losses into unexpected gains. If you lost your job, you can tell yourself that maybe it wasn't such a good job but you were too afraid to quit to look for another, and now you can do so. Even life-shattering events can be viewed in more than one light. A study of 100 spinal-cord-injured people found that two-thirds of them felt the disability had had positive side effects (Schulz & Decker, 1985). They named such benefits as becoming a better person, seeing other people as more important, and gaining a new appreciation of "brain, not brawn." When you are coping with problems, you can also reappraise the actions of others. Instead of becoming angry with a neighbor who is sullen and difficult, for example, you can tell yourself that your neighbor must be deeply unhappy or troubled to behave so badly.

2. *Social comparison.* In a difficult situation, successful copers often compare themselves to others who are (they feel) less fortunate. No matter how bad off they are, even if they have fatal diseases, they find someone who is even worse off (Taylor & Lobel, 1989). One AIDS sufferer said in an interview, "I made a list of all the other diseases I would rather not have than AIDS. Lou Gehrig's disease, being in a wheelchair; rheumatoid arthritis, when you are in knots and in terrible pain. So I said, 'You've got to get some perspective on this, and where you are on the Great Nasty Disease List'" (Reed, 1990). Sometimes successful copers also compare themselves to those who are doing *better* than they are (Collins, 1996). Such comparisons are beneficial when they provide information about how to manage a situation and when the coper feels able to take advantage of such information.

3. *Humor.* "A merry heart doeth good like a medicine," says Proverbs in the Old Testament, and so it does. People who can see the absurd or whimsical aspects of a bad situation are less prone to depression, anger, tension, and fatigue than are people who give in to gloom, moping, and tears

The ultimate example of rethinking your problems.

(P. Fry, 1995; Nezu, Nezu, & Blissett, 1988; Solomon, 1996). In people with serious illnesses, humor reduces distress, improves immune functioning, and hastens recovery from surgery (Carver et al., 1993b; Martin & Dobbin, 1988). Laughter at daily problems may also produce some beneficial biological responses, possibly by stimulating the immune system or starting the flow of endorphins, the painkilling chemicals in the brain (W. Fry, 1994). And humor has mental benefits. When you laugh at a problem, you are seeing it a new way and gaining a sense of control over it (Dixon, 1980). The humor must be good-natured, though; vicious, rude jokes at another person's expense only create more tension and anger.

Looking Outward

A final way to deal with negative emotions and stress is to reach out to others. Think of all the ways in which family members, friends, neighbors, and co-workers can help you. They can offer concern and affection. They can help you evaluate problems and plan a course of action. They can offer resources and services such as lending you money or a car, or taking notes in class for you when you have to go to the doctor. Most of all, they are sources of attachment and connection, which everyone needs throughout life.

Friends can be our greatest source of warmth, support, and fun . . .

Social support turns out to be medically beneficial as well as psychologically helpful. In two major studies that followed thousands of adults for a period of ten years, people who had few friends and relations were more likely to die than those who had many, even when the researchers controlled for physical health at the start of the study, socioeconomic status, age, and risk factors such as smoking (Berkman & Syme, 1979; House, Landis, & Umberson, 1988).

Social support may be related to health because it produces beneficial effects on the cardiovascular, endocrine, and immune systems (Uchino, Cacioppo, & Kiecolt-Glaser, 1996). In some cases, social support groups can even extend the survival time of people with serious illnesses. In a group of 194 older men and women who had had heart attacks, 58 percent of those reporting no close contacts died within the year, compared with only 27 percent of those who said they had two or more people they could count on (Berkman, Leo-Summers, & Horwitz, 1992). Other studies have obtained similar results. Even when social support does not lengthen life, it often lessens the suffering and pain of people with terminal illnesses and enhances their ability to come to terms with death.

Of course, sometimes other people *aren't* helpful; on the contrary, sometimes friends and family are themselves the source of hassles, unhappiness, stress, and anger. When disaster or serious illness strikes, friends and relatives may behave awkwardly, not knowing what to do or say. They may abandon you, try to cut short your feelings of grief, or say something stupid and hurtful. Sometimes they offer the wrong kind of support because they have never been in the same situation or are unwilling to listen to your revelations of fear or sadness (Bolger et al., 1996). And sometimes being in a close network of friends can make it difficult for you to change bad health habits (say, to cut down on drinking when "everyone" else is bingeing).

When thinking about stress and social support, we should also not ignore the benefits of *giving* support, rather than always being on the receiving end. Julius Segal (1986), a psychologist who worked with Holocaust survivors, prisoners of war, hostages, refugees, and other survivors of catastrophe, wrote that a key element in their recovery was compassion, "healing through helping."

Offering support to others can also benefit people with ordinary problems of life: In general, individuals who are highly empathic and cooperative are healthier and happier than those who are self-involved (Crandall, 1984). Why? The ability to look outside yourself is related to virtually all of the successful coping mechanisms we have discussed. It encourages you to solve problems instead of blaming others; helps you reappraise a conflict by seeing conflict as others do; and allows you to gain perspective on a problem instead of exaggerating its importance. Because of its elements of forgiveness, tolerance, and empathy, "looking outward" helps you live with situations that are facts of life.

. . . and also a source of exasperation, headaches, and pressure.

??? QUICK QUIZ

Can you cope with these refresher questions?

1. You accidentally broke your glasses. Which response is an example of cognitive reappraisal? (a) "I am such a stupid clumsy idiot!" (b) "I never do anything right." (c) "What a shame, but I've been wanting new frames anyway." (d) "I'll forget about it in aerobics class."

2. Finding out what your legal and financial resources are when you have been victimized by a crime is an example of (a) problem-focused coping, (b) emotion-focused coping, (c) distraction, (d) reappraisal.

3. "This class drives me crazy, but I'm better off than my friends who aren't in college" is an example of (a) distraction, (b) social comparison, (c) denial, (d) empathy.

4. Your roommate has turned your room into a garbage dump, filled with rotten left-over food and unwashed clothes. Assuming that you don't like living with rotting food and dirty clothes, what coping strategies described in this section might help you?

Answers:

1. c 2. a 3. b 4. You might attack the problem by finding a compromise (e.g., clean the room together); reappraise the seriousness of the problem ("I only have to live with this person until the end of the term"); or compare your roommate to others ("at least mine is generous and friendly"). You might also apply humor (pile everything into a heap, put a flag on top, and add a sign: "Monument to the Battle of the Bilge").

Let us now consider how a better understanding of stress and emotion might help us understand the growing problem of "road rage" and what we can do about it. In a world that is getting noisier and more crowded, getting stuck behind a slow-moving car or caught in an endless traffic jam may feel like the last straw to some people, especially to those who are already anxious, hostile, or impatient. In his testimony to Congress, Ricardo Martinez reported that traffic has increased 35 percent since 1987, but construction of new roads has increased only 1 percent during that time, and resources dedicated to the enforcement of traffic laws have declined.

However, as we have learned, our perceptions of a situation are as important as the situation itself in influencing our emotional response to it and the degree of stress we feel. When you're sitting in traffic, if you tell yourself that being late to your destination will be disastrous, you are likely to feel extremely distressed by those stupid cars that are blocking your way. But if you decide that being stuck in traffic is trivial, as problems go, and that you can't do anything about it anyway, you may take the situation more calmly. If you interpret another person's poor driving habits as a personal insult or challenge ("That guy tried to *kill* me!"), you are likely to be furious at that stupid driver who cut in front of you. But if you interpret the other driver's behavior more empathically— perhaps he or she is racing to a hospital, or just doesn't know any better, poor dolt—you are less likely to feel angry. A therapist we know has a wonderful reappraisal tactic: He helps motorists reduce their stress and rage on the highway by having them visualize other drivers as donkeys— a better technique than *calling* another driver a donkey!

When you're caught in traffic, you might also reduce your physiological arousal by listening to music you enjoy or a book on tape. In "Taking Psychology with You," we offer further suggestions for handling anger, on the road or off. Keep in mind, though, that successful coping does not mean eliminating all sources of stress or all difficult emotions. It does not mean constant happiness or a life without pain and frustration. The healthy person faces problems, deals with them, and gets beyond them, but the problems are necessary if the person is to acquire coping skills that endure. To wish for a life without stress, or a life without emotion, would be like wishing for a life without friends. The result might be calm, but it would be joyless and ultimately hazardous to your health. The stresses and passions of life—the daily hassles, the emotional ups and downs, and the occasional tragedies—force us to grow, and to grow up.

Taking Psychology with You

The Dilemma of Anger: "Let It Out" or "Bottle It Up"?

What do you do when you feel angry? Do you tend to brood and sulk, collecting your righteous complaints like acorns for the winter; erupt, hurling your wrath on anyone or anything at hand; or discuss your feelings after you have calmed down? The answer is crucial for how you get along with your family, neighbors, employers, and strangers. All too often, people freely vent their anger in the home and in public, with rude gestures and insulting remarks. Strangers shoot each other over trivial infractions, and public debate about serious issues often degenerates into name-calling and the exchange of hostilities.

Although some schools of therapy once advised people to "get it out of your system," psychologists have found that this advice often backfires. In contrast to much pop-psych advice, research shows that expressing anger often prolongs it instead of getting rid of it. When people constantly talk about their anger or act on that feeling, they tend to rehearse their grievances, create a hostile dispo-

sition, and pump up their blood pressure (Averill, 1982; Tavris, 1989). Conversely, when people learn to control their tempers and express anger constructively, they usually feel better, not worse; calmer, not angrier.

When people are feeling angry, they can do many things: write letters, play the piano, jog, kick the sofa, abuse their friends or family, or yell. If a particular action soothes their feelings or gets the desired response from other people, they are likely to acquire a habit. Soon that habit feels "natural," as if it could never be changed; indeed, many people justify their violent tempers by saying "I just couldn't help myself." But they can. The research in this chapter offers practical suggestions for relearning constructive ways of managing anger:

• *Don't sound off in the heat of anger; let bodily arousal cool down.* Whether your arousal comes from background stresses such as heat, crowds, or loud noise, or from conflict with another person, take time to relax. Time al-

lows you to decide whether you are really angry or just tired and tense. This is the reason for that sage old advice to count to 10, count to 100, or sleep on it. Other cooling-off strategies include taking a time-out in the middle of an argument, meditating or relaxing, and calming yourself with a distracting activity.

• *Check your perceptions for accuracy, and then see whether you can rethink the problem.* People who are quick to feel anger tend to interpret other people's actions as intentional offenses. People who are slow to anger tend to give others the benefit of the doubt, and they are not as focused on their own injured pride. Empathy ("Poor guy, he's feeling rotten") is usually incompatible with anger, so practice seeing the situation from the other person's perspective (Miller & Eisenberg, 1988; Tangney, 1992).

• *If you decide that expressing anger is appropriate, think carefully about how to do it so that you will get the results you want.* Whoever the target of your anger is, be sure that your feelings and complaints are conveyed clearly so that they will be understood and will have the desired impact.

Ultimately, the best thing you can do before deciding whether to express anger is to ask yourself what you hope to accomplish. Do you just want to feel good? If so, getting angry may not help you much. Do you want to restore your rights, change the other person, improve a bad situation, or achieve justice? If those are your goals, then getting the other person to listen and respond is essential. People who have been the targets of injustice have learned that outbursts of anger may draw society's attention to a problem—but real change requires sustained political effort, challenges to unfair laws, and the use of tactics that persuade rather than alienate the opposition.

Of course, if you just want to blow off steam, go right ahead; but you risk becoming a hothead.

SUMMARY

The Nature of Emotion

1) The complex experience of *emotion* involves physiological changes in the face, brain, and autonomic nervous system; cognitive processes; and cultural conventions.

2) Some basic facial expressions—anger, fear, sadness, happiness, disgust, surprise, contempt—are widely recognized across cultures, although the interpretation of any expression also depends on the context in which it is expressed. The *neurocultural theory* of emotion emphasizes that culture interacts with a universal facial neurophysiology to influence when and how emotions are displayed.

3) Emotional expressions probably evolved to express internal states and communicate with others, functions that are apparent in infancy (although because people can disguise their emotions, their expressions do not always communicate accurately). The *facial feedback* provided by emotional expressions also helps us to identify our own emotional states.

4) Many aspects of emotion are associated with specific parts of the brain. Separate regions of the right hemisphere specialize in recognizing faces and identifying facial expressions. The right hemisphere is specialized for experiencing negative emotions and the left hemisphere for positive ones. The *amygdala* is responsible for initially evaluating the emotional importance of incoming sensory information, and the *cerebral cortex* provides the ability to confirm or override this initial appraisal.

5) During the experience of any emotion, *epinephrine* and *norepinephrine* produce a state of physiological arousal to prepare the body for an output of energy. But different emotions are also associated with somewhat different patterns of autonomic nervous system activity and involve the release of different neurotransmitters in the brain.

6) Schachter and Singer's *two-factor theory* of emotion held that emotions result from arousal and the labeling or interpretation of that arousal. Their research launched many studies designed to identify the cognitive processes involved in different emotions. Emotions result from beliefs, perceptions, expectations, and *attributions* about your own and other people's behavior. When people mislabel their own physical state, making an incorrect attribution, they may feel an emotion that is inappropriate to the situation.

7) Some emotions involve simple, nonconscious reactions. Others, such as shame and guilt, require complex cognitive capacities. As children mature, their cognitions and therefore their emotions become more complex.

Emotions and Culture

8) Some researchers distinguish *primary emotions*, which are thought to be universal, from *secondary emotions*, which are specific to cultures. The list of primary emotions typically includes fear, anger, sadness, joy, surprise, disgust, and contempt. Other psychologists question the effort to find primary emotions. They argue that culture

affects every aspect of emotional experience, including which emotions are considered basic and what people feel emotional about.

9) Cultural *display rules* regulate how, when, and where a person may express or must suppress an emotion, and the *emotion work* a person is expected to do. Cultural differences in the rules governing facial expressions and body language can lead to misunderstandings. In North America, men and women experience the same emotions, but different display rules govern the way they may express those emotions. The influence of a particular situation, however, can often override gender rules.

The Nature of Stress

10) Hans Selye argued that environmental stressors such as heat, pain, and toxins cause the body to respond with fight-or-flight responses, occurring in three stages: *alarm, resistance,* and *exhaustion.* If a stressor persists, it may overwhelm the body's ability to cope, and illness may result. Studies of the immune system have confirmed that stress can suppress the activity of white blood cells and make illness more likely.

11) Stressors especially likely to affect the body include bereavement and loss; uncontrollable, chronic noise and crowding; and poverty and powerlessness. But even these stressors do not have the same effect on everyone. Therefore, modern approaches to stress and illness take into account the psychological factors that mediate between the stressor and physiological reactions to it, especially qualities of the individual (e.g., traits and perceptions) and the individual's coping skills.

12) An *optimistic explanatory style* is better for you in terms of health and longevity than a pessimistic style. Optimists are more likely than pessimists to actively solve their problems, and they may be more likely to take care of themselves when they are ill. However, "defensive pessimism," which is more common in Asian cultures than Western ones, is not associated with poor health outcomes.

13) Another important cognitive element in physical and mental health is having an internal *locus of control* that is realistic and that promotes *self-efficacy.* Health and well-being may depend on the right combination of *primary control* (trying to change the stressful situation) and *secondary control* (learning to accept and accommodate to a stressful situation). Cultures differ in the kind of control they emphasize and value.

Stress and Emotion

14) Researchers have sought links between personality traits and illness. Having a competitive, impatient *Type A personality* is not itself related to heart disease, but *cynical or antagonistic hostility,* which is often part of the Type A pattern, is. Depression is associated with increased risk of heart attack, but its link with other diseases is less clear.

15) "Repressors," people who are emotionally inhibited, are at greater risk of illness than people who can acknowledge and cope with negative emotions. The effort to suppress worries, secrets, and memories of upsetting experiences can paradoxically lead to obsessively ruminating on these thoughts, which can be stressful to the body.

Emotions, Stress, and Health: How to Cope

16) One way to cope with stress and negative emotions is to reduce their physical effects, for example by using relaxation techniques or by exercising. Another is to focus on solving the problem rather than on the emotions caused by the problem. A third is to rethink the problem by reappraising the situation, comparing yourself with others, or applying humor. A fourth is to reach out to friends, family, and other sources of social support.

17) Other people are not always helpful when you are under stress; they can even be a *source* of stress. But in general, social support is associated with health, and even with increased longevity in people with serious illnesses. Giving support—looking outside yourself—is also associated with health and hastens recovery from traumatic experiences.

18) Coping with stress does not mean trying to live without pain, problems, or nuisances. It means learning how to live with them.

KEY TERMS

emotion   400

neurocultural theory of
emotional expressions   400

facial-feedback hypothesis   402

amygdala   403

epinephrine   404

norepinephrine   404

two-factor theory of emotion
405

attributions   405

primary and secondary
emotions   408

display rules   408

body language   409

emotion work   410

stressors   412

alarm, resistance, and
exhaustion phases of stress
412

eustress   412

psychological stress   414

pessimistic and optimistic
explanatory styles   415

positive illusions   416

defensive pessimism   416

internal versus external locus of
control   416

self-efficacy   416

primary control   417

secondary control   417

Type A personality   418

cynical/antagonistic hostility
419

emotional inhibition   419

relaxation training   421

emotion-focused coping   422

problem-focused coping   422

reappraisal   423

social comparison   423

LOOKING BACK

- *Which facial expressions of emotion do people the world over recognize? (p. 400)*

- *Which side of your brain is most active when you're filled with joy—or despair? (p. 403)*

- *Which two hormones can make you "too excited to eat"? (p. 404)*

- *In a competition, who is likely to be happier, the third-place winner or the second-place winner? (p. 406)*

- *Why can't an infant feel shame or guilt? (p. 406)*

- *Are the "basic" emotions basic everywhere? (p. 408)*

- *Do Germans, Japanese, and Americans always mean the same thing when they smile at others? (pp. 408–409)*

- *Why do people feel obliged to show sadness at funerals even when they're not feeling sad? (p. 410)*

- *Are women really more emotional than men? (pp. 410–411)*

- *Why are you more likely to get a cold when you're "stressed out"? (pp. 412–413)*

- *Which stressors pose the greatest hazard to your health? (pp. 413–414)*

- *Why do optimists tend to live longer than pessimists? (pp. 415–416)*

- *When is a sense of control good for you, and when is it not? (pp. 416–417)*

- *Why are people who are chronically angry and mistrustful their own worst enemy? (pp. 418–419)*

- *Which disease is depression most clearly linked to? (p. 419)*

- *How can revealing your unresolved feelings about a past trauma help your health? (p. 420)*

- *When you're feeling overwhelmed, what are some ways to calm yourself? (pp. 421–424)*

- *Why is it important to move beyond the emotions caused by a problem and deal with the problem itself? (p. 422)*

- *How can you learn to rethink your problems? (p. 423)*

- *When do friends reduce your stress, and when do they just make matters worse? (pp. 423–424)*

13

The Major Motives of Life: Love, Sex, Food, and Work

PSYCHOLOGY IN THE NEWS

The romantic story in Titanic has been drawing huge audiences.

Popular Diet Pill Pulled from Market

WASHINGTON, D.C., SEPTEMBER 15, 1997. Wyeth–Ayerst, maker of the diet-pill combination known as "fen-phen," has announced that it is withdrawing the two drugs used as the "fen" half. The ingredients, fenfluramine and dexfenfluramine, are suspected of producing heart-valve problems in up to 25 percent of otherwise healthy users. Because an estimated 6 million Americans have taken the appetite suppressants along with another drug, phentermine, some experts believe the public-health implications could be staggering. Others caution the public not to become alarmed until further research is done.

"Titanic" Refuses to Sink, Draws Huge Repeat Business

LOS ANGELES, CA., MARCH 11, 1998. *Titanic* has passed *Star Wars* as the top moneymaking film of all time, thanks to loyalists who have returned to view it two, three, or even more times. Software engineer Jim Sadur, 42, saw the movie twice and cried both times. "If you didn't," he said, "you may not have a pulse." A 23-year-old teacher, having seen the film a third time with her sister, said, "That's the kind of love I want for myself. Now that I know it exists, I'm going to wait for exactly the right man."

McKinney Demoted, Reprimanded by Army but Acquitted of Misconduct

FORT BELVOIR, VA., MARCH 16, 1998. A military jury, having acquitted Sergeant Major Gene C. McKinney of 18 counts of sexual misconduct and harassment, today imposed a mild sentence on him for the remaining count of obstruction of justice. Sgt. Maj. McKinney will be reprimanded and demoted one rank, but he will retain his pension. The decision ended a high-profile court-martial in which six servicewomen had accused McKinney of sexual harassment.

Hulda Crooks, Oldest Woman to Scale Mt. Whitney, Dies at 101

LOMA LINDA, CA., NOVEMBER 26, 1997. Hulda Crooks, affectionately nicknamed "Grandma Whitney" for her dozens of climbs up 14,495-foot Mt. Whitney and 12,388-foot Mt. Fuji in Japan, has died at the age of 101. At 82, Crooks set a world record in the Senior Olympics in the 1,500-meter run. She began hiking at the age of 54, after the death of her husband. "It's been a great inspiration for me," she told the *Los Angeles Times*. "When I come down from the mountain, I feel like I can battle in the valley again." Last year, Crooks published her memoir, *Conquering Life's Mountains*.

Hulda Crooks, shown here at age 91 climbing Mt. Fuji, inspired many with her energy and determination.

What attracts so many women and men to the love story in *Titanic?* What are the reasons for the misunderstandings and sometimes outright war between men and women about sex? Why do so many people struggle to lose weight, even taking pills with uncertain risks—and why do so many dieters fail? And what motivates people like Hulda Crooks to scale mountains—literal ones and figurative ones—pursuing their dreams in spite of daunting obstacles?

The word *motivation*, like the word *emotion*, comes from the Latin root meaning "to move," and the psychology of motivation is indeed the study of what moves us, why we do what we do. To psychologists, **motivation** refers to an inferred process within a person or animal, which causes that organism to move toward a goal or away from an unpleasant situation. The goal may be to escape a scorpion or to satisfy a biological need, as in eating a sandwich to reduce hunger. Or the goal may be to fulfill a psychological ambition, such as discovering a vaccine for AIDS or winning a Nobel Prize.

For many decades, the study of motivation was dominated by *drive-reduction theory,* which emphasized biological needs resulting from states of physical deprivation, such as a lack of food or water. Such needs create a physiological *drive,* a state of tension that motivates an organism to satisfy the need—for example by eating or drinking. It soon became apparent, however, that drive-reduction theory could not account for the complexity and variety of human motivations. Human beings have only a few primary, unlearned drives, including the reduction of hunger and thirst, and avoidance of excessive cold and pain.

Today, research on motivation emphasizes the fact that people are conscious creatures who think and plan ahead, set goals for themselves, and plot strategies to reach those goals (Dweck, 1992; Pervin, 1992). Unlike the possum or the porpoise, human beings are motivated by many aspirations that are not tied to biology—such as fame, athletic perfection, or being the first to row across the Atlantic Ocean in a dinghy. These *social motives* are learned, in childhood and later life, and they are called "social" because they develop in the context of family, environment, and culture.

In this chapter, we have chosen four examples to illustrate the cognitive, cultural, and biological components of human motivation: love, sex, eating, and work. As you read, see whether this information helps you understand the appeal of *Titanic*, the accusations against Sgt. Maj. McKinney, the reasons that people seek magic pills to lose weight, and the determination of Hulda Crooks to conquer towering mountains.

The gaze of love is unmistakable, even after years together.

have secure attachments, is a fundamental human motivation (Baumeister & Leary, 1995).

While the need for attachment and companionship is universal, however, the meanings and experiences of love—that most intense of attachments—are more diverse. "How do I love thee? Let me count the ways," wrote Elizabeth Barrett Browning in a love sonnet to Robert Browning. Social scientists have also counted the ways of loving, although not as poetically as Browning did. Let's begin our examination of love by defining our terms.

The Varieties of Love

Do you have a favorite love story? Is it one where the couple falls madly in love at first sight, and, after a couple of silly misunderstandings, lives happily ever after, without a single quarrel or miserable moment? Or is your ideal love story captured by Rhett Butler's concluding remark to Scarlett in *Gone with the Wind*: "Frankly, my dear, I don't give a damn"?

Although most people love to talk about love, they often have very different notions of what they are talking about. Perhaps the oldest distinction is that between *passionate ("romantic") love*, characterized by a turmoil of intense emotions, and *companionate love*, characterized by affection and trust (Hatfield & Rapson, 1996). Passionate love is emotionally intense, *the* focus of one's life, and highly sexualized; it often feels unstable and fragile. Companionate love is calmer, *a* focus of one's life, and not necessarily sexualized; it feels stable and reliable—more like liking. Passionate love is the stuff of crushes, infatuations, "love at first sight," and the early stage of love affairs. It

What's Ahead

- *What kind of lover defines love as jealousy and possessiveness, and what kind defines it as just the opposite—calm compatibility?*

- *Do men and women differ in the ability to love?*

THE SOCIAL ANIMAL: MOTIVES FOR LOVE

Everybody needs somebody. One of the deepest and most universal of human motives is the **need for affiliation,** the need to be with others, make friends, cooperate, love. Human survival depends on the child's ability to form attachments and learn from adults and peers, and on the adult's ability to form relationships with intimate partners, family, friends, and colleagues. The need to belong, to

motivation

An inferred process within a person or animal that causes that organism to move toward a goal or away from an unpleasant situation.

need for affiliation

The motive to associate with other people, as by seeking friends, moral support, companionship, or love.

may burn out completely or subside into companionate love.

But most psychologists who study love (it's a tough job, but someone's got to do it) think that love comes in more varieties than two. Here are three leading theories about what they are:

1. *Styles of loving.* Years ago, after surveying hundreds of people, John Alan Lee (1973, 1988) proposed six distinct styles of loving, which he labeled with Greek names. These styles are *ludus,* game-playing love; *eros,* romantic, passionate love; *storge* (STOR-gay), affectionate, friendly love; *mania,* possessive, dependent, "crazy" love; *pragma,* logical, pragmatic love; and *agape* (ah-GAH-pay), unselfish love.

To measure Lee's six types of love, Clyde and Susan Hendrick designed a Love Attitudes Scale that has been given to thousands of adults in such ethnically and culturally diverse cities as Miami (Hendrick & Hendrick, 1986, 1992, 1997) and Toronto (Dion & Dion, 1993). People who score high on eros believe in true love, instant chemistry, and abiding passion; they would agree, for example, that "My lover and I were attracted to each other immediately after we first met." Those who score high on ludic love like to play the game of love with several partners at once; they enjoy

the chase more than the catch, agreeing that "I try to keep my lover a little uncertain about my commitment to him or her." Those who score high on storge believe that true love grows out of friendship; they value companionship and trust, and agree that "It is hard for me to say exactly when our friendship turned into love." Pragmatic lovers choose partners on the basis of a shopping list of compatible traits; for example, they agree that "I considered what my lover was going to become in life before I committed myself to him or her." People who score high on mania yearn desperately for love but suffer from jealousy and worry when they find it: "When things aren't right with my lover and me," they would agree, "my stomach gets upset." And those who score high on agape think of love as a selfless, almost spiritual form of giving to the partner: They will say, "I always try to help my lover through difficult times."

2. *The attachment theory of love.* Phillip Shaver and Cindy Hazan (1993) maintain that, just like babies, adults can be secure, avoidant, or anxious–ambivalent in their attachments (see Chapter 3). Securely attached lovers aren't jealous or worried about being abandoned. Anxious or ambivalent lovers are always fretting about their relationships; they want to be close but worry that their partners will leave them. Avoidant people distrust and avoid all intimate attachments (Brennan & Shaver, 1995). To use Lee's terms, we might say that pragmatic, storgic, and agapic lovers are likely to be securely attached; manic lovers are anxious and ambivalent; and ludic lovers are avoidant.

According to Shaver and Hazan, people acquire these attachment styles in part from how their parents cared for them (Levy, Blatt, & Shaver, 1998). Securely attached individuals report having had warm, close relationships with their parents, whereas avoidant individuals are most likely to report having had cold, rejecting parents or extended periods of separation from their mothers (Feeney & Noller, 1990; Hazan & Shaver, 1994). (Of course, their recall could be biased by their current feelings toward their parents.)

3. *The triangle theory of love.* Robert Sternberg (1997) has argued that the three ingredients of love are *passion* (butterflies in the stomach, euphoria, sexual excitement), *intimacy* (feeling free to talk about anything, being understanding and patient with the loved one), and *commitment* (needing the other person, being loyal). In his view, varieties of love occur because of the ways people combine the three elements: *liking* is intimacy

Drawing by Cline; © 1988 The New Yorker Magazine, Inc.

"Sorry, Eric, but before I commit to anybody I still need about three years of fun."

A "ludic lover" in action. Do you think that gender differences in this style of love are fading?

alone; *companionate love* is intimacy plus commitment, without passion; *romantic love* is intimacy plus passion, without commitment; *infatuation* is passion alone; *"fatuous"* love is passion plus commitment, without intimacy; and *empty love* is commitment alone, without passion or intimacy. In the language of the other theories, Sternberg's "consummate" or ideal form of love combines erotic-passionate love, companionate feelings of closeness, and secure attachment.

When people are asked to define the key ingredients of love, most do agree that love has elements of passion, intimacy, and commitment (Aron & Westbay, 1996). These features of love are consistent across cultures and sexual orientations (Fehr, 1993).

These three theories differ in key ways (see Table 13.1), but the general overlap among them suggests that they are describing many of the same things (Aron & Westbay, 1996). However, a person's style of love is not necessarily permanent. Many people change their styles of love over time and with new partners. People who are in love for the first time are apt to be especially romantic and idealistic, but by their third love relationship they tend to be more realistic and even a touch cynical (Carducci & McGuire, 1990). The most pragmatic

person can have an "erotic" interlude. The most game-playing ludic lover may become committed to an affectionate relationship. Older couples are far less likely to show signs of mania than younger couples are, suggesting that the desperation and insecurity of mania subside with time and experience (Waller & Shaver, 1994).

Most people choose partners who share their fundamental approach to love; individuals who endorse eros, storge, pragma, or agape are likely to marry others who have the same love style (Waller & Shaver, 1994). There are exceptions, however; in studies of dating or married couples, certain combinations rarely turn up: avoidant–avoidant, anxious–anxious, ludic–ludic, or manic–manic (Hendrick, Hendrick, & Adler, 1988; Kirkpatrick & Davis, 1994; Waller & Shaver, 1994). This is hardly surprising; two people who are busy avoiding one another, or who are equally jealous and possessive, are unlikely to stay together for very long! Further, the stability of a relationship does not always depend on the couple's having the same love style. Avoidant men and anxious women can have remarkably stable, successful relationships if they find secure partners (Kirkpatrick & Davis, 1994; Koski & Shaver, 1997).

Many people believe that critical thinking and love are mutually exclusive: If you are thinking

Table 13.1 — Theories of Love Compared

	The six styles of love	Attachment theory	Triangle theory
Definitions of love	A philosophy or an experience	An expression of the need for attachment that begins in infancy	Passion, intimacy, and commitment, in varying combinations
Types of love	Romantic (eros)	—	Romantic (passion + intimacy)
	Game-playing (ludus)	Avoidant	Infatuation (passion only)
	Possessive (mania)	Anxious–ambivalent	Fatuous (passion + commitment)
	Affectionate (storge)	Secure	Companionate (intimacy + commitment)
	Pragmatic (pragma)	Secure	Empty (commitment only)
	Unselfish (agape)	Secure	Liking (intimacy only)
	—	—	Consummate (passion + intimacy + commitment)

Get Involved

What qualities do you look for in a partner in a close relationship? Write down five qualities that matter most to you— intelligence, looks, sexiness, abilities, background, values, income, whatever. Now examine your list. What does it tell you about your own style of love, according to the theories discussed in the text? (If you have a current partner—and have the nerve—ask the person which five qualities are the important ones to him or her. Do your lists match?)

Thinking Critically About Love

critically about love, you kill the emotion; and if you are in love, you stop thinking altogether! Yet psychologists have found repeatedly that the way we define love, and the love stories we choose to guide our lives, deeply affect our satisfaction with relationships— and even whether relationships last. If you believe that love "just happens," that you have no control over it, that love is defined by sexual passion and hot emotion, then you may decide you are "out of love" when the initial phase of attraction fades, as it eventually must—and you will be repeatedly disappointed. Robert Solomon (1994) argues that "We conceive of [love] falsely—as a feeling, as novelty, as bound up with youth and beauty. . . . We expect an explosion at the beginning powerful enough to fuel love through all of its ups and downs instead of viewing love as a process over which we have control, a process that tends to increase with time rather than wane." Perhaps, then, a little critical thinking about love, far from killing it, can make it a truer and richer experience.

Gender, Culture, and Love

Gender stereotypes tell us that men are more ludic and avoidant than women, and that women are more romantic and anxious than men, but like all stereotypes, these oversimplify. Neither sex loves more than the other in terms of "love at first sight," manic (possessive) love, erotic (passionate) love, selfless love, or companionate love over the long haul (Dion & Dion, 1993; Fehr & Russell, 1991; Hatfield & Rapson, 1996; Hendrick & Hendrick, 1992). Both sexes become equally attached and both suffer when a love relationship ends (assuming they did not want it to).

Yet women and men do differ, on average, in certain respects, most notably in how they *express*

love. As we saw in Chapter 12, males in many cultures learn early that revelations of emotion can be construed as evidence of vulnerability and weakness—and that these are terribly unmasculine qualities. So men often develop ways of expressing love that differ from women's. In contemporary Western society, many women express feelings of love in words, whereas many men express these feelings in actions—doing things for the partner, supporting the family financially, or just sharing the same activity, such as watching TV or a game together (Cancian, 1987; Gilmore, 1990; Tavris, 1992). Similarly, many women tend to define "intimacy" as shared revelations of feelings, but many men define intimacy as being together comfortably. As one young man in a study of male friendship explained, his most intimate experiences with other men consisted of "a lot of outdoor-type things—fishing, hunting, Tom Sawyer–type things" (Swain, 1989).

For many years, Western men were more romantic than women in their choice of partner, and women in turn were far more pragmatic than men. One reason was that a woman didn't just marry a man; she married a standard of living. Therefore she could not afford to marry someone "unsuitable" or waste her time in a relationship that was "not going anywhere," even if she loved him. In contrast, a man could afford to be sentimental in his choice of partner. In the 1960s, two-thirds of a sample of college men said they would not marry someone they did not love, but only one-fourth of the women ruled out the possibility (Kephart, 1967).

As women entered the workforce and as two incomes became necessary in most families, however, the gender difference in romantic love waned, and so did pragmatic reasons for marriage—all over the world. Nowadays, in every developed and developing nation, east and west, only tiny numbers of women and men would consider marrying someone who had all the "right" qualities if they weren't in love with the person. Pragmatic reasons for marriage, with romantic love being a remote luxury, persist only in economically underdeveloped countries, such as India and Pakistan, where the extended family still controls the rules of marriage (Hatfield & Rapson, 1996).

As you can see, our beliefs about love, and the kind of love we feel, are influenced by the culture we live in, the historical era that shapes us, and something as unromantic as economic self-sufficiency. How do these influences affect your own style of love?

??? QUICK QUIZ

Are you feeling passionate about quizzes?

A. Of Lee's six styles of loving, which kind does each of the following examples illustrate?

　1. During the nineteenth century, Jane Welsh and historian Thomas Carlyle enjoy exchanging ideas and confidences for years before realizing they love each other.

　2. In choosing his last four wives, Henry VIII makes sure they are likely to bear children and are of suitably high status for his court.

　3. Romeo and Juliet think only of each other and hate to be separated for even an hour.

　4. Casanova tries to seduce every woman he meets for the thrill of the conquest.

B. Tiffany is wildly in love with Timothy, and he with her, but she can't stop worrying about him and doubting his love. She wants to be with him constantly, but when she feels jealous she pushes him away. According to the attachment theory of love, which style of attachment does Tiffany have? In terms of the six styles of love, which style does she have?

Answers:
A. 1. friendship (storge)   2. pragmatic love (pragma)   3. romantic, passionate love (eros)   4. game-playing love (ludus)
B. anxious–ambivalent; mania

What's Ahead

- *What part of the anatomy do psychologists think is the "sexiest sex organ"?*

- *How do the sexual rules for heterosexual couples foster misunderstandings?*

- *Can psychological theories about "smothering mothering" or "absent fathers" explain why some men become gay?*

THE EROTIC ANIMAL: MOTIVES FOR SEX

Most people believe that sex is a matter of doing what comes naturally, that sex is a biological drive like hunger. In fact, people often use the same words in describing food and sex: "She has a strong sexual appetite," someone will say, or "I'm lusting for a hamburger." But psychologists do not agree on whether human sexuality is a primary drive or even whether it is a drive at all. After all, a person will not live long without food and water, but people can survive their whole lives without sex.

In lower species, sexual behavior is genetically programmed. Without instruction, a male stickleback fish knows exactly what to do with a female stickleback, and a whooping crane knows when to whoop. But as sex researcher Leonore Tiefer (1995) has observed, for human beings "sex is not a natural act." People have to learn from experience and culture what they are supposed to do with their sexual desires. Human sexuality is a blend of biological, psychological, and cultural factors.

Desire and sensuality can be lifelong pleasures.

The Biology of Desire

How much of sexual motivation is influenced by physiology? The answer seems to be—some, although not as much as you may think. Nevertheless, biological researchers have made a major contribution to our understanding of sexual motivation by sweeping away the cobwebs of superstition and ignorance about how the body works. They have disproved the idea that the sexes are physically opposite and have documented the capacity for sexual arousal, orgasm, and pleasure in both sexes.

Hormones, Anatomy, and Sexual Response.

One biological factor that seems to promote sexual desire—in both sexes—is the hormone testosterone (McCauley & Ehrhardt, 1980; Sherwin, 1988). The role of testosterone has been documented in studies of men who have been chemically castrated (given synthetic hormones that suppress the production of testosterone) or who have abnormally low testosterone levels; of women who have taken androgens after having their ovaries removed; and of women who kept diaries of their sexual activity while also having their hormone levels periodically measured. However, hormones don't "cause" sexual behavior in a simple direct way, which is why sex offenders who are chemically castrated do not necessarily lose their sexual desires. And hormones and behavior are a two-way street: Testosterone contributes to sexual arousal, but sexual activity also produces higher levels of testosterone (Zilbergeld, 1992).

Physiological research has dispelled a lot of nonsense written about female sexuality. Freud, for example, claimed that when women reach puberty, their locus of sexual sensation shifts from the "childish" clitoris to the "mature" vagina, and women can then have healthy "vaginal" orgasms instead of immature "clitoral" orgasms. (Freud's theory was at least an improvement on the Victorian notion, still held in some cultures, that normal or "good" women don't have orgasms at all.) Freudian ideas caused countless women to worry that they were mentally disturbed or sexually repressed if they were not having the "correct" kind of orgasm (Ehrenreich, 1978).

The first modern attack on these beliefs came from Alfred Kinsey and his associates (1948, 1953), in their pioneering books on male and female sexuality. In *Sexual Behavior in the Human Female*, they observed that "males would be better prepared to understand females, and females to understand males, if they realized that they are alike in their basic anatomy and physiology." For example, the penis and the clitoris develop from the same embryonic tissues; they differ in size, of course, but not in sensitivity.

The idea that men and women are sexually similar was extremely shocking and progressive in 1953, when many people believed that women were not as sexually motivated as men—that orgasm wasn't as important to them, that female sexuality was more "diffuse," and that women cared far more about affection than about sexual satisfaction. Yet Kinsey also tended to attribute the sex differences he did find, such as in frequency of masturbation and orgasm, primarily to biology—specifically, to women's supposedly lesser sexual capacity. Although he acknowledged throughout his books that women are taught to avoid, dislike, or feel ambivalent about sex, he didn't connect these psychological lessons with women's physiological responses.

Kinsey's survey findings were replicated and expanded in the 1960s in the laboratory research of physician William Masters and his associate Virginia Johnson (1966). In studies of physiological changes during sexual arousal and orgasm, they confirmed that male and female arousal and orgasms are indeed remarkably similar and that all orgasms are physiologically the same, regardless of the source of stimulation. But Masters and Johnson disagreed with Kinsey's assertion that women have a lesser sexual capacity than men. On the contrary, they argued, women's capacity for sexual response "infinitely surpasses that of men" because a woman, unlike most men, is physiologically able to have repeated orgasms until exhaustion or a persistent telephone makes her stop.

Masters and Johnson's work, like Kinsey's, had its limitations (Tiefer, 1995). Perhaps the most serious one was that Masters and Johnson did not do research to learn how sexual response might vary among individuals according to age, experience, and culture. They accepted as research subjects only those volunteers who met their predetermined notions of normalcy—for instance, who were readily orgasmic. But not all women, or even all men, are easily orgasmic, let alone multiply orgasmic. Moreover, people's *subjective* experience of sexual arousal does not always correlate strongly with their *physiological* responses (Irvine, 1990). Nonetheless, Masters and Johnson's findings greatly advanced the understanding of human sexual physiology and response.

The Evolutionary View.

Biological approaches to sexuality have had a boost in recent years from *evolutionary psychologists,* who believe that sex differences in courtship and mating practices evolve in response to a species' survival needs (Buss, 1994). In this view, it is evolutionarily adaptive for males to compete with other males for access to young and fertile females, and to try to win and then inseminate as many females as possible. The more females a male mates with, the more genes he can pass along. (The human record in this regard was achieved by a man who fathered 899 children [Daly & Wilson, 1983].) But females need to shop for the best genetic deal, as it were, because they can conceive and bear only a limited number of offspring. Having such a large biological investment in each pregnancy, they can't afford to make mistakes. Besides, mating with a lot of different men would produce no more offspring than staying with just one. So, in the evolutionary view, females try to attach themselves to dominant males, who have resources and status and are likely to have "superior" genes.

The result of these two opposite sexual strategies is that males generally want sex more often than females do; males are fickle and promiscuous, whereas females are devoted and faithful; males are drawn to sexual novelty and even rape, whereas females want stability and security; males are relatively undiscriminating in their choice of

This Kenyan man has 40 wives and 349 children. Although he is unusual, in societies around the world it is far more common for men to have many wives than for women to have many husbands. Evolutionary psychologists attribute this difference to the evolution of different sexual strategies in males and females.

partners, whereas females are cautious and choosy; and males are competitive and concerned about dominance, whereas females are less so (Buss, 1994; Oliver & Hyde, 1993).

Evolutionary psychologists cite evidence from hundreds of studies, such as one massive project in which 50 scientists studied 10,000 people in 37 cultures located on six continents and five islands (Buss, 1994). Around the world, men are more violent than women, more socially dominant, more interested in the youth and beauty of their sexual partners (presumably because youth is associated with fertility), more sexually jealous and possessive (presumably because males can never be 100 percent sure that their children are really theirs genetically), quicker to have sex with partners they don't know well, and more inclined toward polygamy and promiscuity (presumably so that their sperm will be distributed as widely as possible). Women, in contrast, tend to emphasize the financial resources or prospects of a potential mate, his status, and his willingness to commit to a relationship (Bailey et al., 1994; Buss, 1994, 1996; Buunk et al., 1996; Daly & Wilson, 1983; Sprecher, Sullivan, & Hatfield, 1994).

Critics maintain that the evolutionary view is an after-the-fact explanation of a *stereotype*, and that the actual behavior of human beings and other animals often contradicts the image of the sexually promiscuous male and the coy and choosy female (Hrdy, 1988; Hubbard, 1990). In many species—birds, fish, mammals, and primates, including humans—females are sexually ardent and often have many male partners. In these species the female's sexual behavior does not depend only on the goal of being fertilized by the male because females have sex when they are not ovulating and even when they are already pregnant. And in many primate species, males do not just mate and run; they stick around, feeding the infants, carrying them on their backs, and protecting them against predators (Hrdy, 1988; Taub, 1984).

These findings have sent evolutionary theorists scurrying to figure out the evolutionary benefits of female promiscuity and male nurturance. Perhaps, in some species, females need sperm from several males in order to ensure conception by the healthiest sperm (Baker, 1996). Perhaps, in some species, females mate with numerous males precisely to make paternity uncertain; that way, male partners will be more accepting of the female's infants, who could, after all, be their own (Hrdy, 1988). Or perhaps females have multiple partners in order to increase the number of males who will

A basic assumption of evolutionary approaches to sexuality is that females across species have a greater investment in child rearing than males do. But there are many exceptions. Female emperor penguins, for example, take off every winter, leaving behind males like this one to care for the kids.

provide food for the female's offspring. This motive is explicit among the Barí people of Venezuela. There, the man who inseminates a woman is considered the child's primary father, but any lover she takes during her pregnancy (a fairly common practice) is considered a secondary father—and he has the obligation of supplying the child with extra food (Beckerman et al., 1998).

Critics of evolutionary theories, however, think that this entire approach to explaining male–female differences in sexuality doesn't get us very far (Fausto-Sterling, 1997). The reason is that among human beings, sexual behavior is extremely varied and changeable. Cultures range from those in which women have many children to those in which they have very few; from those in which men are intimately involved in child rearing to those in which they do nothing at all; from those in which women may have many lovers to those in which women may be killed if they have sex outside of marriage. Even within a culture, sexual attitudes and practices vary tremendously (Laumann et al., 1994). Such variations, say the critics, argue against a universal, genetically determined sexual strategy.

The Psychology of Desire

Sexual arousal and orgasm may seem to be simple matters of sexual anatomy and response, but researchers have shown repeatedly that the sexiest sex organ is actually the brain, where perceptions begin. People's thoughts, expectations, fantasies, and beliefs profoundly affect sexual desire and responsiveness. This is why a touch on the knee by an exciting new date feels terrifically sexy, but the same touch by a creepy stranger on a bus feels disgusting.

Psychologists and sex therapists have shown, for example, how distracting thoughts can interfere with sexual arousal and pleasure. Most men know what it feels like to lose an erection, and women to lose an imminent orgasm, when their partner says something to break the mood or when a distracting thought or worry crosses their minds. And people who are "thinking too much" during sex play—for example, who are worrying about how they look or whether they are doing the wrong thing—may have difficulty letting go and yielding to sexual sensations (Zilbergeld, 1992).

Surprisingly, people's perceptions and beliefs may also lead them to misinterpret their own physical arousal—which can be caused by many things other than sexual desire. For example, vaginal lubrication is not always a sign of arousal; it is sometimes a response to nervousness, excitement, disgust, or fear. Similarly, a man's erection is not always due to sexual stimulation; a man can also have an erection as a response to fear, anger, exercise, or waking up. If you are thinking critically, you might see the important implications of this information for relationships. For instance, if a man learns to interpret arousal that is actually due to anger as evidence of sexual desire, he may associate sexuality with aggression. And if a woman is embarrassed to acknowledge that she is sexually aroused because she thinks such a revelation will mark her as a bad woman, she may learn to interpret such arousal as love. She may regard her physical reactions as evidence that she was "swept away" by passion only because of her love for her partner (Cassell, 1984).

Thoughts and perceptions also influence sexual motivations. For most people, the primary psychological motives for sex are to express love and intimacy, to feel desirable, and to feel erotic pleasure. And, of course, many people make love for the old-fashioned motive of having children! However, without wishing to discount the many happy motives for sex, psychologists have identified some negative ones as well: to exact revenge on a previous partner, get money or other benefits, dominate the other person, or fulfill a perceived obligation.

On college campuses, large numbers of women *and* men say they have had sex, even when they didn't want to, because of psychological pressures. The percentages vary from school to school but are consistently high; in a typical survey, about half of the women say they have been pressured into kissing, fondling, oral sex, and intercourse (Strong & DeVault, 1994). For their part, many men feel obliged to "make a move" despite a lack of desire. In one survey of 993 college students, fully 63 percent of the men reported having had unwanted intercourse (Muehlenhard & Cook, 1988). The main reasons for doing so, the men said, were peer pressure, inexperience, a desire for popularity, and a fear of seeming homosexual or "unmasculine." Women, too, said they "gave in" for various motives: because it was easier than having an argument; because they didn't want to lose the relationship; because they felt obligated once the partner had spent time and money on them; or because the partner made them feel guilty or inhibited.

The two sexes differ, then, in the reasons they give for having unwanted sex. But nowhere do they differ more dramatically than in their perceptions of outright sexual coercion. In 1994, a research team published the results of a nationally representative survey of more than 3,000 Americans ages 18 to 59 (Laumann et al., 1994). In this survey, 22.8 percent of the women said that men had forced them to do something sexually that they did not want to do. Moreover, these men were usually boyfriends or husbands, not strangers. But only 2.8 percent of the men said they had ever forced a woman into a sexual act. Obviously, what many women regard as coercion is not always seen as such by men.

The most extreme form of sexual coercion, of course, is rape. Although the public image of the rapist tends to be one of a menacing stranger, in most cases the rapist is known to the victim. They may have dated once or a few times; they may have been friends for years; they may even be married (Koss et al., 1988; Russell, 1990). Accord-

In a famous episode from *Gone with the Wind* (left), Rhett Butler (Clark Gable) forcibly carries a protesting Scarlett O'Hara (Vivien Leigh) to bed; she awakes the next morning with a smile on her face. Scenes such as this one, in film and on TV, convey the false impression that women want to be forced into sex. To help counteract this message, men at one college fraternity created an antirape poster of *The Rape of the Sabine Women* (right) and distributed it to other fraternity houses around the country.

ing to a study of a representative sample of 4,008 women in the United States, at least 12 million American women have been the victims of forcible rape at least once in their lives, most before the age of 18. Only 22 percent were assaulted by strangers (National Victim Center, 1992). The survey did not include children or adult men, so the actual number of people who have been raped is even higher.

What motivates some men to rape? In a study of 71 college men who admitted to having physically coerced their dates into having sex with them, these young men had, from early adolescence, been pressured by male friends to "prove their masculinity" by "scoring" (Kanin, 1985). Rape is not only a matter of crossed signals or sexual desire; by its very nature, it implies hostility and a devaluing of the victim. Neil Malamuth and his colleagues (1991, 1995), surveying nearly 3,000 male college students in the 1980s and again 10 years later, found that sexually aggressive males are characterized by a cluster of traits they call *hostile masculinity* (being insecure, defensive, and hostile toward women, and wishing to dominate

women) and by a preference for promiscuous, impersonal sex. Convicted rapists have similarly hostile motives: anger at women or the world, the expression of power, contempt for women, a desire to act out a sexual fantasy, and sometimes sexual sadism (Knight, Prentky, & Cerce, 1994).

The argument that rape is primarily an act of dominance and aggression is also supported by the widespread evidence of soldiers who rape (and often kill) captive women during war and by studies of male victims: Men can be and are raped, usually by anal penetration committed by other men. This form of rape typically occurs in youth gangs, where the intention is to humiliate rival gang members, and in prison, where again the motive is to conquer and degrade the victim (Strong & DeVault, 1994).

Perhaps you can begin to see that the answer to the question "Why do people have sex?" is not obvious after all. In addition to pleasure, passion, procreation, and love, the psychological motives involved can include intimidation, insecurity, and the desire to prove oneself a real man or a desirable woman.

The Culture of Desire

Think about kissing. Westerners like to think about kissing, and to do it, too. But if you think kissing is "natural," try to remember your first serious kiss—and all you had to learn about noses, breathing, and position of teeth and tongue. The sexual kiss is so complicated that some cultures have never even gotten around to it. They think that kissing another person's mouth—the very place that food enters!—is disgusting (Tiefer, 1995). Others have elevated the sexual kiss to high art; why do you suppose one version is called "French" kissing?

Cultural Variations in Sexuality.   As the kiss illustrates, having the physical equipment to perform a sexual act is not all there is to sexual motivation. People acquire their notions of proper sexual behavior from cultural norms and parental lessons (Lottes & Kuriloff, 1994). They learn what is supposed to "turn them on" (and off), what parts of the body and what activities are erotic (or repulsive), and even how to have sexual relations. The range of cultural variations in sexual motivation and response is remarkable:

• Cultures differ in what parts of the body and what style of clothing, if any, are erotic. To men of the Victorian era, the sight of a woman's ankle, let alone an entire leg, was highly arousing; to men of the modern era, an ankle doesn't do it.

• Cultures differ in the sexual acts and sexual positions that are erotic or repulsive. In some, for example, oral sex is regarded as a bizarre sexual deviation; in others, oral sex is considered not only normal but also supremely desirable.

• Cultures differ in whether sex is seen as something joyful and beautiful, an art to be cultivated as one might cultivate the art of cooking or dancing; or as something ugly and dirty, something to "get through" as quickly as possible. These diverse attitudes can occur in the same culture at different times. For example, in ancient China, sexual pleasure was considered one of life's great joys, and a text on sexuality dating back to 168 B.C. reveals that the Chinese had sophisticated knowledge about the sexual response and pleasure of both sexes. But until recently, modern China fostered sexual ignorance and a repressive view of sexuality; surveys suggest that only a minority of Chinese women feel pleasure during intercourse (Hatfield & Rapson, 1996).

Sexual Scripts.   How do cultures transmit their rules and requirements about sex to their members? During childhood and adolescence, people learn their culture's *gender roles*—collections of rules that determine the proper attitudes and behavior for men and women, sexual and otherwise (see Chapter 9). Just as an actor in the role of Hamlet needs a script to learn his part, a person following a gender role needs a *sexual script* that teaches men and women how to behave in sexual matters (Gagnon & Simon, 1973; Laumann et al., 1994). Are women, for example, supposed to be sexually adventurous and assertive or sexually modest and passive? The answers differ from culture to culture, as members act in accordance with the sexual scripts for their gender and age.

In many parts of North America, for example, boys acquire their attitudes about sex in a competitive atmosphere where the goal is to impress other males, talking and joking about masturbation and other sexual experiences with their friends. While boys are learning to value physical sex, however, girls are learning to value relationships and to make themselves attractive. They learn that their role is to be sexually desirable (which is "good"), but not to indulge in their own sexual pleasures (which would be "bad"). As one psychologist, summarizing the different sexual scripts that boys and girls learn, put it: "'Nice women' don't say yes and 'real men' don't say no" (Muehlenhard, 1988). (Is this the script your own culture has written for you? If not, what are your culture's sexual rules? Are they changing?)

In the United States and Canada, the sexual scripts for heterosexual couples are almost guar-

Kissing is a learned skill—and some people start practicing sooner than others.

anteed to create conflicting motives for sexuality and misreadings of one another's behavior. For example, what is a sexual signal? How do you know whether a person is conveying sexual interest in you? Men and women often answer these questions differently: A woman's intent might be to look attractive, but a man may interpret her dress and demeanor as indicating sexual interest. In a study of 400 teenagers ages 14 to 17, boys generally thought that almost everything was a sexual signal! They were more likely to regard tight clothing, certain situations (such as being alone in a room), and affectionate actions (such as a girl's playing with her date's hair or gazing into his eyes) as signs of willingness for sex. The girls were more likely to regard tight clothing as a sign of being fashionable, and being alone with a date or behaving affectionately as signs of—well, affection (Zellman & Goodchilds, 1983).

Is she dressed provocatively or just comfortably? Boys and girls often disagree on the answer.

Gay men and lesbians follow sexual scripts, too. In terms of number of sexual partners, sexual behavior, and acceptance of casual sex, gay men are generally similar to heterosexual men, and lesbians are similar to heterosexual women. But gay men and lesbians tend to be more innovative than heterosexuals in establishing rules for their relationships (Peplau, 1991; Rose, Zand, & Cini, 1993). A review of lesbian romance novels, "how-to" books on dating and relationships, first-person accounts, and empirical research found that emotional intimacy, rather than physical attraction or sexuality, is the basis for many lesbian courtship scripts. These scripts are more open and flexible than heterosexual dating and sexual scripts because neither partner is clearly the pursuer or the pursued or the one who makes the sexual overtures (Rose, Zand, & Cini, 1993).

The Origins of Sexual Attitudes. Finally, where do sexual scripts and gender differences in sexuality come from? In the view of many social and cultural psychologists, the answer has to do with a culture's economic and social arrangements. Historically, for example, when women have needed to find and keep a relationship in order to have financial security, they have tended to regard sex as a bargaining chip—an asset to be rationed, rather than an activity to be enjoyed for its own sake (Cassell, 1984). Women cannot afford to seek and enjoy sex when such behavior means they may get pregnant when they don't want to, or lose the economic security of marriage, their reputations in society, or their physical safety. When women become self-supporting and able to control their own fertility, however, they are more likely to want sex for pleasure rather than as a means to another goal.

In fact, all over the world, as the processes of industrialization and modernization are transforming gender roles, the sexual behavior of women and men is becoming more alike (Laumann et al., 1994). Although this transformation is slow and uneven, and although change always brings protest and confusion in its wake, social scientists have documented a growing endorsement, worldwide, of birth control, premarital sex, sexual freedom in general, and the entitlement of both sexes to love and sexual pleasure (Hatfield & Rapson, 1996).

The Riddle of Sexual Orientation

Why do some people become heterosexual, others homosexual, and still others bisexual? You could not even have asked this question until a century ago. Although same-sex sexual behavior has existed throughout history, the words *homosexual* and *heterosexual* were not invented until the mid-nineteenth century (Katz, 1995). Only then did homosexuality become a "problem" to be studied, an entity distinct from heterosexuality.

Many researchers today are persuaded that sexual orientation is primarily determined by genetics and other biological factors (Bailey & Pillard, 1995; Gladue, 1994). Women with a history of prenatal exposure to high levels of androgen, caused in some cases by a genetic variation, are more likely than others to become bisexual or lesbian (Collaer & Hines, 1995), and so are women with a history of prenatal exposure to synthetic estrogen (Meyer-Bahlburg et al., 1995). Simon LeVay (1991) made national headlines when he announced that he had found a difference in specific brain structures of homosexual and heterosexual men (see also Allen & Gorski, 1992). Others have reported that sexual orientation is moderately heritable both in men and in women (Bailey & Pillard, 1995; Hershberger, Lykken, & McGue, 1995; Whitam, Diamond, & Martin, 1993). And Dean Hamer and his team (1993) caused a stir when they reported a genetic linkage study that found a shared stretch of DNA on the X chromosome in 33 of 40 pairs of gay brothers—a rate significantly above what one would expect in siblings by chance. Two years later, another study by the same group got similar results (Hu et al., 1995).

These findings are especially compelling because exclusively *psychological* theories of homosexuality have never been supported. Homosexuality is unrelated to "smothering mothers," absent fathers, psychopathology, or parental practices and role models (Bailey et al., 1995; Bell, Weinberg, & Hammersmith, 1981; Patterson, 1992).

Other researchers are skeptical of biological explanations for two major reasons. One is that sexual identity and behavior take so many different forms

Many heterosexual people think that all gay men and lesbians live unconventional, flamboyant lives. In reality, as much diversity exists among gays as among straights, and just about everyone, regardless of sexual orientation, seeks the satisfactions of love and companionship.

that no single cause is likely ever to be found (Baumrind, 1995; Byne & Parsons, 1993; Kitzinger & Wilkinson, 1995). Many people are neither exclusively homosexual nor heterosexual, for instance, and their behavior is often at odds with their fantasies. If someone is heterosexual in behavior but has homosexual fantasies, what genetic mechanism explains that? And how can genetics explain the flexible and unpredictable sexual histories of many lesbians (Kitzinger & Wilkinson, 1995)?

Second, critics argue that the existing biological research has too many serious limitations to warrant any firm conclusions. For example, Dean Hamer's genetics study (Hamer et al., 1993) was based on a sample of gay brothers, but the vast majority of gay men and lesbians do *not* have a close gay relative. Likewise, the majority of women with histories of abnormal prenatal exposures to androgens or estrogen do *not* become homosexual. And a key problem in LeVay's study was that all of the gay men in his sample had died of AIDS. AIDS itself, and also some of the medicines given for the disease, create endocrine abnormalities that can affect brain structures. The differences LeVay observed, therefore, might have been a result of AIDS, rather than a cause of sexual orientation (Byne, 1993).

At present, the most reasonable conclusions may be that (1) sexual identity and behavior involve an interaction of biology, culture, and experiences; and (2) the route to sexual identity for one person may not be the same as for another (Gladue, 1994; Patterson, 1995). As Hamer himself told the *New York Times* (July 16, 1993), "Sexual orientation is too complex to be determined by a single gene. The main value of this work is that it opens a window into understanding how genes, the brain and the environment interact to mold human behavior."

What is your response to these findings? Your reactions are probably affected by your feelings about homosexuality and gay rights. Many gay men and lesbians welcome biological research on the grounds that it supports what they have been saying all along: Sexual orientation is not a matter of choice, but a fact of nature. Yet people who are prejudiced against homosexuals have used the same research as evidence that gay people have a biological "defect" that should be eradicated or "cured." Other gay men and lesbians strongly oppose biological arguments because of their potential for misuse. But many antigay people also oppose biological arguments because they want to believe, despite evidence to the contrary, that homosexuality is a "preference" or "choice" that can and should be "unchosen."

Whatever research eventually reveals, however, critically examining our biases and assumptions shows that the *scientific* question of the origins of sexual orientation is logically unrelated to *political and moral* questions of the rights of gay men and lesbians (Strickland, 1995). In a democracy, civil rights do not depend on whether one's beliefs or practices are a matter of choice, nor do they depend on how popular those beliefs are. A person's religion is not biologically inherited, yet America and Canada guarantee freedom of religion to everyone—whether your religion is shared by 75 percent of the population or 2 percent. Research on sexuality can be used for many contradictory purposes and political goals, depending on the values and attitudes of the popular culture in which such findings emerge. As long as a society is uncomfortable about homosexuality, preconceptions and prejudice are likely to cloud its reactions to anything that psychologists learn about it.

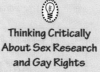

Thinking Critically About Sex Research and Gay Rights

??? QUICK QUIZ

Were you motivated to learn about sexual motivation?

1. Which of the following behaviors would an evolutionary psychologist expect to be more typical of males than of females? (a) promiscuity, (b) choosiness about sexual partners, (c) concern with dominance, (d) interest in young partners, (e) emphasis on physical attractiveness of partners.

2. Biological research finds that (a) male and female sexual responses are physiologically very different, (b) vaginal orgasms are healthier than clitoral ones, (c) testosterone promotes sexual desire in both sexes, (d) all women have multiple orgasms.

3. Research on the motives of rapists finds that rape is usually (a) a result of thwarted sexual desire, (b) the result of hostility or a need for power, (c) a matter of crossed signals.

4. *True or false:* Exclusively psychological theories of the origins of homosexuality have never been supported.

Answers:
1. all but b   2. c   3. b   4. true

What's Ahead

- *Why can some thin people eat anything they want without gaining weight, whereas some heavy people can diet without losing weight?*

- *What disorders can occur when the psychological need to be thin collides with the body's need to store some fat?*

THE HUNGRY ANIMAL: MOTIVES TO EAT

Do you ever eat when you're not hungry—say, to be sociable? Do you ever not eat when you *are* hungry—say, to lose weight or to be polite? You might think that being hungry and eating have a nice, logical connection between them; yet, as we are about to see, the connection is not so obvious.

The Genetics of Weight

At one time, most psychologists thought that being fat was a sign of emotional disturbance. If you were overweight, it was because you hated your mother, feared intimacy, or were trying to fill an emotional hole in your psyche by loading up on rich desserts. The evidence for this belief, however, came mainly from self-reports, and many studies were seriously flawed: They lacked control groups, and they overlooked the possibility that people were saying what they thought researchers wanted to hear (Allison & Heshka, 1993). When researchers put this popular idea to the test, they found no support for it. On average, they discovered, fat people are no more and no less emotionally disturbed than average-weight people (Stunkard, 1980).

Even more surprising, *heaviness is not always caused by overeating* (C. Bouchard et al., 1990).

Many heavy people do eat enormous quantities of food, but so do some very thin people. Many thin people eat very little, but so do some obese people. In one study that carefully monitored everything that subjects were eating, two 260-pound women maintained their weights while consuming only 1,000 calories a day (Wooley, Wooley, & Dyrenforth, 1979). In another study, in which volunteers were required to gorge themselves for months, it was as hard for slender people to gain weight as it is for most heavy people to lose weight. The minute the study was over, the slender people lost weight as fast as dieters gained it back (Sims, 1974).

One theory that integrates such findings holds that a biological mechanism keeps a person's body weight at a genetically influenced **set point**—the weight the person stays at when not consciously trying to gain or lose (Lissner et al., 1991). According to this theory, everyone has a genetically programmed *basal metabolism rate*, the rate at which the body burns calories for energy, and a fixed number of *fat cells*, which store fat for energy. The fat cells can change in size but not in number. A complex interaction of metabolism, fat cells, and hormones keeps people at the weight their bodies are designed to be. When a heavy person diets, the body's metabolism slows down to conserve energy (and fat reserves). When a thin person overeats, metabolism speeds up, burning energy. Set-point theory, which has been supported by dozens of studies of animals and human beings, explains why most people who go on restricted diets eventually gain their weight back: They are returning to their set-point weight (Leibel, Rosenbaum, & Hirsch, 1995; Levitan & Ronan, 1988).

In twin and adoption studies, estimates of the heritability of body weight and shape range from 25 percent to 80 percent (Allison et al., 1994; C. Bouchard et al., 1990; Stunkard et al., 1990). It seems clear, therefore, that genes do contribute to

set point

The genetically influenced weight range for an individual, thought to be maintained by a biological mechanism that regulates food intake, fat reserves, and metabolism.

size and weight differences among people. Consider some further evidence:

• In a study of 171 Pima Indians in Arizona, researchers found that two-thirds of the women and half of the men became obese over time, and the slower their metabolisms, the greater the weight gain. After adding anywhere from 20 to 45 pounds, however, the Pimas stopped gaining weight. Their metabolism rates rose, and their weights stabilized at the new, higher level (Ravussin et al., 1988). Many Pimas apparently have a set point for plumpness.

• In a study of 18 infants at 3 months of age, the babies of overweight mothers generated 21 percent less energy than the babies of normal-weight mothers, although the babies were all eating the same amount. By the age of 1 year, these lower-metabolism babies had become overweight (Roberts et al., 1988).

• Genes also affect whether the body will convert excess calories into fat or muscle, and what the basic body *shape* will be (pear, apple, hourglass, tree trunk, and so on). Pairs of adult identical twins who have been raised in different families are just as similar in body weight and shape as twins raised together. The early family environment has almost no effect at all on body shape, weight gain, or percentage of fat in the body (Stunkard et al., 1990).

In a study of 12 pairs of adult male identical twins, Claude Bouchard and his colleagues (1990) confined the men to a dormitory for 100 days, where they were forbidden to exercise and were given a diet that contained 1,000 extra calories a day. In pairs of twins, both members gained almost exactly the same amount of weight, but the differences *between* twin pairs was astonishing. One pair of twins gained 9½ pounds, but another pair gained almost 30—even though everyone was eating the same number of extra calories. Some twins gained weight on their hips and thighs; others gained weight around the waist.

Enormous progress has been made in identifying the genes involved in some types of obesity. One team of researchers isolated a genetic variation in mice that causes animals with the variation to become obese (Zhang et al., 1994). The usual form of the gene, called "obese," or *ob* for short, causes fat cells to secrete a hormonelike protein, which the researchers named *leptin* (from the Greek *leptos,* "slender"). Leptin travels through the blood to an area in the hypothalamus, the brain structure that regulates appetite. Levels of this substance signal how large or small the body's fat cells are, so that the brain can adjust appetite and metabolism to maintain the animal's or person's set point. Injecting leptin into mice reduces the

Body weight and shape are strongly affected by genetic factors. Set-point theory helps explain why the Pimas of the American Southwest (above) gain weight easily but lose it slowly, whereas the Bororo nomads of Nigeria (right) can eat a lot of food yet remain slender.

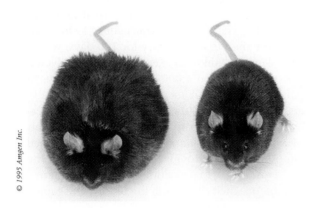

Both of these mice have a mutation in the *ob* gene, which normally directs the synthesis of leptin, a substance that helps regulate appetite and metabolism. The mutation usually makes mice chubby, like the one on the left. But when leptin is injected daily, the mice remain almost normal in weight, like the one on the right, because they eat less and burn more calories.

© 1995 Amgen Inc.

animals' appetites, speeds up their metabolisms, and makes them more active; as a result, the animals shed weight, even if they were not overweight to begin with (Halaas et al., 1995).

The role of leptin in human obesity, though, is more complicated than it is in mice. (We are tempted to say "rats" to this news!) Some obese people may gain weight rapidly because they have the variant form of the *ob* gene and their leptin levels are low (Ravussin et al., 1997). Other obese people, however, have very *high* leptin levels. They produce plenty of leptin, but they are insensitive to it, probably because of a gene that prevents cells in the brain from responding normally to leptin's signals (Chua et al., 1996; Considine et al., 1996; Maffei et al., 1995). As a result, they stay hungry and continue eating even when the body has enough stored fat to meet current energy demands. Other genes and body chemicals, too, are involved in appetite and weight regulation. Genes that predispose individuals to obesity probably exist in our species because, in the past, starvation was all too often a real possibility, so a tendency to store calories in the form of fat provided a definite survival advantage.

Culture, Psychology, and Weight

Hunger may be a primary drive, and eating the way to reduce hunger, but, as with sex, physiology is just the start of the story. For example, when do you eat? Depending on your culture, you might eat lots of little meals throughout the day or only one large meal at noon—or at midnight. What do you eat? People eat what their environment provides: whale meat in Inuit communities, lizards in South America, locusts in Africa, horses in France, dogs in Asia. And they don't eat food their culture calls taboo: pork among Muslims and orthodox Jews, beef in India, horse meat in America (Harris, 1985). With whom do you eat? People tend to eat with those of their own social status or higher. They do not eat with those they regard as their social inferiors, who in various times and places have included servants, children, and women.

Cultures also influence people's notions of what the ideal body should look like—fat, thin, muscular, plump, or gaunt. In many places around the world, such as Tonga, fat is a sign of affluence (in men), sexual desirability (in women), and health (in both). As we saw in Chapter 9, African-Americans and Mexican-Americans are more accepting of fat people and less concerned about their own weight than are white Americans. For many North American whites, fat is a sign of slothfulness, gluttony, and weakness of will, reflecting a cultural ideology that individuals are responsible for what happens to them and for how they look (Crandall & Martinez, 1996).

In recent decades, the cultural ideal for body size in the United States, Canada, and Europe has been getting decidedly thinner, especially for women. Brett Silverstein and his colleagues documented the changing female ideal by computing a bust-to-waist ratio of the measurements of models in women's magazines (Silverstein, Peterson, & Perdue, 1986). The ideal body type became thin, as opposed to voluptuously curvy, twice in this century: first in the mid-1920s and again from the mid-1960s to the present. Some of today's most sought-after fashion models look like they're starving to death—and perhaps they are.

Now, why did these changes occur? Silverstein found that men and women associate the curvy, big-breasted female body with femininity, nurturance, and motherhood. Hence big breasts are fashionable in eras that celebrate women's role as mothers—such as after World War II, when women were encouraged to return home and have many children. But people also, alas, associate femininity and nurturance with incompetence. Thus, in every era in which women have entered traditionally male spheres of education and work, as in the 1920s "flapper" era and again today, ambitious women have tried to look boyishly thin and muscular in order to avoid appearing "feminine" and dumb. Lately, a physically impossible female ideal has appeared, possibly reflecting national ambivalence about whether women's proper role is domestic or professional: big-breasted but narrow-hipped.

The women most likely to be obsessed about achieving a boyishly thin body shape, Silverstein hypothesized, should be those who value achievement, higher education, and careers, especially male-dominated careers. Being thin allows such women to identify with male competence and to distance themselves from the negative associations with "femininity." And that is just what his research finds. College women who develop eating disorders are also more likely than other women to say that their parents believe a woman's place is in the home, that their mothers are unhappy with their lives, that their fathers think their mothers are unintelligent, and that their fathers treat sons as being more intelligent than daughters (Silverstein & Perlick, 1995).

These women, therefore, face a dilemma. Evolution has programmed them for a reserve of fat necessary for the onset of menstruation, healthy childbearing, nursing, and, after menopause, for production and storage of the hormone estrogen. But North American culture tells them they must be thin at all costs. The result of the battle between biological design and cultural norms is that many women today—as in the 1920s—are obsessed with weight and continually dieting.

Sometimes, the obsession goes dangerously far. When cultural pressures to be thin combine with individual psychological needs and perhaps genetic vulnerabilities, eating disorders may result (Holmes, 1997). The two most common ones are *bulimia,* in which the sufferer binges (eating vast quantities of rich food) and then purges by vomiting or using laxatives, and *anorexia nervosa,* in which the sufferer stops eating almost completely because of a delusional belief that she or he is "too fat." These eating disorders are at least ten times more common in women than in men, and they typically begin in late adolescence—as girls' bodies are maturing and conflicts about adult sexuality are emerging (Holmes, 1997). Women who develop eating disorders are also more self-critical than healthy eaters, and they are more likely to use food to soothe hurt feelings and low self-esteem (Lehman & Rodin, 1989). Some anorexics have a single episode and recover completely; some have recurring episodes alternating with periods of normal eating; and some, tragically, die of self-imposed starvation.

The sad revelation in 1992 that Princess Diana suffered from bulimia showed that even women of great beauty, wealth, and power are not immune to cultural pressures to be thin; and even they are vulnerable to the insecurities that can lead to an eating disorder.

Dilemmas of Dieting

The discovery of genetic influences on body weight and shape may help to combat prejudice toward obese individuals—and persuade normal-weight people to accept their bodies. But obesity is a medical concern because it is associated with a higher risk of heart disease, hypertension, diabetes, some cancers, and other diseases. Should seriously overweight people try to fight their set points or should they instead fight society's prejudices? Does the genetic research mean that trying to lose weight is hopeless?

Researchers themselves are divided on these questions. Some believe that dieting is unhealthy and may even contribute to medical problems and eating disorders (Garner & Wooley, 1991). Others conclude that weight loss can help reduce the health risks associated with overweight; even modest losses have medical benefits, such as lowered blood pressure and reduced risk of diabetes

(Brownell & Rodin, 1994). However, all the experts warn against fad diets—in which the dieter is restricted to only a few special foods or put on starvation rations—and *"yo-yo" dieting*—in which people diet and gain it back, diet and gain it back, repeatedly. Yo-yo dieting produces a higher-than-normal risk of cardiovascular disease, hypertension, and other chronic diseases (Brownell & Rodin, 1994; Ernsberger & Nelson, 1988; Lissner et al., 1991).

The behavioral-genetics and cultural research on obesity shows again the danger of either–or thinking. Genes set limits for body weight and

Thinking Critically About Dieting and Weight

shape, but psychological and cultural factors affect weight within that range. One such factor is eating habits. If you consume the high-fat junk-food diet that so many North Americans love (indeed, that human beings might be evolutionarily primed to love), and if you eat such food in the large quantities that most Europeans and Asians find excessive and alarming, you are likely to be heavier than if you eat a low-fat diet in moderate portions. It may not be only a matter of calories: A high-fat diet may actually change an individual's set point for body weight by increasing the body's resistance to leptin (Frederich et al., 1995). As one physician wrote to the *New York Times,* "Perhaps

the flaw lies not so much in our mutations as in McDonald's."

A second factor is exercise, which boosts the body's metabolic rate and may lower its set point. In one study of 18 obese women who were on severely restricted diets, metabolism rates dropped sharply, as set-point theory would predict. But the women who combined the diet with moderate physical activity—daily walking—lost weight, and their metabolic rates rose almost to previous levels (Wadden et al., 1990). This study suggests why changes in weight often accompany major changes in habits and activity levels. People start walking to work (or stop). They become lethargic after losing a job (and gain weight), or excited when they fall in love (and lose weight). One likely contribution to the rising rates of obesity in America is the corresponding rise in energy-saving (fat-conserving!) devices, the popularity of television over active hobbies, and "couch-potato" lifestyles (Brownell & Rodin, 1994).

And yet, even if you make daily trips to the gym and eat a healthy diet, you may never look like the current cultural ideal, which is physically impossible for many people. That's why it is so important to think carefully and critically about the reasons that you are dieting. Are you really overweight? Whose standards are you following, and why?

??? QUICK QUIZ

Is all this information about food making you hungry for knowledge?

1. According to _____ theory, when a thin person overeats, her or his metabolism tends to increase, whereas when a heavy person diets, his or her metabolism tends to slow down.

2. Twin studies indicate that genes contribute not only to differences in weight but also to differences in body _____.

3. Which of the following factors most strongly affect body weight within the set point's range? (a) dieting, (b) the amount of fat in the diet, (c) exercise, (d) nothing can affect the set point.

 4. Bill, who is thin, reads in the paper that genes set the range of body weight and shape. "Oh, good," he exclaims, "now I can eat all the junk food I want; I was born to be skinny." What's wrong with Bill's conclusion?

Answers:
1. set-point 2. shape 3. b, c 4. Bill is right to recognize that there may be limits to how heavy he can become. But he may also be oversimplifying and jumping to conclusions. Even thin people who have a set point for leanness will gain some weight on fatty foods and excess calories, especially if they don't exercise; also, rich junk food is unhealthy for reasons that have nothing to do with overweight.

What's Ahead

- Why is "doing your best" an ineffective goal to set for yourself?
- When you're learning a new skill, should you concentrate on mastering it or on performing it well in front of others?
- What kind of power motivation distinguishes poor leaders from highly effective ones?

THE COMPETENT ANIMAL: MOTIVES TO WORK

Almost every adult works. Most people spend more time at work than they do at play or with their families. "Work" does not mean only paid employment. Students work at studying. Homemakers work, often more hours than salaried employees, at running a household. Artists, poets, and actors work, even if they are paid erratically. What keeps everybody doing it? The obvious answer, of course, is the need for food and shelter. Yet survival does not explain what motivates LeRoy to work for caviar on his table and Duane to work for peanut butter on his. It doesn't explain why some people want to do their work well and others want just to get it done. It doesn't explain the difference between Aristotle's view ("All paid employments absorb and degrade the mind") and Noël Coward's ("Work is more fun than fun").

Psychologists, particularly those in the field of *industrial/organizational psychology*, have studied work motivation in the laboratory, where they have measured internal motives such as the desire for achievement, and in organizations, where they study the conditions that influence productivity and satisfaction.

The Effects of Motivation on Work

Several independent forces keep you working: your expectation of success, the goals you set for yourself, your need to achieve, opportunities in the environment, and the nature of your work. These factors apply to any form of achievement, from running a household to running a marathon.

Expectations and Values. How hard you work for something depends partly on what you expect to accomplish. If you are fairly certain of success, you will work much harder to reach your goal than if you are fairly certain of failure.

A classic experiment showed how quickly experience affects these expectations. Young women were asked to solve 15 anagram puzzles. Before working on each one, they had to estimate their chances of solving it. Half of the women started off with very easy anagrams, but half began with insoluble ones. Sure enough, those who started with the easy ones increased their estimates of success on later ones. Those who began with the impossible ones decided they would all be impossible. These expectations, in turn, affected the young women's ability to actually solve the last 10 anagrams, which were the same for everyone. The higher the expectation of success, the more anagrams the women solved (Feather, 1966).

Once acquired, therefore, expectations can create a **self-fulfilling prophecy,** in which a person predicts how he or she will do and then behaves in such a way as to make the prediction come true (Jones, 1977; Maddux, 1995). You expect to do well, so you study hard, and then you do well. You expect to fail, so you don't do much work, and then you do poorly. In either case, you have fulfilled your expectation of yourself.

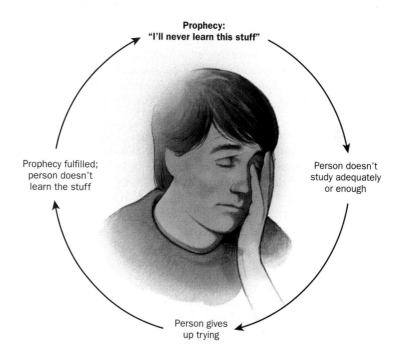

Prophecy: "I'll never learn this stuff"

Person doesn't study adequately or enough

Person gives up trying

Prophecy fulfilled; person doesn't learn the stuff

How hard you work for something, of course, also depends on how much you want it, which in turn depends on your general value system (Feather, 1982). A *value* is a central motivating belief, reflecting a person's fundamental goals and

self-fulfilling prophecy
An expectation that comes true because of the tendency of the person holding it to act in ways that confirm it.

Get Involved

Rank the following values in terms of their importance to you, with 1 the most important and 18 the least, being as honest as you can. Then ask some friends and relatives to do the same. How does your ranking differ from theirs? Do your values affect your goals, relationships, level of community activism, or decisions? Do any of your key values conflict with your daily actions—and if so, does that conflict motivate you to change in any way? (From Rokeach and Ball-Rokeach, 1989.)

_____ A world at peace   _____ Accomplishment

_____ Family security   _____ True friendship

_____ Freedom   _____ National security

_____ Happiness   _____ Inner harmony

_____ Self-respect   _____ Mature love

_____ Wisdom   _____ A world of beauty

_____ Equality   _____ Social recognition

_____ Salvation   _____ Pleasure

_____ A comfortable life   _____ An exciting life

ideals: freedom, beauty, equality, friendship, fame, wisdom, and so on (Rokeach & Ball-Rokeach, 1989). The values that motivate people can themselves have psychological consequences. For example, American culture puts a high value on wealth and financial success. But the pursuit of material wealth for its own sake has a dark side. Young adults whose central value is the acquisition of wealth have poorer overall emotional adjustment and lower well-being than do people whose primary values are self-acceptance, affiliation with others, or wanting to make the world a better place for others (Kasser & Ryan, 1993).

Goals and Aspirations. One of the strongest findings about work motivation is the importance of having goals—but not just any old goals. Goals are most likely to improve performance when three conditions are met (Locke & Latham, 1990; Smither, 1994):

- _The goal is specific._ Defining a goal as "doing your best" is as ineffective as having no goals at all. You need to be specific: "I will write four pages of this assignment today."

- _The goal has a time limit._ If you know you have to meet a goal by a specific date, you are more likely to succeed than if you give yourself an indefinite amount of time ("by next year").

- _The goal is challenging but achievable._ You are apt to work harder for tough but realistic goals that

make you feel gratified when you reach them, than for easy goals that pose no challenge or impossible goals that can never be attained.

But why do some people give up when a goal becomes difficult, whereas others become even more determined to succeed? Why do some people sink into helplessness, doing poorly at solving the problem and eventually giving up, whereas others keep going to master the problem and avoid failure? The crucial fact about these alternatives—helplessness or mastery—is that they are _unrelated to ability._ When people are faced with a frustrating problem, talent or ambition alone does not predict who will push on and who will give up. What does predict success is the way in which people think about the goals they set for themselves and how confident they feel about reaching them.

According to Carol Dweck (1990, 1992), people who are motivated by _performance goals_ are concerned with doing well, being judged favorably, and avoiding criticism. When such people are focused on how well they are performing and then do poorly, they often decide the fault is theirs, and they stop trying to improve. Because their goal is to demonstrate their abilities, they set themselves up for grief when they temporarily fail—as all of us must if we are to learn anything new. In contrast, those who are motivated by _learning and mastery goals_ are concerned with increasing their competence and skills. Therefore, they regard failure as a source of useful information that will help them improve. Failure and criticism do not discourage them because they know that learning takes time. In addition, when most people focus on mastery rather than performance, they feel greater intrinsic pleasure in the task they are doing or the goal they are pursuing. (The opposite is true, however, among highly ambitious, performance-driven people, such as great athletes and musicians. For them, focusing on specific ways of improving their performance raises their intrinsic motivation and satisfaction [Elliot & Harackiewicz, 1994].)

Competence and Self-efficacy.   When people accomplish their goals, they naturally feel competent, and competence is another key motive for everyone—child and adult alike (White, 1959). Albert Bandura (1990, 1994) argues that competence results from **self-efficacy,** the conviction that you can accomplish what you set out to do (see Chapter 12). According to Bandura, self-efficacy is acquired from four sources:

1. *Having experiences in mastering new skills and overcoming obstacles.* Occasional failures are necessary for self-efficacy. Without them, people learn to expect quick results and are easily discouraged by normal difficulties.

2. *Having successful and competent role models.* By observing the competence of persons you identify with, you learn that the task is possible. For example, if an African-American boy learns that a black man, Garrett Morgan, invented the traffic light, his belief that he too could be an engineer may be strengthened. But negative role models can undermine self-efficacy: If other people in your group seem to keep failing, you may come to doubt that you can succeed.

3. *Getting feedback and encouragement from others.* Self-efficacy increases when other people reward your efforts and do not subject you to repeated putdowns and discouragement.

4. *Learning how to read and manage your own physiological state.* You will feel more competent when you are calm and relaxed than when you are tense or under stress. But people with self-efficacy are even able to use nervousness productively. For example, instead of interpreting normal feelings of stage fright as evidence that they are going to make fools of themselves when they give a talk, they regard these jitters as a source of energy that will help them perform better.

Research in North America, Europe, and Russia

Pitcher Jim Abbott was born without a right hand, yet you never would have known it to watch him pitch when he played major-league baseball. His sense of self-efficacy enabled him to achieve a goal that most would have thought impossible.

has found that self-efficacy affects just about every aspect of people's lives: how well they do on a task, how persistently they pursue their goals, the kinds of career choices they make, their ability to solve problems, their motivation to work for political and social goals, their health habits, and even their chances of recovery from a heart attack (Bandura, 1994, 1995; Ewart, 1995; Maddux, 1995). Fortunately, self-efficacy can be acquired through programs and experiences that provide skills and a sense of mastery.

Needs for Achievement and Power.   In the early 1950s, David McClelland and his associates (1953) speculated that some people have a **need for achievement** (often abbreviated *nAch*) that motivates them as much as hunger motivates people to eat. To measure the strength of this motive, McClelland used the *Thematic Apperception Test* (TAT), a projective test that we described in Chapter 10. As we saw, the TAT consists of a set of ambiguous pictures, and the test taker makes up a

self-efficacy

A person's belief that he or she is capable of producing desired results, such as mastering new skills and reaching goals.

need for achievement

A learned motive to meet personal standards of success and excellence in a chosen area (often abbreviated *nAch*).

story about each scene. A standardized scoring system permits the test to be scored for different motives, including the needs for achievement, power, and affiliation. The strength of these internal motives, said McClelland (1961), is captured in the fantasies the test taker reveals. "In fantasy anything is at least symbolically possible," he explained. "A person may rise to great heights, sink to great depths, kill his grandmother, or take off for the South Sea Islands on a pogo stick."

Needless to say, people with high achievement motivation do not fantasize about taking off for the South Seas or sinking to great depths. They tell stories about working hard, becoming rich and famous, and clobbering the opposition with their wit and brilliance; if they don't succeed, they foresee unhappiness. For example, here is what two people wrote in response to a neutral illustration of a man named George at his desk (McClelland, 1985):

High need for achievement: George is an engineer who wants to win a competition in which the man with the most practicable drawing will be awarded the contract to build a bridge. He is taking a moment to think how happy he will be if he wins. He has been baffled by how to make such a long span strong, but remembers to specify a new steel alloy of great strength, submits his entry, but does not win and is very unhappy.

High need for affiliation: George is an engineer who is working late. He is worried that his wife will be annoyed with him for neglecting her. She has been objecting that he cares more about his work than his wife and family. He seems unable to satisfy both his boss and his wife, but he loves her very much, and will do his best to finish up fast and get home to her.

When high achievers are in situations that arouse their competitiveness and desire to succeed—when, for example, they believe that the TAT is measuring their intelligence and leader-

THE MANY MOTIVES OF ACHIEVEMENT

Productivity
Isaac Asimov (1920–1992)
Scientist, writer

"If my doctor told me I had only six minutes to live, I wouldn't brood; I'd type a little faster."

Knowledge
Helen Keller (1880–1968)
Blind/deaf author and lecturer

"Knowledge is happiness, because to have knowledge—broad, deep knowledge—is to know true ends from false, and lofty things from low."

Justice
Martin Luther King, Jr.
(1929–1968)
Civil rights activist

"I have a dream . . . that my four little children will one day live in a nation where they will not be judged by the color of their skin but by the content of their character."

Autonomy
Georgia O'Keeffe (1887–1986)
Artist

"[I] found myself saying to myself—I can't live where I want to, go where I want to, do what I want to . . . I decided I was a very stupid fool not to at least paint as I wanted to."

ship ability—their achievement-related themes increase (Atkinson, 1958). In the laboratory and real life, people who score high on the need for achievement consistently differ from those who score low. High scorers are more likely, for example, to start their own businesses. They set high personal standards and prefer to work with capable colleagues who can help them succeed rather than with co-workers who are merely friendly (McClelland, 1987).

The TAT has also been used to identify people motivated by a **need for power**—the desire to dominate others and to influence people (McClelland, 1975). Men and women who score high on this motive may try to win power by being aggressive and manipulative, or by being inspirational and charismatic (Winter, 1993). They seek prestige and visibility, enter powerful careers, and run for political office. The need for power spurs some people to become leaders, but the *kind* of power that drives them distinguishes effective leaders from ineffective ones. Two researchers systematically examined the speeches, letters, and biogra-

phies of 39 U.S. presidents, from George Washington to Ronald Reagan (Spangler & House, 1991). Using measures of presidential performance, effectiveness, and greatness, they found that great presidents had a lower need for affiliation and even for achievement than did mediocre ones. But they had a higher motivation to use power to improve society rather than to further their own ambitions—the difference between, say, Abraham Lincoln and Herbert Hoover.

In innovative research linking individual motives to national events, David Winter (1993) has measured power and achievement motivation in secret government documents and official speeches by leaders. His work suggests that power motivation may be a crucial psychological cause of war. "When it rises," Winter reports, "war is likely; when it falls, war is less likely and ongoing wars are likely to end." The affiliation motive works in just the opposite fashion: When it rises, wars are averted.

This research raises fascinating questions. What causes power, achievement, and affiliation motives

need for power
A learned motive to dominate or influence others.

Power
Henry Kissinger (b. 1923)
Former Secretary of State

"Power is the ultimate aphrodisiac."

Duty
Eleanor Roosevelt (1884–1962)
Humanitarian, lecturer, stateswoman

"As for accomplishments, I just did what I had to do as things came along."

Excellence
Florence Griffith Joyner (b. 1959)
Olympic gold medalist

"When you've been second best for so long, you can either accept it, or try to become the best. I made the decision to try and be the best."

Greed
Ivan Boesky (b. 1937)
Financier, convicted of insider trading violations

"Greed is all right . . . I think greed is healthy. You can be greedy and still feel good about yourself."

to rise and fall within a society? Do we have any control over them? The evidence that these motives can be scored and measured on a national level—using historical documents, speeches, popular books, and indicators of achievement such as patents and discoveries—suggests not only that historical events can change people's motivations, but also that people's motivations can change the course of history.

The Effects of Work on Motivation

Like all social motives, the motives for achievement or power depend on what is going on in the culture at large. At one time, for example, many people believed that women had an internalized "fear of success," but as opportunities for women improved, this apparent motive faded. Similarly, when the proportion of men and women in an occupation changes, so do people's motivations to work in that field (Kanter, 1977/1993). That is why some psychologists have questioned the assumption that achievement depends on internal "motives"—enduring, unchanging qualities of the individual. This notion, they say, leads to the incorrect inference that if people don't succeed, it is their own fault because they lack the internal drive to make it (Morrison & Von Glinow, 1990).

Thinking Critically About Why People Achieve

An alternative is that accomplishment depends not only on internal motives and cognitive processes, but also on the work you do and the conditions under which you do it.

Working Conditions.   A classic longitudinal study that followed a random sample of American workers for ten years found that aspects of the work (such as fringe benefits, complexity of daily tasks, pace, pressure, and how routine or varied the work was) significantly changed the workers' self-esteem, job commitment, and motivation (Kohn & Schooler, 1983). Two aspects of a job are especially important in enhancing people's pleasure in and commitment to their work: the degree of flexibility and autonomy the job provides (Brown, 1996). People who have a chance to set their own hours, make decisions, vary their tasks, and solve problems become more motivated to work well. They tend to become more creative in their thinking and feel better about themselves and their work than if they feel stuck in a routine, boring job that gives them no control over what they do (Karasek & Theorell, 1990; Locke & Latham, 1990). Conversely, when people with high power or achievement motivation are put in situations that frustrate their desire and ability to express these motives, they become dissatisfied and stressed, and their power and achievement motives decline (Jenkins, 1994).

Although American culture emphasizes money as the great motivator, work motivation is actually related not to the amount of money you get, but to how and when you get it. The strongest motivator is *incentive pay*—bonuses that are given upon completion of a goal and not as an automatic part of salary (Locke et al., 1981). Why? Incentive pay increases people's feelings of self-efficacy and sense of accomplishment ("I got this raise because I deserved it"). This doesn't mean that people should accept low pay so they will like their jobs better, or that they should never demand cost-of-living raises!

Opportunities to Achieve.   Ultimately, ambitions to achieve are related to people's *chances* of achieving. Men and women who work in dead-end jobs with no prospect of promotion tend to play down the importance of achievement, fantasize about quitting, and emphasize the social benefits of their jobs instead of the intellectual benefits (Kanter, 1977/1993). Consider the comments of a man who realized in his mid-30s that he was never going to be promoted to top management and who scaled down his ambitions accordingly (Scofield, 1993). As organizational psychologists would pre-

Like employees, students can have poor working conditions. For example, it can be hard to study in crowded quarters or with small siblings around to distract or interrupt you.

dict, he began to emphasize the benefits of not achieving: "I'm freer to speak my mind," "I can choose not to play office politics," and "I don't volunteer for lousy assignments." He had time, he learned, for coaching Little League and could stay home when the kids were sick. "Of course," he wrote, "if I ever had any chance for upward corporate mobility it's gone now. I couldn't take the grind. Whether real or imagined, that glass ceiling has become an invisible shield."

Women and members of minority groups are especially likely to encounter a "glass ceiling" in management—a barrier to promotion that is so subtle as to be transparent, yet strong enough to prevent advancement. For example, in a study of the banking industry, the three most significant problems that African-Americans reported were not being "in the network," and therefore not being told what was going on; racism; and an inability to find a mentor (Irons & Moore, 1985). Among Asian-Americans in professional and managerial positions, education and work experience do not predict advancement as well as they do for white American men (Cabezas et al., 1989).

It is often said that women are underrepresented in leadership positions because of something about women—their style of managing differs from men's, or they have lower self-esteem and feelings of competence than men, or they have less commitment to the job than men do. None of these popular beliefs has been supported by research (Donnell & Hall, 1980). Women managers are about twice as likely as men to leave an organization, but the reason is not that they lack achievement motivation. Just the opposite: They leave for better jobs, often because of lack of career advancement at the first one (Snyder, 1993).

In sum, work motivation and satisfaction depend on the right fit between qualities of the individual and conditions of the work. This fact raises a host of questions about how best to structure work so that the increasing diversity of workers will lead to worker satisfaction, achievement, and effectiveness, rather than conflict, bitterness, and prejudice. When should people be required to fit into the dominant culture at work, and when should companies become more multicultural, changing themselves to fit their employees?

??? QUICK QUIZ

Work on your understanding of work motivation.

1. Expecting to fail at work and then making no effort to do well can result in a _____.

2. Ramón and Ramona are learning to ski. Every time she falls, Ramona says, "This is the most humiliating experience I've ever had! Everyone is watching me behave like a clumsy dolt!" When Ramón falls, he says, "&*!!@$@! I'll show these dratted skis who's boss!" Why is Ramona more likely than Ramón to give up? (a) She *is* a clumsy dolt; (b) she is less competent at skiing; (c) she is focused on performance; (d) she is focused on learning.

3. Which of these factors significantly increase work motivation? (a) specific goals, (b) regular pay, (c) feedback, (d) general goals, (e) being told what to do, (f) being able to make decisions, (g) the chance of promotion, (h) having routine, predictable work

4. Phyllis works at an umbrella company. Her work is always competent, but she rarely arrives on time, she doesn't seem as motivated as others to do well, and she has begun to take an unusually high number of sick days. Phyllis's employer is irritated by this behavior and is thinking of firing her. What guidelines of critical thinking is the boss overlooking, and what research should the boss consider before taking this step?

Answers:

1. self-fulfilling prophecy 2. c 3. a, c, f, g 4. The boss is jumping to the conclusion that Phyllis has low achievement motivation. This may be true, but because her work is competent, the boss should consider other explanations and examine the evidence. Perhaps the work conditions are unsatisfactory; there may be few opportunities for promotion; she may get no feedback; perhaps the company does not provide child care, so Phyllis arrives late because she has child-care obligations. What other possible explanations come to mind?

What's Ahead

- *What kind of conflict do you have when you want to study for a big exam but you also want to go out partying?*

- *Do you have to satisfy basic needs for security and belonging before you can become "self-actualized"?*

WHEN MOTIVES CONFLICT

The many motives of human life rarely coexist in perfect harmony. Two motives are in conflict when the satisfaction of one leads to the inability to act on the other—when, that is, you want to eat your cake and have it, too. Researchers have identified four kinds of motivational conflicts (Lewin, 1948):

1. *Approach–approach conflicts* occur when you are equally attracted to two or more possible activities or goals. For example, you would like to go out with Tom, Dick, *and* Harry, all at the same time; you would like to be a veterinarian *and* a rock singer; you would like to go out with friends (an affiliation motive) *and* study like mad for an exam (an achievement motive).

2. *Avoidance–avoidance conflicts* require you to choose between "the lesser of two evils" because you dislike both alternatives. Novice parachute jumpers, for example, must choose between the fear of jumping and the fear of losing face if they don't jump.

3. *Approach–avoidance conflicts* occur when one activity or goal has both a positive and a negative aspect. For example, you want to be a powerful executive but you worry about losing your friends if you succeed. You want power and yet you fear it at the same time. In culturally diverse nations, differing cultural values produce many approach–avoidance conflicts, such as the following examples described by some of our students:

- A Chicano student says he wants to succeed and do well in "white" culture, but his parents, valuing the family's closeness, worry that if he goes to college and graduate school, he will become too independent and eventually leave them behind.

- A Pakistani student says she desperately wants an education and a career as a pharmacist, but she also does not want to be disobedient to her parents, who have arranged a marriage for her back home.

- An African-American student from a poor neighborhood is in college on a prestigious scholarship. He is torn between wanting to leave his background behind him forever and returning to help the family and community members who have supported him.

- A white student wants to be a marine biologist, but her friends tell her that only nerdy guys and dweebs go into science.

In many situations in which an approach–avoidance conflict occurs, both attraction and repulsion are strongest when you are nearest the goal. The closer you are to something appealing, the stronger is your desire to approach; and the closer you are to something unpleasant, the stronger is your desire to flee. As you step away from the goal, the two motives change in strength. The attractive aspects of the goal still seem appealing, but the negative ones seem less unpleasant. This may be one reason people often have trouble resolving their ambivalence: When they leave a situation that has some benefits but many problems and observe it from a distance, they see its benefits and overlook the problems, so they approach it again. Up close, the problems appear more clearly, motivating them to avoid the situation once more.

4. *Multiple approach–avoidance conflicts* occur in situations that offer several possible choices, each containing advantages and disadvantages. For ex-

"C'mon, c'mon—it's either one or the other."

ample, you want to marry and settle down while you are still in school, and you think you have found the right person. On the other hand, you also want to establish a career and have some money in the bank, and lately you and the right person have been quarreling a lot.

Internal conflict is inevitable unless you are a tree sloth. But over time, unresolved conflicts have a physical and mental cost. Two psychologists asked students to list their main "personal strivings": *approach* goals such as "trying to be attractive" or "trying to seek new experiences," and *avoidance* goals such as "trying to avoid being noticed by others" or "trying to avoid being dependent on my boyfriend." Students rated these objectives on the amount of conflict they caused and on how ambivalent they felt about them. For example, a student might say that striving "to appear more intelligent than I am" conflicted with striving "to always present myself in an honest light." High levels of conflict and ambivalence were associated with anxiety, depression, headaches and other symptoms, and more visits to the student health center (Emmons & King, 1988).

Conflict and ambivalence, in turn, are affected by how people frame their goals. Those who do so in approach terms (e.g., "I'm going to lose weight by jogging three times a week") feel better about themselves, and are more optimistic and less depressed, than people who frame the same goals in avoidance terms (e.g., "I'm going to lose weight by staying away from rich foods"). The former way of thinking about a goal focuses on what you can actively do to accomplish it, whereas the latter way focuses on what you have to give up (Coats, Janoff-Bulman, & Alpert, 1996).

Another way of thinking about the competing motives in our lives comes from a theory proposed by humanist psychologist Abraham Maslow (1954/1970). Maslow envisioned people's "motivational strivings" on a pyramid that he called a *hierarchy of needs.* At the bottom level of the pyramid were basic *survival needs,* such as for food, sleep, and water; at the next level were *security needs,* such as protection against danger; at the third level were *social needs,* for belonging and affection; at the fourth level were *esteem needs,* for self-respect and the respect of others; and at the top level were *needs for self-actualization* and "self-transcendence." Maslow argued that your needs must be met at each level before you can even think of the matters posed by the level above it. You can't worry about achievement if you are

hungry, cold, and poor. You can't become self-actualized if you haven't satisfied your needs for self-esteem and love. Human beings behave badly, he argued, only when their lower needs are frustrated.

This theory, which is intuitively logical and optimistic about human nature, became immensely popular, but it has not been supported by research (Smither, 1994). People have *simultaneous* needs for comfort and safety and for attachment, self-esteem, and competence. Individuals who have met their "lower" needs do not inevitably seek "higher" ones, nor is it the case that people behave badly only when their lower needs are frustrated. "Higher" needs may take precedence over "lower" ones: History is full of examples of people who would rather starve than be humiliated; who would rather die of torture than sacrifice their convictions; who would rather explore, risk, or create new art than be safe and secure at home.

Understanding the biological, psychological, and cultural influences on motivation can help us understand the stories that opened this chapter—and, for that matter, the stories that fill the newspapers every day.

The love story in *Titanic* appeals most to those whose ideal is romantic or passionate love—the kind that involves emotional turmoil, sexual longing, and idealization of the loved one. As pragmatic reasons for marriage have faded, this ideal has become increasingly popular throughout the world. But as we saw, "eros" is only one kind of love, and it is not the most long-lasting type. It characterizes the early stage of love affairs, when the lovers still don't know much about each other, and it often creates unrealistic expectations that can lead to disappointment. If a relationship is to last, the lovers must also pass the tests of intimacy and commitment. What would have happened to the young couple in *Titanic* if the ship had not gone down? Would they have been as happy clearing the table together and diapering the kids as they were in the swanky salons of a luxury liner? Would the original flame of passion have left a satisfying afterglow? If so, their relationship would probably have endured—but it would no longer be the type that makes grown men cry.

Our second news item, about the court-martial of Sgt. Maj. Gene McKinney, illustrates the misunderstandings and conflicting sexual goals that can occur when women and men learn different sexual scripts regarding the proper sexual behavior for their gender. We saw earlier that women often feel pressured and coerced into sex, whereas men rarely think they have ever pressured or coerced a woman. However, notions about when sexual overtures are proper or improper—when they constitute normal sexual assertiveness and when they become sexual harassment—are changing rapidly as women enter traditionally male domains.

The news item about "fen-phen" reveals the problems that can arise when people turn to appetite suppressants in hopes of a miracle cure for their weight problems. As we saw, some people have a genetic tendency to be plump or obese. So even when they successfully lose weight while taking appetite suppressants, they usually gain it back as soon as they stop the medication. Obesity, of course, carries many health risks of its own, which must be weighed against the unknown long-term risks of drugs. In 1998, a new study reported that fen-phen seemed to be safe after all, but the final word is not in yet. Several research teams are currently studying the possibility of treating obesity with drugs that alter leptin levels,

but it is also too soon to say whether this approach will be safe and effective. For now, therefore, the safest way of altering your set point and maintaining a healthy weight is to eat a healthful diet and get plenty of exercise.

Finally, the remarkable story of Hulda Crooks, setting for herself in middle age new goals to achieve, new mountains to climb, and new records to break, shows how achievement motivation can blossom at any age. Her life illuminates the importance of setting challenging but attainable goals, of valuing competence, and of having a passionate involvement in whatever we choose to do. Because she had a strong sense of self-efficacy, Hulda Crooks was able to go on to do things after her husband's death that many other older people might have considered impossible. She showed that self-actualization is a lifelong process.

Abraham Maslow may have been wrong about a universal hierarchy of motives, but perhaps each of us develops an individual hierarchy in the course of our development from childhood to old age. For some people, the need for love, security, or safety will dominate. For others, the need for achievement or power will rule. Some will wrestle with conflicting motives; for others, one consuming passion, one driving motive, will hold sway over all others. This diversity of motives is inevitable in human personality and in life.

Taking Psychology with You

Improving Your Motivation

Why are you in school? What do you hope to accomplish in your life? Are you motivated primarily by the intrinsic goals of a job well done and the satisfaction of the work itself or by extrinsic goals such as getting a degree, a job, and a salary—or by both? Do you have a burning ambition, or are you burned out? If you are feeling unmotivated these days, research on work motivation suggests some steps you might take:

• *Seek activities that are intrinsically pleasurable, even if they don't "pay off."* If you really, really want to study Swahili or Swedish even though these languages are not in your prelaw requirements, try to find a way to do it. You might also ask yourself whether your major in

school or the kind of work you do is right for you. Are you in this field because you are drawn to it or because others think you should be in it? Remember, though, that even when you are doing the work you most want to do, you will have difficult or boring days.

• *Focus on learning goals rather than performance goals.* In general, you will be better able to cope with inevitable setbacks if your goal is to learn rather than to show off how good you are. It is important to be able to regard failure as a learning experience, rather than as a sure sign of incompetence. Ironically, the more you are able to focus on learning, mastery, and improvement, the better your performance will be. Once you are an accom-

plished performer, focusing on polishing that performance will become intrinsically pleasurable.

• *Get accurate feedback on your performance.* Once you have specified a goal, continued motivation depends in part on getting feedback about your performance. Your employer needs to tell you that you are almost number one in sales. Your piano teacher needs to tell you that your playing has improved. Your statistics instructor needs to tell you what you need to do to raise your grade. When people work or study in environments that do not provide constructive feedback, their motivation to do well is often weakened. If you are not getting enough feedback, ask for it.

• *Assess your working conditions.* How is your job or academic situation structured? Are you getting support from co-workers, employers, or instructors? Do you have opportunities to develop ideas and vary your routine, or are you expected to toe the line and do the same thing day after day? Do you perceive a "glass ceiling" that might limit your advancement in your chosen field, and are you accurate in your perceptions? If you have entered school or a job with enthusiasm, optimism, and expectations of success, only to have these feelings slowly dwindle and dissipate, you might consider whether your working conditions are causing your burnout. And then you might see whether changing some of those conditions could recharge your batteries.

• *Take steps to resolve motivational conflicts.* Many students in an approach–avoidance conflict tend to think a great deal about their conflicts but not do anything to resolve them. A student in one study, for instance, remained unhappily stuck between his goal of achieving independence and his desire to be cared for by his parents (Emmons & King, 1988). The researchers who did this study concluded that the reconciliation of conflicts is a cornerstone of well-being.

At the end of the first chapter of this book, we discussed not only what psychology can do for you but also what it cannot. As we hope this final chapter has shown, psychology can teach us a great deal about the many motives of human life: the meanings of love, the

mysteries of sex, the dilemmas we create for ourselves about eating and weight, and the conditions that enhance or suppress the pursuit of affiliation, achievement, or power.

What psychology cannot tell us is which motives, goals, and values to choose in the first place: love, wealth, security, passion, freedom, fame, the desire to improve the world, or anything else. In a commencement address some years ago, Mario Cuomo, the former governor of New York, had these words of wisdom for the graduating students: "When you've parked the second car in the garage, and installed the hot tub, and skied in Colorado, and wind-surfed in the Caribbean, when you've had your first love affair and your second and your third, the question will remain: Where does the dream end for me?"

SUMMARY

1) *Motivation* refers to an inferred process within a person or animal that causes that organism to move toward a goal—satisfy a biological need or achieve a psychological ambition—or away from an unpleasant situation. A few primary motivating drives are based on physiological needs, but people's cognitive abilities permit them to plan and work for goals that stem from *social motives.*

The Social Animal: Motives for Love

2) Traditionally, *passionate ("romantic") love* has been distinguished from *companionate love.* But psychologists have developed theories to describe other kinds as well, including a theory describing the *six styles of love,* the *attachment theory* of love (love as secure, avoidant, or anxious–ambivalent), and the *triangle theory* of love (love as consisting of different combinations of passion, intimacy, and commitment).

3) People generally choose partners whose style of love matches their own, although there are exceptions, and a person's love style may change over time. The love "stories" that guide our lives affect our satisfaction in relationships; for example, people who expect to feel highly passionate forever are likely to experience repeated disappointment.

4) Men and women are equally likely to feel love and need attachment, but gender roles affect how they experience and express love. In Western societies, women often express love in words, whereas men express it in actions. As women have entered the workforce in large numbers and pragmatic reasons for marriage have faded, the two sexes have become more alike in endorsing romantic love as a requirement for marriage.

The Erotic Animal: Motives for Sex

5) Biological research finds that testosterone influences sexual desire in both sexes, that there is no "right" kind of orgasm for women to have, and that both sexes are capable of sexual arousal and response. Kinsey and, later, Masters and Johnson were the first modern researchers to show that physiologically, male and female sexuality are more similar than different.

6) *Evolutionary psychologists* argue that men and women have evolved different sexual strategies and behavior in response to survival problems faced in the distant past. In this view, it has been more adaptive for males to be promiscuous, to be attracted to young partners, and to want sexual novelty, and for females to be monogamous, to be choosy about partners, and to prefer security to novelty. Critics argue that research on

many species, including primates, does not support these allegedly universal sex differences (for example, females in many species are promiscuous), and that human sexual behavior is too varied and changeable to fit a single evolutionary explanation.

7) Psychological approaches to sexual motivation emphasize the ways in which values, beliefs, perceptions, and fantasies affect sexual desire and response. Although most men and women have sex for intimacy, pleasure, and procreation, they sometimes have negative motives as well: to seek revenge, gain benefits, dominate the other person, or fulfill a perceived obligation. Both sexes may agree to intercourse for nonsexual motives: Men sometimes feel obligated to "make a move" to prove their masculinity, and women sometimes feel obliged to "give in" to preserve the relationship.

8) A major gender difference exists in perceptions of sexual coercion: What many women regard as coercion is not always seen as such by men. Many women have been the victims of forcible rape. Men who rape do so for diverse reasons, including anger at women, a need to express power, and sometimes sadism. Sexually aggressive males typically have a set of qualities called "hostile masculinity" and a preference for impersonal, promiscuous sex.

9) Sexual attitudes and behavior are affected by a culture's *gender roles* and *sexual scripts*. For straight and gay people alike, scripts specify appropriate behavior during courtship and sex. Scripts for heterosexual women and men often lead to misunderstandings over the meaning of sexual signals and the purpose of sex. A society's sexual attitudes are related to its economic and social relationships; as industrialization changes gender roles, the sexual behavior of men and women is becoming more alike.

10) The origins of sexual orientation are still unknown. Traditional psychological explanations do not account for why some people become homosexual or heterosexual. Growing evidence suggests that genetic and hormonal factors are involved. However, biology, culture, learning, and circumstance interact in complex ways to produce a given person's orientation. Research on this issue evokes emotional reactions because people often confuse scientific questions about the origins of homosexuality with political and moral questions about the rights of gay men and lesbians.

The Hungry Animal: Motives to Eat

11) Genetic research is altering our understanding of body weight and shape. According to *set-point theory*, hunger, weight, and eating are regulated by a set of bodily mechanisms that keep people within a genetically influenced weight range. Genes influence body shape, distribution of fat, and whether the body will convert excess calories into fat. Genes may also account for certain types of obesity. Some obese people have low levels of, or are insensitive to, *leptin*, which enables the brain to regulate appetite and metabolism.

12) However, weight is also strongly affected by cultural norms governing when, where, and how much a person should eat; cultural notions of the ideal body shape; the kinds of foods people eat; and exercise. When cultural standards and psychological needs clash with the needs of the body, eating disorders may result, especially *bulimia* and *anorexia*.

The Competent Animal: Motives to Work

13) Motivation to work depends on (a) a person's expectations of success, which can create *self-fulfilling prophecies* of success or failure; and (b) the value the person places on the goal. Success or failure depends not only on ability, but also on whether people set *learning goals*, which can lead to mastery, or *performance goals*, which can lead to helplessness if the person temporarily fails. People are also motivated by a need to feel competent at what they do. Competence results in part from *self-efficacy*, the conviction that you can accomplish your goals. Self-efficacy comes from experience in mastering new skills, having successful role models, encouragement from others, and constructive interpretations of your own emotional state.

14) People who are motivated by a high *need for achievement* set high (but realistic) personal standards for success and excellence. People who are motivated by a *need for power* seek to dominate and influence others. They may use a variety of methods to gain this power, from persuasion to aggression. Patterns of social motives can predict the effectiveness of leaders, including presidential greatness, and national events, such as the outbreak of war.

15) Work motivation also depends on having the right *working conditions*—such as job flexibility, control, and incentive pay—and on having the

opportunity to be promoted and have good work rewarded and recognized.

When Motives Conflict

16) Human motives often conflict. In an *approach–approach conflict*, a person is equally attracted to two goals. In an *avoidance–avoidance conflict*, a person is equally repelled by two goals. An *approach–avoidance* conflict is the most difficult to resolve because the person is both attracted to and repelled by the same goal. Prolonged conflict can lead to physical symptoms and reduced well-being.

17) Abraham Maslow believed that human motives could be ranked from basic biological needs to higher psychological needs, but this popular theory is not supported by evidence. People can have simultaneous motives; "higher" motives can take precedence over "lower" ones; and people do not always become kinder or more self-actualized when their needs for safety and love are met.

KEY TERMS

motivation   431

social motives   432

need for affiliation   432

passionate and companionate love   432

six styles of love   433

attachment theory of love   433

triangle theory of love   433

evolutionary psychology   438

gender roles   442

sexual scripts   442

set point   446

leptin   447

bulimia   449

anorexia   449

self-fulfilling prophecy   451

values   451

performance and learning goals   452

self-efficacy   453

need for achievement (nAch)   453

Thematic Apperception Test (TAT)   453

need for power   455

incentive pay   456

approach and avoidance conflicts   458

Maslow's hierarchy of needs   459

LOOKING BACK

- *What kind of lover defines love as jealousy and possessiveness, and what kind defines it as just the opposite—calm compatibility? (p. 433)*

- *Do men and women differ in the ability to love? (p. 435)*

- *What part of the anatomy do psychologists think is the "sexiest sex organ"? (p. 440)*

- *How do the sexual rules for heterosexual couples foster misunderstandings? (pp. 442–443)*

- *Can psychological theories about "smothering mothering" or "absent fathers" explain why some men become gay? (p. 444)*

- *Why can some thin people eat anything they want without gaining weight, whereas some heavy people can diet without losing weight? (p. 446)*

- *What disorders can occur when the psychological need to be thin collides with the body's need to store some fat? (p. 449)*

- *Why is "doing your best" an ineffective goal to set for yourself? (p. 452)*

- *When you're learning a new skill, should you concentrate on mastering it or on performing it well in front of others? (pp. 452–453)*

- *What kind of power motivation distinguishes poor leaders from highly effective ones? (p. 455)*

- *What kind of conflict do you have when you want to study for a big exam but you also want to go out partying? (p. 458)*

- *Do you have to satisfy basic needs for security and belonging before you can become "self-actualized"? (p. 459)*

APPENDIX: Statistical Methods

Nineteenth-century English statesman Benjamin Disraeli reportedly once named three forms of dishonesty: "lies, damned lies, and statistics." It is certainly true that people can lie with the help of statistics. It happens all the time: Advertisers, politicians, and others with some claim to make either use numbers inappropriately or ignore certain critical ones. (When hearing that "four out of five doctors surveyed" recommended some product, have you ever wondered just how many doctors were surveyed and whether they were representative of all doctors?) People also use numbers to convey a false impression of certainty and objectivity when the true state of affairs is uncertainty or ignorance. But it is people, not statistics, that lie. When statistics are used correctly, they neither confuse nor mislead. On the contrary, they expose unwarranted conclusions, promote clarity and precision, and protect us from our own biases and blind spots.

If statistics are useful anywhere, it is in the study of human behavior. If human beings were all alike, and psychologists could specify all the influences on behavior, there would be no need for statistics. But any time we measure human behavior, we are going to wind up with different observations or scores for different individuals. Statistics can help us spot trends amid the diversity.

This appendix will introduce you to some basic statistical calculations used in psychology. Reading the appendix will not make you into a statistician, but it will acquaint you with some ways of organizing and assessing research data. If you suffer from a "math phobia," relax: You do not need to know much math to understand this material. However, you should have read Chapter 1, which discussed the rationale for using statistics and described various research methods. You may want to review the basic terms and concepts covered in that chapter. Be sure that you can define *hypothesis, sample, correlation, independent variable, dependent variable, random assignment, experimental group, control group, descriptive statistics, inferential statistics* and *test of statistical significance.* (Correlation coefficients, which are described in some detail in Chapter 1, will not be covered here.)

To read the tables in this appendix, you will also need to know the following symbols:

N = the total number of observations or scores in a set

X = an observation or score

Σ = the Greek capital letter sigma, read as "the sum of"

$\sqrt{}$ = the square root of

(*Note:* Boldfaced terms in this appendix are defined in the glossary at the end of the book.)

ORGANIZING DATA

Before we can discuss statistics, we need some numbers. Imagine that you are a psychologist and that you are interested in that most pleasing of human qualities, a sense of humor. You suspect that a well-developed funny bone can protect people from the negative emotional effects of stress. You already know that in the months following a stressful event, people who score high on sense-of-humor tests tend to feel less tense and moody than more sobersided individuals do. You realize, though, that this correlational evidence does not prove cause and effect. Perhaps people with a healthy sense of humor have other traits, such as flexibility or creativity, that act as the true stress buffers. To find out whether humor itself really softens the impact of stress, you do an experiment.

First, you randomly assign subjects to two groups, an experimental group and a control group. To keep our calculations simple, let's assume there are only 15 people per group. Each person individually views a silent film that most North Americans find fairly stressful, one showing Australian aboriginal boys undergoing a puberty rite involving genital mutilation. Subjects in the experimental group are instructed to make up a humorous monologue while watching the film. Those in the control group are told to make up a straightforward narrative. After the film, each person answers a mood questionnaire that measures current feelings of tension, depression, aggressiveness, and anxiety. A person's overall score on the questionnaire can range from 1 (no mood disturbance) to 7 (strong mood disturbance). This procedure provides you with 15 "mood disturbance" scores for each group. Have people who tried to be humorous reported less disturbance than those who did not?

Constructing a Frequency Distribution

Your first step might be to organize and condense the "raw data" (the obtained scores) by constructing a **frequency distribution** for each group. A frequency distribution shows how often each possible score actually occurred. To construct one, you first order all the possible scores from highest to lowest. (Our mood

Table A.1
Some Hypothetical Raw Data

These scores are for the hypothetical humor-and-stress study described in the text.

Experimental group	4,5,4,4,3,6,5,2,4,3,5,4,4,3,4
Control group	6,4,7,6,6,4,6,7,7,5,5,5,7,6,6

Table A.2
Two Frequency Distributions

The scores are from Table A.1.

Experimental Group			Control Group		
Mood Disturbance Score	Tally	Frequency	Mood Disturbance Score	Tally	Frequency
7		0	7	////	4
6	/	1	6	冊 /	6
5	///	3	5	///	3
4	冊 //	7	4	//	2
3	///	3	3		0
2	/	1	2		0
1		0	1		0
		N = 15			N = 15

disturbance scores will be ordered from 7 to 1.) Then you tally how often each score was actually obtained. Table A.1 gives some hypothetical raw data for the two groups, and Table A.2 shows the two frequency distributions based on these data. From these distributions you can see that the two groups differed. In the experimental group, the extreme scores of 7 and 1 did not occur at all, and the most common score was the middle one, 4. In the control group, a score of 7 occurred four times, the most common score was 6, and no one obtained a score lower than 4.

Because our mood scores have only seven possible values, our frequency distributions are quite manageable. Suppose, though, that your questionnaire had yielded scores that could range from 1 to 50. A frequency distribution with 50 entries would be cumbersome and might not reveal trends in the data clearly. A solution would be to construct a *grouped frequency distribution* by grouping adjacent scores into equal-sized *classes* or *intervals*. Each interval could cover, say, five scores (1–5, 6–10, 11–15, and so forth). Then you could tally the frequencies within each *interval*. This procedure would reduce the number of entries in each distribution from 50 to only 10, making the overall results much easier to grasp. However, information would be lost. For example, there would be no way of knowing how many people had a score of 43 versus 44.

Graphing the Data

As everyone knows, a picture is worth a thousand words. The most common statistical picture is a **graph,** a drawing that depicts numerical relationships. Graphs appear at several points in this book, and are routinely used by psychologists to convey their findings to others. From graphs, we can get a general impression of what the data are like, note the relative frequencies of different scores, and see which score was most frequent.

In a graph constructed from a frequency distribution, the possible score values are shown along a horizontal line (the *x-axis* of the graph) and frequencies along a vertical line (the *y-axis*), or vice versa. To construct a **histogram,** or **bar graph,** from our mood

scores, we draw rectangles (bars) above each score, indicating the number of times it occurred by the rectangle's height (see Figure A.1).

A slightly different kind of "picture" is provided by a **frequency polygon,** or **line graph.** In a frequency

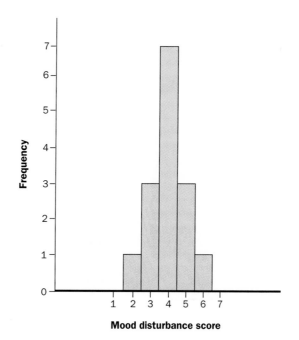

Figure A.1

A Histogram

This graph depicts the distribution of mood disturbance scores shown on the left side of Table A.2.

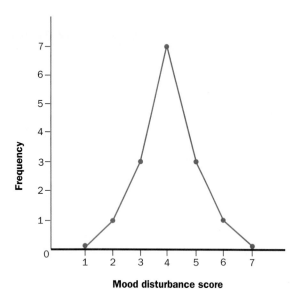

Figure A.2
A Frequency Polygon
This graph depicts the same data as Figure A.1.

polygon, the frequency of each score is indicated by a dot placed directly over the score on the horizontal axis, at the appropriate height on the vertical axis. The dots for the various scores are then joined together by straight lines, as in Figure A.2. When necessary an "extra" score, with a frequency of zero, can be added at each end of the horizontal axis, so that the polygon will rest on this axis instead of floating above it.

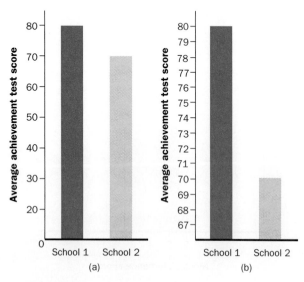

Figure A.3
Same Data, Different Impressions
These two graphs depict the same data, but have different units on the vertical axis.

A word of caution about graphs: They may either exaggerate or mask differences in the data, depending on which units are used on the vertical axis. The two graphs in Figure A.3, although they look quite different, actually depict the same data. Always read the units on the axes of a graph; otherwise, the shape of a histogram or frequency polygon may be misleading.

DESCRIBING DATA

Having organized your data, you are now ready to summarize and describe them. As you will recall from Chapter 1, procedures for doing so are known as *descriptive statistics.* In the following discussion, the word *score* will stand for any numerical observation.

Measuring Central Tendency

Your first step in describing your data might be to compute a **measure of central tendency** for each group. Measures of central tendency characterize an entire set of data in terms of a single representative number.

The Mean. The most popular measure of central tendency is the arithmetic mean, usually called simply the **mean.** It is often expressed by the symbol *M.* Most people are thinking of the mean when they say "average." We run across means all the time: in grade point averages, temperature averages, and batting averages. The mean is valuable to the psychologist because it takes all the data into account and it can be used in further statistical analyses. To compute the mean, you simply add up a set of scores and divide the total by the number of scores in the set. Recall that in mathematical notation, Σ means "the sum of," X stands for the individual scores, and N represents the total number of scores in a set. Thus the formula for calculating the mean is:

$$M = \frac{\Sigma X}{N}$$

Table A.3 shows how to compute the mean for our experimental group. Test your ability to perform this calculation by computing the mean for the control group yourself. (You can find the answer, along with other control group statistics, on page 470.) Later, we will describe how a psychologist would compare the two means statistically to see if there is a significant difference between them.

The Median. Despite its usefulness, sometimes the mean can be misleading, as we noted in Chapter 1. Suppose you piled some children on a seesaw in such a way that it was perfectly balanced, and then a 200-pound adult came and sat on one end. The center of

Table A.3

Calculating a Mean and a Median

The scores are from the left side of Table A.1.

Mean (M)

$$M = \frac{4+5+4+4+3+6+5+2+4+3+5+4+4+3+4}{15}$$

$$= \frac{60}{15}$$

$$= 4$$

Median

Scores, in order: 2, 3, 3, 3, 4, 4, 4, [4,] 4, 4, 4, 5, 5, 5, 6

↑
Median

gravity would quickly shift toward the adult. In the same way, one extremely high score can dramatically raise the mean (and one extremely low score can dramatically lower it). In real life, this can be a serious problem. For example, in the calculation of a town's mean income, one millionaire would offset hundreds of poor people. The mean income would be a misleading indication of the town's actual wealth.

When extreme scores occur, a more representative measure of central tendency is the **median,** or midpoint in a set of scores or observations ordered from highest to lowest. In any set of scores, the same *number* of scores falls above the median as below it. The median is not affected by extreme scores. If you were calculating the *median* income of that same town, the one millionaire would offset only one poor person.

When the number of scores in the set is odd, calculating the median is a simple matter of counting in from the ends to the middle. However, if the number of scores is even, there will be two middle scores. The simplest solution is to find the mean of those two scores and use that number as the median. (When the data are from a grouped frequency distribution, a more complicated procedure is required, one beyond the scope of this appendix.) In our experimental group, the median score is 4 (see Table A.3). What is it for the control group?

The Mode.   A third measure of central tendency is the **mode,** the score that occurs most often. In our experimental group, the modal score is 4. In our control group, it is 6. In some distributions, all scores occur with equal frequency, and there is no mode. In others, two or more scores "tie" for the distinction of being most frequent. Modes are used less often than other measures of central tendency. They do not tell

us anything about the other scores in the distribution; they often are not very "central"; and they tend to fluctuate from one random sample of a population to another more than either the median or the mean.

Measuring Variability

A measure of central tendency may or may not be highly representative of other scores in a distribution. To understand our results, we also need a **measure of variability** that will tell us whether our scores are clustered closely around the mean or widely scattered.

The Range.   The simplest measure of variability is the **range,** which is found by subtracting the lowest score from the highest one. For our hypothetical set of mood disturbance scores, the range in the experimental group is 4 and in the control group it is 3. Unfortunately, though, simplicity is not always a virtue. The range gives us some information about variability but ignores all scores other than the highest and lowest ones.

The Standard Deviation.   A more sophisticated measure of variability is the **standard deviation (SD).** This statistic takes every score in the distribution into account. Loosely speaking, it gives us an idea of how much, on the average, scores in a distribution differ from the mean. If the scores were all the same, the standard deviation would be zero. The higher the standard deviation, the more variability there is among scores.

To compute the standard deviation, we must find out how much each individual score deviates from the mean. To do so we simply subtract the mean from each score. This gives us a set of *deviation scores.* Deviation scores for numbers above the mean will be positive, those for numbers below the mean will be negative, and the positive scores will exactly balance the negative ones. In other words, the sum of the deviation scores will be zero. That is a problem, since the next step in our calculation is to add. The solution is to *square* all the deviation scores (that is, to multiply each score by itself). This step gets rid of negative values. Then we can compute the average of the *squared* deviation scores by adding them up and dividing the sum by the number of scores (N). Finally, we take the square root of the result, which takes us from squared units of measurement back to the same units that were used originally (in this case, mood disturbance levels).

The calculations just described are expressed by the following formula:

$$SD = \sqrt{\frac{\Sigma(X-M)^2}{N}}$$

Table A.4 shows the calculations for computing the standard deviation for our experimental group. Try

Table A.4

Calculating a Standard Deviation

Scores (X)	Deviation scores (X – M)	Squared deviation scores (X – M)²
6	2	4
5	1	1
5	1	1
5	1	1
4	0	0
4	0	0
4	0	0
4	0	0
4	0	0
4	0	0
4	0	0
3	–1	1
3	–1	1
3	–1	1
2	–2	4
	0	14

$$SD = \sqrt{\frac{\Sigma(X-M)^2}{N}} = \sqrt{\frac{14}{15}} = \sqrt{.93} = .97$$

Note: When data from a sample are used to estimate the standard deviation of the population from which the sample was drawn, division is by N – 1 instead of N, for reasons that will not concern us here.

your hand at computing the standard deviation for the control group.

Remember, a large standard deviation signifies that scores are widely scattered, and that therefore the mean is not terribly typical of the entire population. A small standard deviation tells us that most scores are clustered near the mean, and that therefore the mean is representative. Suppose two classes took a psychology exam, and both classes had the same mean score, 75 out of a possible 100. From the means alone, you might conclude that the classes were similar in performance. But if Class A had a standard deviation of 3 and Class B had a standard deviation of 9, you would know that there was much more variability in performance in Class B. This information could be useful to an instructor in planning lectures and making assignments.

Transforming Scores

Sometimes researchers do not wish to work directly with raw scores. They may prefer numbers that are more manageable, such as when the raw scores are tiny fractions. Or they may want to work with scores that reveal where a person stands relative to others. In such cases, raw scores can be transformed to other kinds of scores.

Percentile Scores.   One common transformation converts each raw score to a **percentile score** (also called a *centile rank*). A percentile score gives the percentage of people who scored at or below a given raw score. Suppose you learn that you have scored 37 on a psychology exam. In the absence of any other information, you may not know whether to celebrate or cry. But if you are told that 37 is equivalent to a percentile score of 90, you know that you can be pretty proud of yourself; you have scored as well as, or higher than, 90 percent of those who have taken the test. On the other hand, if you are told that 37 is equivalent to a percentile score of 50, you have scored only at the median—only as well as, or higher than, half of the other students. The highest possible percentile rank is 99, or more precisely, 99.99, because you can never do better than 100 percent of a group when you are a member of the group. (Can you say what the lowest possible percentile score is? The answer is on page 470.) Standardized tests such as those described in previous chapters often come with tables that allow for the easy conversion of any raw score to the appropriate percentile score, based on data from a larger number of people who have already taken the test.

Percentile scores are easy to understand and easy to calculate. However, they also have a drawback: They merely rank people and do *not* tell us how far apart people are in terms of raw scores. Suppose you scored in the 50th percentile on an exam, June scored in the 45th, Tricia scored in the 20th, and Sean scored in the 15th. The difference between you and June may seem identical to that between Tricia and Sean (five percentiles). But in terms of *raw* scores you and June are probably more alike than Tricia and Sean, because exam scores usually cluster closely together around the midpoint of the distribution and are farther apart at the extremes. Because percentile scores do not preserve the spatial relationships in the original distribution of scores, they are inappropriate for computing many kinds of statistics. For example, they cannot be used to calculate means.

Z-scores.   Another common transformation of raw scores is to **z-scores,** or **standard scores.** A z-score tells you how far a given raw score is above or below the mean, using the standard deviation as the unit of measurement. To compute a z-score, you subtract the mean of the distribution from the raw score and divide by the standard deviation:

$$z = \frac{X - M}{SD}$$

Unlike percentile scores, z-scores preserve the relative spacing of the original raw scores. The mean itself always corresponds to a z-score of zero, since it cannot deviate from itself. All scores above the mean have positive z-scores and all scores below the mean have negative ones. When the raw scores form a certain pattern called a *normal distribution* (to be described shortly), a z-score tells you how high or low the corresponding raw score was, relative to the other scores. If your exam score of 37 is equivalent to a z-score of +1.0, you have scored 1 standard deviation above the mean. Assuming a roughly normal distribution, that's pretty good, because in a normal distribution only about 16 percent of all scores fall at or above 1 standard deviation above the mean. But if your 37 is equivalent to a z-score of −1.0, you have scored 1 standard deviation below the mean—a poor score.

Z-scores are sometimes used to compare people's performance on different tests or measures. Say that Elsa earns a score of 64 on her first psychology test and Manuel, who is taking psychology from a different instructor, earns a 62 on his first test. In Elsa's class, the mean score is 50 and the standard deviation is 7, so Elsa's z-score is (64 − 50)/7 = 2.0. In Manuel's class, the mean is also 50, but the standard deviation is 6. Therefore, his z-score is also 2.0 [(62 − 50)/6]. Compared to their respective classmates, Elsa and Manuel did equally well. *But be careful:* This does *not* imply that they are equally able students. Perhaps Elsa's instructor has a reputation for giving easy tests and Manuel's for giving hard ones, so Manuel's instructor has attracted a more industrious group of students. In that case, Manuel faces stiffer competition than Elsa does, and even though he and Elsa have the same z-score, Manuel's performance may be more impressive.

You can see that comparing z-scores from different people or different tests must be done with caution. Standardized tests, such as IQ tests and various personality tests, use z-scores derived from a large sample of people assumed to be representative of the general population taking the tests. When two tests are standardized for similar populations, it is safe to compare z-scores on them. But z-scores derived from special samples, such as students in different psychology classes, may not be comparable.

Curves

In addition to knowing how spread out our scores are, we need to know the *pattern* of their distribution. At this point we come to a rather curious phenomenon. When researchers make a very large number of observations, many of the physical and psychological variables they study have a distribution that approximates a pattern called a **normal distribution.** (We say "approximates" because a *perfect* normal distribution is a theoretical construct and is not actually found in nature.) Plotted in a frequency polygon, a normal distribution has a symmetrical, bell-shaped form known as a **normal curve** (see Figure A.4).

A normal curve has several interesting and convenient properties. The right side is the exact mirror image of the left. The mean, median, and mode all have the same value and are at the exact center of the curve, at the top of the "bell." Most observations or scores cluster around the center of the curve, with far fewer out at the ends, or "tails," of the curve. Most important, as Figure A.4 shows, when standard deviations (or z-scores) are used on the horizontal axis of the curve, the percentage of scores falling between the mean and any given point on the horizontal axis is always the same. For example, 68.26 percent of the scores will fall between plus and minus 1 standard deviation from the mean; 95.44 percent of the scores will fall between plus and minus 2 standard deviations from the mean; and 99.74 percent of the scores will fall between plus and minus 3 standard deviations from the mean. These percentages hold for any normal curve, no matter what the size of the standard deviation. Tables are available showing the percentages of scores in a normal distribution that lie between the mean and various points (as expressed by z-scores).

The normal curve makes life easier for psychologists when they want to compare individuals on some

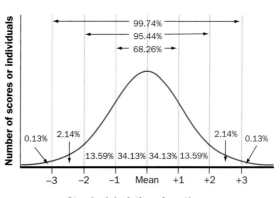

Figure A.4

A Normal Curve

When standard deviations (or z-scores) are used along the horizontal axis of a normal curve, certain fixed percentages of scores fall between the mean and any given point. As you can see, most scores fall in the middle range (between +1 and −1 standard deviations from the mean).

trait or performance. For example, since IQ scores from a population form a roughly normal curve, the mean and standard deviation of a test are all the information you need in order to know how many people score above or below a particular score. On a test with a mean of 100 and a standard deviation of 15, about 68.26 percent of the population scores between 85 and 115—1 standard deviation below and 1 standard deviation above the mean (see Chapter 6).

Not all types of observations, however, are distributed normally. Some curves are lopsided, or *skewed,* with scores clustering at one end or the other of the horizontal axis (see Figure A.5). When the "tail" of the curve is longer on the right than on the left, the curve is said to be positively, or right, skewed. When the opposite is true, the curve is said to be negatively, or left, skewed. In experiments, reaction times typically form a right-skewed distribution. For example, if people must press a button whenever they hear some signal, most will react quite quickly; but a few will take an unusually long time, causing the right "tail" of the curve to be stretched out.

Knowing the shape of a distribution can be extremely valuable. Paleontologist Stephen Jay Gould (1985) has told how such information helped him cope with the news that he had a rare and serious form of cancer. Being a researcher, he immediately headed for the library to learn all he could about his disease. The first thing he found was that it was incurable, with a median mortality of only eight months after discovery. Most people might have assumed that a "median mortality of eight months" means "I will probably be dead in eight months." But Gould realized that although half of all patients died within eight months, the other half survived longer than that. Since his disease had been diagnosed in its early stages, he was getting top-notch medical treatment, and he had a strong will to live, Gould figured he could reasonably expect to be in the half of the distri-

bution that survived beyond eight months. Even more cheering, the distribution of deaths from the disease was right-skewed: The cases to the left of the median of eight months could only extend to zero months, but those to the right could stretch out for years. Gould saw no reason why he should not expect to be in the tip of that right-hand tail.

For Stephen Jay Gould, statistics, properly interpreted, were "profoundly nurturant and life-giving." They offered him hope and inspired him to fight his disease. Today, Gould is as active professionally as he ever was. The initial diagnosis was made in July of 1982.

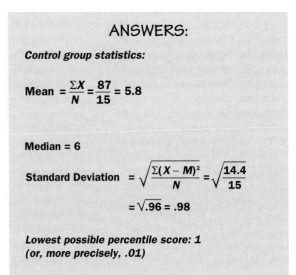

ANSWERS:

Control group statistics:

$$\text{Mean} = \frac{\Sigma X}{N} = \frac{87}{15} = 5.8$$

Median = 6

$$\text{Standard Deviation} = \sqrt{\frac{\Sigma(X - M)^2}{N}} = \sqrt{\frac{14.4}{15}}$$
$$= \sqrt{.96} = .98$$

Lowest possible percentile score: 1 (or, more precisely, .01)

DRAWING INFERENCES

Once data are organized and summarized, the next step is to ask whether they differ from what might have been expected purely by chance (see Chapter 1). A researcher needs to know whether it is safe to infer that the results from a particular sample of people are valid for the entire population from which the sample was drawn. **Inferential statistics** provide this information. They are used in both experimental and correlational studies.

The Null Versus the Alternative Hypothesis

In an experiment, the scientist must assess the possibility that his or her experimental manipulations will have no effect on the subjects' behavior. The statement expressing this possibility is called the **null hypothesis.** In our stress-and-humor study, the null hypothesis states that making up a funny commen-

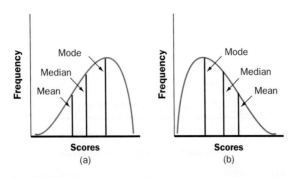

Figure A.5
Skewed Curves

Curve (a) is skewed negatively, to the left. Curve (b) is skewed positively, to the right. The direction of a curve's skewness is determined by the position of the long tail, not by the position of the bulge. In a skewed curve, the mean, median, and mode fall at different points.

tary will not relieve stress any more than making up a straightforward narrative will. In other words, it predicts that the difference between the means of the two groups will not deviate significantly from zero. Any obtained difference will be due solely to chance fluctuations. In contrast, the **alternative hypothesis** (also called the experimental or research hypothesis) states that on the average the experimental group will have lower mood disturbance scores than the control group.

The null hypothesis and the alternative hypothesis cannot both be true. Our goal is to reject the null hypothesis. If our results turn out to be consistent with the null hypothesis, we will not be able to do so. If the data are inconsistent with the null hypothesis, we will be able to reject it with some degree of confidence. Unless we study the entire population, though, we will never be able to say that the alternative hypothesis has been proven. No matter how impressive our results are, there will always be some degree of uncertainty about the inferences we draw from them. Since we cannot prove the alternative hypothesis, we must be satisfied with showing that the null hypothesis is unreasonable.

Students are often surprised to learn that in traditional hypothesis testing it is the null hypothesis, not the alternative hypothesis, that is tested. After all, it is the alternative hypothesis that is actually of interest. But this procedure does make sense. The null hypothesis can be stated precisely and tested directly. In the case of our fictitious study, the null hypothesis predicts that the difference between the two means will be zero. The alternative hypothesis does not permit a precise prediction because we don't know how much the two means might differ (if, in fact, they do differ). Therefore, it cannot be tested directly.

Testing Hypotheses

Many computations are available for testing the null hypothesis. The choice depends on the design of the study, the size of the sample, and other factors. We will not cover any specific tests here. Our purpose is simply to introduce you to the kind of *reasoning* that underlies hypothesis testing. With that in mind, let us return once again to our data. For each of our two groups we have calculated a mean and a standard deviation. Now we want to compare the two sets of data to see if they differ enough for us to reject the null hypothesis. We wish to be reasonably certain that our observed differences did not occur entirely by chance.

What does it mean to be "reasonably certain"? How different from zero must our result be to be taken seriously? Imagine, for a moment, that we had infinite resources and could somehow repeat our experiment, each time using a new pair of groups, until we had "run" the entire population through the study. It can be shown mathematically that if only

chance were operating, our various experimental results would form a normal distribution. This theoretical distribution is called "the sampling distribution of the difference between means," but since that is quite a mouthful, we will simply call it the *sampling distribution* for short. If the null hypothesis were true, the mean of the sampling distribution would be zero. That is, on the average, we would find no difference between the two groups. Often, though, because of chance influences or *random error,* we would get a result that deviated to one degree or another from zero. On rare occasions, the result would deviate a great deal from zero.

We cannot test the entire population, though. All we have are data from a single sample. We would like to know whether the difference between means that we actually obtained would be close to the mean of the theoretical sampling distribution (if we *could* test the entire population) or far away from it, out in one of the "tails" of the curve. Was our result highly likely to occur on the basis of chance alone or highly unlikely?

Before we can answer that question, we must have some precise way to measure distance from the mean of the sampling distribution. We must know exactly how far from the mean our obtained result must be to be considered "far away." If only we knew the standard deviation of the sampling distribution, we could use it as our unit of measurement. We don't know it, but fortunately, we can use the standard deviation of our *sample* to estimate it. (We will not go into the reasons that this is so.)

Now we are in business. We can look at the mean difference between our two groups and figure out how far it is (in terms of standard deviations) from the mean of the sampling distribution. As mentioned earlier, one of the convenient things about a normal distribution is that a certain fixed percentage of all observations falls between the mean of the distribution and any given point above or below the mean. These percentages are available from tables. Therefore, if we know the "distance" of our obtained result from the mean of the theoretical sampling distribution, we automatically know how likely our result is to have occurred strictly by chance.

To give a specific example, if it turns out that our obtained result is 2 standard deviations above the mean of the theoretical sampling distribution, we know that the probability of its having occurred by chance is less than 2.3 percent. If our result is 3 standard deviations above the mean of the sampling distribution, the probability of its having occurred by chance is less than .13 percent—less than 1 in 800. In either case, we might well suspect that our result did not occur entirely by chance after all. We would call the result **statistically significant.** (Psychologists usually consider any highly unlikely result to be of interest, no matter which direction it takes. In other words, the result may be in either "tail" of the sampling distribution.)

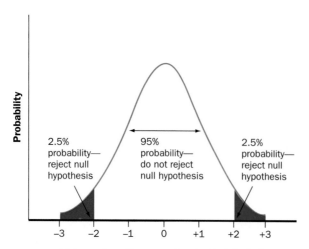

Distance from the mean (in standard deviations)

Figure A.6

Statistical Significance

This curve represents the theoretical sampling distribution discussed in the text. The curve is what we would expect by chance if we did our hypothetical stress-and-humor study many times, testing the entire population. If we used the conventional significance level of .05, we would regard our obtained result as significant only if the probability of getting a result that far from zero by chance (in either direction) totaled 5 percent or less. As shown, the result must fall far out in one of the tails of the sampling distribution. Otherwise, we cannot reject the null hypothesis.

To summarize: Statistical significance means that if only chance were operating, our result would be highly improbable, so we are fairly safe in concluding that more than chance was operating—namely, the influence of our independent variable. We can reject the null hypothesis, and open the champagne. As we noted in Chapter 1, psychologists usually accept a finding as statistically significant if the likelihood of its occurring by chance is 5 percent or less (see Figure A.6). This cutoff point gives the researcher a reason-able chance of confirming reliable results as well as reasonable protection against accepting unreliable ones.

Some cautions are in order, though. As noted in Chapter 1, conventional tests of statistical significance have drawn serious criticisms in recent years. Statistically significant results are not always psychologically interesting or important. Further, statistical significance is related to the size of the sample. A large sample increases the likelihood of reliable results. But there is a trade-off: The larger the sample, the more probable it is that a small result having no practical importance will reach statistical significance. On the other hand, with the sample sizes typically used in psychological research, there is a good chance of falsely concluding that an experimental effect has *not* occurred when one actually has (Hunter, 1997). For these reasons, it is always useful to know how much of the total variability in scores was accounted for by the independent variable (the **effect size**). (The computations are not discussed here.) If only 3 percent of the variance was accounted for, then 97 percent was due either to chance factors or to systematic influences of which the researcher was unaware. Because human behavior is affected by so many factors, the amount of variability accounted for by a single psychological variable is often modest. But sometimes the effect size is considerable even when the results don't quite reach significance.

Oh, yes, about those humor findings: Our fictitious study is similar to two more-complicated ones done by Herbert M. Lefcourt and Rod A. Martin (1986). Women who tried to be funny reported less mood disturbance than women who merely produced a straightforward narrative. They also grimaced and fidgeted less during the film, suggesting that they really did feel less stress. The results were not statistically significant for men. Other findings, however, suggest that humor can shield both sexes from stress (see Chapter 12). *The moral:* When gravity gets you down, try a little levity.

SUMMARY

1) When used correctly, statistics expose un-warranted conclusions, promote precision, and help researchers spot trends amid diversity.

2) Often, the first step in data analysis is to organize and condense data in a *frequency distribution,* a tally showing how often each possible score (or interval of scores) occurred. Such information can also be depicted in a *histogram* (bar graph) or a *frequency polygon* (line graph).

3) Descriptive statistics summarize and describe the data. *Central tendency* is measured by the *mean, median,* or, less frequently, the *mode.* Since a measure of central tendency may or may not be highly representative of other scores in a distribution, it is also important to analyze variability. A large *standard deviation* means that scores are widely scattered about the mean; a small one means that most scores are clustered near the mean.

4) Raw scores can be transformed into other kinds of scores. *Percentile scores* indicate the percentage of people who scored at or below a given raw score. *Z-scores (standard scores)* indicate how far a given raw score is above or below the mean of the distribution.

5) Many variables have a distribution approximating a *normal distribution,* depicted as a *normal curve.* The normal curve has a convenient property: When

standard deviations are used as the units on the horizontal axis, the percentage of scores falling between any two points on the horizontal axis is always the same. Not all types of observations are distributed normally, however. Some distributions are *skewed* to the left or right.

6) Inferential statistics can be used to test the *null hypothesis* and to tell a researcher whether a result differed significantly from what might have been expected purely by chance. Basically, hypothesis testing involves estimating where the obtained result would have fallen in a theoretical *sampling distribution* based on studies of the entire population in question. If the result would have been far out in one of the "tails" of the distribution, it is considered statistically significant. A statistically significant result may or may not be psychologically interesting, important, or informative so many researchers also compute the *effect size*.

KEY TERMS

frequency distribution 464

graph 465

histogram/bar graph 465

frequency polygon/line graph 465

measure of central tendency 466

mean 466

median 466

mode 467

range 467

standard deviation 467

deviation score 467

percentile score 468

z-score (standard score) 468

normal distribution 469

normal curve 469

right- and left-skewed distributions 470

null hypothesis 470

alternative hypothesis 471

sampling distribution 471

statistically significant 471

effect size 472

Glossary

absolute threshold   The smallest quantity of physical energy that can be reliably detected by an observer.

accommodation   In Piaget's theory, the process of modifying existing cognitive structures in response to experience and new information.

acculturation   The process by which members of minority groups in a given society come to identify with and feel part of the mainstream culture.

activation-synthesis theory   The theory that dreaming results from the cortical synthesis and interpretation of neural signals triggered by activity in the lower part of the brain.

adrenal hormones   Hormones that are produced by the adrenal glands and that are involved in emotion and stress; they include cortisol, epinephrine, and norepinephrine.

agoraphobia   A set of phobias, often set off by a panic attack, involving the basic fear of being away from a safe place or person.

algorithm   A problem-solving strategy guaranteed to produce a solution even if the user does not know how it works.

alternative hypothesis   An assertion that the independent variable in a study will have a certain predictable effect on the dependent variable; also called an experimental or research hypothesis.

amnesia (dissociative)   When no organic causes are present, a dissociative disorder involving partial or complete loss of memory for threatening information or traumatic experiences.

amygdala   A brain structure involved in the arousal and regulation of emotion and the initial emotional response to sensory information.

antidepressant drugs   Drugs used primarily in the treatment of mood disorders, especially depression and anxiety.

antipsychotic drugs   Drugs used primarily in the treatment of schizophrenia and other psychotic disorders; also known as *neuroleptics.*

antisocial personality disorder   A disorder (sometimes called psychopathy or sociopathy) characterized by antisocial behavior such as lying, stealing, manipulating others, and sometimes violence; a lack of social emotions (guilt, shame, and empathy); and impulsivity.

applied psychology   The study of psychological issues that have direct practical significance and the application of psychological findings.

archetypes (AR-ki-tipes)   Universal, symbolic images that appear in myths, art, dreams, and other expressions of the collective unconscious, according to Carl Jung.

arithmetic mean   An average that is calculated by adding up a set of quantities and dividing the sum by the total number of quantities in the set.

assimilation   In Piaget's theory, the process of absorbing new information into existing cognitive structures.

attribution theory   The theory that people are motivated to explain their own and other people's' behavior by attributing causes of that behavior to a situation or a disposition.

autonomic nervous system   The subdivision of the peripheral nervous system that regulates the internal organs and glands.

availability heuristic   The tendency to judge the probability of a type of event by how easy it is to think of examples or instances.

axon   A neuron's extending fiber that conducts impulses away from the cell body and transmits them to other neurons.

basic psychology   The study of psychological issues in order to seek knowledge for its own sake rather than for its practical application.

behaviorism   An approach to psychology that emphasizes the study of observable behavior and the role of the environment as a determinant of behavior.

behavior modification   The application of conditioning techniques to teach new responses or to reduce or eliminate maladaptive or problematic behavior.

binocular cues   Visual cues to depth or distance requiring two eyes.

bipolar disorder   A mood disorder in which episodes of both depression and mania (excessive euphoria) occur.

brain stem   The part of the brain at the top of the spinal cord, consisting of the medulla and the pons.

brightness   Lightness or luminance; the dimension of visual experience related to the amount of light emitted from or reflected by an object.

case study   A detailed description of a particular individual being studied or treated.

cell body   The part of the neuron that keeps it alive and determines whether it will fire.

central nervous system (CNS)   The portion of the nervous system consisting of the brain and spinal cord.

cerebellum   A brain structure that regulates movement and balance, and that is involved in the learning of certain kinds of simple responses.

cerebral cortex   A collection of several thin layers of cells covering the cerebrum; it is largely responsible for higher mental functions. *Cortex* is Latin for "bark" or "rind."

cerebral hemispheres   The two halves of the cerebrum.

cerebrum (suh-REE-brum)   The largest brain structure, consisting of the upper part of the brain; divided into two hemispheres, it is in charge of most sensory, motor, and cognitive processes. From the Latin for "brain."

childhood (infantile) amnesia   The inability to remember events and experiences that occurred before ages 2 or 3.

chunk   A meaningful unit of information; may be composed of smaller units.

classical conditioning   The process by which a previously neutral stimulus acquires the capacity to elicit a response through association with a stimulus that already elicits a similar or related response; also called *Pavlovian* and *respondent conditioning.*

cochlea (KOCK-lee-uh)   A snail-shaped, fluid-filled organ in the inner ear, containing the receptors for hearing.

coefficient of correlation   A measure of correlation that ranges in value from –1.00 to +1.00.

cognitive dissonance   A state of tension that occurs when a person simultaneously holds two cognitions that are psychologically inconsistent, or when a person's belief is incongruent with his or her behavior.

cognitive ethology   The study of cognitive processes in nonhuman animals.

cognitive map   A mental representation of the environment.

cognitive schema   An integrated mental network of knowledge, beliefs, and expectations concerning a particular topic or aspect of the world.

collective unconscious   To Carl Jung, the universal memories and experiences of humankind, represented in the unconscious images and symbols of all people.

collectivist cultures   Cultures in which the self is regarded as embedded in relationships, and harmony with one's group is prized above individual goals and wishes.

concept   A mental category that groups objects, relations, activities, abstractions, or qualities having common properties.

conditioned response (CR)   The classical-conditioning term for a response that is elicited by a conditioned stimulus; occurs after the conditioned stimulus is associated with an unconditioned stimulus.

conditioned stimulus (CS)   The classical-conditioning term for an initially neutral stimulus that comes to elicit a conditioned response after being associated with an unconditioned stimulus.

conditioning   A basic kind of learning that involves associations between environmental stimuli and the organism's responses.

cones   Visual receptors involved in color vision.

confirmation bias   The tendency to look for or pay attention only to information that confirms one's own belief.

conservation   The understanding that the physical properties of objects—such as the number of items in a cluster or the amount of liquid in a glass—can remain the same even when their form or appearance changes.

contact comfort   In primates, the innate pleasure derived from physical contact; it is the basis of an infant's first attachment.

continuous reinforcement   A reinforcement schedule in which a particular response is always reinforced.

control condition   In an experiment, a comparison condition in which subjects are not exposed to the same treatment as in the experimental condition.

convergence   The turning inward of the eyes, which occurs when they focus on a nearby object.

corpus callosum   The bundle of nerve fibers connecting the two cerebral hemispheres.

correlation   A measure of how strongly two variables are related to one another.

correlational study   A descriptive study that looks for a consistent relationship between two phenomena.

counterconditioning   In classical conditioning, the process of pairing a conditioned stimulus with a stimulus that elicits a response that is incompatible with an unwanted conditioned response.

critical thinking   The ability and willingness to assess claims and to make objective judgments on the basis of well-supported reasons.

cross-sectional study   A study in which subjects of different ages are compared at a given time.

cue-dependent forgetting   The inability to retrieve information stored in memory because of insufficient cues for recall.

culture   A program of shared rules that govern the behavior of members of a community or society, and a set of values, beliefs, and attitudes shared by most members of that community.

dark adaptation   A process by which visual receptors become maximally sensitive to dim light.

decay theory   The theory that information in memory eventually disappears if it is not accessed; applies more to short-term than to long-term memory.

declarative memories   Memories of facts, rules, concepts, and events ("knowing that"); include semantic and episodic memories.

deductive reasoning   A form of reasoning in which a conclusion follows necessarily from certain premises; if the premises are true, the conclusion must be true.

deep processing   In the encoding of information, the processing of meaning rather than of simply the physical or sensory features of a stimulus.

defense mechanisms   Methods used by the ego to prevent unconscious anxiety or threatening thoughts from entering consciousness.

deindividuation   In groups or crowds, the loss of awareness of one's own individuality and the abdication of mindful action.

dendrites   A neuron's branches that receive information from other neurons and transmit it toward the cell body.

dependent variable   A variable that an experimenter predicts will be affected by manipulations of the independent variable.

descriptive methods   Methods that yield descriptions of behavior but not necessarily causal explanations.

descriptive statistics   Statistics that organize and summarize research data.

dialectical reasoning   A process in which opposing facts or ideas are weighed and compared, with a view to determining the best solution or to resolving differences.

difference threshold   The smallest difference in stimulation that can be reliably detected by an observer when two stimuli are compared; also called *just noticeable difference (jnd)*.

diffusion of responsibility   In organized or anonymous groups, the tendency of members to avoid taking responsibility for actions or decisions, assuming that others will do so.

discriminative stimulus   A stimulus that signals when a particular response is likely to be followed by a certain type of consequence.

display rules   Social and cultural rules that regulate when, how, and where a person may express (or suppress) emotions.

dissociative disorders   Conditions in which consciousness or identity is split or altered.

dissociative identity disorder   A controversial disorder marked by the appearance within one person of two or more distinct personalities, each with its own name and traits; also called *multiple personality disorder*.

dizygotic twins   *See* fraternal twins.

double-blind study   An experiment in which neither the subjects nor the individuals running the study know which subjects are in the control group and which are in the experimental group until after the results are tallied.

effect size   In an experiment, the amount of variance in the data accounted for by the independent variable.

ego   In psychoanalysis, the part of personality that represents reason, good sense, and rational self-control.

egocentric thinking   Seeing the world from only your own point of view; the inability to take another person's perspective.

elaborative rehearsal   Association of new information with already stored knowledge and analysis of the new information to make it memorable.

electroconvulsive therapy (ECT)   A procedure used in cases of prolonged and severe major depression, in which a brief brain seizure is induced.

electroencephalogram (EEG)   A recording of neural activity detected by electrodes.

emotion   A state of arousal involving facial and bodily changes, brain activation, cognitive appraisals, subjective feelings, and tendencies toward action.

emotion work   Expression of an emotion, often because of a role requirement, that a person does not really feel.

empirical   Relying on or derived from observation, experimentation, or measurement.

endocrine glands   Internal organs that produce hormones and release them into the bloodstream.

endorphins (en-DOR-fins)   Chemical substances in the nervous system that are similar in structure and action to opiates; they are involved in pain reduction, pleasure, and memory, and are known technically as *endogenous opioid peptides*.

entrapment   A gradual process in which individuals escalate their commitment to a course of action to justify their investment of time, money, or effort.

episodic memories   Memories of personally experienced events and the contexts in which they occurred.

equilibrium   The sense of balance.

ethnic identity   A person's identification with a racial, religious, or ethnic group.

ethnocentrism   A person's belief that his or her own ethnic group, nation, or religion is superior to all others.

experiment   A controlled test of a hypothesis in which the researcher manipulates one variable to discover its effect on another.

experimenter effects   Unintended changes in subjects' behavior due to cues inadvertently given by the experimenter.

explicit memory   Conscious, intentional recollection of an event or of an item of information.

extinction   The weakening and eventual disappearance of a learned response. In classical conditioning, it occurs when the conditioned stimulus is no longer paired with the unconditioned stimulus. In operant conditioning, it occurs when a response is no longer followed by a reinforcer.

extrinsic reinforcers   Reinforcers that are not inherently related to the activity being reinforced, such as money, prizes, and praise.

factor analysis A statistical method for analyzing the intercorrelations among various measures or test scores; clusters of measures or scores that are highly correlated are assumed to measure the same underlying trait, ability, or aptitude (factor).

feature detectors Cells in the visual cortex that are sensitive to specific features of the environment.

fraternal (dizygotic) twins Twins that develop from two separate eggs fertilized by different sperm; they are no more alike genetically than any other pair of siblings.

free association In psychoanalysis, a method of uncovering unconscious conflicts by saying freely whatever comes to mind.

frequency distribution A summary of how frequently each score in a set occurred.

frequency polygon (line graph) A graph showing a set of points obtained by plotting score values against score frequencies; adjacent points are joined by straight lines.

fugue A dissociative disorder in which a person flees home and forgets his or her identity.

functionalism An early psychological approach that emphasized the function or purpose of behavior and consciousness.

fundamental attribution error In explaining other people's behavior, the tendency to overestimate personality factors and underestimate the influence of the situation.

ganglion cells Neurons in the retina of the eye, which gather information from receptor cells (by way of intermediate bipolar cells); their axons make up the optic nerve.

gate-control theory The theory that the experience of pain depends in part on whether pain impulses get past a neurological "gate" in the spinal cord and thus reach the brain.

gender identity The fundamental sense of being male or female; it is independent of whether the person conforms to the social and cultural rules of gender.

gender role A social position governed by rules and standards for male or female attitudes and behavior.

gender schema A cognitive schema (mental network) of knowledge, beliefs, metaphors, and expectations about what it means to be male or female.

gender socialization The process by which children learn the behaviors, attitudes, and expectations associated with being masculine or feminine in their culture; also called *sex typing*.

generalized anxiety disorder A continuous state of anxiety marked by feelings of worry and dread, apprehension, difficulties in concentration, and signs of motor tension.

genes The functional units of heredity; they are composed of DNA and specify the structure of proteins.

g factor A general intellectual ability assumed by many theorists to underlie specific mental abilities and talents.

glial cells Cells that hold neurons in place, insulate neurons, and provide neurons with nutrients.

graph A drawing that depicts numerical relationships.

groupthink In close-knit groups, the tendency for all members to think alike for the sake of harmony and to suppress dissent.

heritability A statistical estimate of the proportion of the total variance in some trait within a group that is attributable to genetic differences among individuals within the group.

heuristic A rule of thumb that suggests a course of action or guides problem solving but does not guarantee an optimal solution.

higher-order conditioning In classical conditioning, a procedure in which a neutral stimulus becomes a conditioned stimulus through association with an already established conditioned stimulus.

hindsight bias The tendency to overestimate one's ability to have predicted an event once the outcome is known; the "I knew it all along" phenomenon.

hippocampus A brain structure involved in the storage of new information in memory.

histogram (bar graph) A graph in which the heights (or lengths) of bars are proportional to the frequencies of individual scores or classes of scores in a distribution.

hormones Chemical substances, secreted by organs called *glands,* that affect the functioning of other organs.

hue The dimension of visual experience specified by color names and related to the wavelength of light.

humanist psychology A psychological approach that emphasizes personal growth and the achievement of human potential rather than the scientific understanding and assessment of behavior.

hypothalamus A brain structure involved in emotions and drives vital to survival, such as fear, hunger, thirst, and reproduction; it regulates the autonomic nervous system.

hypothesis A statement that attempts to predict or to account for a set of phenomena; scientific hypotheses specify relationships among events or variables and are empirically tested.

id In psychoanalysis, the part of personality containing inherited psychological energy, particularly sexual and aggressive instincts.

identical (monozygotic) twins Twins that develop when a fertilized egg divides into two parts that become separate embryos.

implicit memory Unconscious retention in memory, as evidenced by the effect of a previous experience or previously encountered information on current thoughts or actions.

independent variable A variable that an experimenter manipulates.

individualist cultures Cultures in which the self is regarded as autonomous, and individual goals and wishes are prized above duty and relations with others.

induction A method of child rearing in which the parent appeals to the child's own resources, abilities, sense of responsibility, and feelings for others in correcting the child's misbehavior.

inductive reasoning A form of reasoning in which the premises provide support for a conclusion, but it is still possible for the conclusion to be false.

infantile amnesia *See* childhood amnesia.

inferential statistics Statistical tests that assess how likely it is that a study's results occurred merely by chance.

insight A form of problem solving that appears to involve the (often sudden) understanding of how elements of a situation are related or can be reorganized to achieve a solution.

instinctive drift The tendency of an organism to revert to an instinctive behavior over time; can interfere with learning.

intelligence An inferred characteristic of an individual, usually defined as the ability to profit from experience, acquire knowledge, think abstractly, act purposefully, or adapt to changes in the environment.

intelligence quotient (IQ) A measure of intelligence originally computed by dividing a person's mental age by his or her chronological age and multiplying the result by 100; now derived from norms provided for standardized intelligence tests.

intermittent (partial) schedule of reinforcement A reinforcement schedule in which a particular response is sometimes but not always reinforced.

intrapsychic Within the mind (psyche) or self.

intrinsic reinforcers Reinforcers that are inherently related to the activity being reinforced, such as enjoyment of the task and the satisfaction of accomplishment.

inventories Standardized objective questionnaires requiring written responses; they typically include scales on which people are asked to rate themselves.

just-world hypothesis The notion that many people need to believe that the world is fair and that justice is served; that bad people are punished and good people rewarded.

kinesthesis (KIN-es-THEE-sis) The sense of body position and movement of body parts; also called *kinesthesia*.

latent learning A form of learning that is not immediately expressed in an overt response; occurs without obvious reinforcement.

lateralization Specialization of the two cerebral hemispheres for particular operations.

learning A relatively permanent change in behavior (or behavioral potential) due to experience.

learning disability A difficulty in the performance of a specific mental skill, such as reading or arithmetic; sometimes linked to perceptual or memory problems.

libido In psychoanalysis, the psychic energy that fuels the sexual or life instincts of the id.

limbic system A group of brain areas involved in emotional reactions and motivated behavior.

localization of function Specialization of particular brain areas for particular functions.

locus of control A general expectation about whether the results of your actions are under your own control (internal locus) or beyond your control (external locus).

longitudinal study A study in which subjects are followed and periodically reassessed over a period of time.

long-term memory (LTM) In the three-box model of memory, the memory system involved in the long-term storage of information.

loudness The dimension of auditory experience related to the intensity of a pressure wave.

magnetic resonance imaging *See* MRI.

maintenance rehearsal Rote repetition of material in order to maintain its availability in memory.

major depression A mood disorder involving disturbances in emotion (excessive sadness), behavior (loss of interest in one's usual activities), cognition (thoughts of hopelessness), and body function (fatigue and loss of appetite).

mean *See* arithmetic mean.

measure of central tendency A number intended to characterize an entire set of data.

measure of variability A number that indicates how dispersed scores are around the mean of the distribution. *See also* variance.

median A measure of central tendency; the value at the midpoint of a distribution of scores when the scores are ordered from highest to lowest.

medulla A structure in the brain stem responsible for certain automatic functions, such as breathing and heart rate.

melatonin A hormone, secreted by the pineal gland, that is involved in the regulation of daily biological rhythms.

menarche (men-ARR-kee) The onset of menstruation.

menopause   The cessation of menstruation and of the production of ova; usually a gradual process lasting up to several years.

mental age (MA)   A measure of mental development expressed in terms of the average mental ability at a given age; a child with a mental age of 8 performs on a test of mental ability at the level of the average 8-year-old.

mental disorder   Any behavior or emotional state that causes an individual great suffering or worry; is self-defeating or self-destructive; or is maladaptive and disrupts the person's relationships or the larger community.

mental image   A mental representation that mirrors or resembles the thing it represents; it can occur in many and perhaps all sensory modalities.

mental set   A tendency to solve problems using procedures that worked before on similar problems.

meta-analysis   A procedure for combining and analyzing data from many studies; it determines how much of the variance in scores across all studies can be explained by a particular variable.

metacognition   The knowledge or awareness of one's own cognitive processes.

Minnesota Multiphasic Personality Inventory (MMPI)   A widely used objective personality test.

mnemonics   Strategies and tricks for improving memory, such as the use of a verse or a formula.

mode   A measure of central tendency; the most frequently occurring score in a distribution.

monochronic cultures   Cultures in which time is organized sequentially; schedules and deadlines are valued over people.

monocular cues   Visual cues to depth or distance, which can be used by one eye alone.

monozygotic twins   *See* identical twins.

motivated forgetting   Forgetting that occurs because of a desire to eliminate awareness of painful, embarrassing, or otherwise unpleasant experiences.

motivation   An inferred process within a person or animal that causes that organism to move toward a goal or away from an unpleasant situation.

MRI (magnetic resonance imaging)   A method for studying body and brain tissue using magnetic fields and special radio receivers.

multiple personality disorder   *See* dissociative identity disorder.

myelin sheath   A fatty insulation that may surround the axon of a neuron.

narcissistic personality disorder   A disorder characterized by an exaggerated sense of self-importance and self-absorption.

need for achievement   A learned motive to meet personal standards of success and excellence in a chosen area (often abbreviated *nAch*).

need for affiliation   The motive to associate with other people, as by seeking friends, moral support, companionship, or love.

need for power   A learned motive to dominate or influence others.

negative correlation   An association between increases in one variable and decreases in another.

negative reinforcement   A reinforcement procedure in which a response is followed by the removal, delay, or decrease in intensity of an unpleasant stimulus; as a result, the response becomes stronger or more likely to occur.

nerve   A bundle of nerve fibers (axons and sometimes dendrites) in the peripheral nervous system.

neuron   A cell that conducts electrochemical signals; the basic unit of the nervous system; also called a *nerve cell.*

neurotransmitter   A chemical substance that is released by a transmitting neuron at the synapse and that alters the activity of a receiving neuron.

nonconscious processes   Mental processes occurring outside of and not available to conscious awareness.

normal curve   A symmetrical, bell-shaped frequency polygon representing a normal distribution.

normal distribution   A theoretical frequency distribution having certain special characteristics. For example, the distribution is symmetrical; the mean, mode, and median all have the same value; and the farther a score is from the mean, the less the likelihood of obtaining it.

norms   In test construction, established standards of performance.

norms (social)   Social conventions that regulate human life, including explicit laws and implicit cultural standards.

null hypothesis   An assertion that the independent variable in a study will have no effect on the dependent variable.

object permanence   The understanding, which develops late in the first year after birth, that an object continues to exist even when you can't see it or touch it.

object-relations school   A psychodynamic approach that emphasizes the importance of the infant's first two years of life and the baby's formative relationships.

observational learning   A process in which an individual learns new responses by observing the behavior of another (a model) rather than through direct experience; sometimes called *vicarious conditioning.*

observational study   A study in which the researcher carefully and systematically observes and records behavior without interfering with the behavior; it may involve either naturalistic or laboratory observation.

obsessive–compulsive disorder (OCD) An anxiety disorder in which a person feels trapped in repetitive, persistent thoughts (obsessions) and repetitive, ritualized behaviors (compulsions) designed to reduce anxiety.

Oedipus complex In psychoanalysis, a conflict in which a child desires the parent of the other sex and views the same-sex parent as a rival; this is the key issue in the phallic stage of development.

operant conditioning The process by which a response becomes more likely to occur or less so, depending on its consequences.

operational definition A precise definition of a term in a hypothesis, which specifies the operations for observing and measuring the process or phenomenon being defined.

operations In Piaget's theory, mental actions that are cognitively reversible.

opponent-process theory A theory of color perception that assumes that the visual system treats pairs of colors as opposing or antagonistic.

panic disorder An anxiety disorder in which a person experiences intense periods of fear and feelings of impending doom, accompanied by physiological symptoms such as rapid breathing and pulse, and dizziness.

papillae (pa-PILL-ee) Knoblike elevations on the tongue, containing the taste buds. Singular: *papilla.*

parallel distributed processing (PDP) An alternative to the information-processing model of memory, in which knowledge is represented as connections among thousands of interacting processing units, distributed in a vast network, and all operating in parallel.

paranoid personality disorder A disorder characterized by habitually unreasonable and excessive suspiciousness, jealousy, or mistrust. Paranoid symptoms may also occur in schizophrenia and other psychoses.

parapsychology The study of purported psychic phenomena such as ESP and mental telepathy.

parasympathetic nervous system The subdivision of the autonomic nervous system that operates during relaxed states and that conserves energy.

percentile score A score that indicates the percentage of people who scored at or below a given raw score; also called *centile rank.*

perception The process by which the brain organizes and interprets sensory information.

perceptual constancy The accurate perception of objects as stable or unchanged despite changes in the sensory patterns they produce.

perceptual illusion An erroneous or misleading perception of reality.

perceptual set A habitual way of perceiving, based on expectations.

peripheral nervous system (PNS) All portions of the nervous system outside the brain and spinal cord; it includes sensory and motor nerves.

personality A distinctive and relatively stable pattern of behavior, thoughts, motives, and emotions that characterizes an individual.

personality disorders Rigid, maladaptive personality patterns that cause personal distress or an inability to get along with others.

PET scan (positron-emission tomography) A method for analyzing biochemical activity in the brain, using injections of a glucoselike substance containing a radioactive element.

phobia An exaggerated fear of a specific situation, activity, or object.

pitch The dimension of auditory experience related to the frequency of a pressure wave; height or depth of a tone.

pituitary gland A small endocrine gland at the base of the brain, which releases many hormones and regulates other endocrine glands.

placebo An inactive substance or fake treatment used as a control in an experiment or given by a medical practitioner to a patient.

polychronic cultures Cultures in which time is organized horizontally; people tend to do several things at once and value relationships over schedules.

pons A structure in the brain stem involved in, among other things, sleeping, waking, and dreaming.

positive correlation An association between increases in one variable and increases in another.

positive reinforcement A reinforcement procedure in which a response is followed by the presentation of, or increase in intensity of, a reinforcing stimulus; as a result, the response becomes stronger or more likely to occur.

positron emission tomography *See* PET scan.

posttraumatic stress disorder (PTSD) An anxiety disorder in which a person who has experienced a traumatic or life-threatening event has symptoms such as psychic numbing, reliving of the trauma, and increased physiological arousal.

power assertion A method of child rearing in which the parent uses punishment and authority to correct the child's misbehavior.

primary control An effort to modify reality by changing other people, the situation, or events; a "fighting back" philosophy.

primary emotions Emotions that are considered to be universal and biologically based; they generally include fear, anger, sadness, joy, surprise, disgust, and contempt.

primary punisher A stimulus that is inherently punishing; an example is electric shock.

primary reinforcer A stimulus that is inherently reinforcing, typically satisfying a physiological need; an example is food.

priming A method for measuring implicit memory in which a person reads or listens to information and is later tested to see whether the information affects performance on another type of task.

principle of falsifiability The principle that a scientific theory must make predictions that expose the theory to the possibility of disconfirmation; that is, the theory must predict not only what will happen, but also what will not happen.

proactive interference Forgetting that occurs when previously stored material interferes with the ability to remember similar, more recently learned material.

procedural memories Memories for the performance of actions or skills ("knowing how").

projective tests Psychological tests used to infer a person's motives, conflicts, and unconscious personality dynamics from the person's interpretations of ambiguous or unstructured stimuli.

proposition A unit of meaning that is made up of concepts and expresses a single idea.

prototype An especially representative example of a concept.

psychiatry The medical specialty concerned with mental disorders, maladjustment, and abnormal behavior.

psychoanalysis A theory of personality and a method of psychotherapy developed by Sigmund Freud; it emphasizes unconscious motives and conflicts.

psychodynamic theories Theories that explain behavior and personality in terms of unconscious energy dynamics within the individual.

psychological stress The result of a relationship between the person and the environment, in which the person believes the situation is overwhelming and threatens his or her ability to cope.

psychological tests Procedures used to measure and evaluate personality traits, emotional states, aptitudes, interests, abilities, and values.

psychology The scientific study of behavior and mental processes and how they are affected by an organism's physical state, mental state, and external environment; the term is often represented by ψ, the Greek letter psi (usually pronounced "sy").

psychometrics The measurement of mental abilities, traits, and processes.

psychophysics The area of psychology concerned with the relationship between physical properties of stimuli and sensory experience.

psychosis An extreme mental disturbance involving distorted perceptions and irrational behavior; it may have psychological or organic causes. Plural: *psychoses.*

psychosurgery Any surgical procedure that destroys selected areas of the brain believed to be involved in emotional disorders or violent, impulsive behavior.

puberty The age at which a person becomes capable of sexual reproduction.

punishment The process by which a stimulus or event weakens or reduces the probability of the response that it follows.

range A measure of the spread of scores, calculated by subtracting the lowest score from the highest score.

rapid eye movement (REM) sleep Sleep periods characterized by eye movement, loss of muscle tone, and dreaming.

reasoning The drawing of conclusions or inferences from observations, facts, or assumptions.

recall The ability to retrieve and reproduce from memory previously encountered material.

recognition The ability to identify previously encountered material.

reinforcement The process by which a stimulus or event strengthens or increases the probability of the response that it follows.

reinforcer A stimulus or event that strengthens or increases the probability of the response it follows.

relearning method A method for measuring retention that compares the time required to relearn material with the time used in the initial learning of the material.

reliability In test construction, the consistency of scores derived from a test, from one time and place to another.

REM sleep *See* rapid eye movement (REM) sleep.

representative sample A group of subjects selected from a population for study, which matches the population on important characteristics such as age and sex.

reticular activating system (RAS) A dense network of neurons found in the core of the brain stem; it arouses the cortex and screens incoming information.

retina Neural tissue lining the back of the eyeball's interior, which contains the receptors for vision.

retinal disparity The slight difference in lateral separation between two objects as seen by the left eye and the right eye.

retroactive interference Forgetting that occurs when recently learned material interferes with the ability to remember similar material stored previously.

rods Visual receptors that respond to dim light but are not involved in color vision.

role A given social position that is governed by a set of norms for proper behavior.

Rorschach Inkblot Test A projective test that asks respondents to interpret abstract, symmetrical inkblots.

saturation Vividness or purity of color; the dimension of visual experience related to the complexity of light waves.

schizophrenia A psychotic disorder or group of disorders marked by positive symptoms (e.g., delusions, hallucinations, disorganized and incoherent speech, and inappropriate behavior) and negative symptoms (e.g., emotional flatness and loss of motivation).

secondary control An effort to accept reality by changing your own attitudes, goals, or emotions; a "learn to live with it" philosophy.

secondary emotions Emotions that are specific to certain cultures.

secondary punisher A stimulus that has acquired punishing properties through association with other punishers.

secondary reinforcer A stimulus that has acquired reinforcing properties through association with other reinforcers.

selective attention The focusing of attention on selected aspects of the environment and the blocking out of others.

self-efficacy A person's belief that he or she is capable of producing desired results, such as mastering new skills and reaching goals.

self-fulfilling prophecy An expectation that comes true because of the tendency of the person holding it to act in ways that confirm it.

self-serving bias The tendency, in explaining one's own behavior, to take credit for one's good actions and rationalize one's mistakes.

semantic memories Memories of general knowledge, including facts, rules, concepts, and propositions.

semicircular canals Sense organs in the inner ear that contribute to equilibrium by responding to rotation of the head.

sensation The detection of physical energy emitted or reflected by physical objects; it occurs when energy in the external environment or the body stimulates receptors in the sense organs.

sense receptors Specialized cells that convert physical energy in the environment or the body to electrical energy that can be transmitted as nerve impulses to the brain.

sensory adaptation The reduction or disappearance of sensory responsiveness that occurs when stimulation is unchanging or repetitious.

sensory deprivation The absence of normal levels of sensory stimulation.

sensory memory A memory system that momentarily preserves extremely accurate images of sensory information.

sensory registers Subsystems of sensory memory; most memory models assume a separate register for each sensory modality.

serial-position effect The tendency for recall of the first and the last items on a list to surpass recall of items in the middle of the list.

set point The genetically influenced weight range for an individual, thought to be maintained by a biological mechanism that regulates food intake, fat reserves, and metabolism.

sex hormones Hormones that regulate the development and functioning of reproductive organs and that stimulate the development of male and female sexual characteristics; they include androgens (such as testosterone), estrogens, and progesterone.

sex typing *See* gender socialization.

shaping An operant-conditioning procedure in which successive approximations of a desired response are reinforced; used when the desired response has a low probability of occurring spontaneously.

short-term memory (STM) In the three-box model of memory, a limited-capacity memory system involved in the retention of information for brief periods; also used for holding information retrieved from long-term memory for temporary use.

signal-detection theory A psychophysical theory that divides the detection of a sensory signal into a sensory process and a decision process.

single-blind study An experiment in which subjects do not know whether they are in an experimental or a control group.

social cognition An area in social psychology concerned with social influences on thought, memory, perception, and other cognitive processes.

social identity The part of a person's self-concept that is based on identification with a nation, culture, or ethnic group or with gender or other roles in society.

social-learning theories Theories that emphasize how behavior is learned and maintained through observation and imitation of others, positive consequences, and cognitive processes such as plans, expectations, and motivating beliefs.

somatic nervous system The subdivision of the peripheral nervous system that connects to sensory receptors and to skeletal muscles; sometimes called the *skeletal nervous system*.

source amnesia The inability to distinguish what you originally experienced from what you heard or were told about an event later.

spinal cord A collection of neurons and supportive tissue running from the base of the brain down the center of the back, protected by a column of bones (the spinal column).

spontaneous recovery The reappearance of a learned response after its apparent extinction.

standard deviation A commonly used measure of variability that indicates the average difference between scores in a distribution and their mean; more precisely, the square root of the average squared deviation from the mean.

standardize In test construction, to develop uniform procedures for giving and scoring a test.

state-dependent memory The tendency to remember something when the rememberer is in the same physical or mental state as during the original learning or experience.

statistically significant A term used to refer to a result that is extremely unlikely to have occurred by chance.

stereotype A cognitive schema or a summary impression of a group, in which a person believes that all members of the group share a common trait or traits (positive, negative, or neutral).

stimulus control Control over the occurrence of a response by a discriminative stimulus.

stimulus discrimination The tendency to respond differently to two or more similar stimuli. In classical conditioning, it occurs when a stimulus similar to the conditioned stimulus fails to evoke the conditioned response. In operant conditioning, it occurs when an organism learns to make a response in the presence of one stimulus but not in the presence of other, similar stimuli that differ from it on some dimension.

stimulus generalization After conditioning, the tendency to respond to a stimulus that resembles one involved in the original conditioning. In classical conditioning, it occurs when a stimulus that resembles the conditioned stimulus elicits the conditioned response. In operant conditioning, it occurs when a response that has been reinforced (or punished) in the presence of one stimulus occurs (or is suppressed) in the presence of other, similar stimuli.

stress *See* psychological stress.

subconscious processes Mental processes occurring outside of conscious awareness but accessible to consciousness when necessary.

superego In psychoanalysis, the part of personality that represents conscience, morality, and social standards.

surveys Questionnaires and interviews that ask people directly about their experiences, attitudes, or opinions.

sympathetic nervous system The subdivision of the autonomic nervous system that mobilizes bodily resources and increases the output of energy during emotion and stress.

synapse The site where transmission of a nerve impulse from one nerve cell to another occurs; it includes the axon terminal, the synaptic cleft, and receptor sites in the membrane of the receiving cell.

taste buds Nests of taste-receptor cells.

telegraphic speech A child's first word combinations, which omit (as a telegram does) unnecessary words.

temperaments Characteristic styles of responding to the environment that are present in infancy and are assumed to be innate.

thalamus A brain structure that relays sensory messages to the cerebral cortex.

Thematic Apperception Test (TAT) A projective test that asks respondents to interpret a series of drawings showing ambiguous scenes of people.

theory An organized system of assumptions and principles that purports to explain a specified set of phenomena and their interrelationships.

therapeutic alliance The bond of confidence and mutual understanding established between therapist and client, which allows them to work together to solve the client's problems.

timbre The distinguishing quality of a sound; the dimension of auditory experience related to the complexity of the pressure wave.

token economy A behavior-modification technique in which secondary reinforcers called *tokens*, which can be collected and exchanged for primary or other secondary reinforcers, are used to shape behavior.

trait A descriptive characteristic of an individual, assumed to be stable across situations and time.

tranquilizers Drugs commonly but often inappropriately prescribed for patients who complain of unhappiness, anxiety, or worry.

transference In psychodynamic therapies, a critical step in which the client transfers unconscious emotions or reactions, such as emotional feelings about his or her parents, onto the therapist.

trichromatic theory A theory of color perception that proposes three mechanisms in the visual system, each sensitive to a certain range of wavelengths; their interaction is assumed to produce all the different experiences of hue.

two-factor theory of emotion The theory that emotions depend on both physiological arousal and a cognitive interpretation of that arousal.

unconditional positive regard To Carl Rogers, love or support given to another person, with no conditions attached.

unconditioned response (UR) The classical-conditioning term for a reflexive response elicited by a stimulus in the absence of learning.

unconditioned stimulus (US) The classical-conditioning term for a stimulus that elicits a reflexive response in the absence of learning.

validity The ability of a test to measure what it was designed to measure.

validity effect The tendency of people to believe that a statement is true or valid simply because it has been repeated many times.

variables Characteristics of behavior or experience that can be measured or described by a numeric scale; variables are manipulated and assessed in scientific studies.

variance A measure of the dispersion of scores around the mean.

volunteer bias A shortcoming of findings derived from a sample of volunteers instead of a representative sample.

z-score (standard score) A number that indicates how far a given raw score is above or below the mean, using the standard deviation of the distribution as the unit of measurement.

Bibliography

Abel, Gene G.; Mittelman, Mary; Becker, Judith V.; Rathner, Jerry; et al. (1988). Predicting child molesters' response to treatment: Conference of the New York Academy of Sciences. Human sexual aggression: Current perspectives. *Annals of the New York Academy of Sciences, 528,* 223–234.

Abramson, Lyn Y.; Metalsky, Gerald I.; & Alloy, Lauren B. (1989). Hopelessness depression: A theory-based subtype of depression. *Psychological Review, 96,* 358–372.

Adamopoulos, John, & Lonner, Walter J. (1994). Absolutism, relativism, and universalism in the study of human behavior. In W. J. Lonner & R. S. Malpass (eds.), *Psychology and culture.* Needham Heights, MA: Allyn & Bacon.

Adams, James L. (1986). *Conceptual blockbusting: A guide to better ideas* (3rd ed.). Boston: Addison-Wesley.

Adams, M. J. (1990). *Learning to read: Thinking and learning about print.* Cambridge, MA: MIT Press.

Adler, Nancy E.; Boyce, Thomas; Chesney, Margaret A.; Cohen, Sheldon; Folkman, Susan; Kahn, Robert L.; & Syme, S. Leonard (1994). Socioeconomic status and health: The challenge of the gradient. *American Psychologist, 49,* 15–24.

Affleck, Glenn; Tennen, Howard; Croog, Sydney; & Levine, Sol (1987). Causal attribution, perceived control, and recovery from a heart attack. *Journal of Social and Clinical Psychology, 5,* 339–355.

Ainsworth, Mary D. S. (1973). The development of infant–mother attachment. In B. M. Caldwell & H. N. Ricciuti (eds.), *Review of child development research* (Vol. 3). Chicago: University of Chicago Press.

Ainsworth, Mary D. S. (1979). Infant–mother attachment. *American Psychologist, 34,* 932–937.

Ainsworth, Mary D. S.; Blehar, Mary L.; Waters, Everett; & Wall, Sally (1978). *Patterns of attachment.* Hillsdale, NJ: Erlbaum.

Aldag, Ramon J., & Fuller, Sally R. (1993). Beyond fiasco: A reappraisal of the groupthink phenomenon and a new model of group decision processes. *Psychological Bulletin, 113,* 533–552.

Allen, Laura S., & Gorski, Robert A. (1992). Sexual orientation and the size of the anterior commissure in the human brain. *Proceedings of the National Academy of Sciences, 89,* 7199–7202.

Allison, David B., & Heshka, Stanley (1993). Emotion and eating in obesity? A critical analysis. *International Journal of Eating Disorders, 13,* 289–295.

Allison, David B.; Heshka, Stanley; Neale, Michael C.; Lykken, David T.; et al. (1994). A genetic analysis of relative weight among 4,020 twin pairs, with an emphasis on sex effects. *Health Psychology, 13,* 362–365.

Allport, Gordon W. (1937). *Personality: A psychological interpretation.* New York: Holt, Rinehart and Winston.

Allport, Gordon W. (1954/1979). *The nature of prejudice.* Reading, MA: Addison-Wesley.

Allport, Gordon W. (1961). *Pattern and growth in personality.* New York: Holt, Rinehart and Winston.

Amabile, Teresa M. (1983). *The social psychology of creativity.* New York: Springer-Verlag.

Amabile, Teresa M.; Phillips, Elise D.; & Collins, Mary Ann (1993). Creativity by contract: Social influences on the creativity of professional artists. Paper presented at the annual meeting of the American Psychological Association, Toronto, Canada.

American Psychiatric Association (1994). *The diagnostic and statistical manual of mental disorders* (4th ed.). Washington, DC: Author.

Amering, Michaela, & Katschnig, Heinz (1990). Panic attacks and panic disorder in cross-cultural perspective. *Psychiatric Annals, 20,* 511–516.

Amir, Yehuda (1994). The contact hypothesis in intergroup relations. In W. J. Lonner & R. Malpass (eds.), *Psychology and culture.* Needham Heights, MA: Allyn & Bacon.

Anastasi, Anne (1988). *Psychological testing* (6th ed.). New York: Macmillan.

Anderson, Craig A.; Miller, Rowland S.; Riger, Alice L.; Dill, Jody C.; & Sedikides, Constantine (1994). Behavioral and characterological attributional styles as predictors of depression and loneliness: Review, refinement, and test. *Journal of Personality and Social Psychology, 66,* 549–558.

Anderson, John R. (1990). *The adaptive nature of thought.* Hillsdale, NJ: Erlbaum.

Anderson, Norman B. (1991). Addressing ethnic minority health issues: Behavioral medicine at the forefront of research and practice. Paper presented at the annual meeting of the Society of Behavioral Medicine, Washington, DC.

Andreasen, Nancy C.; Arndt, Stephan; Swayze, Victor, II; Cizadlo, Ted; et al. (1994). Thalamic abnormalities in schizophrenia visualized through magnetic resonance image averaging. *Science, 266,* 294–298.

Anliker, J. A.; Bartoshuk, L. M.; Ferris, A. M.; & Hooks, L. D. (1991). Children's food preferences and genetic sensitivity to the bitter taste of PROP. *American Journal of Clinical Nutrition, 54,* 316–320.

Antonuccio, David; Danton, William G.; & DeNelsky, Garland Y. (1995). Psychotherapy vs. medication for depression: Challenging the conventional wisdom. *Professional Psychology: Research and Practice, 26,* 574–585.

APA Commission on Violence and Youth (1993). *Violence and youth: Psychology's response.* Washington, DC: American Psychological Association.

Apter, Terri (1990). *Altered loves: Mothers and daughters during adolescence.* New York: St. Martin's Press.

Arendt, Hannah (1963). *Eichmann in Jerusalem: A report on the banality of evil.* New York: Viking.

Arkes, Hal R. (1991). Some practical judgment/decision making research. Paper presented at the annual meeting of the American Psychological Association, Boston.

Arkes, Hal R.; Boehm, Lawrence E.; & Xu, Gang (1991). The determinants of judged validity. *Journal of Experimental Social Psychology, 27,* 576–605.

Arkes, Hal R.; Faust, David; Guilmette, Thomas J.; & Hart, Kathleen (1988). Eliminating the hindsight bias. *Journal of Applied Psychology, 73,* 305–307.

Aron, Arthur, & Westbay, Lori (1996). Dimensions of the prototype of love. *Journal of Personality and Social Psychology, 70,* 535–551.

Aronson, Elliot (1995). *The social animal* (7th ed.). New York: Freeman.

Aronson, Elliot, & Mills, Judson (1959). The effect of severity of initiation on liking for a group. *Journal of Abnormal and Social Psychology, 59,* 177–181.

Aronson, Elliot; Stephan, Cookie; Sikes, Jev; Blaney, Nancy; & Snapp, Matthew (1978). *The jigsaw classroom.* Beverly Hills, CA: Sage.

Aronson, Elliot; Wilson, Timothy D.; & Akert, Robin A. (1997). *Social psychology: The heart and the mind* (2nd ed.). New York: Longman.

Asch, Solomon E. (1952). *Social psychology.* Englewood Cliffs, NJ: Prentice-Hall.

Asch, Solomon E. (1965). Effects of group pressure upon the modification and distortion of judgments. In H. Proshansky & B. Seidenberg (eds.), *Basic studies in social psychology.* New York: Holt, Rinehart and Winston.

Aserinsky, Eugene, & Kleitman, Nathaniel (1955). Two types of ocular motility occurring in sleep. *Journal of Applied Physiology, 8,* 1–10.

Aspinwall, Lisa G., & Brunhart, Susanne M. (1996). Distinguishing optimism from denial: Optimistic beliefs predict attention to health threats. *Personality and Social Psychology Bulletin, 22,* 993–1003.

Aspinwall, Lisa G., & Taylor, Shelley E. (1997). A stitch in time: Self-regulation and proactive coping. *Psychological Bulletin, 121,* 417–436.

Atkinson, John W. (ed.) (1958). *Motives in fantasy, action, and society.* Princeton, NJ: Van Nostrand.

Atkinson, Richard C., & Shiffrin, Richard M. (1968). Human memory: A proposed system and its control processes. In K. W. Spence & J. T. Spence (eds.), *The psychology of learning and motivation: Vol. 2. Advances in research and theory.* New York: Academic Press.

Atkinson, Richard C., & Shiffrin, Richard M. (1971, August). The control of short-term memory. *Scientific American, 225*(2), 82–90.

Averill, James R. (1982). *Anger and aggression.* New York: Springer-Verlag.

Azrin, Nathan H., & Foxx, Richard M. (1974). *Toilet training in less than a day.* New York: Simon & Schuster.

Azuma, Hiroshi (1984). Secondary control as a heterogeneous category. *American Psychologist, 39,* 970–971.

Bahill, A. Terry, & Karnavas, William J. (1993). The perceptual illusion of baseball's rising fastball and breaking curveball. *Journal of Experimental Psychology: Human Perception & Performance, 19,* 3–14.

Bahrick, Harry P. (1984). Semantic memory content in permastore: Fifty years of memory for Spanish learned in school. *Journal of Experimental Psychology: General, 113,* 1–29.

Bahrick, Harry P.; Bahrick, Phyllis O.; & Wittlinger, Roy P. (1975). Fifty years of memory for names and faces: A cross-sectional approach. *Journal of Experimental Psychology: General, 104,* 54–75.

Bailey, J. Michael; Bobrow, David; Wolfe, Marilyn; & Mikach, Sarah (1995). Sexual orientation of adult sons of gay fathers. *Developmental Psychology, 31,* 124–129.

Bailey, J. Michael; Gaulin, Steven; Agyei, Yvonne; & Gladue, Brian A. (1994). Effects of gender and sexual orientation on evolutionarily relevant aspects of human mating psychology. *Journal of Personality and Social Psychology, 66,* 1081–1093.

Bailey, J. Michael, & Pillard, Richard C. (1995). Genetics of human sexual orientation. *Annual Review of Sex Research, 6,* 126–150.

Baillargeon, Renée (1994). How do infants learn about the physical world? *Current Directions in Psychological Science, 5,* 133–140.

Baker, Robin (1996). *The sperm wars: The science of sex.* New York: Basic Books.

Baltes, Paul B. (1983). Life-span developmental psychology: Observations on history and theory revisited. In R. M. Lerner (ed.), *Developmental psychology: Historical and philosophical perspectives.* Hillsdale, NJ: Erlbaum.

Baltes, Paul, & Graf, Peter (1996). Psychological aspects of aging: Facts and frontiers. In D. Magnusson (ed.), *The lifespan development of individuals.* Cambridge, England: Cambridge University Press.

Baltes, Paul B.; Sowarka, Doris; & Kliegl, Reinhold (1989). Cognitive training research on fluid intelligence in old age: What can older adults achieve by themselves? *Psychology and Aging, 4,* 217–221.

Bandura, Albert (1977). *Social learning theory.* Englewood Cliffs, NJ: Prentice-Hall.

Bandura, Albert (1986). *Social foundations of thought and action: A social cognitive theory.* Englewood Cliffs, NJ: Prentice-Hall.

Bandura, Albert (1990). Self-regulation of motivation through goal systems. In R. A. Dienstbier (ed.), *Nebraska Symposium on Motivation* (Vol. 38). Lincoln: University of Nebraska Press.

Bandura, Albert (1994). Self-efficacy. In *Encyclopedia of human behavior* (Vol. 4). Orlando, FL: Academic Press.

Bandura, Albert (ed.) (1995). *Self-efficacy in changing societies.* New York: Cambridge University Press.

Bandura, Albert; Ross, Dorothea; & Ross, Sheila A. (1963). Vicarious reinforcement and imitative learning. *Journal of Abnormal and Social Psychology, 67,* 601–607.

Banks, Martin S. (in collaboration with Philip Salapatek) (1984). Infant visual perception. In P. Mussen (series ed.), M. M. Haith & J. J. Campos (vol. eds.), *Handbook of child psychology: Vol. II. Infancy and developmental psychobiology* (4th ed.). New York: Wiley.

Barinaga, Marcia (1992). Challenging the "no new neurons" dogma. *Science, 255,* 1646.

Barlow, David H. (1990). Disorders of emotion. Paper presented at the annual meeting of the American Psychological Association, Boston.

Barlow, David H. (ed.) (1991). Special issue on diagnoses, dimensions, and DSM-IV: The science of classification. *Journal of Abnormal Psychology, 100,* 243–412.

Barlow, David H. (1996). Health care policy, psychotherapy research, and the future of psychotherapy. *American Psychologist, 51,* 1050–1058.

Barnett, Peter A., & Gotlib, Ian H. (1988). Psychosocial functioning and depression: Distinguishing among antecedents, concomitants, and consequences. *Psychological Bulletin, 104,* 97–126.

Baron, Miron (1993). The D2 dopamine receptor gene and alcoholism: A tempest in a wine cup? *Biological Psychiatry, 34,* 821–823.

Bartlett, Frederic C. (1932). *Remembering.* Cambridge, England: Cambridge University Press.

Bartoshuk, Linda M. (1993). Genetic and pathological taste variation: What can we learn from animal models and human disease? In D. J. Chadwick, J. Marsh, & J. Goode (eds.), *The molecular basis of smell and taste transduction.* CIBA Foundation Symposia Series, No. 179. New York: Wiley.

Bartoshuk, Linda M., & Beauchamp, Gary K. (1994). Chemical senses. *Annual Review of Psychology, 45,* 419–449.

Basic Behavioral Science Task Force of the National Advisory Mental Health Council (1996). Basic behavioral science research for mental health: Vulnerability and resilience. *American Psychologist, 51,* 22–28.

Bauer, Patricia J., & Dow, Gina Annunziato (1994). Episodic memory in 16- and 20-month-old children: Specifics are generalized but not forgotten. *Developmental Psychology, 30,* 403–417.

Baum, Andrew; Herberman, Holly; & Cohen, Lorenzo (1995). Managing stress and managing illness: Survival and quality of life in chronic disease. Paper presented at the annual meeting of the American Psychological Association, New York.

Baum, William M. (1994). *Understanding behaviorism: Science, behavior, and culture.* New York: HarperCollins.

Baumeister, Roy F. (1990). Suicide as escape from self. *Psychological Review, 97,* 90–113.

Baumeister, Roy F., & Leary, Mark R. (1995). The need to belong: Desire for interpersonal attachments as a fundamental human motivation. *Psychological Bulletin, 117,* 497–529.

Baumeister, Roy F.; Stillwell, Arlene M.; & Heatherton, Todd F. (1994). Guilt: An interpersonal approach. *Psychological Bulletin, 115,* 243–267.

Baumrind, Diana (1966). Effects of authoritative parental control on child behavior. *Child Development, 37,* 887–907.

Baumrind, Diana (1971). Current patterns of parental authority. *Developmental Psychology Monograph, 4* (1, Part 2).

Baumrind, Diana (1973). The development of instrumental competence through socialization. In A. D. Pick (ed.), *Minnesota Symposium on Child Psychology* (Vol. 7). Minneapolis: University of Minnesota Press.

Baumrind, Diana (1989). Rearing competent children. In W. Damon (ed.), *Child development today and tomorrow.* San Francisco: Jossey-Bass.

Baumrind, Diana (1991). Parenting styles and adolescent development. In R. Lerner, A. C. Petersen, & J. Brooks-Gunn (eds.), *The encyclopedia of adolescence.* New York: Garland.

Baumrind, Diana (1995). Commentary on sexual orientation: Research and social policy implications. *Developmental Psychology, 31,* 130–136.

Baxter, Lewis R.; Schwartz, Jeffrey M.; Bergman, Kenneth S.; Szuba, Martin P.; et al. (1992). Caudate glucose metabolic rate changes with both drug and behavior therapy for obsessive–compulsive disorder. *Archives of General Psychiatry, 49,* 681–689.

Bayer, Ronald (1981). *Homosexuality and American psychiatry.* New York: Basic Books.

Beard, John H.; Propst, Rudyard N.; & Malamud, T. J. (1982). The Fountain House model of psychiatric rehabilitation. *Psychosocial Rehabilitation Journal, 5,* 47–54.

Beck, Aaron T. (1976). *Cognitive therapy and the emotional disorders.* New York: International Universities Press.

Beck, Aaron T. (1988). Cognitive approaches to panic disorder: Theory and therapy. In S. Rachman & J. D. Maser (eds.), *Panic: Psychological perspectives.* Hillsdale, NJ: Erlbaum.

Beck, Aaron T. (1991). Cognitive therapy: A 30-year retrospective. *American Psychologist, 46,* 368–375.

Becker, Judith V.; Skinner, Linda J.; Abel, Gene G.; & Cichon, Joan (1984). Time-limited therapy with sexually dysfunctional sexually assaulted women. *Journal of Social Work and Human Sexuality, 3,* 97–115.

Beckerman, Stephen; Lizarralde, Roberto; Ballew, Carol; Schroeder, Sissel; et al. (1998). The Bari partible paternity project: Preliminary results. *Current Anthropology, 39,* 164–167.

Bee, Helen (1997). *The developing child* (8th ed.). New York: Longman.

Bee, Helen; Barnard, Kathryn E.; et al. (1982). Prediction of IQ and language skill from perinatal status, child performance, family characteristics, and mother–infant interaction. *Child Development, 53,* 1134–1156.

Bekenstein, Jonathan W., & Lothman, Eric W. (1993). Dormancy of inhibitory interneurons in a model of temporal lobe epilepsy. *Science, 259,* 97–100.

Bell, Alan P.; Weinberg, Martin S.; & Hammersmith, Sue K. (1981). *Sexual preference: Its development in men and women.* Bloomington: Indiana University Press.

Bell, Derrick (1992). *Faces at the bottom of the well: The permanence of racism.* New York: Basic Books.

Belmont, Lillian, & Marolla, Francis A. (1973). Birth order, family size, and intelligence. *Science, 182,* 1096–1101.

Belsky, Jay; Hsieh, Kuang-Hua; & Crnic, Keith (1996). Infant positive and negative emotionality: One dimension or two? *Developmental Psychology, 32,* 289–298.

Bem, Daryl J., & Honorton, Charles (1994). Does psi exist? Replicable evidence for an anomalous process of information transfer. *Psychological Bulletin, 115,* 4–18.

Bem, Sandra L. (1985). Androgyny and gender schema theory: A conceptual and empirical integration. In T. B. Sonderegger (ed.), *Nebraska Symposium on Motivation: Vol. 32. Psychology and gender, 1984.* Lincoln: University of Nebraska Press.

Bem, Sandra L. (1993). *The lenses of gender.* New Haven, CT: Yale University Press.

Benet, Verónica, & Waller, Niels G. (1995). The Big Seven factor model of personality description: Evidence for its cross-cultural generality in a Spanish sample. *Journal of Personality and Social Psychology, 69,* 701–718.

Bentall, R. P. (1990). The illusion of reality: A review and integration of psychological research on hallucinations. *Psychological Bulletin, 107,* 82–95.

Bereiter, Carl, & Bird, Marlene (1985). Use of thinking aloud in identification and teaching of reading comprehension strategies. *Cognition and Instruction, 2,* 131–156.

Berenbaum, Sheri A., & Snyder, Elizabeth (1995). Early hormonal influences on childhood sex-typed activity and playmate preferences: Implications for the development of sexual orientation. *Developmental Psychology, 31,* 31–42.

Berkman, L. F.; Leo-Summers, L.; & Horwitz, R. I. (1992). Emotional support and survival after myocardial infarction: A prospective, population-based study of the elderly. *Annals of Internal Medicine, 117,* 1003–1009.

Berkman, Lisa, & Syme, S. Leonard (1979). Social networks, host resistance, and mortality: A nine-year follow-up study of Alameda County residents. *American Journal of Epidemiology, 109,* 186–204.

Berry, John W. (1994). Acculturative stress. In W. J. Lonner & R. S. Malpass (eds.), *Psychology and culture.* Needham Heights, MA: Allyn & Bacon.

Bettelheim, Bruno (1967). *The empty fortress.* New York: Free Press.

Birdwhistell, Ray L. (1970). *Kinesics and context: Essays on body motion communication.* Philadelphia: University of Pennsylvania Press.

Bishop, Katherine M., & Wahlsten, Douglas (1997). Sex differences in the human corpus callosum: Myth or reality? *Neuroscience and Biobehavioral Reviews, 21.*

Bjork, Daniel W. (1993). *B. F. Skinner: A life.* New York: Basic Books.

Black, Donald W.; Wesner, Robert; Bowers, Wayne; & Gabel, Janelle (1993). A comparison of fluvoxamine, cognitive therapy, and placebo in the treatment of panic disorder. *Archives of General Psychiatry, 50,* 44–50.

Blakemore, Colin, & Cooper, Grahame F. (1970). Development of the brain depends on the visual environment. *Nature, 228,* 477–478.

Blass, Thomas (1993). What we know about obedience: Distillations from 30 years of research on the Milgram paradigm. Paper presented at the annual meeting of the American Psychological Association, Toronto.

Bleuler, Eugen (1911/1950). *Dementia praecox or the group of schizophrenias.* New York: International Universities Press.

Blum, Kenneth, with James E. Payne (1991). *Alcohol and the addictive brain.* New York: Free Press/Science News Press.

Boehm, Lawrence E. (1994). The validity effect: A search for mediating variables. *Personality and Social Psychology Bulletin, 20,* 285–293.

Boesch, Cristophe (1991). Teaching among wild chimpanzees. *Animal Behavior, 41,* 530–532.

Bohannon, John N., & Stanowicz, Laura (1988). The issue of negative evidence: Adult responses to children's language errors. *Developmental Psychology, 24,* 684–689.

Bohannon, John N., & Symons, Victoria (1988). Conversational conditions of children's imitation. Paper presented at the biennial Conference on Human Development, Charleston, South Carolina.

Bohman, Michael; Cloninger, R.; Sigvardsson, S.; & von Knorring, Anne-Liis (1987). The genetics of alcoholisms and related disorders. *Journal of Psychiatric Research, 21,* 447–452.

Bolger, Niall; Foster, Mark; Vinokur, Amiram D.; & Ng, Rosanna (1996). Close relationships and adjustment to a life crisis: The case of breast cancer. *Journal of Personality and Social Psychology, 70,* 283–294.

Bond, Rod, & Smith, Peter B. (1996). Culture and conformity: A meta-analysis of studies using Asch's (1952b, 1956) line judgment task. *Psychological Bulletin, 119,* 111–137.

Bornstein, Robert F.; Leone, Dean R.; & Galley, Donna J. (1987). The generalizability of subliminal mere exposure effects: Influence of stimuli perceived without awareness on social behavior. *Journal of Personality and Social Psychology, 53,* 1070–1079.

Borys, Shelley, & Perlman, Daniel (1985). Gender differences in loneliness. *Personality and Social Psychology Bulletin, 11,* 63–74.

Bothwell, R. K., Deffenbacher, K. A., & Brigham, J. C. (1987). Correlation of eyewitness accuracy and confidence: Optimality hypothesis revised. *Journal of Applied Psychology, 72,* 691–698.

Bouchard, Claude; Tremblay, A.; Despres, J. P.; Nadeau, A.; et al. (1990, May 24). The response to long-term overfeeding in identical twins. *New England Journal of Medicine, 322,* 1477–1482.

Bouchard, Thomas J., Jr. (1984). Twins reared together and apart: What they tell us about human diversity. In S. W. Fox (ed.), *Individuality and determinism.* New York: Plenum.

Bouchard, Thomas J., Jr. (1995). Nature's twice-told tale: Identical twins reared apart, what they tell us about human individuality. Paper presented at the annual meeting of the Western Psychological Association, Los Angeles.

Bouchard, Thomas J., Jr. (1997a). IQ similarity in twins reared apart: Findings and responses to critics. In R. J. Sternberg & E. Grigorenko (eds.), *Intelligence: Heredity and environment.* New York: Cambridge University Press.

Bouchard, Thomas J., Jr. (1997b). The genetics of personality. In K. Blum & E. P. Noble (eds.), *Handbook of psychiatric genetics.* Boca Raton, FL: CRC Press.

Bouchard, Thomas J., Jr.; Lykken, David T.; McGue, Matthew; Segal, Nancy L.; et al. (1990). Sources of human psychological differences: The Minnesota Study of Twins Reared Apart. *Science, 250,* 223–228.

Bouchard, Thomas J., Jr.; Lykken, David T.; McGue, Matthew; Segal, Nancy L.; et al. (1991). "Sources of human psychological differences: The Minnesota Study of Twins Reared Apart": Response. *Science, 252,* 191–192.

Bouchard, Thomas J., Jr., & McGue, Matthew (1981). Familial studies of intelligence: A review. *Science, 212,* 1055–1058.

Bousfield, W. A. (1953). The occurrence of clustering in the recall of randomly arranged associates. *Journal of General Psychology, 49,* 229–240.

Bowen, Murray (1978). *Family therapy in clinical practice.* New York: Jason Aronson.

Bower, Gordon H., & Clark, M. C. (1969). Narrative stories as mediators of serial learning. *Psychonomic Science, 14,* 181–182.

Bowers, Kenneth S.; Regehr, Glenn; Balthazard, Claude; & Parker, Kevin (1990). Intuition in the context of discovery. *Cognitive Psychology, 22,* 72–110.

Bowers, Wayne A. (1990). Treatment of depressed inpatients: Cognitive therapy plus medication, relaxation plus medication, and medication alone. *British Journal of Psychiatry, 156,* 73–78.

Bowlby, John (1958). The nature of the child's tie to his mother. *International Journal of Psycho-Analysis, 39,* 350–373.

Bowlby, John (1973). *Attachment and loss: Vol. II. Separation.* New York: Basic Books.

Boyd-Franklin, Nancy (1989). *Black families in therapy: A multisystems approach.* New York: Guilford Press.

Boysen, Sarah T., & Berntson, Gary G. (1989). Numerical competence in a chimpanzee *(Pan troglodytes). Journal of Comparative Psychology, 103,* 23–31.

Bracha, H. Stefan; Torrey, E. Fuller; Bigelow, Llewellyn B.; Lohr, James B.; & Linington, Beverly B. (1991). Subtle signs of prenatal maldevelopment of the hand ectoderm in schizophrenia: A preliminary monozygotic twin study. *Biological Psychiatry, 30,* 719–725.

Bradley, Robert H., & Caldwell, Bettye M. (1984). 174 children: A study of the relationship between home environment and cognitive development during the first 5 years. In Allen W. Gottfried (ed.), *Home environment and early cognitive development: Longitudinal research.* Orlando, FL: Academic Press.

Brainard, David H.; Wandell, Brian A.; & Chichilnisky, Eduardo-Jose (1993). Color constancy: From physics to appearance. *Current Directions in Psychological Science, 2,* 165–170.

Brainerd, C. J. (1996). Piaget: A centennial celebration. *Psychological Science, 7,* 191–195.

Brainerd, C. J.; Reyna, V. F.; & Brandse, E. (1995). Are children's false memories more persistent than their true memories? *Psychological Science, 6,* 359–364.

Breggin, Peter R. (1991). *Toxic psychiatry.* New York: St. Martin's Press.

Breland, Keller, & Breland, Marian (1961). The misbehavior of organisms. *American Psychologist, 16,* 681–684.

Brennan, Kelly A., & Shaver, Phillip R. (1995). Dimensions of adult attachment, affect regulation, and romantic relationship functioning. *Personality and Social Psychology Bulletin, 21,* 267–283.

Brewer, Marilynn B., & Gardner, Wendi (1996). Who is this "we"? Levels of collective identity and self representations. *Journal of Personality and Social Psychology, 71,* 83–93.

Briggs, John (1984, December). The genius mind. *Science Digest, 92*(12), 74–77, 102–103.

Brigham, John C., & Malpass, Roy S. (1985, Fall). The role of experience and contact in the recognition of faces of own- and other-race persons. *Journal of Social Issues, 41,* 139–155.

Brockner, Joel, & Rubin, Jeffrey Z. (1985). *Entrapment in escalating conflicts: A social psychological analysis.* New York: Springer-Verlag.

Brodsky, Annette M. (1982). Sex, race, and class issues in psychotherapy research. In J. H. Harvey & M. M. Parks (eds.), *Psychotherapy research and behavior change: Vol. 1. The APA Master Lecture Series.* Washington, DC: American Psychological Association.

Brody, D. J.; Pirkle, J. L.; Kramer, R. A.; et al. (1994). Blood lead levels in the US population: Phase 1 of the Third National Health and Nutrition Examination Survey (NHANES III, 1988 to 1991). *Journal of the American Medical Association, 272,* 277–283.

Brody, Nathan (1990). Behavior therapy versus placebo: Comment on Bowers and Clum's meta-analysis. *Psychological Bulletin, 107,* 106–109.

Bromberger, Joyce T., & Matthews, Karen A. (1996). A "feminine" model of vulnerability to depressive symptoms: A longitudinal investigation of middle-aged women. *Journal of Personality and Social Psychology, 70,* 591–598.

Brown, Alan S. (1991). A review of the tip-of-the-tongue experience. *Psychological Bulletin, 109,* 204–223.

Brown, George W. (1993). Life events and affective disorder: Replications and limitations. *Psychosomatic Medicine, 55,* 248–259.

Brown, Jonathon D. (1991). Staying fit and staying well. *Journal of Personality and Social Psychology, 60,* 555–561.

Brown, Paul (1994). Toward a psychobiological study of dissociation. In S. J. Lynn & J. Rhue (eds.), *Dissociation: Clinical, theoretical and research perspectives.* New York: Guilford Press.

Brown, Roger (1986). *Social psychology* (2nd ed.). New York: Free Press.

Brown, Roger; Cazden, Courtney; & Bellugi, Ursula (1969). The child's grammar from I to III. In J. P. Hill (ed.), *Minnesota Symposium on Child Psychology* (Vol. 2). Minneapolis: University of Minnesota Press.

Brown, Roger, & Kulik, James (1977). Flashbulb memories. *Cognition, 5,* 73–99.

Brown, Roger, & McNeill, David (1966). The "tip of the tongue" phenomenon. *Journal of Verbal Learning and Verbal Behavior, 5,* 325–337.

Brown, Steven P. (1996). A meta-analysis and review of organizational research on job involvement. *Psychological Bulletin, 120,* 235–255.

Brownell, Kelly D., & Rodin, Judith (1994). The dieting maelstrom: Is it possible and advisable to lose weight? *American Psychologist, 49,* 781–791.

Bryer, Jeffrey; Nelson, Bernadette; Miller, Jean; & Krol, Pamela (1987). Childhood sexual and physical abuse as factors in adult psychiatric illness. *American Journal of Psychiatry, 144,* 1426–1430.

Buck, Linda, & Axel, Richard (1991). A novel multigene family may encode odorant receptors: A molecular basis for odor recognition. *Cell, 65,* 175–187.

Buck, Ross (1984). *The communication of emotion.* New York: Guilford Press.

Buck, Ross, & Teng, Wan-Cheng (1987). Spontaneous emotional communication and social biofeedback: A cross-cultural study of emotional expression and communication in Chinese and Taiwanese students. Paper presented at the annual meeting of the American Psychological Association, New York.

Burgess, C.; Morris, T.; & Pettingale, K. W. (1988). Psychological response to cancer diagnosis: II. Evidence for coping styles (coping styles and cancer diagnosis). *Journal of Psychosomatic Research, 32,* 263–272.

Burgess, Cheryl A.; Kirsch, Irving; Shane, Howard; et al. (1998). Facilitated communication as an ideomotor response. *Psychological Science, 9,* 71–74.

Burke, Deborah M.; MacKay, Donald G.; Worthley, Joanna S.; & Wade, Elizabeth (1991). On the tip of the tongue: What causes word finding failures in young and older adults? *Journal of Memory and Language, 30,* 237–246.

Burnam, M. Audrey; Stein, Judith; Golding, Jacqueline; Siegel, Judith; & Sorenson, Susan (1988). Sexual assault and mental disorders in a community population. *Journal of Counseling and Clinical Psychology, 56,* 843–850.

Bushman, Brad J. (1995). Moderating role of trait aggressiveness in the effects of violent media on aggression. *Journal of Personality and Social Psychology, 69,* 950–960.

Buss, David M. (1994). *The evolution of desire: Strategies of human mating.* New York: Basic Books.

Buss, David M. (1996). Sexual conflict: Can evolutionary and feminist perspectives converge? In D. M. Buss & N. Malamuth (eds.), *Sex, power, conflict: Evolutionary and feminist perspectives.* New York: Oxford University Press.

Bussey, Kay, & Bandura, Albert (1992). Self-regulatory mechanisms governing gender development. *Child Development, 63,* 1236–1250.

Butler, S.; Chalder, T.; Ron, M.; Wessely, S.; et al. (1991). Cognitive behaviour therapy in chronic fatigue syndrome. *Journal of Neurology, Neurosurgery & Psychiatry, 54,* 153–158.

Butterfield, E. C., & Belmont, J. M. (1977). Assessing and improving the executive cognitive functions of mentally retarded people. In I. Bialer & M. Sternlict (eds.), *Psychological issues in mental retardation.* New York: Psychological Dimensions.

Buunk, Bram; Angleitner, Alois; Oubaid, Viktor; & Buss, David M. (1996). Sex differences in jealousy in evolutionary and cultural perspective: Tests from the Netherlands, Germany, and the United States. *Psychological Science, 7,* 359–363.

Byne, William (1993). Sexual orientation and brain structure: Adding up the evidence. Paper presented at the annual meeting of the International Academy of Sex Research, Pacific Grove, CA.

Byne, William, & Parsons, Bruce (1993). Human sexual orientation: The biologic theories reappraised. *Archives of General Psychiatry, 50,* 228–239.

Cabezas, A.; Tam, T. M.; Lowe, B. M.; Wong, A.; & Turner, K. (1989). Empirical study of barriers to upward mobility of Asian Americans in the San Francisco Bay area. In G. Nomura (ed.), *Frontiers of Asian American studies.* Pullman: Washington State University Press.

Cahill, Larry; Prins, Bruce; Weber, Michael; & McGaugh, James L. (1994). J-adrenergic activation and memory for emotional events. *Nature, 371,* 702–704.

Campbell, Frances A., & Ramey, Craig T. (1994). Effects of early intervention on intellectual and academic achievement: A follow-up study of children from low-income families. *Child Development, 65,* 684–698.

Campbell, Frances A., & Ramey, Craig T. (1995). Cognitive and school outcomes for high risk students at middle adolescence: Positive effects of early intervention. *American Educational Research Journal, 32,* 743–772.

Campbell, Jennifer; Trapnell, Paul D.; Heine, Steven J.; Katz, Ilana M.; et al. (1996). Self-concept clarity: Measurement, personality correlates, and cul-tural boundaries. *Journal of Personality and Social Psychology, 70,* 141–156.

Campbell, Joseph (1949/1968). *The hero with 1,000 faces* (2nd ed.). Princeton, NJ: Princeton University Press.

Cancian, Francesca M. (1987). *Love in America: Gender and self-development.* Cambridge, England: Cambridge University Press.

Canetto, Silvia S. (1992). Suicide attempts and substance abuse: Similarities and differences. *Journal of Psychology, 125,* 605–620.

Canino, Glorisa (1994). Alcohol use and misuse among Hispanic women: Selected factors, processes, and studies. [Special Issue: Substance use patterns of Latinas.] *International Journal of the Addictions, 29,* 1083–1100.

Cardeña, Etzel; Lewis-Fernández, Roberto; Bear, David; Pakianathan, Isabel; & Spiegal, David (1994). Dissociative disorders. In *DSM-IV Sourcebook.* Washington, DC: American Psychiatric Press.

Carducci, Bernardo J., & McGuire, Jay C. (1990). Behavior and beliefs characteristic of first-, second-, and third-time lovers. Paper presented at the annual meeting of the American Psychological Association, Boston.

Carr, Edward G., & Durand, V. Mark (1985). Reducing behavior problems through functional communication training. *Journal of Applied Behavior Analysis, 18,* 111–126.

Carroll, James M., & Russell, James A. (1996). Do facial expressions signal specific emotions? Judging emotion from the face in context. *Journal of Personality and Social Psychology, 70,* 203–218.

Carroll, Kathleen M.; Rounsaville, Bruce J.; & Nich, Charla (1994). Blind man's bluff: Effectiveness and significance of psychotherapy and pharmacotherapy blinding procedures in a clinical trial. *Journal of Consulting and Clinical Psychology, 62,* 276–280.

Carson, Robert C. (1989). What happened to schizophrenia? Reflections on a taxonomic absurdity. Paper presented at the annual meeting of the American Psychological Association, New Orleans.

Carson, Robert C.; Butcher, James N.; & Mineka, Susan (1996). *Abnormal psychology and modern life* (10th ed.). New York: HarperCollins.

Carter, Betty, & McGoldrick, Monica (eds.) (1988). *The changing family life cycle: A framework for family therapy* (2nd ed.). New York: Gardner Press.

Cartwright, Rosalind D. (1990). A network model of dreams. In R. R. Bootzin, J. F. Kihlstrom, & D. L. Schacter (eds.), *Sleep and cognition.* Washington, DC: American Psychological Association.

Cartwright, Rosalind, & Lloyd, Stephen R. (1994). Early REM sleep: A compensatory change in depression? *Psychiatry Research, 51,* 245–252.

Carver, Charles S.; Ironson, G.; Wynings, C.; Greenwood, D.; et al. (1993a). Coping with Andrew: How coping responses relate to experience of loss and symptoms of poor adjustment. Paper presented at the annual meeting of the American Psychological Association, Toronto, Canada.

Carver, Charles S.; Pozo, Christina; Harris, Suzanne D.; Noriega, Victoria; et al. (1993b). How coping mediates the effect of optimism on distress: A study of women with early stage breast cancer. *Journal of Personality and Social Psychology, 65,* 375–390.

Caspi, Avshalom, & Moffitt, Terrie E. (1991). Individual differences are accentuated during periods of social change: The sample case of girls at puberty. *Journal of Personality and Social Psychology, 61,* 157–168.

Cassell, Carol (1984). *Swept away: Why women fear their own sexuality.* New York: Simon & Schuster.

Cattell, Raymond B. (1965). *The scientific analysis of personality.* Baltimore, MD: Penguin.

Cattell, Raymond B. (1973). *Personality and mood by questionnaire.* San Francisco: Jossey-Bass.

Ceci, Stephen J. (1996). *On intelligence: A bioecological treatise on intellectual development.* Cambridge, MA: Harvard University Press.

Ceci, Stephen J., & Bruck, Maggie (1993). Suggestibility of the child witness: A historical review and synthesis. *Psychological Bulletin, 113,* 403–439.

Ceci, Stephen J., & Bruck, Maggie (1995). *Jeopardy in the courtroom: A scientific analysis of children's testimony.* Washington, DC: American Psychological Association.

Cermak, Laird S., & Craik, Fergus I. M. (eds.) (1979). *Levels of processing in human memory.* Hillsdale, NJ: Erlbaum.

Chambless, Dianne L. (1988). Cognitive mechanisms in panic disorder. In S. Rachman & J. D. Maser (eds.), *Panic: Psychological perspectives.* Hillsdale, NJ: Erlbaum.

Chambless, Dianne L. (1995). Training in and dissemination of empirically validated psychological treatments: Report and recommendations. *The Clinical Psychologist, 48,* 3–24.

Chambless, Dianne L., & members of the Division 12 Task Force (1996). An update on empirically validated therapies. *The Clinical Psychologist, 49,* 5–18.

Chance, June E., & Goldstein, Alvin G. (1995). The other-race effect in eyewitness identification. In S. L. Sporer, G. Koehnken, & R. S. Malpass (eds.), *Psychological issues in eyewitness identification.* Hillsdale, NJ: Erlbaum.

Chance, Paul (1988, October). Knock wood. *Psychology Today,* 68–69.

Chance, Paul (1994). *Learning and behavior* (3rd ed.). Belmont, CA: Wadsworth.

Chang, Edward C. (1996). Cultural differences in optimism, pessimism, and coping: Predictors of subsequent adjustment in Asian American and Caucasian American college students. *Journal of Counseling Psychology, 43,* 113–123.

Cheney, Dorothy L., & Seyfarth, Robert M. (1990). *How monkeys see the world: Inside the mind of another species.* Chicago: University of Chicago Press.

Chipuer, Heather M.; Rovine, Michael J.; & Plomin, Robert (1990). LISREL modeling: Genetic and environmental influences on IQ revisited. *Intelligence, 14,* 11–29.

Chodorow, Nancy (1978). *The reproduction of mothering.* Berkeley: University of California Press.

Chodorow, Nancy (1992). *Feminism and psychoanalytic theory.* New Haven, CT: Yale University Press.

Chomsky, Noam (1957). *Syntactic structures.* The Hague, Netherlands: Mouton.

Chomsky, Noam (1980). Initial states and steady states. In M. Piatelli-Palmerini (ed.), *Language and learning: The debate between Jean Piaget and Noam Chomsky.* Cambridge, MA: Harvard University Press.

Christensen, Andrew, & Jacobson, Neil S. (1994). Who (or what) can do psychotherapy: The status and challenge of nonprofessional therapies. *Psychological Science, 5,* 8–14.

Christensen, Larry, & Burrows, Ross (1990). Dietary treatment of depression. *Behavior Therapy, 21,* 183–194.

Chua, Streamson C., Jr.; Chung, Wendy K.; Wu-Peng, S. Sharon; et al. (1996). Phenotypes of mouse *diabetes* and rat *fatty* due to mutations in the OB (leptin) receptor. *Science, 271,* 994–996.

Chudacoff, Howard P. (1990). *How old are you? Age consciousness in American culture.* Princeton, NJ: Princeton University Press.

Church, A. Timothy, & Lonner, Walter J. (1998). The cross-cultural perspective in the study of personality: Rationale and current research. *Journal of Cross-Cultural Psychology, 29,* 32–62.

Cialdini, Robert B. (1993). *Influence: The psychology of persuasion.* New York: Quill/Morrow.

Cioffi, Delia, & Holloway, James (1993). Delayed costs of suppressed pain. *Journal of Personality and Social Psychology, 64,* 274–282.

Cioffi, Frank (1974, February 7). Was Freud a liar? *The Listener, 91,* 172–174.

Clark, Margaret S.; Milberg, Sandra; & Erber, Ralph (1987). Arousal state dependent memory: Evidence and some implications for understanding social judgments and social behavior. In K. Fiedler & J. P. Forgas (eds.), *Affect, cognition and social behavior.* Toronto, Canada: Hogrefe.

Clarke-Stewart, K. Alison; VanderStoep, Laima P.; & Killian, Grant A. (1979). Analyses and replication of mother–child relations at two years of age. *Child Development, 50,* 777–793.

Cloninger, C. Robert (1990). *The genetics and biology of alcoholism.* Cold Springs Harbor, ME: Cold Springs Harbor Press.

Clopton, Nancy A., & Sorell, Gwendolyn T. (1993). Gender differences in moral reasoning: Stable or situational? *Psychology of Women Quarterly, 17,* 85–101.

Coats, Erik J.; Janoff-Bulman, Ronnie; & Alpert, Nancy (1996). Approach versus avoidance goals: Differences in self-evaluation and well-being. *Personality and Social Psychology Bulletin, 22,* 1057–1067.

Coffey, C. E. (1993). Structural brain imaging and ECT. In C. E. Coffey (ed.), *The clinical science of electroconvulsive therapy.* Washington, DC: American Psychiatric Association.

Cohen, Sheldon; Evans, Gary W.; Krantz, David S.; & Stokols, Daniel (1980). Physiological, motivational, and cognitive effects of aircraft noise on children. *American Psychologist, 35,* 231–243.

Cohen, Sheldon; Tyrrell, David A.; & Smith, Andrew P. (1993). Negative life events, perceived stress, negative affect, and susceptibility to the common cold. *Journal of Personality and Social Psychology, 64,* 131–140.

Cohn, Lawrence D. (1991). Sex differences in the course of personality development: A meta-analysis. *Psychological Bulletin, 109,* 252–266.

Cole, Michael, & Cole, Sheila R. (1993). *The development of children* (2nd ed.). New York: Freeman.

Collaer, Marcia L., & Hines, Melissa (1995). Human behavioral sex differences: A role for gonadal hormones during early development? *Psychological Bulletin, 118,* 55–107.

Collins, Allan M., & Loftus, Elizabeth F. (1975). A spreading-activation theory of semantic processing. *Psychological Review, 82,* 407–428.

Collins, Barry (1993). Using person perception methodologies to uncover the meanings of the Milgram obedience paradigm. Paper presented at the annual meeting of the American Psychological Association, Toronto, Canada.

Collins, Rebecca L. (1996). For better or worse: The impact of upward social comparison on self-evaluations. *Psychological Bulletin, 119,* 51–69.

Comas-Díaz, Lillian, & Greene, Beverly (1994). *Women of color: Integrating ethnic and gender identities in psychotherapy.* New York: Guilford Press.

Comstock, George; Chaffee, Steven; Katzman, Nathan; McCombs, Maxwell; & Roberts, Donald (1978). *Television and human behavior.* New York: Columbia University Press.

Considine, R. V.; Sinha, M. K.; Heiman, M. L.; et al. (1996). Serum immunoreactive-leptin concentrations in normal-weight and obese humans. *New England Journal of Medicine, 334,* 292–295.

Conway, Martin A.; Anderson, Stephen J.; Larsen, Steen F.; Donnelly, C. M.; et al. (1994). The formation of flashbulb memories. *Memory and Cognition, 22,* 326–343.

Cooper, M. Lynne; Frone, Michael R.; Russell, Marcia; & Mudar, Pamela (1995). Drinking to regulate positive and negative emotions: A motivational model of alcohol use. *Journal of Personality and Social Psychology, 69,* 990–1005.

Coren, Stanley (1996a). Daylight saving time and traffic accidents. *New England Journal of Medicine, 334,* 924.

Coren, Stanley (1996b). *Sleep thieves.* New York: Free Press.

Corkin, Suzanne (1984). Lasting consequences of bilateral medial temporal lobectomy: Clinical course and experimental findings in H. M. *Seminars in Neurology, 4,* 249–259.

Corkin, Suzanne; Amaral, David G.; Gonzalez, R. Gilberto; Johnson, Keith A.; & Hyman, Bradley T. (1997). H. M.'s medial temporal lobe lesion: Findings from magnetic resonance imaging. *Journal of Neuroscience, 17,* 3964–3979.

Cose, Ellis (1994). *The rage of a privileged class.* New York: HarperCollins.

Costa, Paul T., Jr., & McCrae, Robert R. (1994). "Set like plaster"? Evidence for the stability of adult personality. In R. Heatherton & J. Weinberger (eds.), *Can personality change?* Washington, DC: American Psychological Association.

Costantino, Giuseppe; Malgady, Robert G.; & Rogler, Lloyd H. (1986). Cuento therapy: A culturally sensitive modality for Puerto Rican children. *Journal of Consulting and Clinical Psychology, 54,* 639–645.

Coupland, Scott K.; Serovich, Julianne; & Glenn, J. Edgar (1995). Reliability in constructing genograms: A study among marriage and family therapy doctoral students. [Special Section: Genograms in family therapy.] *Journal of Marital and Family Therapy, 21,* 251–263.

Craik, F. I. M., & Salthouse, Timothy A. (eds.) (1992). *The handbook of aging and cognition.* Hillsdale, NJ: Erlbaum.

Craik, Fergus I. M., & Tulving, Endel (1975). Depth of processing and the retention of words in episodic memory. *Journal of Experimental Psychology: General, 104,* 268–294.

Crain, Stephen (1991). Language acquisition in the absence of experience. *Behavioral & Brain Sciences, 14,* 597–650.

Crandall, Christian S., & Martinez, Rebecca (1996). Culture, ideology, and antifat attitudes. *Personality and Social Psychology Bulletin, 22,* 1165–1176.

Crandall, James E. (1984). Social interest as a moderator of life stress. *Journal of Personality and Social Psychology, 47,* 164–174.

Crews, Frederick, and his critics (1995). *The memory wars: Freud's legacy in dispute.* New York: A New York Review Book.

Crick, Francis, & Mitchison, Graeme (1995). REM sleep and neural nets. *Behavioural Brain Research, 69,* 147–155.

Critchlow, Barbara (1986). The powers of John Barleycorn: Beliefs about the effects of alcohol on social behavior. *American Psychologist, 41,* 751–764.

Critser, Greg (1996, June). Oh, how happy we will be: Pills, paradise, and the profits of the drug companies. *Harper's,* 39–48.

Cronbach, Lee J. (1990). *Essentials of psychological testing* (5th ed.). New York: Harper & Row.

Crook, John H. (1987). The nature of conscious awareness. In C. Blakemore & S. Greenfield (eds.), *Mindwaves: Thoughts on intelligence, identity, and consciousness.* Oxford, England: Basil Blackwell.

Cross, William E. (1971). The Negro-to-Black conversion experience: Toward a psychology of Black liberation. *Black World, 20,* 13–27.

Cross, William E., Jr., & Fhagen-Smith, Peony (1996). Nigrescence and ego identity development: Accounting for differential black identity patterns. In P. B. Pedersen, J. G. Draguns, W. J. Lonner, & J. E. Trimble (eds.), *Counseling across cultures* (4th ed.). Thousand Oaks, CA: Sage.

Crystal, David S.; Chen, Chuansheng; Fuligni, Andrew J.; Stevenson, Harold W.; et al. (1994). Psychological maladjustment and academic achievement: A cross-cultural study of Japanese, Chinese, and American high school students. *Child Development, 65,* 738–753.

Csikszentmihalyi, Mihaly, & Larson, Reed (1984). *Being adolescent: Conflict and growth in the teenage years.* New York: Basic Books.

Curtiss, Susan (1977). *Genie: A psycholinguistic study of a modern-day "wild child."* New York: Academic Press.

Curtiss, Susan (1982). Developmental dissociations of language and cognition. In L. Obler & D. Fein (eds.), *Exceptional language and linguistics.* New York: Academic Press.

Cushman, Philip (1995). *Constructing the self, constructing America: A cultural history of psychotherapy.* New York: Addison-Wesley.

Cvetkovich, George T., & Earle, Timothy C. (1994). Risk and culture. In W. J. Lonner & R. Malpass (eds.), *Psychology and culture.* Boston: Allyn & Bacon.

Dagenbach, Dale; Carr, Thomas H.; & Wilhelmsen, AnneLise (1989). Task-induced strategies and near-threshold priming: Conscious influences on unconscious perception. *Journal of Memory and Language, 28,* 412–443.

Daly, Martin, & Wilson, Margo (1983). *Sex, evolution, and behavior* (2nd ed.). Belmont, CA: Wadsworth.

Damasio, Antonio R. (1990). Category-related recognition defects as a clue to the neural substrates of knowledge. *Trends in Neurosciences, 13,* 95–98.

Damasio, Antonio R. (1994). *Descartes' error: Emotion, reason, and the human brain.* New York: Grosset/Putnam.

Damasio, Hanna; Grabowski, Thomas; Frank, Randall; Galaburda, Albert M.; & Damasio, Antonio R. (1994). The return of Phineas Gage: Clues about the brain from the skull of a famous patient. *Science, 264,* 1102–1105.

Damasio, Hanna; Grabowski T. J.; Tranel, Daniel; Hichwa, R. D.; & Damasio, Antonio R. (1996). A neural basis for lexical retrieval. *Nature, 380,* 499–505.

Damon, William (1995). *Greater expectations.* New York: Free Press.

Darley, John M. (1995). Constructive and destructive obedience: A taxonomy of principal agent relationships. In A. G. Miller, B. E. Collins, & D. E. Brief (eds.), Perspectives on obedience to authority: The legacy of the Milgram experiments. *Journal of Social Issues, 51*(3), 125–154.

Darwin, Charles (1872/1965). *The expression of the emotions in man and animals.* Chicago: University of Chicago Press.

Dasen, Pierre R. (1994). Culture and cognitive development from a Piagetian perspective. In W. J. Lonner & R. S. Malpass (eds.), *Psychology and culture.* Needham Heights, MA: Allyn & Bacon.

Davidson, Richard J. (1992). Anterior cerebral asymmetry and the nature of emotion. *Brain and Cognition, 20,* 125–151.

Dawes, Robyn M. (1994). *House of cards: Psychology and psychotherapy built on myth.* New York: Free Press.

Dawit, Seble, & Mekuria, Salem (1993, December 7). The West just doesn't get it (Let Africans fight genital mutilation). *New York Times,* A13.

Dawson, Neal V.; Arkes, Hal R.; Siciliano, C.; et al. (1988). Hindsight bias: An impediment to accurate probability estimation in clinicopathologic conferences. *Medical Decision Making, 8*(4), 259–264.

Dean, Geoffrey (1987, Spring). Does astrology need to be true? Part II. The answer is no. *Skeptical Inquirer, 11,* 257–273.

Deaux, Kay (1985). Sex and gender. *Annual Review of Psychology, 36,* 49–81.

Deci, Edward L., & Ryan, Richard M. (1987). The support of autonomy and the control of behavior. *Journal of Personality and Social Psychology, 53,* 1024–1037.

de Lacoste-Utamsing, Christine, & Holloway, Ralph L. (1982). Sexual dimorphism in the human corpus callosum. *Science, 216,* 1431–1432.

de la Garza, Rodolfo O.; DeSipio, Luis; Garcia, F. Chris; Garcia, John; & Falcon, Angelo (1992). *Latino voices: Mexican, Puerto Rican, & Cuban perspectives on American politics.* Boulder, CO: Westview Press.

DeLeon, Patrick H., & Wiggins, Jack G., Jr. (1996). Prescription privileges for psychologists. *American Psychologist, 51,* 225–229.

DeLoache, Judy S. (1995). Early understanding and use of symbols: The model model. *Current Directions in Psychological Science, 4,* 109–113.

Dement, William (1978). *Some must watch while some must sleep.* New York: Norton.

Dement, William (1992). *The sleepwatchers.* Stanford, CA: Stanford Alumni Association.

DeMyer, Marian K. (1975). Research in infantile autism: A strategy and its results. *Biological Psychiatry, 10,* 433–452.

DeNelsky, Garland Y. (1996). The case against prescription privileges for psychologists. *American Psychologist, 51,* 207–212.

Dennett, Daniel C. (1991). *Consciousness explained.* Boston: Little, Brown.

DePaulo, Bella M. (1992). Nonverbal behavior and self-presentation. *Psychological Bulletin, 111,* 203–243.

de Rivera, Joseph (1989). Comparing experiences across cultures: Shame and guilt in America and Japan. *Hiroshima Forum for Psychology, 14,* 13–20.

Desimone, Robert (1991). Face-selective cells in the temporal cortex of monkeys. *Journal of Cognitive Neuroscience, 3,* 1–8.

Deutsch, Morton, & Collins, Mary Ellen (1951). *Interracial housing: A psychological evaluation of a social experiment.* Minneapolis: University of Minnesota Press.

DeValois, Russell L., & DeValois, Karen K. (1975). Neural coding of color. In E. C. Carterette & M. P. Friedman (eds.), *Handbook of perception* (Vol. 5). New York: Academic Press.

Devanand, Devangere P.; Dwork, Andrew J.; Hutchinson, Edward R.; et al. (1994). Does ECT alter brain structure? *American Journal of Psychiatry, 151,* 957–970.

Devine, Patricia G. (1995). Breaking the prejudice habit: Progress and prospects. Award address paper presented at the annual meeting of the American Psychological Association, New York.

Devine, Patricia G.; Evett, Sophia R.; & Vasquez-Suson, Kristin A. (1996). Exploring the interpersonal dynamics of intergroup contact. In R. M. Sorrentino & E. T. Higgins (eds.), *Handbook of motivation and cognition: Vol. 3. The interpersonal context.* New York: Guilford Press.

Devlin, B.; Daniels, Michael; & Roeder, Kathryn (1997). The heritability of IQ. *Nature, 388,* 468–471.

Devolder, Patricia A., & Pressley, Michael (1989). Metamemory across the adult lifespan. *Canadian Psychology, 30,* 578–587.

Devor, E. J.; Abell, C. W.; Hoffman, P. L.; Tabakoff, B.; & Cloninger, C. R. (1994). Platelet MAO activity in type I and type II alcoholism. *Annals of the New York Academy of Sciences, 708,* 119–128.

Diamond, Marian C. (1993, Winter–Spring). An optimistic view of the aging brain. *Generations, 17,* 31–33.

Dickinson, Alyce M. (1989). The detrimental effects of extrinsic reinforcement on "intrinsic motivation." *The Behavior Analyst, 12,* 1–15.

Digman, John M. (1996). The curious history of the five-factor model. In J. S. Wiggins (ed.), *The five-factor model of personality: Theoretical perspectives.* New York: Guilford Press.

Digman, John M., & Shmelyov, Alexander G. (1996). The structure of temperament and personality in Russian children. *Journal of Personality and Social Psychology, 71,* 341–351.

DiLalla, David.; Carey, Gregory; Gottesman, Irving I.; & Bouchard, Thomas J., Jr. (1996). Heritability of MMPI personality indicators of psychopathology in twins reared apart. *Journal of Abnormal Psychology, 105,* 491–499.

di Leonardo, Micaela (1987). The female world of cards and holidays: Women, families, and the work of kinship. *Signs, 12,* 1–20.

Dinges, David F.; Whitehouse, Wayne G.; Orne, Emily C.; Powell, John W.; Orne, Martin T.; & Erdelyi, Matthew H. (1992). Evaluating hypnotic memory enhancement (hypermnesia and reminiscence) using multitrial forced recall. *Journal of Experimental Psychology: Learning, Memory, and Cognition, 18,* 1139–1147.

Dion, George L., & Anthony, William A. (1987). Research in psychiatric rehabilitation: A review of experimental and quasi-experimental studies. *Rehabilitation Counseling Bulletin, 30,* 177–203.

Dion, Kenneth L., & Dion, Karen K. (1993). Gender and ethnocultural comparisons in style of love. *Psychology of Women Quarterly, 17,* 463–474.

Dixon, N. F. (1980). Humor: A cognitive alternative to stress? In I. G. Sarason & C. D. Spielberger (eds.), *Stress and anxiety* (Vol. 7). Washington, DC: Hemisphere.

Dollard, John, & Miller, Neal E. (1950). *Personality and psychotherapy: An analysis in terms of learning, thinking, and culture.* New York: McGraw-Hill.

Donnell, S. M., & Hall, J. (1980, Spring). Men and women as managers: A significant case of no significant difference. *Organizational Dynamics, 8,* 60–76.

Doty, Richard M.; Peterson, Bill E.; & Winter, David G. (1991). Threat and authoritarianism in the United States, 1978–1987. *Journal of Personality and Social Psychology, 61,* 629–640.

Druckman, Daniel, & Swets, John A. (eds.) (1988). *Enhancing human performance: Issues, theories, and techniques.* Washington, DC: National Academy Press.

Dubbert, Patricia M. (1992). Exercise in behavioral medicine. *Journal of Consulting and Clinical Psychology, 60,* 613–618.

Duncan, Paula D.; Ritter, Philip L.; Dornbusch, Sanford M.; Gross, Ruth T.; & Carlsmith, J. Merrill (1985). The effects of pubertal timing on body image, school behavior, and deviance. *Journal of Youth and Adolescence, 14,* 227–235.

Dunkel-Schetter, Christine (1984). Social support and cancer: Findings based on patient interviews and their implications. *Journal of Social Issues, 40*(4), 77–98.

Dunn, Judy, & Plomin, Robert (1990). *Separate lives: Why siblings are so different.* New York: Basic Books.

du Verglas, Gabrielle; Banks, Steven R.; & Guyer, Kenneth E. (1988). Clinical effects of fenfluramine on children with autism: A review of the research. *Journal of Autism and Developmental Disorders, 18,* 297–308.

Dweck, Carol S. (1990). Toward a theory of goals: Their role in motivation and personality. In R. A. Dienstbier (ed.), *Nebraska Symposium on Motivation* (Vol. 38). Lincoln: University of Nebraska Press.

Dweck, Carol S. (1992). The study of goals in psychology [Commentary to feature review]. *Psychological Science, 3,* 165–167.

D'Zurilla, Thomas J., & Sheedy, Collete F. (1991). Relation between problem-solving ability and subsequent level of psychological stress in college students. *Journal of Personality and Social Psychology, 61,* 841–846.

Eagly, Alice H., & Carli, Linda L. (1981). Sex of researchers and sex-typed communications as determinants of sex differences in influenceability: A meta-analysis of social influence studies. *Psychological Bulletin, 90,* 1–20.

Eagly, Alice H.; Makhijani, M. G.; & Klonsky, B. G. (1990). Gender and the evaluation of leaders: A meta-analysis. *Psychological Bulletin, 111,* 3–22.

Eaton, William W.; Bilker, Warren; Haro, Josep M.; Herrman, Helen; et al. (1992a). Long-term course of hospitalization for schizophrenia: II. Change with passage of time. *Schizophrenia Bulletin, 18,* 229–241.

Eaton, William W.; Mortensen, Preben B.; Herrman, Helen; Freeman, Hugh; et al. (1992b). Long-term course of hospitalization for schizophrenia: I. Risk for rehospitalization. *Schizophrenia Bulletin, 18,* 217–228.

Ebbinghaus, Hermann M. (1885/1913). *Memory: A contribution to experimental psychology* (H. A. Ruger & C. E. Bussenius, trans.). New York: Teachers College Press, Columbia University.

Eccles, Jacquelynne S. (1993). Parents and gender-role socialization during the middle childhood and adolescent years. In S. Oskamp & M. Costanzo (eds.), *The Claremont Symposium on Applied Social Psychology: Gender issues in contemporary society.* Newbury Park, CA: Sage.

Eccles, Jacquelynne S.; Jacobs, Janis E.; & Harold, Rena D. (1990). Gender role stereotypes, expectancy effects, and parents' socialization of gender differences. *Journal of Social Issues, 46,* 183–201.

Eccles, Jacquelynne S.; Midgley, Carol; Wigfield, Allan; Buchanan, Christy M.; et al. (1993). Development during adolescence: The impact of stage–environment fit on young adolescents' experiences in schools and in families. *American Psychologist, 48,* 90–101.

Eckensberger, Lutz H. (1994). Moral development and its measurement across cultures. In W. J. Lonner & R. Malpass (eds.), *Psychology and culture.* Needham Heights, MA: Allyn & Bacon.

Edelson, Marshall (1994). Can psychotherapy research answer this psychotherapist's questions? In P. F. Talley, H. H. Strupp, & S. F. Butler (eds.), *Psychotherapy research and practice: Bridging the gap.* New York: Basic Books.

Edwards, Betty (1986). *Drawing on the artist within.* New York: Simon & Schuster.

Edwards, Kari, & Smith, Edward E. (1996). A disconfirmation bias in the evaluation of arguments. *Journal of Personality and Social Psychology, 71,* 5–24.

Ehrenreich, Barbara (1978). *For her own good: 150 years of the experts' advice to women.* New York: Doubleday.

Eich, Eric (1995). Searching for mood dependent memory. *Psychological Science, 6,* 67–75.

Eich, E., & Hyman, R. (1992). Subliminal self-help. In D. Druckman & R. A. Bjork (eds.), *In the mind's eye: Enhancing human performance.* Washington, DC: National Academy Press.

Eisenberg, Nancy (1995). Prosocial development: A multifaceted model. In W. M. Kurtines & J. L. Gewirtz (eds.), *Moral development: An introduction.* Boston: Allyn & Bacon.

Eisenberg, Nancy; Fabes, Richard A.; Murphy, Bridget; Karbon, Mariss; et al. (1996). The relations of children's dispositional empathy-related responding to their emotionality, regulation, and social functioning. *Developmental Pschology, 32,* 195–209.

Eisenberger, Robert, & Cameron, Judy (1996). Detrimental effects of reward: Reality or myth? *American Psychologist, 51,* 1153–1166.

Ekman, Paul (1994). Strong evidence for universals in facial expressions: A reply to Russell's mistaken critique. *Psychological Bulletin, 115,* 268–287.

Ekman, Paul; Friesen, Wallace V.; & O'Sullivan, Maureen (1988). Smiles when lying. *Journal of Personality and Social Psychology, 54,* 414–420.

Ekman, Paul; Friesen, Wallace V.; O'Sullivan, Maureen; et al. (1987). Universals and cultural differences in the judgments of facial expression of emotion. *Journal of Personality and Social Psychology, 53,* 712–717.

Ekman, Paul, & Heider, Karl G. (1988). The universality of a contempt expression: A replication. *Motivation and Emotion, 12,* 303–308.

Elliot, Andrew J., & Harackiewicz, Judith M. (1994). Goal setting, achievement orientation, and intrinsic motivation: A mediational analysis. *Journal of Personality and Social Psychology, 66,* 968–980.

Elliott, Robert, & Morrow-Bradley, Cheryl (1994). Developing a working marriage between psychotherapists and psychotherapy researchers: Identifying shared purposes. In P. F. Talley, H. H. Strupp, & S. F. Butler (eds.), *Psychotherapy research and practice: Bridging the gap.* New York: Basic Books.

Ellis, Albert (1993). Changing rational-emotive therapy (RET) to rational emotive behavior therapy (REBT). *Behavior Therapist, 16,* 257–258.

Emmons, Robert A., & King, Laura A. (1988). Conflict among personal strivings: Immediate and long-term implications for psychological and physical well-being. *Journal of Personality and Social Psychology, 54,* 1040–1048.

Endler, Norman S. (1991). Electroconvulsive therapy: Myths and realities. Paper presented at the annual meeting of the American Psychological Association, San Francisco.

Ennis, Robert H. (1985). Critical thinking and the curriculum. *National Forum, 65*(1), 28–30.

Entin, Alan D. (1992). Family photographs: Visual icons and emotional history. Paper presented at the annual meeting of the American Psychological Association, Washington, DC.

Epstein, Robert; Kirshnit, C. E.; Lanza, R. P.; & Rubin, L. C. (1984, March 1). "Insight" in the pigeon: Antecedents and determinants of an intelligent performance. *Nature, 308,* 61–62.

Epstein, Seymour (1994). Integration of the cognitive and the psychodynamic unconscious. *American Psychologist, 49,* 709–724.

Erikson, Erik H. (1950/1963). *Childhood and society* (2nd ed.). New York: Norton.

Erikson, Erik H. (1982). *The life cycle completed.* New York: Norton.

Erikson, Erik H. (1987). A way of looking at things: Selected papers from 1930 to 1980 (Stephen Schlein, ed.). New York: Norton.

Ernsberger, Paul, & Nelson, D. O. (1988). Refeeding hypertension in dietary obesity. *American Journal of Physiology, 154,* R47–55.

Eron, Leonard D. (1982). Parent–child interaction, television violence, and aggression of children. *American Psychologist, 37,* 197–211.

Eron, Leonard D. (1995). *Media violence: How it affects kids and what can be done about it.* Invited address presented at the annual meeting of the American Psychological Association, New York.

Ervin-Tripp, Susan (1964). Imitation and structural change in children's language. In E. H. Lenneberg (ed.), *New directions in the study of language.* Cambridge, MA: MIT Press.

Esterson, Allen (1993). *Seductive mirage: An exploration of the work of Sigmund Freud.* New York: Open Court.

Evans, Gary W.; Hygge, Staffan; & Bullinger, Monika (1995). Chronic noise and psychological stress. *Psychological Science, 6,* 333–338.

Evans, Gary W.; Lepore, Stephen J.; & Schroeder, Alex (1996). The role of interior design elements in human responses to crowding. *Journal of Personality and Social Psychology, 70,* 41–46.

Ewart, Craig K. (1995). Self-efficacy and recovery from heart attack. In J. E. Maddux (ed.), *Self-efficacy, adaptation, and adjustment: Theory, research, and application.* New York: Plenum.

Ewart, Craig K., & Kolodner, Kenneth B. (1994). Negative affect, gender, and expressive style predict elevated ambulatory blood pressure in adolescents. *Journal of Personality and Social Psychology, 66,* 596–605.

Eyferth, Klaus (1961). [The performance of different groups of the children of occupation forces on the Hamburg-Wechsler Intelligence Test for Children.] *Archiv für die Gesamte Psychologie, 113,* 222–241.

Eysenck, Hans J. (1993). Prediction of cancer and coronary heart disease mortality by means of a personality inventory: Results of a 15-year follow-up study. *Psychological Reports, 72,* 499–516.

Fagot, Beverly I. (1984). Teacher and peer reactions to boys' and girls' play styles. *Sex Roles, 11,* 691–702.

Fagot, Beverly I. (1985). Beyond the reinforcement principle: Another step toward understanding sex role development. *Developmental Psychology, 2,* 1097–1104.

Fagot, Beverly I. (1993, June). *Gender role development in early childhood: Environmental input, internal construction.* Invited address presented at the annual meeting of the International Academy of Sex Research, Monterey, CA.

Fagot, Beverly I.; Hagan, R.; Leinbach, Mary D.; & Kronsberg, S. (1985). Differential reactions to assertive and communicative acts of toddler boys and girls. *Child Development, 56,* 1499–1505.

Fagot, Beverly I., & Leinbach, Mary D. (1993). Gender-role development in young children: From discrimination to labeling. *Developmental Review, 13,* 205–224.

Falk, Ruma, & Greenbaum, Charles W. (1995). Significance tests die hard: The amazing persistence of a probabilistic misconception. *Theory & Psychology, 5*(1), 75–98.

Fausto-Sterling, Anne (1997, Summer). Beyond difference: A biologist's perspective [Special Issue: J. B. James (ed.), The significance of gender: Theory and research about difference]. *Journal of Social Issues, 53,* 213–232.

Fazio, Russell H.; Jackson, Joni R.; Dunton, Bridget C.; & Williams, Carol J. (1995). Variability in automatic activation as an unobtrusive measure of racial attitudes: A bona fide pipeline? *Journal of Personality and Social Psychology, 69,* 1013–1027.

FDA Drug Bulletin (1990, April). Two new psychiatric drugs. *20*(1), 9.

Feather, N. T. (1966). Effects of prior success and failure on expectations of success and subsequent performance. *Journal of Personality and Social Psychology, 3,* 287–298.

Feather, N. T. (ed.) (1982). *Expectations and actions: Expectancy value models in psychology.* Hillsdale, NJ: Erlbaum.

Feeney, Judith A., & Noller, Patricia (1990). Attachment style as a predictor of adult romantic relationships. *Journal of Personality and Social Psychology, 58,* 281–291.

Fehr, Beverly (1993). How do I love thee . . . ? Let me consult my prototype. In S. Duck (ed.), *Individuals in relationships* (Vol. 1). Newbury Park, CA: Sage.

Fehr, Beverly, & Russell, James A. (1991). The concept of love viewed from a prototype perspective. *Journal of Personality and Social Psychology, 60,* 425–438.

Feingold, Alan (1988). Cognitive gender differences are disappearing. *American Psychologist, 43,* 95–103.

Fernald, Anne (1990). Emotion in the voice: Meaningful melodies in mother's speech to infants. Paper presented at the annual meeting of the American Psychological Association, Boston.

Fernandez, Ephrem, & Turk, Dennis C. (1992). Sensory and affective components of pain: Separation and synthesis. *Psychological Bulletin, 112,* 205–217.

Fernández-Dols, José-Miguel, & Ruiz-Belda, María-Angeles (1995). Are smiles a sign of happiness? Gold medal winners at the Olympic games. *Journal of Personality and Social Psychology, 69,* 1113–1119.

Fernea, Elizabeth, & Fernea, Robert (1994). Cleanliness and culture. In W. J. Lonner & Malpass (eds.), *Psychology and culture.* Boston: Allyn & Bacon.

Feshbach, Seymour, & Feshbach, Norma D. (1986). Aggression and altruism: A personality perspective. In C. Zahn-Waxler, E. M. Cummings, & R. Iannotti (eds.), *Altruism and aggression: Biological and social origins.* Cambridge, England: Cambridge University Press.

Festinger, Leon (1957). *A theory of cognitive dissonance.* Evanston, IL: Row, Peterson.

Festinger, Leon (1980). Looking backward. In L. Festinger (ed.), *Retrospections on social psychology.* New York: Oxford University Press.

Festinger, Leon, & Carlsmith, J. Merrill (1959). Cognitive consequences of forced compliance. *Journal of Abnormal and Social Psychology, 58,* 203–210.

Festinger, Leon; Pepitone, Albert; & Newcomb, Theodore (1952). Some consequences of deindividuation in a group. *Journal of Abnormal and Social Psychology, 47,* 382–389.

Festinger, Leon; Riecken, Henry W.; & Schachter, Stanley (1956). *When prophecy fails.* Minneapolis: University of Minnesota Press.

Feuerstein, Reuven (1980). *Instrumental enrichment: An intervention program for cognitive modifiability.* Baltimore, MD: University Park Press.

Field, Tiffany (1995). Massage therapy for infants and children. Paper presented at the annual meeting of the American Psychological Association, New York.

Fields, Howard (1991). Depression and pain: A neurobiological model. *Neuropsychiatry, Neuropsychology, and Behavioral Neurology, 4,* 83–92.

Fiez, J. A. (1996). Cerebellar contributions to cognition. *Neuron, 16,* 13–15.

Fincham, Frank D., & Bradbury, Thomas N. (1993). Marital satisfaction, depression, and attributions: A longitudinal analysis. *Journal of Personality and Social Psychology, 64,* 442–452.

Fingarette, Herbert (1988). *Heavy drinking: The myth of alcoholism as a disease.* Berkeley: University of California Press.

Fischer, Agneta H. (1993). Sex differences in emotionality: Fact or stereotype? *Feminism & Psychology, 3,* 303–318.

Fischhoff, Baruch (1975). Hindsight is not equal to foresight: The effect of outcome knowledge on judgment under uncertainty. *Journal of Experimental Psychology: Human Perception and Performance, 1,* 288–299.

Fisher, Kathleen (1985, March). ECT: New studies on how, why, who. *APA Monitor, 16,* 18–19.

Fisher, Ronald J. (1994). Generic principles for resolving intergroup conflict. *Journal of Social Issues, 50,* 47–66.

Fiske, Alan P., & Haslam, Nick (1996). Social cognition is thinking about relationships. *Current Directions in Psychological Science, 5,* 143–148.

Fivush, Robyn, & Hamond, Nina R. (1991). Autobiographical memory across the school years: Toward reconceptualizing childhood amnesia. In R. Fivush & J.

A. Hudson (eds.), *Knowing and remembering in young children.* New York: Cambridge University Press.

Flavell, John H. (1993). Young children's understanding of thinking and consciousness. *Current Directions in Psychological Science, 2,* 40–43.

Flavell, John H. (1996). Piaget's legacy. *Psychological Science, 7,* 200–203.

Flor, Herta; Kerns, Robert D.; & Turk, Dennis C. (1987). The role of spouse reinforcement, perceived pain, and activity levels of chronic pain patients. *Journal of Psychosomatic Research, 31,* 251–259.

Flynn, James R. (1987). Massive IQ gains in 14 nations: What IQ tests really measure. *Psychological Bulletin, 95,* 29–51.

Foa, Edna, & Emmelkamp, Paul (eds.) (1983). *Failures in behavior therapy.* New York: Wiley.

Foderaro, Lisa W. (1994, November 8). "Clubhouse" helps mentally ill find the way back. *New York Times,* B1, B3.

Fogelman, Eva (1994). *Conscience and courage: Rescuers of Jews during the Holocaust.* New York: Anchor Books.

Forgas, Joseph, & Bond, Michael H. (1985). Cultural influences on the perception of interaction episodes. *Personality and Social Psychology Bulletin, 11,* 75–88.

Forrest, F.; Florey, C. du V.; Taylor, D.; McPherson, F.; & Young, J. A. (1991, July 6). Reported social alcohol consumption during pregnancy and infants' development at 18 months. *British Medical Journal, 303,* 22–26.

Fouts, Roger S., & Rigby, Randall L. (1977). Man–chimpanzee communication. In T. A. Seboek (ed.), *How animals communicate.* Bloomington: University of Indiana Press.

Fox, Ronald E. (1994). Training professional psychologists for the twenty-first century. *American Psychologist, 49,* 200–206.

Frank, Robert G.; Gluck, John P.; & Buckelew, Susan P. (1990). Rehabilitation: Psychology's greatest opportunity? *American Psychologist, 45,* 757–761.

Franklin, Anderson J. (1993, July/August). The invisibility syndrome. *Family Therapy Networker,* 33–39.

Frederich, R. C.; Hamann, A.; Anderson, S.; et al. (1995). Leptin levels reflect body lipid content in mice: Evidence for diet-induced resistance to leptin action. *Nature Medicine, 1,* 1311–1314.

Freed, C. R.; Breeze, R. E.; Rosenberg, N. L.; & Schneck, S. A. (1993). Embryonic dopamine cell implants as a treatment for the second phase of Parkinson's disease: Replacing failed nerve terminals. *Advances in Neurology, 60,* 721–728.

Freedman, Hill, & Combs, Gene (1996). *Narrative therapy.* New York: Norton.

French, Christopher C.; Fowler, Mandy; McCarthy, Katy; & Peers, Debbie (1991, Winter). Belief in astrology: A test of the Barnum effect. *Skeptical Inquirer, 15,* 166–172.

Freud, Anna (1946). *The ego and the mechanisms of defence.* New York: International Universities Press.

Freud, Sigmund (1900/1953). The interpretation of dreams. In J. Strachey (ed.), *The standard edition of the complete psychological works of Sigmund Freud* (Vols. 4 and 5). London: Hogarth Press.

Freud, Sigmund (1905). Three essays on the theory of sexuality. In J. Strachey (ed.), *Standard edition* (Vol. 7).

Freud, Sigmund (1920/1960). *A general introduction to psychoanalysis* (Joan Riviere, trans.). New York: Washington Square Press.

Freud, Sigmund (1923/1962). *The ego and the id* (Joan Riviere, trans.). New York: Norton.

Freud, Sigmund (1924a). The dissolution of the Oedipus complex. In J. Strachey (ed.), *Standard edition* (Vol. 19).

Freud, Sigmund (1924b). Some psychical consequences of the anatomical distinction between the sexes. In J. Strachey (ed.), *Standard edition* (Vol. 19).

Fridlund, Alan J. (1994). *Human facial expression: An evolutionary view.* San Diego: Academic Press.

Friedman, Meyer, & Rosenman, Ray (1974). *Type A behavior and your heart.* New York: Knopf.

Friedman, William; Robinson, Amy; & Friedman, Britt (1987). Sex differences in moral judgments? A test of Gilligan's theory. *Psychology of Women Quarterly, 11,* 37–46.

Frijda, Nico H. (1988). The laws of emotion. *American Psychologist, 43,* 349–358.

Fry, P. S. (1995). Perfectionism, humor, and optimism as moderators of health outcomes and determinants of coping styles of women executives. *Genetic, Social, and General Psychology Monographs, 121,* 211–245.

Fry, William F. (1994). The biology of humor. *Humor: International Journal of Humor Research, 7,* 111–126.

Frye, Richard E.; Schwartz, B. S.; & Doty, Richard L. (1990). Dose-related effects of cigarette smoking on olfactory function. *Journal of the American Medical Association, 263,* 1233–1236.

Fuchs, C. S.; Stampfer, M. J.; Colditz, G. A.; Giovannucci, E. L.; et al. (1995, May 11). Alcohol consumption and mortality among women. *New England Journal of Medicine, 332,* 1245–1250.

Gabbard, Glen O. (ed.) (1989). Sexual exploitation within professional relationships. Washington, DC: American Psychiatric Association.

Gagnon, John, & Simon, William (1973). *Sexual conduct: The social sources of human sexuality.* Chicago: Aldine.

Galanter, Eugene (1962). Contemporary psychophysics. In R. Brown, E. Galanter, H. Hess, & G. Mandler (eds.), *New directions in psychology*. New York: Holt, Rinehart and Winston.

Galanter, Marc (1989). *Cults: Faith, healing, and coercion.* New York: Oxford University Press.

Gallant, Jack L.; Braun, Jochen; & Van Essen, David C. (1993). Selectivity for polar, hyperbolic, and Cartesian gratings in macaque visual cortex. *Science, 259,* 100–103.

Galotti, Kathleen (1989). Approaches to studying formal and everyday reasoning. *Psychological Bulletin, 105,* 331–351.

Ganaway, George K. (1991). Alternative hypotheses regarding satanic ritual abuse memories. Paper presented at the annual meeting of the American Psychological Association, San Francisco.

Gao, Jia-Hong; Parsons, Lawrence M.; Bower, James M.; et al. (1996). Cerebellum implicated in sensory acquisition and discrimination rather than motor control. *Science, 272,* 545–547.

Garcia, John, & Koelling, Robert A. (1966). Relation of cue to consequence in avoidance learning. *Psychonomic Science, 4,* 23–124.

Gardner, Howard (1983). *Frames of mind: The theory of multiple intelligences.* New York: Basic Books.

Gardner, R. Allen, & Gardner, Beatrice T. (1969). Teaching sign language to a chimpanzee. *Science, 165,* 664–672.

Garfinkel, D.; Laudon, M.; Nof, D.; & Zisapel, N. (1995). Improvement of sleep quality in elderly people by controlled-release melatonin. *Lancet, 346*(8974), 541–544.

Garland, Ann F., & Zigler, Edward (1994). Adolescent suicide prevention: Current research and social policy implications. *American Psychologist, 48,* 169–182.

Garmezy, Norman (1991). Resilience and vulnerability to adverse developmental outcomes associated with poverty. *American Behavioral Scientist, 34,* 416–430.

Garner, David M., & Wooley, Susan C. (1991). Confronting the failure of behavioral and dietary treatments for obesity. *Clinical Psychology Review, 11,* 729–780.

Garnets, Linda; Hancock, Kristin A.; Cochran, Susan D.; Goodchilds, Jacqueline; & Peplau, Letitia A. (1991). Issues in psychotherapy with lesbians and gay men: A survey of psychologists. *American Psychologist, 46,* 964–972.

Garry, Maryanne; Manning, Charles G.; & Loftus, Elizabeth F. (1996). Imagination inflation: Imagining a childhood event inflates confidence that it occurred. *Psychonomic Bulletin & Review, 3,* 208–214.

Gaston, Louise; Marmar, Charles R.; Gallagher, Dolores; & Thompson, Larry W. (1989). Impact of confirming patient expectations of change processes in behavioral, cognitive, and brief dynamic psychotherapy. *Psychotherapy, 26,* 296–302.

Gay, Peter (1988). *Freud: A life for our time.* New York: Norton.

Gazzaniga, Michael S. (1967). The split brain in man. *Scientific American, 217*(2), 24–29.

Gazzaniga, Michael S. (1983). Right hemisphere language following brain bisection: A 20-year perspective. *American Psychologist, 38,* 525–537.

Gazzaniga, Michael S. (1985). *The social brain: Discovering the networks of the mind.* New York: Basic Books.

Gazzaniga, Michael S. (1988). *Mind matters.* Boston: Houghton Mifflin.

Gelernter, David (1997, May 19). How hard is chess? *Time,* 72–73.

Gelernter, Joel; O'Malley, S.; Risch, N.; Kranzler, H. R.; et al. (1991, October 2). No association between an allele at the D2 dopamine receptor gene (DRD2) and alcoholism. *Journal of the American Medical Association, 266,* 1801–1807.

Geller, E. Scott, & Lehman, Galen R. (1988). Drinking–driving intervention strategies: A person–situation–behavior framework. In M. D. Laurence, J. R. Snortum, & F. E. Zimring (eds.), *The social control of drinking and driving.* Chicago: University of Chicago Press.

Gelles, Richard J., & Straus, Murray A. (1988). *Intimate violence: The causes and consequences of abuse in the American family.* New York: Simon & Schuster/Touchstone.

Gerbner, George (1988). Telling stories in the information age. In B. D. Ruben (ed.), *Information and behavior* (Vol. 2). New Brunswick, NJ: Transaction Books.

Gevins, A. S.; Le, J.; Martin, N.; et al. (1994). High resolution EEG: 124-channel recording, spatial enhancement and MRI integration methods. *Electroencephalographic Clinical Neurophysiology, 90,* 337–358.

Gewirtz, Jacob L., & Peláez-Nogueras, Maria (1991). The attachment metaphor and the conditioning of infant separation protests. In J. L. Gewirtz & W. M. Kurtines (eds.), *Intersections with attachment.* Hillsdale, NJ: Erlbaum.

Gibson, Eleanor, & Walk, Richard (1960). The "visual cliff." *Scientific American, 202,* 80–92.

Gillham, Jane E.; Reivich, Karen J.; Jaycox, Lisa H.; & Seligman, Martin E. P. (1995). Prevention of depressive symptoms in schoolchildren: A two-year follow-up. *Psychological Science, 6,* 343–351.

Gilligan, Carol (1982). *In a different voice.* Cambridge, MA: Harvard University Press.

Gilmore, David D. (1990). *Manhood in the making: Cultural concepts of masculinity.* New Haven, CT: Yale University Press.

Gladue, Brian A. (1994). The biopsychology of sexual orientation. *Current Directions in Psychological Science, 3,* 150–154.

Glanzer, Murray, & Cunitz, Anita R. (1966). Two storage mechanisms in free recall. *Journal of Verbal Learning and Verbal Behavior, 5,* 351–360.

Glazer, Myron P., & Glazer, Penina M. (1990). *The whistleblowers: Exposing corruption in government and industry.* New York: Basic Books.

Gleaves, David H. (1996). The sociocognitive model of dissociative identity disorder: A reexamination of the evidence. *Psychological Bulletin, 120,* 42–59.

Goldberg, Lewis R. (1993). The structure of phenotypic personality traits. *American Psychologist, 48,* 26–34.

Golding, Jacqueline M. (1988). Gender differences in depressive symptoms. *Psychology of Women Quarterly, 12,* 61–74.

Goldman-Rakic, Patricia S. (1996). Opening the mind through neurobiology. Invited address at the annual meeting of the American Psychological Association, Toronto, Canada.

Goldstein, Michael J. (1987). Psychosocial issues. *Schizophrenia Bulletin, 13*(1), 157–171.

Goldstein, Michael, & Miklowitz, David (1995). The effectiveness of psychoeducational family therapy in the treatment of schizophrenic disorders. *Journal of Marital and Family Therapy, 21,* 361–376.

Goleman, Daniel (1995). *Emotional intelligence.* New York: Bantam.

Goodison, Tina, & Siegel, Shephard (1995). Learning and tolerance to the intake suppressive effect of cholecystokinin in rats. *Behavioral Neuroscience, 109,* 62–70.

Goodman, Gail S.; Qin, Jianjian; Bottoms, Bette L.; & Shaver, Phillip R. (1995). *Characteristics and sources of allegations of ritualistic child abuse.* Final report to the National Center on Child Abuse and Neglect, Washington, DC. [Executive summary and complete report available from NCCAN, 1-800-394-3366.]

Goodman, Gail S.; Rudy, L.; Bottoms, B.; & Aman, C. (1990). Children's concerns and memory: Issues of ecological validity in the study of children's eyewitness testimony. In R. Fivush & J. Hudson (eds.), *Knowing and remembering in young children.* New York: Cambridge University Press.

Goodman, Gail S.; Wilson, M. E.; Hazan, C.; & Reed, R. S. (1989). Children's testimony nearly four years after an event. Paper presented at the annual meeting of the Eastern Psychological Association, Boston.

Goodwin, Donald W.; Knop, Joachim; Jensen, Per; et al. (1994). Thirty-year follow-up of men at high risk for alcoholism. In Thomas F. Babor & Victor M. Hesselbrock (eds.), *Types of alcoholics: Evidence from clinical, ex-* *perimental, and genetic research.* New York: New York Academy of Sciences.

Goodwyn, Susan W., & Acredolo, Linda P. (1993). Symbolic gesture versus word: Is there a modality advantage for onset of symbol use? *Child Development, 64,* 688–701.

Gore, P. M., & Rotter, Julian B. (1963). A personality correlate of social action. *Journal of Personality, 31,* 58–64.

Gore, Susan, & Mangione, Thomas W. (1983). Social roles, sex roles and psychological distress. *Journal of Health and Social Behavior, 24,* 300–312.

Goren, C. C.; Sarty, J.; & Wu, P. Y. (1975). Visual following and pattern discrimination of face-like stimuli by newborn infants. *Pediatrics, 56,* 544–549.

Gorn, Gerald J. (1982). The effects of music in advertising on choice behavior: A classical conditioning approach. *Journal of Marketing, 46,* 94–101.

Gotlib, Ian H., & Hooley, J. M. (1988). Depression and marital functioning. In S. Duck (ed.), *Handbook of personal relationships: Theory, research and interventions.* Chichester, England: Wiley.

Gottesman, Irving I. (1991). *Schizophrenia genesis: The origins of madness.* New York: Freeman.

Gottesman, Irving I. (1994). Perils and pleasures of genetic psychopathology. Distinguished Scientist Award address presented at the annual meeting of the American Psychological Association, Los Angeles.

Gottfried, Adele Eskeles; Fleming, James S.; & Gottfried, Allen W. (1994). Role of parental motivational practices in children's academic intrinsic motivation and achievement. *Journal of Educational Psychology, 86,* 104–113.

Gould, Elizabeth; Tanapat, Patima; McEwen, Bruce S.; Flügge, Gabriele; & Fuchs, Eberhard (1998). Proliferation of granule cell precursors in the dentate gyrus of adult monkeys is diminished by stress. *Proceedings of the National Academy of Science, 95,* 3168–3171.

Gould, James L., & Gould, Carol G. (1995). *The animal mind.* San Francisco: Freeman.

Gould, Stephen Jay (1981/1996). *The mismeasure of man.* New York: Norton.

Gould, Stephen Jay (1985, June). The median isn't the message. *Discover, 6*(6), 40–42.

Gould, Stephen Jay (1994, November 28). Curveball. [Review of *The Bell Curve,* by Richard J. Herrnstein and Charles Murray.] *New Yorker,* 139–149.

Graf, Peter, & Schacter, Daniel A. (1985). Implicit and explicit memory for new associations in normal and amnesic subjects. *Journal of Experimental Psychology: Learning, Memory, and Cognition, 11,* 501–518.

Graham, Jill W. (1986). Principled organizational dissent: A theoretical essay. *Research in Organizational Behavior, 8,* 1–52.

Greenberg, Roger P.; Bornstein, Robert F.; Greenberg, Michael D.; & Fisher, Seymour (1992). A meta-analysis of antidepressant outcome under "blinder" conditions. *Journal of Consulting and Clinical Psychology, 60,* 664–669.

Greenberg, Roger P.; Bornstein, Robert F.; Zborowski, Michael J.; Fisher, Seymour; et al. (1994). A meta-analysis of fluoxetine outcome in the treatment of depression. *Journal of Nervous and Mental Disease, 182,* 547–551.

Greenberger, Dennis, & Padesky, Christine A. (1995). *Mind over mood: A cognitive therapy treatment manual for clients.* New York: Guilford Press.

Greene, Robert L. (1986). Sources of recency effects in free recall. *Psychological Bulletin, 99,* 221–228.

Greenfield, Patricia (1976). Cross-cultural research and Piagetian theory: Paradox and progress. In K. F. Riegel & J. A. Meacham (eds.), *The developing individual in a changing world: Vol. 1. Historical and cultural issues.* The Hague, Netherlands: Mouton.

Greenough, William T., & Anderson, Brenda J. (1991). Cerebellar synaptic plasticity: Relation to learning vs. neural activity. *Annals of the New York Academy of Sciences, 627,* 231–247.

Greenough, William T., & Black, James E. (1992). Induction of brain structure by experience: Substrates for cognitive development. In M. Gunnar & C. A. Nelson (eds.), *Behavioral developmental neuroscience: Vol. 24. Minnesota Symposia on Child Psychology.* Hillsdale, NJ: Erlbaum.

Greenwald, Anthony G. (1992). New look 3: Unconscious cognition reclaimed. *American Psychologist, 47,* 766–779.

Greenwald, Anthony G.; Draine, Sean C.; & Abrams, Richard L. (1996). Three cognitive markers of unconscious semantic activation. *Science, 273,* 1699–1702.

Greenwald, Anthony G.; Spangenberg, Eric R.; Pratkanis, Anthony R.; & Eskenazi, Jay (1991). Double-blind tests of subliminal self-help audiotapes. *Psychological Science, 2,* 119–122.

Gregory, Richard L. (1963). Distortion of visual space as inappropriate constancy scaling. *Nature, 199,* 678–679.

Greven, Philip (1991). *Spare the child: The religious roots of punishment and the psychological impact of physical abuse.* New York: Knopf.

Griffin, Donald R. (1992). *Animal minds.* Chicago: University of Chicago Press.

Griggs, Richard A., & Cox, J. R. (1982). The elusive thematic-materials effect in Wason's selection task. *British Journal of Psychology, 73,* 407–420.

Grossarth-Maticek, Ronald; Eysenck, Hans J.; Gallasch, G.; Vetter, H.; & Frentzel-Beyme, R. (1991). Changes in degree of sclerosis as a function of prophylactic treatment in cancer-prone and CHD-prone probands. *Behavior Research and Therapy, 29,* 343–351.

Grossman, Michele, & Wood, Wendy (1993). Sex differences in intensity of emotional experience: A social role interpretation. *Journal of Personality and Social Psychology, 65,* 1010–1022.

Gruber, Barry L.; Hersh, Stephen P.; Hall, Nicholas R.; Waletzky, Lucy R.; et al. (1993). Immunological responses of breast cancer patients to behavioral interventions. *Biofeedback and Self-Regulation, 18,* 1–22.

Grusec, Joan E., & Goodnow, Jacqueline J. (1994). Impact of parental discipline methods on child's internalization of values: A reconceptualization of current points of view. *Developmental Psychology, 30,* 4–19.

Grusec, Joan E.; Saas-Kortsaak, P.; & Simutis, Z. M. (1978). The role of example and moral exhortation in the training of altruism. *Child Development, 49,* 920–923.

Guilford, J. P. (1988). Some changes in the structure-of-intellect model. *Educational and Psychological Measurement, 48,* 1–4.

Gutheil, Thomas G. (1993). The psychology of pharmacology. In M. Schacter (ed.), *Psychotherapy and medication.* Worthvale, NJ: Jason Aronson.

Haber, Ralph N. (1970, May). How we remember what we see. *Scientific American, 222,* 104–112.

Haimov, I., & Lavie, P. (1996). Melatonin—A soporific hormone. *Current Directions in Psychological Science, 5,* 106–111.

Halaas, Jeffrey L.; Gajiwala, Ketan S.; & Maffei, Margherita; et al. (1995). Weight-reducing effects of the plasma protein encoded by the *obese gene. Science, 269,* 543–546.

Hall, Edward T. (1959). *The silent language.* Garden City, NY: Doubleday.

Hall, Edward T. (1976). *Beyond culture.* New York: Anchor.

Hall, Edward T. (1983). *The dance of life: The other dimension of time.* Garden City, NY: Anchor Press/Doubleday.

Hall, Edward T., & Hall, Mildred R. (1987). *Hidden differences: Doing business with the Japanese.* Garden City, NY: Anchor Press/Doubleday.

Hall, Edward T., & Hall, Mildred R. (1990). *Understanding cultural differences.* Yarmouth, ME: Intercultural Press.

Hall, G. Stanley (1899). A study of anger. *American Journal of Psychology, 10,* 516–591.

Halpern, Diane (1995). *Thought and knowledge: An introduction to critical thinking* (3rd ed.). Hillsdale, NJ: Erlbaum.

Hamer, Dean H.; Hu, Stella; Magnuson, Victoria L.; et al. (1993). A linkage between DNA markers on the X chromosome and male sexual orientation. *Science, 261,* 321–327.

Hamilton, V. Lee, & Sanders, Joseph (1992). *Everyday justice: Responsibility and the individual in Japan and the United States.* New Haven, CT: Yale University Press.

Haney, Craig; Banks, Curtis; & Zimbardo, Philip (1973). Interpersonal dynamics in a simulated prison. *International Journal of Criminology and Penology, 1,* 69–97.

Harding, Courtenay M.; Zubin, Joseph; & Strauss, John S. (1987). Chronicity in schizophrenia: Fact, partial fact, or artifact? *Hospital and Community Psychiatry, 38,* 477–486.

Harding, Courtenay M.; Zubin, Joseph; & Strauss, John S. (1992). Chronicity in schizophrenia: Revisited. *British Journal of Psychiatry, 161*(Suppl. 18), 27–37.

Hare, Robert D. (1965). Temporal gradient of fear arousal in psychopaths. *Journal of Abnormal Psychology, 70,* 442–445.

Hare, Robert D. (1993). *Without conscience: The disturbing world of the psychopaths among us.* New York: Pocket Books.

Haritos-Fatouros, Mika (1988). The official torturer: A learning model for obedience to the authority of violence. *Journal of Applied Social Psychology, 18,* 1107–1120.

Harkins, Stephen G., & Szymanski, Kate (1989). Social loafing and group evaluation. *Journal of Personality and Social Psychology, 56,* 934–941.

Harlow, Harry F. (1958). The nature of love. *American Psychologist, 13,* 673–685.

Harlow, Harry F., & Harlow, Margaret K. (1966). Learning to love. *American Scientist, 54,* 244–272.

Harmon-Jones, Eddie; Brehm, Jack W.; Greenberg, Jeff; Simon, Linda; & Nelson, David E. (1996). Evidence that the production of aversive consequences is not necessary to create cognitive dissonance. *Journal of Personality and Social Psychology, 70,* 5–16.

Harris, Marvin (1985). *Good to eat: Riddles of food and culture.* New York: Simon & Schuster.

Hart, John, Jr.; Berndt, Rita S.; & Caramazza, Alfonso (1985, August 1). Category-specific naming deficit following cerebral infarction. *Nature, 316,* 339–340.

Harvey, Mary R., & Herman, Judith L. (1994). Amnesia, partial amnesia and delayed recall among adult survivors of childhood trauma.[Special Issue: The recovered memory/false memory debate.] *Consciousness and Cognition, 3,* 295–306.

Hasher, Lynn, & Zacks, Rose T. (1984). Automatic processing of fundamental information: The case of frequency of occurrence. *American Psychologist, 39,* 1372–1388.

Hatfield, Agnes B., & Lefley, Harriet P. (eds.) (1987). *Families of the mentally ill: Coping and adaptation.* New York: Guilford Press.

Hatfield, Elaine, & Rapson, Richard L. (1996). *Love and sex: Cross-cultural perspectives.* Boston: Allyn & Bacon.

Hawkins, Scott A., & Hastie, Reid (1990). Hindsight: Biased judgments of past events after the outcomes are known. *Psychological Bulletin, 107,* 311–327.

Haynes, Suzanne, & Feinleib, Manning (1980). Women, work, and coronary heart disease: Prospective findings from the Framingham heart study. *American Journal of Public Health, 70,* 133–141.

Hazan, Cindy, & Shaver, Phillip R. (1994). Attachment as an organizational framework for research on close relationships. *Psychological Inquiry, 5,* 1–22.

Heath, Shirley B. (1983). *Ways with words: Language, life, and work in communities and classrooms.* New York: Cambridge University Press.

Heinrichs, R. Walter (1993). Schizophrenia and the brain: Conditions for a neuropsychology of madness. *American Psychologist, 48,* 221–233.

Helmes, Edward, & Reddon, John R. (1993). A perspective on developments in assessing psychopathology: A critical review of the MMPI and MMPI-2. *Psychological Bulletin, 113,* 453–471.

Helson, Ravenna, & McCabe, Laurel (1993). The social clock project in middle age. In B. F. Turner & L. E. Troll (eds.), *Women growing older.* Newbury Park, CA: Sage.

Hendrick, Clyde, & Hendrick, Susan S. (1986). A theory and method of love. *Journal of Personality and Social Psychology, 50,* 392–402.

Hendrick, Susan S., & Hendrick, Clyde (1992). *Romantic love.* Newbury Park, CA: Sage.

Hendrick, Susan S., & Hendrick, Clyde (1997). Love and satisfaction. In R. J. Sternberg & M. Hojjat (eds.), *Satisfaction in close relationships.* New York: Guilford Press.

Hendrick, Susan S.; Hendrick, Clyde; & Adler, Nancy L. (1988). Romantic relationships: Love, satisfaction, and staying together. *Journal of Personality and Social Psychology, 54,* 980–988.

Hendrix, William H.; Steel, Robert P.; Leap, Terry L.; & Summers, Timothy P. (1991). Development of a stress-related health promotion model: Antecedents and organizational effectiveness outcomes. [Special Issue: Handbook on job stress.] *Journal of Social Behavior and Personality, 6,* 141–162.

Henley, Nancy (1995). Body politics revisited: What do we know today? In P. J. Kalbfleisch & M. J. Cody (eds.), *Gender, power, and communication in human relationships.* Hillsdale, NJ: Erlbaum.

Henriques, Jeffrey B., & Davidson, Richard J. (1991). Left frontal hypoactivation in depression. *Journal of Abnormal Psychology, 100,* 535–545.

Henry, Bill; Caspi, Avshalom; Moffitt, Terrie E.; & Silva, Phil A. (1996). Temperamental and familial predictors of violent and nonviolent criminal convictions: Age 3 to age 18. *Developmental Psychology, 32,* 614–623.

Hepworth, Joseph T., & West, Stephen G. (1988). Lynchings and the economy: A time-series reanalysis of Hovland and Sears (1940). *Journal of Personality and Social Psychology, 55,* 239–247.

Herman, Louis M. (1987). Receptive competencies of language-trained animals. In J. S. Rosenblatt, C. Beer, M. C. Busnel, & P. J. B. Slater (eds.), *Advances in the study of behavior* (Vol. 17). Petaluma, CA: Academic Press.

Herman, Louis M.; Kuczaj, Stan A.; & Holder, Mark D. (1993). Responses to anomalous gestural sequences by a language-trained dolphin: Evidence for processing of semantic relations and syntactic information. *Journal of Experimental Psychology: General, 122,* 184–194.

Herman-Giddens, Marcia E.; Slora, E. J.; Wasserman, R. C.; et al. (1997). Secondary sexual characteristics and menses in young girls seen in office practice: A study from the Pediatric Research in Office Settings network. *Pediatrics, 99,* 505–512.

Hermans, Hubert J. M. (1996). Voicing the self: From information processing to dialogical interchange. *Psychological Bulletin, 119,* 31–50.

Heron, Woodburn (1957). The pathology of boredom. *Scientific American, 196*(1), 52–56.

Herrnstein, Richard J., & Murray, Charles (1994). *The bell curve: Intelligence and class structure in American life.* New York: Free Press.

Hershberger, Scott L.; Lykken, David T.; & McGue, Matt (1995). A twin registry study of male and female sexual orientation. Paper presented at the annual meeting of the American Psychological Association, New York.

Hicks, Robert D. (1991). The police model of satanism crime. In J. T. Richardson, J. Best, & D. G. Bromley (eds.), *The satanism scare.* New York: Aldine de Gruyter.

Higley, J. D.; Hasert, M. L.; Suomi, S. J.; & Linnoila, M. (1991). A nonhuman primate model of alcohol abuse: Effects of early experience, personality, and stress on alcohol consumption. *Proceedings of the National Academy of Science, 88,* 7261–7265.

Hill, Harlan F.; Chapman, C. Richard; Kornell, Judy A.; Sullivan, Keith M.; et al. (1990). Self-administration of morphine in bone marrow transplant patients reduces drug requirement. *Pain, 40,* 121–129.

Hilsman, Ruth, & Garber, Judy (1995). A test of the cognitive diathesis–stress model of depression in children: Academic stressors, attributional style, perceived competence, and control. *Journal of Personality and Social Psychology, 69,* 370–380.

Hilts, Philip J. (1995). *Memory's ghost: The strange tale of Mr. M. and the nature of memory.* New York: Simon & Schuster.

Hirsch, Helmut V. B., & Spinelli, D. N. (1970). Visual experience modifies distribution of horizontally and vertically oriented receptive fields in cats. *Science, 168,* 869–871.

Hirst, William; Neisser, Ulric; & Spelke, Elizabeth (1978, January). Divided attention. *Human Nature, 1,* 54–61.

Hobson, J. Allan (1988). *The dreaming brain.* New York: Basic Books.

Hobson, J. Allan (1990). Activation, input source, and modulation: A neurocognitive model of the state of the brain–mind. In R. R. Bootzin, J. F. Kihlstrom, & D. L. Schacter (eds.), *Sleep and cognition.* Washington, DC: American Psychological Association.

Hochschild, Arlie (1983). *The managed heart.* Berkeley: University of California Press.

Hoffman, Martin L. (1990). Empathy and justice motivation. [Special Issue: Empathy.] *Motivation and Emotion, 14,* 151–172.

Hoffman, Martin L., & Saltzstein, Herbert (1967). Parent discipline and the child's moral development. *Journal of Personality and Social Psychology, 5,* 45–57.

Hofstede, Geert, & Bond, Michael H. (1988). The Confucius connection: From cultural roots to economic growth. *Organizational Dynamics,* 5–21.

Hogg, Michael A., & Abrams, Dominic (1988). *Social identifications: A social psychology of intergroup relations and group processes.* New York: Routledge.

Holmes, David S. (1997). *Abnormal psychology* (3rd ed.). New York: Longman.

Holzman, Philip S., & Matthysse, Steven (1990). The genetics of schizophrenia: A review. *Psychological Science, 1,* 279–286.

Hooker, Evelyn (1957). The adjustment of the male overt homosexual. *Journal of Projective Techniques, 21,* 18–31.

Hooven, Carole; Gottman, John M.; & Katz, Lynn F. (1995). Parental meta-emotion structure predicts family and child outcomes. *Cognition and Emotion, 9,* 229–269.

Hoptman, Matthew J., & Davidson, Richard J. (1994). How and why do the two cerebral hemispheres interact? *Psychological Bulletin, 116,* 195–219.

Horgan, John (1995, November). Get smart, take a test: A long-term rise in IQ scores baffles intelligence experts. *Scientific American, 273,* 12, 14.

Horn, G., & Hinde, R. A. (eds.) (1970). *Short-term changes in neural activity and behaviour.* New York: Cambridge University Press.

Horn, John L., & Donaldson, Gary (1980). Cognitive development in adulthood. In O. G. Brim, Jr., & J. Kagan (eds.), *Constancy and change in human development.* Cambridge, MA: Harvard University Press.

Horne, J. A. (1988). Sleep loss and "divergent" thinking ability. *Sleep, 11,* 528–536.

Horner, Althea J. (1991). *Psychoanalytic object relations therapy.* New York: Jason Aronson.

Hornstein, Gail (1992). The return of the repressed: Psychology's problematic relations with psychoanalysis, 1909–1960. *American Psychologist, 47,* 254–263.

House, James S.; Landis, Karl R.; & Umberson, Debra (1988, July 19). Social relationships and health. *Science, 241,* 540–545.

Hovland, Carl I., & Sears, Robert R. (1940). Minor studies of aggression: Correlation of lynchings with economic indices. *Journal of Psychology, 9,* 301–310.

Howard, George S. (1991). Culture tales: A narrative approach to thinking, cross-cultural psychology, and psychotherapy. *American Psychologist, 46,* 187–197.

Howard, Kenneth; Kopta, S. Mark; Krause, Merton S.; & Orlinsky, David (1986). The dose–effect relationship in psychotherapy. *American Psychologist, 41,* 159–164.

Howe, Mark L., & Courage, Mary L. (1993). On resolving the enigma of infantile amnesia. *Psychological Bulletin, 113,* 305–326.

Howe, Mark L.; Courage, Mary L.; & Peterson, Carole (1994). How can I remember when "I" wasn't there? Long-term retention of traumatic experiences and emergence of the cognitive self. [Special Issue: The recovered memory/false memory debate.] *Consciousness and Cognition, 3,* 327–355.

Hrdy, Sarah B. (1988). Empathy, polyandry, and the myth of the coy female. In R. Bleier (ed.), *Feminist approaches to science.* New York: Pergamon.

Hu, S.; Pattatucci, A. M.; Patterson C.; et al. (1995). Linkage between sexual orientation and chromosome Xq28 in males but not in females. *Nature Genetics, 11,* 248–256.

Hubbard, Ruth (1990). *The politics of women's biology.* New Brunswick, NJ: Rutgers University Press.

Hubel, David H., & Wiesel, Torsten N. (1962). Receptive fields, binocular interaction and functional architecture in the cat's visual cortex. *Journal of Physiology* (London), *160,* 106–154.

Hubel, David H., & Wiesel, Torsten N. (1968). Receptive fields and functional architecture of monkey striate cortex. *Journal of Physiology* (London), *195,* 215–243.

Hughes, Judith M. (1989). *Reshaping the psychoanalytic domain: The work of Melanie Klein, W. R. D. Fairbairn, & D. W. Winnicott.* Berkeley: University of California Press.

Hunt, Earl; Streissguth, Ann P.; Kerr, Beth; & Olson, Heather C. (1995). Mothers' alcohol consumption during pregnancy: Effects on spatial-visual reasoning in 14-year-old children. *Psychological Science, 6,* 339–342.

Hunt, Morton M. (1993). *The story of psychology.* New York: Doubleday.

Hunter, John E. (1996). Significance tests should be banned. Paper presented at the annual meeting of the American Psychological Society, San Francisco.

Hunter, John E. (1997). Needed: A ban on the significance test. *Psychological Science, 8,* 3–7.

Hupka, Ralph B. (1981). Cultural determinants of jealousy. *Alternative Lifestyles, 4,* 310–356.

Hupka, Ralph B. (1991). The motive for the arousal of romantic jealousy. In P. Salovey (ed.), *The psychology of jealousy and envy.* New York: Guilford Press.

Hyde, Janet S. (1981). How large are cognitive gender differences? A meta-analysis using a2 and d. *American Psychologist, 36,* 892–901.

Hyde, Janet S. (1984). How large are gender differences in aggression? A developmental meta-analysis. *Developmental Psychology, 20,* 722–736.

Hyde, Janet S.; Fennema, Elizabeth; & Lamon, Susan J. (1990). Gender differences in mathematics performance: A meta-analysis. *Psychological Bulletin, 107,* 139–155.

Hyde, Janet S., & Linn, Marcia C. (1988). Gender differences in verbal ability: A meta-analysis. *Psychological Bulletin, 104,* 53–69.

Hyman, Ira E., Jr., & Pentland, Joel (1996). The role of mental imagery in the creation of false childhood memories. *Journal of Memory and Language, 35,* 101–117.

Hyman, Irwin A. (1994). Is spanking child abuse? Conceptualizations, research and policy implications. Paper presented at the annual meeting of the American Psychological Association, Los Angeles.

Hyman, Ray (1994). Anomaly or artifact? Comments on Bem and Honorton. *Psychological Bulletin, 115,* 25–27.

Inglis, James, & Lawson, J. S. (1981). Sex differences in the effects of unilateral brain damage on intelligence. *Science, 212,* 693–695.

Irons, Edward D., & Moore, Gilbert W. (1985). *Black managers: The case of the banking industry.* New York: Praeger/Greenwood.

Irvine, Janice M. (1990). *Disorders of desire: Sex and gender in modern American sexology.* Philadelphia: Temple University Press.

Isen, Alice M.; Daubman, Kimberly A.; & Nowicki, Gary P. (1987). Positive affect facilitates creative problem solving. *Journal of Personality and Social Psychology, 52,* 1122–1131.

Islam, Mir Rabiul, & Hewstone, Miles (1993). Intergroup attributions and affective consequences in majority and minority groups. *Journal of Personality and Social Psychology, 64,* 936–950.

Izard, Carroll E. (1990). Facial expressions and the regulation of emotions. *Journal of Personality and Social Psychology, 58,* 487–498.

Izard, Carroll E. (1994). Innate and universal facial expressions: Evidence from developmental and cross-cultural research. *Psychological Bulletin, 115,* 288–299.

Jacobs, Janis E., & Eccles, Jacquelynne S. (1985). Gender differences in math ability: The impact of media reports on parents. *Educational Researcher, 14,* 20–25.

Jacobsen, Paul B; Bovbjerg, Dana H.; Schwartz, Marc D.; Hudis, Clifford A.; et al. (1995). Conditioned emotional distress in women receiving chemotherapy for breast cancer. *Journal of Consulting & Clinical Psychology, 63,* 108–114.

Jacobsen, Teresa; Edelstein, Wolfgang; & Hofmann, Volker (1994). A longitudinal study of the relation between representations of attachment in childhood and cognitive functioning in childhood and adolescence. *Developmental Psychology, 30,* 112–124.

Jacobson, John W.; Mulick, James A.; & Schwartz, Allen A. (1995). The history of facilitated communication: Science, pseudoscience, and anti-science. *American Psychologist, 50,* 750–765.

James, William (1890/1950). *Principles of psychology* (Vol. 1). New York: Dover.

Janis, Irving L. (1982). *Groupthink: Psychological studies of policy decisions and fiascoes* (2nd ed.). Boston: Houghton Mifflin.

Janis, Irving L. (1989). *Crucial decisions: Leadership in policymaking and crisis management.* New York: Free Press.

Janis, Irving L.; Kaye, Donald; & Kirschner, Paul (1965). Facilitating effects of "eating-while-reading" on responsiveness to persuasive communications. *Journal of Personality and Social Psychology, 1,* 181–186.

Jellinek, E. M. (1960). *The disease concept of alcoholism.* New Haven, CT: Hillhouse Press.

Jenkins, John G., & Dallenbach, Karl M. (1924). Obliviscence during sleep and waking. *American Journal of Psychology, 35,* 605–612.

Jenkins, Sharon Rae (1994). Need for power and women's careers over 14 years: Structural power, job satisfaction, and motive change. *Journal of Personality and Social Psychology, 66,* 155–165.

Jensen, Arthur R. (1969). How much can we boost IQ and scholastic achievement? *Harvard Educational Review, 39,* 1–123.

Jensen, Arthur R. (1981). *Straight talk about mental tests.* New York: Free Press.

Jessor, Richard (1993). Successful adolescent development among youth in high-risk settings. *American Psychologist, 48,* 117–126.

Johnson, Catherine (1988). *When to say goodbye to your therapist.* New York: Simon & Schuster.

Johnson, David W., & Johnson, Roger T. (1989). *A meta-analysis of cooperative, competitive, and individualistic goal structures.* Hillsdale, NJ: Erlbaum.

Johnson, Marcia K. (1995). The relation between memory and reality. Paper presented at the annual meeting of the American Psychological Association, New York.

Johnson, Mark H.; Dziurawiec, Suzanne; Ellis, Hadyn; & Morton, John (1991). Newborns' preferential tracking of face-like stimuli and its subsequent decline. *Cognition, 40,* 1–19.

Johnson-Laird, Philip N. (1988). *The computer and the mind: An introduction to cognitive science.* Cambridge, MA: Harvard University Press.

Joiner, Thomas E., Jr., & Metalsky, Gerald I. (1995). A prospective test of an integrative interpersonal theory of depression: A naturalistic study of college roommates. *Journal of Personality and Social Psychology, 69,* 778–788.

Jones, James M. (1991). Psychological models of race: What have they been and what should they be? In J. D. Goodchilds (ed.), *Psychological perspectives on human diversity in America.* Washington, DC: American Psychological Association.

Jones, Mary Cover (1924). A laboratory study of fear: The case of Peter. *Pedagogical Seminary, 31,* 308–315.

Jones, Russell A. (1977). *Self-fulfilling prophecies.* Hillsdale, NJ: Erlbaum.

Jorgensen, Randall S.; Johnson, Blair T.; Kolodziej, Monika E.; & Schreer, George E. (1996). Elevated blood pressure and personality: A meta-analytic review. *Psychological Bulletin, 120,* 293–320.

Judd, Charles M.; Park, Bernadette; Ryan, Carey S.; Brauer, Markus; & Kraus, Susan (1995). Stereotypes and ethnocentrism: Diverging interethnic perceptions of African American and white American youth. *Journal of Personality and Social Psychology, 69,* 460–481.

Jung, Carl (1967). *Collected works.* Princeton, NJ: Princeton University Press.

Jusczyk, Peter W. (1993). From general to language-specific capacities: The WRAPSA model of how speech perception develops. [Special Issue: Phonetic development.] *Journal of Phonetics, 21,* 3–28.

Jusczyk, Peter W.; Friederici, Angela D.; Wessels, Jeanine M.; Svenkerud, Vigdis Y.; et al. (1993). Infants' sensitivity to the sound patterns of native language words. *Journal of Memory and Language, 32,* 402–420.

Kagan, Jerome (1984). *The nature of the child.* New York: Basic Books.

Kagan, Jerome (1989). *Unstable ideas: Temperament, cognition, and self.* Cambridge, MA: Harvard University Press.

Kagan, Jerome (1993). The meanings of morality. *Psychological Science, 4,* 353, 357–360.

Kagan, Jerome (1994). *Galen's prophecy: Temperament in human nature.* New York: Basic Books.

Kagan, Jerome; Kearsley, Richard B.; & Zelazo, Philip R. (1978). *Infancy: Its place in human development.* Cambridge, MA: Harvard University Press.

Kagan, Jerome, & Snidman, Nancy (1991). Infant predictors of inhibited and uninhibited profiles. *Psychological Science, 2,* 40–44.

Kahneman, Daniel, & Treisman, Anne (1984). Changing views of attention and automaticity. In R. Parasuraman, D. R. Davies, & J. Beatty (eds.), *Varieties of attention.* New York: Academic Press.

Kameda, Tatsuya, & Sugimori, Shinkichi (1993). Psychological entrapment in group decision making: An assigned decision rule and a groupthink phenomenon. *Journal of Personality and Social Psychology, 65,* 282–292.

Kanin, Eugene J. (1985). Date rapists: Differential sexual socialization and relative deprivation. *Archives of Sexual Behavior, 14,* 219–231.

Kanter, Rosabeth Moss (1977/1993). *Men and women of the corporation.* New York: Basic Books.

Kaplan, Abraham (1967). A philosophical discussion of normality. *Archives of General Psychiatry, 17,* 325–330.

Kaplan, Meg S.; Morales, Miguel; & Becker, Judith V. (1993). The impact of verbal satiation of adolescent sex offenders: A preliminary report. *Journal of Child Sexual Abuse, 2,* 81–88.

Kaplan, Stephen L.; Randolph, Stephen W.; & Lemli, James M. (1991). Treatment outcomes in the reduction of fear: A meta-analysis. Paper presented at the annual meeting of the American Psychological Association, San Francisco.

Karasek, Robert, & Theorell, Tores (1990). *Healthy work: Stress, productivity, and the reconstruction of working life.* New York: Basic Books.

Karau, Steven J., & Williams, Kipling D. (1993). Social loafing: A meta-analytic review and theoretical integration. *Journal of Personality and Social Psychology, 65,* 681–706.

Karney, Benjamin R.; Bradbury, Thomas N.; Fincham, Frank D.; & Sullivan, Kieran T. (1994). The role of negative affectivity in the association between attributions and marital satisfaction. *Journal of Personality and Social Psychology, 66,* 413–424.

Karni, Avi; Tanne, David; Rubenstein, Barton S.; Askenasy, Jean J. M.; & Sagi, Dov (1994). Dependence on REM sleep of overnight improvement of a perceptual skill. *Science, 265,* 679–682.

Karon, Bertram P. (1994). Psychotherapy: The appropriate treatment of schizophrenia. Paper presented at the annual meeting of the American Psychological Association, Los Angeles.

Kashima, Yoshihisa; Yamaguchi, Susumu; Kim, Uichol; Choi, Sang-Chin; Gelfand, Michele J.; & Yuki, Masaki (1995). Culture, gender, and self: A perspective from individualism–collectivism research. *Journal of Personality and Social Psychology, 69,* 925–937.

Kasser, Tim, & Ryan, Richard M. (1993). A dark side of the American dream: Correlates of financial success as a central life aspiration. *Journal of Personality and Social Psychology, 65,* 410–422.

Katigbak, Marcia S.; Church, A. Timothy; & Akamine, Toshio X. (1996). Cross-cultural generalizability of personality dimensions: Relating indigenous and imported dimensions in two cultures. *Journal of Personality and Social Psychology, 70,* 99–114.

Katz, Joel, & Melzack, Ronald (1990). Pain "memories" in phantom limbs: Review and clinical observations. *Pain, 43,* 319–336.

Katz, Jonathan Ned (1995). *The invention of heterosexuality.* New York: Dutton.

Katz, Lori, & Epstein, Seymour (1991). Constructive thinking and coping with laboratory-induced stress. *Journal of Personality and Social Psychology, 61,* 789–800.

Katz, Phyllis A., & Ksansnak, Keith R. (1994). Developmental aspects of gender role flexibility and traditionality in middle childhood and adolescence. *Developmental Psychology, 30,* 272–282.

Keating, Caroline F. (1994). World without words: Messages from face and body. In W. J. Lonner & R. Malpass (eds.), *Psychology and culture.* Needham Heights, MA: Allyn & Bacon.

Keck, Paul E.; McElroy, Susan L.; & Pope, Harrison G. (1991). Epidemiology of neuroleptic malignant syndrome. *Psychiatric Annals, 21,* 148–151.

Keefe, Francis J., & Gil, Karen M. (1986). Behavioral concepts in the analysis of chronic pain syndromes. *Journal of Consulting and Clinical Psychology, 54,* 776–783.

Kelly, Anita E., & McKillop, Kevin J. (1996). Consequences of revealing personal secrets. *Psychological Bulletin, 120,* 450–465.

Kelman, Herbert C., & Hamilton, V. Lee (1989). *Crimes of obedience: Toward a social psychology of authority and responsibility.* New Haven, CT: Yale University Press.

Kendler, K. S.; Heath, A. C.; Neale, M. C.; Kessler, R. C.; & Eaves, L. J. (1992, October 14). A population-based twin study of alcoholism in women. *Journal of the American Medical Association, 268,* 1877–1882.

Kephart, William M. (1967). Some correlates of romantic love. *Journal of Marriage and the Family, 29,* 470–474.

Kerr, Michael E., & Bowen, Murray (1988). *Family evaluation: An approach based on Bowen theory.* New York: Norton.

Kerr, Norbert L. (1995). Norms in social dilemmas. In D. Schroeder (ed.), *Social dilemmas: Perspectives on individuals and groups.* Westport, CT: Praeger.

Kessler, Ronald C.; McGonagle, Katherine A.; Zhao, Shanyang; Nelson, Christopher B.; et al. (1994). Lifetime and 12-month prevalence of DSM-III-R psychiatric disorders in the United States: Results from the National Comorbidity Study. *Archives of General Psychiatry, 51,* 8–19.

Kessler, Ronald C.; Sonnega, A.; Bromet, E.; Hughes, M.; & Nelson, C. B. (1995). Posttraumatic stress disorder in the National Comorbidity Survey. *Archives of General Psychiatry, 52,* 1048–1060.

Kiecolt-Glaser, Janice; Garner, Warren; Speicher, Carl; Penn, Gerald; Holliday, Jane; & Glaser, Ronald (1985a). Psychosocial modifiers of immunocompetence in medical students. *Psychosomatic Medicine, 46,* 7–14.

Kiecolt-Glaser, Janice; Glaser, Ronald; Williger, D.; Stout, J. C; et al. (1985b). Psychosocial enhancement of immunocompetence in a geriatric population. *Health Psychology, 4,* 25–41.

Kiecolt-Glaser, Janice; Malarkey, William B.; Chee, MaryAnn; Newton, Tamara; et al. (1993). Negative behavior during marital conflict is associated with immunological down-regulation. *Psychosomatic Medicine, 55,* 395–409.

Kihlstrom, John F. (1994). Hypnosis, delayed recall, and the principles of memory. *International Journal of Clinical and Experimental Hypnosis, 40,* 337–345.

Kihlstrom, John (1995). From a subject's point of view: The experiment as conversation and collaboration between investigator and subject. Invited address presented at the seventh annual meeting of the American Psychological Society, New York.

Kihlstrom, John F.; Barnhardt, Terrence M.; & Tataryn, Douglas J. (1992). The psychological unconscious: Found, lost, and regained. *American Psychologist, 47,* 788–791.

Kihlstrom, John F., & Harackiewicz, Judith M. (1982). The earliest recollection: A new survey. *Journal of Personality, 50,* 134–148.

King, Pamela (1989, October). The chemistry of doubt. *Psychology Today,* 58, 60.

King, Patricia M., & Kitchener, Karen S. (1994). *Developing reflective judgment: Understanding and promoting intellectual growth and critical thinking in adolescents and adults.* San Francisco: Jossey-Bass.

Kinsbourne, Marcel (1982). Hemispheric specialization and the growth of human understanding. *American Psychologist, 37,* 411–420.

Kinsey, Alfred C.; Pomeroy, Wardell B.; & Martin, Clyde E. (1948). *Sexual behavior in the human male.* Philadelphia: Saunders.

Kinsey, Alfred C.; Pomeroy, Wardell B.; Martin, Clyde E.; & Gebhard, Paul H. (1953). *Sexual behavior in the human female.* Philadelphia: Saunders.

Kirkpatrick, Lee A., & Davis, Keith A. (1994). Attachment style, gender, and relationship stability: A longitudinal analysis. *Journal of Personality and Social Psychology, 66,* 502–512.

Kirschenbaum, B.; Nedergaard, M.; Preuss, A.; et al. (1994). In vitro neuronal production and differentiation by precursor cells derived from the adult human forebrain. *Cerebral Cortex, 4,* 576–589.

Kitayama, Shinobu, & Markus, Hazel R. (1994). Introduction to cultural psychology and emotion research. In S. Kitayama & H. R. Markus (eds.), *Emotion and culture: Empirical studies of mutual influence.* Washington, DC: American Psychological Association.

Kitchener, Karen S., & King, Patricia M. (1990). The Reflective Judgment Model: Ten years of research. In M. L. Commons (ed.), *Models and methods in the study of adolescent and adult thought: Vol. 2. Adult development.* Westport, CT: Greenwood Press.

Kitchener, Karen S.; Lynch, Cindy L.; Fischer, Kurt W.; & Wood, Phillip K. (1993). Developmental range of reflective judgment: The effect of contextual support and practice on developmental stage. *Developmental Psychology, 29,* 893–906.

Kitzinger, Celia, & Wilkinson, Sue (1995). Transitions from heterosexuality to lesbianism: The discursive production of lesbian identities. *Developmental Psychology, 31,* 95–104.

Klein, Donald F. (1980). Psychosocial treatment of schizophrenia, or psychosocial help for people with schizophrenia? *Schizophrenia Bulletin, 6,* 122–130.

Kleinman, Arthur (1988). *Rethinking psychiatry: From cultural category to personal experience.* New York: Free Press.

Klerman, Gerald L.; Weissman, Myrna M.; Rounsaville, Bruce J.; & Chevron, Eve S. (1984). *Interpersonal psychotherapy of depression.* New York: Basic Books.

Klima, Edward S., & Bellugi, Ursula (1966). Syntactic regularities in the speech of children. In J. Lyons & R. J. Wales (eds.), *Psycholinguistics papers.* Edinburgh, Scotland: Edinburgh University Press.

Klopfenstein, Glenn D. (1997, May 30). Cheating at chess, 200 million times a second. *Chronicle of Higher Education,* B8.

Kluft, Richard P. (1987). The simulation and dissimulation of multiple personality disorder. *American Journal of Clinical Hypnosis, 30,* 104–118.

Kluft, Richard P. (1993). Multiple personality disorders. In D. Spiegel (ed.), *Dissociative disorders: A clinical review.* Lutherville, MD: Sidran.

Kluger, Richard (1996). *Ashes to ashes: America's hundred-year cigarette war, the public health, and the unabashed triumph of Philip Morris.* New York: Knopf.

Knight, Raymond A.; Prentky, Robert A.; & Cerce, David D. (1994). The development, reliability, and validity of an inventory for the multidimensional assessment of sex and aggression [Special Issue: The assessment and treatment of sex offenders]. *Criminal Justice and Behavior, 21,* 72–94.

Koegel, Robert L.; Schreibman, Laura; O'Neill, Robert E.; & Burke, John C. (1983). The personality and family-interaction characteristics of parents of autistic children. *Journal of Consulting and Clinical Psychology, 51,* 683–692.

Kohlberg, Lawrence (1964). Development of moral character and moral ideology. In M. Hoffman & L. W. Hoffman (eds.), *Review of child development research.* New York: Russell Sage Foundation.

Kohlberg, Lawrence (1966). A cognitive-developmental analysis of children's sex-role concepts and attitudes. In E. E. Maccoby (ed.), *The development of sex differences.* Stanford, CA: Stanford University Press.

Kohlberg, Lawrence (1976). Moral stages and moralization: The cognitive-developmental approach. In T. Lickona (ed.), *Moral development and behavior.* New York: Holt, Rinehart and Winston.

Kohlberg, Lawrence (1984). *Essays on moral development: Vol. 2. The psychology of moral development: The nature and validity of moral stages.* San Francisco: Harper & Row.

Köhler, Wolfgang (1925). *The mentality of apes.* New York: Harcourt, Brace.

Kohn, Melvin, & Schooler, Carmi (1983). *Work and personality: An inquiry into the impact of social stratification.* Norwood, NJ: Ablex.

Kohn, Paul M.; Lafreniere, Kathryn; & Gurevich, Maria (1991). Hassles, health, and personality. *Journal of Personality and Social Psychology, 61,* 478–482.

Kolb, B. (1996). Neural plasticity and behavioural development. [State of the art address.] Paper presented at the International Congress of Psychology, Montreal.

Kolbert, Elizabeth (1995, June 5). Public opinion polls swerve with the turns of a phrase. *New York Times, 144,* A1.

Kopta, Stephen M.; Howard, Kenneth I.; Lowry, Jenny L.; & Beutler, Larry E. (1994). Patterns of symptomatic recovery in psychotherapy. *Journal of Consulting and Clinical Psychology, 62,* 1009–1016.

Koski, Lilah R., & Shaver, Phillip R. (1997). Attachment and relationship satisfaction across the lifespan. In R. J. Sternberg & M. Hojjat (eds.), *Satisfaction in close relationships.* New York: Guilford Press.

Koss, Mary P.; Dinero, Thomas E.; Seibel, Cynthia A.; & Cox, Susan L. (1988). Stranger and acquaintance rape: Are there differences in the victim's experience? *Psychology of Women Quarterly, 12,* 1–24.

Kosslyn, Stephen M. (1980). *Image and mind.* Cambridge, MA: Harvard University Press.

Krantz, David S., & Manuck, Stephen B. (1984). Acute psychophysiologic reactivity and risk of cardiovascular disease: A review and methodological critique. *Psychological Bulletin, 96,* 435–464.

Kraus, Stephen J. (1995). Attitudes and the prediction of behavior: A meta-analysis of the empirical literature. *Personality and Social Psychology Bulletin, 21,* 58–75.

Krieger, Nancy, & Sidney, S. (1996, October). Racial discrimination and blood pressure: The CARDIA study of young black and white adults. *American Journal of Public Health, 86,* 1370–1378.

Kroll, Barry M. (1992). *Teaching hearts and minds: College students reflect on the Vietnam War in literature.* Carbondale: Southern Illinois University Press.

Krupa, David J.; Thompson, Judith K.; & Thompson, Richard F. (1993). Localization of a memory trace in the mammalian brain. *Science, 260,* 989–991.

Kuhl, Patricia K.; Williams, Karen A.; Lacerda, Francisco; Stevens, Kenneth N.; et al. (1992, January 31). Linguistic experience alters phonetic perception in infants by 6 months of age. *Science, 255,* 606–608.

Kuhn, Deanna; Weinstock, Michael; & Flaton, Robin (1994). How well do jurors reason? Competence dimensions of individual variation in a juror reasoning task. *Psychological Science, 5,* 289–296.

Kunda, Ziva (1990). The case for motivated reasoning. *Psychological Bulletin, 108,* 480–498.

Kurtines, William M., & Gewirtz, Jacob J. (eds.) (1995). *Moral development: An introduction.* Boston: Allyn & Bacon.

Kutchins, Herb, & Kirk, Stuart A. (1997). *Making us crazy: DSM. The psychiatric bible and the creation of mental disorders.* New York: Free Press.

Lachman, Sheldon J. (1996). Processes in perception: Psychological transformations of highly structured stimulus material. *Perceptual and Motor Skills, 83,* 411–418.

Lader, Malcolm, & Morton, Sally (1991). Benzodiazepine problems. *British Journal of Addiction, 86,* 823–828.

LaFromboise, Teresa; Coleman, Hardin L. K.; & Gerton, Jennifer (1993). Psychological impact of biculturalism: Evidence and theory. *Psychological Bulletin, 114,* 395–412.

Laird, James D. (1974). Self-attribution of emotion: The effects of expressive behavior on the quality of emotional experience. *Journal of Personality and Social Psychology, 29,* 475–486.

Lakoff, Robin T., & Coyne, James C. (1993). *Father knows best: The use and abuse of power in Freud's case of "Dora."* New York: Teachers College Press.

Lambert, Michael J., & Bergin, Allen E. (1994). The effectiveness of psychotherapy. In A. E. Bergin & S. L. Garfield (eds.), *Handbook of psychotherapy and behavior change* (4th ed.). New York: Wiley.

Lambert, Michael J., & Hill, Clara E. (1994). Assessing psychotherapy outcomes and processes. In A. E. Bergin & S. L. Garfield (eds.), *Handbook of psychotherapy and behavior change* (4th ed.). New York: Wiley.

Land, Edwin H. (1959). Experiments in color vision. *Scientific American, 200*(5), 84–94, 96, 99.

Landrine, Hope (1988). Revising the framework of abnormal psychology. In P. Bronstein & K. Quina (eds.), *Teaching a psychology of people.* Washington, DC: American Psychological Association.

Lang, Peter (1995). The emotion probe: Studies of motivation and attention. *American Psychologist, 50,* 372–385.

Langer, Ellen J. (1983). *The psychology of control.* Beverly Hills, CA: Sage.

Langer, Ellen J. (1989). *Mindfulness.* Reading, MA: Addison-Wesley.

Langer, Ellen J.; Blank, Arthur; & Chanowitz, Benzion (1978). The mindlessness of ostensibly thoughtful action: The role of placebic information in interpersonal interaction. *Journal of Personality and Social Psychology, 36,* 635–642.

Latané, Bibb, & Darley, John (1976). Help in a crisis: Bystander response to an emergency. In J. Thibaut, J. Spence, & R. Carlson (eds.), *Contemporary topics in social psychology.* Morristown, NJ: General Learning Press.

Latané, Bibb; Williams, Kipling; & Harkins, Stephen (1979). Many hands make light the work: The causes and consequences of social loafing. *Journal of Personality and Social Psychology, 37,* 822–832.

Laudenslager, Mark L. (1988). The psychology of loss: Lessons from humans and nonhuman primates. *Journal of Social Issues, 44,* 19–36.

Laumann, Edward O.; Gagnon, John H.; Michael, Robert T.; & Michaels, Stuart (1994). *The social organization of sexuality.* Chicago: University of Chicago Press.

Laursen, Brett, & Collins, W. Andrew (1994). Interpersonal conflict during adolescence. *Psychological Bulletin, 115,* 197–209.

Lazarus, Richard S., & Folkman, Susan (1984). *Stress, appraisal, and coping.* New York: Springer.

LeDoux, Joseph E. (1994, June). Emotion, memory, and the brain. *Scientific American, 220,* 50–57.

LeDoux, Joseph E. (1996). *The emotional brain.* New York: Simon & Schuster.

Lee, Fiona; Hallahan, Mark; & Herzog, Thaddeus (1996). Explaining real-life events: How culture and domain shape attributions. *Personality and Social Psychology Bulletin, 22,* 732–741.

Lee, John Alan (1973). *The colours of love.* Ontario, Canada: New Press.

Lee, John Alan (1988). Love-styles. In R. J. Sternberg & M. L. Barnes (eds.), *The psychology of love.* New Haven, CT: Yale University Press.

Lefcourt, Herbert M., & Martin, Rod A. (1986). *Humor and life stress: Antidote to adversity.* New York: Springer-Verlag.

Lehman, Adam K., & Rodin, Judith (1989). Styles of self-nurturance and disordered eating. *Journal of Consulting and Clinical Psychology, 57,* 117–122.

Leibel, Rudolph L.; Rosenbaum, Michael; & Hirsch, Jules (1995). Changes in energy expenditure resulting from altered body weight. *New England Journal of Medicine, 332,* 621–628.

Lenneberg, Eric H. (1967). *Biological foundations of language.* New York: Wiley.

Lent, James R. (1968, June). Mimosa cottage: Experiment in hope. *Psychology Today,* 51–58.

Leonard, Henrietta L.; Swedo, Susan E.; Lenane, Marge C.; Rettew, David C.; et al. (1993). A 2- to 7-year follow-up study of 54 obsessive–compulsive children and adolescents. *Archives of General Psychiatry, 50,* 429–439.

Lepper, Mark R.; Greene, David; & Nisbett, Richard E. (1973). Undermining children's intrinsic interest with extrinsic rewards. *Journal of Personality and Social Psychology, 28,* 129–137.

Lerner, Melvin J. (1980). *The belief in a just world: A fundamental delusion.* New York: Plenum.

Lesch, Klaus-Peter; Bengel, Dietmar; Heils, Armin; Sabol, Sue Z.; et al. (1996). Association of anxiety-related traits with a polymorphism in the serotonin transporter gene regulatory region. *Science, 274,* 1527–1531.

LeVay, Simon (1991). A difference in hypothalamic structure between heterosexual and homosexual men. *Science, 253,* 1034–1037.

Levenson, Robert W. (1992). Autonomic nervous system differences among emotions. *Psychological Science, 3,* 23–27.

Levenson, Robert W.; Ekman, Paul; & Friesen, Wallace V. (1990). Voluntary facial action generates emotion-specific autonomic nervous system activity. *Psychophysiology, 27,* 363–384.

Leventhal, Howard, & Nerenz, D. R. (1982). A model for stress research and some implications for the control of stress disorders. In D. Meichenbaum & M.

Jaremko (eds.), *Stress prevention and management: A cognitive behavioral approach.* New York: Plenum.

Levine, Robert V.; Martinez, Todd S.; Brase, Gary; & Sorenson, Kerry (1994). Helping in 36 U.S. cities. *Journal of Personality and Social Psychology, 67,* 69–82.

Levitan, Alexander A., & Ronan, William J. (1988). Problems in the treatment of obesity and eating disorders. *Medical Hypnoanalysis Journal, 3,* 131–136.

Levy, David A. (1997). *Tools of critical thinking: Metathoughts for psychology.* Boston: Allyn & Bacon.

Levy, Jerre (1985, May). Right brain, left brain: Fact and fiction. *Psychology Today,* 38–39, 42–44.

Levy, Jerre; Trevarthen, Colwyn; & Sperry, Roger W. (1972). Perception of bilateral chimeric figures following hemispheric deconnection. *Brain, 95,* 61–78.

Levy, Kenneth N.; Blatt, Sidney J.; & Shaver, Phillip R. (1998). Attachment styles and parental representations. *Journal of Personality & Social Psychology, 74,* 407–419.

Lewin, Kurt (1948). *Resolving social conflicts.* New York: Harper.

Lewis, Dorothy O. (ed.) (1981). *Vulnerabilities to delinquency.* New York: Spectrum Medical and Scientific Books.

Lewontin, Richard C. (1970). Race and intelligence. *Bulletin of the Atomic Scientists, 26*(3), 2–8.

Lichtenstein, Sarah; Slovic, Paul; Fischhoff, Baruch; Layman, Mark; & Combs, Barbara (1978). Judged frequency of lethal events. *Journal of Experimental Psychology: Human Learning and Memory, 4,* 551–578.

Lickona, Thomas (1983). *Raising good children.* New York: Bantam.

Lightfoot, Lynn O. (1980). Behavioral tolerance to low doses of alcohol in social drinkers. Unpublished doctoral dissertation, University of Waterloo, Waterloo, Ontario.

Lin, Keh-Ming; Poland, Russell E.; & Chien, C. P. (1990). Ethnicity and psychopharmacology: Recent findings and future research directions. In E. Sorel (ed.), *Family, culture, and psychobiology.* New York: Legas.

Lin, Keh-Ming; Poland, Russell E.; Nuccio, Inocencia; Matsuda, Kazuko; et al. (1989). A longitudinal assessment of haloperidol doses and serum concentrations in Asian and Caucasian schizophrenic patients. *American Journal of Psychiatry, 146,* 1307–1311.

Linday, Linda A. (1994). Maternal reports of pregnancy, genital, and related fantasies in preschool and kindergarten children. *Journal of the American Academy of Child and Adolescent Psychiatry, 33,* 416–423.

Lindvall, O.; Sawle, G.; Widner, H.; et al. (1994). Evidence for long-term survival and function of dopaminergic grafts in progressive Parkinson's disease. *Annals of Neurology, 35,* 172–180.

Linton, Marigold (1978). Real-world memory after six years: An in vivo study of very long-term memory. In M. M. Gruneberg, P. E. Morris, & R. N. Sykes (eds.), *Practical aspects of memory.* London: Academic Press.

Linton, Simi (1998). *Claiming disability: Knowledge and identity.* New York: New York University Press.

Linville, P. W.; Fischer, G. W., & Fischoff, B. (1992). AIDS risk perceptions and decision biases. In J. B. Pryor & G. D. Reeder (eds.), *The social psychology of HIV infection.* Hillsdale, NJ: Erlbaum.

Lipsey, Mark W., & Wilson, David B. (1993). The efficacy of psychological, educational, and behavioral treatment: Confirmation from meta-analysis. *American Psychologist, 48,* 1181–1209.

Lissner, L.; Odell, P. M.; D'Agostino, R. B.; Stokes, J., III; et al. (1991, June 27). Variability of body weight and health outcomes in the Framingham population. *New England Journal of Medicine, 324*(26), 1839–1844.

Locke, Edwin A., & Latham, Gary P. (1991). The fallacies of common sense "truths": A reply to Lamal. *Psychological Science, 2,* 131–132.

Locke, Edwin A.; Shaw, Karyll; Saari, Lise; & Latham, Gary (1981). Goal-setting and task performance: 1969–1980. *Psychological Bulletin, 90,* 125–152.

Loehlin, John C. (1992). *Genes and environment in personality development.* Newbury Park CA: Sage.

Loehlin, John C.; Horn, J. M.; & Willerman, L. (1996). Heredity, environment, and IQ in the Texas adoption study. In R. J. Sternberg & E. Grigorenko (eds.), *Intelligence: Heredity and environment.* New York: Cambridge University Press.

Loewen, E. Ruth; Shaw, Raymond J.; & Craik, Fergus I. (1990). Age differences in components of metamemory. *Experimental Aging Research, 16*(1–2), 43–48.

Loftus, Elizabeth F. (1980). *Memory.* Reading, MA: Addison-Wesley.

Loftus, Elizabeth F. (1995). Memories of childhood trauma or traumas of childhood memory. Paper presented at the annual meeting of the American Psychological Association, New York.

Loftus, Elizabeth F., & Greene, Edith (1980). Warning: Even memory for faces may be contagious. *Law and Human Behavior, 4,* 323–334.

Loftus, Elizabeth F., & Ketcham, Katherine (1994). *The myth of repressed memory.* New York: St. Martin's Press.

Loftus, Elizabeth F.; Miller, David G.; & Burns, Helen J. (1978). Semantic integration of verbal information into a visual memory. *Journal of Experimental Psychology: Human Learning and Memory, 4,* 19–31.

Loftus, Elizabeth F., & Palmer, John C. (1974). Reconstruction of automobile destruction: An example of the interaction between language and memory. *Journal of Verbal Learning and Verbal Behavior, 13,* 585–589.

Loftus, Elizabeth F., & Pickrell, Jacqueline E. (1995). The formation of false memories. [Special Issue: False memories.] *Psychiatric Annals, 25,* 720–725.

Loftus, Elizabeth F., & Zanni, Guido (1975). Eyewitness testimony: The influence of the wording of a question. *Bulletin of the Psychonomic Society, 5,* 86–88.

Lonner, Walter J. (1995). Culture and human diversity. In E. Trickett, R. Watts, & D. Birman (eds.), *Human diversity: Perspectives on people in context.* San Francisco: Jossey-Bass.

López, Steven R. (1989). Patient variable biases in clinical judgment: Conceptual overview and methodological considerations. *Psychological Bulletin, 106,* 184–203.

López, Steven R. (1995). Testing ethnic minority children. In B. B. Wolman (ed.), *The encyclopedia of psychology, psychiatry, and psychoanalysis.* New York: Henry Holt.

Lott, Bernice (1997). The personal and social consequences of a gender difference ideology. *Journal of Social Issues, 53,* 279–298.

Lott, Bernice, & Maluso, Diane (1993). The social learning of gender. In A. E. Beall & R. J. Sternberg (eds.), *The psychology of gender.* New York: Guilford Press.

Lottes, Ilsa L., & Kuriloff, Peter J. (1994). Sexual socialization differences by gender, Greek membership, and religious background. *Psychology of Women Quarterly, 18,* 203–219.

Lovaas, O. Ivar (1977). *The autistic child: Language development through behavior modification.* New York: Halsted Press.

Lovaas, O. Ivar; Schreibman, Laura; & Koegel, Robert L. (1974). A behavior modification approach to the treatment of autistic children. *Journal of Autism and Childhood Schizophrenia, 4,* 111–129.

Luengo, M. A.; Carrillo-de-la-Peña, M. T.; Otero, J. M.; & Romero, E. (1994). A short-term longitudinal study of impulsivity and antisocial behavior. *Journal of Personality and Social Psychology, 66,* 542–548.

Luepnitz, Deborah A. (1988). *The family interpreted: Feminist theory in clinical practice.* New York: Basic Books.

Luria, Alexander (1968). *The mind of a mnemonist* (L. Soltaroff, trans.). New York: Basic Books.

Luria, Alexander R. (1980). *Higher cortical functions in man* (2nd rev. ed.). New York: Basic Books.

Lutz, Catherine (1988). *Unnatural emotions.* Chicago: University of Chicago Press.

Lykken, David, & Tellegen, Auke (1996). Happiness is a stochastic phenomenon. *Psychological Science, 7,* 186–189.

Lytton, Hugh, & Romney, David M. (1991). Parents' differential socialization of boys and girls: A meta-analysis. *Psychological Bulletin, 109,* 267–296.

Maas, James (1998). *Power sleep.* New York: Villard.

Maccoby, Eleanor E. (1990). Gender and relationships: A developmental account. *American Psychologist, 45,* 513–520.

MacKavey, William R.; Malley, Janet E.; & Stewart, Abigail, J. (1991). Remembering autobiographically consequential experiences: Content analysis of psychologists' accounts of their lives. *Psychology and Aging, 6,* 50–59.

MacKinnon, Donald W. (1962). The nature and nurture of creative talent. *American Psychologist, 17,* 484–495.

MacKinnon, Donald W. (1968). Selecting students with creative potential. In P. Heist (ed.), *The creative college student: An unmet challenge.* San Francisco: Jossey-Bass.

MacLean, Paul (1993). Cerebral evolution of emotion. In M. Lewis & J. M. Haviland (eds.), *Handbook of emotions.* New York: Guilford Press.

Macrae, C. Neil; Milne, Alan B.; & Bodenhausen, Galen V. (1994). Stereotypes as energy-saving devices: A peek inside the cognitive toolbox. *Journal of Personality and Social Psychology, 66,* 37–47.

Maddux, James E. (1993, Summer). The mythology of psychopathology: A social cognitive view of deviance, difference, and disorder. *General Psychologist, 29,* 34–45.

Maddux, James E. (ed.) (1995). *Self-efficacy, adaptation, and adjustment: Theory, research, and application.* New York: Plenum.

Maddux, James E. (1996). The social-cognitive construction of difference and disorder. In D. F. Barone, J. E. Maddux, & C. R. Snyder (eds.), *Social cognitive psychology: History and current domains.* New York: Plenum.

Maddux, James E., & Mundell, Clare E. (1997). Disorders of personality. In V. Derlega, B. Winstead, & W. Jones (eds.), *Personality: Contemporary theory and research* (2nd ed.). Chicago: Nelson-Hall.

Maffei, M.; Halaas, J.; Ravussin, E.; et al. (1995). Leptin levels in human and rodent: Measurement of plasma leptin and ob RNA in obese and weight-reduced subjects. *Nature Medicine, 1,* 1155–1161.

Mahoney, Michael J. (1991). *Human change processes: The scientific foundations of psychotherapy.* New York: Basic Books.

Malamuth, Neil, & Dean, Karol (1990). Attraction to sexual aggression. In A. Parrot & L. Bechhofer (eds.), *Acquaintance rape: The hidden crime.* Newark, NJ: Wiley.

Malamuth, Neil M.; Linz, Daniel; Heavey, Christopher L.; Barnes, Gordon; & Acker, Michele (1995). Using the confluence model of sexual aggression to predict men's conflict with women: A 10-year follow-up study. *Journal of Personality and Social Psychology, 69,* 353–369.

Malamuth, Neil M.; Sockloskie, Robert J.; Koss, Mary P.; & Tanaka, J. S. (1991). Characteristics of aggressors against women: Testing a model using a national sample of college students. [Special Section: Theories of sexual aggression.] *Journal of Consulting and Clinical Psychology, 59,* 670–681.

Malatesta, Carol Z. (1990). The role of emotions in the development and organization of personality. In R. A. Thompson (ed.), *Socioemotional development: Nebraska Symposium on Motivation, 1988.* Lincoln: University of Nebraska Press.

Malgady, Robert G.; Rogler, Lloyd; & Costantino, Giuseppe (1987). Ethnocultural and linguistic bias in mental health evaluation of Hispanics. *American Psychologist, 42,* 228–234.

Maling, Michael S., & Howard, Kenneth I. (1994). From research to practice to research to. . . . In P. F. Talley, H. H. Strupp, & S. F. Butler (eds.), *Psychotherapy research and practice: Bridging the gap.* New York: Basic Books.

Manuck, Stephen B.; Cohen, Sheldon; Rabin, Bruce S.; Muldoon, Matthew F.; & Bachen, Elizabeth A. (1991). Individual differences in cellular immune response to stress. *Psychological Science, 2,* 111–115.

Marcus, Gary F.; Pinker, Steven; Ullman, Michael; Hollander, Michelle; et al. (1992). Overregularization in language acquisition. *Monographs of the Society for Research in Child Development, 57* (Serial No. 228), 1–182.

Margo, Geoffrey M.; Greenberg, Roger P.; Fisher, Seymour; & Dewan, Mantosh (1993). A direct comparison of the defense mechanisms of nondepressed people and depressed psychiatric inpatients. *Comprehensive Psychiatry, 34,* 65–69.

Markowitz, Laura M. (1993, July/August). Walking the walk. *Family Therapy Networker,* 19–31.

Markus, Hazel R., & Kitayama, Shinobu (1991). Culture and the self: Implications for cognition, emotion, and motivation. *Psychological Review, 98,* 224–253.

Marlatt, G. Alan (1996). Models of relapse and relapse prevention: A commentary. *Experimental and Clinical Psychopharmacology, 4,* 55–60.

Marriott, Bernadette M. (ed.) (1994). *Food components to enhance performance.* Washington, DC: National Academy Press.

Marshall, Grant N. (1991). A multidimensional analysis of internal health locus of control beliefs: Separating the wheat from the chaff? *Journal of Personality and Social Psychology, 61,* 483–491.

Marshall, Grant N.; Wortman, Camille B.; Vickers, Ross R., Jr.; Kusulas, Jeffrey W.; & Hervig, Linda K. (1994). The five-factor model of personality as a framework for personality health research. *Journal of Personality and Social Psychology, 67,* 278–286.

Martin, Rod A., & Dobbin, James P. (1988). Sense of humor, hassles, and immunoglobulin A: Evidence for a stress-moderating effect of humor. *International Journal of Psychiatry in Medicine, 18,* 93–105.

Maslach, Christina; Stapp, Joy; & Santee, Richard T. (1985). Individuation: Conceptual analysis and assessment. *Journal of Personality and Social Psychology, 49,* 729–738.

Maslow, Abraham H. (1954/1970). *Motivation and personality* (1st and 2nd eds.). New York: Harper & Row.

Maslow, Abraham H. (1971). *The farther reaches of human nature.* New York: Viking.

Masters, William H., & Johnson, Virginia E. (1966). *Human sexual response.* Boston: Little, Brown.

Matthews, Karen A.; Wing, Rena R.; Kuller, Lewis H.; Meilahn, Elaine N.; et al. (1990). Influences of natural menopause on psychological characteristics and symptoms of middle-aged healthy women. *Journal of Consulting and Clinical Psychology, 58,* 345–351.

Mawhinney, T. C. (1990). Decreasing intrinsic "motivation" with extrinsic rewards: Easier said than done. *Journal of Organizational Behavior Management, 11,* 175–191.

May, Ernest R., & Zelikow, Philip D. (eds.) (1997). *The Kennedy tapes: Inside the White House during the Cuban missile crisis.* Cambridge, MA: Belknap/Harvard University Press.

Mayer, John D.; McCormick, Laura J.; & Strong, Sara E. (1995). Mood-congruent memory and natural mood: New evidence. *Personality and Social Psychology Bulletin, 21,* 736–746.

Mayer, John D., & Salovey, Peter (1997). What is emotional intelligence? In P. Salovey & D. Sluyter (eds.), *Emotional development and emotional intelligence: Implications for educators.* New York: Basic Books.

Mazza, James J.; Reynolds, William M.; & Grover, Jennifer H. (1995). Exposure to violence, suicidal ideation and depression in school-based adolescents. Paper presented at the annual meeting of the American Psychological Association, New York.

McAdams, Dan P. (1988). *Power, intimacy, and the life story: Personological inquiries into identity.* New York: Guilford Press.

McCarthy, John (1997). AI as sport. [Review of "Kasparov versus Deep Blue: Computer chess comes of age," by Monty Newborn.] *Science, 276,* 1518–1519.

McCartney, Kathleen; Harris, Monica J.; & Bernieri, Frank (1990). Growing up and growing apart: A developmental meta-analysis of twin studies. *Psychological Bulletin, 107,* 226–237.

McCauley, Elizabeth, & Ehrhardt, Anke (1980). Female sexual response. In D. D. Youngs & A. Ehrhardt (eds.), *Psychosomatic obstetrics and gynecology.* New York: Appleton-Century-Crofts.

McClearn, Gerald E.; Johanson, Boo; Berg, Stig; Pedersen, Nancy L.; et al. (1997). Substantial genetic influence on cognitive abilities in twins 80 or more years old. *Science, 276,* 1560–1563.

McClelland, David C. (1961). *The achieving society.* New York: Free Press.

McClelland, David (1975). *Power: The inner experience.* New York: Irvington.

McClelland, David (1985). *Human motivation.* Glenview, IL: Scott, Foresman.

McClelland, David C. (1987). Characteristics of successful entrepreneurs. *Journal of Creative Behavior, 3,* 219–233.

McClelland, David C.; Atkinson, John W.; Clark, Russell A.; & Lowell, Edgar L. (1953). *The achievement motive.* New York: Appleton-Century-Crofts.

McClelland, James L. (1994). The organization of memory: A parallel distributed processing perspective. *Revue Neurologique, 150,* 570–579.

McClintock, Martha K., & Herdt, Gilbert (1996). Rethinking puberty: The development of sexual attraction. *Current Directions in Psychological Science, 5,* 178–183.

McCord, Joan (1989). Another time, another drug. Paper presented at the conference, Vulnerability to the Transition from Drug Use to Abuse and Dependence, Rockville, MD.

McCord, Joan (1991). Questioning the value of punishment. *Social Problems, 38,* 167–179.

McCrae, Robert R. (1987). Creativity, divergent thinking, and openness to experience. *Journal of Personality and Social Psychology, 52,* 1258–1265.

McCrae, Robert R., & Costa, Paul T., Jr. (1988). Do parental influences matter? A reply to Halverson. *Journal of Personality, 56,* 445–449.

McCrae, Robert R., & Costa, Paul T., Jr. (1996). Toward a new generation of personality theories: Theoretical contexts for the five-factor model. In J. S. Wiggins (ed.), *The five-factor model of personality: Theoretical perspectives.* New York: Guilford Press.

McDonough, Laraine, & Mandler, Jean M. (1994). Very long-term recall in infancy. *Memory, 2,* 339–352.

McEwen, Bruce S. (1983). Gonadal steroid influences on brain development and sexual differentiation. *Reproductive Physiology IV (International Review of Physiology), 27,* 99–145.

McGaugh, James L. (1990). Significance and remembrance: The role of neuromodulatory systems. *Psychological Science, 1,* 15–25.

McGlone, Jeannette (1978). Sex differences in functional brain asymmetry. *Cortex, 14,* 122–128.

McGlynn, Susan M. (1990). Behavioral approaches to neuropsychological rehabilitation. *Psychological Bulletin, 108,* 420–441.

McGoldrick, Monica, & Gerson, Randy (1985). *Genograms in family assessment.* New York: Norton.

McGoldrick, Monica, & Pearce, John K. (1982). Family therapy with Irish Americans. In M. McGoldrick, J. K. Pearce, & J. Giordano (eds.), *Ethnicity and family therapy.* New York: Guilford Press.

McGrath, Ellen; Keita, Gwendolyn P.; Strickland, Bonnie; & Russo, Nancy F. (eds.) (1990). *Women and depression: Risk factors and treatment issues.* Washington, DC: American Psychological Association.

McGue, Matt; Bouchard, Thomas J., Jr.; Iacono, William G.; & Lykken, David T. (1993). Behavioral genetics of cognitive ability: A life-span perspective. In R. Plomin & G. E. McLearn (eds.), *Nature, nurture, and psychology.* Washington, DC: American Psychological Association.

McGue, Matt, & Lykken, David T. (1992). Genetic influence on risk of divorce. *Psychological Science, 3,* 368–373.

McGue, Matt; Pickens, Roy W.; & Svikis, Dace S. (1992). Sex and age effects on the inheritance of alcohol problems: A twin study. *Journal of Abnormal Psychology, 101,* 3–17.

McHugh, Paul R. (1993a). History and the pitfalls of practice. Unpublished paper, Johns Hopkins University.

McHugh, Paul R. (1993b, December). Psychotherapy awry. *American Scholar,* 17–30.

McKee, Richard D., & Squire, Larry R. (1992). Equivalent forgetting rates in long-term memory for diencephalic and medical temporal lobe amnesia. *Journal of Neuroscience, 12,* 3765–3772.

McKee, Richard D., & Squire, Larry R. (1993). On the development of declarative memory. *Journal of Experimental Psychology: Learning, Memory, and Cognition, 19,* 397–404.

McKinlay, John B.; McKinlay, Sonja M.; & Brambilla, Donald (1987). The relative contributions of endocrine changes and social circumstances to depression in mid-aged women. *Journal of Health and Social Behavior, 28,* 345–363.

McLeod, Beverly (1985, March). Real work for real pay. *Psychology Today,* 42–44, 46, 48–50.

McNally, Richard J. (1994). *Panic disorder: A critical analysis.* New York: Guilford Press.

McNaughton, B. L., & Morris, R. G. M. (1987). Hippocampal synaptic enhancement and information storage within a distributed memory system. *Trends in Neuroscience, 10,* 408–415.

McNeill, David (1966). Developmental psycholinguistics. In F. L. Smith & G. A. Miller (eds.), *The genesis of language: A psycholinguistic approach.* Cambridge, MA: MIT Press.

Medawar, Peter B. (1979). *Advice to a young scientist.* New York: Harper & Row.

Mednick, Sarnoff A. (1962). The associative basis of the creative process. *Psychological Review, 69,* 220–232.

Mednick, Sarnoff A.; Huttunen, Matti O.; & Machón, Ricardo (1994). Prenatal influenza infections and adult schizophrenia. *Schizophrenia Bulletin, 20,* 263–267.

Mednick, Sarnoff A.; Parnas, Josef; & Schulsinger, Fini (1987). The Copenhagen High-Risk Project, 1962–86. *Schizophrenia Bulletin, 13,* 485–495.

Medvec, Victoria H.; Madey, Scott F.; & Gilovich, Thomas (1995). When less is more: Counterfactual thinking and satisfaction among Olympic medalists. *Journal of Personality and Social Psychology, 69,* 603–610.

Meeus, Wim H. J., & Raaijmakers, Quinten A.W. (1995). Obedience in modern society: The Utrecht studies. In A. G. Miller, B. E. Collins, & D. E. Brief (eds.), *Perspectives on obedience to authority: The legacy of the Milgram experiments. Journal of Social Issues, 51*(3), 155–175.

Meltzoff, Andrew N., & Gopnik, Alison (1993). The role of imitation in understanding persons and developing a theory of mind. In S. Baron-Cohen, H. Tager-Flusberg, & D. Cohen (eds.), *Understanding other minds.* New York: Oxford University Press.

Melzack, Ronald (1997). Phantom limbs. [Special Issue: Mysteries of the mind]. *Scientific American,* 84–91.

Melzack, Ronald, & Wall, Patrick D. (1965). Pain mechanisms: A new theory. *Science, 13,* 971–979.

Mercer, Jane (1988, May 18). *Racial differences in intelligence: Fact or artifact?* Talk given at San Bernardino Valley College, San Bernardino, CA.

Merikle, Philip M., & Skanes, Heather E. (1992). Subliminal self-help audiotapes: A search for placebo effects. *Journal of Applied Psychology, 77,* 772–776.

Merskey, Harold (1992). The manufacture of personalities: The production of MPD. *British Journal of Psychiatry, 160,* 327–340.

Merskey, Harold (1995). The manufacture of personalities: The production of multiple personality disorder. In L. M. Cohen, J. N. Berzoff, & M. R. Elin (eds.), *Dissociative identity disorder: Theoretical and treatment controversies.* Northvale, NJ: Jason Aronson.

Mesquita, Batja, & Frijda, Nico H. (1993). Cultural variations in emotions: A review. *Psychological Bulletin, 112,* 179–204.

Metalsky, Gerald I.; Joiner, Thomas E., Jr.; Hardin, Tammy S.; & Abramson, Lyn Y. (1993). Depressive reactions to failure in a naturalistic setting: A test of the hopelessness and self-esteem theories of depression. *Journal of Abnormal Psychology, 102,* 101–109.

Meyer-Bahlburg, Heino F. L.; Ehrhardt, Anke A.; Rosen, Laura R.; Gruen, Rhoda S.; Veridiano, Norma P.; Vann, Felix H.; & Neuwalder, Herbert F. (1995). Prenatal estrogens and the development of homosexual orientation. *Developmental Psychology, 31,* 12–21.

Mikulincer, Mario (1995). Attachment style and the mental representations of the self. *Journal of Personality and Social Psychology, 69,* 1203–1215.

Milgram, Stanley (1963). Behavioral study of obedience. *Journal of Abnormal and Social Psychology, 67,* 371–378.

Milgram, Stanley (1974). *Obedience to authority: An experimental view.* New York: Harper & Row.

Miller, George A. (1956). The magical number seven, plus or minus two: Some limits on our capacity for processing information. *Psychological Review, 63,* 81–97.

Miller, George A. (1969, December). On turning psychology over to the unwashed. *Psychology Today,* 53–55, 66–68, 70, 72, 74.

Miller, Inglis J., & Reedy, Frank E. (1990). Variations in human taste bud density and taste intensity perception. *Physiology and Behavior, 47,* 1213–1219.

Miller, Neal E. (1978). Biofeedback and visceral learning. *Annual Review of Psychology, 29,* 421–452.

Miller, Paul A., & Eisenberg, Nancy (1988). The relation of empathy to aggressive and externalizing/antisocial behavior. *Psychological Bulletin, 103,* 324–344.

Miller, Scott D., & Triggiano, Patrick J. (1992). The psychophysiological investigation of multiple personality disorder: Review and update. *American Journal of Clinical Hypnosis, 35,* 47–61.

Miller, Todd Q.; Smith, Timothy W.; Turner, Charles W.; Guijarro, Margarita L.; & Hallet, Amanda J. (1996). A meta-analytic review of research on hostility and physical health. *Psychological Bulletin, 119,* 322–348.

Miller-Jones, Dalton (1989). Culture and testing. *American Psychologist, 44,* 360–366.

Milner, Brenda (1970). Memory and the temporal regions of the brain. In K. H. Pribram & D. E. Broadbent (eds.), *Biology of memory.* New York: Academic Press.

Milner, J. S., & McCanne, T. R. (1991). Neuropsychological correlates of physical child abuse. In J. S. Milner (ed.), *Neuropsychology of aggression.* Norwell, MA: Kluwer Academic.

Minuchin, Salvador (1984). *Family kaleidoscope.* Cambridge, MA: Harvard University Press.

Mischel, Walter (1973). Toward a cognitive social learning reconceptualization of personality. *Psychological Review, 80,* 252–253.

Mischel, Walter, & Shoda, Yuichi (1995). A cognitive affective system theory of personality: Reconceptualizing situations, dispositions, dynamics, and invariance in personality structures. *Psychological Review, 102,* 246–268.

Mishkin, M.; Suzuki, W. A.; Gadian, D. G.; & Vargha-Khadem, F. (1997). Hierarchical organization of cognitive memory. *Philosophical Transactions of the Royal Society of London Series B, 352,* 1461–1467.

Mistry, Jayanthi, & Rogoff, Barbara (1994). Remembering in cultural context. In W. J. Lonner & R. Malpass (eds.), *Psychology and culture.* Needham Heights, MA: Allyn & Bacon.

Mitchell, D. E. (1980). The influence of early visual experience on visual perception. In C. S. Harris (ed.), *Visual coding and adaptability.* Hillsdale, NJ: Erlbaum.

Mitchell, Valory, & Helson, Ravenna (1990). Women's prime of life: Is it the 50s? *Psychology of Women Quarterly, 14,* 451–470.

Mithers, Carol L. (1994). *Reasonable insanity: A true story of the seventies.* Reading, MA: Addison-Wesley.

Modigliani, Andre, & Rochat, François (1995). The role of interaction sequences and the timing of resistance in shaping obedience and defiance to authority. In A. G. Miller, B. E. Collins, & D. E. Brief (eds.), *Perspectives on obedience to authority: The legacy of the Milgram experiments. Journal of Social Issues, 51*(3), 107–125.

Moffitt, Terrie E. (1993). Adolescence-limited and life-course-persistent antisocial behavior: A developmental taxonomy. *Psychological Review, 100,* 674–701.

Monteith, Margo J. (1996). Contemporary forms of prejudice-related conflict: In search of a nutshell. *Personality and Social Psychology Bulletin, 22,* 461–473.

Moore, Timothy E. (1992, Spring). Subliminal perception: Facts and fallacies. *Skeptical Inquirer, 16,* 273–281.

Moore, Timothy E. (1995). Subliminal self-help auditory tapes: An empirical test of perceptual consequences. *Canadian Journal of Behavioural Science, 27,* 9–20.

Morelli, Gilda A.; Rogoff, Barbara; Oppenheim, David; & Goldsmith, Denise (1992). Cultural variation in infants' sleeping arrangements: Questions of independence. [Special Section: Cross-cultural studies of development.] *Developmental Psychology, 28,* 604–613.

Morgan, Christiana D., & Murray, Henry A. (1935). A method for investigating fantasies: The Thematic Apperception Test. *Archives of Neurology and Psychiatry, 34,* 289–306.

Morris, Michael W., & Peng, Kaiping (1994). Culture and cause: American and Chinese attributions for social and physical events. *Journal of Personality and Social Psychology, 67,* 949–971.

Morrison, Ann M., & Von Glinow, Mary Ann (1990). Women and minorities in management. *American Psychologist, 45,* 200–208.

Mozell, Maxwell M.; Smith, Bruce P., Smith, Paul E.; Sullivan, Richard L.; & Swender, Philip (1969). Nasal chemoreception in flavor identification. *Archives of Otolaryngology, 90,* 367–373.

Muehlenhard, Charlene L. (1988). "Nice women" don't say yes and "real men" don't say no: How miscommunication and the double standard can cause sexual problems. [Special Issue: Women and sex therapy.] *Women & Therapy, 7,* 95–108.

Muehlenhard, Charlene, & Cook, Stephen (1988). Men's self-reports of unwanted sexual activity. *Journal of Sex Research, 24,* 58–72.

Murphy, Sheila T.; Monahan, Jennifer L.; & Zajonc, R. B. (1995). Addivity of nonconscious affect: Combined effects of priming and exposure. *Journal of Personality and Social Psychology, 69,* 589–602.

Nadel, Lynn, & Zola-Morgan, Stuart (1984). Infantile amnesia: A neurobiological perspective. In M. Moscovitch (ed.), *Infantile memory: Its relation to normal and pathological memory in humans and other animals.* New York: Plenum.

Nash, Michael R. (1987). What, if anything, is regressed about hypnotic age regression? A review of the empirical literature. *Psychological Bulletin, 102,* 42–52.

Nash, Michael R., & Nadon, Robert (1997). Hypnosis. In D. L. Faigman, D. Kaye, M. J. Saks, & J. Sanders (eds.), *Modern scientific evidence: The law and science of expert testimony.* St. Paul, MN: West.

Nathan, Debbie (1994, Fall). Dividing to conquer? Women, men, and the making of multiple personality disorder. *Social Text, 40,* 77–114.

National Victim Center & Crime Victims Research and Treatment Center (1992). *Rape in America: A report to the nation.* Fort Worth, TX: National Victim Center.

Needleman, Herbert L.; Riess, Julie A.; Tobin, Michael J.; et al. (1996). Bone lead levels and delinquent behavior. *Journal of the American Medical Association, 275,* 363–369.

Needleman, Herbert L.; Schell, Alan; Bellinger, David; Leviton, Alan; et al. (1990). The long-term effects of exposure to low doses of lead in childhood: An 11-year follow-up report. *New England Journal of Medicine, 322,* 83–88.

Neher, Andrew (1996). Jung's theory of archetypes: A critique. *Journal of Humanistic Psychology, 36,* 61–91.

Neisser, Ulric; Boodoo, Gwyneth; Bouchard, Thomas J., Jr.; et al. (1996). Intelligence: Knowns and unknowns. *American Psychologist, 51,* 77–101.

Neisser, Ulric, & Harsch, Nicole (1992). Phantom flashbulbs: False recollections of hearing the news about *Challenger.* In E. Winograd & U. Neisser (eds.), *Affect and accuracy in recall: Studies of "flashbulb memories."* New York: Cambridge University Press.

Neisser, Ulric; Winograd, Eugene; & Weldon, Mary Sue (1991). Remembering the earthquake: "What I experienced" vs. "How I heard the news." Paper presented at the annual meeting of the Psychonomic Society, San Francisco.

Nelson, Thomas O., & Dunlosky, John (1991). When people's judgments of learning (JOLs) are extremely accurate at predicting subsequent recall: The "delayed JOL effect." *Psychological Science, 2,* 267–270.

Nelson, Thomas O., & Leonesio, R. Jacob (1988). Allocation of self-paced study time and the "labor in vain effect." *Journal of Experimental Psychology: Learning, Memory, and Cognition, 14,* 676–686.

Neugarten, Bernice (1979). Time, age, and the life cycle. *American Journal of Psychiatry, 136,* 887–894.

Newman, Joseph P.; Widom, Cathy S.; & Nathan, Stuart (1985). Passive avoidance in syndromes of disinhibition: Psychopathy and extraversion. *Journal of Personality and Social Psychology, 48,* 1316–1327.

Nezu, Arthur M.; Nezu, Christine M.; & Blissett, Sonia E. (1988). Sense of humor as a moderator of the relation between stressful events and psychological distress: A prospective analysis. *Journal of Personality and Social Psychology, 54,* 520–525.

NICHD Early Child Care Research Network (1996, April 20). Infant child care and attachment security: Results of the NICHD study of early child care. Symposium paper presented at the International Conference on Infant Studies, Providence, RI.

Nickerson, Raymond A., & Adams, Marilyn Jager (1979). Long-term memory for a common object. *Cognitive Psychology, 11,* 287–307.

Nigg, Joel T., & Goldsmith, H. Hill (1994). Genetics of personality disorders: Perspectives from personality and psychopathology research. *Psychological Bulletin, 115,* 346–380.

Nisbett, Richard E., & Ross, Lee (1980). *Human inference: Strategies and shortcomings of social judgment.* Englewood Cliffs, NJ: Prentice-Hall.

Noble, Ernest P.; Blum, Kenneth; Ritchie, T.; Montgomery, A.; & Sheridan, P. J. (1991). Allelic association of the D2 dopamine receptor gene with receptor-binding characteristics in alcoholism. *Archives of General Psychiatry, 48,* 648–654.

Nolen-Hoeksema, Susan (1990). *Sex differences in depression.* Stanford, CA: Stanford University Press.

Nolen-Hoeksema, Susan (1991). Responses to depression and their effects on the duration of depressive episodes. *Journal of Abnormal Psychology, 100,* 569–582.

Nolen-Hoeksema, Susan, & Girgus, Joan S. (1994). The emergence of gender differences in depression during adolescence. *Psychological Bulletin, 115,* 424–443.

Norman, Donald A. (1988). *The psychology of everyday things.* New York: Basic Books.

Nowicki, Stephen, & Duke, Marshall P. (1989). A measure of nonverbal social processing ability in children between the ages of 6 and 10. Paper presented at the annual meeting of the American Psychological Society, Alexandria, VA.

Nowicki, Stephen, & Strickland, Bonnie R. (1973). A locus of control scale for children. *Journal of Consulting Psychology, 40,* 148–154.

Nurnberger, John I., & Gershon, Elliot S. (1992). In E. S. Paykel (ed.), *Handbook of affective disorders* (2nd ed.). New York: Guilford Press.

Oatley, Keith (1990). Do emotional states produce irrational thinking? In K. J. Gilhooly, M. T. G. Keane, R. H. Logie, & G. Erdos (eds.), *Lines of thinking* (Vol. 2). New York: Wiley.

Oatley, Keith, & Duncan, Elaine (1994). The experience of emotions in everyday life. *Cognition and Emotion, 8,* 369–381.

Oatley, Keith, & Jenkins, Jennifer M. (1996). *Understanding emotions.* Cambridge, MA: Blackwell.

Offer, Daniel, & Sabshin, Melvin (1984). Adolescence: Empirical perspectives. In D. Offer & M. Sabshin (eds.), *Normality and the life cycle.* New York: Basic Books.

Ofshe, Richard J., & Watters, Ethan (1994). *Making monsters: False memory, psychotherapy, and sexual hysteria.* New York: Scribners.

Ogden, Jenni A., & Corkin, Suzanne (1991). Memories of H. M. In W. C. Abraham, M. C. Corballis, & K. G. White (eds.), *Memory mechanisms: A tribute to G. V. Goddard.* Hillsdale, NJ: Erlbaum.

O'Hanlon, Bill (1994, November/December). The third wave. *Family Therapy Networker,* 18–29.

Olds, James (1975). Mapping the mind onto the brain. In F. G. Worden, J. P. Swazy, & G. Adelman (eds.), *The neurosciences: Paths of discovery.* Cambridge, MA: Colonial Press.

Olds, James, & Milner, Peter (1954). Positive reinforcement produced by electrical stimulation of septal area and other regions of the rat brain. *Journal of Comparative and Physiological Psychology, 47,* 419–429.

Olin, Su-Chin S., & Mednick, Sarnoff A. (1996). Risk factors of psychosis: Identifying vulnerable populations premorbidly. *Schizophrenia Bulletin, 22,* 223–240.

Oliver, Mary Beth, & Hyde, Janet S. (1993). Gender differences in sexuality: A meta-analysis. *Psychological Bulletin, 114,* 29–51.

O'Neil, Harold F., Jr.; Sugrue, Brenda; & Baker, Eva L. (1995/1996). Effects of motivational interventions on the National Assessment of Educational Progress mathematics performance. *Educational Assessment, 3,* 135–157.

Orford, Jim (1992). *Community psychology: Theory and practice.* New York: Wiley.

Orlinsky, David E., & Howard, Kenneth I. (1994). Unity and diversity among psychotherapies: A comparative perspective. In B. Bongar & L. E. Beutler (eds.), *Foundations of psychotherapy: Theory, research, and practice.* New York: Oxford University Press.

Ortar, G. (1963). Is a verbal test cross-cultural? *Scripts Hierosolymitana* (Hebrew University, Jerusalem), *13,* 219–235.

Page, Gayle G.; Ben-Eliyahu, Shamgar; Yirmiya, Raz; & Liebeskind, John C. (1993). Morphine attenuates surgery-induced enhancement of metastatic colonization in rats. *Pain, 54,* 21–28.

Panksepp, Jack; Herman, B. H.; Vilberg, T.; Bishop, P.; & DeEskinazi, F. G. (1980). Endogenous opioids and social behavior. *Neuroscience and Biobehavioral Reviews, 4,* 473–487.

Park, Denise C.; Smith, Anderson D.; & Cavanaugh, John C. (1990). Metamemories of memory researchers. *Memory and Cognition, 18,* 321–327.

Parker, Gwendolyn M. (1997). *Trespassing: My sojourn in the halls of privilege.* Boston: Houghton Mifflin.

Patterson, Charlotte J. (1992). Children of lesbian and gay parents. *Child Development, 63,* 1025–1042.

Patterson, Charlotte J. (1995). Sexual orientation and human development: An overview. *Developmental Psychology, 31,* 3–11.

Patterson, Francine, & Linden, Eugene (1981). *The education of Koko.* New York: Holt, Rinehart and Winston.

Patterson, Gerald R. (1994). Developmental perspectives on violence. Invited address presented at the annual meeting of the American Psychological Association, Los Angeles.

Patterson, Gerald R.; Reid, John; & Dishion, Thomas (1992). *Antisocial boys.* Eugene, OR: Castalia.

Paul, Richard W. (1984, September). Critical thinking: Fundamental to education for a free society. *Educational Leadership,* 4–14.

Peabody, Dean (1985). *National characteristics.* Cambridge, England: Cambridge University Press.

Pearlin, Leonard (1982). Discontinuities in the study of aging. In T. K. Hareven & K. J. Adams (eds.), *Aging and life course transitions: An interdisciplinary perspective.* New York: Guilford Press.

Pedersen, Paul B.; Draguns, Juris G.; Lonner, Walter J.; & Trimble, Joseph E. (eds.) (1996). *Counseling across cultures* (4th ed.). Thousand Oaks, CA: Sage.

Peele, Stanton, & Brodsky, Archie, with Mary Arnold (1991). *The truth about addiction and recovery.* New York: Simon & Schuster.

Pennebaker, James W. (1995). Emotion, disclosure, and health: An overview. In J. W. Pennebaker (ed.), *Emotion, disclosure, and health.* Washington, DC: American Psychological Association.

Pennebaker, James W., & Harber, Kent D. (1993). A social stage model of collective coping: The Loma Prieta earthquake and the Persian Gulf War. *Journal of Social Issues, 49*(4), 125–145.

Pennebaker, James W.; Kiecolt-Glaser, Janice; & Glaser, Ronald (1988). Disclosure of traumas and immune function: Health implications for psychotherapy. *Journal of Consulting and Clinical Psychology, 56,* 239–245.

Peplau, Letitia A. (1991). Lesbian and gay relationships. In J. C. Gonsiorek & J. D. Weinrich (eds.), *Homosexuality: Research findings for social policy.* Newbury Park, CA: Sage.

Peplau, Letitia A., & Gordon, Steven L. (1985). Women and men in love: Gender differences in close heterosexual relationships. In V. O'Leary, R. Unger, & B. Wallston (eds.), *Women, gender, and social psychology.* Hillsdale, NJ: Erlbaum.

Pepperberg, Irene M. (1990). Cognition in an African gray parrot (*Psittacus erithacus*): Further evidence for comprehension of categories and labels. *Journal of Comparative Psychology, 104,* 41–52.

Pepperberg, Irene M. (1994). Numerical competence in an African gray parrot (*Psittacus erithacus*). *Journal of Comparative Psychology, 108,* 36–44.

Perry, Samuel W., & Heidrich, George (1982). Management of pain during debridement: A survey of U.S. burn units. *Pain, 13,* 267–280.

Persons, Ethel S. (1986). Manipulativeness in entrepreneurs and psychopaths. In W. H. Reid, D. Dorr, J. I. Walker, & J. W. Bonner (eds.), *Unmasking the psychopath.* New York: Norton.

Pert, Candace B., & Snyder, Solomon H. (1973). Opiate receptor: Demonstration in nervous tissue. *Science, 179,* 1011–1014.

Pervin, Lawrence A. (1992). The rational mind and the problem of volition [feature review]. *Psychological Science, 3,* 162–164.

Petersen, Anne C. (1989). Developmental transitions and their role in influencing life trajectories. Paper presented at the annual meeting of the American Psychological Association, New Orleans.

Peterson, Bill E., & Stewart, Abigail J. (1993). Generativity and social motives in young adults. *Journal of Personality and Social Psychology, 65,* 186–198.

Peterson, Lloyd R., & Peterson, Margaret J. (1959). Short-term retention of individual verbal items. *Journal of Experimental Psychology, 58,* 193–198.

Peterson, Marilyn R. (1992). *At personal risk: Boundary violations in professional–client relationships.* New York: Norton.

Pfungst, Oskar (1911/1965). *Clever Hans (The horse of Mr. von Osten): A contribution to experimental animal and human psychology.* New York: Holt, Rinehart and Winston.

Phares, E. Jerry (1976). *Locus of control in personality.* Morristown, NJ: General Learning Press.

Phinney, Jean S. (1990). Ethnic identity in adolescents and adults: Review of research. *Psychological Bulletin, 108,* 499–514.

Phinney, Jean S. (1996). When we talk about American ethnic groups, what do we mean? *American Psychologist, 51,* 918–927.

Piaget, Jean (1929/1960). *The child's conception of the world.* Paterson, NJ: Littlefield, Adams.

Piaget, Jean (1932). *The moral judgment of the child.* New York: Macmillan.

Piaget, Jean (1951). *Plays, dreams, and imitation in childhood.* New York: Norton.

Piaget, Jean (1952). *The origins of intelligence in children.* New York: International Universities Press.

Piaget, Jean (1984). Piaget's theory. In P. Mussen (series ed.) & W. Kessen (vol. ed.), *Handbook of child psychology: Vol. 1. History, theory, and methods* (4th ed.). New York: Wiley.

Pickar, David; Owen, Richard R.; & Litman, Robert E. (1991). New developments in the pharmacotherapy of schizophrenia. In A. Tasman & S. M. Goldfinger (eds.), *American Psychiatric Press Review of Psychiatry* (Vol. 10). Washington, DC: American Psychiatric Press.

Pinker, Steven (1994). *The language instinct: How the mind creates language.* New York: Morrow.

Piper, August, Jr. (1997). *Hoax and reality: The bizarre world of multiple personality disorder.* Northvale, NJ: Jason Aronson.

Plomin, Robert (1989). Environment and genes: Determinants of behavior. *American Psychologist, 44,* 105–111.

Plomin, Robert; Corley, Robin; DeFries, J. C.; & Fulker, D. W. (1990). Individual differences in television viewing in early childhood: Nature as well as nurture. *Psychological Science, 1,* 371–377.

Plomin, Robert, & DeFries, John C. (1985). *Origins of individual differences in infancy: The Colorado Adoption Project.* New York: Academic Press.

Plutchik, Robert; Conte, Hope R.; Karasu, Toksoz; & Buckley, Peter (1988, Fall/Winter). The measurement of psychodynamic variables. *Hillside Journal of Clinical Psychology, 10,* 132–147.

Polich, John; Pollock, Vicki E.; & Bloom, Floyd E. (1994). Meta-analysis of P300 amplitude from males at risk for alcoholism. *Psychological Bulletin, 115,* 55–73.

Pollak, Richard (1997). *The creation of Dr. B: A biography of Bruno Bettelheim.* New York: Simon & Schuster.

Poole, Debra A. (1995). Strolling fuzzy-trace theory through eyewitness testimony (or vice versa). *Learning and Individual Differences, 7,* 87–93.

Poole, Debra A.; Lindsay, D. Stephen; Memon, Amina; & Bull, Ray (1995). Psychotherapy and the recovery of memories of childhood sexual abuse: U.S. and British practitioners' opinions, practices, and experiences. *Journal of Consulting and Clinical Psychology, 63,* 426–437.

Portenoy, Russell K. (1994). Opioid therapy for chronic nonmalignant pain: Current status. In H. L. Fields & J. C. Liebeskind (eds.), *Progress in pain research and management: Vol. 1. Pharmacological approaches to the treatment of chronic pain.* Seattle: International Association for the Study of Pain.

Posada, German; Lord, Chiyoko; & Waters, Everett (1995). Secure base behavior and children's misbehavior in three different contexts: Home, neighbors, and school. Paper presented at the annual meeting of the Society for Research in Child Development, Indianapolis.

Potter, W. James (1987). Does television viewing hinder academic achievement among adolescents? *Human Communication Research, 14,* 27–46.

Poulin-Dubois, Diane; Serbin, Lisa A.; Kenyon, Brenda; & Derbyshire, Alison (1994). Infants' intermodal knowledge about gender. *Developmental Psychology, 30,* 436–442.

Poulos, Constantine X., & Cappell, Howard (1991). Homeostatic theory of drug tolerance: A general model of physiological adaptation. *Psychological Review, 98,* 390–408.

Powell, Russell A., & Boer, Douglas P. (1994). Did Freud mislead patients to confabulate memories of abuse? *Psychological Reports, 74,* 1283–1298.

Powell, Russell A., & Boer, Douglas P. (1995). Did Freud misinterpret reported memories of sexual abuse as fantasies? *Psychological Reports, 77,* 563–570.

Pratkanis, Anthony, & Aronson, Elliot (1992). *Age of propaganda: The everyday use and abuse of persuasion.* New York: Freeman.

Pratt, L. A.; Ford, D. E.; Crum, R. M.; et al. (1996, December 15). Depression, psychotropic medication, and risk of myocardial infarction: Prospective data from the Baltimore ECA follow-up. *Circulation, 94,* 3123–3129.

Premack, David, & Premack, Ann James (1983). *The mind of an ape.* New York: Norton.

Prochaska, James O.; Norcross, John C.; & DiClemente, Carlo C. (1994). *Changing for good.* New York: Morrow.

Radetsky, Peter (1991, April). The brainiest cells alive. *Discover, 12,* 82–85, 88, 90.

Radke-Yarrow, Marian; Zahn-Waxler, Carolyn; & Chapman, M. (1983). Prosocial dispositions and behavior. In P. Mussen (ed.), *Manual of child psychology: Vol.*

4. Socialization, personality, and social development. New York: Wiley.

Raine, Adrian; Brennan, Patricia; & Mednick, Sarnoff A. (1994). Birth complications combined with early maternal rejection at age one year predispose to violent crime at age 18 years. *Archives of General Psychiatry, 51*, 984–988.

Ratcliff, Roger (1990). Connectionist models of recognition memory: Constraints imposed by learning and forgetting functions. *Psychological Review, 97*, 285–308.

Ravussin, Eric; Lillioja, Stephen; Knowler, William; Christin, Laurent; et al. (1988). Reduced rate of energy expenditure as a risk factor for body-weight gain. *New England Journal of Medicine, 318*, 467–472.

Ravussin, Eric; Pratley, R. E.; Maffei, M.; et al. (1997). Relatively low plasma leptin concentrations precede weight gain in Pima Indians. *Nature Medicine, 3*, 238–240.

Raz, Sarah, & Raz, Naftali (1990). Structural brain abnormalities in the major psychoses: A quantitative review of the evidence from computerized imaging. *Psychological Bulletin, 108*, 93–108.

Redelmeier, Donald A., & Tversky, Amos (1996). On the belief that arthritis pain is related to the weather. *Proceedings of the National Academy of Sciences, 93*, 2895–2896.

Redmond, D. E., Jr.; Roth, R. H.; Spencer, D. D.; et al. (1993). Neural transplantation for neurodegenerative diseases: Past, present, and future. *Annals of the New York Academy of Sciences, 695*, 258–266.

Reed, Geoffrey M. (1990). Stress, coping, and psychological adaptation in a sample of gay and bisexual men with AIDS. Unpublished doctoral dissertation, University of California, Los Angeles.

Reedy, F. E.; Bartoshuk, L. M.; Miller, I. J.; Duffy, V. B.; Lucchina, L.; & Yanagisawa, K. (1993). Relationships among papillae, taste pores, and 6-n-propylthiouracil (PROP) suprathreshold taste sensitivity. *Chemical Senses, 18*, 618–619.

Regier, Darrel A.; Narrow, William E.; Rae, Donald S.; Manderscheid, Ronald W.; et al. (1993). The de facto US mental and addictive disorders service system: Epidemiologic Catchment Area prospective 1-year prevalence rates of disorders and services. *Archives of General Psychiatry, 50*, 85–94.

Rescorla, Robert A. (1968). Probability of shock in the presence and absence of CS in fear conditioning. *Journal of Comparative and Physiological Psychology, 66*, 1–5.

Rescorla, Robert A. (1988). Pavlovian conditioning: It's not what you think it is. *American Psychologist, 43*, 151–160.

Restak, Richard M. (1994). *The modular brain.* New York: Macmillan.

Reynolds, Brent A., & Weiss, Samuel (1992). Generation of neurons and astrocytes from isolated cells of the adult mammalian central nervous system. *Science, 255*, 1707–1710.

Richards, Ruth L. (1991). Everyday creativity and the arts. Paper presented at the annual meeting of the American Psychological Association, San Francisco.

Richardson-Klavehn, Alan, & Bjork, Robert A. (1988). Measures of memory. *Annual Review of Psychology, 39*, 475–543.

Richmond, Barry J., & Optican, Lance M. (1990). Temporal encoding of two-dimensional patterns by single units in primate primary visual cortex: II. Information transmission. *Journal of Neurophysiology, 64*, 370–380.

Ridley-Johnson, Robyn; Cooper, Harris; & Chance, June (1983). The relation of children's television viewing to school achievement and I.Q. *Journal of Educational Research, 76*, 294–297.

Ristau, Carolyn A. (ed.) (1991). *Cognitive ethology: The minds of other animals.* Hillsdale, NJ: Erlbaum.

Roberts, John E.; Gotlib, Ian H.; & Kassel, Jon D. (1996). Adult attachment security and symptoms of depression: The mediating roles of dysfunctional attitudes and low self-esteem. *Journal of Personality and Social Psychology, 70*, 310–320.

Roberts, Susan B.; Savage, J.; Coward, W. A.; Chew, B.; & Lucas, A. (1988). Energy expenditure and intake in infants born to lean and overweight mothers. *New England Journal of Medicine, 318*, 461–466.

Robertson, Barbara A. (1995). Creating a disability community. Paper presented at the annual meeting of the American Psychological Association, New York.

Robins, Lee N.; Davis, Darlene H.; & Goodwin, Donald W. (1974). Drug use by U.S. Army enlisted men in Vietnam: A follow-up on their return home. *American Journal of Epidemiology, 99*, 235–249.

Robins, Lee N.; Tipp, Jayson; & Przybeck, Thomas R. (1991). Antisocial personality. In L. N. Robins & D. A. Regier (eds.), *Psychiatric disorders in America.* New York: Free Press.

Robinson, Leslie A.; Berman, Jeffrey S.; & Neimeyer, Robert A. (1990). Psychotherapy for the treatment of depression: A comprehensive review of controlled outcome research. *Psychological Bulletin, 108*, 30–49.

Rodgers, Joann (1988, April). Pains of complaint. *Psychology Today*, 26–27.

Rodin, Judith (1988). Control, health, and aging. Invited address presented at the annual meeting of the Society of Behavioral Medicine, Boston.

Roediger, Henry L., III (1990). Implicit memory: Retention without remembering. *American Psychologist, 45*, 1043–1056.

Roediger, Henry L., & McDermott, Kathleen B. (1995). Creating false memories: Remembering words not presented in lists. *Journal of Experimental Psychology; Learning, Memory, and Cognition, 21,* 803–814.

Rogers, Carl (1951). *Client-centered therapy: Its current practice, implications, and theory.* Boston: Houghton Mifflin.

Rogers, Carl (1961). *On becoming a person.* Boston: Houghton Mifflin.

Rogers, Ronald W., & Prentice-Dunn, Steven (1981). Deindividuation and anger-mediated interracial aggression: Unmasking regressive racism. *Journal of Personality and Social Psychology, 41,* 63–73.

Rokeach, Milton, & Ball-Rokeach, Sandra (1989). Stability and change in American value priorities, 1968–1981. *American Psychologist, 44,* 775–784.

Rollin, Henry (ed.) (1980). *Coping with schizophrenia.* London: Burnett.

Rosch, Eleanor H. (1973). Natural categories. *Cognitive Psychology, 4,* 328–350.

Rose, Suzanna; Zand, Debra; & Cini, Marie A. (1993). Lesbian courtship scripts. In E. D. Rothblum & K. A. Brehony (eds.), *Boston marriages.* Amherst: University of Massachusetts Press.

Rosen, B. R.; Aronen, H. J.; Kwong, K. K.; et al. (1993). Advances in clinical neuroimaging: Functional MR imaging techniques. *Radiographics, 13,* 889–896.

Rosen, Gerald M. (1981). Guidelines for the review of do-it-yourself treatment books. *Contemporary Psychology, 26,* 189–191.

Rosen, R. D. (1977). *Psychobabble.* New York: Atheneum.

Rosenberg, Harold (1993). Prediction of controlled drinking by alcoholics and problem drinkers. *Psychological Bulletin, 113,* 129–139.

Rosenhan, David L. (1973). On being sane in insane places. *Science, 179,* 250–258.

Rosenthal, Robert (1966). *Experimenter effects in behavioral research.* New York: Appleton-Century-Crofts.

Rosenthal, Robert (1994). Interpersonal expectancy effects: A 30-year perspective. *Current Directions in Psychological Science, 3,* 176–179.

Rosenzweig, Mark R. (1984). Experience, memory, and the brain. *American Psychologist, 39,* 365–376.

Ross, Colin (1995). The validity and reliability of dissociative identity disorder. In L. M. Cohen, J. N. Berzoff, & M. R. Elin (eds.), *Dissociative identity disorder: Theoretical and treatment controversies.* Northvale, NJ: Jason Aronson.

Roth, David L.; & Holmes, David S. (1985). Influence of physical fitness in determining the impact of stressful life events on physical and psychologic health. *Psychosomatic Medicine, 47,* 164–173.

Rothbaum, Fred M.; Weisz, John R.; & Snyder, Samuel S. (1982). Changing the world and changing the self: A two-process model of perceived control. *Journal of Personality and Social Psychology, 42,* 5–37.

Rotter, Julian B. (1966). Generalized expectancies for internal versus external control of reinforcement. *Psychological Monographs, 80* (Whole No. 609), 1–28.

Rotter, Julian B. (1982). *The development and applications of social learning theory: Selected papers.* New York: Praeger.

Rotter, Julian B. (1990). Internal versus external control of reinforcement: A case history of a variable. *American Psychologist, 45,* 489–493.

Rowe, Walter F. (1993, Winter). Psychic detectives: A critical examination. *Skeptical Inquirer, 17,* 159–165.

Rozin, Paul; Lowery, Laura; & Ebert, Rhonda (1994). Varieties of disgust faces and the structure of disgust. *Journal of Personality and Social Psychology, 66,* 870–881.

Rubin, Jeffrey Z. (1994). Models of conflict management. *Journal of Social Issues, 50,* 33–45.

Ruggiero, Vincent R. (1988). *Teaching thinking across the curriculum.* New York: Harper & Row.

Ruggiero, Vincent R. (1991). *The art of thinking: A guide to critical and creative thought* (3rd ed.). New York: HarperCollins.

Rumbaugh, Duane M. (1977). *Language learning by a chimpanzee: The Lana project.* New York: Academic Press.

Rumbaugh, Duane M.; Savage-Rumbaugh, E. Sue; & Pate, James L. (1988). Addendum to "Summation in the chimpanzee (*Pan troglodytes*)." *Journal of Experimental Psychology: Animal Behavior Processes, 14,* 118–120.

Rumelhart, David E.; McClelland, James L.; & the PDP Research Group (1986). *Parallel distributed processing: Explorations in the microstructure of cognition* (Vols. 1 and 2). Cambridge, MA: MIT Press.

Rushton, J. Philippe (1988). Race differences in behavior: A review and evolutionary analysis. *Personality and Individual Differences, 9,* 1009–1024.

Russell, Diana E. H. (1990). *Rape in marriage* (rev. ed.). Bloomington: Indiana University Press.

Ryff, Carol D., & Keyes, Corey L. M. (1995). The structure of psychological well-being revisited. *Journal of Personality and Social Psychology, 69,* 719–727.

Rymer, Russ (1993). *Genie: An abused child's flight from silence.* New York: HarperCollins.

Sacks, Oliver (1985). *The man who mistook his wife for a hat and other clinical tales.* New York: Simon & Schuster.

Sagan, Eli (1988). *Freud, women, and morality: The psychology of good and evil.* New York: Basic Books.

Sahley, Christie L.; Rudy, Jerry W.; & Gelperin, Alan (1981). An analysis of associative learning in a terrestrial mollusk: 1. Higher-order conditioning, blocking, and a transient US preexposure effect. *Journal of Comparative Physiology, 144,* 1–8.

Saltz, Bruce L.; Woerner, M. G.; Kane, J. M.; Lieberman, J. A.; et al. (1991, November 6). Prospective study of tardive dyskinesia incidence in the elderly. *Journal of the American Medical Association, 266*(17), 2402–2406.

Samelson, Franz (1979). Putting psychology on the map: Ideology and intelligence testing. In A. R. Buss (ed.), *Psychology in social context.* New York: Irvington.

Sameroff, Arnold J., & Seifer, Ronald (1989). Social regulation of developmental continuities. Paper presented at the annual meeting of the American Association for the Advancement of Science, San Francisco.

Sameroff, Arnold J.; Seifer, Ronald; Barocas, Ralph; Zax, Melvin; & Greenspan, Stanley (1987). Intelligence quotient scores of 4-year-old children: Social–environmental risk factors. *Pediatrics, 79,* 343–350.

Sapirstein, Guy, & Kirsch, Irving (1996). Listening to Prozac, but hearing placebo? A meta-analysis of the placebo effect of antidepressant medication. Paper presented at the annual meeting of the American Psychological Association, Toronto, Canada.

Sarbin, Theodore R. (1992). The social construction of schizophrenia. In W. Flack, D. R. Miller, & M. Wiener (eds.), *What is schizophrenia?* New York: Springer-Verlag.

Sáry, Gyula; Vogels, Rufin; & Orban, Guy A. (1993). Cue-invariant shape selectivity of macaque inferior temporal neurons. *Science, 260,* 995–997.

Savage-Rumbaugh, Sue, & Lewin, Roger (1994). *Kanzi: The ape at the brink of the human mind.* New York: Wiley.

Savage-Rumbaugh, Sue; Shanker, Stuart; & Taylor, Talbot (1996). *Apes, language and the human mind.* New York: Oxford University Press.

Saywitz, Karen; Goodman, Gail S.; Nicholas, Elissa; & Moan, Susan (1991). Children's memory for genital exam: Implications for child sexual abuse. *Journal of Consulting and Clinical Psychology, 59,* 682–691.

Scarr, Sandra (1984). Intelligence: What an introductory psychology student might want to know. In A. M. Rogers & C. J. Scheirer (eds.), *The G. Stanley Hall Lecture Series* (Vol. 4). Washington, DC: American Psychological Association.

Scarr, Sandra (1993). Biological and cultural diversity: The legacy of Darwin for development. *Child Development, 64,* 1333–1353.

Scarr, Sandra; Pakstis, Andrew J.; Katz, Soloman H.; & Barker, William B. (1977). Absence of a relationship between degree of white ancestry and intellectual skill in a black population. *Human Genetics, 39,* 69–86.

Scarr, Sandra, & Weinberg, Richard A. (1977). Intellectual similarities within families of both adopted and biological children. *Intelligence, 1,* 170–191.

Scarr, Sandra, & Weinberg, Richard A. (1994). Educational and occupational achievement of brothers and sisters in adoptive and biologically related families. *Behavioral Genetics, 24,* 301–325.

Schachter, Stanley (1971). *Emotion, obesity, and crime.* New York: Academic Press.

Schachter, Stanley, & Singer, Jerome E. (1962). Cognitive, social, and physiological determinants of emotional state. *Psychological Review, 69,* 379–399.

Schacter, Daniel L. (1996). *Searching for memory: The brain, the mind, and the past.* New York: Basic Books.

Schacter, Daniel L.; Chiu, C.-Y. Peter; & Ochsner, Kevin N. (1993). Implicit memory: A selective review. *Annual Review of Neuroscience, 16,* 159–182.

Schacter, Daniel L.; Reiman, E.; Curran, T.; et al. (1996). Neuroanatomical correlates of veridical and illusory recognition memory: Evidence from positron emission tomography. *Neuron, 17,* 267–274.

Schaie, K. Warner (1993). The Seattle longitudinal studies of adult intelligence. *Current Directions in Psychological Science, 2,* 171–175.

Schaie, K. Warner (1994). The course of adult intellectual development. Distinguished scientific contribution award address presented at the annual meeting of the American Psychological Association, Toronto, Canada.

Schank, Roger, with Peter Childers (1988). *The creative attitude.* New York: Macmillan.

Scheier, M. F., & Carver, C. S. (1992). Effects of optimism on psychological and physical well-being: Theoretical overview and empirical update. *Cognitive Therapy and Research, 16,* 201–228.

Schein, Edgar; Schneier, Inge; & Barker, Curtis H. (1961). *Coercive persuasion.* New York: Norton.

Scherer, Klaus R., & Wallbott, Harald G. (1994). Evidence for universality and cultural variation of differential emotion response patterning. *Journal of Personality and Social Psychology, 66,* 310–328.

Schlossberg, Nancy K. (1984). Exploring the adult years. In A. M. Rogers & C. J. Scheirer (eds.), *The G. Stanley Hall Lecture Series* (Vol. 4). Washington, DC: American Psychological Association.

Schlossberg, Nancy K., & Robinson, Susan P. (1996). *Going to plan B.* New York: Simon & Schuster/Fireside.

Schneider, Allen M., & Tarshis, Barry (1986). *An introduction to physiological psychology* (3rd ed.). New York: Random House.

Schnell, Lisa, & Schwab, Martin E. (1990, January 18). Axonal regeneration in the rat spinal cord produced by an antibody against myelin-associated neurite growth inhibitors. *Nature, 343,* 269–272.

Schrader, Harald; Obelieniene, D.; Bovim, G.; et al. (1996). Natural evolution of late whiplash syndrome outside the medicolegal context. *Lancet, 347,* 1207–1211.

Schuckit, Marc A., & Smith, T. L. (1996). An 8-year follow-up of 450 sons of alcoholic and control subjects. *Archives of General Psychiatry, 53,* 202–210.

Schulkin, Jay (1994). Melancholic depression and the hormones of adversity: A role for the amygdala. *Current Directions in Psychological Science, 3,* 41–44.

Schulman, Michael, & Mekler, Eva (1994). *Bringing up a caring child* (rev. ed.). New York: Doubleday.

Schulz, Richard, & Decker, Susan (1985). Long-term adjustment to physical disability: The role of social support, perceived control, and self-blame. *Journal of Personality and Social Psychology, 48,* 1162–1172.

Schuman, Howard, & Scott, Jacqueline (1989). Generations and collective memories. *American Journal of Sociology, 54,* 359–381.

Schwartz, Jeffrey; Stoessel, Paula W.; Baxter, Lewis R.; Martin, Karron M.; & Phelps, Michael E. (1996). Systematic changes in cerebral glucose metabolic rate after successful behavior modification treatment of obsessive–compulsive disorder. *Archives of General Psychiatry, 53,* 109–113.

Scofield, Michael (1993, June 6). About men: Off the ladder. *New York Times Magazine,* 22.

Sears, Pauline, & Barbee, Ann H. (1977). Career and life satisfactions among Terman's gifted women. In J. C. Stanley, W. C. George, & C. H. Solano (eds.), *The gifted and the creative: A fifty-year perspective.* Baltimore, MD: Johns Hopkins University Press.

Seeman, Philip.; Guan, Hong-chang; & Van Tol, Hubert H. (1993). Dopamine D4 receptors elevated in schizophrenia. *Nature, 365,* 441–445.

Segal, Julius (1986). *Winning life's toughest battles.* New York: McGraw-Hill.

Segall, Marshall H. (1994). A cross-cultural research contribution to unraveling the nativist/empiricist controversy. In W. J. Lonner & R. Malpass (eds.), *Psychology and culture.* Needham Heights, MA: Allyn & Bacon.

Segall, Marshall H.; Campbell, Donald T.; & Herskovits, Melville J. (1966). *The influence of culture on visual perception.* Indianapolis: Bobbs-Merrill.

Segall, Marshall H.; Dasen, Pierre R.; Berry, John W.; & Poortinga, Ype H. (1990). *Human behavior in global perspective: An introduction to cross-cultural psychology.* New York: Pergamon.

Seiden, Richard (1978). Where are they now? A follow-up study of suicide attempters from the Golden Gate Bridge. *Suicide and Life-Threatening Behavior, 8,* 203–216.

Seidenberg, Mark S., & Petitto, Laura A. (1979). Signing behavior in apes: A critical review. *Cognition, 7,* 177–215.

Seifer, Ronald; Schiller, Masha; Sameroff, Arnold; Resnick, Staci; & Riordan, Kate (1996). Attachment, maternal sensitivity, and infant temperament during the first year of life. *Developmental Psychology, 32,* 12–25.

Sekuler, Robert, & Blake, Randolph (1994). *Perception* (3rd ed.). New York: Knopf.

Seligman, Martin E. P. (1975). *Helplessness: On depression, development, and death.* San Francisco: Freeman.

Seligman, Martin E. P. (1991). *Learned optimism.* New York: Knopf.

Seligman, Martin E. P., & Hager, Joanne L. (1972, August). Biological boundaries of learning: The sauce-béarnaise syndrome. *Psychology Today, 59–61,* 84–87.

Selye, Hans (1956). *The stress of life.* New York: McGraw-Hill.

Serbin, Lisa A.; Powlishta, Kimberly K.; & Gulko, Judith (1993). The development of sex typing in middle childhood. *Monographs of the Society for Research in Child Development, 58*(2, Serial No. 232), v–74.

Serpell, Robert (1994). The cultural construction of intelligence. In W. J. Lonner & R. S. Malpass (eds.), *Psychology and Culture.* Needham Heights, MA: Allyn & Bacon.

Shadish, William R., Jr.; Lurigio, Arthur J.; & Lewis, Dan A. (1989). After deinstitutionalization: The present and future of mental health long-term care policy. *Journal of Social Issues, 45*(3), 1–16.

Shapiro, A. Eugene, & Wiggins, Jack G. (1994). A PsyD degree for every practitioner. *American Psychologist, 49,* 207–210.

Shapiro, Deane H.; Schwartz, Carolyn E.; & Astin, John A. (1996). Controlling ourselves, controlling our world. *American Psychologist, 51,* 1213–1230.

Shatz, Marilyn, & Gelman, Rochel (1973). The development of communication skills: Modifications in the speech of young children as a function of the listener. *Monographs of the Society for Research in Child Development, 38.*

Shaver, Phillip, & Hazan, Cindy (1987). Romantic love conceptualized as an attachment process. *Journal of Personality and Social Psychology, 52,* 511–524.

Shaver, Phillip R., & Hazan, Cindy (1993). Adult romantic attachment: Theory and evidence. In D. Perlman & W. H. Jones (eds.), *Advances in personal relationships* (Vol. 4). London: Kingsley.

Shaywitz, Bennett A.; Shaywitz, Sally E.; Pugh, Kenneth R.; et al. (1995). Sex differences in the functional organization of the brain for language. *Nature, 373,* 607–609.

Shepard, Roger N., & Metzler, Jacqueline (1971). Mental rotation of three-dimensional objects. *Science, 171,* 701–703.

Shepperd, James A. (1995). Remedying motivation and productivity loss in collective settings. *Current Directions in Psychological Science, 4,* 131–140.

Sherif, Muzafer (1958). Superordinate goals in the reduction of intergroup conflicts. *American Journal of Sociology, 63,* 349–356.

Sherif, Muzafer; Harvey, O. J.; White, B. J.; Hood, William; & Sherif, Carolyn (1961). *Intergroup conflict and cooperation: The Robbers Cave experiment.* Norman: University of Oklahoma Institute of Intergroup Relations.

Sherman, Bonnie R., & Kunda, Ziva (1989). Motivated evaluation of scientific evidence. Paper presented at the annual meeting of the American Psychological Society, Arlington, VA.

Sherwin, Barbara B. (1988). A comparative analysis of the role of androgen in human male and female sexual behavior: Behavioral specificity, critical thresholds, and sensitivity. *Psychobiology, 16,* 416–425.

Shields, Stephanie A. (1975). Functionalism, Darwinism, and the psychology of women: A study in social myth. *American Psychologist, 30,* 739–754.

Shields, Stephanie A. (1991). Gender in the psychology of emotion: A selective research review. In K. T. Strongman (ed.), *International review of studies on emotion* (Vol. 1). New York: Wiley.

Shogren, Elizabeth (1994, August 18). Treatment against their will. *Los Angeles Times,* A1, A14–16.

Shweder, Richard A.; Mahapatra, Manamohan; & Miller, Joan G. (1990). Culture and moral development. In J. W. Stigler, R. A. Shweder, & G. Herdt (eds.), *Cultural psychology: Essays on comparative human development.* Cambridge, England: Cambridge University Press.

Sidanius, Jim; Pratto, Felicia; & Bobo, Lawrence (1996). Racism, conservatism, affirmative action, and intellectual sophistication: A matter of principled conservatism or group dominance? *Journal of Personality and Social Psychology, 70,* 476–490.

Siegel, Alan B. (1991). *Dreams that can change your life.* Los Angeles: Jeremy Tarcher.

Siegel, Shepard (1990). Classical conditioning and opiate tolerance and withdrawal. In D. J. K. Balfour (ed.), *Psychotropic drugs of abuse.* New York: Pergamon.

Siegel, Shepard; Hinson, Riley E.; Krank, Marvin D.; & McCully, Jane (1982). Heroin "overdose" death: Contribution of drug-associated environmental cues. *Science, 216,* 436–437.

Siegler, Robert (1996). *Emerging minds: The process of change in children's thinking.* New York: Oxford University Press.

Silver, Eric; Cirincione, Carmen; & Steadman, Henry J. (1994). Demythologizing inaccurate perceptions of the insanity defense. *Law and Human Behavior, 18,* 63–70.

Silverman, Loyd, & Weinberger, Joel (1985). Mommy and I are one: Implications for psychotherapy. *American Psychologist, 40,* 1296–1308.

Silverstein, Brett, & Perlick, Deborah (1995). *The cost of competence: Why inequality causes depression, eating disorders, and illness in women.* New York: Oxford University Press.

Silverstein, Brett; Peterson, Barbara; & Perdue, Lauren (1986). Some correlates of the thin standard of bodily attractiveness in women. *International Journal of Eating Disorders, 5,* 145–155.

Simon, Herbert A. (1973). The structure of ill-structured problems. *Artificial Intelligence, 4,* 181–202.

Sims, Ethan A. (1974). Studies in human hyperphagia. In G. Bray & J. Bethune (eds.), *Treatment and management of obesity.* New York: Harper & Row.

Sinclair, Robert C.; Hoffman, Curt; Mark, Melvin M.; Martin, Leonard L.; & Pickering, Tracie L. (1994). Construct accessibility and the misattribution of arousal: Schachter and Singer revisited. *Psychological Science, 5,* 15–19.

Singer, Jerome L. (1984). The private personality. *Personality and Social Psychology Bulletin, 10,* 7–30.

Singer, Margaret T.; Temerlin, Maurice K.; & Langone, Michael D. (1990). Psychotherapy cults. *Cultic Studies Journal, 7,* 101–125.

Skinner, B. F. (1938). *The behavior of organisms: An experimental analysis.* New York: Appleton-Century-Crofts.

Skinner, B. F. (1948). Superstition in the pigeon. *Journal of Experimental Psychology, 38,* 168–172.

Skinner, B. F. (1948/1976). *Walden two.* New York: Macmillan.

Skinner, B. F. (1956). A case history in the scientific method. *American Psychologist, 11,* 221–233.

Skinner, B. F. (1968). *The technology of teaching.* New York: Appleton-Century-Crofts.

Skinner, B. F. (1972). The operational analysis of psychological terms. In B. F. Skinner, *Cumulative record* (3rd ed.). New York: Appleton-Century-Crofts.

Skinner, B. F. (1983). *A matter of consequences.* New York: Knopf.

Skinner, B. F. (1990). Can psychology be a science of mind? *American Psychologist, 45,* 1206–1210.

Skinner, Ellen A. (1996). A guide to constructs of control. *Journal of Personality and Social Psychology, 71,* 549–570.

Skinner, J. B.; Erskine, A.; Pearce, S. A.; Rubenstein, I.; et al. (1990). The evaluation of a cognitive behavioural treatment programme in outpatients with chronic pain. *Journal of Psychosomatic Research, 34,* 13–19.

Skreslet, Paula (1987, November 30). The prizes of first grade. *Newsweek,* 8.

Slobin, Daniel I. (ed.) (1985). *The cross-linguistic study of language acquisition* (Vols. 1 and 2). Hillsdale, NJ: Erlbaum.

Smith, James F., & Kida, Thomas (1991). Heuristics and biases: Expertise and task realism in auditing. *Psychological Bulletin, 109,* 472–489.

Smith, Mary Lee; Glass, Gene; & Miller, Thomas I. (1980). *The benefits of psychotherapy.* Baltimore, MD: Johns Hopkins University Press.

Smith, Peter B., & Bond, Michael H. (1993/1994). *Social psychology across cultures: Analysis and perspectives.* Boston: Allyn & Bacon.

Smither, Robert D. (1994). *The psychology of work and human performance* (2nd ed.). New York: HarperCollins.

Snarey, John R. (1985). Cross-cultural universality of social–moral development: A critical review of Kohlbergian research. *Psychological Bulletin, 97,* 202–232.

Snow, Barry R; Pinter, Isaac; Gusmorino, Paul; Jimenez, Arthur; Rosenblum, Andrew; & Adelglass, Howard (1986). Sex differences in chronic pain: Incidence and causal mechanisms. Paper presented at the annual meeting of the American Psychological Association, Washington, DC.

Snyder, C. R., & Shenkel, Randee J. (1975, March). The P. T. Barnum effect. *Psychology Today,* 52–54.

Snyder, Robert A. (1993, Spring). The glass ceiling for women: Things that don't cause it and things that won't break it. *Human Resource Development Quarterly,* 97–106.

Solomon, Jennifer C. (1996). Humor and aging well: A laughing matter or a matter of laughing? [Special Issue: Aging well in contemporary society: II. Choices and processes.] *American Behavioral Scientist, 39,* 249–271.

Solomon, Paul R. (1979). Science and television commercials: Adding relevance to the research methodology course. *Teaching of Psychology, 6,* 26–30.

Solomon, Robert C. (1994). *About love.* Lanham, MD: Littlefield Adams.

Sommer, Robert (1969). *Personal space: The behavioral basis of design.* Englewood Cliffs, NJ: Prentice-Hall.

Sorce, James F.; Emde, Robert N.; Campos, Joseph; & Klinnert, Mary D. (1985). Maternal emotional signaling: Its effect on the visual cliff behavior of 1-year-olds. *Developmental Psychology, 21,* 195–200.

Spangler, William D., & House, Robert J. (1991). Presidential effectiveness and the leadership motive profile. *Journal of Personality and Social Psychology, 60,* 439–455.

Spanos, Nicholas P. (1996). *Multiple identities and false memories: A sociocognitive perspective.* Washington, DC: American Psychological Association.

Spanos, Nicholas P.; Menary, Evelyn; Gabora, Natalie J.; DuBreuil, Susan C.; & Dewhirst, Bridget (1991). Secondary identity enactments during hypnotic past-life regression: A sociocognitive perspective. *Journal of Personality and Social Psychology, 61,* 308–320.

Spearman, Charles (1927). *The abilities of man.* London: Macmillan.

Speltz, Matthew L.; Greenberg, Mark T.; & Deklyen, Michelle (1990). Attachment in preschoolers with disruptive behavior: A comparison of clinic-referred and nonproblem children. *Development and Psychopathology, 2,* 31–46.

Spence, Janet T. (1985). Gender identity and its implications for concepts of masculinity and femininity. In T. Sonderegger (ed.), *Nebraska Symposium on Motivation.* Lincoln: University of Nebraska Press.

Spencer, M. B., & Dornbusch, Sanford M. (1990). Ethnicity. In S. S. Feldman & G. R. Elliott (eds.), *At the threshold: The developing adolescent.* Cambridge, MA: Harvard University Press.

Sperling, George (1960). The information available in brief visual presentations. *Psychological Monographs, 74*(498).

Sperry, Roger W. (1964). The great cerebral commissure. *Scientific American, 210*(1), 42–52.

Sperry, Roger W. (1982). Some effects of disconnecting the cerebral hemispheres. *Science, 217,* 1223–1226.

Spilich, George J.; June, Lorraine; & Renner, Judith (1992). Cigarette smoking and cognitive performance. *British Journal of Addiction, 87,* 113–126.

Spitz, Herman H. (1997). *Nonconscious movements: From mystical messages to facilitated communication.* Mahwah, NJ: Erlbaum.

Spitzer, Robert L., & Williams, Janet B. (1988). Having a dream: A research strategy for DSM-IV. *Archives of General Psychiatry, 45,* 871–874.

Spoont, Michele R. (1992). Modulatory role of serotonin in neural information processing: Implications for human psychopathology. *Psychological Bulletin, 112,* 330–350.

Sporer, Siegfried L.; Penrod, Steven; Read, Don; & Cutler, Brian (1995). Choosing, confidence, and accuracy: A meta-analysis of the confidence–accuracy relation in eyewitness identification studies. *Psychological Bulletin, 118,* 315–327.

Sprecher, Susan; Sullivan, Quintin; & Hatfield, Elaine (1994). Mate selection preferences: Gender differences examined in a national sample. *Journal of Personality and Social Psychology, 66,* 1074–1080.

Spring, Bonnie; Chiodo, June; & Bowen, Deborah J. (1987). Carbohydrates, tryptophan, and behavior: A methodological review. *Psychological Bulletin, 102,* 234–256.

Squire, Larry R. (1987). *Memory and the brain.* New York: Oxford University Press.

Squire, Larry R., & Zola-Morgan, Stuart (1991). The medial temporal lobe memory system. *Science, 253,* 1380–1386.

Staats, Carolyn K., & Staats, Arthur W. (1957). Meaning established by classical conditioning. *Journal of Experimental Psychology, 54,* 74–80.

Stanovich, Keith (1996). *How to think straight about psychology* (4th ed.). New York: HarperCollins.

Staples, Brent (1994). *Parallel time.* New York: Pantheon.

Staples, Susan L. (1996). Human response to environmental noise: Psychological research and public policy. *American Psychologist, 51,* 143–150.

Stattin, Haken, & Magnusson, David (1990). *Pubertal maturation in female development.* Hillsdale, NJ: Erlbaum.

Staub, Ervin (1996). Cultural–social roots of violence. *American Psychologist, 51,* 117–132.

Steinberg, Laurence D. (1990). Interdependence in the family: Autonomy, conflict and harmony in the parent–adolescent relationship. In S. S. Feldman & G. R. Elliott (eds.), *At the threshold: The developing adolescent.* Cambridge, MA: Harvard University Press.

Stenberg, Craig R., & Campos, Joseph (1990). The development of anger expressions in infancy. In N. Stein, B. Leventhal, & T. Trabasso (eds.), *Psychological and biological approaches to emotion.* Hillsdale, NJ: Erlbaum.

Stephan, K. M.; Fink, G. R.; Passingham, R. E.; et al. (1995). Functional anatomy of the mental representation of upper movements in healthy subjects. *Journal of Neurophysiology, 73,* 373–386.

Stephan, Walter G.; Ageyev, Vladimir; Coates-Shrider, Lisa; Stephan, Cookie W.; & Abalakina, Marina (1994). On the relationship between stereotypes and prejudice: An international study. *Personality and Social Psychology Bulletin, 20,* 277–284.

Stephan, Walter, & Brigham, John C. (1985). Intergroup contact: Introduction. *Journal of Social Issues, 41*(3), 1–8.

Stephens, Mitchell (1991, September 20). The death of reading. *Los Angeles Times Magazine,* 10, 12, 16, 42, 44.

Sternberg, Robert J. (1986). *Intelligence applied: Understanding and increasing your intellectual skills.* San Diego: Harcourt Brace Jovanovich.

Sternberg, Robert J. (1988). *The triarchic mind: A new theory of human intelligence.* New York: Viking.

Sternberg Robert J. (1995). *In search of the human mind.* Orlando, FL: Harcourt Brace.

Sternberg, Robert J. (1997). Construct validation of a triangular love scale. *European Journal of Social Psychology, 27,* 313–335.

Sternberg, Robert J., & Wagner, Richard K. (1989). Individual differences in practical knowledge and its acquisition. In P. Ackerman, R. J. Sternberg, & R. Glaser (eds.), *Individual differences.* New York: Freeman.

Sternberg, Robert J.; Wagner, Richard K.; & Okagaki, Lynn (1993). Practical intelligence: The nature and role of tacit knowledge in work and at school. In H. Reese & J. Puckett (eds.), *Advances in lifespan development.* Hillsdale, NJ: Erlbaum.

Sternberg, Robert J.; Wagner, Richard K.; Williams, Wendy M.; & Horvath, Joseph A. (1995). Testing common sense. *American Psychologist, 50,* 912–927.

Sternberg, Robert J., & Williams, Wendy M. (1997). Does the GRE predict meaningful success in the graduate training of psychologists? A case study. *American Psychologist, 52,* 630–641.

Stevenson, Harold W.; Chen, Chuansheng; & Lee, Shin-ying (1993, January 1). Mathematics achievement of Chinese, Japanese, and American children: Ten years later. *Science, 259,* 53–58.

Stevenson, Harold W., & Stigler, James W. (1992). *The learning gap.* New York: Summit.

Stickler, Gunnar B.; Salter, Margery; Broughton, Daniel D.; & Alario, Anthony (1991). Parents' worries about children compared to actual risks. *Clinical Pediatrics, 30,* 522–528.

Stoch, M. B., & Smythe, P. M. (1963). Does undernutrition during infancy inhibit brain growth and subsequent intellectual development? *Archives of Diseases in Childbood, 38,* 546–552.

Strack, Fritz; Martin, Leonard L.; & Stepper, Sabine (1988). Inhibiting and facilitating conditions of the human smile: A nonobtrusive test of the facial-feedback hypothesis. *Journal of Social and Personality Psychology, 54,* 768–777.

Straus, Murray A. (1991). Discipline and deviance: Physical punishment of children and violence and other crime in adulthood. *Social Problems, 38*(2), 133–154.

Streissguth, A. P.; Aase, J. M.; Clarren, S. K.; Randels, S. P.; LaDue, R. A.; & Smith, D. F. (1991). Fetal alcohol syndrome in adolescents and adults. *Journal of the American Medical Association, 265,* 1961–1967.

Strickland, Bonnie R. (1965). The prediction of social action from a dimension of internal–external control. *Journal of Social Psychology, 66,* 353–358.

Strickland, Bonnie R. (1989). Internal–external control expectancies: From contingency to creativity. *American Psychologist, 44,* 1–12.

Strickland, Bonnie R. (1995). Research on sexual orientation and human development: A commentary. *Developmental Psychology, 31,* 137–140.

Strickland, Tony L.; Lin, Keh-Ming; Fu, Paul; Anderson, Dora; & Zheng, Yanping (1995). Comparison of lithium ratio between African-American and Caucasian bipolar patients. *Biological Psychiatry, 37,* 325–330.

Strickland, Tony L.; Ranganath, Vijay; Lin, Keh-Ming; Poland, Russell E.; et al. (1991). Psychopharmacological considerations in the treatment of black American populations. *Psychopharmacology Bulletin, 27,* 441–448.

Stroebe, Wolfgang; Stroebe, Margaret; Abakoumkin, Georgios; & Schut, Henk (1996). The role of loneliness and social support in adjustment to loss: A test of attachment versus stress theory. *Journal of Personality and Social Psychology, 70,* 1241–1249.

Strong, Bryan, & DeVault, Christine (1994). *Human sexuality.* Mountain View, CA: Mayfield.

Strupp, Hans H. (1982). The outcome problem in psychotherapy: Contemporary perspectives. In J. H. Harvey & M. M. Parks (eds.), *Psychotherapy research and behavior change: Vol. 1. The APA Master Lecture Series.* Washington, DC: American Psychological Association.

Strupp, Hans H., & Binder, Jeffrey (1984). *Psychotherapy in a new key.* New York: Basic Books.

Stunkard, Albert J. (ed.) (1980). *Obesity.* Philadelphia: Saunders.

Stunkard, Albert J.; Harris, J. R.; Pedersen, N. L.; & McClearn, G. E. (1990, May 24). The body-mass index of twins who have been reared apart. *New England Journal of Medicine, 322,* 1483–1487.

Sue, Stanley (1991). Ethnicity and culture in psychological research and practice. In J. Goodchilds (ed.), *Psychological perspectives on human diversity in America.* Washington, DC: American Psychological Association.

Suedfeld, Peter (1975). The benefits of boredom: Sensory deprivation reconsidered. *American Scientist, 63*(1), 60–69.

Sulloway, Frank J. (1992). *Freud, biologist of the mind: Beyond the psychoanalytic legend* (rev. ed.). Cambridge, MA: Harvard University Press.

Summerville, Mary B.; Kaslow, Nadine J.; & Doepke, Karla J. (1996). Psychopathology and cognitive and family functioning in suicidal African-American adolescents. *Current Directions in Psychological Science, 5,* 7–11.

Suomi, Stephen J. (1987). Genetic and maternal contributions to individual differences in rhesus monkey biobehavioral development. In N. Krasnegor, E. Blass, M. Hofer, & W. Smotherman (eds.), *Perinatal development: A psychobiological perspective.* New York: Academic Press.

Suomi, Stephen J. (1989). Primate separation models of affective disorders. In J. Madden (ed.), *Adaptation, learning, and affect.* New York: Raven Press.

Suomi, Stephen J. (1991). Uptight and laid-back monkeys: Individual differences in the response to social challenges. In S. Branch, W. Hall, & J. E. Dooling (eds.), *Plasticity of development.* Cambridge, MA: MIT Press.

Super, Charles A., & Harkness, Sara (1994). The developmental niche. In W. J. Lonner & R. Malpass (eds.), *Psychology and culture.* Needham Heights, MA: Allyn & Bacon.

Susser, Ezra; Neugebauer, Richard; Hoek, Hans W.; Brown, Alan S.; et al. (1996). Schizophrenia after prenatal famine: Further evidence. *Archives of General Psychiatry, 53,* 25–31.

Swain, Scott (1989). Covert intimacy: Closeness in men's friendships. In B. J. Risman & P. Schwartz (eds.), *Gender in intimate relationships.* Belmont, CA: Wadsworth.

Szasz, Thomas (1961/1967). *The myth of mental illness.* New York: Dell Delta.

Taffel, Ronald (1990, September/October). The politics of mood. *Family Therapy Networker,* 49–53, 72.

Tajfel, Henri; Billig, M. G.; Bundy, R. P.; & Flament, C. (1971). Social categorization and intergroup behavior. *European Journal of Social Psychology, 1,* 149–178.

Tajfel, Henri, & Turner, John C. (1986). The social identity theory of intergroup behavior. In S. Worchel & W. G. Austin (eds.), *Psychology of intergroup relations.* Chicago: Nelson-Hall.

Tangney, June P. (1992). Constructive vs. destructive responses to anger: The moderating roles of shame and guilt across the lifespan. Paper presented at the annual meeting of the International Congress of Psychology, Brussels, Belgium.

Tangney, June P.; Wagner, Patricia E.; Hill-Barlow, Deborah; Marschall, Donna E.; & Gramzow, Richard (1996). Relation of shame and guilt to constructive versus destructive responses to anger across the lifespan. *Journal of Personality and Social Psychology, 70,* 797–809.

Tartter, Vivien C. (1986). *Language processes.* New York: Holt, Rinehart and Winston.

Taub, David M. (1984). *Primate paternalism.* New York: Van Nostrand Reinhold.

Tavris, Carol (1989). *Anger: The misunderstood emotion* (2nd ed.). New York: Simon & Schuster/Touchstone.

Tavris, Carol (1992). *The mismeasure of woman.* New York: Simon & Schuster/Touchstone.

Taylor, Donald M., & Porter, Lana E. (1994). A multicultural view of stereotyping. In W. J. Lonner & R. Malpass (eds.), *Psychology and culture.* Needham Heights, MA: Allyn & Bacon.

Taylor, Shelley E. (1995). *Health psychology* (3rd ed.). New York: McGraw Hill.

Taylor, Shelley E., & Brown, Jonathon D. (1988). Illusion and well-being: A social psychological perspective on mental health. *Psychological Bulletin, 103,* 193–210.

Taylor, Shelley E., & Brown, Jonathon D. (1994). Positive illusions and well-being revisited: Separating fact from fiction. *Psychological Bulletin, 116,* 21–27.

Taylor, Shelley E.; Lichtman, Rosemary R.; & Wood, Joanne V. (1984). Attributions, beliefs about control, and adjustment to breast cancer. *Journal of Personality and Social Psychology, 46,* 489–502.

Taylor, Shelley E., & Lobel, Marci (1989). Social comparison activity under threat: Downward evaluation and upward contacts. *Psychological Review, 96,* 569–575.

Taylor, Shelley E.; Peplau, Letitia A.; & Sears, David O. (1997). *Social psychology* (9th ed.). Englewood Cliffs, NJ: Prentice-Hall.

Taylor, Shelley E.; Repetti, Rena; & Seeman, Teresa (1997). Health psychology: What is an unhealthy environment and how does it get under the skin? *Annual Review of Psychology* (Vol. 48). Palo Alto, CA: Annual Reviews.

Tellegen, Auke; Lykken, David T.; Bouchard, Thomas J., Jr.; et al. (1988). Personality similarity in twins reared apart and together. *Journal of Personality and Social Psychology, 54,* 1031–1039.

Temerlin, Jane W., & Temerlin, Maurice K. (1986). Some hazards of the therapeutic relationship. *Cultic Studies Journal, 3,* 234–242.

Terman, Lewis M., & Oden, Melita H. (1959). *Genetic studies of genius: Vol. 5. The gifted group at mid-life.* Stanford, CA: Stanford University Press.

Terrace, H. S. (1985). In the beginning was the "name." *American Psychologist, 40,* 1011–1028.

Thibodeau, Ruth, & Aronson, Elliot (1992). Taking a closer look: Reasserting the role of the self-concept in dissonance theory. *Personality and Social Psychology Bulletin, 18,* 591–602.

Thiriart, Philippe (1991, Winter). Acceptance of personality test results. *Skeptical Inquirer, 15,* 161–165.

Thoma, Stephen J. (1986). Estimating gender differences in the comprehension and preference of moral issues. *Developmental Review, 6,* 165–180.

Thomas, Sandra P. (1993). Introduction. In S. P. Thomas (ed.), *Women and anger.* New York: Springer.

Thompson, Richard F. (1986). The neurobiology of learning and memory. *Science, 233,* 941–947.

Thompson, Suzanne C.; Nanni, Christopher; & Levine, Alexandra (1994). Primary versus secondary and central versus consequence-related control in HIV-positive men. *Journal of Personality and Social Psychology, 67,* 540–547.

Thorndike, Edward L. (1898). Animal intelligence: An experimental study of the associative processes in animals. *Psychological Review Monograph Supplement, 2* (Whole No. 8).

Tice, Dianne M., & Baumeister, Roy F. (1997). Longitudinal study of procrastination, performance, stress, and health: The costs and benefits of dawdling. *Pschological Science, 8,* 454–458.

Tiefer, Leonore (1995). *Sex is not a natural act and other essays.* Boulder, CO: Westview Press.

Tolman, Edward C. (1938). The determiners of behavior at a choice point. *Psychological Review, 45,* 1–35.

Tolman, Edward C. (1948). Cognitive maps in rats and men. *Psychological Review, 55,* 189–208.

Tolman, Edward C., & Honzik, Chase H. (1930). Introduction and removal of reward and maze performance in rats. *University of California Publications in Psychology, 4,* 257–275.

Tomkins, Silvan S. (1981). The role of facial response in the experience of emotion: A reply to Tourangeau and Ellsworth. *Journal of Personality and Social Psychology, 40,* 355–357.

Torrey, E. Fuller (1988). *Surviving schizophrenia* (rev. ed.). New York: Harper & Row.

Torrey, E. Fuller; Bowler, Ann E.; Taylor, Edward H.; & Gottesman, Irving I. (1994). *Schizophrenia and manic–depressive disorder.* New York: Basic Books.

Tougas, Francine; Brown, Rupert; Beaton, Ann M.; & Joly, Stéphane (1995). Neosexism: Plus ça change, plus c'est pareil. *Personality and Social Psychology Bulletin, 21,* 842–849.

Triandis, Harry C. (1994). *Culture and social behavior.* New York: McGraw-Hill.

Triandis, Harry C. (1995). *Individualism and collectivism.* Boulder, CO: Westview Press.

Triandis, Harry C. (1996). The psychological measurement of cultural syndromes. *American Psychologist, 51,* 407–415.

Tronick, Edward Z.; Morelli, Gilda A.; & Ivey, Paula K. (1992). The Efe forager infant and toddler's pattern of social relationships: Multiple and simultaneous. [Special Section: Cross-cultural studies of development.] *Developmental Psychology, 28,* 568–577.

Tsuang, Ming T., & Faraone, Stephen V. (1990). *The genetics of mood disorder.* Baltimore, MD: Johns Hopkins University Press.

Tulving, Endel (1985). How many memory systems are there? *American Psychologist, 40,* 385–398.

Tversky, Amos, & Kahneman, Daniel (1973). Availability: A heuristic for judging frequency and probability. *Cognitive Psychology, 5,* 207–232.

Tversky, Amos, & Kahneman, Daniel (1981). The framing of decisions and the psychology of choice. *Science, 211,* 453–458.

Tversky, Amos, & Kahneman, Daniel (1986). Rational choice and the framing of decisions. *Journal of Business, 59,* S251–S278.

Twenge, Jean M. (1996). Attitudes toward women, 1970–1995: A meta-analysis. Paper presented at the annual meeting of the American Psychological Association, Toronto, Canada.

Tzischinsky, Orna; Pal, I.; Epstein, Rachel; Dagan, Y.; & Lavie, Peretz (1992). The importance of timing in melatonin administration in a blind man. *Journal of Pineal Research, 12,* 105–108.

Uchida, K., & Toya, S. (1996). Grafting of genetically manipulated cells into adult brain: Toward graft-gene therapy. *Keio Journal of Medicine* (Japan), *45,* 81–89.

Uchino, Bert N.; Cacioppo, John T.; & Kiecolt-Glaser, Janice K. (1996). The relationship between social support and physiological processes: A review with emphasis on underlying mechanisms and implications for health. *Psychological Bulletin, 119,* 488–531.

Uchino, Bert N.; Cacioppo, John T.; Malarkey, William; & Glaser, Ronald (1995). Individual differences in cardiac sympathetic control predict endocrine and immune responses to acute psychological stress. *Journal of Personality and Social Psychology, 69,* 736–743.

Usher, JoNell A., & Neisser, Ulric (1993). Childhood amnesia and the beginnings of memory for four early life events. *Journal of Experimental Psychology: General, 122,* 155–165.

Vaillant, George E. (1983). *The natural history of alcoholism: Causes, patterns, and paths to recovery.* Cambridge, MA: Harvard University Press.

Vaillant, George E. (ed.) (1992). *Ego mechanisms of defense.* Washington, DC: American Psychiatric Press.

Vaillant, George E. (1995). *The natural history of alcoholism revisited.* Cambridge, MA: Harvard University Press.

Valenstein, Elliot (1986). *Great and desperate cures: The rise and decline of psychosurgery and other radical treatments for mental illness.* New York: Basic Books.

Van Cantfort, Thomas E., & Rimpau, James B. (1982). Sign language studies with children and chimpanzees. *Sign Language Studies, 34,* 15–72.

Viken, Richard J.; Rose, Richard J.; Kaprio, Jaakko; & Koskenvuo, Markku (1994). A developmental genetic analysis of adult personality: Extraversion and neuroticism from 18 to 59 years of age. *Journal of Personality and Social Psychology, 66,* 722–730.

Voyer, Daniel; Voyer, Susan; & Bryden, M. P. (1995). Magnitude of sex differences in spatial abilities: A meta-analysis and consideration of critical variables. *Psychological Bulletin, 117,* 250–270.

Wadden, Thomas A.; Foster, G. D.; Letizia, K. A.; & Mullen, J. L. (1990, August 8). Long-term effects of dieting on resting metabolic rate in obese outpatients. *Journal of the American Medical Association, 264,* 707–711.

Wagenaar, Willem A. (1986). My memory: A study of autobiographical memory over six years. *Cognitive Psychology, 18,* 225–252.

Wakefield, Jerome C. (1992). The concept of mental disorder: On the boundary between biological facts and social values. *American Psychologist, 47,* 373–388.

Walker, Lawrence J.; de Vries, Brian; & Trevethan, Shelley D. (1987). Moral stages and moral orientations in real-life and hypothetical dilemmas. *Child Development, 58,* 842–858.

Wallbott, Harald G.; Ricci-Bitti, Pio; & Bänninger-Huber, Eva (1986). Non-verbal reactions to emotional experiences. In K. R. Scherer, H. G. Wallbott, & A. B. Summerfield (eds.), *Experiencing emotion: A cross-cultural study.* Cambridge, England: Cambridge University Press.

Waller, Niels G.; Kojetin, Brian A.; Bouchard, Thomas J., Jr.; Lykken, David T.; & Tellegen, Auke (1990). Genetic and environmental influences on religious interests, attitudes, and values: A study of twins reared apart and together. *Psychological Science, 1,* 138–142.

Waller, Niels G., & Shaver, Phillip (1994). The importance of nongenetic influences on romantic love styles: A twin-family study. *Psychological Science, 5,* 268–274.

Wang, Alvin Y.; Thomas, Margaret H.; & Ouellette, Judith A. (1992). The keyword mnemonic and retention of second-language vocabulary words. *Journal of Educational Psychology, 84,* 520–528.

Ward, L. Monique (1994). Preschoolers' awareness of associations between gender and societal status. Paper presented at the annual meeting of the American Psychological Association, Los Angeles.

Wark, Gillian R., & Krebs, Dennis (1996). Gender and dilemma differences in real-life moral judgment. *Developmental Psychology, 32,* 220–230.

Washburn, David A., & Rumbaugh, Duane M. (1991). Ordinal judgments of numerical symbols by macaques *(Macaca mulatta). Psychological Science, 2,* 190–193.

Waters, Everett; Merrick, Susan K.; Albersheim, Leah J.; & Treboux, Dominique (1995). Attachment security from infancy to early adulthood: A 20-year-longitudinal study. Paper presented at the annual meeting of the Society for Research in Child Development, Indianapolis.

Watson, David, & Clark, Lee Anna (1992). On traits and temperament: General and specific factors of emotional experience and their relation to the five-factor model. *Journal of Personality, 60,* 441–476.

Watson, John B. (1913). Psychology as the behaviorist views it. *Psychological Review, 20,* 158–177.

Watson, John B., & Rayner, Rosalie (1920). Conditioned emotional reactions. *Journal of Experimental Psychology, 3,* 1–14.

Webb, Wilse B., & Cartwright, Rosalind D. (1978). Sleep and dreams. In M. Rosenzweig & L. Porter (eds.), *Annual Review of Psychology, 29,* 223–252.

Webster, Richard (1995). *Why Freud was wrong.* New York: Basic Books.

Wechsler, David (1955). *Manual for the Wechsler Adult Intelligence Scale.* New York: Psychological Corporation.

Weder, Alan B., & Schork, Nicholas J. (1994). Adaptation, allometry, and hypertension. *Hypertension, 24,* 145–156.

Wegner, Daniel M., & Gold, Daniel B. (1995). Fanning old flames: Emotional and cognitive effects of suppressing thoughts of a past relationship. *Journal of Personality and Social Psychology, 68,* 782–792.

Weil, Andrew T. (1974a, June). Parapsychology: Andrew Weil's search for the true Geller. *Psychology Today,* 45–50.

Weil, Andrew T. (1974b, July). Parapsychology: Andrew Weil's search for the true Geller, Part II. The letdown. *Psychology Today,* 74–78, 82.

Weiner, Bernard (1986). *An attributional theory of motivation and emotion.* New York: Springer-Verlag.

Weiss, Bahr; Dodge, Kenneth A.; Bates, John E.; & Petitt, Gregory S. (1992). Some consequences of early harsh discipline: Child aggression and a maladaptive social information processing style. *Child Development, 63,* 1321–1335.

Weisz, John R.; Weiss, Bahr; Alicke, Mark D.; & Klotz, M. L. (1987). Effectiveness of psychotherapy with children and adolescents: A meta-analysis for clinicians. *Journal of Consulting and Clinical Psychology, 55,* 542–549.

Weisz, John R.; Weiss, Bahr; Han, Susan S.; Granger, Douglas A.; & Morton, Todd (1995). Effects of psychotherapy with children and adolescents revisited: A meta-analysis of treatment outcome studies. *Psychological Bulletin, 117,* 450–468.

Weiten, Wayne, & Wight, Randall D. (1992). Portraits of a discipline: An examination of introductory psychology textbooks in America. In A. E. Puente, J. R. Matthews, & C. L. Brewer (eds.), *Teaching psychology in America: A history.* Washington, DC: American Psychological Association.

Wender, Paul H., & Klein, Donald F. (1981). *Mind, mood, and medicine: A guide to the new biopsychiatry.* New York: Farrar, Straus & Giroux.

Werner, Emmy E. (1989). High-risk children in young adulthood: A longitudinal study from birth to 32 years. *American Journal of Orthopsychiatry, 59,* 72–81.

Westermeyer, Joseph (1995). Cultural aspects of substance abuse and alcoholism: Assessment and management. *Psychiatric Clinics of North America, 18,* 589–605.

Whisman, Mark A. (1993). Mediators and moderators of change in cognitive therapy of depression. *Psychological Bulletin, 114,* 248–265.

Whitam, Frederick L.; Diamond, Milton; & Martin, James (1993). Homosexual orientation in twins: A report on 61 pairs and 3 triplet sets. *Archives of Sexual Behavior, 22,* 187–206.

White, Michael, & Epston, David (1990). *Narrative means to therapeutic ends.* New York: Norton.

White, Robert W. (1959). Motivation reconsidered: The concept of competence. *Psychological Review, 66,* 297–333.

White, Sheldon H., & Pillemer, David B. (1979). Childhood amnesia and the development of a socially accessible memory system. In J. F. Kihlstrom & F. J. Evans (eds.), *Functional disorders of memory.* Hillsdale, NJ: Erlbaum.

Whitehurst, Grover J.; Arnold, David S.; Epstein, Jeffery N.; Angell, Andrea L.; Smith, Meagan; & Fischel, Janet E. (1994). A picture book reading intervention in day care and home for children from low-income families. *Developmental Psychology, 30,* 679–689.

Whitehurst, Grover J.; Falco, F. L.; Lonigan, C. J.; Fischel, J. E.; et al. (1988). Accelerating language development through picture book reading. *Developmental Psychology, 24,* 552–559.

Whiting, Beatrice B., & Edwards, Carolyn P. (1988). *Children of different worlds: The formation of social behavior.* Cambridge, MA: Harvard University Press.

Whiting, Beatrice, & Whiting, John (1975). *Children of six cultures.* Cambridge, MA: Harvard University Press.

Widner, H.; Tetrud, J.; Rehncrona, S.; et al. (1993). Fifteen months' follow-up on bilateral embryonic mesencephalic grafts in two cases of severe MPTP-induced Parkinsonism. *Advances in Neurology, 60,* 729–733.

Wiggins, Jerry S. (ed.) (1996). *The five-factor model of personality: Theoretical perspectives.* New York: Guilford Press.

Williams, Kipling D., & Karau, Steven J. (1991). Social loafing and social compensation: The effects of expectations of co-worker performance. *Journal of Personality and Social Psychology, 61,* 570–581.

Williams, Redford B., Jr.; Barefoot, John C.; & Shekelle, Richard B. (1985). The health consequences of hostility. In M. A. Chesney & R. H. Rosenman (eds.), *Anger and hostility in cardiovascular and behavioral disorders.* New York: Hemisphere.

Willie, Charles V.; Rieker, Patricia P.; Kramer, Bernard M.; & Brown, Bertram S. (eds.) (1995). *Mental health, racism, and sexism* (rev. ed.). Pittsburgh: University of Pittsburgh Press.

Willis, Sherry L. (1987). Cognitive training and everyday competence. In K. W. Schaie (ed.), *Annual review of gerontology and geriatrics* (Vol. 7). New York: Springer.

Wilner, Daniel; Walkley, Rosabelle; & Cook, Stuart (1955). *Human relations in interracial housing.* Minneapolis: University of Minnesota Press.

Wilson, G. Terence, & Fairburn, Christopher G. (1993). Cognitive treatments for eating disorders. [Special Section: Recent developments in cognitive and constructivist psychotherapies.] *Journal of Consulting and Clinical Psychology, 61,* 261–269.

Windholz, George, & Lamal, P. A. (1985). Köhler's insight revisited. *Teaching of Psychology, 12,* 165–167.

Winick, Myron; Meyer, Knarig Katchadurian; & Harris, Ruth C. (1975). Malnutrition and environmental enrichment by early adoption. *Science, 190,* 1173–1175.

Winnicott, D. W. (1957/1990). *Home is where we start from.* New York: Norton.

Winter, David G. (1993). Power, affiliation, and war: Three tests of a motivational model. *Journal of Personality and Social Psychology, 65,* 532–545.

Wispé, Lauren G., & Drambarean, Nicholas C. (1953). Physiological need, word frequency, and visual duration thresholds. *Journal of Experimental Psychology, 46,* 25–31.

Witelson, Sandra F.; Glazer, I. I., & Kigar, D. L. (1994). Sex differences in numerical density of neurons in human auditory association cortex. *Society for Neuroscience Abstracts, 30* (Abstr. No. 582.12).

Wittchen, Hans-Ulrich; Kessler, Ronald C.; Zhao, Shanyang; & Abelson, Jamie (1995). Reliability and clinical validity of UM-CIDI DSM-III-R generalized anxiety disorder. *Journal of Psychiatric Research, 29,* 95–110.

Wong, Dean F.; Wagner, Henry N.; Tune, Larry E.; et al. (1986). Positron emission tomography reveals elevated D-sub-2 dopamine receptors in drug-naïve schizophrenics. *Science, 234,* 1558–1563.

Wood, James M.; Nezworski, Teresa; & Stejskal, William J. (1996). The comprehensive system for the Rorschach: A critical examination. *Psychological Science, 7,* 3–10.

Wood, Wendy; Lundgren, Sharon; Ouellette, Judith A.; Busceme, Shelly; & Blackstone, Tamela (1994). Minority influence: A meta-analytic review of social influence processes. *Psychological Bulletin, 115,* 323–345.

Wooley, Susan; Wooley, O. Wayne; & Dyrenforth, Susan (1979). Theoretical, practical, and social issues in behavioral treatments of obesity. *Journal of Applied Behavior Analysis, 12,* 3–25.

Wright, Daniel B. (1993). Recall of the Hillsborough disaster over time: Systematic biases of "flashbulb" memories. *Applied Cognitive Psychology, 7,* 129–138.

Wright, R. L. D. (1976). *Understanding statistics: An informal introduction for the behavioral sciences.* New York: Harcourt Brace Jovanovich.

Wurtman, Richard J. (1982). Nutrients that modify brain function. *Scientific American, 264*(4), 50–59.

Wurtman, Richard J., & Lieberman, Harris R. (eds.) (1982–1983). Research strategies for assessing the behavioral effects of foods and nutrients. *Journal of Psychiatric Research, 17*(2) [whole issue].

Wuthnow, Robert (1995). *Sharing the journey: Support groups and America's new quest for community.* New York: Free Press.

Wyatt, Gail E., & Mickey, M. Ray (1987). Ameliorating the effects of child sexual abuse: An exploratory study of support by parents and others. *Journal of Interpersonal Violence, 2,* 403–414.

Yalom, Irvin D. (1989). *Love's executioner and other tales of psychotherapy.* New York: Basic Books.

Yalom, Irvin D. (1995). *The theory and practice of group psychotherapy* (4th ed.). New York: Basic Books.

Yang, Kuo-shu, & Bond, Michael H. (1990). Exploring implicit personality theories with indigenous or imported constructs: The Chinese case. *Journal of Personality and Social Psychology, 58,* 1087–1095.

Yapko, Michael (1994). *Suggestions of abuse: True and false memories of childhood sexual trauma.* New York: Simon & Schuster.

Yazigi, R. A.; Odem, R. R.; & Polakoski, K. L. (1991, October 9). Demonstration of specific binding of cocaine to human spermatozoa. *Journal of the American Medical Association, 266*(14), 1956–1959.

Young, Malcolm P., & Yamane, Shigeru (1992). Sparse population coding of faces in the inferotemporal cortex. *Science, 256,* 1327–1331.

Young-Eisendrath, Polly (1993). *You're not what I expected: Learning to love the opposite sex.* New York: Morrow.

Zahn-Waxler, Carolyn (1996). Environment, biology, and culture: Implications for adolescent development. *Developmental Psychology, 32,* 571–573.

Zajonc, Robert B. (1968). Attitudinal effects of mere exposure. *Journal of Personality and Social Psychology, 9, Monograph Supplement 2,* 1–27.

Zajonc, Robert B., & Markus, Gregory B. (1975). Birth order and intellectual development. *Psychological Review, 82,* 74–88.

Zellman, Gail, & Goodchilds, Jacqueline (1983). Becoming sexual in adolescence. In E. R. Allgeier & N. B. McCormick (eds.), *Changing boundaries: Gender roles and sexual behavior.* Palo Alto, CA: Mayfield.

Zhang, Yiying; Proenca, Ricardo; Maffei, Margherita; et al. (1994). Positional cloning of the mouse obese gene and its human homologue. *Nature, 372*(6505), 425–432.

Zilbergeld, Bernie (1992). *The new male sexuality.* New York: Bantam.

Zillmann, Dolf (1983). Transfer of excitation in emotional behavior. In J. T. Cacioppo & R. E. Petty (eds.), *Social psychophysiology: A sourcebook.* New York: Guilford Press.

Zimbardo, Philip G. (1970). The human choice: Individuation, reason, and order versus deindividuation, impulse, and chaos. In W. J. Arnold & D. Levine (eds.), *Nebraska Symposium on Motivation, 1969.* Lincoln: University of Nebraska Press.

Zimbardo, Philip (1996). Reflections on the Stanford prison experiment 25 years later: Genesis, transformations, and positive consequences. Paper presented at the annual meeting of the American Psychological Association, Toronto, Canada.

Zimbardo, Philip G., & Leippe, M. R. (1991). *The psychology of attitude change and social influence.* New York: McGraw-Hill.

Zinberg, Norman (1974). The search for rational approaches to heroin use. In P. G. Bourne (ed.), *Addiction.* New York: Academic Press.

Credits

CHAPTER 1 Figure 1.2, from R. L. Wright, "Correlations in understanding statistics," *Understanding Statistics: An Informal Introduction for the Behavioral Sciences.* © 1976 by Harcourt Brace & Company. Reprinted by permission of the publisher.

CHAPTER 2 Figure 2.1, from Jerome Kagan and William James Hall, *Galen's Prophecy.* © 1994 by Basic Books Inc. Reprinted by permission of BasicBooks, a division of HarperCollins Publishers, Inc. / Table 2.1, from Harry C. Triandis, "The psychological measurement of cultural syndrome," *American Psychologist, 51,* 407–415, 1996. Copyright © 1996 by the American Psychological Association. Adapted with permission / p. 56, from Sigmund Freud, *The Ego and the Id,* trans. by James Strachey. © 1960 by James Strachey. Reprinted by permission of W. W. Norton and Co., Inc. / p. 68, from C. R. Snyder and Randee J. Shenkel, "The P. T. Barnum effect," *Psychology Today.* © 1989 by Sussex Publishers. Reprinted by permission of Psychology Today Magazine.

CHAPTER 3 Table 3.1, from Helen Bee, *The Developing Child.* © 1989 by Harper & Row, Publishers, Inc. Reprinted by permission of Harper & Row, Publishers / Figure 3.4, from René Baillargeon, "How do infants learn about the physical world?" *Current Directions in Psychological Science,* Vol. 5 (1994). Reprinted by permission of Cambridge University Press and the author / Figure 3.5, from Kay Bussey and Albert Bandura, "Gender-linked activities," *Child Development,* 63. © The Society for Research in Child Development, Inc. Reprinted by permission.

CHAPTER 4 Figure 4.6, Orietta Agostoni

CHAPTER 5 Figure 5.2, from Tom N. Cornsweet, "Information processing in human visual systems," *The SRI Journal,* Issue 5, January 1969. © 1969 by SRI Journal. Reprinted by permssion of SRI International / Table 5.1, reprinted with permission from the American Academy of Otolaryngology–Head and Neck Surgery, Washington, D.C.

CHAPTER 6 Table 6.1, from Kathleen Galotti, "Two kinds of reasoning," *Psychological Bulletin,* 105, 1989. Copyright © 1989 by the American Psychological Association. Adapted with permission / pp. 194–195, from Patricia King and Karen Kitchener, *Developing Reflective Judgment: Understanding and Promoting Intellectual Growth and Critical Thinking in Adolescents and Adults.* © 1994 by Jossey-Bass Inc., Publishers. Reprinted by permission / Table 6.2, Copyright © 1972 by The Riverside Publishing Company. Reproduced from *Stanford Binet Intelligence Scale, Form L-M Manual for 3rd Revision, Part 2,* pages 68–111 by Lewis M. Terman and Maud A. Merrill, with permission of the publisher. All rights reserved / Figure 6.3, from Lee J. Cronbach, "Performance tasks on the Weschler tests," *Essentials of Psychological Testing,* 4th edition, p. 208. © 1984 by HarperCollins Publishers.

Reprinted by permission / Figure 6.6, from Arnold Sameroff and Ronald Seifer, "Intelligent quotient scores of 4-year-old children: Social-environmental risk factors," *Pediatrics, 79,* pp. 343–350. Reprinted by permission of the authors / Figure 6.7, from J. Horgan, "Get smart, take a test: A long-term rise in IQ scores baffles intelligence experts," *Scientific American,* November 1995. © 1995 by Scientific American, Inc. Reprinted by permission of Scientific American, Inc. All rights reserved.

CHAPTER 7 Figure 7.2, from "A piece of the semantic memory network—a later view," in *Cognitive Psychology and Information processing: An Introduction* by Lachman et al., 1979. Reprinted by permission of Lawrence Erlbaum Associates, Inc / Figure 7.4, from Elizabeth Loftus, "Serial position effect," *Memory,* p. 25. © 1980 by Addison Wesley Publishing Co. Reprinted by permission / Figure 7.5, from Michael G. Wesell, "Retention in short term memory," *Cognitive Psychology,* p. 98. © 1982 by Harper & Row, Publishers, Inc. Reprinted by permission / Figure 7.7a, from Hermann Ebbinghaus, *Memory: A Contribution to Experimental Psychology.* © 1964 by Dover Publications, Inc. Reprinted by permission / Figure 7.7b, from Marigold Linton, "I remember it well," *Psychology Today.* © 1979 by Sussex Publishers, Inc. Reprinted by permission of Psychology Today Magazine.

CHAPTER 8 Figure 8.2, from Ivan P. Pavlov, "Acquisition and extinction of a salivary response," *Conditioned Reflexes.* Copyright 1927. Reprinted by permission of Oxford University Press / Figure 8.6, from Carl Cheney, "A rat's route," *Learning and Behavior.* © 1979 by Wadsworth Publishing Co., Inc. Reprinted by permission of the publisher / p. 279, from Paul Chance, "Knock wood," *Psychology Today,* October 1988. © 1988 by P. T. Partners, L. P. Reprinted by permission of Psychology Today Magazine / Figure 8.7, from David Greene and Mark R. Lepper, "Turning play into work," *Psychology Today,* September 1974. © 1974 by Sussex Publishers, Inc. Reprinted by permission of Psychology Today Magazine / Figure 8.8, from E. C. Tolman and C. H. Honzik, "Introduction and removal of reward and maze performance in rats," *Psychology,* 4 (1930). Reprinted by permission of University of California Publications.

CHAPTER 9 p. 300, from Stanley Milgram, *Obedience to Authority.* © 1974 by Stanley Milgram. Reprinted by permission of HarperCollins Publishers / p. 320, G. Allport, *The Nature of Prejudice,* pp. 13–14. © 1979 by Addison Wesley Publishing Company, Inc. Reprinted by permission of Addison Wesley Longman.

CHAPTER 10 pp. 335, 336, drawing recreated by Daniel John Del Ben / Figure 10.2, from Robert Hare, "Antisocial personality disorder," *Journal of Psychology,* 1965, p. 369, Fig. 1-A. © 1965. Reprinted by permission of the Helen Dwight Reid Educational Foundation. Published by Heldref Publications, 1319 Eighteenth St., N.W., Washington, D.C., 20036-1802 / Table 10.2, reprinted with permission of Simon & Schuster from *The Truth About Addiction and Recovery* by Stanton Peele and Archie Brodsky with Mary Arnold. Copyright © 1991 by Stanton Peele and Archie Brodsky with Mary Arnold / p. 359, from Eugen Bleuler, *Dementia Praecox or the Group of Schizophrenias*, 1950, International Universities Press, Madison, CT. Reprinted by permission.

CHAPTER 11 Figure 11.2, from Jane Gillham et al., "Prevention of depressive symptoms in school children: A two-year follow-up," *Psychological Science, 6,* 1995, pp. 343–351. © 1995 by Psychological Science. Reprinted by permission of Cambridge University Press / Figure 11.3, from Monica McGoldrick and Randy Gerson, "O'Neill family—repetitive functioning patterns," *Genograms in Family Assessment.* © 1985 by Monica McGoldrick and Randy Gerson. Reprinted by permission of W. W. Norton & Company, Inc. / Figure 11.4, from Kenneth Howard et al., "The dose-effect relationship in psychotherapy," *American Psychologist, 41,* February 1986, p. 160. © 1986 by the American Psychological Association. Reprinted by permission of the publisher and the author.

CHAPTER 12 Figure 12.3, from David Holmes, "Fitness and health," *Abnormal Psychology.* © 1991 by Addison Wesley Longman Publishers. Reprinted by permission of Addison Wesley Longman Publishers.

Photographs and Cartoons

Unless otherwise acknowledged, all photographs are the property of Addison Wesley Educational Publishers, Inc. Page abbreviations are as follows: (T) top, (C) center, (B) bottom, (L) left, (R) right.

CHAPTER OPENERS Page 3 (T) Elizabeth Darwin Gatlin/*Fayetteville Observer-Times* / p. 3 (BL) Michael Schumann/SABA / p. 3 (BR) AP/Wide World Photos / p. 39 © A. Berliner/Gamma Liaison / p. 72 *National Enquirer* / p. 113 Deborah Booker/*The Honolulu Advertiser* / p. 149 AP/Wide World Photos / p. 187 AP/Wide World Photos / p. 227 Rick Martin/*San Jose Mercury News* / p. 261 Reuters/Jonathan Drake/Archive Photos / p. 297 James W. Terry/ Sipa Press / p. 333 (L) Carol Halebian/ Gamma Liaison / p. 333 (R) Scott Audette/Sipa Press / p. 369 Thomas Kelsey/*Los Angeles Times* / p. 399 Tony Freeman/PhotoEdit / p. 431 Everett Collection

CHAPTER 1 Page 5 © Punch/Rothco / p. 6 Hand-colored for Addison Wesley Educational Publishers, Inc. by Cheryl Kucharzak / p. 7 Les Jorgensen/Photonica / p. 11 (TL) Michael Newman/Photo Edit / p. 11 (BL) Roe Di Bona / p. 11 (R) Ed Kashi / p. 13 The "BIZARRO" cartoon by Dan Piraro is reprinted by permission of Chronicle Features, San Francisco, California / p. 14 Courtesy of André Kole Productions / p. 16 Tannenbaum/Sygma / p. 18 From Susan Curtiss, *Genie: A Modern Day Wild Child*, Academic Press, used by permission / p. 19 Charles Moore/Black Star / p. 21 Copyright 1994, Los Angeles Times Syndicate. Reprinted with permission / p. 26 Alan Carey/The Image Works / p. 30 *Miss Peach* by Mell Lazarus. By permission of Mell Lazarus and Creators Syndicate / p. 32 (L) Mark E. Gibson/The Stock Market / p. 32 (CT) David Young-Wolff/Photo Edit / p. 32 (R) William Thompson/Picture Cube / p. 32 (CB) Sankei Shimbun

CHAPTER 2 Page 40 *The Far Side* © 1990 Farworks, Inc./Dist. by Universal Press Syndicate. Reprinted with permission. All rights reserved / p. 41 Ed Kashi / p. 43 M. Siluk/The Image Works / p. 44 Evan Byrne, Laboratory of Comparative Ethnology, National Institute of Child Health and Human Development / p. 45 Peter Byron / p. 46 Drawing by Charles Addams; © 1981 The New Yorker Magazine, Inc. / p. 48 Herman Kokojan/Black Star / p. 50 Lisa Quinones/Black Star / p. 53 (L) Wally McNamee/ Woodfin Camp & Associates / p. 53 (R) Timothy Egan/ Woodfin Camp & Associates / p. 58 (T) Joe Mirachi/ © 1985 The New Yorker Magazine, Inc. / p. 58 (B) Innervisions / p. 61 Photofest / p. 62 Donna Day/Tony Stone Images / p. 63 S. Franklin/Sygma / p. 65 Catherine Ursillo/Photo Researchers

CHAPTER 3 Page 74 National Portrait Gallery, London / p. 75 Russell D. Curtis/Photo Researchers, Inc. / p. 77 (T) Marina Raith/Gruner & Jahr / p. 77 (B) Dorris Pinney Brenner / p. 78 Harlow Primate Laboratory, University of Wisconsin / p. 82 (L) Mimi Forsyth/Monkmeyer Press Photo Service / p. 82 (R) Marcia Weinstein / p. 84 Mandal Ranjiz/Photo Researchers / p. 85 Erika Stone / p. 86 Bill Bachmann/Stock Boston / p. 87 Cartoonists & Writers Syndicate / p. 89 (T) Laura Dwight / p. 89 (B) *Cathy* © Cathy Guisewite. Reprinted with permission of Universal Press Syndicate. All rights reserved / p. 93 UPI/Corbis-Bettmann / p. 95 (L) Tony Freeman/Photo Edit / p. 95 (R) Robert Brenner/Photo Edit / p. 96 (L) Diane M. Lowe/Stock Boston, Inc. / p. 96 (R) Betsy Lee / p. 98 Richard Hutchings/Photo Researchers / p. 99 (L) Phil McCarten/PhotoEdit / p. 99 (R) James D. Wilson/Gamma Liaison / p. 103 (L) Ira Wyman/ Sygma / p. 103 (R) Dan McCoy/Rainbow / p. 104 Tom McCarthy/Picture Cube / p. 105 *Doonesbury* © G. C. Trudeau. Reprinted with permission of Universal Press Syndicate. All rights reserved.

CHAPTER 4 Page 114 Sidney Harris / p. 119 Biophoto Associates/Photo Researchers / p. 123 Yale/Axion Neural Transplant Program / p. 125 Dan McCoy/Rainbow / p. 126 (L) Fritz Goro, *Life* Magazine, Time Warner Inc. / p. 126 (R) Courtesy of Dr. Michael E. Phelps and Dr. John C. Mazziotta, UCLA School of Medicine / p. 127 (T) Howard Sochurek / p. 127 (B) Alan Gevins, EEG Systems Laboratory, San Francisco / p. 133 from "The return of Phineas Gage: Clues about the brain from the skull of a famous patient" by Hanna Damasio, Thomas Grabowski, Randall Frank, Albert M. Galaburda, Antonio R. Damasio. *Science*, May 20, 1994. Courtesy Hanna Damasio, M.D. / p. 137 Courtesy of Natural Nectar Corp. / p. 139 Walter Chandoha / p. 142 B. A. Shaywitz et al., 1995 NMR/Yale Medical School / p. 143 Copyright © 1992 The Time Inc. Magazine Company. Reprinted by permission.

CHAPTER 5 Page 152 Gary Retherford / p. 153 Tom N. Cornsweet, "Information processing in human visual systems." Reprinted by permission from Issue 5, *The SRI Journal.* © January 1969, SRI International / p. 154 B.

Press Syndicate. All rights reserved / p. 381 Alan D. Entin, Ph. D. / p. 385 Christopher Morris/Black Star / p. 386 Michael Schuman/SABA / p. 387 Drawing by M. Twohy; © 1991 The New Yorker Magazine, Inc. / p. 388 Michael Newman/PhotoEdit / p. 390 (L) Courtesy of Dr. Giuseppe Costantino / p. 390 (R) Xan Lopez

CHAPTER 12 Page 401 (TL) Barry Lewis/Network/Matrix / p. 401 (TCL) Erika Stone / p. 401 (TCR) Laura Dwight / p. 401 (TR) Francie Manning/The Picture Cube / p. 401 (BL) John Giordano/SABA / p. 401 (BC) Bridgeman/Art Resource, NY / p. 401 (BR) The New York Public Library, Astor, Lenox and Tilden Foundations / p. 402 (T) A. Knudsen/Sygma / p. 402 (B) David Matsumoto, Department of Psychology, San Francisco State University / p. 403 Heidi Stetson Mario / p. 406 (T) Duomo / p. 406 (B) Laura Dwight / p. 409 Philip J. Griffiths/Magnum Photos / p. 410 Tom McCarthy/The Picture Cube / p. 411 William Karel/Sygma / p. 413 Manfred Kage/Peter Arnold, Inc. / p. 414 (L) Stephen Agricola/The Image Works / p. 414 (R) Michael Greenlar/The Image Works / p. 415 National Baseball Library & Archive, Cooperstown, NY / p. 417 Roy Roper/Zuma Images / p. 418 Tom Sobolik/Black Star / p. 420 Barbara Singer/Photonica / p. 423 Malcolm Hancock / p. 424 The Museum of Modern Art/Film Stills Archive / p. 425 Culver Pictures

CHAPTER 13 Page 432 Harry Groom/Photo Researchers / p. 433 Drawing by Cline; © 1988 The New Yorker Magazine, Inc. / p. 437 Bruce Ayers/Tony Stone Images / p. 438 Alex Webb/Magnum Photos / p. 439 Art Wolfe/Tony Stone Images / p. 441 (L) Photofest / p. 441 (R) The poster "The Rape of the Sabine Women" was created by the Pi Kappa Phi fraternity in 1987 to raise sexual abuse awareness among its undergraduate members / p. 442 Les Van/Unicorn Stock Photos / p. 443 Eric Kroll / p. 444 (L) Deborah Davis/Photo Edit / p. 444 (R) Zigy Kaluzny/Tony Stone Images / p. 447 (L) Dennis Stock/Magnum Photos / p. 447 (R) Victor Englebert/Photo Researchers / p. 448 © 1995 Amgen Inc. / p. 449 Spooner/Gamma Liaison / p. 453 Focus on Sports / p. 454 (L) Rick Friedman/Black Star / p. 454 (CL) American Foundation for the Blind Helen Keller Archives / p. 454 (CR) Flip Shulke/Black Star / p. 454 (R) Dennis Brack/Black Star / p. 455 (L) Owen Franken/Sygma / p. 455 (CL) Marvin Koner/Black Star / p. 455 (CR) Duran/Giansanti/Perin/Sygma / p. 455 (R) Carol Halebian/Gamma-Liaison / p. 456 Spencer Grant/The Picture Cube / p. 458 *The Far Side* © 1985 Farworks, Inc./Dist. by Universal Press Syndicate. Reprinted with permission. All rights reserved.

Author Index

Subject Index